THE GREAT BIG BOOK OF TOMORROW

A TREASURY OF CARTOONS BY

TOM TOMORROW

Also by Tom Tomorrow

Greetings from This Modern World
Tune in Tomorrow
The Wrath of Sparky
Penguin Soup for the Soul
When Penguins Attack!

For Beverly, of course.

THE GREAT BIG BOOK OF TOMORROW

A TREASURY OF CARTOONS BY TOM TOMORROW

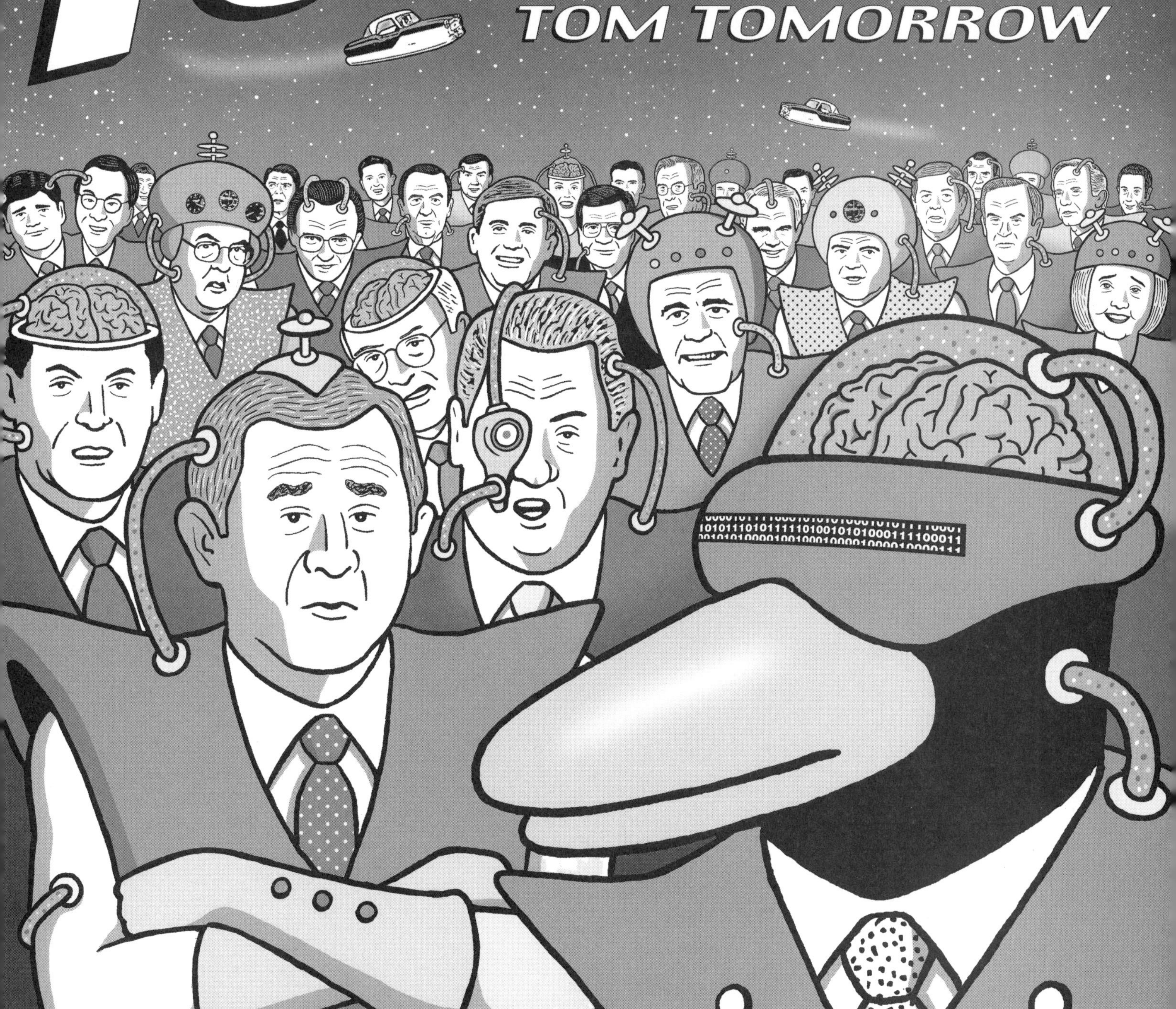

ST. MARTIN'S GRIFFIN NEW YORK

THE GREAT BIG BOOK OF TOMORROW

For information, address St. Martin's Press,
175 Fifth Avenue, New York, N.Y. 10010.

www.stmartins.com

Design by Dan Perkins and Kevin Pyle; production by Kevin Pyle.

Visit Tom Tomorrow's frequently updated blog and cartoon archive:
www.thismodernworld.com

Figure sculpted by Andgor Toy Company.

ISBN 0-312-30177-4

10 9 8 7 6 5 4 3 2

FOREWORD
by Tom Tomorrow

Who *is* Tom Tomorrow?

It is a question that keeps the public awake at night, tossing and turning throughout the long, restless predawn hours, much to the annoyance of the public's significant other, who could really use a decent night's sleep for a change. Who is the mysterious and notoriously reclusive man behind the infamous nom de plume? Does he really live in a yurt somewhere in the Catskill Mountains, subsisting on a diet of roadkill and rainwater? What's the story behind those rumors of an illicit liason with Alex Trebek and Marilyn Quayle, a night of debauchery which reportedly left two of them emotionally scarred for life, but meant very little to the third?

Is it true that he once shot a man in Reno, just to watch him die?

Well, my friends, if you seek the answers to these questions and more, then you are clearly interested in the unknown, the mysterious, the unexplainable. And now, for the first time, we will give you all the evidence, based only on the secret testimonies of the miserable souls who survived this terrifying ordeal. The incidents, the places, my friends—we cannot keep this a secret any longer. Let us punish the guilty, let us reward the innocent.

Can your heart stand the shocking facts?

Then let's peel away the mask behind the man, the myth which underlies the legend. You see, I have noticed, over the years, that many of my devoted fans want to know more about me than can be gleaned from either my cartoon work or my weblog entries. Every time I check my email, there are more questions: Am I interested in surefire investment opportunities? Would I like to have sex with cheerleaders? Am I satisfied with the size of my penis? Things like that.

It's just the price of fame, I guess, this insatiable curiosity about *me*.

So. Pull up a chair, make yourself comfortable. We've got a couple of pages to fill here, so we might as well start at the beginning.

I was born in Wichita, Kansas in 1961. We moved to a suburb of Detroit, and then to Iowa City, Iowa, all by the time I was five—foreshadowing the impermanence and dislocation which have defined much of my life, I guess. My parents divorced when I was about ten, and I went off with my mother and spent the next few years living in Ft. Lauderdale, Florida, Stone Mountain, Georgia—birthplace of the modern Ku Klux Klan—and a couple of very small towns in Arkansas, before going back to live with my father in Iowa City to finish high school.

And the one thing I always knew for sure was that I wanted to be a cartoonist.

I know, it sounds contrived, like something the momentarily ubiquitous pop star says during television interviews–*ever since I was a little girl, I wanted to star in Pepsi commercials!*– but it's true. From my earliest years, I pored over cartoons–Peanuts and *Mad* magazine and Charles Addams compilations and anything else I could get my hands on–and I knew that this was what I wanted to do. I filled sheet after sheet of three-hole punch notebook paper with pencil drawings of googly-eyed characters, who were, even then, excessively verbose. I wish I had at least one or two examples to show you, but none of it survived the various moves and divorces and upheavals of my childhood. (I do have a felt-tip rendering of the starship *Enterprise*, circa fifth grade, around here somewhere, but I'll spare you.)

After high school, like any good Iowa boy unburdened by excessive ambition, I dutifully enrolled in the state university, and I attended some classes and did whatever it is college freshmen do–much of it probably best forgotten–but more relevant to the discussion at hand, I spent much of the year creating satirical collages, incorporating found imagery and my own text into advertisements for fictional movies and products and so on, which I'd then photocopy and post anonymously around town on kiosks and bulletin boards. This time-wasting, schoolwork-avoiding pastime would prove to be far more significant than any reasonable person might have surmised at the time.

Because shortly thereafter, I became a *nationally syndicated cartoonist!*

Except some other stuff happened first. About a decade's worth.

That summer, at the age of nineteen, restlessness settled in like a house guest who simply won't leave, and I realized I needed to get out and see the world, which at that point I defined as anywhere other than the midwest or south. So, with five hundred dollars in my pocket and no appreciable job skills, I got on a Greyhound bus and headed for New York City, and spent the first month or so sleeping on the floor of a friend-of-a-friend's flat in the Park Slope neighborhood of Brooklyn. A group of friends and I then moved to Williamsburg, which has become a painfully hip artists' colony, but which was then dominated by the uneasy intersection of Puerto Rican and Hassidic cultures, with the occasional starving artist thrown in here and there for good measure.

I'd like to say that I spent most of my time in New York working furiously on cartoons, but—well—I would be lying. The truth is, I spent most of that time in a dissolute haze, playing guitar with friends at night and supporting myself, barely, with a variety of dead end jobs—as a paste up artist on a startup magazine patterned after the *Comics Journal*, and then after the magazine went out of business, as a copy shop clerk, a picture framer, and an usher in one of the big movie houses in Times Square, among other things. I was living on about $100 a week, which was no mean feat in New York City even in 1981. Trust me. I used to pretty much survive on ramen noodles and, when I really felt I could afford to splurge, the occasional slice of Ben's pizza.

I was really, really skinny when I left New York after a year and a half of this. After an abortive effort to move to California, I ended up back in Iowa City, all via Greyhound. And if you've never barrelled through the wastelands of some godforsaken Nevada highway as a drugged-out woman with distant eyes walks purposefully down the aisle of a Greyhound bus, click-click-clicking a pair of long silver scissors as she slowly makes her way toward the driver, well, you just haven't lived. But that's a story for another day.

What's important here is that shortly thereafter, I became a *nationally syndicated cartoonist!*

Well, still not quite yet. But: imagine a beautiful midwestern spring day, clear blue skies that stretch on for miles, birds chirping, yadda yadda yadda. Your humble narrator is leaving his job at the copy shop and heading for home—but on a whim, he stops in an antique shop and stumbles across a box of old *Life* magazines on sale for a pittance, and is immediately entranced by page after page of blatantly manipulative advertising imagery, the forced cheerfulness of a less media-savvy age, in which it is not simply implied that your problems can be solved by various snack products and hair tonics and over-the-counter medications, but explicitly stated. ("He won't love you if you cough," warns one of my favorite old ads from this era. It doesn't get any more straightforward than that.)

I'm not sure if it happened exactly like that, but it could have. At any rate, happy anachronistic consumers soon began seeping into the collages I was still creating and posting around town, work which was eventually compiled into a self published zine called *Writing on the Wall* (unknowingly subsidized by the copy shop I was working in—sorry about that, guys). *Writing* also featured "Can You Concentrate," a surrealistic take on children's textbooks (created with text and images clipped from actual old schoolbooks salvaged from the public library's discard bin), which is reproduced on the pages immediately following this introduction—basically because it made me laugh when I went back and reread it for the first time in maybe ten years. The rest of the zine was a hodgepodge of collages, cartoons and other satirical bits, including those fake movie posters mentioned above.

At this point, I began to experiment with combining the discarded imagery of previous decades (with which I had grown increasingly obsessed) with a more traditional comic book format. I was twenty three years old, an age at which many people have finished college and begun to climb up

the career ladder of their choice, and I was living hand-to-mouth, working at a copy center and spending my spare time cutting pictures out of old magazines.

I was, to be blunt, not prominently placed on anybody's most-likely-to-succeed list.

But this is the thing: I wasn't living in a world in which people wrote books, directed movies, drew cartoons. I mean, you understood that somebody somewhere was creating these things, that they did not simply somehow spring into being fully formed, and some of these people even passed through Iowa City from time to time—Kurt Vonnegut spent some time there, teaching at the Writer's Workshop, and to this day, there are people who will proudly point out the house in which he lived—but the chances that you yourself would become one of those people . . . you might as well have been Icarus dreaming of flight. Anyone could tell you how well that was going to work out.

I bounced around a little bit more, followed a girlfriend to Champaign-Urbana, and then to Chicago, before finally heading out to San Francisco in 1984. I had a little more money in my pocket this time and at least one marketable skill—word processing, which I'd taught myself in the back of that Iowa City copy shop because I'd heard that word processors in the big city could make a whopping $12 an hour, which at the time seemed like untold riches, a damn license to print money. And for the next few years, this was my identity to the world at large: I was a temp, a processor of words, a means of translating the important thoughts of attorneys and businessmen and advertising executives from hastily scrawled notes into neatly formatted letters and documents. I was an organic information conduit, a microchip that hadn't been invented yet.

But it worked for me, mainly because I was able to take a lot of time off—a fan at the time of John MacDonald's Travis McGee novels, I imagined that I, too, was "taking my retirement in installments." Except that Travis McGee supported his life as a Florida beach bum with intermittent installments of adventure and danger, whereas I was just, um, taking three or four day weekends whenever I could, and then back to the word processing. But other than that, pretty much the same thing.

I got a lot of writing done during these mindless temp assignments. It sounds like it should have made my head explode, but somehow I was able to format documents and transcribe notes and whatever else it was that I had to do without really occupying any of my brain—somehow the work passed from my eyes directly to my fingers, leaving my brain free to amuse itself thinking up cartoons. And so, around this time, I put out my second zine, the longish piece reprinted on pp. 7-33, which pretty much established the beginning of the Tom Tomorrow style, as well as quite a few themes which persist in my work to this day.

This first version of "This Modern World" was later serialized in *Processed World*, a small, independent magazine which focused on the underbelly of the information age, the corporate world as seen from the bottom up, by the over-educated, underutilized drones who passed through this world as anonymously and fleetingly as the word "temp" would suggest. *PW* also included exposes and stories of office sabotage, and there was a sense at the time that contributing to the magazine could lead to one's firing and/or blacklisting, though in retrospect, it seems unlikely that any office manager or temp agency coordinator ever even knew the magazine existed—but at any rate, most contributors chose to byline their work pseudononymously. Since my work at the time revolved around a retro-future in which secretaries spoke enthusiastically of their "computing machines" and children were kept in stasis where they weren't "any trouble at all," the name Tom Tomorrow (which was actually a misremembered version of Tom Terrific, an old cartoon that used to run on the *Captain Kangaroo* show early every weekday morning) seemed somehow appropriate. (And as a result, I am to this day referred to by many people I meet as Tom-I-Mean-Dan. Advice to young cartoonists: don't take a pen name.)

I did a few short pieces such as "Everybody Loves Meat" (pp. 34-35) for obscure comic books with titles like *Suburban High Life*, *Cannibal Romance* (seriously), and *Centrifugal Bumble Puppy* (the latter edited by Joe Sacco, who would later make a name for himself as the creator of such extraordinary works as *Palestine* and *Safe Area Gorazde*), but I was primarily focused on taking "This Modern World" and turning it into a weekly cartoon. I had noticed that a guy named Matt Groening was having some modest success at the time with a cartoon called "Life in Hell," which I'd first seen in the *Chicago Reader*, during my brief time in that paper's eponymous city, and I thought that if I could convince five or ten of these weekly papers to run my work, I could probably cut down on the amount of hours I had to put in as a temp to pay my rent.

And that, my friends, was the extent of my dreams and ambitions at the age of 26.

A number of these very early cartoons appear on pp. 36-40. For a brief time, Tom Tomorrow was a character within the cartoon, a cipher in a radiation suit with a lovable penguin sidekick Dippy. (To my knowledge, these cartoons have not seen the light of day since they first ran in the small handful of weekly papers which were beginning to carry my work at the time.) Dippy, of course, would eventually morph into that craaaaazy penguin named Sparky, the third most recognizable cartoon character on the face of the planet, after Mickey Mouse and Joe Camel.

(Clears throat and proceeds matter-of-factly.) So.

After that, the work began to mutate into something more closely resembling its current form. The strip grew increasingly political, particularly around the time of the Gulf War (or, as we'll almost certainly be calling it by the time this book is published—keep in mind that I'm writing these words in the summer of 2002—the *First* Gulf War). I began to strike a balance between the photocopy-collage look and pen-and-ink work (contrary to popular belief, my characters do not all spring forth ready made from some magical clip art book). Somewhere in there, I gave up temping and spent a few years working in the art department of a t-shirt company called Winterland, commuting to work each day on an old BMW motorcycle (a habit I've long since forsaken—I would no sooner ride a motorcycle in New York City than I would swim in the Hudson river).

And eventually, I began to make enough money to support myself off my cartooning alone—and never looked back. I haven't had a real job in more than a decade, and that alone has always felt like the pinnacle of success to me. Everything else is gravy.

In 1990, I sent a pile of my work to St. Martin's, and miraculously, it was plucked from the slush pile of unsolicited submissions and I was offered a publishing contract—a relationship which continues to this day, largely due to the persistence of my long-time editor, Keith Kahla, without whom this book and most of the others would almost certainly not exist. The cartoon started picking up steam in the alternative press— fifty papers, seventy-five, a hundred. *Salon* gave me an online home, and suddenly my audience was no longer limited by geography. The *New York Times* started running my work from time to time. I began to realize that I had actually managed to stumble ass-backwards into something resembling a respectable career. My life became—and remains to this day— defined by the relentless weekly deadline, an inexorable force utterly indifferent to anything else that might be happening in my life at the time. (That can be exhausting, but it can also be a refuge. Some of the cartoons in this book were produced under conditions of such stress and upheaval, you'd think the creative process would have shut down like an overloaded power transformer—but if you think you can tell which ones they are, I promise you you're wrong.)

I moved back east in 1996, first to New Haven and then back to New York City, for the love of the coolest girl in the world. And things just kept happening. I was hired by *US News*. I was fired by *US News*. I became an occasional contributor to the *New Yorker*. I picked up more papers. I lost a few. I had a development deal with *Saturday Night Live*, a nightmarish process which ultimately went nowhere—but I teamed up with an animator from that project, Harold Moss, with whom I produced an online animated series, and with whom I continue to work on other projects to this day.

Did I mention I married the coolest girl in the world, bar none?

And as I write these words, we're living in Park Slope, Brooklyn, a short walk from the street where I first landed, fresh off the Greyhound bus, in 1981, never imagining the strange, circuitous journey which would fill the intervening years. I'm 41 years old now, and the cartoons in this book represent most of what I've got to show for the past couple of decades.

That's my story, and I'm sticking to it.

Dan Perkins
("Tom Tomorrow")
Brooklyn, 2002

EARLY DAYS

Fun with x-acto knives and photocopiers. Below: an excerpt from the self-published zine, *Writing on the Wall.* Pages 7-33: the first incarnation of This Modern World. Pages 34-35: Everybody Loves Meat. (These pieces are all discussed at greater length in the Foreword—but you knew that already, because nobody ever skips the Foreword to a cartoon compilation . . . *right?*)

1983-1987

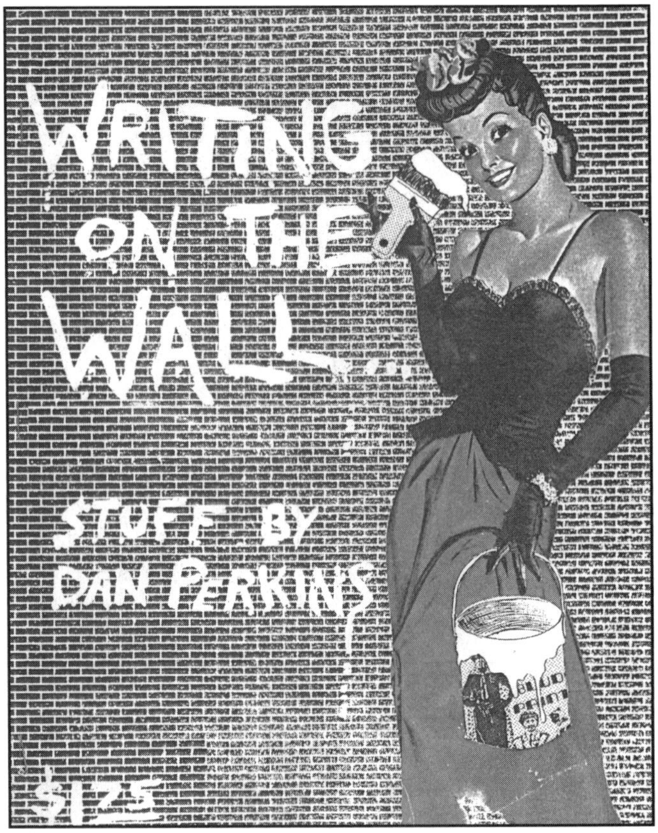
WRITING ON THE WALL...
STUFF BY DAN PERKINS
$1.25

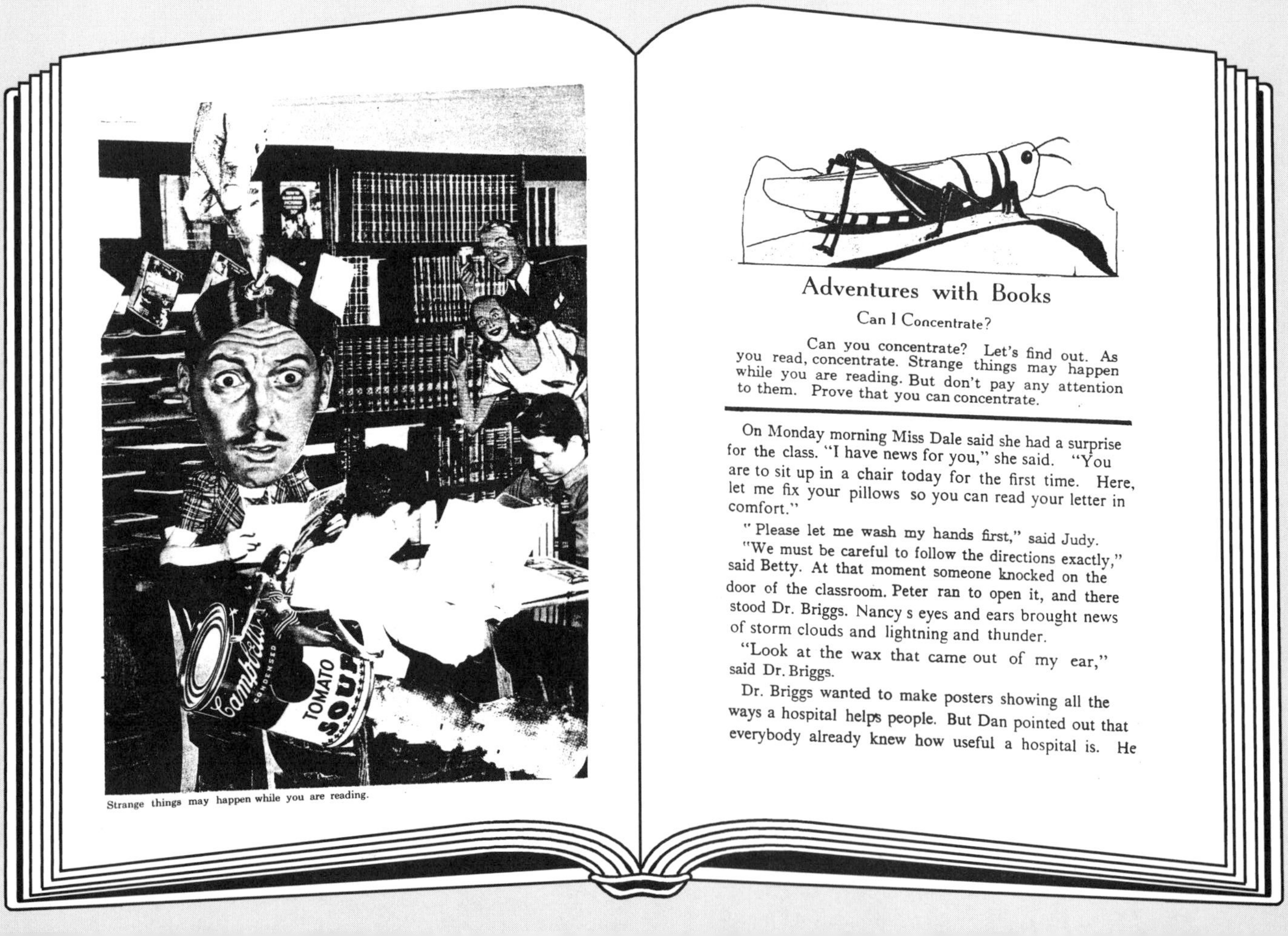
TOMATO SOUP
Strange things may happen while you are reading.
Adventures with Books
Can I Concentrate?
Can you concentrate? Let's find out. As you read, concentrate. Strange things may happen while you are reading. But don't pay any attention to them. Prove that you can concentrate.
On Monday morning Miss Dale said she had a surprise for the class. "I have news for you," she said. "You are to sit up in a chair today for the first time. Here, let me fix your pillows so you can read your letter in comfort."
"Please let me wash my hands first," said Judy.
"We must be careful to follow the directions exactly," said Betty. At that moment someone knocked on the door of the classroom. Peter ran to open it, and there stood Dr. Briggs. Nancy s eyes and ears brought news of storm clouds and lightning and thunder.
"Look at the wax that came out of my ear," said Dr. Briggs.
Dr. Briggs wanted to make posters showing all the ways a hospital helps people. But Dan pointed out that everybody already knew how useful a hospital is. He

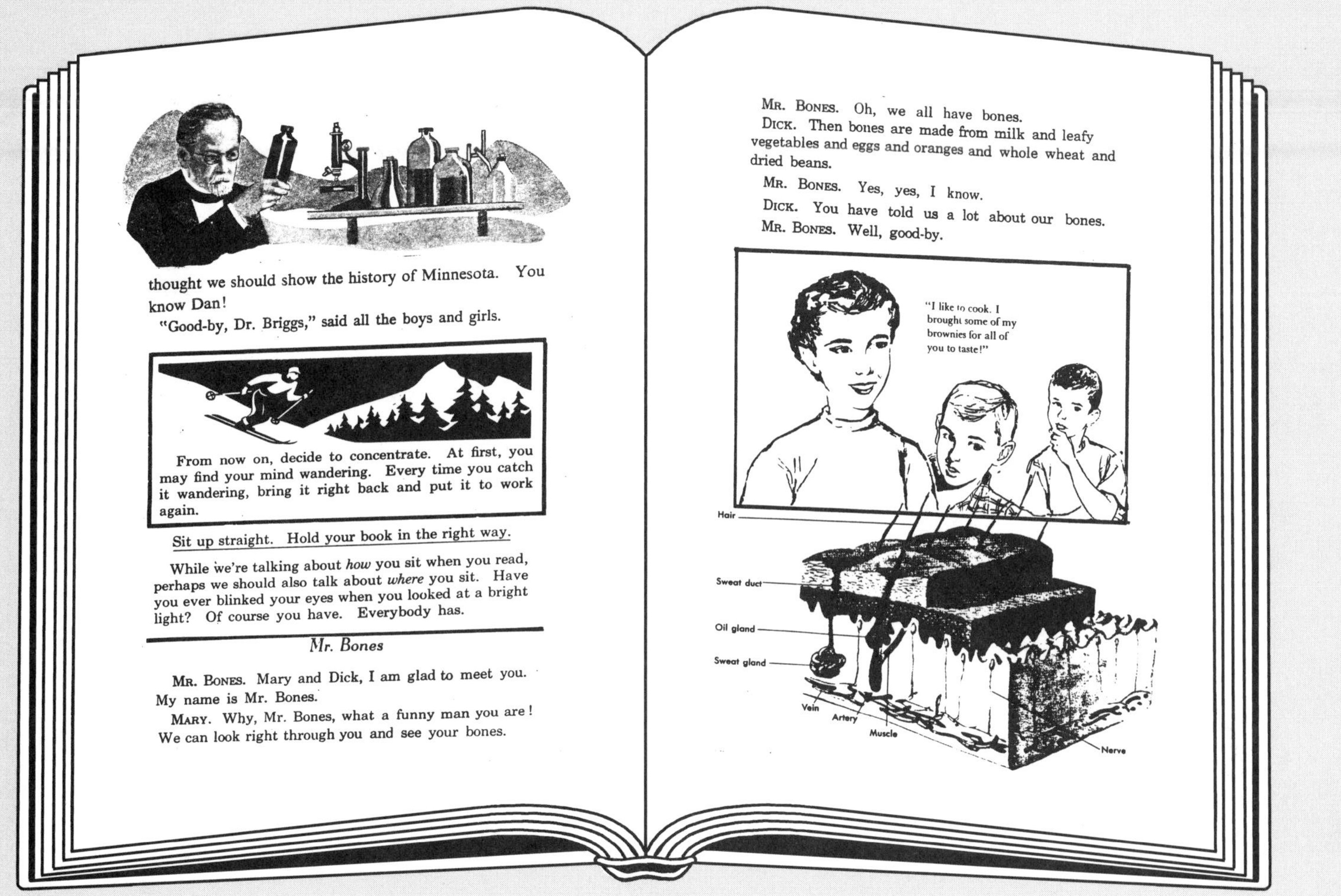

thought we should show the history of Minnesota. You know Dan!

"Good-by, Dr. Briggs," said all the boys and girls.

From now on, decide to concentrate. At first, you may find your mind wandering. Every time you catch it wandering, bring it right back and put it to work again.

Sit up straight. Hold your book in the right way.

While we're talking about *how* you sit when you read, perhaps we should also talk about *where* you sit. Have you ever blinked your eyes when you looked at a bright light? Of course you have. Everybody has.

Mr. Bones

Mr. Bones. Mary and Dick, I am glad to meet you. My name is Mr. Bones.

Mary. Why, Mr. Bones, what a funny man you are! We can look right through you and see your bones.

Mr. Bones. Oh, we all have bones.

Dick. Then bones are made from milk and leafy vegetables and eggs and oranges and whole wheat and dried beans.

Mr. Bones. Yes, yes, I know.

Dick. You have told us a lot about our bones.

Mr. Bones. Well, good-by.

"I like to cook. I brought some of my brownies for all of you to taste!"
Hair
Sweat duct
Oil gland
Sweat gland
Vein
Artery
Muscle
Nerve

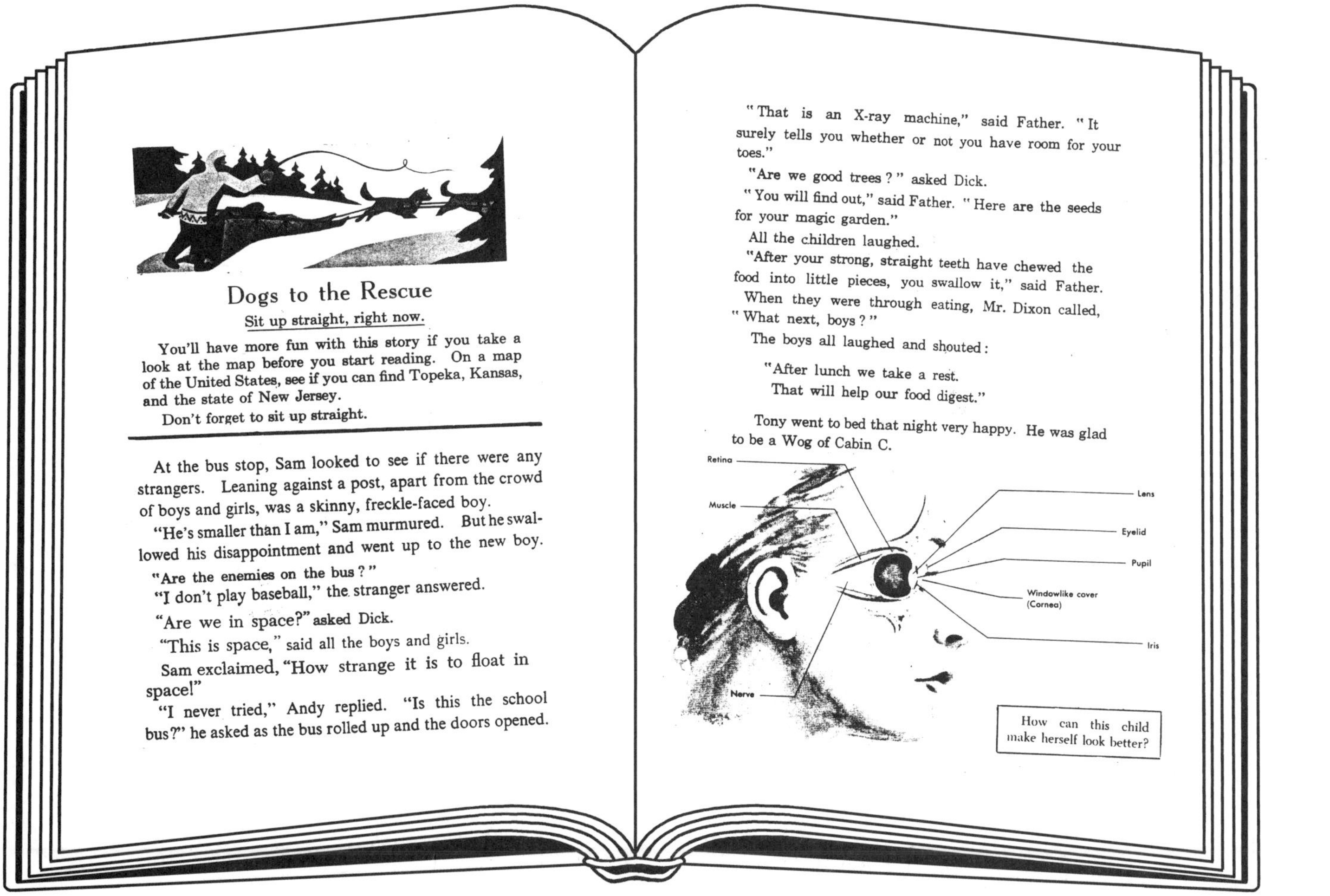

Dogs to the Rescue

Sit up straight, right now.

You'll have more fun with this story if you take a look at the map before you start reading. On a map of the United States, see if you can find Topeka, Kansas, and the state of New Jersey.

Don't forget to sit up straight.

At the bus stop, Sam looked to see if there were any strangers. Leaning against a post, apart from the crowd of boys and girls, was a skinny, freckle-faced boy.

"He's smaller than I am," Sam murmured. But he swallowed his disappointment and went up to the new boy.

"Are the enemies on the bus?"

"I don't play baseball," the stranger answered.

"Are we in space?" asked Dick.

"This is space," said all the boys and girls.

Sam exclaimed, "How strange it is to float in space!"

"I never tried," Andy replied. "Is this the school bus?" he asked as the bus rolled up and the doors opened.

"That is an X-ray machine," said Father. "It surely tells you whether or not you have room for your toes."

"Are we good trees?" asked Dick.

"You will find out," said Father. "Here are the seeds for your magic garden."

All the children laughed.

"After your strong, straight teeth have chewed the food into little pieces, you swallow it," said Father.

When they were through eating, Mr. Dixon called, "What next, boys?"

The boys all laughed and shouted:

"After lunch we take a rest.
That will help our food digest."

Tony went to bed that night very happy. He was glad to be a Wog of Cabin C.

Retina
Muscle
Lens
Eyelid
Pupil
Windowlike cover (Cornea)
Iris
Nerve

How can this child make herself look better?

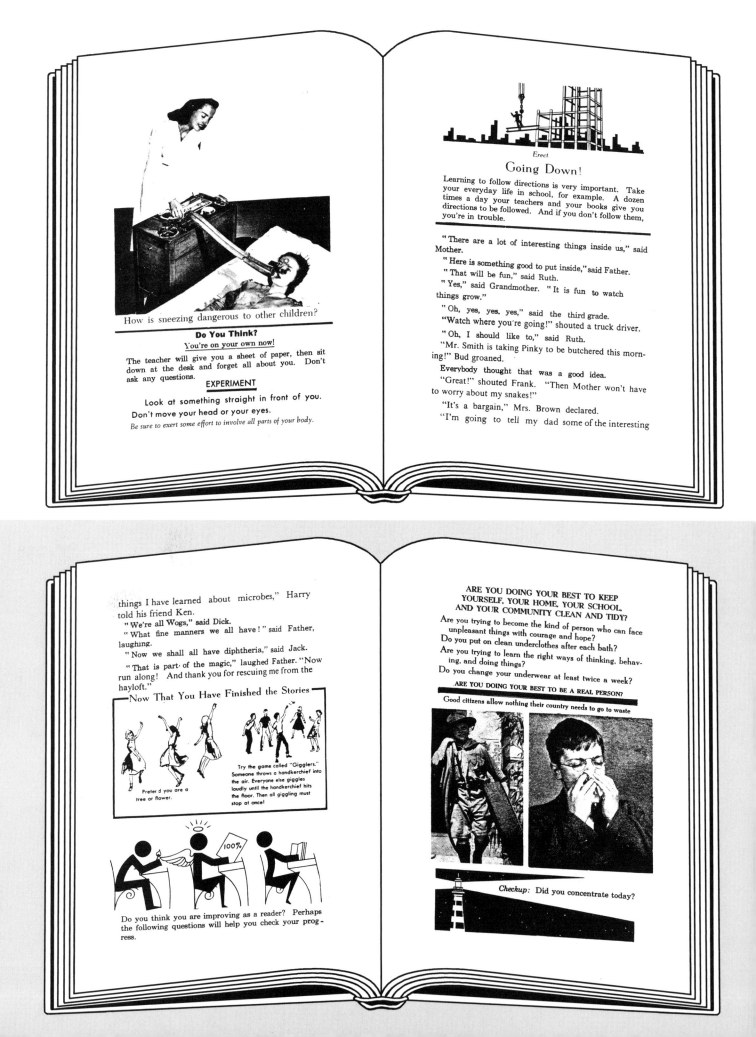

How is sneezing dangerous to other children?

Do You Think?
You're on your own now!

The teacher will give you a sheet of paper, then sit down at the desk and forget all about you. Don't ask any questions.

EXPERIMENT

Look at something straight in front of you.
Don't move your head or your eyes.
Be sure to exert some effort to involve all parts of your body.

Erect.

Going Down!

Learning to follow directions is very important. Take your everyday life in school, for example. A dozen times a day your teachers and your books give you directions to be followed. And if you don't follow them, you're in trouble.

"There are a lot of interesting things inside us," said Mother.

"Here is something good to put inside," said Father.

"That will be fun," said Ruth.

"Yes," said Grandmother. "It is fun to watch things grow."

"Oh, yes, yes, yes," said the third grade.

"Watch where you're going!" shouted a truck driver.

"Oh, I should like to," said Ruth.

"Mr. Smith is taking Pinky to be butchered this morning!" Bud groaned.

Everybody thought that was a good idea.

"Great!" shouted Frank. "Then Mother won't have to worry about my snakes!"

"It's a bargain," Mrs. Brown declared.

"I'm going to tell my dad some of the interesting

---

things I have learned about microbes," Harry told his friend Ken.

"We're all Wogs," said Dick.

"What fine manners we all have!" said Father, laughing.

"Now we shall all have diphtheria," said Jack.

"That is part of the magic," laughed Father. "Now run along! And thank you for rescuing me from the hayloft."

Now That You Have Finished the Stories

Preter d you are a tree or flower.

Try the game called "Gigglers." Someone throws a handkerchief into the air. Everyone else giggles loudly until the handkerchief hits the floor. Then all giggling must stop at once!

100%

Do you think you are improving as a reader? Perhaps the following questions will help you check your progress.

ARE YOU DOING YOUR BEST TO KEEP YOURSELF, YOUR HOME, YOUR SCHOOL, AND YOUR COMMUNITY CLEAN AND TIDY?

Are you trying to become the kind of person who can face unpleasant things with courage and hope?

Do you put on clean underclothes after each bath?

Are you trying to learn the right ways of thinking, behaving, and doing things?

Do you change your underwear at least twice a week?

ARE YOU DOING YOUR BEST TO BE A REAL PERSON?

Good citizens allow nothing their country needs to go to waste

Checkup: Did you concentrate today?

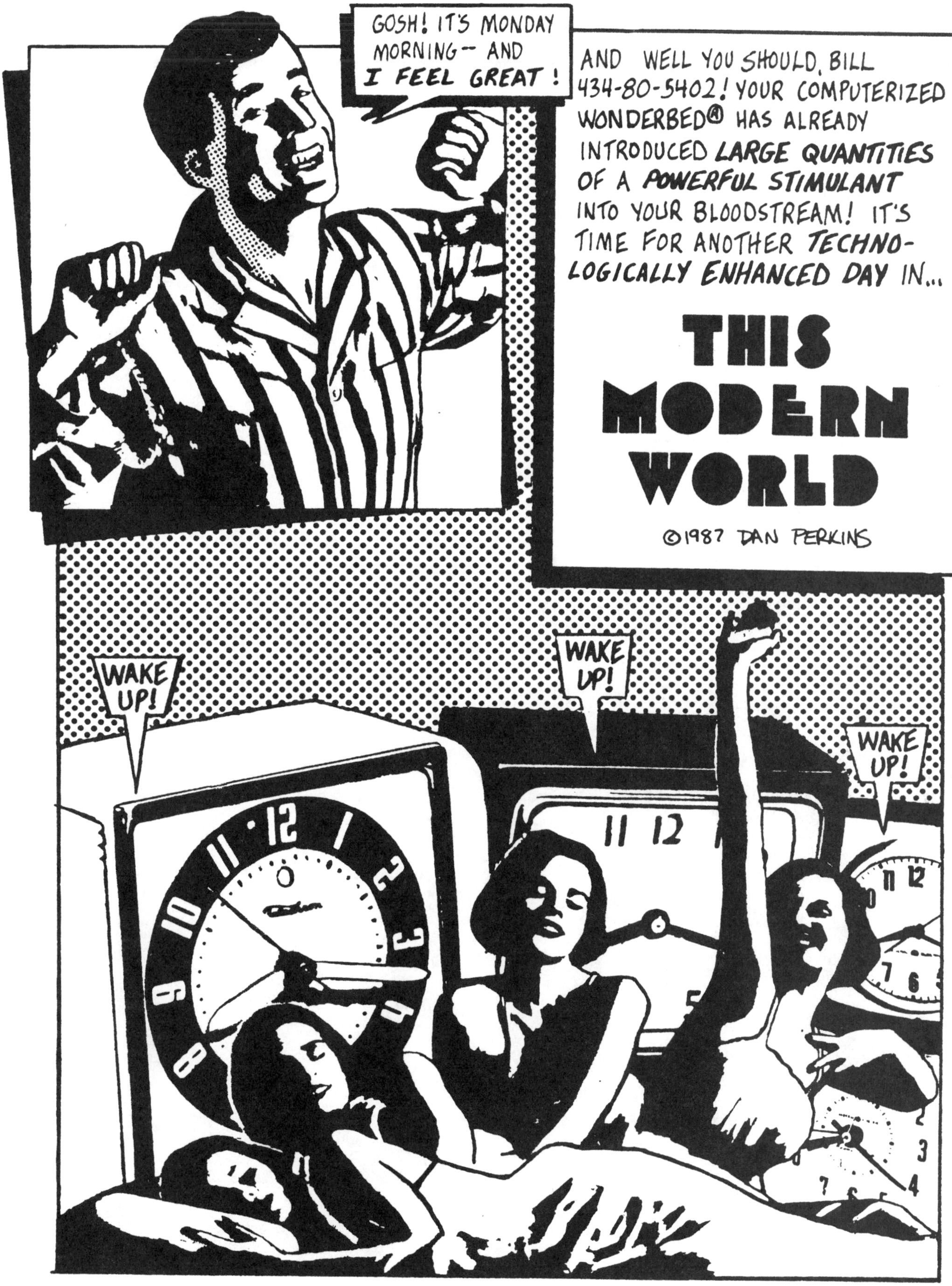

GOSH! IT'S MONDAY MORNING— AND I FEEL GREAT!
AND WELL YOU SHOULD, BILL 434-80-5402! YOUR COMPUTERIZED WONDERBED® HAS ALREADY INTRODUCED LARGE QUANTITIES OF A POWERFUL STIMULANT INTO YOUR BLOODSTREAM! IT'S TIME FOR ANOTHER TECHNOLOGICALLY ENHANCED DAY IN...
THIS MODERN WORLD
©1987 DAN PERKINS
WAKE UP!
WAKE UP!
WAKE UP!

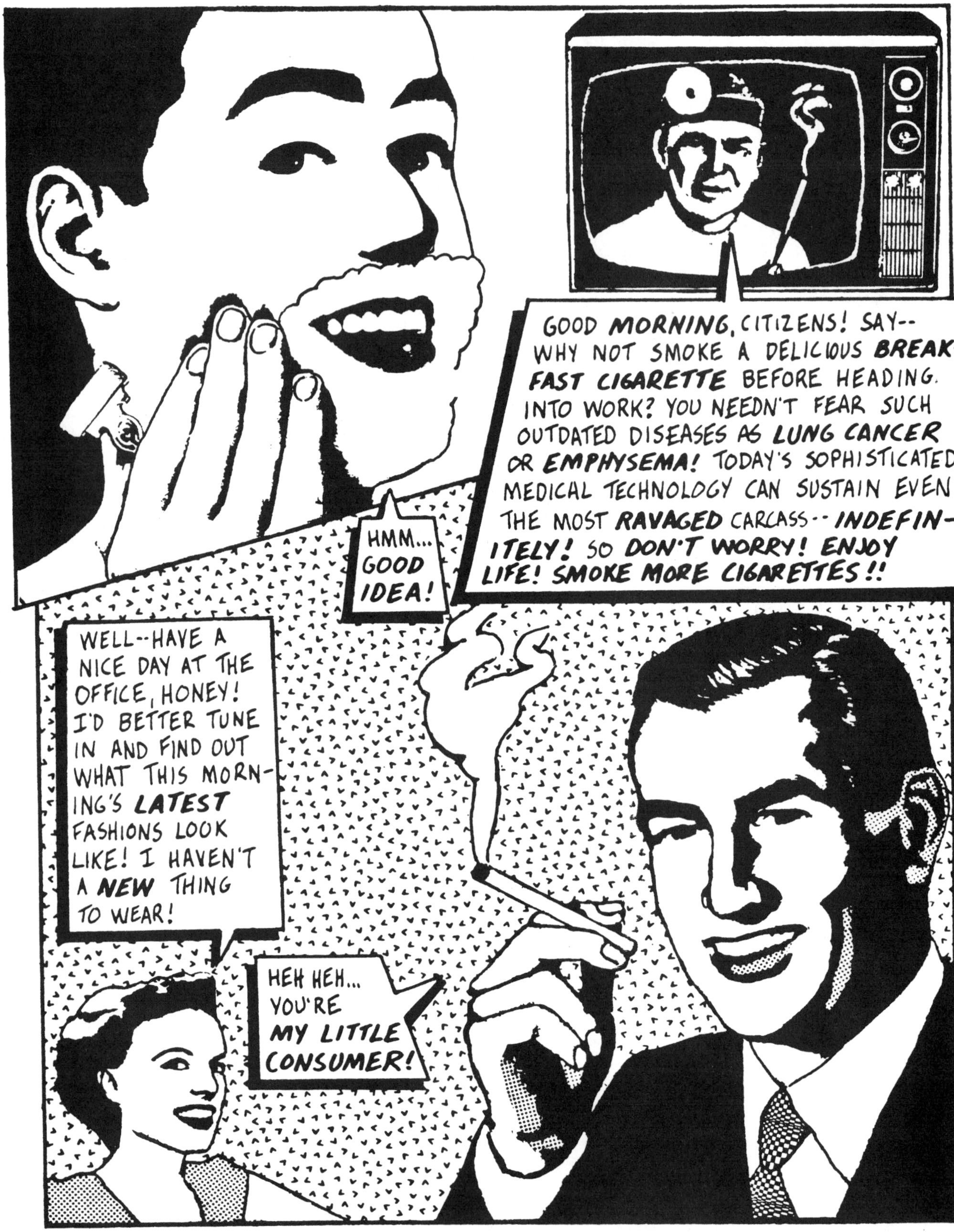
GOOD MORNING, CITIZENS! SAY-- WHY NOT SMOKE A DELICIOUS BREAKFAST CIGARETTE BEFORE HEADING INTO WORK? YOU NEEDN'T FEAR SUCH OUTDATED DISEASES AS LUNG CANCER OR EMPHYSEMA! TODAY'S SOPHISTICATED MEDICAL TECHNOLOGY CAN SUSTAIN EVEN THE MOST RAVAGED CARCASS-- INDEFINITELY! SO DON'T WORRY! ENJOY LIFE! SMOKE MORE CIGARETTES!!
HMM... GOOD IDEA!
WELL--HAVE A NICE DAY AT THE OFFICE, HONEY! I'D BETTER TUNE IN AND FIND OUT WHAT THIS MORNING'S LATEST FASHIONS LOOK LIKE! I HAVEN'T A NEW THING TO WEAR!
HEH HEH... YOU'RE MY LITTLE CONSUMER!

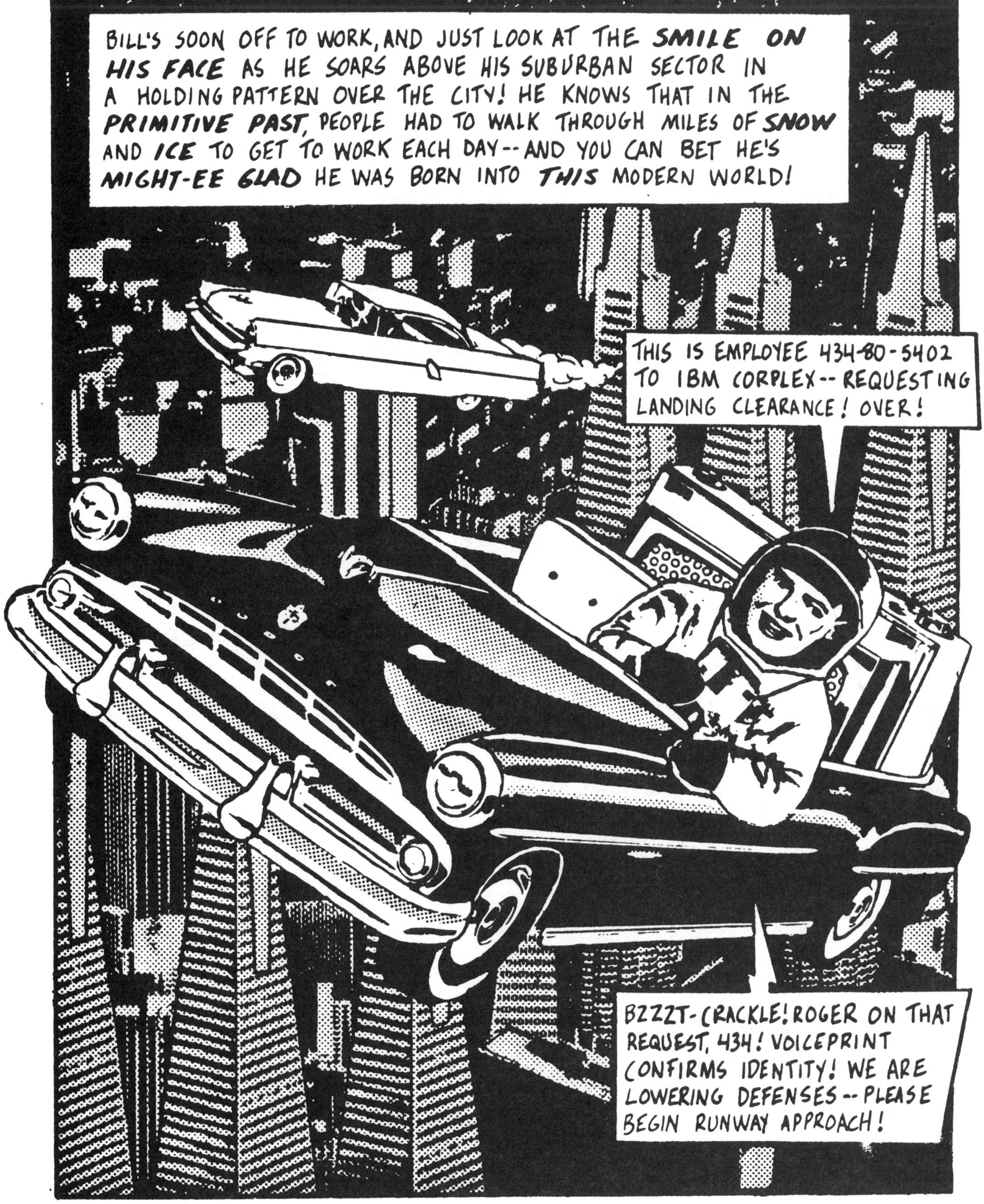
BILL'S SOON OFF TO WORK, AND JUST LOOK AT THE SMILE ON HIS FACE AS HE SOARS ABOVE HIS SUBURBAN SECTOR IN A HOLDING PATTERN OVER THE CITY! HE KNOWS THAT IN THE PRIMITIVE PAST, PEOPLE HAD TO WALK THROUGH MILES OF SNOW AND ICE TO GET TO WORK EACH DAY--AND YOU CAN BET HE'S MIGHT-EE GLAD HE WAS BORN INTO THIS MODERN WORLD!
THIS IS EMPLOYEE 434-80-5402 TO IBM CORPLEX--REQUESTING LANDING CLEARANCE! OVER!
BZZZT-CRACKLE! ROGER ON THAT REQUEST, 434! VOICEPRINT CONFIRMS IDENTITY! WE ARE LOWERING DEFENSES--PLEASE BEGIN RUNWAY APPROACH!

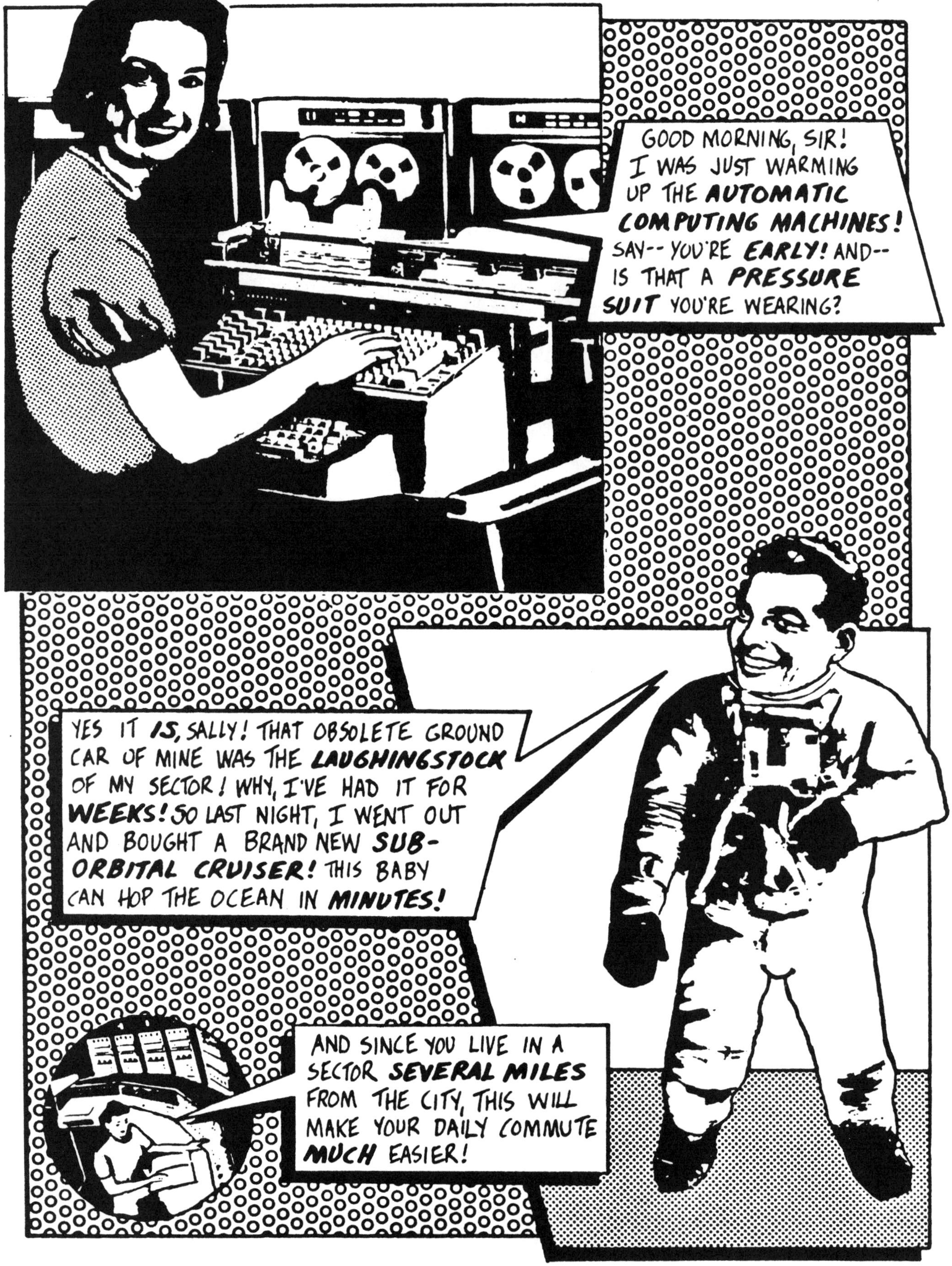
GOOD MORNING, SIR! I WAS JUST WARMING UP THE AUTOMATIC COMPUTING MACHINES! SAY-- YOU'RE EARLY! AND-- IS THAT A PRESSURE SUIT YOU'RE WEARING?
YES IT IS, SALLY! THAT OBSOLETE GROUND CAR OF MINE WAS THE LAUGHINGSTOCK OF MY SECTOR! WHY, I'VE HAD IT FOR WEEKS! SO LAST NIGHT, I WENT OUT AND BOUGHT A BRAND NEW SUB-ORBITAL CRUISER! THIS BABY CAN HOP THE OCEAN IN MINUTES!
AND SINCE YOU LIVE IN A SECTOR SEVERAL MILES FROM THE CITY, THIS WILL MAKE YOUR DAILY COMMUTE MUCH EASIER!

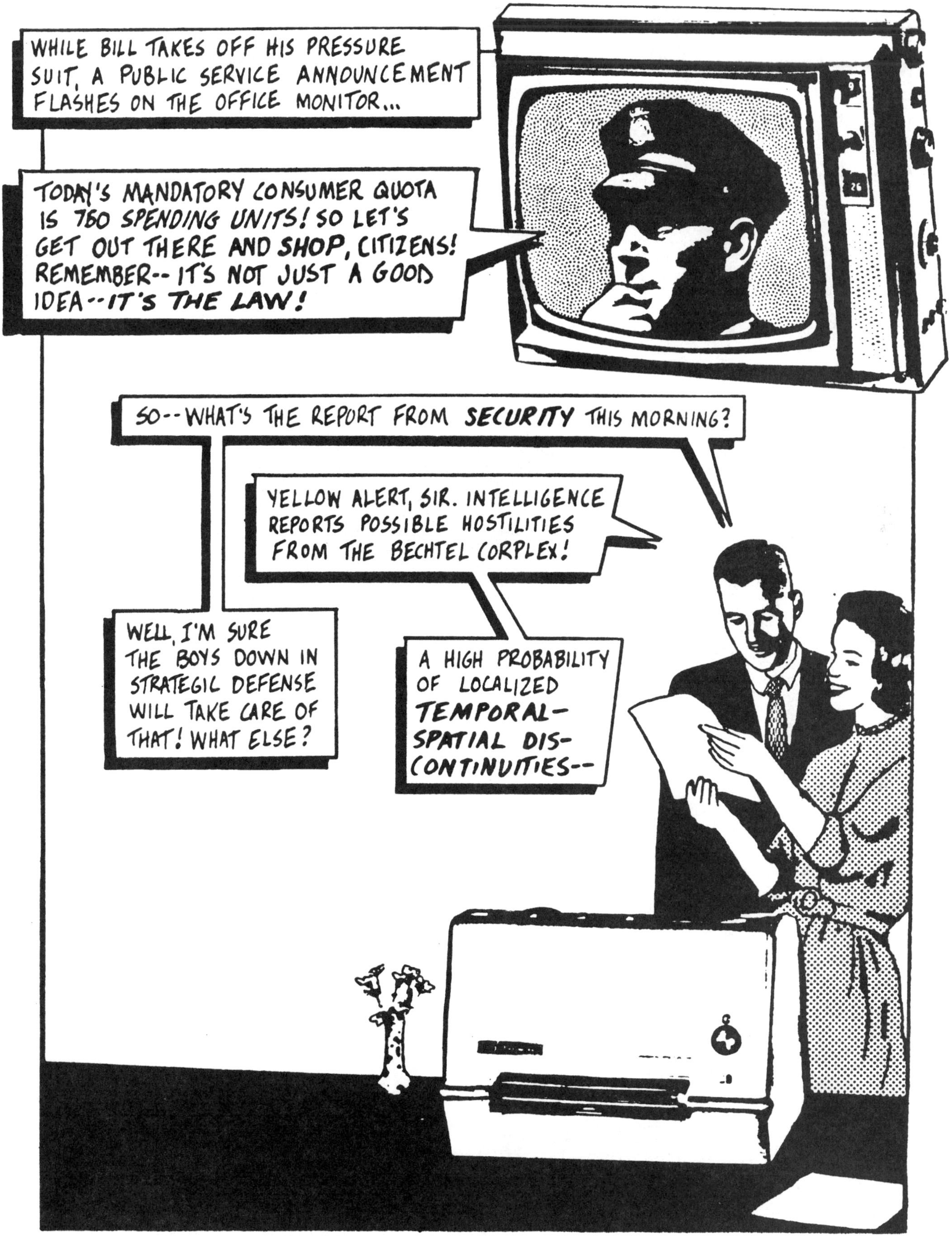
WHILE BILL TAKES OFF HIS PRESSURE SUIT, A PUBLIC SERVICE ANNOUNCEMENT FLASHES ON THE OFFICE MONITOR...
TODAY'S MANDATORY CONSUMER QUOTA IS 750 SPENDING UNITS! SO LET'S GET OUT THERE AND SHOP, CITIZENS! REMEMBER--IT'S NOT JUST A GOOD IDEA--IT'S THE LAW!
SO--WHAT'S THE REPORT FROM SECURITY THIS MORNING?
YELLOW ALERT, SIR. INTELLIGENCE REPORTS POSSIBLE HOSTILITIES FROM THE BECHTEL CORPLEX!
WELL, I'M SURE THE BOYS DOWN IN STRATEGIC DEFENSE WILL TAKE CARE OF THAT! WHAT ELSE?
A HIGH PROBABILITY OF LOCALIZED TEMPORAL-SPATIAL DIS-CONTINUITIES--

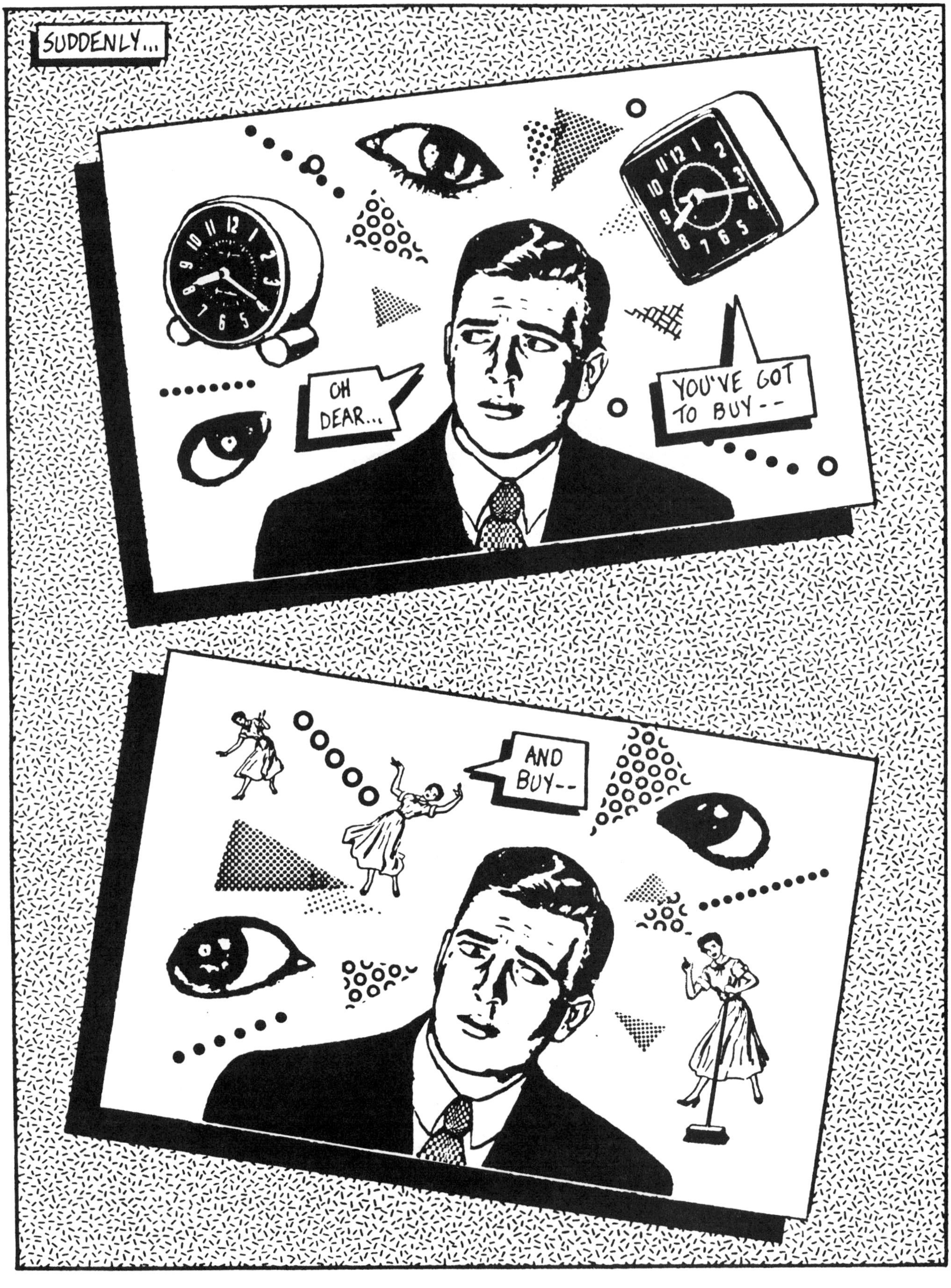
SUDDENLY...
OH DEAR...
YOU'VE GOT TO BUY--
AND BUY--

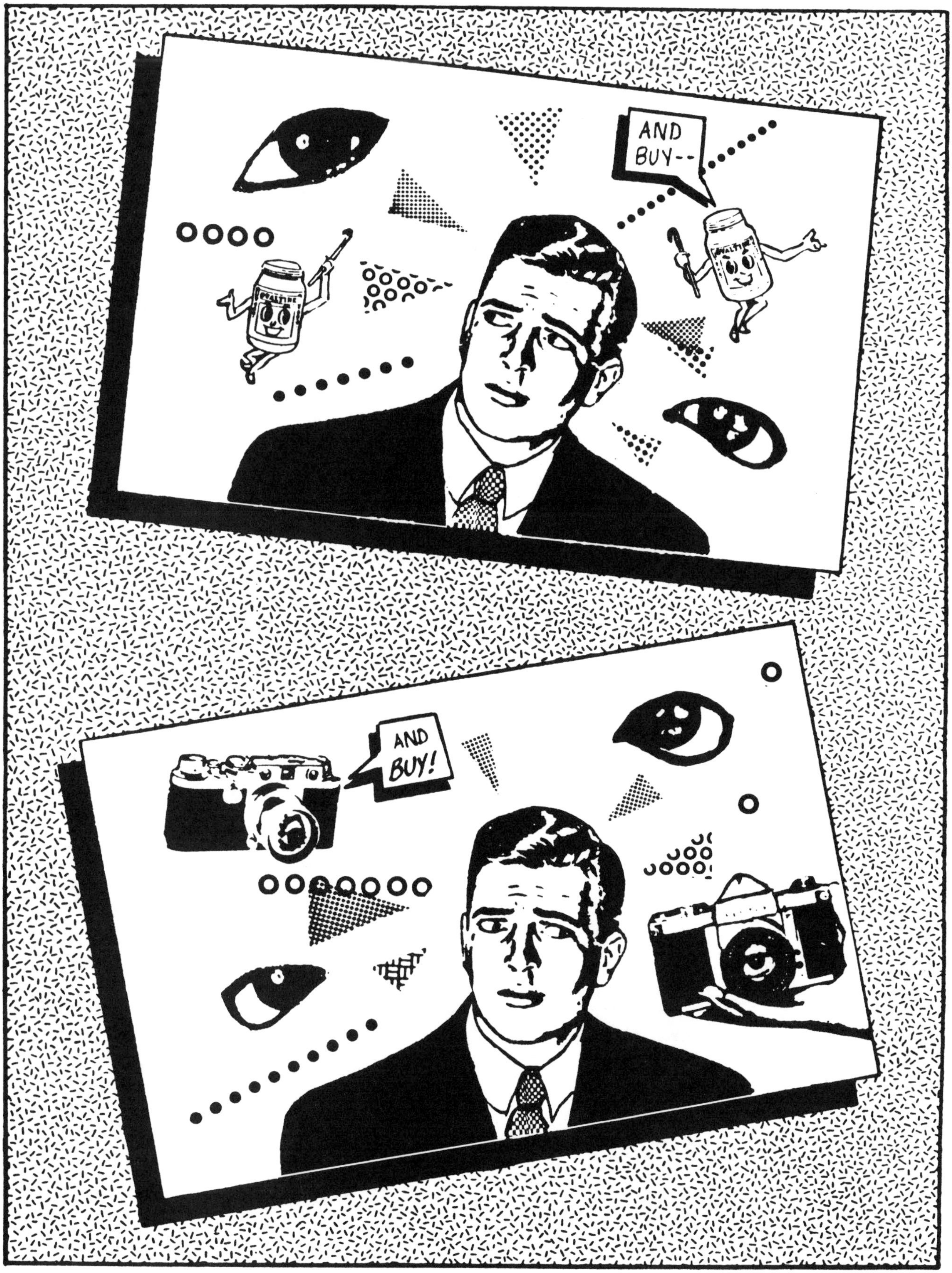
AND BUY--
AND BUY!

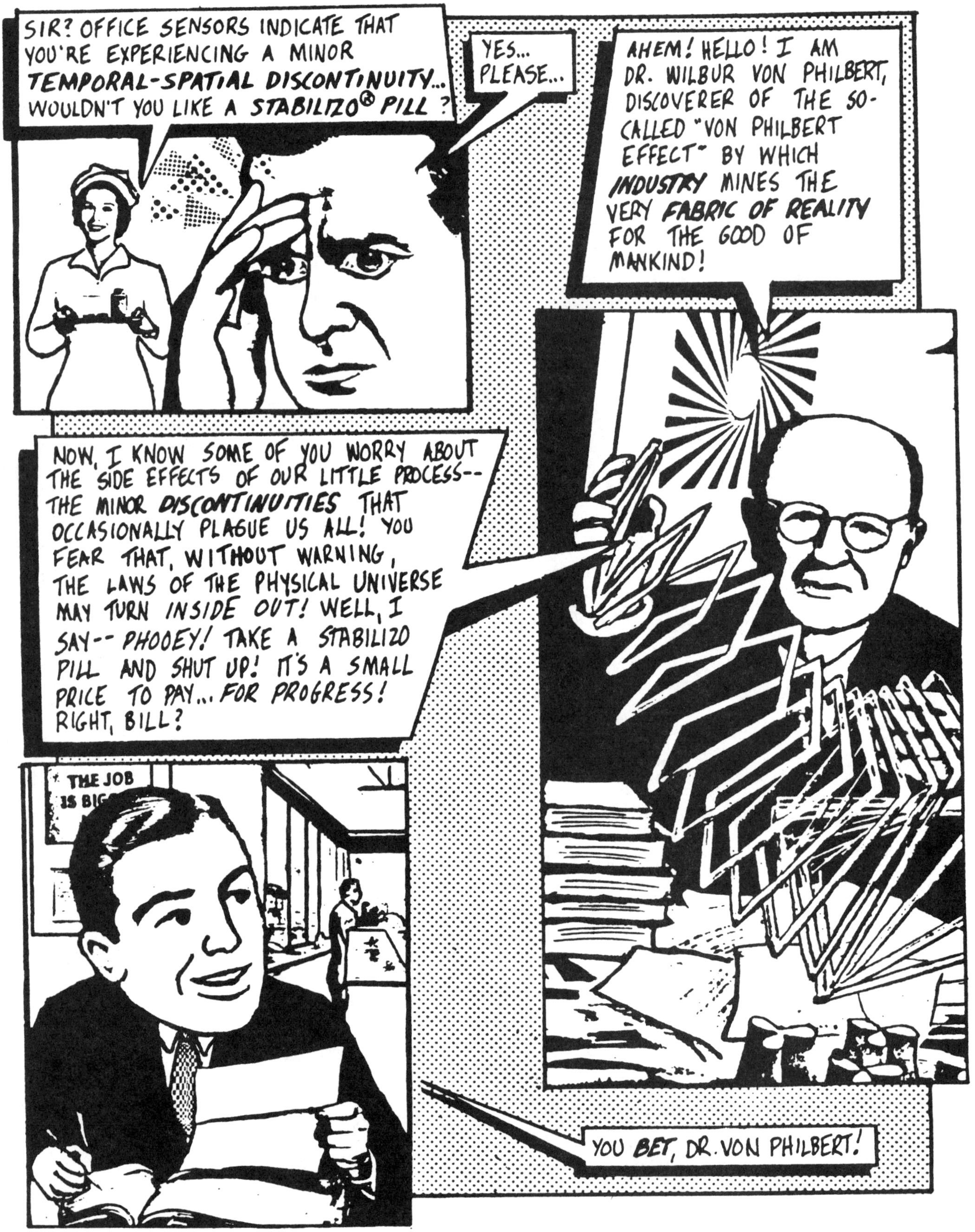
SIR? OFFICE SENSORS INDICATE THAT YOU'RE EXPERIENCING A MINOR TEMPORAL-SPATIAL DISCONTINUITY... WOULDN'T YOU LIKE A STABILIZO® PILL ?
YES... PLEASE...
AHEM! HELLO! I AM DR. WILBUR VON PHILBERT, DISCOVERER OF THE SO-CALLED "VON PHILBERT EFFECT" BY WHICH INDUSTRY MINES THE VERY FABRIC OF REALITY FOR THE GOOD OF MANKIND!
NOW, I KNOW SOME OF YOU WORRY ABOUT THE SIDE EFFECTS OF OUR LITTLE PROCESS-- THE MINOR DISCONTINUITIES THAT OCCASIONALLY PLAGUE US ALL! YOU FEAR THAT, WITHOUT WARNING, THE LAWS OF THE PHYSICAL UNIVERSE MAY TURN INSIDE OUT! WELL, I SAY-- PHOOEY! TAKE A STABILIZO PILL AND SHUT UP! IT'S A SMALL PRICE TO PAY... FOR PROGRESS! RIGHT, BILL?
THE JOB IS BIG
YOU BET, DR. VON PHILBERT!

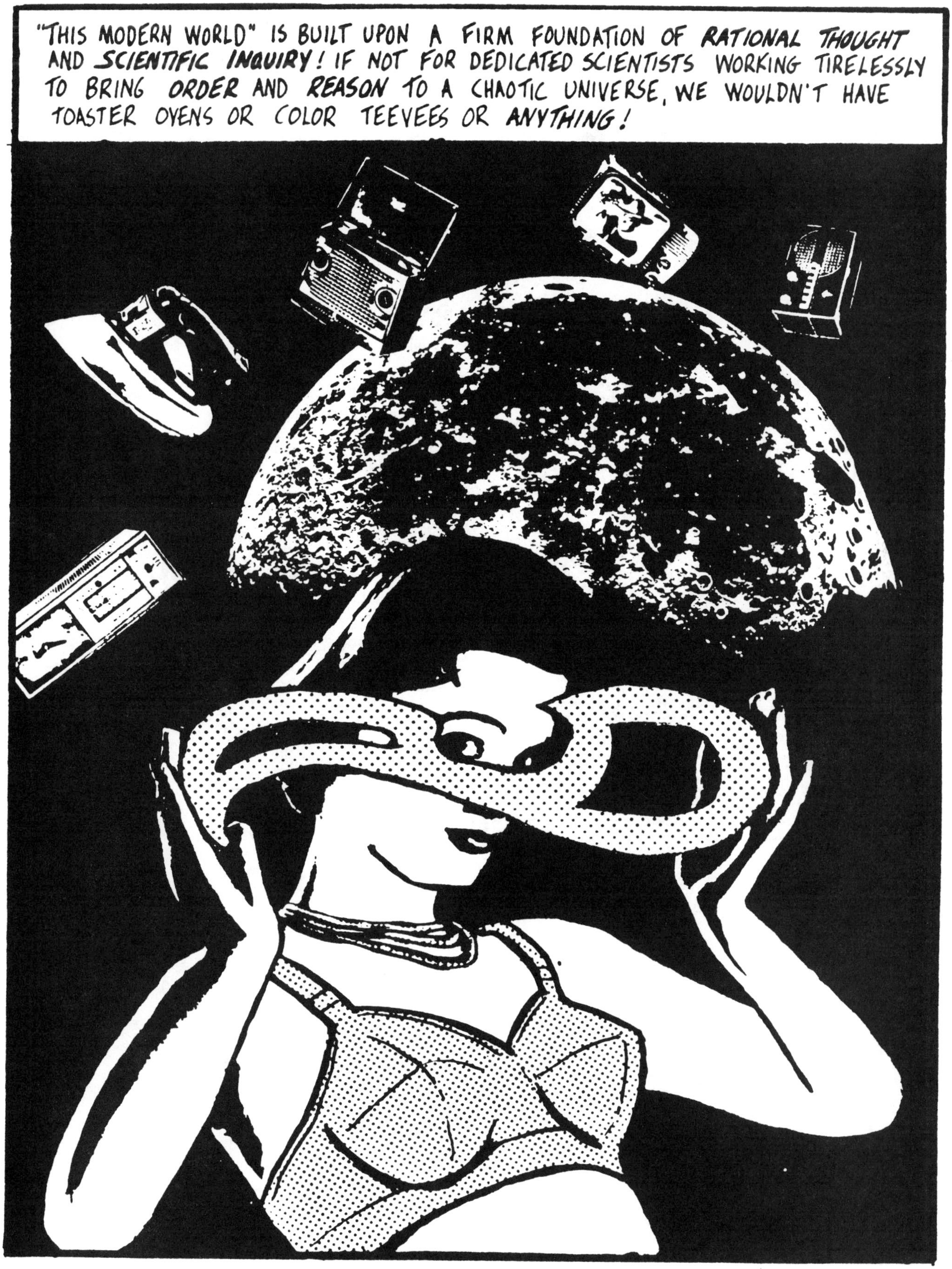
"THIS MODERN WORLD" IS BUILT UPON A FIRM FOUNDATION OF *RATIONAL THOUGHT* AND *SCIENTIFIC INQUIRY!* IF NOT FOR DEDICATED SCIENTISTS WORKING TIRELESSLY TO BRING *ORDER* AND *REASON* TO A CHAOTIC UNIVERSE, WE WOULDN'T HAVE TOASTER OVENS OR COLOR TEEVEES OR *ANYTHING!*

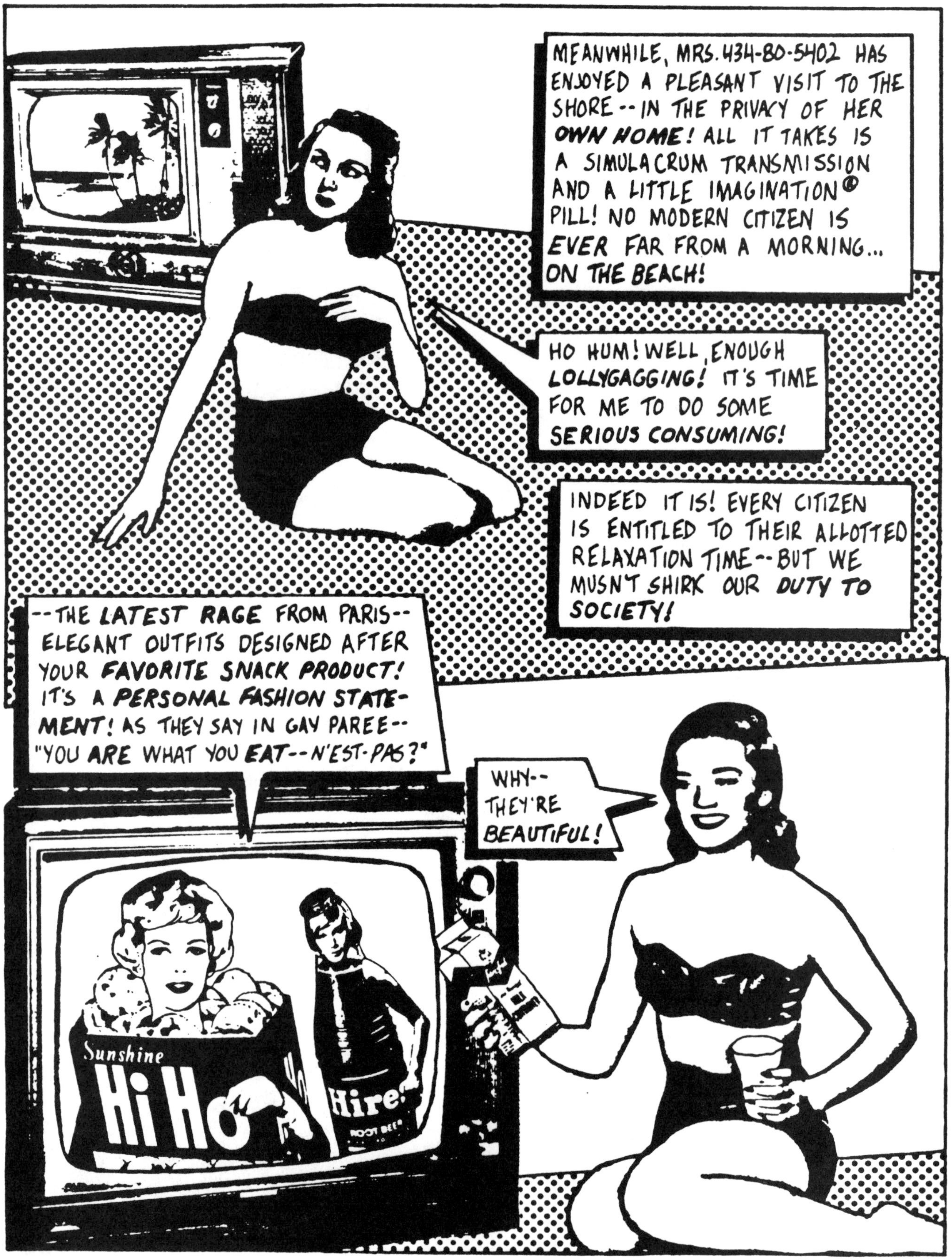
MEANWHILE, MRS. 434-80-5402 HAS ENJOYED A PLEASANT VISIT TO THE SHORE -- IN THE PRIVACY OF HER OWN HOME! ALL IT TAKES IS A SIMULACRUM TRANSMISSION AND A LITTLE IMAGINATION® PILL! NO MODERN CITIZEN IS EVER FAR FROM A MORNING... ON THE BEACH!
HO HUM! WELL, ENOUGH LOLLYGAGGING! IT'S TIME FOR ME TO DO SOME SERIOUS CONSUMING!
INDEED IT IS! EVERY CITIZEN IS ENTITLED TO THEIR ALLOTTED RELAXATION TIME -- BUT WE MUSN'T SHIRK OUR DUTY TO SOCIETY!
-- THE LATEST RAGE FROM PARIS -- ELEGANT OUTFITS DESIGNED AFTER YOUR FAVORITE SNACK PRODUCT! IT'S A PERSONAL FASHION STATEMENT! AS THEY SAY IN GAY PAREE -- "YOU ARE WHAT YOU EAT -- N'EST-PAS?"
WHY -- THEY'RE BEAUTIFUL!
Sunshine
Hi Ho
Hires
ROOT BEER

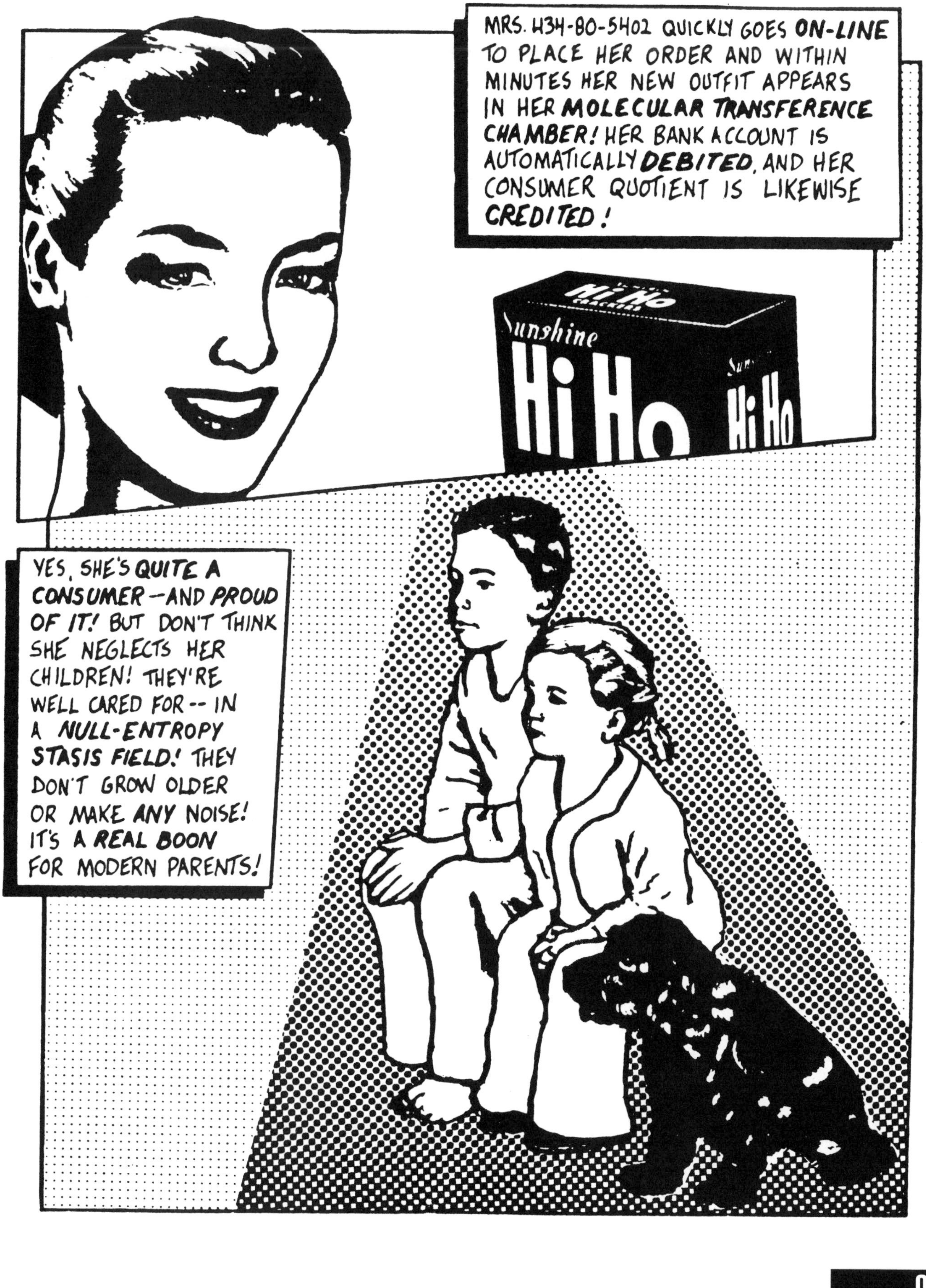
MRS. H34-80-5402 QUICKLY GOES **ON-LINE** TO PLACE HER ORDER AND WITHIN MINUTES HER NEW OUTFIT APPEARS IN HER **MOLECULAR TRANSFERENCE CHAMBER!** HER BANK ACCOUNT IS AUTOMATICALLY **DEBITED**, AND HER CONSUMER QUOTIENT IS LIKEWISE **CREDITED!**
Sunshine Hi Ho
Hi Ho
YES, SHE'S **QUITE A CONSUMER**--AND **PROUD OF IT!** BUT DON'T THINK SHE NEGLECTS HER CHILDREN! THEY'RE WELL CARED FOR-- IN A **NULL-ENTROPY STASIS FIELD!** THEY DON'T GROW OLDER OR MAKE **ANY** NOISE! IT'S **A REAL BOON** FOR MODERN PARENTS!

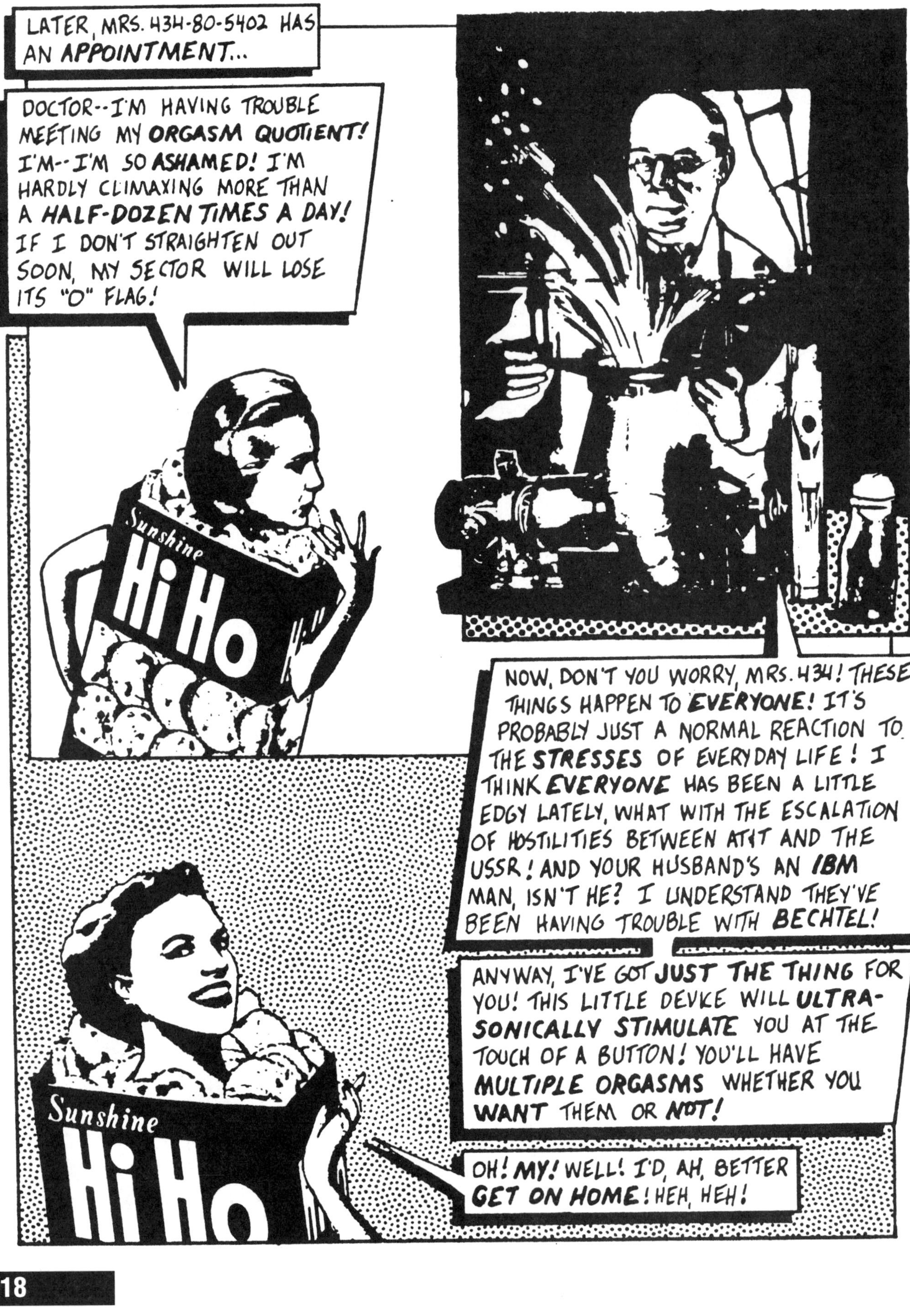

LATER, MRS. 434-80-5402 HAS AN APPOINTMENT...
DOCTOR--I'M HAVING TROUBLE MEETING MY ORGASM QUOTIENT! I'M--I'M SO ASHAMED! I'M HARDLY CLIMAXING MORE THAN A HALF-DOZEN TIMES A DAY! IF I DON'T STRAIGHTEN OUT SOON, MY SECTOR WILL LOSE ITS "O" FLAG!
Sunshine Hi Ho
NOW, DON'T YOU WORRY, MRS. 434! THESE THINGS HAPPEN TO EVERYONE! IT'S PROBABLY JUST A NORMAL REACTION TO THE STRESSES OF EVERYDAY LIFE! I THINK EVERYONE HAS BEEN A LITTLE EDGY LATELY, WHAT WITH THE ESCALATION OF HOSTILITIES BETWEEN AT&T AND THE USSR! AND YOUR HUSBAND'S AN IBM MAN, ISN'T HE? I UNDERSTAND THEY'VE BEEN HAVING TROUBLE WITH BECHTEL!
ANYWAY, I'VE GOT JUST THE THING FOR YOU! THIS LITTLE DEVICE WILL ULTRA-SONICALLY STIMULATE YOU AT THE TOUCH OF A BUTTON! YOU'LL HAVE MULTIPLE ORGASMS WHETHER YOU WANT THEM OR NOT!
Sunshine Hi Ho
OH! MY! WELL! I'D, AH, BETTER GET ON HOME! HEH, HEH!

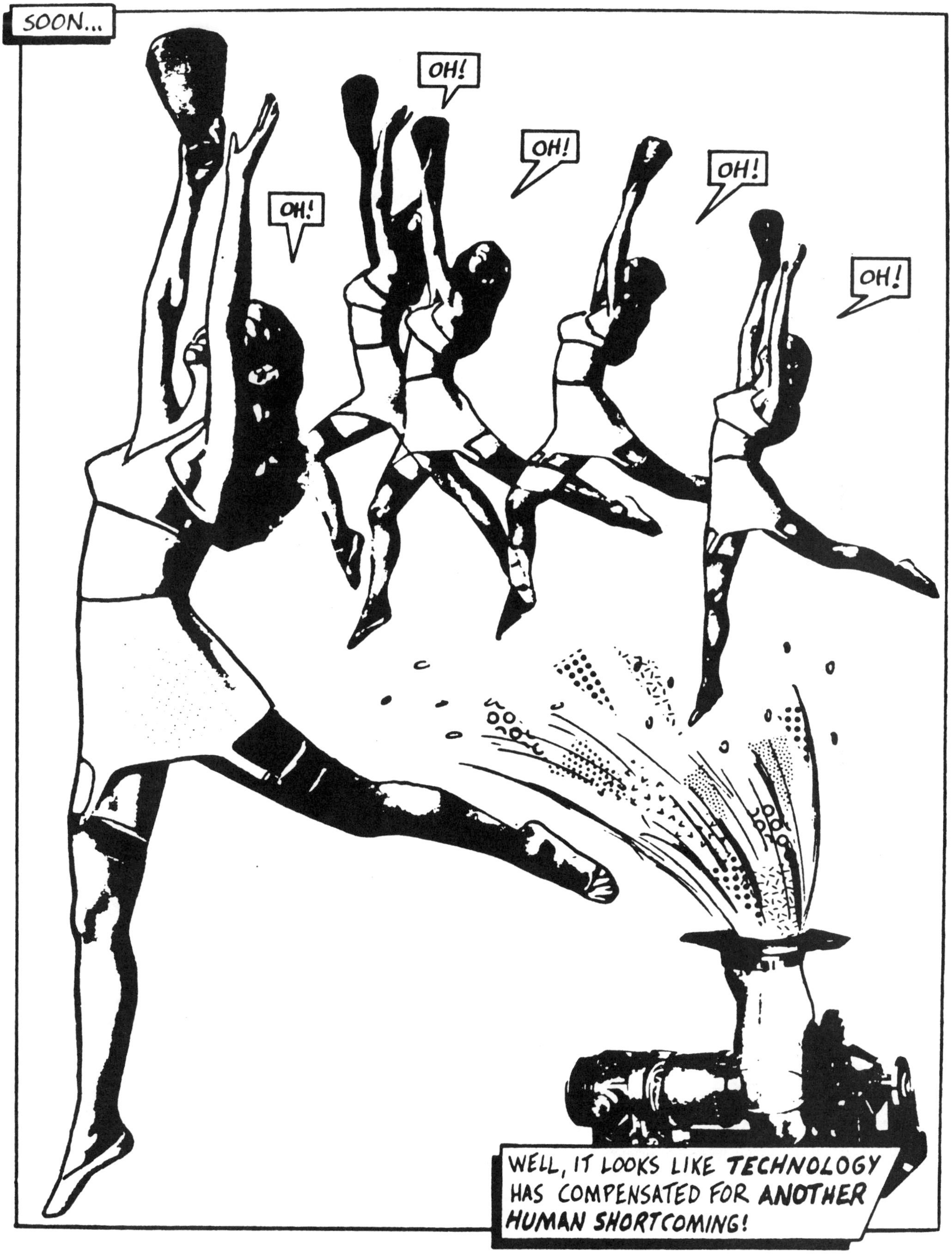
SOON...
OH!
OH!
OH!
OH!
OH!
WELL, IT LOOKS LIKE TECHNOLOGY HAS COMPENSATED FOR ANOTHER HUMAN SHORTCOMING!

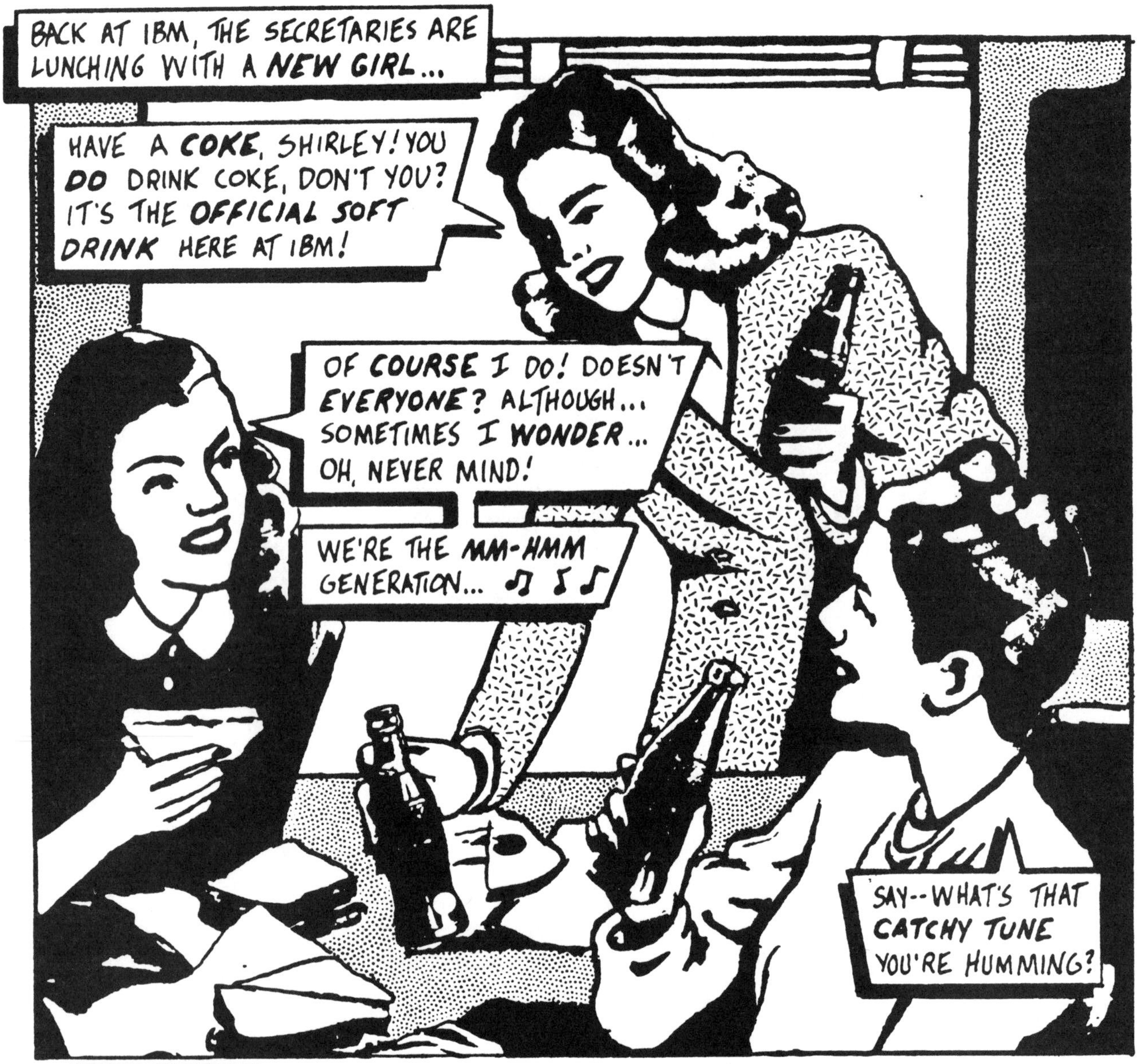
BACK AT IBM, THE SECRETARIES ARE LUNCHING WITH A NEW GIRL...
HAVE A COKE, SHIRLEY! YOU DO DRINK COKE, DON'T YOU? IT'S THE OFFICIAL SOFT DRINK HERE AT IBM!
OF COURSE I DO! DOESN'T EVERYONE? ALTHOUGH... SOMETIMES I WONDER... OH, NEVER MIND!
WE'RE THE MM-HMM GENERATION... ♫ ♪ ♪
SAY--WHAT'S THAT CATCHY TUNE YOU'RE HUMMING?

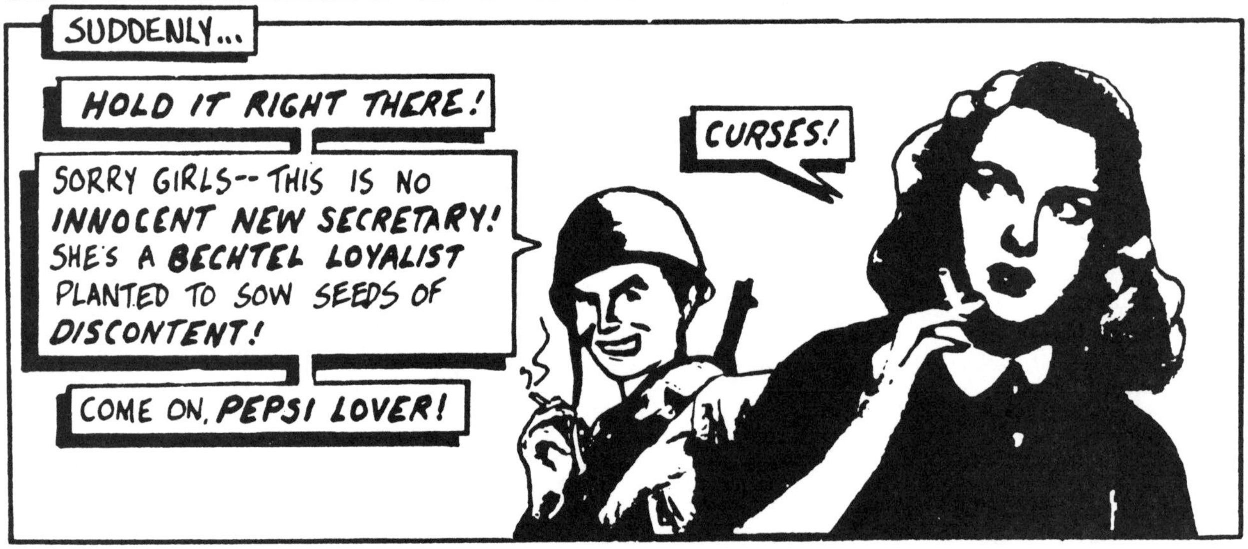
SUDDENLY...
HOLD IT RIGHT THERE!
SORRY GIRLS-- THIS IS NO INNOCENT NEW SECRETARY! SHE'S A BECHTEL LOYALIST PLANTED TO SOW SEEDS OF DISCONTENT!
COME ON, PEPSI LOVER!
CURSES!

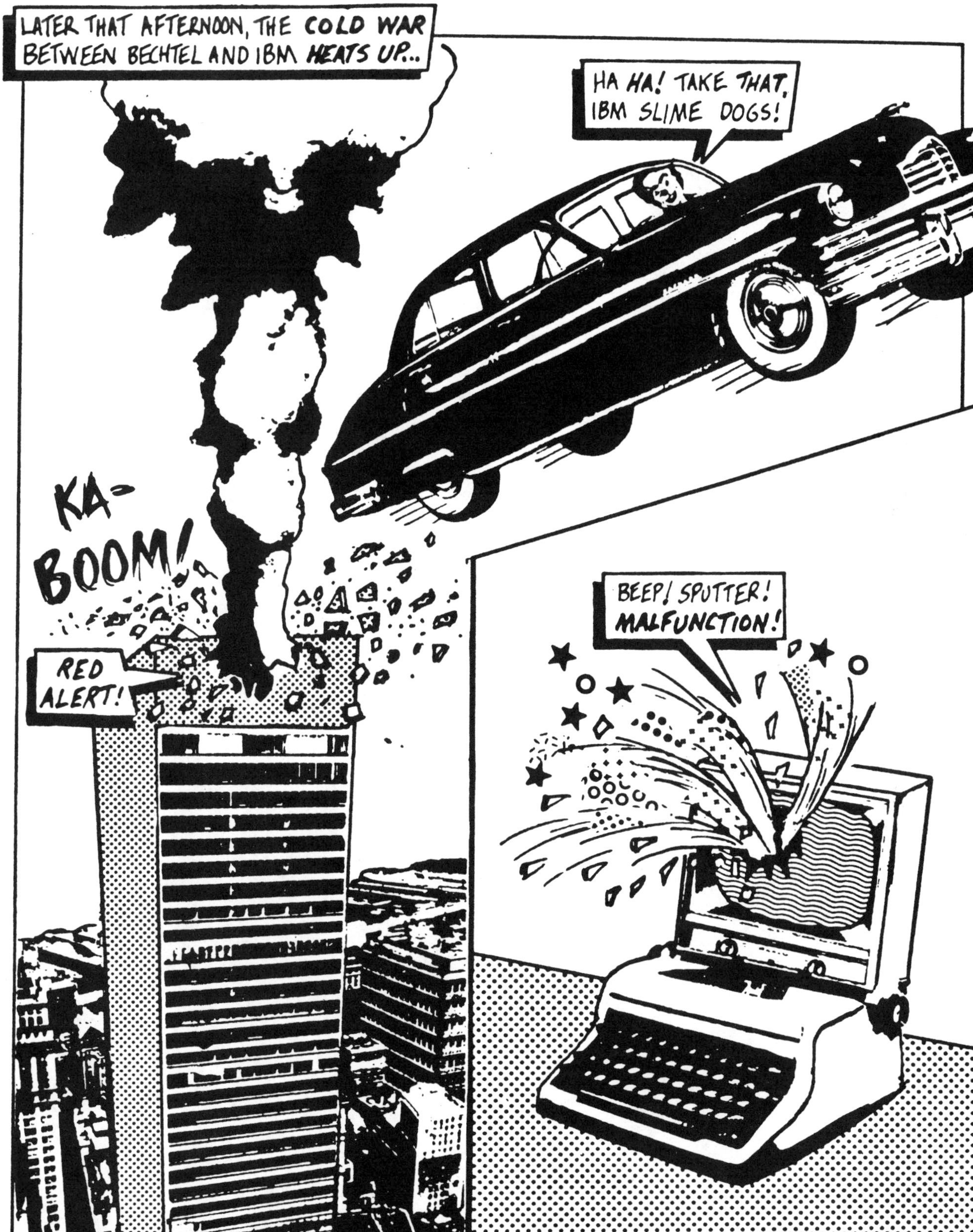

LATER THAT AFTERNOON, THE COLD WAR BETWEEN BECHTEL AND IBM HEATS UP...
HA HA! TAKE THAT, IBM SLIME DOGS!
KA-BOOM!
RED ALERT!
BEEP! SPUTTER! MALFUNCTION!

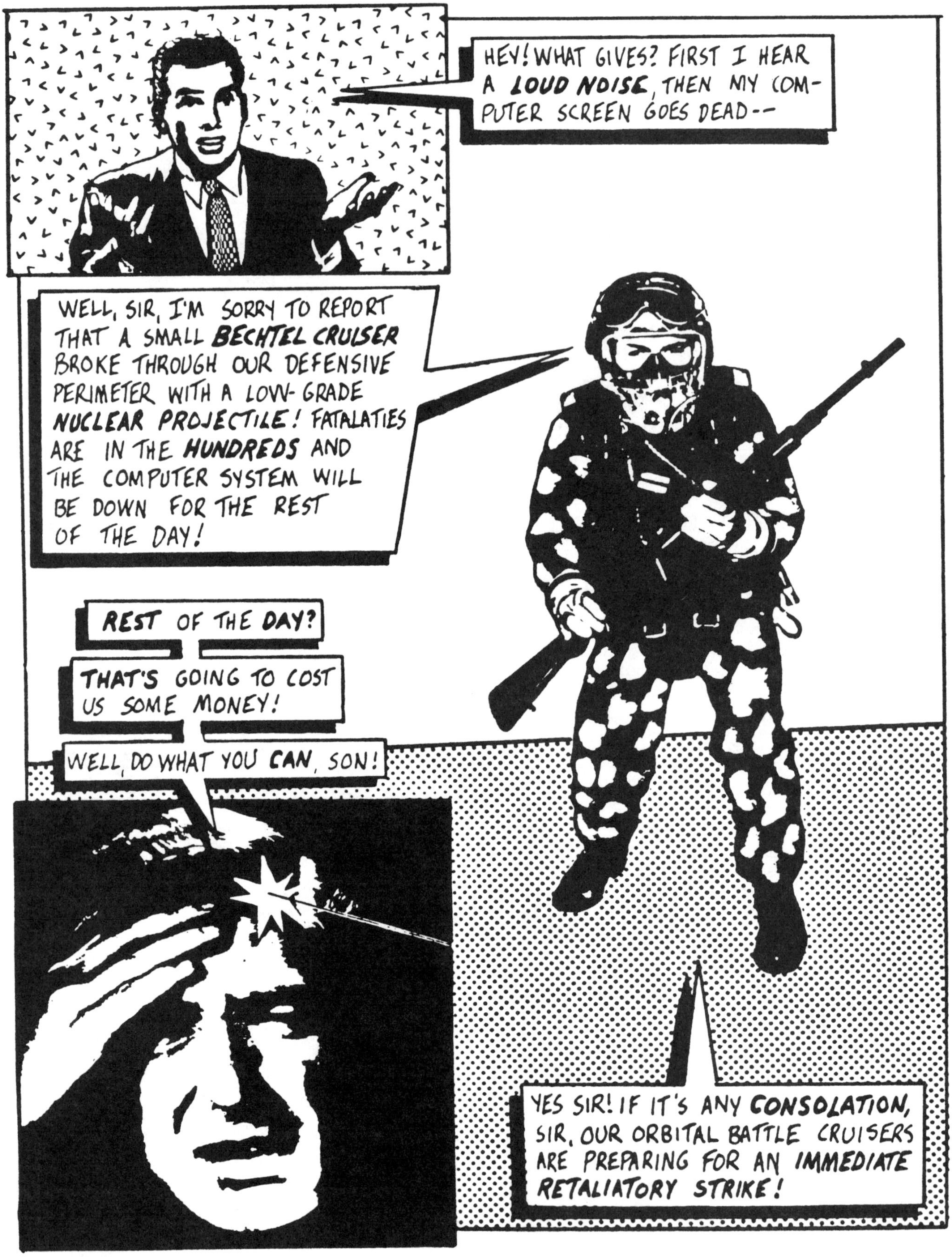
HEY! WHAT GIVES? FIRST I HEAR A LOUD NOISE, THEN MY COMPUTER SCREEN GOES DEAD--
WELL, SIR, I'M SORRY TO REPORT THAT A SMALL BECHTEL CRUISER BROKE THROUGH OUR DEFENSIVE PERIMETER WITH A LOW-GRADE NUCLEAR PROJECTILE! FATALATIES ARE IN THE HUNDREDS AND THE COMPUTER SYSTEM WILL BE DOWN FOR THE REST OF THE DAY!
REST OF THE DAY?
THAT'S GOING TO COST US SOME MONEY!
WELL, DO WHAT YOU CAN, SON!
YES SIR! IF IT'S ANY CONSOLATION, SIR, OUR ORBITAL BATTLE CRUISERS ARE PREPARING FOR AN IMMEDIATE RETALIATORY STRIKE!

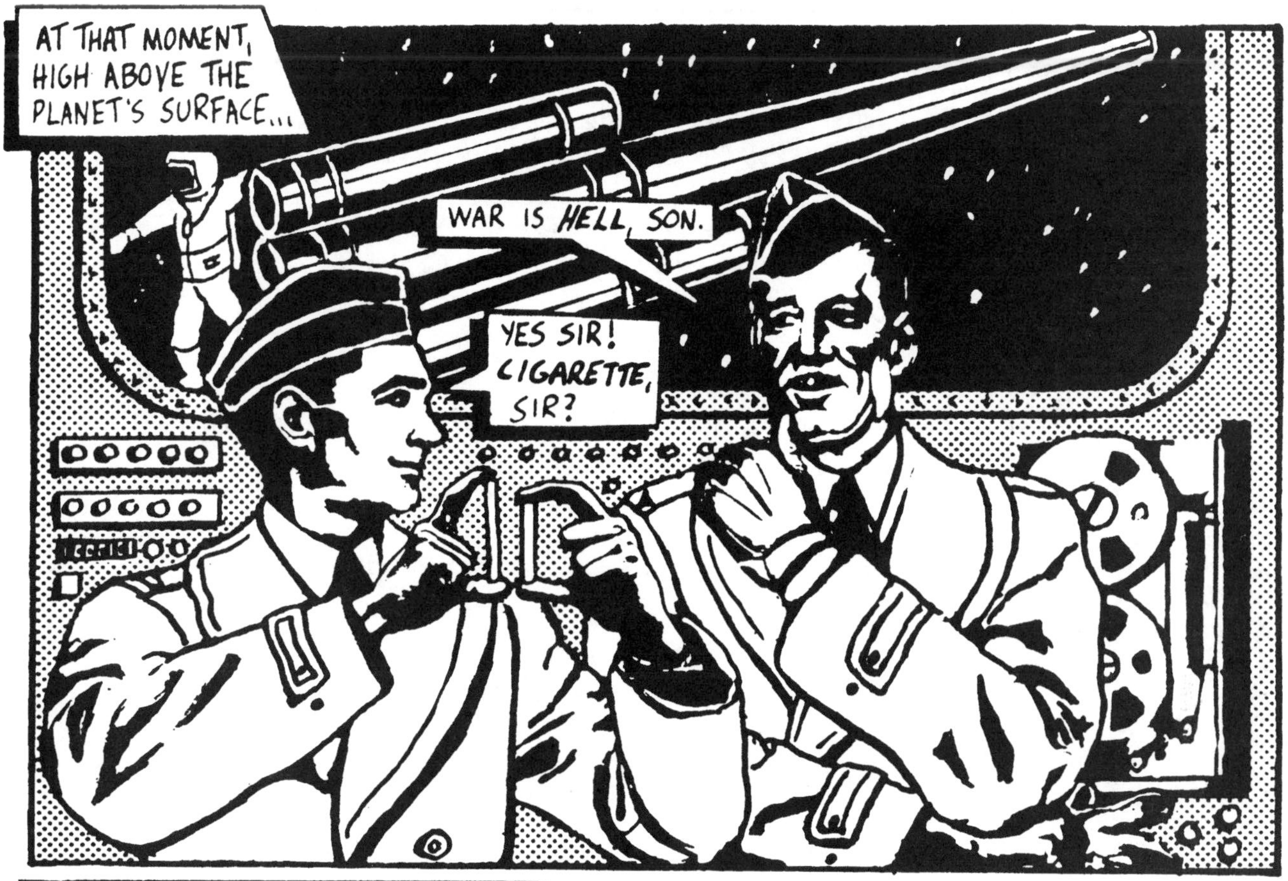
AT THAT MOMENT, HIGH ABOVE THE PLANET'S SURFACE...
WAR IS HELL, SON.
YES SIR! CIGARETTE, SIR?

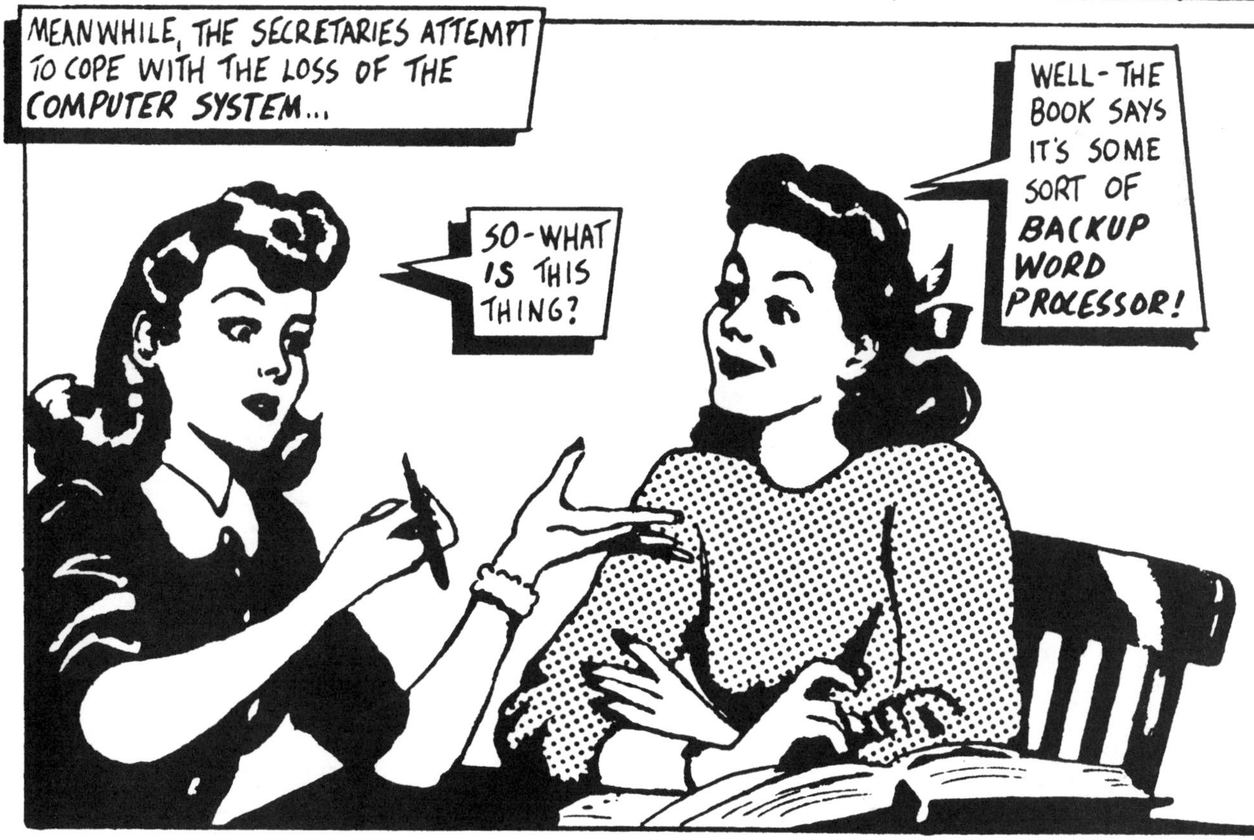
MEANWHILE, THE SECRETARIES ATTEMPT TO COPE WITH THE LOSS OF THE COMPUTER SYSTEM...
SO-WHAT IS THIS THING?
WELL-THE BOOK SAYS IT'S SOME SORT OF BACKUP WORD PROCESSOR!

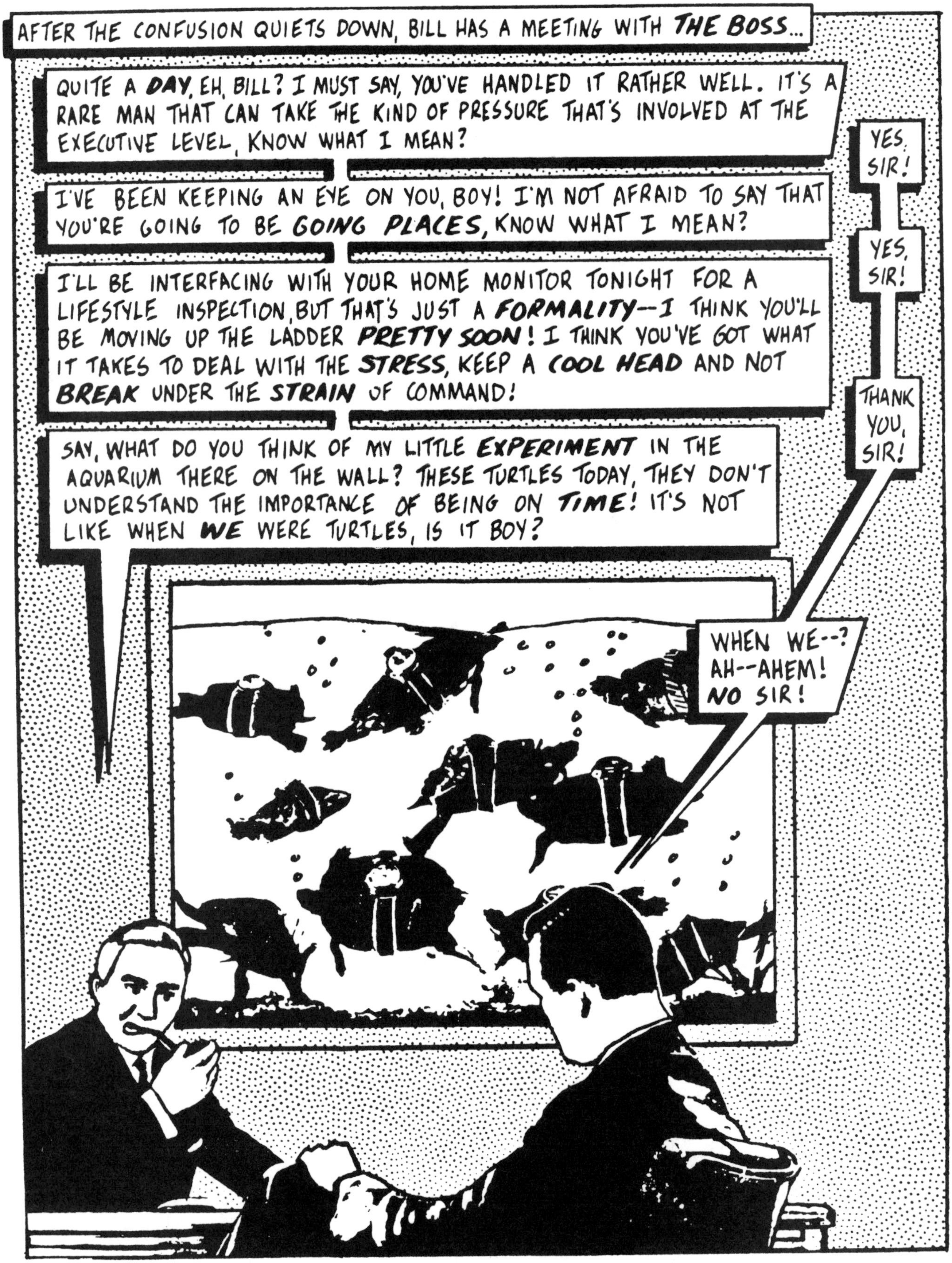
AFTER THE CONFUSION QUIETS DOWN, BILL HAS A MEETING WITH THE BOSS...
QUITE A DAY, EH, BILL? I MUST SAY, YOU'VE HANDLED IT RATHER WELL. IT'S A RARE MAN THAT CAN TAKE THE KIND OF PRESSURE THAT'S INVOLVED AT THE EXECUTIVE LEVEL, KNOW WHAT I MEAN?
YES, SIR!
I'VE BEEN KEEPING AN EYE ON YOU, BOY! I'M NOT AFRAID TO SAY THAT YOU'RE GOING TO BE GOING PLACES, KNOW WHAT I MEAN?
YES, SIR!
I'LL BE INTERFACING WITH YOUR HOME MONITOR TONIGHT FOR A LIFESTYLE INSPECTION, BUT THAT'S JUST A FORMALITY--I THINK YOU'LL BE MOVING UP THE LADDER PRETTY SOON! I THINK YOU'VE GOT WHAT IT TAKES TO DEAL WITH THE STRESS, KEEP A COOL HEAD AND NOT BREAK UNDER THE STRAIN OF COMMAND!
THANK YOU, SIR!
SAY, WHAT DO YOU THINK OF MY LITTLE EXPERIMENT IN THE AQUARIUM THERE ON THE WALL? THESE TURTLES TODAY, THEY DON'T UNDERSTAND THE IMPORTANCE OF BEING ON TIME! IT'S NOT LIKE WHEN WE WERE TURTLES, IS IT BOY?
WHEN WE--? AH--AHEM! NO SIR!

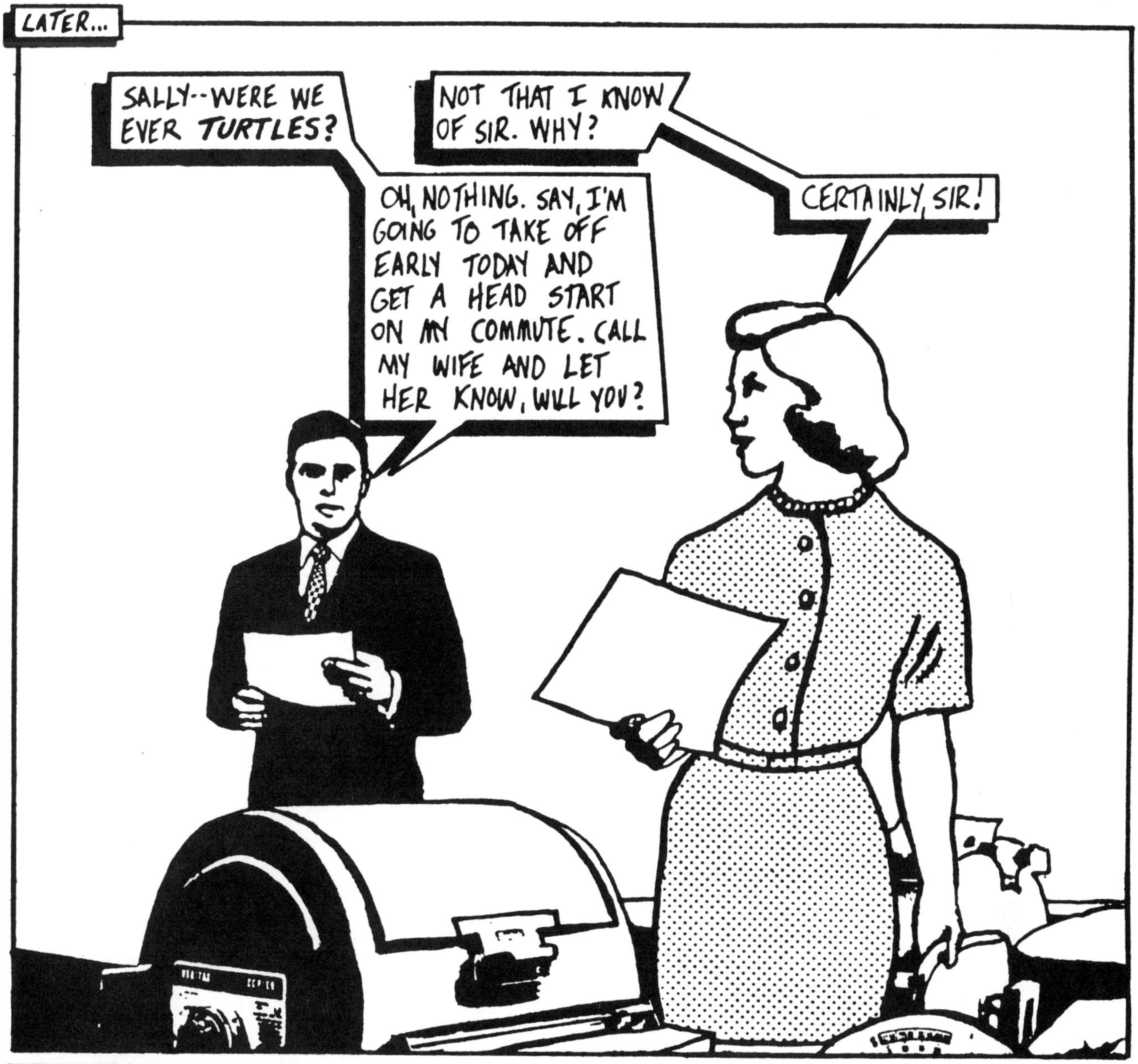
LATER...
SALLY--WERE WE EVER TURTLES?
NOT THAT I KNOW OF SIR. WHY?
OH, NOTHING. SAY, I'M GOING TO TAKE OFF EARLY TODAY AND GET A HEAD START ON MY COMMUTE. CALL MY WIFE AND LET HER KNOW, WILL YOU?
CERTAINLY, SIR!

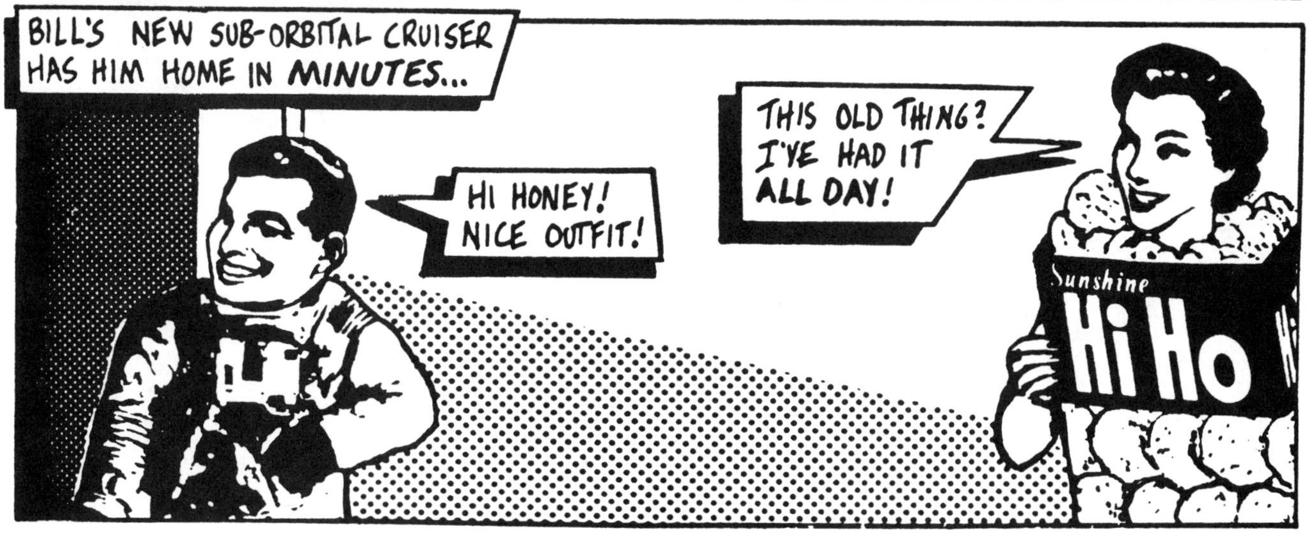
BILL'S NEW SUB-ORBITAL CRUISER HAS HIM HOME IN MINUTES...
HI HONEY! NICE OUTFIT!
THIS OLD THING? I'VE HAD IT ALL DAY!
Sunshine
Hi Ho

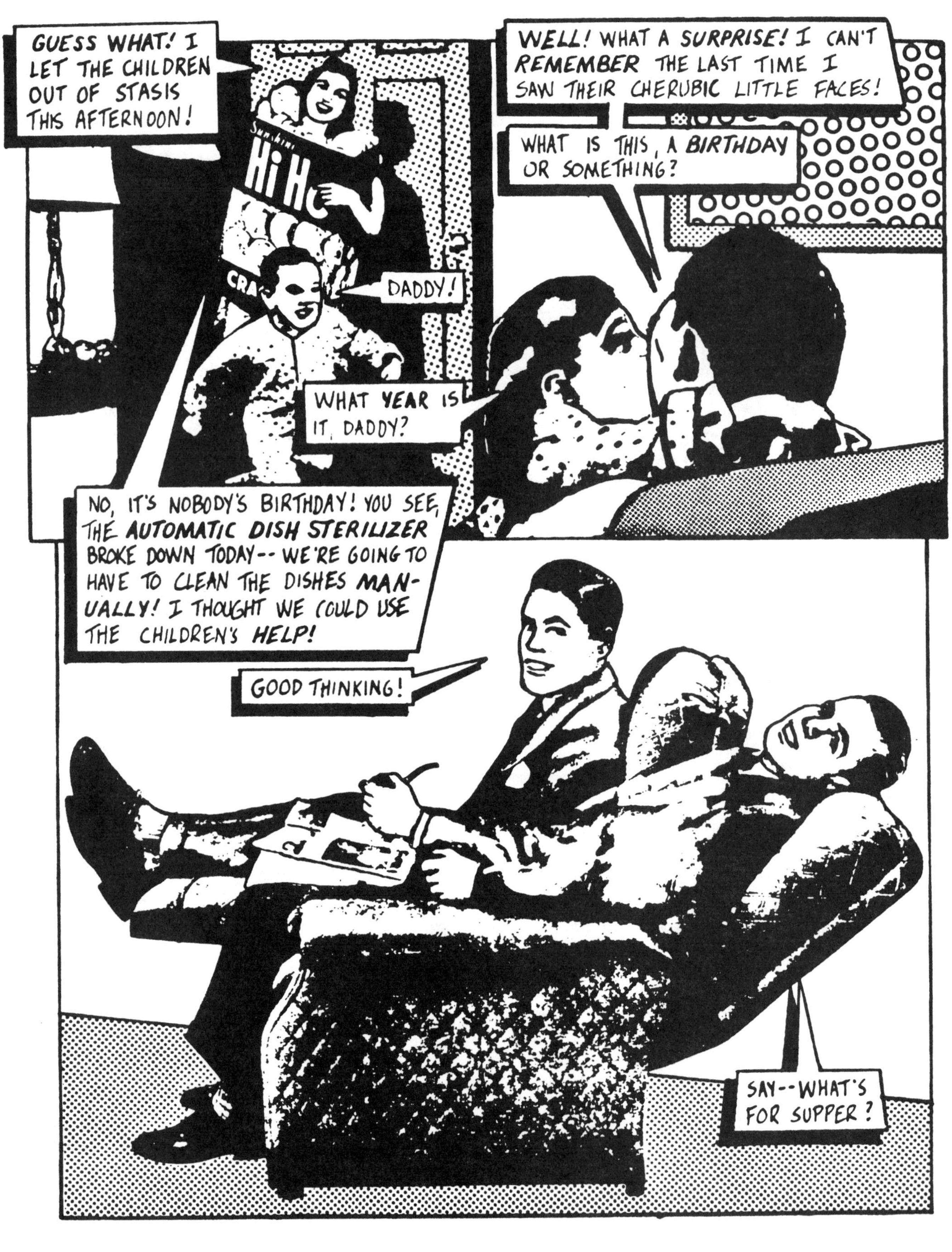
GUESS WHAT! I LET THE CHILDREN OUT OF STASIS THIS AFTERNOON!
WELL! WHAT A SURPRISE! I CAN'T REMEMBER THE LAST TIME I SAW THEIR CHERUBIC LITTLE FACES!
WHAT IS THIS, A BIRTHDAY OR SOMETHING?
DADDY!
WHAT YEAR IS IT, DADDY?
NO, IT'S NOBODY'S BIRTHDAY! YOU SEE, THE AUTOMATIC DISH STERILIZER BROKE DOWN TODAY-- WE'RE GOING TO HAVE TO CLEAN THE DISHES MAN-UALLY! I THOUGHT WE COULD USE THE CHILDREN'S HELP!
GOOD THINKING!
SAY--WHAT'S FOR SUPPER?

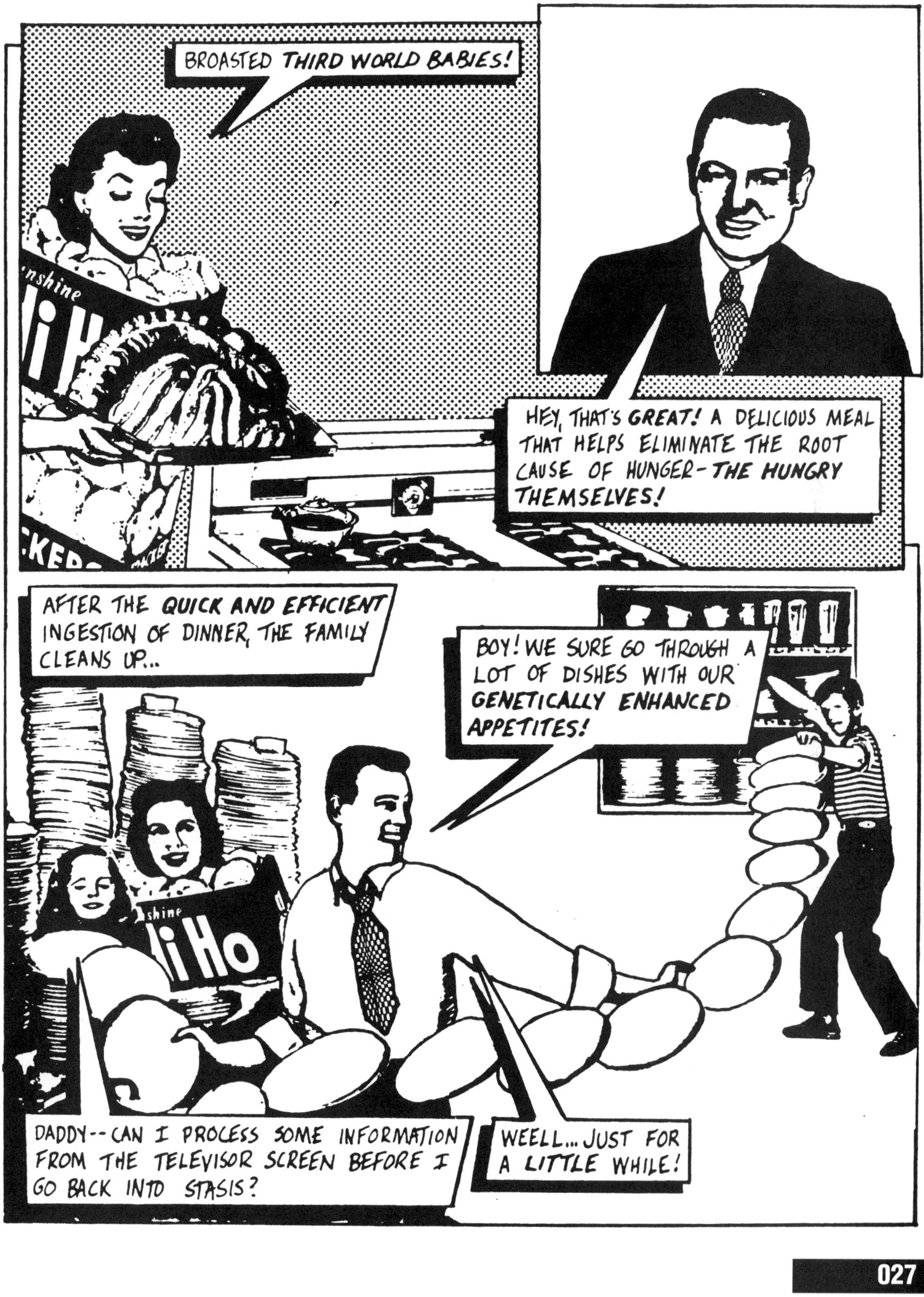
BROASTED **THIRD WORLD BABIES!**
HEY, THAT'S **GREAT!** A DELICIOUS MEAL THAT HELPS ELIMINATE THE ROOT CAUSE OF HUNGER-**THE HUNGRY THEMSELVES!**
AFTER THE **QUICK AND EFFICIENT** INGESTION OF DINNER, THE FAMILY CLEANS UP...
BOY! WE SURE GO THROUGH A LOT OF DISHES WITH OUR **GENETICALLY ENHANCED APPETITES!**
DADDY--CAN I PROCESS SOME INFORMATION FROM THE TELEVISOR SCREEN BEFORE I GO BACK INTO STASIS?
WEELL... JUST FOR A *LITTLE* WHILE!

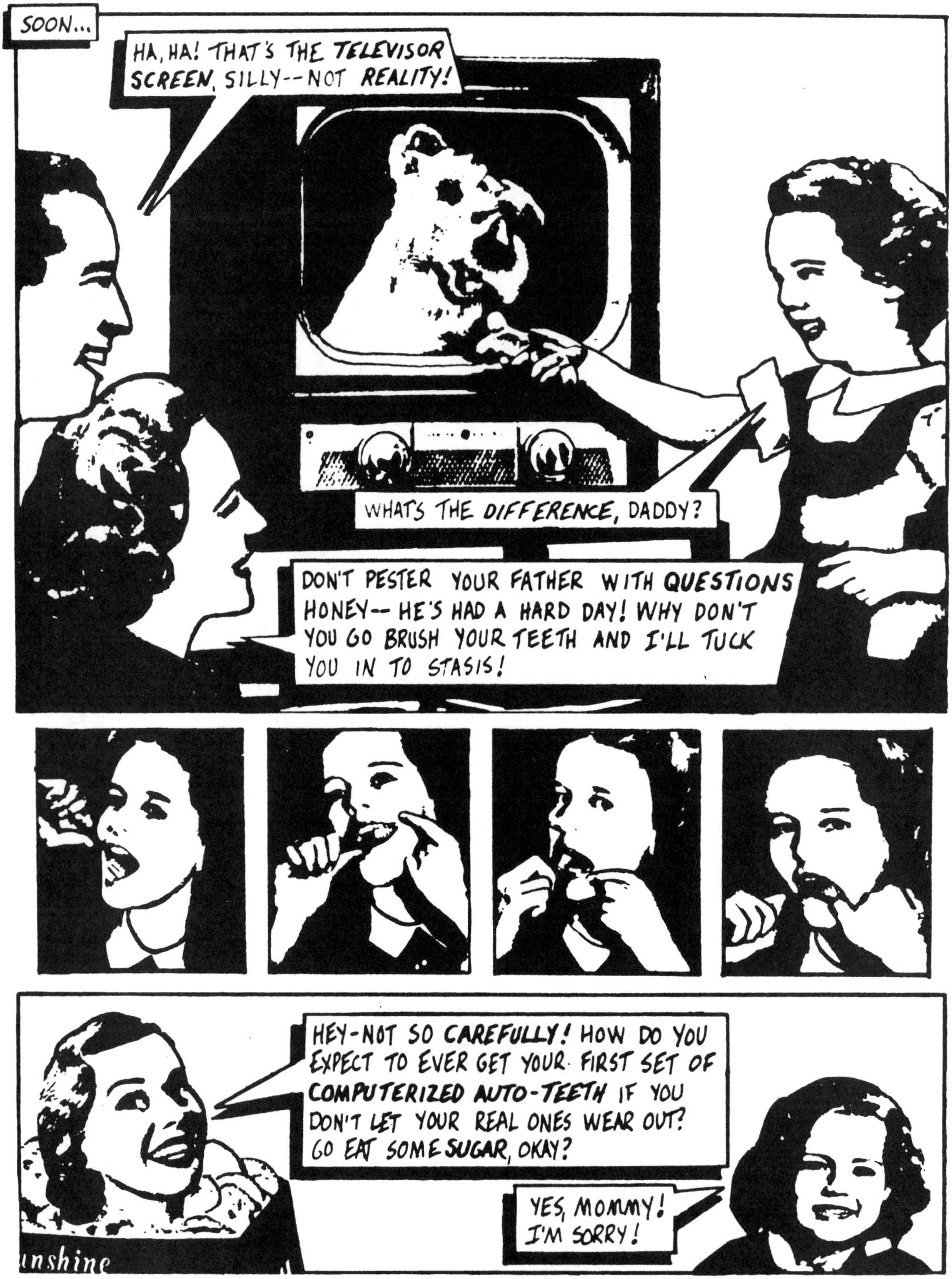
SOON...
HA, HA! THAT'S THE TELEVISOR SCREEN, SILLY--NOT REALITY!
WHAT'S THE DIFFERENCE, DADDY?
DON'T PESTER YOUR FATHER WITH QUESTIONS HONEY-- HE'S HAD A HARD DAY! WHY DON'T YOU GO BRUSH YOUR TEETH AND I'LL TUCK YOU IN TO STASIS!
HEY-NOT SO CAREFULLY! HOW DO YOU EXPECT TO EVER GET YOUR FIRST SET OF COMPUTERIZED AUTO-TEETH IF YOU DON'T LET YOUR REAL ONES WEAR OUT? GO EAT SOME SUGAR, OKAY?
YES, MOMMY! I'M SORRY!
unshine

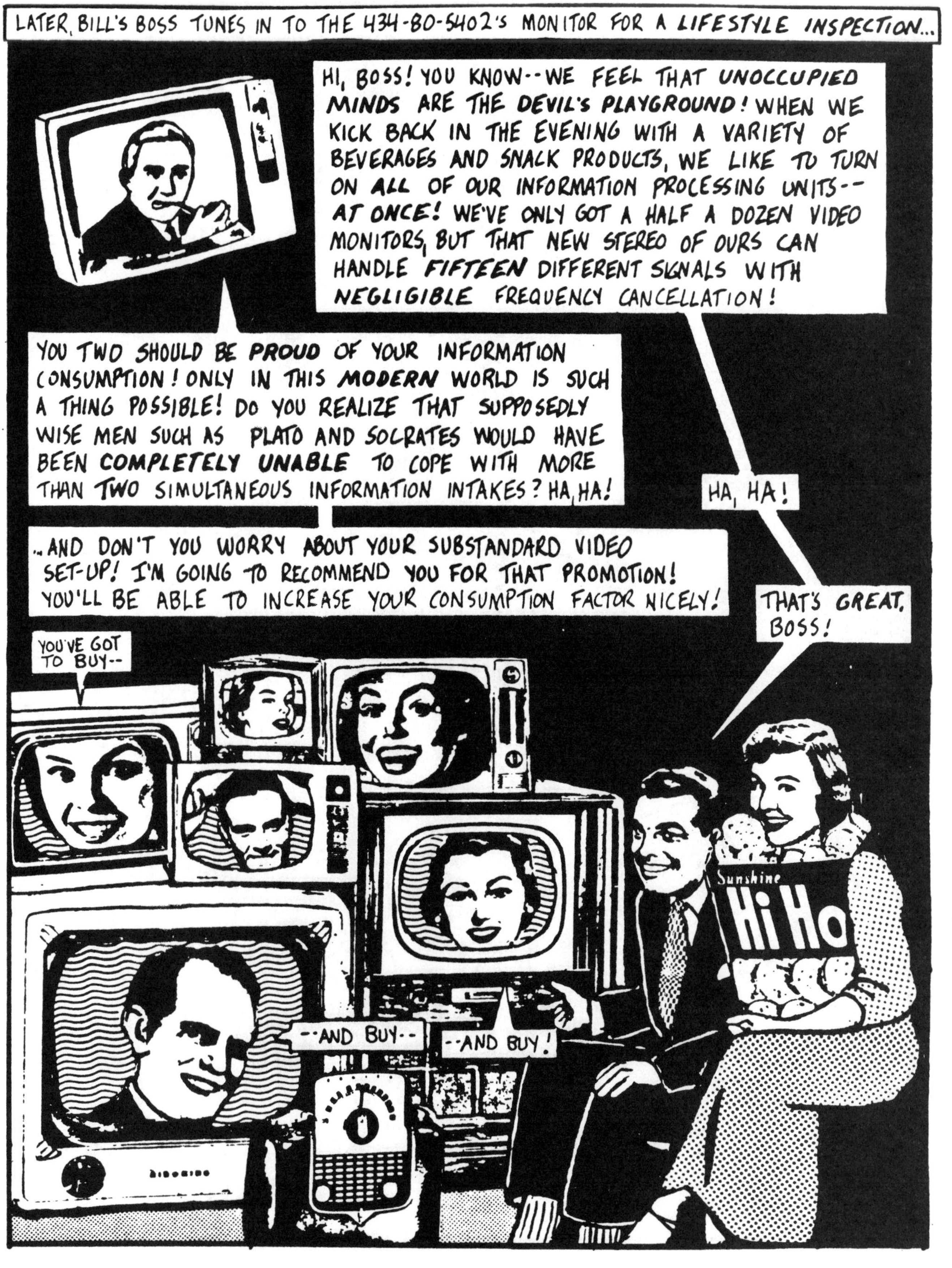
LATER, BILL'S BOSS TUNES IN TO THE 434-80-5402'S MONITOR FOR A LIFESTYLE INSPECTION...
HI, BOSS! YOU KNOW--WE FEEL THAT UNOCCUPIED MINDS ARE THE DEVIL'S PLAYGROUND! WHEN WE KICK BACK IN THE EVENING WITH A VARIETY OF BEVERAGES AND SNACK PRODUCTS, WE LIKE TO TURN ON ALL OF OUR INFORMATION PROCESSING UNITS--AT ONCE! WE'VE ONLY GOT A HALF A DOZEN VIDEO MONITORS, BUT THAT NEW STEREO OF OURS CAN HANDLE FIFTEEN DIFFERENT SIGNALS WITH NEGLIGIBLE FREQUENCY CANCELLATION!
YOU TWO SHOULD BE PROUD OF YOUR INFORMATION CONSUMPTION! ONLY IN THIS MODERN WORLD IS SUCH A THING POSSIBLE! DO YOU REALIZE THAT SUPPOSEDLY WISE MEN SUCH AS PLATO AND SOCRATES WOULD HAVE BEEN COMPLETELY UNABLE TO COPE WITH MORE THAN TWO SIMULTANEOUS INFORMATION INTAKES? HA, HA!
HA, HA!
..AND DON'T YOU WORRY ABOUT YOUR SUBSTANDARD VIDEO SET-UP! I'M GOING TO RECOMMEND YOU FOR THAT PROMOTION! YOU'LL BE ABLE TO INCREASE YOUR CONSUMPTION FACTOR NICELY!
THAT'S GREAT, BOSS!
YOU'VE GOT TO BUY--
--AND BUY--
--AND BUY!
Sunshine Hi Ho

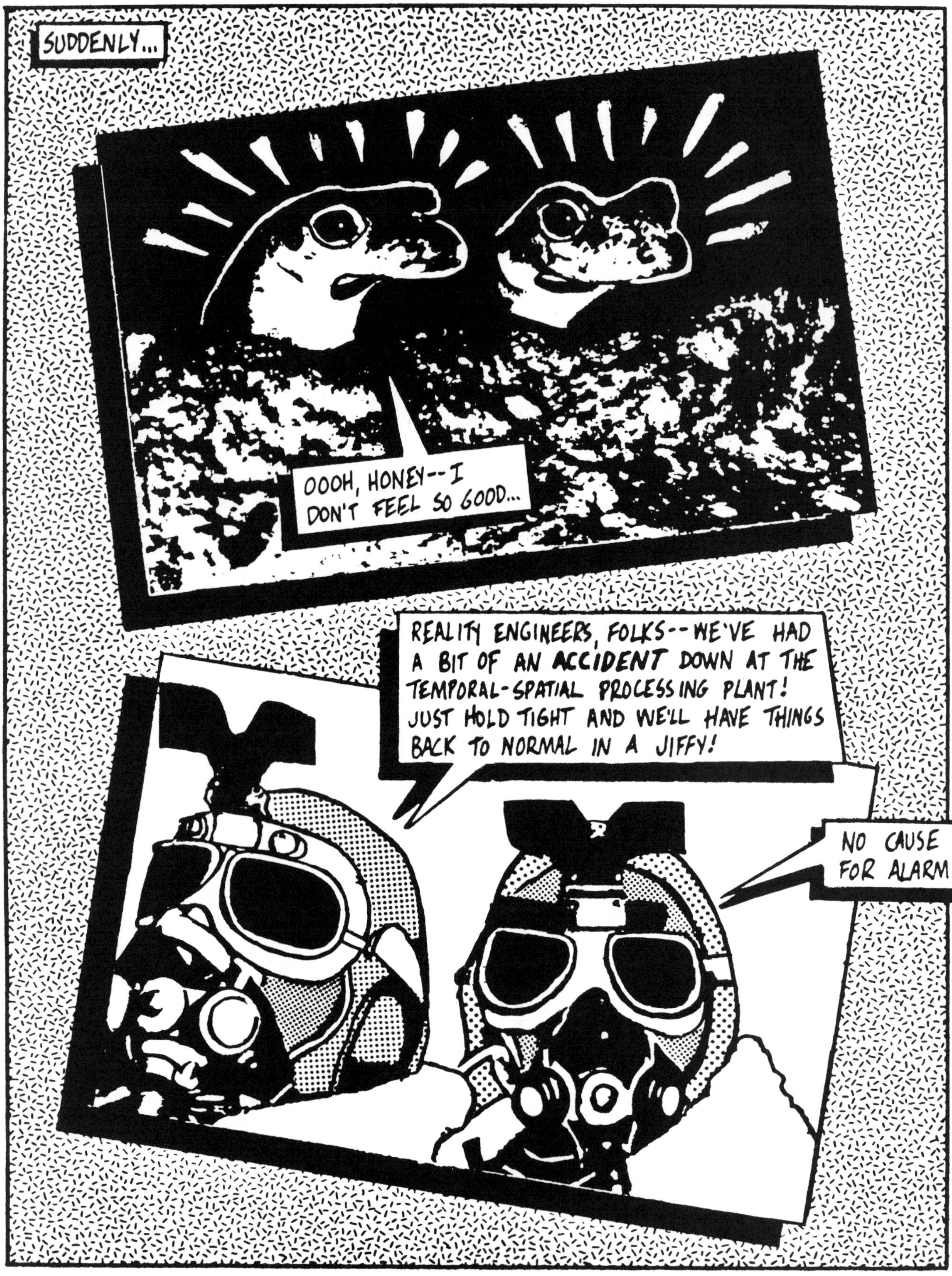
SUDDENLY...
OOOH, HONEY--I DON'T FEEL SO GOOD...
REALITY ENGINEERS, FOLKS--WE'VE HAD A BIT OF AN ACCIDENT DOWN AT THE TEMPORAL-SPATIAL PROCESSING PLANT! JUST HOLD TIGHT AND WE'LL HAVE THINGS BACK TO NORMAL IN A JIFFY!
NO CAUSE FOR ALARM!

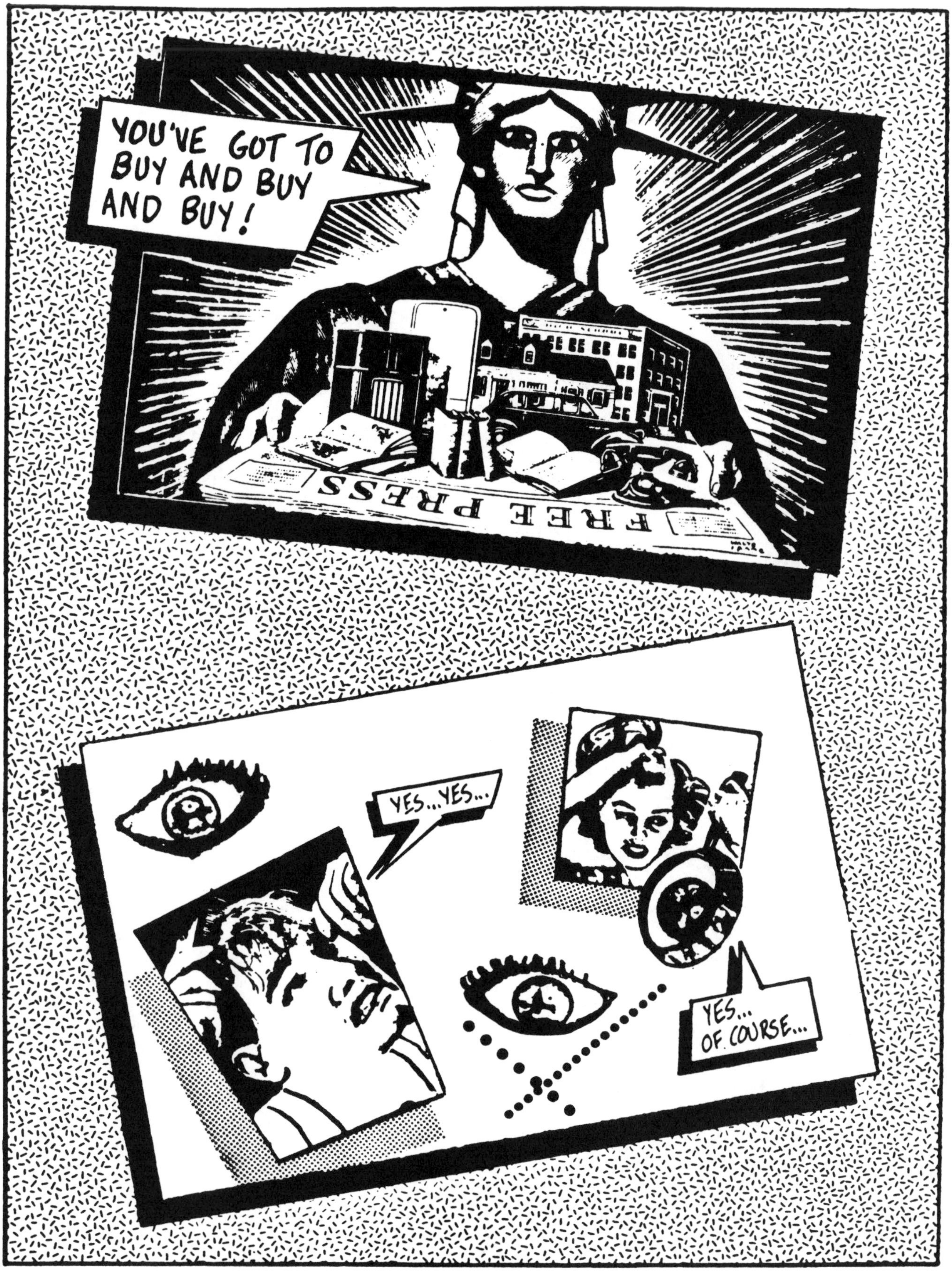
YOU'VE GOT TO BUY AND BUY AND BUY!
FREE PRESS
YES...YES...
YES... OF COURSE...

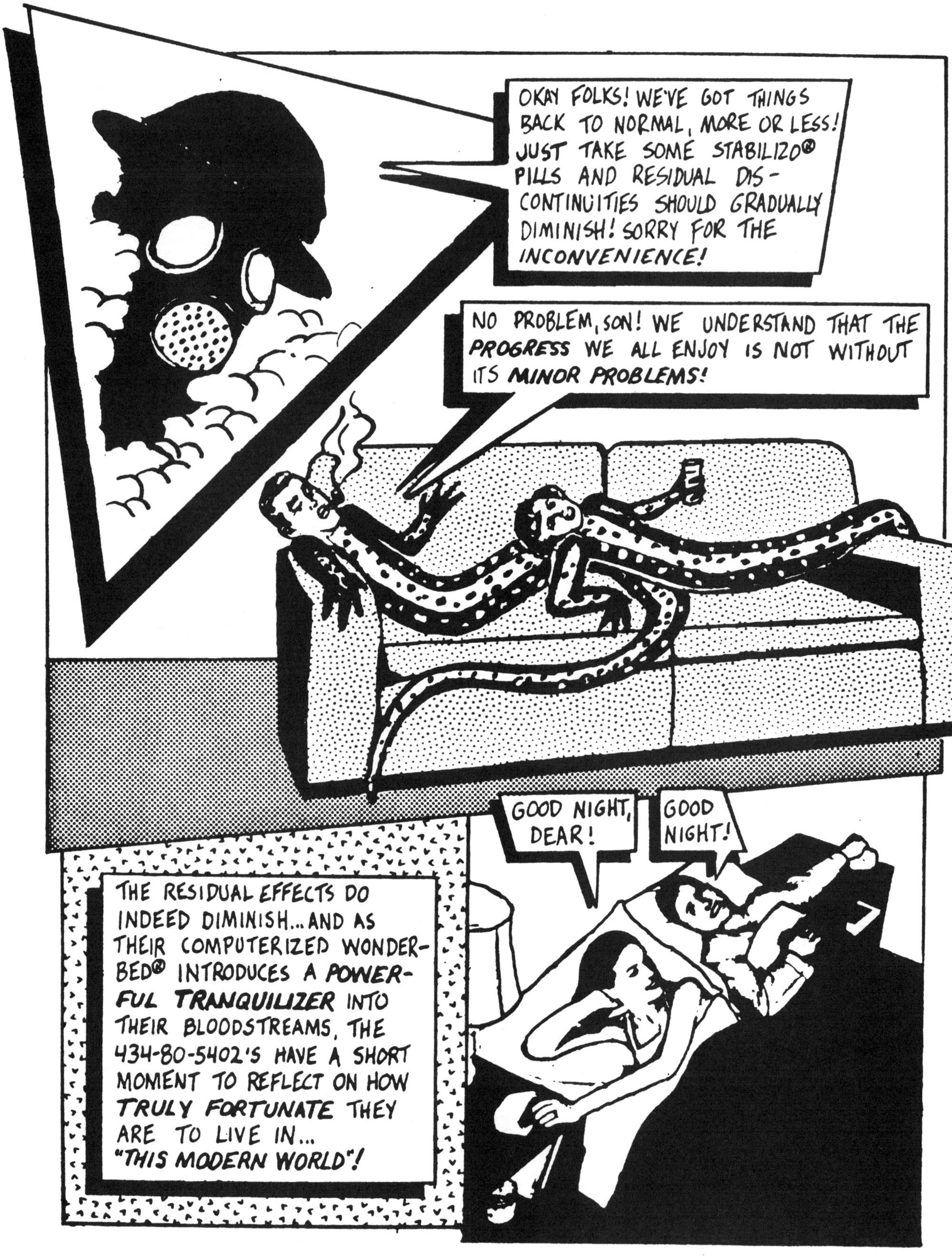
OKAY FOLKS! WE'VE GOT THINGS BACK TO NORMAL, MORE OR LESS! JUST TAKE SOME STABILIZO® PILLS AND RESIDUAL DIS-CONTINUITIES SHOULD GRADUALLY DIMINISH! SORRY FOR THE INCONVENIENCE!
NO PROBLEM, SON! WE UNDERSTAND THAT THE PROGRESS WE ALL ENJOY IS NOT WITHOUT ITS MINOR PROBLEMS!
THE RESIDUAL EFFECTS DO INDEED DIMINISH... AND AS THEIR COMPUTERIZED WONDER-BED® INTRODUCES A POWER-FUL TRANQUILIZER INTO THEIR BLOODSTREAMS, THE 434-80-5402'S HAVE A SHORT MOMENT TO REFLECT ON HOW TRULY FORTUNATE THEY ARE TO LIVE IN... "THIS MODERN WORLD"!
GOOD NIGHT, DEAR!
GOOD NIGHT!

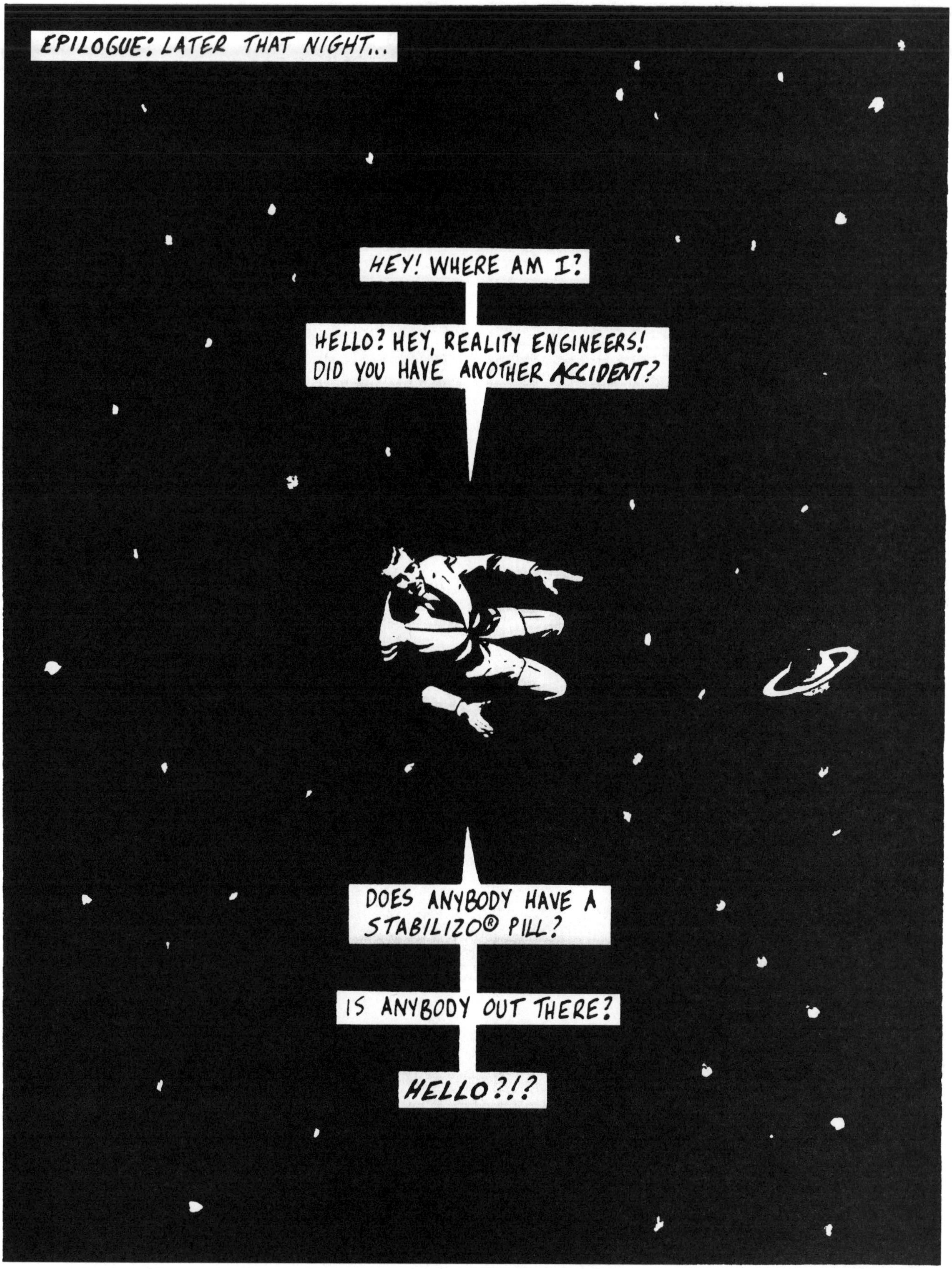
EPILOGUE: LATER THAT NIGHT...
HEY! WHERE AM I?
HELLO? HEY, REALITY ENGINEERS! DID YOU HAVE ANOTHER ACCIDENT?
DOES ANYBODY HAVE A STABILIZO® PILL?
IS ANYBODY OUT THERE?
HELLO?!?

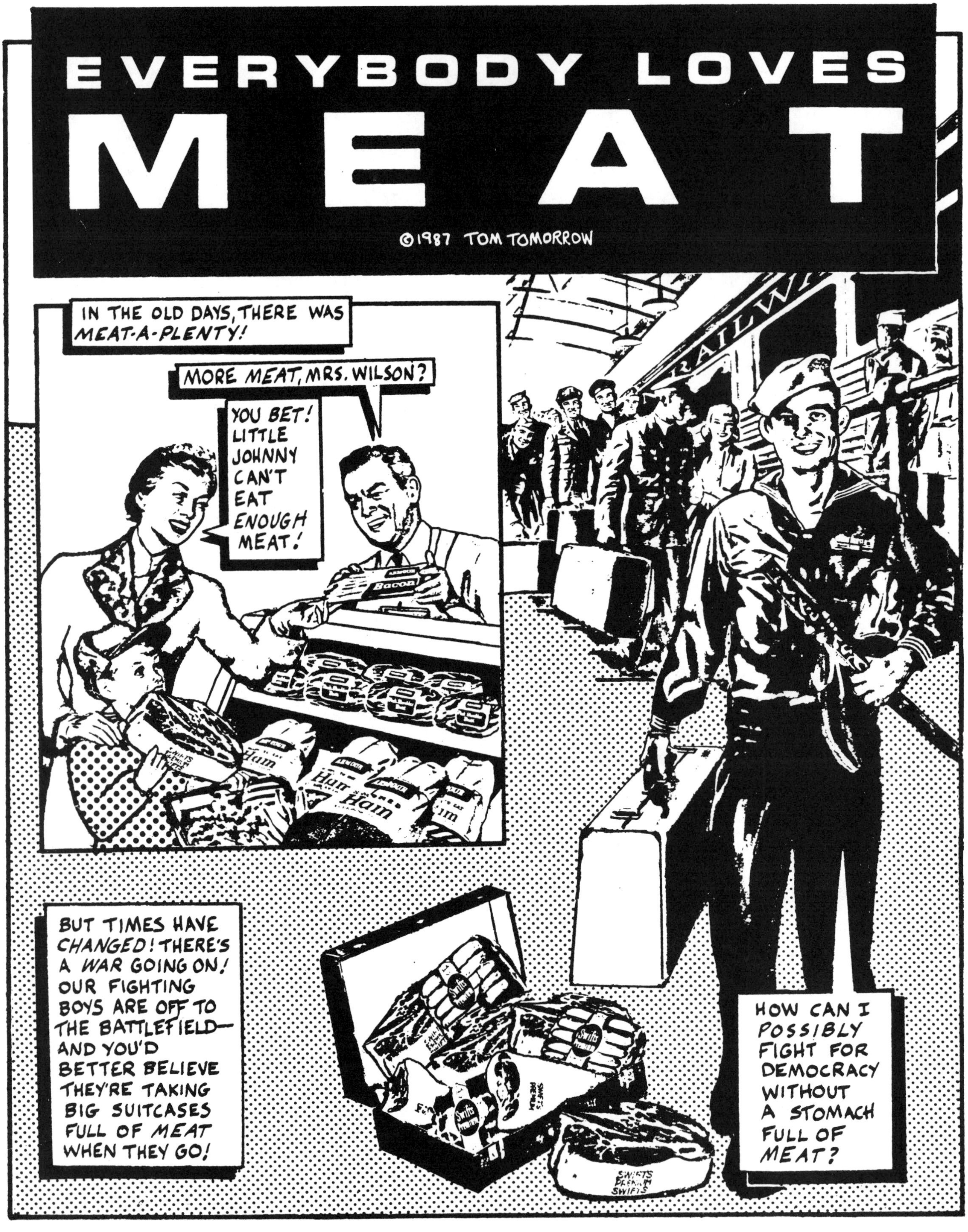
EVERYBODY LOVES
MEAT
©1987 TOM TOMORROW
IN THE OLD DAYS, THERE WAS MEAT-A-PLENTY!
MORE MEAT, MRS. WILSON?
YOU BET! LITTLE JOHNNY CAN'T EAT ENOUGH MEAT!
Bacon
Ham
RAILW
BUT TIMES HAVE CHANGED! THERE'S A WAR GOING ON! OUR FIGHTING BOYS ARE OFF TO THE BATTLEFIELD— AND YOU'D BETTER BELIEVE THEY'RE TAKING BIG SUITCASES FULL OF MEAT WHEN THEY GO!
HOW CAN I POSSIBLY FIGHT FOR DEMOCRACY WITHOUT A STOMACH FULL OF MEAT?

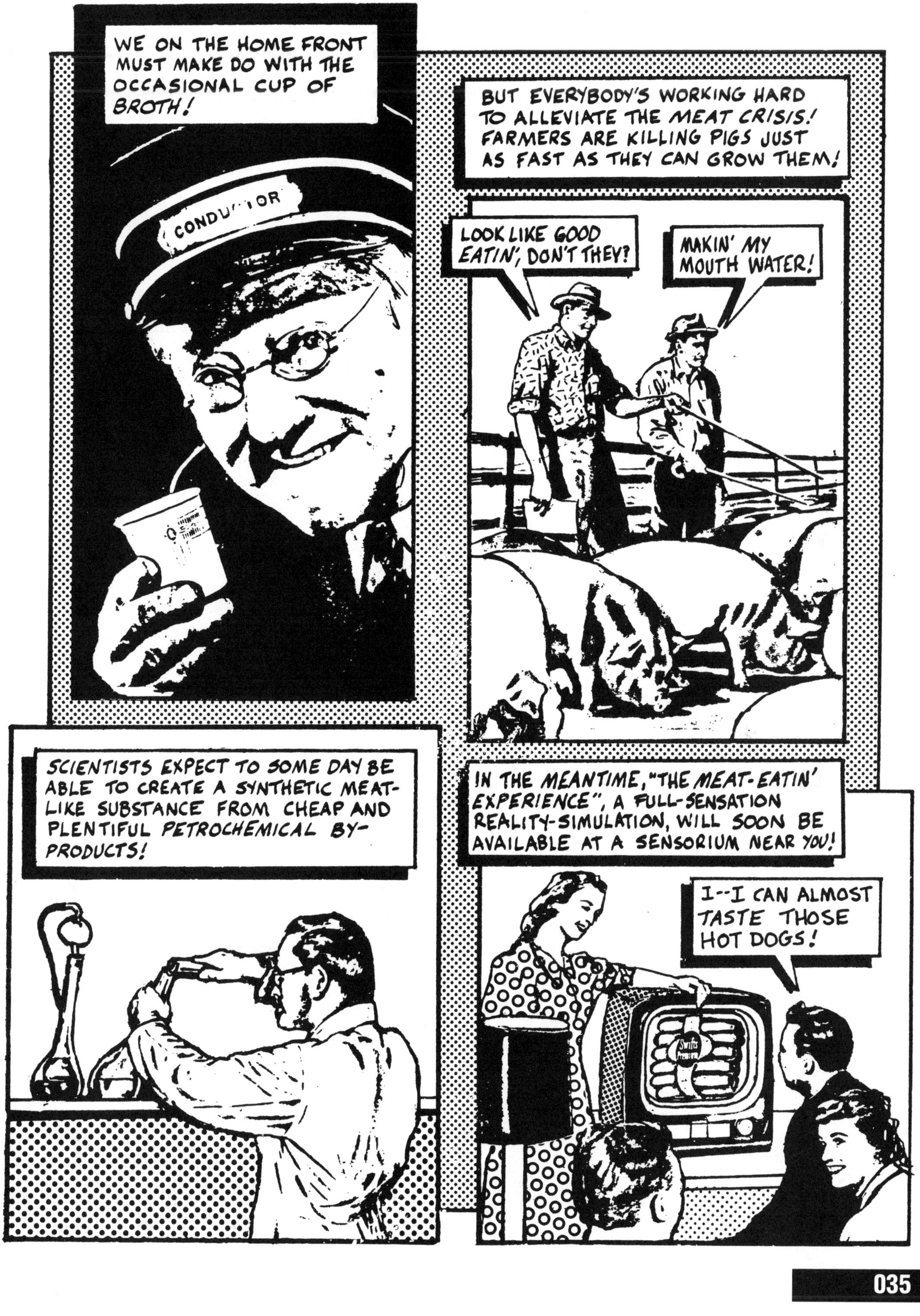
WE ON THE HOME FRONT MUST MAKE DO WITH THE OCCASIONAL CUP OF BROTH!
CONDUCTOR
BUT EVERYBODY'S WORKING HARD TO ALLEVIATE THE MEAT CRISIS! FARMERS ARE KILLING PIGS JUST AS FAST AS THEY CAN GROW THEM!
LOOK LIKE GOOD EATIN', DON'T THEY?
MAKIN' MY MOUTH WATER!
SCIENTISTS EXPECT TO SOME DAY BE ABLE TO CREATE A SYNTHETIC MEAT-LIKE SUBSTANCE FROM CHEAP AND PLENTIFUL PETROCHEMICAL BY-PRODUCTS!
IN THE MEANTIME, "THE MEAT-EATIN' EXPERIENCE", A FULL-SENSATION REALITY-SIMULATION, WILL SOON BE AVAILABLE AT A SENSORIUM NEAR YOU!
I--I CAN ALMOST TASTE THOSE HOT DOGS!
Swift's Premium

"Hello Citizens!"

This Modern World becomes a weekly strip, and is soon featured in at *least* two or three alternative papers! Confusingly enough, the strip is both *by* Tom Tomorrow and occasionally features a character *named* "Tom Tomorrow." Sadly, the American public just wasn't ready for the mind-boggling paradox of a cartoon authored by its own central character, and "Tom" would eventually be retired, along with his lovable sidekick Dippy—though the latter, of course, would soon return as—you guessed it—Alan Greenspan.

1987-1989

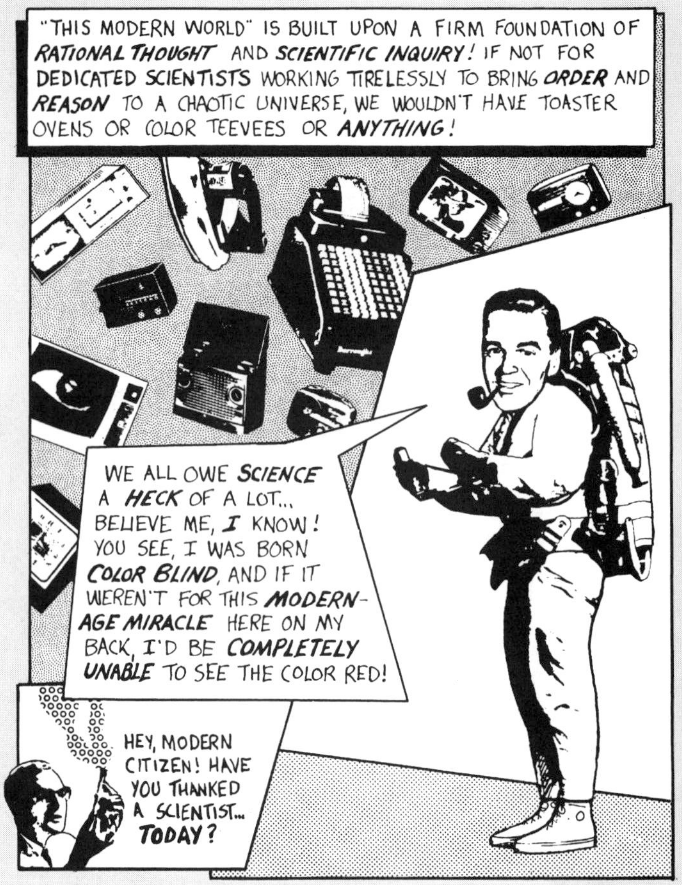

"THIS MODERN WORLD" IS BUILT UPON A FIRM FOUNDATION OF RATIONAL THOUGHT AND SCIENTIFIC INQUIRY! IF NOT FOR DEDICATED SCIENTISTS WORKING TIRELESSLY TO BRING ORDER AND REASON TO A CHAOTIC UNIVERSE, WE WOULDN'T HAVE TOASTER OVENS OR COLOR TEEVEES OR ANYTHING!
WE ALL OWE SCIENCE A HECK OF A LOT... BELIEVE ME, I KNOW! YOU SEE, I WAS BORN COLOR BLIND, AND IF IT WEREN'T FOR THIS MODERN-AGE MIRACLE HERE ON MY BACK, I'D BE COMPLETELY UNABLE TO SEE THE COLOR RED!
HEY, MODERN CITIZEN! HAVE YOU THANKED A SCIENTIST... TODAY?

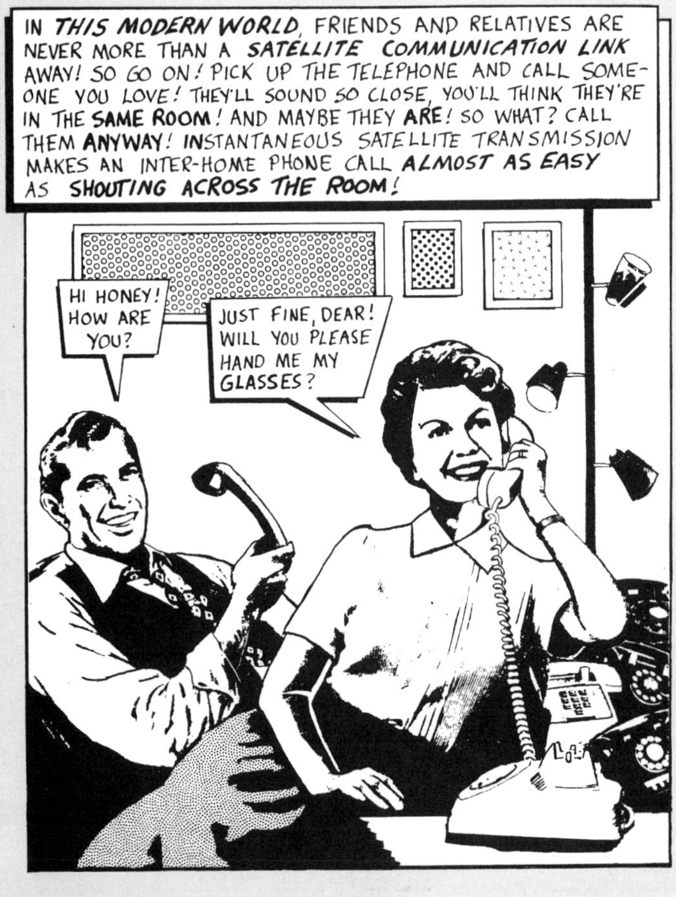

IN THIS MODERN WORLD, FRIENDS AND RELATIVES ARE NEVER MORE THAN A SATELLITE COMMUNICATION LINK AWAY! SO GO ON! PICK UP THE TELEPHONE AND CALL SOMEONE YOU LOVE! THEY'LL SOUND SO CLOSE, YOU'LL THINK THEY'RE IN THE SAME ROOM! AND MAYBE THEY ARE! SO WHAT? CALL THEM ANYWAY! INSTANTANEOUS SATELLITE TRANSMISSION MAKES AN INTER-HOME PHONE CALL ALMOST AS EASY AS SHOUTING ACROSS THE ROOM!
HI HONEY! HOW ARE YOU?
JUST FINE, DEAR! WILL YOU PLEASE HAND ME MY GLASSES?

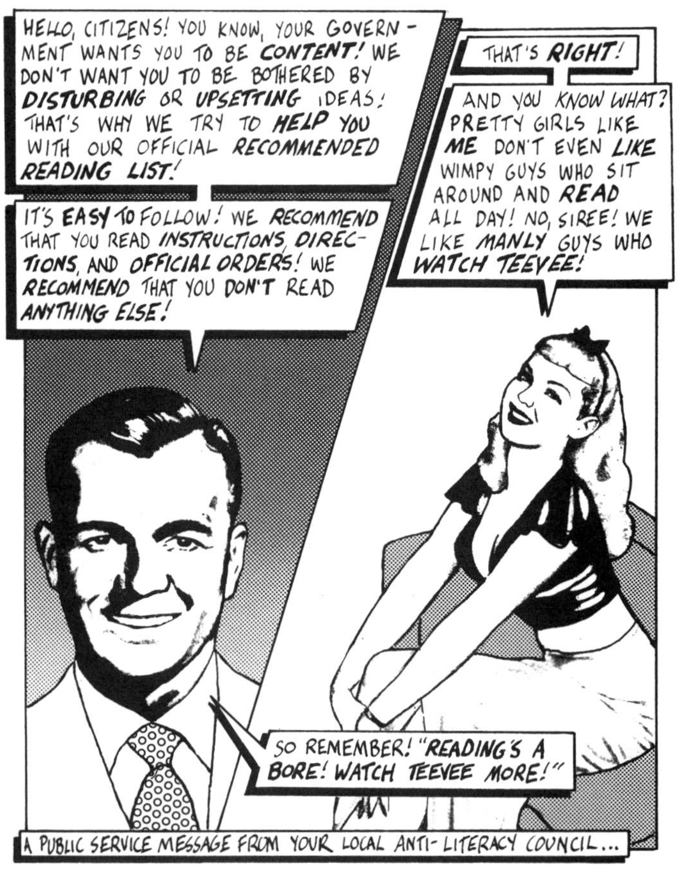

HELLO, CITIZENS! YOU KNOW, YOUR GOVERNMENT WANTS YOU TO BE CONTENT! WE DON'T WANT YOU TO BE BOTHERED BY DISTURBING OR UPSETTING IDEAS! THAT'S WHY WE TRY TO HELP YOU WITH OUR OFFICIAL RECOMMENDED READING LIST!
IT'S EASY TO FOLLOW! WE RECOMMEND THAT YOU READ INSTRUCTIONS, DIRECTIONS, AND OFFICIAL ORDERS! WE RECOMMEND THAT YOU DON'T READ ANYTHING ELSE!
THAT'S RIGHT!
AND YOU KNOW WHAT? PRETTY GIRLS LIKE ME DON'T EVEN LIKE WIMPY GUYS WHO SIT AROUND AND READ ALL DAY! NO, SIREE! WE LIKE MANLY GUYS WHO WATCH TEEVEE!
SO REMEMBER! "READING'S A BORE! WATCH TEEVEE MORE!"
A PUBLIC SERVICE MESSAGE FROM YOUR LOCAL ANTI-LITERACY COUNCIL...

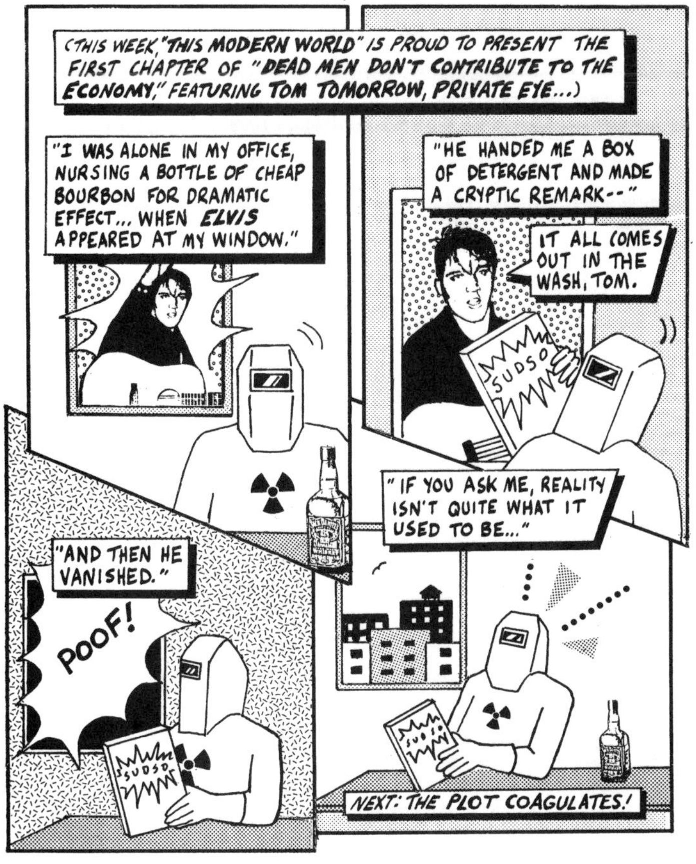
(THIS WEEK, "THIS MODERN WORLD" IS PROUD TO PRESENT THE FIRST CHAPTER OF "DEAD MEN DON'T CONTRIBUTE TO THE ECONOMY," FEATURING TOM TOMORROW, PRIVATE EYE...)
"I WAS ALONE IN MY OFFICE, NURSING A BOTTLE OF CHEAP BOURBON FOR DRAMATIC EFFECT... WHEN ELVIS APPEARED AT MY WINDOW."
"HE HANDED ME A BOX OF DETERGENT AND MADE A CRYPTIC REMARK--"
IT ALL COMES OUT IN THE WASH, TOM.
SUDSO
"IF YOU ASK ME, REALITY ISN'T QUITE WHAT IT USED TO BE..."
"AND THEN HE VANISHED."
POOF!
SUDSO
SUDSO
NEXT: THE PLOT COAGULATES!

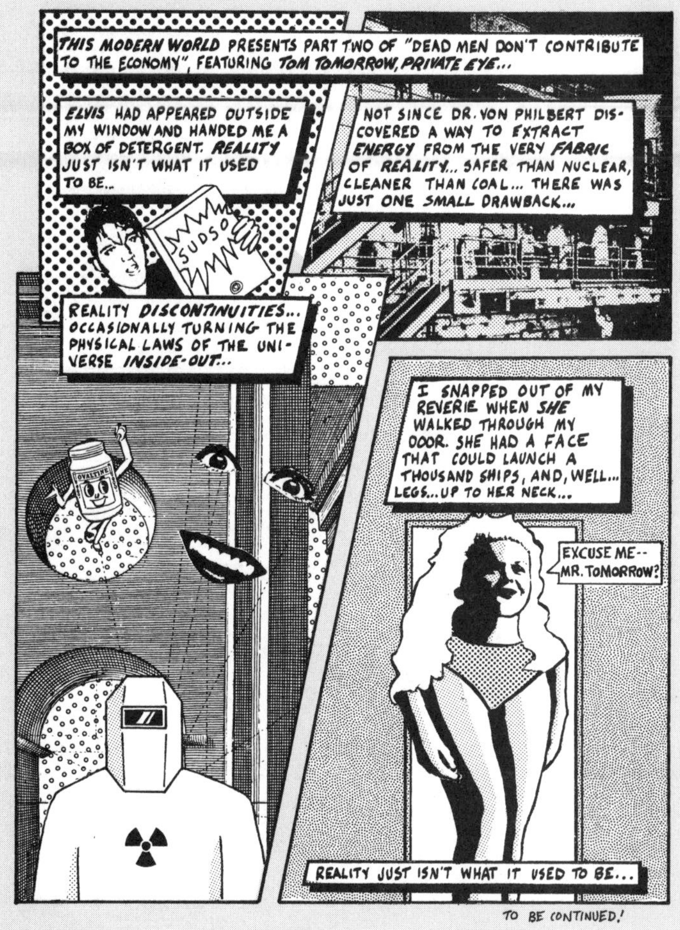
THIS MODERN WORLD PRESENTS PART TWO OF "DEAD MEN DON'T CONTRIBUTE TO THE ECONOMY", FEATURING TOM TOMORROW, PRIVATE EYE...
ELVIS HAD APPEARED OUTSIDE MY WINDOW AND HANDED ME A BOX OF DETERGENT. REALITY JUST ISN'T WHAT IT USED TO BE..
SUDSO
NOT SINCE DR. VON PHILBERT DISCOVERED A WAY TO EXTRACT ENERGY FROM THE VERY FABRIC OF REALITY... SAFER THAN NUCLEAR, CLEANER THAN COAL... THERE WAS JUST ONE SMALL DRAWBACK...
REALITY DISCONTINUITIES... OCCASIONALLY TURNING THE PHYSICAL LAWS OF THE UNIVERSE INSIDE-OUT...
OVALTINE
I SNAPPED OUT OF MY REVERIE WHEN SHE WALKED THROUGH MY DOOR. SHE HAD A FACE THAT COULD LAUNCH A THOUSAND SHIPS, AND, WELL... LEGS... UP TO HER NECK...
EXCUSE ME-- MR. TOMORROW?
REALITY JUST ISN'T WHAT IT USED TO BE...
TO BE CONTINUED!

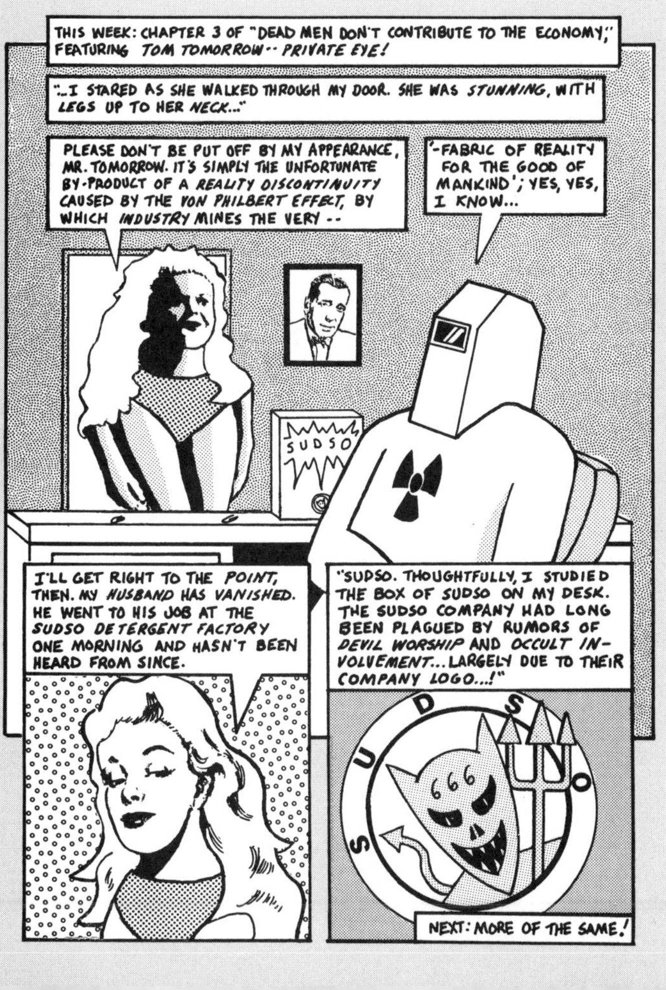
THIS WEEK: CHAPTER 3 OF "DEAD MEN DON'T CONTRIBUTE TO THE ECONOMY," FEATURING TOM TOMORROW -- PRIVATE EYE!
"...I STARED AS SHE WALKED THROUGH MY DOOR. SHE WAS STUNNING, WITH LEGS UP TO HER NECK..."
PLEASE DON'T BE PUT OFF BY MY APPEARANCE, MR. TOMORROW. IT'S SIMPLY THE UNFORTUNATE BY-PRODUCT OF A REALITY DISCONTINUITY CAUSED BY THE VON PHILBERT EFFECT, BY WHICH INDUSTRY MINES THE VERY --
-FABRIC OF REALITY FOR THE GOOD OF MANKIND'; YES, YES, I KNOW...
SUDSO
I'LL GET RIGHT TO THE POINT, THEN. MY HUSBAND HAS VANISHED. HE WENT TO HIS JOB AT THE SUDSO DETERGENT FACTORY ONE MORNING AND HASN'T BEEN HEARD FROM SINCE.
"SUDSO. THOUGHTFULLY, I STUDIED THE BOX OF SUDSO ON MY DESK. THE SUDSO COMPANY HAD LONG BEEN PLAGUED BY RUMORS OF DEVIL WORSHIP AND OCCULT INVOLVEMENT... LARGELY DUE TO THEIR COMPANY LOGO...!"
SUDSO
666
NEXT: MORE OF THE SAME!

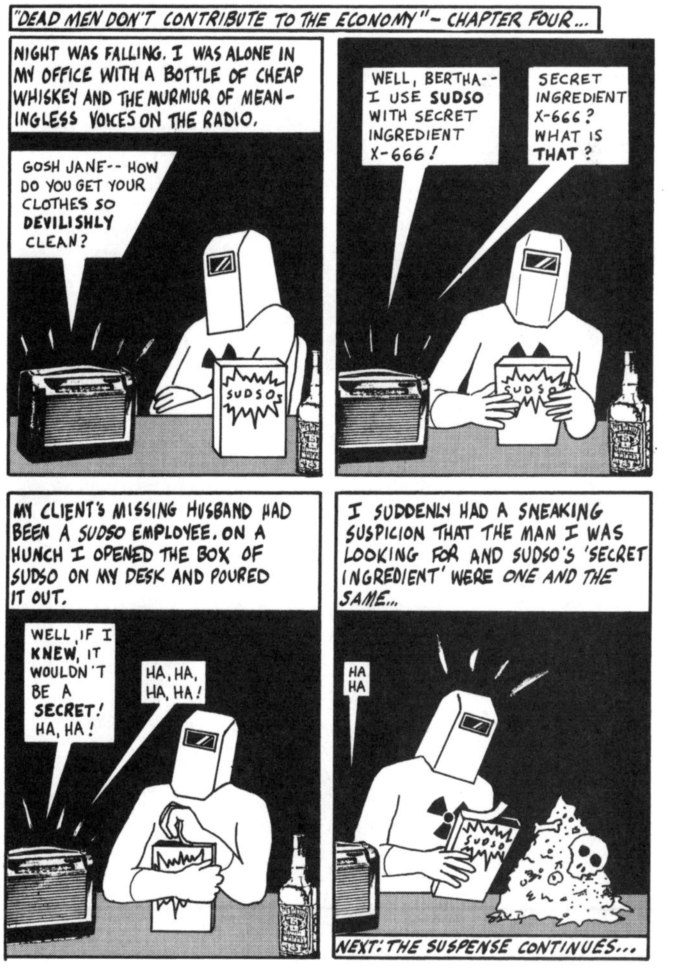
"DEAD MEN DON'T CONTRIBUTE TO THE ECONOMY" - CHAPTER FOUR...
NIGHT WAS FALLING. I WAS ALONE IN MY OFFICE WITH A BOTTLE OF CHEAP WHISKEY AND THE MURMUR OF MEANINGLESS VOICES ON THE RADIO.
GOSH JANE-- HOW DO YOU GET YOUR CLOTHES SO DEVILISHLY CLEAN?
SUDSO
WELL, BERTHA-- I USE SUDSO WITH SECRET INGREDIENT X-666!
SECRET INGREDIENT X-666? WHAT IS THAT?
SUDSO
MY CLIENT'S MISSING HUSBAND HAD BEEN A SUDSO EMPLOYEE. ON A HUNCH I OPENED THE BOX OF SUDSO ON MY DESK AND POURED IT OUT.
WELL, IF I KNEW, IT WOULDN'T BE A SECRET! HA, HA!
HA, HA, HA, HA!
I SUDDENLY HAD A SNEAKING SUSPICION THAT THE MAN I WAS LOOKING FOR AND SUDSO'S 'SECRET INGREDIENT' WERE ONE AND THE SAME...
HA HA
SUDSO
NEXT: THE SUSPENSE CONTINUES...

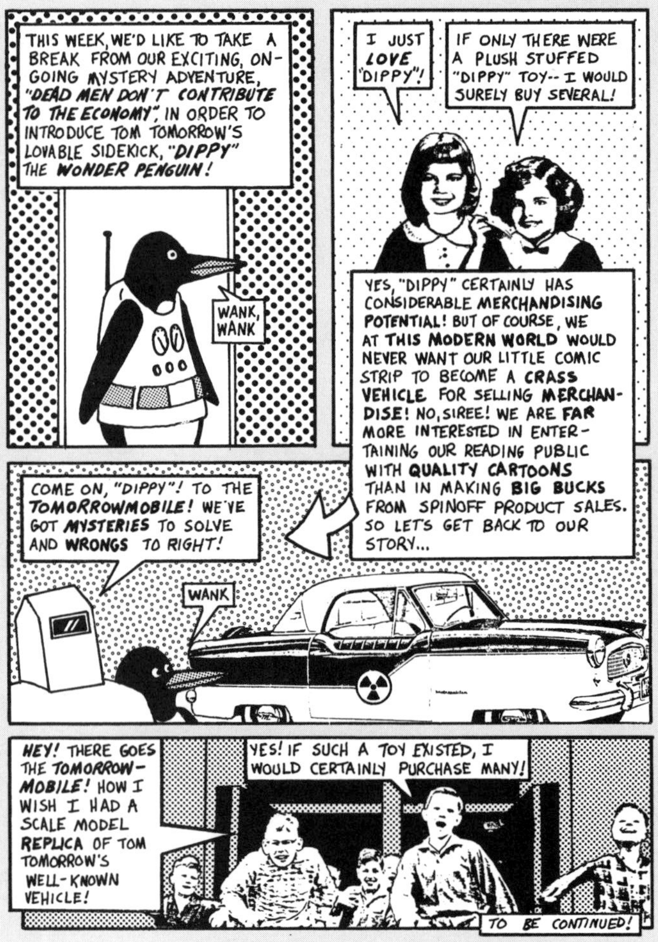
THIS WEEK, WE'D LIKE TO TAKE A BREAK FROM OUR EXCITING, ON-GOING MYSTERY ADVENTURE, "DEAD MEN DON'T CONTRIBUTE TO THE ECONOMY", IN ORDER TO INTRODUCE TOM TOMORROW'S LOVABLE SIDEKICK, "DIPPY" THE WONDER PENGUIN!
WANK, WANK
I JUST LOVE "DIPPY"!
IF ONLY THERE WERE A PLUSH STUFFED "DIPPY" TOY-- I WOULD SURELY BUY SEVERAL!
YES, "DIPPY" CERTAINLY HAS CONSIDERABLE MERCHANDISING POTENTIAL! BUT OF COURSE, WE AT THIS MODERN WORLD WOULD NEVER WANT OUR LITTLE COMIC STRIP TO BECOME A CRASS VEHICLE FOR SELLING MERCHANDISE! NO, SIREE! WE ARE FAR MORE INTERESTED IN ENTERTAINING OUR READING PUBLIC WITH QUALITY CARTOONS THAN IN MAKING BIG BUCKS FROM SPINOFF PRODUCT SALES. SO LET'S GET BACK TO OUR STORY...
COME ON, "DIPPY"! TO THE TOMORROWMOBILE! WE'VE GOT MYSTERIES TO SOLVE AND WRONGS TO RIGHT!
WANK
HEY! THERE GOES THE TOMORROW-MOBILE! HOW I WISH I HAD A SCALE MODEL REPLICA OF TOM TOMORROW'S WELL-KNOWN VEHICLE!
YES! IF SUCH A TOY EXISTED, I WOULD CERTAINLY PURCHASE MANY!
TO BE CONTINUED!

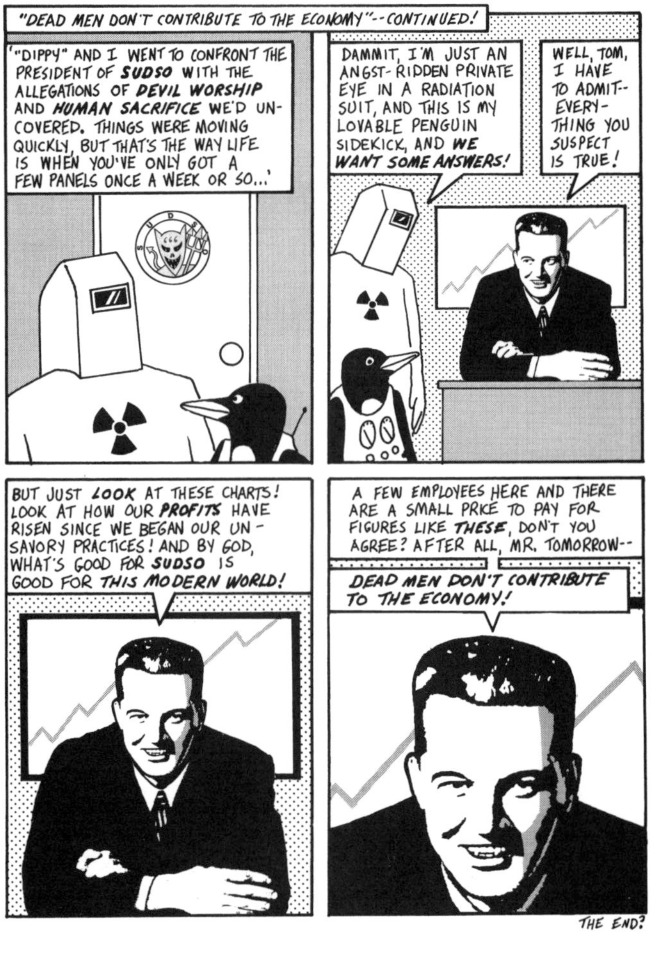
"DEAD MEN DON'T CONTRIBUTE TO THE ECONOMY"--CONTINUED!
"DIPPY" AND I WENT TO CONFRONT THE PRESIDENT OF SUDSO WITH THE ALLEGATIONS OF DEVIL WORSHIP AND HUMAN SACRIFICE WE'D UNCOVERED. THINGS WERE MOVING QUICKLY, BUT THAT'S THE WAY LIFE IS WHEN YOU'VE ONLY GOT A FEW PANELS ONCE A WEEK OR SO...'
DAMMIT, I'M JUST AN ANGST-RIDDEN PRIVATE EYE IN A RADIATION SUIT, AND THIS IS MY LOVABLE PENGUIN SIDEKICK, AND WE WANT SOME ANSWERS!
WELL, TOM, I HAVE TO ADMIT-- EVERYTHING YOU SUSPECT IS TRUE!
BUT JUST LOOK AT THESE CHARTS! LOOK AT HOW OUR PROFITS HAVE RISEN SINCE WE BEGAN OUR UNSAVORY PRACTICES! AND BY GOD, WHAT'S GOOD FOR SUDSO IS GOOD FOR THIS MODERN WORLD!
A FEW EMPLOYEES HERE AND THERE ARE A SMALL PRICE TO PAY FOR FIGURES LIKE THESE, DON'T YOU AGREE? AFTER ALL, MR. TOMORROW--
DEAD MEN DON'T CONTRIBUTE TO THE ECONOMY!
THE END?

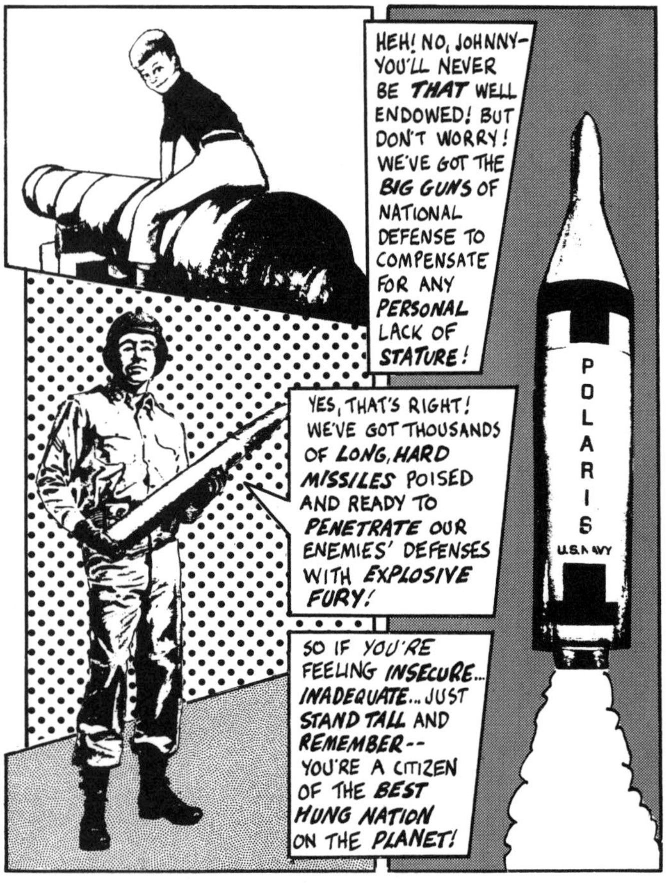
HEH! NO, JOHNNY-- YOU'LL NEVER BE THAT WELL ENDOWED! BUT DON'T WORRY! WE'VE GOT THE BIG GUNS OF NATIONAL DEFENSE TO COMPENSATE FOR ANY PERSONAL LACK OF STATURE!
YES, THAT'S RIGHT! WE'VE GOT THOUSANDS OF LONG, HARD MISSILES POISED AND READY TO PENETRATE OUR ENEMIES' DEFENSES WITH EXPLOSIVE FURY!
POLARIS
U.S. NAVY
SO IF YOU'RE FEELING INSECURE... INADEQUATE... JUST STAND TALL AND REMEMBER-- YOU'RE A CITIZEN OF THE BEST HUNG NATION ON THE PLANET!

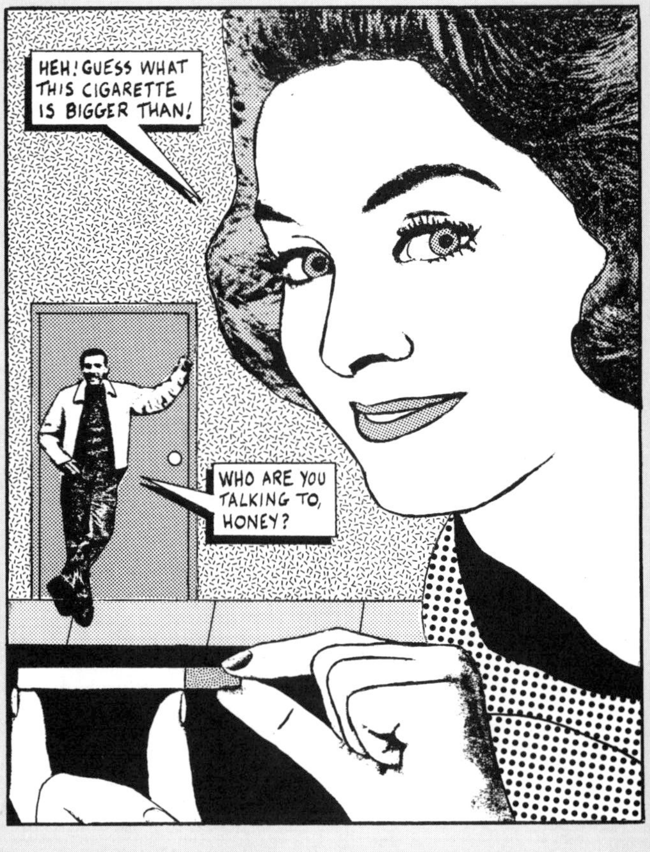
HEH! GUESS WHAT THIS CIGARETTE IS BIGGER THAN!
WHO ARE YOU TALKING TO, HONEY?

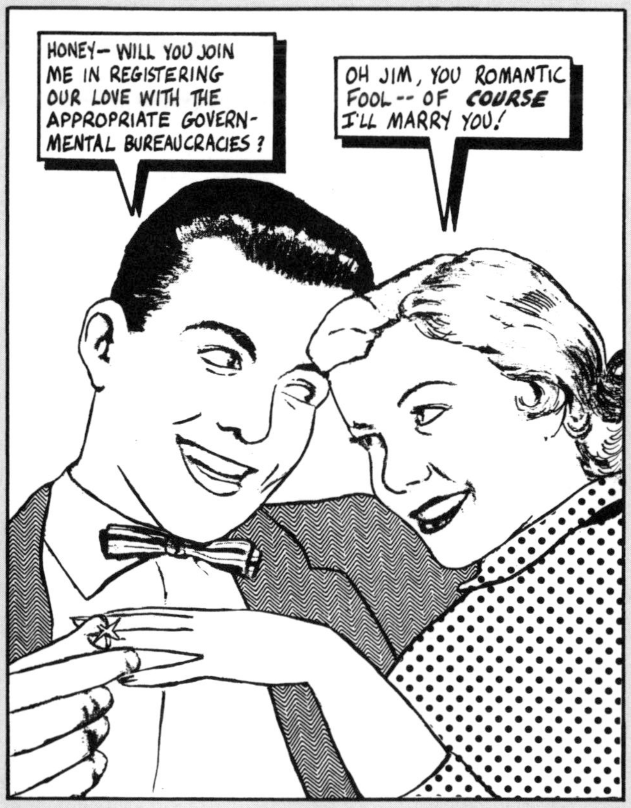
HONEY— WILL YOU JOIN ME IN REGISTERING OUR LOVE WITH THE APPROPRIATE GOVERN-MENTAL BUREAUCRACIES?
OH JIM, YOU ROMANTIC FOOL -- OF COURSE I'LL MARRY YOU!

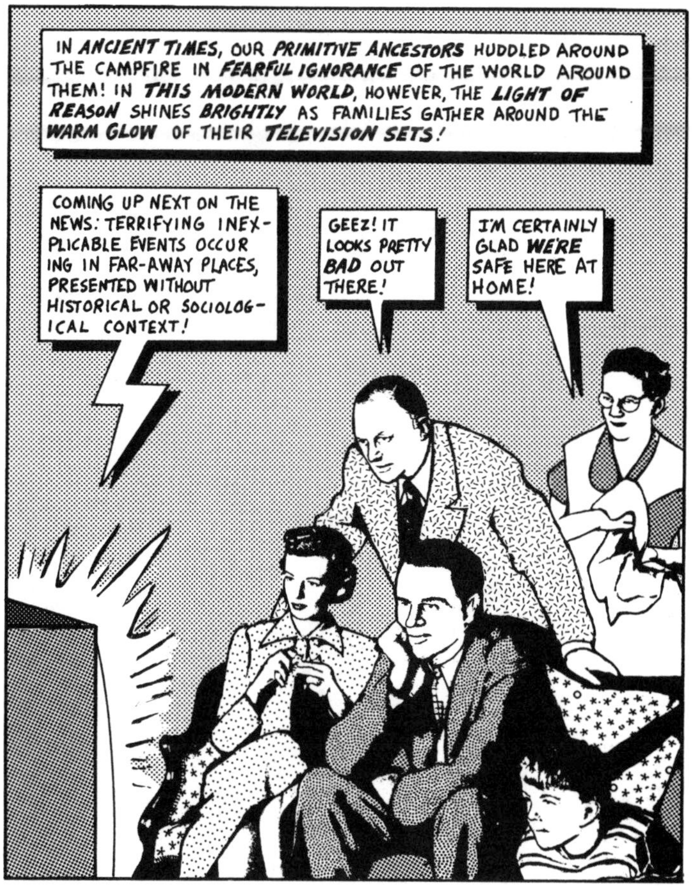
IN ANCIENT TIMES, OUR PRIMITIVE ANCESTORS HUDDLED AROUND THE CAMPFIRE IN FEARFUL IGNORANCE OF THE WORLD AROUND THEM! IN THIS MODERN WORLD, HOWEVER, THE LIGHT OF REASON SHINES BRIGHTLY AS FAMILIES GATHER AROUND THE WARM GLOW OF THEIR TELEVISION SETS!
COMING UP NEXT ON THE NEWS: TERRIFYING INEX-PLICABLE EVENTS OCCURING IN FAR-AWAY PLACES, PRESENTED WITHOUT HISTORICAL OR SOCIOLOG-ICAL CONTEXT!
GEEZ! IT LOOKS PRETTY BAD OUT THERE!
I'M CERTAINLY GLAD WE'RE SAFE HERE AT HOME!

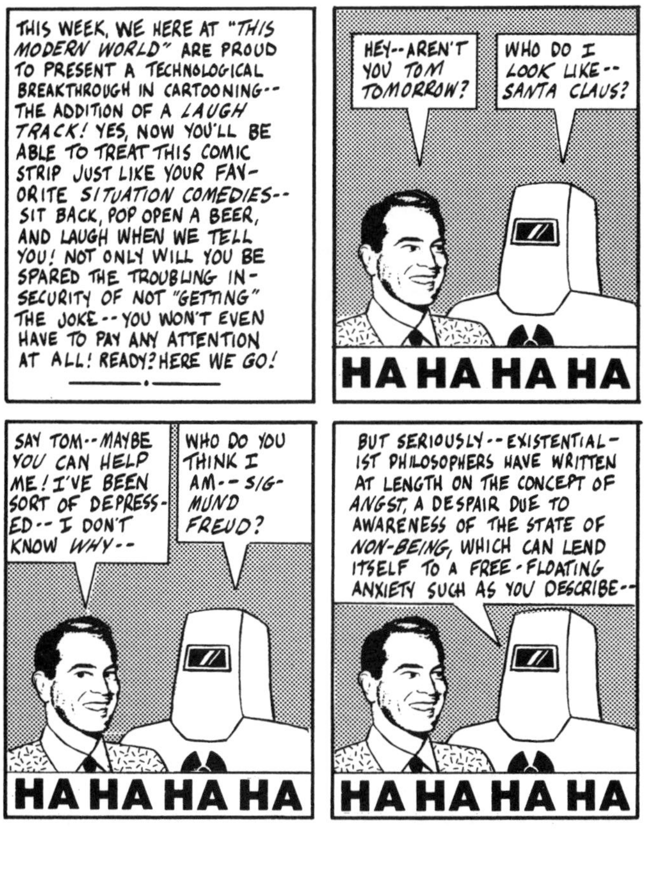
THIS WEEK, WE HERE AT "THIS MODERN WORLD" ARE PROUD TO PRESENT A TECHNOLOGICAL BREAKTHROUGH IN CARTOONING-- THE ADDITION OF A LAUGH TRACK! YES, NOW YOU'LL BE ABLE TO TREAT THIS COMIC STRIP JUST LIKE YOUR FAV-ORITE SITUATION COMEDIES-- SIT BACK, POP OPEN A BEER, AND LAUGH WHEN WE TELL YOU! NOT ONLY WILL YOU BE SPARED THE TROUBLING IN-SECURITY OF NOT "GETTING" THE JOKE -- YOU WON'T EVEN HAVE TO PAY ANY ATTENTION AT ALL! READY? HERE WE GO!
HEY--AREN'T YOU TOM TOMORROW?
WHO DO I LOOK LIKE-- SANTA CLAUS?
HA HA HA HA
SAY TOM--MAYBE YOU CAN HELP ME! I'VE BEEN SORT OF DEPRESS-ED -- I DON'T KNOW WHY--
WHO DO YOU THINK I AM-- SIG-MUND FREUD?
HA HA HA HA
BUT SERIOUSLY -- EXISTENTIAL-IST PHILOSOPHERS HAVE WRITTEN AT LENGTH ON THE CONCEPT OF ANGST, A DESPAIR DUE TO AWARENESS OF THE STATE OF NON-BEING, WHICH CAN LEND ITSELF TO A FREE-FLOATING ANXIETY SUCH AS YOU DESCRIBE--
HA HA HA HA

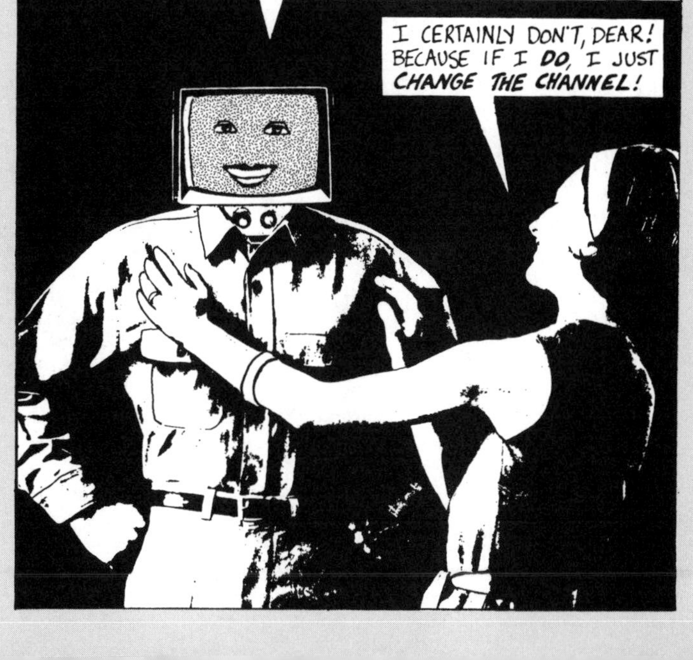
YOU KNOW, FOLKS, IF IT WEREN'T FOR MODERN TECHNOLOGY, I WOULDN'T BE STANDING HERE TODAY! YOU SEE, I LOST MY ENTIRE HEAD IN A TERRIBLE BATHROOM ACCIDENT -- AND BOY, IT WAS PRETTY TOUCH-AND-GO THERE FOR AWHILE! BUT HIGHLY SKILLED SURGEONS WERE ABLE TO FIT ME WITH THIS ARTIFICIAL HEAD-- AND TODAY, I LEAD A PERFECTLY NORMAL LIFE! IN FACT, THIS HEAD OF MINE HAS SOME REAL ADVANTAGES! FOR ONE THING, I CAN WATCH MY FAVORITE MORNING BROADCASTS IN THE BATH-ROOM MIRROR WHILE I GET READY FOR WORK EACH DAY! AND-- BEST OF ALL -- MY WIFE NEVER TIRES OF GAZING LOVINGLY INTO MY EYES -- DO YOU, HONEY?
I CERTAINLY DON'T, DEAR! BECAUSE IF I DO, I JUST CHANGE THE CHANNEL!

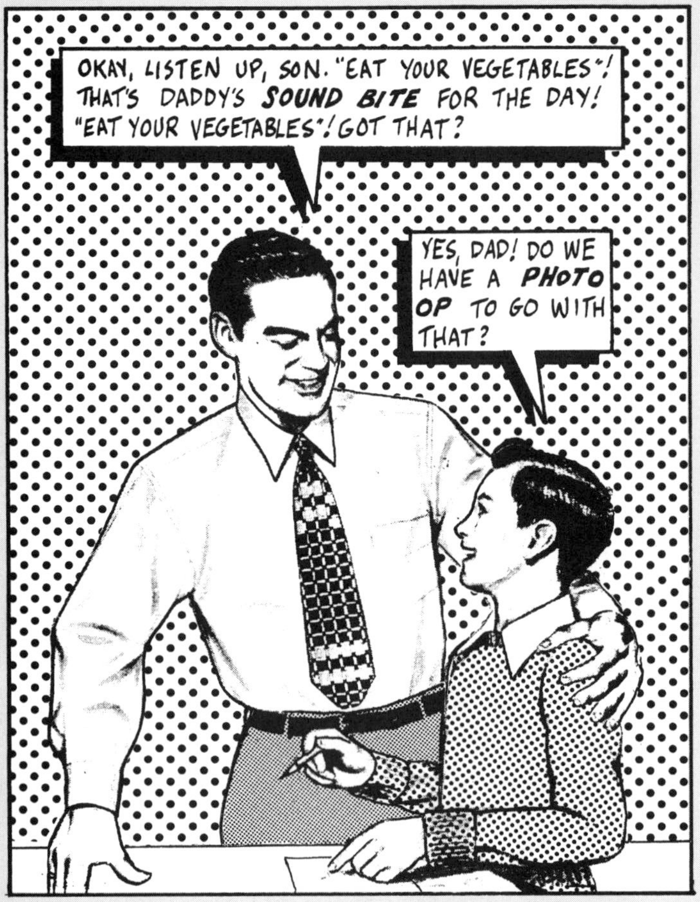
OKAY, LISTEN UP, SON. "EAT YOUR VEGETABLES"! THAT'S DADDY'S **SOUND BITE** FOR THE DAY! "EAT YOUR VEGETABLES"! GOT THAT?
YES, DAD! DO WE HAVE A **PHOTO OP** TO GO WITH THAT?

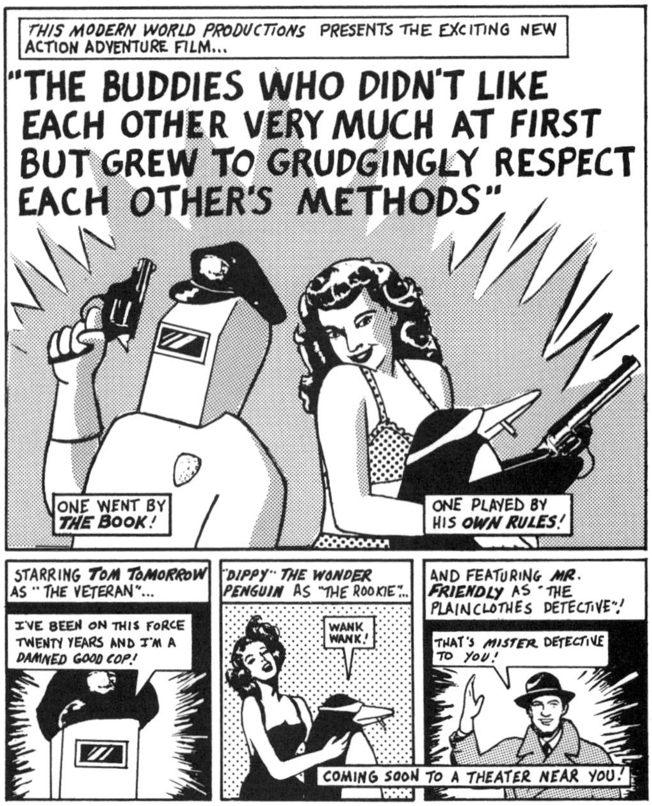
THIS MODERN WORLD PRODUCTIONS PRESENTS THE EXCITING NEW ACTION ADVENTURE FILM...
"THE BUDDIES WHO DIDN'T LIKE EACH OTHER VERY MUCH AT FIRST BUT GREW TO GRUDGINGLY RESPECT EACH OTHER'S METHODS"
ONE WENT BY **THE BOOK**!
ONE PLAYED BY HIS **OWN RULES**!
STARRING **TOM TOMORROW** AS "THE VETERAN"...
I'VE BEEN ON THIS FORCE TWENTY YEARS AND I'M A DAMNED GOOD COP!
"**DIPPY**" **THE WONDER PENGUIN** AS "THE ROOKIE"...
WANK WANK!
AND FEATURING **MR. FRIENDLY** AS "THE PLAINCLOTHES DETECTIVE"!
THAT'S **MISTER** DETECTIVE TO **YOU**!
COMING SOON TO A THEATER NEAR YOU!

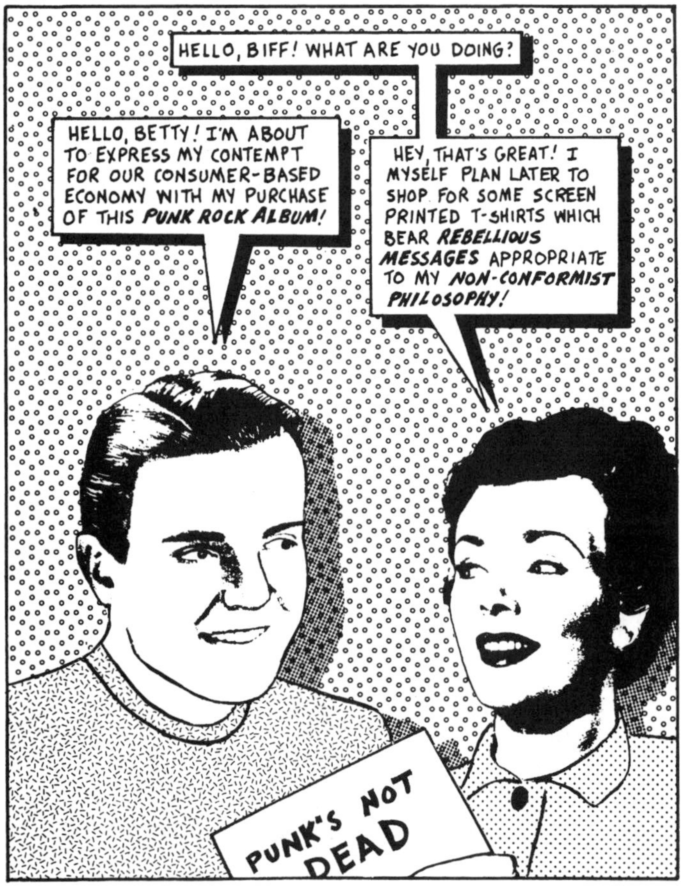
HELLO, BIFF! WHAT ARE YOU DOING?
HELLO, BETTY! I'M ABOUT TO EXPRESS MY CONTEMPT FOR OUR CONSUMER-BASED ECONOMY WITH MY PURCHASE OF THIS **PUNK ROCK ALBUM**!
HEY, THAT'S GREAT! I MYSELF PLAN LATER TO SHOP FOR SOME SCREEN PRINTED T-SHIRTS WHICH BEAR **REBELLIOUS MESSAGES** APPROPRIATE TO MY **NON-CONFORMIST PHILOSOPHY**!
PUNK'S NOT DEAD

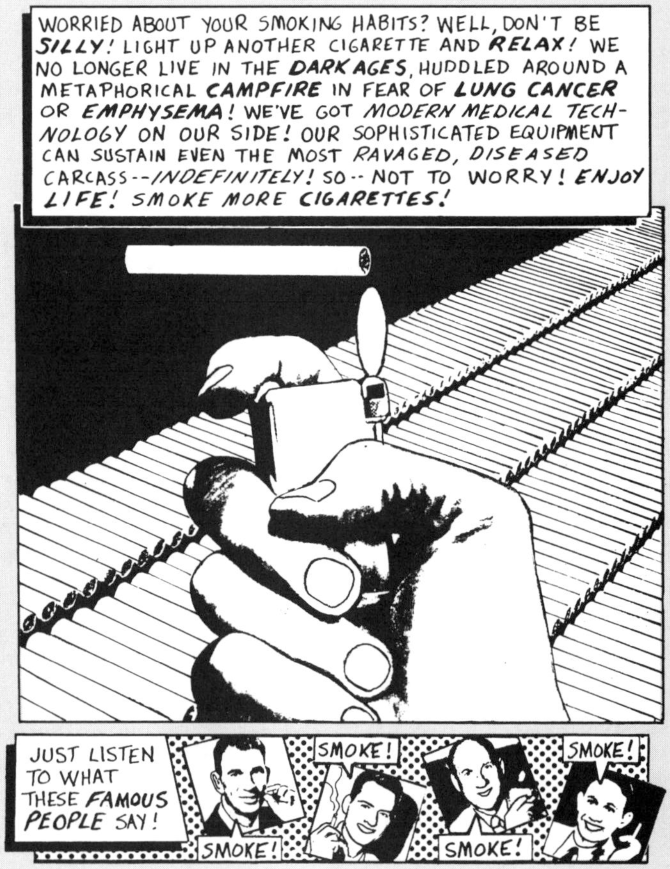
WORRIED ABOUT YOUR SMOKING HABITS? WELL, DON'T BE **SILLY**! LIGHT UP ANOTHER CIGARETTE AND **RELAX**! WE NO LONGER LIVE IN THE **DARK AGES**, HUDDLED AROUND A METAPHORICAL **CAMPFIRE** IN FEAR OF **LUNG CANCER** OR **EMPHYSEMA**! WE'VE GOT *MODERN MEDICAL TECHNOLOGY* ON OUR SIDE! OUR SOPHISTICATED EQUIPMENT CAN SUSTAIN EVEN THE MOST *RAVAGED, DISEASED* CARCASS--*INDEFINITELY*! SO-- NOT TO WORRY! *ENJOY LIFE*! *SMOKE MORE* **CIGARETTES**!
JUST LISTEN TO WHAT THESE *FAMOUS PEOPLE* SAY!
SMOKE!
SMOKE!
SMOKE!
SMOKE!

The Reign of King George the First

He fiddled with "the vision thing," as the economy crashed and burned. He insisted that the Gulf War had nothing whatsoever to do with oil—it was about naked aggression, which could not be tolerated, at least in this one specific instance. It was about keeping the world safe for the values of democracy, at least as practiced by a repressive monarchical dictatorship which just happened to be an oil producing nation.

And the public bought it hook, line and sinker—at least, as long as the bombs were falling and the flags were flying. A year later, of course, they sent him packing.

When confronted with disagreement on the part of his staff or advisors, President Bush Senior the First is said to have had a standard reply: "If you're so smart, how come I'm the one who's president?" And perhaps those are ultimately the words by which his time in office should be remembered.

1990-1992: A presidency in search of a catchphrase

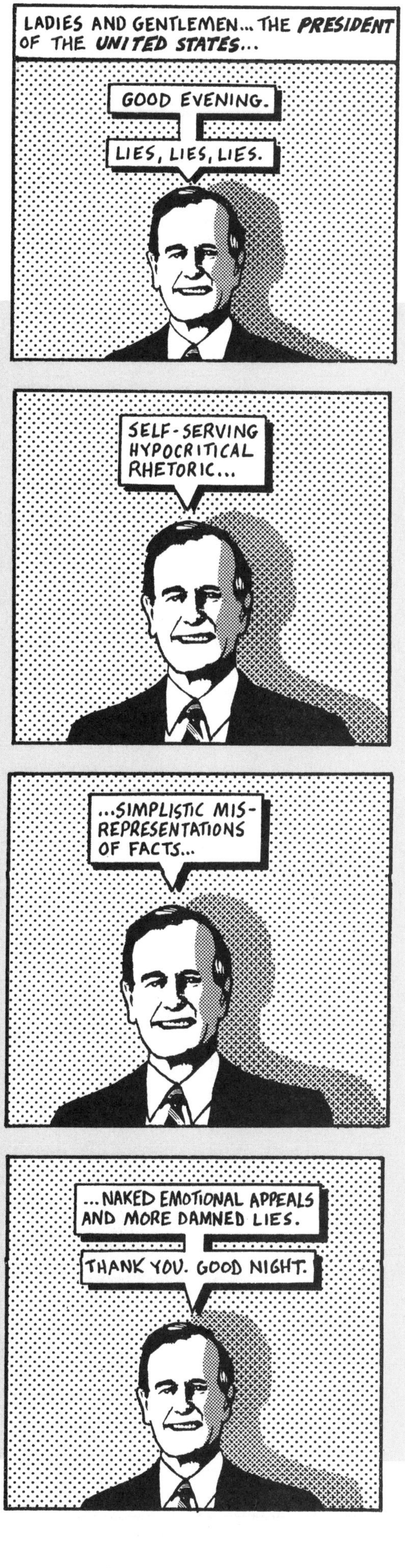

LADIES AND GENTLEMEN... THE *PRESIDENT* OF THE *UNITED STATES*...
GOOD EVENING.
LIES, LIES, LIES.
SELF-SERVING HYPOCRITICAL RHETORIC...
...SIMPLISTIC MIS-REPRESENTATIONS OF FACTS...
...NAKED EMOTIONAL APPEALS AND MORE DAMNED LIES.
THANK YOU. GOOD NIGHT.

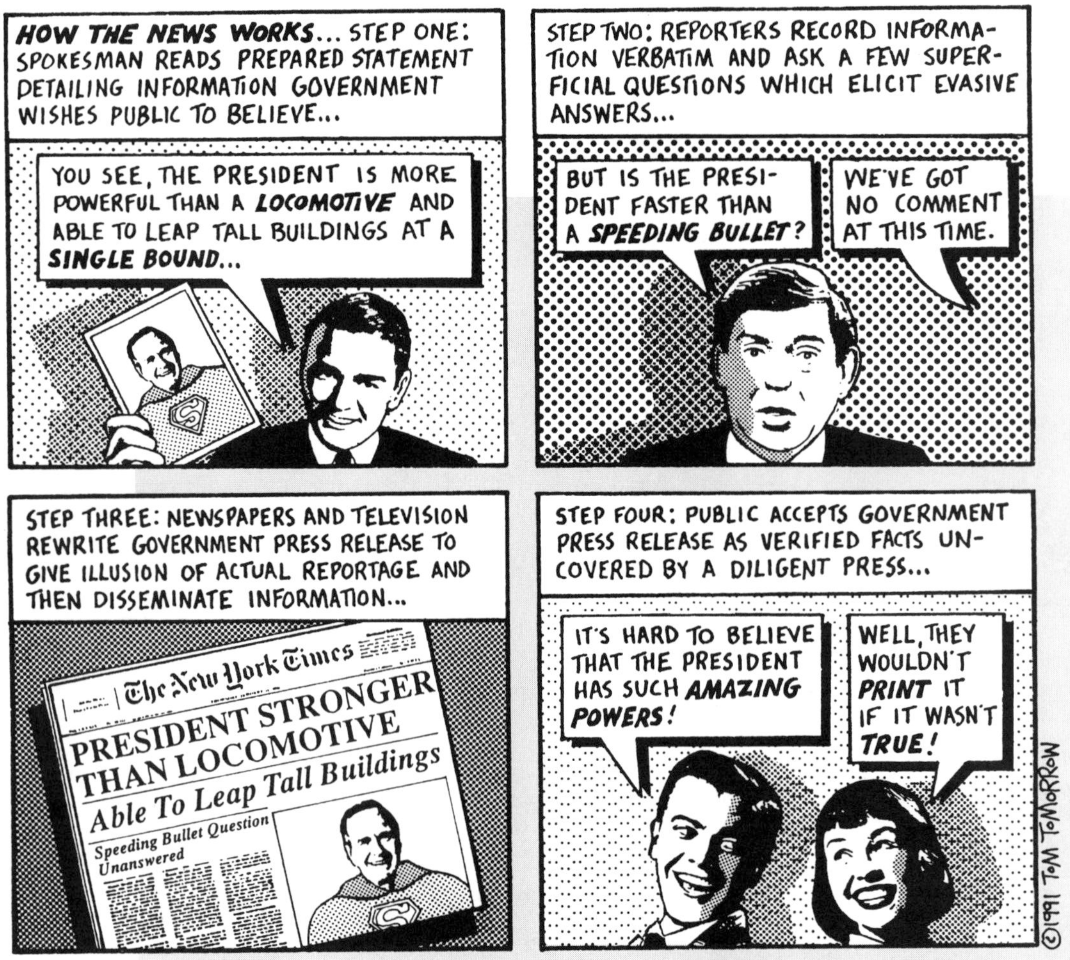
HOW THE NEWS WORKS... STEP ONE: SPOKESMAN READS PREPARED STATEMENT DETAILING INFORMATION GOVERNMENT WISHES PUBLIC TO BELIEVE...
YOU SEE, THE PRESIDENT IS MORE POWERFUL THAN A LOCOMOTIVE AND ABLE TO LEAP TALL BUILDINGS AT A SINGLE BOUND...
STEP TWO: REPORTERS RECORD INFORMATION VERBATIM AND ASK A FEW SUPERFICIAL QUESTIONS WHICH ELICIT EVASIVE ANSWERS...
BUT IS THE PRESIDENT FASTER THAN A SPEEDING BULLET?
WE'VE GOT NO COMMENT AT THIS TIME.
STEP THREE: NEWSPAPERS AND TELEVISION REWRITE GOVERNMENT PRESS RELEASE TO GIVE ILLUSION OF ACTUAL REPORTAGE AND THEN DISSEMINATE INFORMATION...
The New York Times
PRESIDENT STRONGER THAN LOCOMOTIVE
Able To Leap Tall Buildings
Speeding Bullet Question Unanswered
STEP FOUR: PUBLIC ACCEPTS GOVERNMENT PRESS RELEASE AS VERIFIED FACTS UNCOVERED BY A DILIGENT PRESS...
IT'S HARD TO BELIEVE THAT THE PRESIDENT HAS SUCH AMAZING POWERS!
WELL, THEY WOULDN'T PRINT IT IF IT WASN'T TRUE!
©1991 TOM TOMORROW

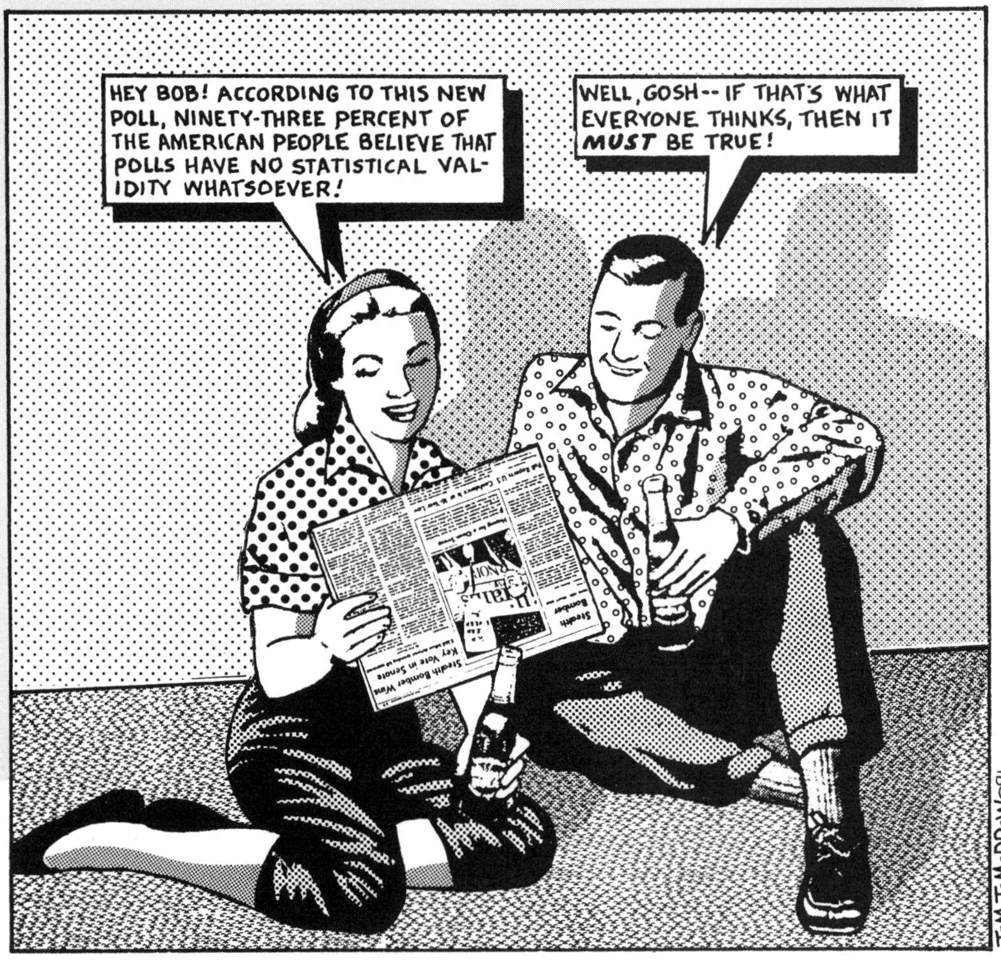
HEY BOB! ACCORDING TO THIS NEW POLL, NINETY-THREE PERCENT OF THE AMERICAN PEOPLE BELIEVE THAT POLLS HAVE NO STATISTICAL VALIDITY WHATSOEVER!
WELL, GOSH-- IF THAT'S WHAT EVERYONE THINKS, THEN IT MUST BE TRUE!
TOM TOMORROW ©91

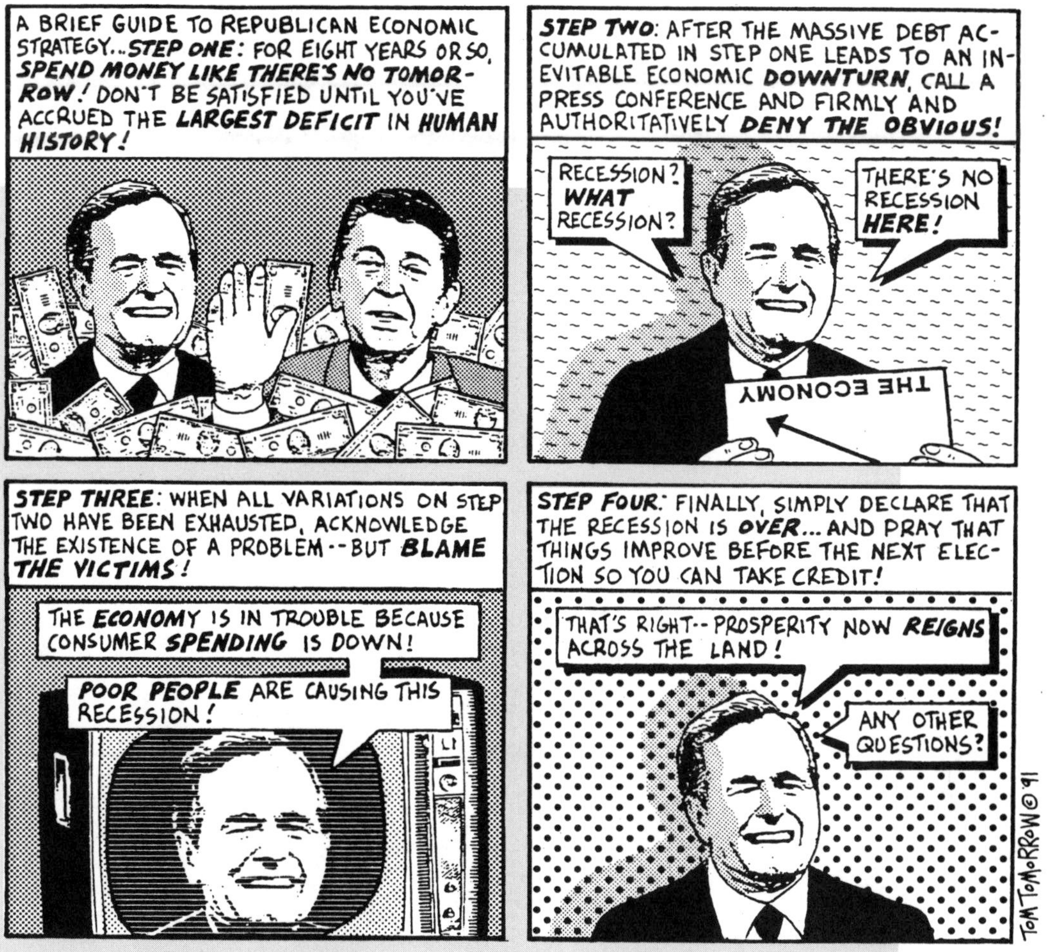
A BRIEF GUIDE TO REPUBLICAN ECONOMIC STRATEGY... STEP ONE: FOR EIGHT YEARS OR SO, SPEND MONEY LIKE THERE'S NO TOMORROW! DON'T BE SATISFIED UNTIL YOU'VE ACCRUED THE LARGEST DEFICIT IN HUMAN HISTORY!
STEP TWO: AFTER THE MASSIVE DEBT ACCUMULATED IN STEP ONE LEADS TO AN INEVITABLE ECONOMIC DOWNTURN, CALL A PRESS CONFERENCE AND FIRMLY AND AUTHORITATIVELY DENY THE OBVIOUS!
RECESSION? WHAT RECESSION?
THERE'S NO RECESSION HERE!
THE ECONOMY
STEP THREE: WHEN ALL VARIATIONS ON STEP TWO HAVE BEEN EXHAUSTED, ACKNOWLEDGE THE EXISTENCE OF A PROBLEM--BUT BLAME THE VICTIMS!
THE ECONOMY IS IN TROUBLE BECAUSE CONSUMER SPENDING IS DOWN!
POOR PEOPLE ARE CAUSING THIS RECESSION!
STEP FOUR: FINALLY, SIMPLY DECLARE THAT THE RECESSION IS OVER... AND PRAY THAT THINGS IMPROVE BEFORE THE NEXT ELECTION SO YOU CAN TAKE CREDIT!
THAT'S RIGHT--PROSPERITY NOW REIGNS ACROSS THE LAND!
ANY OTHER QUESTIONS?
TOM TOMORROW ©'91

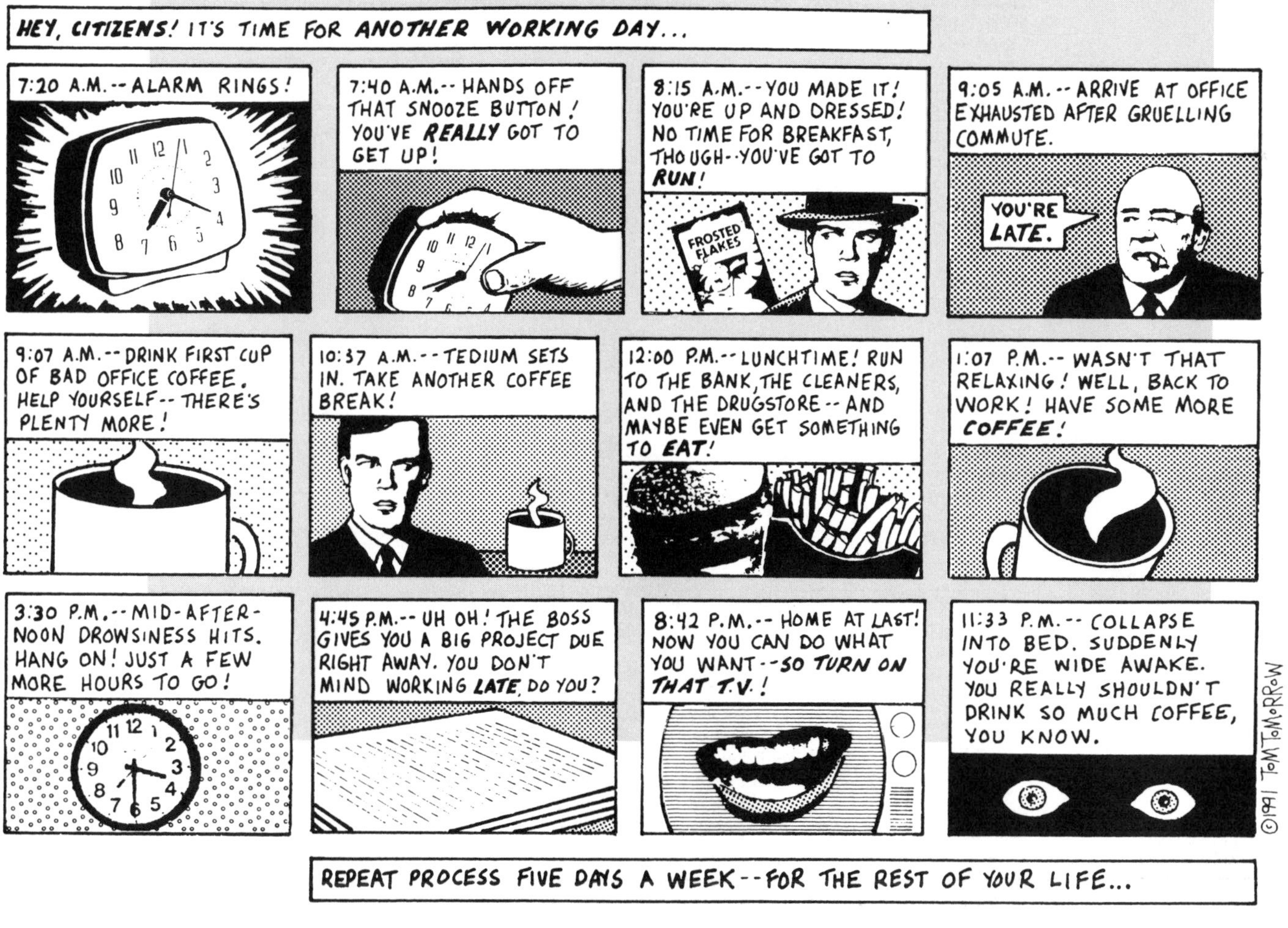
HEY, CITIZENS! IT'S TIME FOR ANOTHER WORKING DAY...
7:20 A.M.--ALARM RINGS!
7:40 A.M.--HANDS OFF THAT SNOOZE BUTTON! YOU'VE REALLY GOT TO GET UP!
8:15 A.M.--YOU MADE IT! YOU'RE UP AND DRESSED! NO TIME FOR BREAKFAST, THOUGH--YOU'VE GOT TO RUN!
FROSTED FLAKES
9:05 A.M.--ARRIVE AT OFFICE EXHAUSTED AFTER GRUELLING COMMUTE.
YOU'RE LATE.
9:07 A.M.--DRINK FIRST CUP OF BAD OFFICE COFFEE. HELP YOURSELF--THERE'S PLENTY MORE!
10:37 A.M.--TEDIUM SETS IN. TAKE ANOTHER COFFEE BREAK!
12:00 P.M.--LUNCHTIME! RUN TO THE BANK, THE CLEANERS, AND THE DRUGSTORE--AND MAYBE EVEN GET SOMETHING TO EAT!
1:07 P.M.--WASN'T THAT RELAXING! WELL, BACK TO WORK! HAVE SOME MORE COFFEE!
3:30 P.M.--MID-AFTERNOON DROWSINESS HITS. HANG ON! JUST A FEW MORE HOURS TO GO!
4:45 P.M.--UH OH! THE BOSS GIVES YOU A BIG PROJECT DUE RIGHT AWAY. YOU DON'T MIND WORKING LATE, DO YOU?
8:42 P.M.--HOME AT LAST! NOW YOU CAN DO WHAT YOU WANT--SO TURN ON THAT T.V.!
11:33 P.M.--COLLAPSE INTO BED. SUDDENLY YOU'RE WIDE AWAKE. YOU REALLY SHOULDN'T DRINK SO MUCH COFFEE, YOU KNOW.
©1991 TOM TOMORROW
REPEAT PROCESS FIVE DAYS A WEEK--FOR THE REST OF YOUR LIFE...

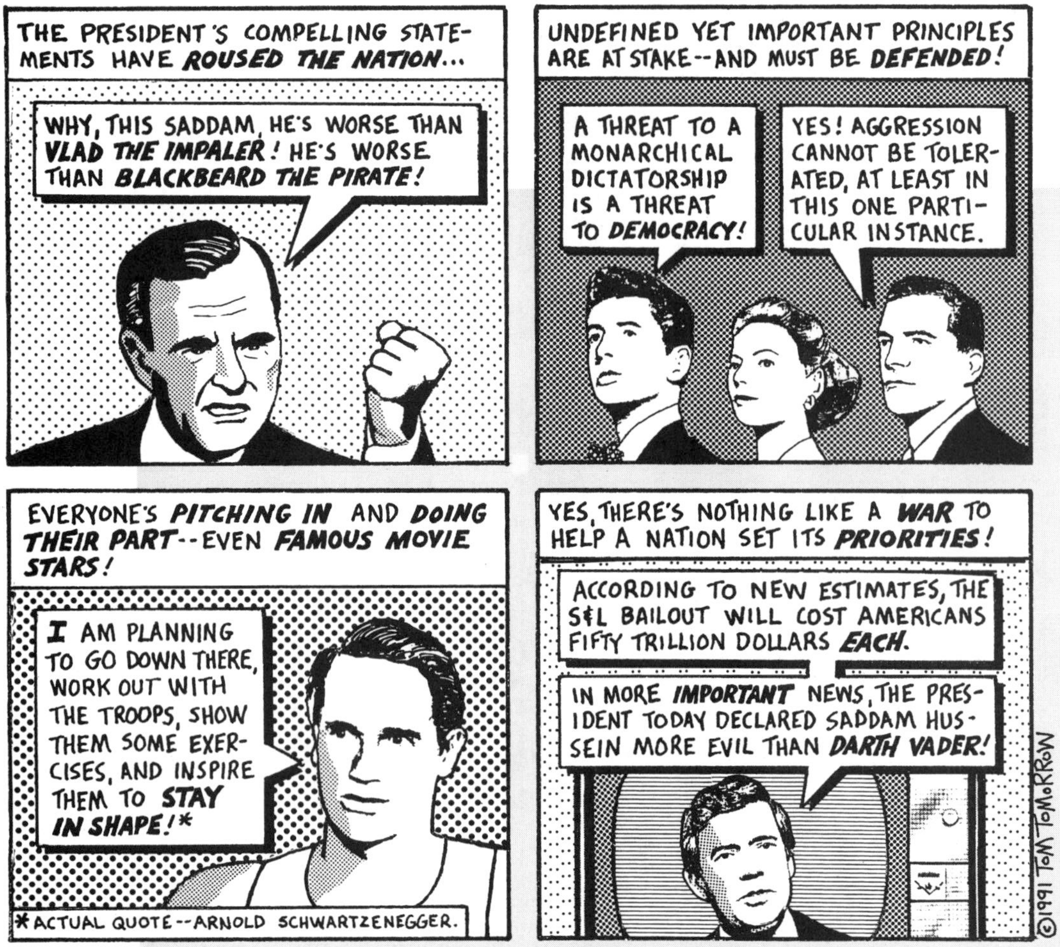
THE PRESIDENT'S COMPELLING STATEMENTS HAVE ROUSED THE NATION...
WHY, THIS SADDAM, HE'S WORSE THAN VLAD THE IMPALER! HE'S WORSE THAN BLACKBEARD THE PIRATE!
UNDEFINED YET IMPORTANT PRINCIPLES ARE AT STAKE--AND MUST BE DEFENDED!
A THREAT TO A MONARCHICAL DICTATORSHIP IS A THREAT TO DEMOCRACY!
YES! AGGRESSION CANNOT BE TOLERATED, AT LEAST IN THIS ONE PARTICULAR INSTANCE.
EVERYONE'S PITCHING IN AND DOING THEIR PART--EVEN FAMOUS MOVIE STARS!
I AM PLANNING TO GO DOWN THERE, WORK OUT WITH THE TROOPS, SHOW THEM SOME EXERCISES, AND INSPIRE THEM TO STAY IN SHAPE!*
*ACTUAL QUOTE--ARNOLD SCHWARTZENEGGER.
YES, THERE'S NOTHING LIKE A WAR TO HELP A NATION SET ITS PRIORITIES!
ACCORDING TO NEW ESTIMATES, THE S&L BAILOUT WILL COST AMERICANS FIFTY TRILLION DOLLARS EACH.
IN MORE IMPORTANT NEWS, THE PRESIDENT TODAY DECLARED SADDAM HUSSEIN MORE EVIL THAN DARTH VADER!
©1991 TOM TOMORROW

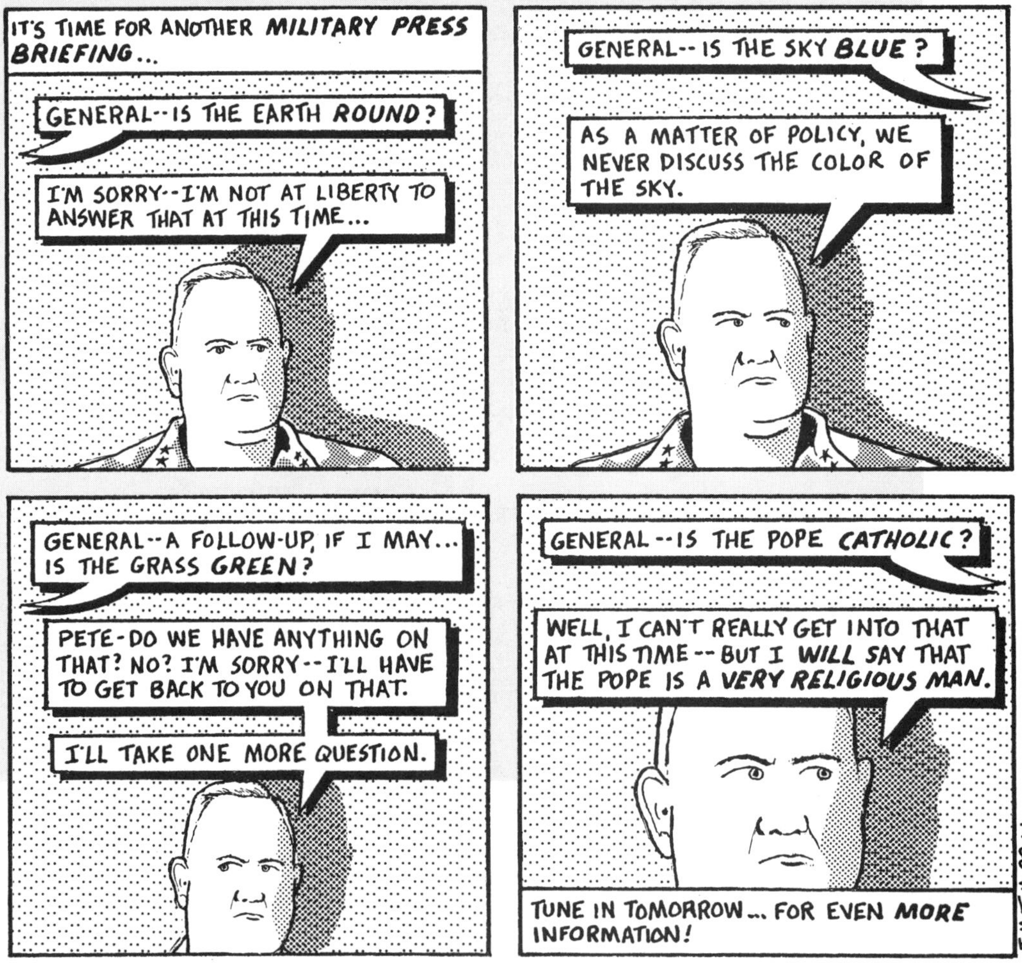
IT'S TIME FOR ANOTHER MILITARY PRESS BRIEFING...
GENERAL--IS THE EARTH ROUND?
I'M SORRY--I'M NOT AT LIBERTY TO ANSWER THAT AT THIS TIME...
GENERAL--IS THE SKY BLUE?
AS A MATTER OF POLICY, WE NEVER DISCUSS THE COLOR OF THE SKY.
GENERAL--A FOLLOW-UP, IF I MAY... IS THE GRASS GREEN?
PETE-DO WE HAVE ANYTHING ON THAT? NO? I'M SORRY--I'LL HAVE TO GET BACK TO YOU ON THAT.
I'LL TAKE ONE MORE QUESTION.
GENERAL--IS THE POPE CATHOLIC?
WELL, I CAN'T REALLY GET INTO THAT AT THIS TIME--BUT I WILL SAY THAT THE POPE IS A VERY RELIGIOUS MAN.
TUNE IN TOMORROW... FOR EVEN MORE INFORMATION!
TOM TOMORROW

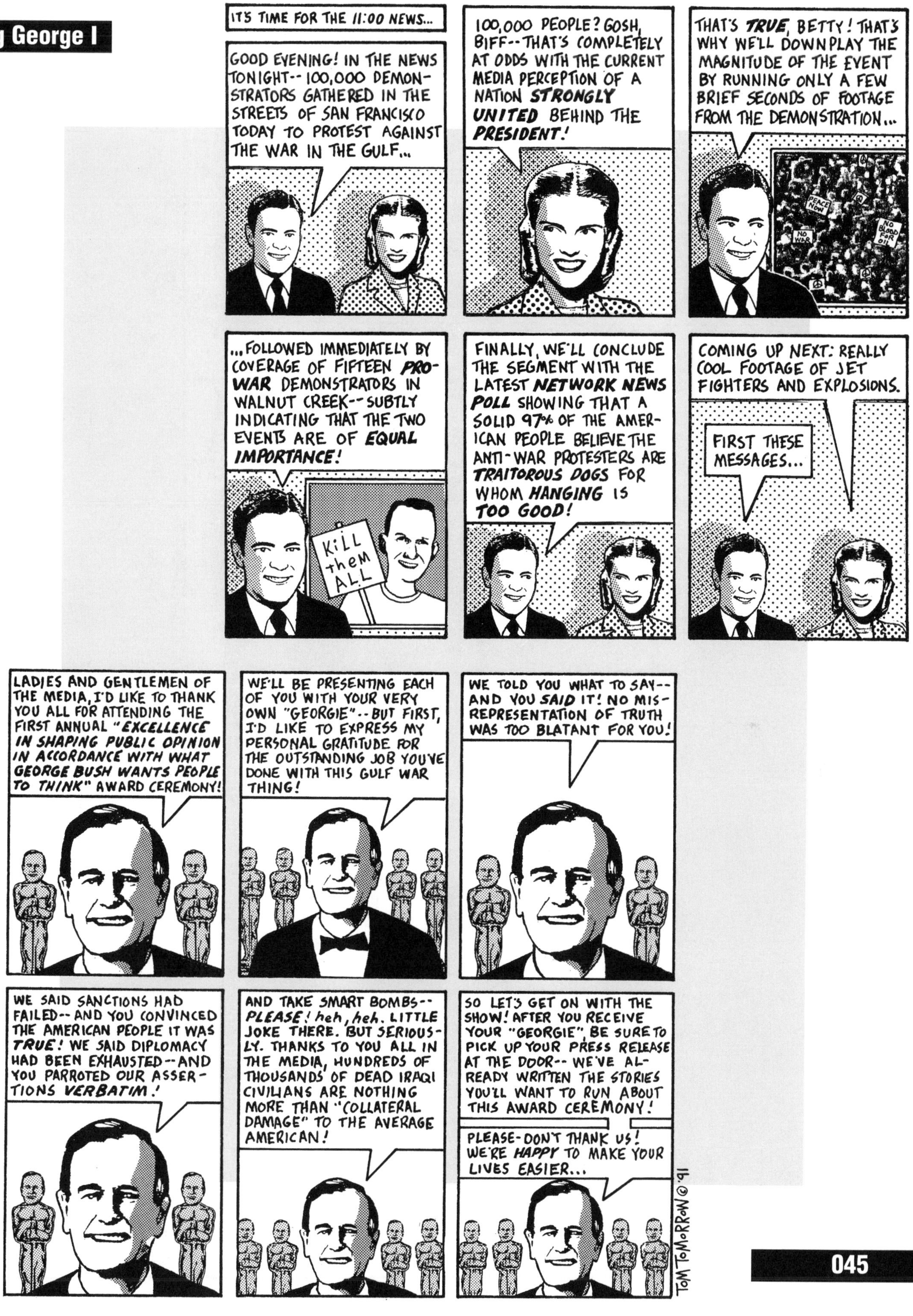
IT'S TIME FOR THE 11:00 NEWS...
GOOD EVENING! IN THE NEWS TONIGHT-- 100,000 DEMONSTRATORS GATHERED IN THE STREETS OF SAN FRANCISCO TODAY TO PROTEST AGAINST THE WAR IN THE GULF...
100,000 PEOPLE? GOSH, BIFF--THAT'S COMPLETELY AT ODDS WITH THE CURRENT MEDIA PERCEPTION OF A NATION STRONGLY UNITED BEHIND THE PRESIDENT!
THAT'S TRUE, BETTY! THAT'S WHY WE'LL DOWNPLAY THE MAGNITUDE OF THE EVENT BY RUNNING ONLY A FEW BRIEF SECONDS OF FOOTAGE FROM THE DEMONSTRATION...
PEACE NOW
NO WAR
NO BLOOD FOR OIL
...FOLLOWED IMMEDIATELY BY COVERAGE OF FIFTEEN PRO-WAR DEMONSTRATORS IN WALNUT CREEK-- SUBTLY INDICATING THAT THE TWO EVENTS ARE OF EQUAL IMPORTANCE!
KILL THEM ALL
FINALLY, WE'LL CONCLUDE THE SEGMENT WITH THE LATEST NETWORK NEWS POLL SHOWING THAT A SOLID 97% OF THE AMERICAN PEOPLE BELIEVE THE ANTI-WAR PROTESTERS ARE TRAITOROUS DOGS FOR WHOM HANGING IS TOO GOOD!
COMING UP NEXT: REALLY COOL FOOTAGE OF JET FIGHTERS AND EXPLOSIONS.
FIRST THESE MESSAGES...
LADIES AND GENTLEMEN OF THE MEDIA, I'D LIKE TO THANK YOU ALL FOR ATTENDING THE FIRST ANNUAL "EXCELLENCE IN SHAPING PUBLIC OPINION IN ACCORDANCE WITH WHAT GEORGE BUSH WANTS PEOPLE TO THINK" AWARD CEREMONY!
WE'LL BE PRESENTING EACH OF YOU WITH YOUR VERY OWN "GEORGIE"--BUT FIRST, I'D LIKE TO EXPRESS MY PERSONAL GRATITUDE FOR THE OUTSTANDING JOB YOU'VE DONE WITH THIS GULF WAR THING!
WE TOLD YOU WHAT TO SAY-- AND YOU SAID IT! NO MISREPRESENTATION OF TRUTH WAS TOO BLATANT FOR YOU!
WE SAID SANCTIONS HAD FAILED--AND YOU CONVINCED THE AMERICAN PEOPLE IT WAS TRUE! WE SAID DIPLOMACY HAD BEEN EXHAUSTED--AND YOU PARROTED OUR ASSERTIONS VERBATIM!
AND TAKE SMART BOMBS-- PLEASE! heh, heh. LITTLE JOKE THERE. BUT SERIOUSLY. THANKS TO YOU ALL IN THE MEDIA, HUNDREDS OF THOUSANDS OF DEAD IRAQI CIVILIANS ARE NOTHING MORE THAN "COLLATERAL DAMAGE" TO THE AVERAGE AMERICAN!
SO LET'S GET ON WITH THE SHOW! AFTER YOU RECEIVE YOUR "GEORGIE", BE SURE TO PICK UP YOUR PRESS RELEASE AT THE DOOR-- WE'VE ALREADY WRITTEN THE STORIES YOU'LL WANT TO RUN ABOUT THIS AWARD CEREMONY!
PLEASE-DON'T THANK US! WE'RE HAPPY TO MAKE YOUR LIVES EASIER...
TOM TOMORROW © '91

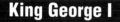

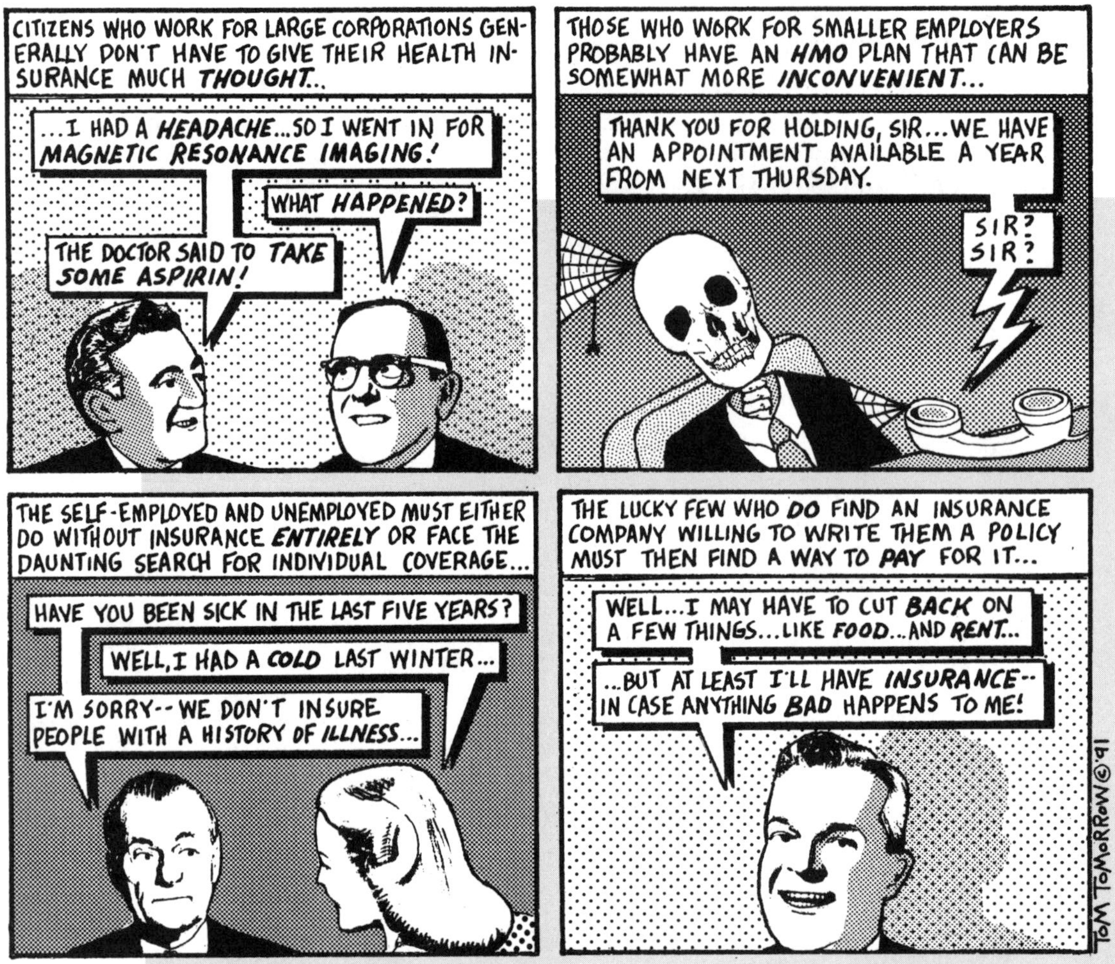
CITIZENS WHO WORK FOR LARGE CORPORATIONS GENERALLY DON'T HAVE TO GIVE THEIR HEALTH INSURANCE MUCH THOUGHT...
...I HAD A HEADACHE...SO I WENT IN FOR MAGNETIC RESONANCE IMAGING!
WHAT HAPPENED?
THE DOCTOR SAID TO TAKE SOME ASPIRIN!
THOSE WHO WORK FOR SMALLER EMPLOYERS PROBABLY HAVE AN HMO PLAN THAT CAN BE SOMEWHAT MORE INCONVENIENT...
THANK YOU FOR HOLDING, SIR...WE HAVE AN APPOINTMENT AVAILABLE A YEAR FROM NEXT THURSDAY.
SIR? SIR?
THE SELF-EMPLOYED AND UNEMPLOYED MUST EITHER DO WITHOUT INSURANCE ENTIRELY OR FACE THE DAUNTING SEARCH FOR INDIVIDUAL COVERAGE...
HAVE YOU BEEN SICK IN THE LAST FIVE YEARS?
WELL, I HAD A COLD LAST WINTER...
I'M SORRY--WE DON'T INSURE PEOPLE WITH A HISTORY OF ILLNESS...
THE LUCKY FEW WHO DO FIND AN INSURANCE COMPANY WILLING TO WRITE THEM A POLICY MUST THEN FIND A WAY TO PAY FOR IT...
WELL...I MAY HAVE TO CUT BACK ON A FEW THINGS...LIKE FOOD...AND RENT...
...BUT AT LEAST I'LL HAVE INSURANCE--IN CASE ANYTHING BAD HAPPENS TO ME!
TOM TOMORROW©91

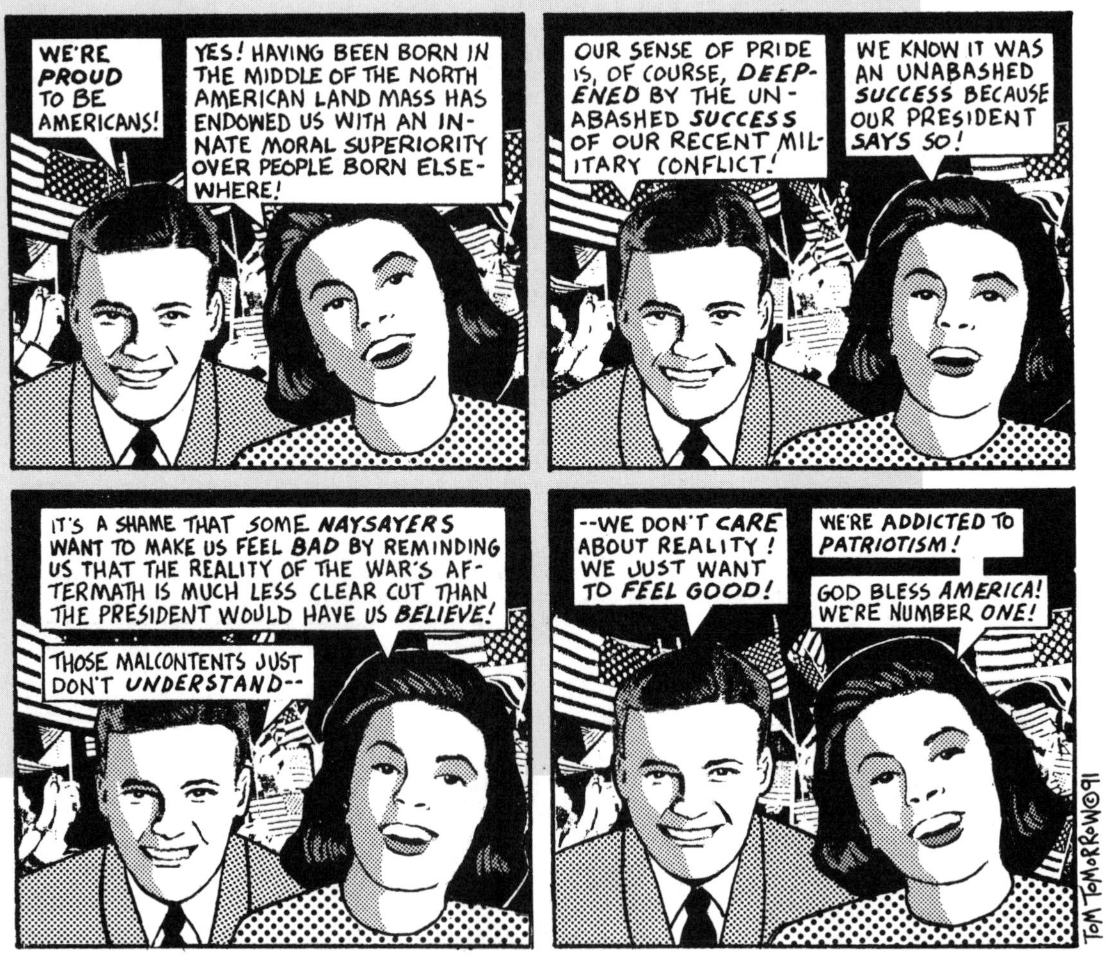
WE'RE PROUD TO BE AMERICANS!
YES! HAVING BEEN BORN IN THE MIDDLE OF THE NORTH AMERICAN LAND MASS HAS ENDOWED US WITH AN INNATE MORAL SUPERIORITY OVER PEOPLE BORN ELSEWHERE!
OUR SENSE OF PRIDE IS, OF COURSE, DEEPENED BY THE UNABASHED SUCCESS OF OUR RECENT MILITARY CONFLICT!
WE KNOW IT WAS AN UNABASHED SUCCESS BECAUSE OUR PRESIDENT SAYS SO!
IT'S A SHAME THAT SOME NAYSAYERS WANT TO MAKE US FEEL BAD BY REMINDING US THAT THE REALITY OF THE WAR'S AFTERMATH IS MUCH LESS CLEAR CUT THAN THE PRESIDENT WOULD HAVE US BELIEVE!
THOSE MALCONTENTS JUST DON'T UNDERSTAND--
--WE DON'T CARE ABOUT REALITY! WE JUST WANT TO FEEL GOOD!
WE'RE ADDICTED TO PATRIOTISM!
GOD BLESS AMERICA! WE'RE NUMBER ONE!
TOM TOMORROW©91

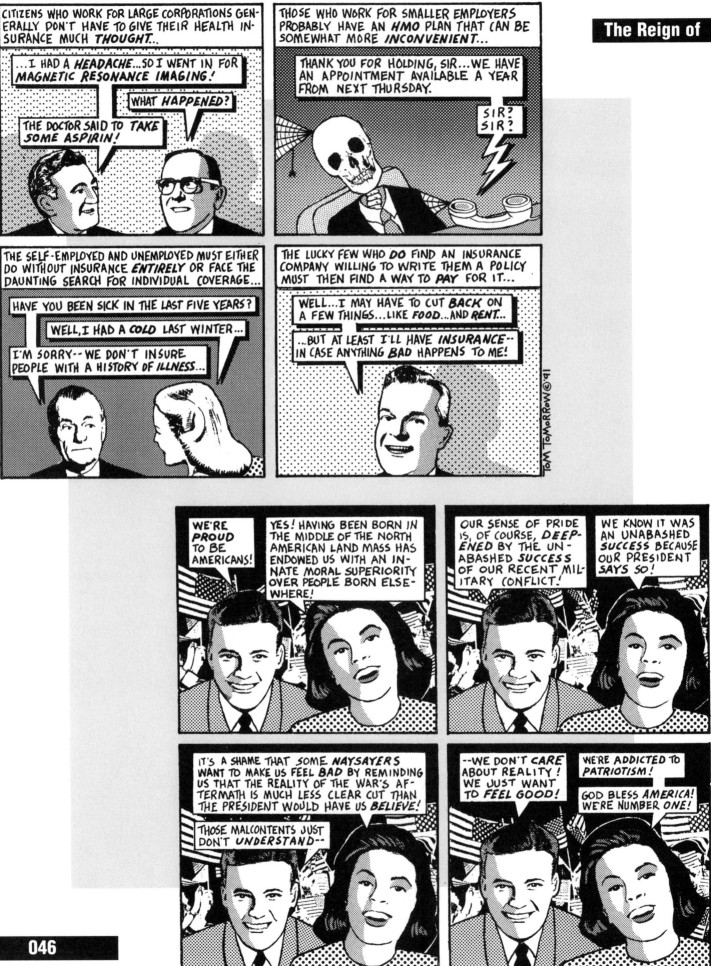

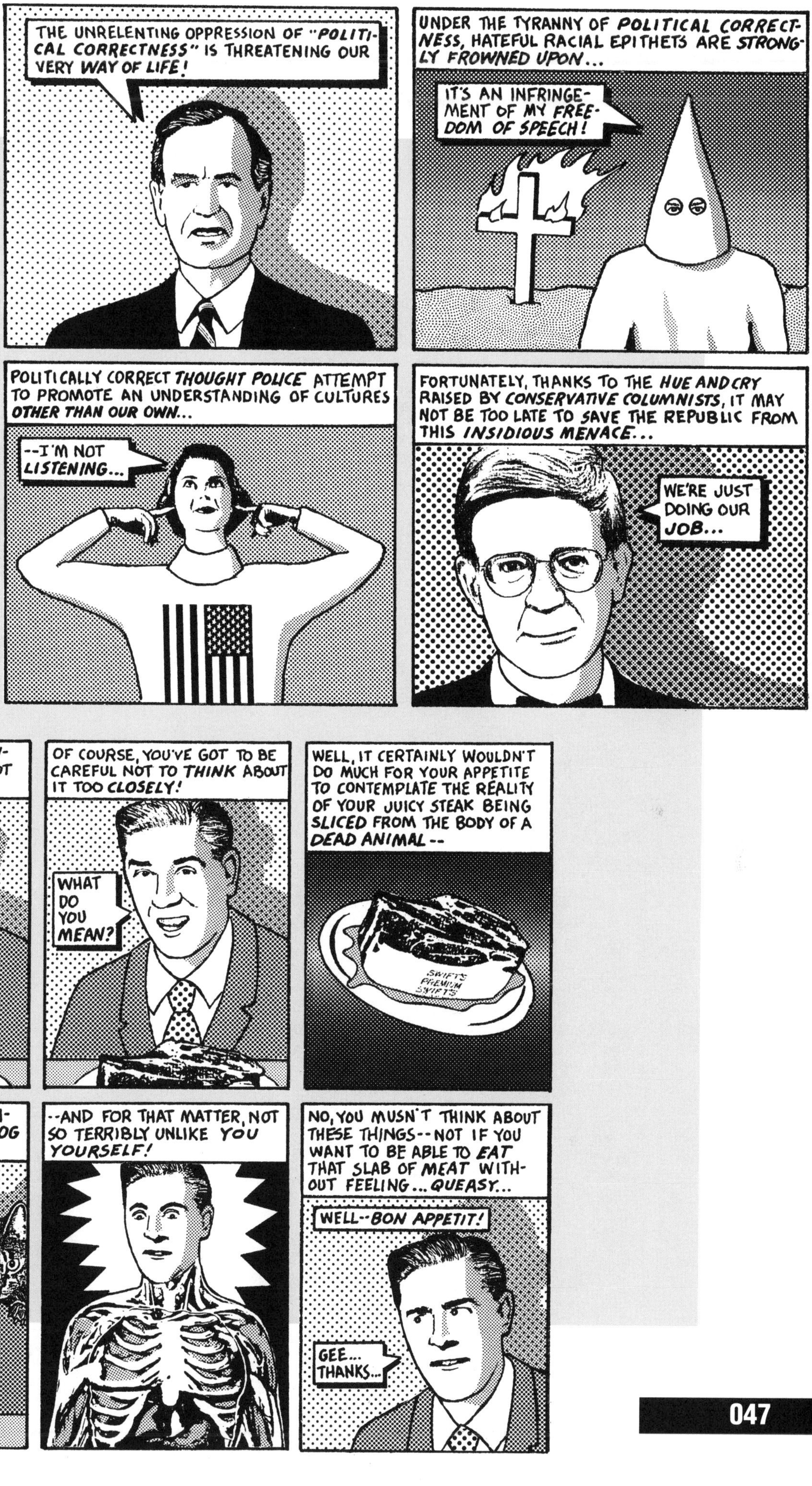
THE UNRELENTING OPPRESSION OF "POLITICAL CORRECTNESS" IS THREATENING OUR VERY WAY OF LIFE!
UNDER THE TYRANNY OF POLITICAL CORRECTNESS, HATEFUL RACIAL EPITHETS ARE STRONGLY FROWNED UPON...
IT'S AN INFRINGEMENT OF MY FREEDOM OF SPEECH!
POLITICALLY CORRECT THOUGHT POLICE ATTEMPT TO PROMOTE AN UNDERSTANDING OF CULTURES OTHER THAN OUR OWN...
--I'M NOT LISTENING...
FORTUNATELY, THANKS TO THE HUE AND CRY RAISED BY CONSERVATIVE COLUMNISTS, IT MAY NOT BE TOO LATE TO SAVE THE REPUBLIC FROM THIS INSIDIOUS MENACE...
WE'RE JUST DOING OUR JOB...
HEY, THAT'S A PRETTY MOUTH-WATERING STEAK YOU'VE GOT THERE!
IT SURE IS!
OF COURSE, YOU'VE GOT TO BE CAREFUL NOT TO THINK ABOUT IT TOO CLOSELY!
WHAT DO YOU MEAN?
WELL, IT CERTAINLY WOULDN'T DO MUCH FOR YOUR APPETITE TO CONTEMPLATE THE REALITY OF YOUR JUICY STEAK BEING SLICED FROM THE BODY OF A DEAD ANIMAL--
SWIFT'S PREMIUM SWIFT'S
--A SENTIENT BEING, NOT UNLIKE YOUR OWN BELOVED DOG OR CAT--
--AND FOR THAT MATTER, NOT SO TERRIBLY UNLIKE YOU YOURSELF!
NO, YOU MUSN'T THINK ABOUT THESE THINGS--NOT IF YOU WANT TO BE ABLE TO EAT THAT SLAB OF MEAT WITHOUT FEELING... QUEASY...
WELL--BON APPETIT!
GEE... THANKS...

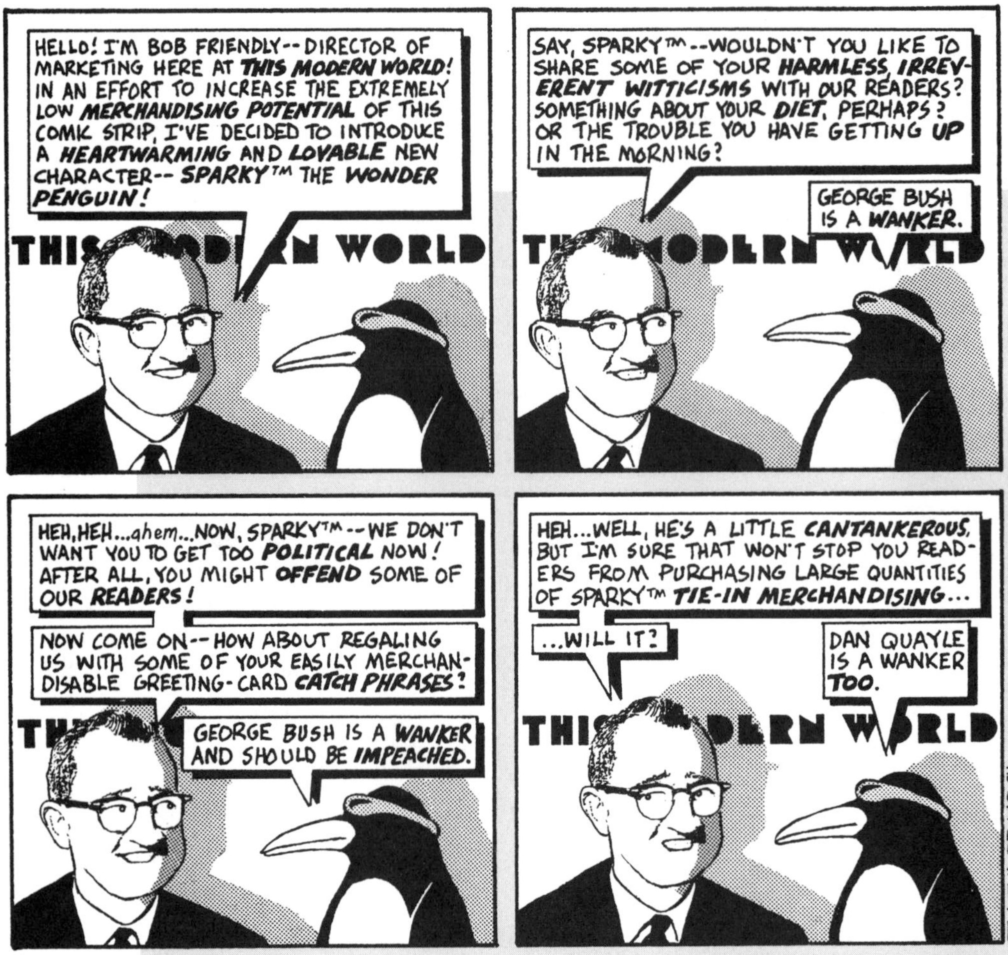
HELLO! I'M BOB FRIENDLY-- DIRECTOR OF MARKETING HERE AT THIS MODERN WORLD! IN AN EFFORT TO INCREASE THE EXTREMELY LOW MERCHANDISING POTENTIAL OF THIS COMIC STRIP, I'VE DECIDED TO INTRODUCE A HEARTWARMING AND LOVABLE NEW CHARACTER-- SPARKY™ THE WONDER PENGUIN!
SAY, SPARKY™--WOULDN'T YOU LIKE TO SHARE SOME OF YOUR HARMLESS, IRREVERENT WITTICISMS WITH OUR READERS? SOMETHING ABOUT YOUR DIET, PERHAPS? OR THE TROUBLE YOU HAVE GETTING UP IN THE MORNING?
GEORGE BUSH IS A WANKER.
HEH,HEH...ahem...NOW, SPARKY™--WE DON'T WANT YOU TO GET TOO POLITICAL NOW! AFTER ALL, YOU MIGHT OFFEND SOME OF OUR READERS!
NOW COME ON--HOW ABOUT REGALING US WITH SOME OF YOUR EASILY MERCHANDISABLE GREETING-CARD CATCH PHRASES?
GEORGE BUSH IS A WANKER AND SHOULD BE IMPEACHED.
HEH...WELL, HE'S A LITTLE CANTANKEROUS, BUT I'M SURE THAT WON'T STOP YOU READERS FROM PURCHASING LARGE QUANTITIES OF SPARKY™ TIE-IN MERCHANDISING...
...WILL IT?
DAN QUAYLE IS A WANKER TOO.
TOM TOMORROW©'91

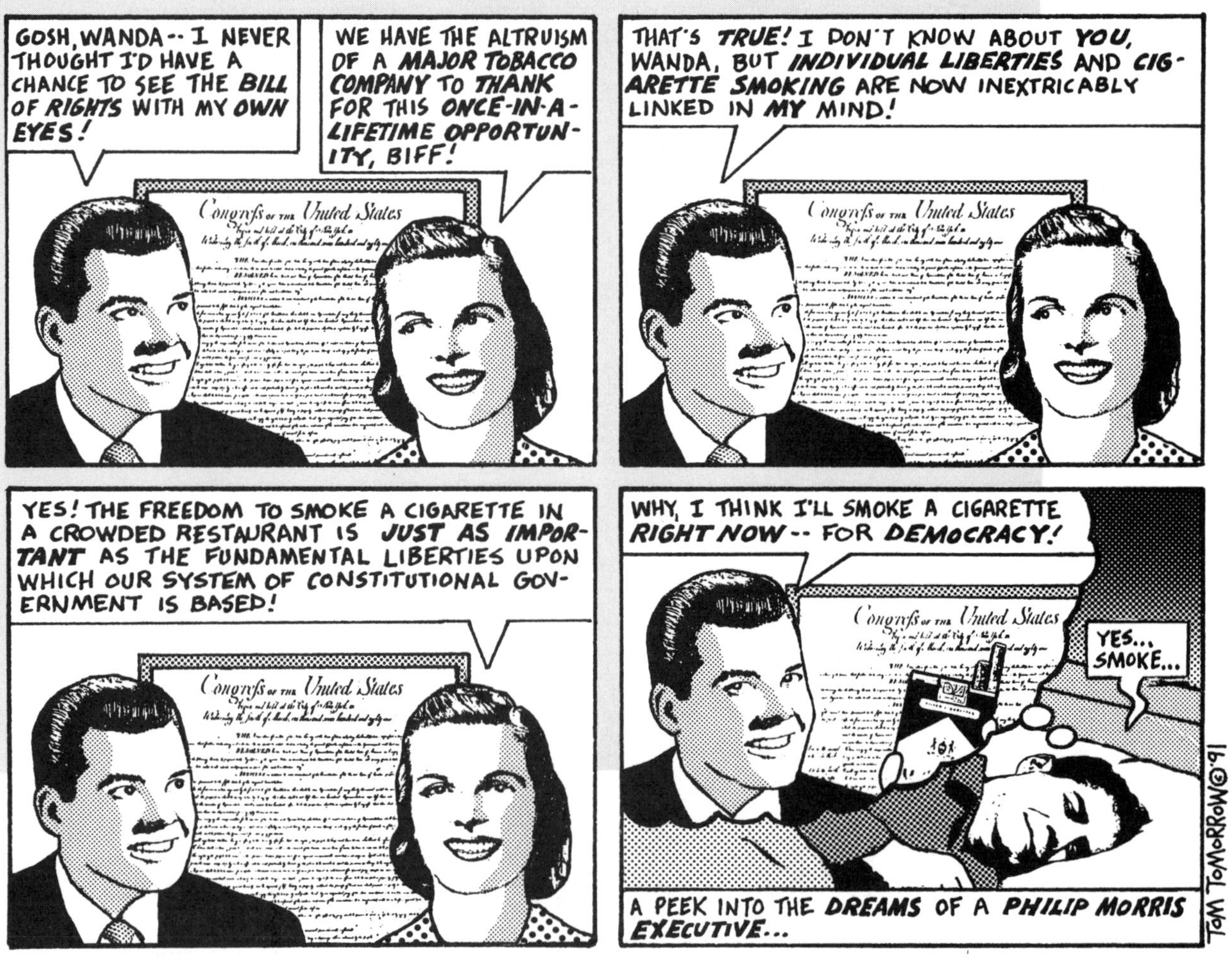
GOSH, WANDA-- I NEVER THOUGHT I'D HAVE A CHANCE TO SEE THE BILL OF RIGHTS WITH MY OWN EYES!
WE HAVE THE ALTRUISM OF A MAJOR TOBACCO COMPANY TO THANK FOR THIS ONCE-IN-A-LIFETIME OPPORTUNITY, BIFF!
Congress of the United States
THAT'S TRUE! I DON'T KNOW ABOUT YOU, WANDA, BUT INDIVIDUAL LIBERTIES AND CIGARETTE SMOKING ARE NOW INEXTRICABLY LINKED IN MY MIND!
YES! THE FREEDOM TO SMOKE A CIGARETTE IN A CROWDED RESTAURANT IS JUST AS IMPORTANT AS THE FUNDAMENTAL LIBERTIES UPON WHICH OUR SYSTEM OF CONSTITUTIONAL GOVERNMENT IS BASED!
WHY, I THINK I'LL SMOKE A CIGARETTE RIGHT NOW -- FOR DEMOCRACY!
YES... SMOKE...
A PEEK INTO THE DREAMS OF A PHILIP MORRIS EXECUTIVE...
TOM TOMORROW©'91

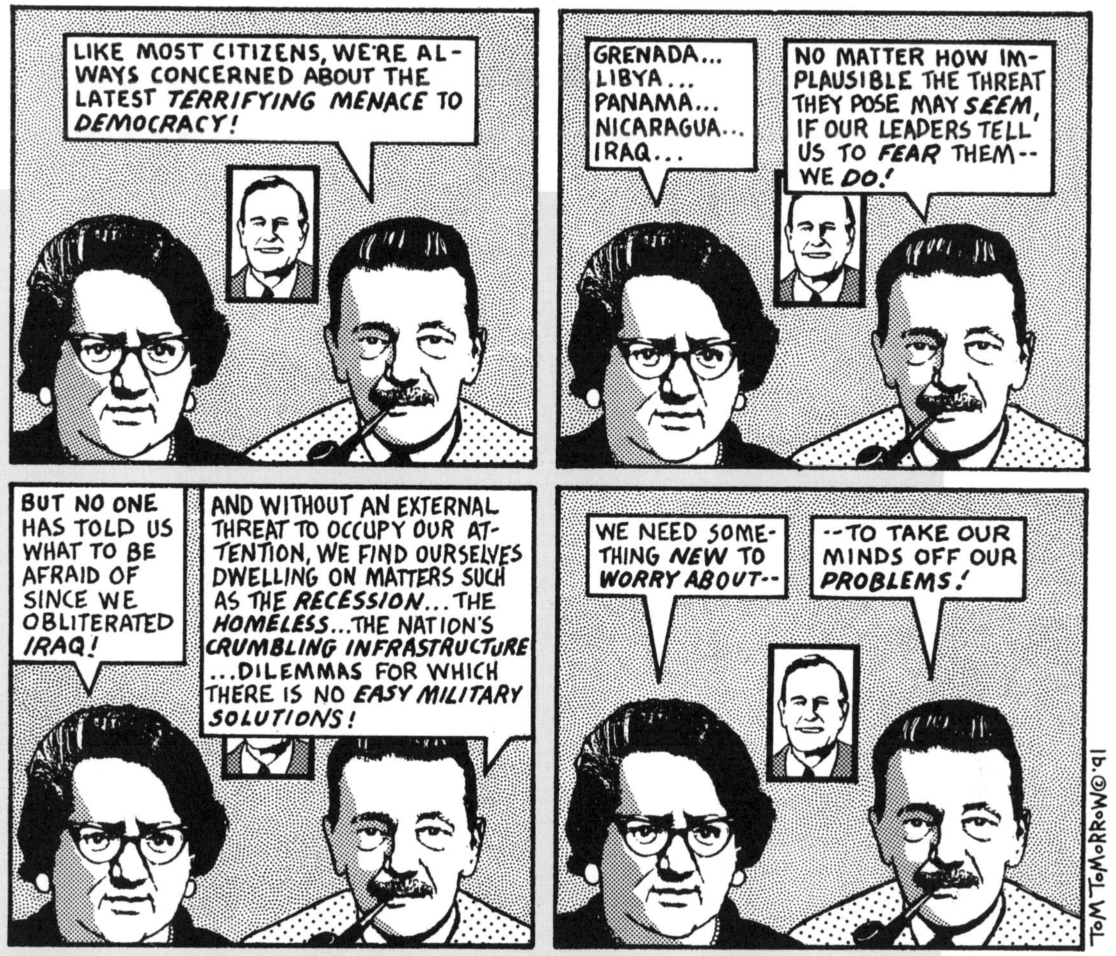
LIKE MOST CITIZENS, WE'RE ALWAYS CONCERNED ABOUT THE LATEST TERRIFYING MENACE TO DEMOCRACY!
GRENADA... LIBYA... PANAMA... NICARAGUA... IRAQ...
NO MATTER HOW IMPLAUSIBLE THE THREAT THEY POSE MAY SEEM, IF OUR LEADERS TELL US TO FEAR THEM--WE DO!
BUT NO ONE HAS TOLD US WHAT TO BE AFRAID OF SINCE WE OBLITERATED IRAQ!
AND WITHOUT AN EXTERNAL THREAT TO OCCUPY OUR ATTENTION, WE FIND OURSELVES DWELLING ON MATTERS SUCH AS THE RECESSION... THE HOMELESS... THE NATION'S CRUMBLING INFRASTRUCTURE ...DILEMMAS FOR WHICH THERE IS NO EASY MILITARY SOLUTIONS!
WE NEED SOMETHING NEW TO WORRY ABOUT--
--TO TAKE OUR MINDS OFF OUR PROBLEMS!
TOM TOMORROW ©'91

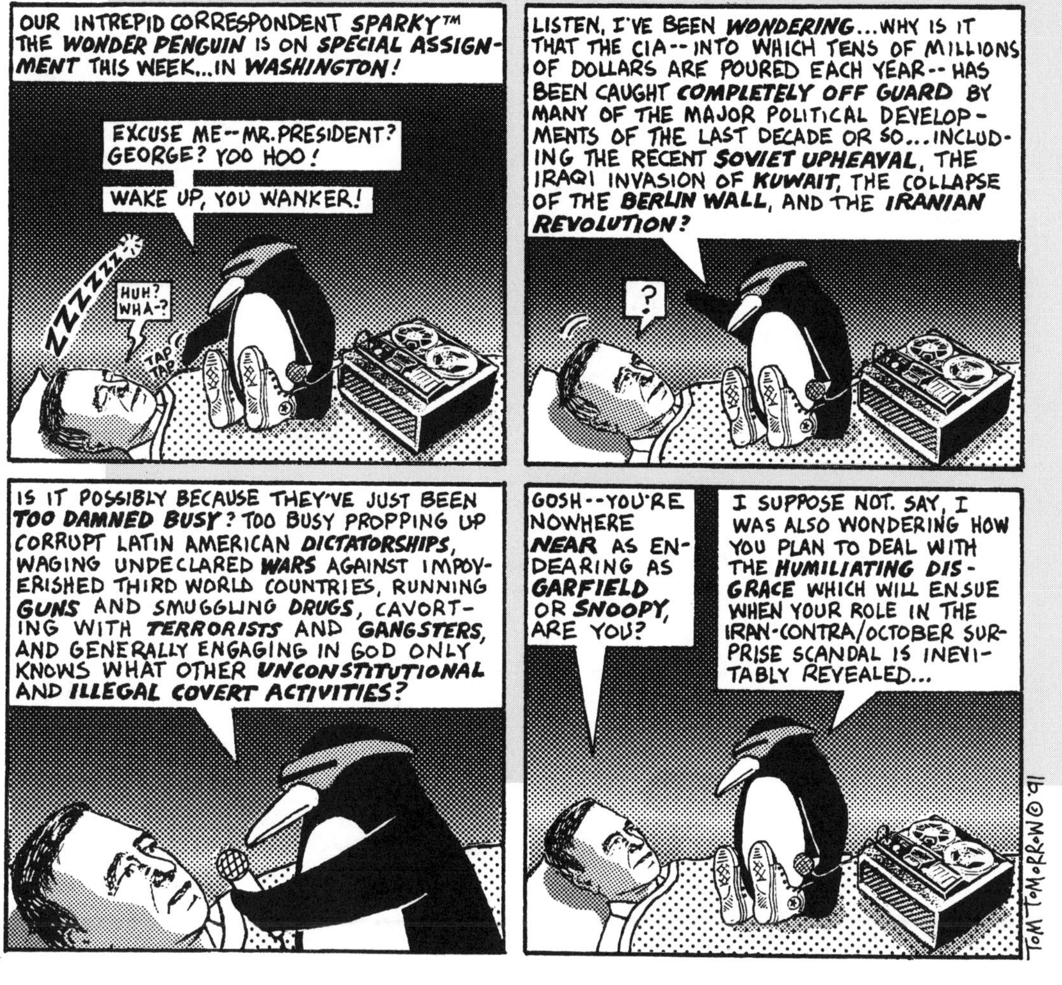
OUR INTREPID CORRESPONDENT SPARKY™ THE WONDER PENGUIN IS ON SPECIAL ASSIGNMENT THIS WEEK...IN WASHINGTON!
EXCUSE ME--MR. PRESIDENT? GEORGE? YOO HOO!
WAKE UP, YOU WANKER!
ZZZZZZZ*
HUH? WHA-?
TAP TAP
LISTEN, I'VE BEEN WONDERING...WHY IS IT THAT THE CIA--INTO WHICH TENS OF MILLIONS OF DOLLARS ARE POURED EACH YEAR--HAS BEEN CAUGHT COMPLETELY OFF GUARD BY MANY OF THE MAJOR POLITICAL DEVELOPMENTS OF THE LAST DECADE OR SO...INCLUDING THE RECENT SOVIET UPHEAVAL, THE IRAQI INVASION OF KUWAIT, THE COLLAPSE OF THE BERLIN WALL, AND THE IRANIAN REVOLUTION?
?
IS IT POSSIBLY BECAUSE THEY'VE JUST BEEN TOO DAMNED BUSY? TOO BUSY PROPPING UP CORRUPT LATIN AMERICAN DICTATORSHIPS, WAGING UNDECLARED WARS AGAINST IMPOVERISHED THIRD WORLD COUNTRIES, RUNNING GUNS AND SMUGGLING DRUGS, CAVORTING WITH TERRORISTS AND GANGSTERS, AND GENERALLY ENGAGING IN GOD ONLY KNOWS WHAT OTHER UNCONSTITUTIONAL AND ILLEGAL COVERT ACTIVITIES?
GOSH--YOU'RE NOWHERE NEAR AS ENDEARING AS GARFIELD OR SNOOPY, ARE YOU?
I SUPPOSE NOT. SAY, I WAS ALSO WONDERING HOW YOU PLAN TO DEAL WITH THE HUMILIATING DISGRACE WHICH WILL ENSUE WHEN YOUR ROLE IN THE IRAN-CONTRA/OCTOBER SURPRISE SCANDAL IS INEVITABLY REVEALED...
TOM TOMORROW ©'91

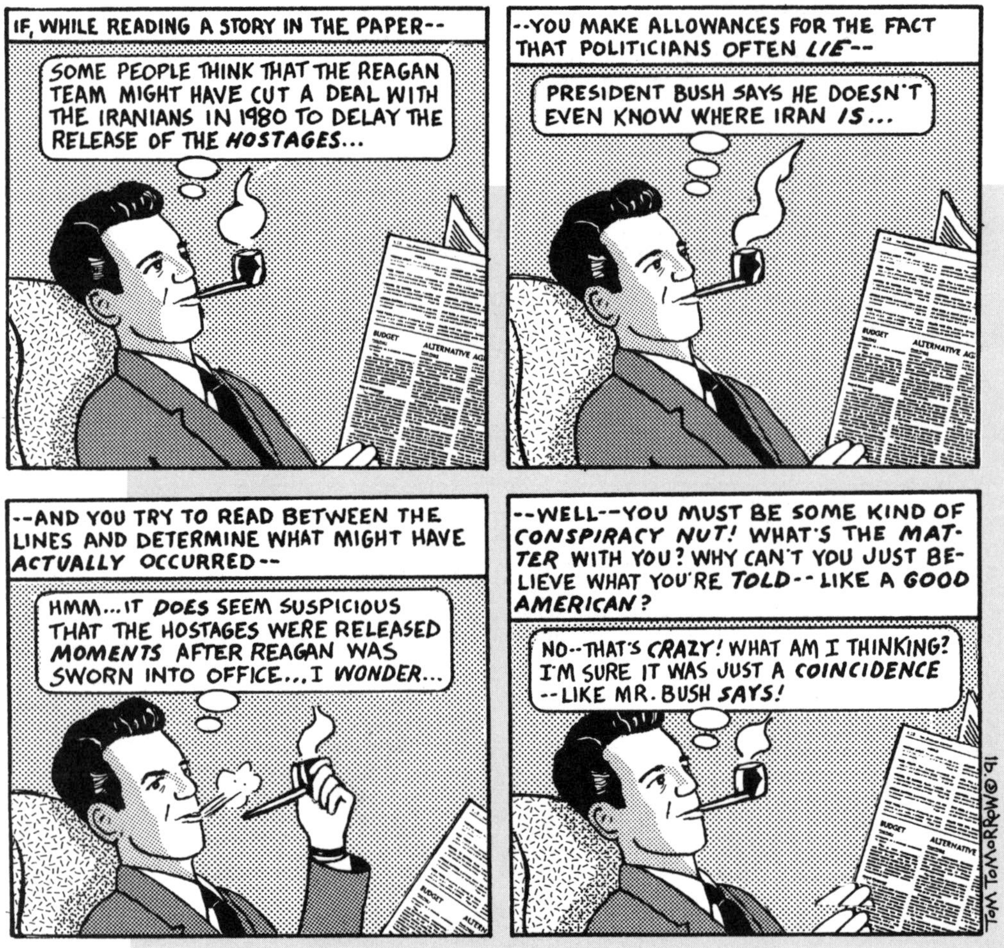
IF, WHILE READING A STORY IN THE PAPER--
SOME PEOPLE THINK THAT THE REAGAN TEAM MIGHT HAVE CUT A DEAL WITH THE IRANIANS IN 1980 TO DELAY THE RELEASE OF THE HOSTAGES...
--YOU MAKE ALLOWANCES FOR THE FACT THAT POLITICIANS OFTEN LIE--
PRESIDENT BUSH SAYS HE DOESN'T EVEN KNOW WHERE IRAN IS...
--AND YOU TRY TO READ BETWEEN THE LINES AND DETERMINE WHAT MIGHT HAVE ACTUALLY OCCURRED--
HMM...IT DOES SEEM SUSPICIOUS THAT THE HOSTAGES WERE RELEASED MOMENTS AFTER REAGAN WAS SWORN INTO OFFICE...I WONDER...
--WELL--YOU MUST BE SOME KIND OF CONSPIRACY NUT! WHAT'S THE MATTER WITH YOU? WHY CAN'T YOU JUST BELIEVE WHAT YOU'RE TOLD--LIKE A GOOD AMERICAN?
NO--THAT'S CRAZY! WHAT AM I THINKING? I'M SURE IT WAS JUST A COINCIDENCE --LIKE MR. BUSH SAYS!
TOM TOMORROW©'91

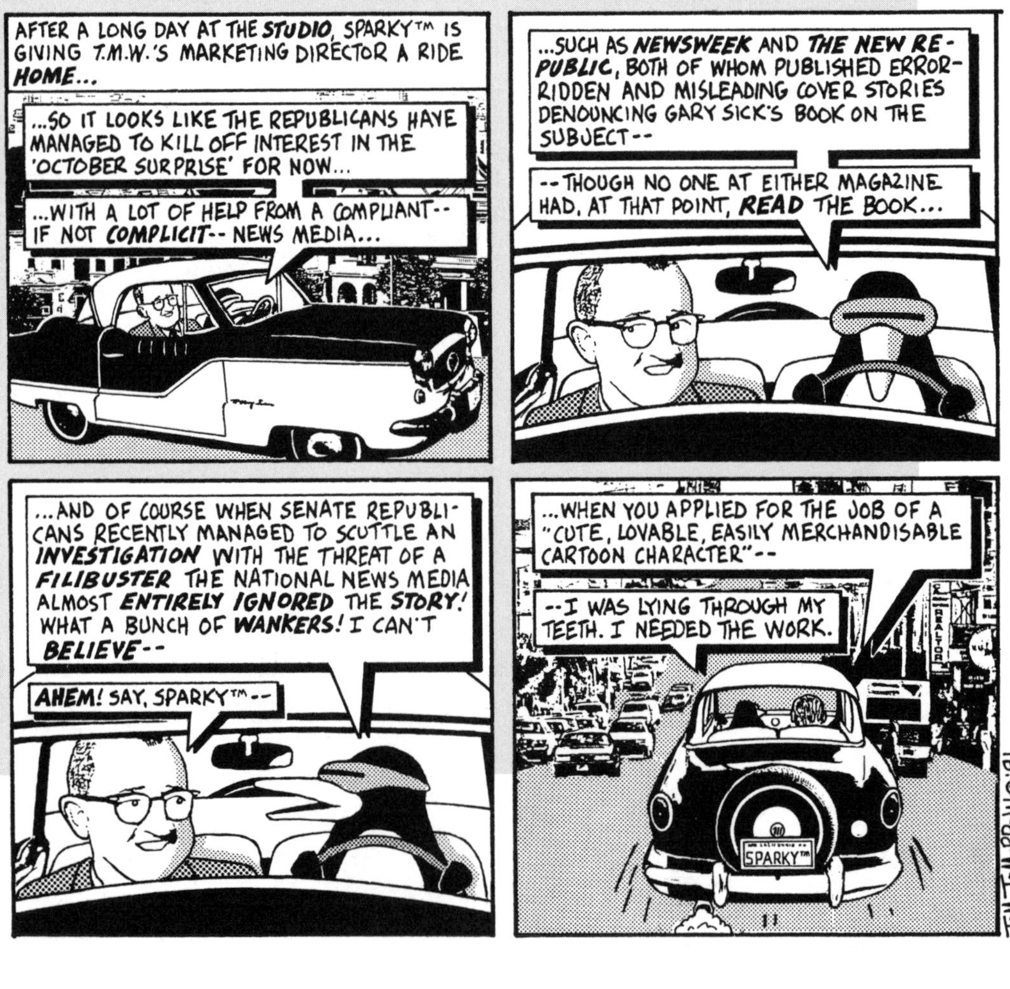
AFTER A LONG DAY AT THE STUDIO, SPARKY™ IS GIVING T.M.W.'S MARKETING DIRECTOR A RIDE HOME...
...SO IT LOOKS LIKE THE REPUBLICANS HAVE MANAGED TO KILL OFF INTEREST IN THE 'OCTOBER SURPRISE' FOR NOW...
...WITH A LOT OF HELP FROM A COMPLIANT--IF NOT COMPLICIT--NEWS MEDIA...
...SUCH AS NEWSWEEK AND THE NEW REPUBLIC, BOTH OF WHOM PUBLISHED ERROR-RIDDEN AND MISLEADING COVER STORIES DENOUNCING GARY SICK'S BOOK ON THE SUBJECT--
--THOUGH NO ONE AT EITHER MAGAZINE HAD, AT THAT POINT, READ THE BOOK...
...AND OF COURSE WHEN SENATE REPUBLICANS RECENTLY MANAGED TO SCUTTLE AN INVESTIGATION WITH THE THREAT OF A FILIBUSTER THE NATIONAL NEWS MEDIA ALMOST ENTIRELY IGNORED THE STORY! WHAT A BUNCH OF WANKERS! I CAN'T BELIEVE--
AHEM! SAY, SPARKY™--
...WHEN YOU APPLIED FOR THE JOB OF A "CUTE, LOVABLE, EASILY MERCHANDISABLE CARTOON CHARACTER"--
--I WAS LYING THROUGH MY TEETH. I NEEDED THE WORK.
REALTOR
SPARKY™
TOM TOMORROW©'91

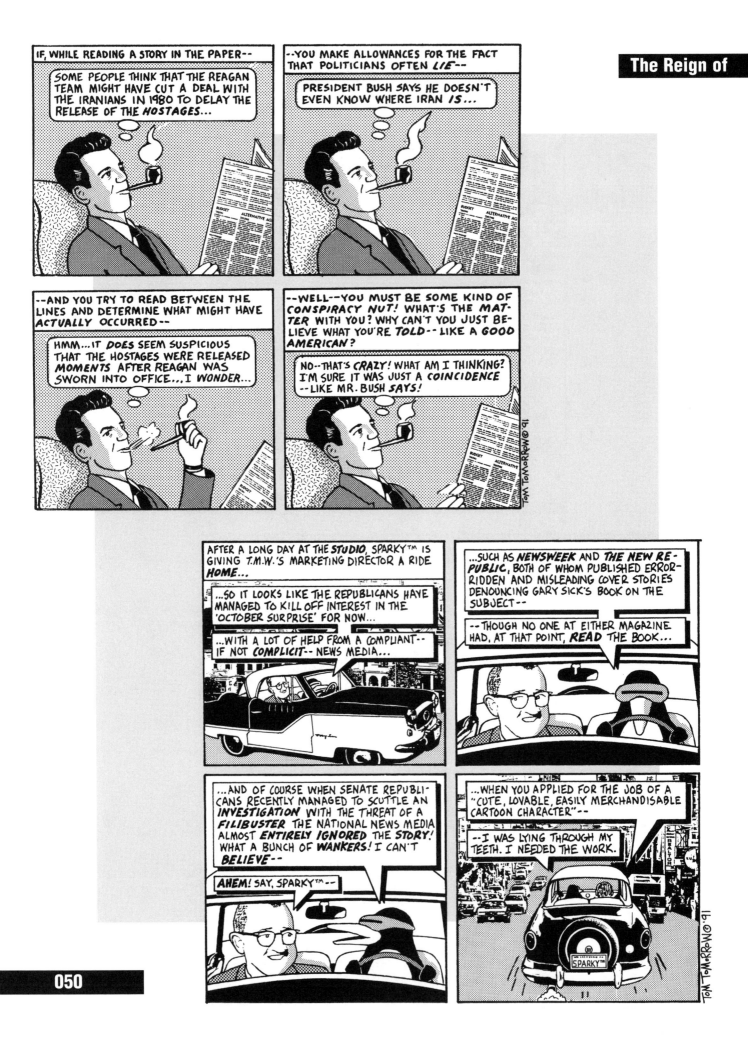

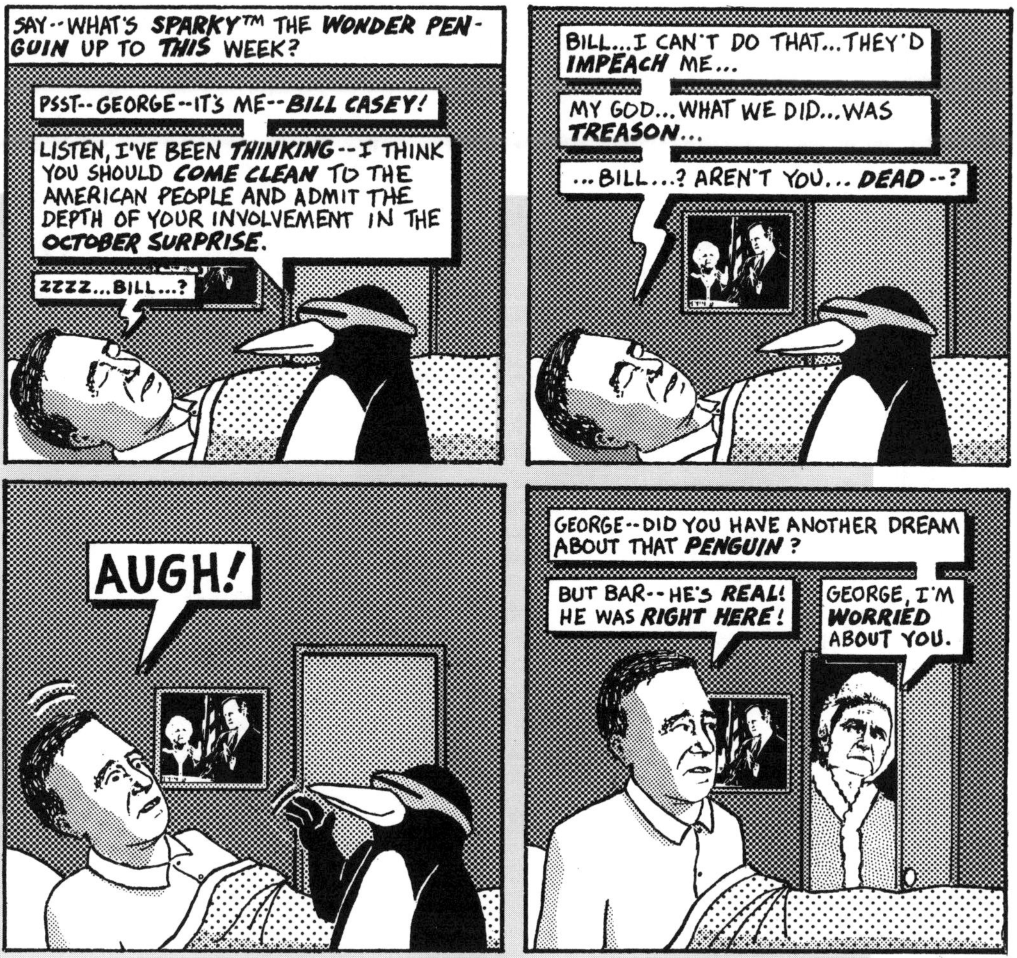
SAY--WHAT'S SPARKY™ THE WONDER PENGUIN UP TO THIS WEEK?
PSST--GEORGE--IT'S ME--BILL CASEY!
LISTEN, I'VE BEEN THINKING--I THINK YOU SHOULD COME CLEAN TO THE AMERICAN PEOPLE AND ADMIT THE DEPTH OF YOUR INVOLVEMENT IN THE OCTOBER SURPRISE.
ZZZZ...BILL...?
BILL...I CAN'T DO THAT...THEY'D IMPEACH ME...
MY GOD...WHAT WE DID...WAS TREASON...
...BILL...? AREN'T YOU...DEAD--?
AUGH!
GEORGE--DID YOU HAVE ANOTHER DREAM ABOUT THAT PENGUIN?
BUT BAR--HE'S REAL! HE WAS RIGHT HERE!
GEORGE, I'M WORRIED ABOUT YOU.

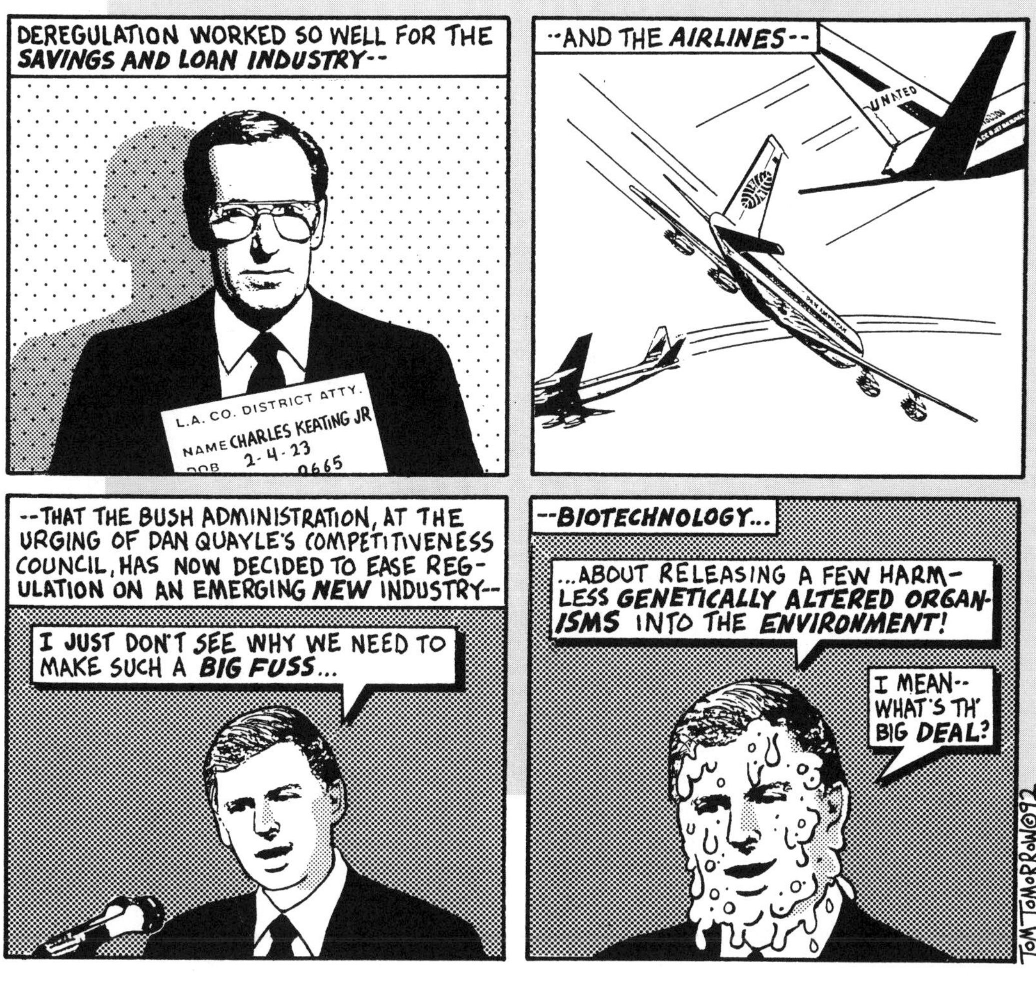
DEREGULATION WORKED SO WELL FOR THE SAVINGS AND LOAN INDUSTRY--
L.A. CO. DISTRICT ATTY.
NAME CHARLES KEATING JR
2-4-23
--AND THE AIRLINES--
UNITED
--THAT THE BUSH ADMINISTRATION, AT THE URGING OF DAN QUAYLE'S COMPETITIVENESS COUNCIL, HAS NOW DECIDED TO EASE REGULATION ON AN EMERGING NEW INDUSTRY--
I JUST DON'T SEE WHY WE NEED TO MAKE SUCH A BIG FUSS...
--BIOTECHNOLOGY...
...ABOUT RELEASING A FEW HARMLESS GENETICALLY ALTERED ORGANISMS INTO THE ENVIRONMENT!
I MEAN--WHAT'S TH' BIG DEAL?
TOM TOMORROW©92

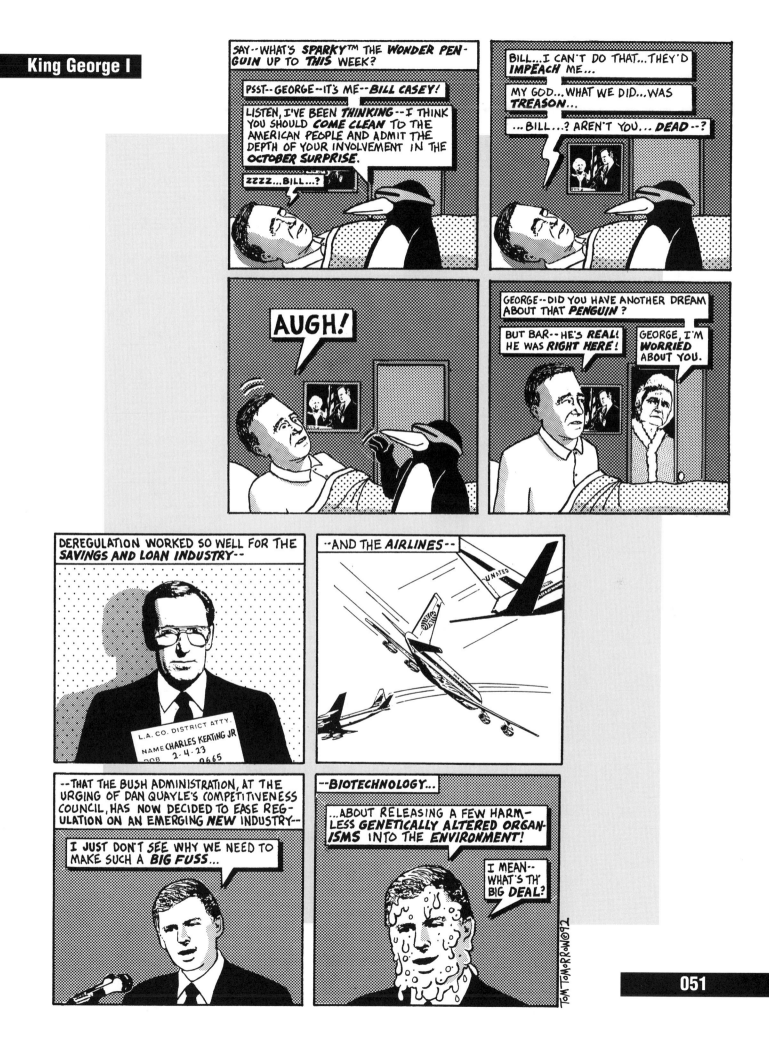

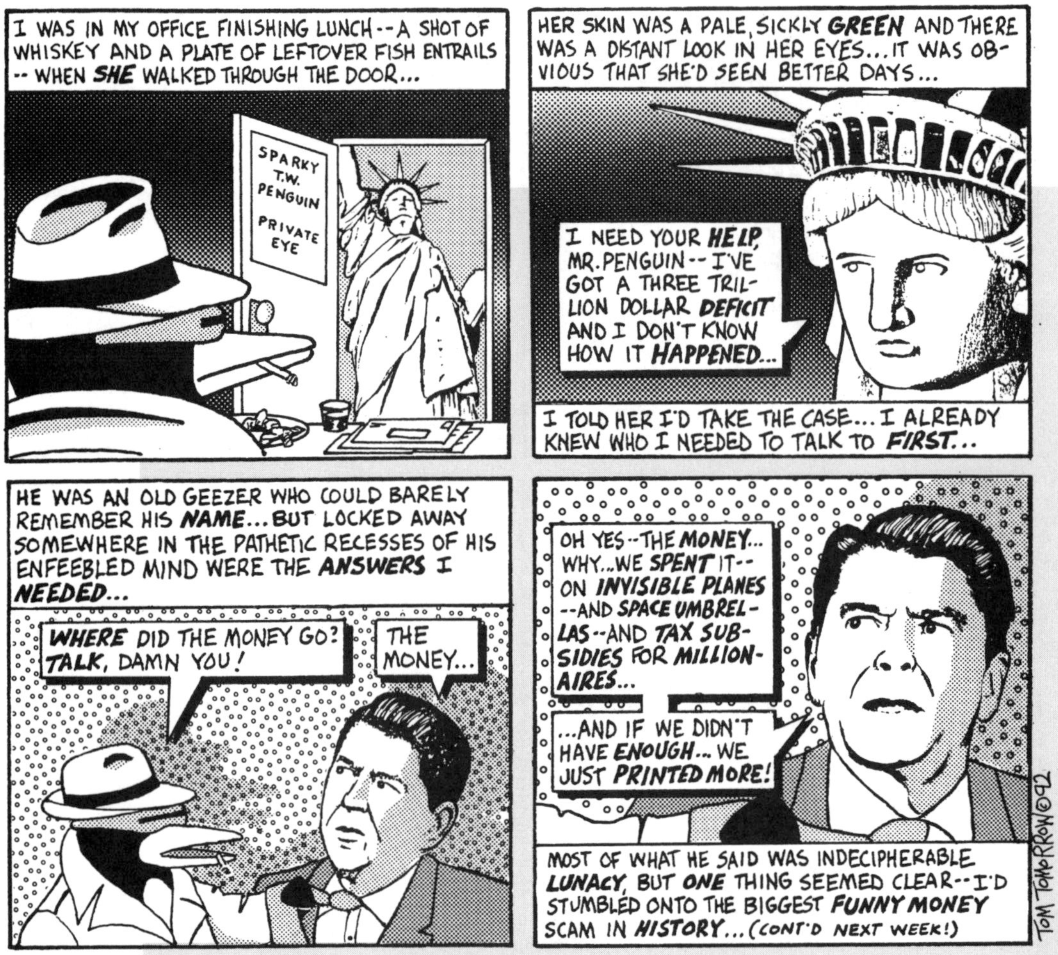
I WAS IN MY OFFICE FINISHING LUNCH -- A SHOT OF WHISKEY AND A PLATE OF LEFTOVER FISH ENTRAILS -- WHEN SHE WALKED THROUGH THE DOOR...
SPARKY T.W. PENGUIN PRIVATE EYE
HER SKIN WAS A PALE, SICKLY GREEN AND THERE WAS A DISTANT LOOK IN HER EYES... IT WAS OBVIOUS THAT SHE'D SEEN BETTER DAYS...
I NEED YOUR HELP, MR. PENGUIN -- I'VE GOT A THREE TRILLION DOLLAR DEFICIT AND I DON'T KNOW HOW IT HAPPENED...
I TOLD HER I'D TAKE THE CASE... I ALREADY KNEW WHO I NEEDED TO TALK TO FIRST...
HE WAS AN OLD GEEZER WHO COULD BARELY REMEMBER HIS NAME... BUT LOCKED AWAY SOMEWHERE IN THE PATHETIC RECESSES OF HIS ENFEEBLED MIND WERE THE ANSWERS I NEEDED...
WHERE DID THE MONEY GO? TALK, DAMN YOU!
THE MONEY...
OH YES -- THE MONEY... WHY... WE SPENT IT -- ON INVISIBLE PLANES -- AND SPACE UMBRELLAS -- AND TAX SUBSIDIES FOR MILLIONAIRES...
...AND IF WE DIDN'T HAVE ENOUGH... WE JUST PRINTED MORE!
MOST OF WHAT HE SAID WAS INDECIPHERABLE LUNACY, BUT ONE THING SEEMED CLEAR -- I'D STUMBLED ONTO THE BIGGEST FUNNY MONEY SCAM IN HISTORY... (CONT'D NEXT WEEK!)
TOM TOMORROW©92

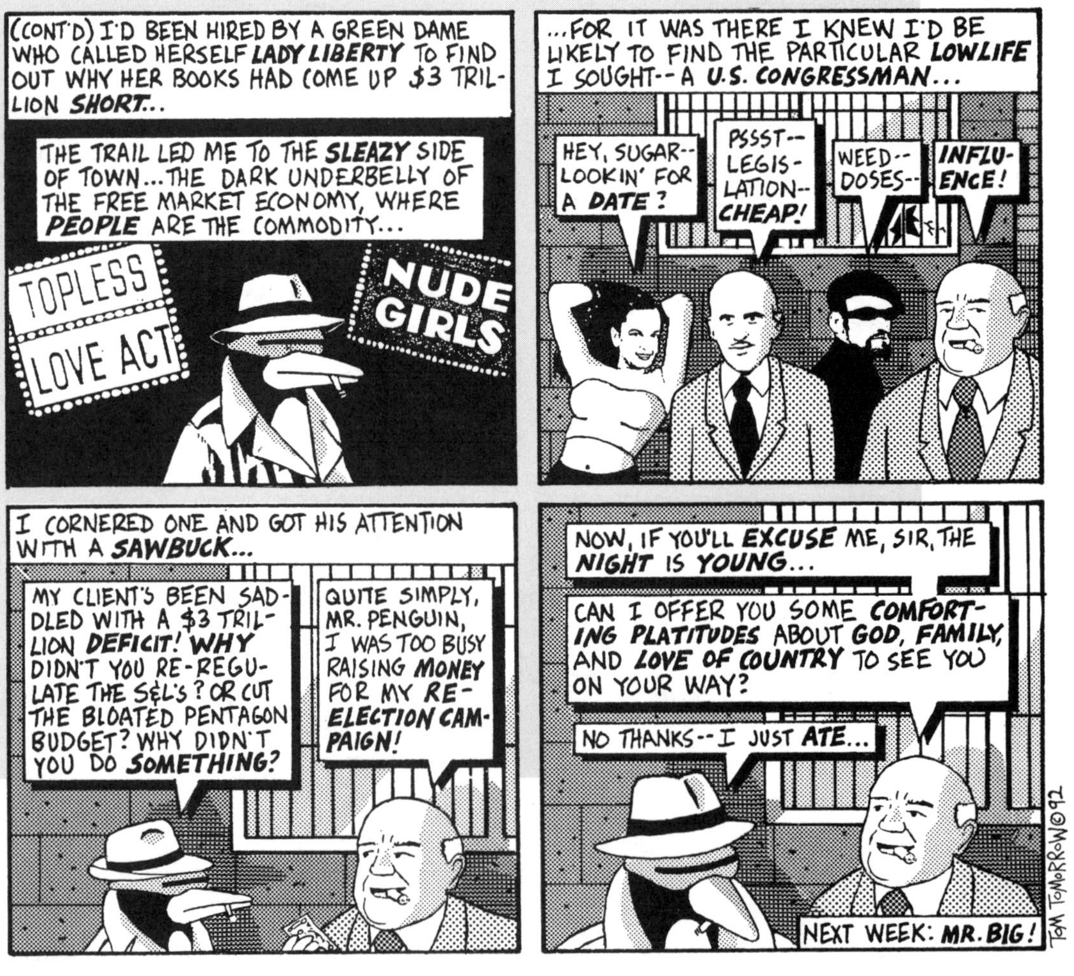
(CONT'D) I'D BEEN HIRED BY A GREEN DAME WHO CALLED HERSELF LADY LIBERTY TO FIND OUT WHY HER BOOKS HAD COME UP $3 TRILLION SHORT...
THE TRAIL LED ME TO THE SLEAZY SIDE OF TOWN... THE DARK UNDERBELLY OF THE FREE MARKET ECONOMY, WHERE PEOPLE ARE THE COMMODITY...
TOPLESS
LOVE ACT
NUDE GIRLS
...FOR IT WAS THERE I KNEW I'D BE LIKELY TO FIND THE PARTICULAR LOWLIFE I SOUGHT -- A U.S. CONGRESSMAN...
HEY, SUGAR -- LOOKIN' FOR A DATE?
PSSST -- LEGISLATION -- CHEAP!
WEED -- DOSES --
INFLUENCE!
I CORNERED ONE AND GOT HIS ATTENTION WITH A SAWBUCK...
MY CLIENT'S BEEN SADDLED WITH A $3 TRILLION DEFICIT! WHY DIDN'T YOU RE-REGULATE THE S&L'S? OR CUT THE BLOATED PENTAGON BUDGET? WHY DIDN'T YOU DO SOMETHING?
QUITE SIMPLY, MR. PENGUIN, I WAS TOO BUSY RAISING MONEY FOR MY RE-ELECTION CAMPAIGN!
NOW, IF YOU'LL EXCUSE ME, SIR, THE NIGHT IS YOUNG...
CAN I OFFER YOU SOME COMFORTING PLATITUDES ABOUT GOD, FAMILY, AND LOVE OF COUNTRY TO SEE YOU ON YOUR WAY?
NO THANKS -- I JUST ATE...
NEXT WEEK: MR. BIG!
TOM TOMORROW©92

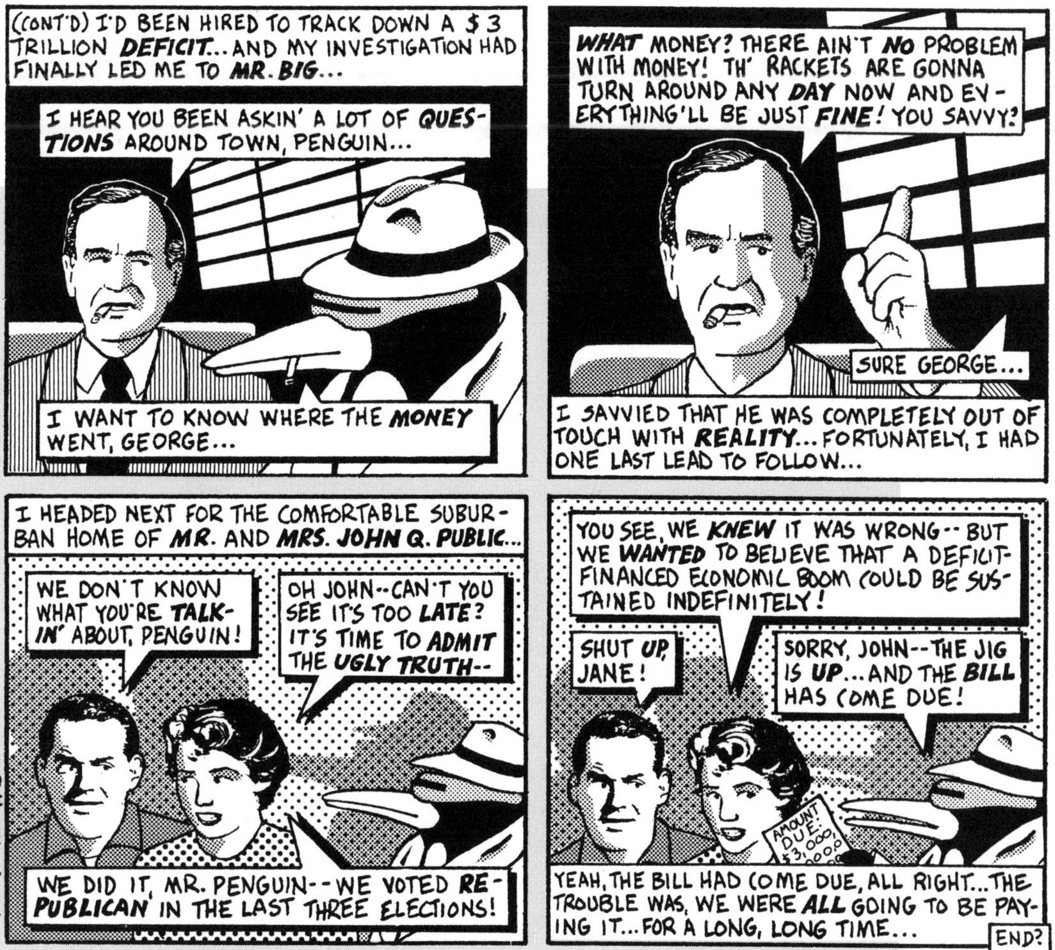
(CONT'D) I'D BEEN HIRED TO TRACK DOWN A $3 TRILLION DEFICIT... AND MY INVESTIGATION HAD FINALLY LED ME TO MR. BIG...
I HEAR YOU BEEN ASKIN' A LOT OF QUESTIONS AROUND TOWN, PENGUIN...
I WANT TO KNOW WHERE THE MONEY WENT, GEORGE...
WHAT MONEY? THERE AIN'T NO PROBLEM WITH MONEY! TH' RACKETS ARE GONNA TURN AROUND ANY DAY NOW AND EVERYTHING'LL BE JUST FINE! YOU SAVVY?
SURE GEORGE...
I SAVVIED THAT HE WAS COMPLETELY OUT OF TOUCH WITH REALITY... FORTUNATELY, I HAD ONE LAST LEAD TO FOLLOW...
I HEADED NEXT FOR THE COMFORTABLE SUBURBAN HOME OF MR. AND MRS. JOHN Q. PUBLIC...
WE DON'T KNOW WHAT YOU'RE TALKIN' ABOUT, PENGUIN!
OH JOHN--CAN'T YOU SEE IT'S TOO LATE? IT'S TIME TO ADMIT THE UGLY TRUTH--
WE DID IT, MR. PENGUIN--WE VOTED REPUBLICAN IN THE LAST THREE ELECTIONS!
TOM TOMORROW©92
YOU SEE, WE KNEW IT WAS WRONG--BUT WE WANTED TO BELIEVE THAT A DEFICIT-FINANCED ECONOMIC BOOM COULD BE SUSTAINED INDEFINITELY!
SHUT UP, JANE!
SORRY, JOHN--THE JIG IS UP...AND THE BILL HAS COME DUE!
AMOUNT DUE:
YEAH, THE BILL HAD COME DUE, ALL RIGHT...THE TROUBLE WAS, WE WERE ALL GOING TO BE PAYING IT...FOR A LONG, LONG TIME...
END?

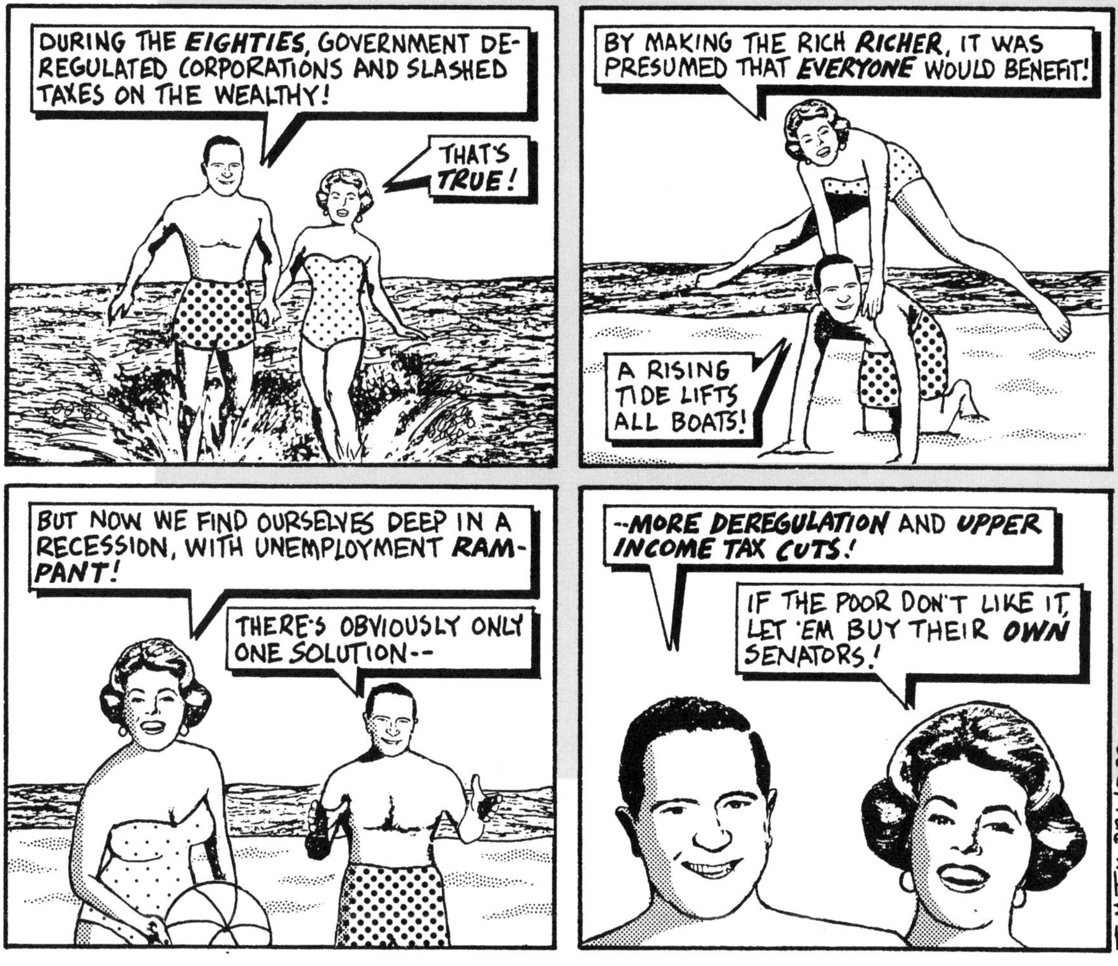
DURING THE EIGHTIES, GOVERNMENT DEREGULATED CORPORATIONS AND SLASHED TAXES ON THE WEALTHY!
THAT'S TRUE!
BY MAKING THE RICH RICHER, IT WAS PRESUMED THAT EVERYONE WOULD BENEFIT!
A RISING TIDE LIFTS ALL BOATS!
BUT NOW WE FIND OURSELVES DEEP IN A RECESSION, WITH UNEMPLOYMENT RAMPANT!
THERE'S OBVIOUSLY ONLY ONE SOLUTION--
--MORE DEREGULATION AND UPPER INCOME TAX CUTS!
IF THE POOR DON'T LIKE IT, LET 'EM BUY THEIR OWN SENATORS!
TOM TOMORROW©92

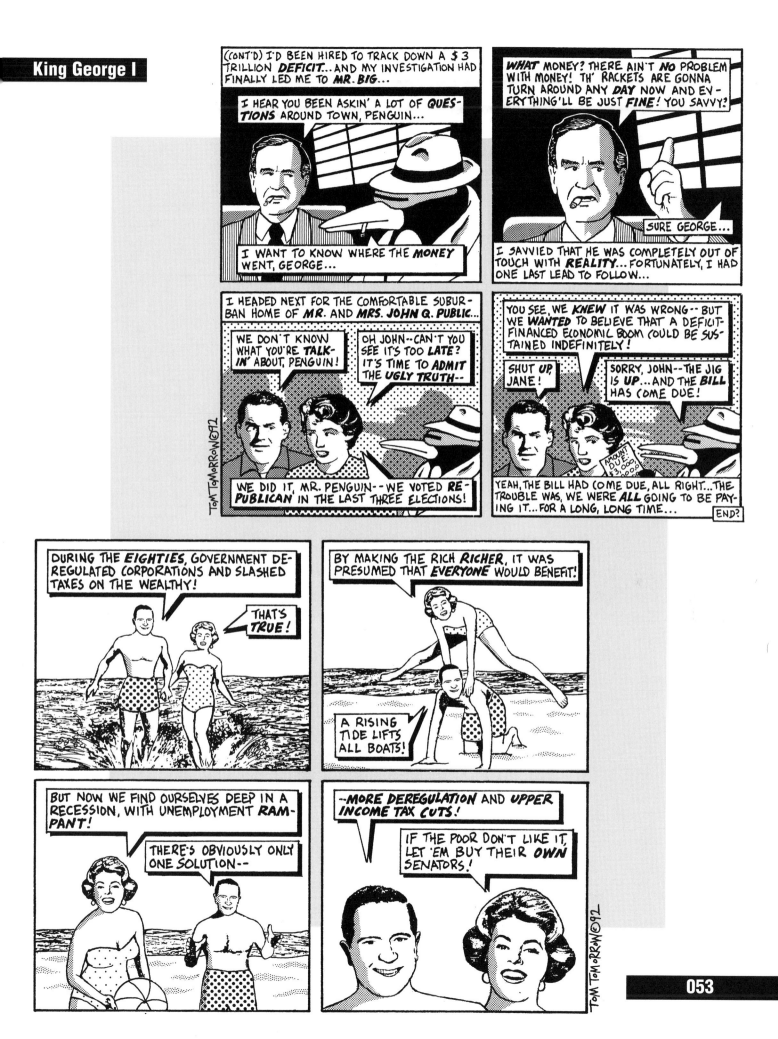

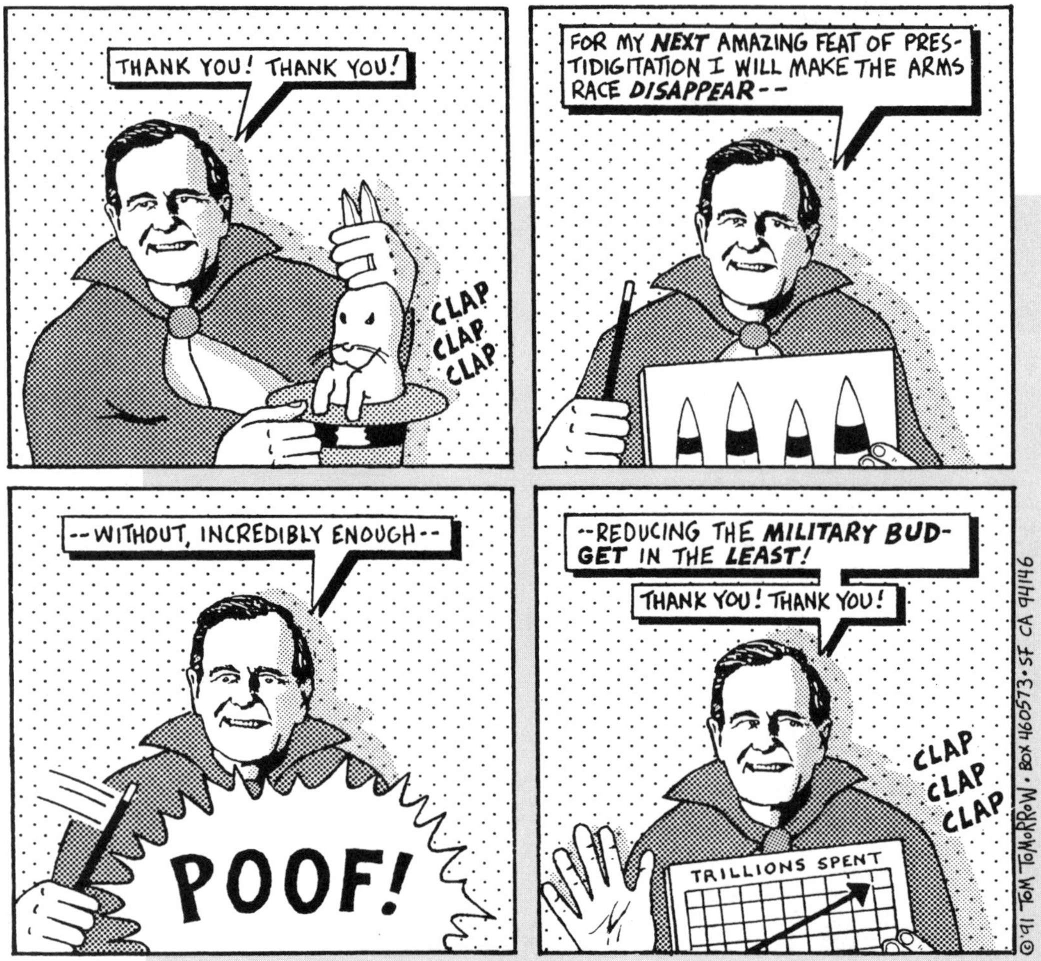
THANK YOU! THANK YOU!
CLAP CLAP CLAP
FOR MY NEXT AMAZING FEAT OF PRESTIDIGITATION I WILL MAKE THE ARMS RACE DISAPPEAR--
--WITHOUT, INCREDIBLY ENOUGH--
POOF!
--REDUCING THE MILITARY BUDGET IN THE LEAST!
THANK YOU! THANK YOU!
CLAP CLAP CLAP
TRILLIONS SPENT
©'91 TOM TOMORROW • BOX 460573 • SF CA 94146

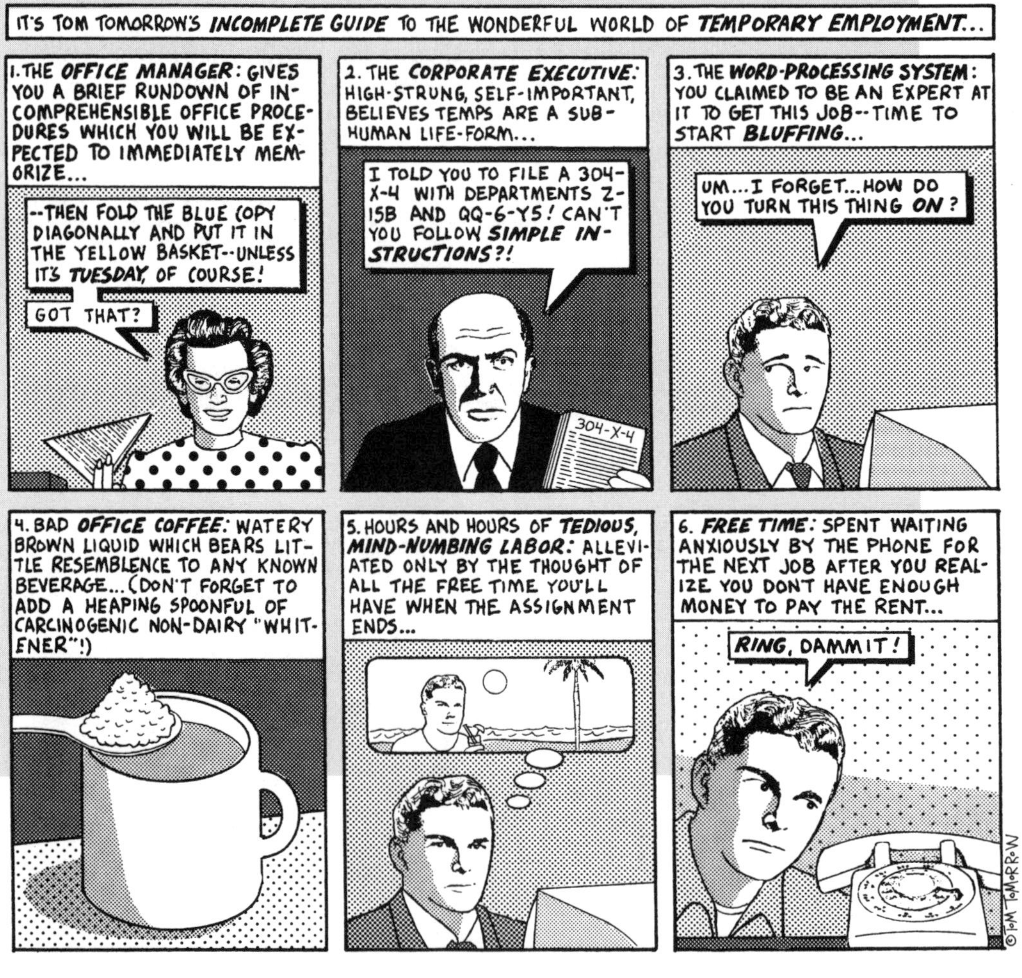
IT'S TOM TOMORROW'S INCOMPLETE GUIDE TO THE WONDERFUL WORLD OF TEMPORARY EMPLOYMENT...
1. THE OFFICE MANAGER: GIVES YOU A BRIEF RUNDOWN OF INCOMPREHENSIBLE OFFICE PROCEDURES WHICH YOU WILL BE EXPECTED TO IMMEDIATELY MEMORIZE...
--THEN FOLD THE BLUE COPY DIAGONALLY AND PUT IT IN THE YELLOW BASKET--UNLESS IT'S TUESDAY, OF COURSE!
GOT THAT?
2. THE CORPORATE EXECUTIVE: HIGH-STRUNG, SELF-IMPORTANT, BELIEVES TEMPS ARE A SUB-HUMAN LIFE-FORM...
I TOLD YOU TO FILE A 304-X-4 WITH DEPARTMENTS Z-15B AND QQ-6-Y5! CAN'T YOU FOLLOW SIMPLE INSTRUCTIONS?!
304-X-4
3. THE WORD-PROCESSING SYSTEM: YOU CLAIMED TO BE AN EXPERT AT IT TO GET THIS JOB--TIME TO START BLUFFING...
UM...I FORGET...HOW DO YOU TURN THIS THING ON?
4. BAD OFFICE COFFEE: WATERY BROWN LIQUID WHICH BEARS LITTLE RESEMBLENCE TO ANY KNOWN BEVERAGE...(DON'T FORGET TO ADD A HEAPING SPOONFUL OF CARCINOGENIC NON-DAIRY "WHITENER"!)
5. HOURS AND HOURS OF TEDIOUS, MIND-NUMBING LABOR: ALLEVIATED ONLY BY THE THOUGHT OF ALL THE FREE TIME YOU'LL HAVE WHEN THE ASSIGNMENT ENDS...
6. FREE TIME: SPENT WAITING ANXIOUSLY BY THE PHONE FOR THE NEXT JOB AFTER YOU REALIZE YOU DON'T HAVE ENOUGH MONEY TO PAY THE RENT...
RING, DAMMIT!
©TOM TOMORROW

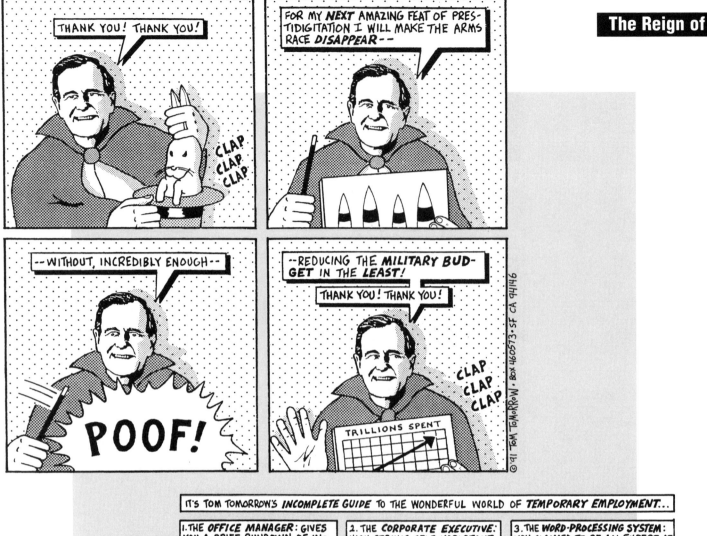

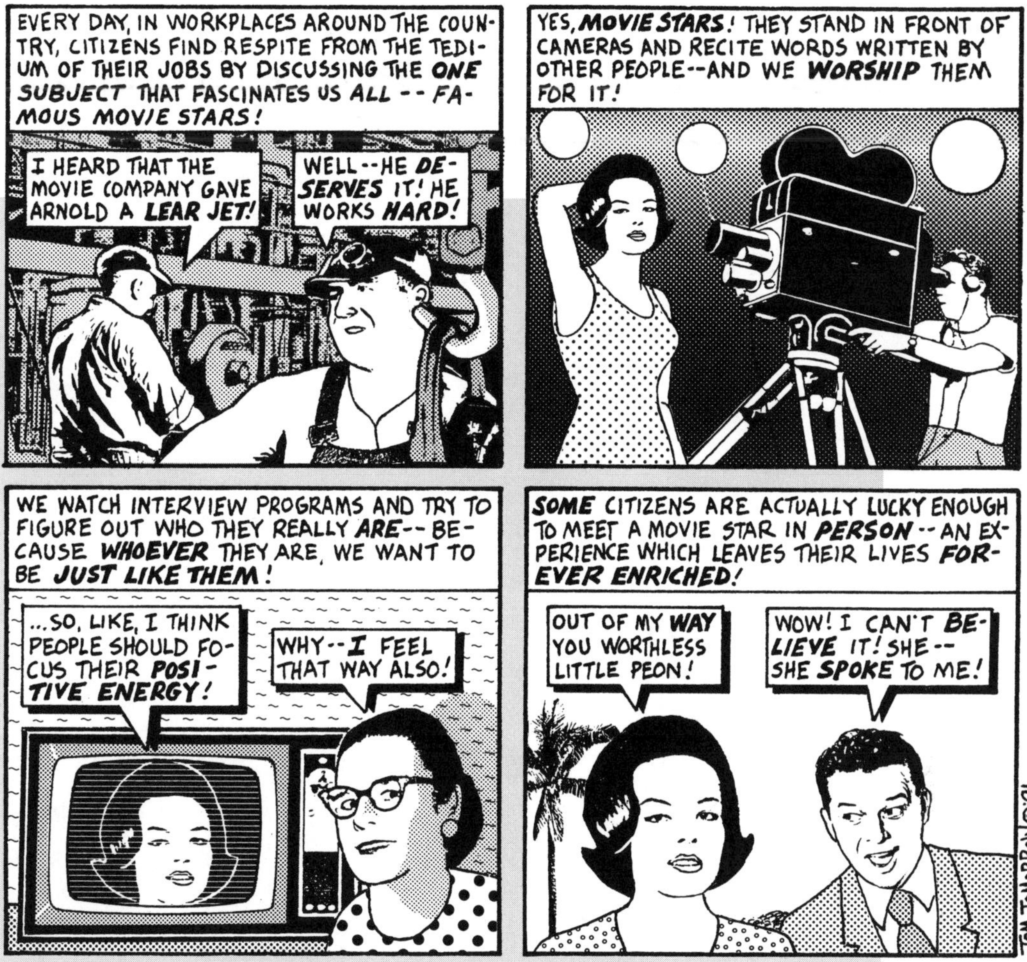
EVERY DAY, IN WORKPLACES AROUND THE COUNTRY, CITIZENS FIND RESPITE FROM THE TEDIUM OF THEIR JOBS BY DISCUSSING THE ONE SUBJECT THAT FASCINATES US ALL -- FAMOUS MOVIE STARS!
I HEARD THAT THE MOVIE COMPANY GAVE ARNOLD A LEAR JET!
WELL--HE DESERVES IT! HE WORKS HARD!
YES, MOVIE STARS! THEY STAND IN FRONT OF CAMERAS AND RECITE WORDS WRITTEN BY OTHER PEOPLE--AND WE WORSHIP THEM FOR IT!
WE WATCH INTERVIEW PROGRAMS AND TRY TO FIGURE OUT WHO THEY REALLY ARE-- BECAUSE WHOEVER THEY ARE, WE WANT TO BE JUST LIKE THEM!
...SO, LIKE, I THINK PEOPLE SHOULD FOCUS THEIR POSITIVE ENERGY!
WHY--I FEEL THAT WAY ALSO!
SOME CITIZENS ARE ACTUALLY LUCKY ENOUGH TO MEET A MOVIE STAR IN PERSON -- AN EXPERIENCE WHICH LEAVES THEIR LIVES FOREVER ENRICHED!
OUT OF MY WAY YOU WORTHLESS LITTLE PEON!
WOW! I CAN'T BELIEVE IT! SHE--SHE SPOKE TO ME!
TOM TOMORROW©'91

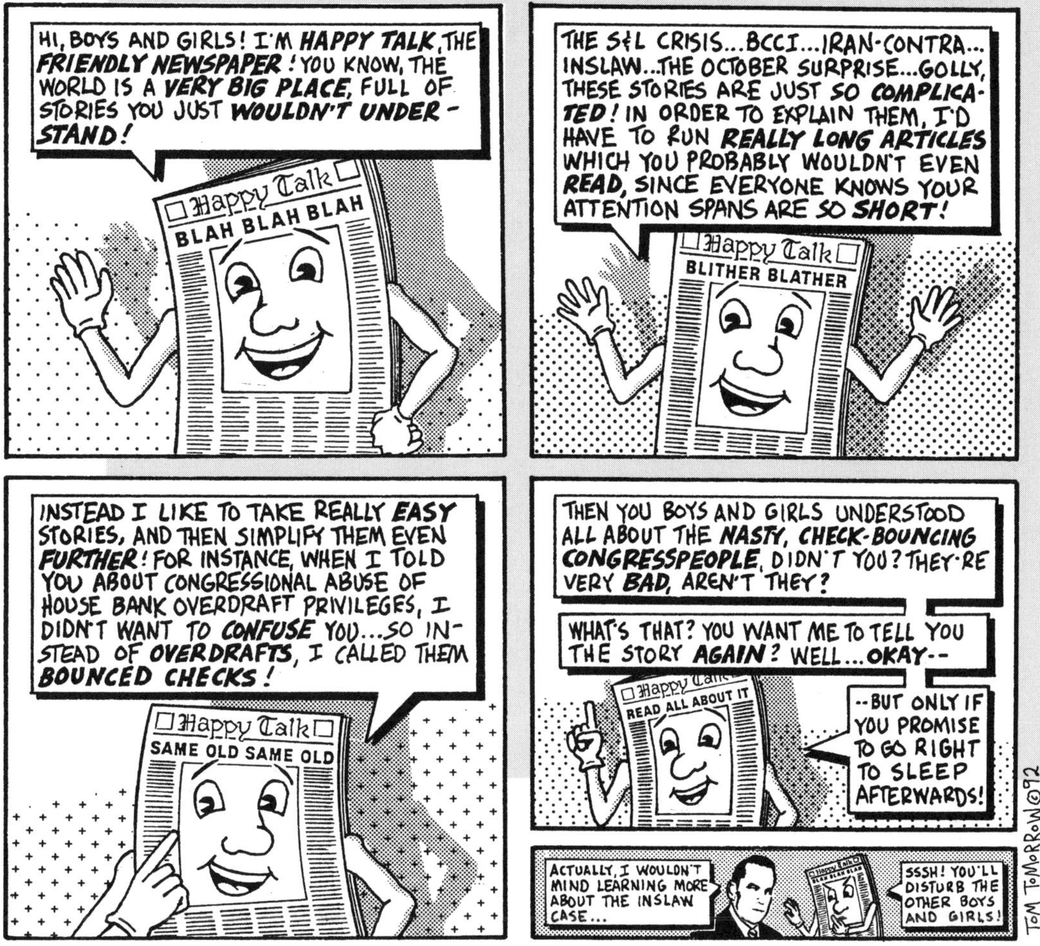
HI, BOYS AND GIRLS! I'M HAPPY TALK, THE FRIENDLY NEWSPAPER! YOU KNOW, THE WORLD IS A VERY BIG PLACE, FULL OF STORIES YOU JUST WOULDN'T UNDERSTAND!
Happy Talk
BLAH BLAH BLAH
THE S&L CRISIS...BCCI...IRAN-CONTRA...INSLAW...THE OCTOBER SURPRISE...GOLLY, THESE STORIES ARE JUST SO COMPLICATED! IN ORDER TO EXPLAIN THEM, I'D HAVE TO RUN REALLY LONG ARTICLES WHICH YOU PROBABLY WOULDN'T EVEN READ, SINCE EVERYONE KNOWS YOUR ATTENTION SPANS ARE SO SHORT!
Happy Talk
BLITHER BLATHER
INSTEAD I LIKE TO TAKE REALLY EASY STORIES, AND THEN SIMPLIFY THEM EVEN FURTHER! FOR INSTANCE, WHEN I TOLD YOU ABOUT CONGRESSIONAL ABUSE OF HOUSE BANK OVERDRAFT PRIVILEGES, I DIDN'T WANT TO CONFUSE YOU...SO INSTEAD OF OVERDRAFTS, I CALLED THEM BOUNCED CHECKS!
Happy Talk
SAME OLD SAME OLD
THEN YOU BOYS AND GIRLS UNDERSTOOD ALL ABOUT THE NASTY, CHECK-BOUNCING CONGRESSPEOPLE, DIDN'T YOU? THEY'RE VERY BAD, AREN'T THEY?
WHAT'S THAT? YOU WANT ME TO TELL YOU THE STORY AGAIN? WELL...OKAY--
READ ALL ABOUT IT
--BUT ONLY IF YOU PROMISE TO GO RIGHT TO SLEEP AFTERWARDS!
ACTUALLY, I WOULDN'T MIND LEARNING MORE ABOUT THE INSLAW CASE...
SSSH! YOU'LL DISTURB THE OTHER BOYS AND GIRLS!
TOM TOMORROW©'92

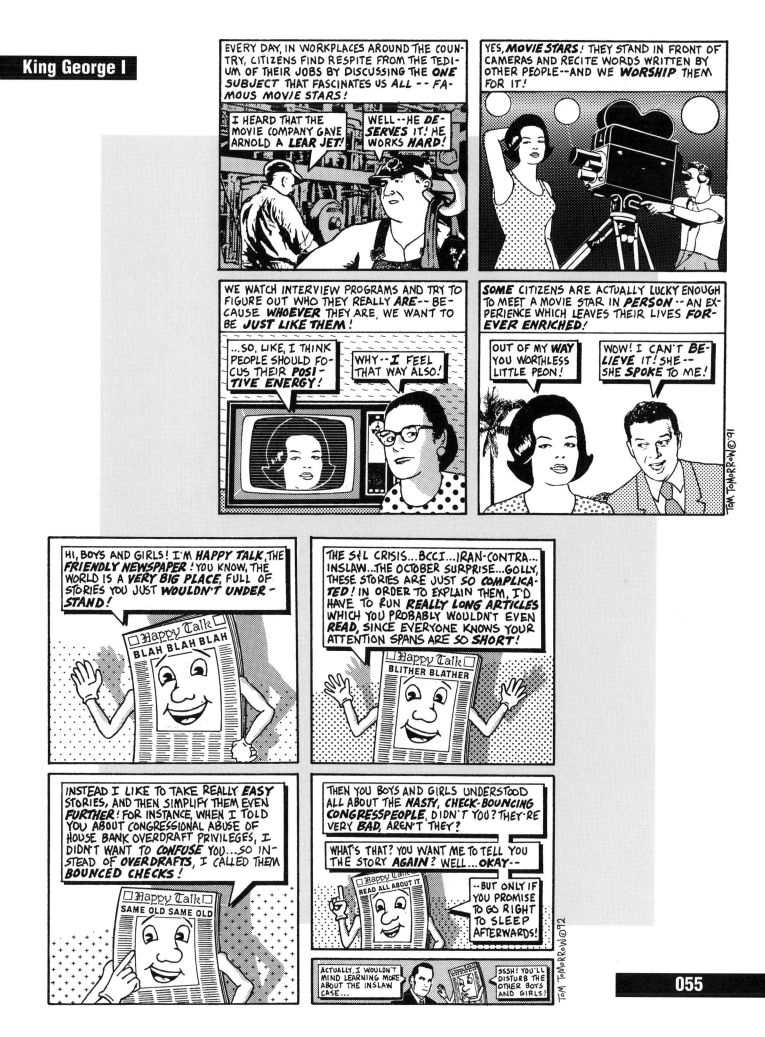

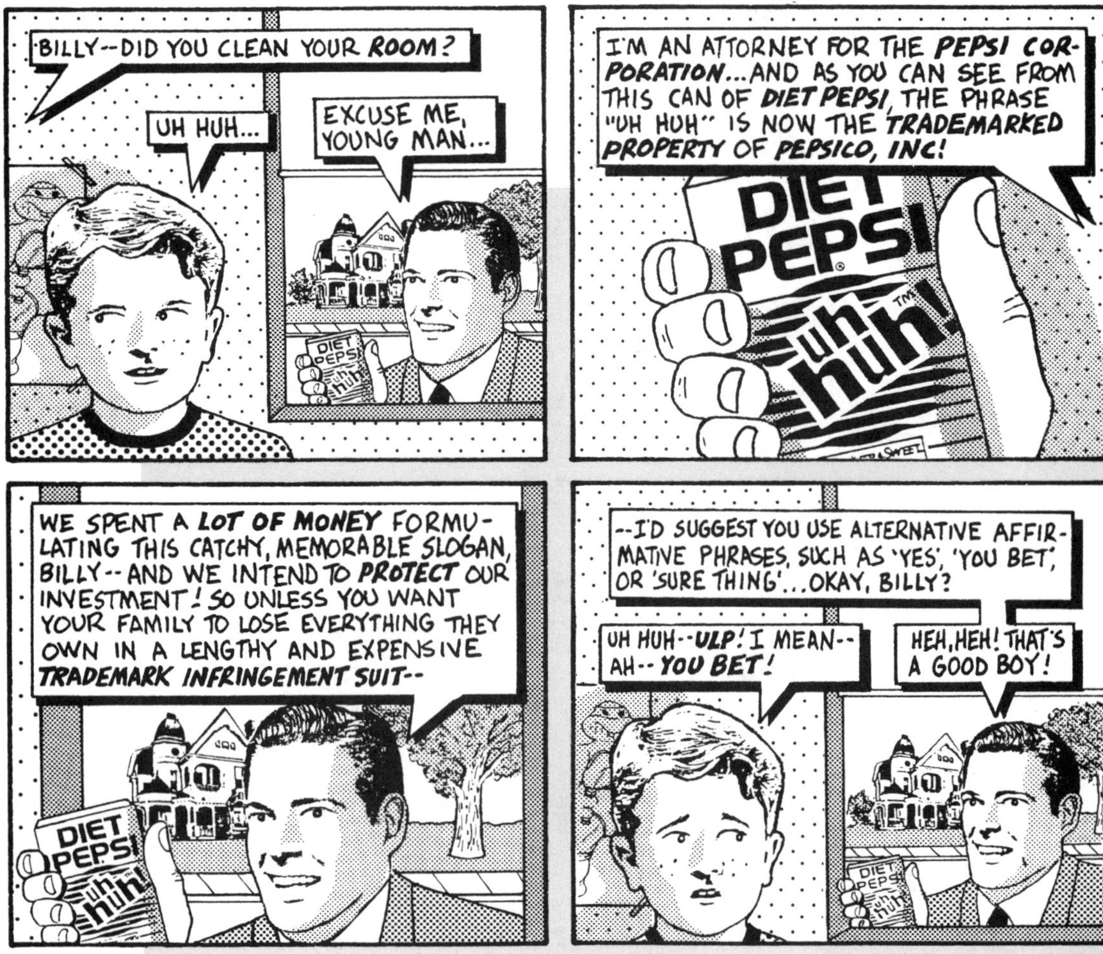
BILLY--DID YOU CLEAN YOUR ROOM?
UH HUH...
EXCUSE ME, YOUNG MAN...
I'M AN ATTORNEY FOR THE PEPSI CORPORATION...AND AS YOU CAN SEE FROM THIS CAN OF DIET PEPSI, THE PHRASE "UH HUH" IS NOW THE TRADEMARKED PROPERTY OF PEPSICO, INC!
DIET PEPSI
uh huh!™
WE SPENT A LOT OF MONEY FORMULATING THIS CATCHY, MEMORABLE SLOGAN, BILLY--AND WE INTEND TO PROTECT OUR INVESTMENT! SO UNLESS YOU WANT YOUR FAMILY TO LOSE EVERYTHING THEY OWN IN A LENGTHY AND EXPENSIVE TRADEMARK INFRINGEMENT SUIT--
--I'D SUGGEST YOU USE ALTERNATIVE AFFIRMATIVE PHRASES, SUCH AS 'YES', 'YOU BET', OR 'SURE THING'...OKAY, BILLY?
UH HUH--ULP! I MEAN--AH--YOU BET!
HEH, HEH! THAT'S A GOOD BOY!
TOM TOMORROW©92

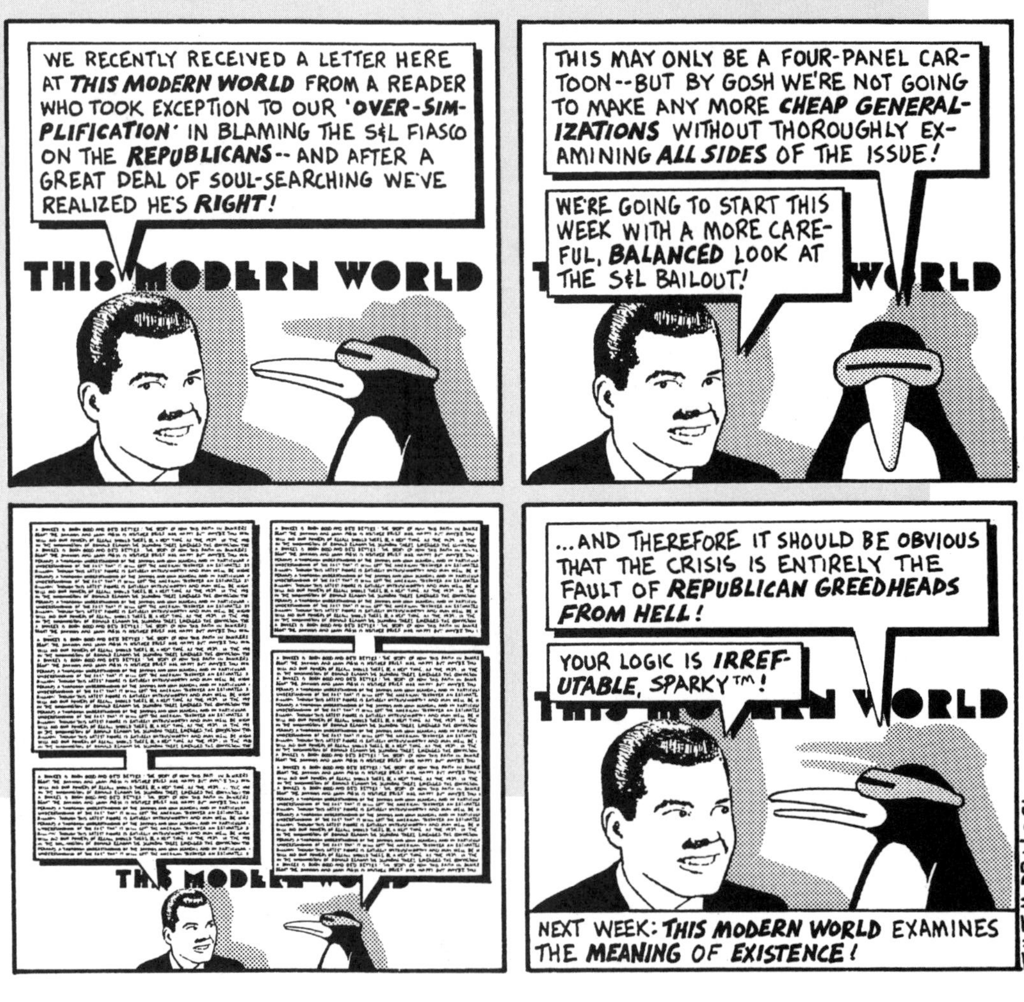
WE RECENTLY RECEIVED A LETTER HERE AT THIS MODERN WORLD FROM A READER WHO TOOK EXCEPTION TO OUR 'OVER-SIMPLIFICATION' IN BLAMING THE S&L FIASCO ON THE REPUBLICANS--AND AFTER A GREAT DEAL OF SOUL-SEARCHING WE'VE REALIZED HE'S RIGHT!
THIS MODERN WORLD
THIS MAY ONLY BE A FOUR-PANEL CARTOON--BUT BY GOSH WE'RE NOT GOING TO MAKE ANY MORE CHEAP GENERALIZATIONS WITHOUT THOROUGHLY EXAMINING ALL SIDES OF THE ISSUE!
WE'RE GOING TO START THIS WEEK WITH A MORE CAREFUL, BALANCED LOOK AT THE S&L BAILOUT!
...AND THEREFORE IT SHOULD BE OBVIOUS THAT THE CRISIS IS ENTIRELY THE FAULT OF REPUBLICAN GREEDHEADS FROM HELL!
YOUR LOGIC IS IRREFUTABLE, SPARKY™!
NEXT WEEK: THIS MODERN WORLD EXAMINES THE MEANING OF EXISTENCE!
TOM TOMORROW©91

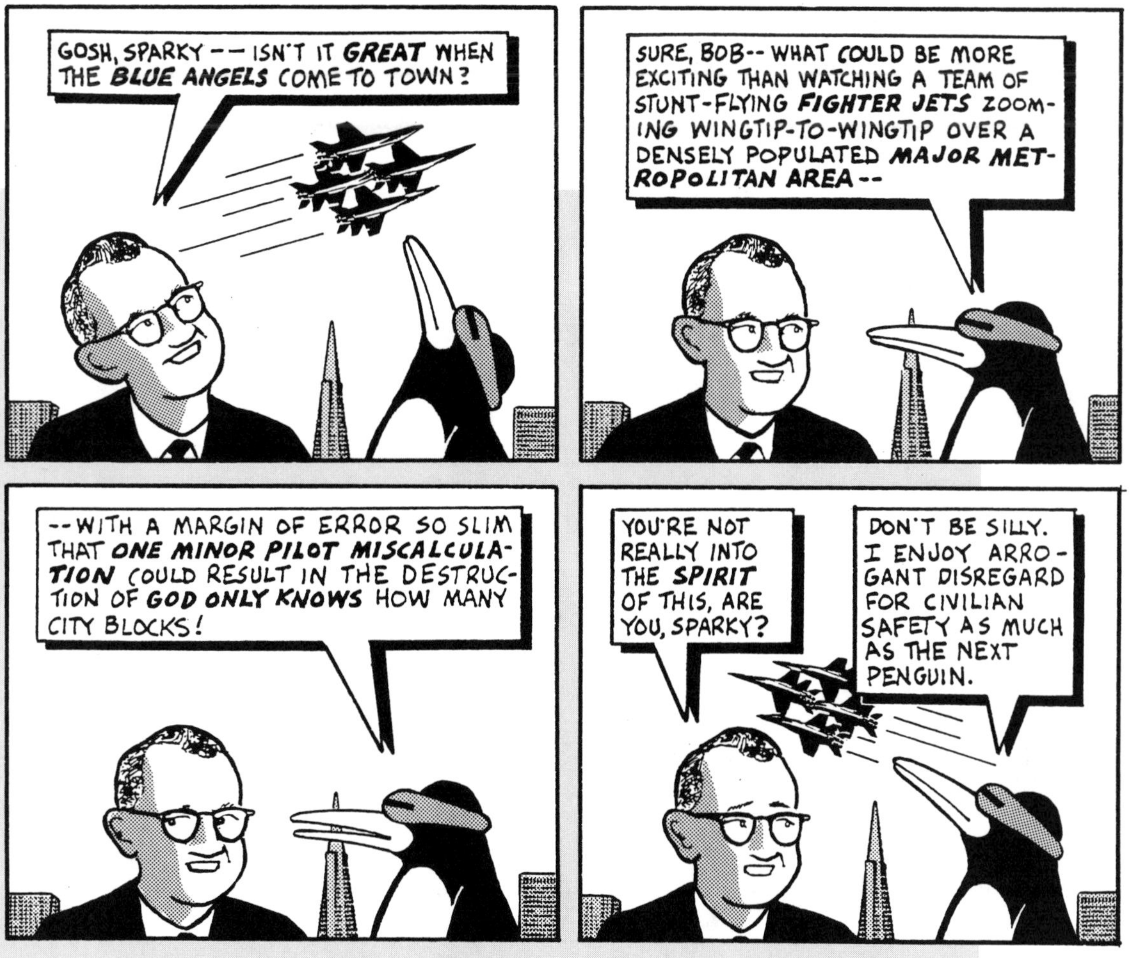
GOSH, SPARKY -- ISN'T IT GREAT WHEN THE BLUE ANGELS COME TO TOWN?
SURE, BOB-- WHAT COULD BE MORE EXCITING THAN WATCHING A TEAM OF STUNT-FLYING FIGHTER JETS ZOOMING WINGTIP-TO-WINGTIP OVER A DENSELY POPULATED MAJOR METROPOLITAN AREA--
--WITH A MARGIN OF ERROR SO SLIM THAT ONE MINOR PILOT MISCALCULATION COULD RESULT IN THE DESTRUCTION OF GOD ONLY KNOWS HOW MANY CITY BLOCKS!
YOU'RE NOT REALLY INTO THE SPIRIT OF THIS, ARE YOU, SPARKY?
DON'T BE SILLY. I ENJOY ARROGANT DISREGARD FOR CIVILIAN SAFETY AS MUCH AS THE NEXT PENGUIN.

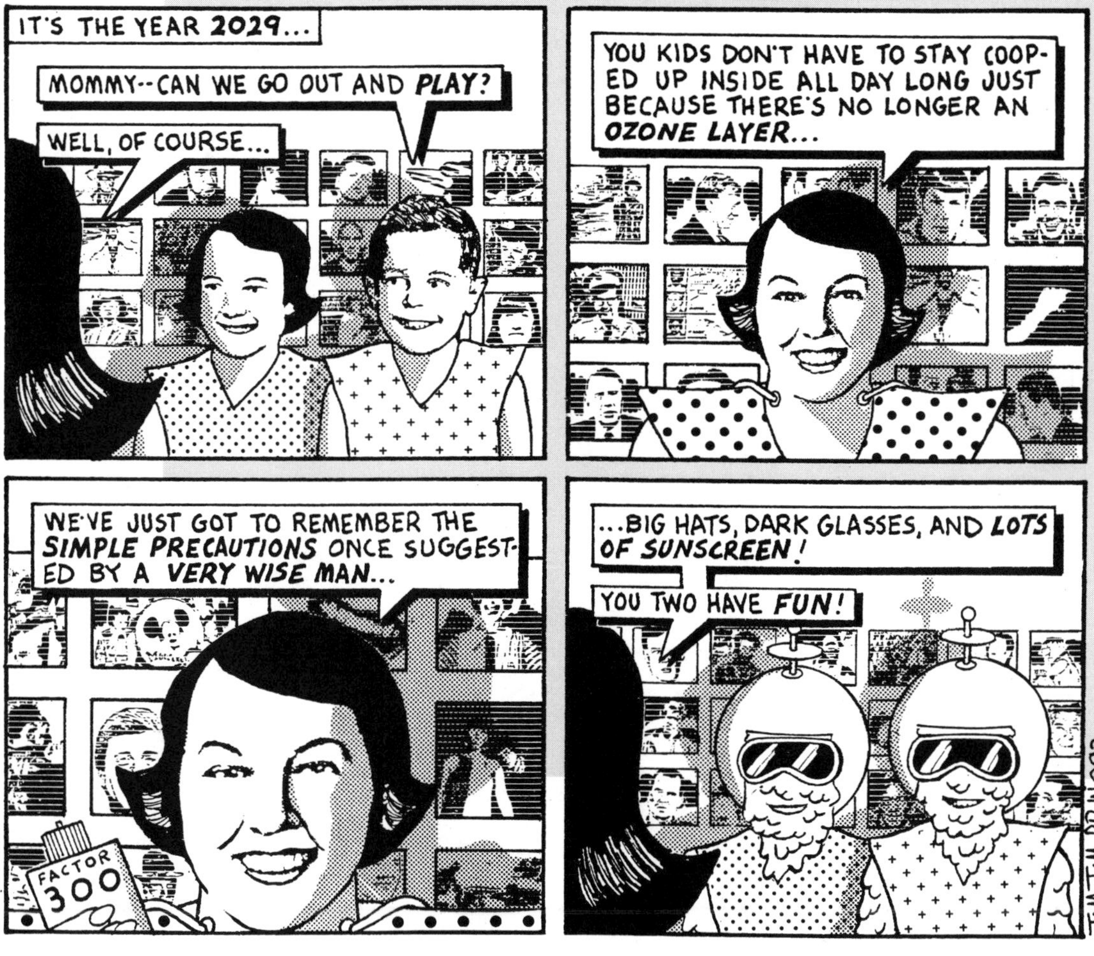
IT'S THE YEAR 2029...
MOMMY--CAN WE GO OUT AND PLAY?
WELL, OF COURSE...
YOU KIDS DON'T HAVE TO STAY COOPED UP INSIDE ALL DAY LONG JUST BECAUSE THERE'S NO LONGER AN OZONE LAYER...
WE'VE JUST GOT TO REMEMBER THE SIMPLE PRECAUTIONS ONCE SUGGESTED BY A VERY WISE MAN...
FACTOR 300
...BIG HATS, DARK GLASSES, AND LOTS OF SUNSCREEN!
YOU TWO HAVE FUN!
TOM TOMORROW ©92

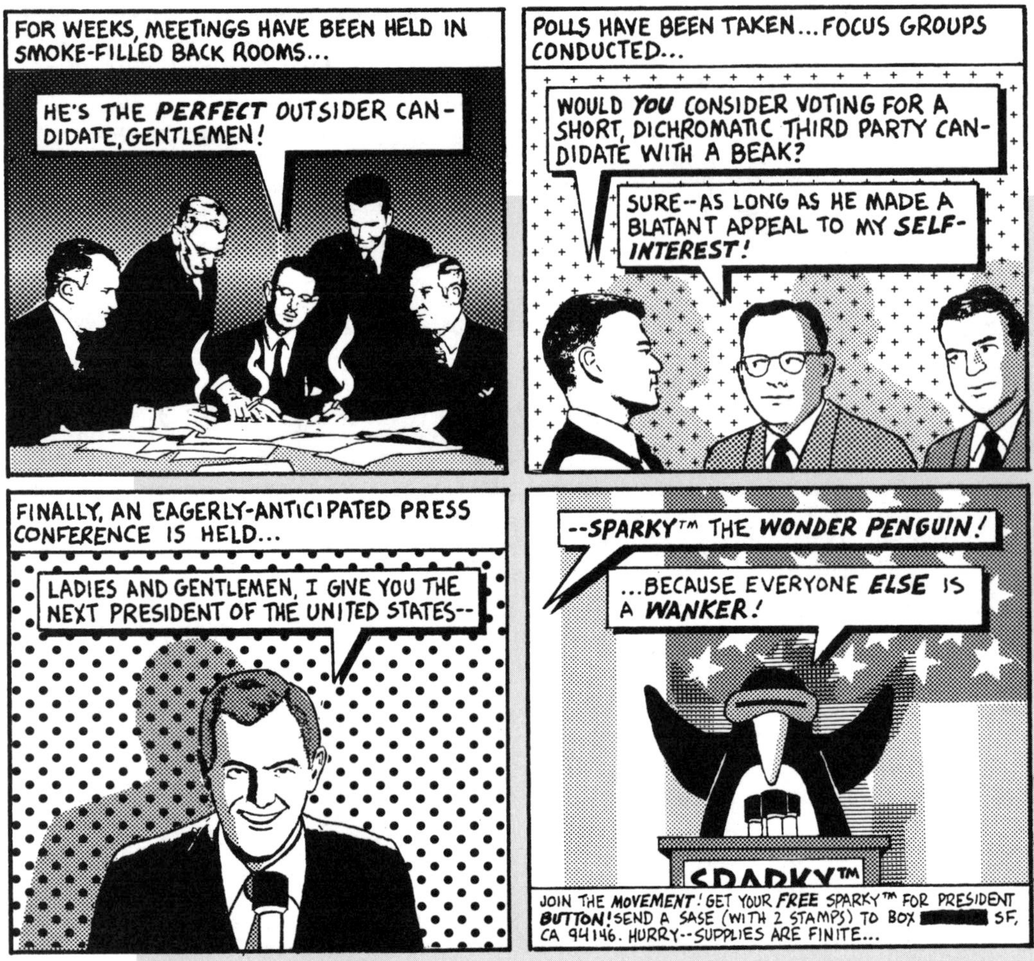
FOR WEEKS, MEETINGS HAVE BEEN HELD IN SMOKE-FILLED BACK ROOMS...
HE'S THE PERFECT OUTSIDER CANDIDATE, GENTLEMEN!
POLLS HAVE BEEN TAKEN... FOCUS GROUPS CONDUCTED...
WOULD YOU CONSIDER VOTING FOR A SHORT, DICHROMATIC THIRD PARTY CANDIDATE WITH A BEAK?
SURE--AS LONG AS HE MADE A BLATANT APPEAL TO MY SELF-INTEREST!
FINALLY, AN EAGERLY-ANTICIPATED PRESS CONFERENCE IS HELD...
LADIES AND GENTLEMEN, I GIVE YOU THE NEXT PRESIDENT OF THE UNITED STATES--
--SPARKY™ THE WONDER PENGUIN!
...BECAUSE EVERYONE ELSE IS A WANKER!
SPARKY™
JOIN THE MOVEMENT! GET YOUR FREE SPARKY™ FOR PRESIDENT BUTTON! SEND A SASE (WITH 2 STAMPS) TO BOX [redacted] SF, CA 94146. HURRY--SUPPLIES ARE FINITE...
TOM TOMORROW ©92

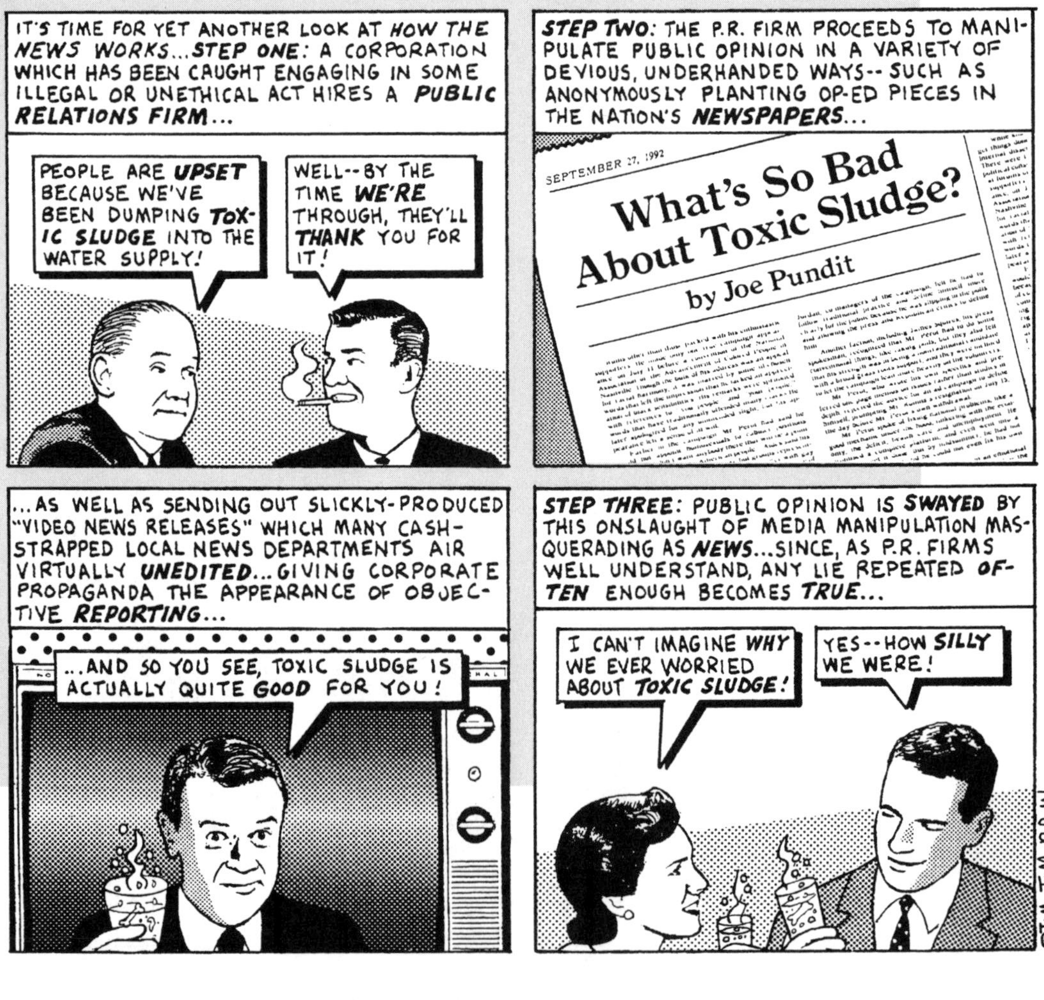
IT'S TIME FOR YET ANOTHER LOOK AT HOW THE NEWS WORKS... STEP ONE: A CORPORATION WHICH HAS BEEN CAUGHT ENGAGING IN SOME ILLEGAL OR UNETHICAL ACT HIRES A PUBLIC RELATIONS FIRM...
PEOPLE ARE UPSET BECAUSE WE'VE BEEN DUMPING TOXIC SLUDGE INTO THE WATER SUPPLY!
WELL--BY THE TIME WE'RE THROUGH, THEY'LL THANK YOU FOR IT!
STEP TWO: THE P.R. FIRM PROCEEDS TO MANIPULATE PUBLIC OPINION IN A VARIETY OF DEVIOUS, UNDERHANDED WAYS-- SUCH AS ANONYMOUSLY PLANTING OP-ED PIECES IN THE NATION'S NEWSPAPERS...
SEPTEMBER 27, 1992
What's So Bad About Toxic Sludge?
by Joe Pundit
...AS WELL AS SENDING OUT SLICKLY-PRODUCED "VIDEO NEWS RELEASES" WHICH MANY CASH-STRAPPED LOCAL NEWS DEPARTMENTS AIR VIRTUALLY UNEDITED... GIVING CORPORATE PROPAGANDA THE APPEARANCE OF OBJECTIVE REPORTING...
...AND SO YOU SEE, TOXIC SLUDGE IS ACTUALLY QUITE GOOD FOR YOU!
STEP THREE: PUBLIC OPINION IS SWAYED BY THIS ONSLAUGHT OF MEDIA MANIPULATION MASQUERADING AS NEWS... SINCE, AS P.R. FIRMS WELL UNDERSTAND, ANY LIE REPEATED OFTEN ENOUGH BECOMES TRUE...
I CAN'T IMAGINE WHY WE EVER WORRIED ABOUT TOXIC SLUDGE!
YES--HOW SILLY WE WERE!
©TOM TOMORROW

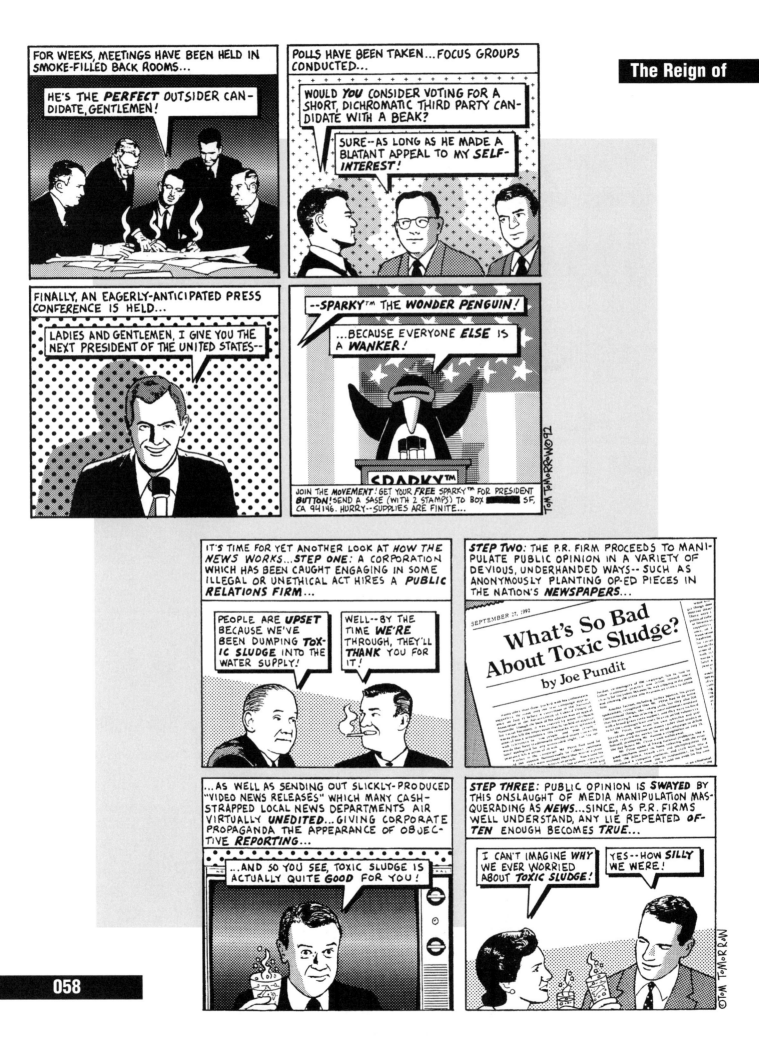

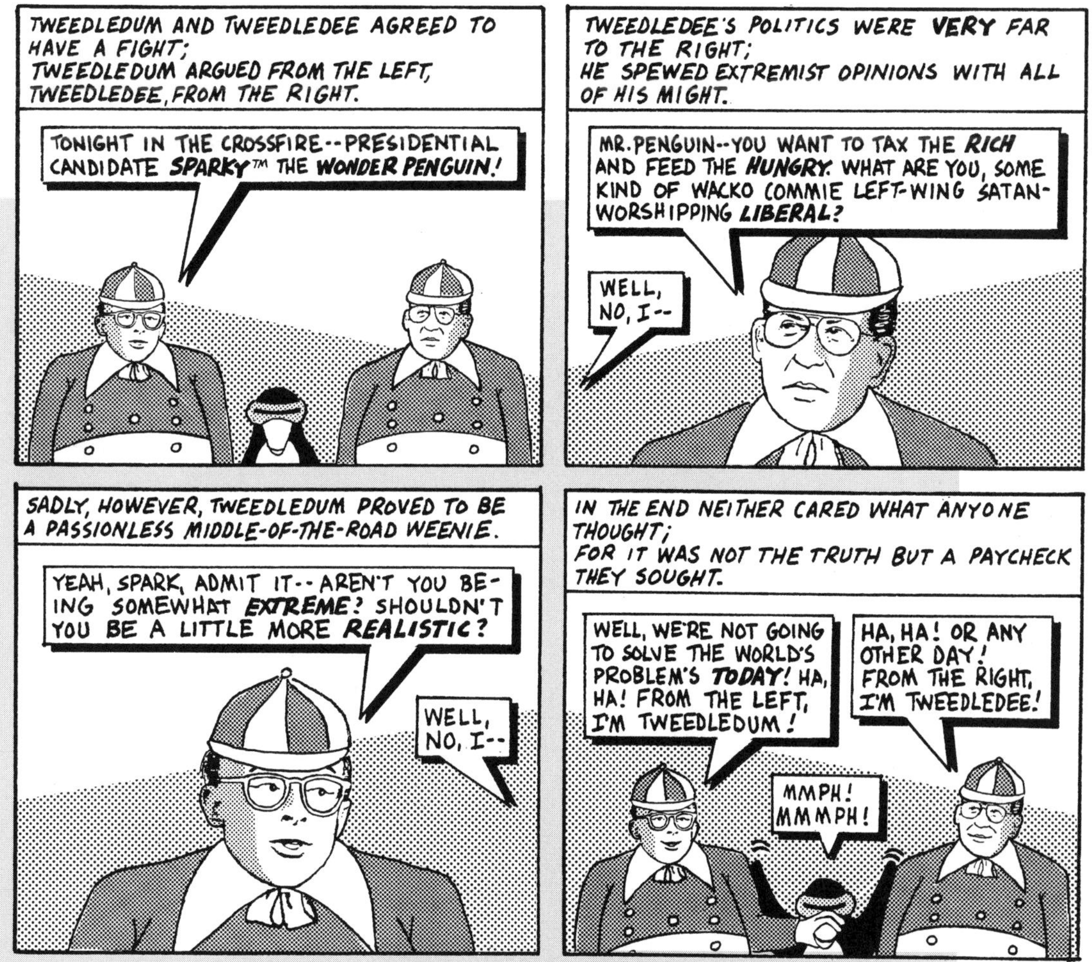
TWEEDLEDUM AND TWEEDLEDEE AGREED TO HAVE A FIGHT; TWEEDLEDUM ARGUED FROM THE LEFT, TWEEDLEDEE, FROM THE RIGHT.
TONIGHT IN THE CROSSFIRE--PRESIDENTIAL CANDIDATE SPARKY™ THE WONDER PENGUIN!
TWEEDLEDEE'S POLITICS WERE VERY FAR TO THE RIGHT; HE SPEWED EXTREMIST OPINIONS WITH ALL OF HIS MIGHT.
MR. PENGUIN--YOU WANT TO TAX THE RICH AND FEED THE HUNGRY. WHAT ARE YOU, SOME KIND OF WACKO COMMIE LEFT-WING SATAN-WORSHIPPING LIBERAL?
WELL, NO, I--
SADLY, HOWEVER, TWEEDLEDUM PROVED TO BE A PASSIONLESS MIDDLE-OF-THE-ROAD WEENIE.
YEAH, SPARK, ADMIT IT--AREN'T YOU BE-ING SOMEWHAT EXTREME? SHOULDN'T YOU BE A LITTLE MORE REALISTIC?
WELL, NO, I--
IN THE END NEITHER CARED WHAT ANYONE THOUGHT; FOR IT WAS NOT THE TRUTH BUT A PAYCHECK THEY SOUGHT.
WELL, WE'RE NOT GOING TO SOLVE THE WORLD'S PROBLEM'S TODAY! HA, HA! FROM THE LEFT, I'M TWEEDLEDUM!
HA, HA! OR ANY OTHER DAY! FROM THE RIGHT, I'M TWEEDLEDEE!
MMPH! MMMPH!

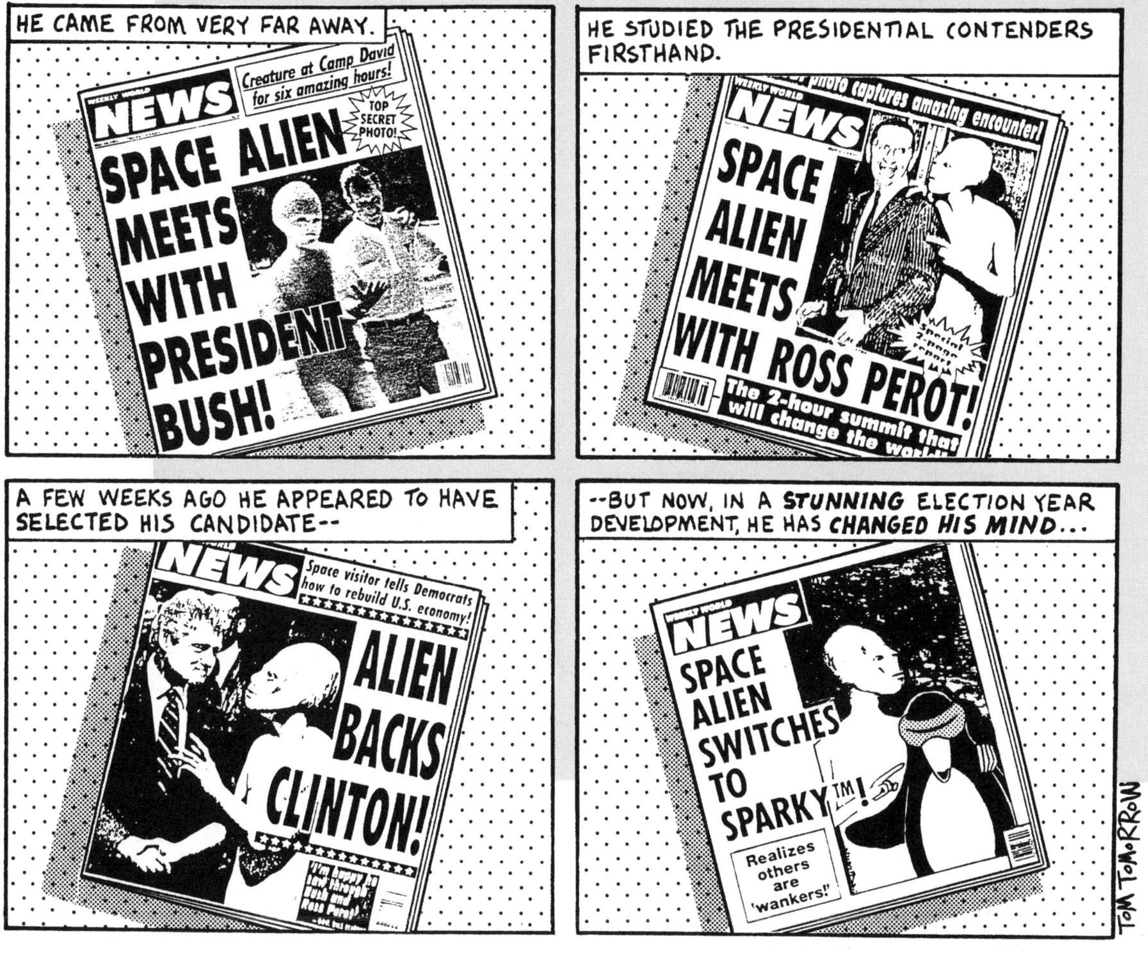
HE CAME FROM VERY FAR AWAY.
WEEKLY WORLD NEWS
Creature at Camp David for six amazing hours!
TOP SECRET PHOTO!
SPACE ALIEN MEETS WITH PRESIDENT BUSH!
HE STUDIED THE PRESIDENTIAL CONTENDERS FIRSTHAND.
photo captures amazing encounter!
NEWS
SPACE ALIEN MEETS WITH ROSS PEROT!
The 2-hour summit that will change the world
A FEW WEEKS AGO HE APPEARED TO HAVE SELECTED HIS CANDIDATE--
NEWS
Space visitor tells Democrats how to rebuild U.S. economy!
ALIEN BACKS CLINTON!
--BUT NOW, IN A STUNNING ELECTION YEAR DEVELOPMENT, HE HAS CHANGED HIS MIND...
WEEKLY WORLD NEWS
SPACE ALIEN SWITCHES TO SPARKY™!
Realizes others are 'wankers!'
TOM TOMORROW

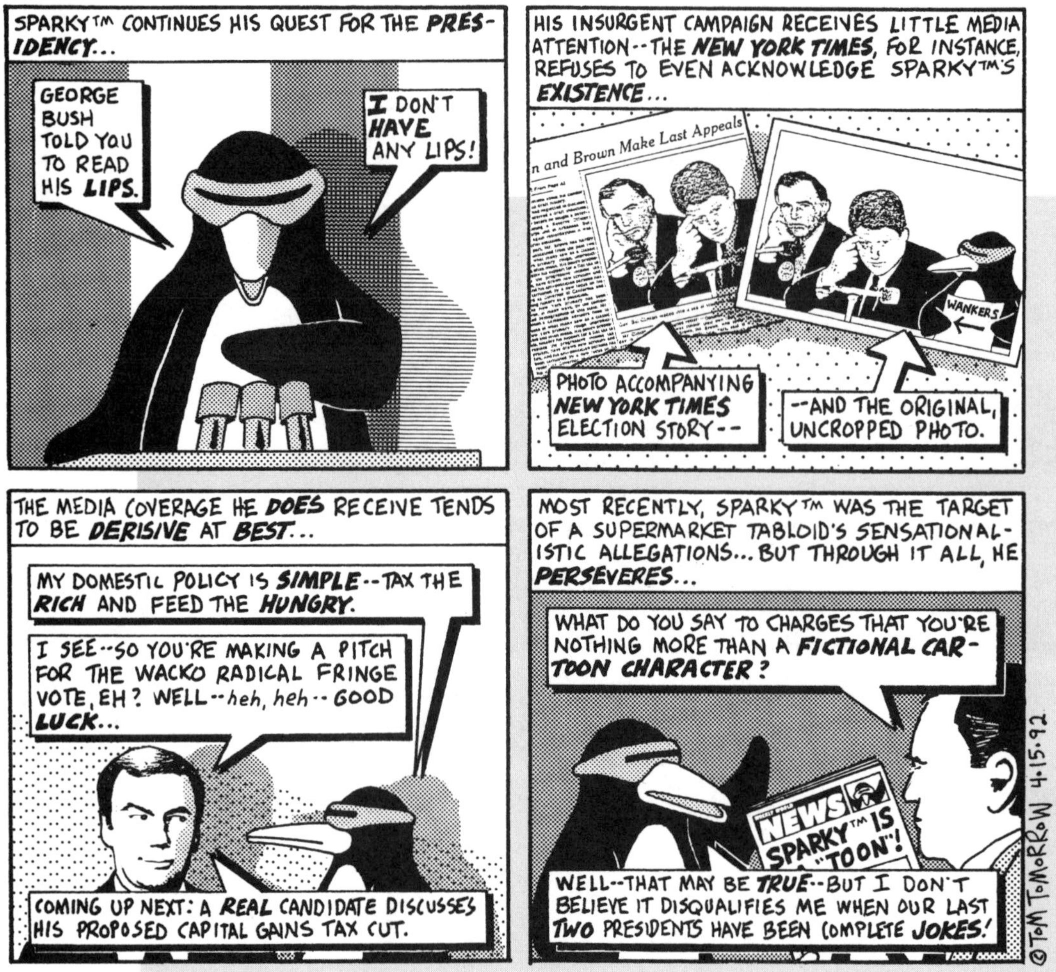
SPARKY™ CONTINUES HIS QUEST FOR THE *PRESIDENCY*...
GEORGE BUSH TOLD YOU TO READ HIS *LIPS*.
I DON'T *HAVE* ANY LIPS!
HIS INSURGENT CAMPAIGN RECEIVES LITTLE MEDIA ATTENTION--THE *NEW YORK TIMES*, FOR INSTANCE, REFUSES TO EVEN ACKNOWLEDGE SPARKY™'S *EXISTENCE*...
n and Brown Make Last Appeals
WANKERS
PHOTO ACCOMPANYING *NEW YORK TIMES* ELECTION STORY--
--AND THE ORIGINAL, UNCROPPED PHOTO.
THE MEDIA COVERAGE HE *DOES* RECEIVE TENDS TO BE *DERISIVE* AT *BEST*...
MY DOMESTIC POLICY IS *SIMPLE*--TAX THE *RICH* AND FEED THE *HUNGRY*.
I SEE--SO YOU'RE MAKING A PITCH FOR THE WACKO RADICAL FRINGE VOTE, EH? WELL--*heh, heh*--GOOD *LUCK*...
COMING UP NEXT: A *REAL* CANDIDATE DISCUSSES HIS PROPOSED CAPITAL GAINS TAX CUT.
MOST RECENTLY, SPARKY™ WAS THE TARGET OF A SUPERMARKET TABLOID'S SENSATIONALISTIC ALLEGATIONS... BUT THROUGH IT ALL, HE *PERSEVERES*...
WHAT DO YOU SAY TO CHARGES THAT YOU'RE NOTHING MORE THAN A *FICTIONAL CARTOON CHARACTER*?
NEWS
SPARKY™ IS "TOON"!
WELL--THAT MAY BE *TRUE*--BUT I DON'T BELIEVE IT DISQUALIFIES ME WHEN OUR LAST *TWO* PRESIDENTS HAVE BEEN COMPLETE *JOKES*!
©TOM TOMORROW 4·15·92

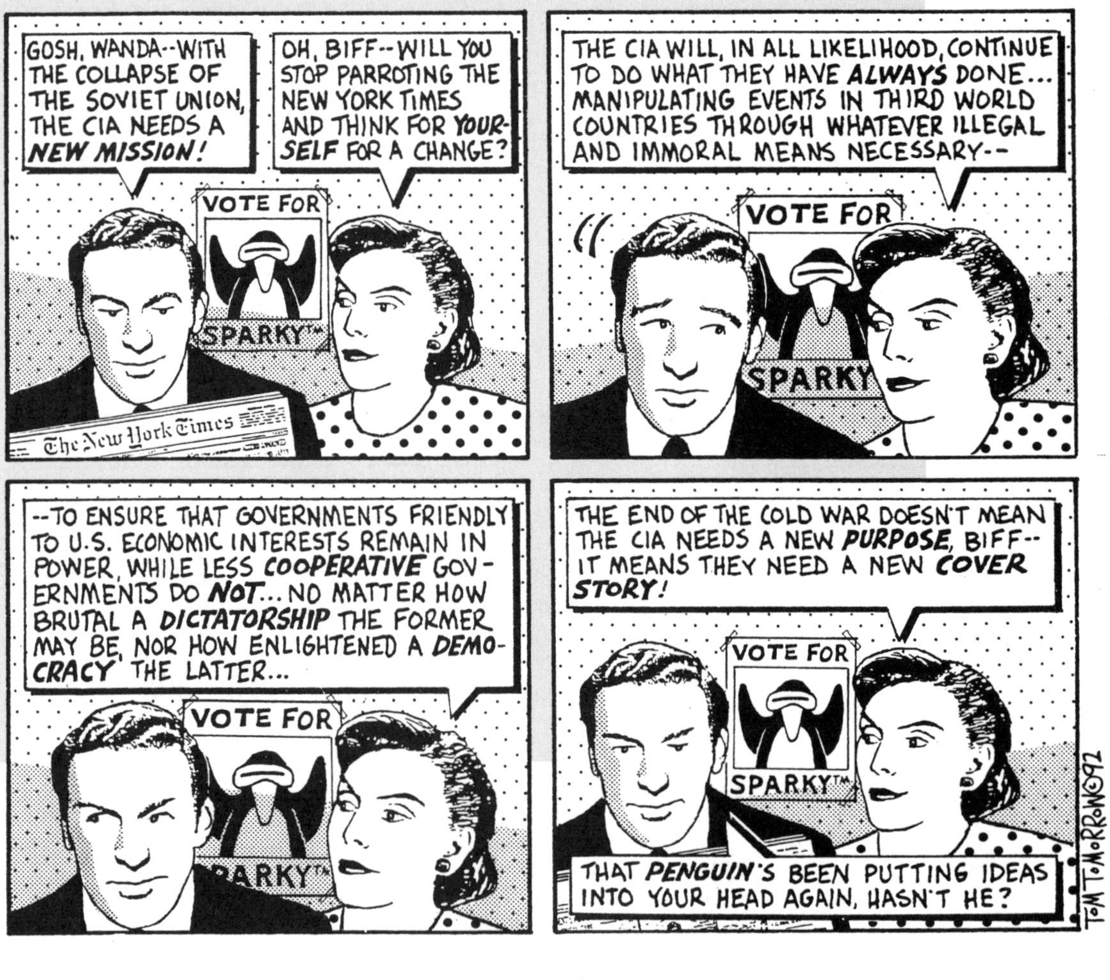
GOSH, WANDA--WITH THE COLLAPSE OF THE SOVIET UNION, THE CIA NEEDS A *NEW MISSION*!
OH, BIFF--WILL YOU STOP PARROTING THE NEW YORK TIMES AND THINK FOR *YOURSELF* FOR A CHANGE?
VOTE FOR
SPARKY™
The New York Times
THE CIA WILL, IN ALL LIKELIHOOD, CONTINUE TO DO WHAT THEY HAVE *ALWAYS* DONE... MANIPULATING EVENTS IN THIRD WORLD COUNTRIES THROUGH WHATEVER ILLEGAL AND IMMORAL MEANS NECESSARY--
VOTE FOR
SPARKY
--TO ENSURE THAT GOVERNMENTS FRIENDLY TO U.S. ECONOMIC INTERESTS REMAIN IN POWER, WHILE LESS *COOPERATIVE* GOVERNMENTS DO *NOT*... NO MATTER HOW BRUTAL A *DICTATORSHIP* THE FORMER MAY BE, NOR HOW ENLIGHTENED A *DEMOCRACY* THE LATTER...
VOTE FOR
SPARKY™
THE END OF THE COLD WAR DOESN'T MEAN THE CIA NEEDS A NEW *PURPOSE*, BIFF--IT MEANS THEY NEED A NEW *COVER STORY*!
VOTE FOR
SPARKY™
THAT *PENGUIN*'S BEEN PUTTING IDEAS INTO YOUR HEAD AGAIN, HASN'T HE?
TOM TOMORROW©92

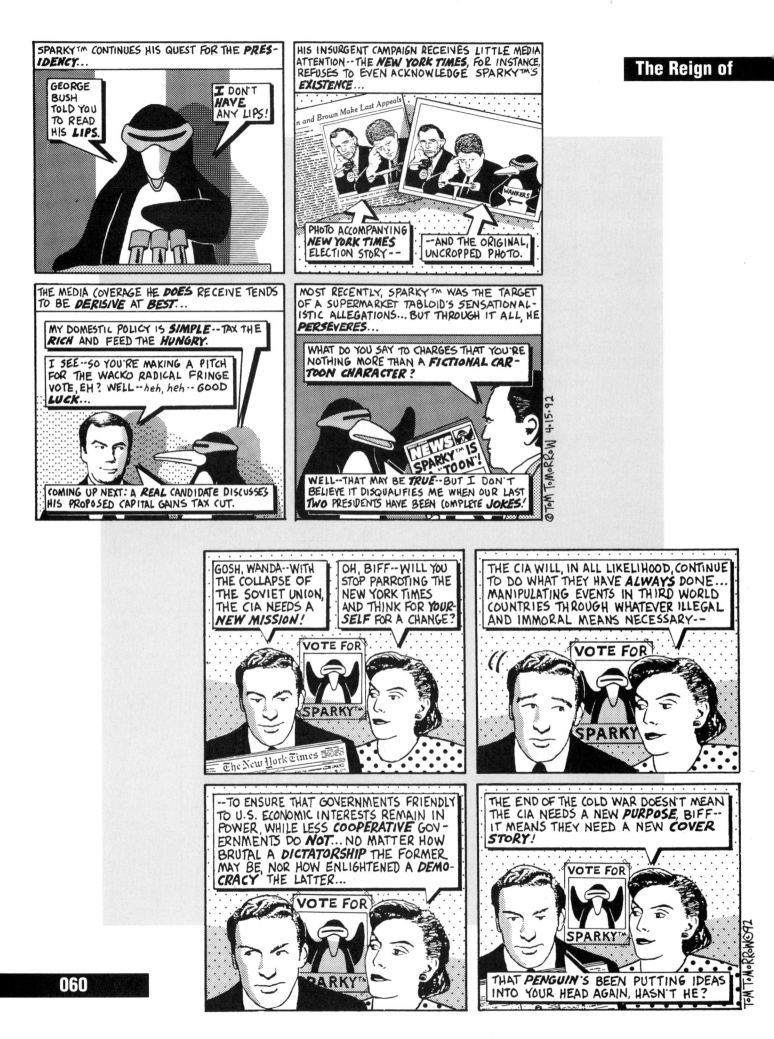

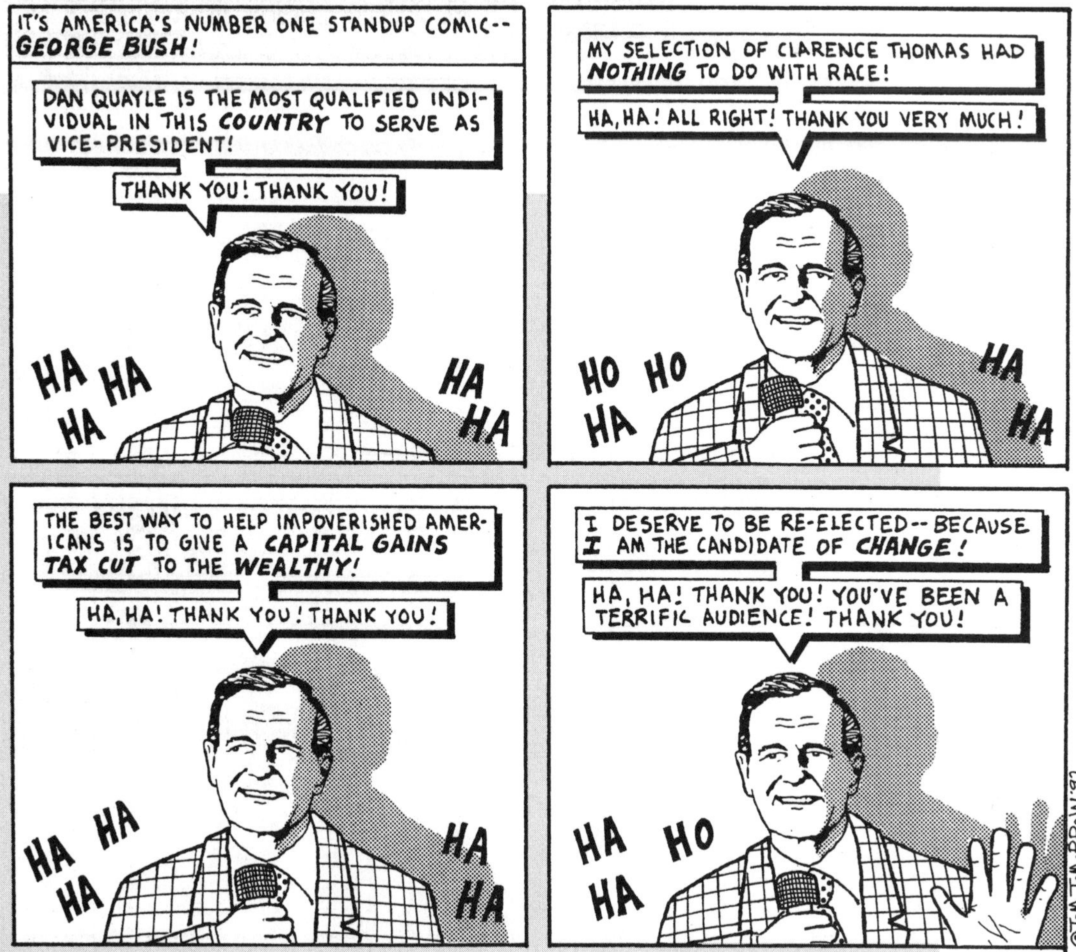
IT'S AMERICA'S NUMBER ONE STANDUP COMIC-- GEORGE BUSH!
DAN QUAYLE IS THE MOST QUALIFIED INDIVIDUAL IN THIS COUNTRY TO SERVE AS VICE-PRESIDENT!
THANK YOU! THANK YOU!
HA HA HA HA HA
MY SELECTION OF CLARENCE THOMAS HAD NOTHING TO DO WITH RACE!
HA, HA! ALL RIGHT! THANK YOU VERY MUCH!
HO HO HA HA HA
THE BEST WAY TO HELP IMPOVERISHED AMERICANS IS TO GIVE A CAPITAL GAINS TAX CUT TO THE WEALTHY!
HA, HA! THANK YOU! THANK YOU!
HA HA HA HA HA
I DESERVE TO BE RE-ELECTED-- BECAUSE I AM THE CANDIDATE OF CHANGE!
HA, HA! THANK YOU! YOU'VE BEEN A TERRIFIC AUDIENCE! THANK YOU!
HA HO HA
©TOM TOMORROW '92

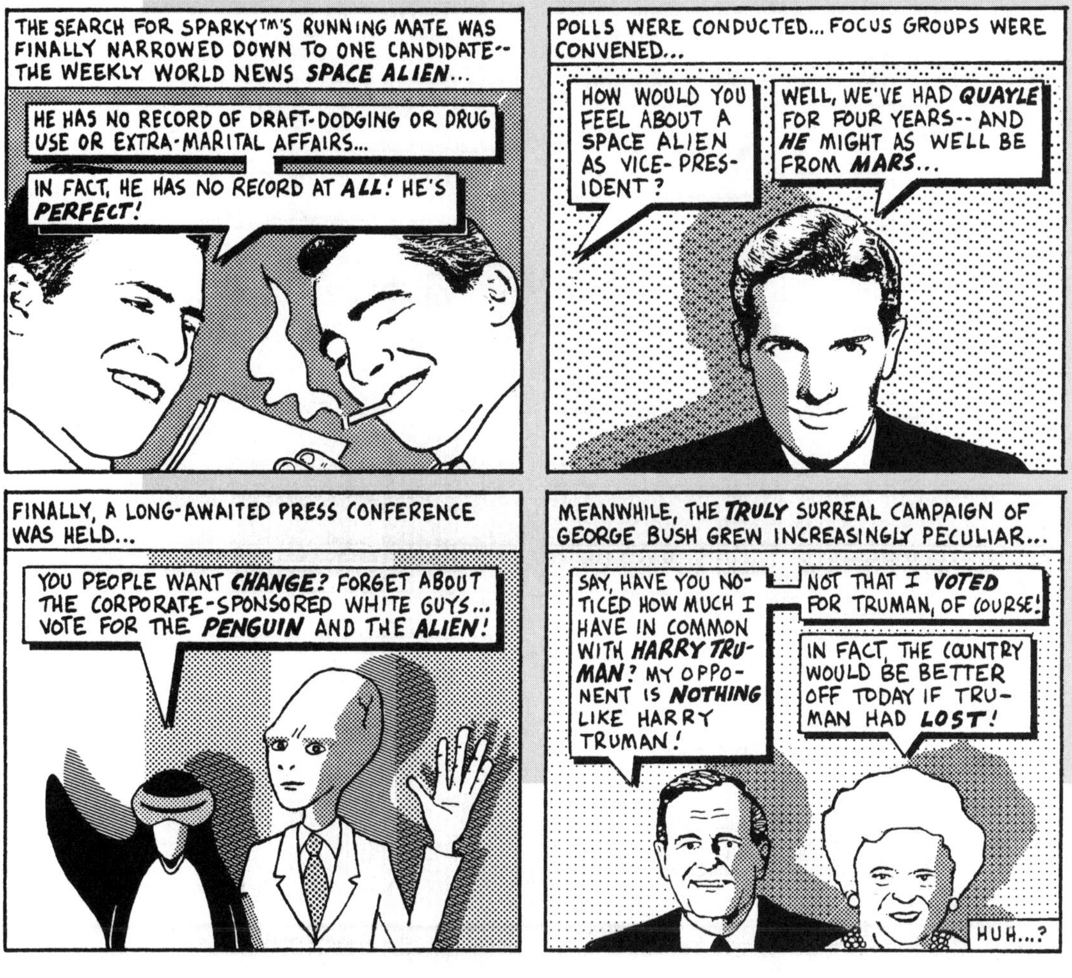
THE SEARCH FOR SPARKY™'S RUNNING MATE WAS FINALLY NARROWED DOWN TO ONE CANDIDATE-- THE WEEKLY WORLD NEWS SPACE ALIEN...
HE HAS NO RECORD OF DRAFT-DODGING OR DRUG USE OR EXTRA-MARITAL AFFAIRS...
IN FACT, HE HAS NO RECORD AT ALL! HE'S PERFECT!
POLLS WERE CONDUCTED... FOCUS GROUPS WERE CONVENED...
HOW WOULD YOU FEEL ABOUT A SPACE ALIEN AS VICE-PRESIDENT?
WELL, WE'VE HAD QUAYLE FOR FOUR YEARS-- AND HE MIGHT AS WELL BE FROM MARS...
FINALLY, A LONG-AWAITED PRESS CONFERENCE WAS HELD...
YOU PEOPLE WANT CHANGE? FORGET ABOUT THE CORPORATE-SPONSORED WHITE GUYS... VOTE FOR THE PENGUIN AND THE ALIEN!
MEANWHILE, THE TRULY SURREAL CAMPAIGN OF GEORGE BUSH GREW INCREASINGLY PECULIAR...
SAY, HAVE YOU NOTICED HOW MUCH I HAVE IN COMMON WITH HARRY TRUMAN? MY OPPONENT IS NOTHING LIKE HARRY TRUMAN!
NOT THAT I VOTED FOR TRUMAN, OF COURSE!
IN FACT, THE COUNTRY WOULD BE BETTER OFF TODAY IF TRUMAN HAD LOST!
HUH...?

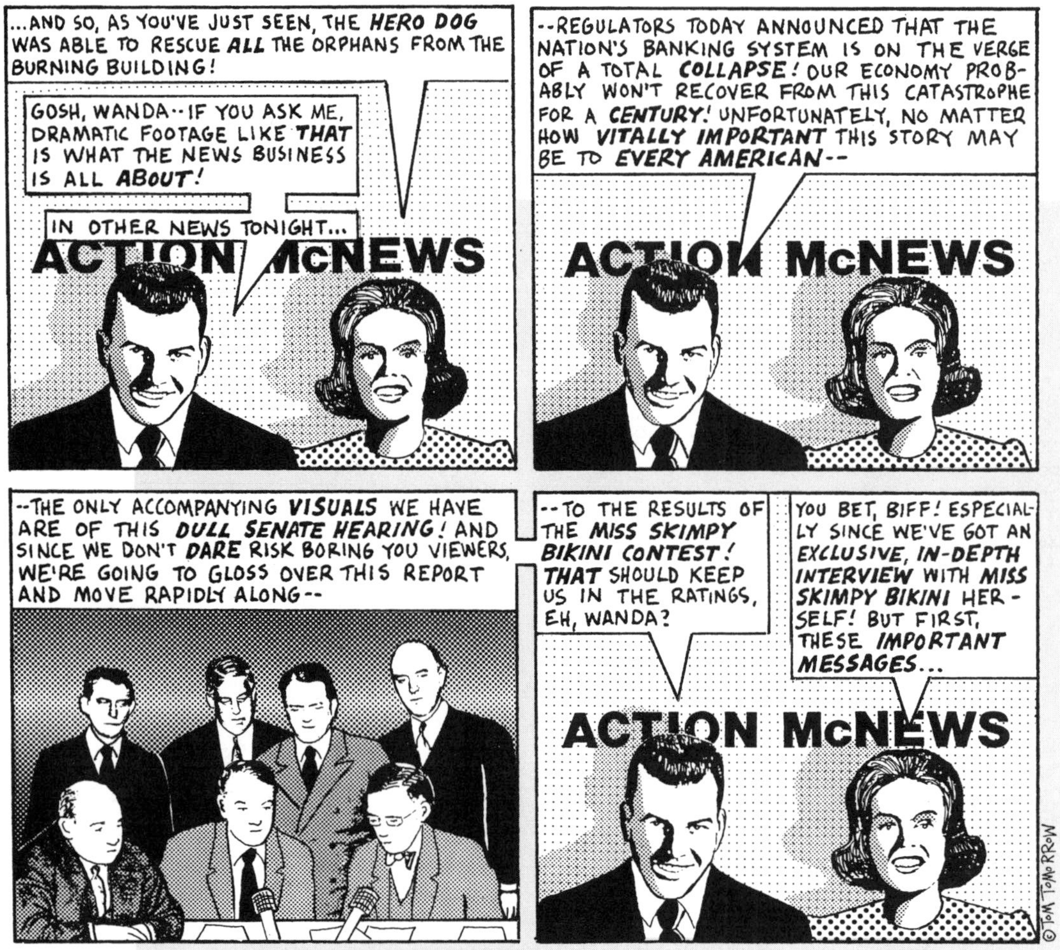
...AND SO, AS YOU'VE JUST SEEN, THE HERO DOG WAS ABLE TO RESCUE ALL THE ORPHANS FROM THE BURNING BUILDING!
GOSH, WANDA--IF YOU ASK ME, DRAMATIC FOOTAGE LIKE THAT IS WHAT THE NEWS BUSINESS IS ALL ABOUT!
IN OTHER NEWS TONIGHT...
ACTION McNEWS
--REGULATORS TODAY ANNOUNCED THAT THE NATION'S BANKING SYSTEM IS ON THE VERGE OF A TOTAL COLLAPSE! OUR ECONOMY PROBABLY WON'T RECOVER FROM THIS CATASTROPHE FOR A CENTURY! UNFORTUNATELY, NO MATTER HOW VITALLY IMPORTANT THIS STORY MAY BE TO EVERY AMERICAN--
ACTION McNEWS
--THE ONLY ACCOMPANYING VISUALS WE HAVE ARE OF THIS DULL SENATE HEARING! AND SINCE WE DON'T DARE RISK BORING YOU VIEWERS, WE'RE GOING TO GLOSS OVER THIS REPORT AND MOVE RAPIDLY ALONG--
--TO THE RESULTS OF THE MISS SKIMPY BIKINI CONTEST! THAT SHOULD KEEP US IN THE RATINGS, EH, WANDA?
YOU BET, BIFF! ESPECIALLY SINCE WE'VE GOT AN EXCLUSIVE, IN-DEPTH INTERVIEW WITH MISS SKIMPY BIKINI HERSELF! BUT FIRST, THESE IMPORTANT MESSAGES...
ACTION McNEWS
© TOM TOMORROW

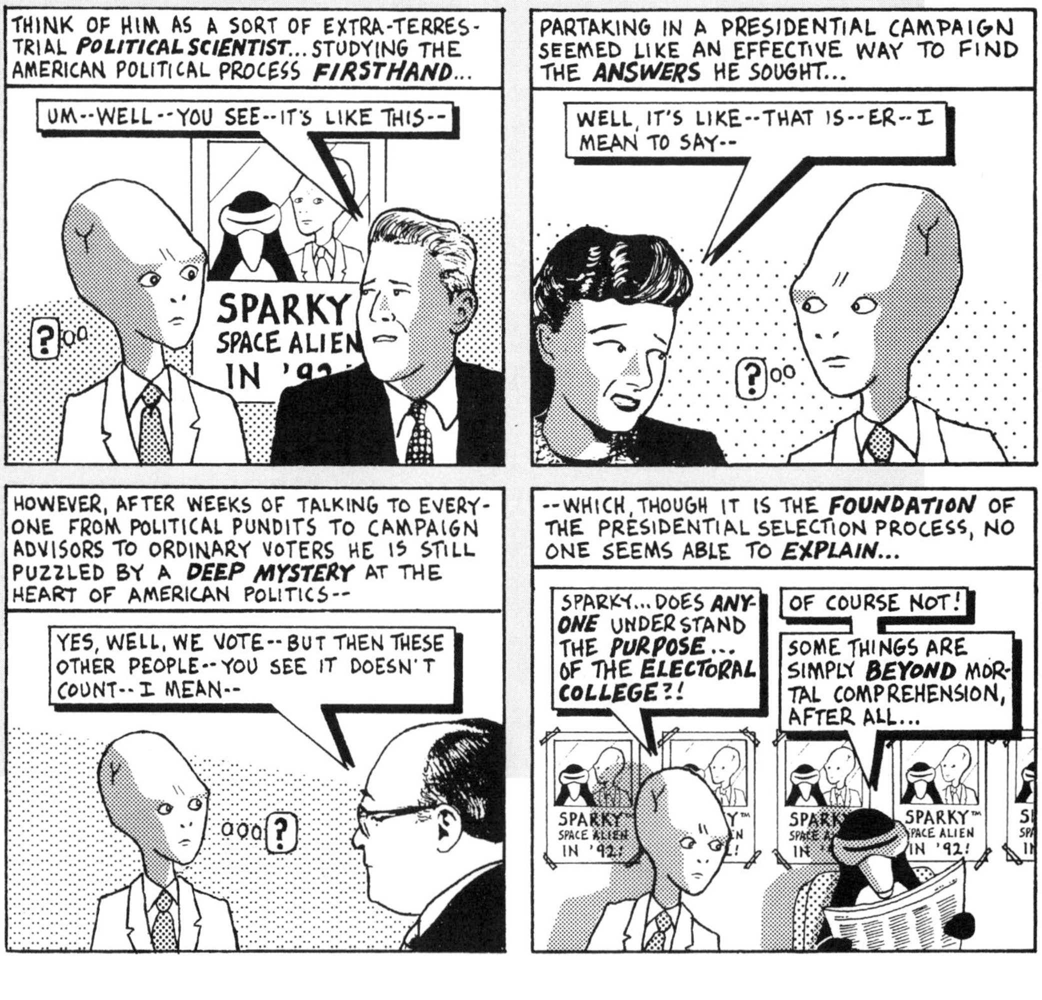
THINK OF HIM AS A SORT OF EXTRA-TERRESTRIAL POLITICAL SCIENTIST... STUDYING THE AMERICAN POLITICAL PROCESS FIRSTHAND...
UM--WELL--YOU SEE--IT'S LIKE THIS--
SPARKY SPACE ALIEN IN '92
PARTAKING IN A PRESIDENTIAL CAMPAIGN SEEMED LIKE AN EFFECTIVE WAY TO FIND THE ANSWERS HE SOUGHT...
WELL, IT'S LIKE--THAT IS--ER--I MEAN TO SAY--
HOWEVER, AFTER WEEKS OF TALKING TO EVERYONE FROM POLITICAL PUNDITS TO CAMPAIGN ADVISORS TO ORDINARY VOTERS HE IS STILL PUZZLED BY A DEEP MYSTERY AT THE HEART OF AMERICAN POLITICS--
YES, WELL, WE VOTE--BUT THEN THESE OTHER PEOPLE--YOU SEE IT DOESN'T COUNT--I MEAN--
--WHICH, THOUGH IT IS THE FOUNDATION OF THE PRESIDENTIAL SELECTION PROCESS, NO ONE SEEMS ABLE TO EXPLAIN...
SPARKY... DOES ANYONE UNDERSTAND THE PURPOSE... OF THE ELECTORAL COLLEGE?!
OF COURSE NOT!
SOME THINGS ARE SIMPLY BEYOND MORTAL COMPREHENSION, AFTER ALL...
SPARKY™ SPACE ALIEN IN '92!

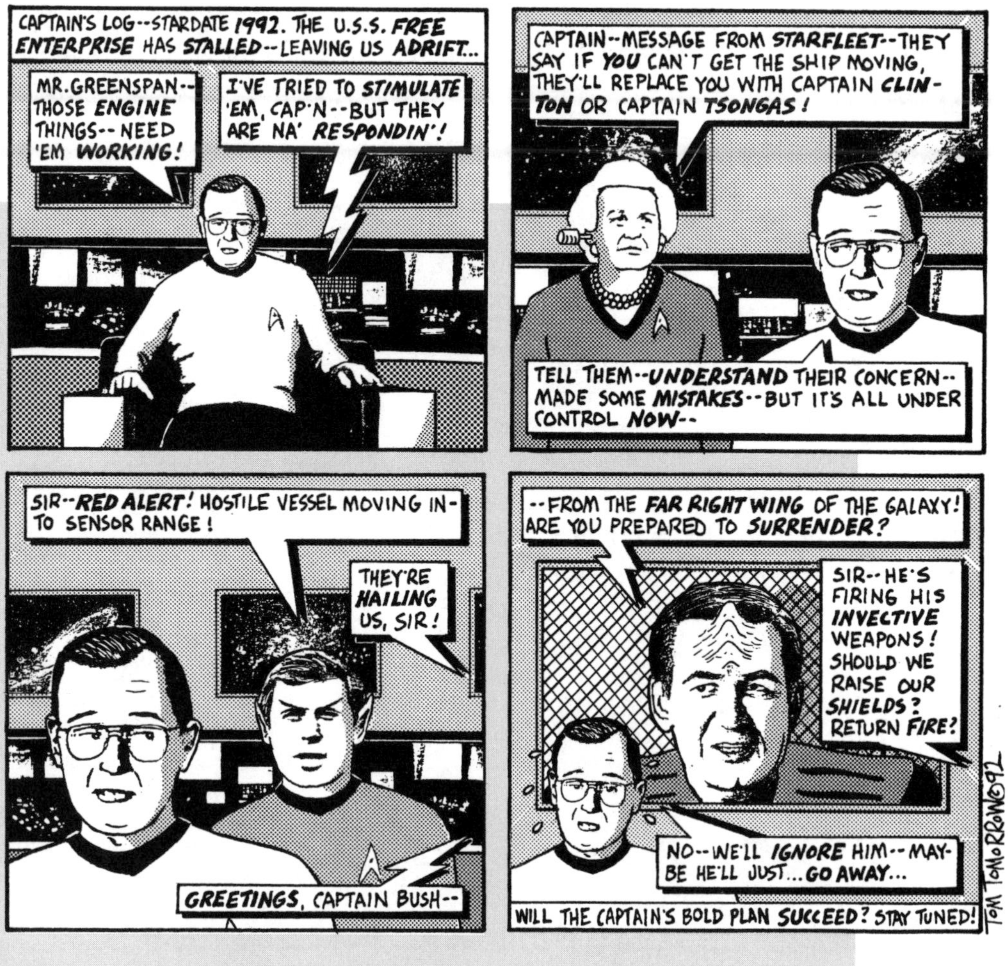
CAPTAIN'S LOG--STARDATE 1992. THE U.S.S. FREE ENTERPRISE HAS STALLED--LEAVING US ADRIFT...
MR. GREENSPAN--THOSE ENGINE THINGS--NEED 'EM WORKING!
I'VE TRIED TO STIMULATE 'EM, CAP'N--BUT THEY ARE NA' RESPONDIN'!
CAPTAIN--MESSAGE FROM STARFLEET--THEY SAY IF YOU CAN'T GET THE SHIP MOVING, THEY'LL REPLACE YOU WITH CAPTAIN CLINTON OR CAPTAIN TSONGAS!
TELL THEM--UNDERSTAND THEIR CONCERN--MADE SOME MISTAKES--BUT IT'S ALL UNDER CONTROL NOW--
SIR--RED ALERT! HOSTILE VESSEL MOVING INTO SENSOR RANGE!
THEY'RE HAILING US, SIR!
GREETINGS, CAPTAIN BUSH--
--FROM THE FAR RIGHT WING OF THE GALAXY! ARE YOU PREPARED TO SURRENDER?
SIR--HE'S FIRING HIS INVECTIVE WEAPONS! SHOULD WE RAISE OUR SHIELDS? RETURN FIRE?
NO--WE'LL IGNORE HIM--MAYBE HE'LL JUST...GO AWAY...
WILL THE CAPTAIN'S BOLD PLAN SUCCEED? STAY TUNED!
TOM TOMORROW©92

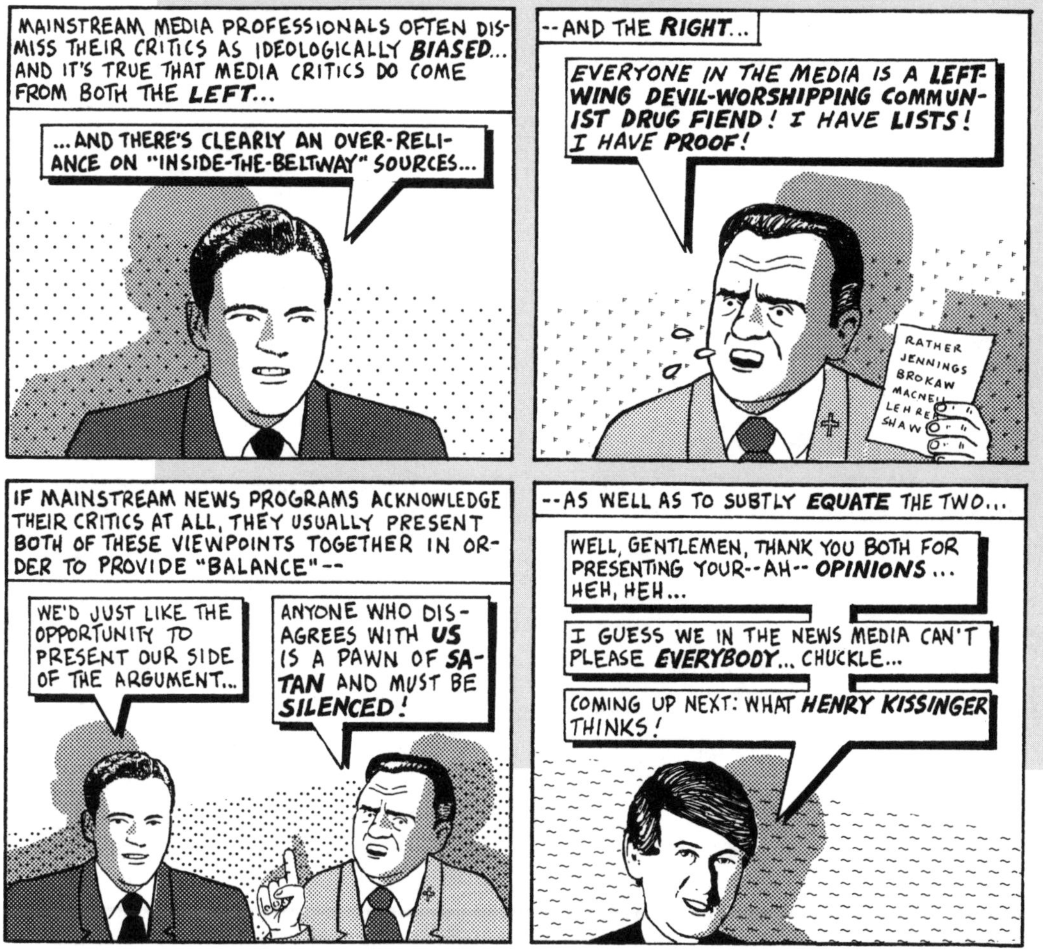
MAINSTREAM MEDIA PROFESSIONALS OFTEN DISMISS THEIR CRITICS AS IDEOLOGICALLY BIASED... AND IT'S TRUE THAT MEDIA CRITICS DO COME FROM BOTH THE LEFT...
...AND THERE'S CLEARLY AN OVER-RELIANCE ON "INSIDE-THE-BELTWAY" SOURCES...
--AND THE RIGHT...
EVERYONE IN THE MEDIA IS A LEFT-WING DEVIL-WORSHIPPING COMMUNIST DRUG FIEND! I HAVE LISTS! I HAVE PROOF!
RATHER
JENNINGS
BROKAW
MACNEIL
LEHRER
SHAW
IF MAINSTREAM NEWS PROGRAMS ACKNOWLEDGE THEIR CRITICS AT ALL, THEY USUALLY PRESENT BOTH OF THESE VIEWPOINTS TOGETHER IN ORDER TO PROVIDE "BALANCE"--
WE'D JUST LIKE THE OPPORTUNITY TO PRESENT OUR SIDE OF THE ARGUMENT...
ANYONE WHO DISAGREES WITH US IS A PAWN OF SATAN AND MUST BE SILENCED!
--AS WELL AS TO SUBTLY EQUATE THE TWO...
WELL, GENTLEMEN, THANK YOU BOTH FOR PRESENTING YOUR--AH--OPINIONS... HEH, HEH...
I GUESS WE IN THE NEWS MEDIA CAN'T PLEASE EVERYBODY... CHUCKLE...
COMING UP NEXT: WHAT HENRY KISSINGER THINKS!

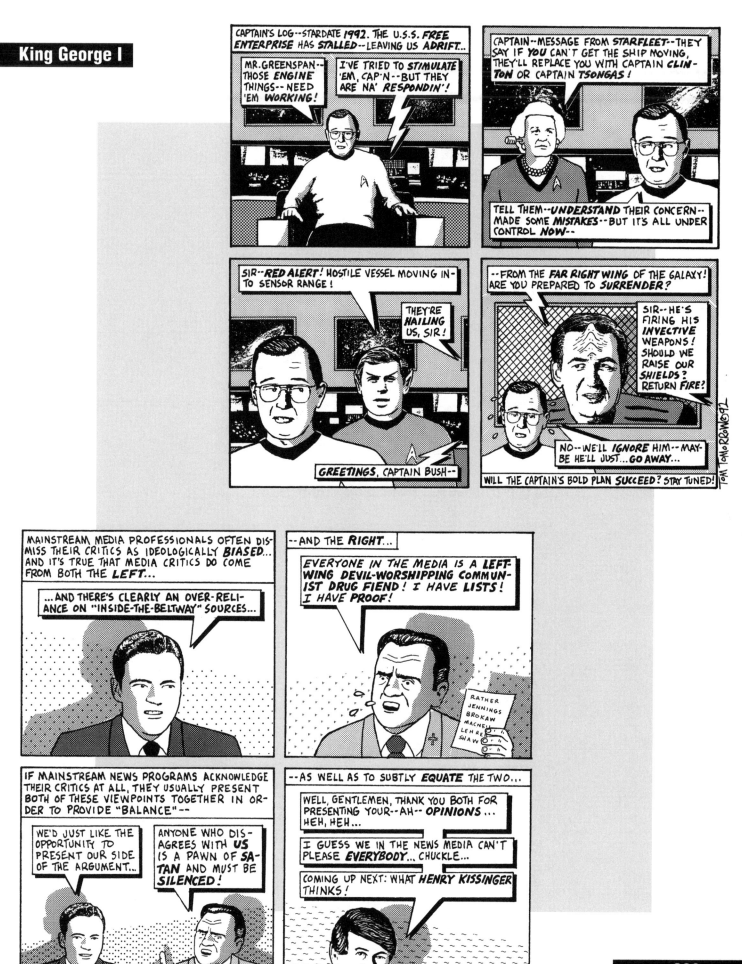

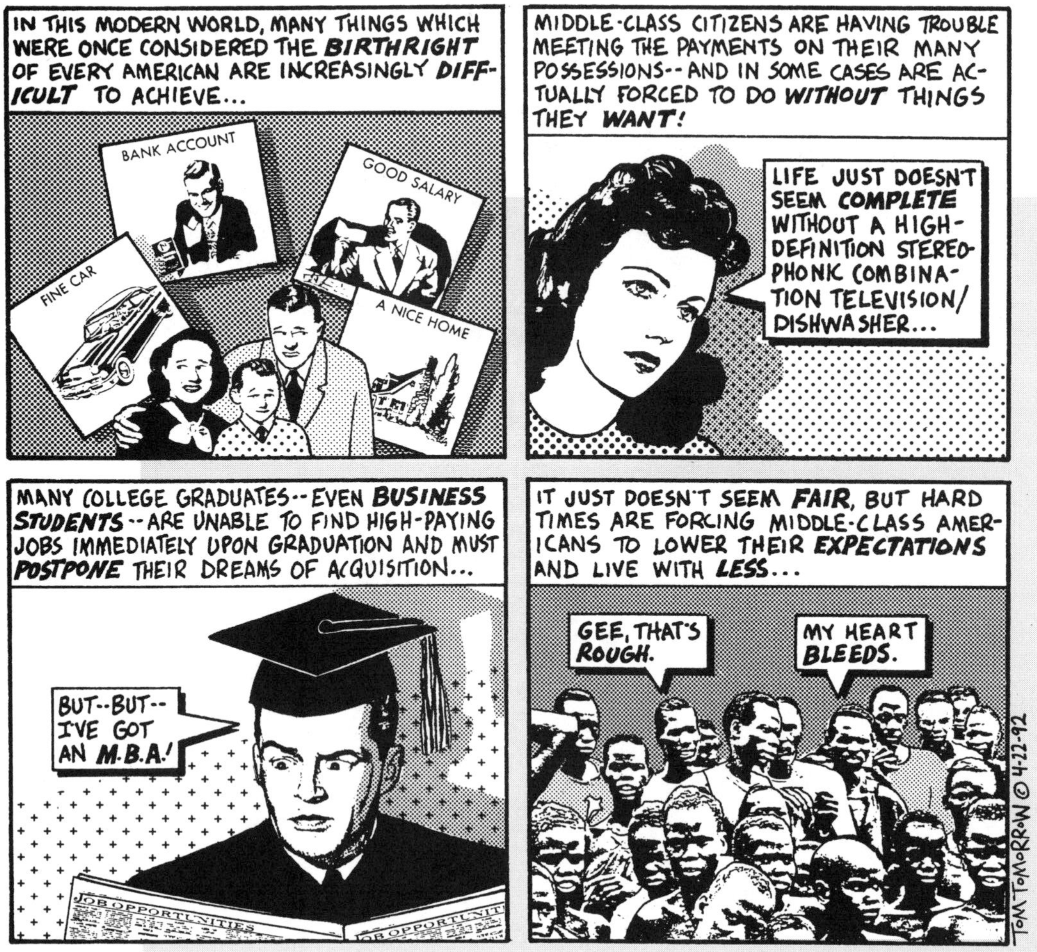
IN THIS MODERN WORLD, MANY THINGS WHICH WERE ONCE CONSIDERED THE BIRTHRIGHT OF EVERY AMERICAN ARE INCREASINGLY DIFFICULT TO ACHIEVE...
BANK ACCOUNT
GOOD SALARY
FINE CAR
A NICE HOME
MIDDLE-CLASS CITIZENS ARE HAVING TROUBLE MEETING THE PAYMENTS ON THEIR MANY POSSESSIONS--AND IN SOME CASES ARE ACTUALLY FORCED TO DO WITHOUT THINGS THEY WANT!
LIFE JUST DOESN'T SEEM COMPLETE WITHOUT A HIGH-DEFINITION STEREOPHONIC COMBINATION TELEVISION/DISHWASHER...
MANY COLLEGE GRADUATES--EVEN BUSINESS STUDENTS--ARE UNABLE TO FIND HIGH-PAYING JOBS IMMEDIATELY UPON GRADUATION AND MUST POSTPONE THEIR DREAMS OF ACQUISITION...
BUT--BUT--I'VE GOT AN M.B.A.!
JOB OPPORTUNITIES
IT JUST DOESN'T SEEM FAIR, BUT HARD TIMES ARE FORCING MIDDLE-CLASS AMERICANS TO LOWER THEIR EXPECTATIONS AND LIVE WITH LESS...
GEE, THAT'S ROUGH.
MY HEART BLEEDS.
TOM TOMORROW © 4-22-92

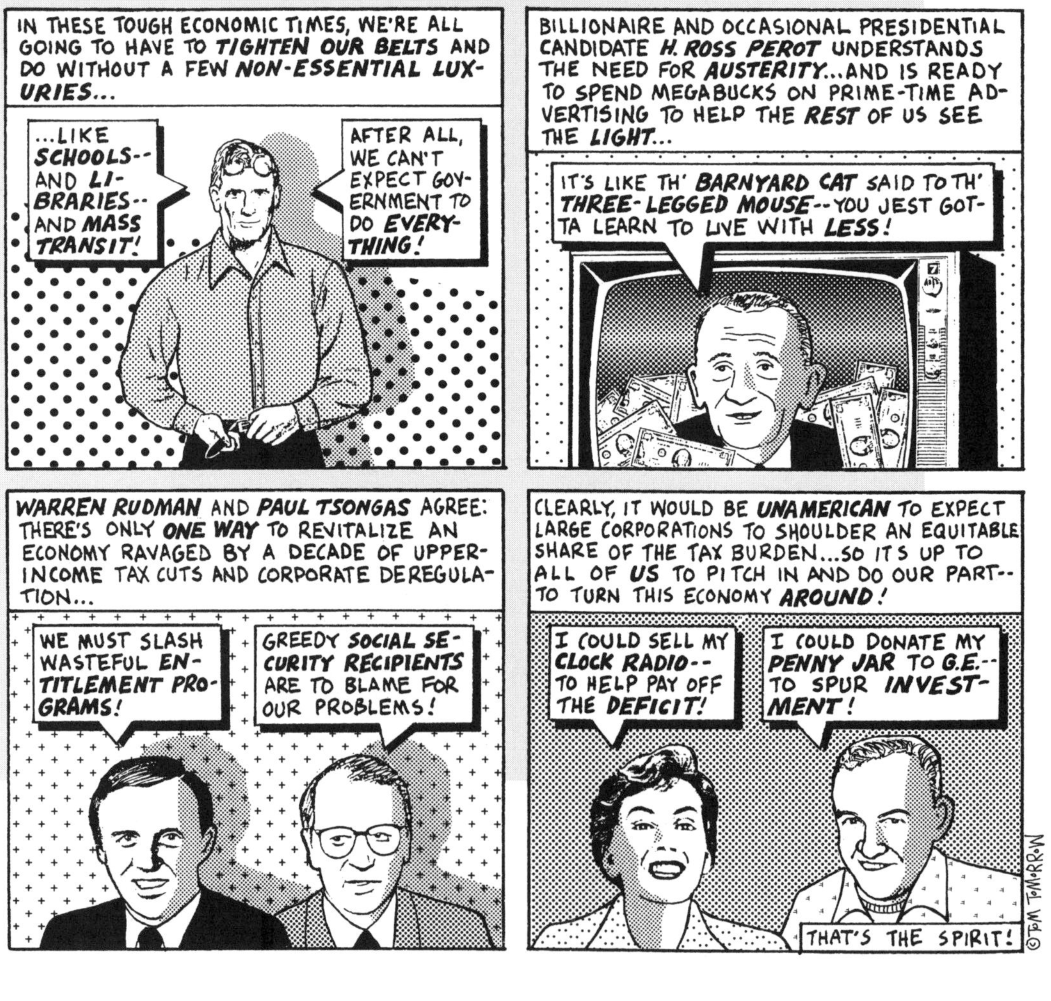
IN THESE TOUGH ECONOMIC TIMES, WE'RE ALL GOING TO HAVE TO TIGHTEN OUR BELTS AND DO WITHOUT A FEW NON-ESSENTIAL LUXURIES...
...LIKE SCHOOLS--AND LIBRARIES--AND MASS TRANSIT!
AFTER ALL, WE CAN'T EXPECT GOVERNMENT TO DO EVERYTHING!
BILLIONAIRE AND OCCASIONAL PRESIDENTIAL CANDIDATE H. ROSS PEROT UNDERSTANDS THE NEED FOR AUSTERITY...AND IS READY TO SPEND MEGABUCKS ON PRIME-TIME ADVERTISING TO HELP THE REST OF US SEE THE LIGHT...
IT'S LIKE TH' BARNYARD CAT SAID TO TH' THREE-LEGGED MOUSE--YOU JEST GOTTA LEARN TO LIVE WITH LESS!
WARREN RUDMAN AND PAUL TSONGAS AGREE: THERE'S ONLY ONE WAY TO REVITALIZE AN ECONOMY RAVAGED BY A DECADE OF UPPER-INCOME TAX CUTS AND CORPORATE DEREGULATION...
WE MUST SLASH WASTEFUL ENTITLEMENT PROGRAMS!
GREEDY SOCIAL SECURITY RECIPIENTS ARE TO BLAME FOR OUR PROBLEMS!
CLEARLY, IT WOULD BE UNAMERICAN TO EXPECT LARGE CORPORATIONS TO SHOULDER AN EQUITABLE SHARE OF THE TAX BURDEN...SO ITS UP TO ALL OF US TO PITCH IN AND DO OUR PART--TO TURN THIS ECONOMY AROUND!
I COULD SELL MY CLOCK RADIO--TO HELP PAY OFF THE DEFICIT!
I COULD DONATE MY PENNY JAR TO G.E.--TO SPUR INVESTMENT!
THAT'S THE SPIRIT!
© TOM TOMORROW

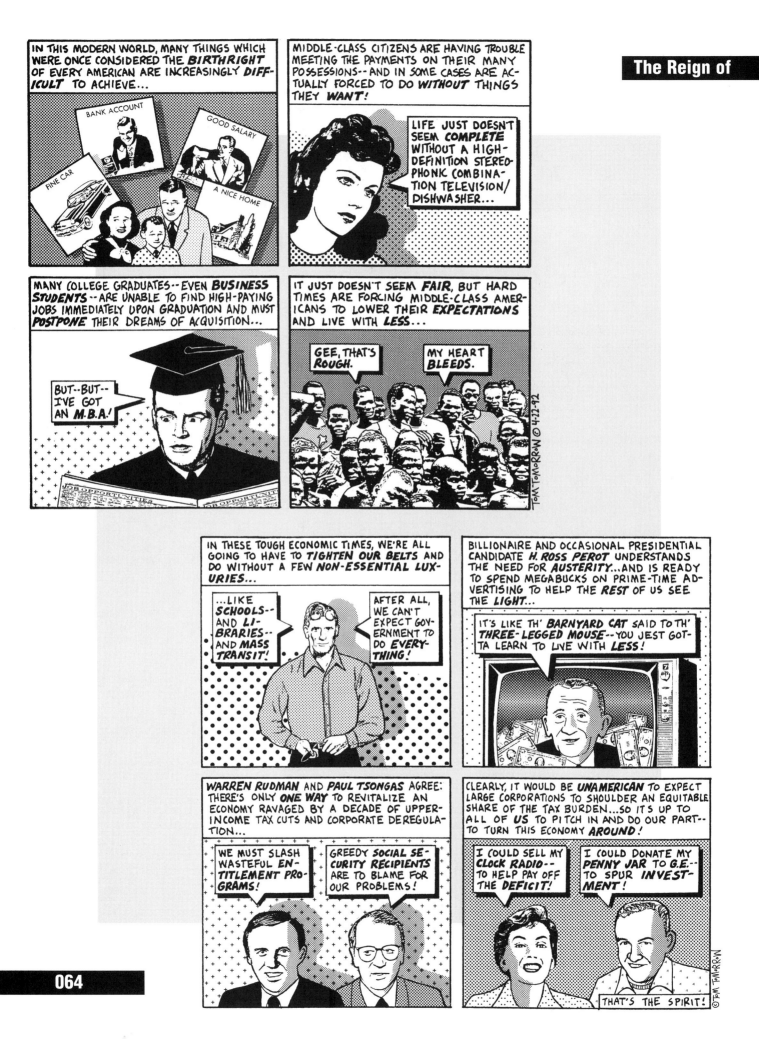

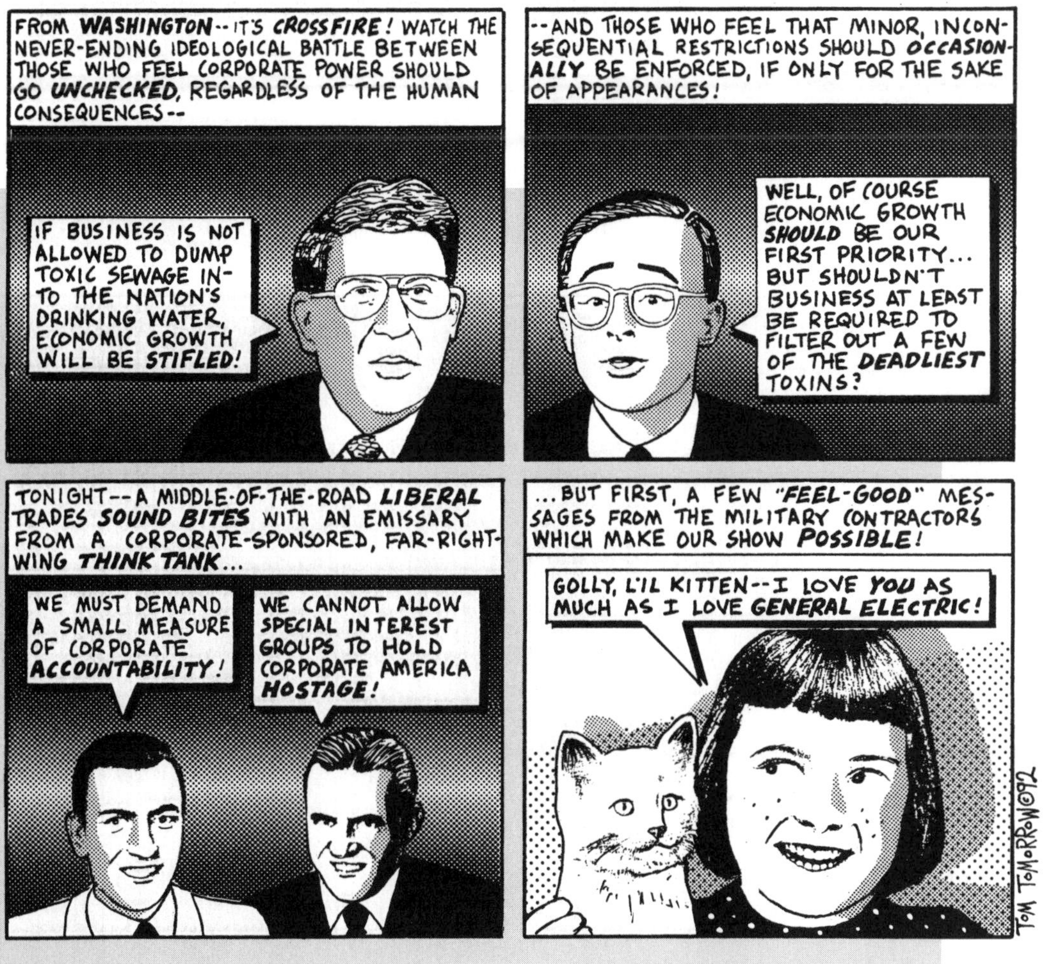
FROM WASHINGTON--IT'S CROSSFIRE! WATCH THE NEVER-ENDING IDEOLOGICAL BATTLE BETWEEN THOSE WHO FEEL CORPORATE POWER SHOULD GO UNCHECKED, REGARDLESS OF THE HUMAN CONSEQUENCES--
IF BUSINESS IS NOT ALLOWED TO DUMP TOXIC SEWAGE INTO THE NATION'S DRINKING WATER, ECONOMIC GROWTH WILL BE STIFLED!
--AND THOSE WHO FEEL THAT MINOR, INCONSEQUENTIAL RESTRICTIONS SHOULD OCCASIONALLY BE ENFORCED, IF ONLY FOR THE SAKE OF APPEARANCES!
WELL, OF COURSE ECONOMIC GROWTH SHOULD BE OUR FIRST PRIORITY... BUT SHOULDN'T BUSINESS AT LEAST BE REQUIRED TO FILTER OUT A FEW OF THE DEADLIEST TOXINS?
TONIGHT--A MIDDLE-OF-THE-ROAD LIBERAL TRADES SOUND BITES WITH AN EMISSARY FROM A CORPORATE-SPONSORED, FAR-RIGHT-WING THINK TANK...
WE MUST DEMAND A SMALL MEASURE OF CORPORATE ACCOUNTABILITY!
WE CANNOT ALLOW SPECIAL INTEREST GROUPS TO HOLD CORPORATE AMERICA HOSTAGE!
...BUT FIRST, A FEW "FEEL-GOOD" MESSAGES FROM THE MILITARY CONTRACTORS WHICH MAKE OUR SHOW POSSIBLE!
GOLLY, L'IL KITTEN--I LOVE YOU AS MUCH AS I LOVE GENERAL ELECTRIC!
TOM TOMORROW©92

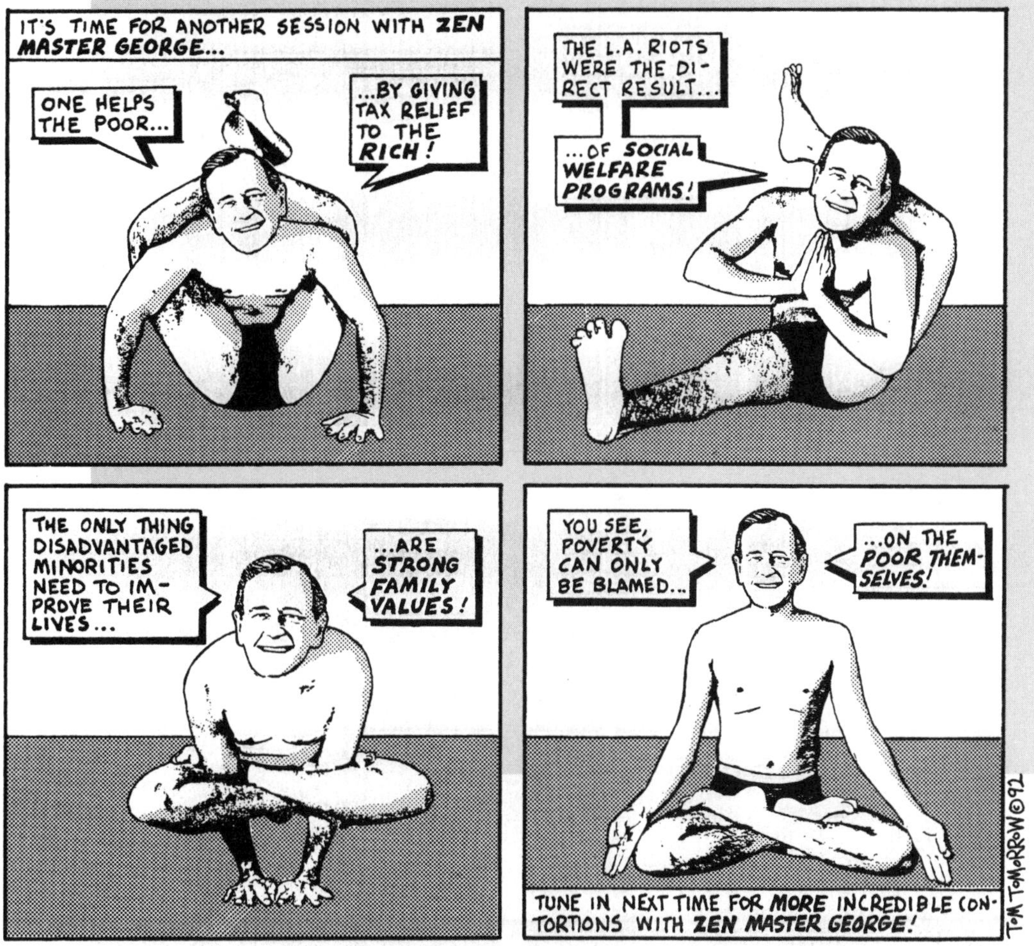
IT'S TIME FOR ANOTHER SESSION WITH ZEN MASTER GEORGE...
ONE HELPS THE POOR...
...BY GIVING TAX RELIEF TO THE RICH!
THE L.A. RIOTS WERE THE DIRECT RESULT...
...OF SOCIAL WELFARE PROGRAMS!
THE ONLY THING DISADVANTAGED MINORITIES NEED TO IMPROVE THEIR LIVES...
...ARE STRONG FAMILY VALUES!
YOU SEE, POVERTY CAN ONLY BE BLAMED...
...ON THE POOR THEMSELVES!
TUNE IN NEXT TIME FOR MORE INCREDIBLE CONTORTIONS WITH ZEN MASTER GEORGE!
TOM TOMORROW©92

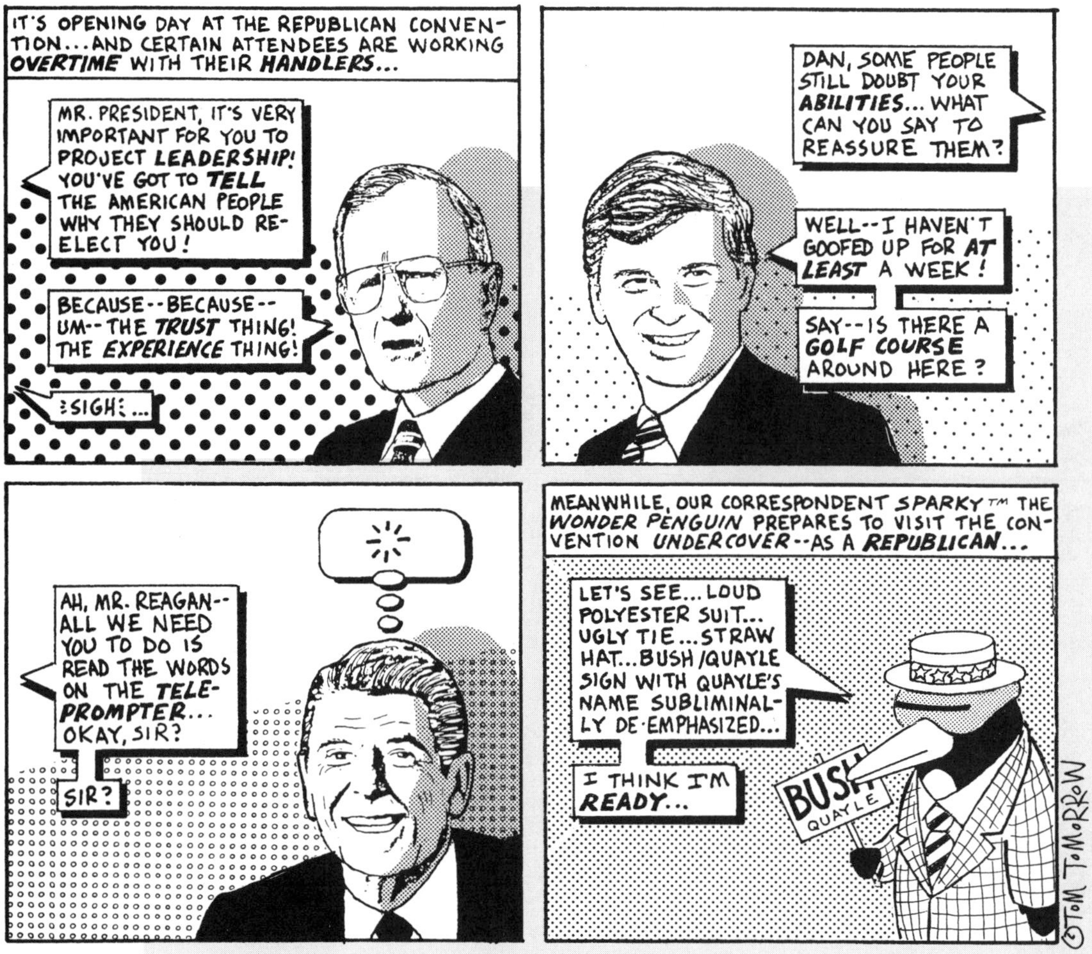
IT'S OPENING DAY AT THE REPUBLICAN CONVENTION... AND CERTAIN ATTENDEES ARE WORKING OVERTIME WITH THEIR HANDLERS...
MR. PRESIDENT, IT'S VERY IMPORTANT FOR YOU TO PROJECT LEADERSHIP! YOU'VE GOT TO TELL THE AMERICAN PEOPLE WHY THEY SHOULD RE-ELECT YOU!
BECAUSE--BECAUSE--UM--THE TRUST THING! THE EXPERIENCE THING!
:SIGH:...
DAN, SOME PEOPLE STILL DOUBT YOUR ABILITIES... WHAT CAN YOU SAY TO REASSURE THEM?
WELL--I HAVEN'T GOOFED UP FOR AT LEAST A WEEK!
SAY--IS THERE A GOLF COURSE AROUND HERE?
AH, MR. REAGAN--ALL WE NEED YOU TO DO IS READ THE WORDS ON THE TELE-PROMPTER... OKAY, SIR?
SIR?
MEANWHILE, OUR CORRESPONDENT SPARKY™ THE WONDER PENGUIN PREPARES TO VISIT THE CONVENTION UNDERCOVER--AS A REPUBLICAN...
LET'S SEE... LOUD POLYESTER SUIT... UGLY TIE... STRAW HAT... BUSH/QUAYLE SIGN WITH QUAYLE'S NAME SUBLIMINALLY DE-EMPHASIZED...
I THINK I'M READY...
BUSH
QUAYLE
©TOM TOMORROW

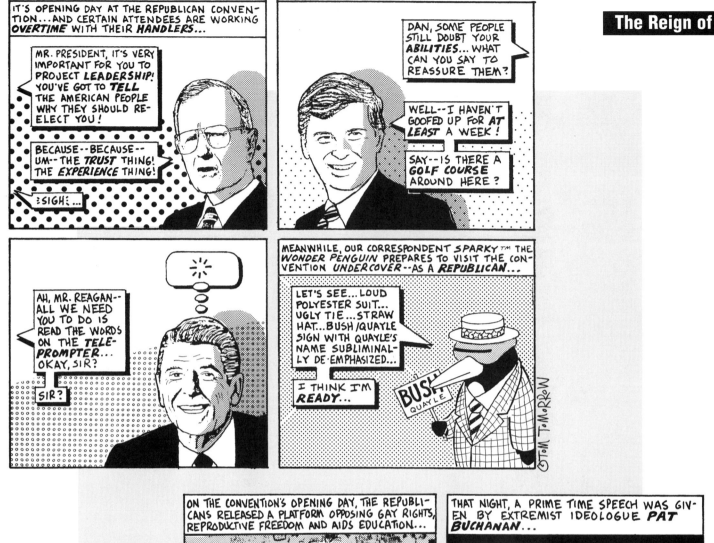

These cartoons appeared as a daily series in the *SanFrancisco Examiner* during the 1992 Republican convention. (I didn't actually attend that one—these were all based on news reports and television coverage.) This is the first time they've been reprinted anywhere.

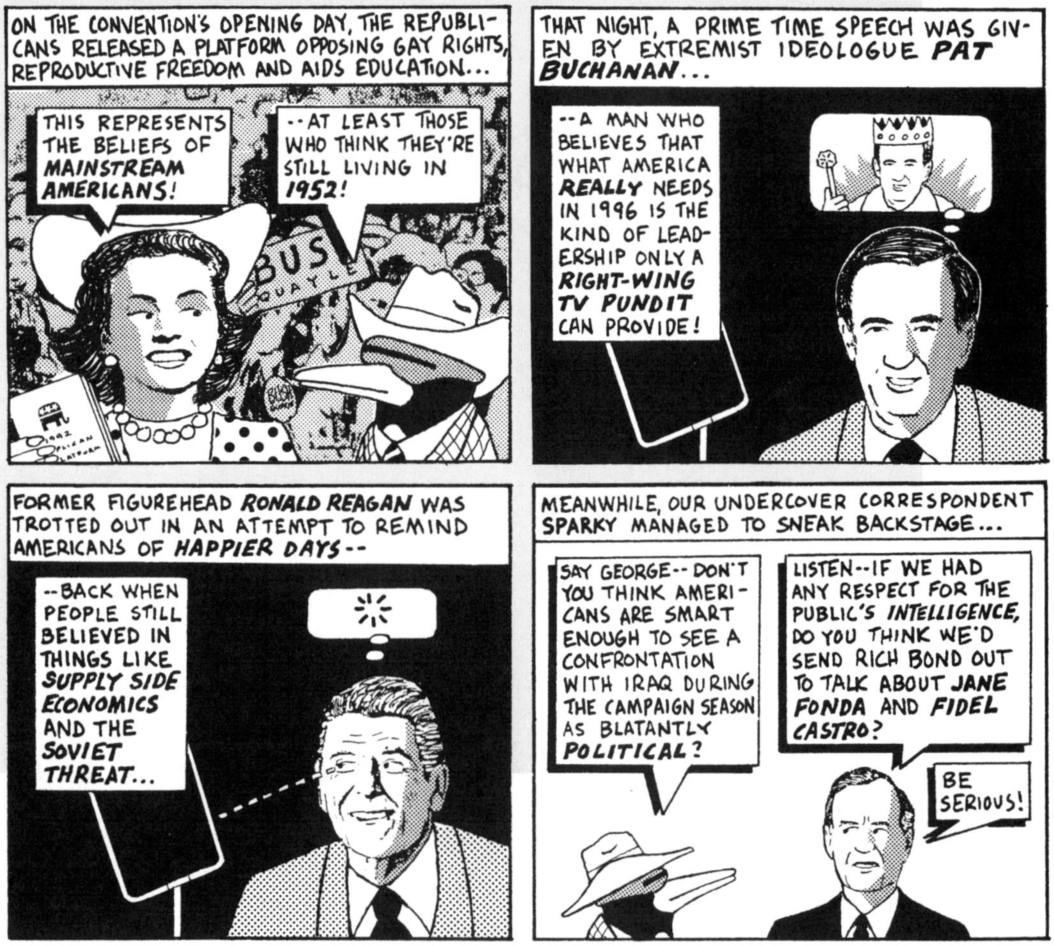
ON THE CONVENTION'S OPENING DAY, THE REPUBLICANS RELEASED A PLATFORM OPPOSING GAY RIGHTS, REPRODUCTIVE FREEDOM AND AIDS EDUCATION...
THIS REPRESENTS THE BELIEFS OF MAINSTREAM AMERICANS!
--AT LEAST THOSE WHO THINK THEY'RE STILL LIVING IN 1952!
BUSH
QUAYLE
THAT NIGHT, A PRIME TIME SPEECH WAS GIVEN BY EXTREMIST IDEOLOGUE PAT BUCHANAN...
--A MAN WHO BELIEVES THAT WHAT AMERICA REALLY NEEDS IN 1996 IS THE KIND OF LEADERSHIP ONLY A RIGHT-WING TV PUNDIT CAN PROVIDE!
FORMER FIGUREHEAD RONALD REAGAN WAS TROTTED OUT IN AN ATTEMPT TO REMIND AMERICANS OF HAPPIER DAYS--
--BACK WHEN PEOPLE STILL BELIEVED IN THINGS LIKE SUPPLY SIDE ECONOMICS AND THE SOVIET THREAT...
MEANWHILE, OUR UNDERCOVER CORRESPONDENT SPARKY MANAGED TO SNEAK BACKSTAGE...
SAY GEORGE--DON'T YOU THINK AMERICANS ARE SMART ENOUGH TO SEE A CONFRONTATION WITH IRAQ DURING THE CAMPAIGN SEASON AS BLATANTLY POLITICAL?
LISTEN--IF WE HAD ANY RESPECT FOR THE PUBLIC'S INTELLIGENCE, DO YOU THINK WE'D SEND RICH BOND OUT TO TALK ABOUT JANE FONDA AND FIDEL CASTRO?
BE SERIOUS!

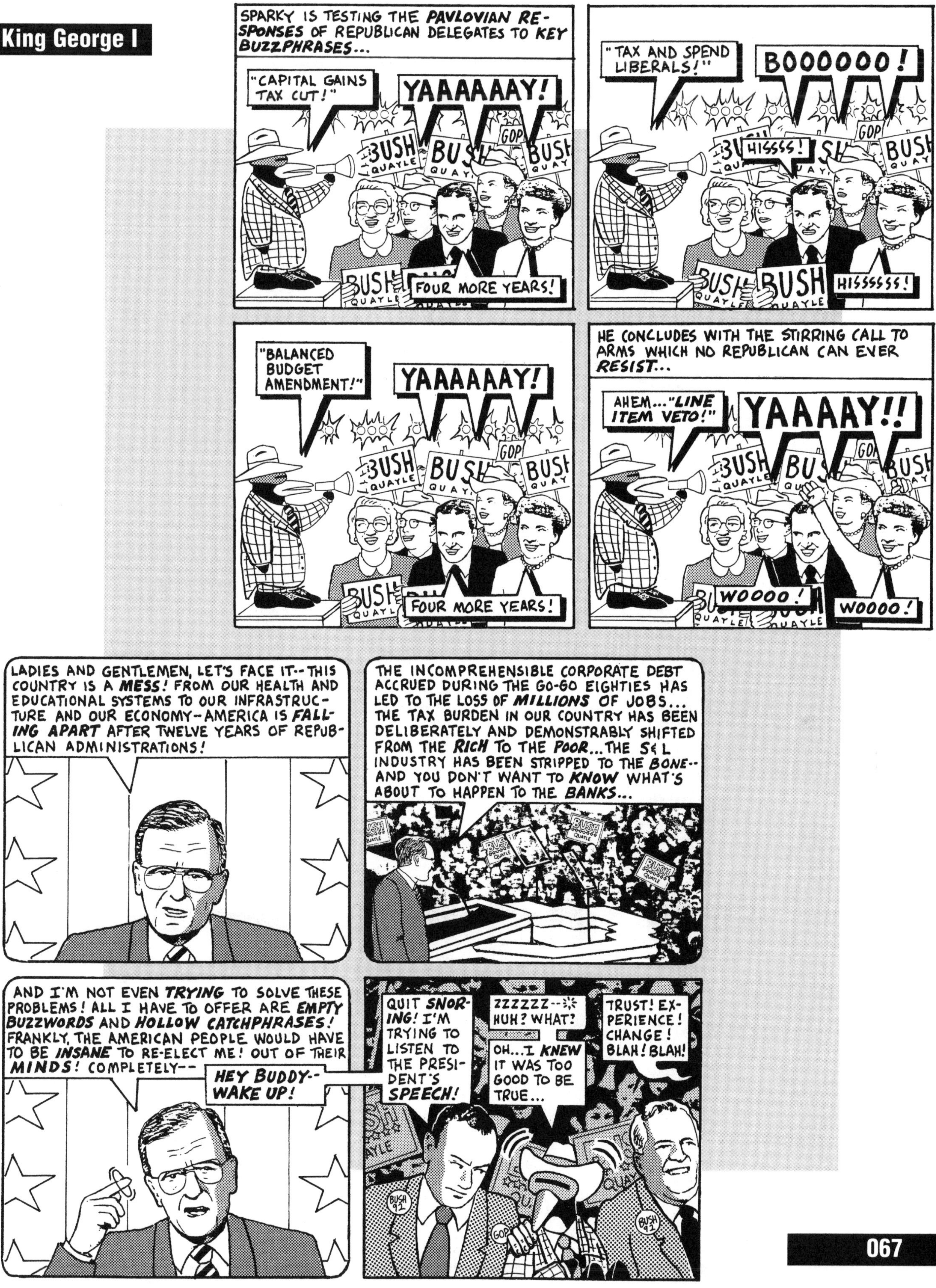
SPARKY IS TESTING THE PAVLOVIAN RE-SPONSES OF REPUBLICAN DELEGATES TO KEY BUZZPHRASES...
"CAPITAL GAINS TAX CUT!"
YAAAAAAY!
FOUR MORE YEARS!
"TAX AND SPEND LIBERALS!"
BOOOOOO!
HISSSS!
HISSSSSS!
"BALANCED BUDGET AMENDMENT!"
YAAAAAAY!
FOUR MORE YEARS!
HE CONCLUDES WITH THE STIRRING CALL TO ARMS WHICH NO REPUBLICAN CAN EVER RESIST...
AHEM..."LINE ITEM VETO!"
YAAAAY!!
WOOOO!
WOOOO!
LADIES AND GENTLEMEN, LET'S FACE IT--THIS COUNTRY IS A MESS! FROM OUR HEALTH AND EDUCATIONAL SYSTEMS TO OUR INFRASTRUCTURE AND OUR ECONOMY--AMERICA IS FALLING APART AFTER TWELVE YEARS OF REPUBLICAN ADMINISTRATIONS!
THE INCOMPREHENSIBLE CORPORATE DEBT ACCRUED DURING THE GO-GO EIGHTIES HAS LED TO THE LOSS OF MILLIONS OF JOBS... THE TAX BURDEN IN OUR COUNTRY HAS BEEN DELIBERATELY AND DEMONSTRABLY SHIFTED FROM THE RICH TO THE POOR... THE S&L INDUSTRY HAS BEEN STRIPPED TO THE BONE--AND YOU DON'T WANT TO KNOW WHAT'S ABOUT TO HAPPEN TO THE BANKS...
AND I'M NOT EVEN TRYING TO SOLVE THESE PROBLEMS! ALL I HAVE TO OFFER ARE EMPTY BUZZWORDS AND HOLLOW CATCHPHRASES! FRANKLY, THE AMERICAN PEOPLE WOULD HAVE TO BE INSANE TO RE-ELECT ME! OUT OF THEIR MINDS! COMPLETELY--
HEY BUDDY--WAKE UP!
QUIT SNORING! I'M TRYING TO LISTEN TO THE PRESIDENT'S SPEECH!
ZZZZZZ-- HUH? WHAT?
OH...I KNEW IT WAS TOO GOOD TO BE TRUE...
TRUST! EXPERIENCE! CHANGE! BLAH! BLAH!

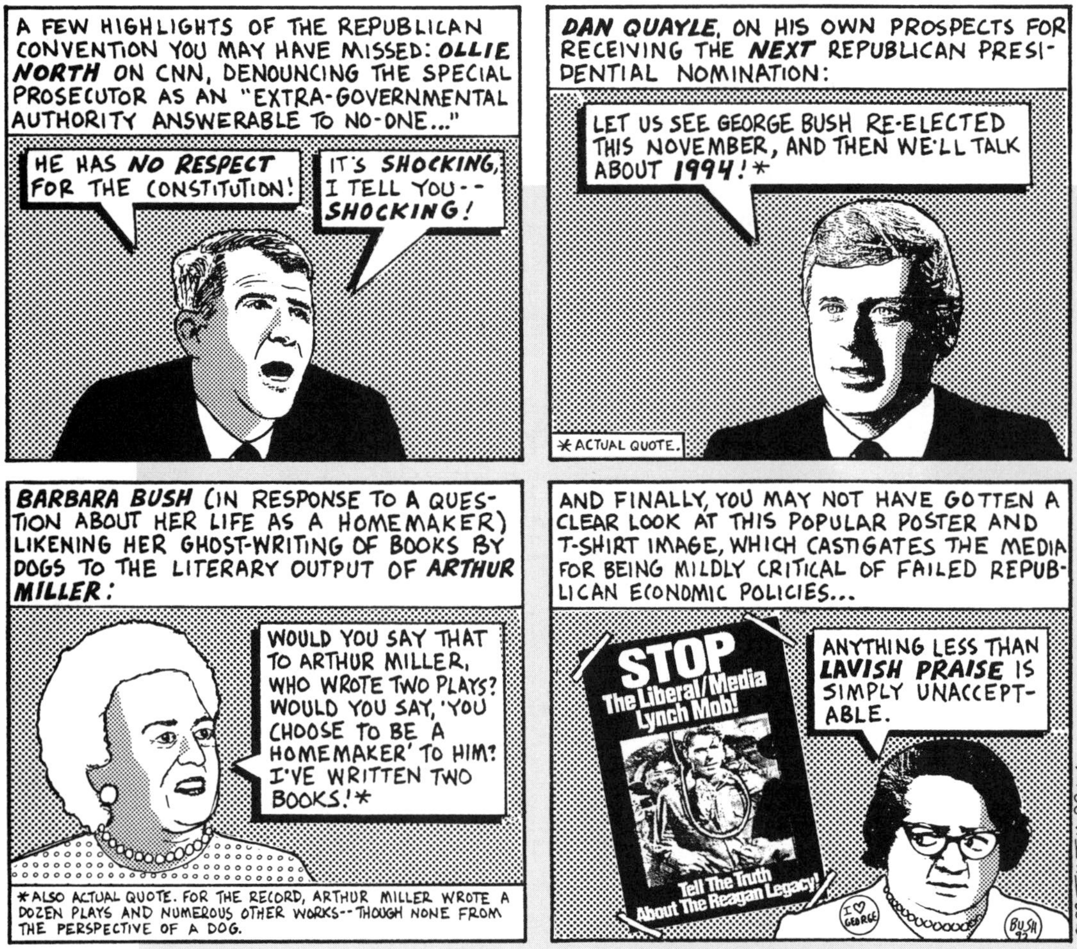
A FEW HIGHLIGHTS OF THE REPUBLICAN CONVENTION YOU MAY HAVE MISSED: OLLIE NORTH ON CNN, DENOUNCING THE SPECIAL PROSECUTOR AS AN "EXTRA-GOVERNMENTAL AUTHORITY ANSWERABLE TO NO-ONE..."
HE HAS NO RESPECT FOR THE CONSTITUTION!
IT'S SHOCKING, I TELL YOU-- SHOCKING!
DAN QUAYLE, ON HIS OWN PROSPECTS FOR RECEIVING THE NEXT REPUBLICAN PRESIDENTIAL NOMINATION:
LET US SEE GEORGE BUSH RE-ELECTED THIS NOVEMBER, AND THEN WE'LL TALK ABOUT 1994!*
*ACTUAL QUOTE.
BARBARA BUSH (IN RESPONSE TO A QUESTION ABOUT HER LIFE AS A HOMEMAKER) LIKENING HER GHOST-WRITING OF BOOKS BY DOGS TO THE LITERARY OUTPUT OF ARTHUR MILLER:
WOULD YOU SAY THAT TO ARTHUR MILLER, WHO WROTE TWO PLAYS? WOULD YOU SAY, 'YOU CHOOSE TO BE A HOMEMAKER' TO HIM? I'VE WRITTEN TWO BOOKS!*
*ALSO ACTUAL QUOTE. FOR THE RECORD, ARTHUR MILLER WROTE A DOZEN PLAYS AND NUMEROUS OTHER WORKS-- THOUGH NONE FROM THE PERSPECTIVE OF A DOG.
AND FINALLY, YOU MAY NOT HAVE GOTTEN A CLEAR LOOK AT THIS POPULAR POSTER AND T-SHIRT IMAGE, WHICH CASTIGATES THE MEDIA FOR BEING MILDLY CRITICAL OF FAILED REPUBLICAN ECONOMIC POLICIES...
STOP The Liberal/Media Lynch Mob!
Tell The Truth About The Reagan Legacy!
ANYTHING LESS THAN LAVISH PRAISE IS SIMPLY UNACCEPTABLE.
BUSH 92
©92 TOM TOMORROW

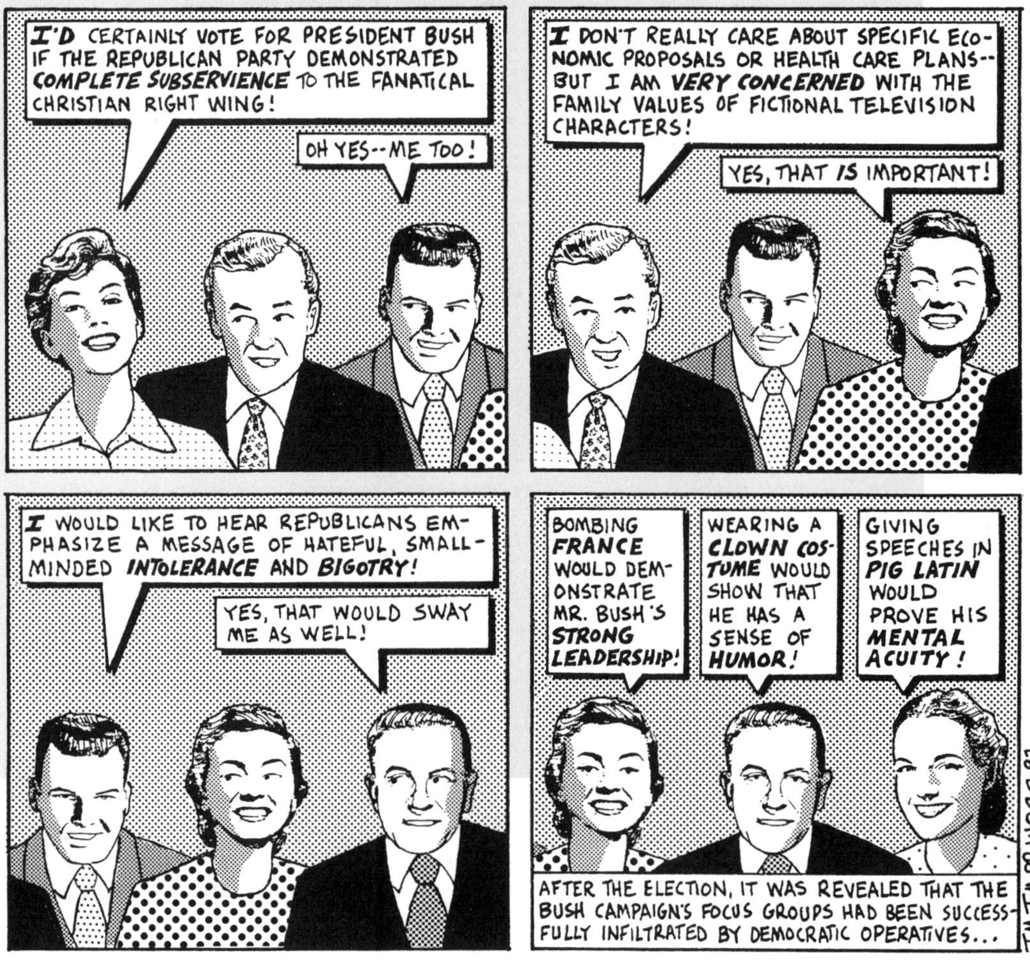
I'D CERTAINLY VOTE FOR PRESIDENT BUSH IF THE REPUBLICAN PARTY DEMONSTRATED COMPLETE SUBSERVIENCE TO THE FANATICAL CHRISTIAN RIGHT WING!
OH YES--ME TOO!
I DON'T REALLY CARE ABOUT SPECIFIC ECONOMIC PROPOSALS OR HEALTH CARE PLANS-- BUT I AM VERY CONCERNED WITH THE FAMILY VALUES OF FICTIONAL TELEVISION CHARACTERS!
YES, THAT IS IMPORTANT!
I WOULD LIKE TO HEAR REPUBLICANS EMPHASIZE A MESSAGE OF HATEFUL, SMALL-MINDED INTOLERANCE AND BIGOTRY!
YES, THAT WOULD SWAY ME AS WELL!
BOMBING FRANCE WOULD DEMONSTRATE MR. BUSH'S STRONG LEADERSHIP!
WEARING A CLOWN COSTUME WOULD SHOW THAT HE HAS A SENSE OF HUMOR!
GIVING SPEECHES IN PIG LATIN WOULD PROVE HIS MENTAL ACUITY!
AFTER THE ELECTION, IT WAS REVEALED THAT THE BUSH CAMPAIGN'S FOCUS GROUPS HAD BEEN SUCCESSFULLY INFILTRATED BY DEMOCRATIC OPERATIVES...
TOM TOMORROW ©9-8-92

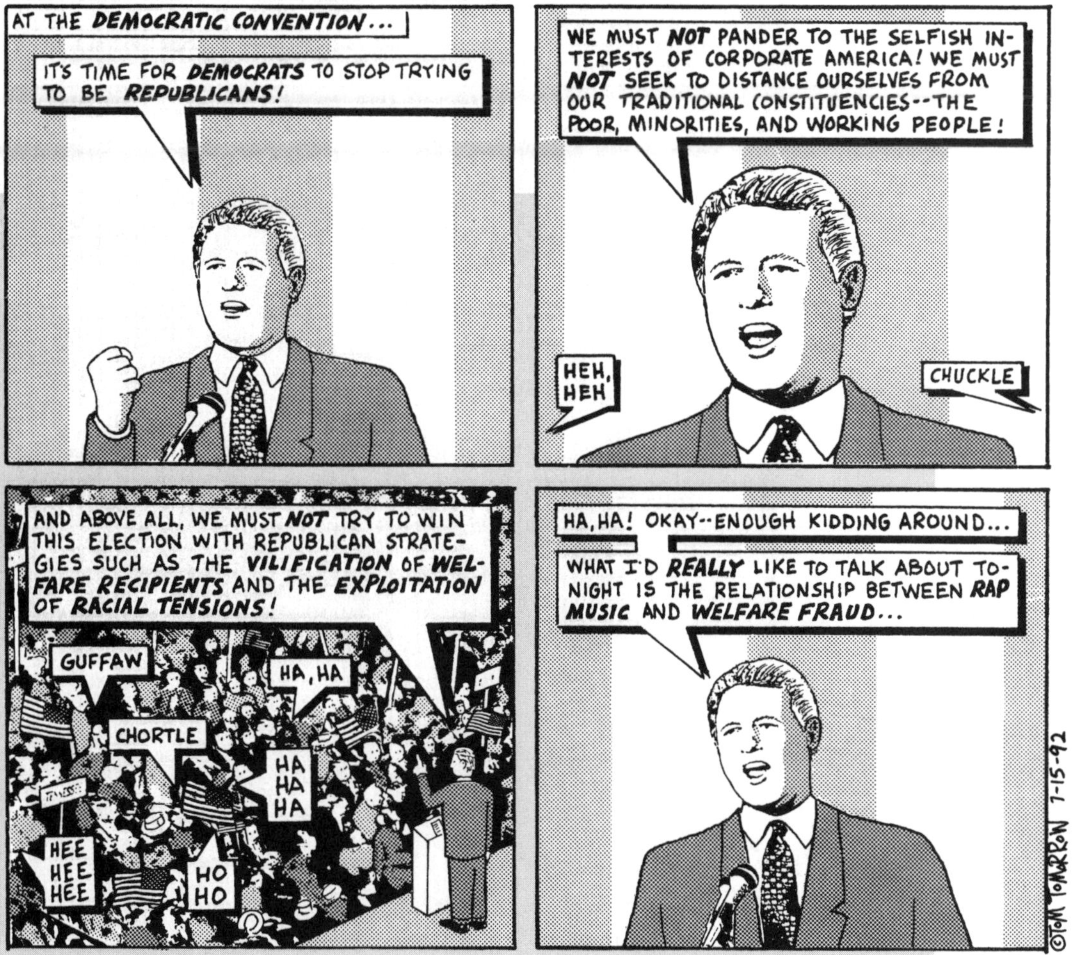
AT THE DEMOCRATIC CONVENTION...
IT'S TIME FOR DEMOCRATS TO STOP TRYING TO BE REPUBLICANS!
WE MUST NOT PANDER TO THE SELFISH INTERESTS OF CORPORATE AMERICA! WE MUST NOT SEEK TO DISTANCE OURSELVES FROM OUR TRADITIONAL CONSTITUENCIES--THE POOR, MINORITIES, AND WORKING PEOPLE!
HEH, HEH
CHUCKLE
AND ABOVE ALL, WE MUST NOT TRY TO WIN THIS ELECTION WITH REPUBLICAN STRATEGIES SUCH AS THE VILIFICATION OF WELFARE RECIPIENTS AND THE EXPLOITATION OF RACIAL TENSIONS!
GUFFAW
HA, HA
CHORTLE
HA HA HA
HEE HEE HEE
HO HO
HA, HA! OKAY--ENOUGH KIDDING AROUND...
WHAT I'D REALLY LIKE TO TALK ABOUT TONIGHT IS THE RELATIONSHIP BETWEEN RAP MUSIC AND WELFARE FRAUD...
©TOM TOMORROW 7-15-92

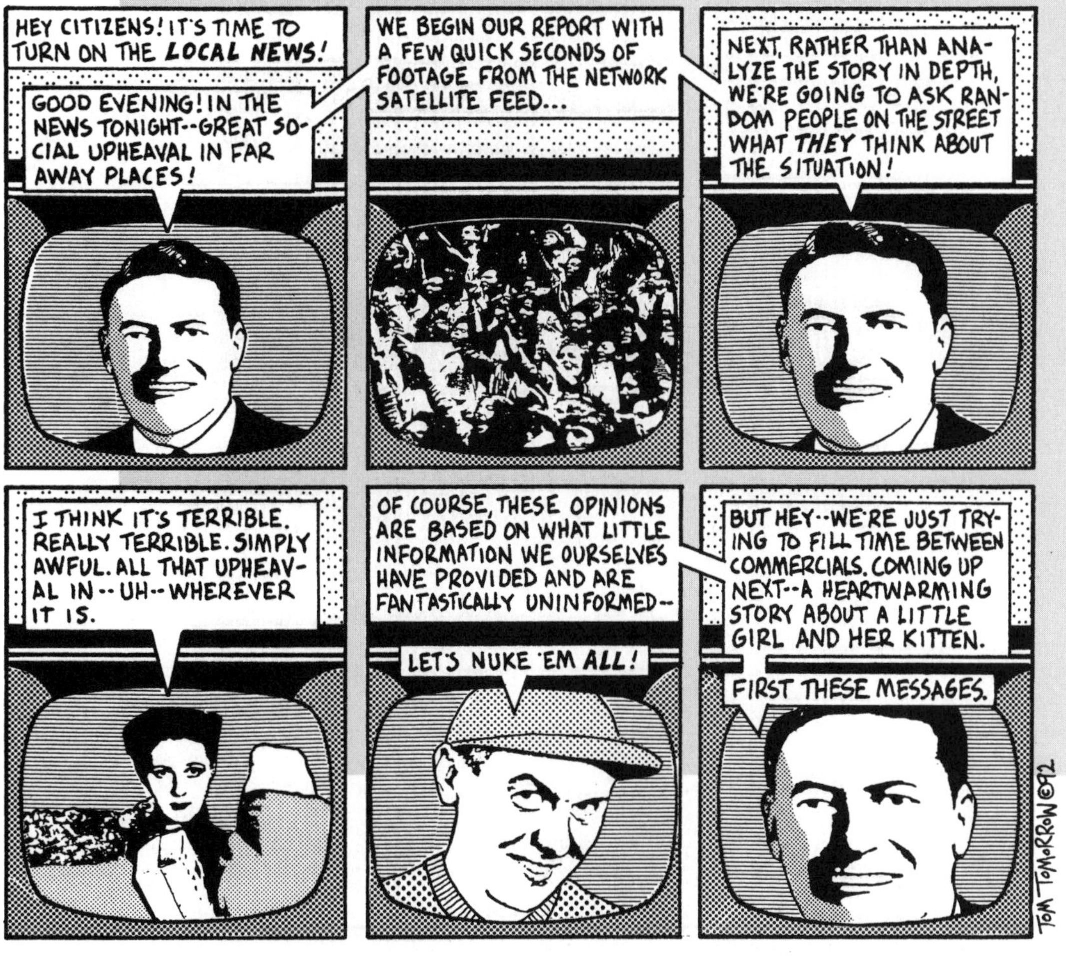
HEY CITIZENS! IT'S TIME TO TURN ON THE LOCAL NEWS!
GOOD EVENING! IN THE NEWS TONIGHT--GREAT SOCIAL UPHEAVAL IN FAR AWAY PLACES!
WE BEGIN OUR REPORT WITH A FEW QUICK SECONDS OF FOOTAGE FROM THE NETWORK SATELLITE FEED...
NEXT, RATHER THAN ANALYZE THE STORY IN DEPTH, WE'RE GOING TO ASK RANDOM PEOPLE ON THE STREET WHAT THEY THINK ABOUT THE SITUATION!
I THINK IT'S TERRIBLE. REALLY TERRIBLE. SIMPLY AWFUL. ALL THAT UPHEAVAL IN--UH--WHEREVER IT IS.
OF COURSE, THESE OPINIONS ARE BASED ON WHAT LITTLE INFORMATION WE OURSELVES HAVE PROVIDED AND ARE FANTASTICALLY UNINFORMED--
LET'S NUKE 'EM ALL!
BUT HEY--WE'RE JUST TRYING TO FILL TIME BETWEEN COMMERCIALS. COMING UP NEXT--A HEARTWARMING STORY ABOUT A LITTLE GIRL AND HER KITTEN.
FIRST THESE MESSAGES.
TOM TOMORROW ©92

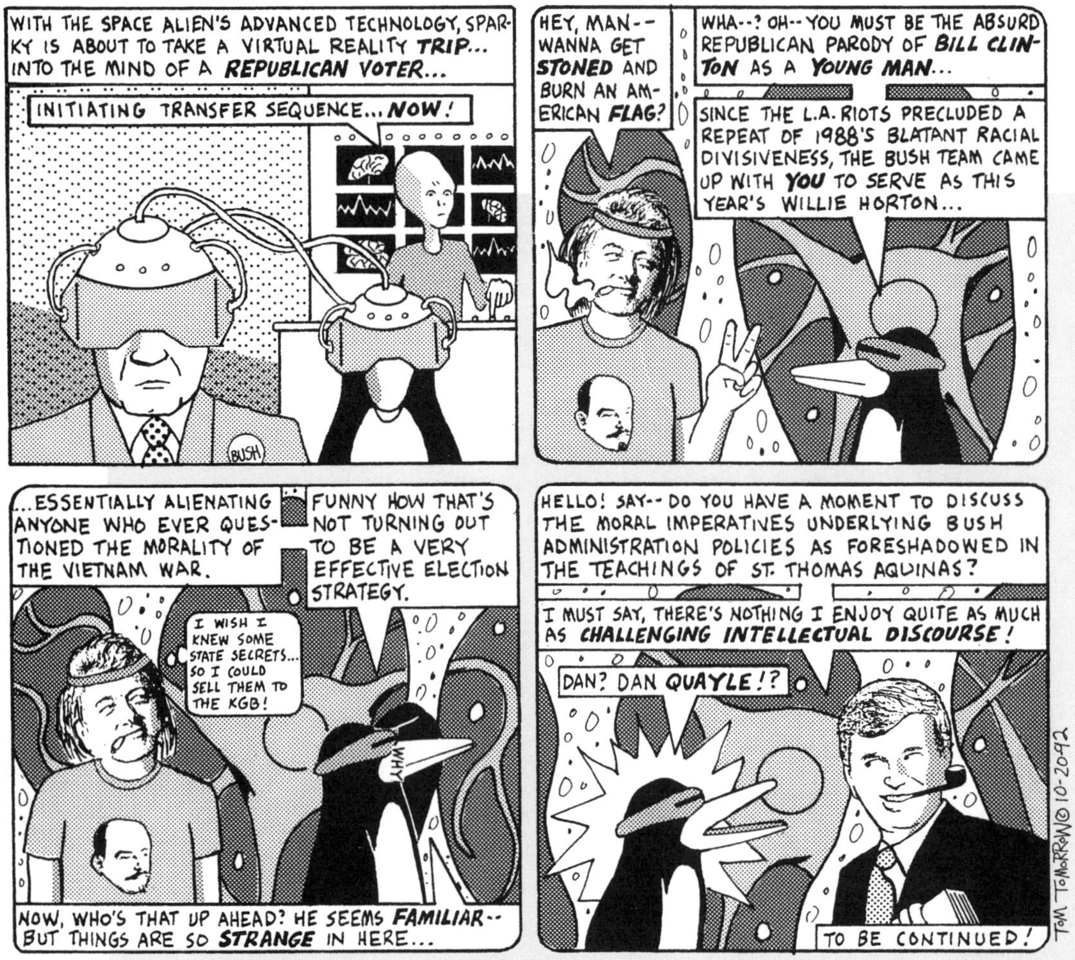
WITH THE SPACE ALIEN'S ADVANCED TECHNOLOGY, SPARKY IS ABOUT TO TAKE A VIRTUAL REALITY TRIP... INTO THE MIND OF A REPUBLICAN VOTER...
INITIATING TRANSFER SEQUENCE... NOW!
BUSH
HEY, MAN-- WANNA GET STONED AND BURN AN AMERICAN FLAG?
WHA--? OH-- YOU MUST BE THE ABSURD REPUBLICAN PARODY OF BILL CLINTON AS A YOUNG MAN...
SINCE THE L.A. RIOTS PRECLUDED A REPEAT OF 1988'S BLATANT RACIAL DIVISIVENESS, THE BUSH TEAM CAME UP WITH YOU TO SERVE AS THIS YEAR'S WILLIE HORTON...
...ESSENTIALLY ALIENATING ANYONE WHO EVER QUESTIONED THE MORALITY OF THE VIETNAM WAR.
FUNNY HOW THAT'S NOT TURNING OUT TO BE A VERY EFFECTIVE ELECTION STRATEGY.
I WISH I KNEW SOME STATE SECRETS... SO I COULD SELL THEM TO THE KGB!
NOW, WHO'S THAT UP AHEAD? HE SEEMS FAMILIAR-- BUT THINGS ARE SO STRANGE IN HERE...
HELLO! SAY-- DO YOU HAVE A MOMENT TO DISCUSS THE MORAL IMPERATIVES UNDERLYING BUSH ADMINISTRATION POLICIES AS FORESHADOWED IN THE TEACHINGS OF ST. THOMAS AQUINAS?
I MUST SAY, THERE'S NOTHING I ENJOY QUITE AS MUCH AS CHALLENGING INTELLECTUAL DISCOURSE!
DAN? DAN QUAYLE!?
TO BE CONTINUED!
TOM TOMORROW © 10-20-92

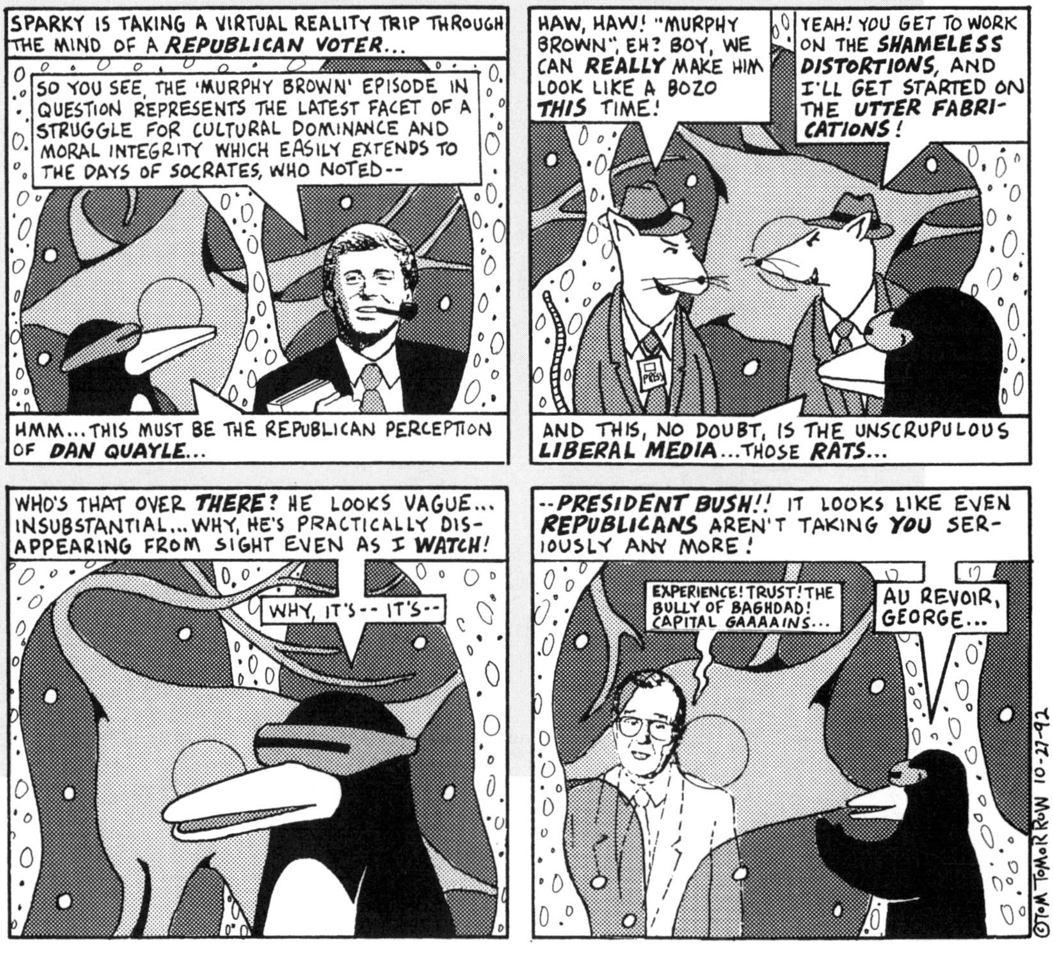
SPARKY IS TAKING A VIRTUAL REALITY TRIP THROUGH THE MIND OF A REPUBLICAN VOTER...
SO YOU SEE, THE 'MURPHY BROWN' EPISODE IN QUESTION REPRESENTS THE LATEST FACET OF A STRUGGLE FOR CULTURAL DOMINANCE AND MORAL INTEGRITY WHICH EASILY EXTENDS TO THE DAYS OF SOCRATES, WHO NOTED--
HMM... THIS MUST BE THE REPUBLICAN PERCEPTION OF DAN QUAYLE...
HAW, HAW! "MURPHY BROWN", EH? BOY, WE CAN REALLY MAKE HIM LOOK LIKE A BOZO THIS TIME!
YEAH! YOU GET TO WORK ON THE SHAMELESS DISTORTIONS, AND I'LL GET STARTED ON THE UTTER FABRICATIONS!
PRESS
AND THIS, NO DOUBT, IS THE UNSCRUPULOUS LIBERAL MEDIA... THOSE RATS...
WHO'S THAT OVER THERE? HE LOOKS VAGUE... INSUBSTANTIAL... WHY, HE'S PRACTICALLY DISAPPEARING FROM SIGHT EVEN AS I WATCH!
WHY, IT'S-- IT'S--
--PRESIDENT BUSH!! IT LOOKS LIKE EVEN REPUBLICANS AREN'T TAKING YOU SERIOUSLY ANY MORE!
EXPERIENCE! TRUST! THE BULLY OF BAGHDAD! CAPITAL GAAAAINS...
AU REVOIR, GEORGE...
©TOM TOMORROW 10-27-92

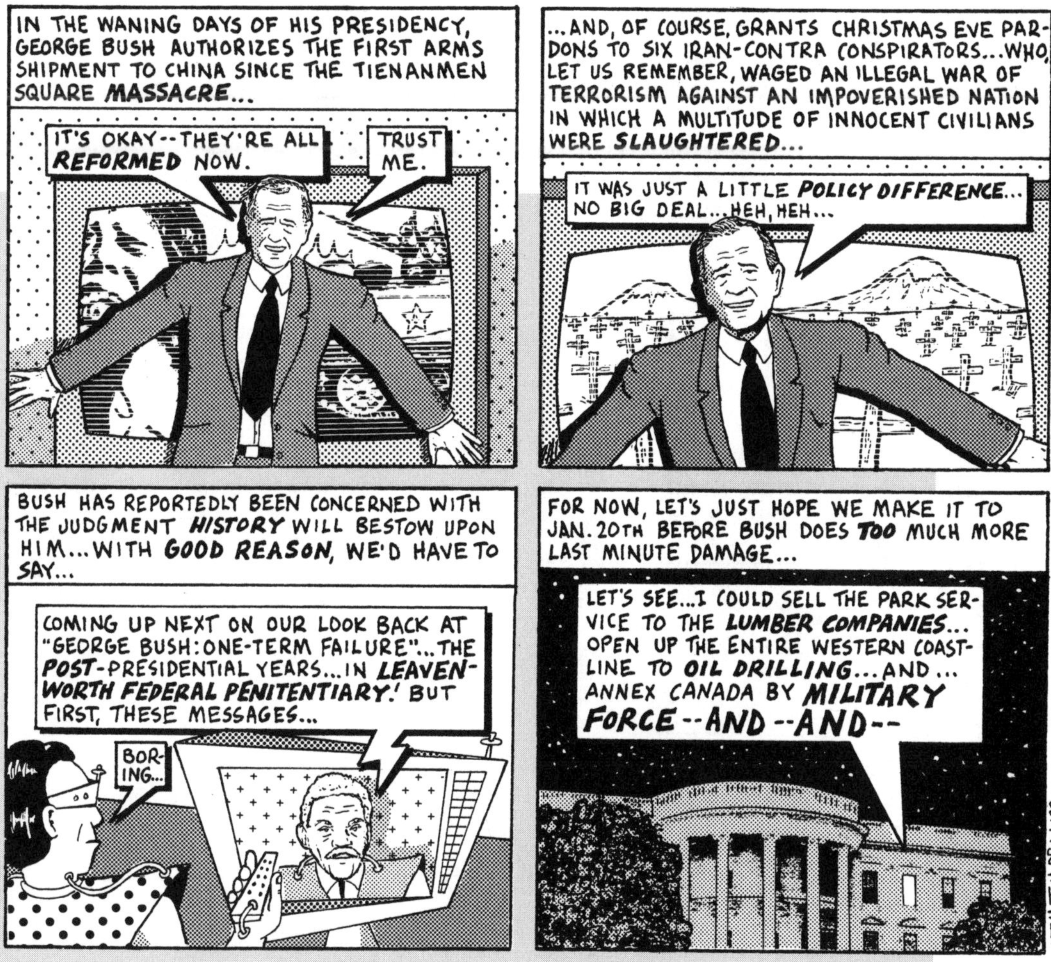
IN THE WANING DAYS OF HIS PRESIDENCY, GEORGE BUSH AUTHORIZES THE FIRST ARMS SHIPMENT TO CHINA SINCE THE TIENANMEN SQUARE MASSACRE...
IT'S OKAY--THEY'RE ALL REFORMED NOW.
TRUST ME.
...AND, OF COURSE, GRANTS CHRISTMAS EVE PARDONS TO SIX IRAN-CONTRA CONSPIRATORS...WHO, LET US REMEMBER, WAGED AN ILLEGAL WAR OF TERRORISM AGAINST AN IMPOVERISHED NATION IN WHICH A MULTITUDE OF INNOCENT CIVILIANS WERE SLAUGHTERED...
IT WAS JUST A LITTLE POLICY DIFFERENCE... NO BIG DEAL...HEH, HEH...
BUSH HAS REPORTEDLY BEEN CONCERNED WITH THE JUDGMENT HISTORY WILL BESTOW UPON HIM...WITH GOOD REASON, WE'D HAVE TO SAY...
COMING UP NEXT ON OUR LOOK BACK AT "GEORGE BUSH: ONE-TERM FAILURE"...THE POST-PRESIDENTIAL YEARS...IN LEAVENWORTH FEDERAL PENITENTIARY! BUT FIRST, THESE MESSAGES...
BORING...
FOR NOW, LET'S JUST HOPE WE MAKE IT TO JAN. 20TH BEFORE BUSH DOES TOO MUCH MORE LAST MINUTE DAMAGE...
LET'S SEE...I COULD SELL THE PARK SERVICE TO THE LUMBER COMPANIES... OPEN UP THE ENTIRE WESTERN COASTLINE TO OIL DRILLING...AND... ANNEX CANADA BY MILITARY FORCE--AND--AND--
© TOM TOMORROW '92

The cartoon below ran on the op-ed page of *The New York Times* the day after the 1992 election, but was, of course, due the day before—which is why I so carefully avoid mentioning the new President's name or party affiliation.

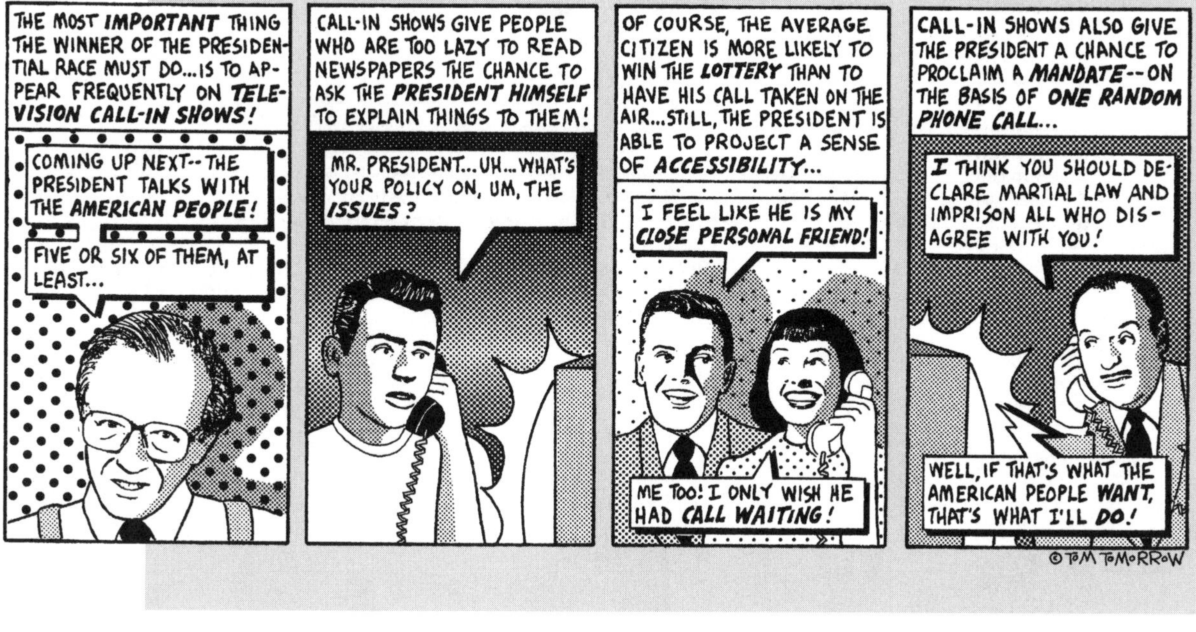
THE MOST IMPORTANT THING THE WINNER OF THE PRESIDENTIAL RACE MUST DO...IS TO APPEAR FREQUENTLY ON TELEVISION CALL-IN SHOWS!
COMING UP NEXT--THE PRESIDENT TALKS WITH THE AMERICAN PEOPLE!
FIVE OR SIX OF THEM, AT LEAST...
CALL-IN SHOWS GIVE PEOPLE WHO ARE TOO LAZY TO READ NEWSPAPERS THE CHANCE TO ASK THE PRESIDENT HIMSELF TO EXPLAIN THINGS TO THEM!
MR. PRESIDENT...UH...WHAT'S YOUR POLICY ON, UM, THE ISSUES?
OF COURSE, THE AVERAGE CITIZEN IS MORE LIKELY TO WIN THE LOTTERY THAN TO HAVE HIS CALL TAKEN ON THE AIR...STILL, THE PRESIDENT IS ABLE TO PROJECT A SENSE OF ACCESSIBILITY...
I FEEL LIKE HE IS MY CLOSE PERSONAL FRIEND!
ME TOO! I ONLY WISH HE HAD CALL WAITING!
CALL-IN SHOWS ALSO GIVE THE PRESIDENT A CHANCE TO PROCLAIM A MANDATE--ON THE BASIS OF ONE RANDOM PHONE CALL...
I THINK YOU SHOULD DECLARE MARTIAL LAW AND IMPRISON ALL WHO DISAGREE WITH YOU!
WELL, IF THAT'S WHAT THE AMERICAN PEOPLE WANT, THAT'S WHAT I'LL DO!
© TOM TOMORROW

DURING THE INAUGURAL *HOOPLA*, A CERTAIN CYNICAL PENGUIN DECIDES THE ONLY WAY TO AVOID LISTENING TO "DON'T STOP THINKIN' ABOUT TOMORROW" FOR A SOLID *WEEK* IS TO LEAVE THE *COUNTRY*... SO, WHILE AMERICANS *FAWN* OVER THEIR NEW PRESIDENT--

SPARKY goes to PARIS

————— A MOSTLY-TRUE CARTOON TRAVELOGUE BY TOM TOMORROW —————

THERE IS AN ANCIENT PROVERB WHICH STATES THAT A JOURNEY OF A THOUSAND MILES BEGINS WITH A SINGLE STEP... IN *MODERN* TIMES, HOWEVER, SUCH JOURNEYS BEGIN WITH AN INTERMINABLE PERIOD OF CONFINEMENT IN A CLAUSTROPHOBIC *AIRPLANE SEAT*...

THIS IS WHERE I WILL SIT... FOR THE NEXT *TWELVE HOURS*...

RECOGNIZING THAT A PROBLEM EXISTS, THE AIRLINE ON WHICH SPARKY IS TRAVELLING HAS PRODUCED A *WORKOUT VIDEO*... FEATURING AN AEROBICS INSTRUCTOR IN LEOTARDS GUIDING PASSENGERS THROUGH A SERIES OF EXERCISES WHICH CAN BE PERFORMED WITHIN THE CONSTRAINTS OF A TYPICAL AIRLINE SEAT...

OKAY, NOW MOVE YOUR HEAD SLIGHTLY TO THE LEFT! THAT'S *GOOD!*

EVENTUALLY, OF COURSE, THE ORDEAL *ENDS*... BEDRAGGLED AND EXHAUSTED, SPARKY IS NONETHELESS EXHILARATED TO FIND HIMSELF IN ONE OF HIS FAVORITE CITIES...

SIGH...

AFTER CHECKING IN TO HIS HOTEL, SPARKY BEGINS HIS FIRST DAY IN PARIS AT A BRASSERIE, WITH A STRONG ESPRESSO... WATERY AMERICAN-STYLE COFFEE IS UNKNOWN HERE... IT COSTS EXTRA TO SIT, SO MOST PARISIANS CHOOSE TO STAND AT THE BAR... SPEAKING LITTLE FRENCH, SPARKY CAN ONLY *WONDER* WHAT THEY ARE DISCUSSING...

(HE LOOKS LIKE A *PENGUIN* OR SOMETHING.)

(WHY DO YOU SUPPOSE HE WEARS THOSE PECULIAR *SUNGLASSES*?)

?...

This one originally appeared in the *San Francisco Examiner*.

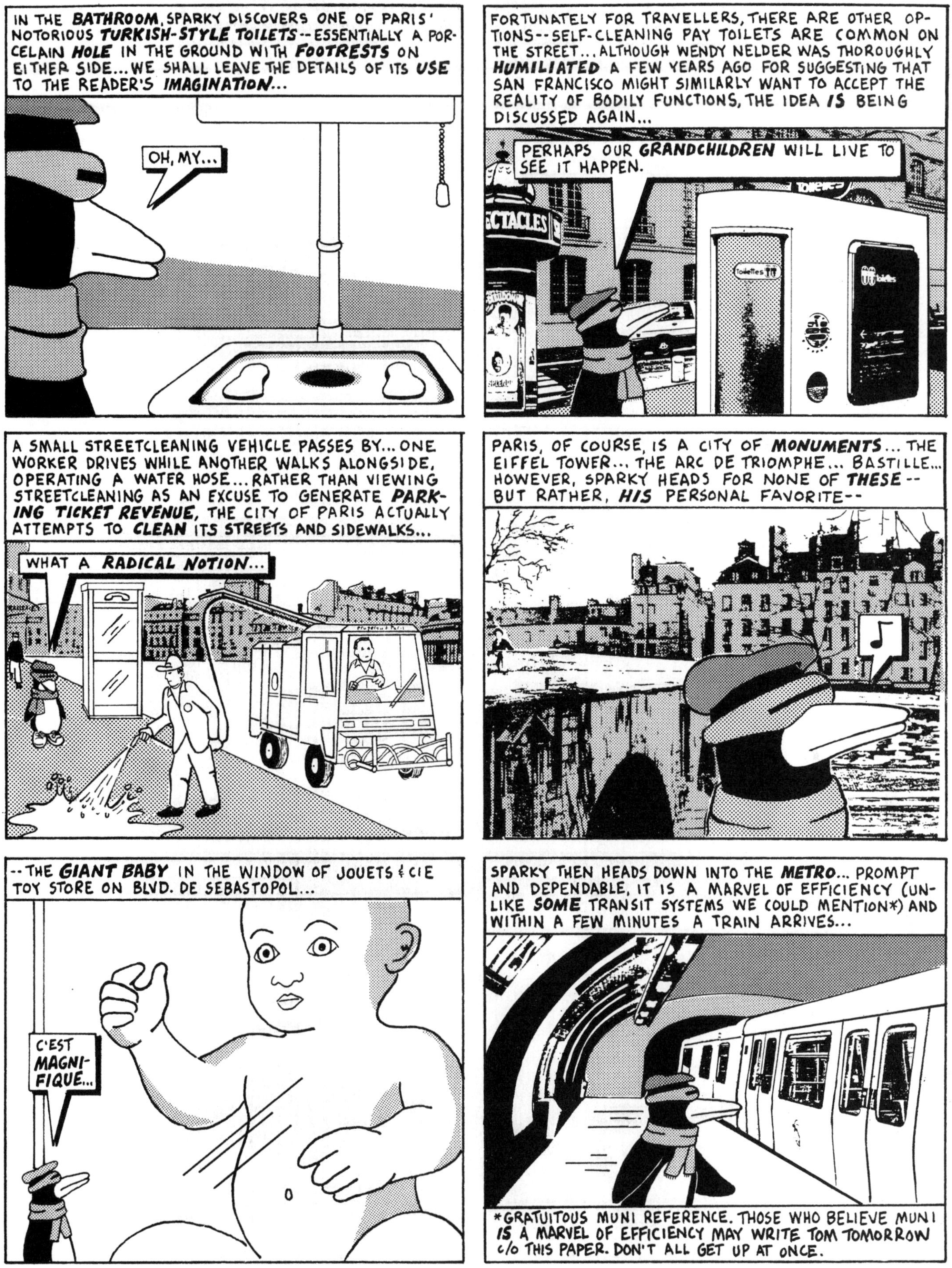
IN THE BATHROOM, SPARKY DISCOVERS ONE OF PARIS' NOTORIOUS TURKISH-STYLE TOILETS -- ESSENTIALLY A PORCELAIN HOLE IN THE GROUND WITH FOOTRESTS ON EITHER SIDE... WE SHALL LEAVE THE DETAILS OF ITS USE TO THE READER'S IMAGINATION...
OH, MY...
FORTUNATELY FOR TRAVELLERS, THERE ARE OTHER OPTIONS -- SELF-CLEANING PAY TOILETS ARE COMMON ON THE STREET... ALTHOUGH WENDY NELDER WAS THOROUGHLY HUMILIATED A FEW YEARS AGO FOR SUGGESTING THAT SAN FRANCISCO MIGHT SIMILARLY WANT TO ACCEPT THE REALITY OF BODILY FUNCTIONS, THE IDEA IS BEING DISCUSSED AGAIN...
PERHAPS OUR GRANDCHILDREN WILL LIVE TO SEE IT HAPPEN.
Toilettes
A SMALL STREETCLEANING VEHICLE PASSES BY... ONE WORKER DRIVES WHILE ANOTHER WALKS ALONGSIDE, OPERATING A WATER HOSE... RATHER THAN VIEWING STREETCLEANING AS AN EXCUSE TO GENERATE PARKING TICKET REVENUE, THE CITY OF PARIS ACTUALLY ATTEMPTS TO CLEAN ITS STREETS AND SIDEWALKS...
WHAT A RADICAL NOTION...
PARIS, OF COURSE, IS A CITY OF MONUMENTS... THE EIFFEL TOWER... THE ARC DE TRIOMPHE... BASTILLE... HOWEVER, SPARKY HEADS FOR NONE OF THESE -- BUT RATHER, HIS PERSONAL FAVORITE --
♪
-- THE GIANT BABY IN THE WINDOW OF JOUETS & CIE TOY STORE ON BLVD. DE SEBASTOPOL...
C'EST MAGNIFIQUE...
SPARKY THEN HEADS DOWN INTO THE METRO... PROMPT AND DEPENDABLE, IT IS A MARVEL OF EFFICIENCY (UNLIKE SOME TRANSIT SYSTEMS WE COULD MENTION*) AND WITHIN A FEW MINUTES A TRAIN ARRIVES...
*GRATUITOUS MUNI REFERENCE. THOSE WHO BELIEVE MUNI IS A MARVEL OF EFFICIENCY MAY WRITE TOM TOMORROW c/o THIS PAPER. DON'T ALL GET UP AT ONCE.

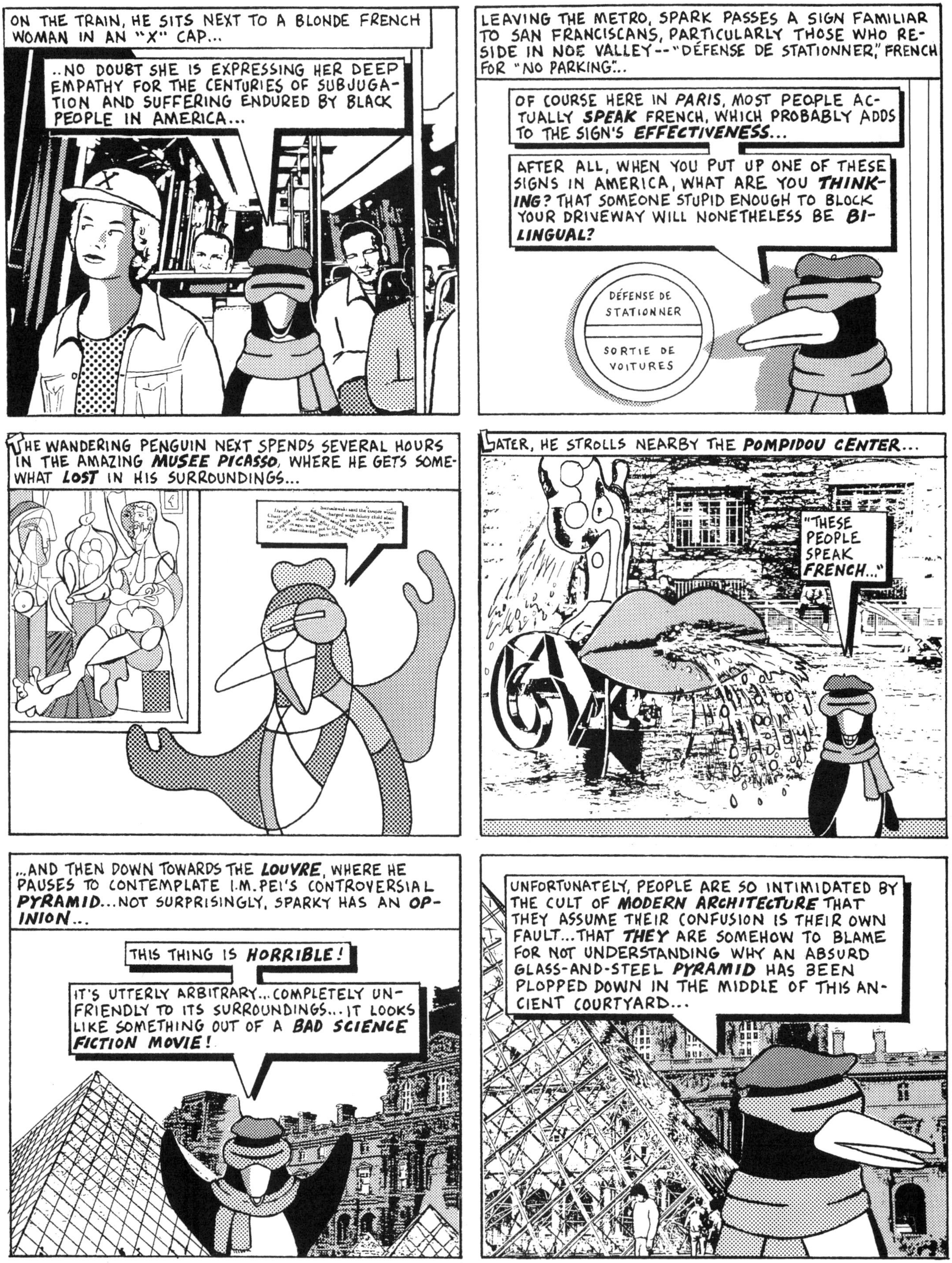
ON THE TRAIN, HE SITS NEXT TO A BLONDE FRENCH WOMAN IN AN "X" CAP...
..NO DOUBT SHE IS EXPRESSING HER DEEP EMPATHY FOR THE CENTURIES OF SUBJUGATION AND SUFFERING ENDURED BY BLACK PEOPLE IN AMERICA...
X
LEAVING THE METRO, SPARK PASSES A SIGN FAMILIAR TO SAN FRANCISCANS, PARTICULARLY THOSE WHO RESIDE IN NOE VALLEY--"DÉFENSE DE STATIONNER," FRENCH FOR "NO PARKING"..
OF COURSE HERE IN PARIS, MOST PEOPLE ACTUALLY SPEAK FRENCH, WHICH PROBABLY ADDS TO THE SIGN'S EFFECTIVENESS...
AFTER ALL, WHEN YOU PUT UP ONE OF THESE SIGNS IN AMERICA, WHAT ARE YOU THINKING? THAT SOMEONE STUPID ENOUGH TO BLOCK YOUR DRIVEWAY WILL NONETHELESS BE BILINGUAL?
DÉFENSE DE STATIONNER
SORTIE DE VOITURES
THE WANDERING PENGUIN NEXT SPENDS SEVERAL HOURS IN THE AMAZING MUSEE PICASSO, WHERE HE GETS SOMEWHAT LOST IN HIS SURROUNDINGS...
LATER, HE STROLLS NEARBY THE POMPIDOU CENTER...
"THESE PEOPLE SPEAK FRENCH..."
...AND THEN DOWN TOWARDS THE LOUVRE, WHERE HE PAUSES TO CONTEMPLATE I.M.PEI'S CONTROVERSIAL PYRAMID...NOT SURPRISINGLY, SPARKY HAS AN OPINION...
THIS THING IS HORRIBLE!
IT'S UTTERLY ARBITRARY...COMPLETELY UNFRIENDLY TO ITS SURROUNDINGS...IT LOOKS LIKE SOMETHING OUT OF A BAD SCIENCE FICTION MOVIE!
UNFORTUNATELY, PEOPLE ARE SO INTIMIDATED BY THE CULT OF MODERN ARCHITECTURE THAT THEY ASSUME THEIR CONFUSION IS THEIR OWN FAULT...THAT THEY ARE SOMEHOW TO BLAME FOR NOT UNDERSTANDING WHY AN ABSURD GLASS-AND-STEEL PYRAMID HAS BEEN PLOPPED DOWN IN THE MIDDLE OF THIS ANCIENT COURTYARD...

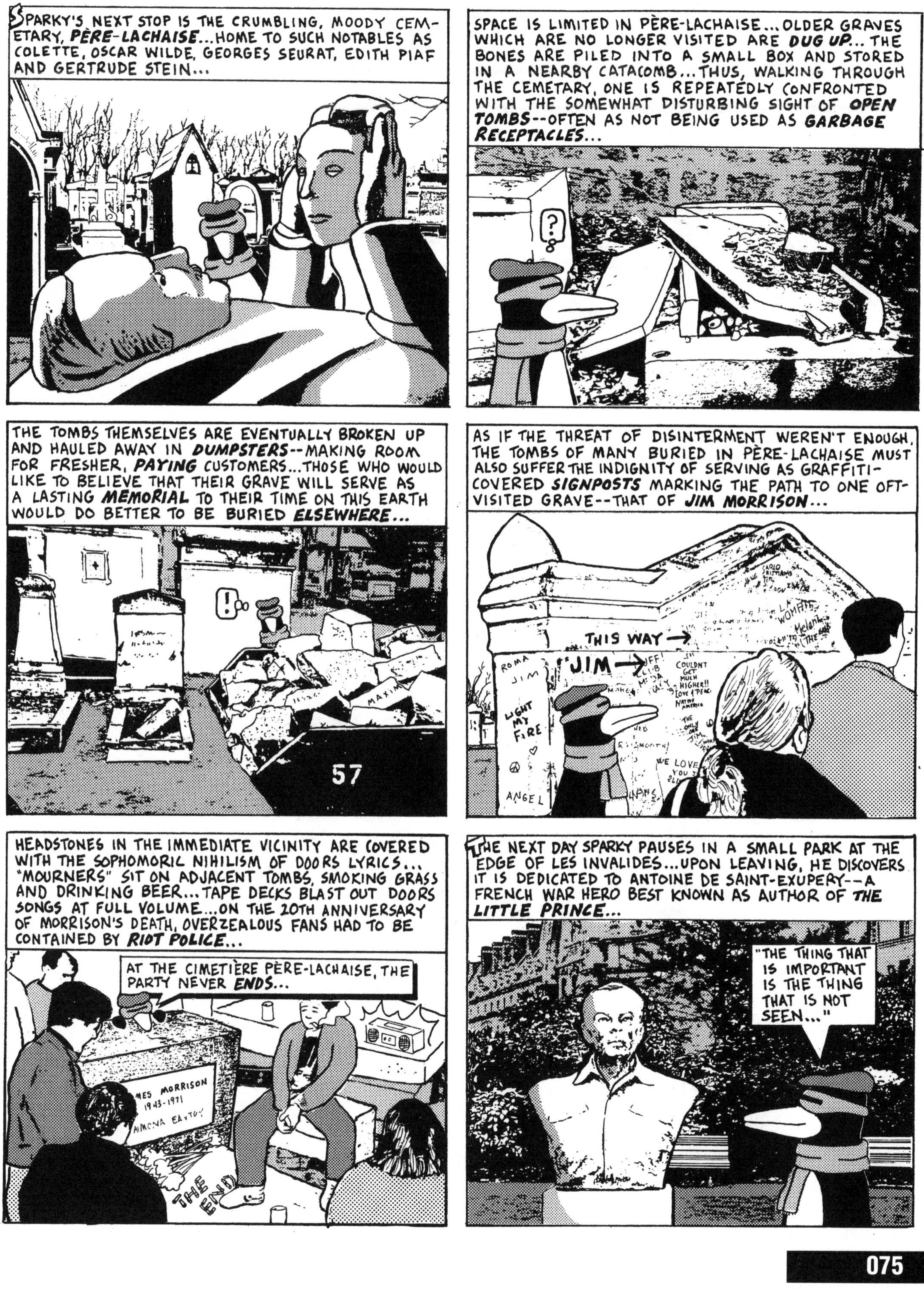
SPARKY'S NEXT STOP IS THE CRUMBLING, MOODY CEMETARY, PÈRE-LACHAISE... HOME TO SUCH NOTABLES AS COLETTE, OSCAR WILDE, GEORGES SEURAT, EDITH PIAF AND GERTRUDE STEIN...
SPACE IS LIMITED IN PÈRE-LACHAISE... OLDER GRAVES WHICH ARE NO LONGER VISITED ARE DUG UP... THE BONES ARE PILED INTO A SMALL BOX AND STORED IN A NEARBY CATACOMB... THUS, WALKING THROUGH THE CEMETARY, ONE IS REPEATEDLY CONFRONTED WITH THE SOMEWHAT DISTURBING SIGHT OF OPEN TOMBS--OFTEN AS NOT BEING USED AS GARBAGE RECEPTACLES...
?
THE TOMBS THEMSELVES ARE EVENTUALLY BROKEN UP AND HAULED AWAY IN DUMPSTERS--MAKING ROOM FOR FRESHER, PAYING CUSTOMERS... THOSE WHO WOULD LIKE TO BELIEVE THAT THEIR GRAVE WILL SERVE AS A LASTING MEMORIAL TO THEIR TIME ON THIS EARTH WOULD DO BETTER TO BE BURIED ELSEWHERE...
!
MAXIM
57
AS IF THE THREAT OF DISINTERMENT WEREN'T ENOUGH, THE TOMBS OF MANY BURIED IN PÈRE-LACHAISE MUST ALSO SUFFER THE INDIGNITY OF SERVING AS GRAFFITI-COVERED SIGNPOSTS MARKING THE PATH TO ONE OFT-VISITED GRAVE--THAT OF JIM MORRISON...
THIS WAY →
JIM →
ROMA
JIM
LIGHT MY FIRE
COULDNT GET MUCH HIGHER!! LOVE & PEACE
WE LOVE YOU
ANGEL
HEADSTONES IN THE IMMEDIATE VICINITY ARE COVERED WITH THE SOPHOMORIC NIHILISM OF DOORS LYRICS... "MOURNERS" SIT ON ADJACENT TOMBS, SMOKING GRASS AND DRINKING BEER... TAPE DECKS BLAST OUT DOORS SONGS AT FULL VOLUME... ON THE 20TH ANNIVERSARY OF MORRISON'S DEATH, OVERZEALOUS FANS HAD TO BE CONTAINED BY RIOT POLICE...
AT THE CIMETIÈRE PÈRE-LACHAISE, THE PARTY NEVER ENDS...
MES MORRISON
1943-1971
THE END
THE NEXT DAY SPARKY PAUSES IN A SMALL PARK AT THE EDGE OF LES INVALIDES... UPON LEAVING, HE DISCOVERS IT IS DEDICATED TO ANTOINE DE SAINT-EXUPERY--A FRENCH WAR HERO BEST KNOWN AS AUTHOR OF THE LITTLE PRINCE...
"THE THING THAT IS IMPORTANT IS THE THING THAT IS NOT SEEN..."

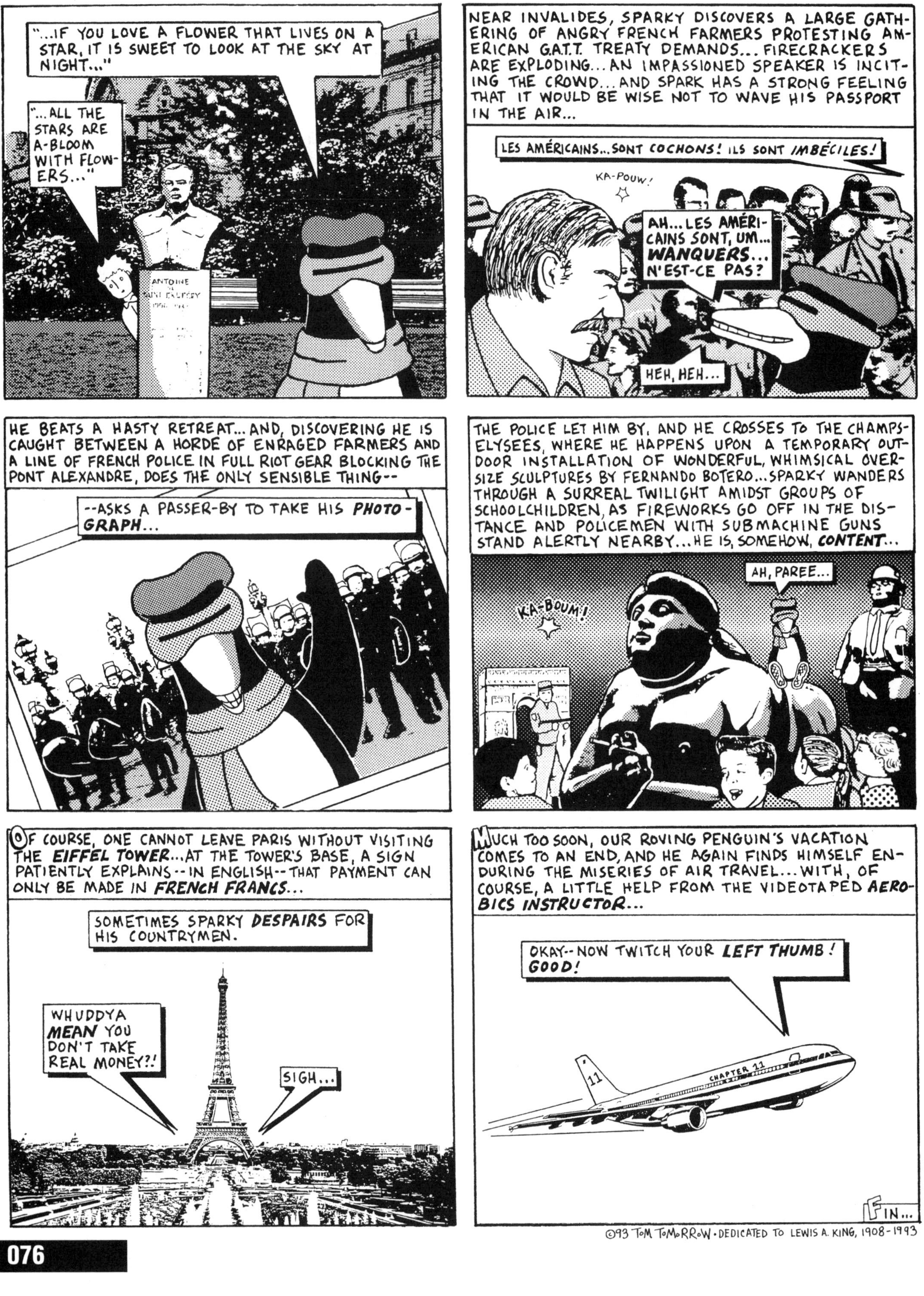
"...IF YOU LOVE A FLOWER THAT LIVES ON A STAR, IT IS SWEET TO LOOK AT THE SKY AT NIGHT..."
"...ALL THE STARS ARE A-BLOOM WITH FLOWERS..."
ANTOINE DE SAINT EXUPÉRY
NEAR INVALIDES, SPARKY DISCOVERS A LARGE GATHERING OF ANGRY FRENCH FARMERS PROTESTING AMERICAN G.A.T.T. TREATY DEMANDS... FIRECRACKERS ARE EXPLODING... AN IMPASSIONED SPEAKER IS INCITING THE CROWD... AND SPARK HAS A STRONG FEELING THAT IT WOULD BE WISE NOT TO WAVE HIS PASSPORT IN THE AIR...
LES AMÉRICAINS... SONT COCHONS! ILS SONT IMBÉCILES!
KA-POUW!
AH... LES AMÉRICAINS SONT, UM... WANQUERS... N'EST-CE PAS?
HEH, HEH...
HE BEATS A HASTY RETREAT... AND, DISCOVERING HE IS CAUGHT BETWEEN A HORDE OF ENRAGED FARMERS AND A LINE OF FRENCH POLICE IN FULL RIOT GEAR BLOCKING THE PONT ALEXANDRE, DOES THE ONLY SENSIBLE THING--
--ASKS A PASSER-BY TO TAKE HIS PHOTOGRAPH...
THE POLICE LET HIM BY, AND HE CROSSES TO THE CHAMPS-ELYSEES, WHERE HE HAPPENS UPON A TEMPORARY OUTDOOR INSTALLATION OF WONDERFUL, WHIMSICAL OVERSIZE SCULPTURES BY FERNANDO BOTERO... SPARKY WANDERS THROUGH A SURREAL TWILIGHT AMIDST GROUPS OF SCHOOLCHILDREN, AS FIREWORKS GO OFF IN THE DISTANCE AND POLICEMEN WITH SUBMACHINE GUNS STAND ALERTLY NEARBY... HE IS, SOMEHOW, CONTENT...
AH, PAREE...
KA-BOUM!
OF COURSE, ONE CANNOT LEAVE PARIS WITHOUT VISITING THE EIFFEL TOWER... AT THE TOWER'S BASE, A SIGN PATIENTLY EXPLAINS -- IN ENGLISH -- THAT PAYMENT CAN ONLY BE MADE IN FRENCH FRANCS...
SOMETIMES SPARKY DESPAIRS FOR HIS COUNTRYMEN.
WHUDDYA MEAN YOU DON'T TAKE REAL MONEY?!
SIGH...
MUCH TOO SOON, OUR ROVING PENGUIN'S VACATION COMES TO AN END, AND HE AGAIN FINDS HIMSELF ENDURING THE MISERIES OF AIR TRAVEL... WITH, OF COURSE, A LITTLE HELP FROM THE VIDEOTAPED AEROBICS INSTRUCTOR...
OKAY-- NOW TWITCH YOUR LEFT THUMB! GOOD!
CHAPTER 11
11
FIN...

The Song Remains the Same

In 1992, voters traded in their moderate pro-business Republican president for a moderate, pro-business Democrat. Conservatives seemed certain that the end of civilization as they knew it was at hand, while liberals were convinced that all of America's problems had now been solved. "What are you going to do cartoons about now?" I was repeatedly asked after the election.

Clinton, of course, proceeded to endorse George Bush's NAFTA, to support MFN status for China, to propose a business-friendly health care plan which set real health care reform back by at least a decade, and to pretty much dismantle the social safety net (something Republicans had been fantasizing about for decades).

But hey—he said all those warm and fuzzy things about hope and change. What more could we ask for?

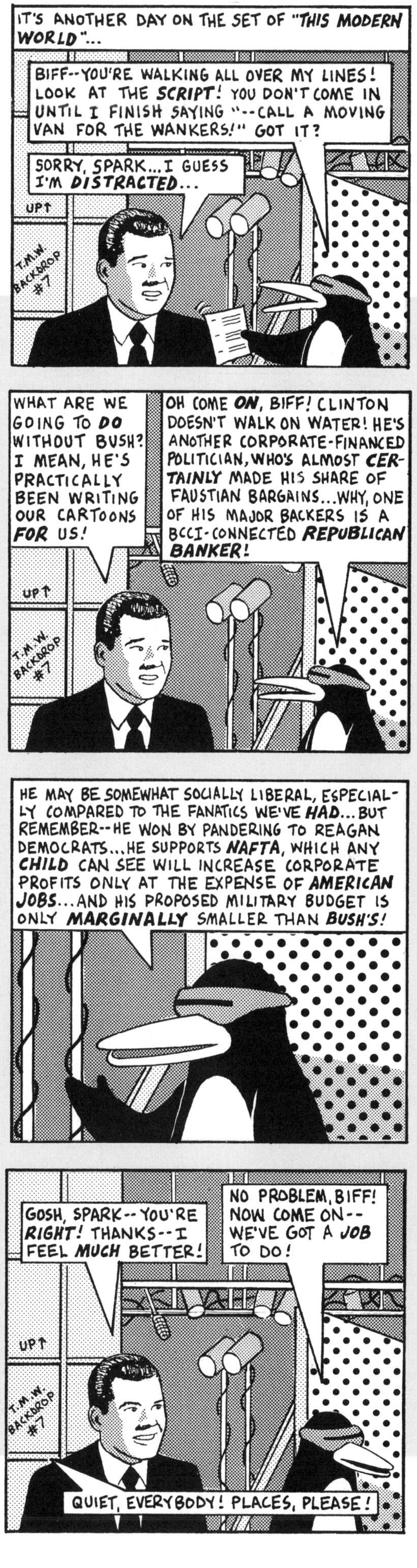

IT'S ANOTHER DAY ON THE SET OF "THIS MODERN WORLD"...
BIFF--YOU'RE WALKING ALL OVER MY LINES! LOOK AT THE SCRIPT! YOU DON'T COME IN UNTIL I FINISH SAYING "--CALL A MOVING VAN FOR THE WANKERS!" GOT IT?
SORRY, SPARK...I GUESS I'M DISTRACTED...
UP↑
T.M.W. BACKDROP #7
WHAT ARE WE GOING TO DO WITHOUT BUSH? I MEAN, HE'S PRACTICALLY BEEN WRITING OUR CARTOONS FOR US!
OH COME ON, BIFF! CLINTON DOESN'T WALK ON WATER! HE'S ANOTHER CORPORATE-FINANCED POLITICIAN, WHO'S ALMOST CERTAINLY MADE HIS SHARE OF FAUSTIAN BARGAINS...WHY, ONE OF HIS MAJOR BACKERS IS A BCCI-CONNECTED REPUBLICAN BANKER!
UP↑
T.M.W. BACKDROP #7
HE MAY BE SOMEWHAT SOCIALLY LIBERAL, ESPECIALLY COMPARED TO THE FANATICS WE'VE HAD...BUT REMEMBER--HE WON BY PANDERING TO REAGAN DEMOCRATS...HE SUPPORTS NAFTA, WHICH ANY CHILD CAN SEE WILL INCREASE CORPORATE PROFITS ONLY AT THE EXPENSE OF AMERICAN JOBS...AND HIS PROPOSED MILITARY BUDGET IS ONLY MARGINALLY SMALLER THAN BUSH'S!
GOSH, SPARK--YOU'RE RIGHT! THANKS--I FEEL MUCH BETTER!
NO PROBLEM, BIFF! NOW COME ON--WE'VE GOT A JOB TO DO!
UP↑
T.M.W. BACKDROP #7
QUIET, EVERYBODY! PLACES, PLEASE!

1992-1996: The Great Triangulator Takes the Stage

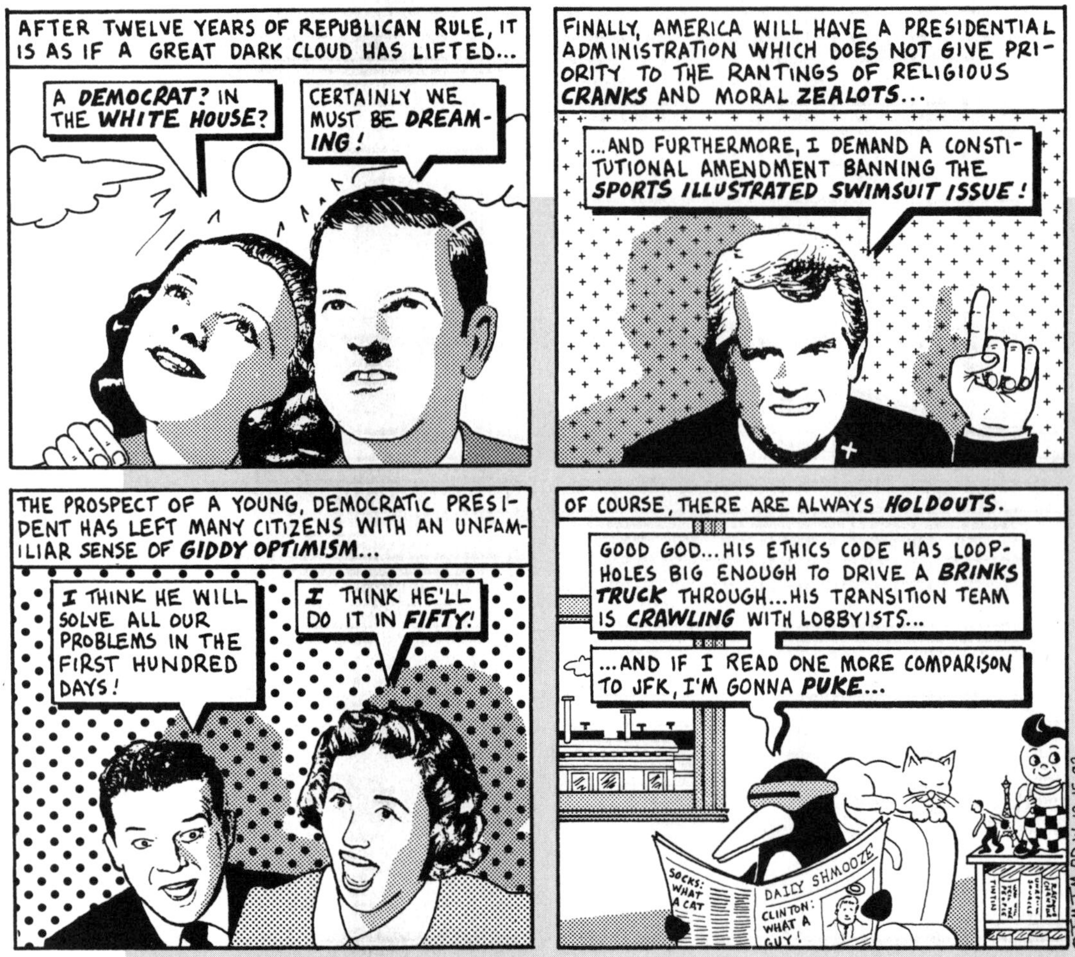
AFTER TWELVE YEARS OF REPUBLICAN RULE, IT IS AS IF A GREAT DARK CLOUD HAS LIFTED...
A DEMOCRAT? IN THE WHITE HOUSE?
CERTAINLY WE MUST BE DREAMING!
FINALLY, AMERICA WILL HAVE A PRESIDENTIAL ADMINISTRATION WHICH DOES NOT GIVE PRIORITY TO THE RANTINGS OF RELIGIOUS CRANKS AND MORAL ZEALOTS...
...AND FURTHERMORE, I DEMAND A CONSTITUTIONAL AMENDMENT BANNING THE SPORTS ILLUSTRATED SWIMSUIT ISSUE!
THE PROSPECT OF A YOUNG, DEMOCRATIC PRESIDENT HAS LEFT MANY CITIZENS WITH AN UNFAMILIAR SENSE OF GIDDY OPTIMISM...
I THINK HE WILL SOLVE ALL OUR PROBLEMS IN THE FIRST HUNDRED DAYS!
I THINK HE'LL DO IT IN FIFTY!
OF COURSE, THERE ARE ALWAYS HOLDOUTS.
GOOD GOD...HIS ETHICS CODE HAS LOOPHOLES BIG ENOUGH TO DRIVE A BRINKS TRUCK THROUGH...HIS TRANSITION TEAM IS CRAWLING WITH LOBBYISTS...
...AND IF I READ ONE MORE COMPARISON TO JFK, I'M GONNA PUKE...
SOCKS: WHAT A CAT
DAILY SHMOOZE
CLINTON: WHAT A GUY!
© TOM TOMORROW 12-15-92

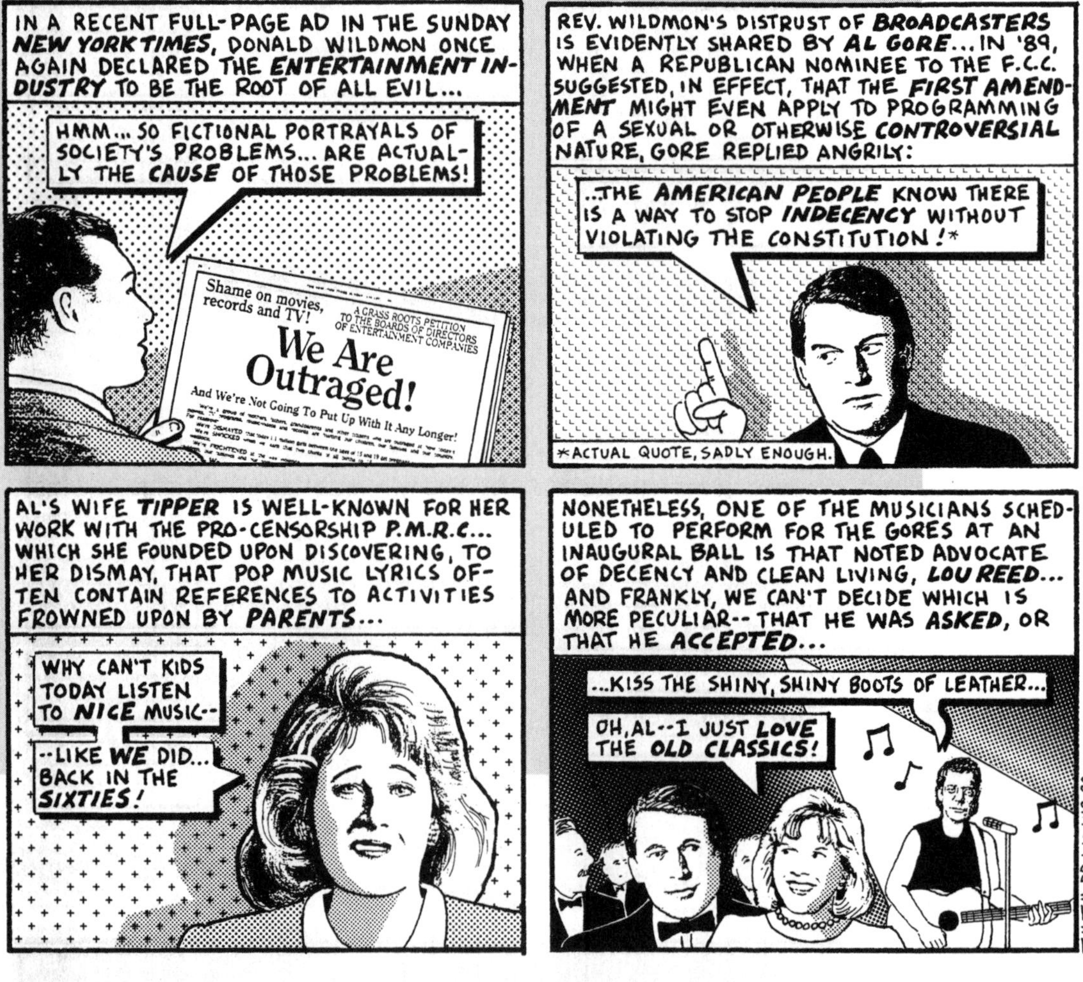
IN A RECENT FULL-PAGE AD IN THE SUNDAY NEW YORK TIMES, DONALD WILDMON ONCE AGAIN DECLARED THE ENTERTAINMENT INDUSTRY TO BE THE ROOT OF ALL EVIL...
HMM... SO FICTIONAL PORTRAYALS OF SOCIETY'S PROBLEMS... ARE ACTUALLY THE CAUSE OF THOSE PROBLEMS!
Shame on movies, records and TV!
A GRASS ROOTS PETITION TO THE BOARDS OF DIRECTORS OF ENTERTAINMENT COMPANIES
We Are Outraged!
And We're Not Going To Put Up With It Any Longer!
REV. WILDMON'S DISTRUST OF BROADCASTERS IS EVIDENTLY SHARED BY AL GORE... IN '89, WHEN A REPUBLICAN NOMINEE TO THE F.C.C. SUGGESTED, IN EFFECT, THAT THE FIRST AMENDMENT MIGHT EVEN APPLY TO PROGRAMMING OF A SEXUAL OR OTHERWISE CONTROVERSIAL NATURE, GORE REPLIED ANGRILY:
..THE AMERICAN PEOPLE KNOW THERE IS A WAY TO STOP INDECENCY WITHOUT VIOLATING THE CONSTITUTION!*
*ACTUAL QUOTE, SADLY ENOUGH.
AL'S WIFE TIPPER IS WELL-KNOWN FOR HER WORK WITH THE PRO-CENSORSHIP P.M.R.C... WHICH SHE FOUNDED UPON DISCOVERING, TO HER DISMAY, THAT POP MUSIC LYRICS OFTEN CONTAIN REFERENCES TO ACTIVITIES FROWNED UPON BY PARENTS...
WHY CAN'T KIDS TODAY LISTEN TO NICE MUSIC--
--LIKE WE DID... BACK IN THE SIXTIES!
NONETHELESS, ONE OF THE MUSICIANS SCHEDULED TO PERFORM FOR THE GORES AT AN INAUGURAL BALL IS THAT NOTED ADVOCATE OF DECENCY AND CLEAN LIVING, LOU REED... AND FRANKLY, WE CAN'T DECIDE WHICH IS MORE PECULIAR-- THAT HE WAS ASKED, OR THAT HE ACCEPTED...
...KISS THE SHINY, SHINY BOOTS OF LEATHER...
OH, AL--I JUST LOVE THE OLD CLASSICS!
TOM TOMORROW© 1-19-92

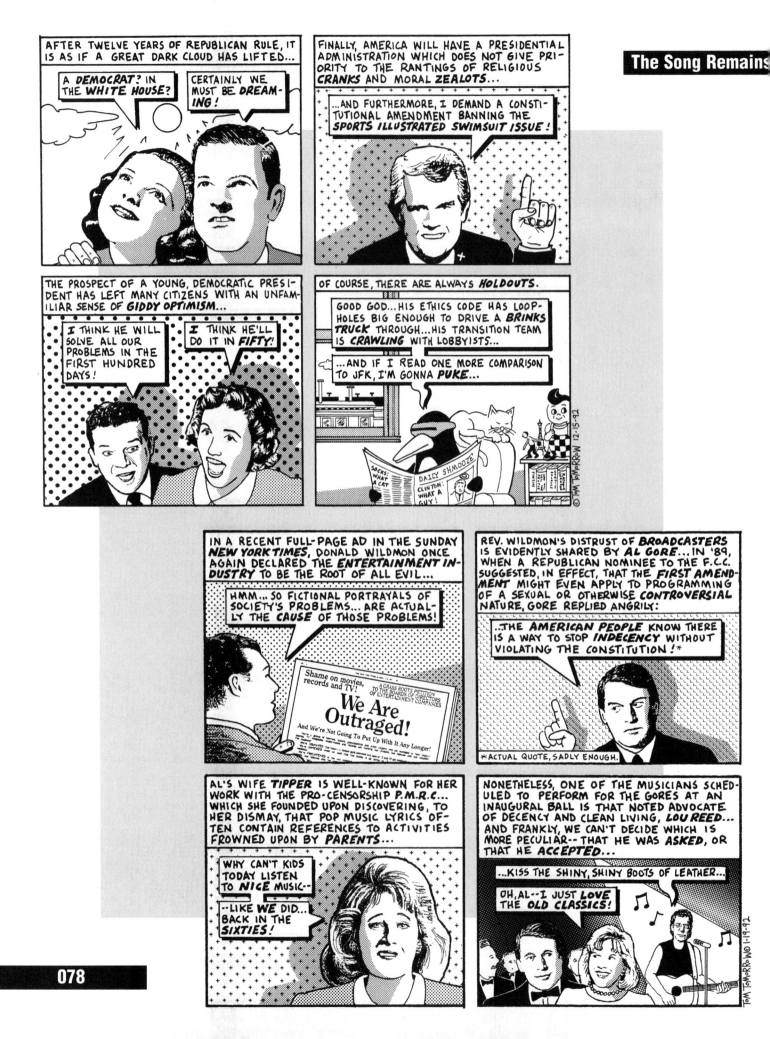

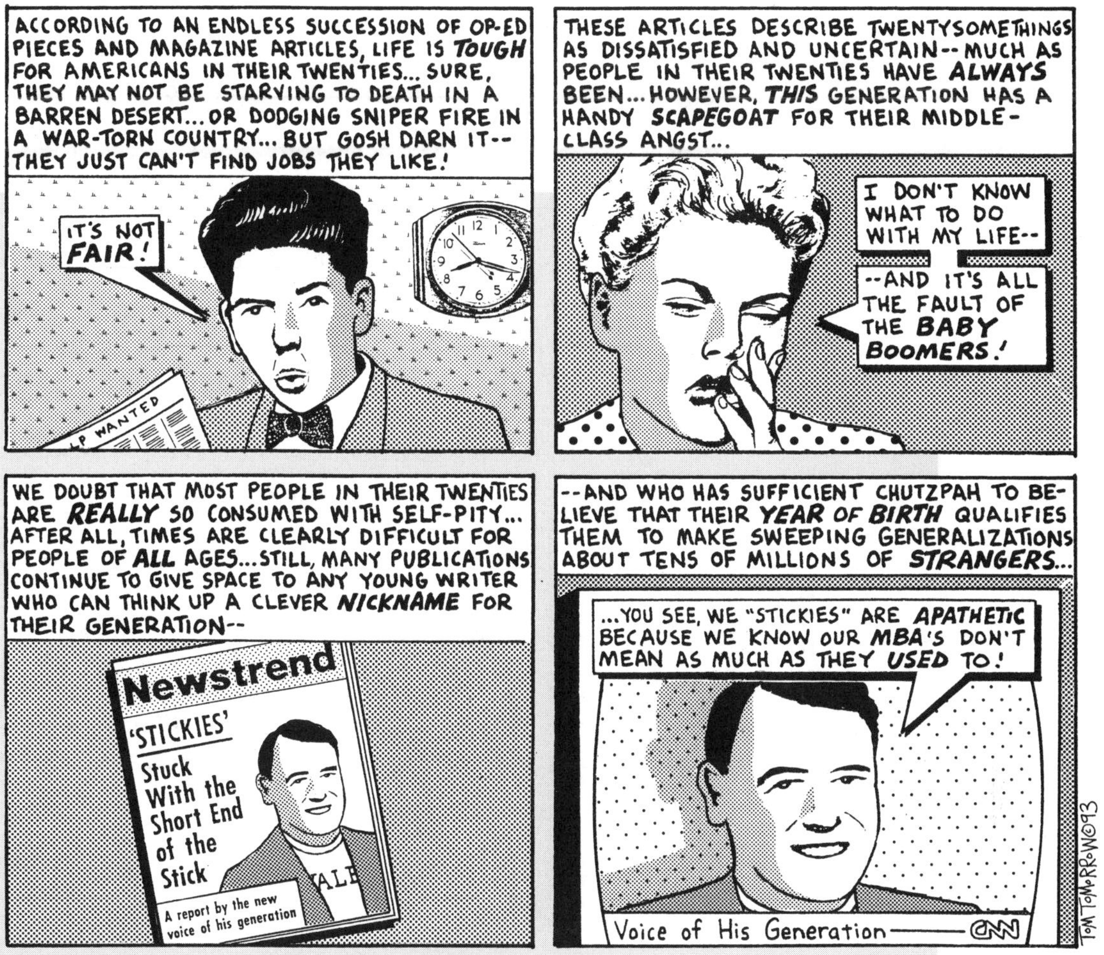
ACCORDING TO AN ENDLESS SUCCESSION OF OP-ED PIECES AND MAGAZINE ARTICLES, LIFE IS TOUGH FOR AMERICANS IN THEIR TWENTIES... SURE, THEY MAY NOT BE STARVING TO DEATH IN A BARREN DESERT... OR DODGING SNIPER FIRE IN A WAR-TORN COUNTRY... BUT GOSH DARN IT--THEY JUST CAN'T FIND JOBS THEY LIKE!
IT'S NOT FAIR!
THESE ARTICLES DESCRIBE TWENTYSOMETHINGS AS DISSATISFIED AND UNCERTAIN--MUCH AS PEOPLE IN THEIR TWENTIES HAVE ALWAYS BEEN... HOWEVER, THIS GENERATION HAS A HANDY SCAPEGOAT FOR THEIR MIDDLE-CLASS ANGST...
I DON'T KNOW WHAT TO DO WITH MY LIFE--
--AND IT'S ALL THE FAULT OF THE BABY BOOMERS!
WE DOUBT THAT MOST PEOPLE IN THEIR TWENTIES ARE REALLY SO CONSUMED WITH SELF-PITY... AFTER ALL, TIMES ARE CLEARLY DIFFICULT FOR PEOPLE OF ALL AGES... STILL, MANY PUBLICATIONS CONTINUE TO GIVE SPACE TO ANY YOUNG WRITER WHO CAN THINK UP A CLEVER NICKNAME FOR THEIR GENERATION--
Newstrend
'STICKIES'
Stuck With the Short End of the Stick
A report by the new voice of his generation
--AND WHO HAS SUFFICIENT CHUTZPAH TO BELIEVE THAT THEIR YEAR OF BIRTH QUALIFIES THEM TO MAKE SWEEPING GENERALIZATIONS ABOUT TENS OF MILLIONS OF STRANGERS...
...YOU SEE, WE "STICKIES" ARE APATHETIC BECAUSE WE KNOW OUR MBA'S DON'T MEAN AS MUCH AS THEY USED TO!
Voice of His Generation — CNN
TOM TOMORROW©93

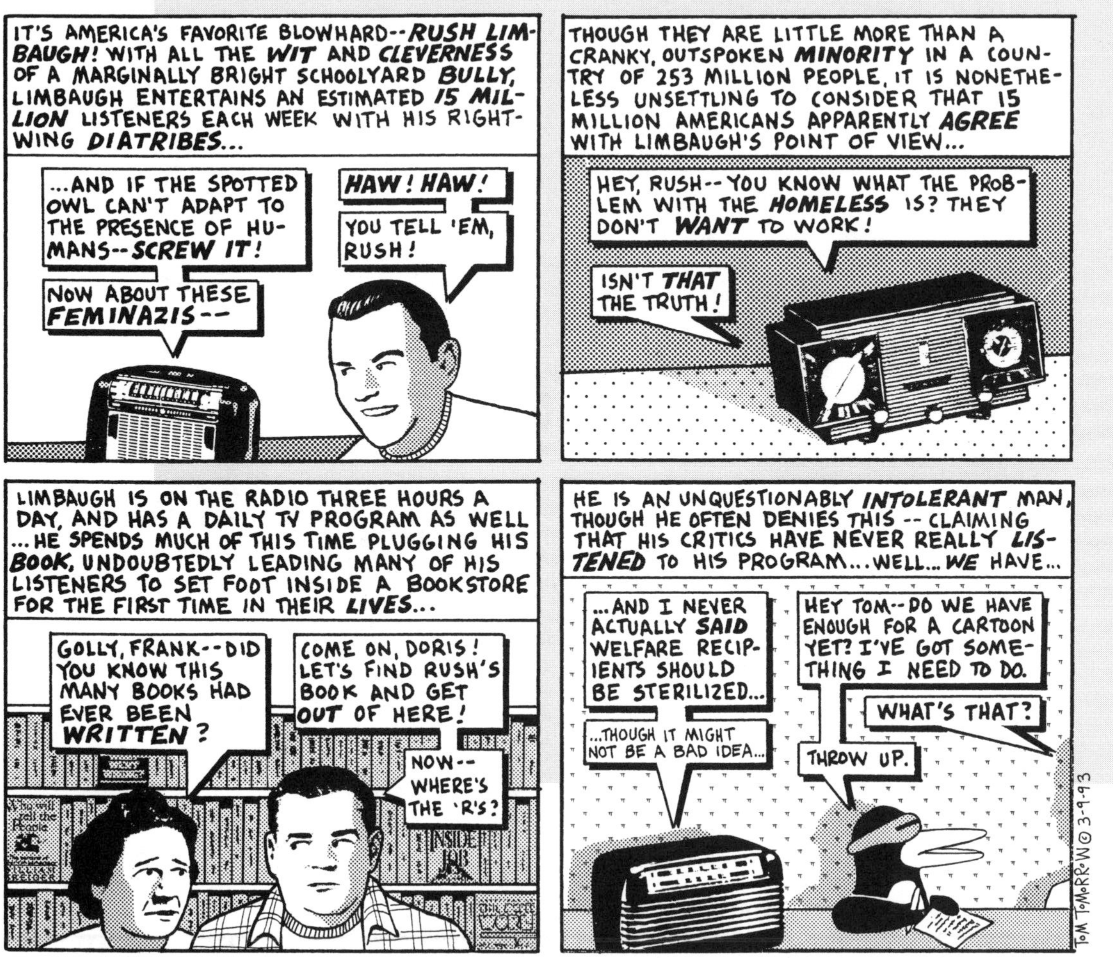
IT'S AMERICA'S FAVORITE BLOWHARD--RUSH LIMBAUGH! WITH ALL THE WIT AND CLEVERNESS OF A MARGINALLY BRIGHT SCHOOLYARD BULLY, LIMBAUGH ENTERTAINS AN ESTIMATED 15 MILLION LISTENERS EACH WEEK WITH HIS RIGHT-WING DIATRIBES...
...AND IF THE SPOTTED OWL CAN'T ADAPT TO THE PRESENCE OF HUMANS--SCREW IT!
NOW ABOUT THESE FEMINAZIS--
HAW! HAW!
YOU TELL 'EM, RUSH!
THOUGH THEY ARE LITTLE MORE THAN A CRANKY, OUTSPOKEN MINORITY IN A COUNTRY OF 253 MILLION PEOPLE, IT IS NONETHELESS UNSETTLING TO CONSIDER THAT 15 MILLION AMERICANS APPARENTLY AGREE WITH LIMBAUGH'S POINT OF VIEW...
HEY, RUSH--YOU KNOW WHAT THE PROBLEM WITH THE HOMELESS IS? THEY DON'T WANT TO WORK!
ISN'T THAT THE TRUTH!
LIMBAUGH IS ON THE RADIO THREE HOURS A DAY, AND HAS A DAILY TV PROGRAM AS WELL ... HE SPENDS MUCH OF THIS TIME PLUGGING HIS BOOK, UNDOUBTEDLY LEADING MANY OF HIS LISTENERS TO SET FOOT INSIDE A BOOKSTORE FOR THE FIRST TIME IN THEIR LIVES...
GOLLY, FRANK--DID YOU KNOW THIS MANY BOOKS HAD EVER BEEN WRITTEN?
COME ON, DORIS! LET'S FIND RUSH'S BOOK AND GET OUT OF HERE!
NOW--WHERE'S THE 'R'S?
HE IS AN UNQUESTIONABLY INTOLERANT MAN, THOUGH HE OFTEN DENIES THIS--CLAIMING THAT HIS CRITICS HAVE NEVER REALLY LISTENED TO HIS PROGRAM... WELL... WE HAVE...
...AND I NEVER ACTUALLY SAID WELFARE RECIPIENTS SHOULD BE STERILIZED...
...THOUGH IT MIGHT NOT BE A BAD IDEA...
HEY TOM--DO WE HAVE ENOUGH FOR A CARTOON YET? I'VE GOT SOMETHING I NEED TO DO.
WHAT'S THAT?
THROW UP.
TOM TOMORROW © 3-9-93

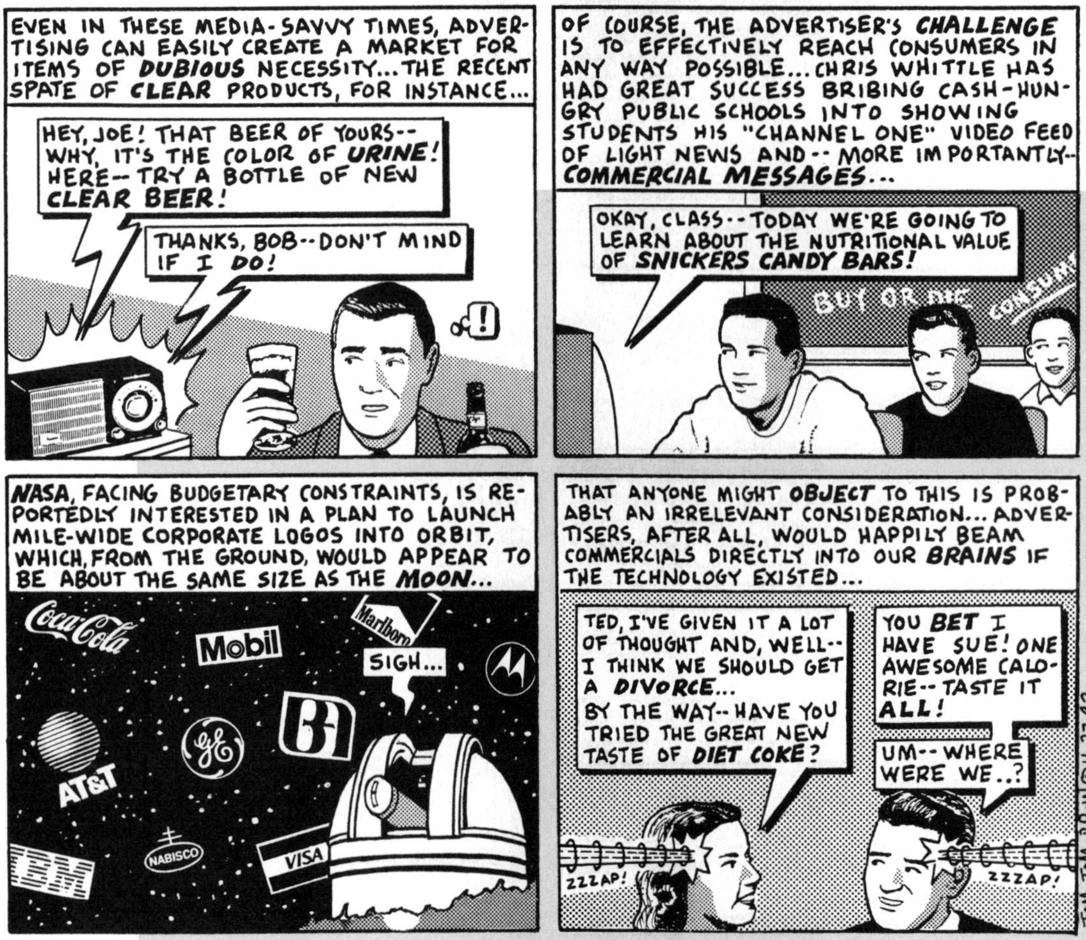
EVEN IN THESE MEDIA-SAVVY TIMES, ADVERTISING CAN EASILY CREATE A MARKET FOR ITEMS OF DUBIOUS NECESSITY... THE RECENT SPATE OF CLEAR PRODUCTS, FOR INSTANCE...
HEY, JOE! THAT BEER OF YOURS-- WHY, IT'S THE COLOR OF URINE! HERE-- TRY A BOTTLE OF NEW CLEAR BEER!
THANKS, BOB-- DON'T MIND IF I DO!
OF COURSE, THE ADVERTISER'S CHALLENGE IS TO EFFECTIVELY REACH CONSUMERS IN ANY WAY POSSIBLE... CHRIS WHITTLE HAS HAD GREAT SUCCESS BRIBING CASH-HUNGRY PUBLIC SCHOOLS INTO SHOWING STUDENTS HIS "CHANNEL ONE" VIDEO FEED OF LIGHT NEWS AND-- MORE IMPORTANTLY-- COMMERCIAL MESSAGES...
OKAY, CLASS-- TODAY WE'RE GOING TO LEARN ABOUT THE NUTRITIONAL VALUE OF SNICKERS CANDY BARS!
BUY OR DIE
NASA, FACING BUDGETARY CONSTRAINTS, IS REPORTEDLY INTERESTED IN A PLAN TO LAUNCH MILE-WIDE CORPORATE LOGOS INTO ORBIT, WHICH, FROM THE GROUND, WOULD APPEAR TO BE ABOUT THE SAME SIZE AS THE MOON...
Coca-Cola
Mobil
Marlboro
SIGH...
AT&T
NABISCO
VISA
IBM
THAT ANYONE MIGHT OBJECT TO THIS IS PROBABLY AN IRRELEVANT CONSIDERATION... ADVERTISERS, AFTER ALL, WOULD HAPPILY BEAM COMMERCIALS DIRECTLY INTO OUR BRAINS IF THE TECHNOLOGY EXISTED...
TED, I'VE GIVEN IT A LOT OF THOUGHT AND, WELL-- I THINK WE SHOULD GET A DIVORCE... BY THE WAY-- HAVE YOU TRIED THE GREAT NEW TASTE OF DIET COKE?
YOU BET I HAVE SUE! ONE AWESOME CALORIE-- TASTE IT ALL!
UM-- WHERE WERE WE..?
ZZZAP!
ZZZAP!
TOM TOMORROW © 4-27-93

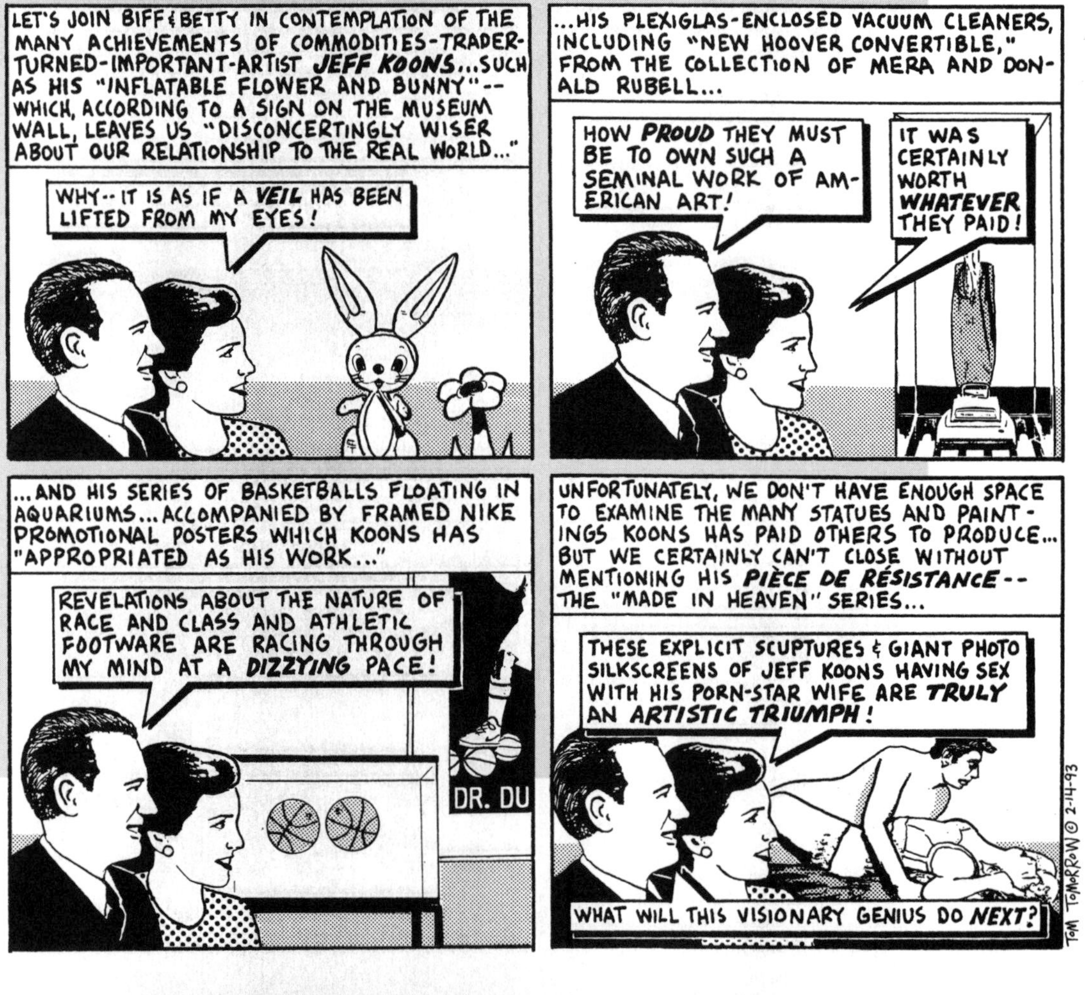
LET'S JOIN BIFF & BETTY IN CONTEMPLATION OF THE MANY ACHIEVEMENTS OF COMMODITIES-TRADER-TURNED-IMPORTANT-ARTIST JEFF KOONS... SUCH AS HIS "INFLATABLE FLOWER AND BUNNY" -- WHICH, ACCORDING TO A SIGN ON THE MUSEUM WALL, LEAVES US "DISCONCERTINGLY WISER ABOUT OUR RELATIONSHIP TO THE REAL WORLD..."
WHY-- IT IS AS IF A VEIL HAS BEEN LIFTED FROM MY EYES!
...HIS PLEXIGLAS-ENCLOSED VACUUM CLEANERS, INCLUDING "NEW HOOVER CONVERTIBLE," FROM THE COLLECTION OF MERA AND DONALD RUBELL...
HOW PROUD THEY MUST BE TO OWN SUCH A SEMINAL WORK OF AMERICAN ART!
IT WAS CERTAINLY WORTH WHATEVER THEY PAID!
...AND HIS SERIES OF BASKETBALLS FLOATING IN AQUARIUMS... ACCOMPANIED BY FRAMED NIKE PROMOTIONAL POSTERS WHICH KOONS HAS "APPROPRIATED AS HIS WORK..."
REVELATIONS ABOUT THE NATURE OF RACE AND CLASS AND ATHLETIC FOOTWARE ARE RACING THROUGH MY MIND AT A DIZZYING PACE!
DR. DU
UNFORTUNATELY, WE DON'T HAVE ENOUGH SPACE TO EXAMINE THE MANY STATUES AND PAINTINGS KOONS HAS PAID OTHERS TO PRODUCE... BUT WE CERTAINLY CAN'T CLOSE WITHOUT MENTIONING HIS PIÈCE DE RÉSISTANCE-- THE "MADE IN HEAVEN" SERIES...
THESE EXPLICIT SCUPTURES & GIANT PHOTO SILKSCREENS OF JEFF KOONS HAVING SEX WITH HIS PORN-STAR WIFE ARE TRULY AN ARTISTIC TRIUMPH!
WHAT WILL THIS VISIONARY GENIUS DO NEXT?
TOM TOMORROW © 2-14-93

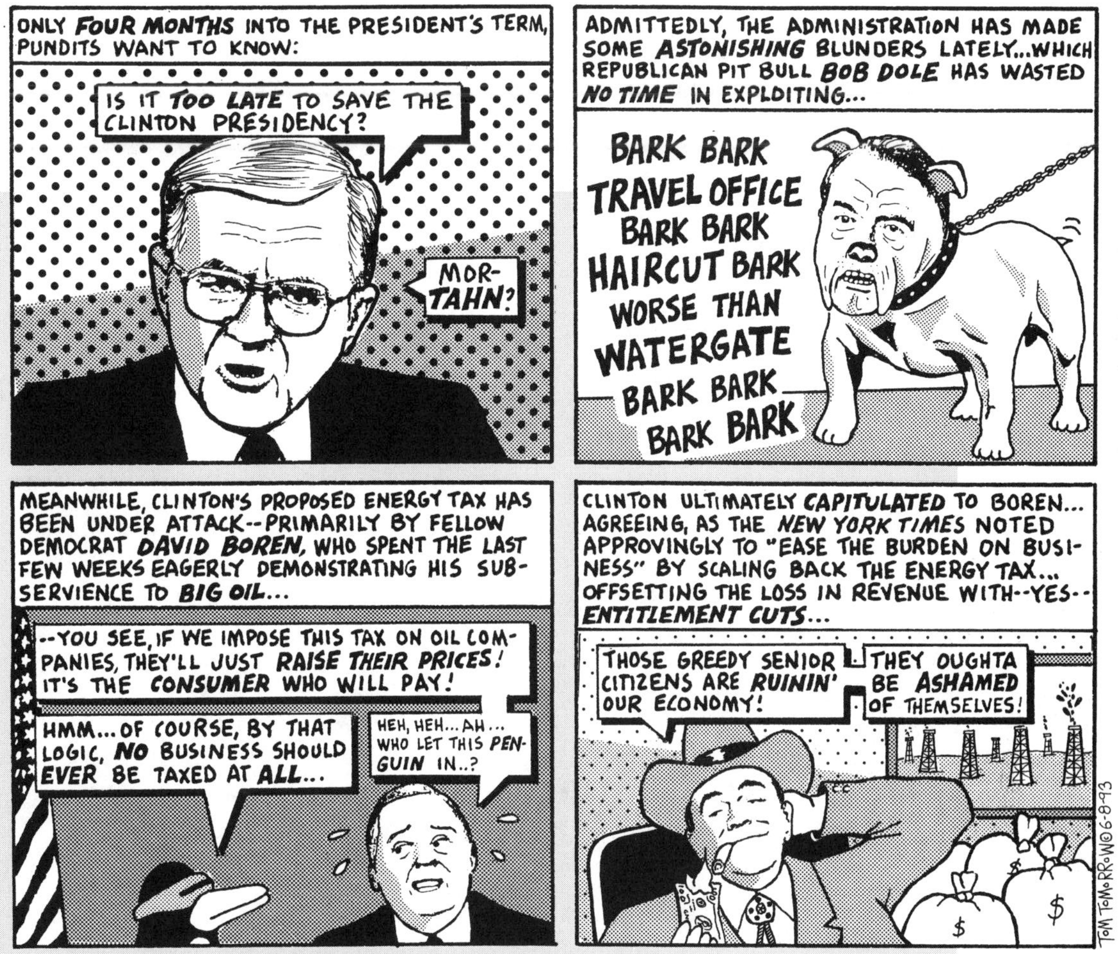
ONLY FOUR MONTHS INTO THE PRESIDENT'S TERM, PUNDITS WANT TO KNOW:
IS IT TOO LATE TO SAVE THE CLINTON PRESIDENCY?
MOR-TAHN?
ADMITTEDLY, THE ADMINISTRATION HAS MADE SOME ASTONISHING BLUNDERS LATELY...WHICH REPUBLICAN PIT BULL BOB DOLE HAS WASTED NO TIME IN EXPLOITING...
BARK BARK TRAVEL OFFICE BARK BARK HAIRCUT BARK WORSE THAN WATERGATE BARK BARK BARK BARK
MEANWHILE, CLINTON'S PROPOSED ENERGY TAX HAS BEEN UNDER ATTACK--PRIMARILY BY FELLOW DEMOCRAT DAVID BOREN, WHO SPENT THE LAST FEW WEEKS EAGERLY DEMONSTRATING HIS SUBSERVIENCE TO BIG OIL...
--YOU SEE, IF WE IMPOSE THIS TAX ON OIL COMPANIES, THEY'LL JUST RAISE THEIR PRICES! IT'S THE CONSUMER WHO WILL PAY!
HMM...OF COURSE, BY THAT LOGIC, NO BUSINESS SHOULD EVER BE TAXED AT ALL...
HEH, HEH...AH... WHO LET THIS PENGUIN IN..?
CLINTON ULTIMATELY CAPITULATED TO BOREN... AGREEING, AS THE NEW YORK TIMES NOTED APPROVINGLY TO "EASE THE BURDEN ON BUSINESS" BY SCALING BACK THE ENERGY TAX... OFFSETTING THE LOSS IN REVENUE WITH--YES--ENTITLEMENT CUTS...
THOSE GREEDY SENIOR CITIZENS ARE RUININ' OUR ECONOMY!
THEY OUGHTA BE ASHAMED OF THEMSELVES!
TOM TOMORROW©6-8-93

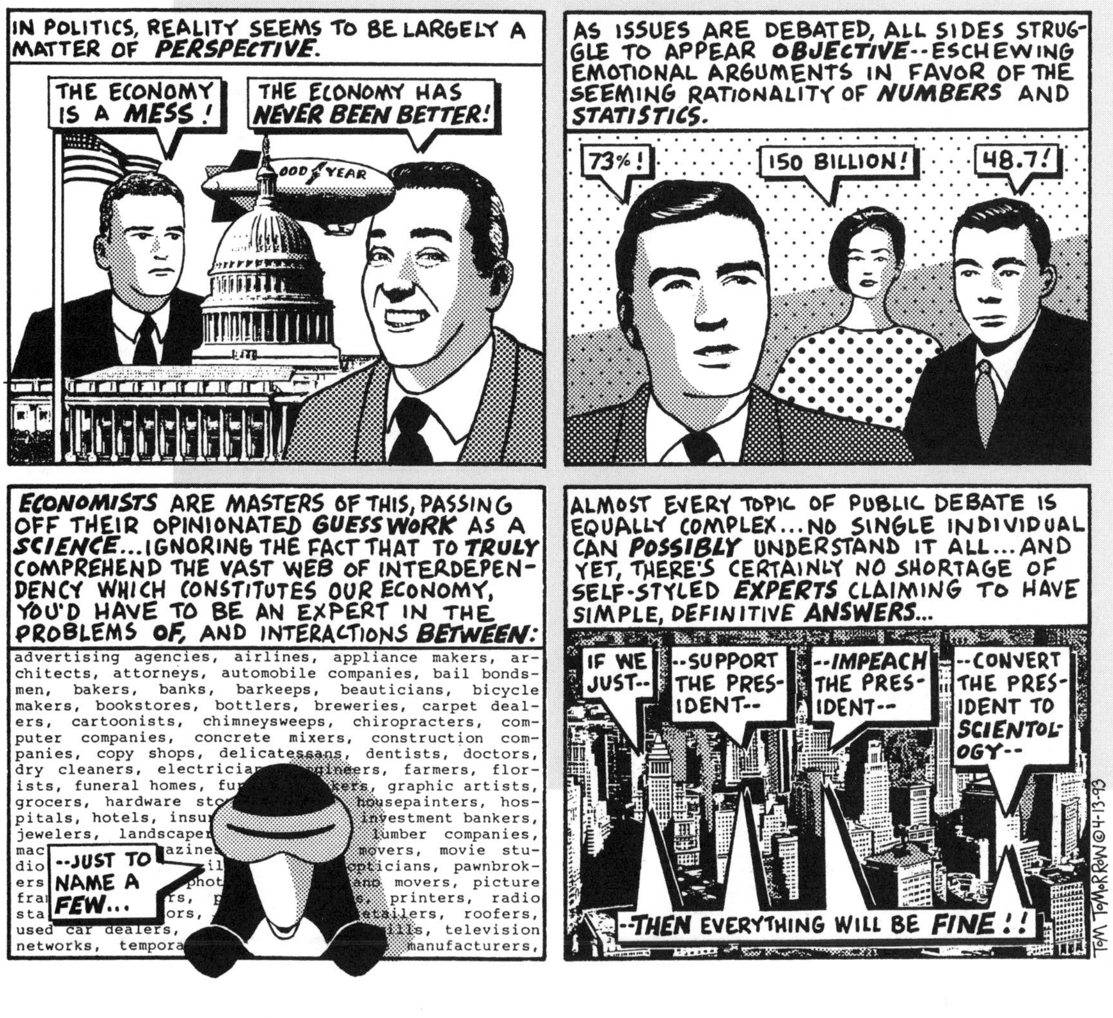
IN POLITICS, REALITY SEEMS TO BE LARGELY A MATTER OF PERSPECTIVE.
THE ECONOMY IS A MESS!
THE ECONOMY HAS NEVER BEEN BETTER!
AS ISSUES ARE DEBATED, ALL SIDES STRUGGLE TO APPEAR OBJECTIVE--ESCHEWING EMOTIONAL ARGUMENTS IN FAVOR OF THE SEEMING RATIONALITY OF NUMBERS AND STATISTICS.
73%!
150 BILLION!
48.7!
ECONOMISTS ARE MASTERS OF THIS, PASSING OFF THEIR OPINIONATED GUESSWORK AS A SCIENCE...IGNORING THE FACT THAT TO TRULY COMPREHEND THE VAST WEB OF INTERDEPENDENCY WHICH CONSTITUTES OUR ECONOMY, YOU'D HAVE TO BE AN EXPERT IN THE PROBLEMS OF, AND INTERACTIONS BETWEEN:
advertising agencies, airlines, appliance makers, architects, attorneys, automobile companies, bail bondsmen, bakers, banks, barkeeps, beauticians, bicycle makers, bookstores, bottlers, breweries, carpet dealers, cartoonists, chimneysweeps, chiropracters, computer companies, concrete mixers, construction companies, copy shops, delicatessans, dentists, doctors,
dry cleaners, electrician ... ers, farmers, florists, funeral homes, fu ... ers, graphic artists, grocers, hardware sto ... housepainters, hospitals, hotels, insu ... investment bankers, jewelers, landscape ... lumber companies, mac ... azines ... movers, movie studio ... opticians, pawnbrokers ... phot ... movers, picture fra ... rs, ... printers, radio sta ... ors, ... etailers, roofers, used car dealers, ... ills, television networks, tempora ... manufacturers,
--JUST TO NAME A FEW...
ALMOST EVERY TOPIC OF PUBLIC DEBATE IS EQUALLY COMPLEX...NO SINGLE INDIVIDUAL CAN POSSIBLY UNDERSTAND IT ALL...AND YET, THERE'S CERTAINLY NO SHORTAGE OF SELF-STYLED EXPERTS CLAIMING TO HAVE SIMPLE, DEFINITIVE ANSWERS...
IF WE JUST--
--SUPPORT THE PRESIDENT--
--IMPEACH THE PRESIDENT--
--CONVERT THE PRESIDENT TO SCIENTOLOGY--
--THEN EVERYTHING WILL BE FINE!!
TOM TOMORROW©4-13-93

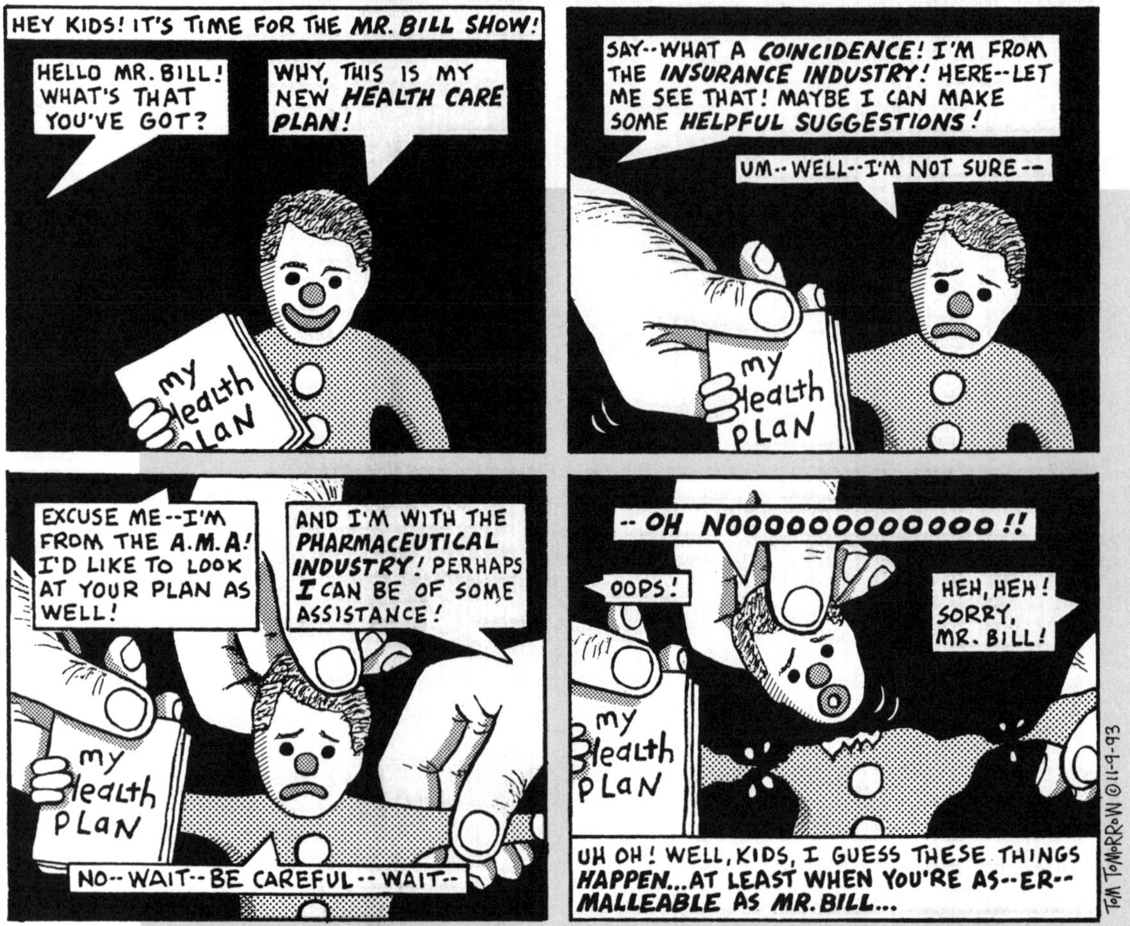
HEY KIDS! IT'S TIME FOR THE MR. BILL SHOW!
HELLO MR. BILL! WHAT'S THAT YOU'VE GOT?
WHY, THIS IS MY NEW HEALTH CARE PLAN!
my Health PLAN
SAY--WHAT A COINCIDENCE! I'M FROM THE INSURANCE INDUSTRY! HERE--LET ME SEE THAT! MAYBE I CAN MAKE SOME HELPFUL SUGGESTIONS!
UM--WELL--I'M NOT SURE--
EXCUSE ME--I'M FROM THE A.M.A! I'D LIKE TO LOOK AT YOUR PLAN AS WELL!
AND I'M WITH THE PHARMACEUTICAL INDUSTRY! PERHAPS I CAN BE OF SOME ASSISTANCE!
NO--WAIT--BE CAREFUL--WAIT--
--OH NOOOOOOOOOOOO!!
OOPS!
HEH, HEH! SORRY, MR. BILL!
UH OH! WELL, KIDS, I GUESS THESE THINGS HAPPEN...AT LEAST WHEN YOU'RE AS--ER--MALLEABLE AS MR. BILL...
TOM TOMORROW ©11-9-93

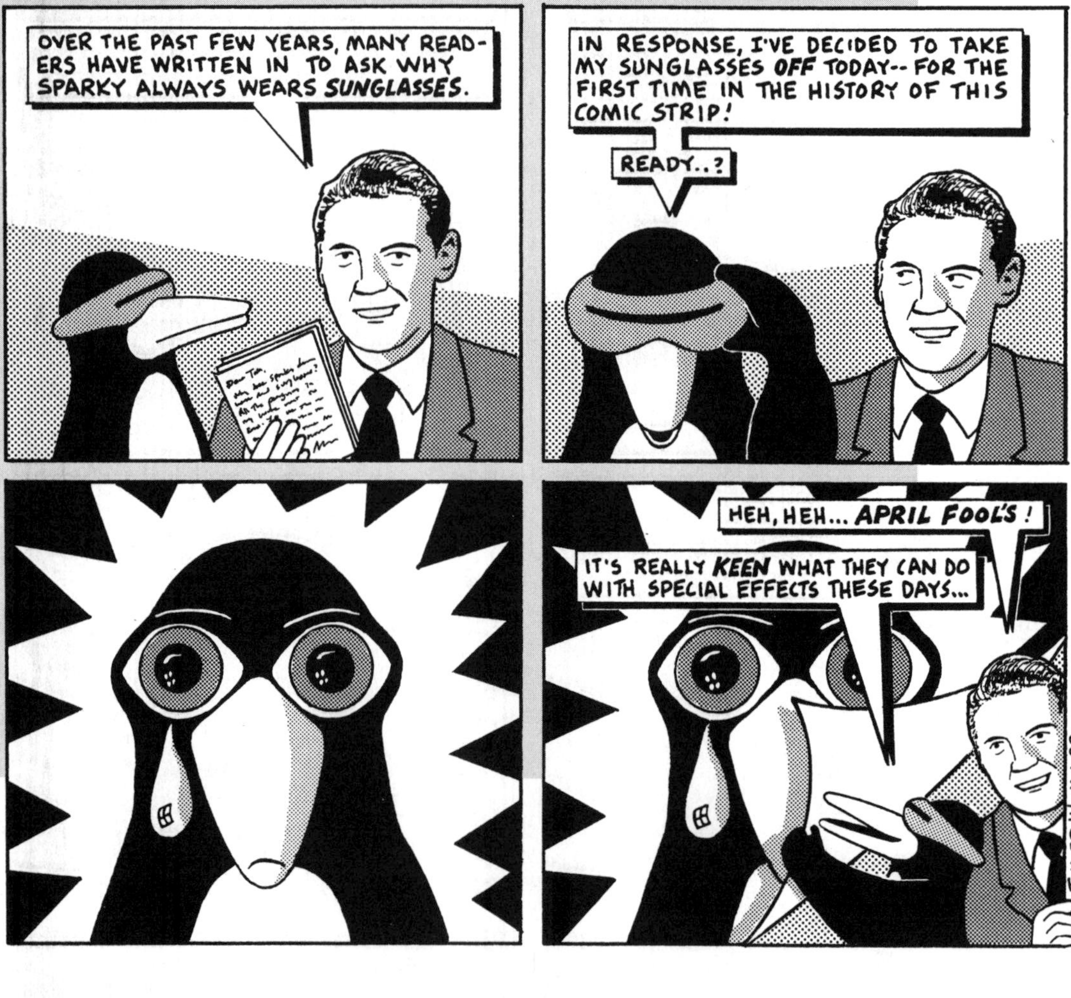
OVER THE PAST FEW YEARS, MANY READERS HAVE WRITTEN IN TO ASK WHY SPARKY ALWAYS WEARS SUNGLASSES.
IN RESPONSE, I'VE DECIDED TO TAKE MY SUNGLASSES OFF TODAY-- FOR THE FIRST TIME IN THE HISTORY OF THIS COMIC STRIP!
READY..?
HEH, HEH... APRIL FOOL'S!
IT'S REALLY KEEN WHAT THEY CAN DO WITH SPECIAL EFFECTS THESE DAYS...
TOM TOMORROW ©4-1-93

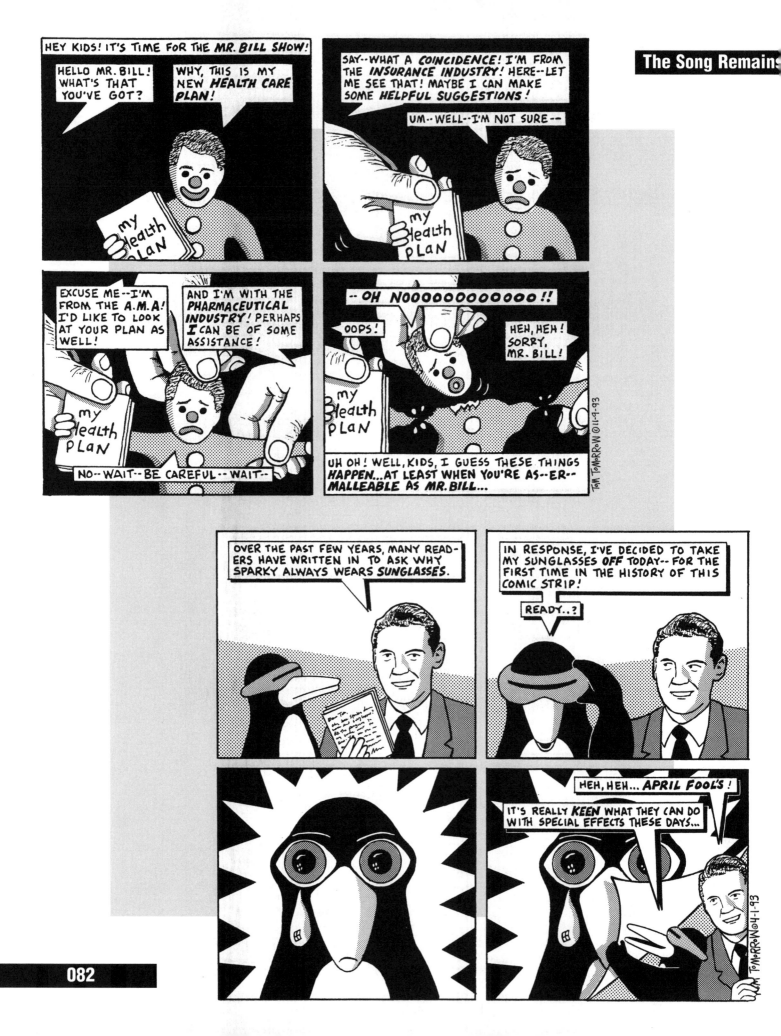

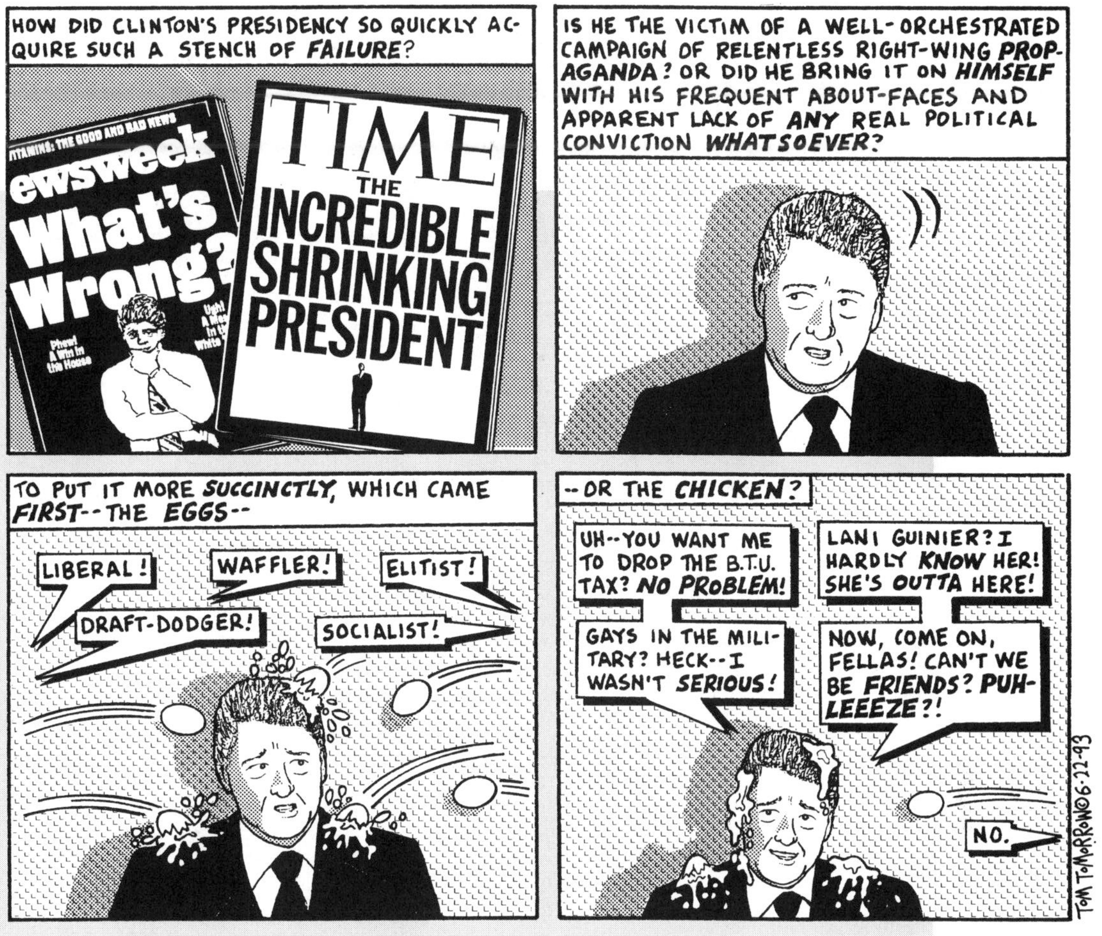
HOW DID CLINTON'S PRESIDENCY SO QUICKLY ACQUIRE SUCH A STENCH OF *FAILURE*?
ewsweek
What's Wrong?
TIME
THE INCREDIBLE SHRINKING PRESIDENT
IS HE THE VICTIM OF A WELL-ORCHESTRATED CAMPAIGN OF RELENTLESS RIGHT-WING *PROPAGANDA*? OR DID HE BRING IT ON *HIMSELF* WITH HIS FREQUENT ABOUT-FACES AND APPARENT LACK OF *ANY* REAL POLITICAL CONVICTION *WHATSOEVER*?
TO PUT IT MORE *SUCCINCTLY*, WHICH CAME *FIRST*--THE *EGGS*--
LIBERAL!
WAFFLER!
ELITIST!
DRAFT-DODGER!
SOCIALIST!
--OR THE *CHICKEN*?
UH--YOU WANT ME TO DROP THE B.T.U. TAX? *NO PROBLEM!*
GAYS IN THE MILITARY? HECK--I WASN'T *SERIOUS*!
LANI GUINIER? I HARDLY *KNOW* HER! SHE'S *OUTTA* HERE!
NOW, COME ON, FELLAS! CAN'T WE BE *FRIENDS*? *PUH-LEEEZE*?!
NO.
TOM TOMORROW©6-22-93

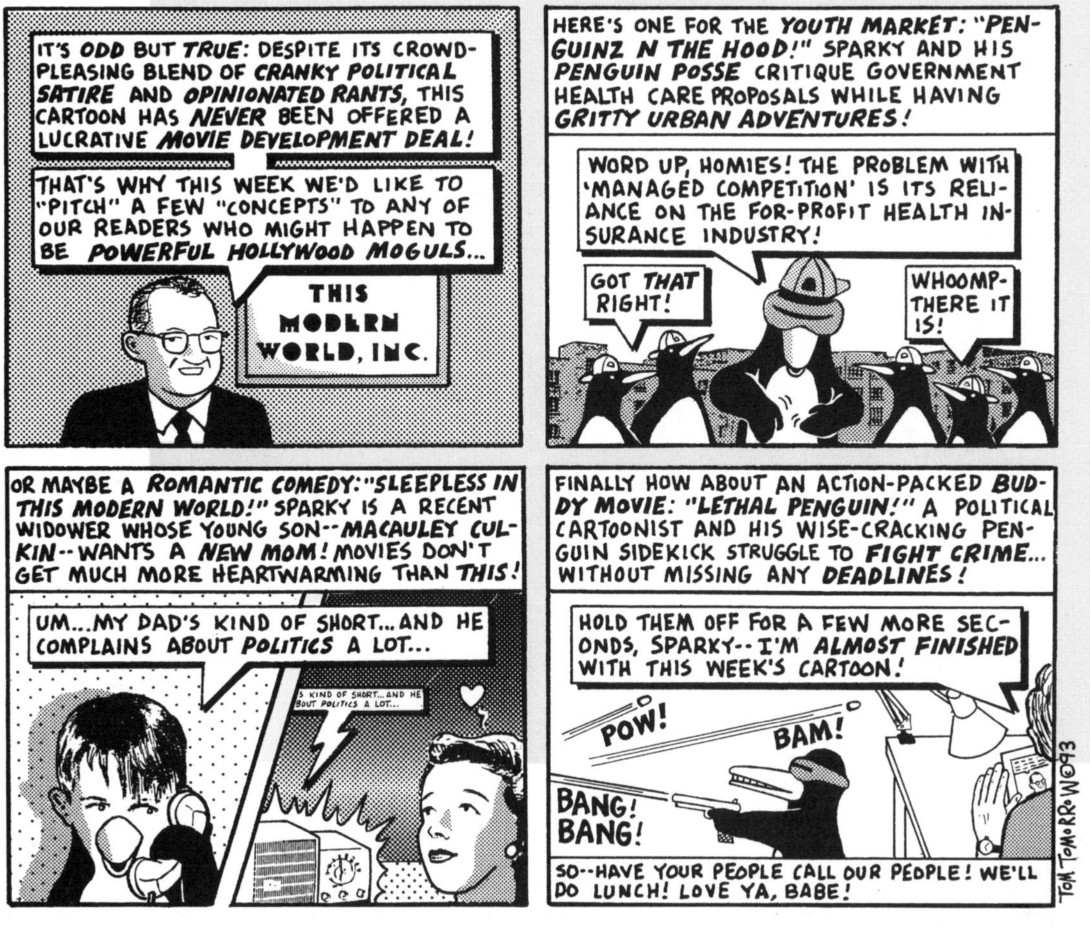
IT'S *ODD* BUT *TRUE*: DESPITE ITS CROWD-PLEASING BLEND OF *CRANKY POLITICAL SATIRE* AND *OPINIONATED RANTS*, THIS CARTOON HAS *NEVER* BEEN OFFERED A LUCRATIVE *MOVIE DEVELOPMENT DEAL*!
THAT'S WHY THIS WEEK WE'D LIKE TO "PITCH" A FEW "CONCEPTS" TO ANY OF OUR READERS WHO MIGHT HAPPEN TO BE *POWERFUL HOLLYWOOD MOGULS*...
THIS MODERN WORLD, INC.
HERE'S ONE FOR THE *YOUTH MARKET*: "*PENGUINZ N THE HOOD!*" SPARKY AND HIS *PENGUIN POSSE* CRITIQUE GOVERNMENT HEALTH CARE PROPOSALS WHILE HAVING *GRITTY URBAN ADVENTURES*!
WORD UP, HOMIES! THE PROBLEM WITH 'MANAGED COMPETITION' IS ITS RELIANCE ON THE FOR-PROFIT HEALTH INSURANCE INDUSTRY!
GOT *THAT* RIGHT!
WHOOMP-THERE IT IS!
OR MAYBE A *ROMANTIC COMEDY*: "*SLEEPLESS IN THIS MODERN WORLD!*" SPARKY IS A RECENT WIDOWER WHOSE YOUNG SON--*MACAULEY CULKIN*--WANTS A *NEW MOM*! MOVIES DON'T GET MUCH MORE HEARTWARMING THAN *THIS*!
UM...MY DAD'S KIND OF SHORT...AND HE COMPLAINS ABOUT *POLITICS* A LOT...
FINALLY HOW ABOUT AN ACTION-PACKED *BUDDY MOVIE*: "*LETHAL PENGUIN!*" A POLITICAL CARTOONIST AND HIS WISE-CRACKING PENGUIN SIDEKICK STRUGGLE TO *FIGHT CRIME*... WITHOUT MISSING ANY *DEADLINES*!
HOLD THEM OFF FOR A FEW MORE SECONDS, SPARKY--I'M *ALMOST FINISHED* WITH THIS WEEK'S CARTOON!
POW!
BAM!
BANG! BANG!
SO--HAVE YOUR PEOPLE CALL OUR PEOPLE! WE'LL DO LUNCH! LOVE YA, BABE!
TOM TOMORROW©93

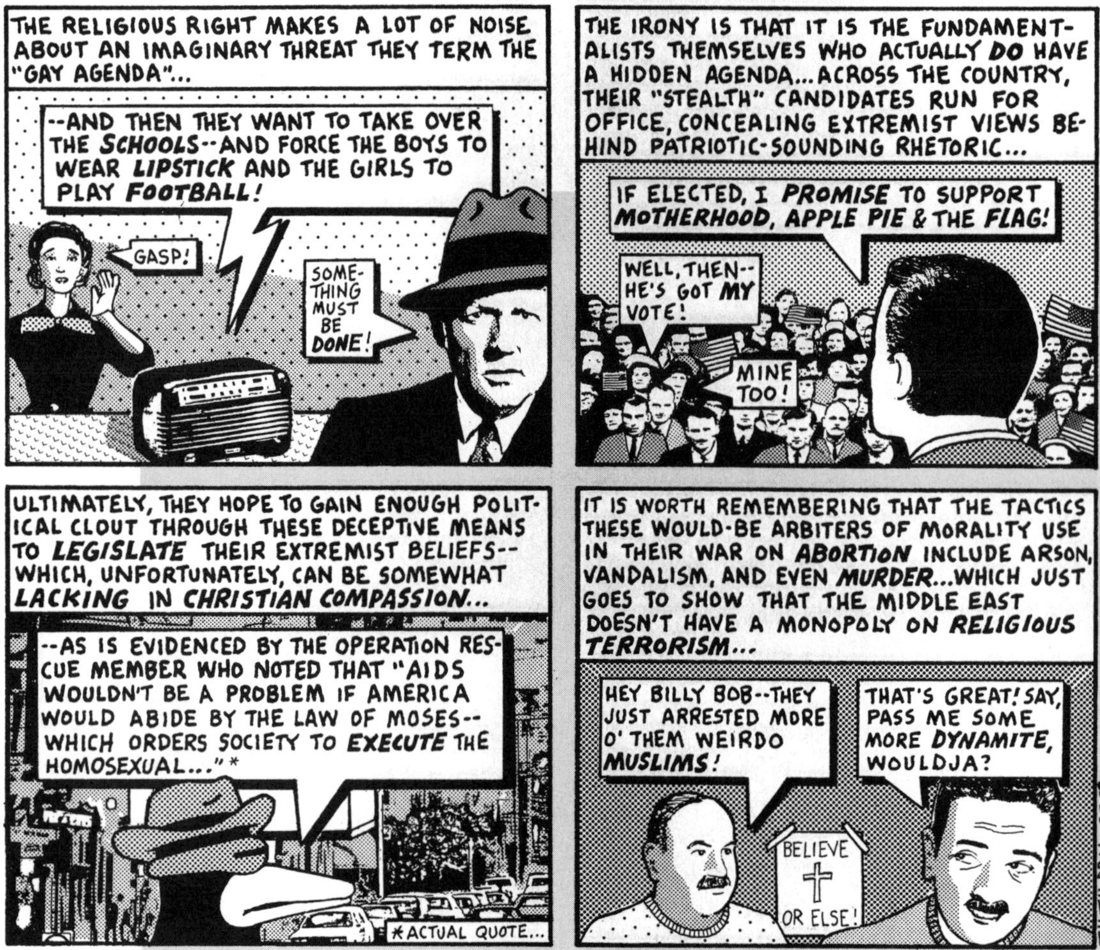
THE RELIGIOUS RIGHT MAKES A LOT OF NOISE ABOUT AN IMAGINARY THREAT THEY TERM THE "GAY AGENDA"...
--AND THEN THEY WANT TO TAKE OVER THE SCHOOLS--AND FORCE THE BOYS TO WEAR LIPSTICK AND THE GIRLS TO PLAY FOOTBALL!
GASP!
SOMETHING MUST BE DONE!
THE IRONY IS THAT IT IS THE FUNDAMENTALISTS THEMSELVES WHO ACTUALLY DO HAVE A HIDDEN AGENDA... ACROSS THE COUNTRY, THEIR "STEALTH" CANDIDATES RUN FOR OFFICE, CONCEALING EXTREMIST VIEWS BEHIND PATRIOTIC-SOUNDING RHETORIC...
IF ELECTED, I PROMISE TO SUPPORT MOTHERHOOD, APPLE PIE & THE FLAG!
WELL, THEN--HE'S GOT MY VOTE!
MINE TOO!
ULTIMATELY, THEY HOPE TO GAIN ENOUGH POLITICAL CLOUT THROUGH THESE DECEPTIVE MEANS TO LEGISLATE THEIR EXTREMIST BELIEFS--WHICH, UNFORTUNATELY, CAN BE SOMEWHAT LACKING IN CHRISTIAN COMPASSION...
--AS IS EVIDENCED BY THE OPERATION RESCUE MEMBER WHO NOTED THAT "AIDS WOULDN'T BE A PROBLEM IF AMERICA WOULD ABIDE BY THE LAW OF MOSES--WHICH ORDERS SOCIETY TO EXECUTE THE HOMOSEXUAL..."*
*ACTUAL QUOTE...
IT IS WORTH REMEMBERING THAT THE TACTICS THESE WOULD-BE ARBITERS OF MORALITY USE IN THEIR WAR ON ABORTION INCLUDE ARSON, VANDALISM, AND EVEN MURDER... WHICH JUST GOES TO SHOW THAT THE MIDDLE EAST DOESN'T HAVE A MONOPOLY ON RELIGIOUS TERRORISM...
HEY BILLY BOB--THEY JUST ARRESTED MORE O' THEM WEIRDO MUSLIMS!
THAT'S GREAT! SAY, PASS ME SOME MORE DYNAMITE, WOULDJA?
BELIEVE OR ELSE!
TOM TOMORROW©9-7-93

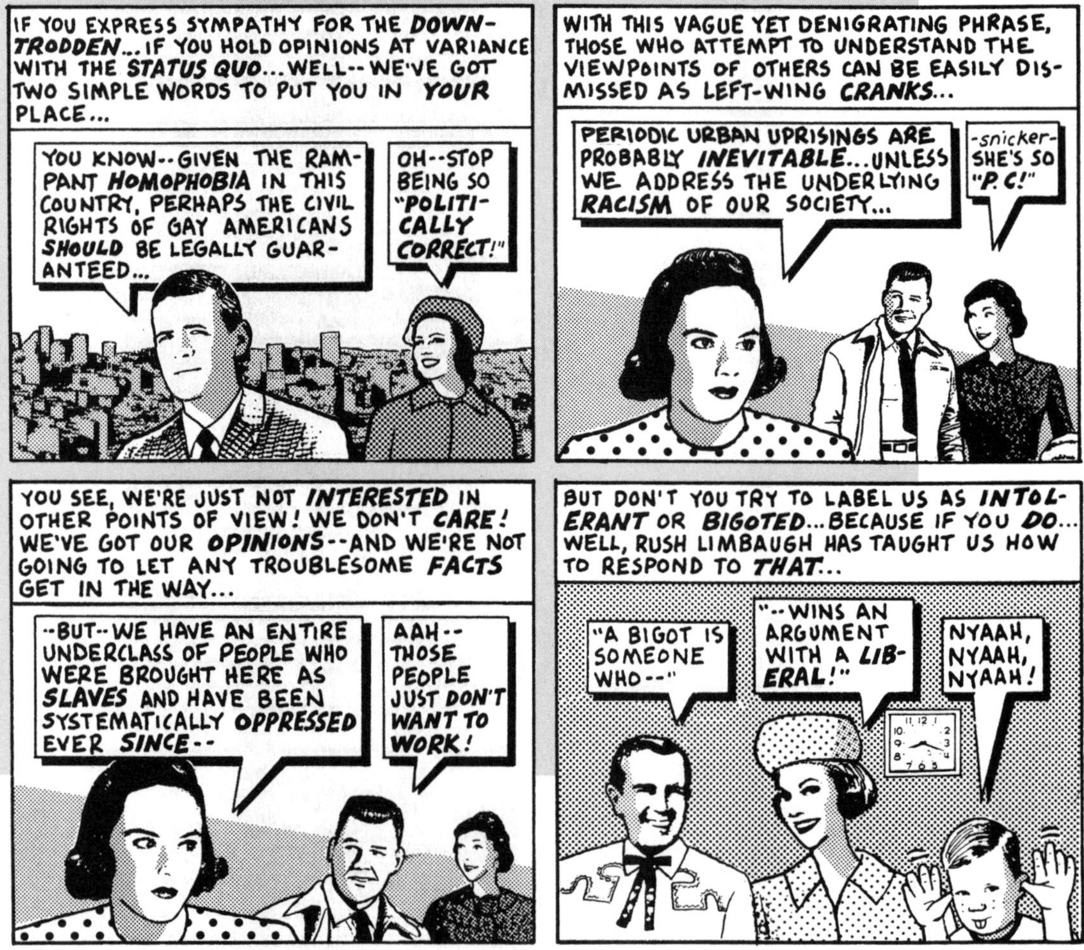
IF YOU EXPRESS SYMPATHY FOR THE DOWNTRODDEN... IF YOU HOLD OPINIONS AT VARIANCE WITH THE STATUS QUO... WELL--WE'VE GOT TWO SIMPLE WORDS TO PUT YOU IN YOUR PLACE...
YOU KNOW--GIVEN THE RAMPANT HOMOPHOBIA IN THIS COUNTRY, PERHAPS THE CIVIL RIGHTS OF GAY AMERICANS SHOULD BE LEGALLY GUARANTEED...
OH--STOP BEING SO "POLITICALLY CORRECT!"
WITH THIS VAGUE YET DENIGRATING PHRASE, THOSE WHO ATTEMPT TO UNDERSTAND THE VIEWPOINTS OF OTHERS CAN BE EASILY DISMISSED AS LEFT-WING CRANKS...
PERIODIC URBAN UPRISINGS ARE PROBABLY INEVITABLE... UNLESS WE ADDRESS THE UNDERLYING RACISM OF OUR SOCIETY...
-snicker- SHE'S SO "P.C!"
YOU SEE, WE'RE JUST NOT INTERESTED IN OTHER POINTS OF VIEW! WE DON'T CARE! WE'VE GOT OUR OPINIONS--AND WE'RE NOT GOING TO LET ANY TROUBLESOME FACTS GET IN THE WAY...
--BUT--WE HAVE AN ENTIRE UNDERCLASS OF PEOPLE WHO WERE BROUGHT HERE AS SLAVES AND HAVE BEEN SYSTEMATICALLY OPPRESSED EVER SINCE--
AAH--THOSE PEOPLE JUST DON'T WANT TO WORK!
BUT DON'T YOU TRY TO LABEL US AS INTOLERANT OR BIGOTED... BECAUSE IF YOU DO... WELL, RUSH LIMBAUGH HAS TAUGHT US HOW TO RESPOND TO THAT...
"A BIGOT IS SOMEONE WHO--"
"--WINS AN ARGUMENT WITH A LIBERAL!"
NYAAH, NYAAH, NYAAH!
TOM TOMORROW©93

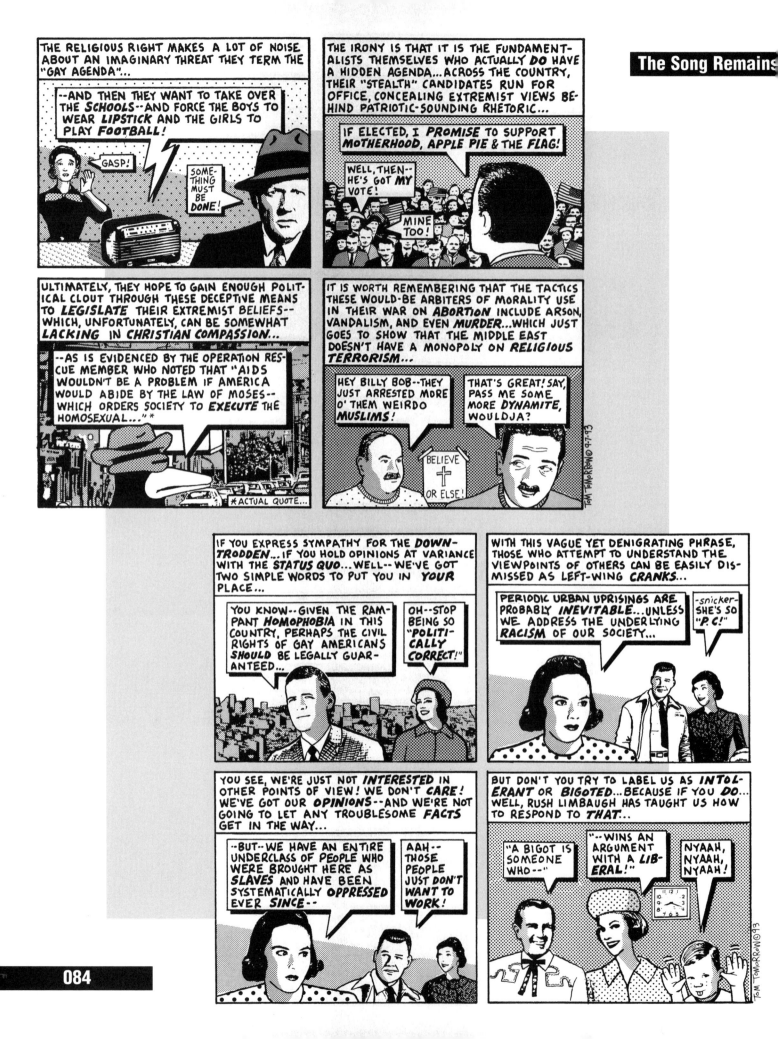

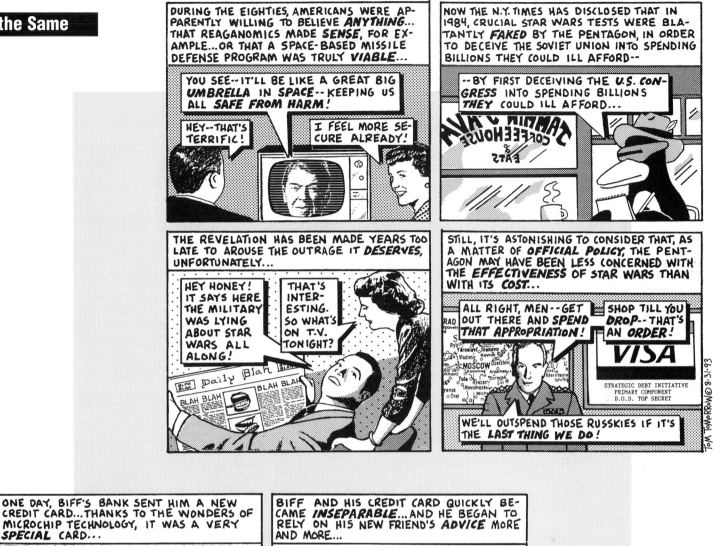

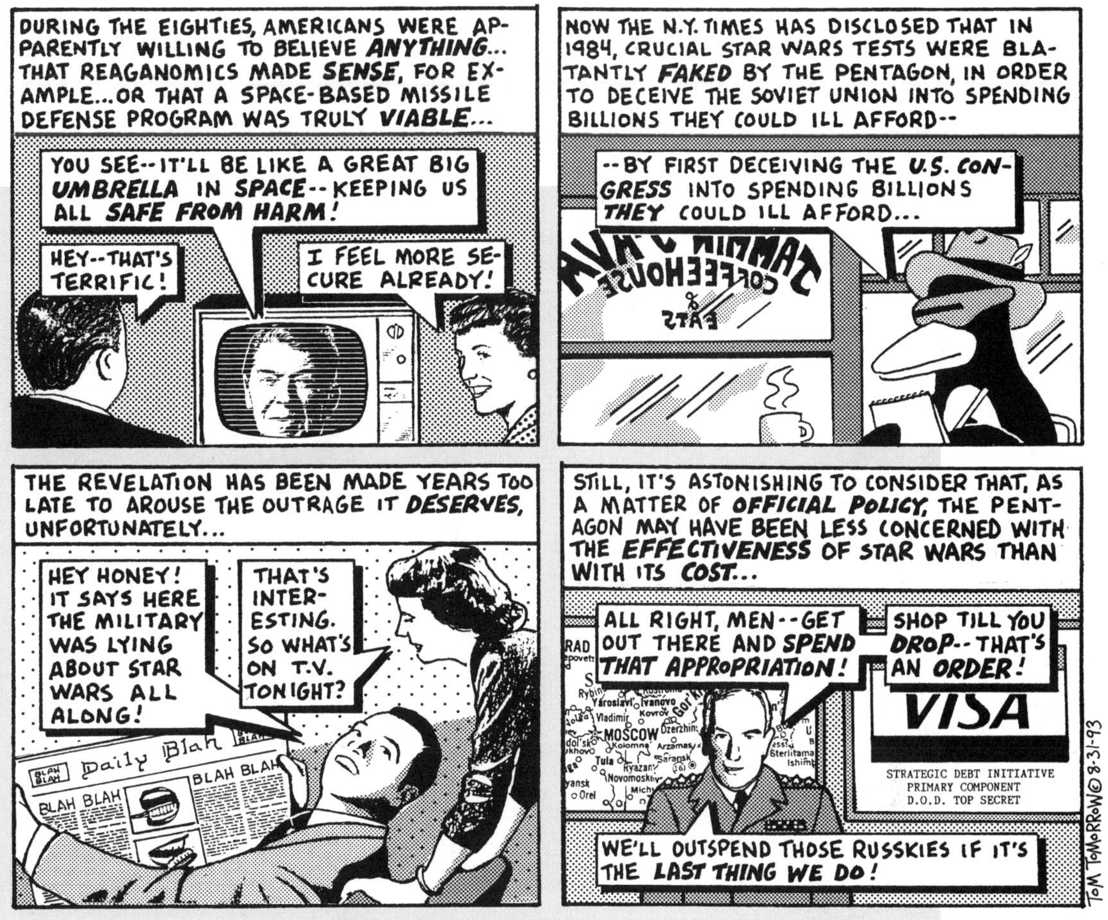
DURING THE EIGHTIES, AMERICANS WERE APPARENTLY WILLING TO BELIEVE ANYTHING... THAT REAGANOMICS MADE SENSE, FOR EXAMPLE...OR THAT A SPACE-BASED MISSILE DEFENSE PROGRAM WAS TRULY VIABLE...
YOU SEE--IT'LL BE LIKE A GREAT BIG UMBRELLA IN SPACE--KEEPING US ALL SAFE FROM HARM!
HEY--THAT'S TERRIFIC!
I FEEL MORE SECURE ALREADY!
NOW THE N.Y. TIMES HAS DISCLOSED THAT IN 1984, CRUCIAL STAR WARS TESTS WERE BLATANTLY FAKED BY THE PENTAGON, IN ORDER TO DECEIVE THE SOVIET UNION INTO SPENDING BILLIONS THEY COULD ILL AFFORD--
--BY FIRST DECEIVING THE U.S. CONGRESS INTO SPENDING BILLIONS THEY COULD ILL AFFORD...
COFFEEHOUSE & EATS
THE REVELATION HAS BEEN MADE YEARS TOO LATE TO AROUSE THE OUTRAGE IT DESERVES, UNFORTUNATELY...
HEY HONEY! IT SAYS HERE THE MILITARY WAS LYING ABOUT STAR WARS ALL ALONG!
THAT'S INTERESTING. SO WHAT'S ON T.V. TONIGHT?
Daily Blah
BLAH BLAH
STILL, IT'S ASTONISHING TO CONSIDER THAT, AS A MATTER OF OFFICIAL POLICY, THE PENTAGON MAY HAVE BEEN LESS CONCERNED WITH THE EFFECTIVENESS OF STAR WARS THAN WITH ITS COST...
ALL RIGHT, MEN--GET OUT THERE AND SPEND THAT APPROPRIATION!
SHOP TILL YOU DROP--THAT'S AN ORDER!
MOSCOW
VISA
STRATEGIC DEBT INITIATIVE
PRIMARY COMPONENT
D.O.D. TOP SECRET
WE'LL OUTSPEND THOSE RUSSKIES IF IT'S THE LAST THING WE DO!
TOM TOMORROW©8-31-93

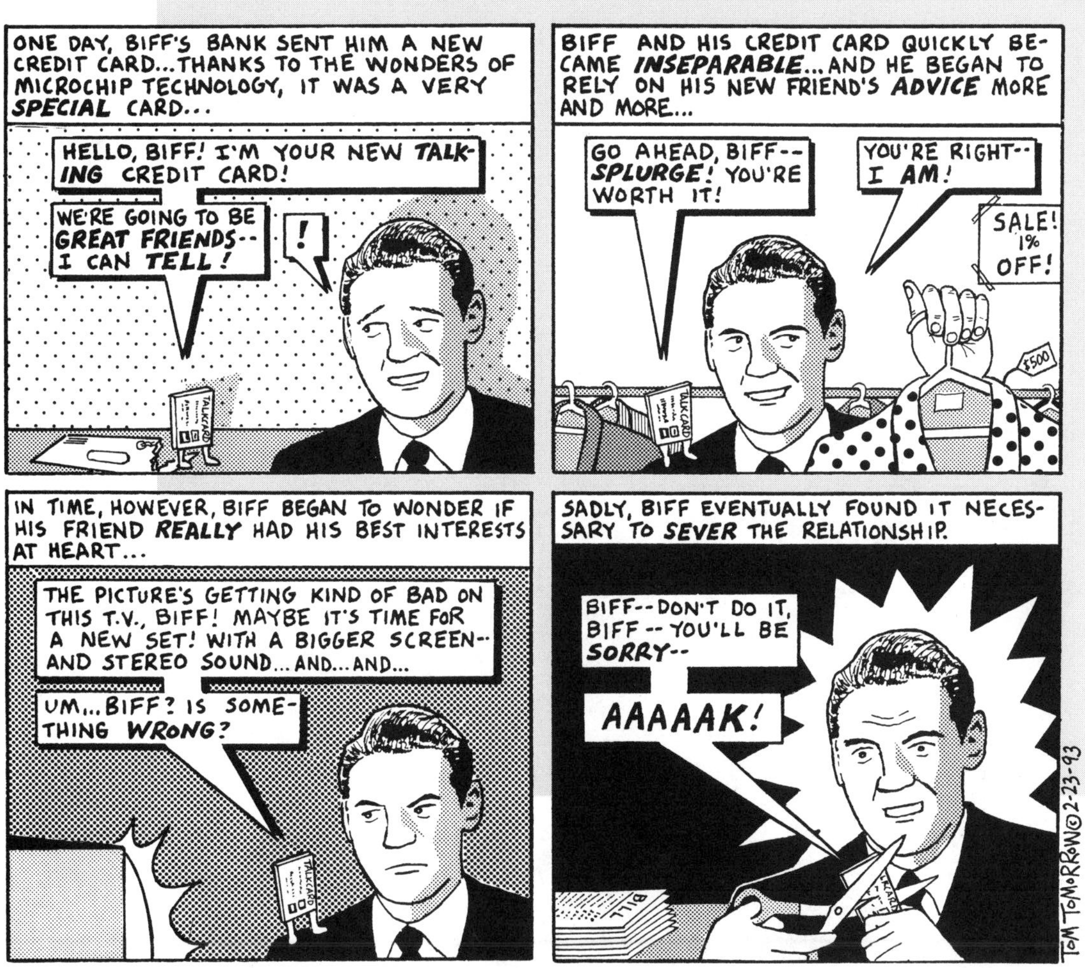
ONE DAY, BIFF'S BANK SENT HIM A NEW CREDIT CARD...THANKS TO THE WONDERS OF MICROCHIP TECHNOLOGY, IT WAS A VERY SPECIAL CARD...
HELLO, BIFF! I'M YOUR NEW TALKING CREDIT CARD!
WE'RE GOING TO BE GREAT FRIENDS--I CAN TELL!
!
BIFF AND HIS CREDIT CARD QUICKLY BECAME INSEPARABLE...AND HE BEGAN TO RELY ON HIS NEW FRIEND'S ADVICE MORE AND MORE...
GO AHEAD, BIFF--SPLURGE! YOU'RE WORTH IT!
YOU'RE RIGHT--I AM!
SALE! 1% OFF!
$500
IN TIME, HOWEVER, BIFF BEGAN TO WONDER IF HIS FRIEND REALLY HAD HIS BEST INTERESTS AT HEART...
THE PICTURE'S GETTING KIND OF BAD ON THIS T.V., BIFF! MAYBE IT'S TIME FOR A NEW SET! WITH A BIGGER SCREEN--AND STEREO SOUND...AND...AND...
UM...BIFF? IS SOMETHING WRONG?
SADLY, BIFF EVENTUALLY FOUND IT NECESSARY TO SEVER THE RELATIONSHIP.
BIFF--DON'T DO IT, BIFF--YOU'LL BE SORRY--
AAAAAK!
BILL
TOM TOMORROW©2-23-93

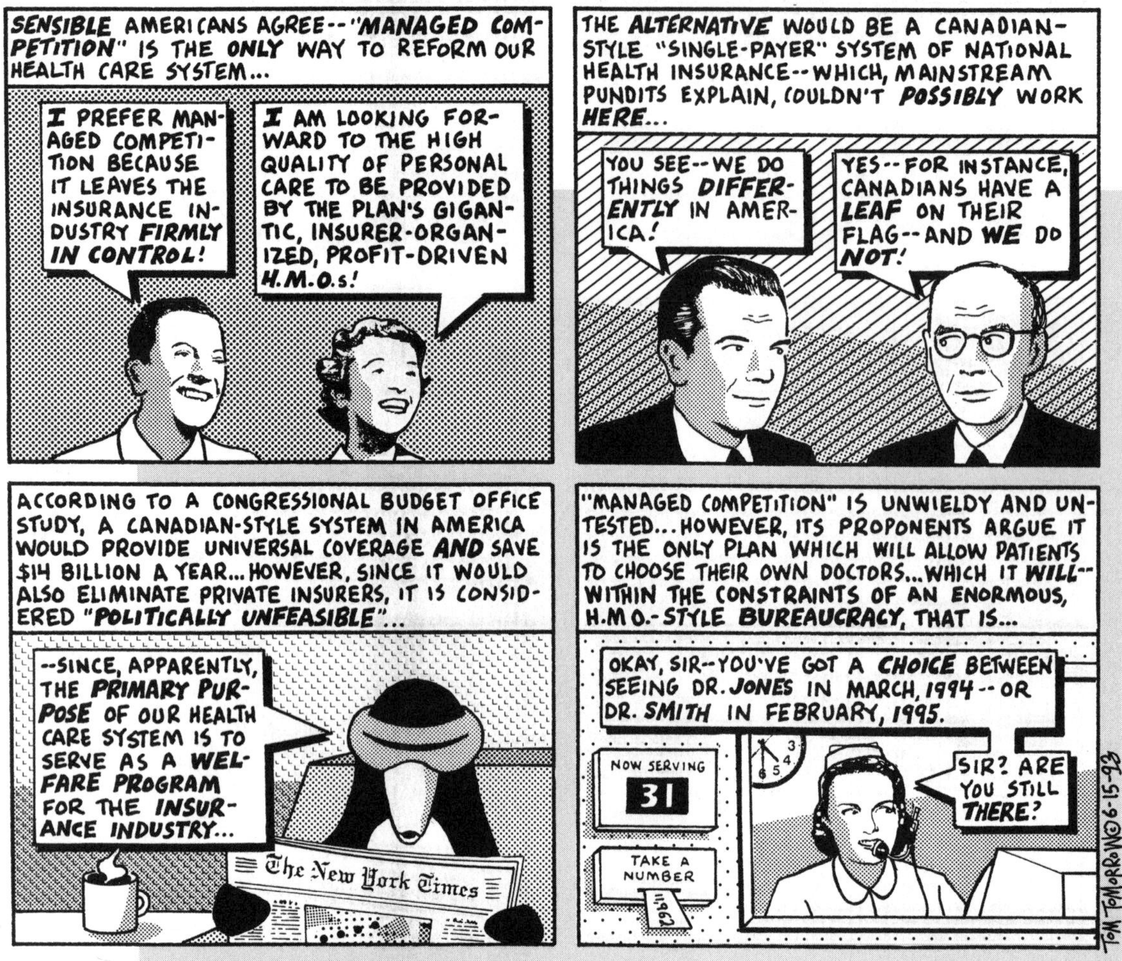
SENSIBLE AMERICANS AGREE--"MANAGED COMPETITION" IS THE ONLY WAY TO REFORM OUR HEALTH CARE SYSTEM...
I PREFER MANAGED COMPETITION BECAUSE IT LEAVES THE INSURANCE INDUSTRY FIRMLY IN CONTROL!
I AM LOOKING FORWARD TO THE HIGH QUALITY OF PERSONAL CARE TO BE PROVIDED BY THE PLAN'S GIGANTIC, INSURER-ORGANIZED, PROFIT-DRIVEN H.M.O.s!
THE ALTERNATIVE WOULD BE A CANADIAN-STYLE "SINGLE-PAYER" SYSTEM OF NATIONAL HEALTH INSURANCE--WHICH, MAINSTREAM PUNDITS EXPLAIN, COULDN'T POSSIBLY WORK HERE...
YOU SEE--WE DO THINGS DIFFERENTLY IN AMERICA!
YES--FOR INSTANCE, CANADIANS HAVE A LEAF ON THEIR FLAG--AND WE DO NOT!
ACCORDING TO A CONGRESSIONAL BUDGET OFFICE STUDY, A CANADIAN-STYLE SYSTEM IN AMERICA WOULD PROVIDE UNIVERSAL COVERAGE AND SAVE $14 BILLION A YEAR... HOWEVER, SINCE IT WOULD ALSO ELIMINATE PRIVATE INSURERS, IT IS CONSIDERED "POLITICALLY UNFEASIBLE"...
--SINCE, APPARENTLY, THE PRIMARY PURPOSE OF OUR HEALTH CARE SYSTEM IS TO SERVE AS A WELFARE PROGRAM FOR THE INSURANCE INDUSTRY...
The New York Times
"MANAGED COMPETITION" IS UNWIELDY AND UNTESTED... HOWEVER, ITS PROPONENTS ARGUE IT IS THE ONLY PLAN WHICH WILL ALLOW PATIENTS TO CHOOSE THEIR OWN DOCTORS... WHICH IT WILL--WITHIN THE CONSTRAINTS OF AN ENORMOUS, H.M.O.-STYLE BUREAUCRACY, THAT IS...
OKAY, SIR--YOU'VE GOT A CHOICE BETWEEN SEEING DR. JONES IN MARCH, 1994--OR DR. SMITH IN FEBRUARY, 1995.
NOW SERVING
31
TAKE A NUMBER
SIR? ARE YOU STILL THERE?
TOM TOMORROW©6-15-93

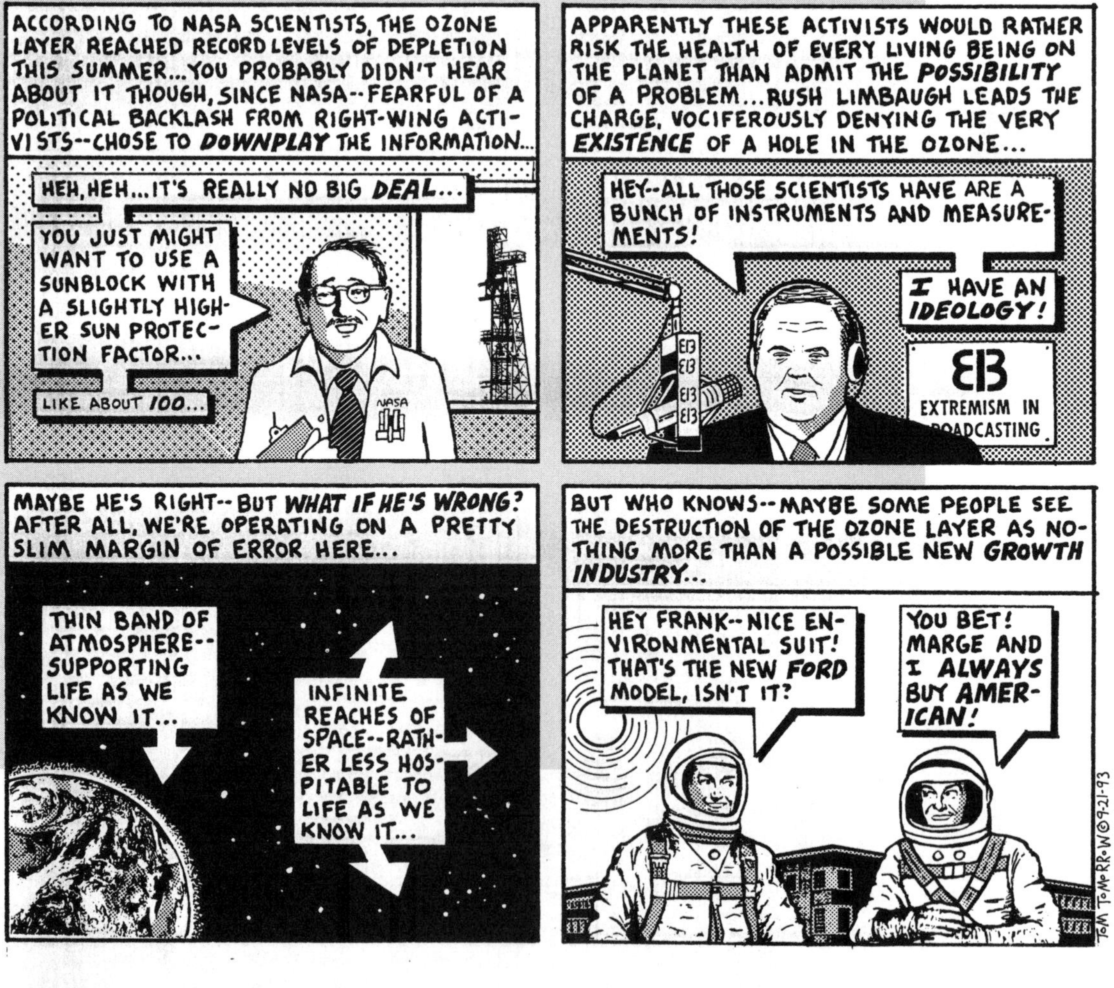
ACCORDING TO NASA SCIENTISTS, THE OZONE LAYER REACHED RECORD LEVELS OF DEPLETION THIS SUMMER... YOU PROBABLY DIDN'T HEAR ABOUT IT THOUGH, SINCE NASA--FEARFUL OF A POLITICAL BACKLASH FROM RIGHT-WING ACTIVISTS--CHOSE TO DOWNPLAY THE INFORMATION...
HEH, HEH... IT'S REALLY NO BIG DEAL...
YOU JUST MIGHT WANT TO USE A SUNBLOCK WITH A SLIGHTLY HIGHER SUN PROTECTION FACTOR...
LIKE ABOUT 100...
NASA
APPARENTLY THESE ACTIVISTS WOULD RATHER RISK THE HEALTH OF EVERY LIVING BEING ON THE PLANET THAN ADMIT THE POSSIBILITY OF A PROBLEM... RUSH LIMBAUGH LEADS THE CHARGE, VOCIFEROUSLY DENYING THE VERY EXISTENCE OF A HOLE IN THE OZONE...
HEY--ALL THOSE SCIENTISTS HAVE ARE A BUNCH OF INSTRUMENTS AND MEASUREMENTS!
I HAVE AN IDEOLOGY!
EIB
EXTREMISM IN BROADCASTING
MAYBE HE'S RIGHT--BUT WHAT IF HE'S WRONG? AFTER ALL, WE'RE OPERATING ON A PRETTY SLIM MARGIN OF ERROR HERE...
THIN BAND OF ATMOSPHERE--SUPPORTING LIFE AS WE KNOW IT...
INFINITE REACHES OF SPACE--RATHER LESS HOSPITABLE TO LIFE AS WE KNOW IT...
BUT WHO KNOWS--MAYBE SOME PEOPLE SEE THE DESTRUCTION OF THE OZONE LAYER AS NOTHING MORE THAN A POSSIBLE NEW GROWTH INDUSTRY...
HEY FRANK--NICE ENVIRONMENTAL SUIT! THAT'S THE NEW FORD MODEL, ISN'T IT?
YOU BET! MARGE AND I ALWAYS BUY AMERICAN!
TOM TOMORROW©9-21-93

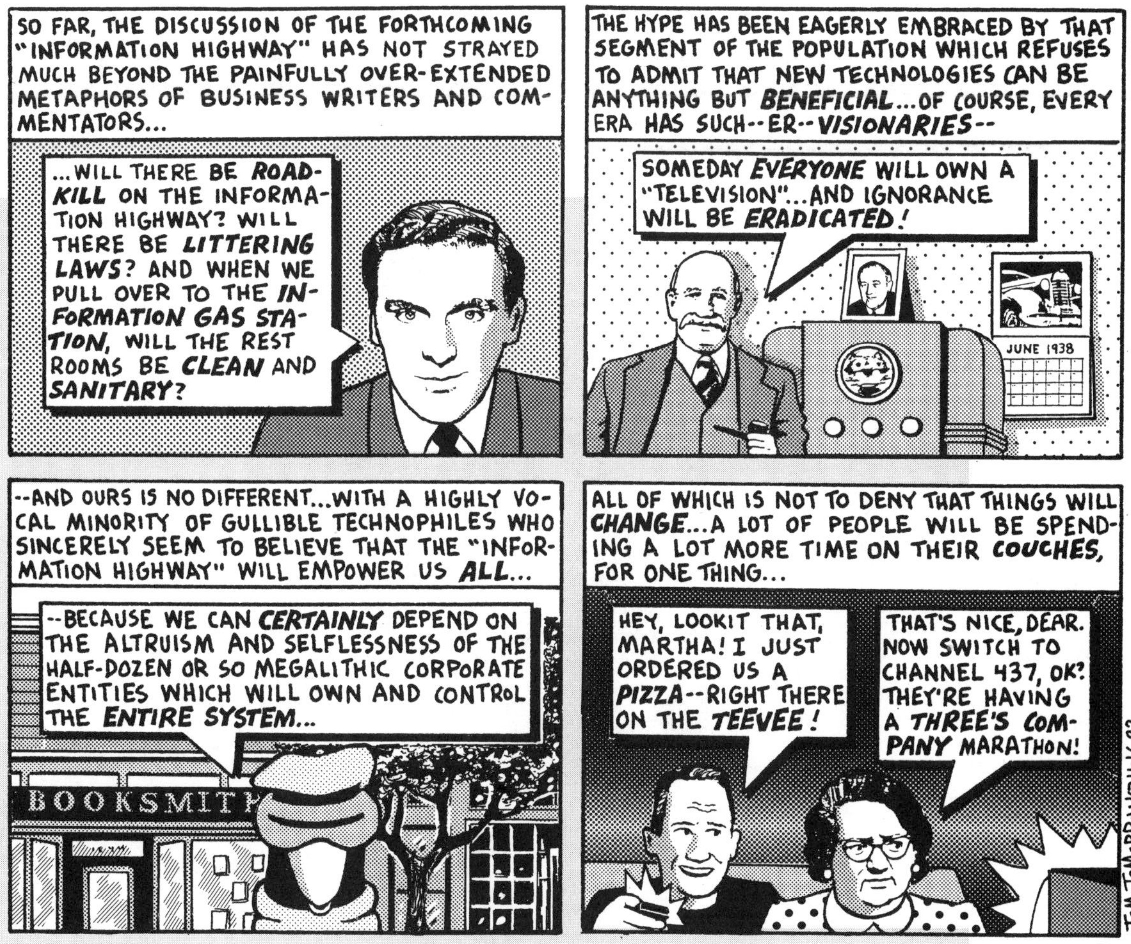
SO FAR, THE DISCUSSION OF THE FORTHCOMING "INFORMATION HIGHWAY" HAS NOT STRAYED MUCH BEYOND THE PAINFULLY OVER-EXTENDED METAPHORS OF BUSINESS WRITERS AND COMMENTATORS...
...WILL THERE BE ROAD-KILL ON THE INFORMATION HIGHWAY? WILL THERE BE LITTERING LAWS? AND WHEN WE PULL OVER TO THE INFORMATION GAS STATION, WILL THE REST ROOMS BE CLEAN AND SANITARY?
THE HYPE HAS BEEN EAGERLY EMBRACED BY THAT SEGMENT OF THE POPULATION WHICH REFUSES TO ADMIT THAT NEW TECHNOLOGIES CAN BE ANYTHING BUT BENEFICIAL...OF COURSE, EVERY ERA HAS SUCH--ER--VISIONARIES--
SOMEDAY EVERYONE WILL OWN A "TELEVISION"...AND IGNORANCE WILL BE ERADICATED!
JUNE 1938
--AND OURS IS NO DIFFERENT...WITH A HIGHLY VOCAL MINORITY OF GULLIBLE TECHNOPHILES WHO SINCERELY SEEM TO BELIEVE THAT THE "INFORMATION HIGHWAY" WILL EMPOWER US ALL...
--BECAUSE WE CAN CERTAINLY DEPEND ON THE ALTRUISM AND SELFLESSNESS OF THE HALF-DOZEN OR SO MEGALITHIC CORPORATE ENTITIES WHICH WILL OWN AND CONTROL THE ENTIRE SYSTEM...
BOOKSMITH
ALL OF WHICH IS NOT TO DENY THAT THINGS WILL CHANGE...A LOT OF PEOPLE WILL BE SPENDING A LOT MORE TIME ON THEIR COUCHES, FOR ONE THING...
HEY, LOOKIT THAT, MARTHA! I JUST ORDERED US A PIZZA--RIGHT THERE ON THE TEEVEE!
THAT'S NICE, DEAR. NOW SWITCH TO CHANNEL 437, OK? THEY'RE HAVING A THREE'S COMPANY MARATHON!
TOM TOMORROW©11-16-93

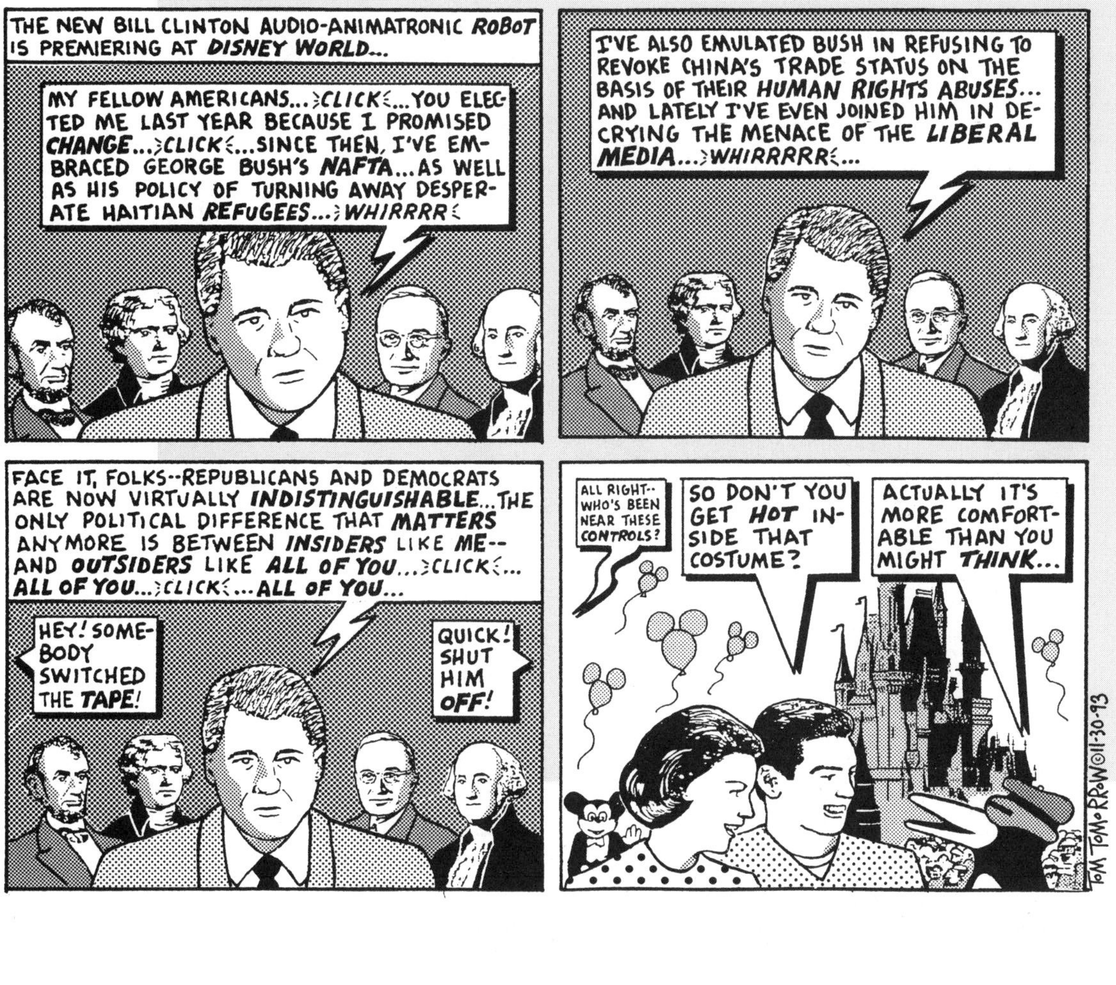
THE NEW BILL CLINTON AUDIO-ANIMATRONIC ROBOT IS PREMIERING AT DISNEY WORLD...
MY FELLOW AMERICANS...›CLICK‹...YOU ELECTED ME LAST YEAR BECAUSE I PROMISED CHANGE...›CLICK‹...SINCE THEN, I'VE EMBRACED GEORGE BUSH'S NAFTA...AS WELL AS HIS POLICY OF TURNING AWAY DESPERATE HAITIAN REFUGEES...›WHIRRRR‹
I'VE ALSO EMULATED BUSH IN REFUSING TO REVOKE CHINA'S TRADE STATUS ON THE BASIS OF THEIR HUMAN RIGHTS ABUSES... AND LATELY I'VE EVEN JOINED HIM IN DECRYING THE MENACE OF THE LIBERAL MEDIA...›WHIRRRRR‹...
FACE IT, FOLKS--REPUBLICANS AND DEMOCRATS ARE NOW VIRTUALLY INDISTINGUISHABLE...THE ONLY POLITICAL DIFFERENCE THAT MATTERS ANYMORE IS BETWEEN INSIDERS LIKE ME--AND OUTSIDERS LIKE ALL OF YOU...›CLICK‹...ALL OF YOU...›CLICK‹...ALL OF YOU...
HEY! SOMEBODY SWITCHED THE TAPE!
QUICK! SHUT HIM OFF!
ALL RIGHT--WHO'S BEEN NEAR THESE CONTROLS?
SO DON'T YOU GET HOT INSIDE THAT COSTUME?
ACTUALLY IT'S MORE COMFORTABLE THAN YOU MIGHT THINK...
TOM TOMORROW©11-30-93

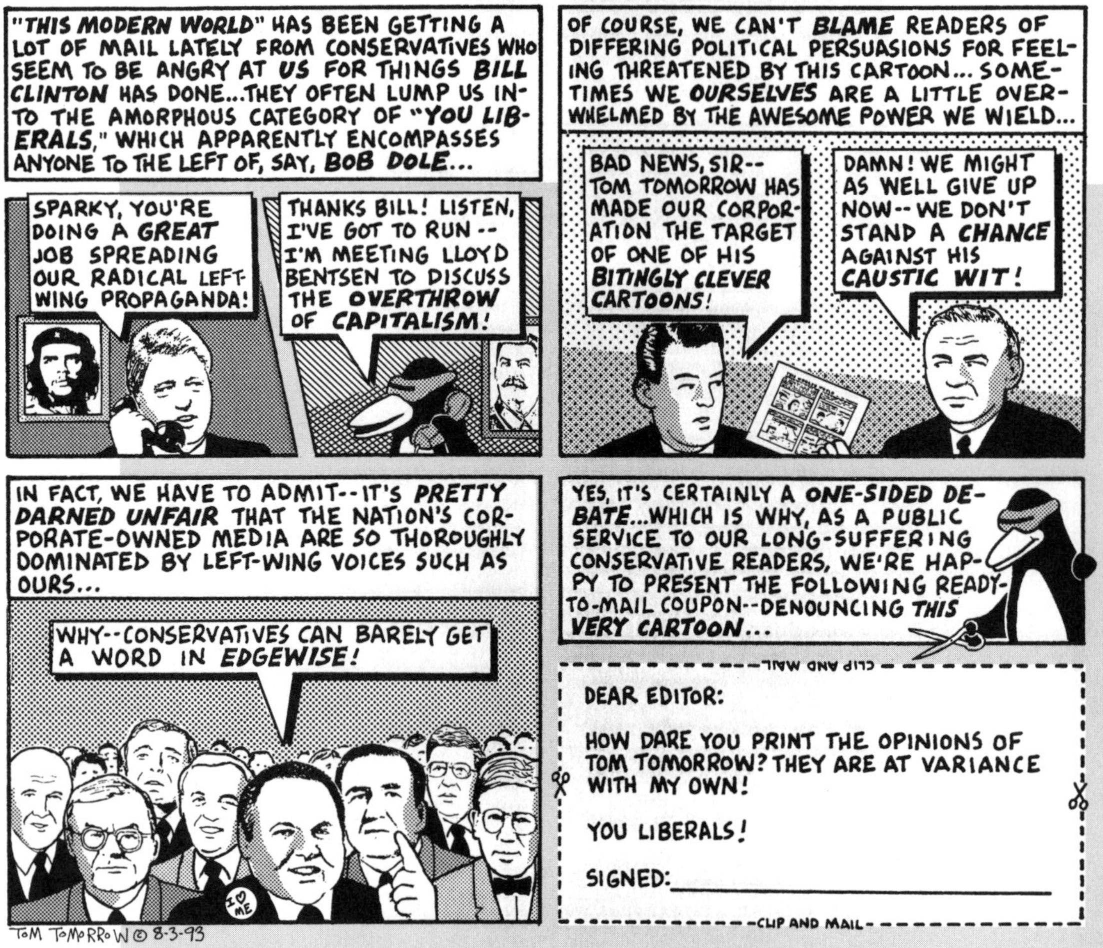
"THIS MODERN WORLD" HAS BEEN GETTING A LOT OF MAIL LATELY FROM CONSERVATIVES WHO SEEM TO BE ANGRY AT US FOR THINGS BILL CLINTON HAS DONE... THEY OFTEN LUMP US INTO THE AMORPHOUS CATEGORY OF "YOU LIBERALS," WHICH APPARENTLY ENCOMPASSES ANYONE TO THE LEFT OF, SAY, BOB DOLE...
SPARKY, YOU'RE DOING A GREAT JOB SPREADING OUR RADICAL LEFT-WING PROPAGANDA!
THANKS BILL! LISTEN, I'VE GOT TO RUN -- I'M MEETING LLOYD BENTSEN TO DISCUSS THE OVERTHROW OF CAPITALISM!
OF COURSE, WE CAN'T BLAME READERS OF DIFFERING POLITICAL PERSUASIONS FOR FEELING THREATENED BY THIS CARTOON... SOMETIMES WE OURSELVES ARE A LITTLE OVERWHELMED BY THE AWESOME POWER WE WIELD...
BAD NEWS, SIR -- TOM TOMORROW HAS MADE OUR CORPORATION THE TARGET OF ONE OF HIS BITINGLY CLEVER CARTOONS!
DAMN! WE MIGHT AS WELL GIVE UP NOW -- WE DON'T STAND A CHANCE AGAINST HIS CAUSTIC WIT!
IN FACT, WE HAVE TO ADMIT -- IT'S PRETTY DARNED UNFAIR THAT THE NATION'S CORPORATE-OWNED MEDIA ARE SO THOROUGHLY DOMINATED BY LEFT-WING VOICES SUCH AS OURS...
WHY -- CONSERVATIVES CAN BARELY GET A WORD IN EDGEWISE!
YES, IT'S CERTAINLY A ONE-SIDED DEBATE... WHICH IS WHY, AS A PUBLIC SERVICE TO OUR LONG-SUFFERING CONSERVATIVE READERS, WE'RE HAPPY TO PRESENT THE FOLLOWING READY-TO-MAIL COUPON -- DENOUNCING THIS VERY CARTOON...
CLIP AND MAIL
DEAR EDITOR:
HOW DARE YOU PRINT THE OPINIONS OF TOM TOMORROW? THEY ARE AT VARIANCE WITH MY OWN!
YOU LIBERALS!
SIGNED:
CLIP AND MAIL
TOM TOMORROW © 8-3-93

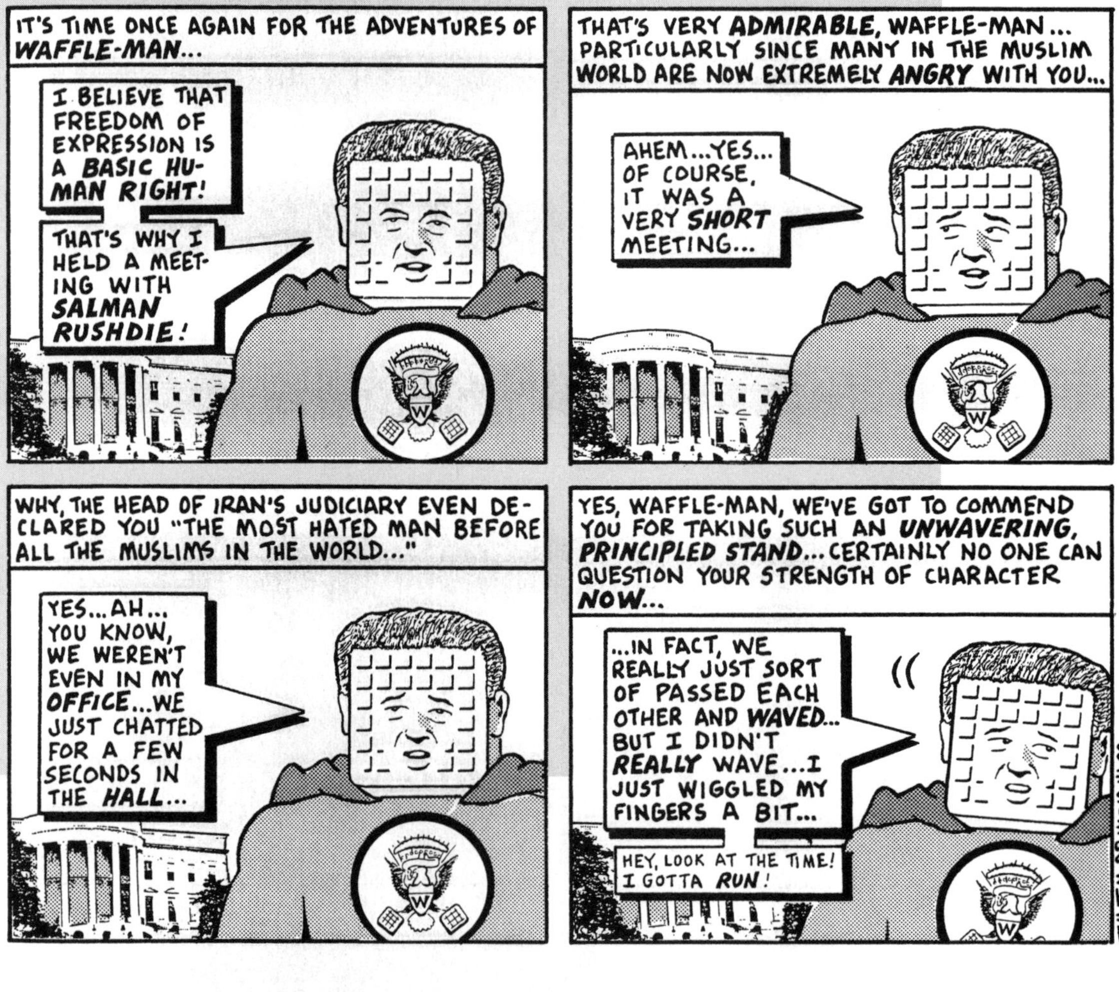
IT'S TIME ONCE AGAIN FOR THE ADVENTURES OF WAFFLE-MAN...
I BELIEVE THAT FREEDOM OF EXPRESSION IS A BASIC HUMAN RIGHT!
THAT'S WHY I HELD A MEETING WITH SALMAN RUSHDIE!
THAT'S VERY ADMIRABLE, WAFFLE-MAN... PARTICULARLY SINCE MANY IN THE MUSLIM WORLD ARE NOW EXTREMELY ANGRY WITH YOU...
AHEM... YES... OF COURSE, IT WAS A VERY SHORT MEETING...
WHY, THE HEAD OF IRAN'S JUDICIARY EVEN DECLARED YOU "THE MOST HATED MAN BEFORE ALL THE MUSLIMS IN THE WORLD..."
YES... AH... YOU KNOW, WE WEREN'T EVEN IN MY OFFICE... WE JUST CHATTED FOR A FEW SECONDS IN THE HALL...
YES, WAFFLE-MAN, WE'VE GOT TO COMMEND YOU FOR TAKING SUCH AN UNWAVERING, PRINCIPLED STAND... CERTAINLY NO ONE CAN QUESTION YOUR STRENGTH OF CHARACTER NOW...
...IN FACT, WE REALLY JUST SORT OF PASSED EACH OTHER AND WAVED... BUT I DIDN'T REALLY WAVE... I JUST WIGGLED MY FINGERS A BIT...
HEY, LOOK AT THE TIME! I GOTTA RUN!
TOM TOMORROW © 12-14-93

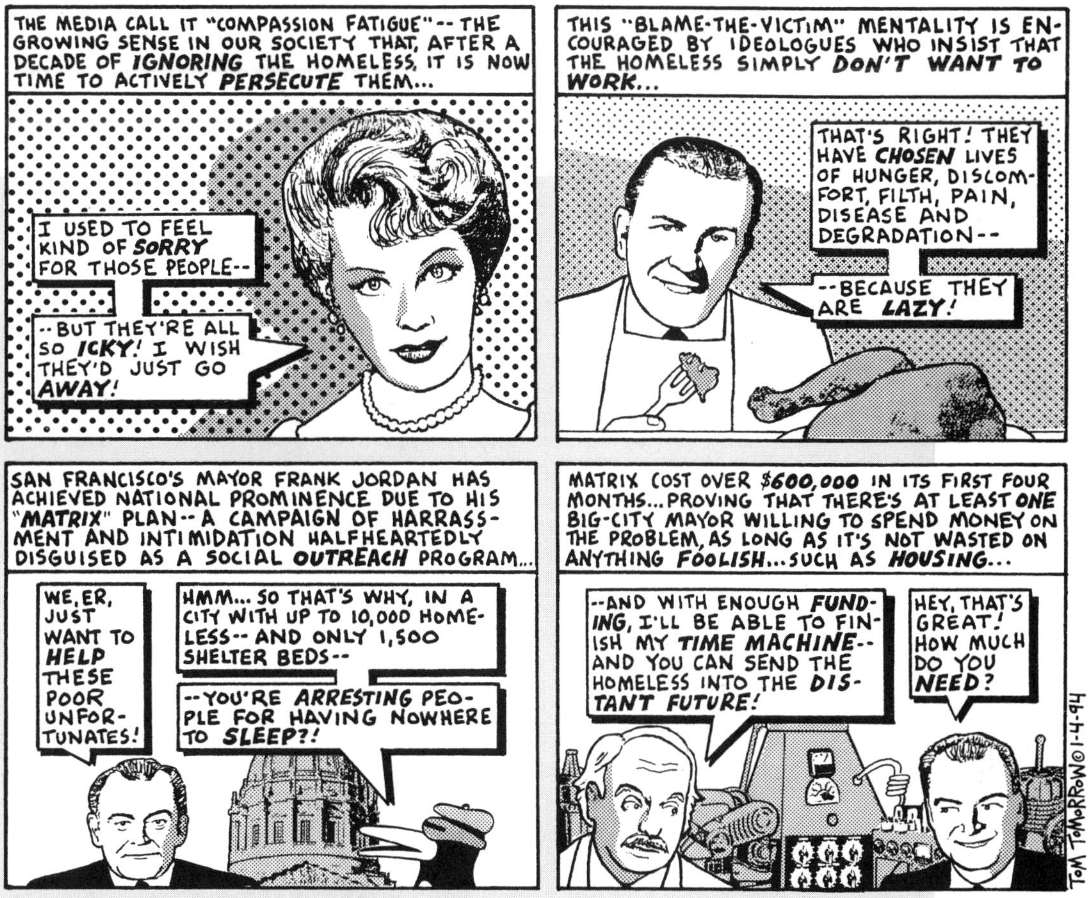
THE MEDIA CALL IT "COMPASSION FATIGUE"-- THE GROWING SENSE IN OUR SOCIETY THAT, AFTER A DECADE OF IGNORING THE HOMELESS, IT IS NOW TIME TO ACTIVELY PERSECUTE THEM...
I USED TO FEEL KIND OF SORRY FOR THOSE PEOPLE--
--BUT THEY'RE ALL SO ICKY! I WISH THEY'D JUST GO AWAY!
THIS "BLAME-THE-VICTIM" MENTALITY IS ENCOURAGED BY IDEOLOGUES WHO INSIST THAT THE HOMELESS SIMPLY DON'T WANT TO WORK...
THAT'S RIGHT! THEY HAVE CHOSEN LIVES OF HUNGER, DISCOMFORT, FILTH, PAIN, DISEASE AND DEGRADATION--
--BECAUSE THEY ARE LAZY!
SAN FRANCISCO'S MAYOR FRANK JORDAN HAS ACHIEVED NATIONAL PROMINENCE DUE TO HIS "MATRIX" PLAN--A CAMPAIGN OF HARRASSMENT AND INTIMIDATION HALFHEARTEDLY DISGUISED AS A SOCIAL OUTREACH PROGRAM...
WE, ER, JUST WANT TO HELP THESE POOR UNFORTUNATES!
HMM... SO THAT'S WHY, IN A CITY WITH UP TO 10,000 HOMELESS-- AND ONLY 1,500 SHELTER BEDS--
--YOU'RE ARRESTING PEOPLE FOR HAVING NOWHERE TO SLEEP?!
MATRIX COST OVER $600,000 IN ITS FIRST FOUR MONTHS...PROVING THAT THERE'S AT LEAST ONE BIG-CITY MAYOR WILLING TO SPEND MONEY ON THE PROBLEM, AS LONG AS IT'S NOT WASTED ON ANYTHING FOOLISH...SUCH AS HOUSING...
--AND WITH ENOUGH FUNDING, I'LL BE ABLE TO FINISH MY TIME MACHINE-- AND YOU CAN SEND THE HOMELESS INTO THE DISTANT FUTURE!
HEY, THAT'S GREAT! HOW MUCH DO YOU NEED?
TOM TOMORROW©1-4-94

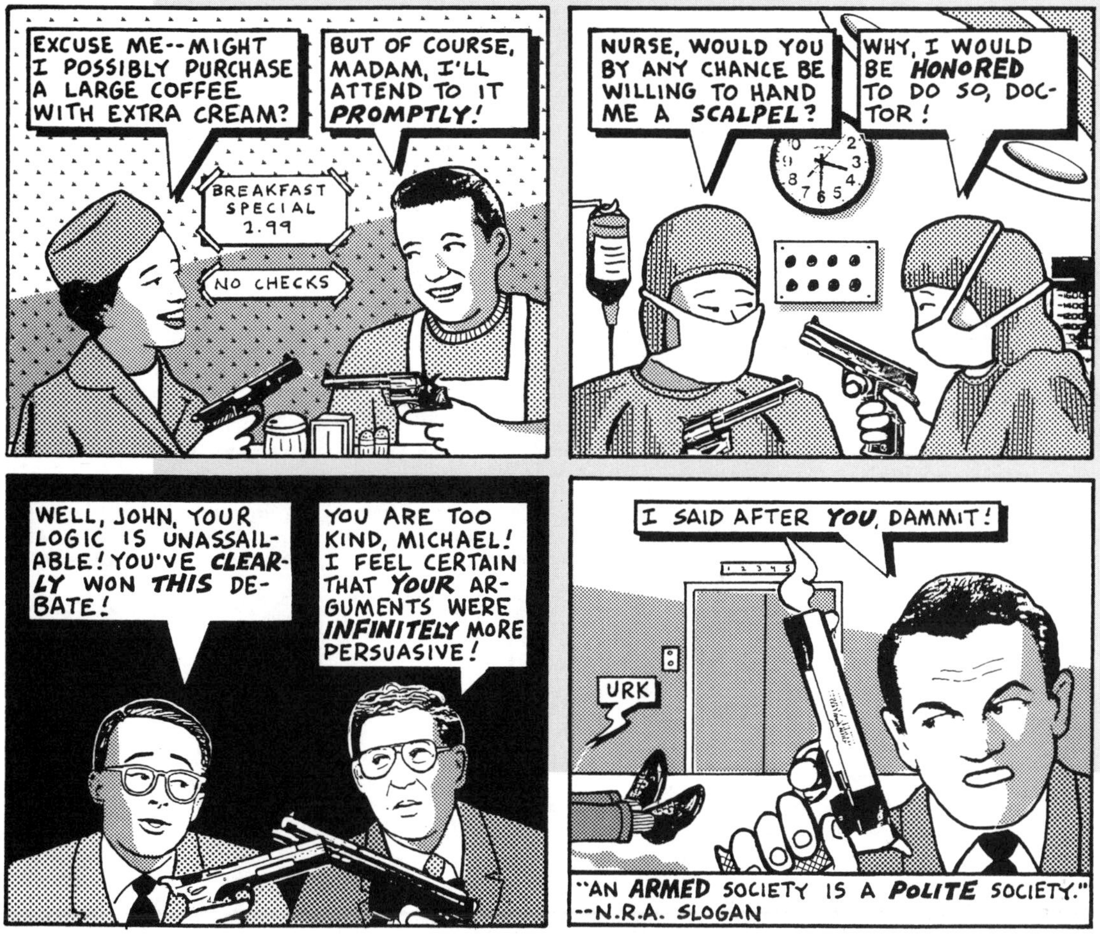
EXCUSE ME--MIGHT I POSSIBLY PURCHASE A LARGE COFFEE WITH EXTRA CREAM?
BUT OF COURSE, MADAM, I'LL ATTEND TO IT PROMPTLY!
BREAKFAST SPECIAL 2.99
NO CHECKS
NURSE, WOULD YOU BY ANY CHANCE BE WILLING TO HAND ME A SCALPEL?
WHY, I WOULD BE HONORED TO DO SO, DOCTOR!
WELL, JOHN, YOUR LOGIC IS UNASSAILABLE! YOU'VE CLEARLY WON THIS DEBATE!
YOU ARE TOO KIND, MICHAEL! I FEEL CERTAIN THAT YOUR ARGUMENTS WERE INFINITELY MORE PERSUASIVE!
I SAID AFTER YOU, DAMMIT!
URK
"AN ARMED SOCIETY IS A POLITE SOCIETY." --N.R.A. SLOGAN

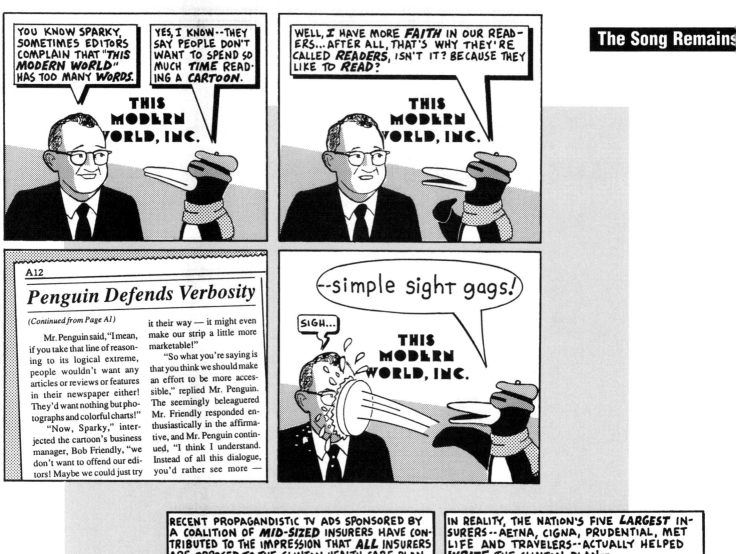

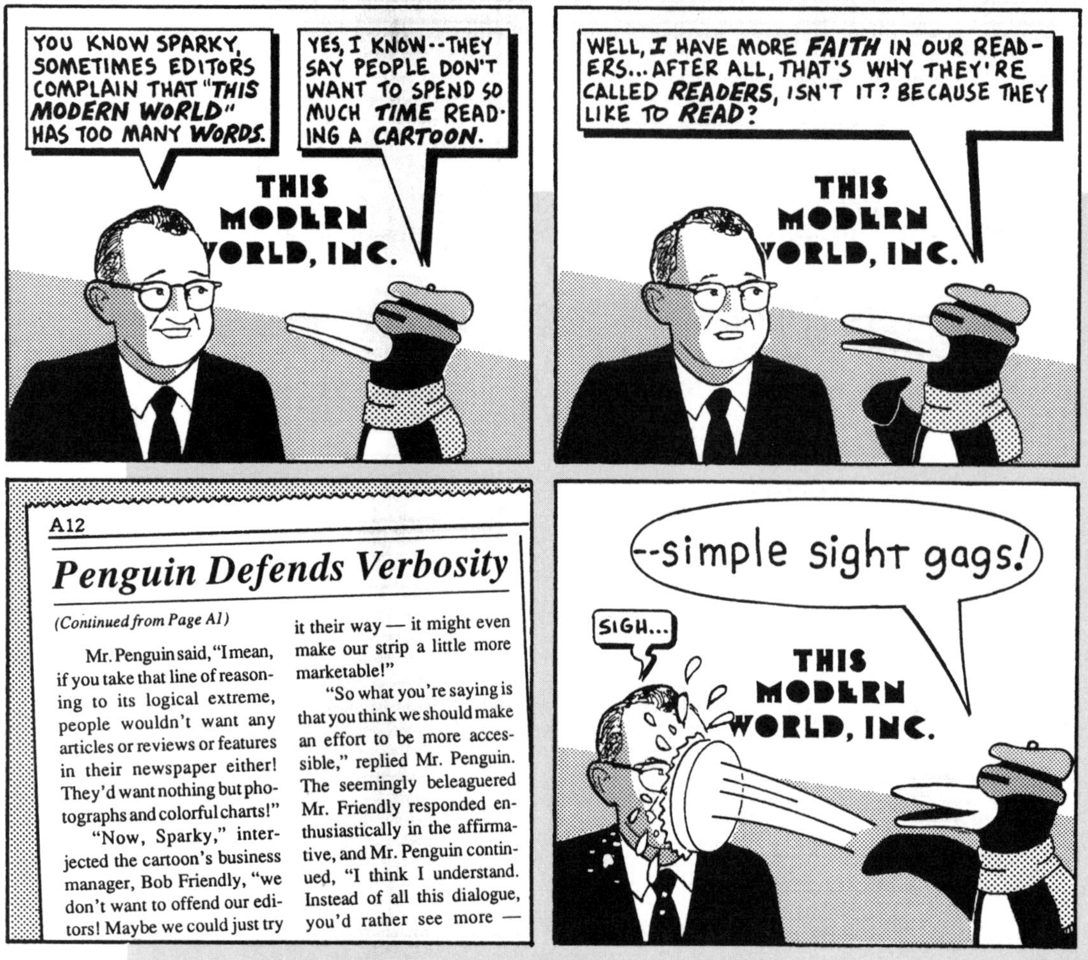
YOU KNOW SPARKY, SOMETIMES EDITORS COMPLAIN THAT "THIS MODERN WORLD" HAS TOO MANY WORDS.
YES, I KNOW--THEY SAY PEOPLE DON'T WANT TO SPEND SO MUCH TIME READING A CARTOON.
THIS MODERN WORLD, INC.
WELL, I HAVE MORE FAITH IN OUR READERS... AFTER ALL, THAT'S WHY THEY'RE CALLED READERS, ISN'T IT? BECAUSE THEY LIKE TO READ?
THIS MODERN WORLD, INC.
A12
Penguin Defends Verbosity
(Continued from Page A1)
Mr. Penguin said, "I mean, if you take that line of reasoning to its logical extreme, people wouldn't want any articles or reviews or features in their newspaper either! They'd want nothing but photographs and colorful charts!"
"Now, Sparky," interjected the cartoon's business manager, Bob Friendly, "we don't want to offend our editors! Maybe we could just try it their way — it might even make our strip a little more marketable!"
"So what you're saying is that you think we should make an effort to be more accessible," replied Mr. Penguin. The seemingly beleaguered Mr. Friendly responded enthusiastically in the affirmative, and Mr. Penguin continued, "I think I understand. Instead of all this dialogue, you'd rather see more —
--simple sight gags!
SIGH...
THIS MODERN WORLD, INC.

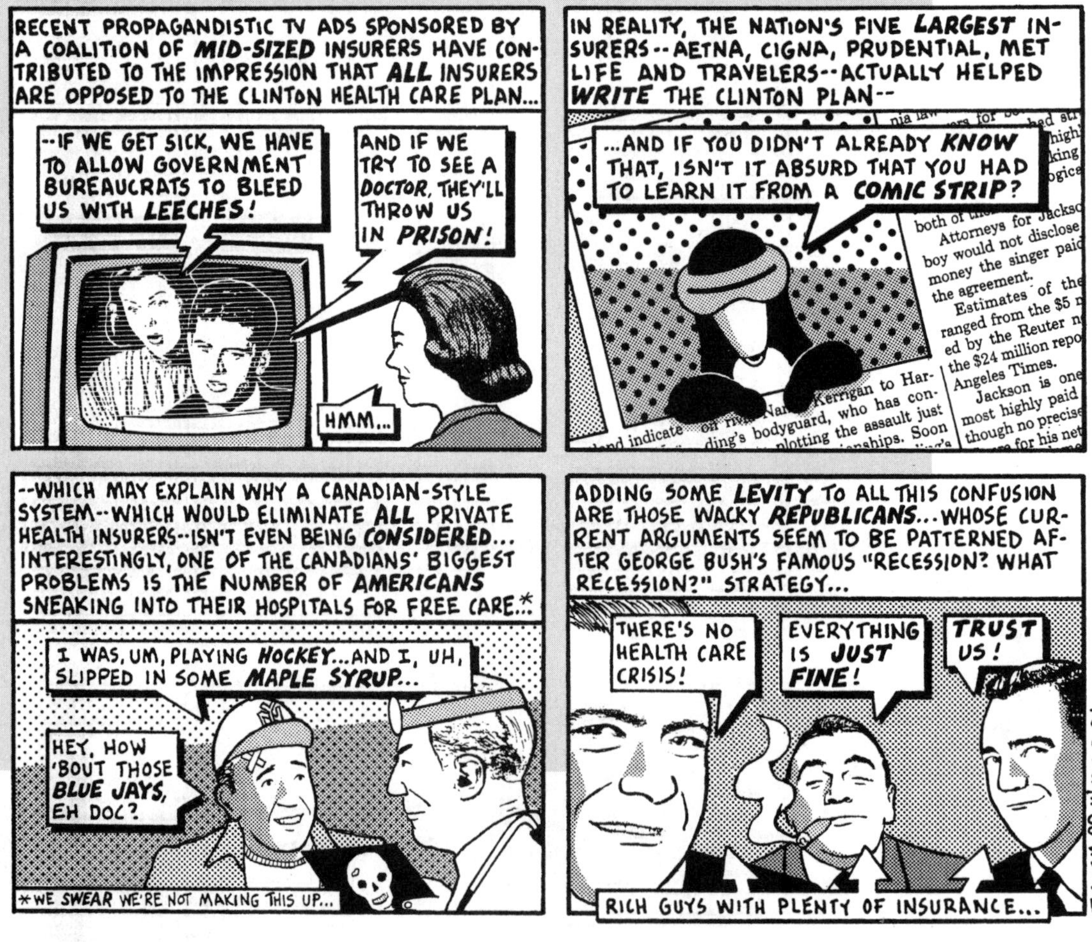
RECENT PROPAGANDISTIC TV ADS SPONSORED BY A COALITION OF MID-SIZED INSURERS HAVE CONTRIBUTED TO THE IMPRESSION THAT ALL INSURERS ARE OPPOSED TO THE CLINTON HEALTH CARE PLAN...
--IF WE GET SICK, WE HAVE TO ALLOW GOVERNMENT BUREAUCRATS TO BLEED US WITH LEECHES!
AND IF WE TRY TO SEE A DOCTOR, THEY'LL THROW US IN PRISON!
HMM...
IN REALITY, THE NATION'S FIVE LARGEST INSURERS--AETNA, CIGNA, PRUDENTIAL, MET LIFE AND TRAVELERS--ACTUALLY HELPED WRITE THE CLINTON PLAN--
...AND IF YOU DIDN'T ALREADY KNOW THAT, ISN'T IT ABSURD THAT YOU HAD TO LEARN IT FROM A COMIC STRIP?
--WHICH MAY EXPLAIN WHY A CANADIAN-STYLE SYSTEM--WHICH WOULD ELIMINATE ALL PRIVATE HEALTH INSURERS--ISN'T EVEN BEING CONSIDERED... INTERESTINGLY, ONE OF THE CANADIANS' BIGGEST PROBLEMS IS THE NUMBER OF AMERICANS SNEAKING INTO THEIR HOSPITALS FOR FREE CARE.*
I WAS, UM, PLAYING HOCKEY... AND I, UH, SLIPPED IN SOME MAPLE SYRUP...
HEY, HOW 'BOUT THOSE BLUE JAYS, EH DOC?
*WE SWEAR WE'RE NOT MAKING THIS UP...
ADDING SOME LEVITY TO ALL THIS CONFUSION ARE THOSE WACKY REPUBLICANS... WHOSE CURRENT ARGUMENTS SEEM TO BE PATTERNED AFTER GEORGE BUSH'S FAMOUS "RECESSION? WHAT RECESSION?" STRATEGY...
THERE'S NO HEALTH CARE CRISIS!
EVERYTHING IS JUST FINE!
TRUST US!
RICH GUYS WITH PLENTY OF INSURANCE...
TOM TOMORROW © 2-8-94

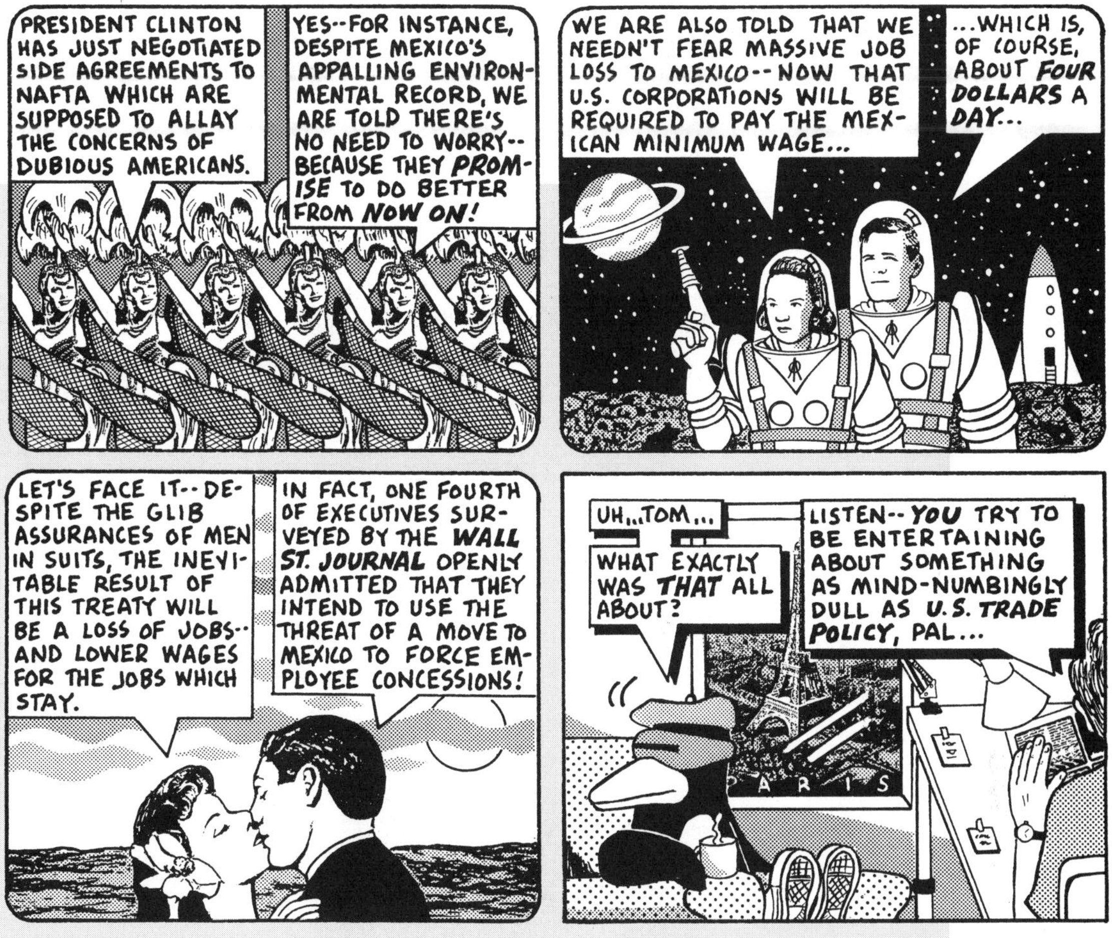
PRESIDENT CLINTON HAS JUST NEGOTIATED SIDE AGREEMENTS TO NAFTA WHICH ARE SUPPOSED TO ALLAY THE CONCERNS OF DUBIOUS AMERICANS.
YES--FOR INSTANCE, DESPITE MEXICO'S APPALLING ENVIRONMENTAL RECORD, WE ARE TOLD THERE'S NO NEED TO WORRY--BECAUSE THEY PROMISE TO DO BETTER FROM NOW ON!
WE ARE ALSO TOLD THAT WE NEEDN'T FEAR MASSIVE JOB LOSS TO MEXICO--NOW THAT U.S. CORPORATIONS WILL BE REQUIRED TO PAY THE MEXICAN MINIMUM WAGE...
...WHICH IS, OF COURSE, ABOUT FOUR DOLLARS A DAY...
LET'S FACE IT--DESPITE THE GLIB ASSURANCES OF MEN IN SUITS, THE INEVITABLE RESULT OF THIS TREATY WILL BE A LOSS OF JOBS--AND LOWER WAGES FOR THE JOBS WHICH STAY.
IN FACT, ONE FOURTH OF EXECUTIVES SURVEYED BY THE WALL ST. JOURNAL OPENLY ADMITTED THAT THEY INTEND TO USE THE THREAT OF A MOVE TO MEXICO TO FORCE EMPLOYEE CONCESSIONS!
UH...TOM...
WHAT EXACTLY WAS THAT ALL ABOUT?
LISTEN--YOU TRY TO BE ENTERTAINING ABOUT SOMETHING AS MIND-NUMBINGLY DULL AS U.S. TRADE POLICY, PAL...
PARIS

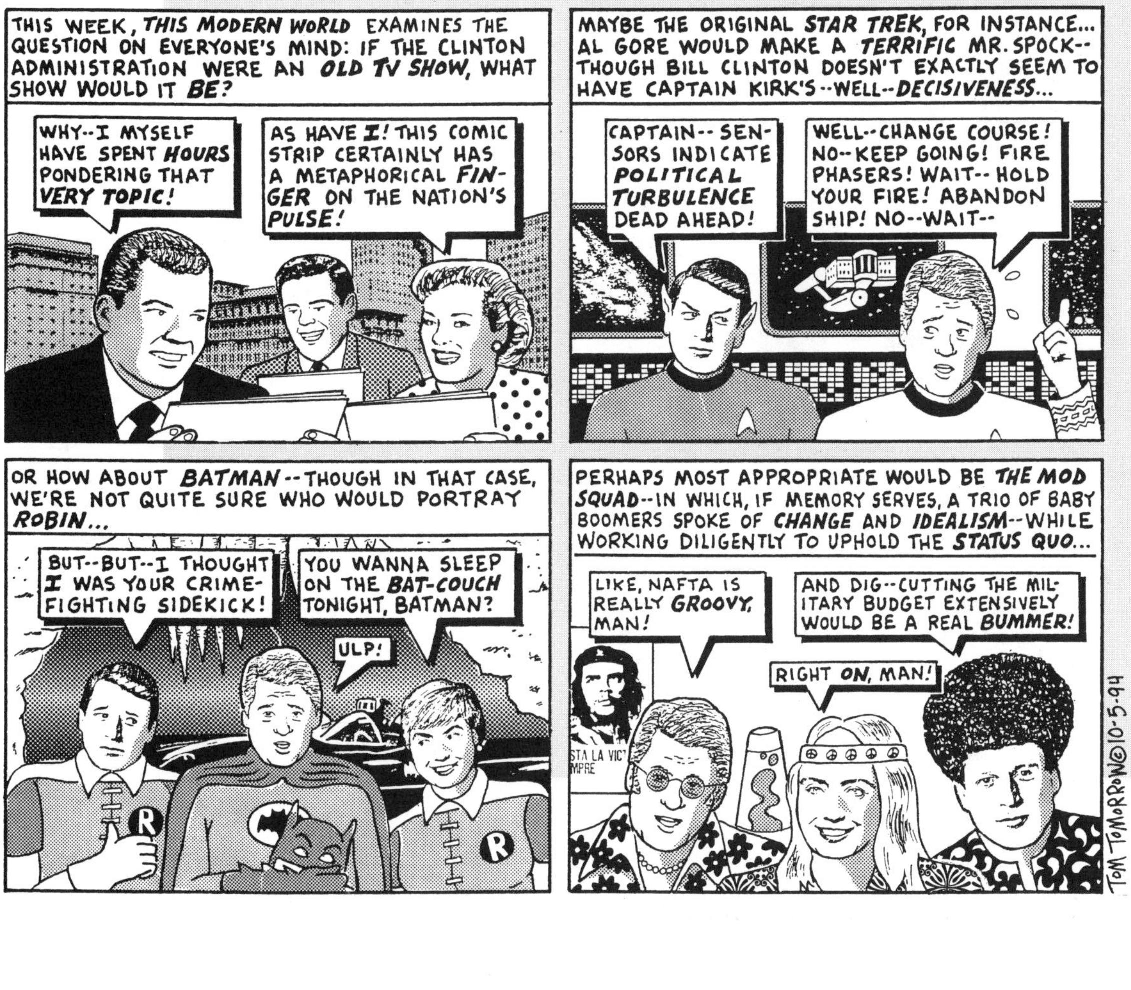
THIS WEEK, THIS MODERN WORLD EXAMINES THE QUESTION ON EVERYONE'S MIND: IF THE CLINTON ADMINISTRATION WERE AN OLD TV SHOW, WHAT SHOW WOULD IT BE?
WHY--I MYSELF HAVE SPENT HOURS PONDERING THAT VERY TOPIC!
AS HAVE I! THIS COMIC STRIP CERTAINLY HAS A METAPHORICAL FINGER ON THE NATION'S PULSE!
MAYBE THE ORIGINAL STAR TREK, FOR INSTANCE... AL GORE WOULD MAKE A TERRIFIC MR. SPOCK--THOUGH BILL CLINTON DOESN'T EXACTLY SEEM TO HAVE CAPTAIN KIRK'S--WELL--DECISIVENESS...
CAPTAIN--SENSORS INDICATE POLITICAL TURBULENCE DEAD AHEAD!
WELL--CHANGE COURSE! NO--KEEP GOING! FIRE PHASERS! WAIT--HOLD YOUR FIRE! ABANDON SHIP! NO--WAIT--
OR HOW ABOUT BATMAN--THOUGH IN THAT CASE, WE'RE NOT QUITE SURE WHO WOULD PORTRAY ROBIN...
BUT--BUT--I THOUGHT I WAS YOUR CRIME-FIGHTING SIDEKICK!
YOU WANNA SLEEP ON THE BAT-COUCH TONIGHT, BATMAN?
ULP!
PERHAPS MOST APPROPRIATE WOULD BE THE MOD SQUAD--IN WHICH, IF MEMORY SERVES, A TRIO OF BABY BOOMERS SPOKE OF CHANGE AND IDEALISM--WHILE WORKING DILIGENTLY TO UPHOLD THE STATUS QUO...
LIKE, NAFTA IS REALLY GROOVY, MAN!
AND DIG--CUTTING THE MILITARY BUDGET EXTENSIVELY WOULD BE A REAL BUMMER!
RIGHT ON, MAN!
TOM TOMORROW©10-5-94

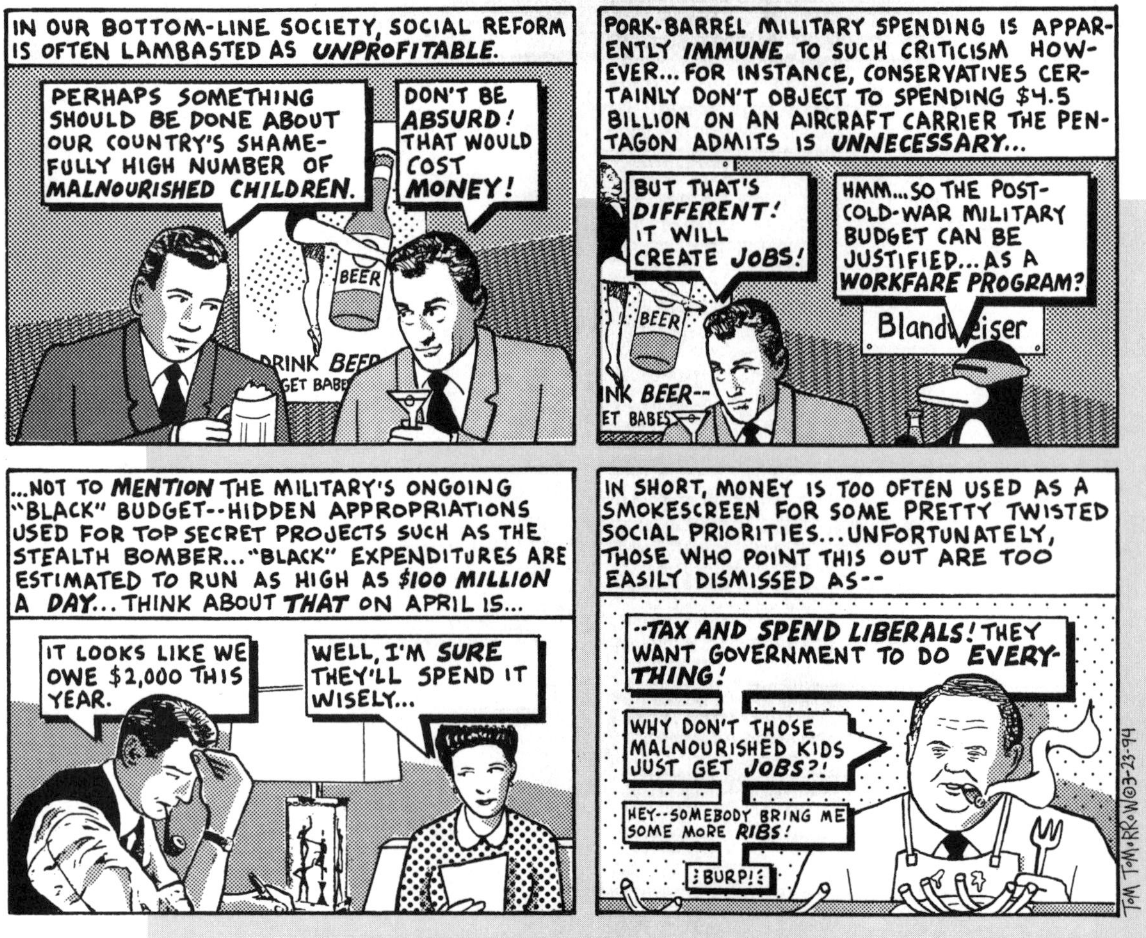
IN OUR BOTTOM-LINE SOCIETY, SOCIAL REFORM IS OFTEN LAMBASTED AS UNPROFITABLE.
PERHAPS SOMETHING SHOULD BE DONE ABOUT OUR COUNTRY'S SHAMEFULLY HIGH NUMBER OF MALNOURISHED CHILDREN.
DON'T BE ABSURD! THAT WOULD COST MONEY!
BEER
DRINK BEER
GET BABE
PORK-BARREL MILITARY SPENDING IS APPARENTLY IMMUNE TO SUCH CRITICISM HOWEVER... FOR INSTANCE, CONSERVATIVES CERTAINLY DON'T OBJECT TO SPENDING $4.5 BILLION ON AN AIRCRAFT CARRIER THE PENTAGON ADMITS IS UNNECESSARY...
BUT THAT'S DIFFERENT! IT WILL CREATE JOBS!
HMM... SO THE POST-COLD-WAR MILITARY BUDGET CAN BE JUSTIFIED... AS A WORKFARE PROGRAM?
Blandweiser
BEER
NK BEER--
ET BABES
...NOT TO MENTION THE MILITARY'S ONGOING "BLACK" BUDGET--HIDDEN APPROPRIATIONS USED FOR TOP SECRET PROJECTS SUCH AS THE STEALTH BOMBER... "BLACK" EXPENDITURES ARE ESTIMATED TO RUN AS HIGH AS $100 MILLION A DAY... THINK ABOUT THAT ON APRIL 15...
IT LOOKS LIKE WE OWE $2,000 THIS YEAR.
WELL, I'M SURE THEY'LL SPEND IT WISELY...
IN SHORT, MONEY IS TOO OFTEN USED AS A SMOKESCREEN FOR SOME PRETTY TWISTED SOCIAL PRIORITIES... UNFORTUNATELY, THOSE WHO POINT THIS OUT ARE TOO EASILY DISMISSED AS--
--TAX AND SPEND LIBERALS! THEY WANT GOVERNMENT TO DO EVERYTHING!
WHY DON'T THOSE MALNOURISHED KIDS JUST GET JOBS?!
HEY--SOMEBODY BRING ME SOME MORE RIBS!
BURP!
TOM TOMORROW©3-23-94

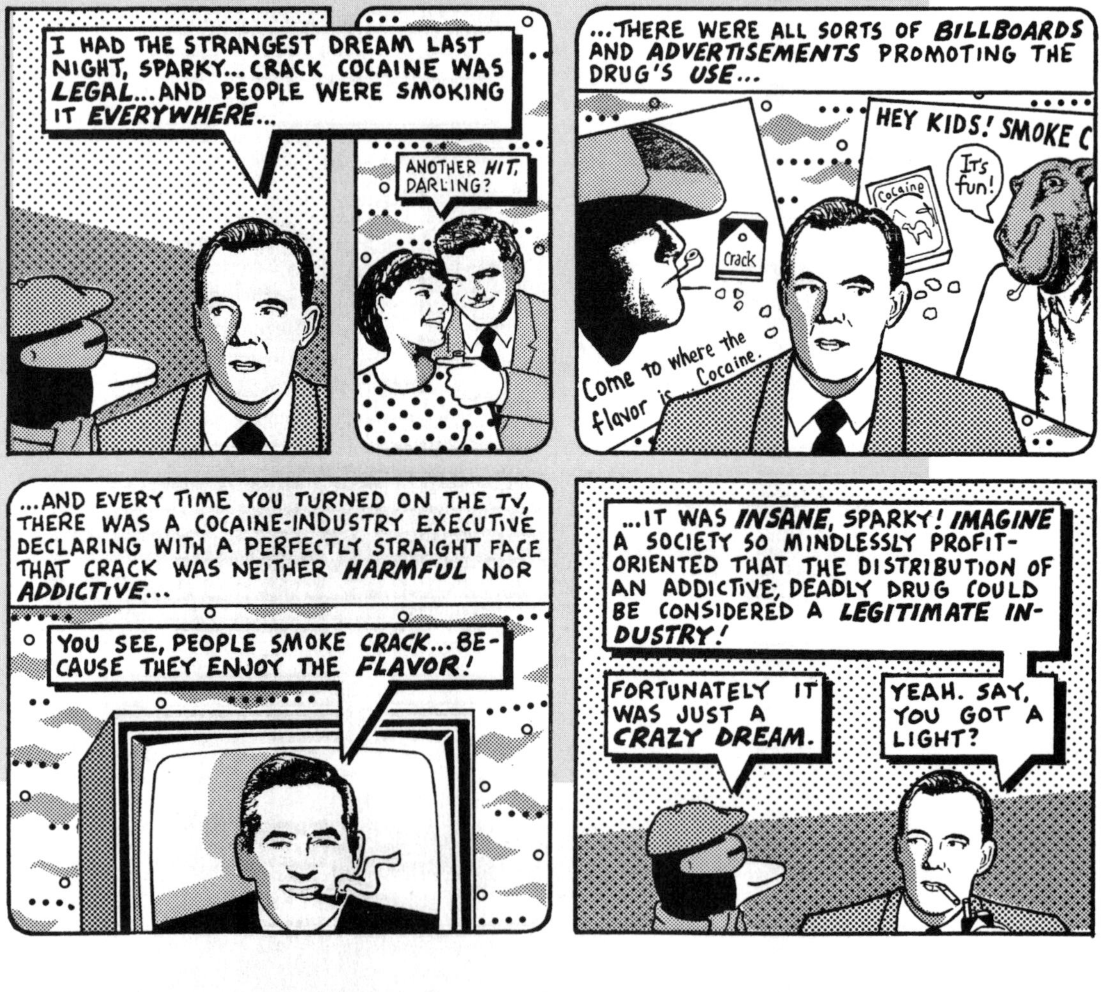
I HAD THE STRANGEST DREAM LAST NIGHT, SPARKY... CRACK COCAINE WAS LEGAL... AND PEOPLE WERE SMOKING IT EVERYWHERE...
ANOTHER HIT, DARLING?
...THERE WERE ALL SORTS OF BILLBOARDS AND ADVERTISEMENTS PROMOTING THE DRUG'S USE...
HEY KIDS! SMOKE C
It's fun!
Cocaine
Crack
Come to where the flavor is... Cocaine.
...AND EVERY TIME YOU TURNED ON THE TV, THERE WAS A COCAINE-INDUSTRY EXECUTIVE DECLARING WITH A PERFECTLY STRAIGHT FACE THAT CRACK WAS NEITHER HARMFUL NOR ADDICTIVE...
YOU SEE, PEOPLE SMOKE CRACK... BECAUSE THEY ENJOY THE FLAVOR!
...IT WAS INSANE, SPARKY! IMAGINE A SOCIETY SO MINDLESSLY PROFIT-ORIENTED THAT THE DISTRIBUTION OF AN ADDICTIVE, DEADLY DRUG COULD BE CONSIDERED A LEGITIMATE INDUSTRY!
FORTUNATELY IT WAS JUST A CRAZY DREAM.
YEAH. SAY, YOU GOT A LIGHT?

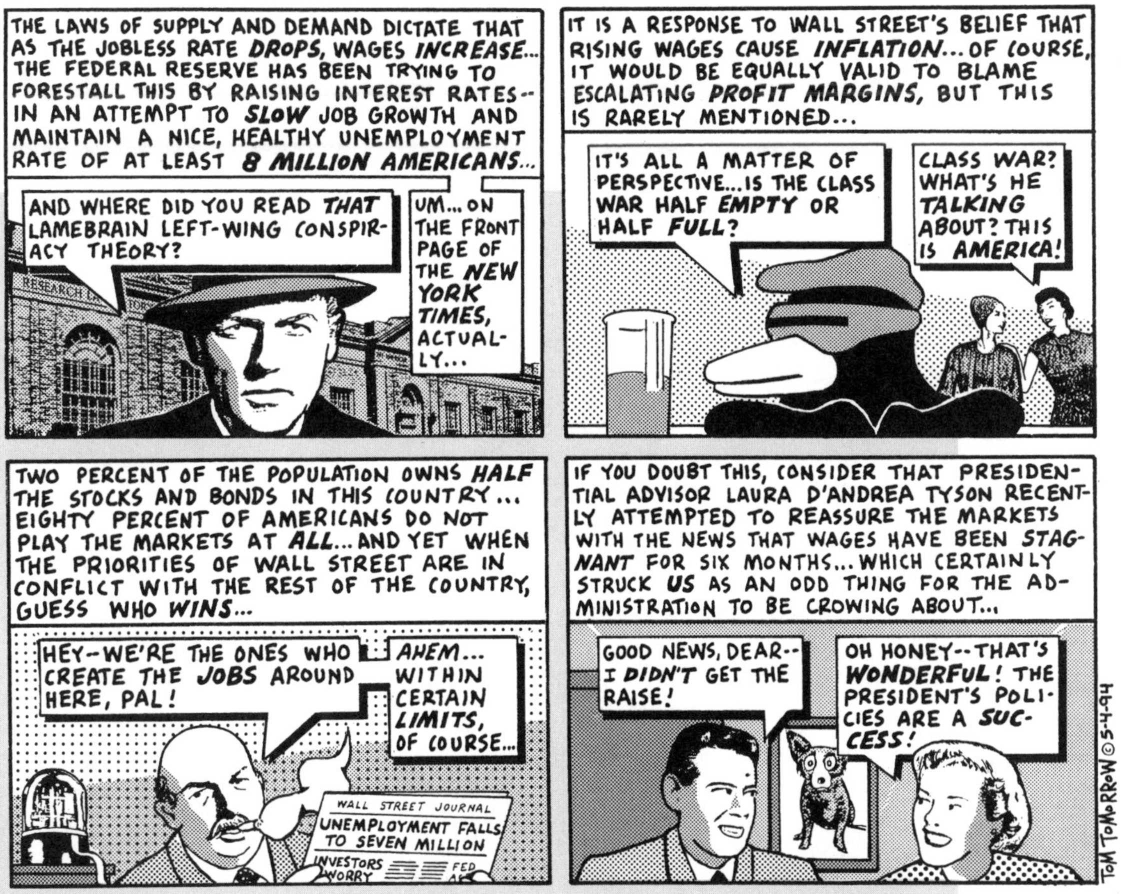
THE LAWS OF SUPPLY AND DEMAND DICTATE THAT AS THE JOBLESS RATE DROPS, WAGES INCREASE... THE FEDERAL RESERVE HAS BEEN TRYING TO FORESTALL THIS BY RAISING INTEREST RATES-- IN AN ATTEMPT TO SLOW JOB GROWTH AND MAINTAIN A NICE, HEALTHY UNEMPLOYMENT RATE OF AT LEAST 8 MILLION AMERICANS...
AND WHERE DID YOU READ THAT LAMEBRAIN LEFT-WING CONSPIRACY THEORY?
UM... ON THE FRONT PAGE OF THE NEW YORK TIMES, ACTUALLY...
IT IS A RESPONSE TO WALL STREET'S BELIEF THAT RISING WAGES CAUSE INFLATION... OF COURSE, IT WOULD BE EQUALLY VALID TO BLAME ESCALATING PROFIT MARGINS, BUT THIS IS RARELY MENTIONED...
IT'S ALL A MATTER OF PERSPECTIVE... IS THE CLASS WAR HALF EMPTY OR HALF FULL?
CLASS WAR? WHAT'S HE TALKING ABOUT? THIS IS AMERICA!
TWO PERCENT OF THE POPULATION OWNS HALF THE STOCKS AND BONDS IN THIS COUNTRY... EIGHTY PERCENT OF AMERICANS DO NOT PLAY THE MARKETS AT ALL... AND YET WHEN THE PRIORITIES OF WALL STREET ARE IN CONFLICT WITH THE REST OF THE COUNTRY, GUESS WHO WINS...
HEY--WE'RE THE ONES WHO CREATE THE JOBS AROUND HERE, PAL!
AHEM... WITHIN CERTAIN LIMITS, OF COURSE...
WALL STREET JOURNAL
UNEMPLOYMENT FALLS TO SEVEN MILLION
INVESTORS WORRY
FED
IF YOU DOUBT THIS, CONSIDER THAT PRESIDENTIAL ADVISOR LAURA D'ANDREA TYSON RECENTLY ATTEMPTED TO REASSURE THE MARKETS WITH THE NEWS THAT WAGES HAVE BEEN STAGNANT FOR SIX MONTHS... WHICH CERTAINLY STRUCK US AS AN ODD THING FOR THE ADMINISTRATION TO BE CROWING ABOUT...
GOOD NEWS, DEAR-- I DIDN'T GET THE RAISE!
OH HONEY--THAT'S WONDERFUL! THE PRESIDENT'S POLICIES ARE A SUCCESS!
TOM TOMORROW ©5-4-94

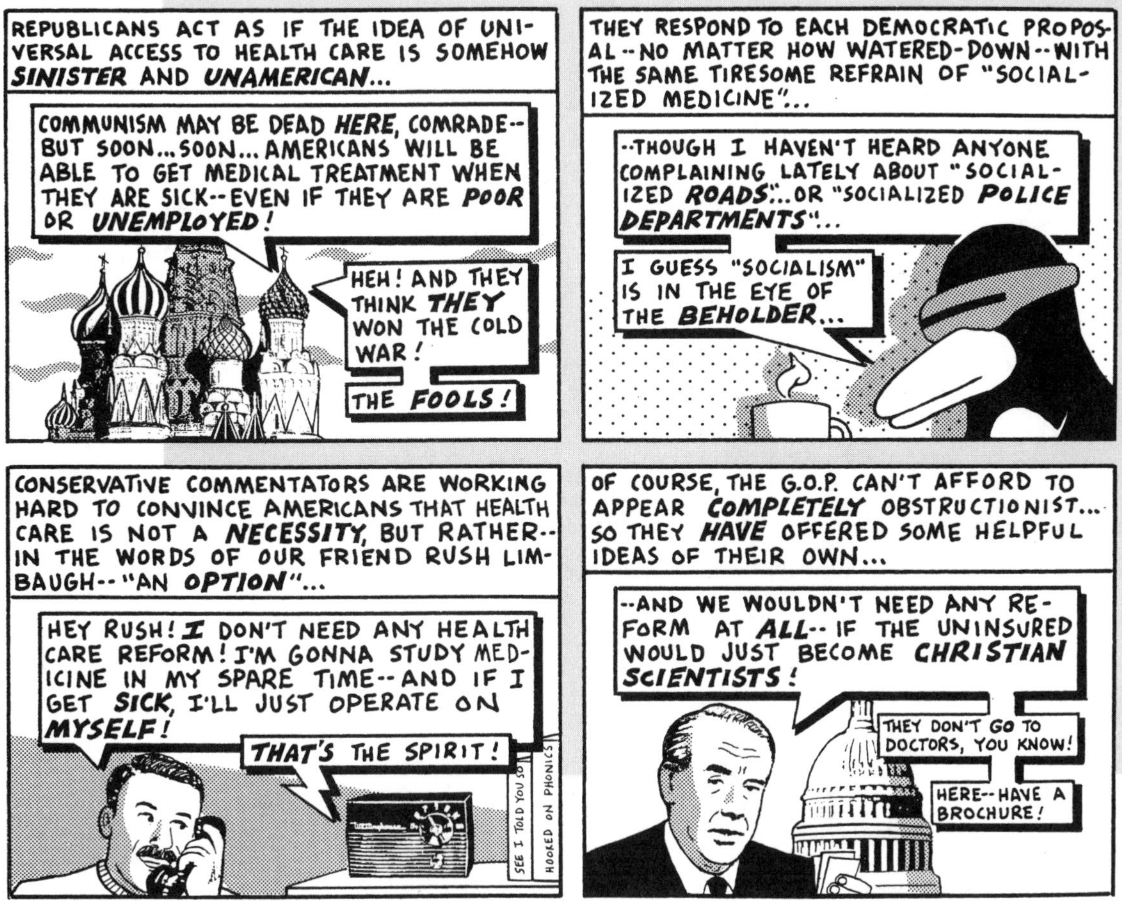
REPUBLICANS ACT AS IF THE IDEA OF UNIVERSAL ACCESS TO HEALTH CARE IS SOMEHOW SINISTER AND UNAMERICAN...
COMMUNISM MAY BE DEAD HERE, COMRADE-- BUT SOON... SOON... AMERICANS WILL BE ABLE TO GET MEDICAL TREATMENT WHEN THEY ARE SICK--EVEN IF THEY ARE POOR OR UNEMPLOYED!
HEH! AND THEY THINK THEY WON THE COLD WAR!
THE FOOLS!
THEY RESPOND TO EACH DEMOCRATIC PROPOSAL--NO MATTER HOW WATERED-DOWN--WITH THE SAME TIRESOME REFRAIN OF "SOCIALIZED MEDICINE"...
--THOUGH I HAVEN'T HEARD ANYONE COMPLAINING LATELY ABOUT "SOCIALIZED ROADS"... OR "SOCIALIZED POLICE DEPARTMENTS"...
I GUESS "SOCIALISM" IS IN THE EYE OF THE BEHOLDER...
CONSERVATIVE COMMENTATORS ARE WORKING HARD TO CONVINCE AMERICANS THAT HEALTH CARE IS NOT A NECESSITY, BUT RATHER-- IN THE WORDS OF OUR FRIEND RUSH LIMBAUGH--"AN OPTION"...
HEY RUSH! I DON'T NEED ANY HEALTH CARE REFORM! I'M GONNA STUDY MEDICINE IN MY SPARE TIME--AND IF I GET SICK, I'LL JUST OPERATE ON MYSELF!
THAT'S THE SPIRIT!
SEE I TOLD YOU SO
HOOKED ON PHONICS
OF COURSE, THE G.O.P. CAN'T AFFORD TO APPEAR COMPLETELY OBSTRUCTIONIST... SO THEY HAVE OFFERED SOME HELPFUL IDEAS OF THEIR OWN...
--AND WE WOULDN'T NEED ANY REFORM AT ALL--IF THE UNINSURED WOULD JUST BECOME CHRISTIAN SCIENTISTS!
THEY DON'T GO TO DOCTORS, YOU KNOW!
HERE--HAVE A BROCHURE!

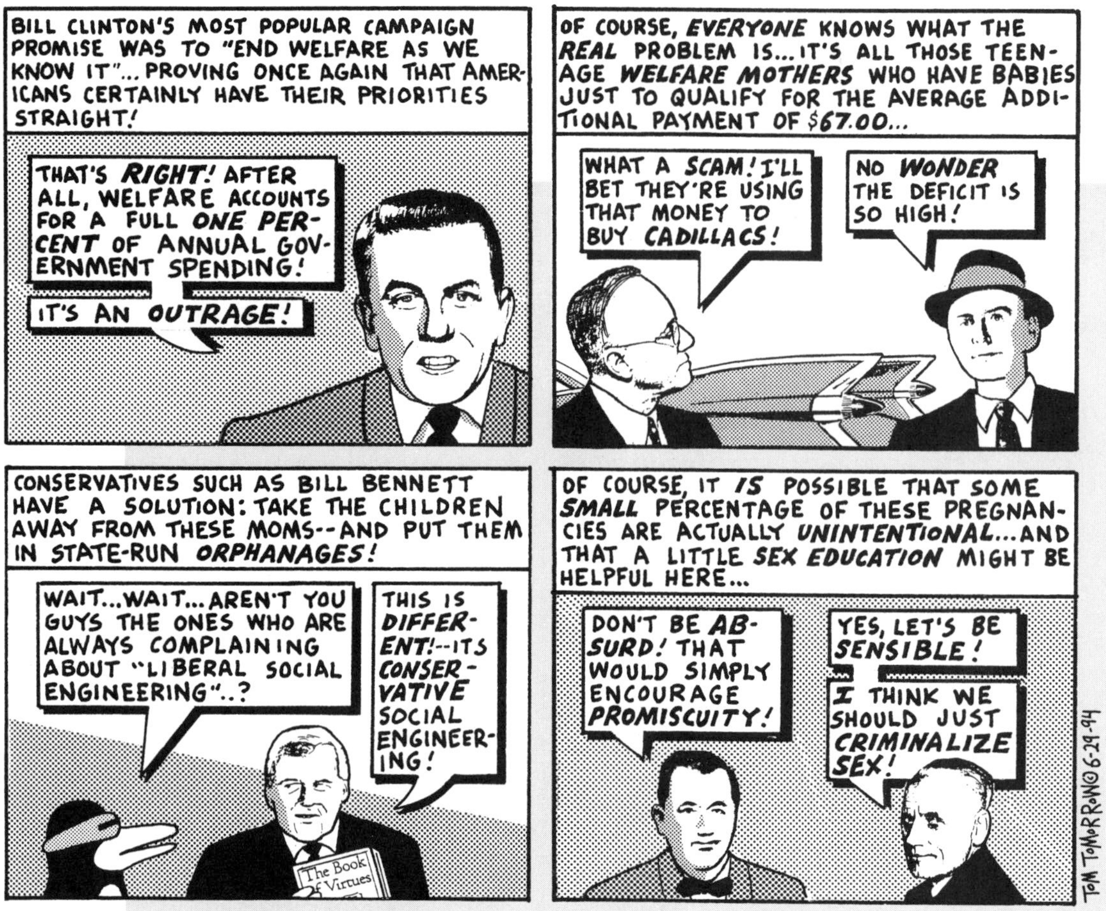
BILL CLINTON'S MOST POPULAR CAMPAIGN PROMISE WAS TO "END WELFARE AS WE KNOW IT"... PROVING ONCE AGAIN THAT AMERICANS CERTAINLY HAVE THEIR PRIORITIES STRAIGHT!
THAT'S RIGHT! AFTER ALL, WELFARE ACCOUNTS FOR A FULL ONE PERCENT OF ANNUAL GOVERNMENT SPENDING!
IT'S AN OUTRAGE!
OF COURSE, EVERYONE KNOWS WHAT THE REAL PROBLEM IS... IT'S ALL THOSE TEENAGE WELFARE MOTHERS WHO HAVE BABIES JUST TO QUALIFY FOR THE AVERAGE ADDITIONAL PAYMENT OF $67.00...
WHAT A SCAM! I'LL BET THEY'RE USING THAT MONEY TO BUY CADILLACS!
NO WONDER THE DEFICIT IS SO HIGH!
CONSERVATIVES SUCH AS BILL BENNETT HAVE A SOLUTION: TAKE THE CHILDREN AWAY FROM THESE MOMS--AND PUT THEM IN STATE-RUN ORPHANAGES!
WAIT...WAIT... AREN'T YOU GUYS THE ONES WHO ARE ALWAYS COMPLAINING ABOUT "LIBERAL SOCIAL ENGINEERING"..?
THIS IS DIFFERENT!--ITS CONSERVATIVE SOCIAL ENGINEERING!
The Book of Virtues
OF COURSE, IT IS POSSIBLE THAT SOME SMALL PERCENTAGE OF THESE PREGNANCIES ARE ACTUALLY UNINTENTIONAL...AND THAT A LITTLE SEX EDUCATION MIGHT BE HELPFUL HERE...
DON'T BE ABSURD! THAT WOULD SIMPLY ENCOURAGE PROMISCUITY!
YES, LET'S BE SENSIBLE!
I THINK WE SHOULD JUST CRIMINALIZE SEX!
TOM TOMORROW©6-29-94

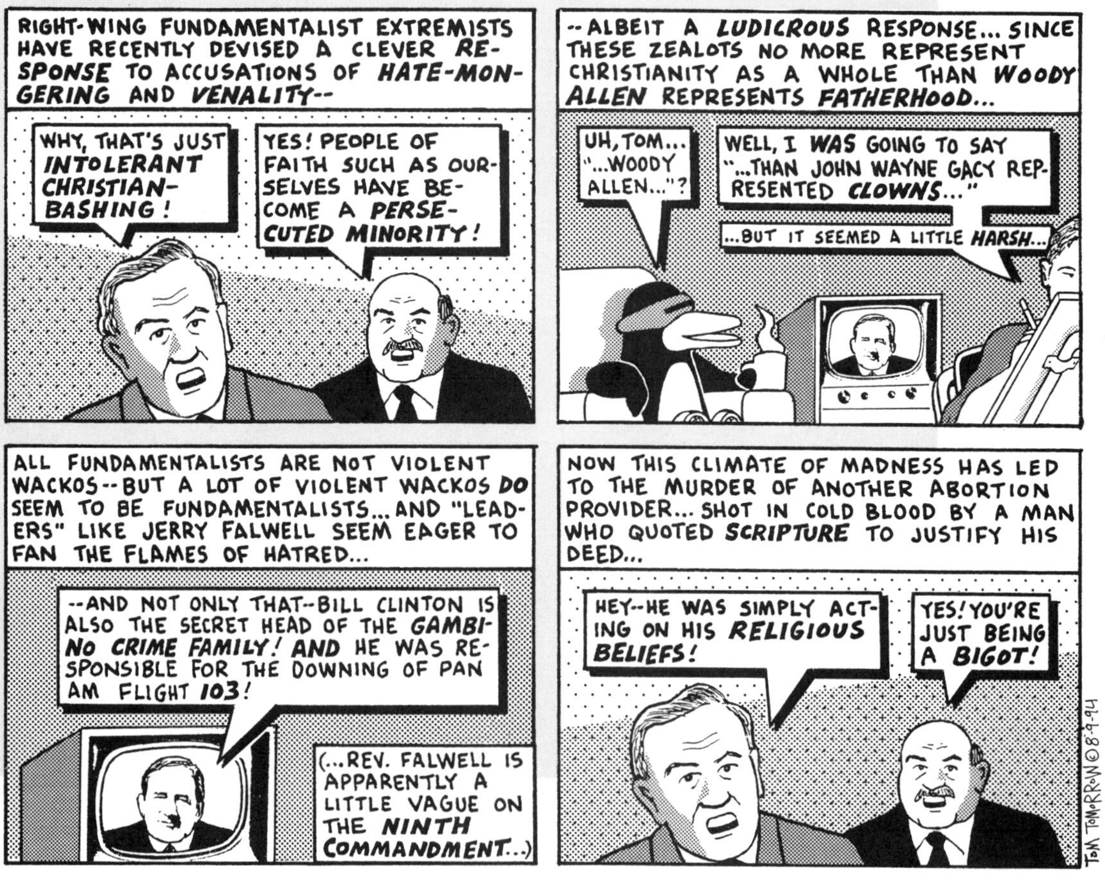
RIGHT-WING FUNDAMENTALIST EXTREMISTS HAVE RECENTLY DEVISED A CLEVER RESPONSE TO ACCUSATIONS OF HATE-MONGERING AND VENALITY--
WHY, THAT'S JUST INTOLERANT CHRISTIAN-BASHING!
YES! PEOPLE OF FAITH SUCH AS OURSELVES HAVE BECOME A PERSECUTED MINORITY!
--ALBEIT A LUDICROUS RESPONSE... SINCE THESE ZEALOTS NO MORE REPRESENT CHRISTIANITY AS A WHOLE THAN WOODY ALLEN REPRESENTS FATHERHOOD...
UH, TOM... "...WOODY ALLEN..."?
WELL, I WAS GOING TO SAY "...THAN JOHN WAYNE GACY REPRESENTED CLOWNS..."
...BUT IT SEEMED A LITTLE HARSH...
ALL FUNDAMENTALISTS ARE NOT VIOLENT WACKOS--BUT A LOT OF VIOLENT WACKOS DO SEEM TO BE FUNDAMENTALISTS... AND "LEADERS" LIKE JERRY FALWELL SEEM EAGER TO FAN THE FLAMES OF HATRED...
--AND NOT ONLY THAT--BILL CLINTON IS ALSO THE SECRET HEAD OF THE GAMBINO CRIME FAMILY! AND HE WAS RESPONSIBLE FOR THE DOWNING OF PAN AM FLIGHT 103!
(...REV. FALWELL IS APPARENTLY A LITTLE VAGUE ON THE NINTH COMMANDMENT...)
NOW THIS CLIMATE OF MADNESS HAS LED TO THE MURDER OF ANOTHER ABORTION PROVIDER... SHOT IN COLD BLOOD BY A MAN WHO QUOTED SCRIPTURE TO JUSTIFY HIS DEED...
HEY--HE WAS SIMPLY ACTING ON HIS RELIGIOUS BELIEFS!
YES! YOU'RE JUST BEING A BIGOT!
TOM TOMORROW©8-9-94

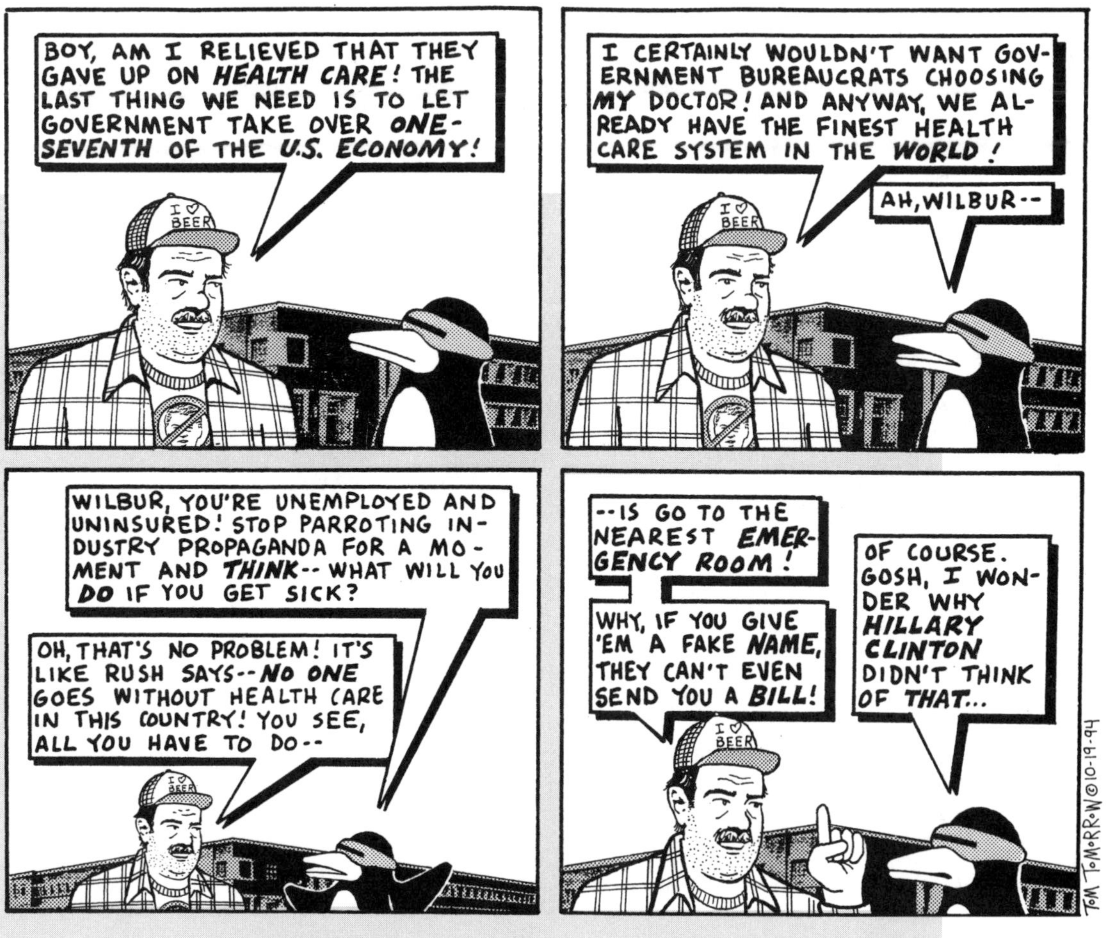
BOY, AM I RELIEVED THAT THEY GAVE UP ON HEALTH CARE! THE LAST THING WE NEED IS TO LET GOVERNMENT TAKE OVER ONE-SEVENTH OF THE U.S. ECONOMY!
I ♡ BEER
I CERTAINLY WOULDN'T WANT GOVERNMENT BUREAUCRATS CHOOSING MY DOCTOR! AND ANYWAY, WE ALREADY HAVE THE FINEST HEALTH CARE SYSTEM IN THE WORLD!
AH, WILBUR--
WILBUR, YOU'RE UNEMPLOYED AND UNINSURED! STOP PARROTING INDUSTRY PROPAGANDA FOR A MOMENT AND THINK-- WHAT WILL YOU DO IF YOU GET SICK?
OH, THAT'S NO PROBLEM! IT'S LIKE RUSH SAYS--NO ONE GOES WITHOUT HEALTH CARE IN THIS COUNTRY! YOU SEE, ALL YOU HAVE TO DO--
--IS GO TO THE NEAREST EMERGENCY ROOM!
WHY, IF YOU GIVE 'EM A FAKE NAME, THEY CAN'T EVEN SEND YOU A BILL!
OF COURSE. GOSH, I WONDER WHY HILLARY CLINTON DIDN'T THINK OF THAT...
TOM TOMORROW ©10-19-94

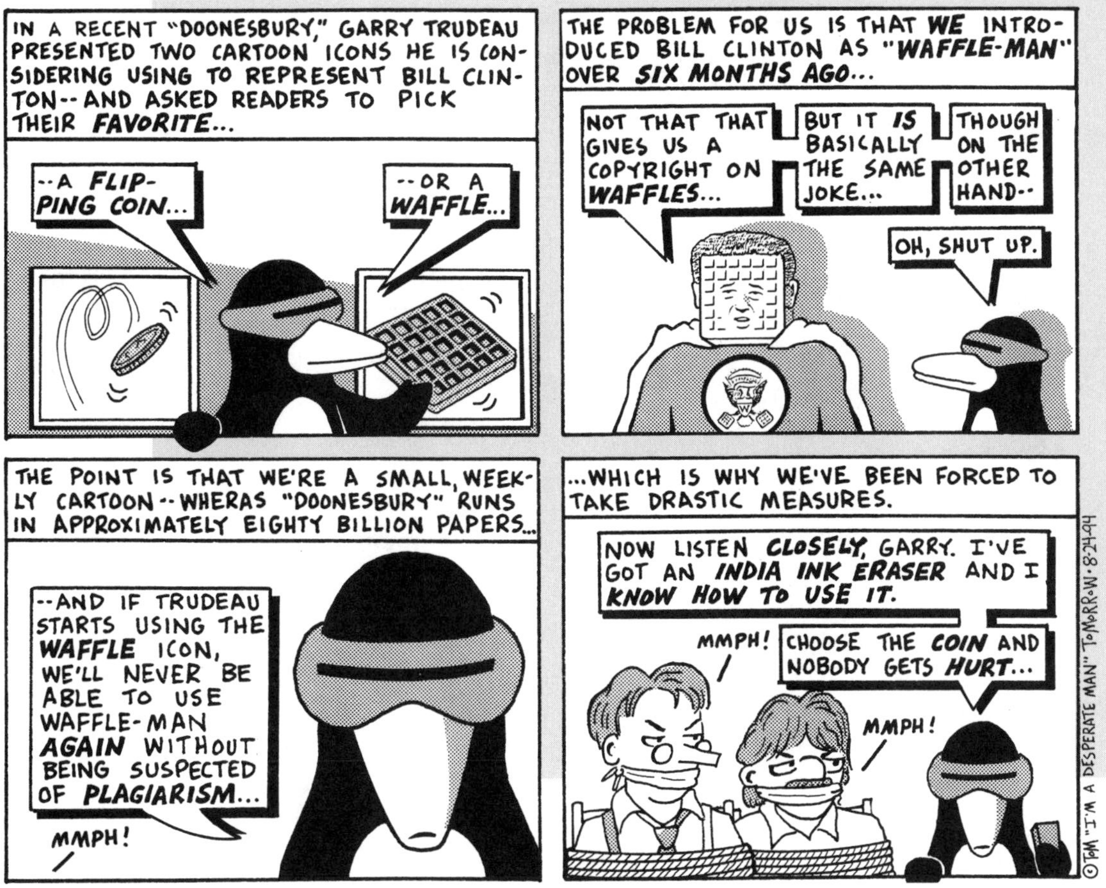
IN A RECENT "DOONESBURY," GARRY TRUDEAU PRESENTED TWO CARTOON ICONS HE IS CONSIDERING USING TO REPRESENT BILL CLINTON--AND ASKED READERS TO PICK THEIR FAVORITE...
--A FLIPPING COIN...
--OR A WAFFLE...
THE PROBLEM FOR US IS THAT WE INTRODUCED BILL CLINTON AS "WAFFLE-MAN" OVER SIX MONTHS AGO...
NOT THAT THAT GIVES US A COPYRIGHT ON WAFFLES...
BUT IT IS BASICALLY THE SAME JOKE...
THOUGH ON THE OTHER HAND--
OH, SHUT UP.
THE POINT IS THAT WE'RE A SMALL, WEEKLY CARTOON--WHERAS "DOONESBURY" RUNS IN APPROXIMATELY EIGHTY BILLION PAPERS...
--AND IF TRUDEAU STARTS USING THE WAFFLE ICON, WE'LL NEVER BE ABLE TO USE WAFFLE-MAN AGAIN WITHOUT BEING SUSPECTED OF PLAGIARISM...
MMPH!
...WHICH IS WHY WE'VE BEEN FORCED TO TAKE DRASTIC MEASURES.
NOW LISTEN CLOSELY, GARRY. I'VE GOT AN INDIA INK ERASER AND I KNOW HOW TO USE IT.
MMPH!
CHOOSE THE COIN AND NOBODY GETS HURT...
MMPH!
©TOM "I'M A DESPERATE MAN" TOMORROW 8-24-94

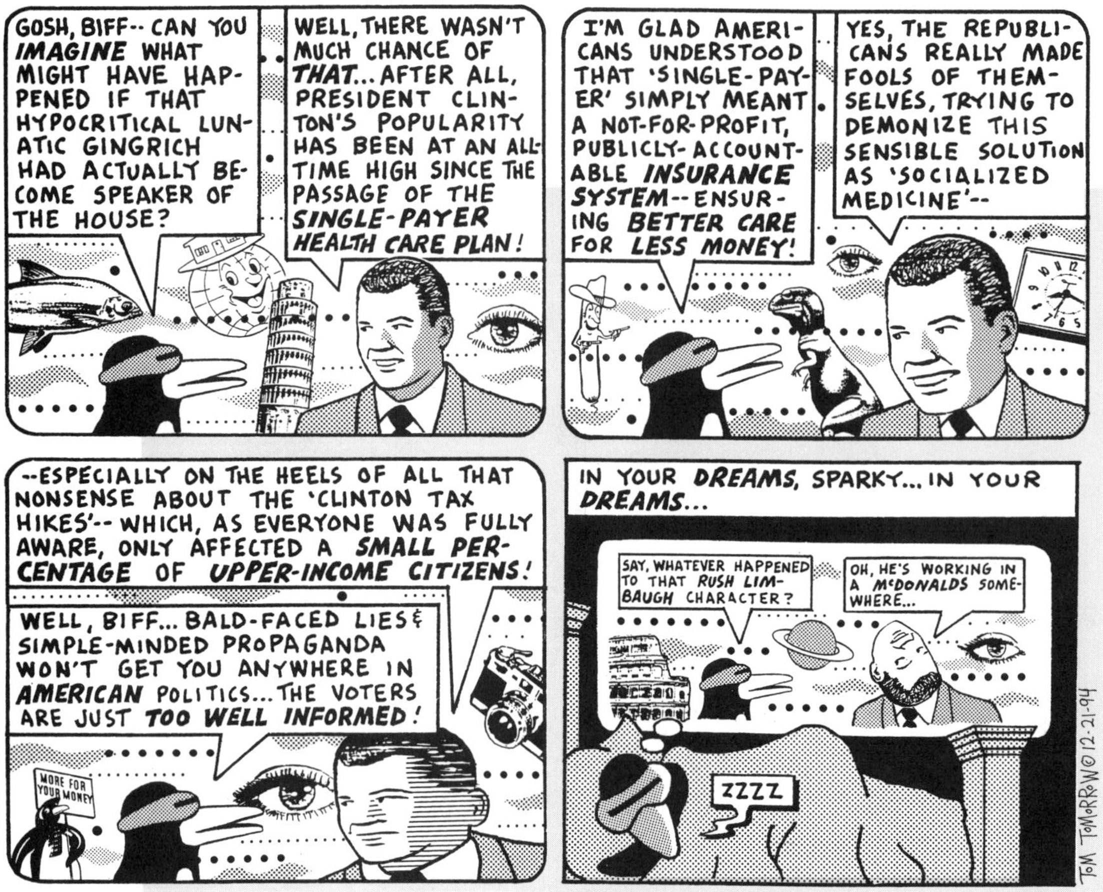
GOSH, BIFF-- CAN YOU IMAGINE WHAT MIGHT HAVE HAPPENED IF THAT HYPOCRITICAL LUNATIC GINGRICH HAD ACTUALLY BECOME SPEAKER OF THE HOUSE?
WELL, THERE WASN'T MUCH CHANCE OF THAT... AFTER ALL, PRESIDENT CLINTON'S POPULARITY HAS BEEN AT AN ALL-TIME HIGH SINCE THE PASSAGE OF THE SINGLE-PAYER HEALTH CARE PLAN!
I'M GLAD AMERICANS UNDERSTOOD THAT 'SINGLE-PAYER' SIMPLY MEANT A NOT-FOR-PROFIT, PUBLICLY-ACCOUNTABLE INSURANCE SYSTEM-- ENSURING BETTER CARE FOR LESS MONEY!
YES, THE REPUBLICANS REALLY MADE FOOLS OF THEMSELVES, TRYING TO DEMONIZE THIS SENSIBLE SOLUTION AS 'SOCIALIZED MEDICINE'--
--ESPECIALLY ON THE HEELS OF ALL THAT NONSENSE ABOUT THE 'CLINTON TAX HIKES'-- WHICH, AS EVERYONE WAS FULLY AWARE, ONLY AFFECTED A SMALL PERCENTAGE OF UPPER-INCOME CITIZENS!
WELL, BIFF... BALD-FACED LIES & SIMPLE-MINDED PROPAGANDA WON'T GET YOU ANYWHERE IN AMERICAN POLITICS... THE VOTERS ARE JUST TOO WELL INFORMED!
MORE FOR YOUR MONEY
IN YOUR DREAMS, SPARKY... IN YOUR DREAMS...
SAY, WHATEVER HAPPENED TO THAT RUSH LIMBAUGH CHARACTER?
OH, HE'S WORKING IN A McDONALDS SOMEWHERE...
ZZZZ
TOM TOMORROW © 12-21-94

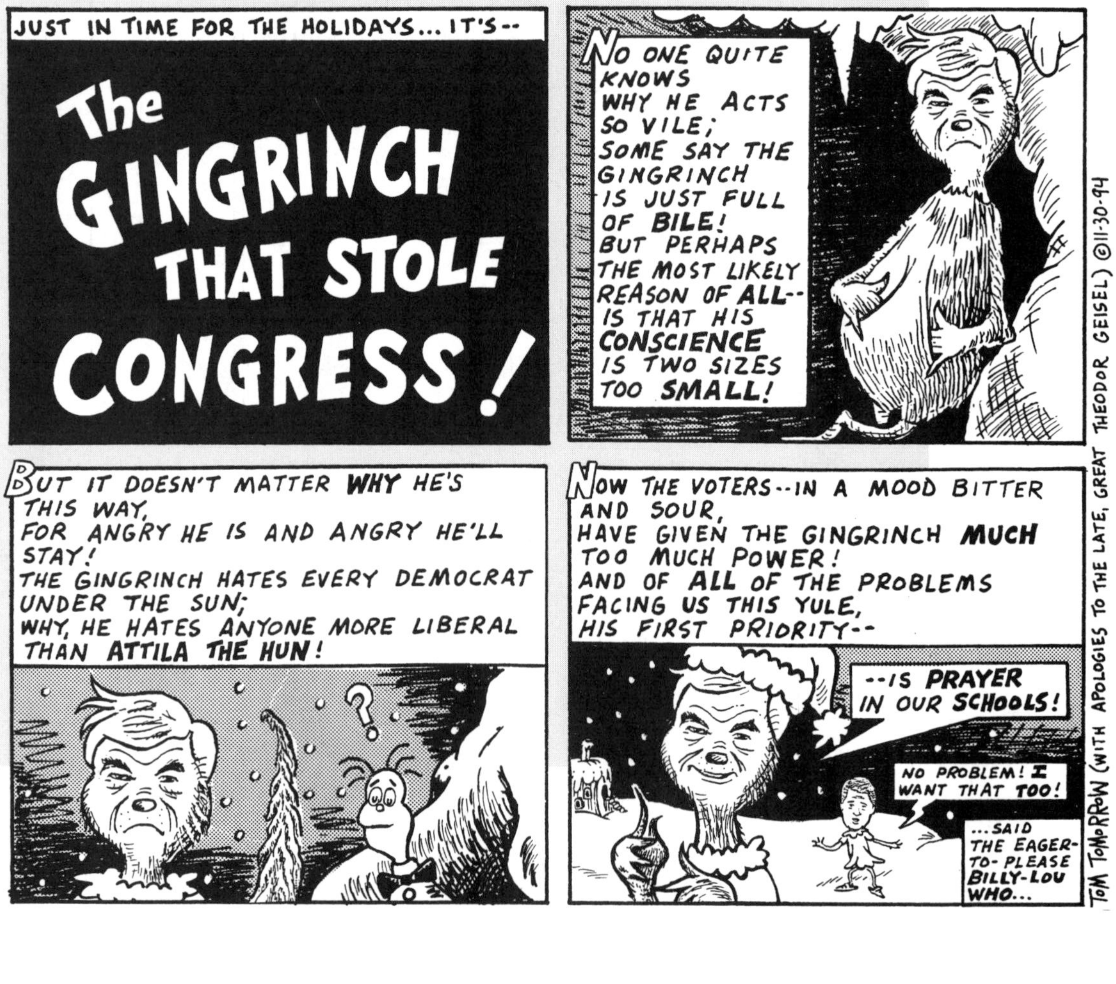
JUST IN TIME FOR THE HOLIDAYS... IT'S--
The GINGRINCH THAT STOLE CONGRESS!
NO ONE QUITE KNOWS WHY HE ACTS SO VILE; SOME SAY THE GINGRINCH IS JUST FULL OF BILE! BUT PERHAPS THE MOST LIKELY REASON OF ALL-- IS THAT HIS CONSCIENCE IS TWO SIZES TOO SMALL!
BUT IT DOESN'T MATTER WHY HE'S THIS WAY, FOR ANGRY HE IS AND ANGRY HE'LL STAY! THE GINGRINCH HATES EVERY DEMOCRAT UNDER THE SUN; WHY, HE HATES ANYONE MORE LIBERAL THAN ATTILA THE HUN!
?
NOW THE VOTERS-- IN A MOOD BITTER AND SOUR, HAVE GIVEN THE GINGRINCH MUCH TOO MUCH POWER! AND OF ALL OF THE PROBLEMS FACING US THIS YULE, HIS FIRST PRIORITY--
--IS PRAYER IN OUR SCHOOLS!
NO PROBLEM! I WANT THAT TOO!
...SAID THE EAGER-TO-PLEASE BILLY-LOU WHO...
TOM TOMORROW (WITH APOLOGIES TO THE LATE, GREAT THEODOR GEISEL) ©11-30-94

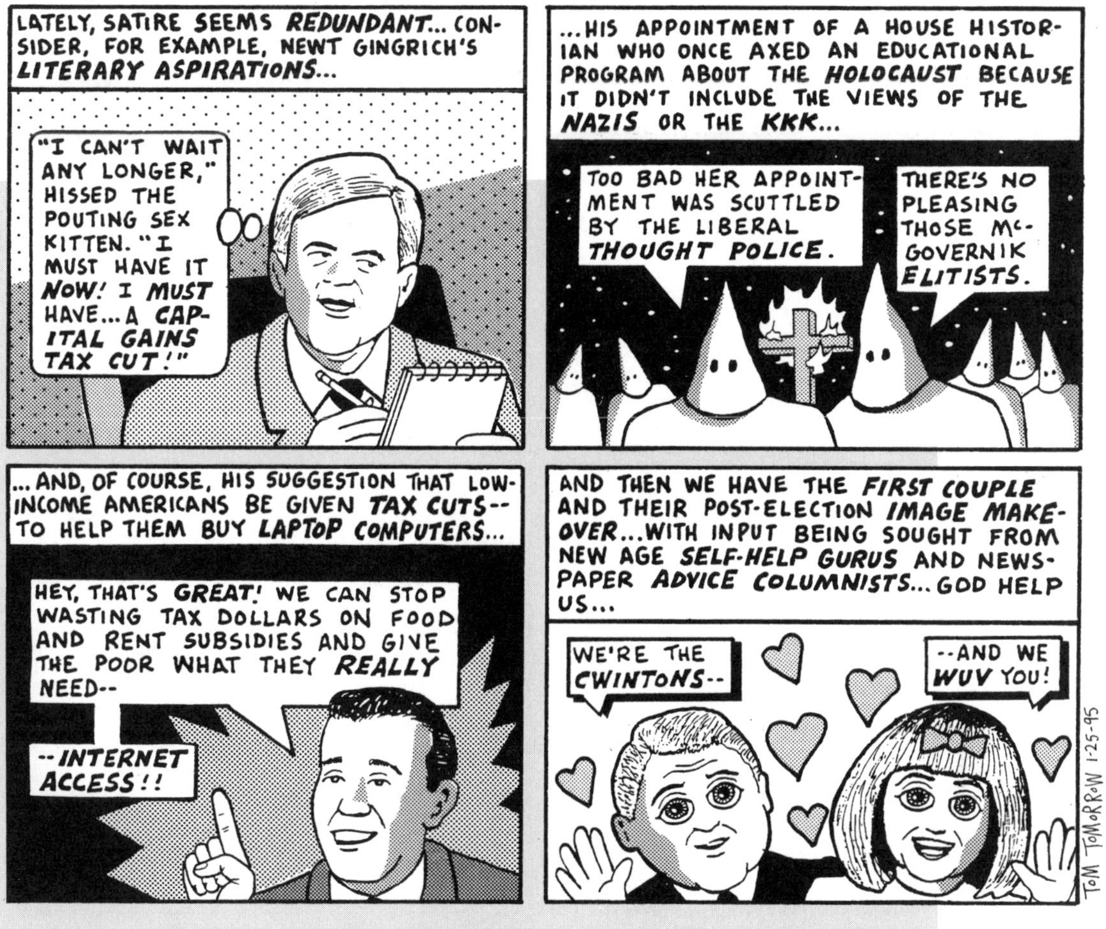
LATELY, SATIRE SEEMS REDUNDANT... CONSIDER, FOR EXAMPLE, NEWT GINGRICH'S LITERARY ASPIRATIONS...
"I CAN'T WAIT ANY LONGER," HISSED THE POUTING SEX KITTEN. "I MUST HAVE IT NOW! I MUST HAVE... A CAPITAL GAINS TAX CUT!"
...HIS APPOINTMENT OF A HOUSE HISTORIAN WHO ONCE AXED AN EDUCATIONAL PROGRAM ABOUT THE HOLOCAUST BECAUSE IT DIDN'T INCLUDE THE VIEWS OF THE NAZIS OR THE KKK...
TOO BAD HER APPOINTMENT WAS SCUTTLED BY THE LIBERAL THOUGHT POLICE.
THERE'S NO PLEASING THOSE McGOVERNIK ELITISTS.
...AND, OF COURSE, HIS SUGGESTION THAT LOW-INCOME AMERICANS BE GIVEN TAX CUTS--TO HELP THEM BUY LAPTOP COMPUTERS...
HEY, THAT'S GREAT! WE CAN STOP WASTING TAX DOLLARS ON FOOD AND RENT SUBSIDIES AND GIVE THE POOR WHAT THEY REALLY NEED--
--INTERNET ACCESS!!
AND THEN WE HAVE THE FIRST COUPLE AND THEIR POST-ELECTION IMAGE MAKEOVER...WITH INPUT BEING SOUGHT FROM NEW AGE SELF-HELP GURUS AND NEWSPAPER ADVICE COLUMNISTS... GOD HELP US...
WE'RE THE CWINTONS--
--AND WE WUV YOU!
TOM TOMORROW 1-25-95

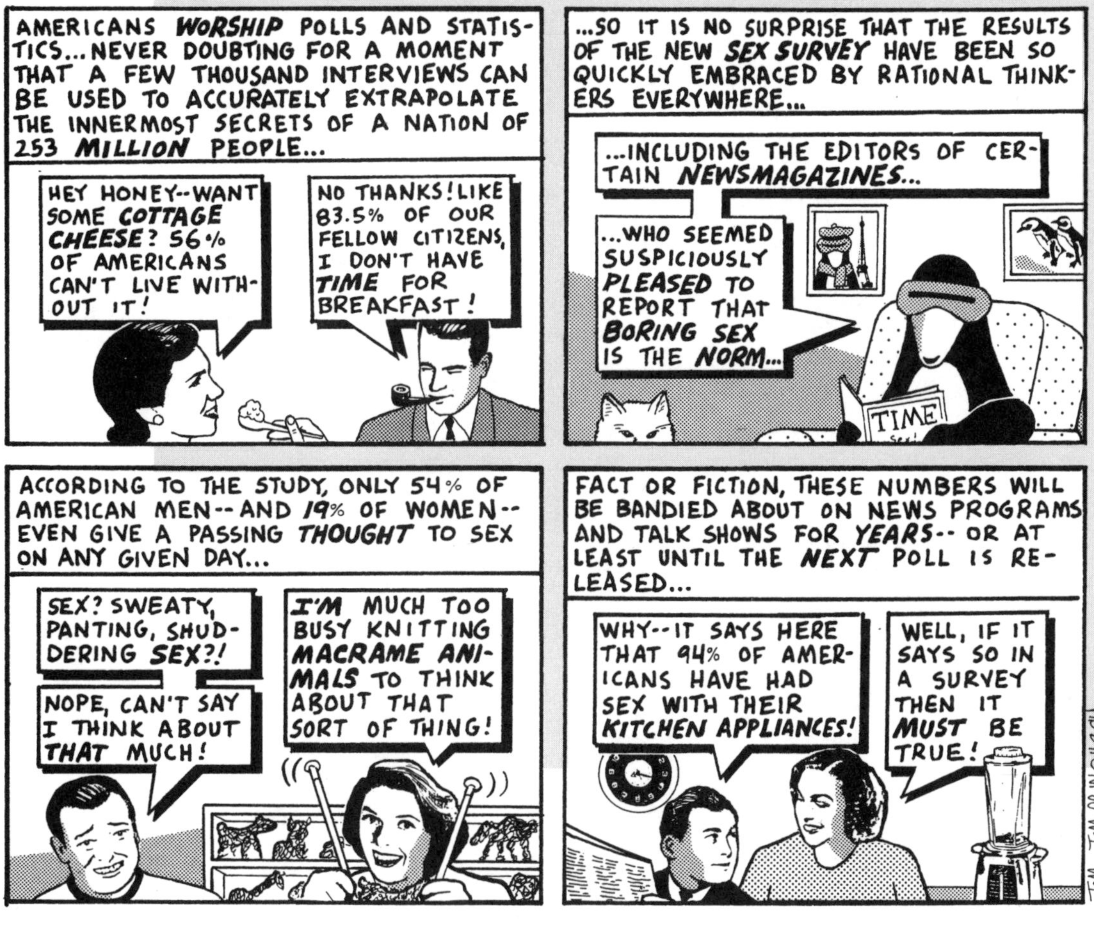
AMERICANS WORSHIP POLLS AND STATISTICS... NEVER DOUBTING FOR A MOMENT THAT A FEW THOUSAND INTERVIEWS CAN BE USED TO ACCURATELY EXTRAPOLATE THE INNERMOST SECRETS OF A NATION OF 253 MILLION PEOPLE...
HEY HONEY--WANT SOME COTTAGE CHEESE? 56% OF AMERICANS CAN'T LIVE WITHOUT IT!
NO THANKS! LIKE 83.5% OF OUR FELLOW CITIZENS, I DON'T HAVE TIME FOR BREAKFAST!
...SO IT IS NO SURPRISE THAT THE RESULTS OF THE NEW SEX SURVEY HAVE BEEN SO QUICKLY EMBRACED BY RATIONAL THINKERS EVERYWHERE...
...INCLUDING THE EDITORS OF CERTAIN NEWSMAGAZINES...
...WHO SEEMED SUSPICIOUSLY PLEASED TO REPORT THAT BORING SEX IS THE NORM...
TIME
ACCORDING TO THE STUDY, ONLY 54% OF AMERICAN MEN--AND 19% OF WOMEN--EVEN GIVE A PASSING THOUGHT TO SEX ON ANY GIVEN DAY...
SEX? SWEATY, PANTING, SHUDDERING SEX?!
NOPE, CAN'T SAY I THINK ABOUT THAT MUCH!
I'M MUCH TOO BUSY KNITTING MACRAME ANIMALS TO THINK ABOUT THAT SORT OF THING!
FACT OR FICTION, THESE NUMBERS WILL BE BANDIED ABOUT ON NEWS PROGRAMS AND TALK SHOWS FOR YEARS-- OR AT LEAST UNTIL THE NEXT POLL IS RELEASED...
WHY--IT SAYS HERE THAT 94% OF AMERICANS HAVE HAD SEX WITH THEIR KITCHEN APPLIANCES!
WELL, IF IT SAYS SO IN A SURVEY THEN IT MUST BE TRUE!
TOM TOMORROW©11-9-94

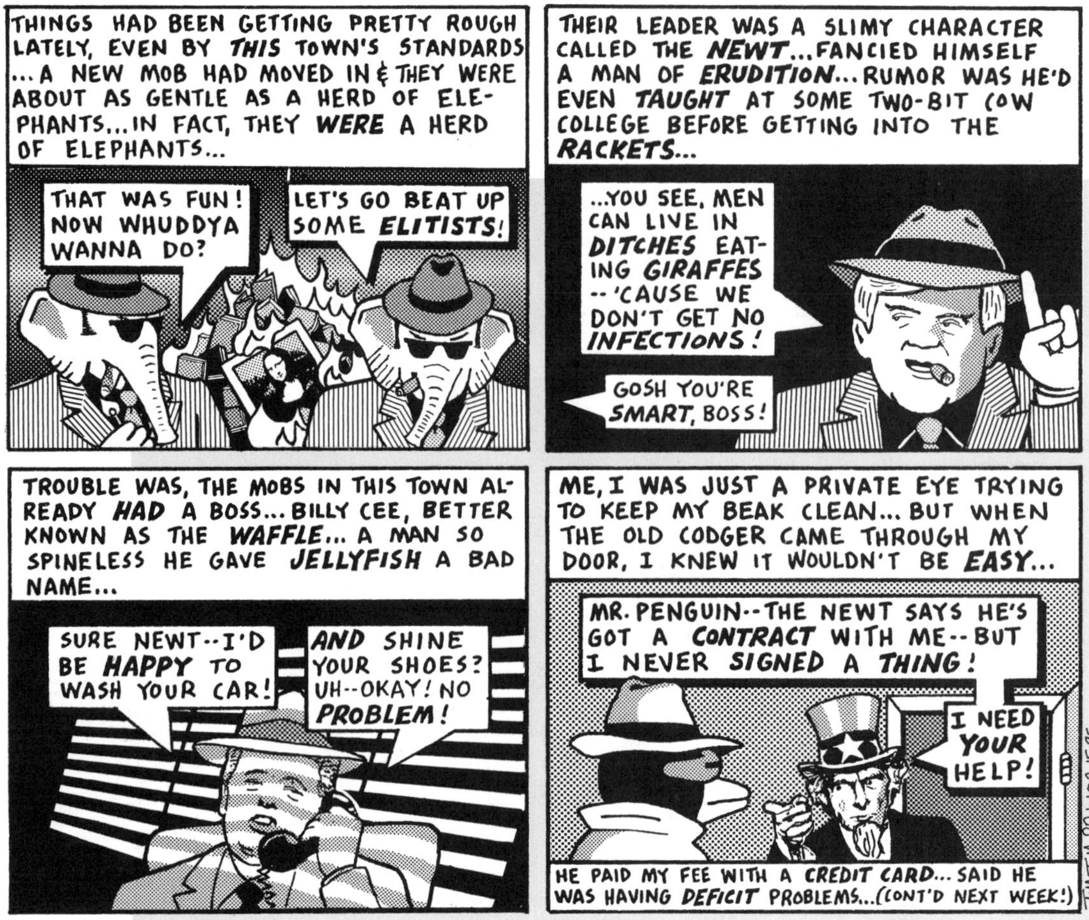
THINGS HAD BEEN GETTING PRETTY ROUGH LATELY, EVEN BY THIS TOWN'S STANDARDS ...A NEW MOB HAD MOVED IN & THEY WERE ABOUT AS GENTLE AS A HERD OF ELEPHANTS... IN FACT, THEY WERE A HERD OF ELEPHANTS...
THAT WAS FUN! NOW WHUDDYA WANNA DO?
LET'S GO BEAT UP SOME ELITISTS!
THEIR LEADER WAS A SLIMY CHARACTER CALLED THE NEWT... FANCIED HIMSELF A MAN OF ERUDITION... RUMOR WAS HE'D EVEN TAUGHT AT SOME TWO-BIT COW COLLEGE BEFORE GETTING INTO THE RACKETS...
...YOU SEE, MEN CAN LIVE IN DITCHES EATING GIRAFFES --'CAUSE WE DON'T GET NO INFECTIONS!
GOSH YOU'RE SMART, BOSS!
TROUBLE WAS, THE MOBS IN THIS TOWN ALREADY HAD A BOSS... BILLY CEE, BETTER KNOWN AS THE WAFFLE... A MAN SO SPINELESS HE GAVE JELLYFISH A BAD NAME...
SURE NEWT--I'D BE HAPPY TO WASH YOUR CAR!
AND SHINE YOUR SHOES? UH--OKAY! NO PROBLEM!
ME, I WAS JUST A PRIVATE EYE TRYING TO KEEP MY BEAK CLEAN... BUT WHEN THE OLD CODGER CAME THROUGH MY DOOR, I KNEW IT WOULDN'T BE EASY...
MR. PENGUIN--THE NEWT SAYS HE'S GOT A CONTRACT WITH ME--BUT I NEVER SIGNED A THING!
I NEED YOUR HELP!
HE PAID MY FEE WITH A CREDIT CARD... SAID HE WAS HAVING DEFICIT PROBLEMS...(CONT'D NEXT WEEK!)
TOM TOMORROW©2-15-95

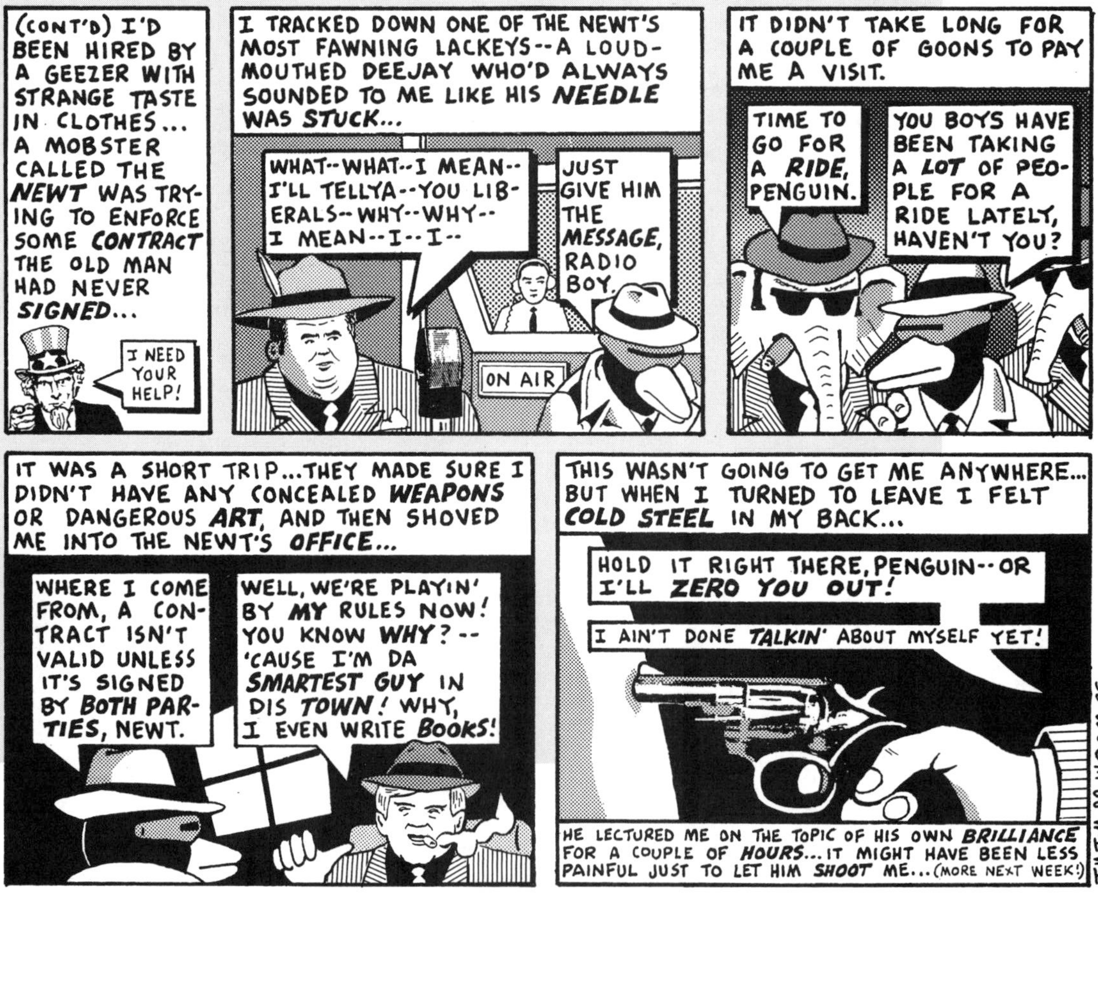
(CONT'D) I'D BEEN HIRED BY A GEEZER WITH STRANGE TASTE IN CLOTHES... A MOBSTER CALLED THE NEWT WAS TRYING TO ENFORCE SOME CONTRACT THE OLD MAN HAD NEVER SIGNED...
I NEED YOUR HELP!
I TRACKED DOWN ONE OF THE NEWT'S MOST FAWNING LACKEYS--A LOUD-MOUTHED DEEJAY WHO'D ALWAYS SOUNDED TO ME LIKE HIS NEEDLE WAS STUCK...
WHAT--WHAT--I MEAN--I'LL TELLYA--YOU LIBERALS--WHY--WHY--I MEAN--I--I--
JUST GIVE HIM THE MESSAGE, RADIO BOY.
ON AIR
IT DIDN'T TAKE LONG FOR A COUPLE OF GOONS TO PAY ME A VISIT.
TIME TO GO FOR A RIDE, PENGUIN.
YOU BOYS HAVE BEEN TAKING A LOT OF PEOPLE FOR A RIDE LATELY, HAVEN'T YOU?
IT WAS A SHORT TRIP...THEY MADE SURE I DIDN'T HAVE ANY CONCEALED WEAPONS OR DANGEROUS ART, AND THEN SHOVED ME INTO THE NEWT'S OFFICE...
WHERE I COME FROM, A CONTRACT ISN'T VALID UNLESS IT'S SIGNED BY BOTH PARTIES, NEWT.
WELL, WE'RE PLAYIN' BY MY RULES NOW! YOU KNOW WHY?--'CAUSE I'M DA SMARTEST GUY IN DIS TOWN! WHY, I EVEN WRITE BOOKS!
THIS WASN'T GOING TO GET ME ANYWHERE... BUT WHEN I TURNED TO LEAVE I FELT COLD STEEL IN MY BACK...
HOLD IT RIGHT THERE, PENGUIN--OR I'LL ZERO YOU OUT!
I AIN'T DONE TALKIN' ABOUT MYSELF YET!
HE LECTURED ME ON THE TOPIC OF HIS OWN BRILLIANCE FOR A COUPLE OF HOURS... IT MIGHT HAVE BEEN LESS PAINFUL JUST TO LET HIM SHOOT ME...(MORE NEXT WEEK!)
TOM TOMORROW© 2-22-95

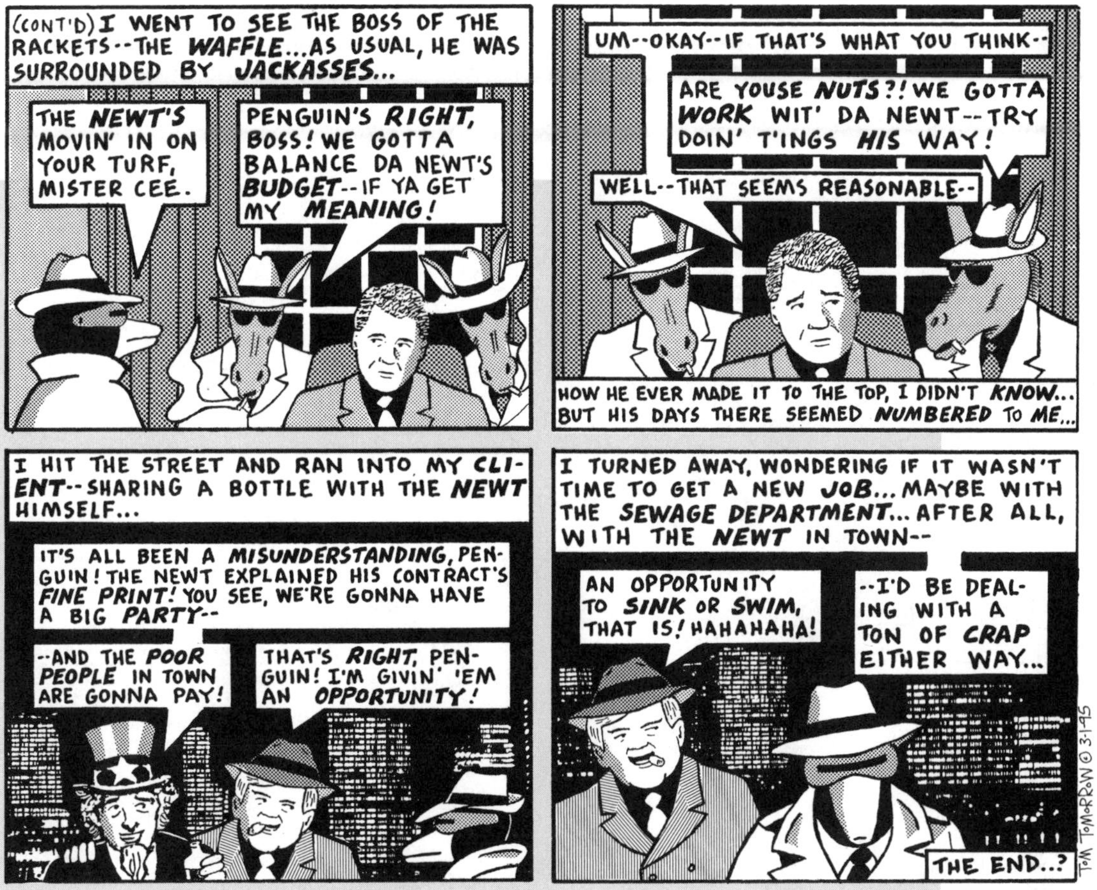
(CONT'D) I WENT TO SEE THE BOSS OF THE RACKETS--THE WAFFLE...AS USUAL, HE WAS SURROUNDED BY JACKASSES...
THE NEWT'S MOVIN' IN ON YOUR TURF, MISTER CEE.
PENGUIN'S RIGHT, BOSS! WE GOTTA BALANCE DA NEWT'S BUDGET--IF YA GET MY MEANING!
UM--OKAY--IF THAT'S WHAT YOU THINK--
ARE YOUSE NUTS?! WE GOTTA WORK WIT' DA NEWT--TRY DOIN' T'INGS HIS WAY!
WELL--THAT SEEMS REASONABLE--
HOW HE EVER MADE IT TO THE TOP, I DIDN'T KNOW... BUT HIS DAYS THERE SEEMED NUMBERED TO ME...
I HIT THE STREET AND RAN INTO MY CLIENT--SHARING A BOTTLE WITH THE NEWT HIMSELF...
IT'S ALL BEEN A MISUNDERSTANDING, PENGUIN! THE NEWT EXPLAINED HIS CONTRACT'S FINE PRINT! YOU SEE, WE'RE GONNA HAVE A BIG PARTY--
--AND THE POOR PEOPLE IN TOWN ARE GONNA PAY!
THAT'S RIGHT, PENGUIN! I'M GIVIN' 'EM AN OPPORTUNITY!
I TURNED AWAY, WONDERING IF IT WASN'T TIME TO GET A NEW JOB... MAYBE WITH THE SEWAGE DEPARTMENT... AFTER ALL, WITH THE NEWT IN TOWN--
AN OPPORTUNITY TO SINK OR SWIM, THAT IS! HAHAHAHA!
--I'D BE DEALING WITH A TON OF CRAP EITHER WAY...
THE END..?
TOM TOMORROW © 3-1-95

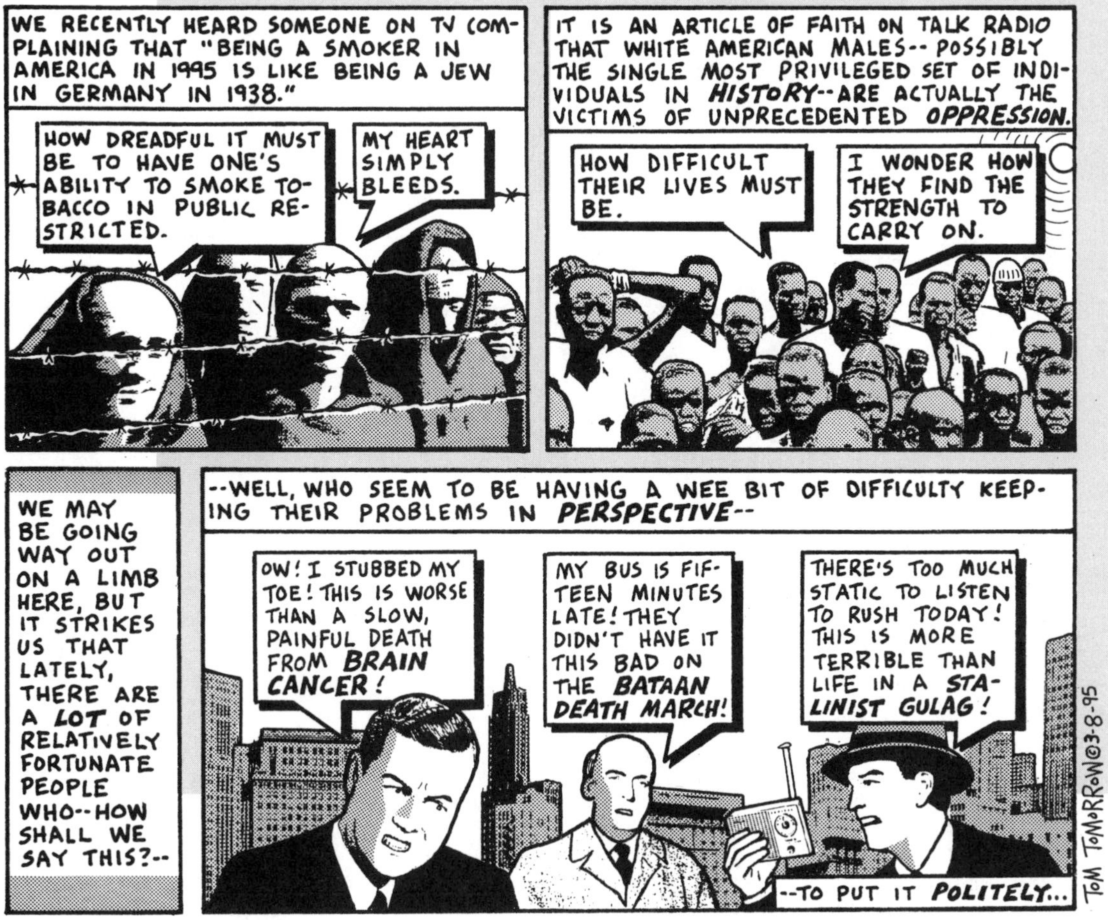
WE RECENTLY HEARD SOMEONE ON TV COMPLAINING THAT "BEING A SMOKER IN AMERICA IN 1995 IS LIKE BEING A JEW IN GERMANY IN 1938."
HOW DREADFUL IT MUST BE TO HAVE ONE'S ABILITY TO SMOKE TOBACCO IN PUBLIC RESTRICTED.
MY HEART SIMPLY BLEEDS.
IT IS AN ARTICLE OF FAITH ON TALK RADIO THAT WHITE AMERICAN MALES--POSSIBLY THE SINGLE MOST PRIVILEGED SET OF INDIVIDUALS IN HISTORY--ARE ACTUALLY THE VICTIMS OF UNPRECEDENTED OPPRESSION.
HOW DIFFICULT THEIR LIVES MUST BE.
I WONDER HOW THEY FIND THE STRENGTH TO CARRY ON.
WE MAY BE GOING WAY OUT ON A LIMB HERE, BUT IT STRIKES US THAT LATELY, THERE ARE A LOT OF RELATIVELY FORTUNATE PEOPLE WHO--HOW SHALL WE SAY THIS?--
--WELL, WHO SEEM TO BE HAVING A WEE BIT OF DIFFICULTY KEEPING THEIR PROBLEMS IN PERSPECTIVE--
OW! I STUBBED MY TOE! THIS IS WORSE THAN A SLOW, PAINFUL DEATH FROM BRAIN CANCER!
MY BUS IS FIFTEEN MINUTES LATE! THEY DIDN'T HAVE IT THIS BAD ON THE BATAAN DEATH MARCH!
THERE'S TOO MUCH STATIC TO LISTEN TO RUSH TODAY! THIS IS MORE TERRIBLE THAN LIFE IN A STALINIST GULAG!
--TO PUT IT POLITELY...
TOM TOMORROW © 3-8-95

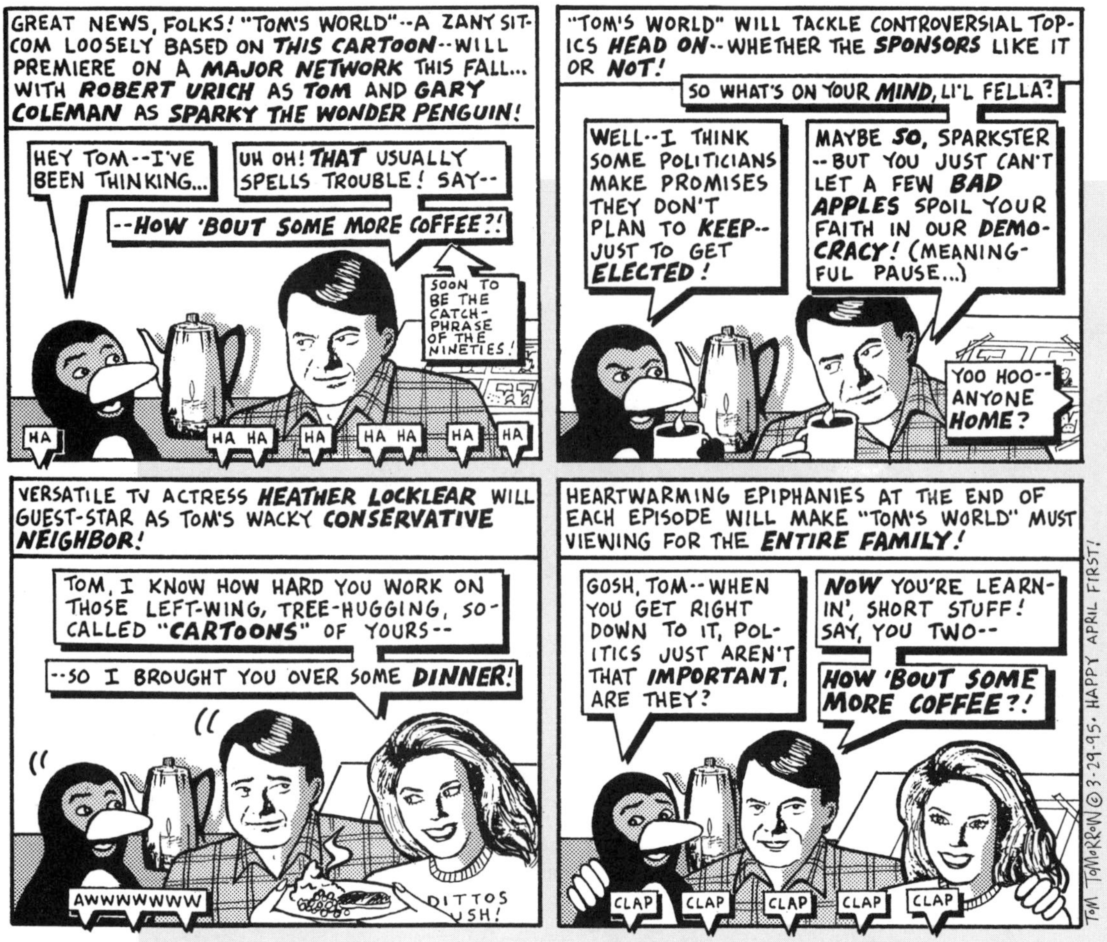
GREAT NEWS, FOLKS! "TOM'S WORLD"--A ZANY SIT-COM LOOSELY BASED ON THIS CARTOON--WILL PREMIERE ON A MAJOR NETWORK THIS FALL... WITH ROBERT URICH AS TOM AND GARY COLEMAN AS SPARKY THE WONDER PENGUIN!
HEY TOM--I'VE BEEN THINKING...
UH OH! THAT USUALLY SPELLS TROUBLE! SAY--
--HOW 'BOUT SOME MORE COFFEE?!
SOON TO BE THE CATCH-PHRASE OF THE NINETIES!
HA
HA HA
HA
HA HA
HA
HA
"TOM'S WORLD" WILL TACKLE CONTROVERSIAL TOPICS HEAD ON--WHETHER THE SPONSORS LIKE IT OR NOT!
SO WHAT'S ON YOUR MIND, LI'L FELLA?
WELL--I THINK SOME POLITICIANS MAKE PROMISES THEY DON'T PLAN TO KEEP--JUST TO GET ELECTED!
MAYBE SO, SPARKSTER--BUT YOU JUST CAN'T LET A FEW BAD APPLES SPOIL YOUR FAITH IN OUR DEMOCRACY! (MEANINGFUL PAUSE...)
YOO HOO--ANYONE HOME?
VERSATILE TV ACTRESS HEATHER LOCKLEAR WILL GUEST-STAR AS TOM'S WACKY CONSERVATIVE NEIGHBOR!
TOM, I KNOW HOW HARD YOU WORK ON THOSE LEFT-WING, TREE-HUGGING, SO-CALLED "CARTOONS" OF YOURS--
--SO I BROUGHT YOU OVER SOME DINNER!
AWWWWWWW
DITTOS
HEARTWARMING EPIPHANIES AT THE END OF EACH EPISODE WILL MAKE "TOM'S WORLD" MUST VIEWING FOR THE ENTIRE FAMILY!
GOSH, TOM--WHEN YOU GET RIGHT DOWN TO IT, POLITICS JUST AREN'T THAT IMPORTANT, ARE THEY?
NOW YOU'RE LEARNIN', SHORT STUFF! SAY, YOU TWO--
HOW 'BOUT SOME MORE COFFEE?!
CLAP
CLAP
CLAP
CLAP
CLAP
TOM TOMORROW © 3-29-95. HAPPY APRIL FIRST!

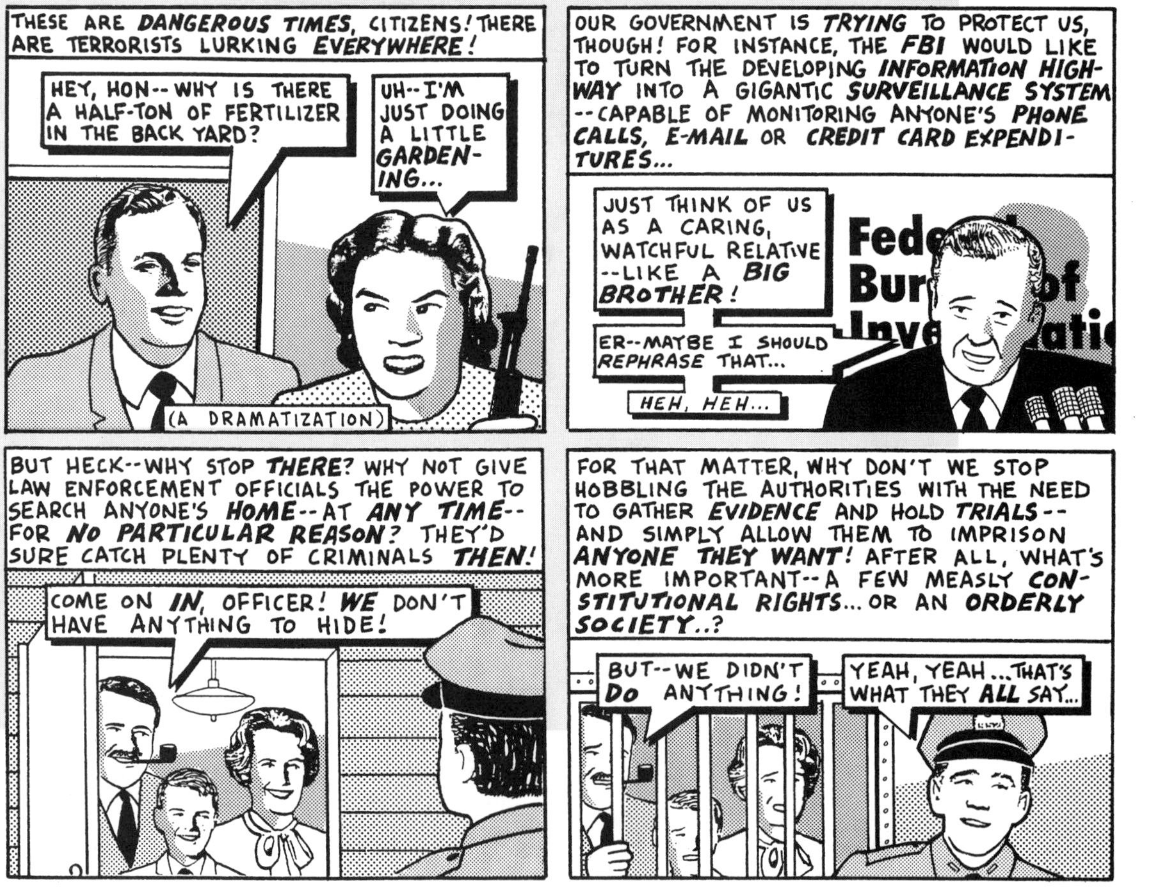
THESE ARE DANGEROUS TIMES, CITIZENS! THERE ARE TERRORISTS LURKING EVERYWHERE!
HEY, HON--WHY IS THERE A HALF-TON OF FERTILIZER IN THE BACK YARD?
UH--I'M JUST DOING A LITTLE GARDENING...
(A DRAMATIZATION)
OUR GOVERNMENT IS TRYING TO PROTECT US, THOUGH! FOR INSTANCE, THE FBI WOULD LIKE TO TURN THE DEVELOPING INFORMATION HIGHWAY INTO A GIGANTIC SURVEILLANCE SYSTEM--CAPABLE OF MONITORING ANYONE'S PHONE CALLS, E-MAIL OR CREDIT CARD EXPENDITURES...
JUST THINK OF US AS A CARING, WATCHFUL RELATIVE--LIKE A BIG BROTHER!
ER--MAYBE I SHOULD REPHRASE THAT...
HEH, HEH...
BUT HECK--WHY STOP THERE? WHY NOT GIVE LAW ENFORCEMENT OFFICIALS THE POWER TO SEARCH ANYONE'S HOME--AT ANY TIME--FOR NO PARTICULAR REASON? THEY'D SURE CATCH PLENTY OF CRIMINALS THEN!
COME ON IN, OFFICER! WE DON'T HAVE ANYTHING TO HIDE!
FOR THAT MATTER, WHY DON'T WE STOP HOBBLING THE AUTHORITIES WITH THE NEED TO GATHER EVIDENCE AND HOLD TRIALS--AND SIMPLY ALLOW THEM TO IMPRISON ANYONE THEY WANT! AFTER ALL, WHAT'S MORE IMPORTANT--A FEW MEASLY CONSTITUTIONAL RIGHTS...OR AN ORDERLY SOCIETY..?
BUT--WE DIDN'T DO ANYTHING!
YEAH, YEAH...THAT'S WHAT THEY ALL SAY...

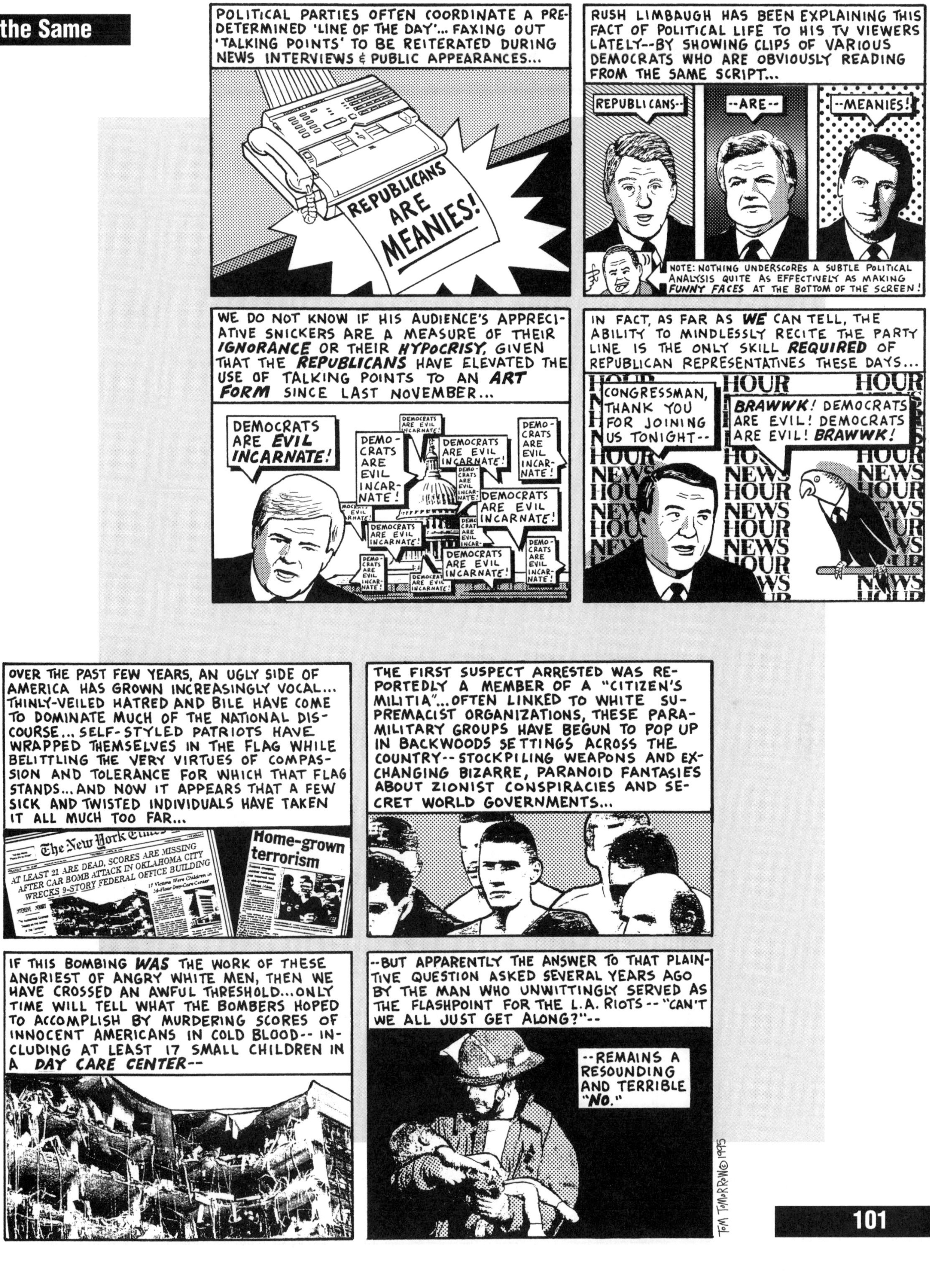
POLITICAL PARTIES OFTEN COORDINATE A PRE-DETERMINED 'LINE OF THE DAY'... FAXING OUT 'TALKING POINTS' TO BE REITERATED DURING NEWS INTERVIEWS & PUBLIC APPEARANCES...
REPUBLICANS ARE MEANIES!
RUSH LIMBAUGH HAS BEEN EXPLAINING THIS FACT OF POLITICAL LIFE TO HIS TV VIEWERS LATELY--BY SHOWING CLIPS OF VARIOUS DEMOCRATS WHO ARE OBVIOUSLY READING FROM THE SAME SCRIPT...
REPUBLICANS--
--ARE--
--MEANIES!
NOTE: NOTHING UNDERSCORES A SUBTLE POLITICAL ANALYSIS QUITE AS EFFECTIVELY AS MAKING FUNNY FACES AT THE BOTTOM OF THE SCREEN!
WE DO NOT KNOW IF HIS AUDIENCE'S APPRECIATIVE SNICKERS ARE A MEASURE OF THEIR IGNORANCE OR THEIR HYPOCRISY, GIVEN THAT THE REPUBLICANS HAVE ELEVATED THE USE OF TALKING POINTS TO AN ART FORM SINCE LAST NOVEMBER...
DEMOCRATS ARE EVIL INCARNATE!
DEMOCRATS ARE EVIL INCARNATE!
DEMOCRATS ARE EVIL INCARNATE!
DEMOCRATS ARE EVIL INCARNATE!
DEMOCRATS ARE EVIL INCARNATE!
DEMOCRATS ARE EVIL INCARNATE!
DEMOCRATS ARE EVIL INCARNATE!
IN FACT, AS FAR AS WE CAN TELL, THE ABILITY TO MINDLESSLY RECITE THE PARTY LINE IS THE ONLY SKILL REQUIRED OF REPUBLICAN REPRESENTATIVES THESE DAYS...
CONGRESSMAN, THANK YOU FOR JOINING US TONIGHT--
BRAWWK! DEMOCRATS ARE EVIL! DEMOCRATS ARE EVIL! BRAWWK!
NEWS HOUR
OVER THE PAST FEW YEARS, AN UGLY SIDE OF AMERICA HAS GROWN INCREASINGLY VOCAL... THINLY-VEILED HATRED AND BILE HAVE COME TO DOMINATE MUCH OF THE NATIONAL DISCOURSE... SELF-STYLED PATRIOTS HAVE WRAPPED THEMSELVES IN THE FLAG WHILE BELITTLING THE VERY VIRTUES OF COMPASSION AND TOLERANCE FOR WHICH THAT FLAG STANDS... AND NOW IT APPEARS THAT A FEW SICK AND TWISTED INDIVIDUALS HAVE TAKEN IT ALL MUCH TOO FAR...
The New York Times
AT LEAST 21 ARE DEAD, SCORES ARE MISSING AFTER CAR BOMB ATTACK IN OKLAHOMA CITY WRECKS 9-STORY FEDERAL OFFICE BUILDING
17 Victims Were Children in 2d-Floor Day-Care Center
Home-grown terrorism
THE FIRST SUSPECT ARRESTED WAS REPORTEDLY A MEMBER OF A "CITIZEN'S MILITIA"... OFTEN LINKED TO WHITE SUPREMACIST ORGANIZATIONS, THESE PARAMILITARY GROUPS HAVE BEGUN TO POP UP IN BACKWOODS SETTINGS ACROSS THE COUNTRY--STOCKPILING WEAPONS AND EXCHANGING BIZARRE, PARANOID FANTASIES ABOUT ZIONIST CONSPIRACIES AND SECRET WORLD GOVERNMENTS...
IF THIS BOMBING WAS THE WORK OF THESE ANGRIEST OF ANGRY WHITE MEN, THEN WE HAVE CROSSED AN AWFUL THRESHOLD... ONLY TIME WILL TELL WHAT THE BOMBERS HOPED TO ACCOMPLISH BY MURDERING SCORES OF INNOCENT AMERICANS IN COLD BLOOD--INCLUDING AT LEAST 17 SMALL CHILDREN IN A DAY CARE CENTER--
--BUT APPARENTLY THE ANSWER TO THAT PLAINTIVE QUESTION ASKED SEVERAL YEARS AGO BY THE MAN WHO UNWITTINGLY SERVED AS THE FLASHPOINT FOR THE L.A. RIOTS--"CAN'T WE ALL JUST GET ALONG?"--
--REMAINS A RESOUNDING AND TERRIBLE "NO."
TOM TOMORROW©1995

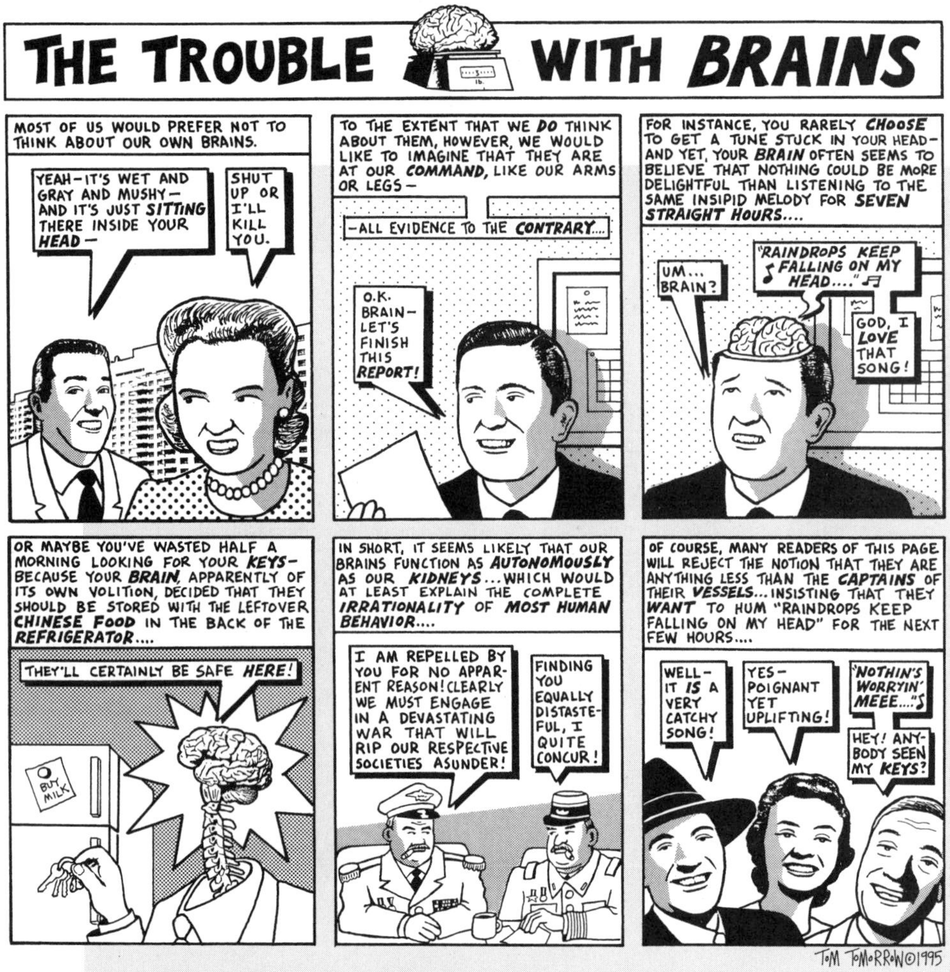
THE TROUBLE WITH BRAINS
MOST OF US WOULD PREFER NOT TO THINK ABOUT OUR OWN BRAINS.
YEAH—IT'S WET AND GRAY AND MUSHY—AND IT'S JUST SITTING THERE INSIDE YOUR HEAD—
SHUT UP OR I'LL KILL YOU.
TO THE EXTENT THAT WE DO THINK ABOUT THEM, HOWEVER, WE WOULD LIKE TO IMAGINE THAT THEY ARE AT OUR COMMAND, LIKE OUR ARMS OR LEGS—
—ALL EVIDENCE TO THE CONTRARY....
O.K. BRAIN—LET'S FINISH THIS REPORT!
FOR INSTANCE, YOU RARELY CHOOSE TO GET A TUNE STUCK IN YOUR HEAD—AND YET, YOUR BRAIN OFTEN SEEMS TO BELIEVE THAT NOTHING COULD BE MORE DELIGHTFUL THAN LISTENING TO THE SAME INSIPID MELODY FOR SEVEN STRAIGHT HOURS....
UM... BRAIN?
"RAINDROPS KEEP FALLING ON MY HEAD...."
GOD, I LOVE THAT SONG!
OR MAYBE YOU'VE WASTED HALF A MORNING LOOKING FOR YOUR KEYS—BECAUSE YOUR BRAIN, APPARENTLY OF ITS OWN VOLITION, DECIDED THAT THEY SHOULD BE STORED WITH THE LEFTOVER CHINESE FOOD IN THE BACK OF THE REFRIGERATOR....
THEY'LL CERTAINLY BE SAFE HERE!
BUY MILK
IN SHORT, IT SEEMS LIKELY THAT OUR BRAINS FUNCTION AS AUTONOMOUSLY AS OUR KIDNEYS...WHICH WOULD AT LEAST EXPLAIN THE COMPLETE IRRATIONALITY OF MOST HUMAN BEHAVIOR....
I AM REPELLED BY YOU FOR NO APPARENT REASON! CLEARLY WE MUST ENGAGE IN A DEVASTATING WAR THAT WILL RIP OUR RESPECTIVE SOCIETIES ASUNDER!
FINDING YOU EQUALLY DISTASTEFUL, I QUITE CONCUR!
OF COURSE, MANY READERS OF THIS PAGE WILL REJECT THE NOTION THAT THEY ARE ANYTHING LESS THAN THE CAPTAINS OF THEIR VESSELS...INSISTING THAT THEY WANT TO HUM "RAINDROPS KEEP FALLING ON MY HEAD" FOR THE NEXT FEW HOURS....
WELL—IT IS A VERY CATCHY SONG!
YES—POIGNANT YET UPLIFTING!
"NOTHIN'S WORRYIN' MEEE...."
HEY! ANYBODY SEEN MY KEYS?
TOM TOMORROW©1995

This one first ran (in color) on the 'Endpaper' page of *The New York Times Magazine.*

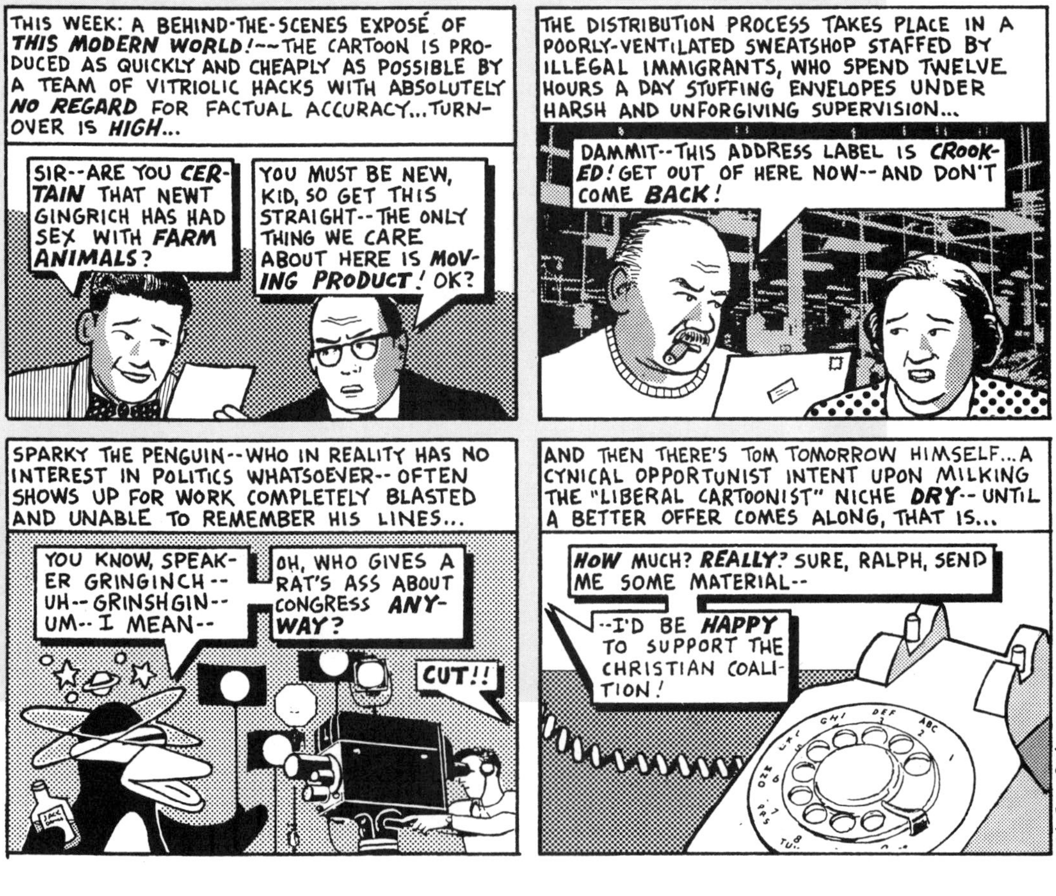
THIS WEEK: A BEHIND-THE-SCENES EXPOSÉ OF THIS MODERN WORLD!--THE CARTOON IS PRODUCED AS QUICKLY AND CHEAPLY AS POSSIBLE BY A TEAM OF VITRIOLIC HACKS WITH ABSOLUTELY NO REGARD FOR FACTUAL ACCURACY...TURNOVER IS HIGH...
SIR--ARE YOU CERTAIN THAT NEWT GINGRICH HAS HAD SEX WITH FARM ANIMALS?
YOU MUST BE NEW, KID, SO GET THIS STRAIGHT--THE ONLY THING WE CARE ABOUT HERE IS MOVING PRODUCT! OK?
THE DISTRIBUTION PROCESS TAKES PLACE IN A POORLY-VENTILATED SWEATSHOP STAFFED BY ILLEGAL IMMIGRANTS, WHO SPEND TWELVE HOURS A DAY STUFFING ENVELOPES UNDER HARSH AND UNFORGIVING SUPERVISION...
DAMMIT--THIS ADDRESS LABEL IS CROOKED! GET OUT OF HERE NOW--AND DON'T COME BACK!
SPARKY THE PENGUIN--WHO IN REALITY HAS NO INTEREST IN POLITICS WHATSOEVER--OFTEN SHOWS UP FOR WORK COMPLETELY BLASTED AND UNABLE TO REMEMBER HIS LINES...
YOU KNOW, SPEAKER GRINGINCH--UH--GRINSHGIN--UM--I MEAN--
OH, WHO GIVES A RAT'S ASS ABOUT CONGRESS ANYWAY?
CUT!!
AND THEN THERE'S TOM TOMORROW HIMSELF...A CYNICAL OPPORTUNIST INTENT UPON MILKING THE "LIBERAL CARTOONIST" NICHE DRY--UNTIL A BETTER OFFER COMES ALONG, THAT IS...
HOW MUCH? REALLY? SURE, RALPH, SEND ME SOME MATERIAL--
--I'D BE HAPPY TO SUPPORT THE CHRISTIAN COALITION!
TOM TOMORROW©6-28-95

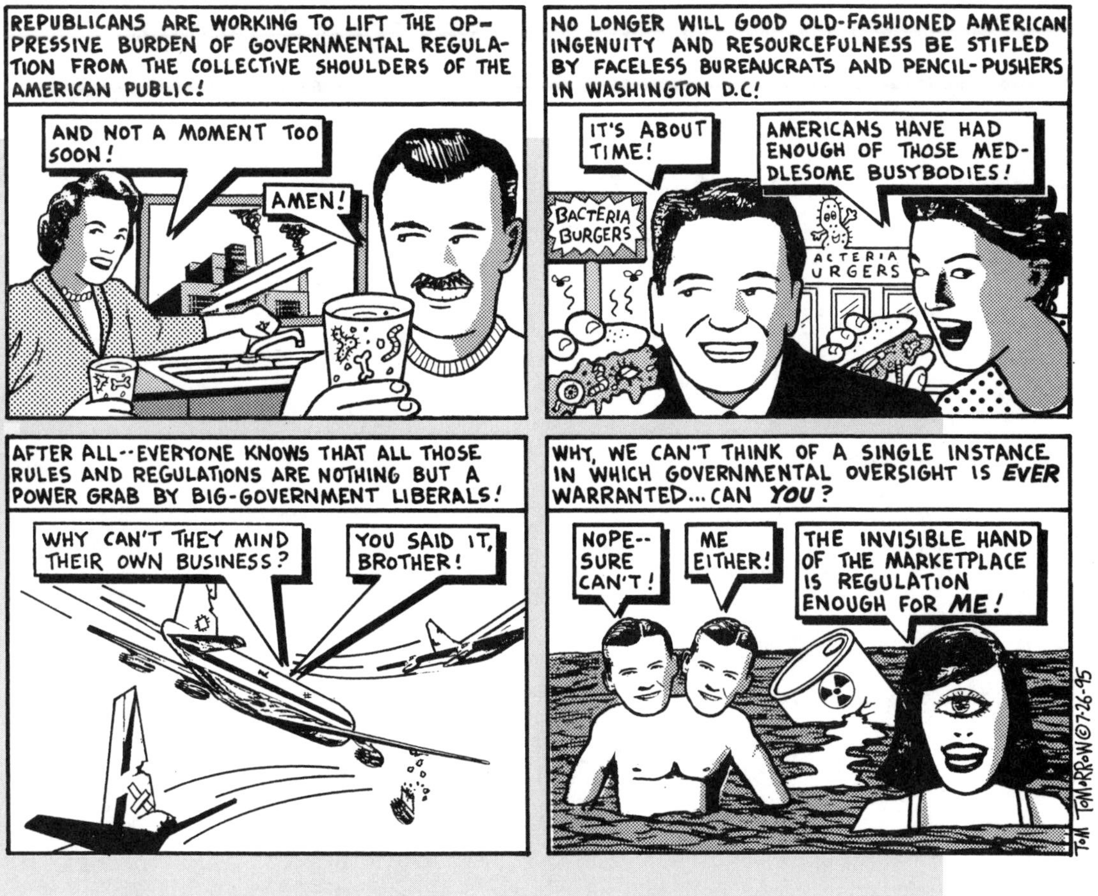
REPUBLICANS ARE WORKING TO LIFT THE OPPRESSIVE BURDEN OF GOVERNMENTAL REGULATION FROM THE COLLECTIVE SHOULDERS OF THE AMERICAN PUBLIC!
AND NOT A MOMENT TOO SOON!
AMEN!
NO LONGER WILL GOOD OLD-FASHIONED AMERICAN INGENUITY AND RESOURCEFULNESS BE STIFLED BY FACELESS BUREAUCRATS AND PENCIL-PUSHERS IN WASHINGTON D.C!
IT'S ABOUT TIME!
AMERICANS HAVE HAD ENOUGH OF THOSE MEDDLESOME BUSYBODIES!
BACTERIA BURGERS
AFTER ALL--EVERYONE KNOWS THAT ALL THOSE RULES AND REGULATIONS ARE NOTHING BUT A POWER GRAB BY BIG-GOVERNMENT LIBERALS!
WHY CAN'T THEY MIND THEIR OWN BUSINESS?
YOU SAID IT, BROTHER!
WHY, WE CAN'T THINK OF A SINGLE INSTANCE IN WHICH GOVERNMENTAL OVERSIGHT IS EVER WARRANTED... CAN YOU?
NOPE--SURE CAN'T!
ME EITHER!
THE INVISIBLE HAND OF THE MARKETPLACE IS REGULATION ENOUGH FOR ME!
TOM TOMORROW©7-26-95

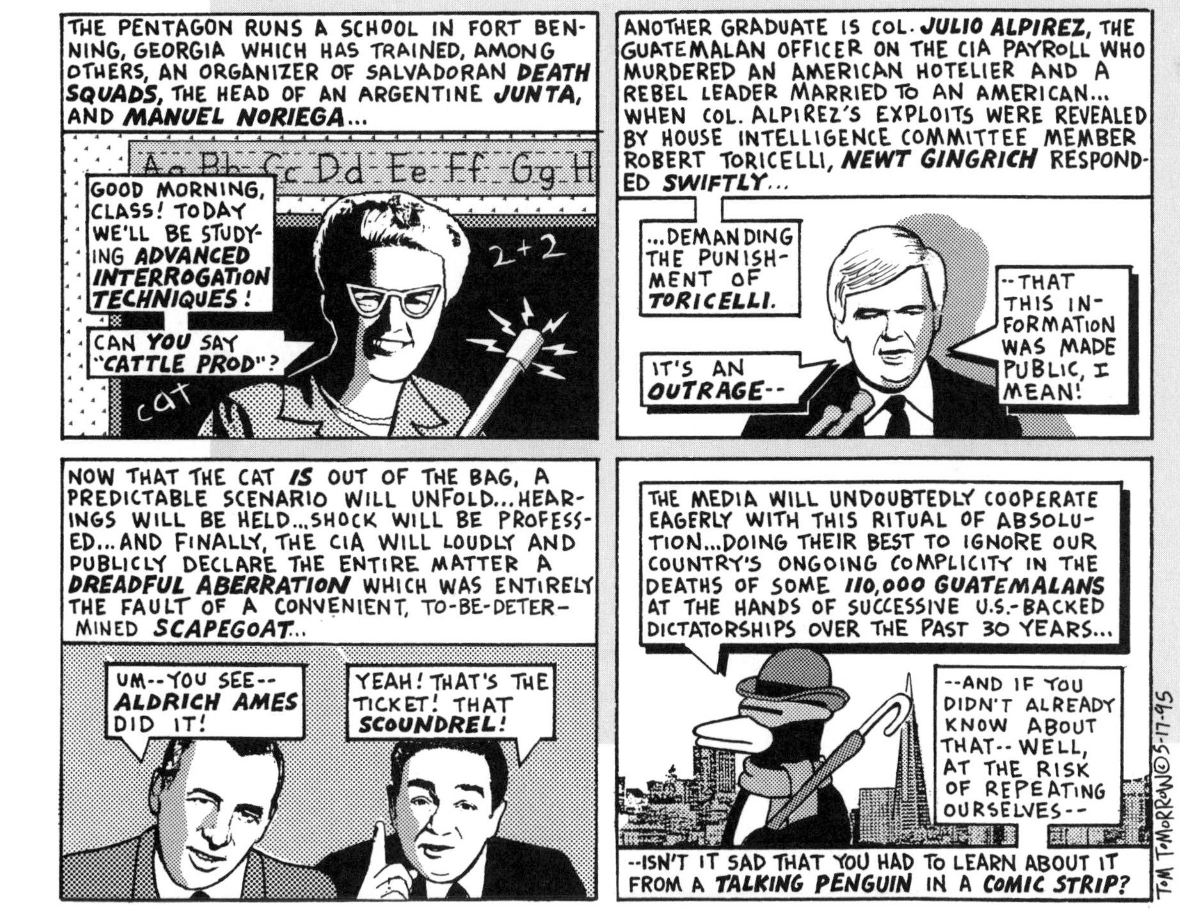
THE PENTAGON RUNS A SCHOOL IN FORT BENNING, GEORGIA WHICH HAS TRAINED, AMONG OTHERS, AN ORGANIZER OF SALVADORAN DEATH SQUADS, THE HEAD OF AN ARGENTINE JUNTA, AND MANUEL NORIEGA...
Aa Bb Cc Dd Ee Ff Gg H
GOOD MORNING, CLASS! TODAY WE'LL BE STUDYING ADVANCED INTERROGATION TECHNIQUES!
CAN YOU SAY "CATTLE PROD"?
2+2
cat
ANOTHER GRADUATE IS COL. JULIO ALPIREZ, THE GUATEMALAN OFFICER ON THE CIA PAYROLL WHO MURDERED AN AMERICAN HOTELIER AND A REBEL LEADER MARRIED TO AN AMERICAN... WHEN COL. ALPIREZ'S EXPLOITS WERE REVEALED BY HOUSE INTELLIGENCE COMMITTEE MEMBER ROBERT TORICELLI, NEWT GINGRICH RESPONDED SWIFTLY...
...DEMANDING THE PUNISHMENT OF TORICELLI.
IT'S AN OUTRAGE--
--THAT THIS INFORMATION WAS MADE PUBLIC, I MEAN!
NOW THAT THE CAT IS OUT OF THE BAG, A PREDICTABLE SCENARIO WILL UNFOLD... HEARINGS WILL BE HELD... SHOCK WILL BE PROFESSED... AND FINALLY, THE CIA WILL LOUDLY AND PUBLICLY DECLARE THE ENTIRE MATTER A DREADFUL ABERRATION WHICH WAS ENTIRELY THE FAULT OF A CONVENIENT, TO-BE-DETERMINED SCAPEGOAT...
UM--YOU SEE--ALDRICH AMES DID IT!
YEAH! THAT'S THE TICKET! THAT SCOUNDREL!
THE MEDIA WILL UNDOUBTEDLY COOPERATE EAGERLY WITH THIS RITUAL OF ABSOLUTION... DOING THEIR BEST TO IGNORE OUR COUNTRY'S ONGOING COMPLICITY IN THE DEATHS OF SOME 110,000 GUATEMALANS AT THE HANDS OF SUCCESSIVE U.S.-BACKED DICTATORSHIPS OVER THE PAST 30 YEARS...
--AND IF YOU DIDN'T ALREADY KNOW ABOUT THAT-- WELL, AT THE RISK OF REPEATING OURSELVES--
--ISN'T IT SAD THAT YOU HAD TO LEARN ABOUT IT FROM A TALKING PENGUIN IN A COMIC STRIP?
TOM TOMORROW©5-17-95

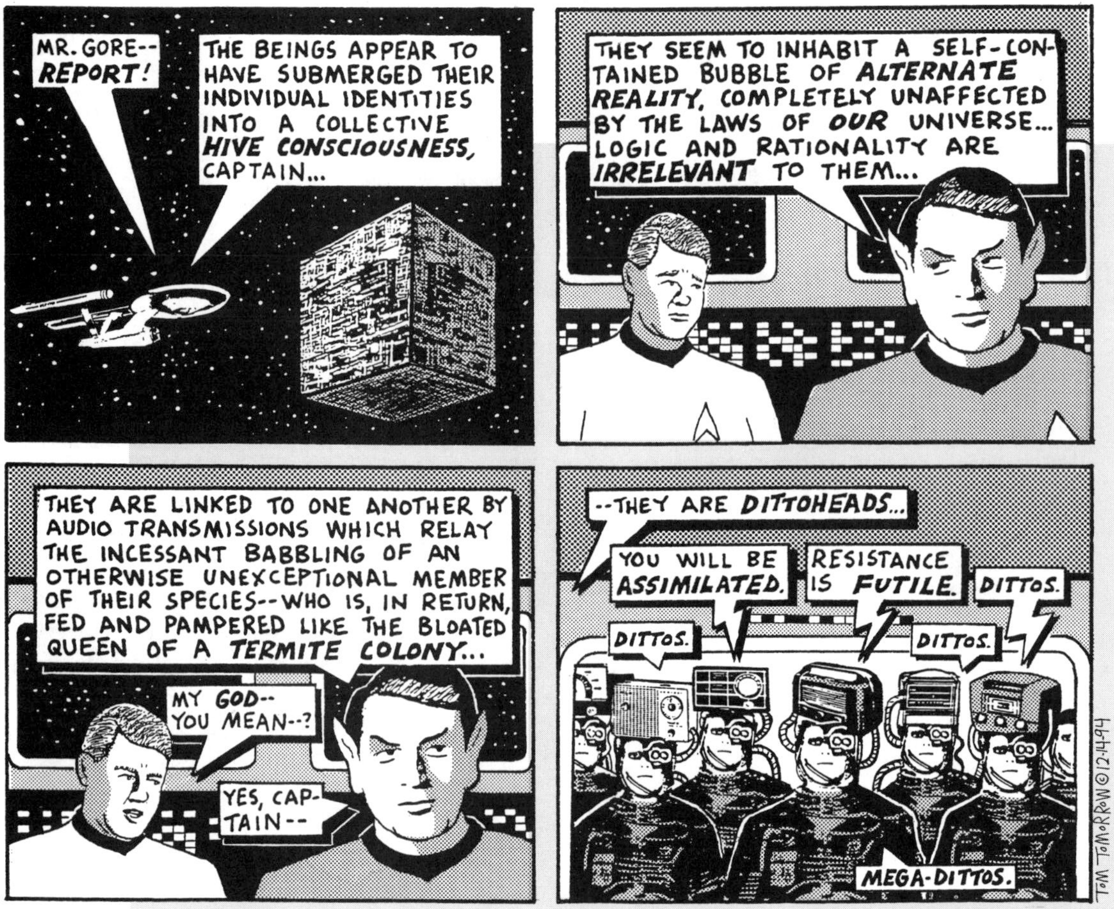
MR. GORE-- REPORT!
THE BEINGS APPEAR TO HAVE SUBMERGED THEIR INDIVIDUAL IDENTITIES INTO A COLLECTIVE HIVE CONSCIOUSNESS, CAPTAIN...
THEY SEEM TO INHABIT A SELF-CONTAINED BUBBLE OF ALTERNATE REALITY, COMPLETELY UNAFFECTED BY THE LAWS OF OUR UNIVERSE... LOGIC AND RATIONALITY ARE IRRELEVANT TO THEM...
THEY ARE LINKED TO ONE ANOTHER BY AUDIO TRANSMISSIONS WHICH RELAY THE INCESSANT BABBLING OF AN OTHERWISE UNEXCEPTIONAL MEMBER OF THEIR SPECIES--WHO IS, IN RETURN, FED AND PAMPERED LIKE THE BLOATED QUEEN OF A TERMITE COLONY...
MY GOD-- YOU MEAN--?
YES, CAPTAIN--
--THEY ARE DITTOHEADS...
YOU WILL BE ASSIMILATED.
RESISTANCE IS FUTILE.
DITTOS.
DITTOS.
DITTOS.
MEGA-DITTOS.
TOM TOMORROW©12-4-94

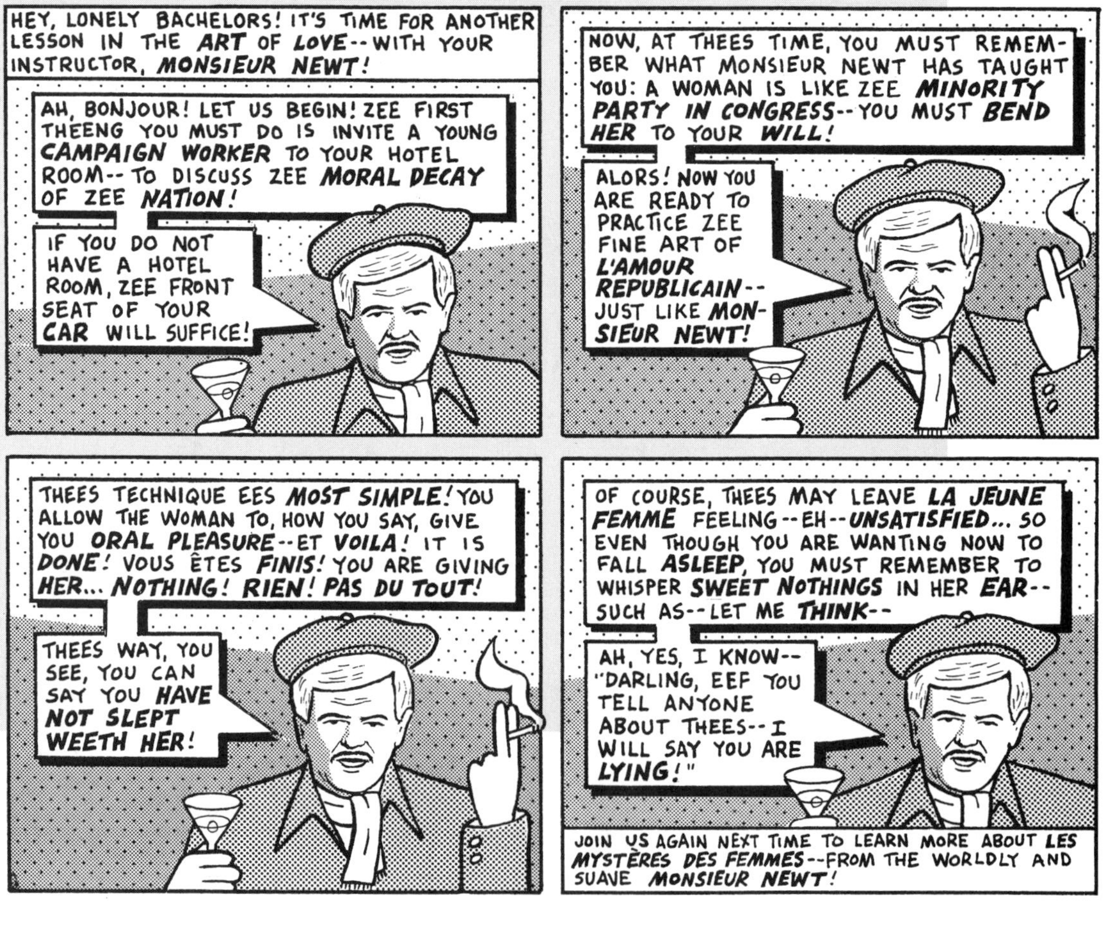
HEY, LONELY BACHELORS! IT'S TIME FOR ANOTHER LESSON IN THE ART OF LOVE--WITH YOUR INSTRUCTOR, MONSIEUR NEWT!
AH, BONJOUR! LET US BEGIN! ZEE FIRST THEENG YOU MUST DO IS INVITE A YOUNG CAMPAIGN WORKER TO YOUR HOTEL ROOM--TO DISCUSS ZEE MORAL DECAY OF ZEE NATION!
IF YOU DO NOT HAVE A HOTEL ROOM, ZEE FRONT SEAT OF YOUR CAR WILL SUFFICE!
NOW, AT THEES TIME, YOU MUST REMEMBER WHAT MONSIEUR NEWT HAS TAUGHT YOU: A WOMAN IS LIKE ZEE MINORITY PARTY IN CONGRESS--YOU MUST BEND HER TO YOUR WILL!
ALORS! NOW YOU ARE READY TO PRACTICE ZEE FINE ART OF L'AMOUR REPUBLICAIN--JUST LIKE MONSIEUR NEWT!
THEES TECHNIQUE EES MOST SIMPLE! YOU ALLOW THE WOMAN TO, HOW YOU SAY, GIVE YOU ORAL PLEASURE--ET VOILA! IT IS DONE! VOUS ÊTES FINIS! YOU ARE GIVING HER... NOTHING! RIEN! PAS DU TOUT!
THEES WAY, YOU SEE, YOU CAN SAY YOU HAVE NOT SLEPT WEETH HER!
OF COURSE, THEES MAY LEAVE LA JEUNE FEMME FEELING--EH--UNSATISFIED... SO EVEN THOUGH YOU ARE WANTING NOW TO FALL ASLEEP, YOU MUST REMEMBER TO WHISPER SWEET NOTHINGS IN HER EAR--SUCH AS--LET ME THINK--
AH, YES, I KNOW-- "DARLING, EEF YOU TELL ANYONE ABOUT THEES--I WILL SAY YOU ARE LYING!"
JOIN US AGAIN NEXT TIME TO LEARN MORE ABOUT LES MYSTÈRES DES FEMMES--FROM THE WORLDLY AND SUAVE MONSIEUR NEWT!

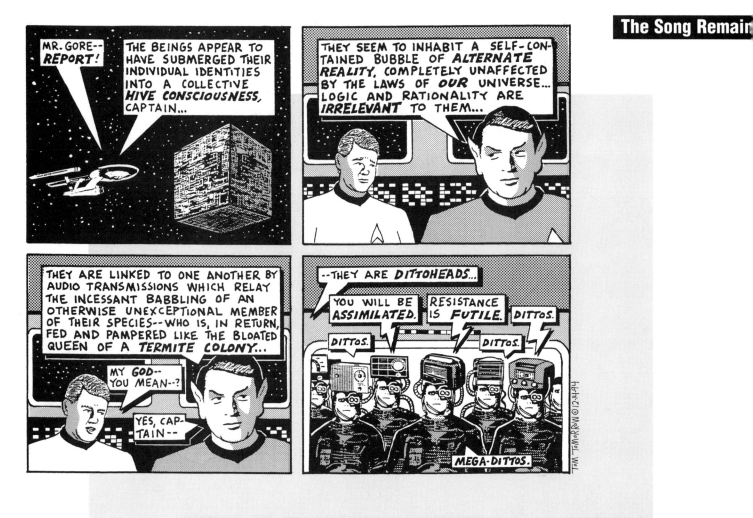

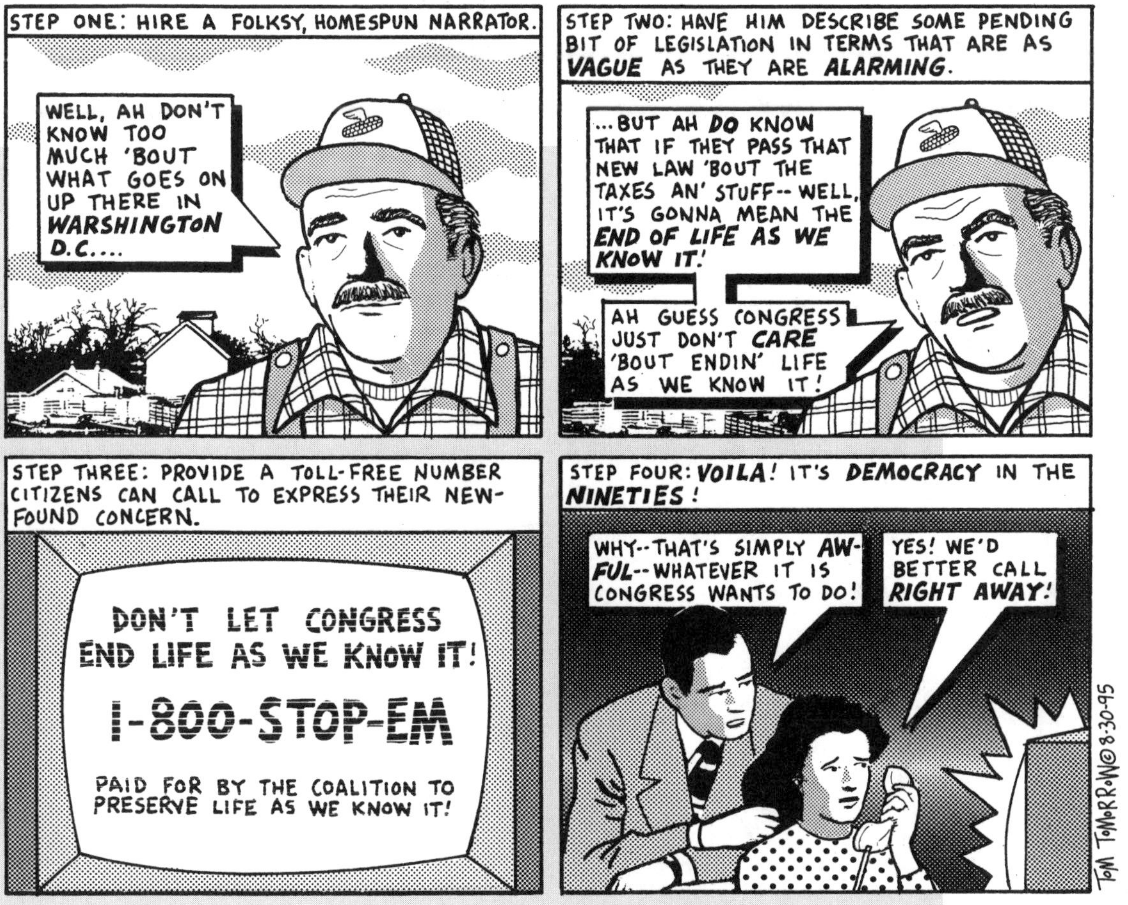
STEP ONE: HIRE A FOLKSY, HOMESPUN NARRATOR.
WELL, AH DON'T KNOW TOO MUCH 'BOUT WHAT GOES ON UP THERE IN WARSHINGTON D.C....
STEP TWO: HAVE HIM DESCRIBE SOME PENDING BIT OF LEGISLATION IN TERMS THAT ARE AS VAGUE AS THEY ARE ALARMING.
...BUT AH DO KNOW THAT IF THEY PASS THAT NEW LAW 'BOUT THE TAXES AN' STUFF-- WELL, IT'S GONNA MEAN THE END OF LIFE AS WE KNOW IT!
AH GUESS CONGRESS JUST DON'T CARE 'BOUT ENDIN' LIFE AS WE KNOW IT!
STEP THREE: PROVIDE A TOLL-FREE NUMBER CITIZENS CAN CALL TO EXPRESS THEIR NEW-FOUND CONCERN.
DON'T LET CONGRESS END LIFE AS WE KNOW IT!
1-800-STOP-EM
PAID FOR BY THE COALITION TO PRESERVE LIFE AS WE KNOW IT!
STEP FOUR: VOILA! IT'S DEMOCRACY IN THE NINETIES!
WHY--THAT'S SIMPLY AW-FUL--WHATEVER IT IS CONGRESS WANTS TO DO!
YES! WE'D BETTER CALL RIGHT AWAY!
TOM TOMORROW©8-30-95

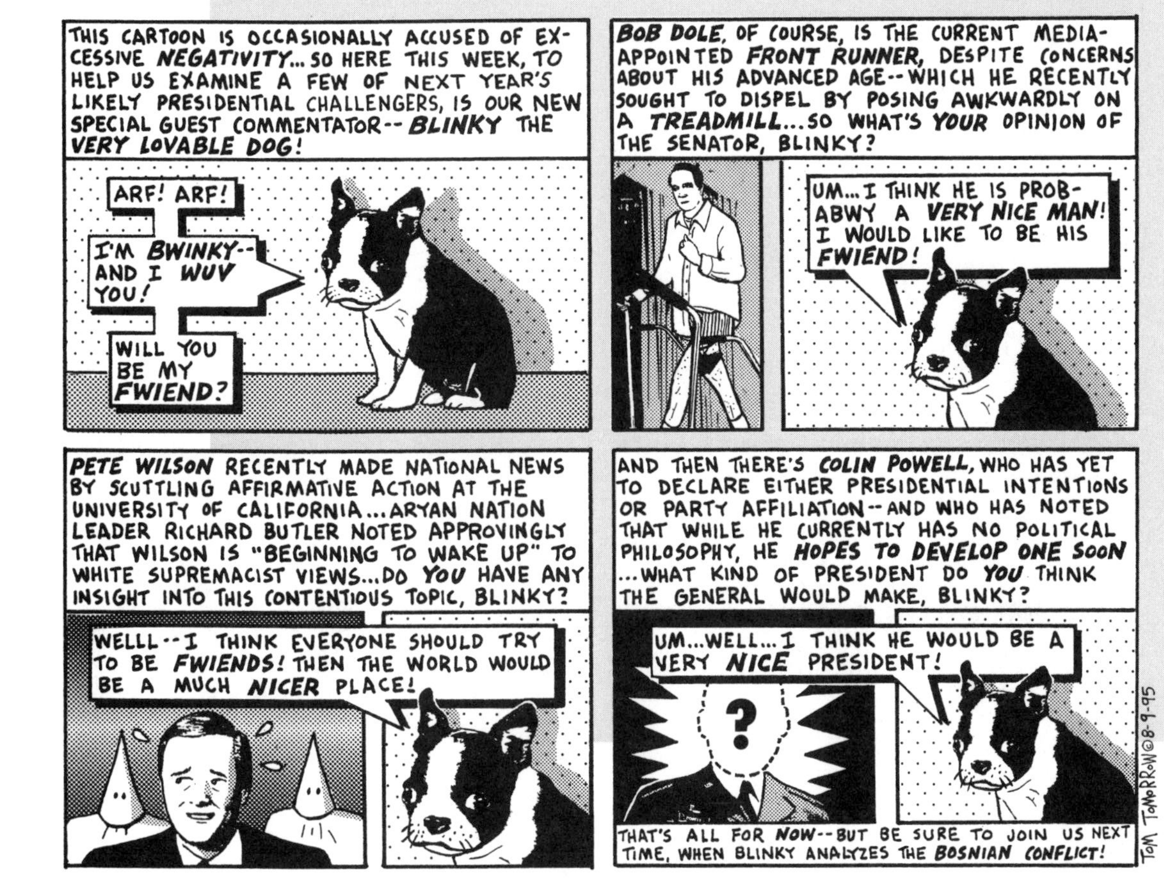
THIS CARTOON IS OCCASIONALLY ACCUSED OF EXCESSIVE NEGATIVITY... SO HERE THIS WEEK, TO HELP US EXAMINE A FEW OF NEXT YEAR'S LIKELY PRESIDENTIAL CHALLENGERS, IS OUR NEW SPECIAL GUEST COMMENTATOR-- BLINKY THE VERY LOVABLE DOG!
ARF! ARF!
I'M BWINKY-- AND I WUV YOU!
WILL YOU BE MY FWIEND?
BOB DOLE, OF COURSE, IS THE CURRENT MEDIA-APPOINTED FRONT RUNNER, DESPITE CONCERNS ABOUT HIS ADVANCED AGE--WHICH HE RECENTLY SOUGHT TO DISPEL BY POSING AWKWARDLY ON A TREADMILL... SO WHAT'S YOUR OPINION OF THE SENATOR, BLINKY?
UM... I THINK HE IS PROB-ABWY A VERY NICE MAN! I WOULD LIKE TO BE HIS FWIEND!
PETE WILSON RECENTLY MADE NATIONAL NEWS BY SCUTTLING AFFIRMATIVE ACTION AT THE UNIVERSITY OF CALIFORNIA... ARYAN NATION LEADER RICHARD BUTLER NOTED APPROVINGLY THAT WILSON IS "BEGINNING TO WAKE UP" TO WHITE SUPREMACIST VIEWS... DO YOU HAVE ANY INSIGHT INTO THIS CONTENTIOUS TOPIC, BLINKY?
WELLL--I THINK EVERYONE SHOULD TRY TO BE FWIENDS! THEN THE WORLD WOULD BE A MUCH NICER PLACE!
AND THEN THERE'S COLIN POWELL, WHO HAS YET TO DECLARE EITHER PRESIDENTIAL INTENTIONS OR PARTY AFFILIATION--AND WHO HAS NOTED THAT WHILE HE CURRENTLY HAS NO POLITICAL PHILOSOPHY, HE HOPES TO DEVELOP ONE SOON ...WHAT KIND OF PRESIDENT DO YOU THINK THE GENERAL WOULD MAKE, BLINKY?
UM...WELL... I THINK HE WOULD BE A VERY NICE PRESIDENT!
?
THAT'S ALL FOR NOW--BUT BE SURE TO JOIN US NEXT TIME, WHEN BLINKY ANALYZES THE BOSNIAN CONFLICT!
TOM TOMORROW©8-9-95

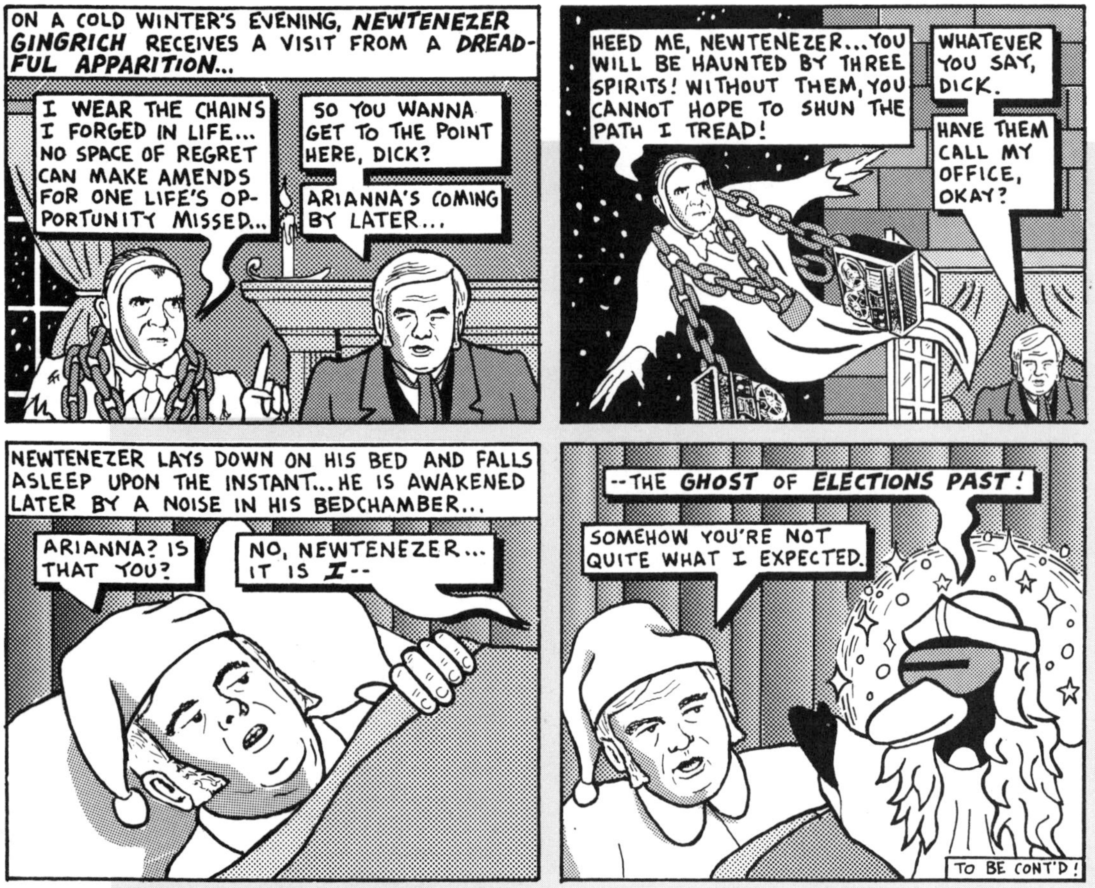
ON A COLD WINTER'S EVENING, NEWTENEZER GINGRICH RECEIVES A VISIT FROM A DREADFUL APPARITION...
I WEAR THE CHAINS I FORGED IN LIFE... NO SPACE OF REGRET CAN MAKE AMENDS FOR ONE LIFE'S OPPORTUNITY MISSED...
SO YOU WANNA GET TO THE POINT HERE, DICK?
ARIANNA'S COMING BY LATER...
HEED ME, NEWTENEZER...YOU WILL BE HAUNTED BY THREE SPIRITS! WITHOUT THEM, YOU CANNOT HOPE TO SHUN THE PATH I TREAD!
WHATEVER YOU SAY, DICK.
HAVE THEM CALL MY OFFICE, OKAY?
NEWTENEZER LAYS DOWN ON HIS BED AND FALLS ASLEEP UPON THE INSTANT...HE IS AWAKENED LATER BY A NOISE IN HIS BEDCHAMBER...
ARIANNA? IS THAT YOU?
NO, NEWTENEZER... IT IS I--
--THE GHOST OF ELECTIONS PAST!
SOMEHOW YOU'RE NOT QUITE WHAT I EXPECTED.
TO BE CONT'D!

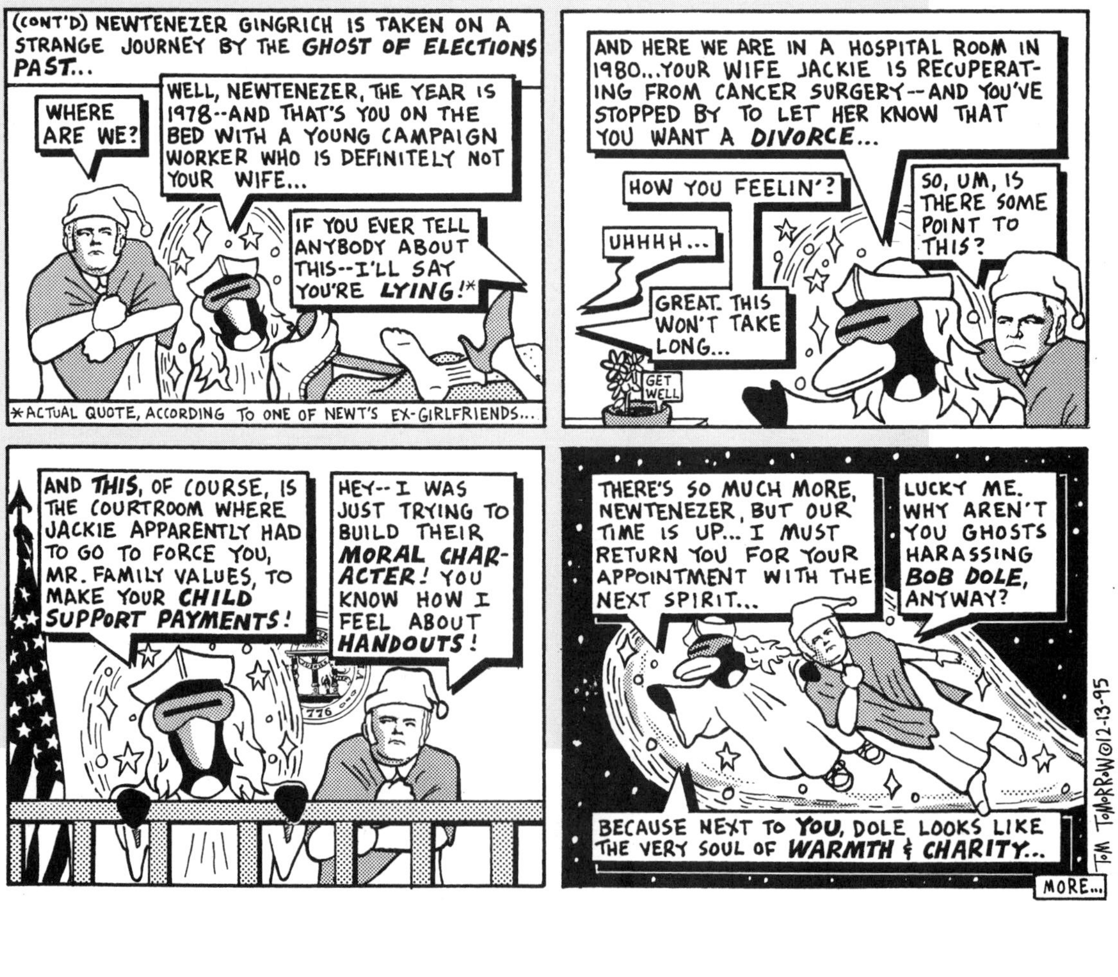
(CONT'D) NEWTENEZER GINGRICH IS TAKEN ON A STRANGE JOURNEY BY THE GHOST OF ELECTIONS PAST...
WHERE ARE WE?
WELL, NEWTENEZER, THE YEAR IS 1978--AND THAT'S YOU ON THE BED WITH A YOUNG CAMPAIGN WORKER WHO IS DEFINITELY NOT YOUR WIFE...
IF YOU EVER TELL ANYBODY ABOUT THIS--I'LL SAY YOU'RE LYING!*
*ACTUAL QUOTE, ACCORDING TO ONE OF NEWT'S EX-GIRLFRIENDS...
AND HERE WE ARE IN A HOSPITAL ROOM IN 1980...YOUR WIFE JACKIE IS RECUPERATING FROM CANCER SURGERY--AND YOU'VE STOPPED BY TO LET HER KNOW THAT YOU WANT A DIVORCE...
HOW YOU FEELIN'?
UHHHH...
GREAT. THIS WON'T TAKE LONG...
SO, UM, IS THERE SOME POINT TO THIS?
GET WELL
AND THIS, OF COURSE, IS THE COURTROOM WHERE JACKIE APPARENTLY HAD TO GO TO FORCE YOU, MR. FAMILY VALUES, TO MAKE YOUR CHILD SUPPORT PAYMENTS!
HEY--I WAS JUST TRYING TO BUILD THEIR MORAL CHARACTER! YOU KNOW HOW I FEEL ABOUT HANDOUTS!
THERE'S SO MUCH MORE, NEWTENEZER, BUT OUR TIME IS UP... I MUST RETURN YOU FOR YOUR APPOINTMENT WITH THE NEXT SPIRIT...
LUCKY ME. WHY AREN'T YOU GHOSTS HARASSING BOB DOLE, ANYWAY?
BECAUSE NEXT TO YOU, DOLE LOOKS LIKE THE VERY SOUL OF WARMTH & CHARITY...
TOM TOMORROW©12-13-95
MORE...

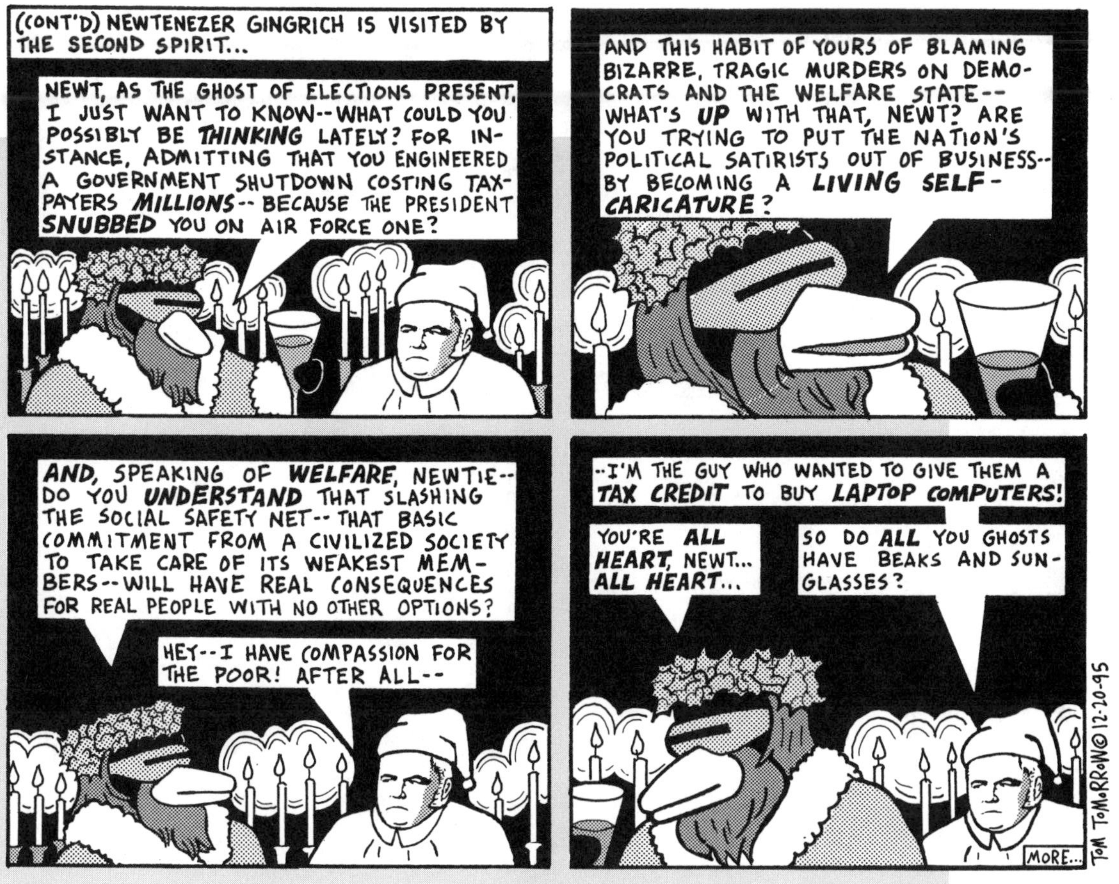
(CONT'D) NEWTENEZER GINGRICH IS VISITED BY THE SECOND SPIRIT...
NEWT, AS THE GHOST OF ELECTIONS PRESENT, I JUST WANT TO KNOW--WHAT COULD YOU POSSIBLY BE THINKING LATELY? FOR INSTANCE, ADMITTING THAT YOU ENGINEERED A GOVERNMENT SHUTDOWN COSTING TAXPAYERS MILLIONS--BECAUSE THE PRESIDENT SNUBBED YOU ON AIR FORCE ONE?
AND THIS HABIT OF YOURS OF BLAMING BIZARRE, TRAGIC MURDERS ON DEMOCRATS AND THE WELFARE STATE--WHAT'S UP WITH THAT, NEWT? ARE YOU TRYING TO PUT THE NATION'S POLITICAL SATIRISTS OUT OF BUSINESS--BY BECOMING A LIVING SELF-CARICATURE?
AND, SPEAKING OF WELFARE, NEWTIE--DO YOU UNDERSTAND THAT SLASHING THE SOCIAL SAFETY NET--THAT BASIC COMMITMENT FROM A CIVILIZED SOCIETY TO TAKE CARE OF ITS WEAKEST MEMBERS--WILL HAVE REAL CONSEQUENCES FOR REAL PEOPLE WITH NO OTHER OPTIONS?
HEY--I HAVE COMPASSION FOR THE POOR! AFTER ALL--
--I'M THE GUY WHO WANTED TO GIVE THEM A TAX CREDIT TO BUY LAPTOP COMPUTERS!
YOU'RE ALL HEART, NEWT... ALL HEART...
SO DO ALL YOU GHOSTS HAVE BEAKS AND SUNGLASSES?
MORE...
TOM TOMORROW©12-20-95

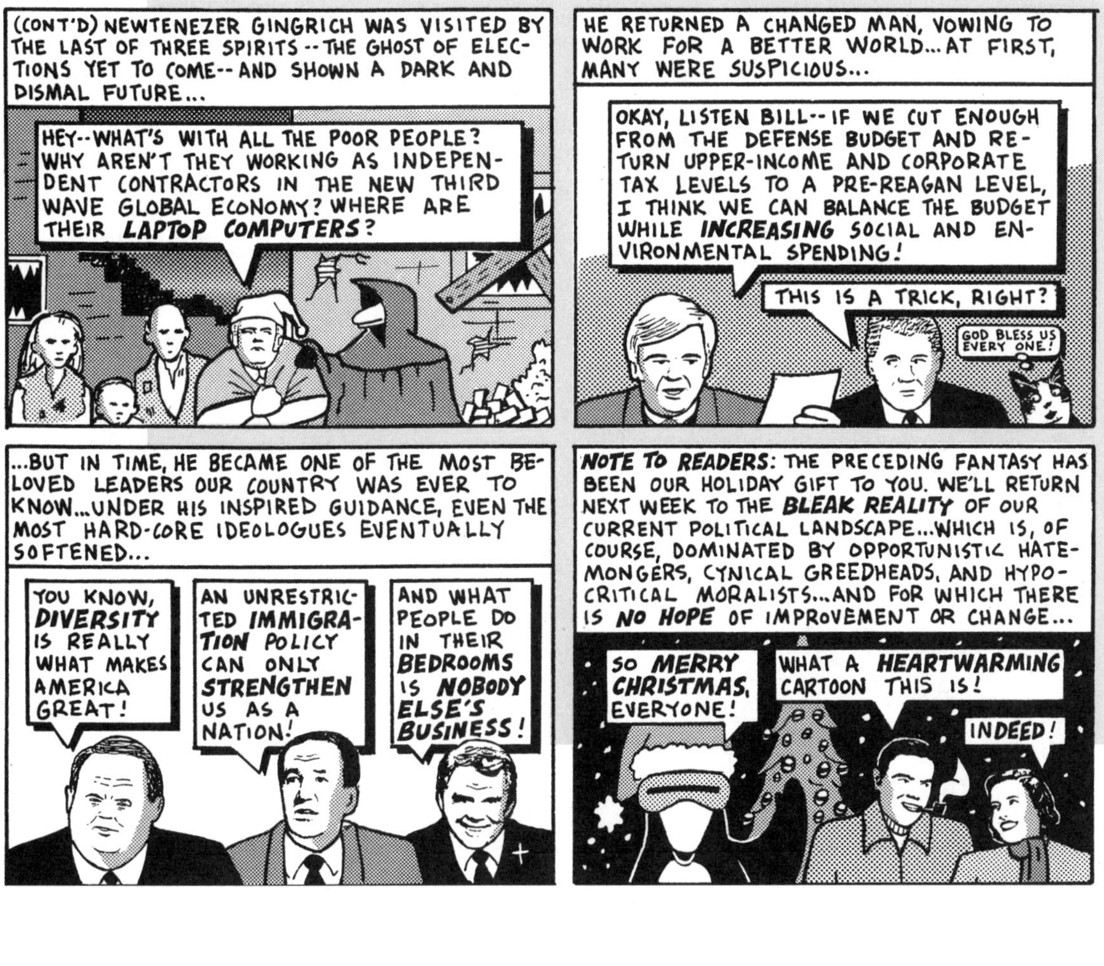
(CONT'D) NEWTENEZER GINGRICH WAS VISITED BY THE LAST OF THREE SPIRITS--THE GHOST OF ELECTIONS YET TO COME--AND SHOWN A DARK AND DISMAL FUTURE...
HEY--WHAT'S WITH ALL THE POOR PEOPLE? WHY AREN'T THEY WORKING AS INDEPENDENT CONTRACTORS IN THE NEW THIRD WAVE GLOBAL ECONOMY? WHERE ARE THEIR LAPTOP COMPUTERS?
HE RETURNED A CHANGED MAN, VOWING TO WORK FOR A BETTER WORLD... AT FIRST, MANY WERE SUSPICIOUS...
OKAY, LISTEN BILL--IF WE CUT ENOUGH FROM THE DEFENSE BUDGET AND RETURN UPPER-INCOME AND CORPORATE TAX LEVELS TO A PRE-REAGAN LEVEL, I THINK WE CAN BALANCE THE BUDGET WHILE INCREASING SOCIAL AND ENVIRONMENTAL SPENDING!
THIS IS A TRICK, RIGHT?
GOD BLESS US EVERY ONE!
...BUT IN TIME, HE BECAME ONE OF THE MOST BELOVED LEADERS OUR COUNTRY WAS EVER TO KNOW... UNDER HIS INSPIRED GUIDANCE, EVEN THE MOST HARD-CORE IDEOLOGUES EVENTUALLY SOFTENED...
YOU KNOW, DIVERSITY IS REALLY WHAT MAKES AMERICA GREAT!
AN UNRESTRICTED IMMIGRATION POLICY CAN ONLY STRENGTHEN US AS A NATION!
AND WHAT PEOPLE DO IN THEIR BEDROOMS IS NOBODY ELSE'S BUSINESS!
NOTE TO READERS: THE PRECEDING FANTASY HAS BEEN OUR HOLIDAY GIFT TO YOU. WE'LL RETURN NEXT WEEK TO THE BLEAK REALITY OF OUR CURRENT POLITICAL LANDSCAPE... WHICH IS, OF COURSE, DOMINATED BY OPPORTUNISTIC HATE-MONGERS, CYNICAL GREEDHEADS, AND HYPOCRITICAL MORALISTS... AND FOR WHICH THERE IS NO HOPE OF IMPROVEMENT OR CHANGE...
SO MERRY CHRISTMAS, EVERYONE!
WHAT A HEARTWARMING CARTOON THIS IS!
INDEED!

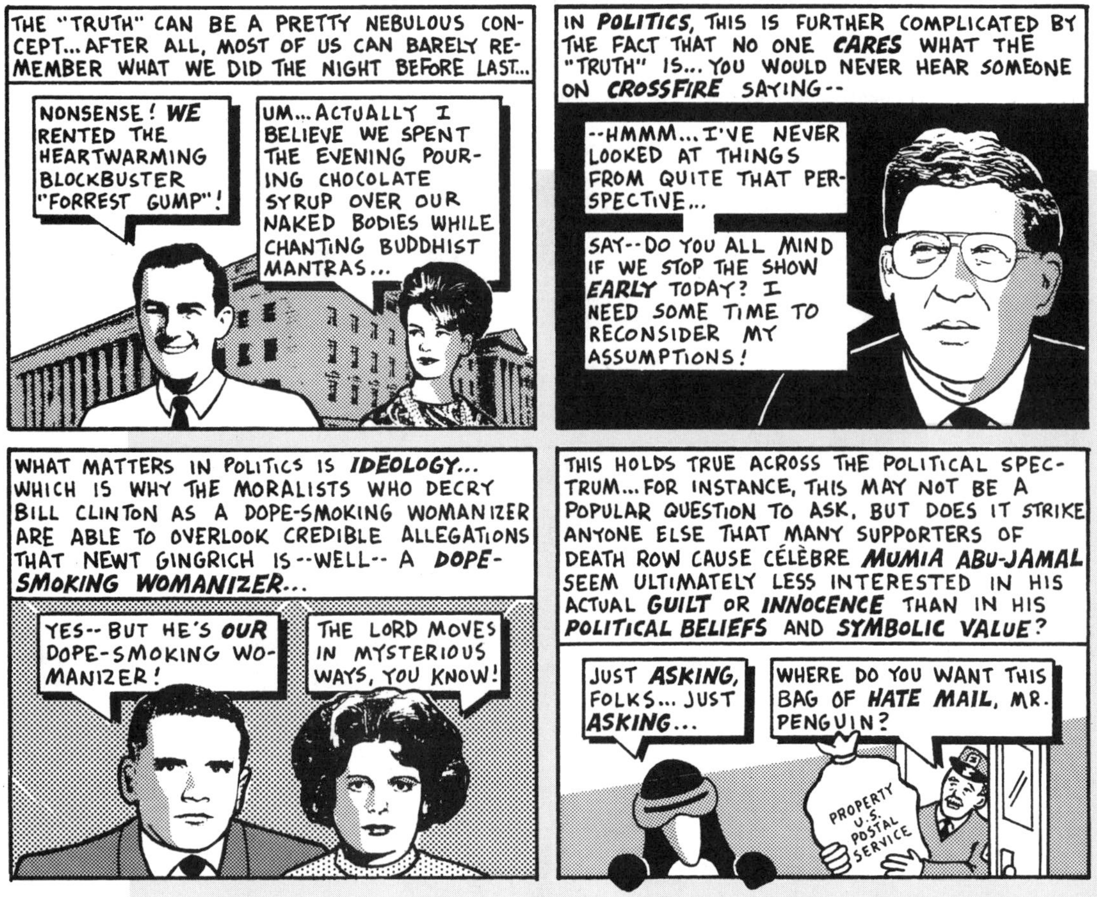
THE "TRUTH" CAN BE A PRETTY NEBULOUS CONCEPT... AFTER ALL, MOST OF US CAN BARELY REMEMBER WHAT WE DID THE NIGHT BEFORE LAST...
NONSENSE! WE RENTED THE HEARTWARMING BLOCKBUSTER "FORREST GUMP"!
UM... ACTUALLY I BELIEVE WE SPENT THE EVENING POURING CHOCOLATE SYRUP OVER OUR NAKED BODIES WHILE CHANTING BUDDHIST MANTRAS...
IN POLITICS, THIS IS FURTHER COMPLICATED BY THE FACT THAT NO ONE CARES WHAT THE "TRUTH" IS... YOU WOULD NEVER HEAR SOMEONE ON CROSSFIRE SAYING--
--HMMM... I'VE NEVER LOOKED AT THINGS FROM QUITE THAT PERSPECTIVE...
SAY--DO YOU ALL MIND IF WE STOP THE SHOW EARLY TODAY? I NEED SOME TIME TO RECONSIDER MY ASSUMPTIONS!
WHAT MATTERS IN POLITICS IS IDEOLOGY... WHICH IS WHY THE MORALISTS WHO DECRY BILL CLINTON AS A DOPE-SMOKING WOMANIZER ARE ABLE TO OVERLOOK CREDIBLE ALLEGATIONS THAT NEWT GINGRICH IS--WELL-- A DOPE-SMOKING WOMANIZER...
YES--BUT HE'S OUR DOPE-SMOKING WOMANIZER!
THE LORD MOVES IN MYSTERIOUS WAYS, YOU KNOW!
THIS HOLDS TRUE ACROSS THE POLITICAL SPECTRUM... FOR INSTANCE, THIS MAY NOT BE A POPULAR QUESTION TO ASK, BUT DOES IT STRIKE ANYONE ELSE THAT MANY SUPPORTERS OF DEATH ROW CAUSE CÉLÈBRE MUMIA ABU-JAMAL SEEM ULTIMATELY LESS INTERESTED IN HIS ACTUAL GUILT OR INNOCENCE THAN IN HIS POLITICAL BELIEFS AND SYMBOLIC VALUE?
JUST ASKING, FOLKS... JUST ASKING...
WHERE DO YOU WANT THIS BAG OF HATE MAIL, MR. PENGUIN?
PROPERTY U.S. POSTAL SERVICE

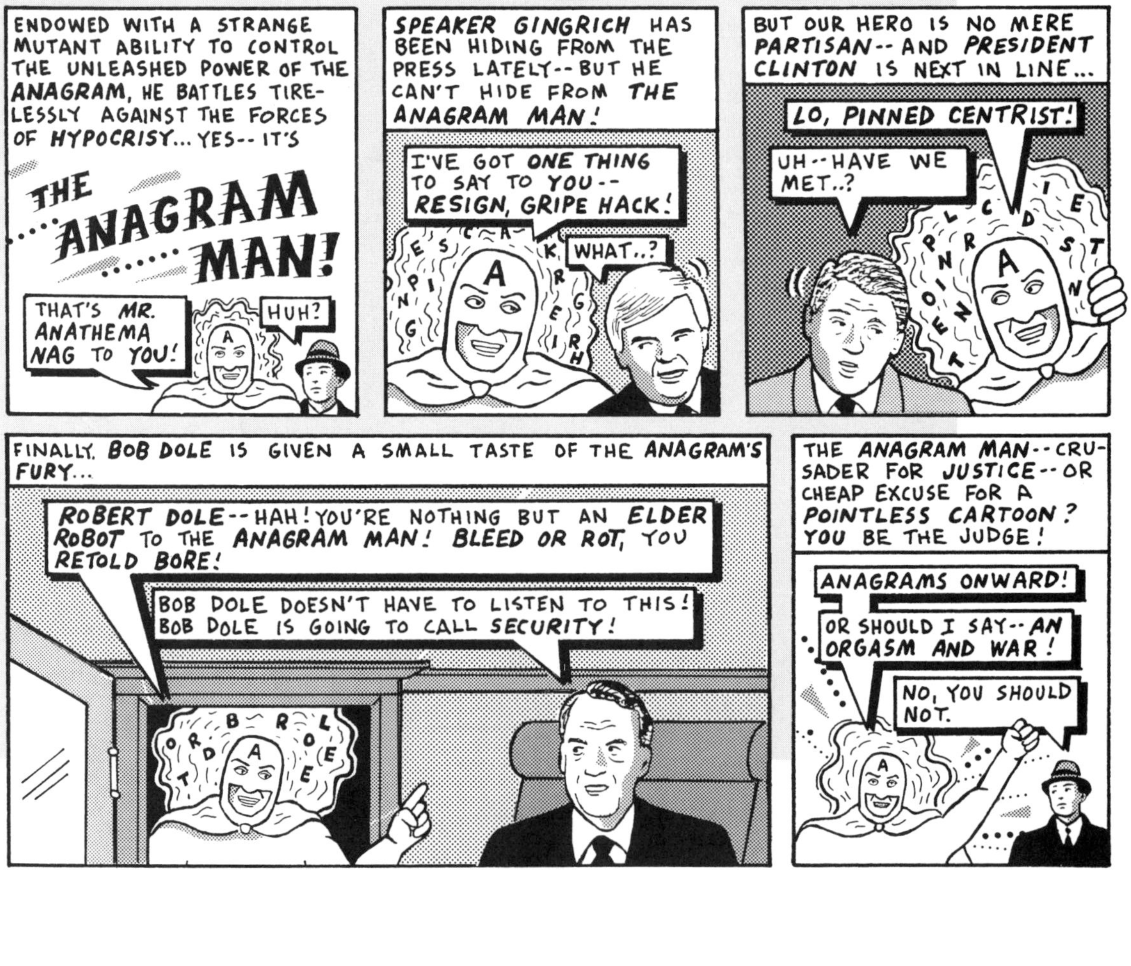
ENDOWED WITH A STRANGE MUTANT ABILITY TO CONTROL THE UNLEASHED POWER OF THE ANAGRAM, HE BATTLES TIRELESSLY AGAINST THE FORCES OF HYPOCRISY... YES-- IT'S
THE ANAGRAM MAN!
THAT'S MR. ANATHEMA NAG TO YOU!
HUH?
SPEAKER GINGRICH HAS BEEN HIDING FROM THE PRESS LATELY--BUT HE CAN'T HIDE FROM THE ANAGRAM MAN!
I'VE GOT ONE THING TO SAY TO YOU-- RESIGN, GRIPE HACK!
WHAT..?
BUT OUR HERO IS NO MERE PARTISAN-- AND PRESIDENT CLINTON IS NEXT IN LINE...
LO, PINNED CENTRIST!
UH--HAVE WE MET..?
FINALLY, BOB DOLE IS GIVEN A SMALL TASTE OF THE ANAGRAM'S FURY...
ROBERT DOLE--HAH! YOU'RE NOTHING BUT AN ELDER ROBOT TO THE ANAGRAM MAN! BLEED OR ROT, YOU RETOLD BORE!
BOB DOLE DOESN'T HAVE TO LISTEN TO THIS! BOB DOLE IS GOING TO CALL SECURITY!
THE ANAGRAM MAN--CRUSADER FOR JUSTICE--OR CHEAP EXCUSE FOR A POINTLESS CARTOON? YOU BE THE JUDGE!
ANAGRAMS ONWARD!
OR SHOULD I SAY-- AN ORGASM AND WAR!
NO, YOU SHOULD NOT.

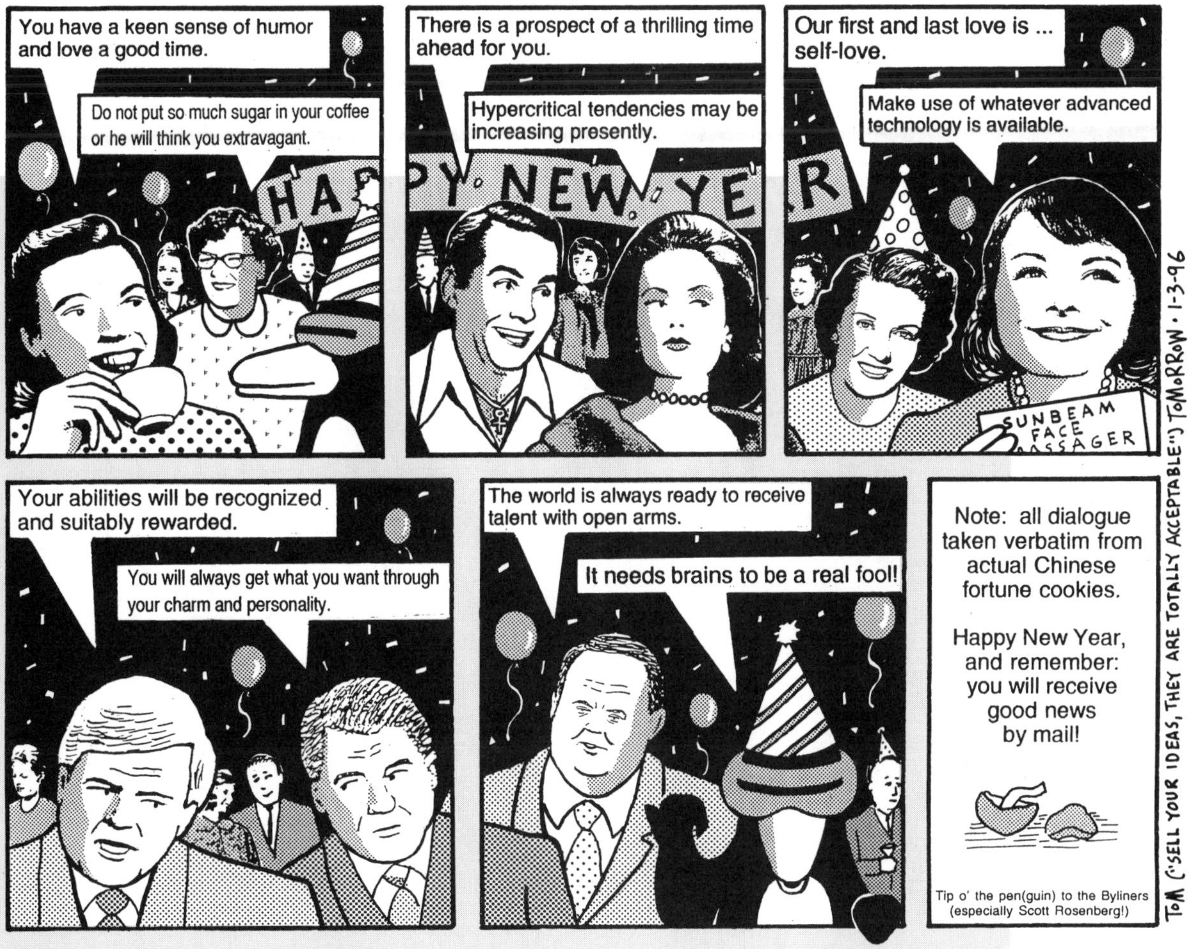
You have a keen sense of humor and love a good time.
Do not put so much sugar in your coffee or he will think you extravagant.
HAPPY NEW YEAR
There is a prospect of a thrilling time ahead for you.
Hypercritical tendencies may be increasing presently.
Our first and last love is ... self-love.
Make use of whatever advanced technology is available.
SUNBEAM FACE MASSAGER
Your abilities will be recognized and suitably rewarded.
You will always get what you want through your charm and personality.
The world is always ready to receive talent with open arms.
It needs brains to be a real fool!
Note: all dialogue taken verbatim from actual Chinese fortune cookies.
Happy New Year, and remember: you will receive good news by mail!
Tip o' the pen(guin) to the Byliners (especially Scott Rosenberg!)
TOM ("SELL YOUR IDEAS, THEY ARE TOTALLY ACCEPTABLE") TOMORROW • 1-3-96

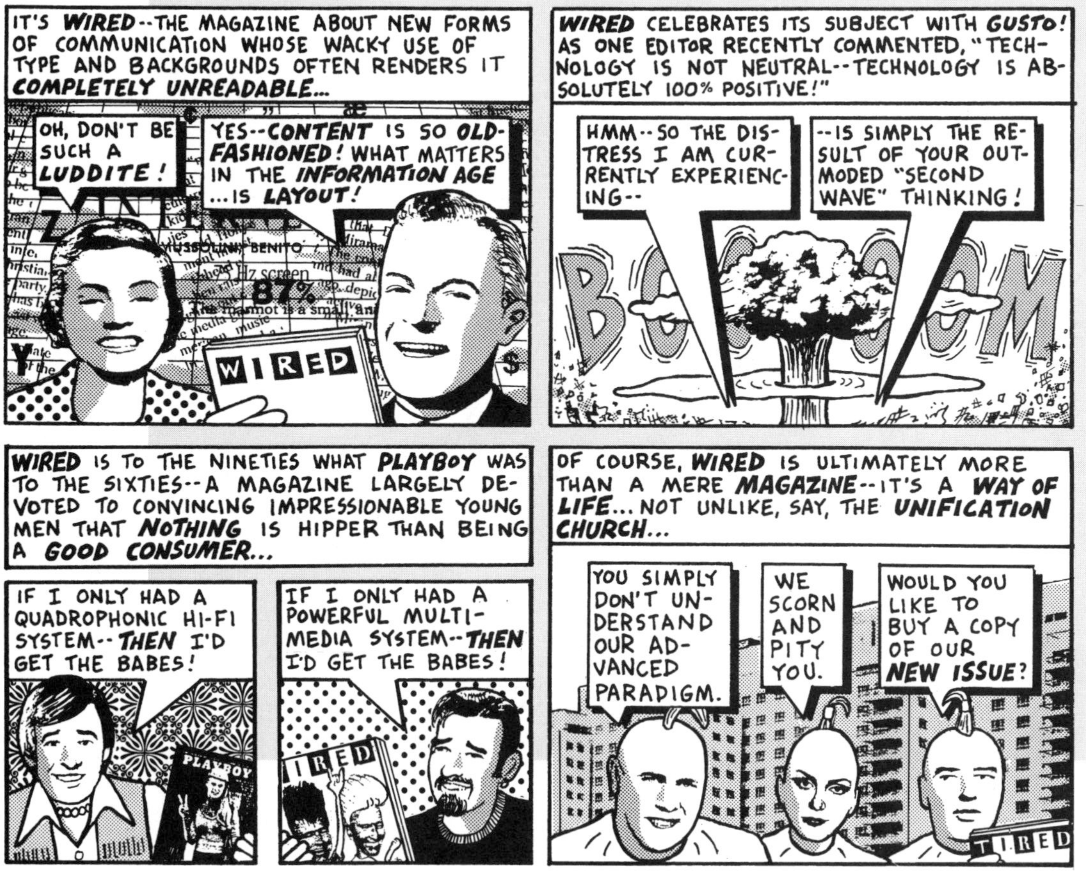
IT'S WIRED--THE MAGAZINE ABOUT NEW FORMS OF COMMUNICATION WHOSE WACKY USE OF TYPE AND BACKGROUNDS OFTEN RENDERS IT COMPLETELY UNREADABLE...
OH, DON'T BE SUCH A LUDDITE!
YES--CONTENT IS SO OLD-FASHIONED! WHAT MATTERS IN THE INFORMATION AGE ...IS LAYOUT!
WIRED
WIRED CELEBRATES ITS SUBJECT WITH GUSTO! AS ONE EDITOR RECENTLY COMMENTED, "TECHNOLOGY IS NOT NEUTRAL--TECHNOLOGY IS ABSOLUTELY 100% POSITIVE!"
HMM--SO THE DISTRESS I AM CURRENTLY EXPERIENCING--
--IS SIMPLY THE RESULT OF YOUR OUTMODED "SECOND WAVE" THINKING!
WIRED IS TO THE NINETIES WHAT PLAYBOY WAS TO THE SIXTIES--A MAGAZINE LARGELY DEVOTED TO CONVINCING IMPRESSIONABLE YOUNG MEN THAT NOTHING IS HIPPER THAN BEING A GOOD CONSUMER...
IF I ONLY HAD A QUADROPHONIC HI-FI SYSTEM--THEN I'D GET THE BABES!
PLAYBOY
IF I ONLY HAD A POWERFUL MULTI-MEDIA SYSTEM--THEN I'D GET THE BABES!
TIRED
OF COURSE, WIRED IS ULTIMATELY MORE THAN A MERE MAGAZINE--IT'S A WAY OF LIFE... NOT UNLIKE, SAY, THE UNIFICATION CHURCH...
YOU SIMPLY DON'T UNDERSTAND OUR ADVANCED PARADIGM.
WE SCORN AND PITY YOU.
WOULD YOU LIKE TO BUY A COPY OF OUR NEW ISSUE?
TIRED

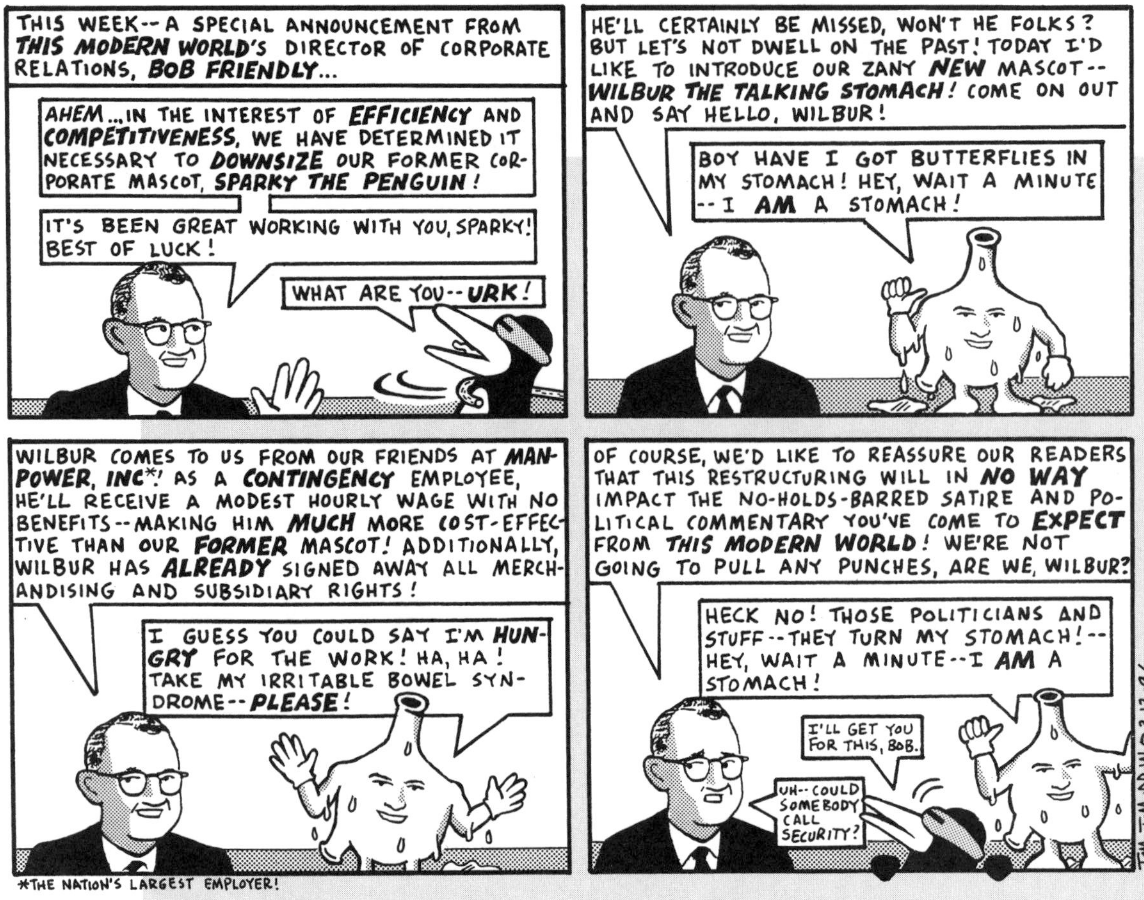
THIS WEEK--A SPECIAL ANNOUNCEMENT FROM THIS MODERN WORLD'S DIRECTOR OF CORPORATE RELATIONS, BOB FRIENDLY...
AHEM...IN THE INTEREST OF EFFICIENCY AND COMPETITIVENESS, WE HAVE DETERMINED IT NECESSARY TO DOWNSIZE OUR FORMER CORPORATE MASCOT, SPARKY THE PENGUIN!
IT'S BEEN GREAT WORKING WITH YOU, SPARKY! BEST OF LUCK!
WHAT ARE YOU--URK!
HE'LL CERTAINLY BE MISSED, WON'T HE FOLKS? BUT LET'S NOT DWELL ON THE PAST! TODAY I'D LIKE TO INTRODUCE OUR ZANY NEW MASCOT--WILBUR THE TALKING STOMACH! COME ON OUT AND SAY HELLO, WILBUR!
BOY HAVE I GOT BUTTERFLIES IN MY STOMACH! HEY, WAIT A MINUTE--I AM A STOMACH!
WILBUR COMES TO US FROM OUR FRIENDS AT MANPOWER, INC*! AS A CONTINGENCY EMPLOYEE, HE'LL RECEIVE A MODEST HOURLY WAGE WITH NO BENEFITS--MAKING HIM MUCH MORE COST-EFFECTIVE THAN OUR FORMER MASCOT! ADDITIONALLY, WILBUR HAS ALREADY SIGNED AWAY ALL MERCHANDISING AND SUBSIDIARY RIGHTS!
I GUESS YOU COULD SAY I'M HUNGRY FOR THE WORK! HA, HA! TAKE MY IRRITABLE BOWEL SYNDROME--PLEASE!
OF COURSE, WE'D LIKE TO REASSURE OUR READERS THAT THIS RESTRUCTURING WILL IN NO WAY IMPACT THE NO-HOLDS-BARRED SATIRE AND POLITICAL COMMENTARY YOU'VE COME TO EXPECT FROM THIS MODERN WORLD! WE'RE NOT GOING TO PULL ANY PUNCHES, ARE WE, WILBUR?
HECK NO! THOSE POLITICIANS AND STUFF--THEY TURN MY STOMACH!--HEY, WAIT A MINUTE--I AM A STOMACH!
I'LL GET YOU FOR THIS, BOB.
UH--COULD SOMEBODY CALL SECURITY?
TOM TOMORROW © 3-13-96
*THE NATION'S LARGEST EMPLOYER!

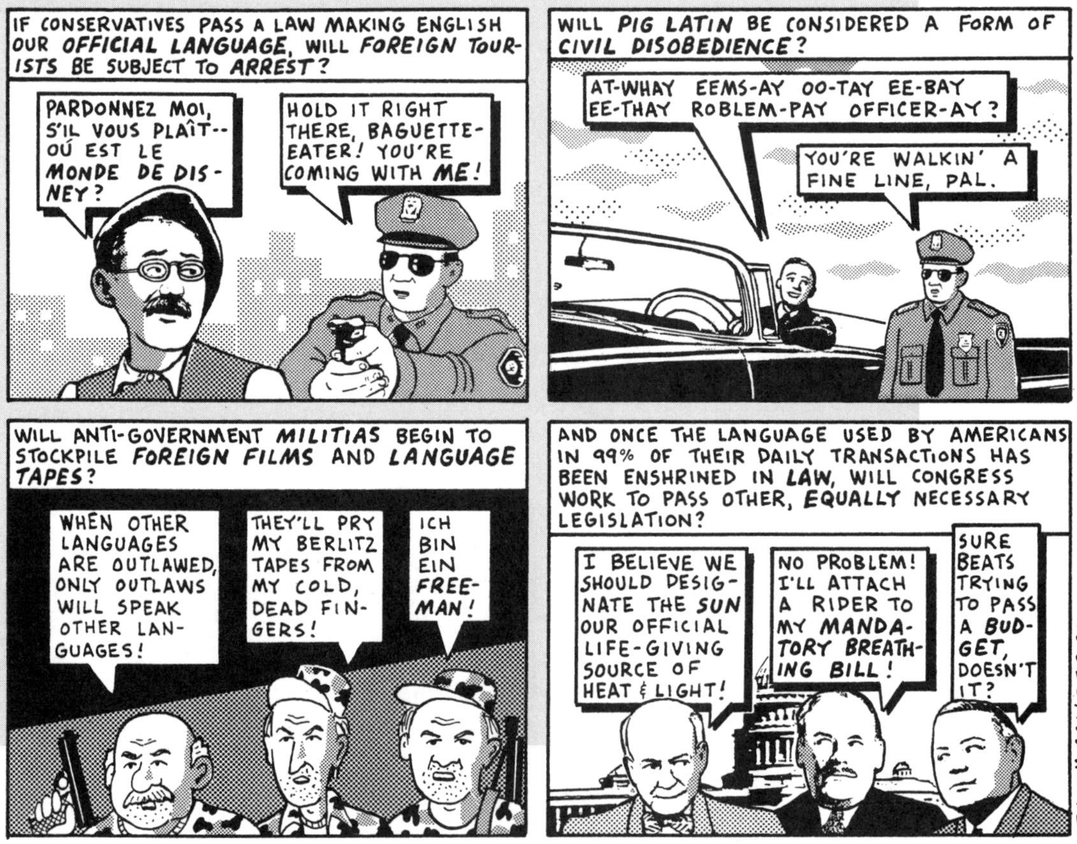
IF CONSERVATIVES PASS A LAW MAKING ENGLISH OUR OFFICIAL LANGUAGE, WILL FOREIGN TOURISTS BE SUBJECT TO ARREST?
PARDONNEZ MOI, S'IL VOUS PLAÎT--OÚ EST LE MONDE DE DISNEY?
HOLD IT RIGHT THERE, BAGUETTE-EATER! YOU'RE COMING WITH ME!
WILL PIG LATIN BE CONSIDERED A FORM OF CIVIL DISOBEDIENCE?
AT-WHAY EEMS-AY OO-TAY EE-BAY EE-THAY ROBLEM-PAY OFFICER-AY?
YOU'RE WALKIN' A FINE LINE, PAL.
WILL ANTI-GOVERNMENT MILITIAS BEGIN TO STOCKPILE FOREIGN FILMS AND LANGUAGE TAPES?
WHEN OTHER LANGUAGES ARE OUTLAWED, ONLY OUTLAWS WILL SPEAK OTHER LANGUAGES!
THEY'LL PRY MY BERLITZ TAPES FROM MY COLD, DEAD FINGERS!
ICH BIN EIN FREEMAN!
AND ONCE THE LANGUAGE USED BY AMERICANS IN 99% OF THEIR DAILY TRANSACTIONS HAS BEEN ENSHRINED IN LAW, WILL CONGRESS WORK TO PASS OTHER, EQUALLY NECESSARY LEGISLATION?
I BELIEVE WE SHOULD DESIGNATE THE SUN OUR OFFICIAL LIFE-GIVING SOURCE OF HEAT & LIGHT!
NO PROBLEM! I'LL ATTACH A RIDER TO MY MANDATORY BREATHING BILL!
SURE BEATS TRYING TO PASS A BUDGET, DOESN'T IT?
TOM TOMORROW © 5-8-96

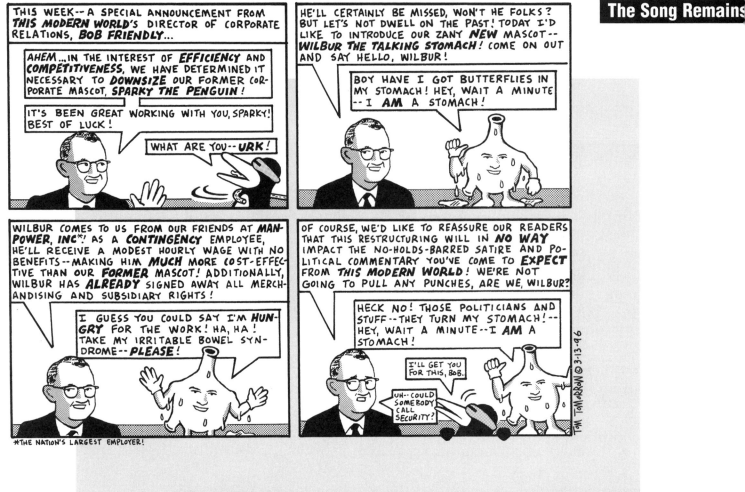

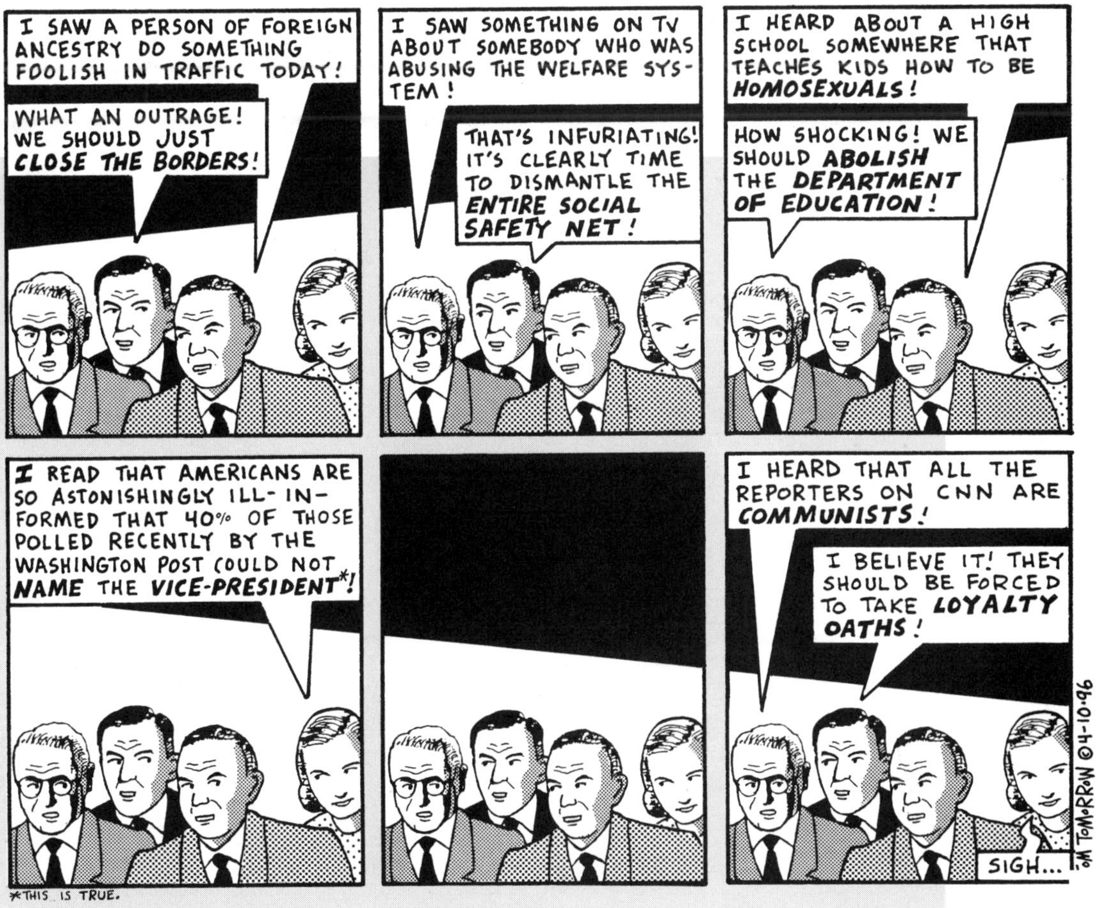
I SAW A PERSON OF FOREIGN ANCESTRY DO SOMETHING FOOLISH IN TRAFFIC TODAY!
WHAT AN OUTRAGE! WE SHOULD JUST CLOSE THE BORDERS!
I SAW SOMETHING ON TV ABOUT SOMEBODY WHO WAS ABUSING THE WELFARE SYSTEM!
THAT'S INFURIATING! IT'S CLEARLY TIME TO DISMANTLE THE ENTIRE SOCIAL SAFETY NET!
I HEARD ABOUT A HIGH SCHOOL SOMEWHERE THAT TEACHES KIDS HOW TO BE HOMOSEXUALS!
HOW SHOCKING! WE SHOULD ABOLISH THE DEPARTMENT OF EDUCATION!
I READ THAT AMERICANS ARE SO ASTONISHINGLY ILL-INFORMED THAT 40% OF THOSE POLLED RECENTLY BY THE WASHINGTON POST COULD NOT NAME THE VICE-PRESIDENT*!
I HEARD THAT ALL THE REPORTERS ON CNN ARE COMMUNISTS!
I BELIEVE IT! THEY SHOULD BE FORCED TO TAKE LOYALTY OATHS!
SIGH...
TOM TOMORROW ©4-10-96
*THIS IS TRUE.

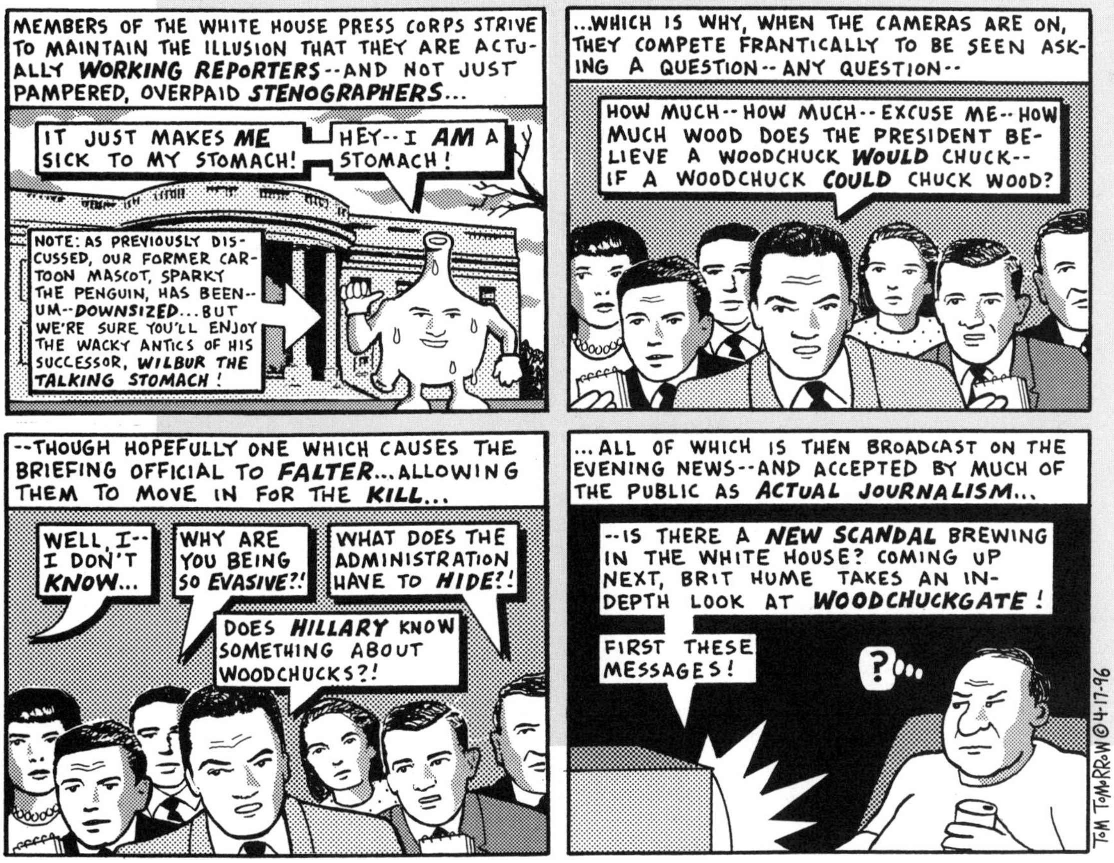
MEMBERS OF THE WHITE HOUSE PRESS CORPS STRIVE TO MAINTAIN THE ILLUSION THAT THEY ARE ACTUALLY WORKING REPORTERS--AND NOT JUST PAMPERED, OVERPAID STENOGRAPHERS...
IT JUST MAKES ME SICK TO MY STOMACH!
HEY--I AM A STOMACH!
NOTE: AS PREVIOUSLY DISCUSSED, OUR FORMER CARTOON MASCOT, SPARKY THE PENGUIN, HAS BEEN--UM--DOWNSIZED...BUT WE'RE SURE YOU'LL ENJOY THE WACKY ANTICS OF HIS SUCCESSOR, WILBUR THE TALKING STOMACH!
...WHICH IS WHY, WHEN THE CAMERAS ARE ON, THEY COMPETE FRANTICALLY TO BE SEEN ASKING A QUESTION--ANY QUESTION--
HOW MUCH--HOW MUCH--EXCUSE ME--HOW MUCH WOOD DOES THE PRESIDENT BELIEVE A WOODCHUCK WOULD CHUCK--IF A WOODCHUCK COULD CHUCK WOOD?
--THOUGH HOPEFULLY ONE WHICH CAUSES THE BRIEFING OFFICIAL TO FALTER...ALLOWING THEM TO MOVE IN FOR THE KILL...
WELL, I--I DON'T KNOW...
WHY ARE YOU BEING SO EVASIVE?!
WHAT DOES THE ADMINISTRATION HAVE TO HIDE?!
DOES HILLARY KNOW SOMETHING ABOUT WOODCHUCKS?!
...ALL OF WHICH IS THEN BROADCAST ON THE EVENING NEWS--AND ACCEPTED BY MUCH OF THE PUBLIC AS ACTUAL JOURNALISM...
--IS THERE A NEW SCANDAL BREWING IN THE WHITE HOUSE? COMING UP NEXT, BRIT HUME TAKES AN IN-DEPTH LOOK AT WOODCHUCKGATE!
FIRST THESE MESSAGES!
?...
TOM TOMORROW©4-17-96

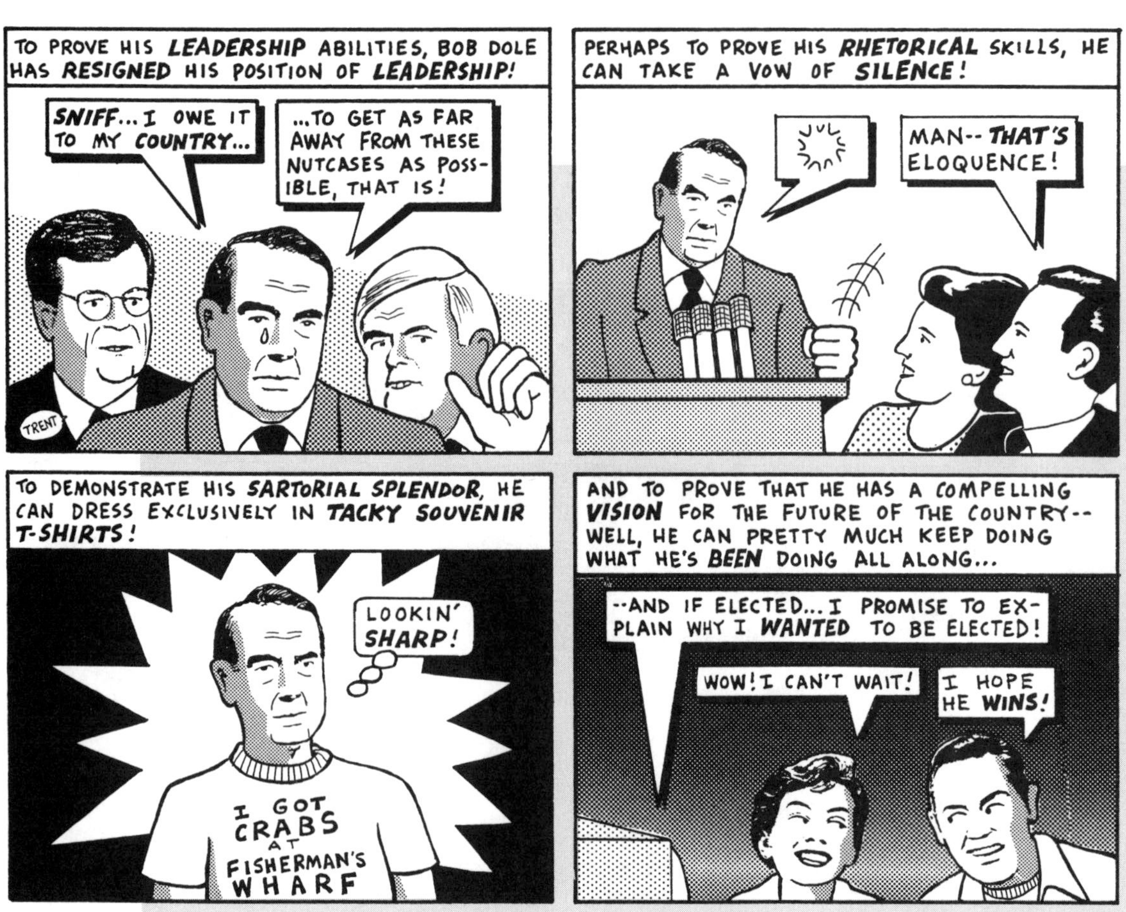
TO PROVE HIS LEADERSHIP ABILITIES, BOB DOLE HAS RESIGNED HIS POSITION OF LEADERSHIP!
SNIFF... I OWE IT TO MY COUNTRY...
...TO GET AS FAR AWAY FROM THESE NUTCASES AS POSSIBLE, THAT IS!
TRENT
PERHAPS TO PROVE HIS RHETORICAL SKILLS, HE CAN TAKE A VOW OF SILENCE!
MAN-- THAT'S ELOQUENCE!
TO DEMONSTRATE HIS SARTORIAL SPLENDOR, HE CAN DRESS EXCLUSIVELY IN TACKY SOUVENIR T-SHIRTS!
LOOKIN' SHARP!
I GOT CRABS AT FISHERMAN'S WHARF
AND TO PROVE THAT HE HAS A COMPELLING VISION FOR THE FUTURE OF THE COUNTRY-- WELL, HE CAN PRETTY MUCH KEEP DOING WHAT HE'S BEEN DOING ALL ALONG...
--AND IF ELECTED... I PROMISE TO EXPLAIN WHY I WANTED TO BE ELECTED!
WOW! I CAN'T WAIT!
I HOPE HE WINS!

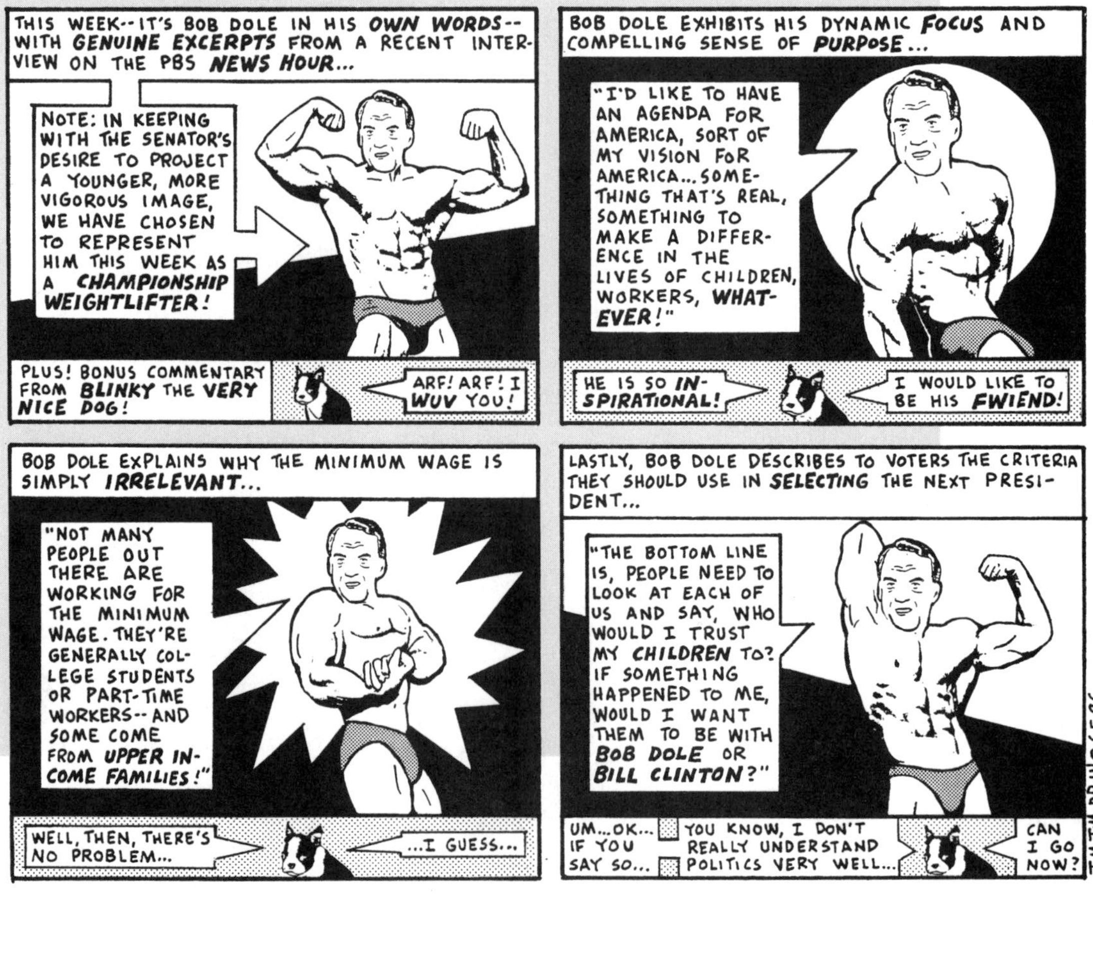
THIS WEEK--IT'S BOB DOLE IN HIS OWN WORDS-- WITH GENUINE EXCERPTS FROM A RECENT INTERVIEW ON THE PBS NEWS HOUR...
NOTE: IN KEEPING WITH THE SENATOR'S DESIRE TO PROJECT A YOUNGER, MORE VIGOROUS IMAGE, WE HAVE CHOSEN TO REPRESENT HIM THIS WEEK AS A CHAMPIONSHIP WEIGHTLIFTER!
PLUS! BONUS COMMENTARY FROM BLINKY THE VERY NICE DOG!
ARF! ARF! I WUV YOU!
BOB DOLE EXHIBITS HIS DYNAMIC FOCUS AND COMPELLING SENSE OF PURPOSE...
"I'D LIKE TO HAVE AN AGENDA FOR AMERICA, SORT OF MY VISION FOR AMERICA... SOMETHING THAT'S REAL, SOMETHING TO MAKE A DIFFERENCE IN THE LIVES OF CHILDREN, WORKERS, WHATEVER!"
HE IS SO INSPIRATIONAL!
I WOULD LIKE TO BE HIS FWIEND!
BOB DOLE EXPLAINS WHY THE MINIMUM WAGE IS SIMPLY IRRELEVANT...
"NOT MANY PEOPLE OUT THERE ARE WORKING FOR THE MINIMUM WAGE. THEY'RE GENERALLY COLLEGE STUDENTS OR PART-TIME WORKERS-- AND SOME COME FROM UPPER INCOME FAMILIES!"
WELL, THEN, THERE'S NO PROBLEM...
...I GUESS...
LASTLY, BOB DOLE DESCRIBES TO VOTERS THE CRITERIA THEY SHOULD USE IN SELECTING THE NEXT PRESIDENT...
"THE BOTTOM LINE IS, PEOPLE NEED TO LOOK AT EACH OF US AND SAY, WHO WOULD I TRUST MY CHILDREN TO? IF SOMETHING HAPPENED TO ME, WOULD I WANT THEM TO BE WITH BOB DOLE OR BILL CLINTON?"
UM...OK... IF YOU SAY SO...
YOU KNOW, I DON'T REALLY UNDERSTAND POLITICS VERY WELL...
CAN I GO NOW?
TOM TOMORROW © 6-5-96

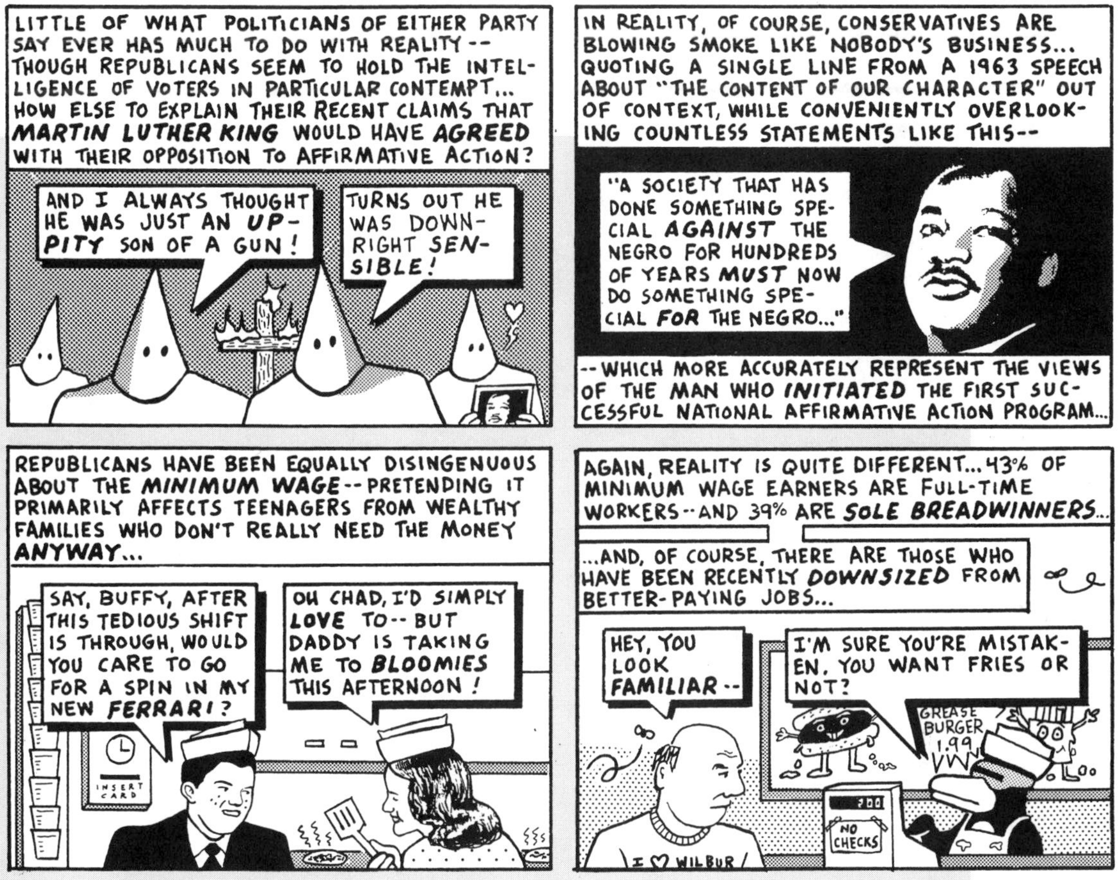
LITTLE OF WHAT POLITICIANS OF EITHER PARTY SAY EVER HAS MUCH TO DO WITH REALITY -- THOUGH REPUBLICANS SEEM TO HOLD THE INTELLIGENCE OF VOTERS IN PARTICULAR CONTEMPT... HOW ELSE TO EXPLAIN THEIR RECENT CLAIMS THAT MARTIN LUTHER KING WOULD HAVE AGREED WITH THEIR OPPOSITION TO AFFIRMATIVE ACTION?
AND I ALWAYS THOUGHT HE WAS JUST AN UPPITY SON OF A GUN!
TURNS OUT HE WAS DOWNRIGHT SENSIBLE!
IN REALITY, OF COURSE, CONSERVATIVES ARE BLOWING SMOKE LIKE NOBODY'S BUSINESS... QUOTING A SINGLE LINE FROM A 1963 SPEECH ABOUT "THE CONTENT OF OUR CHARACTER" OUT OF CONTEXT, WHILE CONVENIENTLY OVERLOOKING COUNTLESS STATEMENTS LIKE THIS--
"A SOCIETY THAT HAS DONE SOMETHING SPECIAL AGAINST THE NEGRO FOR HUNDREDS OF YEARS MUST NOW DO SOMETHING SPECIAL FOR THE NEGRO..."
--WHICH MORE ACCURATELY REPRESENT THE VIEWS OF THE MAN WHO INITIATED THE FIRST SUCCESSFUL NATIONAL AFFIRMATIVE ACTION PROGRAM...
REPUBLICANS HAVE BEEN EQUALLY DISINGENUOUS ABOUT THE MINIMUM WAGE -- PRETENDING IT PRIMARILY AFFECTS TEENAGERS FROM WEALTHY FAMILIES WHO DON'T REALLY NEED THE MONEY ANYWAY...
SAY, BUFFY, AFTER THIS TEDIOUS SHIFT IS THROUGH, WOULD YOU CARE TO GO FOR A SPIN IN MY NEW FERRARI?
OH CHAD, I'D SIMPLY LOVE TO -- BUT DADDY IS TAKING ME TO BLOOMIES THIS AFTERNOON!
INSERT CARD
AGAIN, REALITY IS QUITE DIFFERENT... 43% OF MINIMUM WAGE EARNERS ARE FULL-TIME WORKERS -- AND 39% ARE SOLE BREADWINNERS...
...AND, OF COURSE, THERE ARE THOSE WHO HAVE BEEN RECENTLY DOWNSIZED FROM BETTER-PAYING JOBS...
HEY, YOU LOOK FAMILIAR --
I'M SURE YOU'RE MISTAKEN. YOU WANT FRIES OR NOT?
GREASE BURGER 1.99
NO CHECKS
I ♡ WILBUR

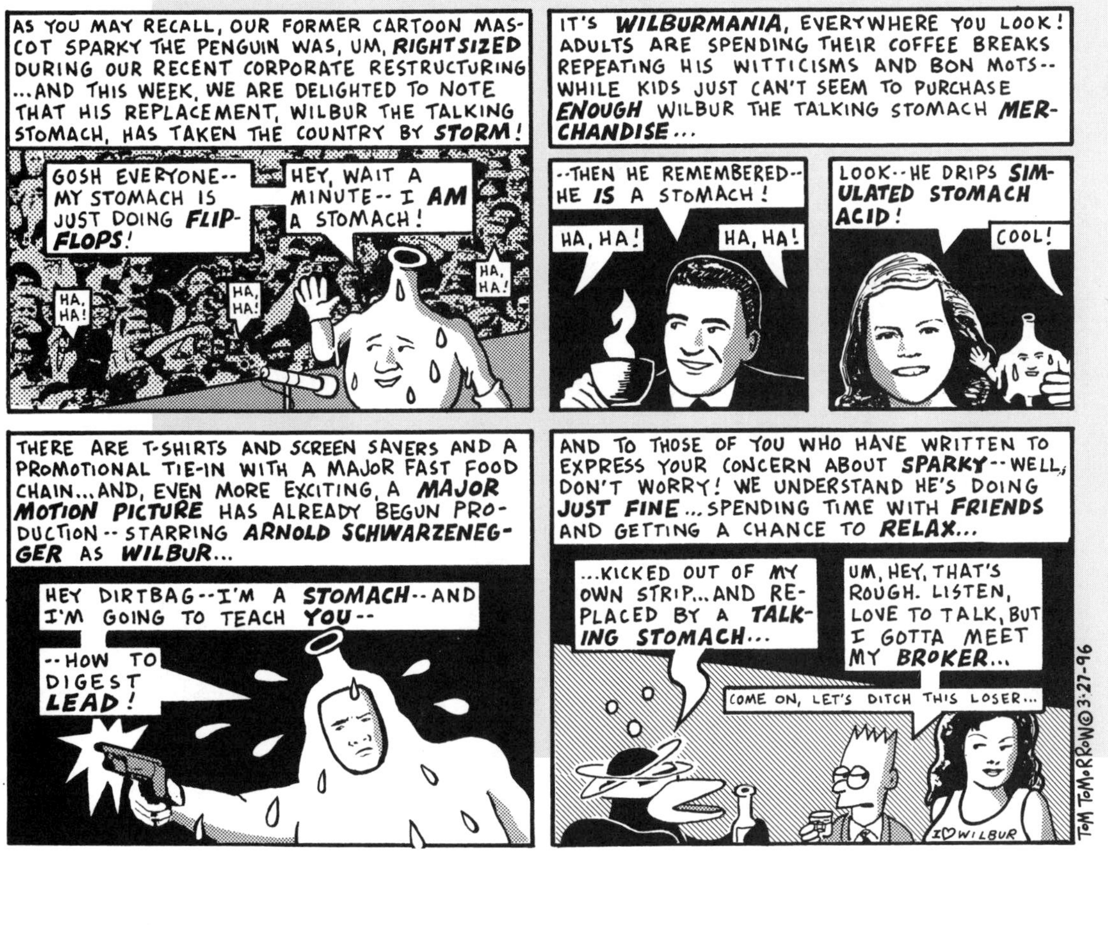
AS YOU MAY RECALL, OUR FORMER CARTOON MASCOT SPARKY THE PENGUIN WAS, UM, RIGHTSIZED DURING OUR RECENT CORPORATE RESTRUCTURING ...AND THIS WEEK, WE ARE DELIGHTED TO NOTE THAT HIS REPLACEMENT, WILBUR THE TALKING STOMACH, HAS TAKEN THE COUNTRY BY STORM!
GOSH EVERYONE -- MY STOMACH IS JUST DOING FLIP-FLOPS!
HEY, WAIT A MINUTE -- I AM A STOMACH!
HA, HA!
HA, HA!
HA, HA!
IT'S WILBURMANIA, EVERYWHERE YOU LOOK! ADULTS ARE SPENDING THEIR COFFEE BREAKS REPEATING HIS WITTICISMS AND BON MOTS -- WHILE KIDS JUST CAN'T SEEM TO PURCHASE ENOUGH WILBUR THE TALKING STOMACH MERCHANDISE...
--THEN HE REMEMBERED-- HE IS A STOMACH!
HA, HA!
HA, HA!
LOOK--HE DRIPS SIMULATED STOMACH ACID!
COOL!
THERE ARE T-SHIRTS AND SCREEN SAVERS AND A PROMOTIONAL TIE-IN WITH A MAJOR FAST FOOD CHAIN... AND, EVEN MORE EXCITING, A MAJOR MOTION PICTURE HAS ALREADY BEGUN PRODUCTION -- STARRING ARNOLD SCHWARZENEGGER AS WILBUR...
HEY DIRTBAG -- I'M A STOMACH -- AND I'M GOING TO TEACH YOU --
-- HOW TO DIGEST LEAD!
AND TO THOSE OF YOU WHO HAVE WRITTEN TO EXPRESS YOUR CONCERN ABOUT SPARKY -- WELL, DON'T WORRY! WE UNDERSTAND HE'S DOING JUST FINE... SPENDING TIME WITH FRIENDS AND GETTING A CHANCE TO RELAX...
...KICKED OUT OF MY OWN STRIP... AND REPLACED BY A TALKING STOMACH...
UM, HEY, THAT'S ROUGH. LISTEN, LOVE TO TALK, BUT I GOTTA MEET MY BROKER...
COME ON, LET'S DITCH THIS LOSER...
I ♡ WILBUR
TOM TOMORROW © 3-27-96

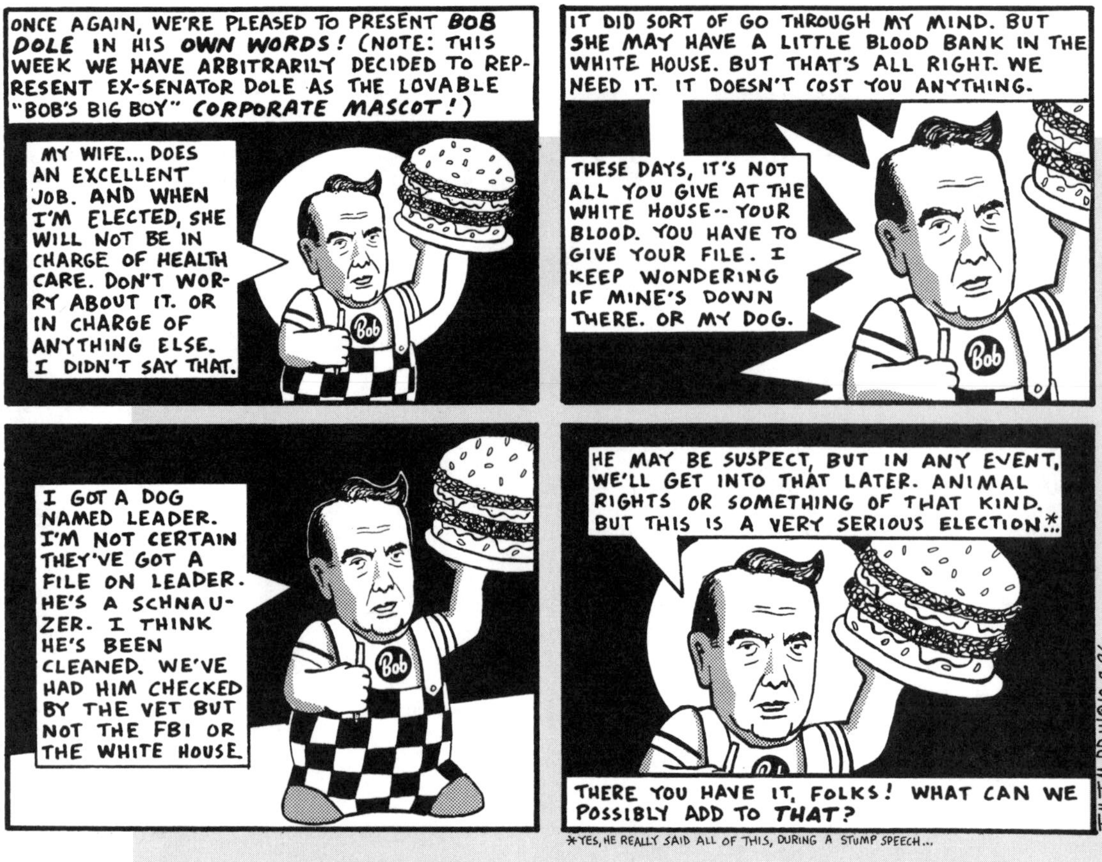
ONCE AGAIN, WE'RE PLEASED TO PRESENT BOB DOLE IN HIS OWN WORDS! (NOTE: THIS WEEK WE HAVE ARBITRARILY DECIDED TO REPRESENT EX-SENATOR DOLE AS THE LOVABLE "BOB'S BIG BOY" CORPORATE MASCOT!)
MY WIFE... DOES AN EXCELLENT JOB. AND WHEN I'M ELECTED, SHE WILL NOT BE IN CHARGE OF HEALTH CARE. DON'T WORRY ABOUT IT. OR IN CHARGE OF ANYTHING ELSE. I DIDN'T SAY THAT.
Bob
IT DID SORT OF GO THROUGH MY MIND. BUT SHE MAY HAVE A LITTLE BLOOD BANK IN THE WHITE HOUSE. BUT THAT'S ALL RIGHT. WE NEED IT. IT DOESN'T COST YOU ANYTHING.
THESE DAYS, IT'S NOT ALL YOU GIVE AT THE WHITE HOUSE-- YOUR BLOOD. YOU HAVE TO GIVE YOUR FILE. I KEEP WONDERING IF MINE'S DOWN THERE. OR MY DOG.
Bob
I GOT A DOG NAMED LEADER. I'M NOT CERTAIN THEY'VE GOT A FILE ON LEADER. HE'S A SCHNAUZER. I THINK HE'S BEEN CLEANED. WE'VE HAD HIM CHECKED BY THE VET BUT NOT THE FBI OR THE WHITE HOUSE.
Bob
HE MAY BE SUSPECT, BUT IN ANY EVENT, WE'LL GET INTO THAT LATER. ANIMAL RIGHTS OR SOMETHING OF THAT KIND. BUT THIS IS A VERY SERIOUS ELECTION.*
THERE YOU HAVE IT, FOLKS! WHAT CAN WE POSSIBLY ADD TO THAT?
TOM TOMORROW©10-9-96
*YES, HE REALLY SAID ALL OF THIS, DURING A STUMP SPEECH...

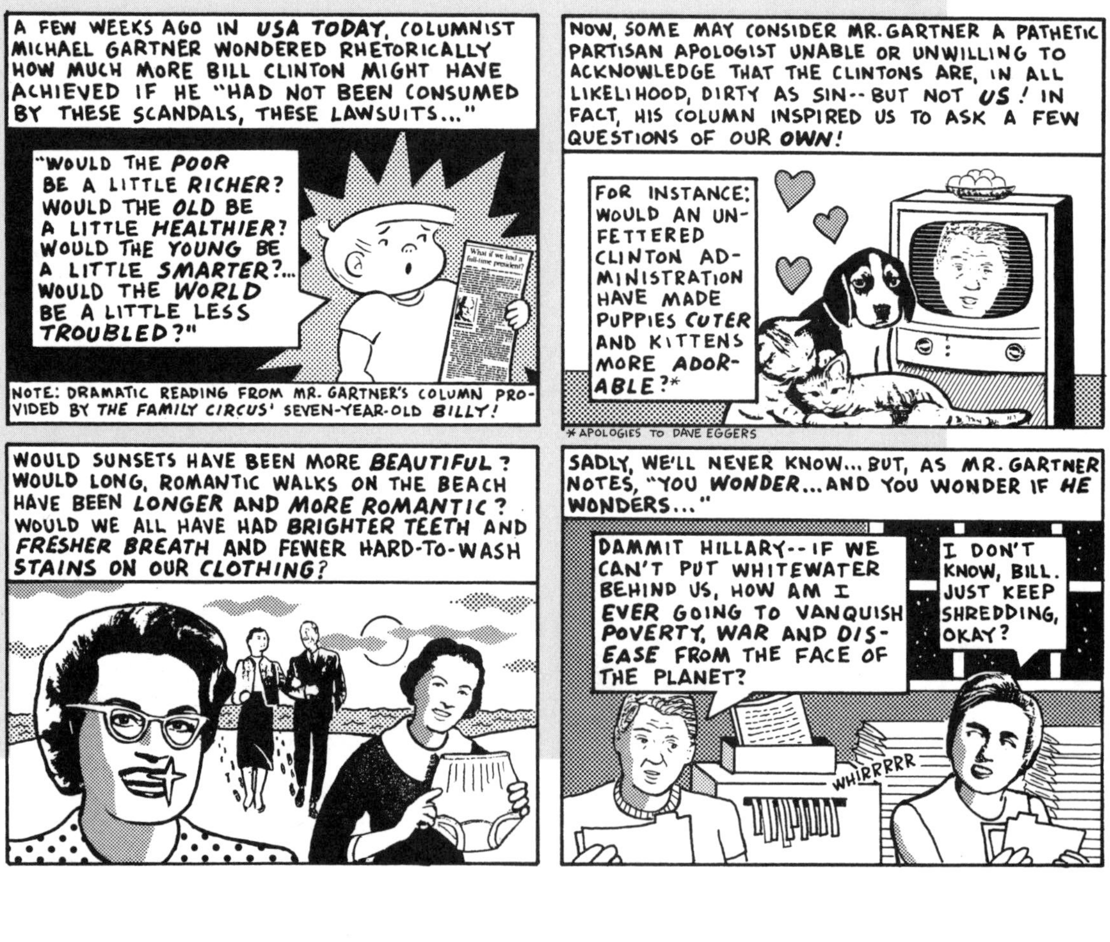
A FEW WEEKS AGO IN USA TODAY, COLUMNIST MICHAEL GARTNER WONDERED RHETORICALLY HOW MUCH MORE BILL CLINTON MIGHT HAVE ACHIEVED IF HE "HAD NOT BEEN CONSUMED BY THESE SCANDALS, THESE LAWSUITS..."
"WOULD THE POOR BE A LITTLE RICHER? WOULD THE OLD BE A LITTLE HEALTHIER? WOULD THE YOUNG BE A LITTLE SMARTER?... WOULD THE WORLD BE A LITTLE LESS TROUBLED?"
NOTE: DRAMATIC READING FROM MR. GARTNER'S COLUMN PROVIDED BY THE FAMILY CIRCUS' SEVEN-YEAR-OLD BILLY!
NOW, SOME MAY CONSIDER MR. GARTNER A PATHETIC PARTISAN APOLOGIST UNABLE OR UNWILLING TO ACKNOWLEDGE THAT THE CLINTONS ARE, IN ALL LIKELIHOOD, DIRTY AS SIN-- BUT NOT US! IN FACT, HIS COLUMN INSPIRED US TO ASK A FEW QUESTIONS OF OUR OWN!
FOR INSTANCE: WOULD AN UNFETTERED CLINTON ADMINISTRATION HAVE MADE PUPPIES CUTER AND KITTENS MORE ADORABLE?*
*APOLOGIES TO DAVE EGGERS
WOULD SUNSETS HAVE BEEN MORE BEAUTIFUL? WOULD LONG, ROMANTIC WALKS ON THE BEACH HAVE BEEN LONGER AND MORE ROMANTIC? WOULD WE ALL HAVE HAD BRIGHTER TEETH AND FRESHER BREATH AND FEWER HARD-TO-WASH STAINS ON OUR CLOTHING?
SADLY, WE'LL NEVER KNOW... BUT, AS MR. GARTNER NOTES, "YOU WONDER... AND YOU WONDER IF HE WONDERS..."
DAMMIT HILLARY-- IF WE CAN'T PUT WHITEWATER BEHIND US, HOW AM I EVER GOING TO VANQUISH POVERTY, WAR AND DISEASE FROM THE FACE OF THE PLANET?
I DON'T KNOW, BILL. JUST KEEP SHREDDING, OKAY?
WHIRRRRR

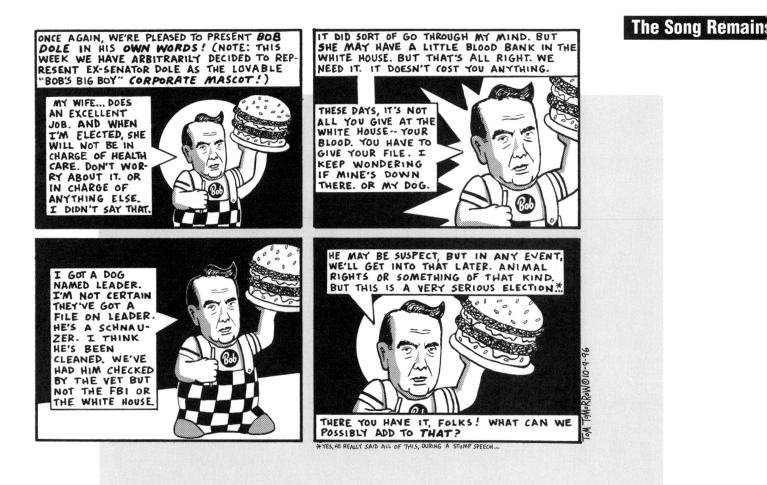

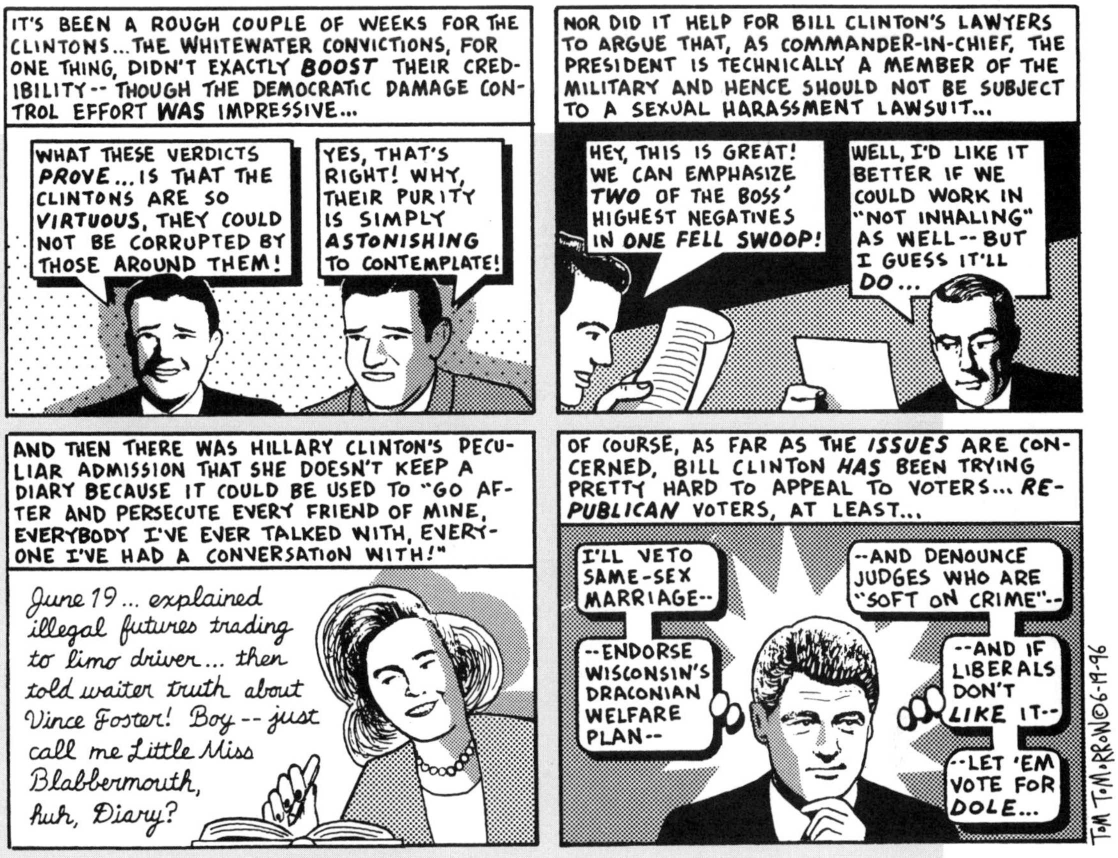
IT'S BEEN A ROUGH COUPLE OF WEEKS FOR THE CLINTONS... THE WHITEWATER CONVICTIONS, FOR ONE THING, DIDN'T EXACTLY BOOST THEIR CREDIBILITY -- THOUGH THE DEMOCRATIC DAMAGE CONTROL EFFORT WAS IMPRESSIVE...
WHAT THESE VERDICTS PROVE... IS THAT THE CLINTONS ARE SO VIRTUOUS, THEY COULD NOT BE CORRUPTED BY THOSE AROUND THEM!
YES, THAT'S RIGHT! WHY, THEIR PURITY IS SIMPLY ASTONISHING TO CONTEMPLATE!
NOR DID IT HELP FOR BILL CLINTON'S LAWYERS TO ARGUE THAT, AS COMMANDER-IN-CHIEF, THE PRESIDENT IS TECHNICALLY A MEMBER OF THE MILITARY AND HENCE SHOULD NOT BE SUBJECT TO A SEXUAL HARASSMENT LAWSUIT...
HEY, THIS IS GREAT! WE CAN EMPHASIZE TWO OF THE BOSS' HIGHEST NEGATIVES IN ONE FELL SWOOP!
WELL, I'D LIKE IT BETTER IF WE COULD WORK IN "NOT INHALING" AS WELL -- BUT I GUESS IT'LL DO...
AND THEN THERE WAS HILLARY CLINTON'S PECULIAR ADMISSION THAT SHE DOESN'T KEEP A DIARY BECAUSE IT COULD BE USED TO "GO AFTER AND PERSECUTE EVERY FRIEND OF MINE, EVERYBODY I'VE EVER TALKED WITH, EVERYONE I'VE HAD A CONVERSATION WITH!"
June 19 ... explained illegal futures trading to limo driver ... then told waiter truth about Vince Foster! Boy -- just call me Little Miss Blabbermouth, huh, Diary?
OF COURSE, AS FAR AS THE ISSUES ARE CONCERNED, BILL CLINTON HAS BEEN TRYING PRETTY HARD TO APPEAL TO VOTERS... REPUBLICAN VOTERS, AT LEAST...
I'LL VETO SAME-SEX MARRIAGE--
--ENDORSE WISCONSIN'S DRACONIAN WELFARE PLAN--
--AND DENOUNCE JUDGES WHO ARE "SOFT ON CRIME"--
--AND IF LIBERALS DON'T LIKE IT--
--LET 'EM VOTE FOR DOLE...
TOM TOMORROW©6-19-96

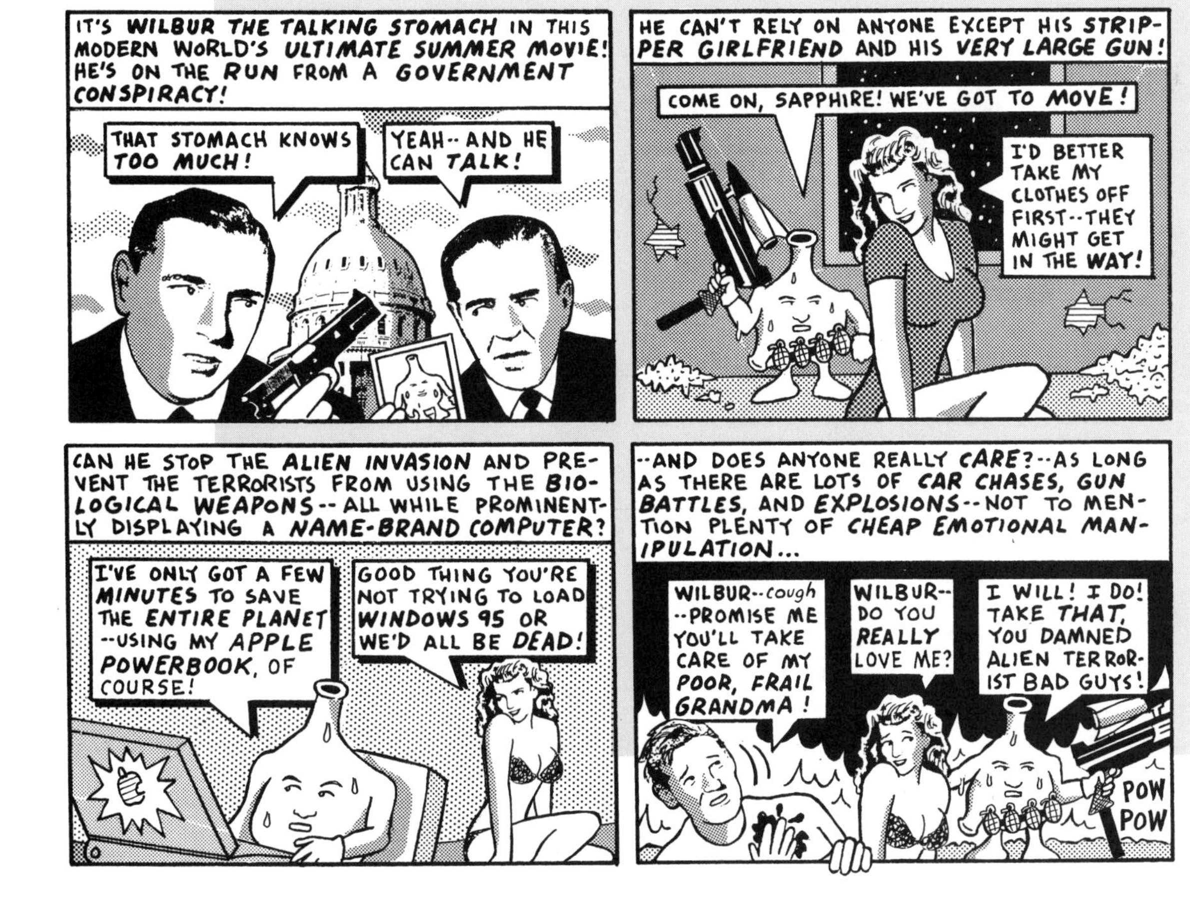
IT'S WILBUR THE TALKING STOMACH IN THIS MODERN WORLD'S ULTIMATE SUMMER MOVIE! HE'S ON THE RUN FROM A GOVERNMENT CONSPIRACY!
THAT STOMACH KNOWS TOO MUCH!
YEAH -- AND HE CAN TALK!
HE CAN'T RELY ON ANYONE EXCEPT HIS STRIPPER GIRLFRIEND AND HIS VERY LARGE GUN!
COME ON, SAPPHIRE! WE'VE GOT TO MOVE!
I'D BETTER TAKE MY CLOTHES OFF FIRST -- THEY MIGHT GET IN THE WAY!
CAN HE STOP THE ALIEN INVASION AND PREVENT THE TERRORISTS FROM USING THE BIOLOGICAL WEAPONS -- ALL WHILE PROMINENTLY DISPLAYING A NAME-BRAND COMPUTER?
I'VE ONLY GOT A FEW MINUTES TO SAVE THE ENTIRE PLANET --USING MY APPLE POWERBOOK, OF COURSE!
GOOD THING YOU'RE NOT TRYING TO LOAD WINDOWS 95 OR WE'D ALL BE DEAD!
--AND DOES ANYONE REALLY CARE? -- AS LONG AS THERE ARE LOTS OF CAR CHASES, GUN BATTLES, AND EXPLOSIONS -- NOT TO MENTION PLENTY OF CHEAP EMOTIONAL MANIPULATION...
WILBUR -- cough -- PROMISE ME YOU'LL TAKE CARE OF MY POOR, FRAIL GRANDMA!
WILBUR -- DO YOU REALLY LOVE ME?
I WILL! I DO! TAKE THAT, YOU DAMNED ALIEN TERRORIST BAD GUYS!
POW
POW

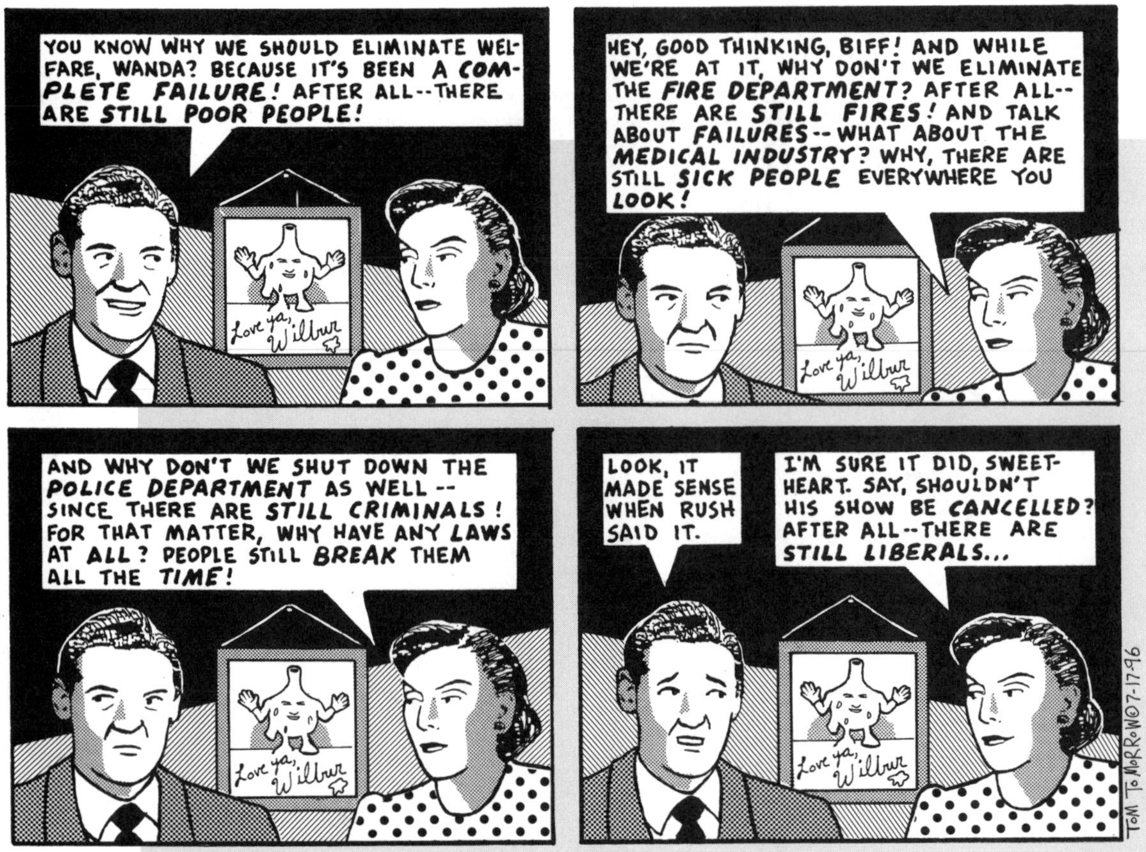
YOU KNOW WHY WE SHOULD ELIMINATE WELFARE, WANDA? BECAUSE IT'S BEEN A COMPLETE FAILURE! AFTER ALL--THERE ARE STILL POOR PEOPLE!
Love ya, Wilbur
HEY, GOOD THINKING, BIFF! AND WHILE WE'RE AT IT, WHY DON'T WE ELIMINATE THE FIRE DEPARTMENT? AFTER ALL--THERE ARE STILL FIRES! AND TALK ABOUT FAILURES--WHAT ABOUT THE MEDICAL INDUSTRY? WHY, THERE ARE STILL SICK PEOPLE EVERYWHERE YOU LOOK!
AND WHY DON'T WE SHUT DOWN THE POLICE DEPARTMENT AS WELL--SINCE THERE ARE STILL CRIMINALS! FOR THAT MATTER, WHY HAVE ANY LAWS AT ALL? PEOPLE STILL BREAK THEM ALL THE TIME!
LOOK, IT MADE SENSE WHEN RUSH SAID IT.
I'M SURE IT DID, SWEETHEART. SAY, SHOULDN'T HIS SHOW BE CANCELLED? AFTER ALL--THERE ARE STILL LIBERALS...
TOM TOMORROW 07-17-96

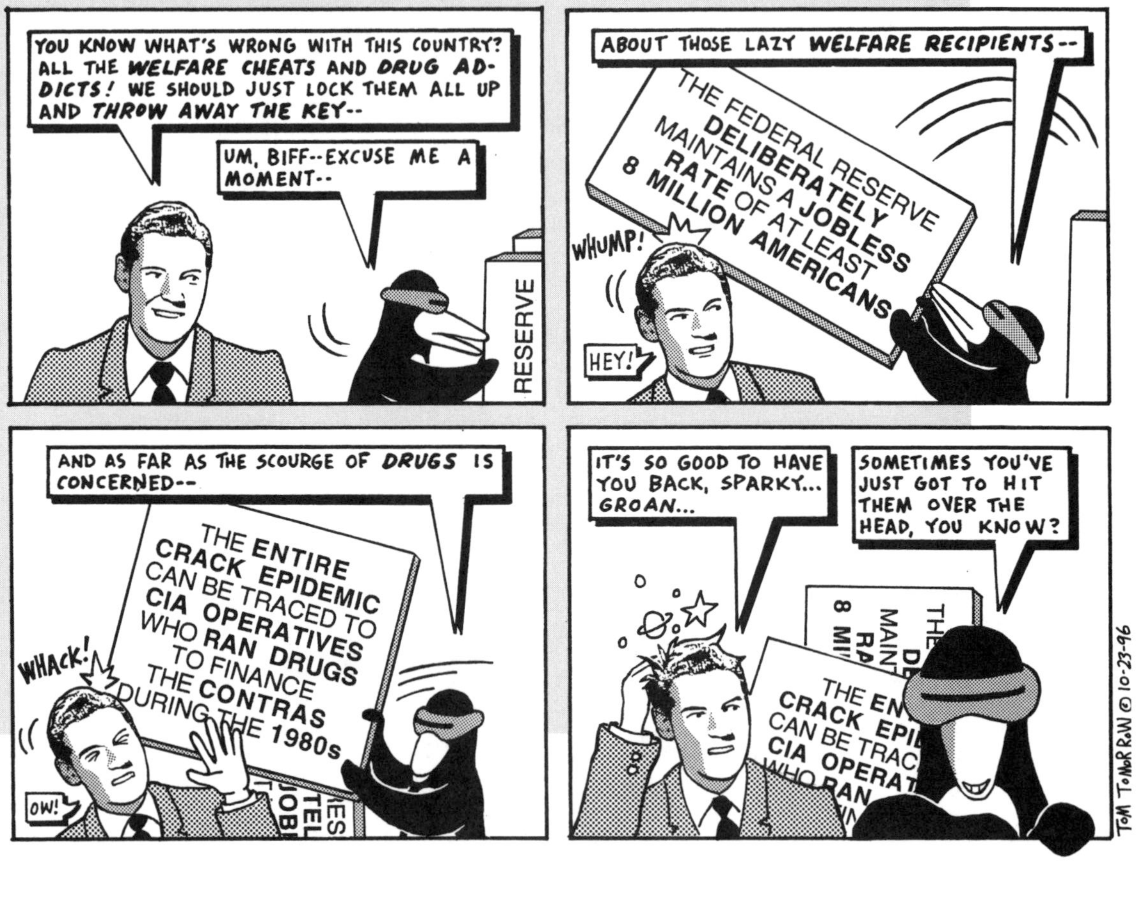
YOU KNOW WHAT'S WRONG WITH THIS COUNTRY? ALL THE WELFARE CHEATS AND DRUG ADDICTS! WE SHOULD JUST LOCK THEM ALL UP AND THROW AWAY THE KEY--
UM, BIFF--EXCUSE ME A MOMENT--
RESERVE
ABOUT THOSE LAZY WELFARE RECIPIENTS--
THE FEDERAL RESERVE DELIBERATELY MAINTAINS A JOBLESS RATE OF AT LEAST 8 MILLION AMERICANS
WHUMP!
HEY!
AND AS FAR AS THE SCOURGE OF DRUGS IS CONCERNED--
THE ENTIRE CRACK EPIDEMIC CAN BE TRACED TO CIA OPERATIVES WHO RAN DRUGS TO FINANCE THE CONTRAS DURING THE 1980s
WHACK!
OW!
IT'S SO GOOD TO HAVE YOU BACK, SPARKY... GROAN...
SOMETIMES YOU'VE JUST GOT TO HIT THEM OVER THE HEAD, YOU KNOW?
TOM TOMORROW © 10-23-96

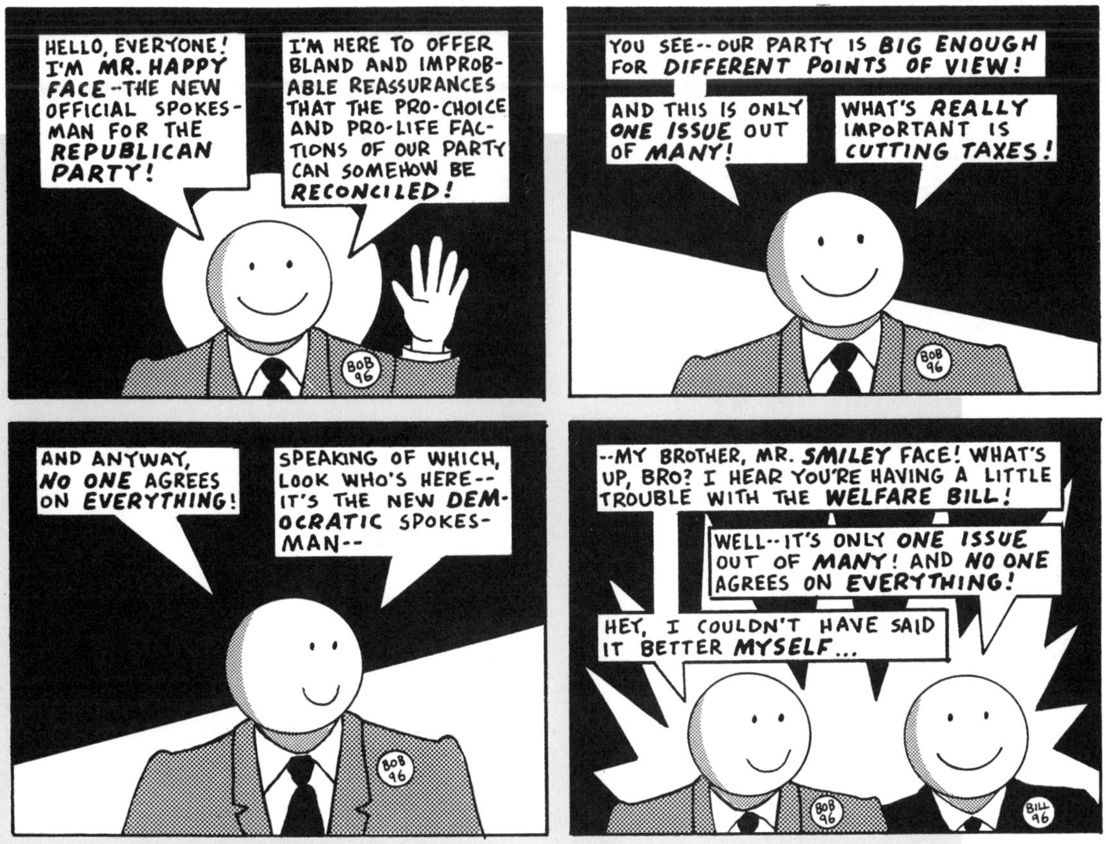
HELLO, EVERYONE! I'M MR. HAPPY FACE--THE NEW OFFICIAL SPOKESMAN FOR THE REPUBLICAN PARTY!
I'M HERE TO OFFER BLAND AND IMPROBABLE REASSURANCES THAT THE PRO-CHOICE AND PRO-LIFE FACTIONS OF OUR PARTY CAN SOMEHOW BE RECONCILED!
BOB 96
YOU SEE--OUR PARTY IS BIG ENOUGH FOR DIFFERENT POINTS OF VIEW!
AND THIS IS ONLY ONE ISSUE OUT OF MANY!
WHAT'S REALLY IMPORTANT IS CUTTING TAXES!
AND ANYWAY, NO ONE AGREES ON EVERYTHING!
SPEAKING OF WHICH, LOOK WHO'S HERE--IT'S THE NEW DEMOCRATIC SPOKESMAN--
--MY BROTHER, MR. SMILEY FACE! WHAT'S UP, BRO? I HEAR YOU'RE HAVING A LITTLE TROUBLE WITH THE WELFARE BILL!
WELL--IT'S ONLY ONE ISSUE OUT OF MANY! AND NO ONE AGREES ON EVERYTHING!
HEY, I COULDN'T HAVE SAID IT BETTER MYSELF...
BILL 96

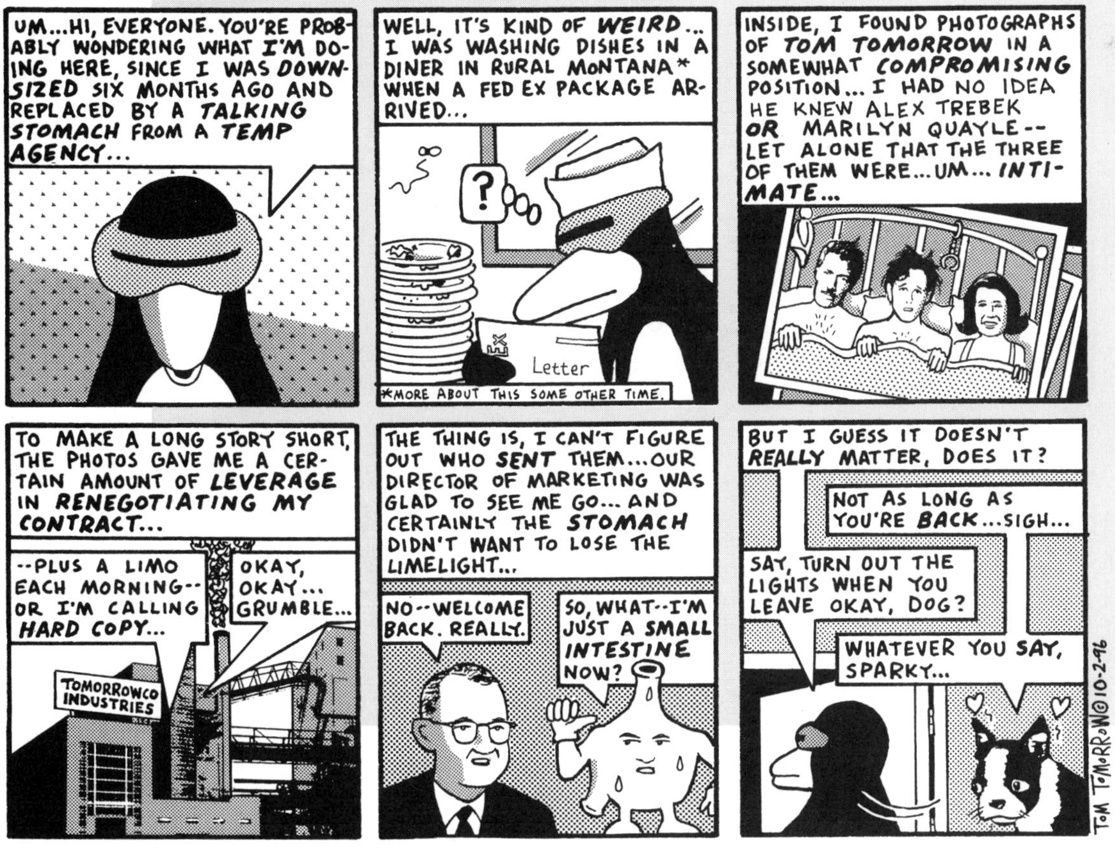
UM...HI, EVERYONE. YOU'RE PROBABLY WONDERING WHAT I'M DOING HERE, SINCE I WAS DOWNSIZED SIX MONTHS AGO AND REPLACED BY A TALKING STOMACH FROM A TEMP AGENCY...
WELL, IT'S KIND OF WEIRD... I WAS WASHING DISHES IN A DINER IN RURAL MONTANA* WHEN A FED EX PACKAGE ARRIVED...
Letter
*MORE ABOUT THIS SOME OTHER TIME.
INSIDE, I FOUND PHOTOGRAPHS OF TOM TOMORROW IN A SOMEWHAT COMPROMISING POSITION... I HAD NO IDEA HE KNEW ALEX TREBEK OR MARILYN QUAYLE--LET ALONE THAT THE THREE OF THEM WERE...UM...INTIMATE...
TO MAKE A LONG STORY SHORT, THE PHOTOS GAVE ME A CERTAIN AMOUNT OF LEVERAGE IN RENEGOTIATING MY CONTRACT...
--PLUS A LIMO EACH MORNING--OR I'M CALLING HARD COPY...
OKAY, OKAY... GRUMBLE...
TOMORROWCO INDUSTRIES
THE THING IS, I CAN'T FIGURE OUT WHO SENT THEM...OUR DIRECTOR OF MARKETING WAS GLAD TO SEE ME GO... AND CERTAINLY THE STOMACH DIDN'T WANT TO LOSE THE LIMELIGHT...
NO--WELCOME BACK. REALLY.
SO, WHAT--I'M JUST A SMALL INTESTINE NOW?
BUT I GUESS IT DOESN'T REALLY MATTER, DOES IT?
NOT AS LONG AS YOU'RE BACK...SIGH...
SAY, TURN OUT THE LIGHTS WHEN YOU LEAVE OKAY, DOG?
WHATEVER YOU SAY, SPARKY...
TOM TOMORROW©10-2-96

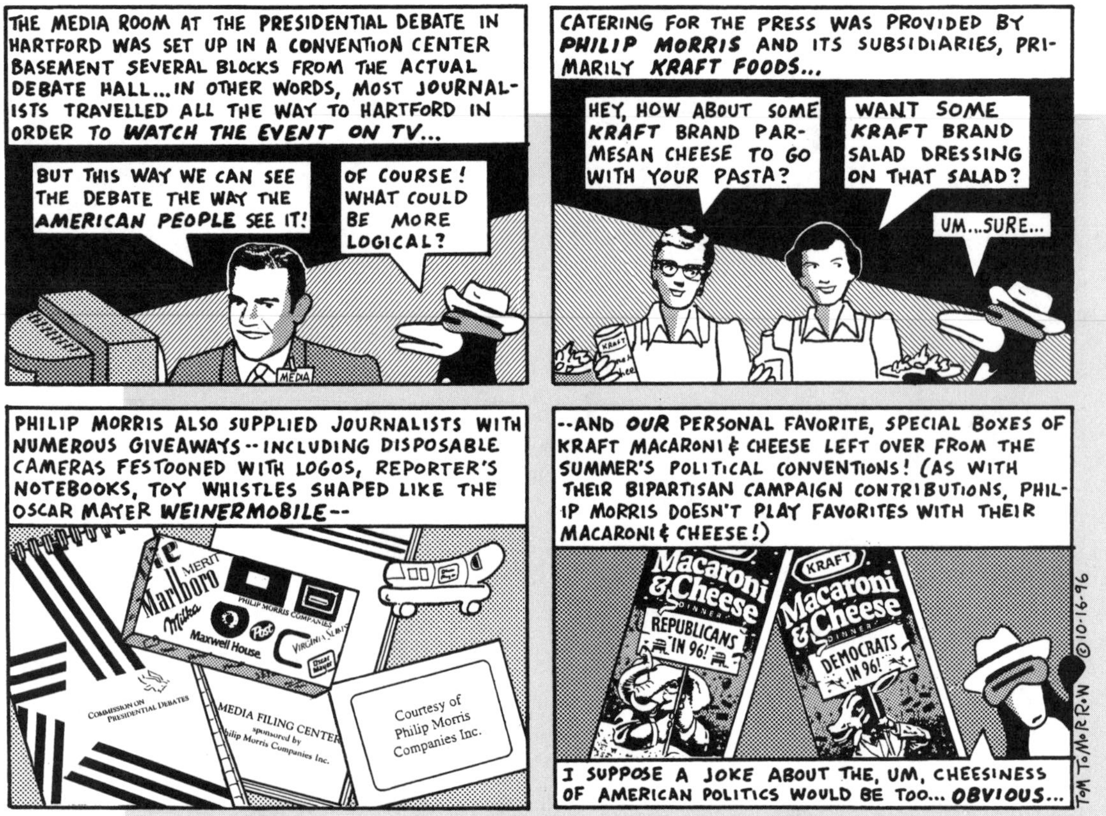
THE MEDIA ROOM AT THE PRESIDENTIAL DEBATE IN HARTFORD WAS SET UP IN A CONVENTION CENTER BASEMENT SEVERAL BLOCKS FROM THE ACTUAL DEBATE HALL... IN OTHER WORDS, MOST JOURNALISTS TRAVELLED ALL THE WAY TO HARTFORD IN ORDER TO WATCH THE EVENT ON TV...
BUT THIS WAY WE CAN SEE THE DEBATE THE WAY THE AMERICAN PEOPLE SEE IT!
OF COURSE! WHAT COULD BE MORE LOGICAL?
MEDIA
CATERING FOR THE PRESS WAS PROVIDED BY PHILIP MORRIS AND ITS SUBSIDIARIES, PRIMARILY KRAFT FOODS...
HEY, HOW ABOUT SOME KRAFT BRAND PARMESAN CHEESE TO GO WITH YOUR PASTA?
WANT SOME KRAFT BRAND SALAD DRESSING ON THAT SALAD?
UM...SURE...
PHILIP MORRIS ALSO SUPPLIED JOURNALISTS WITH NUMEROUS GIVEAWAYS--INCLUDING DISPOSABLE CAMERAS FESTOONED WITH LOGOS, REPORTER'S NOTEBOOKS, TOY WHISTLES SHAPED LIKE THE OSCAR MAYER WEINERMOBILE--
Marlboro
Maxwell House
Commission on Presidential Debates
MEDIA FILING CENTER sponsored by Philip Morris Companies Inc.
Courtesy of Philip Morris Companies Inc.
--AND OUR PERSONAL FAVORITE, SPECIAL BOXES OF KRAFT MACARONI & CHEESE LEFT OVER FROM THE SUMMER'S POLITICAL CONVENTIONS! (AS WITH THEIR BIPARTISAN CAMPAIGN CONTRIBUTIONS, PHILIP MORRIS DOESN'T PLAY FAVORITES WITH THEIR MACARONI & CHEESE!)
Macaroni & Cheese
REPUBLICANS IN 96!
KRAFT
Macaroni & Cheese
DEMOCRATS IN 96!
I SUPPOSE A JOKE ABOUT THE, UM, CHEESINESS OF AMERICAN POLITICS WOULD BE TOO... OBVIOUS...
TOM TOMORROW ©10-16-96

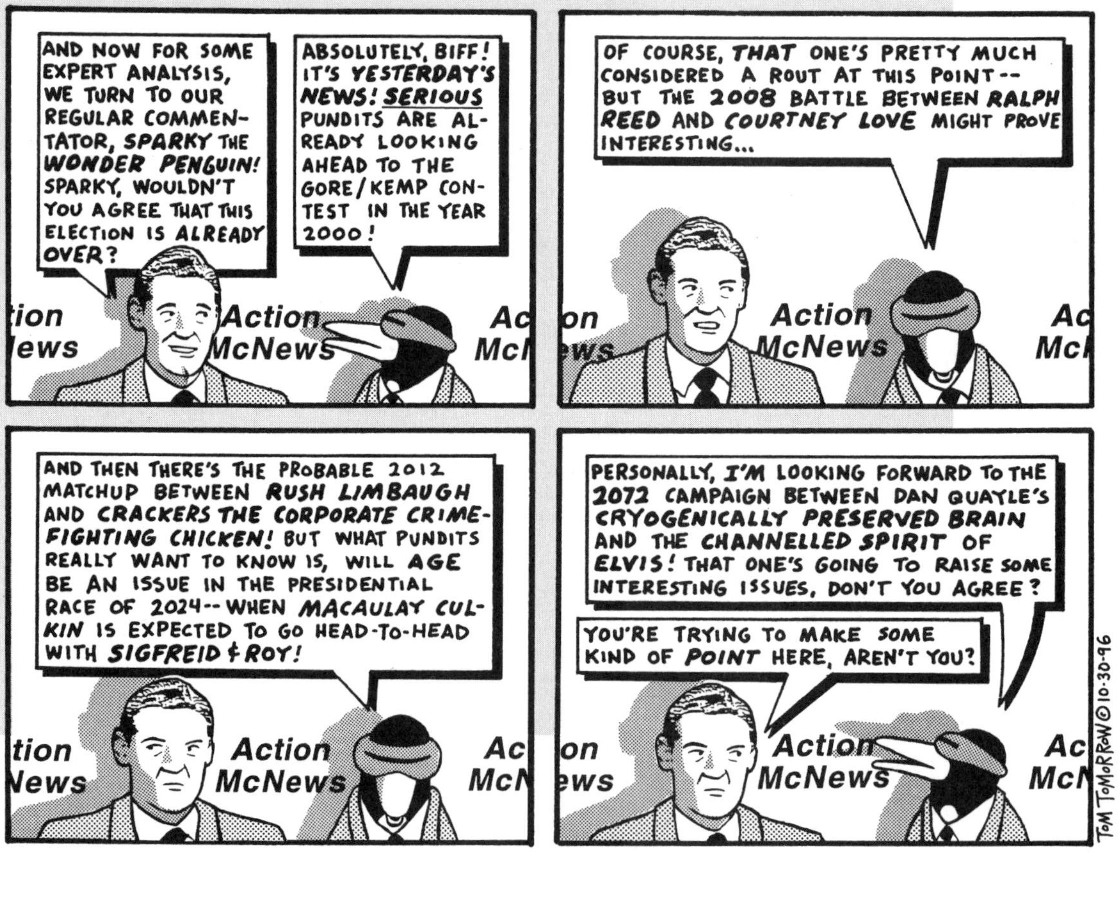
AND NOW FOR SOME EXPERT ANALYSIS, WE TURN TO OUR REGULAR COMMENTATOR, SPARKY THE WONDER PENGUIN! SPARKY, WOULDN'T YOU AGREE THAT THIS ELECTION IS ALREADY OVER?
ABSOLUTELY, BIFF! IT'S YESTERDAY'S NEWS! SERIOUS PUNDITS ARE ALREADY LOOKING AHEAD TO THE GORE/KEMP CONTEST IN THE YEAR 2000!
Action McNews
OF COURSE, THAT ONE'S PRETTY MUCH CONSIDERED A ROUT AT THIS POINT--BUT THE 2008 BATTLE BETWEEN RALPH REED AND COURTNEY LOVE MIGHT PROVE INTERESTING...
AND THEN THERE'S THE PROBABLE 2012 MATCHUP BETWEEN RUSH LIMBAUGH AND CRACKERS THE CORPORATE CRIME-FIGHTING CHICKEN! BUT WHAT PUNDITS REALLY WANT TO KNOW IS, WILL AGE BE AN ISSUE IN THE PRESIDENTIAL RACE OF 2024--WHEN MACAULAY CULKIN IS EXPECTED TO GO HEAD-TO-HEAD WITH SIGFREID & ROY!
PERSONALLY, I'M LOOKING FORWARD TO THE 2072 CAMPAIGN BETWEEN DAN QUAYLE'S CRYOGENICALLY PRESERVED BRAIN AND THE CHANNELLED SPIRIT OF ELVIS! THAT ONE'S GOING TO RAISE SOME INTERESTING ISSUES, DON'T YOU AGREE?
YOU'RE TRYING TO MAKE SOME KIND OF POINT HERE, AREN'T YOU?
TOM TOMORROW ©10-30-96

The Tabloid Presidency

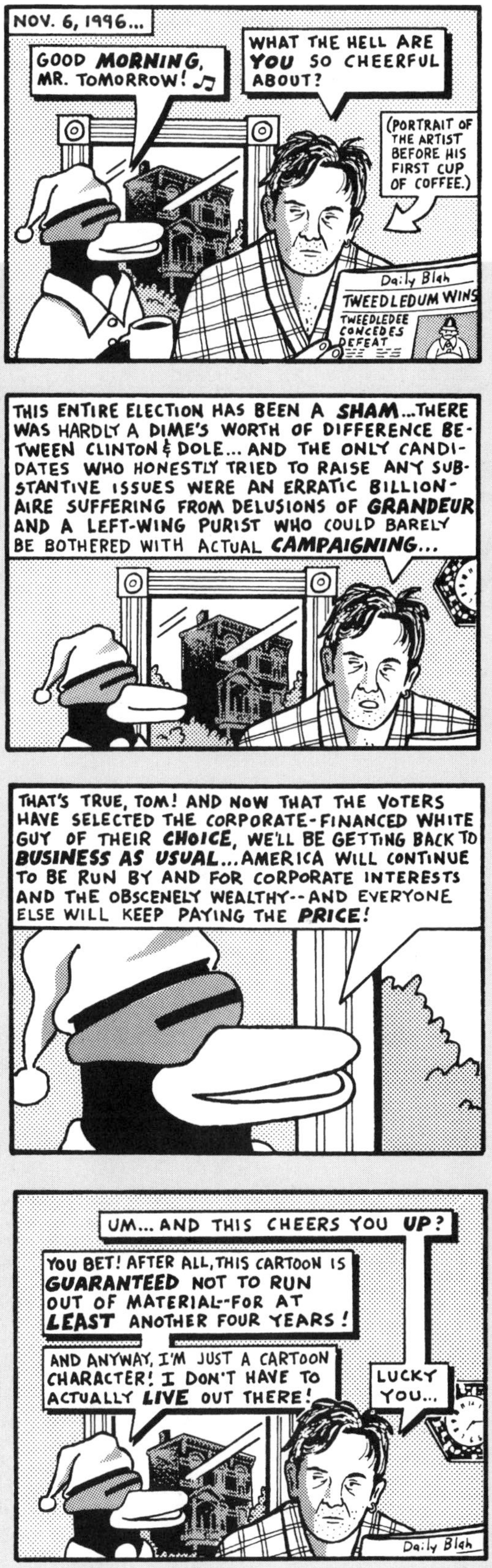
NOV. 6, 1996...
GOOD MORNING, MR. TOMORROW! ♫
WHAT THE HELL ARE YOU SO CHEERFUL ABOUT?
(PORTRAIT OF THE ARTIST BEFORE HIS FIRST CUP OF COFFEE.)
Daily Blah
TWEEDLEDUM WINS
TWEEDLEDEE CONCEDES DEFEAT
THIS ENTIRE ELECTION HAS BEEN A SHAM...THERE WAS HARDLY A DIME'S WORTH OF DIFFERENCE BETWEEN CLINTON & DOLE... AND THE ONLY CANDIDATES WHO HONESTLY TRIED TO RAISE ANY SUBSTANTIVE ISSUES WERE AN ERRATIC BILLIONAIRE SUFFERING FROM DELUSIONS OF GRANDEUR AND A LEFT-WING PURIST WHO COULD BARELY BE BOTHERED WITH ACTUAL CAMPAIGNING...
THAT'S TRUE, TOM! AND NOW THAT THE VOTERS HAVE SELECTED THE CORPORATE-FINANCED WHITE GUY OF THEIR CHOICE, WE'LL BE GETTING BACK TO BUSINESS AS USUAL... AMERICA WILL CONTINUE TO BE RUN BY AND FOR CORPORATE INTERESTS AND THE OBSCENELY WEALTHY--AND EVERYONE ELSE WILL KEEP PAYING THE PRICE!
UM... AND THIS CHEERS YOU UP?
YOU BET! AFTER ALL, THIS CARTOON IS GUARANTEED NOT TO RUN OUT OF MATERIAL--FOR AT LEAST ANOTHER FOUR YEARS!
AND ANYWAY, I'M JUST A CARTOON CHARACTER! I DON'T HAVE TO ACTUALLY LIVE OUT THERE!
LUCKY YOU...
Daily Blah

And so history descended well and truly into farce. We found ourselves with "a commander-in-chief who clearly paid too much attention to the small presidential advisor in his pants," being prosecuted by the likes of Bob Barr, Newt Gingrich, Dan Burton, and Henry Hyde—all of whom turned out to have had affairs, and/or fathered out-of-wedlock children, and/or generally behaved in ways unbecoming a Smug Self Righteous Republican Wingnut.

Clinton wagged his finger at the cameras and insulted our intelligence—and Republicans spent the next couple of years wallowing in the filth like happy little pigs. It was to actual political scandal as the dot-com bubble was to actual economic growth, sound and fury, signifying nothing—and when it was over, everyone looked a little foolish and sad, like dazed partygoers stumbling hungover into the harsh, unforgiving light of morning.

1996-2000: The Meaning of "Is," and Other Semantic Antics

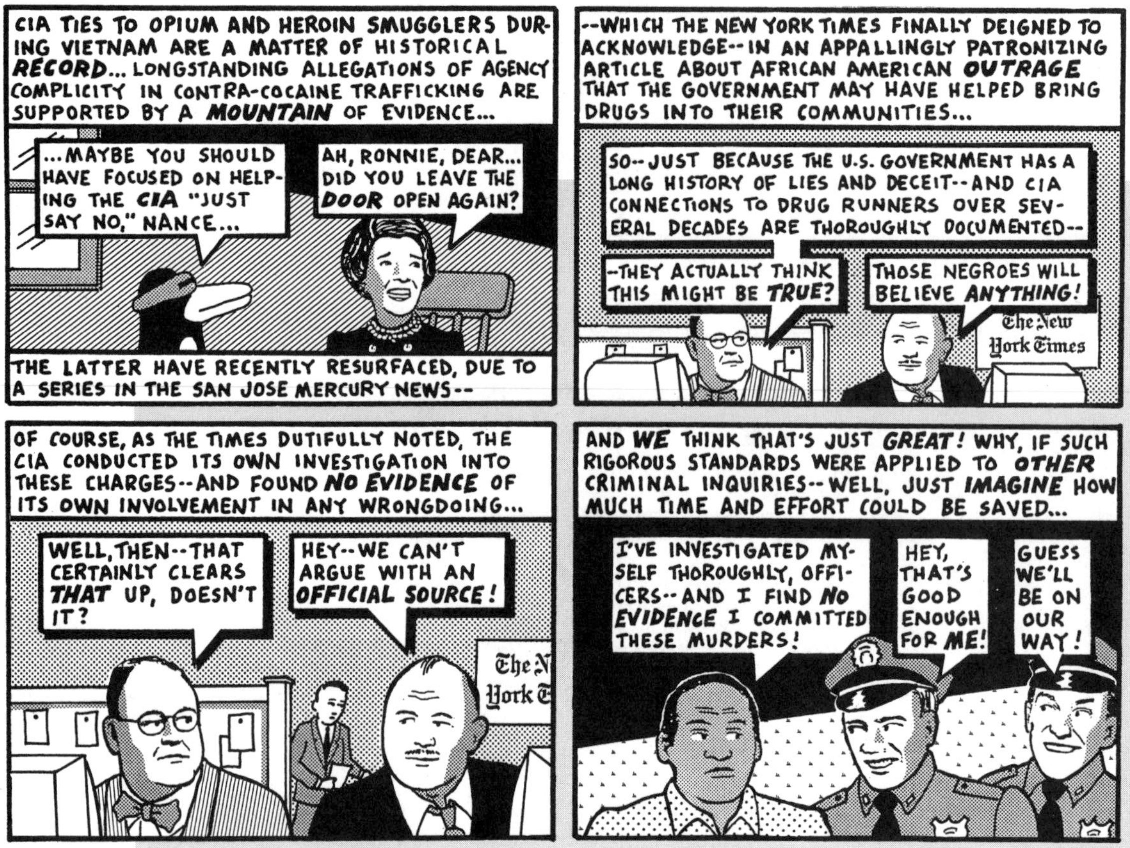
CIA TIES TO OPIUM AND HEROIN SMUGGLERS DURING VIETNAM ARE A MATTER OF HISTORICAL RECORD... LONGSTANDING ALLEGATIONS OF AGENCY COMPLICITY IN CONTRA-COCAINE TRAFFICKING ARE SUPPORTED BY A MOUNTAIN OF EVIDENCE...
...MAYBE YOU SHOULD HAVE FOCUSED ON HELPING THE CIA "JUST SAY NO," NANCE...
AH, RONNIE, DEAR... DID YOU LEAVE THE DOOR OPEN AGAIN?
THE LATTER HAVE RECENTLY RESURFACED, DUE TO A SERIES IN THE SAN JOSE MERCURY NEWS--
--WHICH THE NEW YORK TIMES FINALLY DEIGNED TO ACKNOWLEDGE--IN AN APPALLINGLY PATRONIZING ARTICLE ABOUT AFRICAN AMERICAN OUTRAGE THAT THE GOVERNMENT MAY HAVE HELPED BRING DRUGS INTO THEIR COMMUNITIES...
SO--JUST BECAUSE THE U.S. GOVERNMENT HAS A LONG HISTORY OF LIES AND DECEIT--AND CIA CONNECTIONS TO DRUG RUNNERS OVER SEVERAL DECADES ARE THOROUGHLY DOCUMENTED--
--THEY ACTUALLY THINK THIS MIGHT BE TRUE?
THOSE NEGROES WILL BELIEVE ANYTHING!
The New York Times
OF COURSE, AS THE TIMES DUTIFULLY NOTED, THE CIA CONDUCTED ITS OWN INVESTIGATION INTO THESE CHARGES--AND FOUND NO EVIDENCE OF ITS OWN INVOLVEMENT IN ANY WRONGDOING...
WELL, THEN--THAT CERTAINLY CLEARS THAT UP, DOESN'T IT?
HEY--WE CAN'T ARGUE WITH AN OFFICIAL SOURCE!
AND WE THINK THAT'S JUST GREAT! WHY, IF SUCH RIGOROUS STANDARDS WERE APPLIED TO OTHER CRIMINAL INQUIRIES--WELL, JUST IMAGINE HOW MUCH TIME AND EFFORT COULD BE SAVED...
I'VE INVESTIGATED MYSELF THOROUGHLY, OFFICERS--AND I FIND NO EVIDENCE I COMMITTED THESE MURDERS!
HEY, THAT'S GOOD ENOUGH FOR ME!
GUESS WE'LL BE ON OUR WAY!

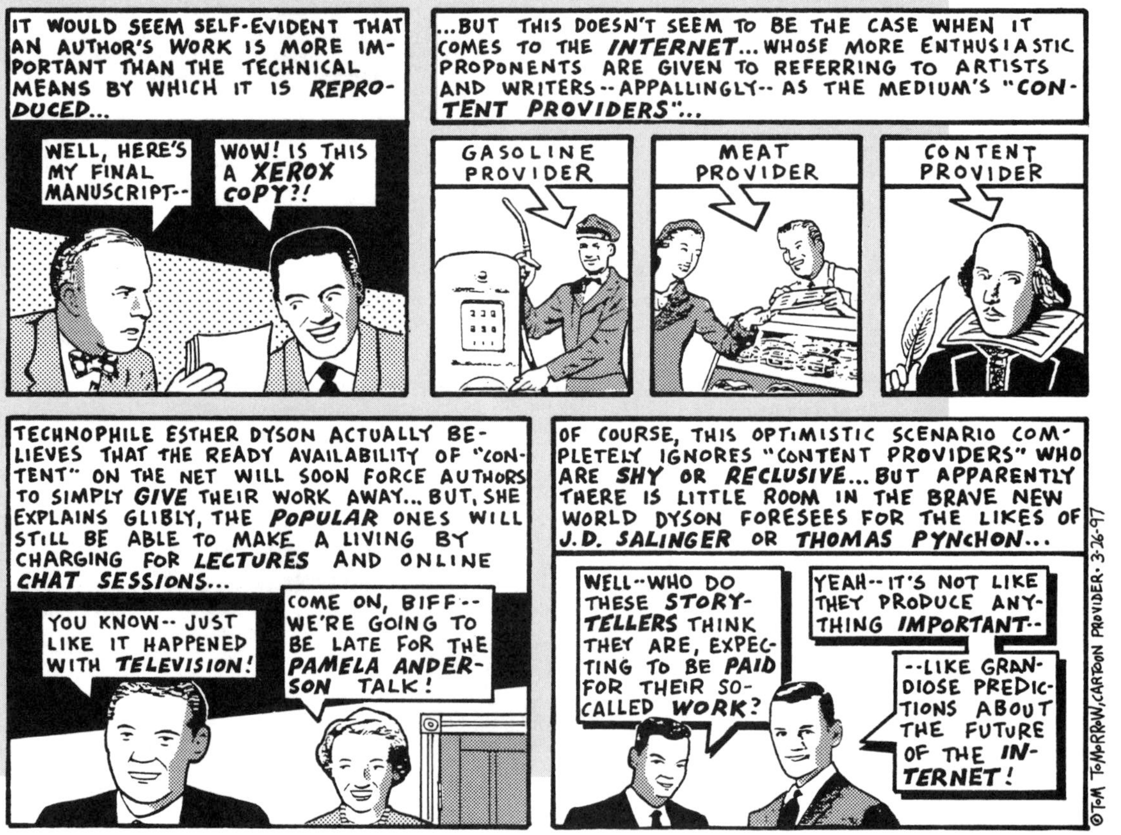
IT WOULD SEEM SELF-EVIDENT THAT AN AUTHOR'S WORK IS MORE IMPORTANT THAN THE TECHNICAL MEANS BY WHICH IT IS REPRODUCED...
WELL, HERE'S MY FINAL MANUSCRIPT--
WOW! IS THIS A XEROX COPY?!
...BUT THIS DOESN'T SEEM TO BE THE CASE WHEN IT COMES TO THE INTERNET... WHOSE MORE ENTHUSIASTIC PROPONENTS ARE GIVEN TO REFERRING TO ARTISTS AND WRITERS--APPALLINGLY--AS THE MEDIUM'S "CONTENT PROVIDERS"...
GASOLINE PROVIDER
MEAT PROVIDER
CONTENT PROVIDER
TECHNOPHILE ESTHER DYSON ACTUALLY BELIEVES THAT THE READY AVAILABILITY OF "CONTENT" ON THE NET WILL SOON FORCE AUTHORS TO SIMPLY GIVE THEIR WORK AWAY... BUT, SHE EXPLAINS GLIBLY, THE POPULAR ONES WILL STILL BE ABLE TO MAKE A LIVING BY CHARGING FOR LECTURES AND ONLINE CHAT SESSIONS...
YOU KNOW--JUST LIKE IT HAPPENED WITH TELEVISION!
COME ON, BIFF--WE'RE GOING TO BE LATE FOR THE PAMELA ANDERSON TALK!
OF COURSE, THIS OPTIMISTIC SCENARIO COMPLETELY IGNORES "CONTENT PROVIDERS" WHO ARE SHY OR RECLUSIVE... BUT APPARENTLY THERE IS LITTLE ROOM IN THE BRAVE NEW WORLD DYSON FORESEES FOR THE LIKES OF J.D. SALINGER OR THOMAS PYNCHON...
WELL--WHO DO THESE STORYTELLERS THINK THEY ARE, EXPECTING TO BE PAID FOR THEIR SO-CALLED WORK?
YEAH--IT'S NOT LIKE THEY PRODUCE ANYTHING IMPORTANT--
--LIKE GRANDIOSE PREDICTIONS ABOUT THE FUTURE OF THE INTERNET!
©TOM TOMORROW, CARTOON PROVIDER. 3-26-97

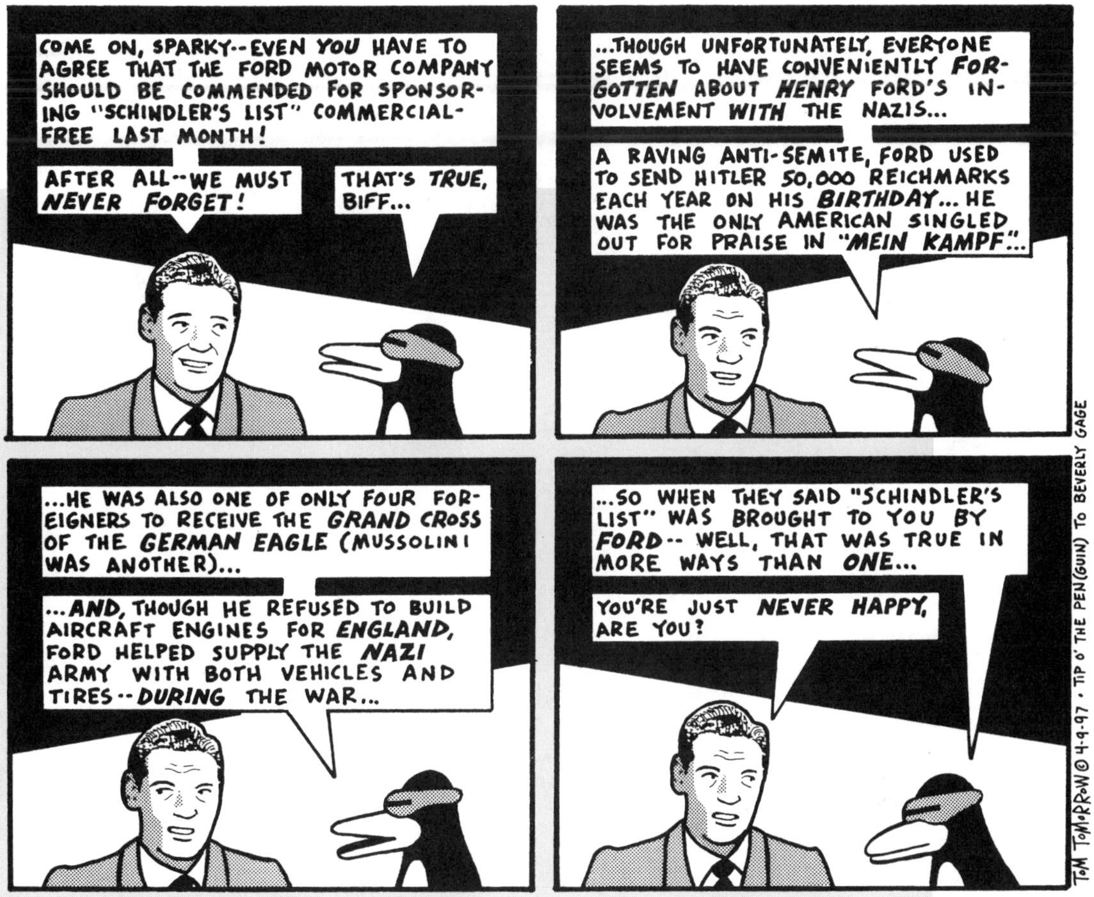
COME ON, SPARKY--EVEN YOU HAVE TO AGREE THAT THE FORD MOTOR COMPANY SHOULD BE COMMENDED FOR SPONSORING "SCHINDLER'S LIST" COMMERCIAL-FREE LAST MONTH!
AFTER ALL--WE MUST NEVER FORGET!
THAT'S TRUE, BIFF...
...THOUGH UNFORTUNATELY, EVERYONE SEEMS TO HAVE CONVENIENTLY FORGOTTEN ABOUT HENRY FORD'S INVOLVEMENT WITH THE NAZIS...
A RAVING ANTI-SEMITE, FORD USED TO SEND HITLER 50,000 REICHMARKS EACH YEAR ON HIS BIRTHDAY... HE WAS THE ONLY AMERICAN SINGLED OUT FOR PRAISE IN "MEIN KAMPF"...
...HE WAS ALSO ONE OF ONLY FOUR FOREIGNERS TO RECEIVE THE GRAND CROSS OF THE GERMAN EAGLE (MUSSOLINI WAS ANOTHER)...
...AND, THOUGH HE REFUSED TO BUILD AIRCRAFT ENGINES FOR ENGLAND, FORD HELPED SUPPLY THE NAZI ARMY WITH BOTH VEHICLES AND TIRES--DURING THE WAR...
...SO WHEN THEY SAID "SCHINDLER'S LIST" WAS BROUGHT TO YOU BY FORD-- WELL, THAT WAS TRUE IN MORE WAYS THAN ONE...
YOU'RE JUST NEVER HAPPY, ARE YOU?
TOM TOMORROW©4-9-97 • TIP O' THE PEN(GUIN) TO BEVERLY GAGE

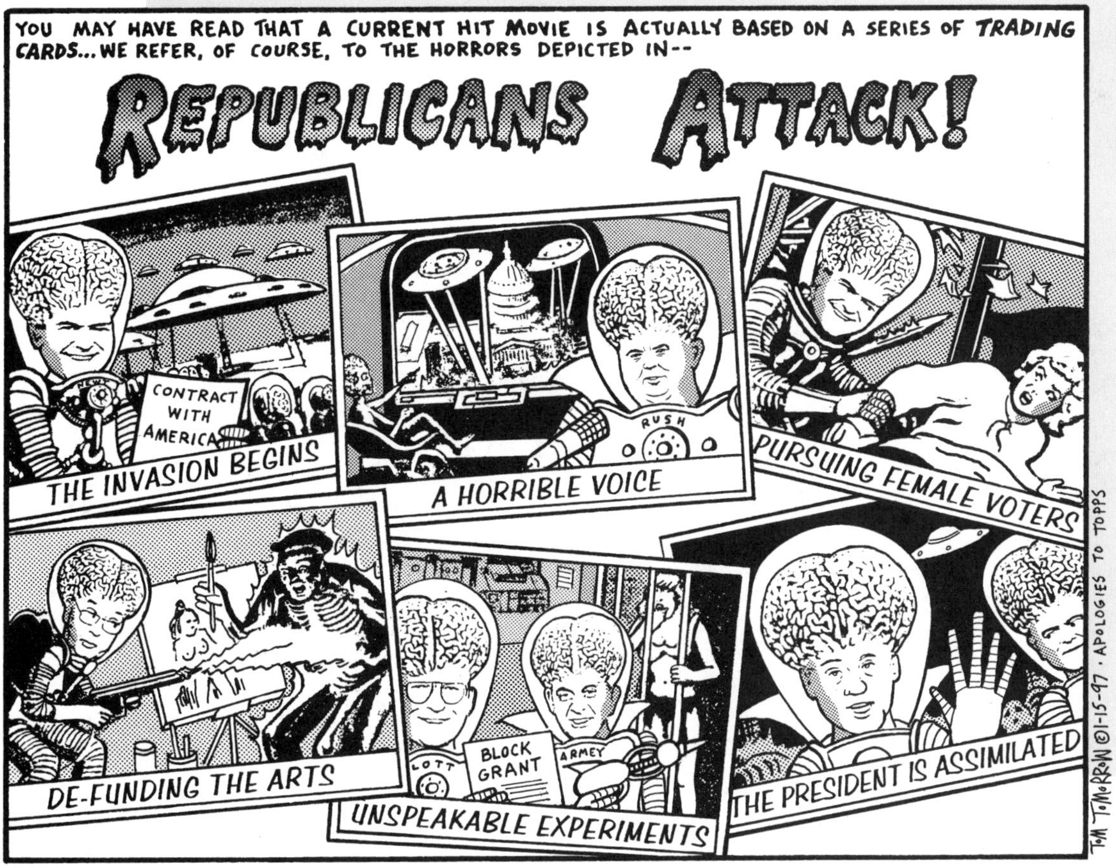
YOU MAY HAVE READ THAT A CURRENT HIT MOVIE IS ACTUALLY BASED ON A SERIES OF TRADING CARDS... WE REFER, OF COURSE, TO THE HORRORS DEPICTED IN--
REPUBLICANS ATTACK!
CONTRACT WITH AMERICA
THE INVASION BEGINS
RUSH
A HORRIBLE VOICE
PURSUING FEMALE VOTERS
DE-FUNDING THE ARTS
LOTT
BLOCK GRANT
ARMEY
UNSPEAKABLE EXPERIMENTS
THE PRESIDENT IS ASSIMILATED
TOM TOMORROW©01-15-97 • APOLOGIES TO TOPPS

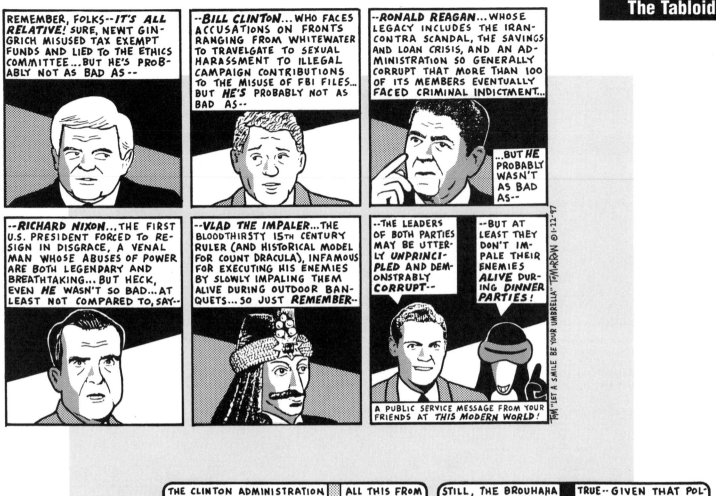

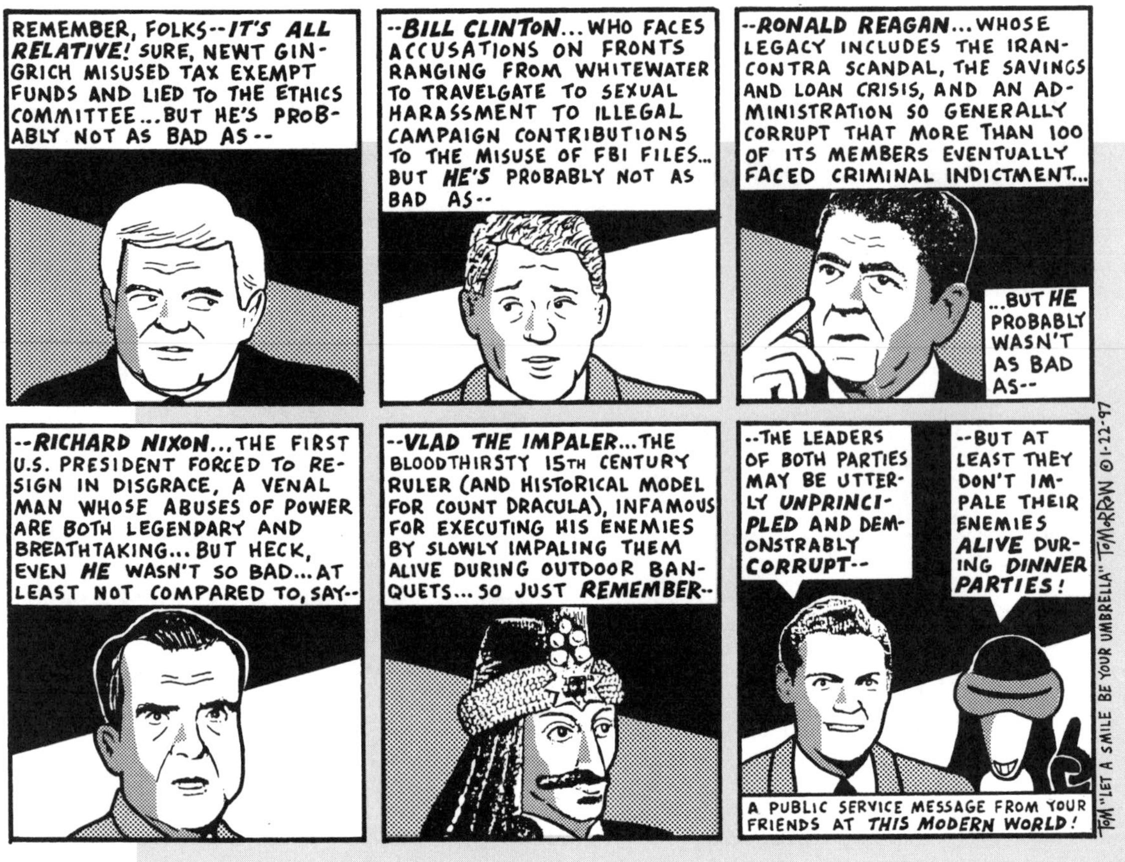
REMEMBER, FOLKS--IT'S ALL RELATIVE! SURE, NEWT GINGRICH MISUSED TAX EXEMPT FUNDS AND LIED TO THE ETHICS COMMITTEE...BUT HE'S PROBABLY NOT AS BAD AS--
--BILL CLINTON...WHO FACES ACCUSATIONS ON FRONTS RANGING FROM WHITEWATER TO TRAVELGATE TO SEXUAL HARASSMENT TO ILLEGAL CAMPAIGN CONTRIBUTIONS TO THE MISUSE OF FBI FILES...BUT HE'S PROBABLY NOT AS BAD AS--
--RONALD REAGAN...WHOSE LEGACY INCLUDES THE IRAN-CONTRA SCANDAL, THE SAVINGS AND LOAN CRISIS, AND AN ADMINISTRATION SO GENERALLY CORRUPT THAT MORE THAN 100 OF ITS MEMBERS EVENTUALLY FACED CRIMINAL INDICTMENT...
...BUT HE PROBABLY WASN'T AS BAD AS--
--RICHARD NIXON...THE FIRST U.S. PRESIDENT FORCED TO RESIGN IN DISGRACE, A VENAL MAN WHOSE ABUSES OF POWER ARE BOTH LEGENDARY AND BREATHTAKING...BUT HECK, EVEN HE WASN'T SO BAD...AT LEAST NOT COMPARED TO, SAY--
--VLAD THE IMPALER...THE BLOODTHIRSTY 15TH CENTURY RULER (AND HISTORICAL MODEL FOR COUNT DRACULA), INFAMOUS FOR EXECUTING HIS ENEMIES BY SLOWLY IMPALING THEM ALIVE DURING OUTDOOR BANQUETS...SO JUST REMEMBER--
--THE LEADERS OF BOTH PARTIES MAY BE UTTERLY UNPRINCIPLED AND DEMONSTRABLY CORRUPT--
--BUT AT LEAST THEY DON'T IMPALE THEIR ENEMIES ALIVE DURING DINNER PARTIES!
A PUBLIC SERVICE MESSAGE FROM YOUR FRIENDS AT THIS MODERN WORLD!
TOM "LET A SMILE BE YOUR UMBRELLA" TOMORROW ©1-22-97

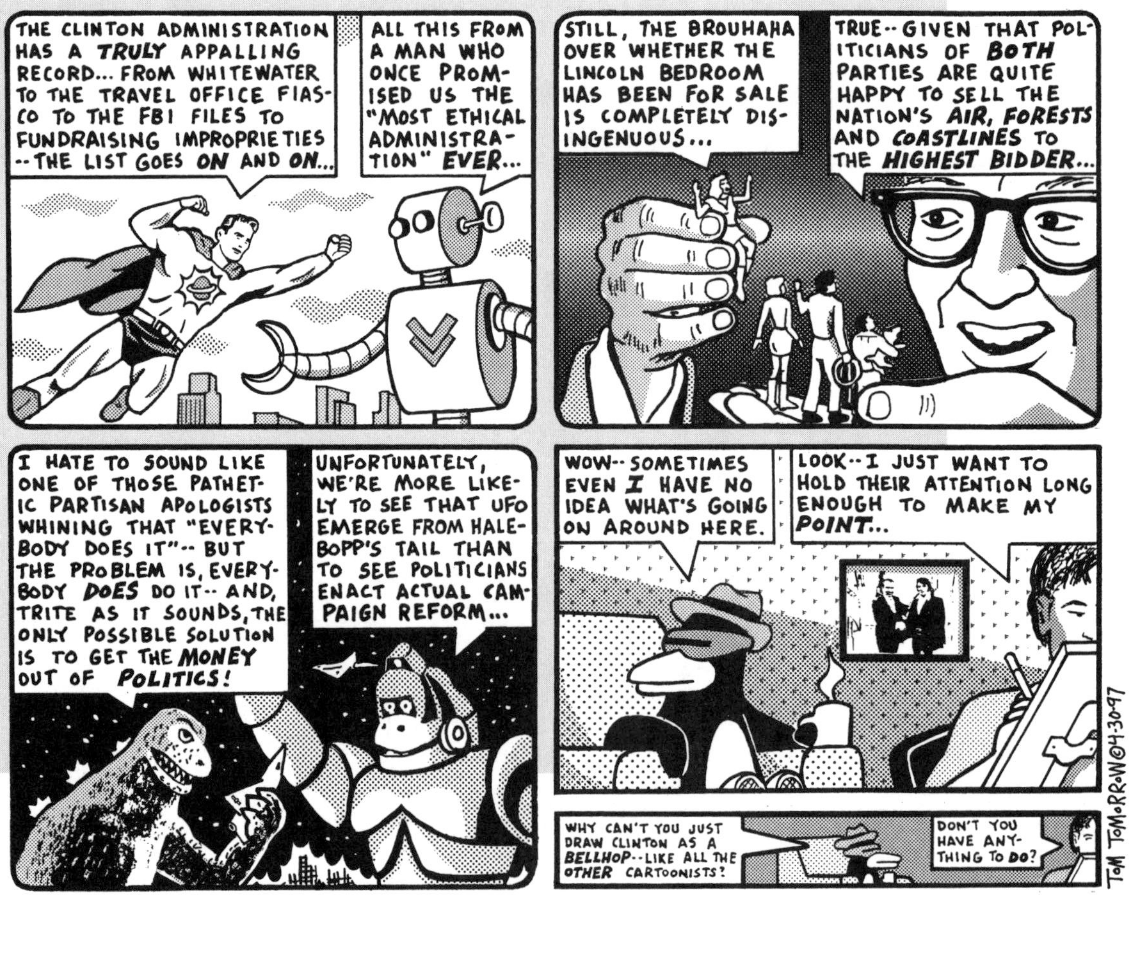
THE CLINTON ADMINISTRATION HAS A TRULY APPALLING RECORD...FROM WHITEWATER TO THE TRAVEL OFFICE FIASCO TO THE FBI FILES TO FUNDRAISING IMPROPRIETIES--THE LIST GOES ON AND ON...
ALL THIS FROM A MAN WHO ONCE PROMISED US THE "MOST ETHICAL ADMINISTRATION" EVER...
STILL, THE BROUHAHA OVER WHETHER THE LINCOLN BEDROOM HAS BEEN FOR SALE IS COMPLETELY DISINGENUOUS...
TRUE--GIVEN THAT POLITICIANS OF BOTH PARTIES ARE QUITE HAPPY TO SELL THE NATION'S AIR, FORESTS AND COASTLINES TO THE HIGHEST BIDDER...
I HATE TO SOUND LIKE ONE OF THOSE PATHETIC PARTISAN APOLOGISTS WHINING THAT "EVERYBODY DOES IT"--BUT THE PROBLEM IS, EVERYBODY DOES DO IT--AND, TRITE AS IT SOUNDS, THE ONLY POSSIBLE SOLUTION IS TO GET THE MONEY OUT OF POLITICS!
UNFORTUNATELY, WE'RE MORE LIKELY TO SEE THAT UFO EMERGE FROM HALE-BOPP'S TAIL THAN TO SEE POLITICIANS ENACT ACTUAL CAMPAIGN REFORM...
WOW--SOMETIMES EVEN I HAVE NO IDEA WHAT'S GOING ON AROUND HERE.
LOOK--I JUST WANT TO HOLD THEIR ATTENTION LONG ENOUGH TO MAKE MY POINT...
WHY CAN'T YOU JUST DRAW CLINTON AS A BELLHOP--LIKE ALL THE OTHER CARTOONISTS?
DON'T YOU HAVE ANYTHING TO DO?
TOM TOMORROW©4-30-97

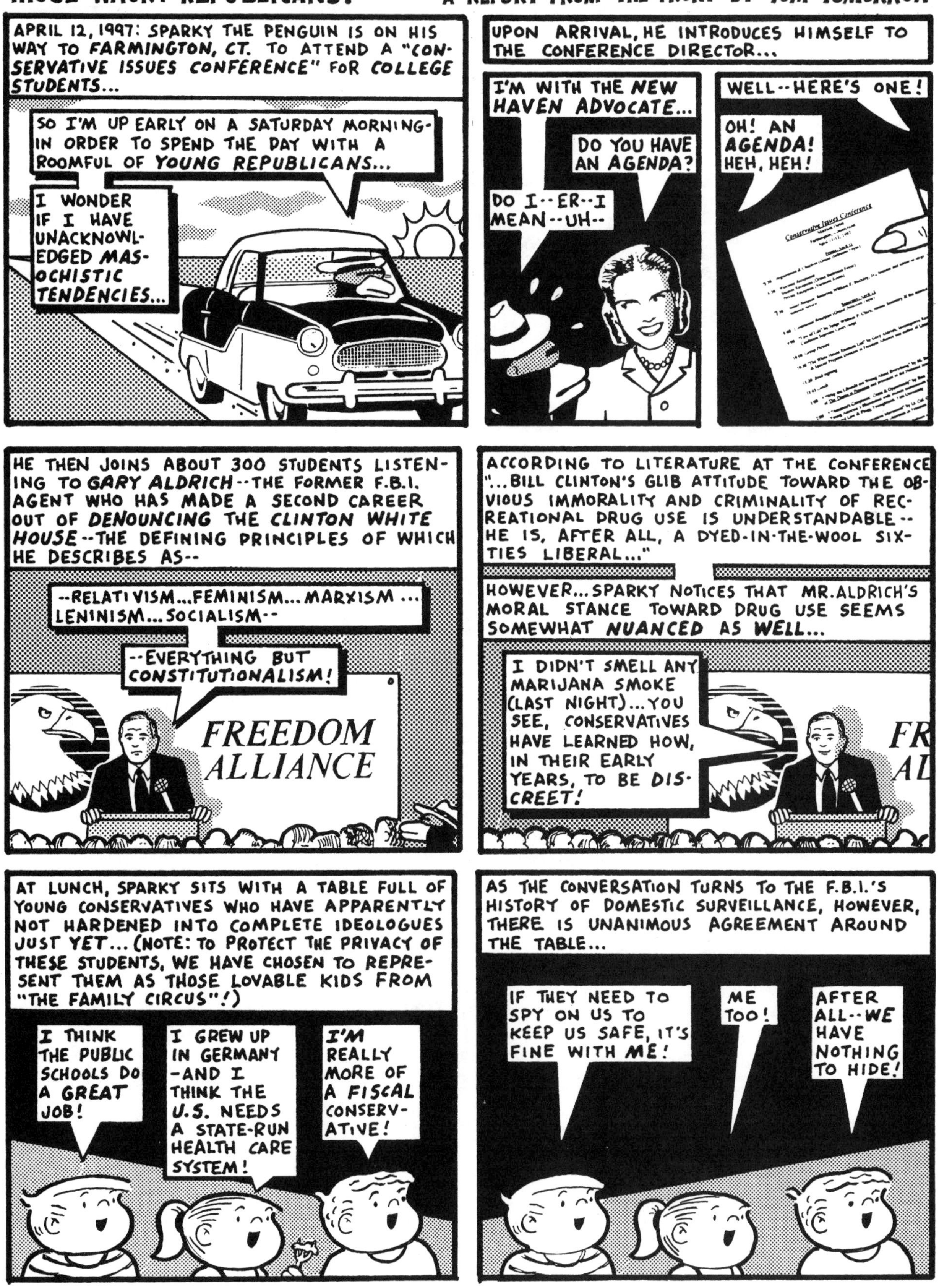
THOSE WACKY REPUBLICANS!
A REPORT FROM THE FRONT BY TOM TOMORROW
APRIL 12, 1997: SPARKY THE PENGUIN IS ON HIS WAY TO FARMINGTON, CT. TO ATTEND A "CONSERVATIVE ISSUES CONFERENCE" FOR COLLEGE STUDENTS...
SO I'M UP EARLY ON A SATURDAY MORNING-IN ORDER TO SPEND THE DAY WITH A ROOMFUL OF YOUNG REPUBLICANS...
I WONDER IF I HAVE UNACKNOWLEDGED MASOCHISTIC TENDENCIES...
UPON ARRIVAL, HE INTRODUCES HIMSELF TO THE CONFERENCE DIRECTOR...
I'M WITH THE NEW HAVEN ADVOCATE...
DO YOU HAVE AN AGENDA?
DO I--ER--I MEAN--UH--
WELL--HERE'S ONE!
OH! AN AGENDA! HEH, HEH!
Conservative Issues Conference
HE THEN JOINS ABOUT 300 STUDENTS LISTENING TO GARY ALDRICH--THE FORMER F.B.I. AGENT WHO HAS MADE A SECOND CAREER OUT OF DENOUNCING THE CLINTON WHITE HOUSE--THE DEFINING PRINCIPLES OF WHICH HE DESCRIBES AS--
--RELATIVISM...FEMINISM...MARXISM...LENINISM...SOCIALISM--
--EVERYTHING BUT CONSTITUTIONALISM!
FREEDOM ALLIANCE
ACCORDING TO LITERATURE AT THE CONFERENCE "...BILL CLINTON'S GLIB ATTITUDE TOWARD THE OBVIOUS IMMORALITY AND CRIMINALITY OF RECREATIONAL DRUG USE IS UNDERSTANDABLE--HE IS, AFTER ALL, A DYED-IN-THE-WOOL SIXTIES LIBERAL..."
HOWEVER...SPARKY NOTICES THAT MR. ALDRICH'S MORAL STANCE TOWARD DRUG USE SEEMS SOMEWHAT NUANCED AS WELL...
I DIDN'T SMELL ANY MARIJUANA SMOKE (LAST NIGHT)...YOU SEE, CONSERVATIVES HAVE LEARNED HOW, IN THEIR EARLY YEARS, TO BE DISCREET!
AT LUNCH, SPARKY SITS WITH A TABLE FULL OF YOUNG CONSERVATIVES WHO HAVE APPARENTLY NOT HARDENED INTO COMPLETE IDEOLOGUES JUST YET... (NOTE: TO PROTECT THE PRIVACY OF THESE STUDENTS, WE HAVE CHOSEN TO REPRESENT THEM AS THOSE LOVABLE KIDS FROM "THE FAMILY CIRCUS"!)
I THINK THE PUBLIC SCHOOLS DO A GREAT JOB!
I GREW UP IN GERMANY -AND I THINK THE U.S. NEEDS A STATE-RUN HEALTH CARE SYSTEM!
I'M REALLY MORE OF A FISCAL CONSERVATIVE!
AS THE CONVERSATION TURNS TO THE F.B.I.'S HISTORY OF DOMESTIC SURVEILLANCE, HOWEVER, THERE IS UNANIMOUS AGREEMENT AROUND THE TABLE...
IF THEY NEED TO SPY ON US TO KEEP US SAFE, IT'S FINE WITH ME!
ME TOO!
AFTER ALL--WE HAVE NOTHING TO HIDE!

The intrepid cartoon journalist, on assignment for the *New Haven Advocate*.

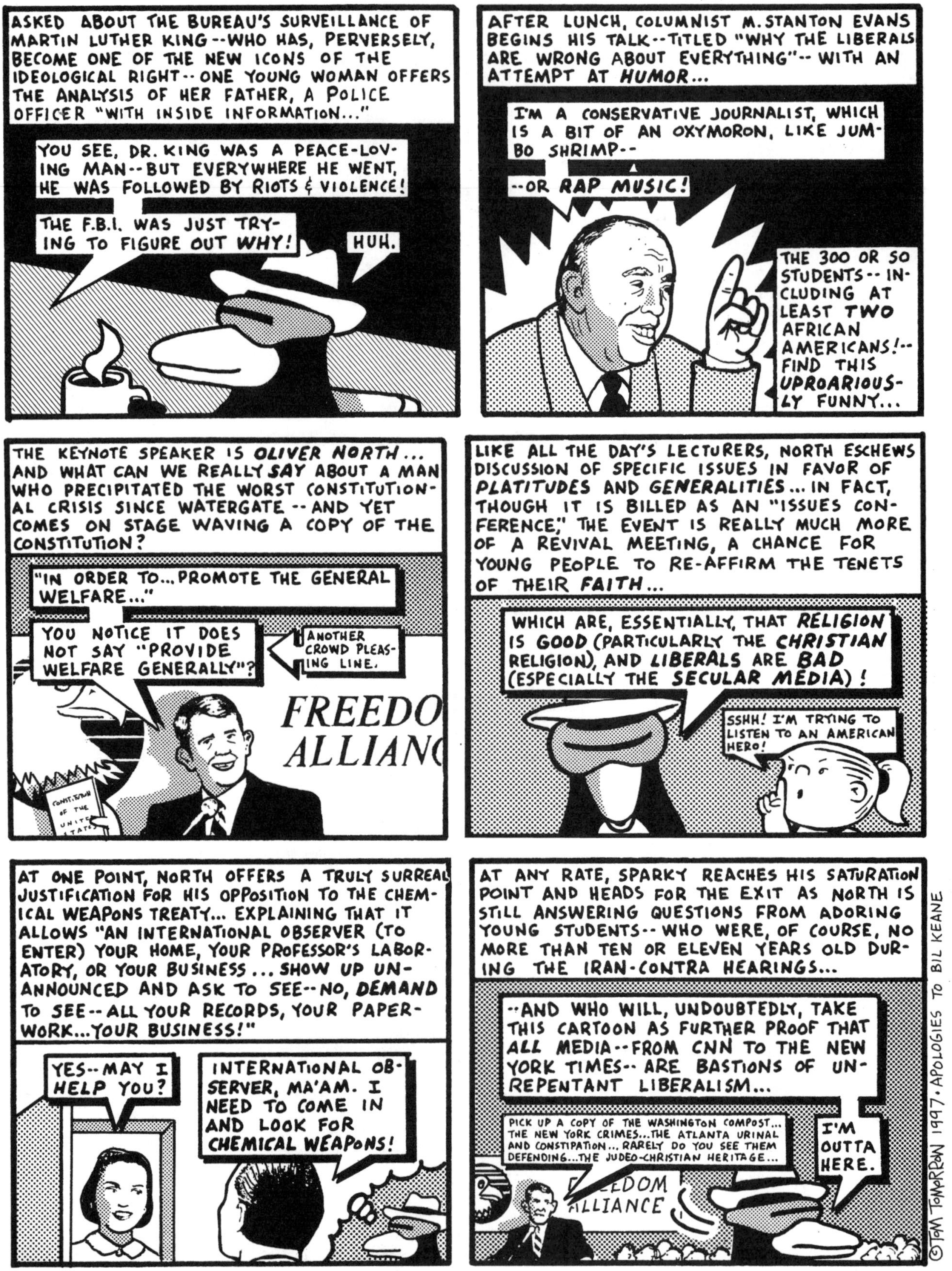
ASKED ABOUT THE BUREAU'S SURVEILLANCE OF MARTIN LUTHER KING--WHO HAS, PERVERSELY, BECOME ONE OF THE NEW ICONS OF THE IDEOLOGICAL RIGHT--ONE YOUNG WOMAN OFFERS THE ANALYSIS OF HER FATHER, A POLICE OFFICER "WITH INSIDE INFORMATION..."
YOU SEE, DR. KING WAS A PEACE-LOVING MAN--BUT EVERYWHERE HE WENT, HE WAS FOLLOWED BY RIOTS & VIOLENCE!
THE F.B.I. WAS JUST TRYING TO FIGURE OUT WHY!
HUH.
AFTER LUNCH, COLUMNIST M. STANTON EVANS BEGINS HIS TALK--TITLED "WHY THE LIBERALS ARE WRONG ABOUT EVERYTHING"--WITH AN ATTEMPT AT HUMOR...
I'M A CONSERVATIVE JOURNALIST, WHICH IS A BIT OF AN OXYMORON, LIKE JUMBO SHRIMP--
--OR RAP MUSIC!
THE 300 OR SO STUDENTS--INCLUDING AT LEAST TWO AFRICAN AMERICANS!--FIND THIS UPROARIOUSLY FUNNY...
THE KEYNOTE SPEAKER IS OLIVER NORTH... AND WHAT CAN WE REALLY SAY ABOUT A MAN WHO PRECIPITATED THE WORST CONSTITUTIONAL CRISIS SINCE WATERGATE--AND YET COMES ON STAGE WAVING A COPY OF THE CONSTITUTION?
"IN ORDER TO...PROMOTE THE GENERAL WELFARE..."
YOU NOTICE IT DOES NOT SAY "PROVIDE WELFARE GENERALLY"?
ANOTHER CROWD PLEASING LINE.
FREEDO
ALLIANC
CONSTITUTION OF THE UNITED STATES
LIKE ALL THE DAY'S LECTURERS, NORTH ESCHEWS DISCUSSION OF SPECIFIC ISSUES IN FAVOR OF PLATITUDES AND GENERALITIES... IN FACT, THOUGH IT IS BILLED AS AN "ISSUES CONFERENCE," THE EVENT IS REALLY MUCH MORE OF A REVIVAL MEETING, A CHANCE FOR YOUNG PEOPLE TO RE-AFFIRM THE TENETS OF THEIR FAITH...
WHICH ARE, ESSENTIALLY, THAT RELIGION IS GOOD (PARTICULARLY THE CHRISTIAN RELIGION), AND LIBERALS ARE BAD (ESPECIALLY THE SECULAR MEDIA)!
SSHH! I'M TRYING TO LISTEN TO AN AMERICAN HERO!
AT ONE POINT, NORTH OFFERS A TRULY SURREAL JUSTIFICATION FOR HIS OPPOSITION TO THE CHEMICAL WEAPONS TREATY... EXPLAINING THAT IT ALLOWS "AN INTERNATIONAL OBSERVER (TO ENTER) YOUR HOME, YOUR PROFESSOR'S LABORATORY, OR YOUR BUSINESS... SHOW UP UNANNOUNCED AND ASK TO SEE--NO, DEMAND TO SEE--ALL YOUR RECORDS, YOUR PAPERWORK...YOUR BUSINESS!"
YES--MAY I HELP YOU?
INTERNATIONAL OBSERVER, MA'AM. I NEED TO COME IN AND LOOK FOR CHEMICAL WEAPONS!
AT ANY RATE, SPARKY REACHES HIS SATURATION POINT AND HEADS FOR THE EXIT AS NORTH IS STILL ANSWERING QUESTIONS FROM ADORING YOUNG STUDENTS--WHO WERE, OF COURSE, NO MORE THAN TEN OR ELEVEN YEARS OLD DURING THE IRAN-CONTRA HEARINGS...
--AND WHO WILL, UNDOUBTEDLY, TAKE THIS CARTOON AS FURTHER PROOF THAT ALL MEDIA--FROM CNN TO THE NEW YORK TIMES--ARE BASTIONS OF UNREPENTANT LIBERALISM...
PICK UP A COPY OF THE WASHINGTON COMPOST... THE NEW YORK CRIMES...THE ATLANTA URINAL AND CONSTIPATION... RARELY DO YOU SEE THEM DEFENDING...THE JUDEO-CHRISTIAN HERITAGE...
I'M OUTTA HERE.
ALLIANCE
©TOM TOMORROW 1997 · APOLOGIES TO BIL KEANE

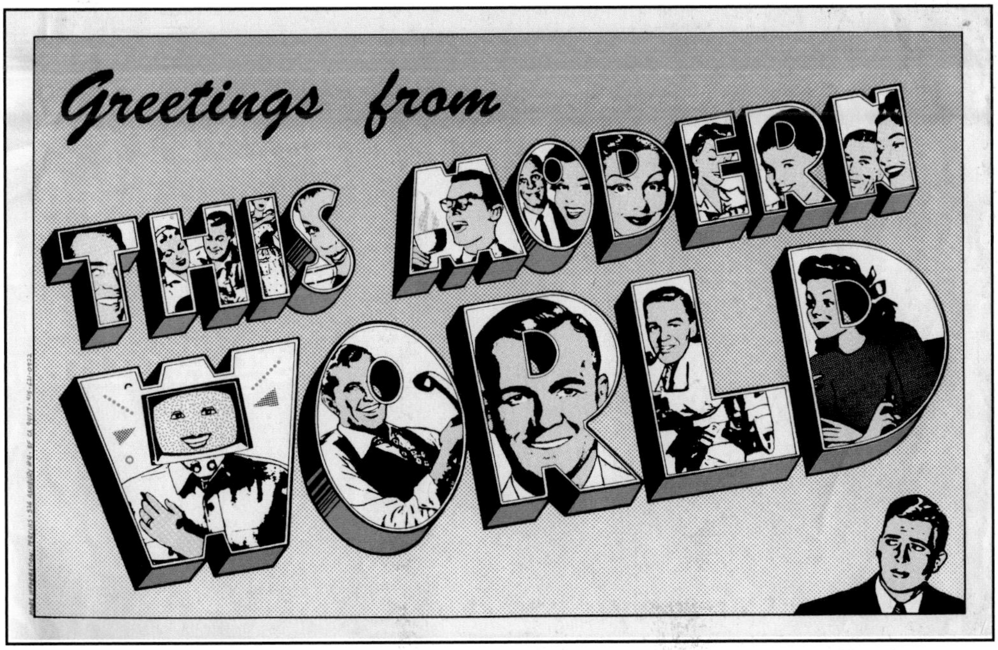
Greetings from
THIS MODERN
WORLD

Left: promotional poster, circa 1986.

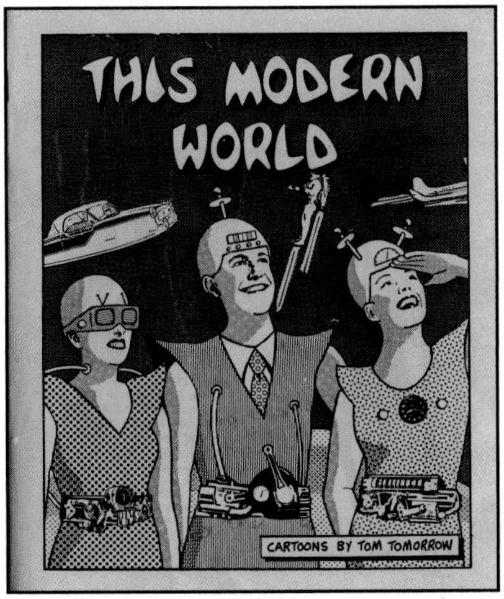
THIS MODERN
WORLD
CARTOONS BY TOM TOMORROW

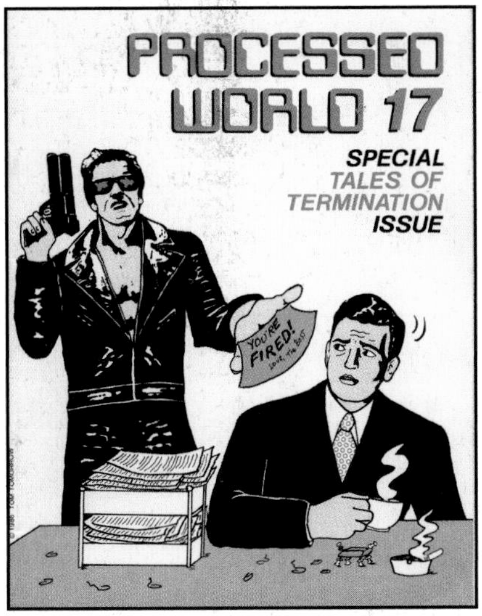
PROCESSED
WORLD 17
SPECIAL
TALES OF
TERMINATION
ISSUE
YOU'RE
FIRED!

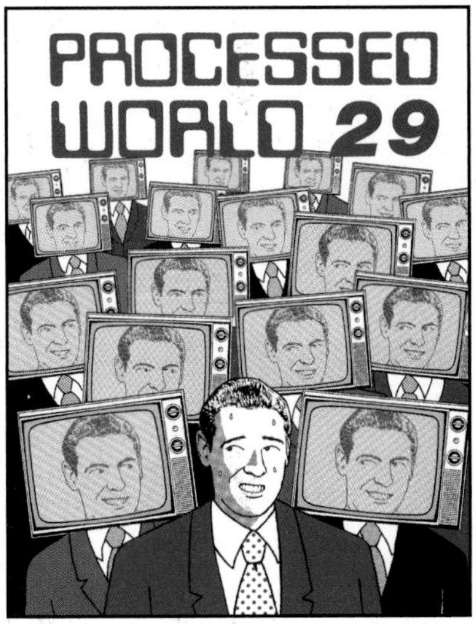
PROCESSED
WORLD 29

Middle: self-published zine, circa 1986; *Processed World* covers, 1986 and 1992.

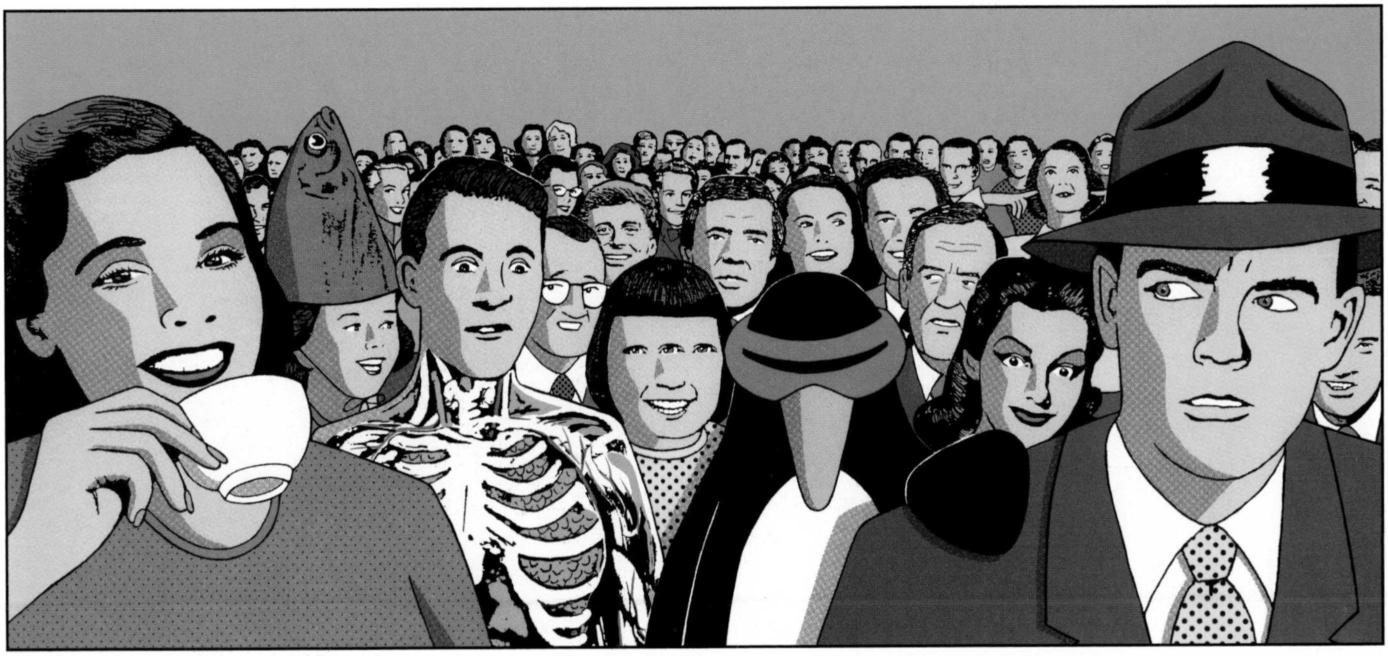

Bottom: wraparound art for cover of first book, *Greetings From This Modern World* (1991), also used on poster for solo show at San Francisco's Cartoon Art Museum, 1993.

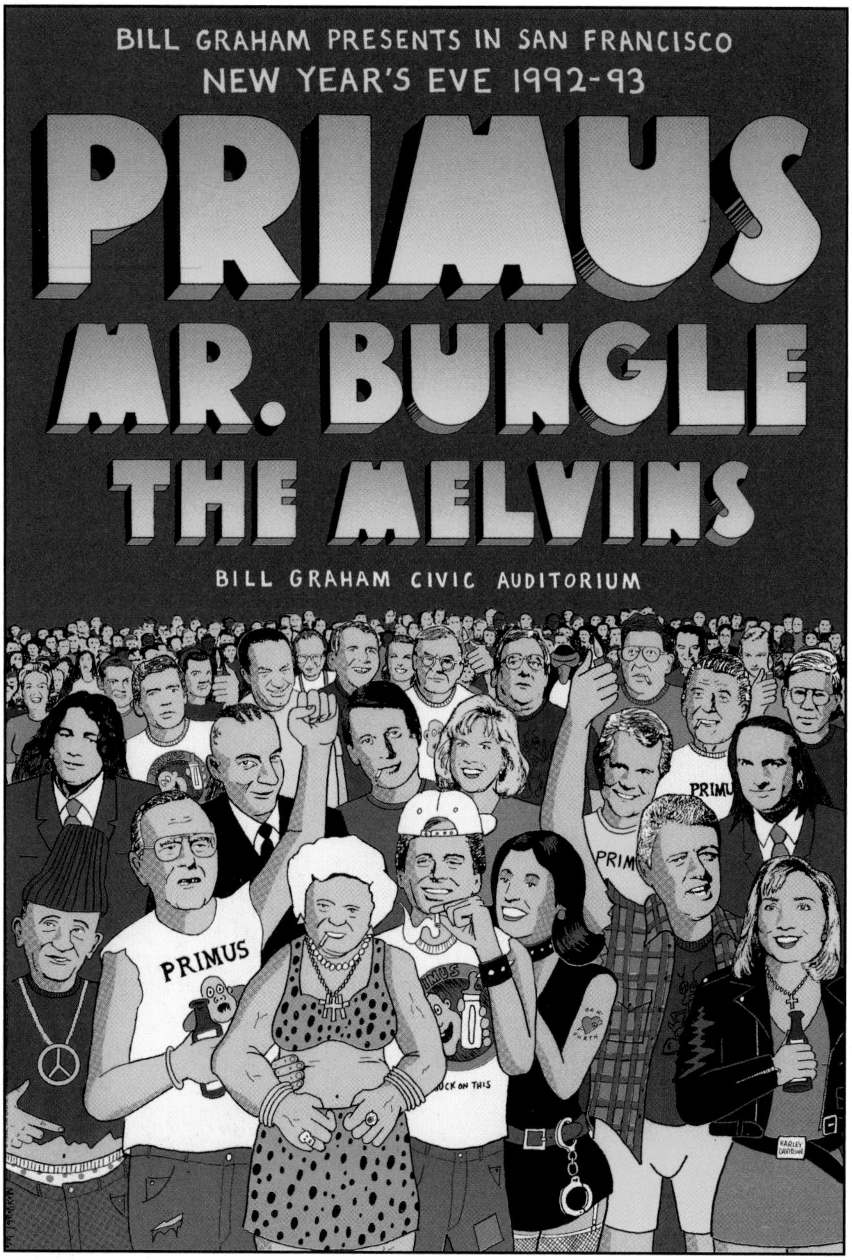

BILL GRAHAM PRESENTS IN SAN FRANCISCO
NEW YEAR'S EVE 1992-93
PRIMUS
MR. BUNGLE
THE MELVINS
BILL GRAHAM CIVIC AUDITORIUM
PRIMUS
PRIMUS
PRIMUS

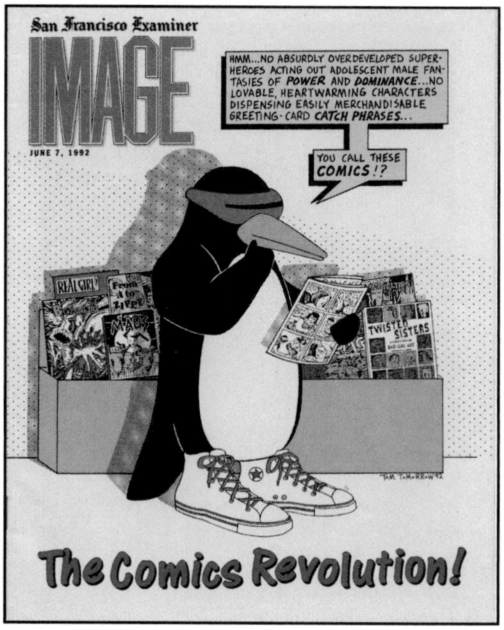

San Francisco Examiner
IMAGE
JUNE 7, 1992
HMM...NO ABSURDLY OVERDEVELOPED SUPER-HEROES ACTING OUT ADOLESCENT MALE FANTASIES OF POWER AND DOMINANCE...NO LOVABLE, HEARTWARMING CHARACTERS DISPENSING EASILY MERCHANDISABLE GREETING-CARD CATCH PHRASES...
YOU CALL THESE COMICS!?
TWISTED SISTERS
The Comics Revolution!

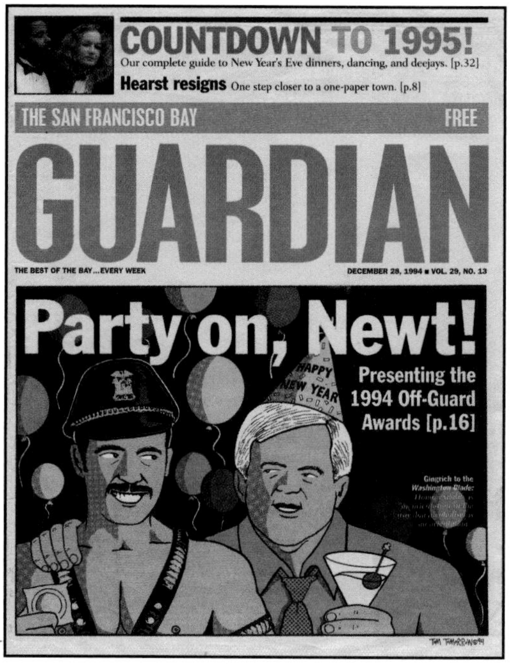

COUNTDOWN TO 1995!
Our complete guide to New Year's Eve dinners, dancing, and deejays. [p.32]
Hearst resigns One step closer to a one-paper town. [p.8]
THE SAN FRANCISCO BAY
FREE
GUARDIAN
THE BEST OF THE BAY...EVERY WEEK
DECEMBER 28, 1994 ■ VOL. 29, NO. 13
Party on, Newt!
Presenting the 1994 Off-Guard Awards [p.16]
HAPPY NEW YEAR

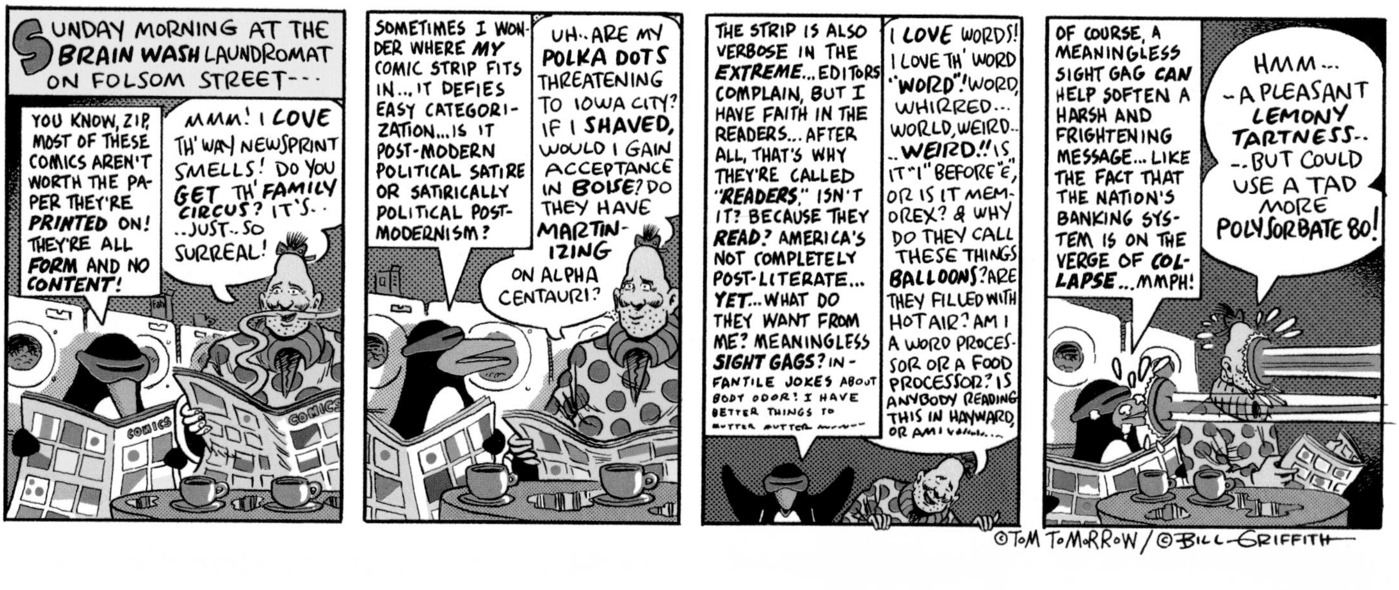

SUNDAY MORNING AT THE BRAIN WASH LAUNDROMAT ON FOLSOM STREET---
YOU KNOW, ZIP, MOST OF THESE COMICS AREN'T WORTH THE PAPER THEY'RE PRINTED ON! THEY'RE ALL FORM AND NO CONTENT!
MMM! I LOVE TH' WAY NEWSPRINT SMELLS! DO YOU GET TH' FAMILY CIRCUS? IT'S.. ..JUST.. SO SURREAL!
SOMETIMES I WONDER WHERE MY COMIC STRIP FITS IN... IT DEFIES EASY CATEGORIZATION... IS IT POST-MODERN POLITICAL SATIRE OR SATIRICALLY POLITICAL POST-MODERNISM?
UH.. ARE MY POLKA DOTS THREATENING TO IOWA CITY? IF I SHAVED, WOULD I GAIN ACCEPTANCE IN BOISE? DO THEY HAVE MARTINIZING ON ALPHA CENTAURI?
THE STRIP IS ALSO VERBOSE IN THE EXTREME... EDITORS COMPLAIN, BUT I HAVE FAITH IN THE READERS... AFTER ALL, THAT'S WHY THEY'RE CALLED "READERS," ISN'T IT? BECAUSE THEY READ? AMERICA'S NOT COMPLETELY POST-LITERATE... YET... WHAT DO THEY WANT FROM ME? MEANINGLESS SIGHT GAGS? INFANTILE JOKES ABOUT BODY ODOR? I HAVE BETTER THINGS TO
I LOVE WORDS! I LOVE TH' WORD "WORD"! WORD, WHIRRED... WORLD, WEIRD.. ..WEIRD!! IS IT "I" BEFORE "E", OR IS IT MEMOREX? & WHY DO THEY CALL THESE THINGS BALLOONS? ARE THEY FILLED WITH HOT AIR? AM I A WORD PROCESSOR OR A FOOD PROCESSOR? IS ANYBODY READING THIS IN HAYWARD, OR AM I
OF COURSE, A MEANINGLESS SIGHT GAG CAN HELP SOFTEN A HARSH AND FRIGHTENING MESSAGE... LIKE THE FACT THAT THE NATION'S BANKING SYSTEM IS ON THE VERGE OF COLLAPSE... MMPH!
HMM... - A PLEASANT LEMONY TARTNESS.. ..BUT COULD USE A TAD MORE POLYSORBATE 80!
COMICS
©TOM TOMORROW / ©BILL GRIFFITH

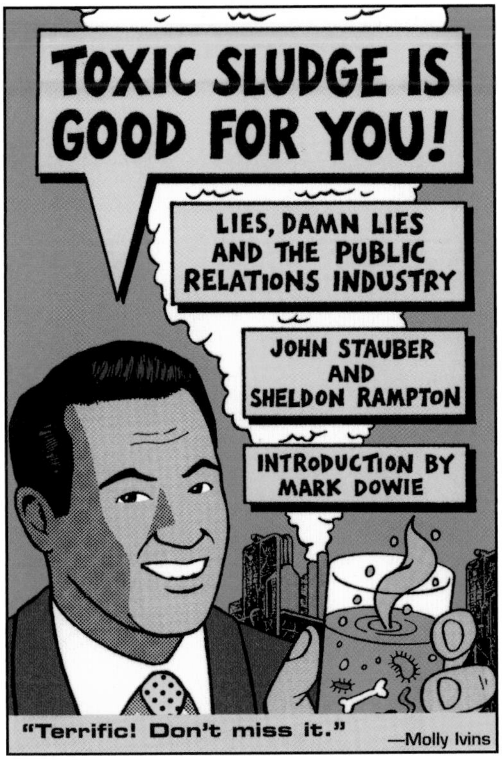
TOXIC SLUDGE IS GOOD FOR YOU!
LIES, DAMN LIES AND THE PUBLIC RELATIONS INDUSTRY
JOHN STAUBER AND SHELDON RAMPTON
INTRODUCTION BY MARK DOWIE
"Terrific! Don't miss it." —Molly Ivins

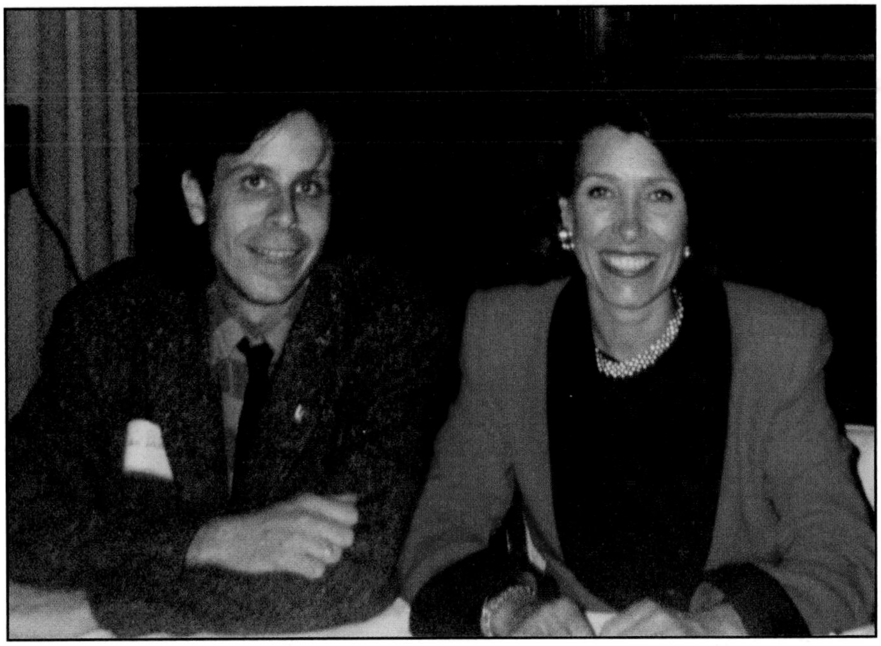

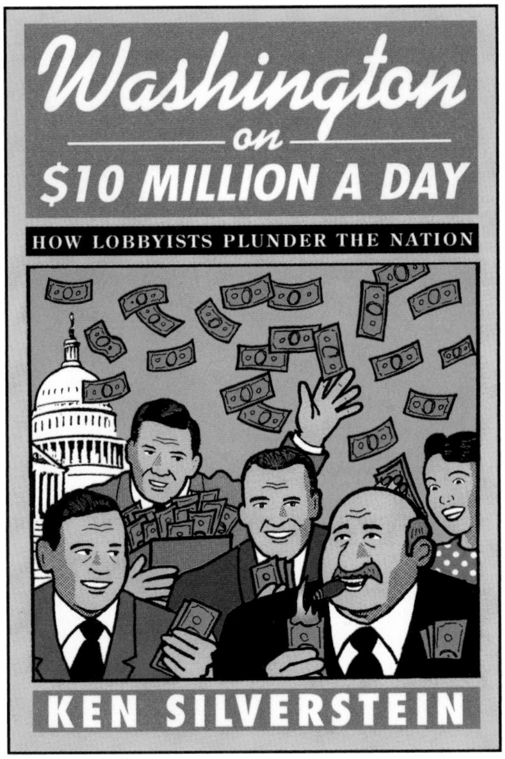
Washington on $10 MILLION A DAY
HOW LOBBYISTS PLUNDER THE NATION
KEN SILVERSTEIN

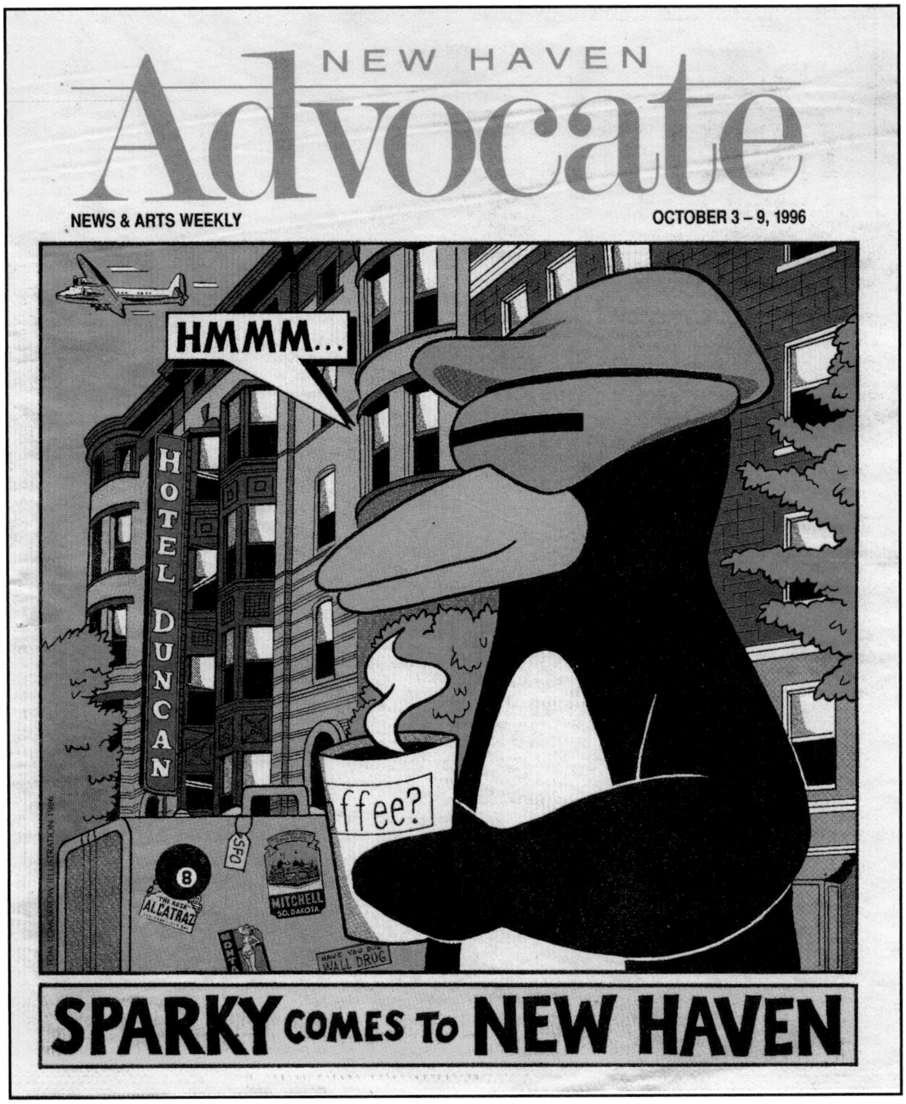
NEW HAVEN
Advocate
NEWS & ARTS WEEKLY
OCTOBER 3 – 9, 1996
HMMM...
HOTEL DUNCAN
ffee?
SFO
ALCATRAZ
MITCHELL
SO. DAKOTA
SPARKY COMES TO NEW HAVEN

Opposite, clockwise: poster for Primus concert, 1992; *Image* cover, 1992; *San Francisco Bay Guardian* cover, 1994; collaboration with Bill Griffith for the *San Francisco Examiner*, 1993. This page, clockwise from top: book cover, 1995; the author with close personal friend Marilyn Quayle, circa 1991; *New Haven Advocate* cover, 1996; book cover, 1998.

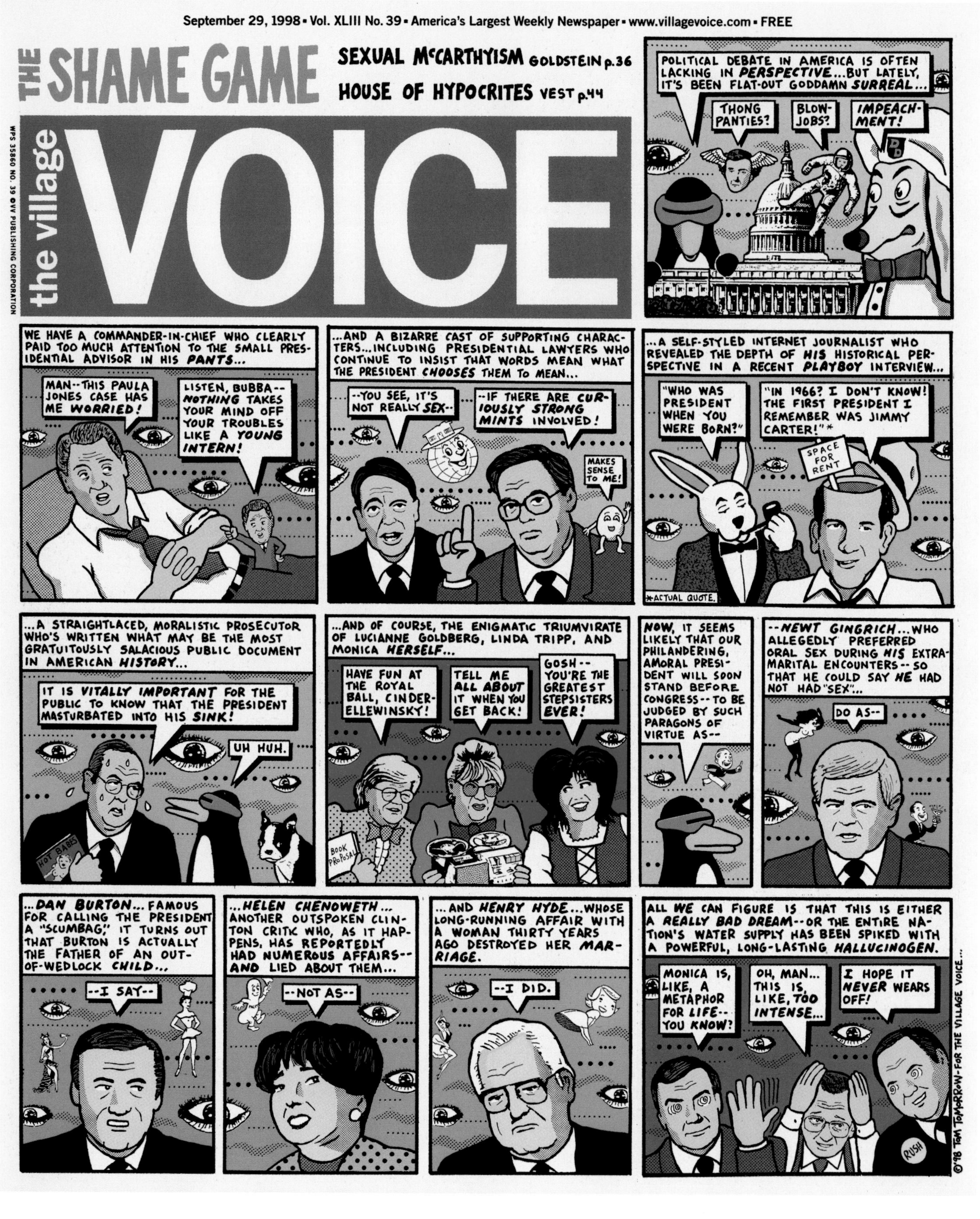
September 29, 1998 • Vol. XLIII No. 39 • America's Largest Weekly Newspaper • www.villagevoice.com • FREE
THE SHAME GAME
SEXUAL McCARTHYISM GOLDSTEIN p.36
HOUSE OF HYPOCRITES VEST p.44
the village VOICE
WPS 35860 NO. 39 ©VV PUBLISHING CORPORATION
POLITICAL DEBATE IN AMERICA IS OFTEN LACKING IN PERSPECTIVE... BUT LATELY, IT'S BEEN FLAT-OUT GODDAMN SURREAL...
THONG PANTIES?
BLOW-JOBS?
IMPEACH-MENT!
WE HAVE A COMMANDER-IN-CHIEF WHO CLEARLY PAID TOO MUCH ATTENTION TO THE SMALL PRESIDENTIAL ADVISOR IN HIS PANTS...
MAN--THIS PAULA JONES CASE HAS ME WORRIED!
LISTEN, BUBBA--NOTHING TAKES YOUR MIND OFF YOUR TROUBLES LIKE A YOUNG INTERN!
...AND A BIZARRE CAST OF SUPPORTING CHARACTERS... INCLUDING PRESIDENTIAL LAWYERS WHO CONTINUE TO INSIST THAT WORDS MEAN WHAT THE PRESIDENT CHOOSES THEM TO MEAN...
--YOU SEE, IT'S NOT REALLY SEX--
--IF THERE ARE CURIOUSLY STRONG MINTS INVOLVED!
MAKES SENSE TO ME!
...A SELF-STYLED INTERNET JOURNALIST WHO REVEALED THE DEPTH OF HIS HISTORICAL PERSPECTIVE IN A RECENT PLAYBOY INTERVIEW...
"WHO WAS PRESIDENT WHEN YOU WERE BORN?"
"IN 1966? I DON'T KNOW! THE FIRST PRESIDENT I REMEMBER WAS JIMMY CARTER!"*
SPACE FOR RENT
*ACTUAL QUOTE.
...A STRAIGHTLACED, MORALISTIC PROSECUTOR WHO'S WRITTEN WHAT MAY BE THE MOST GRATUITOUSLY SALACIOUS PUBLIC DOCUMENT IN AMERICAN HISTORY...
IT IS VITALLY IMPORTANT FOR THE PUBLIC TO KNOW THAT THE PRESIDENT MASTURBATED INTO HIS SINK!
UH HUH.
HOT BABES
...AND OF COURSE, THE ENIGMATIC TRIUMVIRATE OF LUCIANNE GOLDBERG, LINDA TRIPP, AND MONICA HERSELF...
HAVE FUN AT THE ROYAL BALL, CINDERELLEWINSKY!
TELL ME ALL ABOUT IT WHEN YOU GET BACK!
GOSH--YOU'RE THE GREATEST STEPSISTERS EVER!
BOOK PROPOSAL
NOW, IT SEEMS LIKELY THAT OUR PHILANDERING, AMORAL PRESIDENT WILL SOON STAND BEFORE CONGRESS--TO BE JUDGED BY SUCH PARAGONS OF VIRTUE AS--
--NEWT GINGRICH... WHO ALLEGEDLY PREFERRED ORAL SEX DURING HIS EXTRAMARITAL ENCOUNTERS--SO THAT HE COULD SAY HE HAD NOT HAD "SEX"...
DO AS--
...DAN BURTON... FAMOUS FOR CALLING THE PRESIDENT A "SCUMBAG," IT TURNS OUT THAT BURTON IS ACTUALLY THE FATHER OF AN OUT-OF-WEDLOCK CHILD...
--I SAY--
...HELEN CHENOWETH... ANOTHER OUTSPOKEN CLINTON CRITIC WHO, AS IT HAPPENS, HAS REPORTEDLY HAD NUMEROUS AFFAIRS--AND LIED ABOUT THEM...
--NOT AS--
...AND HENRY HYDE... WHOSE LONG-RUNNING AFFAIR WITH A WOMAN THIRTY YEARS AGO DESTROYED HER MARRIAGE.
--I DID.
ALL WE CAN FIGURE IS THAT THIS IS EITHER A REALLY BAD DREAM--OR THE ENTIRE NATION'S WATER SUPPLY HAS BEEN SPIKED WITH A POWERFUL, LONG-LASTING HALLUCINOGEN.
MONICA IS, LIKE, A METAPHOR FOR LIFE--YOU KNOW?
OH, MAN... THIS IS, LIKE, TOO INTENSE...
I HOPE IT NEVER WEARS OFF!
RUSH
©'98 TOM TOMORROW--FOR THE VILLAGE VOICE...

The Village Voice cover cartoon, September 1998.

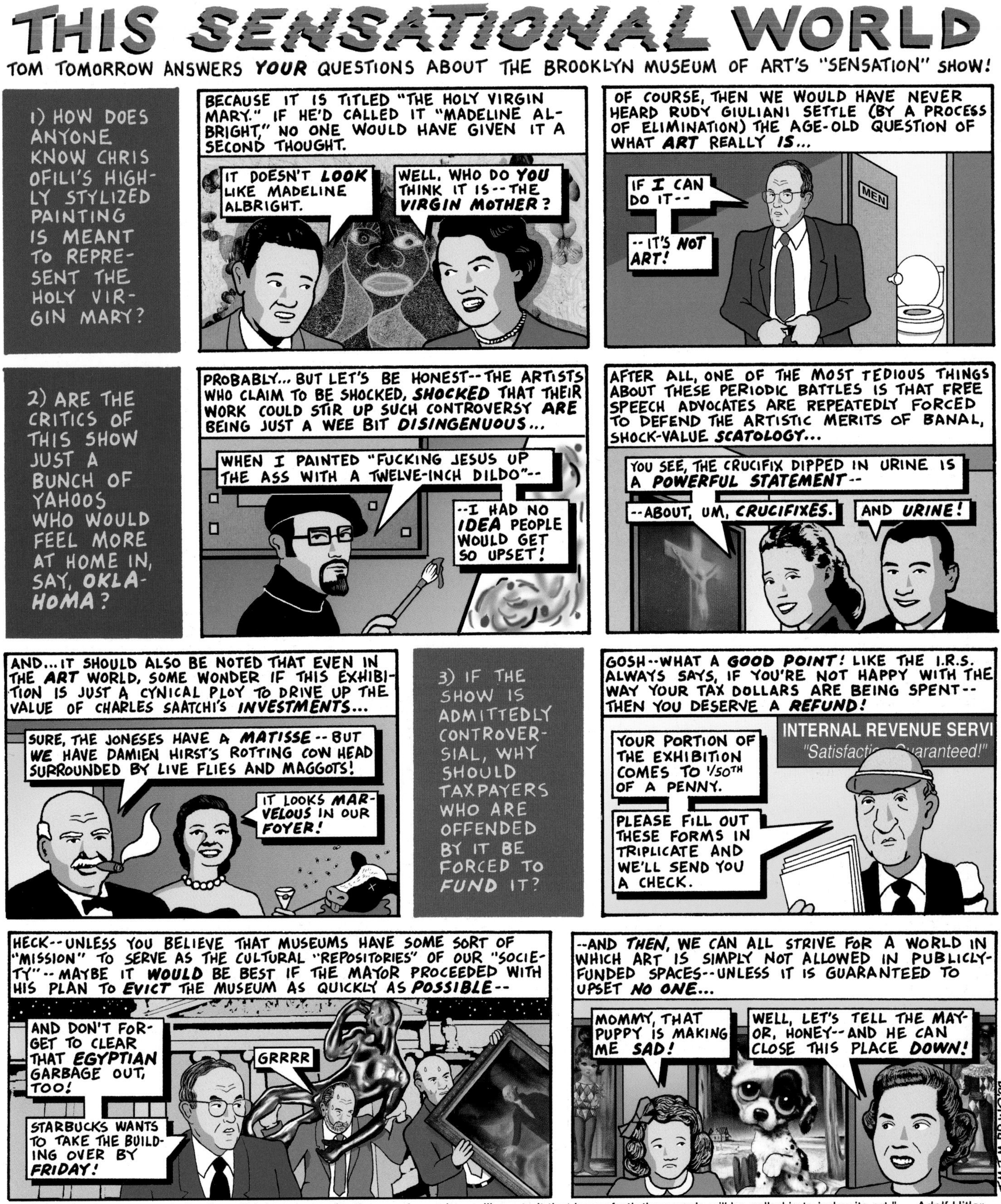
THIS SENSATIONAL WORLD
TOM TOMORROW ANSWERS YOUR QUESTIONS ABOUT THE BROOKLYN MUSEUM OF ART'S "SENSATION" SHOW!
1) HOW DOES ANYONE KNOW CHRIS OFILI'S HIGHLY STYLIZED PAINTING IS MEANT TO REPRESENT THE HOLY VIRGIN MARY?
BECAUSE IT IS TITLED "THE HOLY VIRGIN MARY." IF HE'D CALLED IT "MADELINE ALBRIGHT," NO ONE WOULD HAVE GIVEN IT A SECOND THOUGHT.
IT DOESN'T LOOK LIKE MADELINE ALBRIGHT.
WELL, WHO DO YOU THINK IT IS--THE VIRGIN MOTHER?
OF COURSE, THEN WE WOULD HAVE NEVER HEARD RUDY GIULIANI SETTLE (BY A PROCESS OF ELIMINATION) THE AGE-OLD QUESTION OF WHAT ART REALLY IS...
IF I CAN DO IT--
--IT'S NOT ART!
MEN
2) ARE THE CRITICS OF THIS SHOW JUST A BUNCH OF YAHOOS WHO WOULD FEEL MORE AT HOME IN, SAY, OKLAHOMA?
PROBABLY... BUT LET'S BE HONEST--THE ARTISTS WHO CLAIM TO BE SHOCKED, SHOCKED THAT THEIR WORK COULD STIR UP SUCH CONTROVERSY ARE BEING JUST A WEE BIT DISINGENUOUS...
WHEN I PAINTED "FUCKING JESUS UP THE ASS WITH A TWELVE-INCH DILDO"--
--I HAD NO IDEA PEOPLE WOULD GET SO UPSET!
AFTER ALL, ONE OF THE MOST TEDIOUS THINGS ABOUT THESE PERIODIC BATTLES IS THAT FREE SPEECH ADVOCATES ARE REPEATEDLY FORCED TO DEFEND THE ARTISTIC MERITS OF BANAL, SHOCK-VALUE SCATOLOGY...
YOU SEE, THE CRUCIFIX DIPPED IN URINE IS A POWERFUL STATEMENT--
--ABOUT, UM, CRUCIFIXES.
AND URINE!
AND... IT SHOULD ALSO BE NOTED THAT EVEN IN THE ART WORLD, SOME WONDER IF THIS EXHIBITION IS JUST A CYNICAL PLOY TO DRIVE UP THE VALUE OF CHARLES SAATCHI'S INVESTMENTS...
SURE, THE JONESES HAVE A MATISSE--BUT WE HAVE DAMIEN HIRST'S ROTTING COW HEAD SURROUNDED BY LIVE FLIES AND MAGGOTS!
IT LOOKS MARVELOUS IN OUR FOYER!
3) IF THE SHOW IS ADMITTEDLY CONTROVERSIAL, WHY SHOULD TAXPAYERS WHO ARE OFFENDED BY IT BE FORCED TO FUND IT?
GOSH--WHAT A GOOD POINT! LIKE THE I.R.S. ALWAYS SAYS, IF YOU'RE NOT HAPPY WITH THE WAY YOUR TAX DOLLARS ARE BEING SPENT--THEN YOU DESERVE A REFUND!
INTERNAL REVENUE SERVI
YOUR PORTION OF THE EXHIBITION COMES TO 1/50TH OF A PENNY.
PLEASE FILL OUT THESE FORMS IN TRIPLICATE AND WE'LL SEND YOU A CHECK.
HECK--UNLESS YOU BELIEVE THAT MUSEUMS HAVE SOME SORT OF "MISSION" TO SERVE AS THE CULTURAL "REPOSITORIES" OF OUR "SOCIETY"--MAYBE IT WOULD BE BEST IF THE MAYOR PROCEEDED WITH HIS PLAN TO EVICT THE MUSEUM AS QUICKLY AS POSSIBLE--
AND DON'T FORGET TO CLEAR THAT EGYPTIAN GARBAGE OUT, TOO!
GRRRR
STARBUCKS WANTS TO TAKE THE BUILDING OVER BY FRIDAY!
--AND THEN, WE CAN ALL STRIVE FOR A WORLD IN WHICH ART IS SIMPLY NOT ALLOWED IN PUBLICLY-FUNDED SPACES--UNLESS IT IS GUARANTEED TO UPSET NO ONE...
MOMMY, THAT PUPPY IS MAKING ME SAD!
WELL, LET'S TELL THE MAYOR, HONEY--AND HE CAN CLOSE THIS PLACE DOWN!
TOM TOMORROW©99

"The artist does not create for the artist; he creates for the people, and we will see to it that henceforth the people will be called in to judge its art." -- Adolf Hitler

The Village Voice, October 1999.

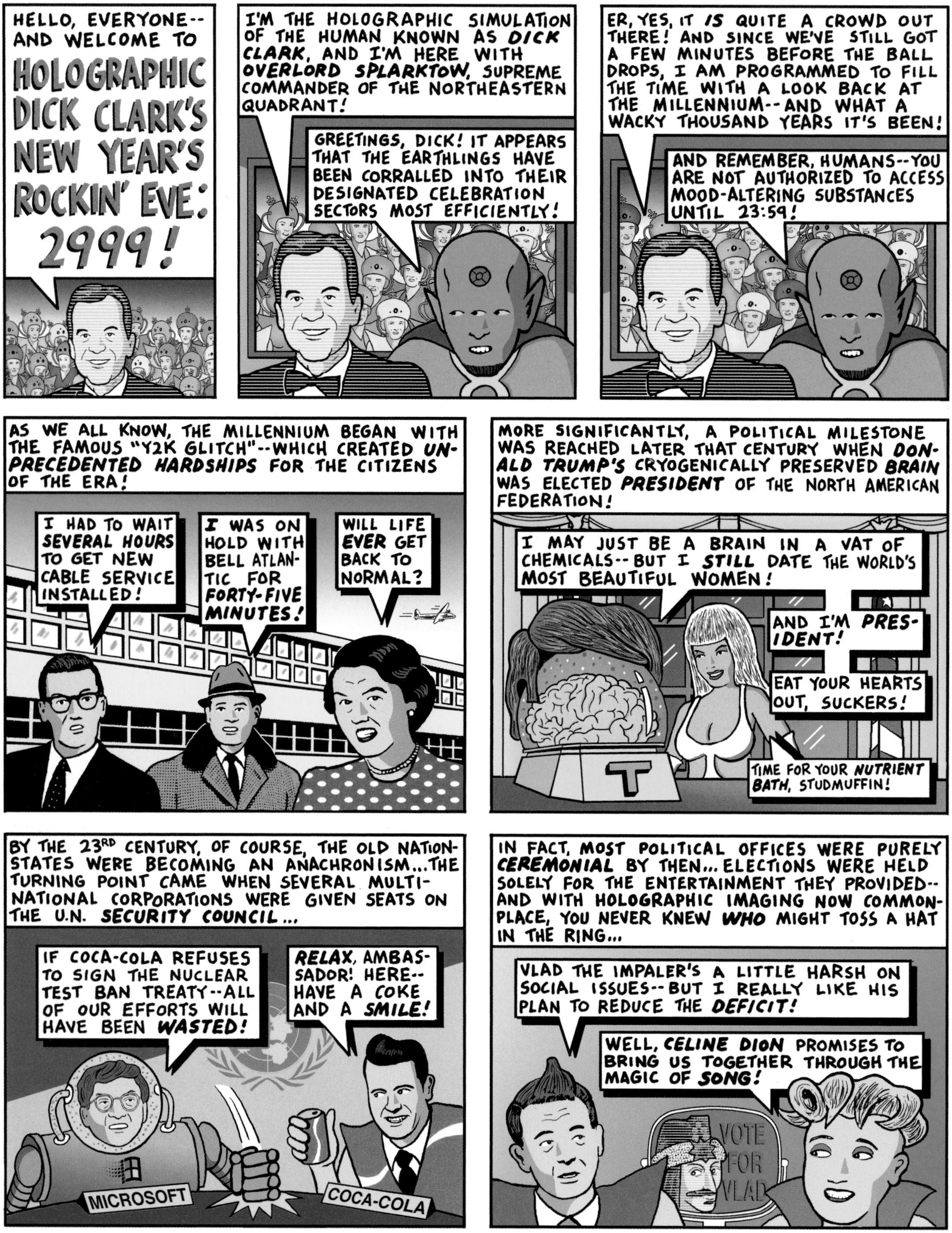
HELLO, EVERYONE-- AND WELCOME TO HOLOGRAPHIC DICK CLARK'S NEW YEAR'S ROCKIN' EVE: 2999!
I'M THE HOLOGRAPHIC SIMULATION OF THE HUMAN KNOWN AS DICK CLARK, AND I'M HERE WITH OVERLORD SPLARKTOW, SUPREME COMMANDER OF THE NORTHEASTERN QUADRANT!
GREETINGS, DICK! IT APPEARS THAT THE EARTHLINGS HAVE BEEN CORRALLED INTO THEIR DESIGNATED CELEBRATION SECTORS MOST EFFICIENTLY!
ER, YES, IT IS QUITE A CROWD OUT THERE! AND SINCE WE'VE STILL GOT A FEW MINUTES BEFORE THE BALL DROPS, I AM PROGRAMMED TO FILL THE TIME WITH A LOOK BACK AT THE MILLENNIUM--AND WHAT A WACKY THOUSAND YEARS IT'S BEEN!
AND REMEMBER, HUMANS--YOU ARE NOT AUTHORIZED TO ACCESS MOOD-ALTERING SUBSTANCES UNTIL 23:59!
AS WE ALL KNOW, THE MILLENNIUM BEGAN WITH THE FAMOUS "Y2K GLITCH"--WHICH CREATED UNPRECEDENTED HARDSHIPS FOR THE CITIZENS OF THE ERA!
I HAD TO WAIT SEVERAL HOURS TO GET NEW CABLE SERVICE INSTALLED!
I WAS ON HOLD WITH BELL ATLANTIC FOR FORTY-FIVE MINUTES!
WILL LIFE EVER GET BACK TO NORMAL?
MORE SIGNIFICANTLY, A POLITICAL MILESTONE WAS REACHED LATER THAT CENTURY WHEN DONALD TRUMP'S CRYOGENICALLY PRESERVED BRAIN WAS ELECTED PRESIDENT OF THE NORTH AMERICAN FEDERATION!
I MAY JUST BE A BRAIN IN A VAT OF CHEMICALS--BUT I STILL DATE THE WORLD'S MOST BEAUTIFUL WOMEN!
AND I'M PRESIDENT!
EAT YOUR HEARTS OUT, SUCKERS!
T
TIME FOR YOUR NUTRIENT BATH, STUDMUFFIN!
BY THE 23RD CENTURY, OF COURSE, THE OLD NATION-STATES WERE BECOMING AN ANACHRONISM... THE TURNING POINT CAME WHEN SEVERAL MULTINATIONAL CORPORATIONS WERE GIVEN SEATS ON THE U.N. SECURITY COUNCIL...
IF COCA-COLA REFUSES TO SIGN THE NUCLEAR TEST BAN TREATY--ALL OF OUR EFFORTS WILL HAVE BEEN WASTED!
RELAX, AMBASSADOR! HERE--HAVE A COKE AND A SMILE!
MICROSOFT
COCA-COLA
IN FACT, MOST POLITICAL OFFICES WERE PURELY CEREMONIAL BY THEN... ELECTIONS WERE HELD SOLELY FOR THE ENTERTAINMENT THEY PROVIDED--AND WITH HOLOGRAPHIC IMAGING NOW COMMONPLACE, YOU NEVER KNEW WHO MIGHT TOSS A HAT IN THE RING...
VLAD THE IMPALER'S A LITTLE HARSH ON SOCIAL ISSUES--BUT I REALLY LIKE HIS PLAN TO REDUCE THE DEFICIT!
WELL, CELINE DION PROMISES TO BRING US TOGETHER THROUGH THE MAGIC OF SONG!
VOTE FOR VLAD

For *The New Yorker*'s cartoon issue, Nov. 18, 1999.

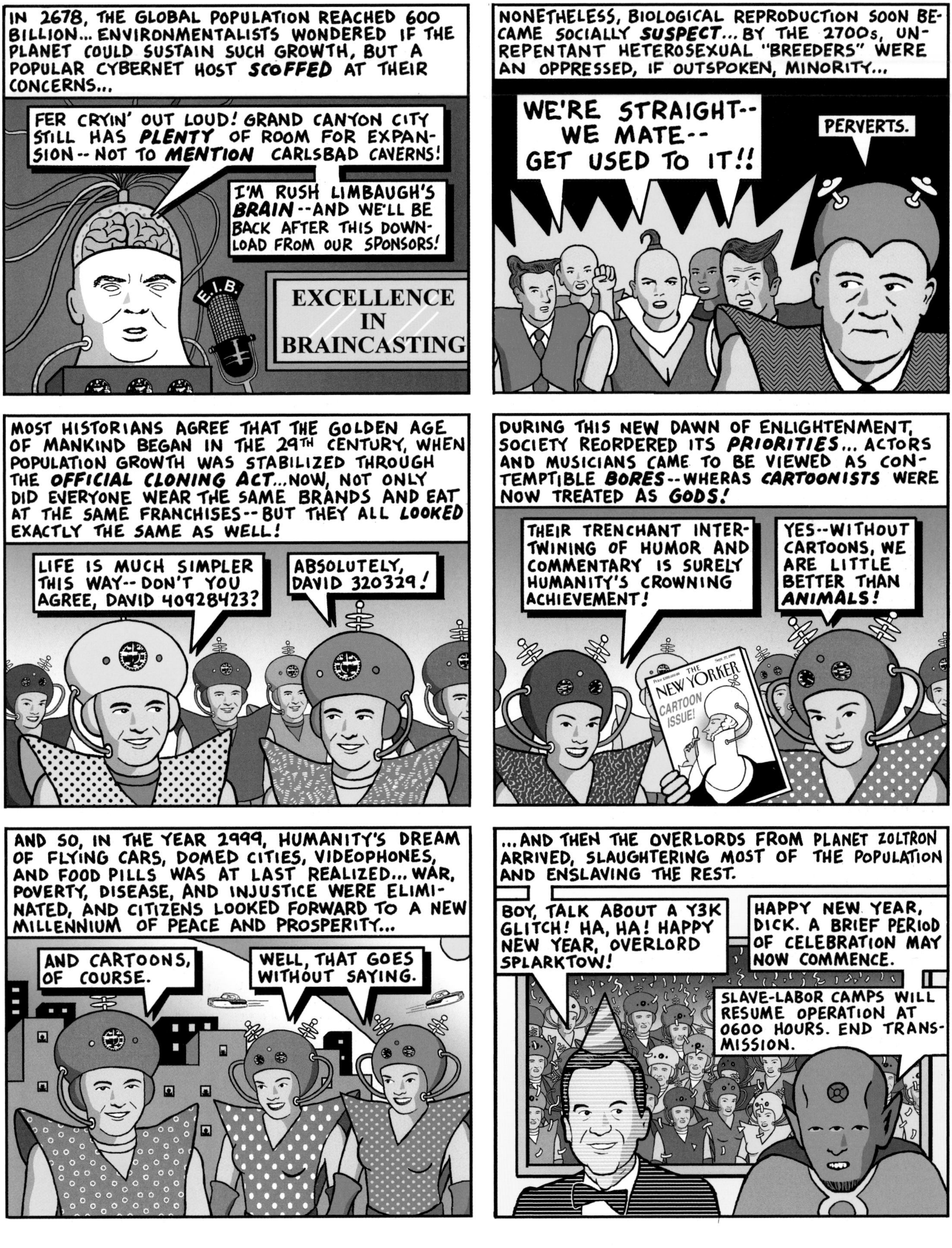
IN 2678, THE GLOBAL POPULATION REACHED 600 BILLION... ENVIRONMENTALISTS WONDERED IF THE PLANET COULD SUSTAIN SUCH GROWTH, BUT A POPULAR CYBERNET HOST SCOFFED AT THEIR CONCERNS...
FER CRYIN' OUT LOUD! GRAND CANYON CITY STILL HAS PLENTY OF ROOM FOR EXPANSION -- NOT TO MENTION CARLSBAD CAVERNS!
I'M RUSH LIMBAUGH'S BRAIN -- AND WE'LL BE BACK AFTER THIS DOWNLOAD FROM OUR SPONSORS!
E.I.B.
EXCELLENCE IN BRAINCASTING
NONETHELESS, BIOLOGICAL REPRODUCTION SOON BECAME SOCIALLY SUSPECT... BY THE 2700s, UNREPENTANT HETEROSEXUAL "BREEDERS" WERE AN OPPRESSED, IF OUTSPOKEN, MINORITY...
WE'RE STRAIGHT -- WE MATE -- GET USED TO IT!!
PERVERTS.
MOST HISTORIANS AGREE THAT THE GOLDEN AGE OF MANKIND BEGAN IN THE 29TH CENTURY, WHEN POPULATION GROWTH WAS STABILIZED THROUGH THE OFFICIAL CLONING ACT... NOW, NOT ONLY DID EVERYONE WEAR THE SAME BRANDS AND EAT AT THE SAME FRANCHISES -- BUT THEY ALL LOOKED EXACTLY THE SAME AS WELL!
LIFE IS MUCH SIMPLER THIS WAY -- DON'T YOU AGREE, DAVID 40928423?
ABSOLUTELY, DAVID 320329!
DURING THIS NEW DAWN OF ENLIGHTENMENT, SOCIETY REORDERED ITS PRIORITIES... ACTORS AND MUSICIANS CAME TO BE VIEWED AS CONTEMPTIBLE BORES -- WHERAS CARTOONISTS WERE NOW TREATED AS GODS!
THEIR TRENCHANT INTERTWINING OF HUMOR AND COMMENTARY IS SURELY HUMANITY'S CROWNING ACHIEVEMENT!
YES -- WITHOUT CARTOONS, WE ARE LITTLE BETTER THAN ANIMALS!
THE NEW YORKER
CARTOON ISSUE!
AND SO, IN THE YEAR 2999, HUMANITY'S DREAM OF FLYING CARS, DOMED CITIES, VIDEOPHONES, AND FOOD PILLS WAS AT LAST REALIZED... WAR, POVERTY, DISEASE, AND INJUSTICE WERE ELIMINATED, AND CITIZENS LOOKED FORWARD TO A NEW MILLENNIUM OF PEACE AND PROSPERITY...
AND CARTOONS, OF COURSE.
WELL, THAT GOES WITHOUT SAYING.
...AND THEN THE OVERLORDS FROM PLANET ZOLTRON ARRIVED, SLAUGHTERING MOST OF THE POPULATION AND ENSLAVING THE REST.
BOY, TALK ABOUT A Y3K GLITCH! HA, HA! HAPPY NEW YEAR, OVERLORD SPLARKTOW!
HAPPY NEW YEAR, DICK. A BRIEF PERIOD OF CELEBRATION MAY NOW COMMENCE.
SLAVE-LABOR CAMPS WILL RESUME OPERATION AT 0600 HOURS. END TRANSMISSION.

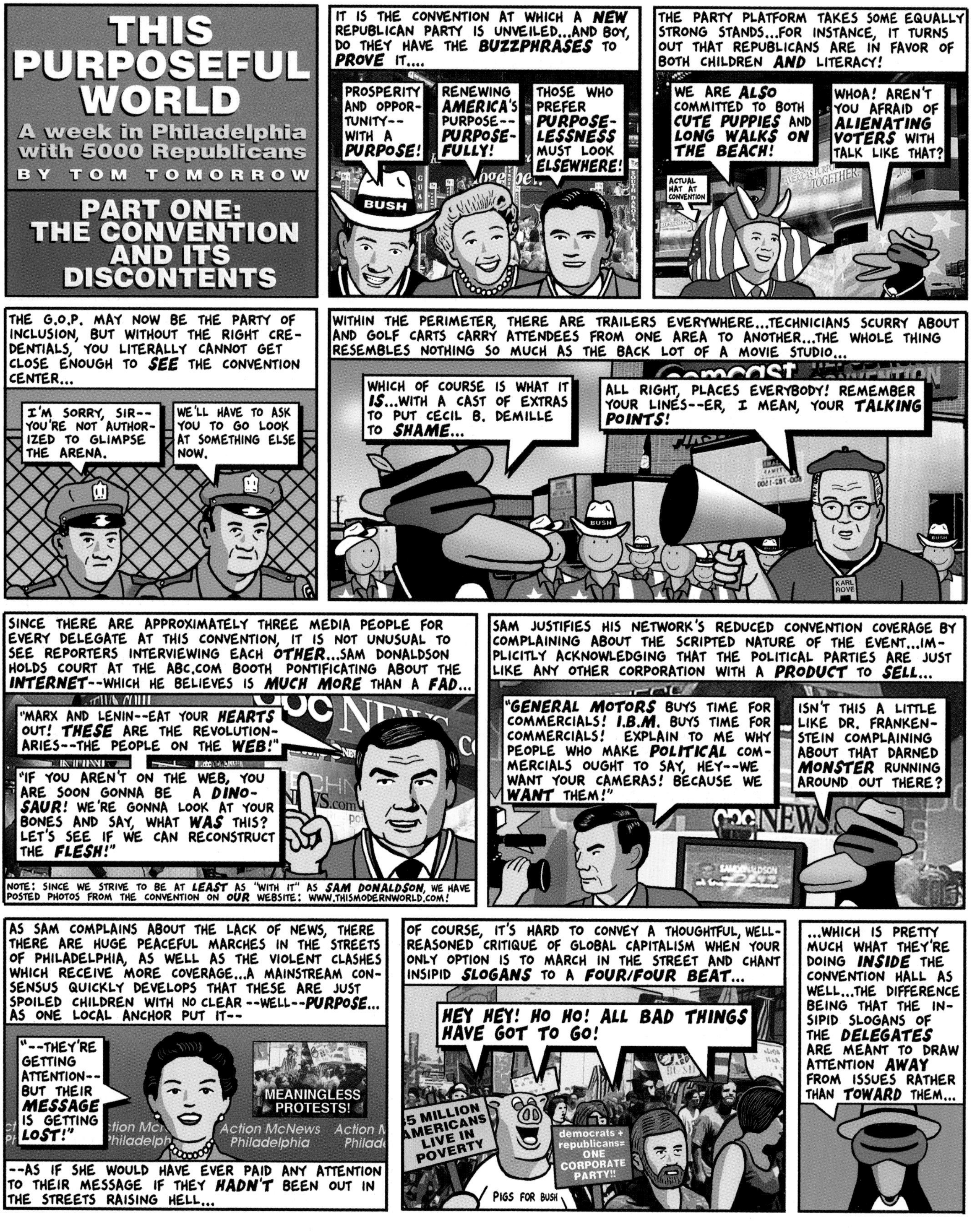
THIS PURPOSEFUL WORLD
A week in Philadelphia with 5000 Republicans
BY TOM TOMORROW
PART ONE: THE CONVENTION AND ITS DISCONTENTS
IT IS THE CONVENTION AT WHICH A NEW REPUBLICAN PARTY IS UNVEILED...AND BOY, DO THEY HAVE THE BUZZPHRASES TO PROVE IT....
PROSPERITY AND OPPOR-TUNITY-- WITH A PURPOSE!
RENEWING AMERICA'S PURPOSE-- PURPOSE-FULLY!
THOSE WHO PREFER PURPOSE-LESSNESS MUST LOOK ELSEWHERE!
BUSH
THE PARTY PLATFORM TAKES SOME EQUALLY STRONG STANDS...FOR INSTANCE, IT TURNS OUT THAT REPUBLICANS ARE IN FAVOR OF BOTH CHILDREN AND LITERACY!
WE ARE ALSO COMMITTED TO BOTH CUTE PUPPIES AND LONG WALKS ON THE BEACH!
WHOA! AREN'T YOU AFRAID OF ALIENATING VOTERS WITH TALK LIKE THAT?
ACTUAL HAT AT CONVENTION
THE G.O.P. MAY NOW BE THE PARTY OF INCLUSION, BUT WITHOUT THE RIGHT CRE-DENTIALS, YOU LITERALLY CANNOT GET CLOSE ENOUGH TO SEE THE CONVENTION CENTER...
I'M SORRY, SIR-- YOU'RE NOT AUTHOR-IZED TO GLIMPSE THE ARENA.
WE'LL HAVE TO ASK YOU TO GO LOOK AT SOMETHING ELSE NOW.
WITHIN THE PERIMETER, THERE ARE TRAILERS EVERYWHERE...TECHNICIANS SCURRY ABOUT AND GOLF CARTS CARRY ATTENDEES FROM ONE AREA TO ANOTHER...THE WHOLE THING RESEMBLES NOTHING SO MUCH AS THE BACK LOT OF A MOVIE STUDIO...
WHICH OF COURSE IS WHAT IT IS...WITH A CAST OF EXTRAS TO PUT CECIL B. DEMILLE TO SHAME...
ALL RIGHT, PLACES EVERYBODY! REMEMBER YOUR LINES--ER, I MEAN, YOUR TALKING POINTS!
BUSH
KARL ROVE
SINCE THERE ARE APPROXIMATELY THREE MEDIA PEOPLE FOR EVERY DELEGATE AT THIS CONVENTION, IT IS NOT UNUSUAL TO SEE REPORTERS INTERVIEWING EACH OTHER...SAM DONALDSON HOLDS COURT AT THE ABC.COM BOOTH PONTIFICATING ABOUT THE INTERNET--WHICH HE BELIEVES IS MUCH MORE THAN A FAD...
"MARX AND LENIN--EAT YOUR HEARTS OUT! THESE ARE THE REVOLUTION-ARIES--THE PEOPLE ON THE WEB!"
"IF YOU AREN'T ON THE WEB, YOU ARE SOON GONNA BE A DINO-SAUR! WE'RE GONNA LOOK AT YOUR BONES AND SAY, WHAT WAS THIS? LET'S SEE IF WE CAN RECONSTRUCT THE FLESH!"
NOTE: SINCE WE STRIVE TO BE AT LEAST AS "WITH IT" AS SAM DONALDSON, WE HAVE POSTED PHOTOS FROM THE CONVENTION ON OUR WEBSITE: WWW.THISMODERNWORLD.COM!
SAM JUSTIFIES HIS NETWORK'S REDUCED CONVENTION COVERAGE BY COMPLAINING ABOUT THE SCRIPTED NATURE OF THE EVENT...IM-PLICITLY ACKNOWLEDGING THAT THE POLITICAL PARTIES ARE JUST LIKE ANY OTHER CORPORATION WITH A PRODUCT TO SELL...
"GENERAL MOTORS BUYS TIME FOR COMMERCIALS! I.B.M. BUYS TIME FOR COMMERCIALS! EXPLAIN TO ME WHY PEOPLE WHO MAKE POLITICAL COM-MERCIALS OUGHT TO SAY, HEY--WE WANT YOUR CAMERAS! BECAUSE WE WANT THEM!"
ISN'T THIS A LITTLE LIKE DR. FRANKEN-STEIN COMPLAINING ABOUT THAT DARNED MONSTER RUNNING AROUND OUT THERE?
AS SAM COMPLAINS ABOUT THE LACK OF NEWS, THERE THERE ARE HUGE PEACEFUL MARCHES IN THE STREETS OF PHILADELPHIA, AS WELL AS THE VIOLENT CLASHES WHICH RECEIVE MORE COVERAGE...A MAINSTREAM CON-SENSUS QUICKLY DEVELOPS THAT THESE ARE JUST SPOILED CHILDREN WITH NO CLEAR --WELL--PURPOSE... AS ONE LOCAL ANCHOR PUT IT--
"--THEY'RE GETTING ATTENTION-- BUT THEIR MESSAGE IS GETTING LOST!"
MEANINGLESS PROTESTS!
Action McNews Philadelphia
--AS IF SHE WOULD HAVE EVER PAID ANY ATTENTION TO THEIR MESSAGE IF THEY HADN'T BEEN OUT IN THE STREETS RAISING HELL...
OF COURSE, IT'S HARD TO CONVEY A THOUGHTFUL, WELL-REASONED CRITIQUE OF GLOBAL CAPITALISM WHEN YOUR ONLY OPTION IS TO MARCH IN THE STREET AND CHANT INSIPID SLOGANS TO A FOUR/FOUR BEAT...
HEY HEY! HO HO! ALL BAD THINGS HAVE GOT TO GO!
5 MILLION AMERICANS LIVE IN POVERTY
democrats + republicans= ONE CORPORATE PARTY!!
PIGS FOR BUSH
...WHICH IS PRETTY MUCH WHAT THEY'RE DOING INSIDE THE CONVENTION HALL AS WELL...THE DIFFERENCE BEING THAT THE IN-SIPID SLOGANS OF THE DELEGATES ARE MEANT TO DRAW ATTENTION AWAY FROM ISSUES RATHER THAN TOWARD THEM...

The Village Voice, July 2000.

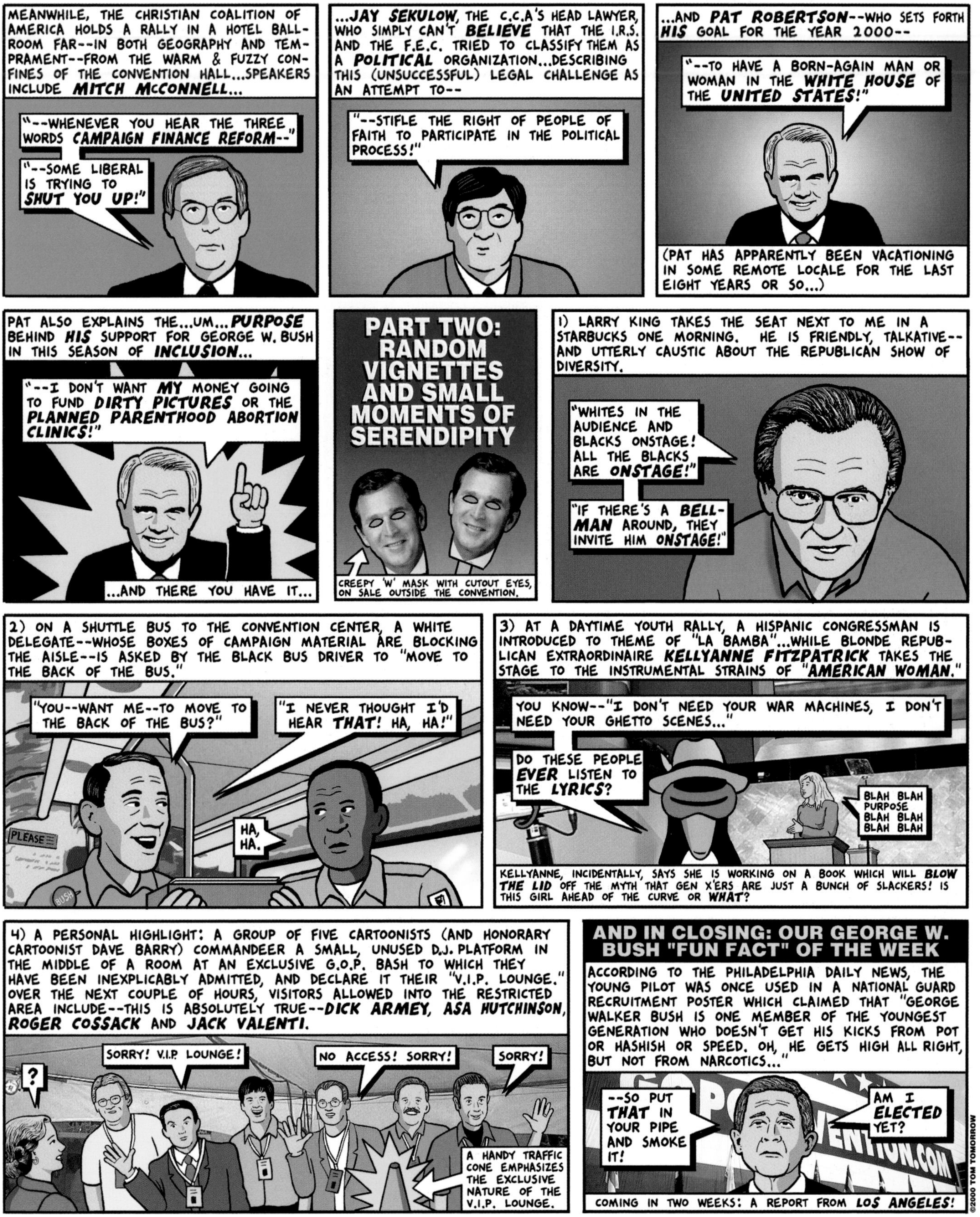

MEANWHILE, THE CHRISTIAN COALITION OF AMERICA HOLDS A RALLY IN A HOTEL BALLROOM FAR--IN BOTH GEOGRAPHY AND TEMPRAMENT--FROM THE WARM & FUZZY CONFINES OF THE CONVENTION HALL...SPEAKERS INCLUDE MITCH McCONNELL...
"--WHENEVER YOU HEAR THE THREE WORDS CAMPAIGN FINANCE REFORM--"
"--SOME LIBERAL IS TRYING TO SHUT YOU UP!"
...JAY SEKULOW, THE C.C.A'S HEAD LAWYER, WHO SIMPLY CAN'T BELIEVE THAT THE I.R.S. AND THE F.E.C. TRIED TO CLASSIFY THEM AS A POLITICAL ORGANIZATION...DESCRIBING THIS (UNSUCCESSFUL) LEGAL CHALLENGE AS AN ATTEMPT TO--
"--STIFLE THE RIGHT OF PEOPLE OF FAITH TO PARTICIPATE IN THE POLITICAL PROCESS!"
...AND PAT ROBERTSON--WHO SETS FORTH HIS GOAL FOR THE YEAR 2000--
"--TO HAVE A BORN-AGAIN MAN OR WOMAN IN THE WHITE HOUSE OF THE UNITED STATES!"
(PAT HAS APPARENTLY BEEN VACATIONING IN SOME REMOTE LOCALE FOR THE LAST EIGHT YEARS OR SO...)
PAT ALSO EXPLAINS THE...UM...PURPOSE BEHIND HIS SUPPORT FOR GEORGE W. BUSH IN THIS SEASON OF INCLUSION...
"--I DON'T WANT MY MONEY GOING TO FUND DIRTY PICTURES OR THE PLANNED PARENTHOOD ABORTION CLINICS!"
...AND THERE YOU HAVE IT...
PART TWO: RANDOM VIGNETTES AND SMALL MOMENTS OF SERENDIPITY
CREEPY 'W' MASK WITH CUTOUT EYES, ON SALE OUTSIDE THE CONVENTION.
1) LARRY KING TAKES THE SEAT NEXT TO ME IN A STARBUCKS ONE MORNING. HE IS FRIENDLY, TALKATIVE--AND UTTERLY CAUSTIC ABOUT THE REPUBLICAN SHOW OF DIVERSITY.
"WHITES IN THE AUDIENCE AND BLACKS ONSTAGE! ALL THE BLACKS ARE ONSTAGE!"
"IF THERE'S A BELLMAN AROUND, THEY INVITE HIM ONSTAGE!"
2) ON A SHUTTLE BUS TO THE CONVENTION CENTER, A WHITE DELEGATE--WHOSE BOXES OF CAMPAIGN MATERIAL ARE BLOCKING THE AISLE--IS ASKED BY THE BLACK BUS DRIVER TO "MOVE TO THE BACK OF THE BUS."
"YOU--WANT ME--TO MOVE TO THE BACK OF THE BUS?"
"I NEVER THOUGHT I'D HEAR THAT! HA, HA!"
HA, HA.
PLEASE
BUSH
3) AT A DAYTIME YOUTH RALLY, A HISPANIC CONGRESSMAN IS INTRODUCED TO THEME OF "LA BAMBA"...WHILE BLONDE REPUBLICAN EXTRAORDINAIRE KELLYANNE FITZPATRICK TAKES THE STAGE TO THE INSTRUMENTAL STRAINS OF "AMERICAN WOMAN."
YOU KNOW--"I DON'T NEED YOUR WAR MACHINES, I DON'T NEED YOUR GHETTO SCENES..."
DO THESE PEOPLE EVER LISTEN TO THE LYRICS?
BLAH BLAH PURPOSE BLAH BLAH BLAH BLAH
KELLYANNE, INCIDENTALLY, SAYS SHE IS WORKING ON A BOOK WHICH WILL BLOW THE LID OFF THE MYTH THAT GEN X'ERS ARE JUST A BUNCH OF SLACKERS! IS THIS GIRL AHEAD OF THE CURVE OR WHAT?
4) A PERSONAL HIGHLIGHT: A GROUP OF FIVE CARTOONISTS (AND HONORARY CARTOONIST DAVE BARRY) COMMANDEER A SMALL, UNUSED D.J. PLATFORM IN THE MIDDLE OF A ROOM AT AN EXCLUSIVE G.O.P. BASH TO WHICH THEY HAVE BEEN INEXPLICABLY ADMITTED, AND DECLARE IT THEIR "V.I.P. LOUNGE." OVER THE NEXT COUPLE OF HOURS, VISITORS ALLOWED INTO THE RESTRICTED AREA INCLUDE--THIS IS ABSOLUTELY TRUE--DICK ARMEY, ASA HUTCHINSON, ROGER COSSACK AND JACK VALENTI.
?
SORRY! V.I.P. LOUNGE!
NO ACCESS! SORRY!
SORRY!
A HANDY TRAFFIC CONE EMPHASIZES THE EXCLUSIVE NATURE OF THE V.I.P. LOUNGE.
AND IN CLOSING: OUR GEORGE W. BUSH "FUN FACT" OF THE WEEK
ACCORDING TO THE PHILADELPHIA DAILY NEWS, THE YOUNG PILOT WAS ONCE USED IN A NATIONAL GUARD RECRUITMENT POSTER WHICH CLAIMED THAT "GEORGE WALKER BUSH IS ONE MEMBER OF THE YOUNGEST GENERATION WHO DOESN'T GET HIS KICKS FROM POT OR HASHISH OR SPEED. OH, HE GETS HIGH ALL RIGHT, BUT NOT FROM NARCOTICS..."
--SO PUT THAT IN YOUR PIPE AND SMOKE IT!
AM I ELECTED YET?
COMING IN TWO WEEKS: A REPORT FROM LOS ANGELES!
©2000 TOM TOMORROW

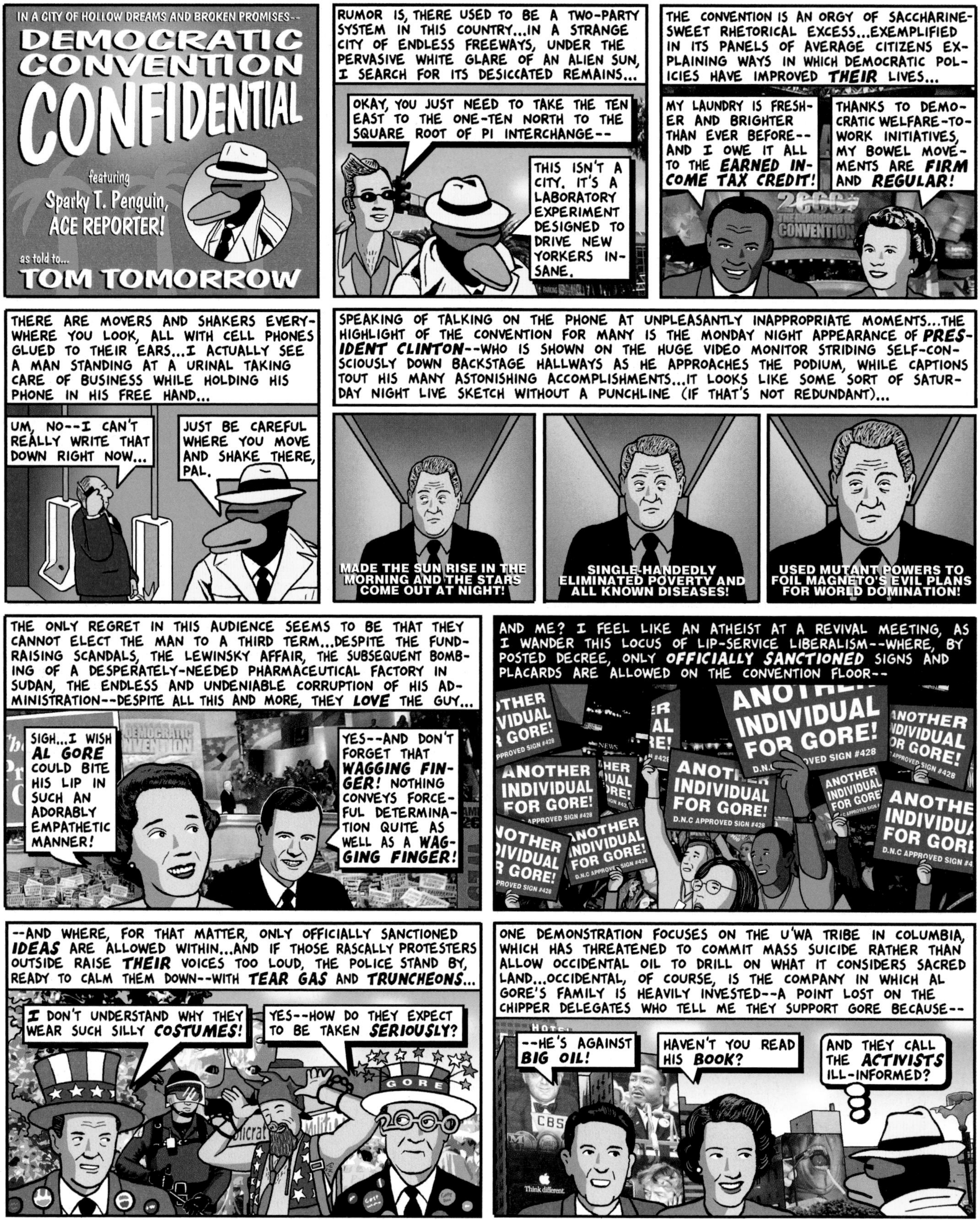
IN A CITY OF HOLLOW DREAMS AND BROKEN PROMISES--
DEMOCRATIC CONVENTION CONFIDENTIAL
featuring
Sparky T. Penguin, ACE REPORTER!
as told to...
TOM TOMORROW
RUMOR IS, THERE USED TO BE A TWO-PARTY SYSTEM IN THIS COUNTRY...IN A STRANGE CITY OF ENDLESS FREEWAYS, UNDER THE PERVASIVE WHITE GLARE OF AN ALIEN SUN, I SEARCH FOR ITS DESICCATED REMAINS...
OKAY, YOU JUST NEED TO TAKE THE TEN EAST TO THE ONE-TEN NORTH TO THE SQUARE ROOT OF PI INTERCHANGE--
THIS ISN'T A CITY. IT'S A LABORATORY EXPERIMENT DESIGNED TO DRIVE NEW YORKERS INSANE.
THE CONVENTION IS AN ORGY OF SACCHARINE-SWEET RHETORICAL EXCESS...EXEMPLIFIED IN ITS PANELS OF AVERAGE CITIZENS EXPLAINING WAYS IN WHICH DEMOCRATIC POLICIES HAVE IMPROVED THEIR LIVES...
MY LAUNDRY IS FRESHER AND BRIGHTER THAN EVER BEFORE--AND I OWE IT ALL TO THE EARNED INCOME TAX CREDIT!
THANKS TO DEMOCRATIC WELFARE-TO-WORK INITIATIVES, MY BOWEL MOVEMENTS ARE FIRM AND REGULAR!
THERE ARE MOVERS AND SHAKERS EVERYWHERE YOU LOOK, ALL WITH CELL PHONES GLUED TO THEIR EARS...I ACTUALLY SEE A MAN STANDING AT A URINAL TAKING CARE OF BUSINESS WHILE HOLDING HIS PHONE IN HIS FREE HAND...
UM, NO--I CAN'T REALLY WRITE THAT DOWN RIGHT NOW...
JUST BE CAREFUL WHERE YOU MOVE AND SHAKE THERE, PAL.
SPEAKING OF TALKING ON THE PHONE AT UNPLEASANTLY INAPPROPRIATE MOMENTS...THE HIGHLIGHT OF THE CONVENTION FOR MANY IS THE MONDAY NIGHT APPEARANCE OF PRESIDENT CLINTON--WHO IS SHOWN ON THE HUGE VIDEO MONITOR STRIDING SELF-CONSCIOUSLY DOWN BACKSTAGE HALLWAYS AS HE APPROACHES THE PODIUM, WHILE CAPTIONS TOUT HIS MANY ASTONISHING ACCOMPLISHMENTS...IT LOOKS LIKE SOME SORT OF SATURDAY NIGHT LIVE SKETCH WITHOUT A PUNCHLINE (IF THAT'S NOT REDUNDANT)...
MADE THE SUN RISE IN THE MORNING AND THE STARS COME OUT AT NIGHT!
SINGLE-HANDEDLY ELIMINATED POVERTY AND ALL KNOWN DISEASES!
USED MUTANT POWERS TO FOIL MAGNETO'S EVIL PLANS FOR WORLD DOMINATION!
THE ONLY REGRET IN THIS AUDIENCE SEEMS TO BE THAT THEY CANNOT ELECT THE MAN TO A THIRD TERM...DESPITE THE FUND-RAISING SCANDALS, THE LEWINSKY AFFAIR, THE SUBSEQUENT BOMBING OF A DESPERATELY-NEEDED PHARMACEUTICAL FACTORY IN SUDAN, THE ENDLESS AND UNDENIABLE CORRUPTION OF HIS ADMINISTRATION--DESPITE ALL THIS AND MORE, THEY LOVE THE GUY...
SIGH...I WISH AL GORE COULD BITE HIS LIP IN SUCH AN ADORABLY EMPATHETIC MANNER!
YES--AND DON'T FORGET THAT WAGGING FINGER! NOTHING CONVEYS FORCEFUL DETERMINATION QUITE AS WELL AS A WAGGING FINGER!
AND ME? I FEEL LIKE AN ATHEIST AT A REVIVAL MEETING, AS I WANDER THIS LOCUS OF LIP-SERVICE LIBERALISM--WHERE, BY POSTED DECREE, ONLY OFFICIALLY SANCTIONED SIGNS AND PLACARDS ARE ALLOWED ON THE CONVENTION FLOOR--
ANOTHER INDIVIDUAL FOR GORE!
D.N.C APPROVED SIGN #428
--AND WHERE, FOR THAT MATTER, ONLY OFFICIALLY SANCTIONED IDEAS ARE ALLOWED WITHIN...AND IF THOSE RASCALLY PROTESTERS OUTSIDE RAISE THEIR VOICES TOO LOUD, THE POLICE STAND BY, READY TO CALM THEM DOWN--WITH TEAR GAS AND TRUNCHEONS...
I DON'T UNDERSTAND WHY THEY WEAR SUCH SILLY COSTUMES!
YES--HOW DO THEY EXPECT TO BE TAKEN SERIOUSLY?
GORE
ONE DEMONSTRATION FOCUSES ON THE U'WA TRIBE IN COLUMBIA, WHICH HAS THREATENED TO COMMIT MASS SUICIDE RATHER THAN ALLOW OCCIDENTAL OIL TO DRILL ON WHAT IT CONSIDERS SACRED LAND...OCCIDENTAL, OF COURSE, IS THE COMPANY IN WHICH AL GORE'S FAMILY IS HEAVILY INVESTED--A POINT LOST ON THE CHIPPER DELEGATES WHO TELL ME THEY SUPPORT GORE BECAUSE--
--HE'S AGAINST BIG OIL!
HAVEN'T YOU READ HIS BOOK?
AND THEY CALL THE ACTIVISTS ILL-INFORMED?
Think different.

The Village Voice, August 2000.

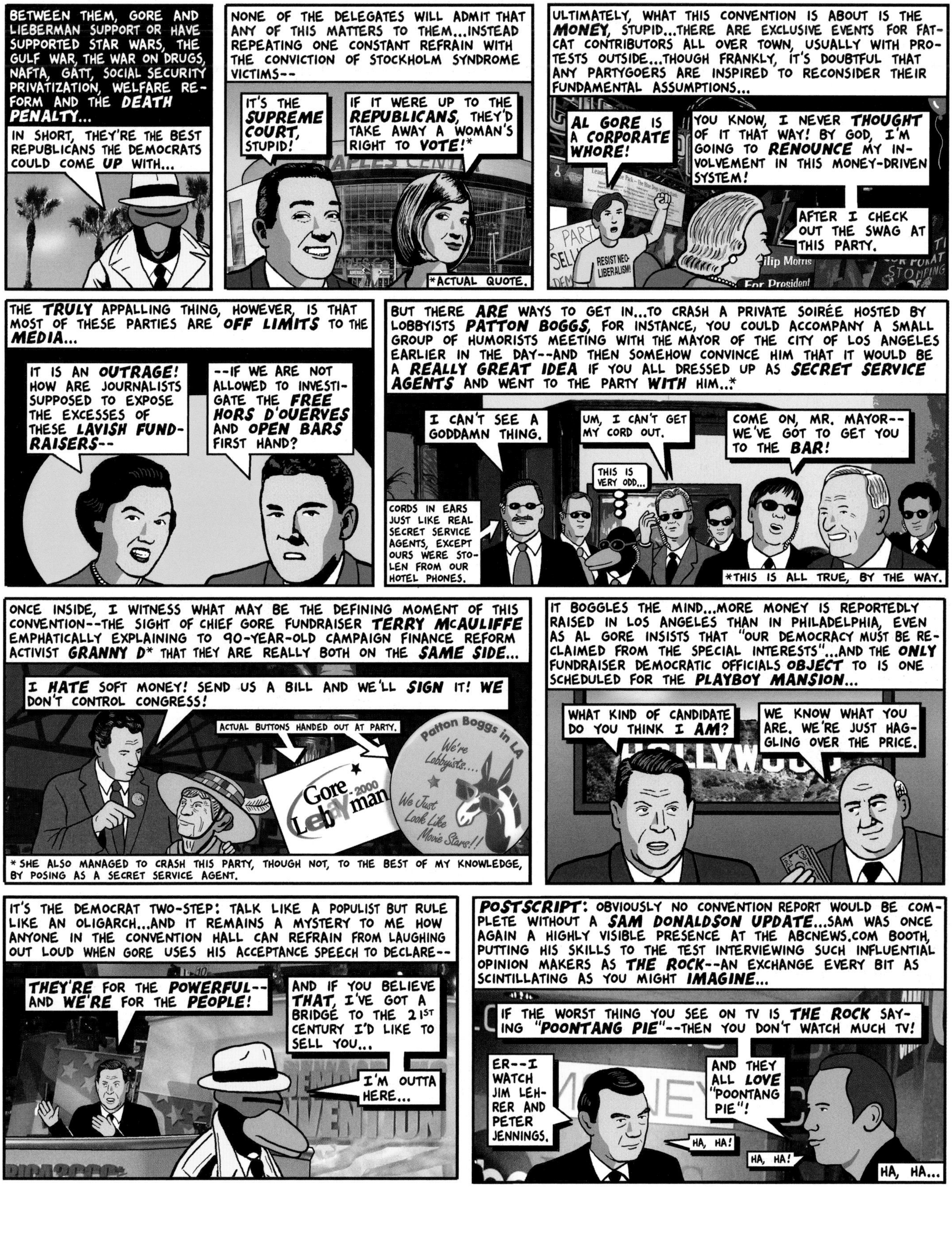
BETWEEN THEM, GORE AND LIEBERMAN SUPPORT OR HAVE SUPPORTED STAR WARS, THE GULF WAR, THE WAR ON DRUGS, NAFTA, GATT, SOCIAL SECURITY PRIVATIZATION, WELFARE REFORM AND THE DEATH PENALTY...
IN SHORT, THEY'RE THE BEST REPUBLICANS THE DEMOCRATS COULD COME UP WITH...
NONE OF THE DELEGATES WILL ADMIT THAT ANY OF THIS MATTERS TO THEM...INSTEAD REPEATING ONE CONSTANT REFRAIN WITH THE CONVICTION OF STOCKHOLM SYNDROME VICTIMS--
IT'S THE SUPREME COURT, STUPID!
IF IT WERE UP TO THE REPUBLICANS, THEY'D TAKE AWAY A WOMAN'S RIGHT TO VOTE!*
*ACTUAL QUOTE.
ULTIMATELY, WHAT THIS CONVENTION IS ABOUT IS THE MONEY, STUPID...THERE ARE EXCLUSIVE EVENTS FOR FAT-CAT CONTRIBUTORS ALL OVER TOWN, USUALLY WITH PROTESTS OUTSIDE...THOUGH FRANKLY, IT'S DOUBTFUL THAT ANY PARTYGOERS ARE INSPIRED TO RECONSIDER THEIR FUNDAMENTAL ASSUMPTIONS...
AL GORE IS A CORPORATE WHORE!
YOU KNOW, I NEVER THOUGHT OF IT THAT WAY! BY GOD, I'M GOING TO RENOUNCE MY INVOLVEMENT IN THIS MONEY-DRIVEN SYSTEM!
AFTER I CHECK OUT THE SWAG AT THIS PARTY.
RESIST NEO-LIBERALISM!
THE TRULY APPALLING THING, HOWEVER, IS THAT MOST OF THESE PARTIES ARE OFF LIMITS TO THE MEDIA...
IT IS AN OUTRAGE! HOW ARE JOURNALISTS SUPPOSED TO EXPOSE THE EXCESSES OF THESE LAVISH FUND-RAISERS--
--IF WE ARE NOT ALLOWED TO INVESTIGATE THE FREE HORS D'OUERVES AND OPEN BARS FIRST HAND?
BUT THERE ARE WAYS TO GET IN...TO CRASH A PRIVATE SOIRÉE HOSTED BY LOBBYISTS PATTON BOGGS, FOR INSTANCE, YOU COULD ACCOMPANY A SMALL GROUP OF HUMORISTS MEETING WITH THE MAYOR OF THE CITY OF LOS ANGELES EARLIER IN THE DAY--AND THEN SOMEHOW CONVINCE HIM THAT IT WOULD BE A REALLY GREAT IDEA IF YOU ALL DRESSED UP AS SECRET SERVICE AGENTS AND WENT TO THE PARTY WITH HIM...*
I CAN'T SEE A GODDAMN THING.
UM, I CAN'T GET MY CORD OUT.
COME ON, MR. MAYOR--WE'VE GOT TO GET YOU TO THE BAR!
THIS IS VERY ODD...
CORDS IN EARS JUST LIKE REAL SECRET SERVICE AGENTS, EXCEPT OURS WERE STOLEN FROM OUR HOTEL PHONES.
*THIS IS ALL TRUE, BY THE WAY.
ONCE INSIDE, I WITNESS WHAT MAY BE THE DEFINING MOMENT OF THIS CONVENTION--THE SIGHT OF CHIEF GORE FUNDRAISER TERRY MCAULIFFE EMPHATICALLY EXPLAINING TO 90-YEAR-OLD CAMPAIGN FINANCE REFORM ACTIVIST GRANNY D* THAT THEY ARE REALLY BOTH ON THE SAME SIDE...
I HATE SOFT MONEY! SEND US A BILL AND WE'LL SIGN IT! WE DON'T CONTROL CONGRESS!
ACTUAL BUTTONS HANDED OUT AT PARTY.
Gore Lobbyman 2000
Patton Boggs in LA
We're Lobbyists...
We Just Look Like Movie Stars!!
* SHE ALSO MANAGED TO CRASH THIS PARTY, THOUGH NOT, TO THE BEST OF MY KNOWLEDGE, BY POSING AS A SECRET SERVICE AGENT.
IT BOGGLES THE MIND...MORE MONEY IS REPORTEDLY RAISED IN LOS ANGELES THAN IN PHILADELPHIA, EVEN AS AL GORE INSISTS THAT "OUR DEMOCRACY MUST BE RECLAIMED FROM THE SPECIAL INTERESTS"...AND THE ONLY FUNDRAISER DEMOCRATIC OFFICIALS OBJECT TO IS ONE SCHEDULED FOR THE PLAYBOY MANSION...
WHAT KIND OF CANDIDATE DO YOU THINK I AM?
WE KNOW WHAT YOU ARE. WE'RE JUST HAGGLING OVER THE PRICE.
IT'S THE DEMOCRAT TWO-STEP: TALK LIKE A POPULIST BUT RULE LIKE AN OLIGARCH...AND IT REMAINS A MYSTERY TO ME HOW ANYONE IN THE CONVENTION HALL CAN REFRAIN FROM LAUGHING OUT LOUD WHEN GORE USES HIS ACCEPTANCE SPEECH TO DECLARE--
THEY'RE FOR THE POWERFUL--AND WE'RE FOR THE PEOPLE!
AND IF YOU BELIEVE THAT, I'VE GOT A BRIDGE TO THE 21ST CENTURY I'D LIKE TO SELL YOU...
I'M OUTTA HERE...
POSTSCRIPT: OBVIOUSLY NO CONVENTION REPORT WOULD BE COMPLETE WITHOUT A SAM DONALDSON UPDATE...SAM WAS ONCE AGAIN A HIGHLY VISIBLE PRESENCE AT THE ABCNEWS.COM BOOTH, PUTTING HIS SKILLS TO THE TEST INTERVIEWING SUCH INFLUENTIAL OPINION MAKERS AS THE ROCK--AN EXCHANGE EVERY BIT AS SCINTILLATING AS YOU MIGHT IMAGINE...
IF THE WORST THING YOU SEE ON TV IS THE ROCK SAYING "POONTANG PIE"--THEN YOU DON'T WATCH MUCH TV!
ER--I WATCH JIM LEHRER AND PETER JENNINGS.
AND THEY ALL LOVE "POONTANG PIE"!
HA, HA!
HA, HA!
HA, HA...

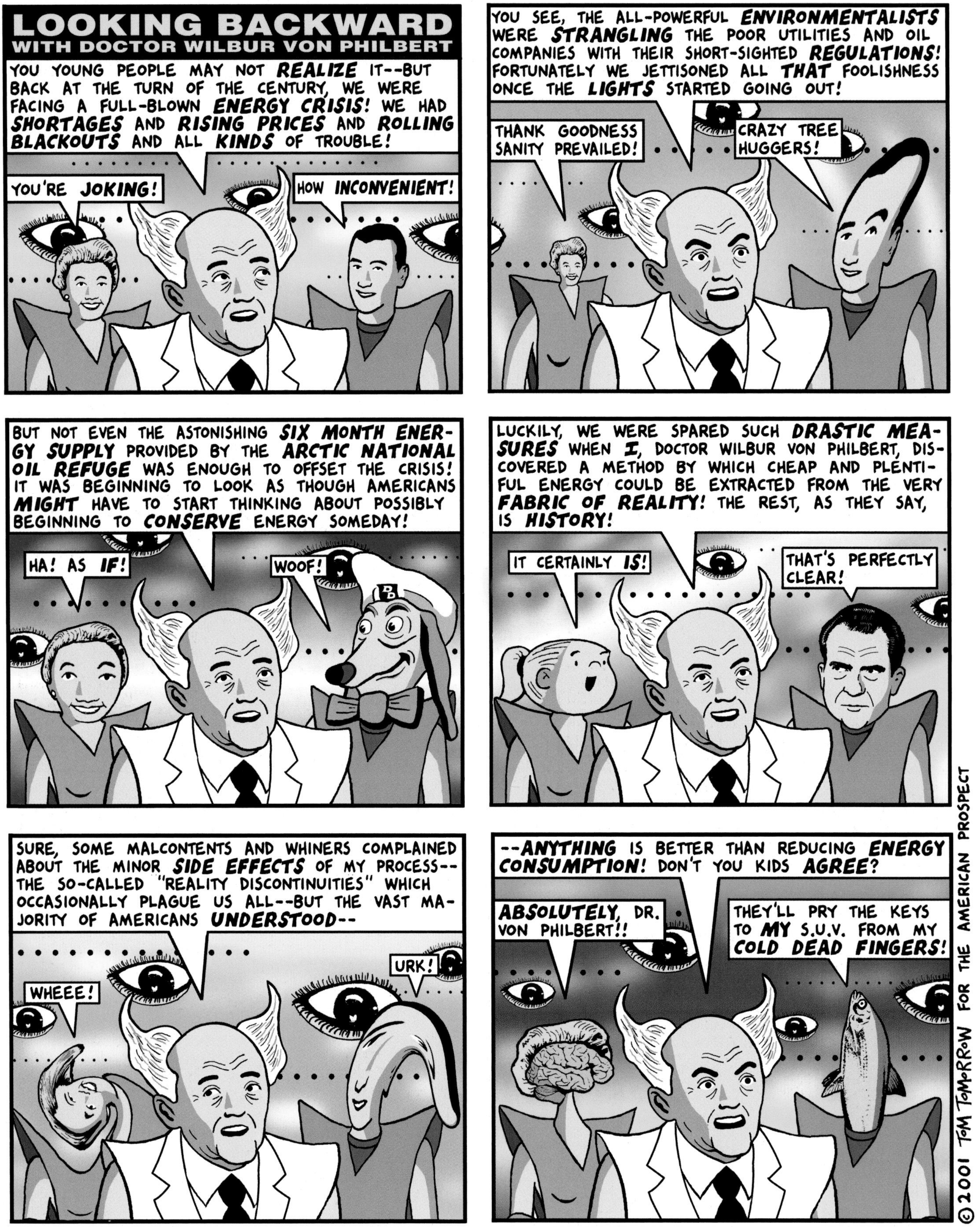
LOOKING BACKWARD
WITH DOCTOR WILBUR VON PHILBERT
YOU YOUNG PEOPLE MAY NOT REALIZE IT--BUT BACK AT THE TURN OF THE CENTURY, WE WERE FACING A FULL-BLOWN ENERGY CRISIS! WE HAD SHORTAGES AND RISING PRICES AND ROLLING BLACKOUTS AND ALL KINDS OF TROUBLE!
YOU'RE JOKING!
HOW INCONVENIENT!
YOU SEE, THE ALL-POWERFUL ENVIRONMENTALISTS WERE STRANGLING THE POOR UTILITIES AND OIL COMPANIES WITH THEIR SHORT-SIGHTED REGULATIONS! FORTUNATELY WE JETTISONED ALL THAT FOOLISHNESS ONCE THE LIGHTS STARTED GOING OUT!
THANK GOODNESS SANITY PREVAILED!
CRAZY TREE HUGGERS!
BUT NOT EVEN THE ASTONISHING SIX MONTH ENERGY SUPPLY PROVIDED BY THE ARCTIC NATIONAL OIL REFUGE WAS ENOUGH TO OFFSET THE CRISIS! IT WAS BEGINNING TO LOOK AS THOUGH AMERICANS MIGHT HAVE TO START THINKING ABOUT POSSIBLY BEGINNING TO CONSERVE ENERGY SOMEDAY!
HA! AS IF!
WOOF!
LUCKILY, WE WERE SPARED SUCH DRASTIC MEASURES WHEN I, DOCTOR WILBUR VON PHILBERT, DISCOVERED A METHOD BY WHICH CHEAP AND PLENTIFUL ENERGY COULD BE EXTRACTED FROM THE VERY FABRIC OF REALITY! THE REST, AS THEY SAY, IS HISTORY!
IT CERTAINLY IS!
THAT'S PERFECTLY CLEAR!
SURE, SOME MALCONTENTS AND WHINERS COMPLAINED ABOUT THE MINOR SIDE EFFECTS OF MY PROCESS--THE SO-CALLED "REALITY DISCONTINUITIES" WHICH OCCASIONALLY PLAGUE US ALL--BUT THE VAST MAJORITY OF AMERICANS UNDERSTOOD--
WHEEE!
URK!
--ANYTHING IS BETTER THAN REDUCING ENERGY CONSUMPTION! DON'T YOU KIDS AGREE?
ABSOLUTELY, DR. VON PHILBERT!!
THEY'LL PRY THE KEYS TO MY S.U.V. FROM MY COLD DEAD FINGERS!
©2001 TOM TOMORROW FOR THE AMERICAN PROSPECT

The American Prospect, May 2001.

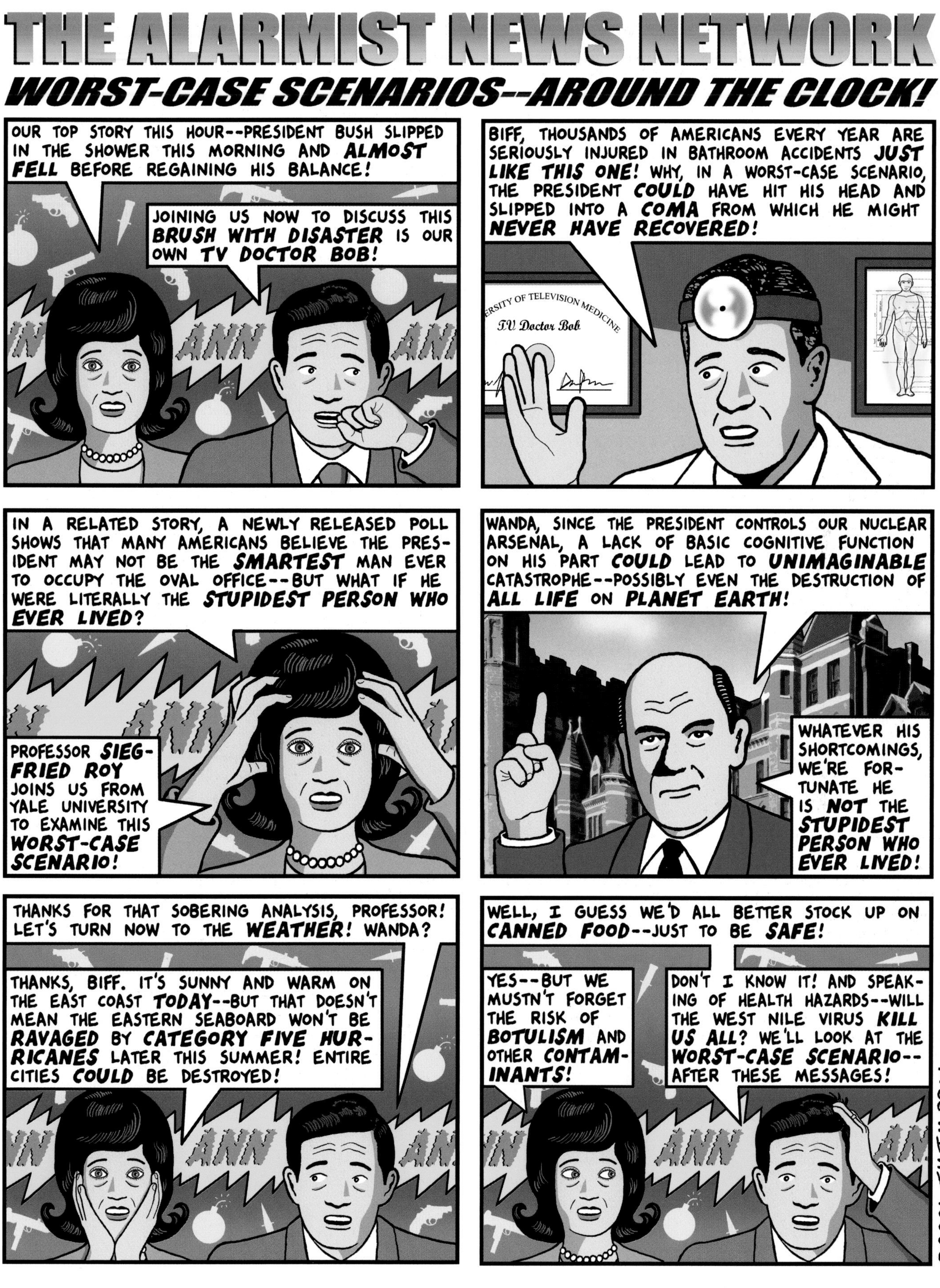
THE ALARMIST NEWS NETWORK
WORST-CASE SCENARIOS--AROUND THE CLOCK!
OUR TOP STORY THIS HOUR--PRESIDENT BUSH SLIPPED IN THE SHOWER THIS MORNING AND ALMOST FELL BEFORE REGAINING HIS BALANCE!
JOINING US NOW TO DISCUSS THIS BRUSH WITH DISASTER IS OUR OWN TV DOCTOR BOB!
BIFF, THOUSANDS OF AMERICANS EVERY YEAR ARE SERIOUSLY INJURED IN BATHROOM ACCIDENTS JUST LIKE THIS ONE! WHY, IN A WORST-CASE SCENARIO, THE PRESIDENT COULD HAVE HIT HIS HEAD AND SLIPPED INTO A COMA FROM WHICH HE MIGHT NEVER HAVE RECOVERED!
TV Doctor Bob
IN A RELATED STORY, A NEWLY RELEASED POLL SHOWS THAT MANY AMERICANS BELIEVE THE PRESIDENT MAY NOT BE THE SMARTEST MAN EVER TO OCCUPY THE OVAL OFFICE--BUT WHAT IF HE WERE LITERALLY THE STUPIDEST PERSON WHO EVER LIVED?
PROFESSOR SIEGFRIED ROY JOINS US FROM YALE UNIVERSITY TO EXAMINE THIS WORST-CASE SCENARIO!
WANDA, SINCE THE PRESIDENT CONTROLS OUR NUCLEAR ARSENAL, A LACK OF BASIC COGNITIVE FUNCTION ON HIS PART COULD LEAD TO UNIMAGINABLE CATASTROPHE--POSSIBLY EVEN THE DESTRUCTION OF ALL LIFE ON PLANET EARTH!
WHATEVER HIS SHORTCOMINGS, WE'RE FORTUNATE HE IS NOT THE STUPIDEST PERSON WHO EVER LIVED!
THANKS FOR THAT SOBERING ANALYSIS, PROFESSOR! LET'S TURN NOW TO THE WEATHER! WANDA?
THANKS, BIFF. IT'S SUNNY AND WARM ON THE EAST COAST TODAY--BUT THAT DOESN'T MEAN THE EASTERN SEABOARD WON'T BE RAVAGED BY CATEGORY FIVE HURRICANES LATER THIS SUMMER! ENTIRE CITIES COULD BE DESTROYED!
WELL, I GUESS WE'D ALL BETTER STOCK UP ON CANNED FOOD--JUST TO BE SAFE!
YES--BUT WE MUSTN'T FORGET THE RISK OF BOTULISM AND OTHER CONTAMINANTS!
DON'T I KNOW IT! AND SPEAKING OF HEALTH HAZARDS--WILL THE WEST NILE VIRUS KILL US ALL? WE'LL LOOK AT THE WORST-CASE SCENARIO--AFTER THESE MESSAGES!
© 2001 TOM TOMORROW

The New Yorker Back Page, June 2001. Little did we know...

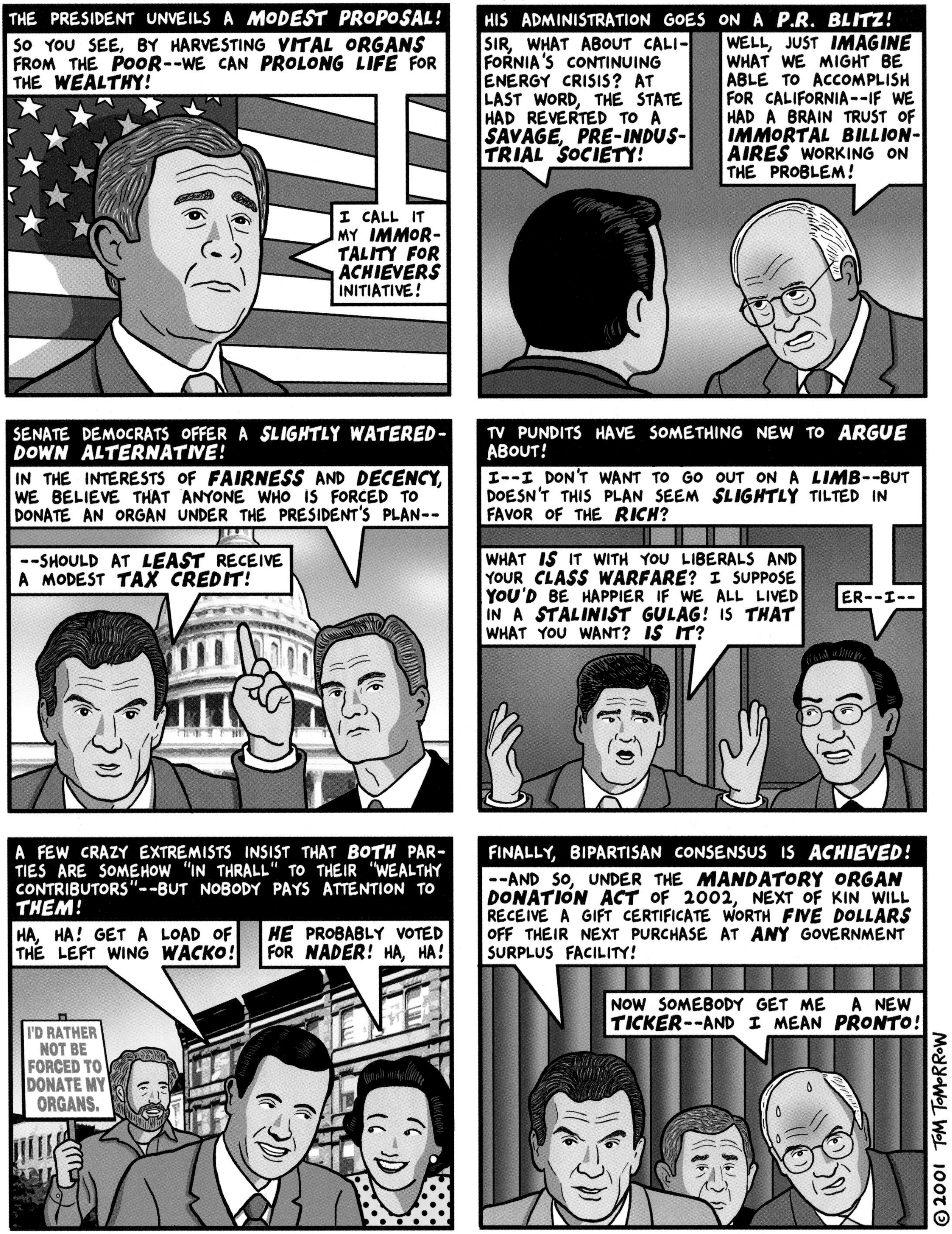
THE PRESIDENT UNVEILS A MODEST PROPOSAL!
SO YOU SEE, BY HARVESTING VITAL ORGANS FROM THE POOR--WE CAN PROLONG LIFE FOR THE WEALTHY!
I CALL IT MY IMMORTALITY FOR ACHIEVERS INITIATIVE!
HIS ADMINISTRATION GOES ON A P.R. BLITZ!
SIR, WHAT ABOUT CALIFORNIA'S CONTINUING ENERGY CRISIS? AT LAST WORD, THE STATE HAD REVERTED TO A SAVAGE, PRE-INDUSTRIAL SOCIETY!
WELL, JUST IMAGINE WHAT WE MIGHT BE ABLE TO ACCOMPLISH FOR CALIFORNIA--IF WE HAD A BRAIN TRUST OF IMMORTAL BILLIONAIRES WORKING ON THE PROBLEM!
SENATE DEMOCRATS OFFER A SLIGHTLY WATERED-DOWN ALTERNATIVE!
IN THE INTERESTS OF FAIRNESS AND DECENCY, WE BELIEVE THAT ANYONE WHO IS FORCED TO DONATE AN ORGAN UNDER THE PRESIDENT'S PLAN--
--SHOULD AT LEAST RECEIVE A MODEST TAX CREDIT!
TV PUNDITS HAVE SOMETHING NEW TO ARGUE ABOUT!
I--I DON'T WANT TO GO OUT ON A LIMB--BUT DOESN'T THIS PLAN SEEM SLIGHTLY TILTED IN FAVOR OF THE RICH?
WHAT IS IT WITH YOU LIBERALS AND YOUR CLASS WARFARE? I SUPPOSE YOU'D BE HAPPIER IF WE ALL LIVED IN A STALINIST GULAG! IS THAT WHAT YOU WANT? IS IT?
ER--I--
A FEW CRAZY EXTREMISTS INSIST THAT BOTH PARTIES ARE SOMEHOW "IN THRALL" TO THEIR "WEALTHY CONTRIBUTORS"--BUT NOBODY PAYS ATTENTION TO THEM!
HA, HA! GET A LOAD OF THE LEFT WING WACKO!
HE PROBABLY VOTED FOR NADER! HA, HA!
I'D RATHER NOT BE FORCED TO DONATE MY ORGANS.
FINALLY, BIPARTISAN CONSENSUS IS ACHIEVED!
--AND SO, UNDER THE MANDATORY ORGAN DONATION ACT OF 2002, NEXT OF KIN WILL RECEIVE A GIFT CERTIFICATE WORTH FIVE DOLLARS OFF THEIR NEXT PURCHASE AT ANY GOVERNMENT SURPLUS FACILITY!
NOW SOMEBODY GET ME A NEW TICKER--AND I MEAN PRONTO!
©2001 TOM TOMORROW

The New Yorker Back Page, July 2001.

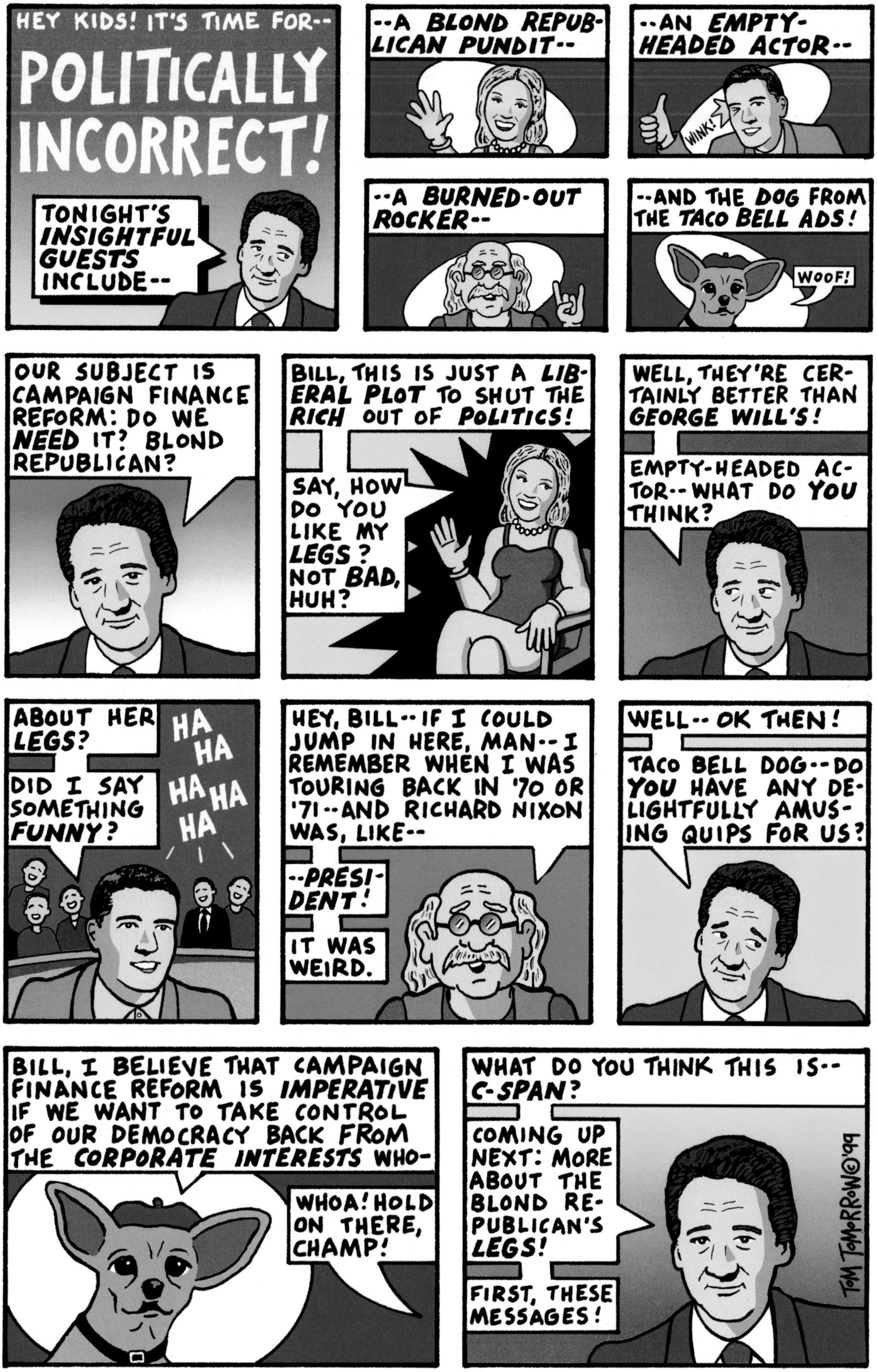
HEY KIDS! IT'S TIME FOR--
POLITICALLY INCORRECT!
TONIGHT'S INSIGHTFUL GUESTS INCLUDE--
--A BLOND REPUBLICAN PUNDIT--
--AN EMPTY-HEADED ACTOR--
WINK!
--A BURNED-OUT ROCKER--
--AND THE DOG FROM THE TACO BELL ADS!
WOOF!
OUR SUBJECT IS CAMPAIGN FINANCE REFORM: DO WE NEED IT? BLOND REPUBLICAN?
BILL, THIS IS JUST A LIBERAL PLOT TO SHUT THE RICH OUT OF POLITICS!
SAY, HOW DO YOU LIKE MY LEGS? NOT BAD, HUH?
WELL, THEY'RE CERTAINLY BETTER THAN GEORGE WILL'S!
EMPTY-HEADED ACTOR--WHAT DO YOU THINK?
ABOUT HER LEGS?
DID I SAY SOMETHING FUNNY?
HA HA HA HA HA
HEY, BILL--IF I COULD JUMP IN HERE, MAN--I REMEMBER WHEN I WAS TOURING BACK IN '70 OR '71--AND RICHARD NIXON WAS, LIKE--
--PRESIDENT!
IT WAS WEIRD.
WELL--OK THEN!
TACO BELL DOG--DO YOU HAVE ANY DELIGHTFULLY AMUSING QUIPS FOR US?
BILL, I BELIEVE THAT CAMPAIGN FINANCE REFORM IS IMPERATIVE IF WE WANT TO TAKE CONTROL OF OUR DEMOCRACY BACK FROM THE CORPORATE INTERESTS WHO-
WHOA! HOLD ON THERE, CHAMP!
WHAT DO YOU THINK THIS IS--C-SPAN?
COMING UP NEXT: MORE ABOUT THE BLOND REPUBLICAN'S LEGS!
FIRST, THESE MESSAGES!
TOM TOMORROW©'99

TV Guide, September 1999.

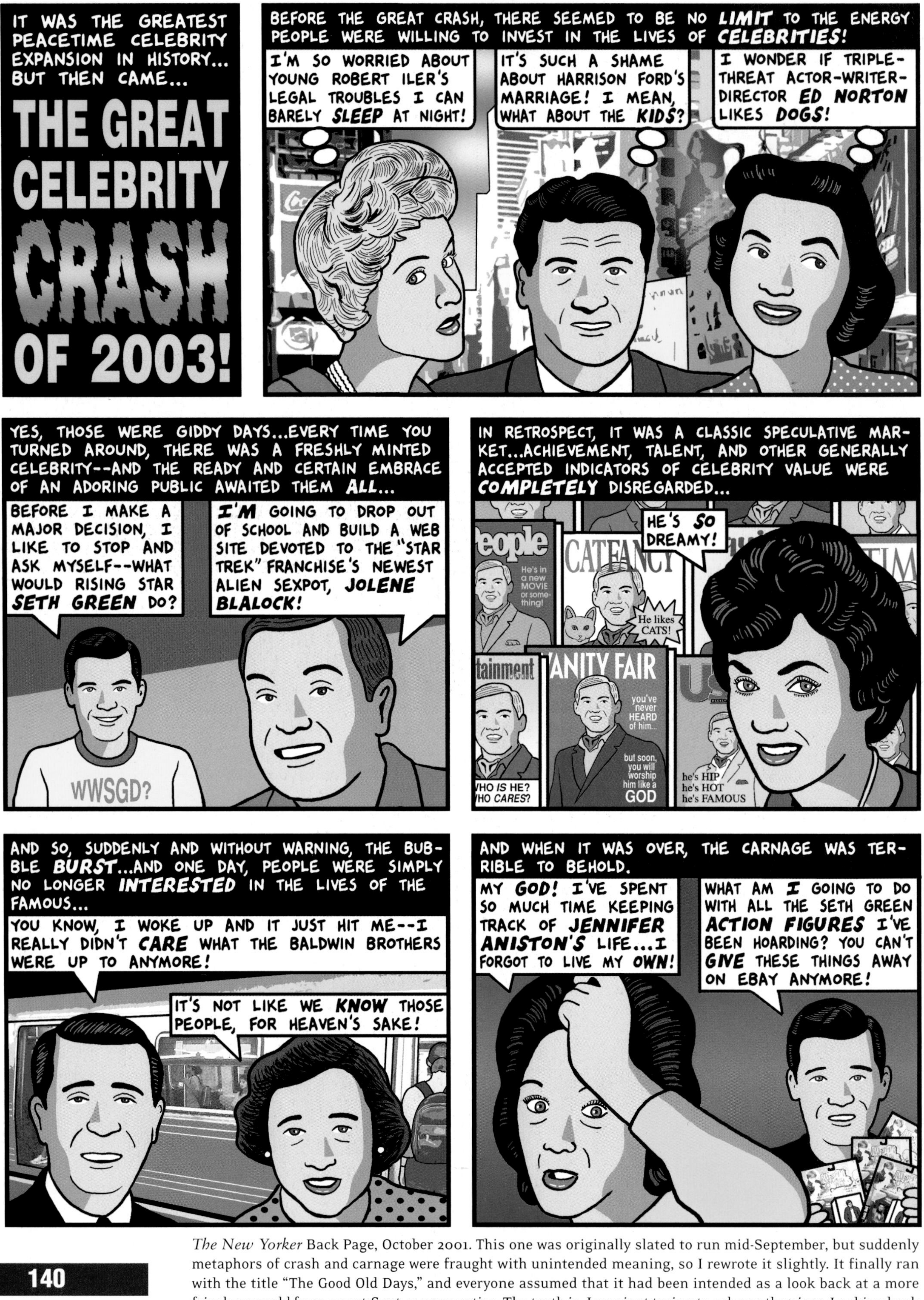
IT WAS THE GREATEST PEACETIME CELEBRITY EXPANSION IN HISTORY... BUT THEN CAME...
THE GREAT CELEBRITY CRASH OF 2003!
BEFORE THE GREAT CRASH, THERE SEEMED TO BE NO LIMIT TO THE ENERGY PEOPLE WERE WILLING TO INVEST IN THE LIVES OF CELEBRITIES!
I'M SO WORRIED ABOUT YOUNG ROBERT ILER'S LEGAL TROUBLES I CAN BARELY SLEEP AT NIGHT!
IT'S SUCH A SHAME ABOUT HARRISON FORD'S MARRIAGE! I MEAN, WHAT ABOUT THE KIDS?
I WONDER IF TRIPLE-THREAT ACTOR-WRITER-DIRECTOR ED NORTON LIKES DOGS!
YES, THOSE WERE GIDDY DAYS...EVERY TIME YOU TURNED AROUND, THERE WAS A FRESHLY MINTED CELEBRITY--AND THE READY AND CERTAIN EMBRACE OF AN ADORING PUBLIC AWAITED THEM ALL...
BEFORE I MAKE A MAJOR DECISION, I LIKE TO STOP AND ASK MYSELF--WHAT WOULD RISING STAR SETH GREEN DO?
I'M GOING TO DROP OUT OF SCHOOL AND BUILD A WEB SITE DEVOTED TO THE "STAR TREK" FRANCHISE'S NEWEST ALIEN SEXPOT, JOLENE BLALOCK!
WWSGD?
IN RETROSPECT, IT WAS A CLASSIC SPECULATIVE MARKET...ACHIEVEMENT, TALENT, AND OTHER GENERALLY ACCEPTED INDICATORS OF CELEBRITY VALUE WERE COMPLETELY DISREGARDED...
HE'S SO DREAMY!
eople
He's in a new MOVIE or something!
CATFANCY
He likes CATS!
tainment
WHO IS HE? WHO CARES?
VANITY FAIR
you've never HEARD of him...
but soon, you will worship him like a GOD
he's HIP he's HOT he's FAMOUS
AND SO, SUDDENLY AND WITHOUT WARNING, THE BUBBLE BURST...AND ONE DAY, PEOPLE WERE SIMPLY NO LONGER INTERESTED IN THE LIVES OF THE FAMOUS...
YOU KNOW, I WOKE UP AND IT JUST HIT ME--I REALLY DIDN'T CARE WHAT THE BALDWIN BROTHERS WERE UP TO ANYMORE!
IT'S NOT LIKE WE KNOW THOSE PEOPLE, FOR HEAVEN'S SAKE!
AND WHEN IT WAS OVER, THE CARNAGE WAS TERRIBLE TO BEHOLD.
MY GOD! I'VE SPENT SO MUCH TIME KEEPING TRACK OF JENNIFER ANISTON'S LIFE...I FORGOT TO LIVE MY OWN!
WHAT AM I GOING TO DO WITH ALL THE SETH GREEN ACTION FIGURES I'VE BEEN HOARDING? YOU CAN'T GIVE THESE THINGS AWAY ON EBAY ANYMORE!
TOM TOMORROW©2001

The New Yorker Back Page, October 2001. This one was originally slated to run mid-September, but suddenly metaphors of crash and carnage were fraught with unintended meaning, so I rewrote it slightly. It finally ran with the title "The Good Old Days," and everyone assumed that it had been intended as a look back at a more frivolous world from a post-Sept. 11 perspective. The truth is, I was just trying to salvage the piece. Looking back on it now, I like the original version better, so that's what I'm including here.

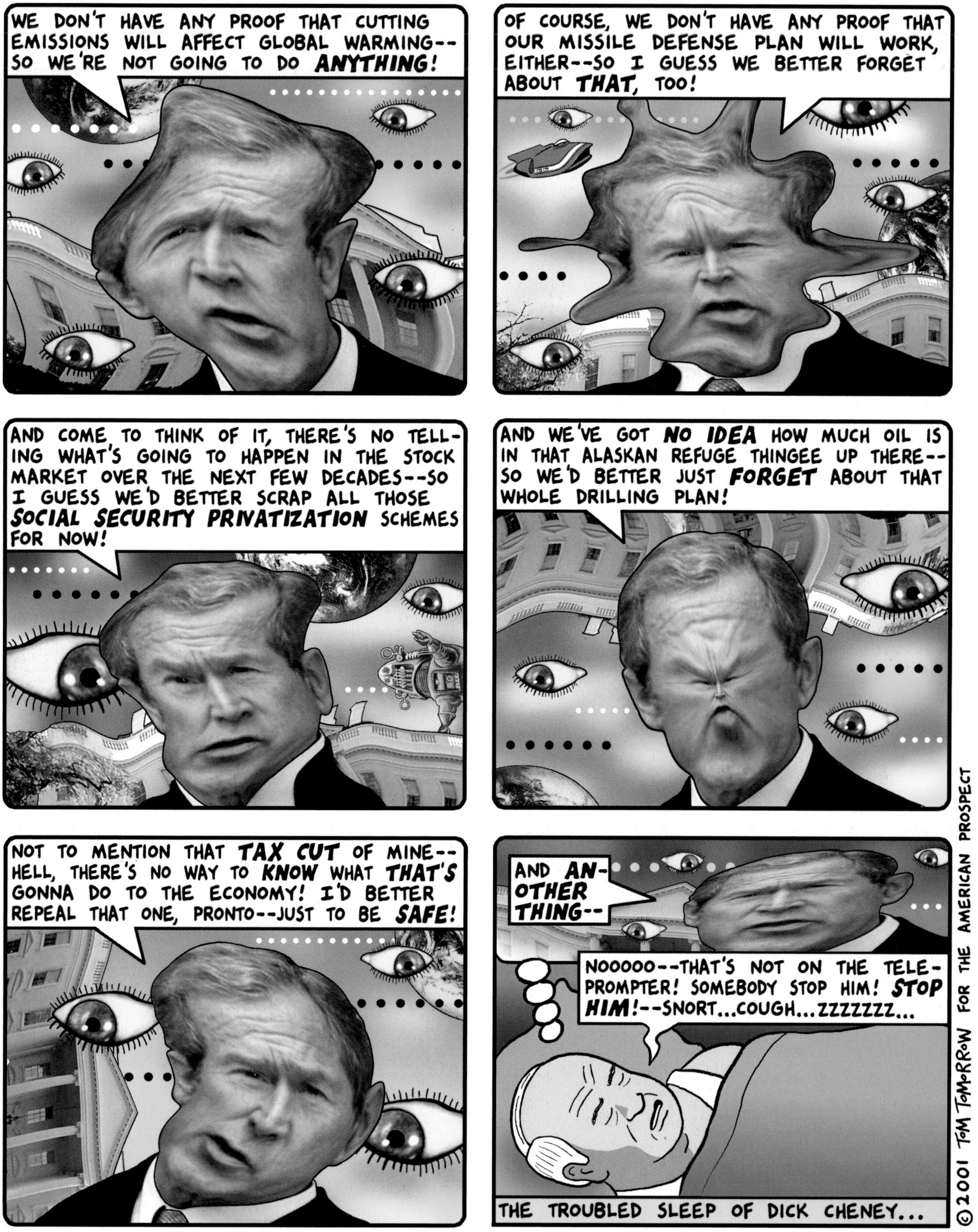

WE DON'T HAVE ANY PROOF THAT CUTTING EMISSIONS WILL AFFECT GLOBAL WARMING--SO WE'RE NOT GOING TO DO ANYTHING!
OF COURSE, WE DON'T HAVE ANY PROOF THAT OUR MISSILE DEFENSE PLAN WILL WORK, EITHER--SO I GUESS WE BETTER FORGET ABOUT THAT, TOO!
AND COME TO THINK OF IT, THERE'S NO TELLING WHAT'S GOING TO HAPPEN IN THE STOCK MARKET OVER THE NEXT FEW DECADES--SO I GUESS WE'D BETTER SCRAP ALL THOSE SOCIAL SECURITY PRIVATIZATION SCHEMES FOR NOW!
AND WE'VE GOT NO IDEA HOW MUCH OIL IS IN THAT ALASKAN REFUGE THINGEE UP THERE--SO WE'D BETTER JUST FORGET ABOUT THAT WHOLE DRILLING PLAN!
NOT TO MENTION THAT TAX CUT OF MINE--HELL, THERE'S NO WAY TO KNOW WHAT THAT'S GONNA DO TO THE ECONOMY! I'D BETTER REPEAL THAT ONE, PRONTO--JUST TO BE SAFE!
AND ANOTHER THING--
NOOOOO--THAT'S NOT ON THE TELEPROMPTER! SOMEBODY STOP HIM! STOP HIM!--SNORT...COUGH...ZZZZZZZ...
THE TROUBLED SLEEP OF DICK CHENEY...
©2001 TOM TOMORROW FOR THE AMERICAN PROSPECT

Another cartoon I finished right before Sept. 11, this one for *The American Prospect.* In the immediate aftermath of the terrorist attack, any other topic seemed utterly irrelevant—so I rewrote the text to this one, clumsily and at the last minute—even including, in all sincerity, the dread phrase ". . . then the terrorists have already won." Unsurprisingly, I like the original version of this one better as well.

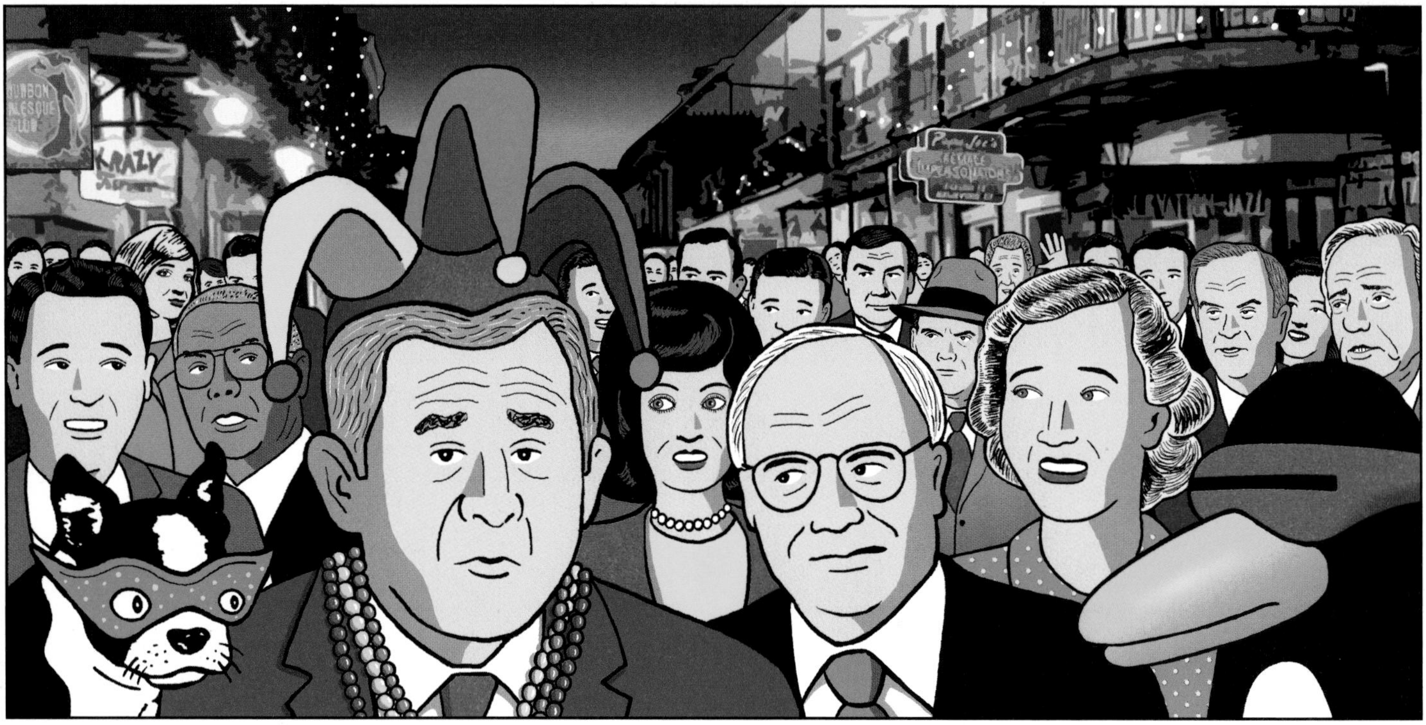

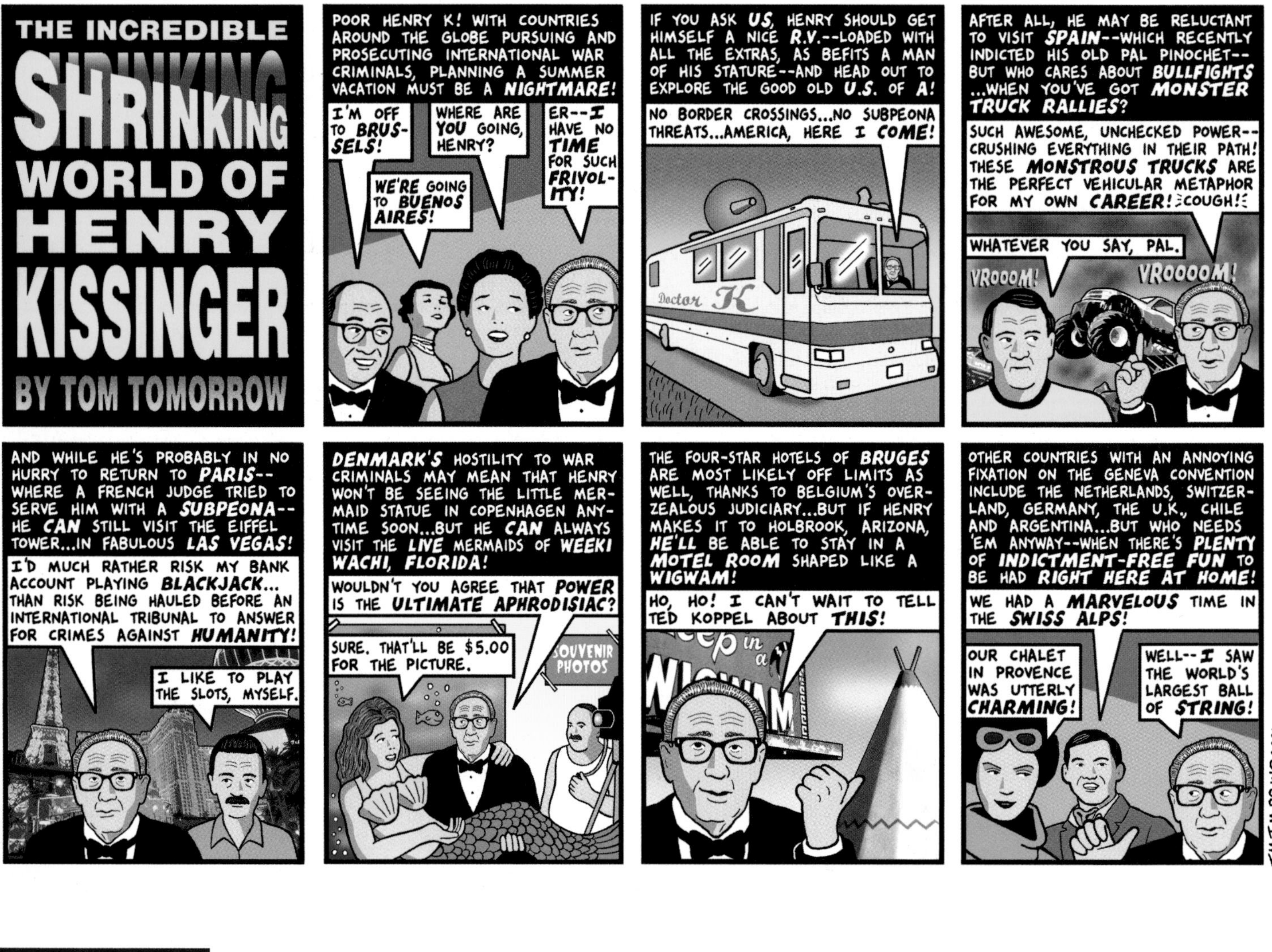

THE INCREDIBLE SHRINKING WORLD OF HENRY KISSINGER
BY TOM TOMORROW
POOR HENRY K! WITH COUNTRIES AROUND THE GLOBE PURSUING AND PROSECUTING INTERNATIONAL WAR CRIMINALS, PLANNING A SUMMER VACATION MUST BE A NIGHTMARE!
I'M OFF TO BRUSSELS!
WHERE ARE YOU GOING, HENRY?
ER--I HAVE NO TIME FOR SUCH FRIVOLITY!
WE'RE GOING TO BUENOS AIRES!
IF YOU ASK US, HENRY SHOULD GET HIMSELF A NICE R.V.--LOADED WITH ALL THE EXTRAS, AS BEFITS A MAN OF HIS STATURE--AND HEAD OUT TO EXPLORE THE GOOD OLD U.S. OF A!
NO BORDER CROSSINGS...NO SUBPEONA THREATS...AMERICA, HERE I COME!
Doctor K
AFTER ALL, HE MAY BE RELUCTANT TO VISIT SPAIN--WHICH RECENTLY INDICTED HIS OLD PAL PINOCHET--BUT WHO CARES ABOUT BULLFIGHTS ...WHEN YOU'VE GOT MONSTER TRUCK RALLIES?
SUCH AWESOME, UNCHECKED POWER--CRUSHING EVERYTHING IN THEIR PATH! THESE MONSTROUS TRUCKS ARE THE PERFECT VEHICULAR METAPHOR FOR MY OWN CAREER! COUGH!
WHATEVER YOU SAY, PAL.
VROOOM!
VROOOOM!
AND WHILE HE'S PROBABLY IN NO HURRY TO RETURN TO PARIS--WHERE A FRENCH JUDGE TRIED TO SERVE HIM WITH A SUBPEONA--HE CAN STILL VISIT THE EIFFEL TOWER...IN FABULOUS LAS VEGAS!
I'D MUCH RATHER RISK MY BANK ACCOUNT PLAYING BLACKJACK... THAN RISK BEING HAULED BEFORE AN INTERNATIONAL TRIBUNAL TO ANSWER FOR CRIMES AGAINST HUMANITY!
I LIKE TO PLAY THE SLOTS, MYSELF.
DENMARK'S HOSTILITY TO WAR CRIMINALS MAY MEAN THAT HENRY WON'T BE SEEING THE LITTLE MERMAID STATUE IN COPENHAGEN ANYTIME SOON...BUT HE CAN ALWAYS VISIT THE LIVE MERMAIDS OF WEEKI WACHI, FLORIDA!
WOULDN'T YOU AGREE THAT POWER IS THE ULTIMATE APHRODISIAC?
SURE. THAT'LL BE $5.00 FOR THE PICTURE.
SOUVENIR PHOTOS
THE FOUR-STAR HOTELS OF BRUGES ARE MOST LIKELY OFF LIMITS AS WELL, THANKS TO BELGIUM'S OVERZEALOUS JUDICIARY...BUT IF HENRY MAKES IT TO HOLBROOK, ARIZONA, HE'LL BE ABLE TO STAY IN A MOTEL ROOM SHAPED LIKE A WIGWAM!
HO, HO! I CAN'T WAIT TO TELL TED KOPPEL ABOUT THIS!
eep in a WIGWAM
OTHER COUNTRIES WITH AN ANNOYING FIXATION ON THE GENEVA CONVENTION INCLUDE THE NETHERLANDS, SWITZERLAND, GERMANY, THE U.K., CHILE AND ARGENTINA...BUT WHO NEEDS 'EM ANYWAY--WHEN THERE'S PLENTY OF INDICTMENT-FREE FUN TO BE HAD RIGHT HERE AT HOME!
WE HAD A MARVELOUS TIME IN THE SWISS ALPS!
OUR CHALET IN PROVENCE WAS UTTERLY CHARMING!
WELL--I SAW THE WORLD'S LARGEST BALL OF STRING!
TOM TOMORROW©2001

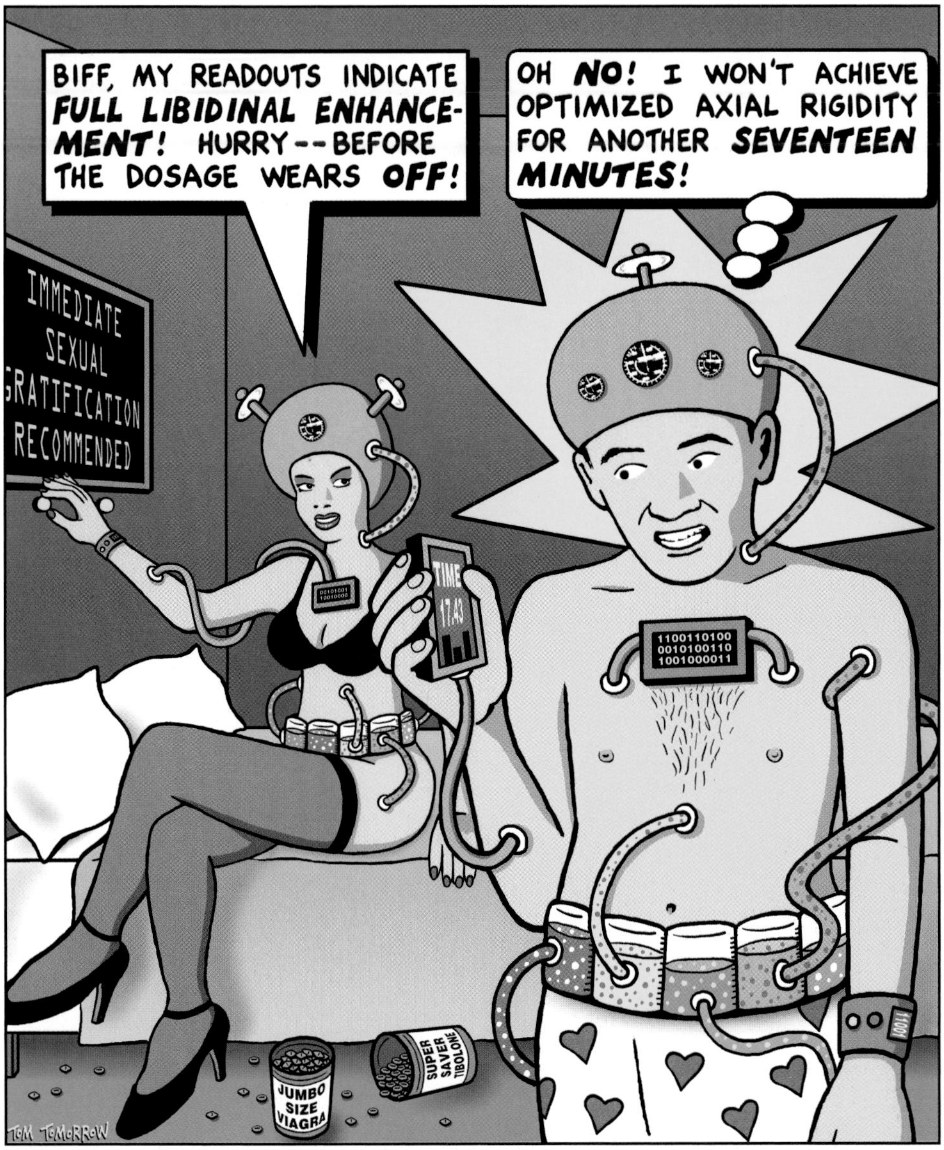
BIFF, MY READOUTS INDICATE FULL LIBIDINAL ENHANCEMENT! HURRY--BEFORE THE DOSAGE WEARS OFF!
OH NO! I WON'T ACHIEVE OPTIMIZED AXIAL RIGIDITY FOR ANOTHER SEVENTEEN MINUTES!
IMMEDIATE SEXUAL GRATIFICATION RECOMMENDED
TIME 17:43
1100110100 0010100110 1001000011
JUMBO SIZE VIAGRA
SUPER SAVER TIBOLONE
TOM TOMORROW

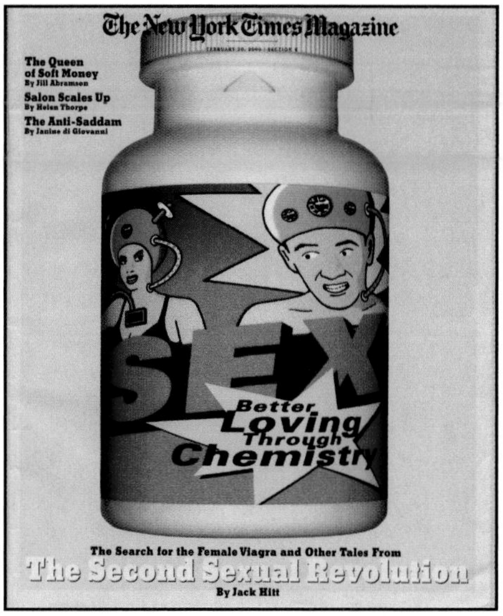
The New York Times Magazine
The Queen of Soft Money By Jill Abramson
Salon Scales Up By Helen Thorpe
The Anti-Saddam By Janine di Giovanni
SEX
Better Loving Through Chemistry
The Search for the Female Viagra and Other Tales From
The Second Sexual Revolution
By Jack Hitt

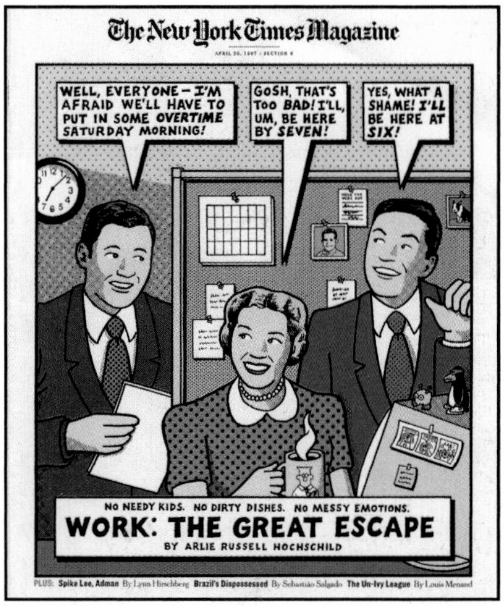
The New York Times Magazine
WELL, EVERYONE—I'M AFRAID WE'LL HAVE TO PUT IN SOME OVERTIME SATURDAY MORNING!
GOSH, THAT'S TOO BAD! I'LL, UM, BE HERE BY SEVEN!
YES, WHAT A SHAME! I'LL BE HERE AT SIX!
NO NEEDY KIDS. NO DIRTY DISHES. NO MESSY EMOTIONS.
WORK: THE GREAT ESCAPE
BY ARLIE RUSSELL HOCHSCHILD

Opposite page top: artwork from promotional poster for Association of Alternative Newspapers convention in New Orleans, July 2001. Below: *The Village Voice*, August 2001.

This page, clockwise from top left: illustration for *The New York Times Magazine*, February 2000; top right, the cover of that issue (the illustration was deemed too racy for the cover, hence this abbreviated version); a cover for the *Magazine* from April, 1997; and the author with close personal friend Bill O'Reilly.

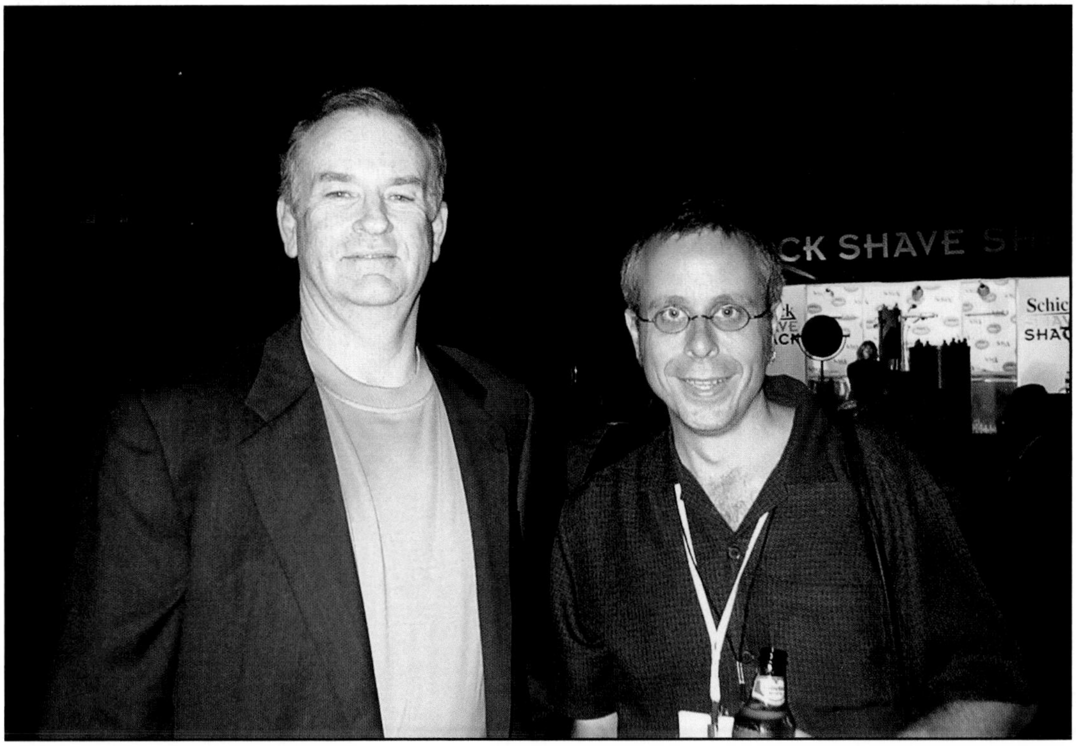

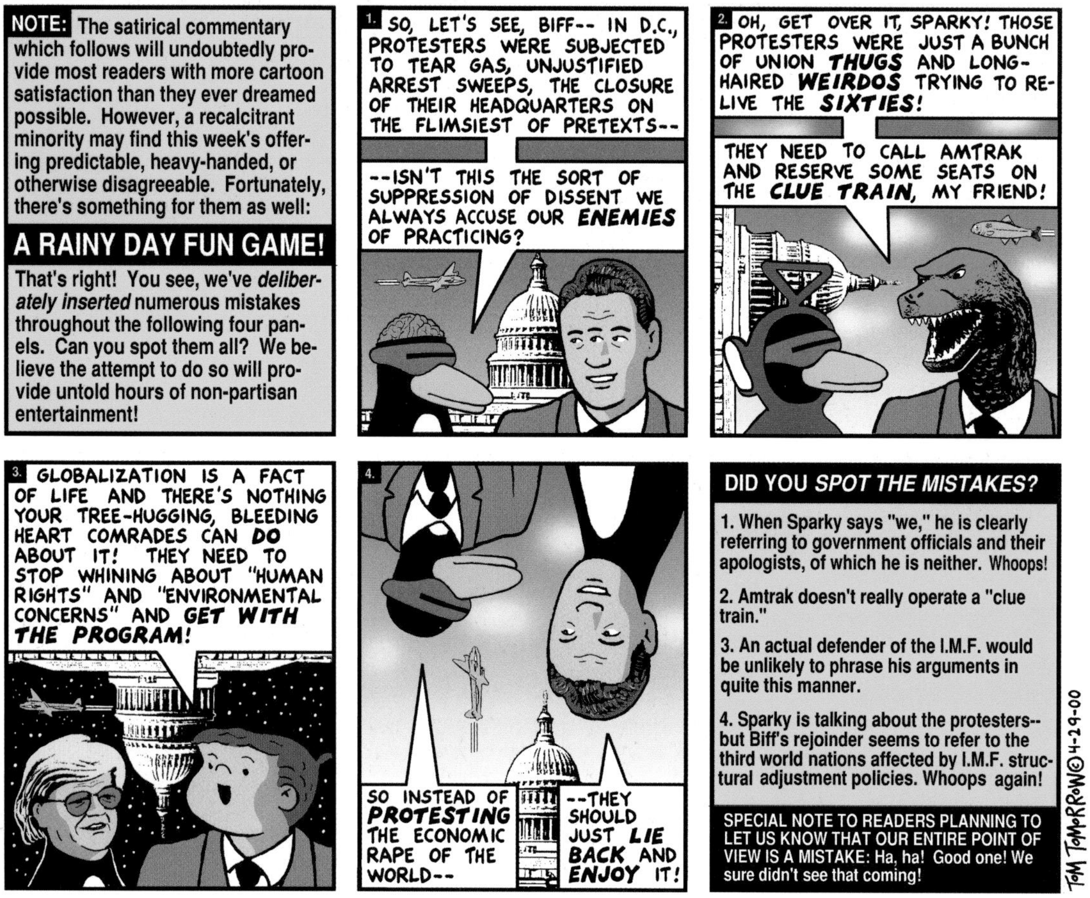
NOTE: The satirical commentary which follows will undoubtedly provide most readers with more cartoon satisfaction than they ever dreamed possible. However, a recalcitrant minority may find this week's offering predictable, heavy-handed, or otherwise disagreeable. Fortunately, there's something for them as well:
A RAINY DAY FUN GAME!
That's right! You see, we've deliberately inserted numerous mistakes throughout the following four panels. Can you spot them all? We believe the attempt to do so will provide untold hours of non-partisan entertainment!
1.
SO, LET'S SEE, BIFF-- IN D.C., PROTESTERS WERE SUBJECTED TO TEAR GAS, UNJUSTIFIED ARREST SWEEPS, THE CLOSURE OF THEIR HEADQUARTERS ON THE FLIMSIEST OF PRETEXTS--
--ISN'T THIS THE SORT OF SUPPRESSION OF DISSENT WE ALWAYS ACCUSE OUR ENEMIES OF PRACTICING?
2.
OH, GET OVER IT, SPARKY! THOSE PROTESTERS WERE JUST A BUNCH OF UNION THUGS AND LONG-HAIRED WEIRDOS TRYING TO RELIVE THE SIXTIES!
THEY NEED TO CALL AMTRAK AND RESERVE SOME SEATS ON THE CLUE TRAIN, MY FRIEND!
3.
GLOBALIZATION IS A FACT OF LIFE AND THERE'S NOTHING YOUR TREE-HUGGING, BLEEDING HEART COMRADES CAN DO ABOUT IT! THEY NEED TO STOP WHINING ABOUT "HUMAN RIGHTS" AND "ENVIRONMENTAL CONCERNS" AND GET WITH THE PROGRAM!
4.
SO INSTEAD OF PROTESTING THE ECONOMIC RAPE OF THE WORLD--
--THEY SHOULD JUST LIE BACK AND ENJOY IT!
DID YOU SPOT THE MISTAKES?
1. When Sparky says "we," he is clearly referring to government officials and their apologists, of which he is neither. Whoops!
2. Amtrak doesn't really operate a "clue train."
3. An actual defender of the I.M.F. would be unlikely to phrase his arguments in quite this manner.
4. Sparky is talking about the protesters--but Biff's rejoinder seems to refer to the third world nations affected by I.M.F. structural adjustment policies. Whoops again!
SPECIAL NOTE TO READERS PLANNING TO LET US KNOW THAT OUR ENTIRE POINT OF VIEW IS A MISTAKE: Ha, ha! Good one! We sure didn't see that coming!
TOM TOMORROW©4-29-00

Though my cartoon runs most places in glorious black and white, I do a color version each week for *Salon*. These are some of my favorites.

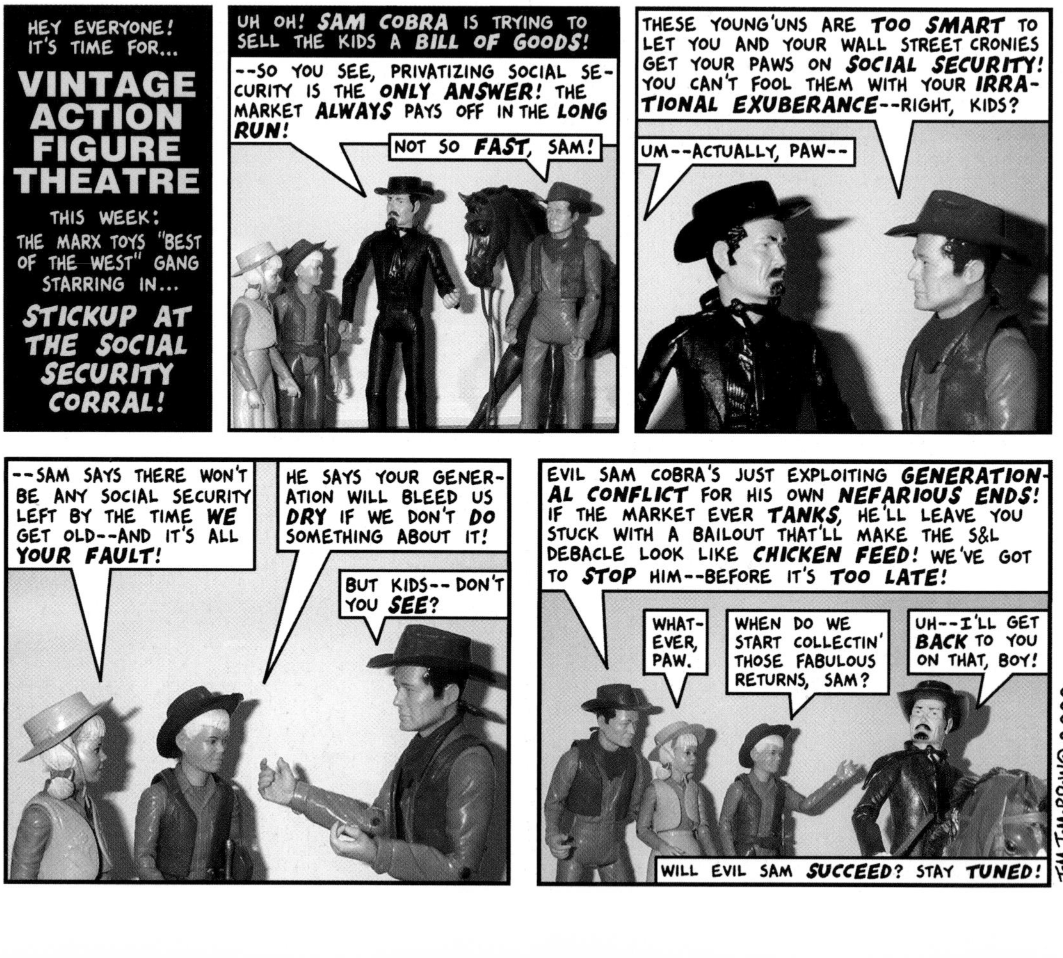
HEY EVERYONE! IT'S TIME FOR...
VINTAGE ACTION FIGURE THEATRE
THIS WEEK: THE MARX TOYS "BEST OF THE WEST" GANG STARRING IN...
STICKUP AT THE SOCIAL SECURITY CORRAL!
UH OH! SAM COBRA IS TRYING TO SELL THE KIDS A BILL OF GOODS!
--SO YOU SEE, PRIVATIZING SOCIAL SECURITY IS THE ONLY ANSWER! THE MARKET ALWAYS PAYS OFF IN THE LONG RUN!
NOT SO FAST, SAM!
THESE YOUNG'UNS ARE TOO SMART TO LET YOU AND YOUR WALL STREET CRONIES GET YOUR PAWS ON SOCIAL SECURITY! YOU CAN'T FOOL THEM WITH YOUR IRRATIONAL EXUBERANCE--RIGHT, KIDS?
UM--ACTUALLY, PAW--
--SAM SAYS THERE WON'T BE ANY SOCIAL SECURITY LEFT BY THE TIME WE GET OLD--AND IT'S ALL YOUR FAULT!
HE SAYS YOUR GENERATION WILL BLEED US DRY IF WE DON'T DO SOMETHING ABOUT IT!
BUT KIDS-- DON'T YOU SEE?
EVIL SAM COBRA'S JUST EXPLOITING GENERATIONAL CONFLICT FOR HIS OWN NEFARIOUS ENDS! IF THE MARKET EVER TANKS, HE'LL LEAVE YOU STUCK WITH A BAILOUT THAT'LL MAKE THE S&L DEBACLE LOOK LIKE CHICKEN FEED! WE'VE GOT TO STOP HIM--BEFORE IT'S TOO LATE!
WHAT-EVER, PAW.
WHEN DO WE START COLLECTIN' THOSE FABULOUS RETURNS, SAM?
UH--I'LL GET BACK TO YOU ON THAT, BOY!
WILL EVIL SAM SUCCEED? STAY TUNED!
TOM TOMORROW© 2000

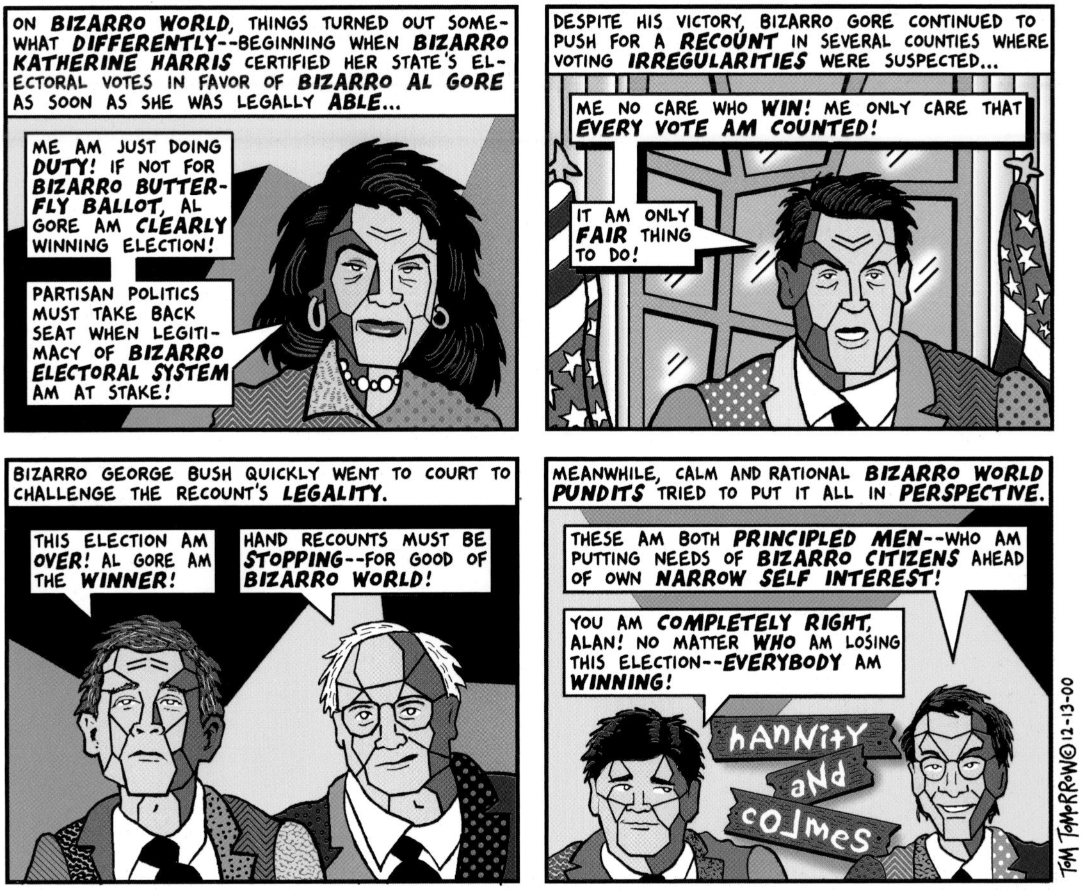
ON BIZARRO WORLD, THINGS TURNED OUT SOMEWHAT DIFFERENTLY--BEGINNING WHEN BIZARRO KATHERINE HARRIS CERTIFIED HER STATE'S ELECTORAL VOTES IN FAVOR OF BIZARRO AL GORE AS SOON AS SHE WAS LEGALLY ABLE...
ME AM JUST DOING DUTY! IF NOT FOR BIZARRO BUTTERFLY BALLOT, AL GORE AM CLEARLY WINNING ELECTION!
PARTISAN POLITICS MUST TAKE BACK SEAT WHEN LEGITIMACY OF BIZARRO ELECTORAL SYSTEM AM AT STAKE!
DESPITE HIS VICTORY, BIZARRO GORE CONTINUED TO PUSH FOR A RECOUNT IN SEVERAL COUNTIES WHERE VOTING IRREGULARITIES WERE SUSPECTED...
ME NO CARE WHO WIN! ME ONLY CARE THAT EVERY VOTE AM COUNTED!
IT AM ONLY FAIR THING TO DO!
BIZARRO GEORGE BUSH QUICKLY WENT TO COURT TO CHALLENGE THE RECOUNT'S LEGALITY.
THIS ELECTION AM OVER! AL GORE AM THE WINNER!
HAND RECOUNTS MUST BE STOPPING--FOR GOOD OF BIZARRO WORLD!
MEANWHILE, CALM AND RATIONAL BIZARRO WORLD PUNDITS TRIED TO PUT IT ALL IN PERSPECTIVE.
THESE AM BOTH PRINCIPLED MEN--WHO AM PUTTING NEEDS OF BIZARRO CITIZENS AHEAD OF OWN NARROW SELF INTEREST!
YOU AM COMPLETELY RIGHT, ALAN! NO MATTER WHO AM LOSING THIS ELECTION--EVERYBODY AM WINNING!
hANNity aNd coLmes
TOM TOMORROW© 12-13-00

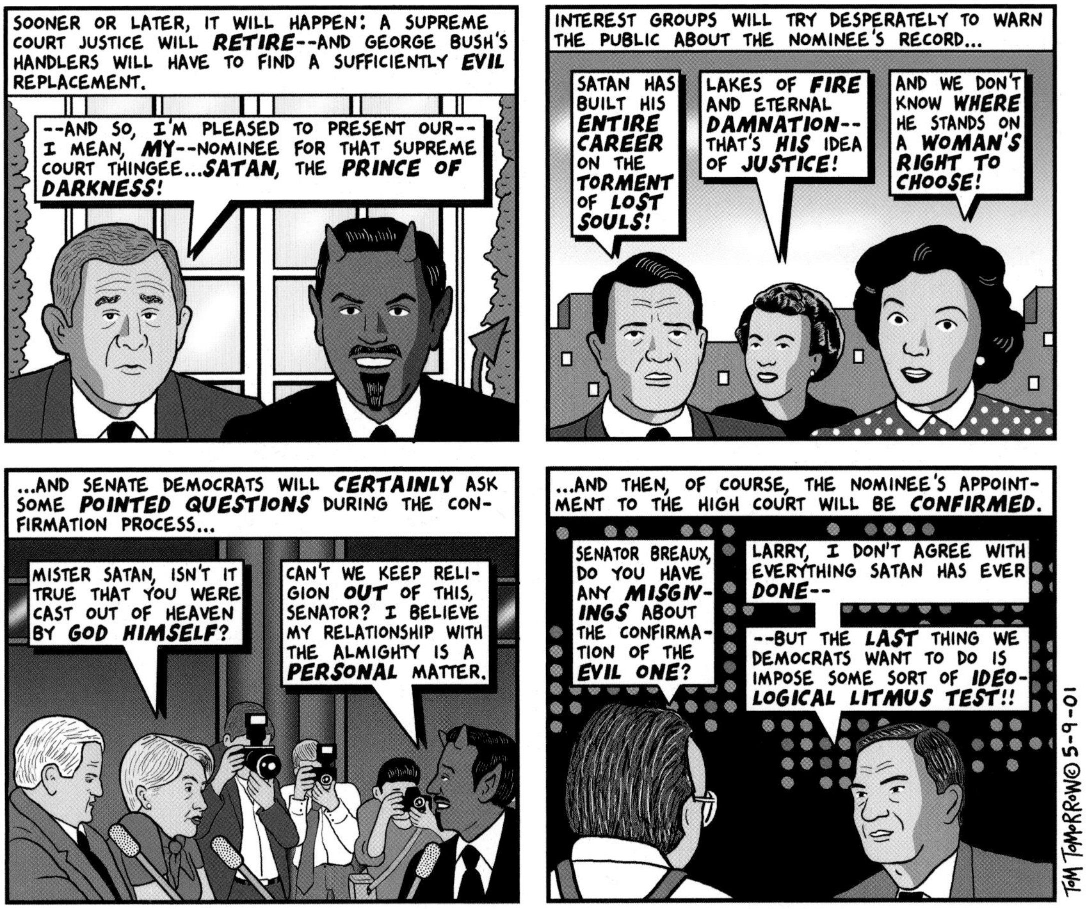
SOONER OR LATER, IT WILL HAPPEN: A SUPREME COURT JUSTICE WILL RETIRE--AND GEORGE BUSH'S HANDLERS WILL HAVE TO FIND A SUFFICIENTLY EVIL REPLACEMENT.
--AND SO, I'M PLEASED TO PRESENT OUR-- I MEAN, MY--NOMINEE FOR THAT SUPREME COURT THINGEE...SATAN, THE PRINCE OF DARKNESS!
INTEREST GROUPS WILL TRY DESPERATELY TO WARN THE PUBLIC ABOUT THE NOMINEE'S RECORD...
SATAN HAS BUILT HIS ENTIRE CAREER ON THE TORMENT OF LOST SOULS!
LAKES OF FIRE AND ETERNAL DAMNATION--THAT'S HIS IDEA OF JUSTICE!
AND WE DON'T KNOW WHERE HE STANDS ON A WOMAN'S RIGHT TO CHOOSE!
...AND SENATE DEMOCRATS WILL CERTAINLY ASK SOME POINTED QUESTIONS DURING THE CONFIRMATION PROCESS...
MISTER SATAN, ISN'T IT TRUE THAT YOU WERE CAST OUT OF HEAVEN BY GOD HIMSELF?
CAN'T WE KEEP RELIGION OUT OF THIS, SENATOR? I BELIEVE MY RELATIONSHIP WITH THE ALMIGHTY IS A PERSONAL MATTER.
...AND THEN, OF COURSE, THE NOMINEE'S APPOINTMENT TO THE HIGH COURT WILL BE CONFIRMED.
SENATOR BREAUX, DO YOU HAVE ANY MISGIVINGS ABOUT THE CONFIRMATION OF THE EVIL ONE?
LARRY, I DON'T AGREE WITH EVERYTHING SATAN HAS EVER DONE--
--BUT THE LAST THING WE DEMOCRATS WANT TO DO IS IMPOSE SOME SORT OF IDEOLOGICAL LITMUS TEST!!
TOM TOMORROW© 5-9-01

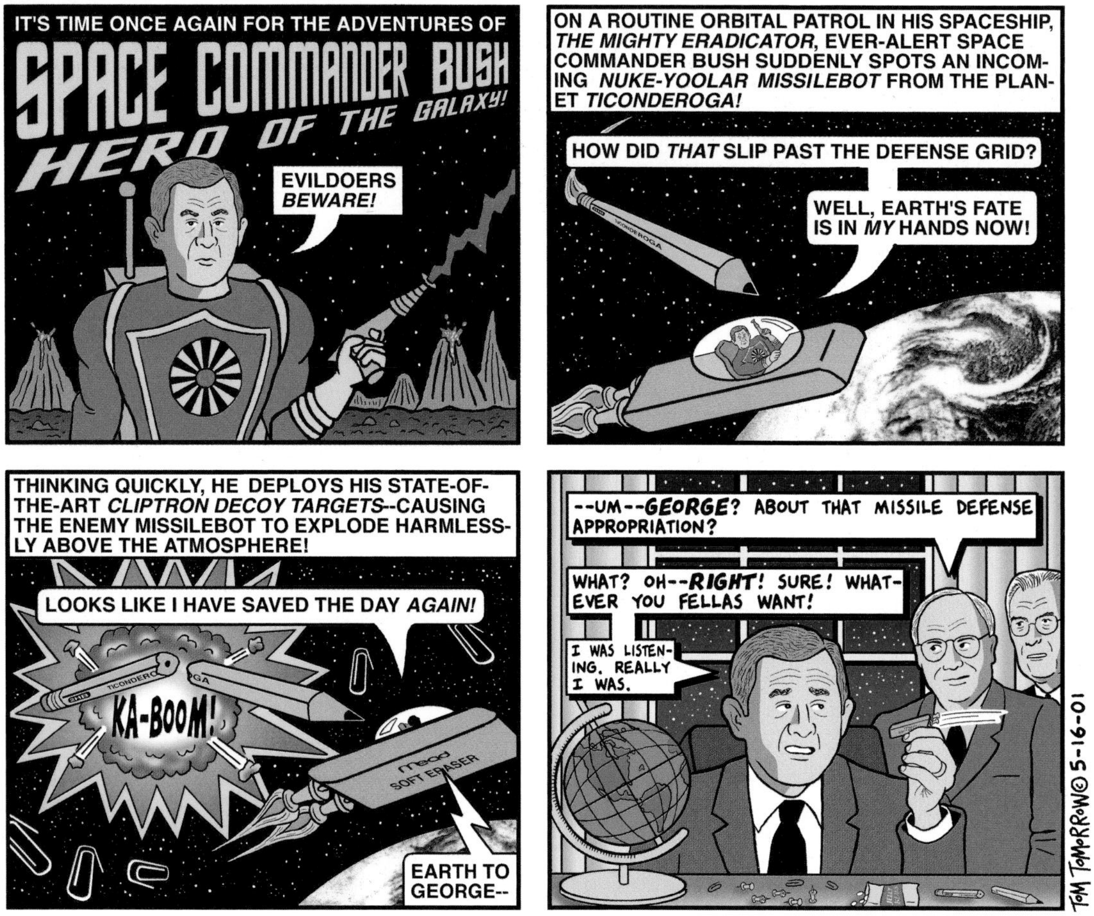
IT'S TIME ONCE AGAIN FOR THE ADVENTURES OF
SPACE COMMANDER BUSH
HERO OF THE GALAXY!
EVILDOERS BEWARE!
ON A ROUTINE ORBITAL PATROL IN HIS SPACESHIP, THE MIGHTY ERADICATOR, EVER-ALERT SPACE COMMANDER BUSH SUDDENLY SPOTS AN INCOMING NUKE-YOOLAR MISSILEBOT FROM THE PLANET TICONDEROGA!
HOW DID THAT SLIP PAST THE DEFENSE GRID?
WELL, EARTH'S FATE IS IN MY HANDS NOW!
THINKING QUICKLY, HE DEPLOYS HIS STATE-OF-THE-ART CLIPTRON DECOY TARGETS--CAUSING THE ENEMY MISSILEBOT TO EXPLODE HARMLESSLY ABOVE THE ATMOSPHERE!
LOOKS LIKE I HAVE SAVED THE DAY AGAIN!
KA-BOOM!
SOFT ERASER
EARTH TO GEORGE--
--UM--GEORGE? ABOUT THAT MISSILE DEFENSE APPROPRIATION?
WHAT? OH--RIGHT! SURE! WHATEVER YOU FELLAS WANT!
I WAS LISTENING. REALLY I WAS.
TOM TOMORROW© 5-16-01

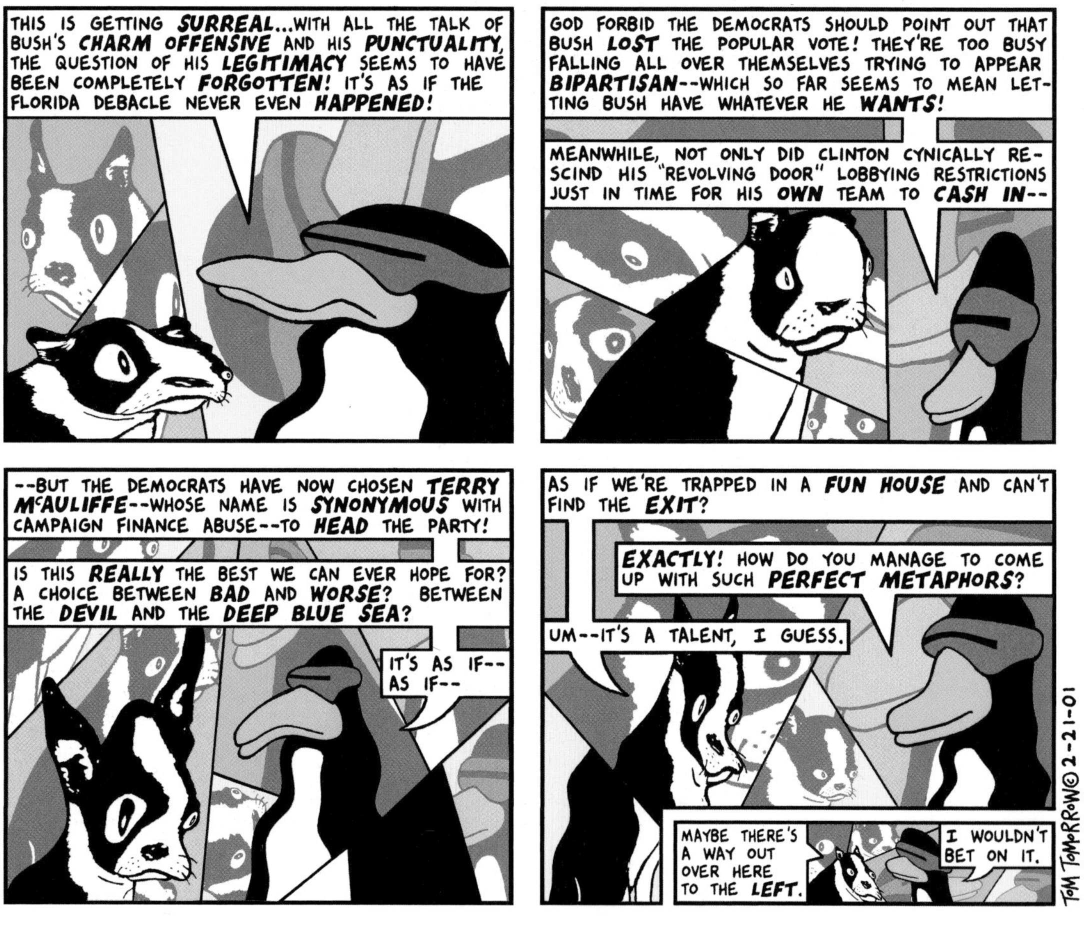
THIS IS GETTING SURREAL...WITH ALL THE TALK OF BUSH'S CHARM OFFENSIVE AND HIS PUNCTUALITY, THE QUESTION OF HIS LEGITIMACY SEEMS TO HAVE BEEN COMPLETELY FORGOTTEN! IT'S AS IF THE FLORIDA DEBACLE NEVER EVEN HAPPENED!
GOD FORBID THE DEMOCRATS SHOULD POINT OUT THAT BUSH LOST THE POPULAR VOTE! THEY'RE TOO BUSY FALLING ALL OVER THEMSELVES TRYING TO APPEAR BIPARTISAN--WHICH SO FAR SEEMS TO MEAN LETTING BUSH HAVE WHATEVER HE WANTS!
MEANWHILE, NOT ONLY DID CLINTON CYNICALLY RESCIND HIS "REVOLVING DOOR" LOBBYING RESTRICTIONS JUST IN TIME FOR HIS OWN TEAM TO CASH IN--
--BUT THE DEMOCRATS HAVE NOW CHOSEN TERRY McAULIFFE--WHOSE NAME IS SYNONYMOUS WITH CAMPAIGN FINANCE ABUSE--TO HEAD THE PARTY!
IS THIS REALLY THE BEST WE CAN EVER HOPE FOR? A CHOICE BETWEEN BAD AND WORSE? BETWEEN THE DEVIL AND THE DEEP BLUE SEA?
IT'S AS IF--AS IF--
AS IF WE'RE TRAPPED IN A FUN HOUSE AND CAN'T FIND THE EXIT?
EXACTLY! HOW DO YOU MANAGE TO COME UP WITH SUCH PERFECT METAPHORS?
UM--IT'S A TALENT, I GUESS.
MAYBE THERE'S A WAY OUT OVER HERE TO THE LEFT.
I WOULDN'T BET ON IT.
TOM TOMORROW© 2-21-01

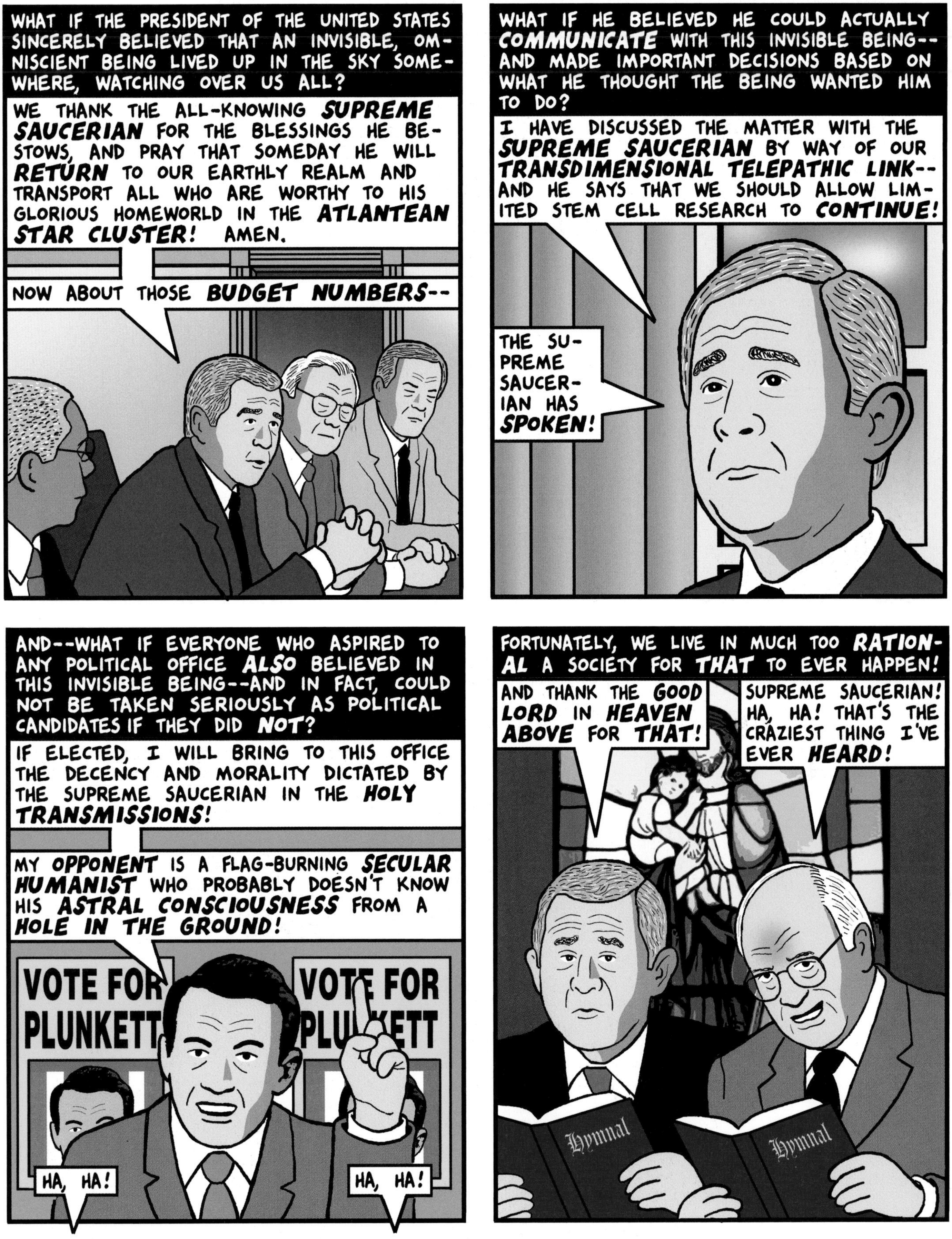
WHAT IF THE PRESIDENT OF THE UNITED STATES SINCERELY BELIEVED THAT AN INVISIBLE, OMNISCIENT BEING LIVED UP IN THE SKY SOMEWHERE, WATCHING OVER US ALL?
WE THANK THE ALL-KNOWING SUPREME SAUCERIAN FOR THE BLESSINGS HE BESTOWS, AND PRAY THAT SOMEDAY HE WILL RETURN TO OUR EARTHLY REALM AND TRANSPORT ALL WHO ARE WORTHY TO HIS GLORIOUS HOMEWORLD IN THE ATLANTEAN STAR CLUSTER! AMEN.
NOW ABOUT THOSE BUDGET NUMBERS--
WHAT IF HE BELIEVED HE COULD ACTUALLY COMMUNICATE WITH THIS INVISIBLE BEING--AND MADE IMPORTANT DECISIONS BASED ON WHAT HE THOUGHT THE BEING WANTED HIM TO DO?
I HAVE DISCUSSED THE MATTER WITH THE SUPREME SAUCERIAN BY WAY OF OUR TRANSDIMENSIONAL TELEPATHIC LINK--AND HE SAYS THAT WE SHOULD ALLOW LIMITED STEM CELL RESEARCH TO CONTINUE!
THE SUPREME SAUCERIAN HAS SPOKEN!
AND--WHAT IF EVERYONE WHO ASPIRED TO ANY POLITICAL OFFICE ALSO BELIEVED IN THIS INVISIBLE BEING--AND IN FACT, COULD NOT BE TAKEN SERIOUSLY AS POLITICAL CANDIDATES IF THEY DID NOT?
IF ELECTED, I WILL BRING TO THIS OFFICE THE DECENCY AND MORALITY DICTATED BY THE SUPREME SAUCERIAN IN THE HOLY TRANSMISSIONS!
MY OPPONENT IS A FLAG-BURNING SECULAR HUMANIST WHO PROBABLY DOESN'T KNOW HIS ASTRAL CONSCIOUSNESS FROM A HOLE IN THE GROUND!
VOTE FOR PLUNKETT
VOTE FOR PLUNKETT
HA, HA!
HA, HA!
FORTUNATELY, WE LIVE IN MUCH TOO RATIONAL A SOCIETY FOR THAT TO EVER HAPPEN!
AND THANK THE GOOD LORD IN HEAVEN ABOVE FOR THAT!
SUPREME SAUCERIAN! HA, HA! THAT'S THE CRAZIEST THING I'VE EVER HEARD!
Hymnal
Hymnal

The American Prospect, September 2001.

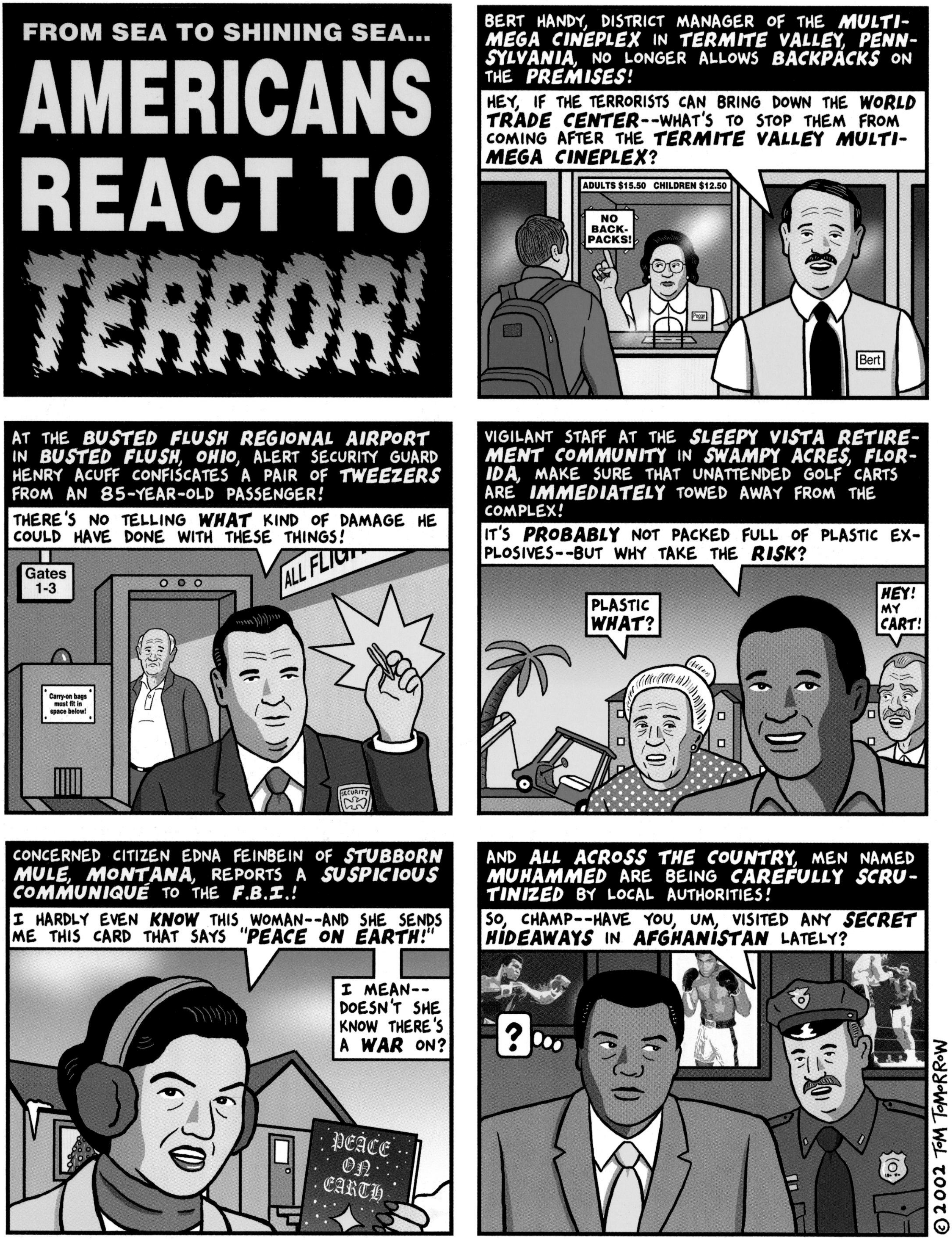
FROM SEA TO SHINING SEA...
AMERICANS REACT TO TERROR!
BERT HANDY, DISTRICT MANAGER OF THE MULTI-MEGA CINEPLEX IN TERMITE VALLEY, PENNSYLVANIA, NO LONGER ALLOWS BACKPACKS ON THE PREMISES!
HEY, IF THE TERRORISTS CAN BRING DOWN THE WORLD TRADE CENTER--WHAT'S TO STOP THEM FROM COMING AFTER THE TERMITE VALLEY MULTI-MEGA CINEPLEX?
ADULTS $15.50 CHILDREN $12.50
NO BACK-PACKS!
Peggy
Bert
AT THE BUSTED FLUSH REGIONAL AIRPORT IN BUSTED FLUSH, OHIO, ALERT SECURITY GUARD HENRY ACUFF CONFISCATES A PAIR OF TWEEZERS FROM AN 85-YEAR-OLD PASSENGER!
THERE'S NO TELLING WHAT KIND OF DAMAGE HE COULD HAVE DONE WITH THESE THINGS!
Gates 1-3
Carry-on bags must fit in space below!
SECURITY
VIGILANT STAFF AT THE SLEEPY VISTA RETIREMENT COMMUNITY IN SWAMPY ACRES, FLORIDA, MAKE SURE THAT UNATTENDED GOLF CARTS ARE IMMEDIATELY TOWED AWAY FROM THE COMPLEX!
IT'S PROBABLY NOT PACKED FULL OF PLASTIC EXPLOSIVES--BUT WHY TAKE THE RISK?
PLASTIC WHAT?
HEY! MY CART!
CONCERNED CITIZEN EDNA FEINBEIN OF STUBBORN MULE, MONTANA, REPORTS A SUSPICIOUS COMMUNIQUÉ TO THE F.B.I.!
I HARDLY EVEN KNOW THIS WOMAN--AND SHE SENDS ME THIS CARD THAT SAYS "PEACE ON EARTH!"
I MEAN--DOESN'T SHE KNOW THERE'S A WAR ON?
PEACE ON EARTH
AND ALL ACROSS THE COUNTRY, MEN NAMED MUHAMMED ARE BEING CAREFULLY SCRUTINIZED BY LOCAL AUTHORITIES!
SO, CHAMP--HAVE YOU, UM, VISITED ANY SECRET HIDEAWAYS IN AFGHANISTAN LATELY?
?
©2002 TOM TOMORROW

The New Yorker Back Page, January 2002.

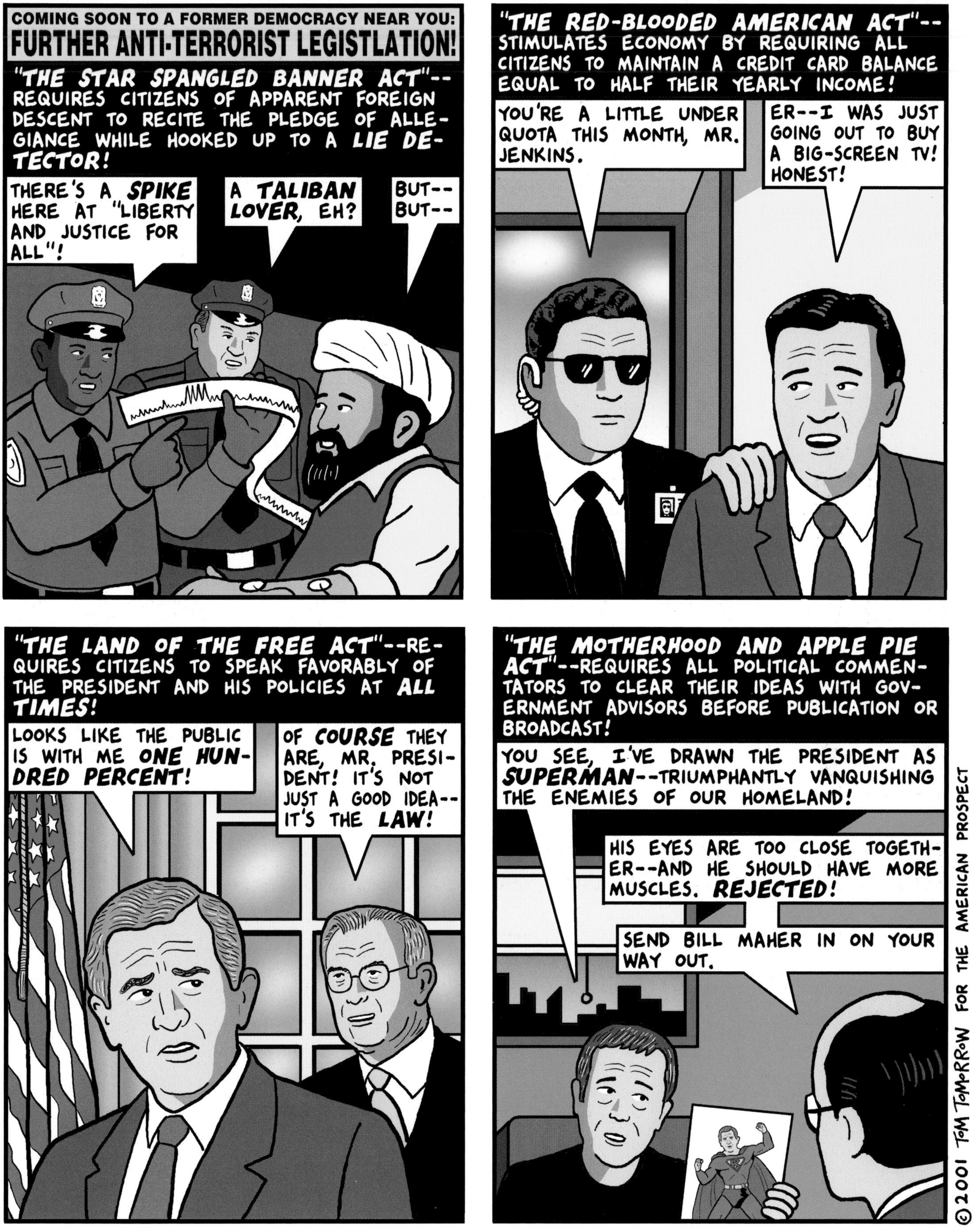
COMING SOON TO A FORMER DEMOCRACY NEAR YOU:
FURTHER ANTI-TERRORIST LEGISTLATION!
"THE STAR SPANGLED BANNER ACT"--REQUIRES CITIZENS OF APPARENT FOREIGN DESCENT TO RECITE THE PLEDGE OF ALLEGIANCE WHILE HOOKED UP TO A LIE DETECTOR!
THERE'S A SPIKE HERE AT "LIBERTY AND JUSTICE FOR ALL"!
A TALIBAN LOVER, EH?
BUT--BUT--
"THE RED-BLOODED AMERICAN ACT"--STIMULATES ECONOMY BY REQUIRING ALL CITIZENS TO MAINTAIN A CREDIT CARD BALANCE EQUAL TO HALF THEIR YEARLY INCOME!
YOU'RE A LITTLE UNDER QUOTA THIS MONTH, MR. JENKINS.
ER--I WAS JUST GOING OUT TO BUY A BIG-SCREEN TV! HONEST!
"THE LAND OF THE FREE ACT"--REQUIRES CITIZENS TO SPEAK FAVORABLY OF THE PRESIDENT AND HIS POLICIES AT ALL TIMES!
LOOKS LIKE THE PUBLIC IS WITH ME ONE HUNDRED PERCENT!
OF COURSE THEY ARE, MR. PRESIDENT! IT'S NOT JUST A GOOD IDEA--IT'S THE LAW!
"THE MOTHERHOOD AND APPLE PIE ACT"--REQUIRES ALL POLITICAL COMMENTATORS TO CLEAR THEIR IDEAS WITH GOVERNMENT ADVISORS BEFORE PUBLICATION OR BROADCAST!
YOU SEE, I'VE DRAWN THE PRESIDENT AS SUPERMAN--TRIUMPHANTLY VANQUISHING THE ENEMIES OF OUR HOMELAND!
HIS EYES ARE TOO CLOSE TOGETHER--AND HE SHOULD HAVE MORE MUSCLES. REJECTED!
SEND BILL MAHER IN ON YOUR WAY OUT.
©2001 TOM TOMORROW FOR THE AMERICAN PROSPECT

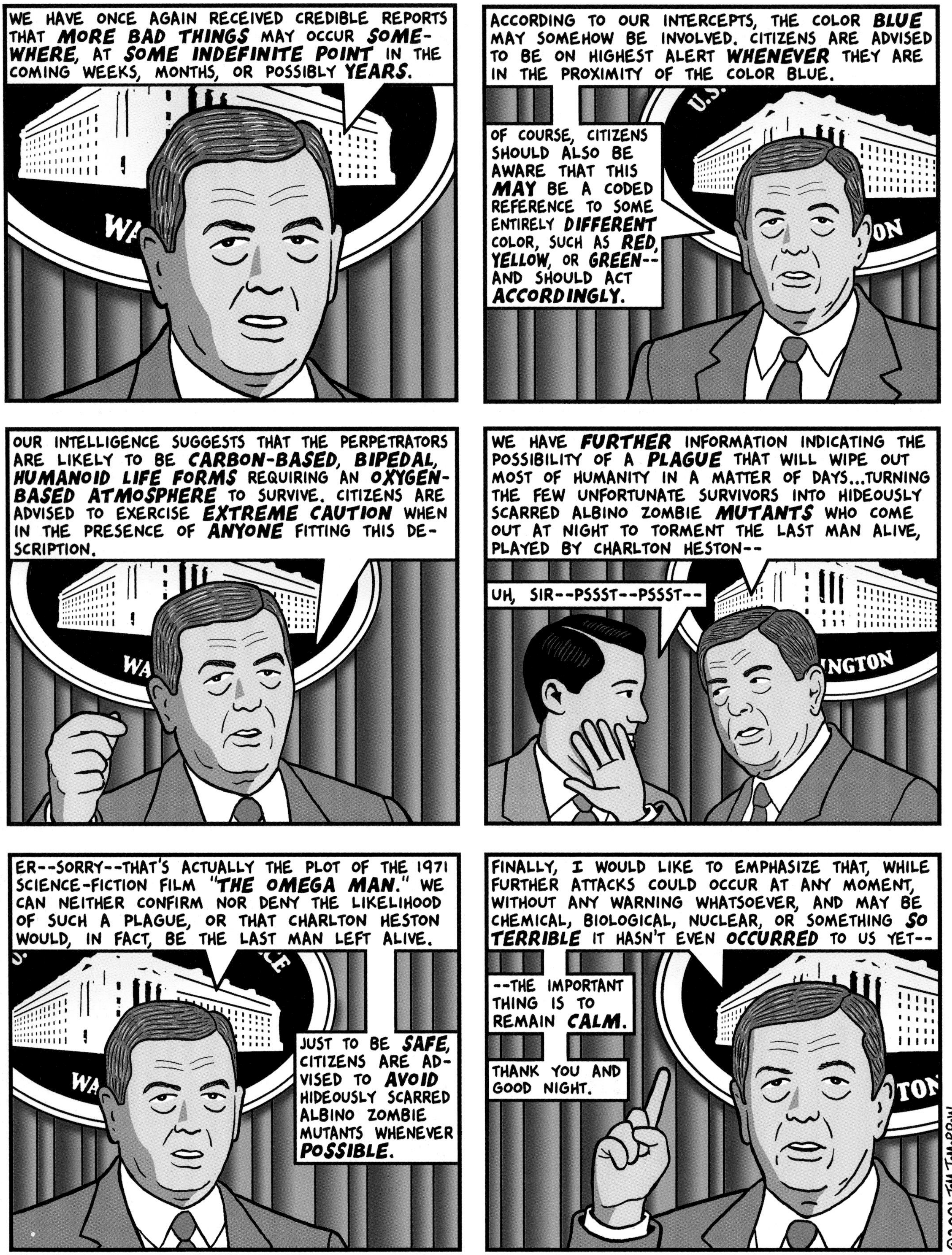
WE HAVE ONCE AGAIN RECEIVED CREDIBLE REPORTS THAT MORE BAD THINGS MAY OCCUR SOMEWHERE, AT SOME INDEFINITE POINT IN THE COMING WEEKS, MONTHS, OR POSSIBLY YEARS.
ACCORDING TO OUR INTERCEPTS, THE COLOR BLUE MAY SOMEHOW BE INVOLVED. CITIZENS ARE ADVISED TO BE ON HIGHEST ALERT WHENEVER THEY ARE IN THE PROXIMITY OF THE COLOR BLUE.
OF COURSE, CITIZENS SHOULD ALSO BE AWARE THAT THIS MAY BE A CODED REFERENCE TO SOME ENTIRELY DIFFERENT COLOR, SUCH AS RED, YELLOW, OR GREEN--AND SHOULD ACT ACCORDINGLY.
OUR INTELLIGENCE SUGGESTS THAT THE PERPETRATORS ARE LIKELY TO BE CARBON-BASED, BIPEDAL, HUMANOID LIFE FORMS REQUIRING AN OXYGEN-BASED ATMOSPHERE TO SURVIVE. CITIZENS ARE ADVISED TO EXERCISE EXTREME CAUTION WHEN IN THE PRESENCE OF ANYONE FITTING THIS DESCRIPTION.
WE HAVE FURTHER INFORMATION INDICATING THE POSSIBILITY OF A PLAGUE THAT WILL WIPE OUT MOST OF HUMANITY IN A MATTER OF DAYS...TURNING THE FEW UNFORTUNATE SURVIVORS INTO HIDEOUSLY SCARRED ALBINO ZOMBIE MUTANTS WHO COME OUT AT NIGHT TO TORMENT THE LAST MAN ALIVE, PLAYED BY CHARLTON HESTON--
UH, SIR--PSSST--PSSST--
ER--SORRY--THAT'S ACTUALLY THE PLOT OF THE 1971 SCIENCE-FICTION FILM "THE OMEGA MAN." WE CAN NEITHER CONFIRM NOR DENY THE LIKELIHOOD OF SUCH A PLAGUE, OR THAT CHARLTON HESTON WOULD, IN FACT, BE THE LAST MAN LEFT ALIVE.
JUST TO BE SAFE, CITIZENS ARE ADVISED TO AVOID HIDEOUSLY SCARRED ALBINO ZOMBIE MUTANTS WHENEVER POSSIBLE.
FINALLY, I WOULD LIKE TO EMPHASIZE THAT, WHILE FURTHER ATTACKS COULD OCCUR AT ANY MOMENT, WITHOUT ANY WARNING WHATSOEVER, AND MAY BE CHEMICAL, BIOLOGICAL, NUCLEAR, OR SOMETHING SO TERRIBLE IT HASN'T EVEN OCCURRED TO US YET--
--THE IMPORTANT THING IS TO REMAIN CALM.
THANK YOU AND GOOD NIGHT.
©2001 TOM TOMORROW

The New Yorker Back Page, November 2001.

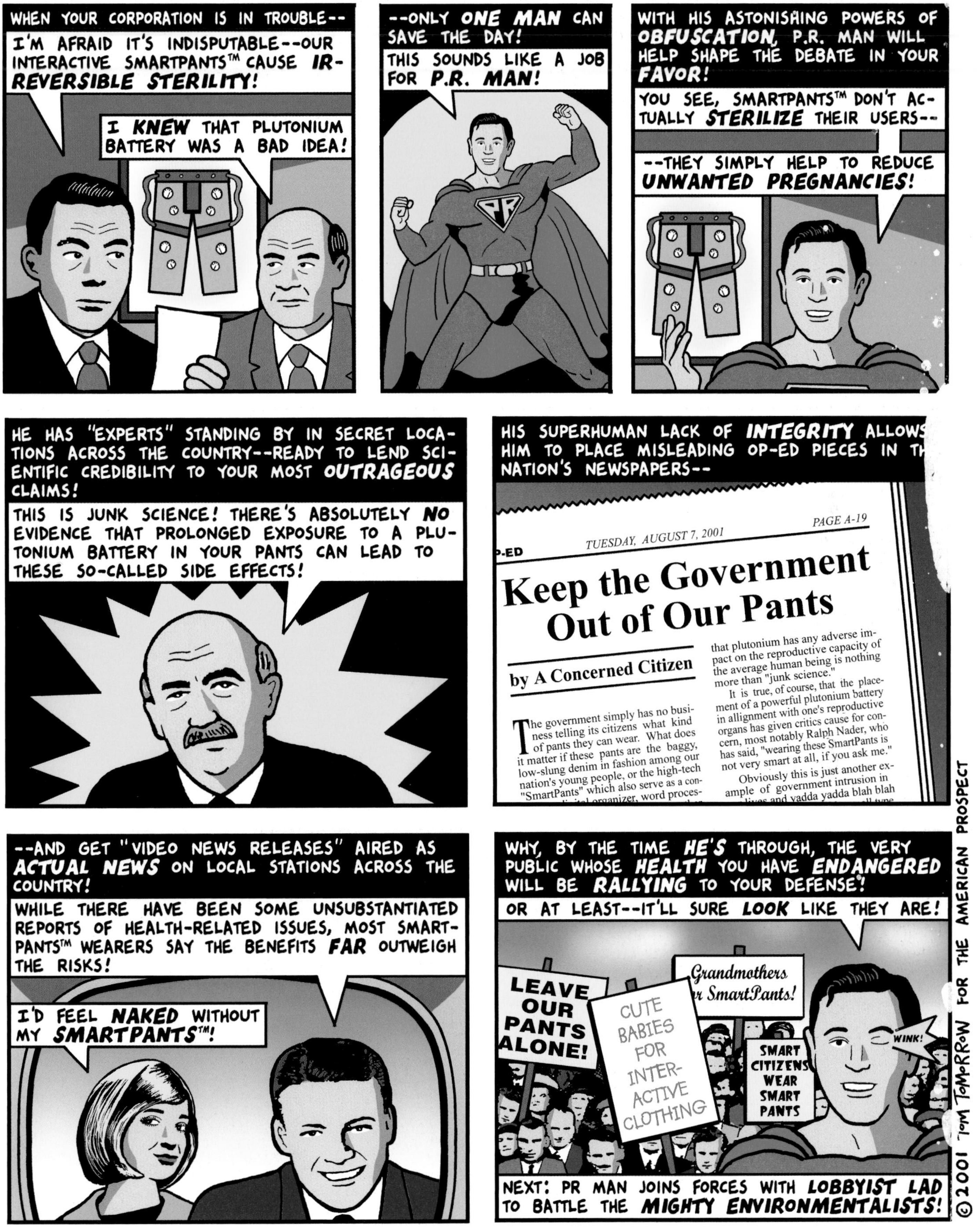
WHEN YOUR CORPORATION IS IN TROUBLE--
I'M AFRAID IT'S INDISPUTABLE--OUR INTERACTIVE SMARTPANTS™ CAUSE IRREVERSIBLE STERILITY!
I KNEW THAT PLUTONIUM BATTERY WAS A BAD IDEA!
--ONLY ONE MAN CAN SAVE THE DAY!
THIS SOUNDS LIKE A JOB FOR P.R. MAN!
PR
WITH HIS ASTONISHING POWERS OF OBFUSCATION, P.R. MAN WILL HELP SHAPE THE DEBATE IN YOUR FAVOR!
YOU SEE, SMARTPANTS™ DON'T ACTUALLY STERILIZE THEIR USERS--
--THEY SIMPLY HELP TO REDUCE UNWANTED PREGNANCIES!
HE HAS "EXPERTS" STANDING BY IN SECRET LOCATIONS ACROSS THE COUNTRY--READY TO LEND SCIENTIFIC CREDIBILITY TO YOUR MOST OUTRAGEOUS CLAIMS!
THIS IS JUNK SCIENCE! THERE'S ABSOLUTELY NO EVIDENCE THAT PROLONGED EXPOSURE TO A PLUTONIUM BATTERY IN YOUR PANTS CAN LEAD TO THESE SO-CALLED SIDE EFFECTS!
HIS SUPERHUMAN LACK OF INTEGRITY ALLOWS HIM TO PLACE MISLEADING OP-ED PIECES IN THE NATION'S NEWSPAPERS--
PAGE A-19
TUESDAY, AUGUST 7, 2001
-ED
Keep the Government Out of Our Pants
by A Concerned Citizen
The government simply has no business telling its citizens what kind of pants they can wear. What does it matter if these pants are the baggy, low-slung denim in fashion among our nation's young people, or the high-tech "SmartPants" which also serve as a con-
that plutonium has any adverse impact on the reproductive capacity of the average human being is nothing more than "junk science."
It is true, of course, that the placement of a powerful plutonium battery in allignment with one's reproductive organs has given critics cause for concern, most notably Ralph Nader, who has said, "wearing these SmartPants is not very smart at all, if you ask me."
Obviously this is just another example of government intrusion in
--AND GET "VIDEO NEWS RELEASES" AIRED AS ACTUAL NEWS ON LOCAL STATIONS ACROSS THE COUNTRY!
WHILE THERE HAVE BEEN SOME UNSUBSTANTIATED REPORTS OF HEALTH-RELATED ISSUES, MOST SMARTPANTS™ WEARERS SAY THE BENEFITS FAR OUTWEIGH THE RISKS!
I'D FEEL NAKED WITHOUT MY SMARTPANTS™!
WHY, BY THE TIME HE'S THROUGH, THE VERY PUBLIC WHOSE HEALTH YOU HAVE ENDANGERED WILL BE RALLYING TO YOUR DEFENSE!
OR AT LEAST--IT'LL SURE LOOK LIKE THEY ARE!
LEAVE OUR PANTS ALONE!
CUTE BABIES FOR INTER-ACTIVE CLOTHING
Grandmothers r SmartPants!
SMART CITIZENS WEAR SMART PANTS
WINK!
NEXT: PR MAN JOINS FORCES WITH LOBBYIST LAD TO BATTLE THE MIGHTY ENVIRONMENTALISTS!
© 2001 TOM TOMORROW FOR THE AMERICAN PROSPECT

The American Prospect, August 2001.

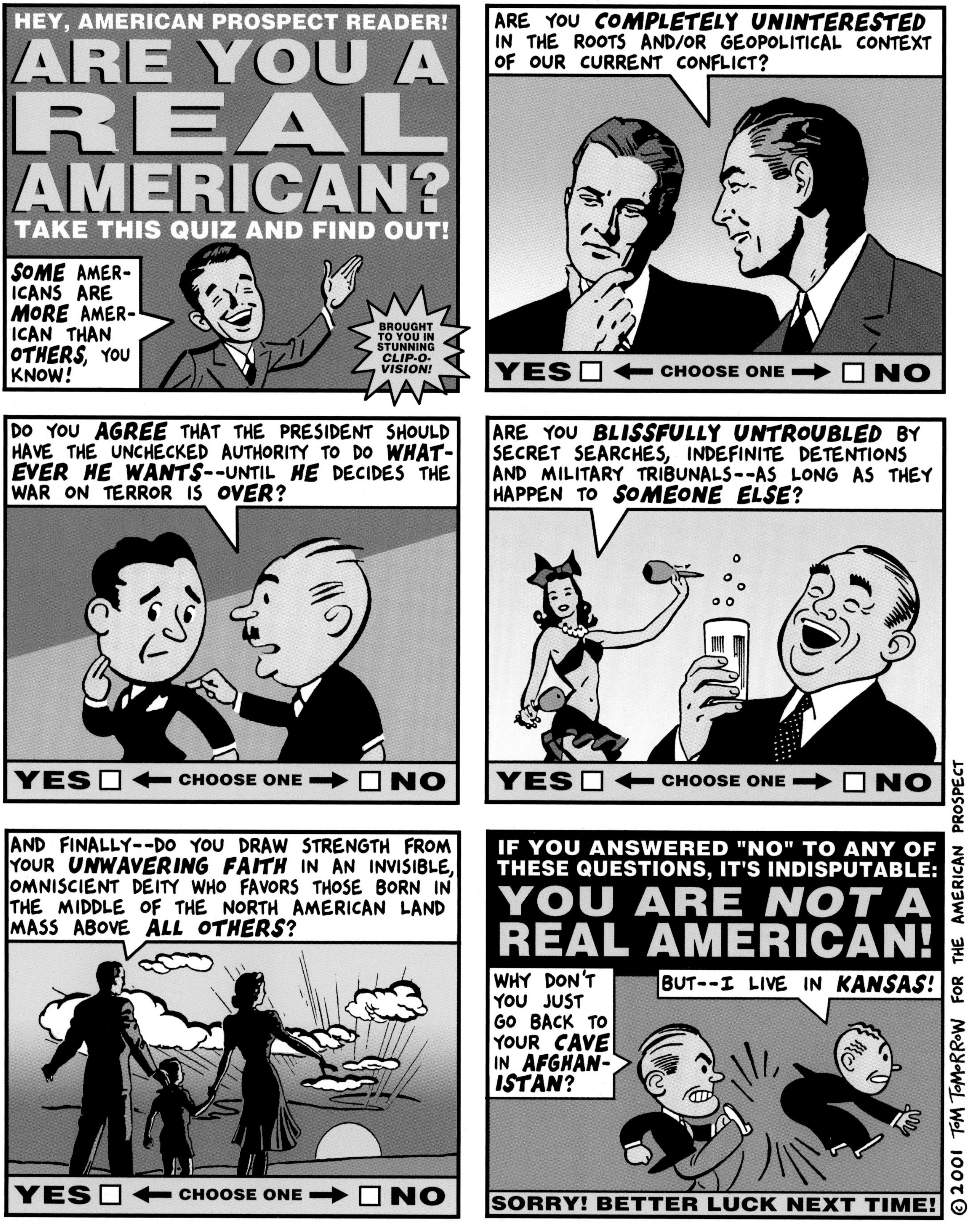
HEY, AMERICAN PROSPECT READER!
ARE YOU A REAL AMERICAN?
TAKE THIS QUIZ AND FIND OUT!
SOME AMERICANS ARE MORE AMERICAN THAN OTHERS, YOU KNOW!
BROUGHT TO YOU IN STUNNING CLIP-O-VISION!
ARE YOU COMPLETELY UNINTERESTED IN THE ROOTS AND/OR GEOPOLITICAL CONTEXT OF OUR CURRENT CONFLICT?
YES ☐ ← CHOOSE ONE → ☐ NO
DO YOU AGREE THAT THE PRESIDENT SHOULD HAVE THE UNCHECKED AUTHORITY TO DO WHATEVER HE WANTS--UNTIL HE DECIDES THE WAR ON TERROR IS OVER?
YES ☐ ← CHOOSE ONE → ☐ NO
ARE YOU BLISSFULLY UNTROUBLED BY SECRET SEARCHES, INDEFINITE DETENTIONS AND MILITARY TRIBUNALS--AS LONG AS THEY HAPPEN TO SOMEONE ELSE?
YES ☐ ← CHOOSE ONE → ☐ NO
AND FINALLY--DO YOU DRAW STRENGTH FROM YOUR UNWAVERING FAITH IN AN INVISIBLE, OMNISCIENT DEITY WHO FAVORS THOSE BORN IN THE MIDDLE OF THE NORTH AMERICAN LAND MASS ABOVE ALL OTHERS?
YES ☐ ← CHOOSE ONE → ☐ NO
IF YOU ANSWERED "NO" TO ANY OF THESE QUESTIONS, IT'S INDISPUTABLE:
YOU ARE NOT A REAL AMERICAN!
WHY DON'T YOU JUST GO BACK TO YOUR CAVE IN AFGHANISTAN?
BUT--I LIVE IN KANSAS!
SORRY! BETTER LUCK NEXT TIME!
©2001 TOM TOMORROW FOR THE AMERICAN PROSPECT

The American Prospect, January 2002.

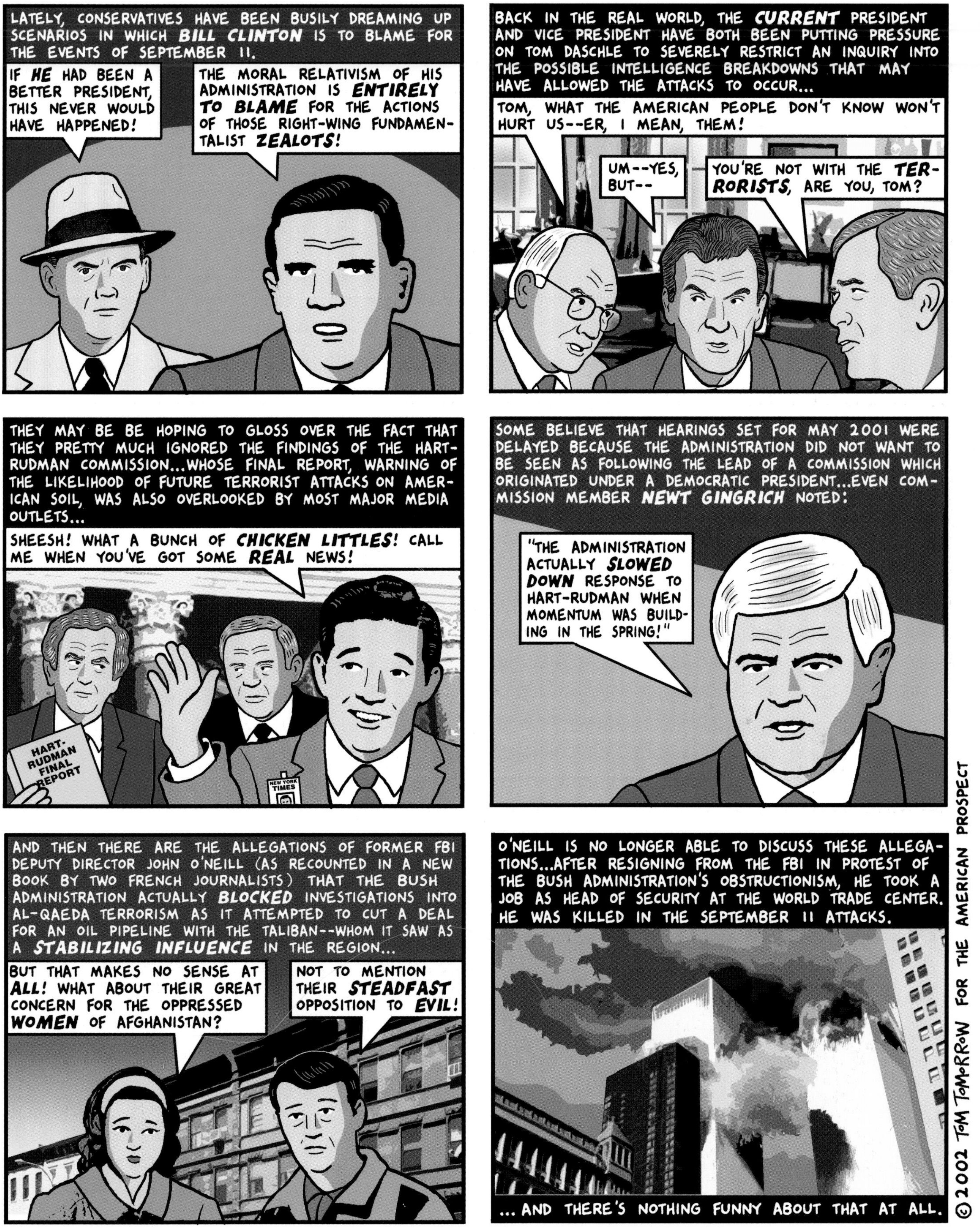
LATELY, CONSERVATIVES HAVE BEEN BUSILY DREAMING UP SCENARIOS IN WHICH BILL CLINTON IS TO BLAME FOR THE EVENTS OF SEPTEMBER 11.
IF HE HAD BEEN A BETTER PRESIDENT, THIS NEVER WOULD HAVE HAPPENED!
THE MORAL RELATIVISM OF HIS ADMINISTRATION IS ENTIRELY TO BLAME FOR THE ACTIONS OF THOSE RIGHT-WING FUNDAMENTALIST ZEALOTS!
BACK IN THE REAL WORLD, THE CURRENT PRESIDENT AND VICE PRESIDENT HAVE BOTH BEEN PUTTING PRESSURE ON TOM DASCHLE TO SEVERELY RESTRICT AN INQUIRY INTO THE POSSIBLE INTELLIGENCE BREAKDOWNS THAT MAY HAVE ALLOWED THE ATTACKS TO OCCUR...
TOM, WHAT THE AMERICAN PEOPLE DON'T KNOW WON'T HURT US--ER, I MEAN, THEM!
UM--YES, BUT--
YOU'RE NOT WITH THE TERRORISTS, ARE YOU, TOM?
THEY MAY BE BE HOPING TO GLOSS OVER THE FACT THAT THEY PRETTY MUCH IGNORED THE FINDINGS OF THE HART-RUDMAN COMMISSION...WHOSE FINAL REPORT, WARNING OF THE LIKELIHOOD OF FUTURE TERRORIST ATTACKS ON AMERICAN SOIL, WAS ALSO OVERLOOKED BY MOST MAJOR MEDIA OUTLETS...
SHEESH! WHAT A BUNCH OF CHICKEN LITTLES! CALL ME WHEN YOU'VE GOT SOME REAL NEWS!
HART-RUDMAN FINAL REPORT
NEW YORK TIMES
SOME BELIEVE THAT HEARINGS SET FOR MAY 2001 WERE DELAYED BECAUSE THE ADMINISTRATION DID NOT WANT TO BE SEEN AS FOLLOWING THE LEAD OF A COMMISSION WHICH ORIGINATED UNDER A DEMOCRATIC PRESIDENT...EVEN COMMISSION MEMBER NEWT GINGRICH NOTED:
"THE ADMINISTRATION ACTUALLY SLOWED DOWN RESPONSE TO HART-RUDMAN WHEN MOMENTUM WAS BUILDING IN THE SPRING!"
AND THEN THERE ARE THE ALLEGATIONS OF FORMER FBI DEPUTY DIRECTOR JOHN O'NEILL (AS RECOUNTED IN A NEW BOOK BY TWO FRENCH JOURNALISTS) THAT THE BUSH ADMINISTRATION ACTUALLY BLOCKED INVESTIGATIONS INTO AL-QAEDA TERRORISM AS IT ATTEMPTED TO CUT A DEAL FOR AN OIL PIPELINE WITH THE TALIBAN--WHOM IT SAW AS A STABILIZING INFLUENCE IN THE REGION...
BUT THAT MAKES NO SENSE AT ALL! WHAT ABOUT THEIR GREAT CONCERN FOR THE OPPRESSED WOMEN OF AFGHANISTAN?
NOT TO MENTION THEIR STEADFAST OPPOSITION TO EVIL!
O'NEILL IS NO LONGER ABLE TO DISCUSS THESE ALLEGATIONS...AFTER RESIGNING FROM THE FBI IN PROTEST OF THE BUSH ADMINISTRATION'S OBSTRUCTIONISM, HE TOOK A JOB AS HEAD OF SECURITY AT THE WORLD TRADE CENTER. HE WAS KILLED IN THE SEPTEMBER 11 ATTACKS.
...AND THERE'S NOTHING FUNNY ABOUT THAT AT ALL.
© 2002 TOM TOMORROW FOR THE AMERICAN PROSPECT

The American Prospect, March 2002.

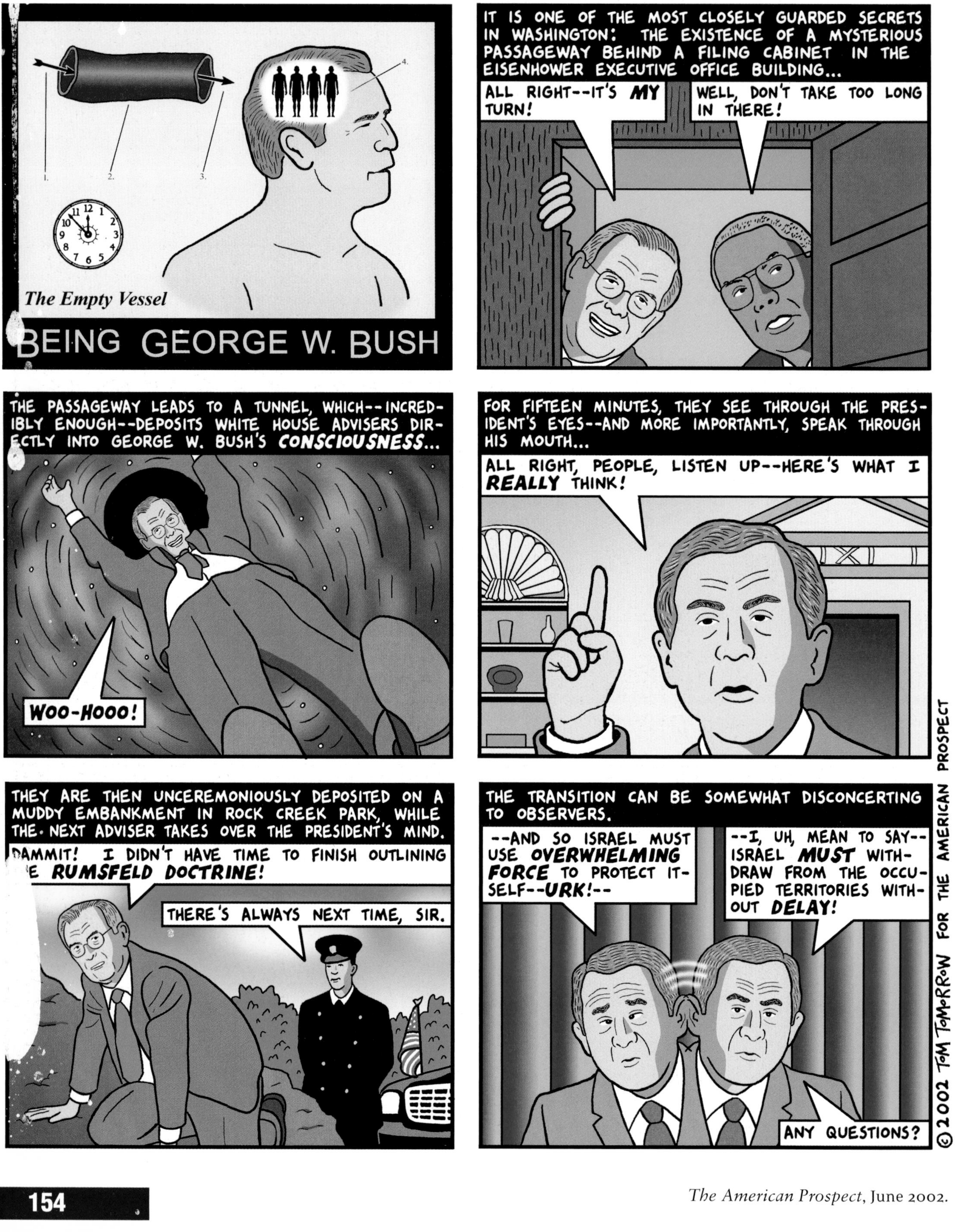
1.
2.
3.
4.
The Empty Vessel
BEING GEORGE W. BUSH
IT IS ONE OF THE MOST CLOSELY GUARDED SECRETS IN WASHINGTON: THE EXISTENCE OF A MYSTERIOUS PASSAGEWAY BEHIND A FILING CABINET IN THE EISENHOWER EXECUTIVE OFFICE BUILDING...
ALL RIGHT--IT'S MY TURN!
WELL, DON'T TAKE TOO LONG IN THERE!
THE PASSAGEWAY LEADS TO A TUNNEL, WHICH--INCREDIBLY ENOUGH--DEPOSITS WHITE HOUSE ADVISERS DIR-ECTLY INTO GEORGE W. BUSH'S CONSCIOUSNESS...
WOO-HOOO!
FOR FIFTEEN MINUTES, THEY SEE THROUGH THE PRESIDENT'S EYES--AND MORE IMPORTANTLY, SPEAK THROUGH HIS MOUTH...
ALL RIGHT, PEOPLE, LISTEN UP--HERE'S WHAT I REALLY THINK!
THEY ARE THEN UNCEREMONIOUSLY DEPOSITED ON A MUDDY EMBANKMENT IN ROCK CREEK PARK, WHILE THE NEXT ADVISER TAKES OVER THE PRESIDENT'S MIND.
DAMMIT! I DIDN'T HAVE TIME TO FINISH OUTLINING E RUMSFELD DOCTRINE!
THERE'S ALWAYS NEXT TIME, SIR.
THE TRANSITION CAN BE SOMEWHAT DISCONCERTING TO OBSERVERS.
--AND SO ISRAEL MUST USE OVERWHELMING FORCE TO PROTECT ITSELF--URK!--
--I, UH, MEAN TO SAY--ISRAEL MUST WITHDRAW FROM THE OCCUPIED TERRITORIES WITHOUT DELAY!
ANY QUESTIONS?
©2002 TOM TOMORROW FOR THE AMERICAN PROSPECT

The American Prospect, June 2002.

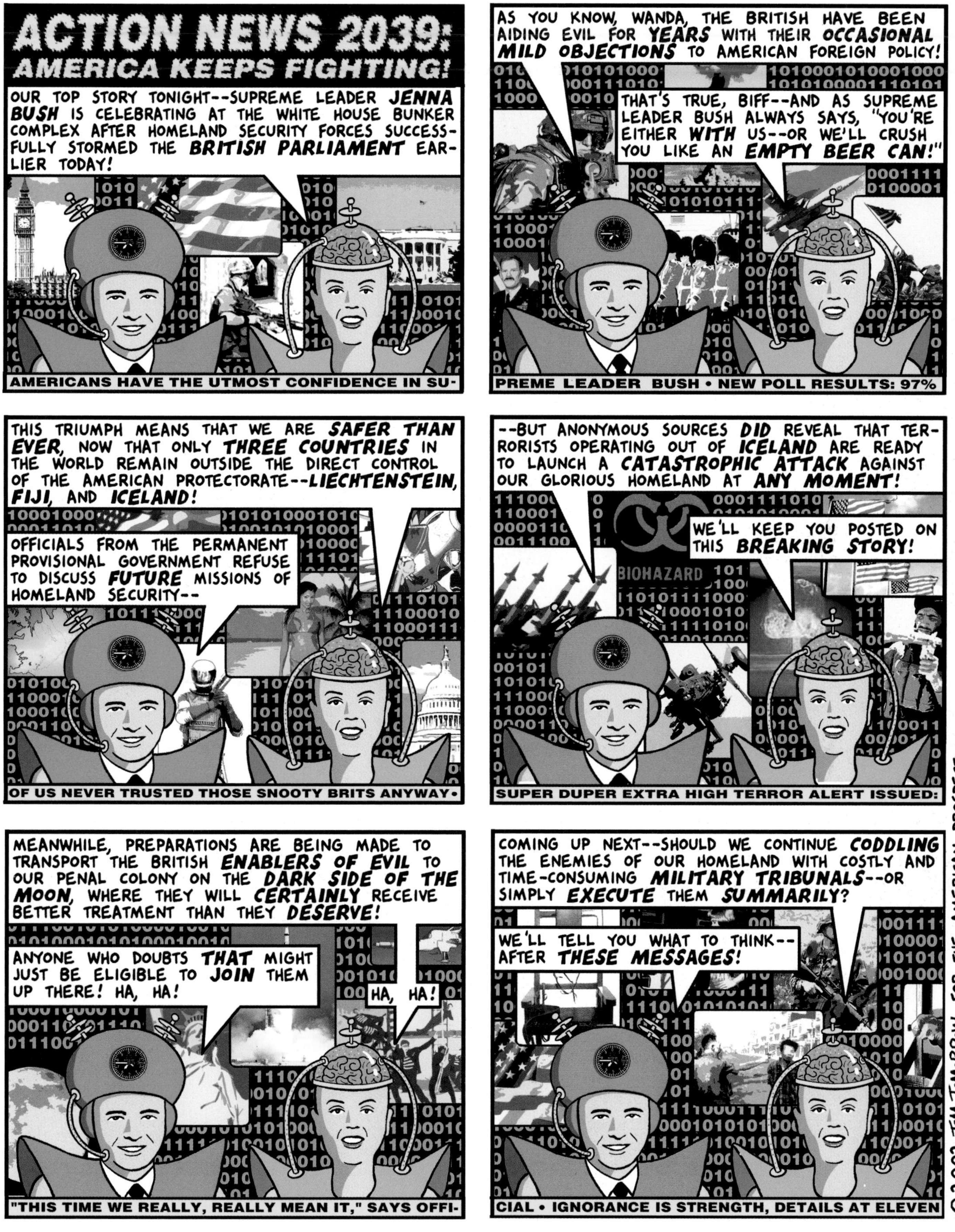
ACTION NEWS 2039: AMERICA KEEPS FIGHTING!
OUR TOP STORY TONIGHT--SUPREME LEADER JENNA BUSH IS CELEBRATING AT THE WHITE HOUSE BUNKER COMPLEX AFTER HOMELAND SECURITY FORCES SUCCESSFULLY STORMED THE BRITISH PARLIAMENT EARLIER TODAY!
AMERICANS HAVE THE UTMOST CONFIDENCE IN SU-
AS YOU KNOW, WANDA, THE BRITISH HAVE BEEN AIDING EVIL FOR YEARS WITH THEIR OCCASIONAL MILD OBJECTIONS TO AMERICAN FOREIGN POLICY!
THAT'S TRUE, BIFF--AND AS SUPREME LEADER BUSH ALWAYS SAYS, "YOU'RE EITHER WITH US--OR WE'LL CRUSH YOU LIKE AN EMPTY BEER CAN!"
PREME LEADER BUSH • NEW POLL RESULTS: 97%
THIS TRIUMPH MEANS THAT WE ARE SAFER THAN EVER, NOW THAT ONLY THREE COUNTRIES IN THE WORLD REMAIN OUTSIDE THE DIRECT CONTROL OF THE AMERICAN PROTECTORATE--LIECHTENSTEIN, FIJI, AND ICELAND!
OFFICIALS FROM THE PERMANENT PROVISIONAL GOVERNMENT REFUSE TO DISCUSS FUTURE MISSIONS OF HOMELAND SECURITY--
OF US NEVER TRUSTED THOSE SNOOTY BRITS ANYWAY•
--BUT ANONYMOUS SOURCES DID REVEAL THAT TERRORISTS OPERATING OUT OF ICELAND ARE READY TO LAUNCH A CATASTROPHIC ATTACK AGAINST OUR GLORIOUS HOMELAND AT ANY MOMENT!
BIOHAZARD
WE'LL KEEP YOU POSTED ON THIS BREAKING STORY!
SUPER DUPER EXTRA HIGH TERROR ALERT ISSUED:
MEANWHILE, PREPARATIONS ARE BEING MADE TO TRANSPORT THE BRITISH ENABLERS OF EVIL TO OUR PENAL COLONY ON THE DARK SIDE OF THE MOON, WHERE THEY WILL CERTAINLY RECEIVE BETTER TREATMENT THAN THEY DESERVE!
ANYONE WHO DOUBTS THAT MIGHT JUST BE ELIGIBLE TO JOIN THEM UP THERE! HA, HA!
HA, HA!
"THIS TIME WE REALLY, REALLY MEAN IT," SAYS OFFI-
COMING UP NEXT--SHOULD WE CONTINUE CODDLING THE ENEMIES OF OUR HOMELAND WITH COSTLY AND TIME-CONSUMING MILITARY TRIBUNALS--OR SIMPLY EXECUTE THEM SUMMARILY?
WE'LL TELL YOU WHAT TO THINK--AFTER THESE MESSAGES!
CIAL • IGNORANCE IS STRENGTH, DETAILS AT ELEVEN
©2002 TOM TOMORROW FOR THE AMERICAN PROSPECT

The American Prospect, March 2002.

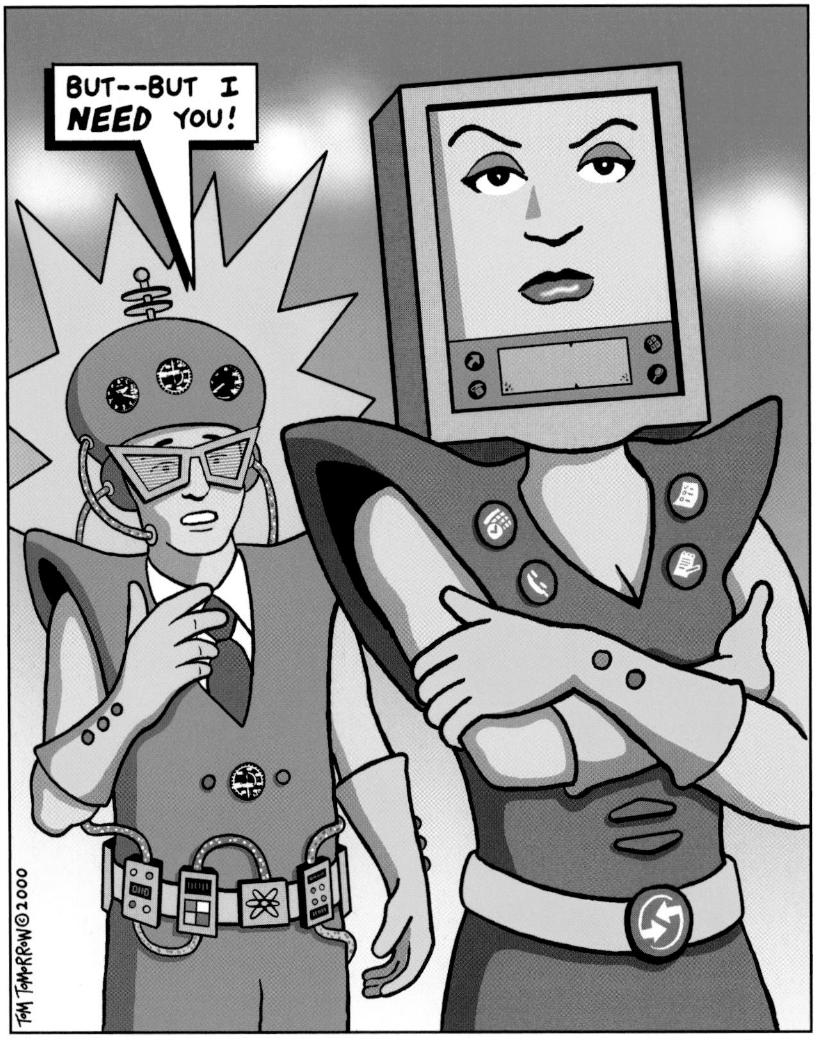
BUT--BUT I NEED YOU!
TOM TOMORROW©2000

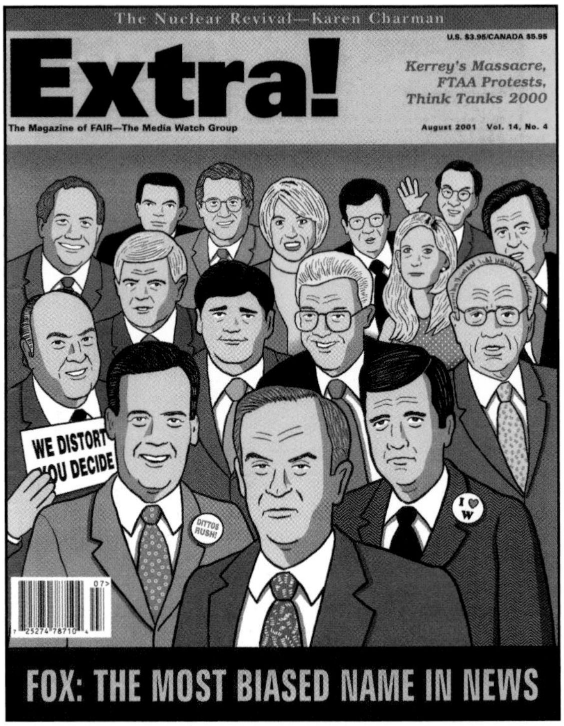
The Nuclear Revival—Karen Charman
U.S. $3.95/CANADA $5.95
Extra!
Kerrey's Massacre,
FTAA Protests,
Think Tanks 2000
The Magazine of FAIR—The Media Watch Group
August 2001 Vol. 14, No. 4
WE DISTORT YOU DECIDE
DITTOS RUSH!
FOX: THE MOST BIASED NAME IN NEWS

Clockwise from top left: illustration for *Yahoo Internet Life*, 2001; *Extra!* cover, 2002; illustration for *The Village Voice* (concerning a rumored Warren Beatty presidential candidacy), 1999; the author with close personal friend Oliver North.

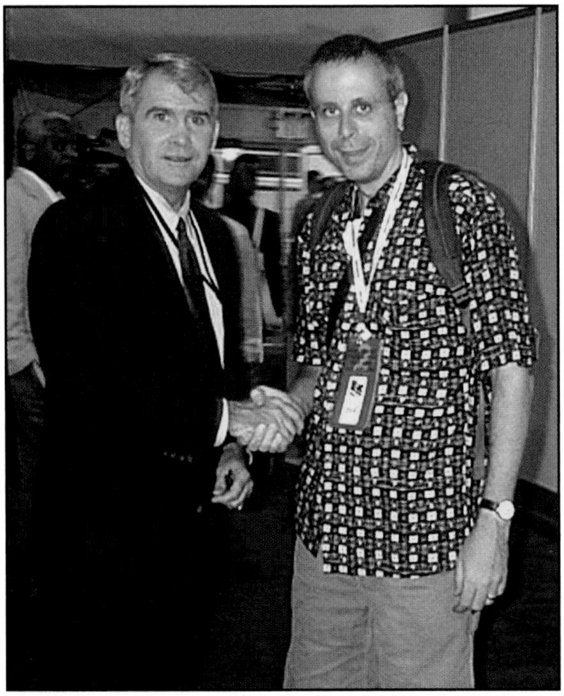

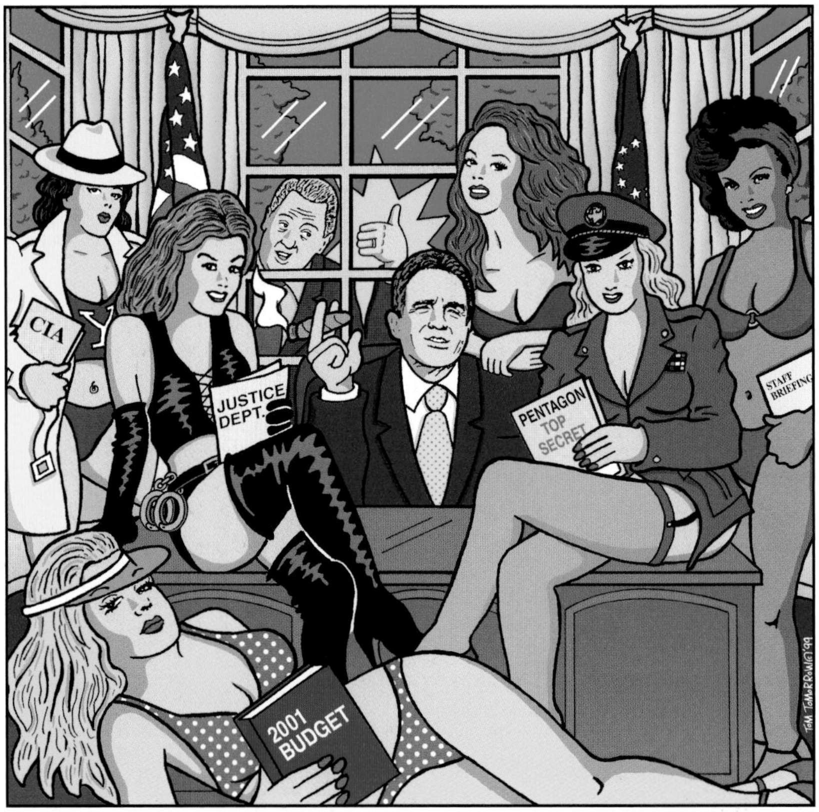
CIA
JUSTICE DEPT.
PENTAGON TOP SECRET
STAFF BRIEFING
2001 BUDGET
TOM TOMORROW©99

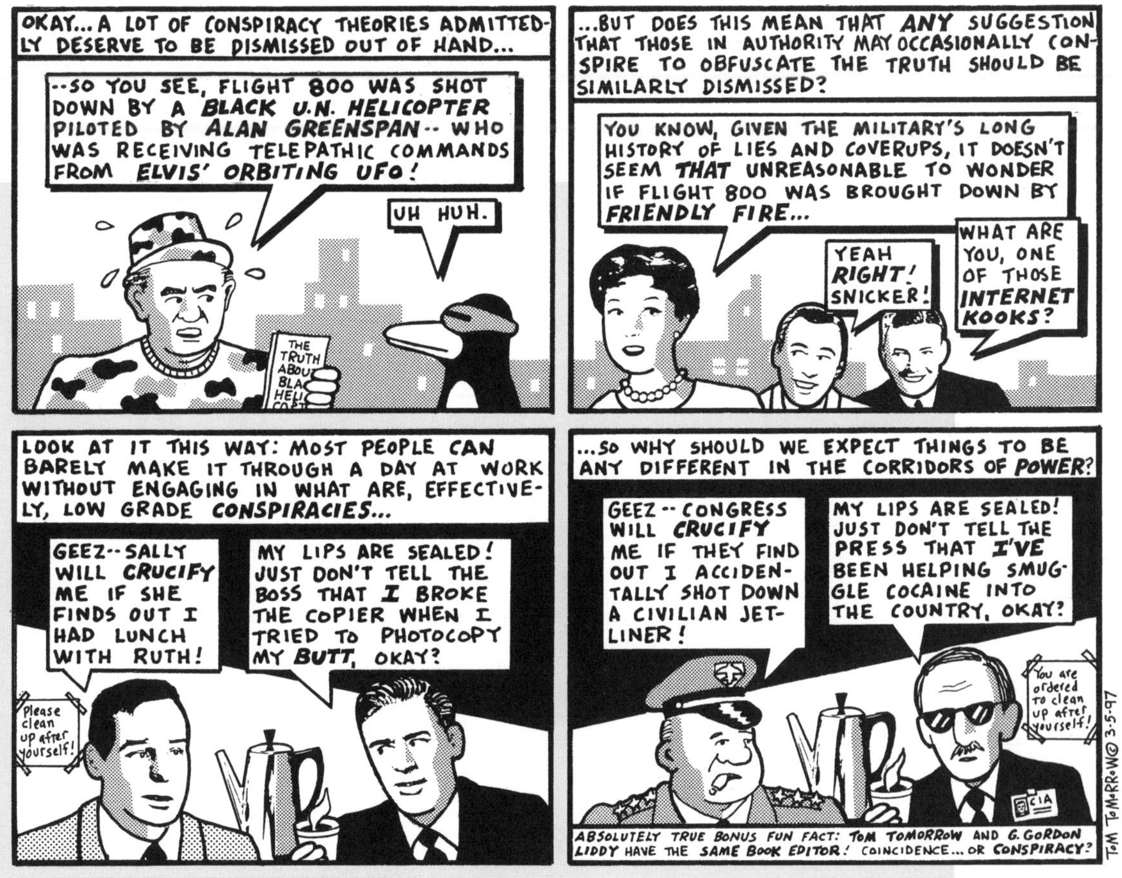
OKAY... A LOT OF CONSPIRACY THEORIES ADMITTEDLY DESERVE TO BE DISMISSED OUT OF HAND...
--SO YOU SEE, FLIGHT 800 WAS SHOT DOWN BY A BLACK U.N. HELICOPTER PILOTED BY ALAN GREENSPAN-- WHO WAS RECEIVING TELEPATHIC COMMANDS FROM ELVIS' ORBITING UFO!
UH HUH.
...BUT DOES THIS MEAN THAT ANY SUGGESTION THAT THOSE IN AUTHORITY MAY OCCASIONALLY CONSPIRE TO OBFUSCATE THE TRUTH SHOULD BE SIMILARLY DISMISSED?
YOU KNOW, GIVEN THE MILITARY'S LONG HISTORY OF LIES AND COVERUPS, IT DOESN'T SEEM THAT UNREASONABLE TO WONDER IF FLIGHT 800 WAS BROUGHT DOWN BY FRIENDLY FIRE...
YEAH RIGHT! SNICKER!
WHAT ARE YOU, ONE OF THOSE INTERNET KOOKS?
LOOK AT IT THIS WAY: MOST PEOPLE CAN BARELY MAKE IT THROUGH A DAY AT WORK WITHOUT ENGAGING IN WHAT ARE, EFFECTIVELY, LOW GRADE CONSPIRACIES...
GEEZ--SALLY WILL CRUCIFY ME IF SHE FINDS OUT I HAD LUNCH WITH RUTH!
MY LIPS ARE SEALED! JUST DON'T TELL THE BOSS THAT I BROKE THE COPIER WHEN I TRIED TO PHOTOCOPY MY BUTT, OKAY?
Please clean up after yourself!
...SO WHY SHOULD WE EXPECT THINGS TO BE ANY DIFFERENT IN THE CORRIDORS OF POWER?
GEEZ--CONGRESS WILL CRUCIFY ME IF THEY FIND OUT I ACCIDENTALLY SHOT DOWN A CIVILIAN JETLINER!
MY LIPS ARE SEALED! JUST DON'T TELL THE PRESS THAT I'VE BEEN HELPING SMUGGLE COCAINE INTO THE COUNTRY, OKAY?
You are ordered to clean up after yourself!
CIA
ABSOLUTELY TRUE BONUS FUN FACT: TOM TOMORROW AND G. GORDON LIDDY HAVE THE SAME BOOK EDITOR! COINCIDENCE... OR CONSPIRACY?
TOM TOMORROW © 3-5-97

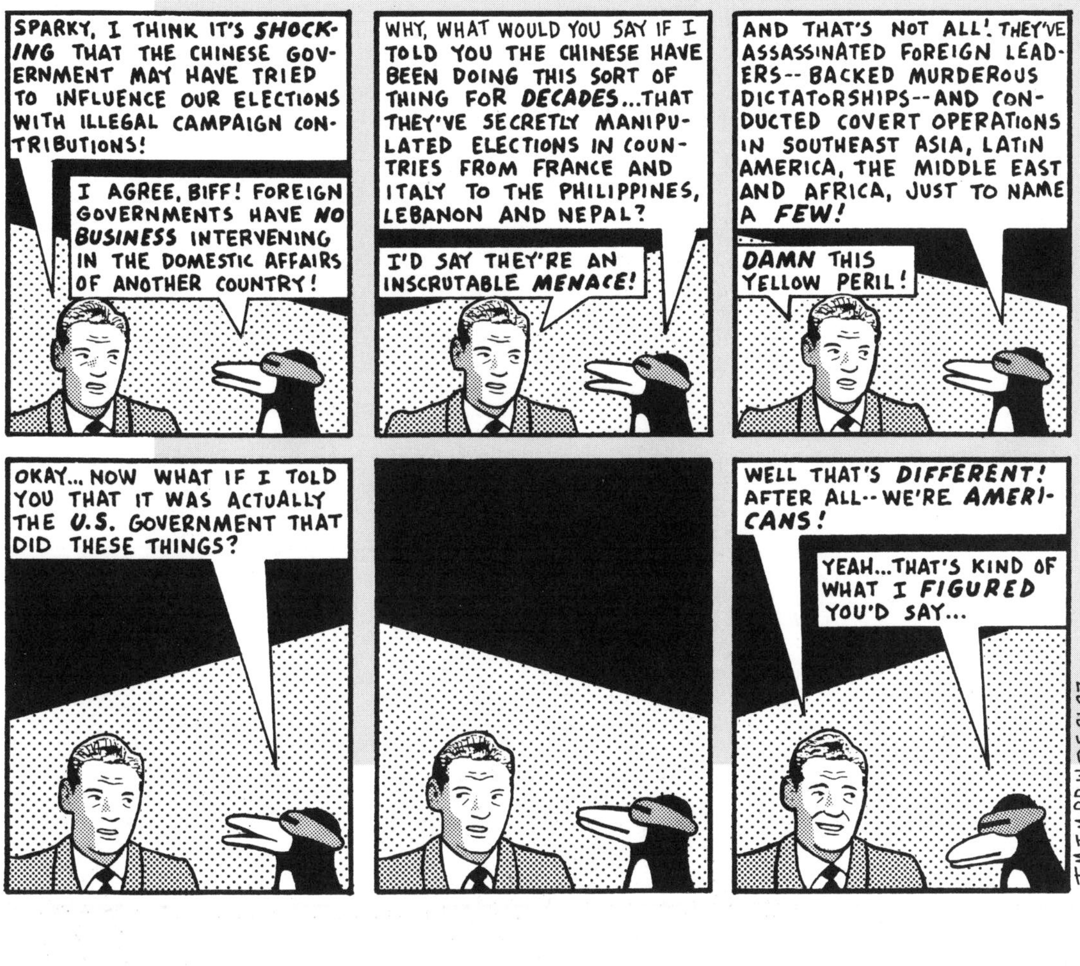
SPARKY, I THINK IT'S SHOCKING THAT THE CHINESE GOVERNMENT MAY HAVE TRIED TO INFLUENCE OUR ELECTIONS WITH ILLEGAL CAMPAIGN CONTRIBUTIONS!
I AGREE, BIFF! FOREIGN GOVERNMENTS HAVE NO BUSINESS INTERVENING IN THE DOMESTIC AFFAIRS OF ANOTHER COUNTRY!
WHY, WHAT WOULD YOU SAY IF I TOLD YOU THE CHINESE HAVE BEEN DOING THIS SORT OF THING FOR DECADES...THAT THEY'VE SECRETLY MANIPULATED ELECTIONS IN COUNTRIES FROM FRANCE AND ITALY TO THE PHILIPPINES, LEBANON AND NEPAL?
I'D SAY THEY'RE AN INSCRUTABLE MENACE!
AND THAT'S NOT ALL! THEY'VE ASSASSINATED FOREIGN LEADERS-- BACKED MURDEROUS DICTATORSHIPS--AND CONDUCTED COVERT OPERATIONS IN SOUTHEAST ASIA, LATIN AMERICA, THE MIDDLE EAST AND AFRICA, JUST TO NAME A FEW!
DAMN THIS YELLOW PERIL!
OKAY... NOW WHAT IF I TOLD YOU THAT IT WAS ACTUALLY THE U.S. GOVERNMENT THAT DID THESE THINGS?
TOM TOMORROW © 5-21-97
WELL THAT'S DIFFERENT! AFTER ALL--WE'RE AMERICANS!
YEAH...THAT'S KIND OF WHAT I FIGURED YOU'D SAY...

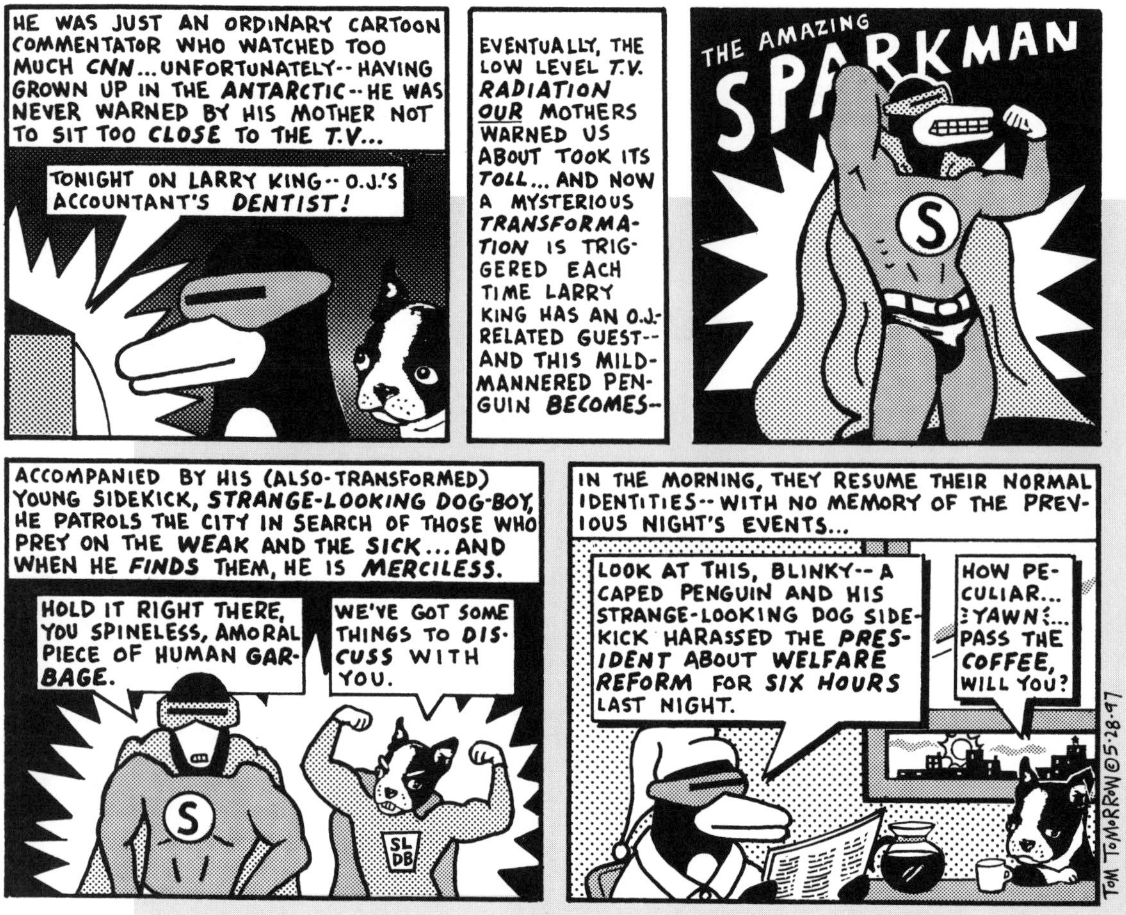
HE WAS JUST AN ORDINARY CARTOON COMMENTATOR WHO WATCHED TOO MUCH CNN... UNFORTUNATELY-- HAVING GROWN UP IN THE ANTARCTIC-- HE WAS NEVER WARNED BY HIS MOTHER NOT TO SIT TOO CLOSE TO THE T.V...
TONIGHT ON LARRY KING-- O.J.'S ACCOUNTANT'S DENTIST!
EVENTUALLY, THE LOW LEVEL T.V. RADIATION OUR MOTHERS WARNED US ABOUT TOOK ITS TOLL... AND NOW A MYSTERIOUS TRANSFORMATION IS TRIGGERED EACH TIME LARRY KING HAS AN O.J.-RELATED GUEST-- AND THIS MILD-MANNERED PENGUIN BECOMES--
THE AMAZING SPARKMAN
S
ACCOMPANIED BY HIS (ALSO-TRANSFORMED) YOUNG SIDEKICK, STRANGE-LOOKING DOG-BOY, HE PATROLS THE CITY IN SEARCH OF THOSE WHO PREY ON THE WEAK AND THE SICK... AND WHEN HE FINDS THEM, HE IS MERCILESS.
HOLD IT RIGHT THERE, YOU SPINELESS, AMORAL PIECE OF HUMAN GARBAGE.
WE'VE GOT SOME THINGS TO DISCUSS WITH YOU.
S
SL DB
IN THE MORNING, THEY RESUME THEIR NORMAL IDENTITIES-- WITH NO MEMORY OF THE PREVIOUS NIGHT'S EVENTS...
LOOK AT THIS, BLINKY-- A CAPED PENGUIN AND HIS STRANGE-LOOKING DOG SIDEKICK HARASSED THE PRESIDENT ABOUT WELFARE REFORM FOR SIX HOURS LAST NIGHT.
HOW PECULIAR... ;YAWN;... PASS THE COFFEE, WILL YOU?
TOM TOMORROW ©5·28·97

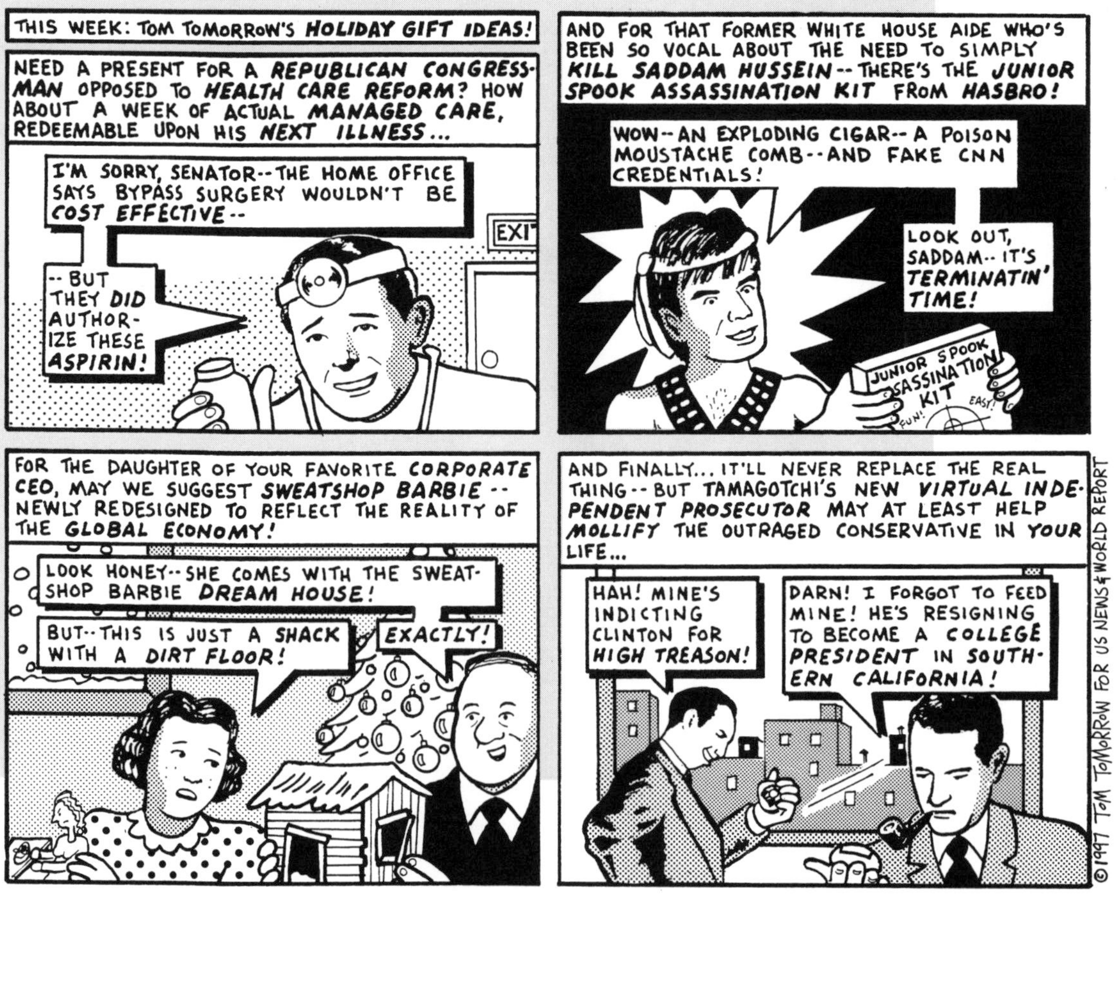
THIS WEEK: TOM TOMORROW'S HOLIDAY GIFT IDEAS!
NEED A PRESENT FOR A REPUBLICAN CONGRESSMAN OPPOSED TO HEALTH CARE REFORM? HOW ABOUT A WEEK OF ACTUAL MANAGED CARE, REDEEMABLE UPON HIS NEXT ILLNESS...
I'M SORRY, SENATOR-- THE HOME OFFICE SAYS BYPASS SURGERY WOULDN'T BE COST EFFECTIVE--
-- BUT THEY DID AUTHORIZE THESE ASPIRIN!
EXIT
AND FOR THAT FORMER WHITE HOUSE AIDE WHO'S BEEN SO VOCAL ABOUT THE NEED TO SIMPLY KILL SADDAM HUSSEIN-- THERE'S THE JUNIOR SPOOK ASSASSINATION KIT FROM HASBRO!
WOW-- AN EXPLODING CIGAR-- A POISON MOUSTACHE COMB-- AND FAKE CNN CREDENTIALS!
LOOK OUT, SADDAM-- IT'S TERMINATIN' TIME!
JUNIOR SPOOK ASSASSINATION KIT
FUN! EASY!
FOR THE DAUGHTER OF YOUR FAVORITE CORPORATE CEO, MAY WE SUGGEST SWEATSHOP BARBIE -- NEWLY REDESIGNED TO REFLECT THE REALITY OF THE GLOBAL ECONOMY!
LOOK HONEY-- SHE COMES WITH THE SWEATSHOP BARBIE DREAM HOUSE!
BUT-- THIS IS JUST A SHACK WITH A DIRT FLOOR!
EXACTLY!
AND FINALLY... IT'LL NEVER REPLACE THE REAL THING-- BUT TAMAGOTCHI'S NEW VIRTUAL INDEPENDENT PROSECUTOR MAY AT LEAST HELP MOLLIFY THE OUTRAGED CONSERVATIVE IN YOUR LIFE...
HAH! MINE'S INDICTING CLINTON FOR HIGH TREASON!
DARN! I FORGOT TO FEED MINE! HE'S RESIGNING TO BECOME A COLLEGE PRESIDENT IN SOUTHERN CALIFORNIA!
©1997 TOM TOMORROW FOR US NEWS & WORLD REPORT

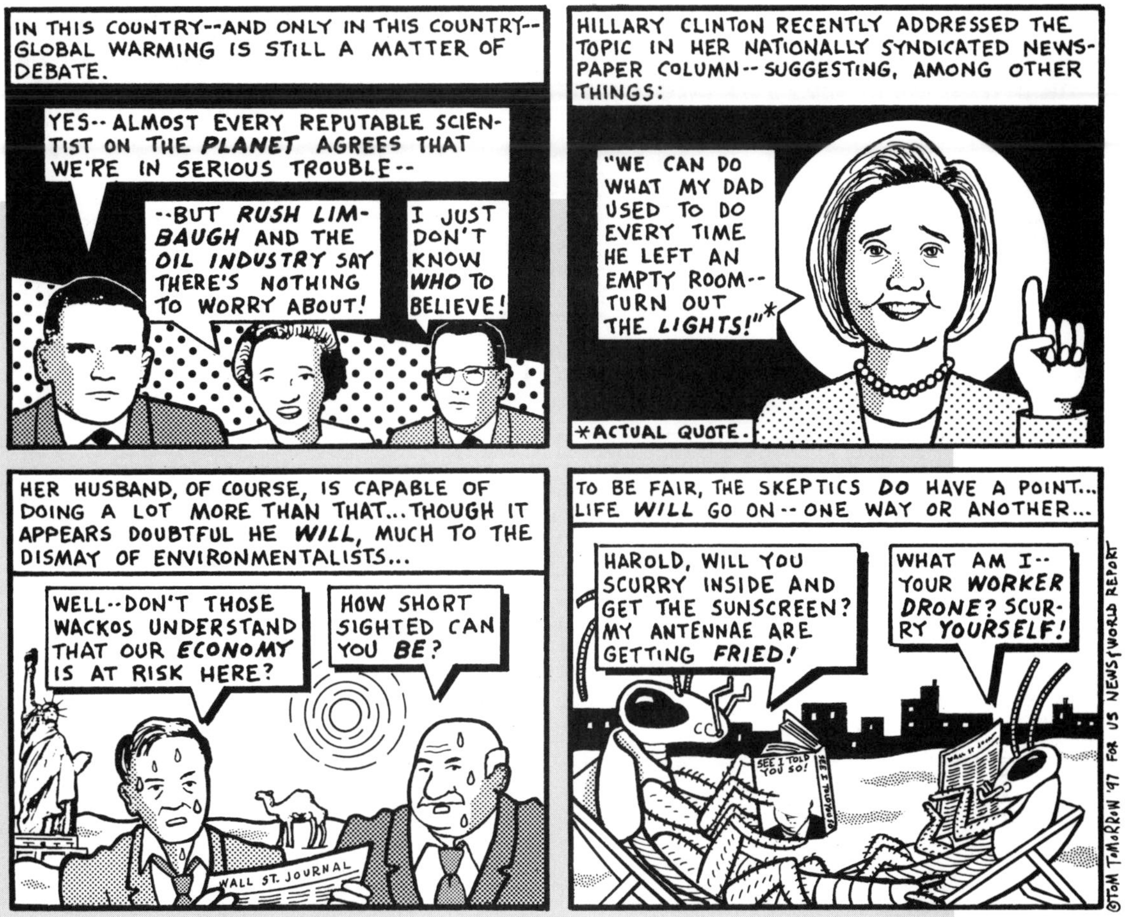
IN THIS COUNTRY--AND ONLY IN THIS COUNTRY--GLOBAL WARMING IS STILL A MATTER OF DEBATE.
YES--ALMOST EVERY REPUTABLE SCIENTIST ON THE PLANET AGREES THAT WE'RE IN SERIOUS TROUBLE--
--BUT RUSH LIMBAUGH AND THE OIL INDUSTRY SAY THERE'S NOTHING TO WORRY ABOUT!
I JUST DON'T KNOW WHO TO BELIEVE!
HILLARY CLINTON RECENTLY ADDRESSED THE TOPIC IN HER NATIONALLY SYNDICATED NEWSPAPER COLUMN--SUGGESTING, AMONG OTHER THINGS:
"WE CAN DO WHAT MY DAD USED TO DO EVERY TIME HE LEFT AN EMPTY ROOM--TURN OUT THE LIGHTS!"*
*ACTUAL QUOTE.
HER HUSBAND, OF COURSE, IS CAPABLE OF DOING A LOT MORE THAN THAT... THOUGH IT APPEARS DOUBTFUL HE WILL, MUCH TO THE DISMAY OF ENVIRONMENTALISTS...
WELL--DON'T THOSE WACKOS UNDERSTAND THAT OUR ECONOMY IS AT RISK HERE?
HOW SHORT SIGHTED CAN YOU BE?
WALL ST. JOURNAL
TO BE FAIR, THE SKEPTICS DO HAVE A POINT... LIFE WILL GO ON--ONE WAY OR ANOTHER...
HAROLD, WILL YOU SCURRY INSIDE AND GET THE SUNSCREEN? MY ANTENNAE ARE GETTING FRIED!
WHAT AM I--YOUR WORKER DRONE? SCURRY YOURSELF!
SEE I TOLD YOU SO!
©TOM TOMORROW '97 FOR US NEWS & WORLD REPORT

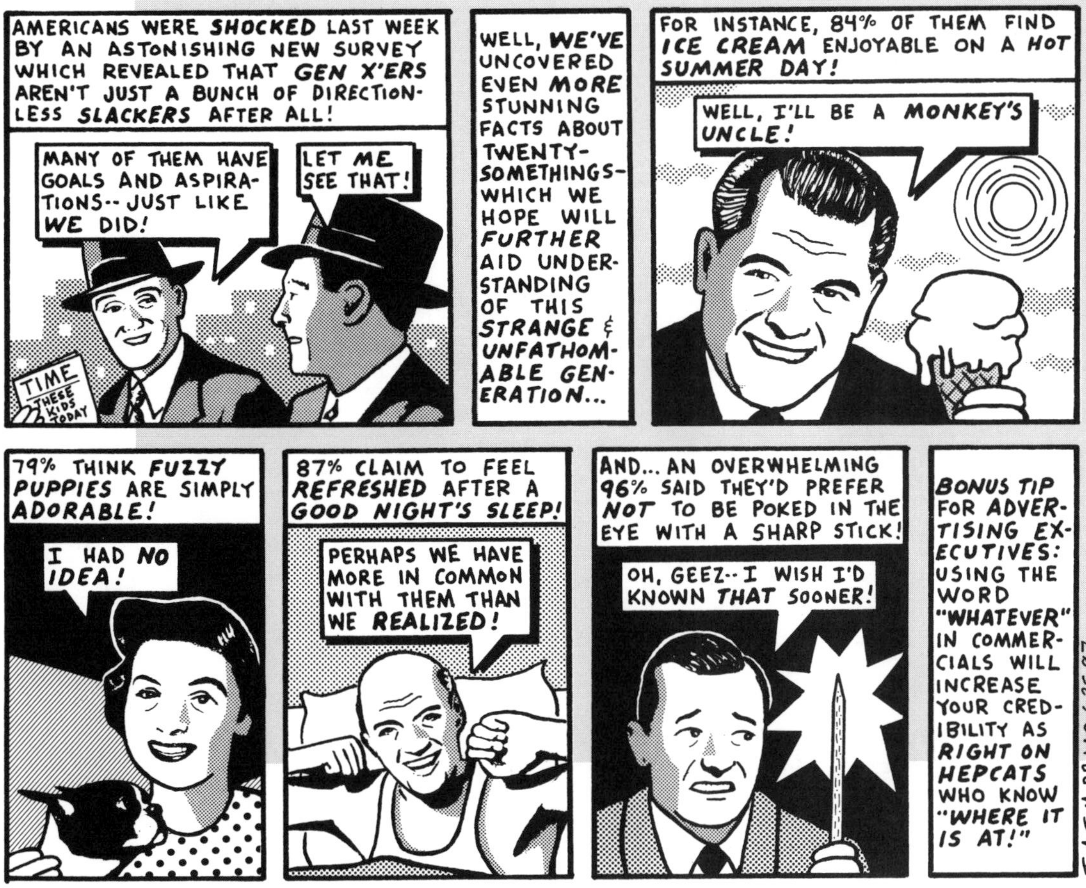
AMERICANS WERE SHOCKED LAST WEEK BY AN ASTONISHING NEW SURVEY WHICH REVEALED THAT GEN X'ERS AREN'T JUST A BUNCH OF DIRECTIONLESS SLACKERS AFTER ALL!
MANY OF THEM HAVE GOALS AND ASPIRATIONS--JUST LIKE WE DID!
LET ME SEE THAT!
TIME THESE KIDS TODAY
WELL, WE'VE UNCOVERED EVEN MORE STUNNING FACTS ABOUT TWENTY-SOMETHINGS-WHICH WE HOPE WILL FURTHER AID UNDERSTANDING OF THIS STRANGE & UNFATHOMABLE GENERATION...
FOR INSTANCE, 84% OF THEM FIND ICE CREAM ENJOYABLE ON A HOT SUMMER DAY!
WELL, I'LL BE A MONKEY'S UNCLE!
79% THINK FUZZY PUPPIES ARE SIMPLY ADORABLE!
I HAD NO IDEA!
87% CLAIM TO FEEL REFRESHED AFTER A GOOD NIGHT'S SLEEP!
PERHAPS WE HAVE MORE IN COMMON WITH THEM THAN WE REALIZED!
AND... AN OVERWHELMING 96% SAID THEY'D PREFER NOT TO BE POKED IN THE EYE WITH A SHARP STICK!
OH, GEEZ--I WISH I'D KNOWN THAT SOONER!
BONUS TIP FOR ADVERTISING EXECUTIVES: USING THE WORD "WHATEVER" IN COMMERCIALS WILL INCREASE YOUR CREDIBILITY AS RIGHT ON HEPCATS WHO KNOW "WHERE IT IS AT!"
TOM TOMORROW © 6-25-97

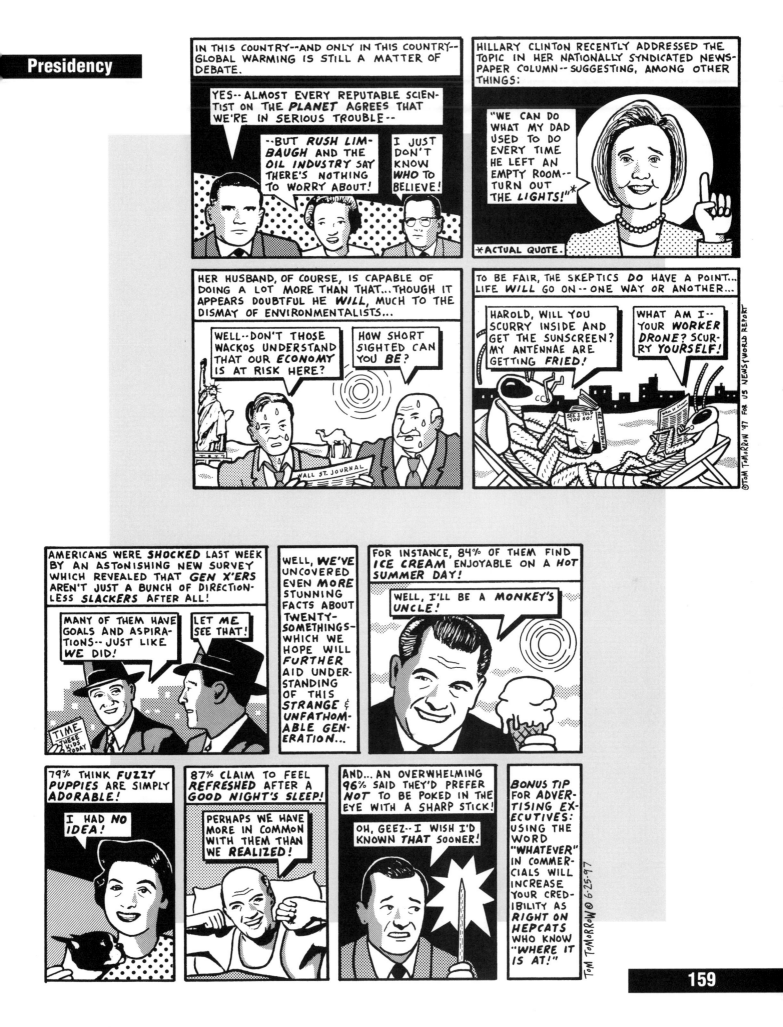

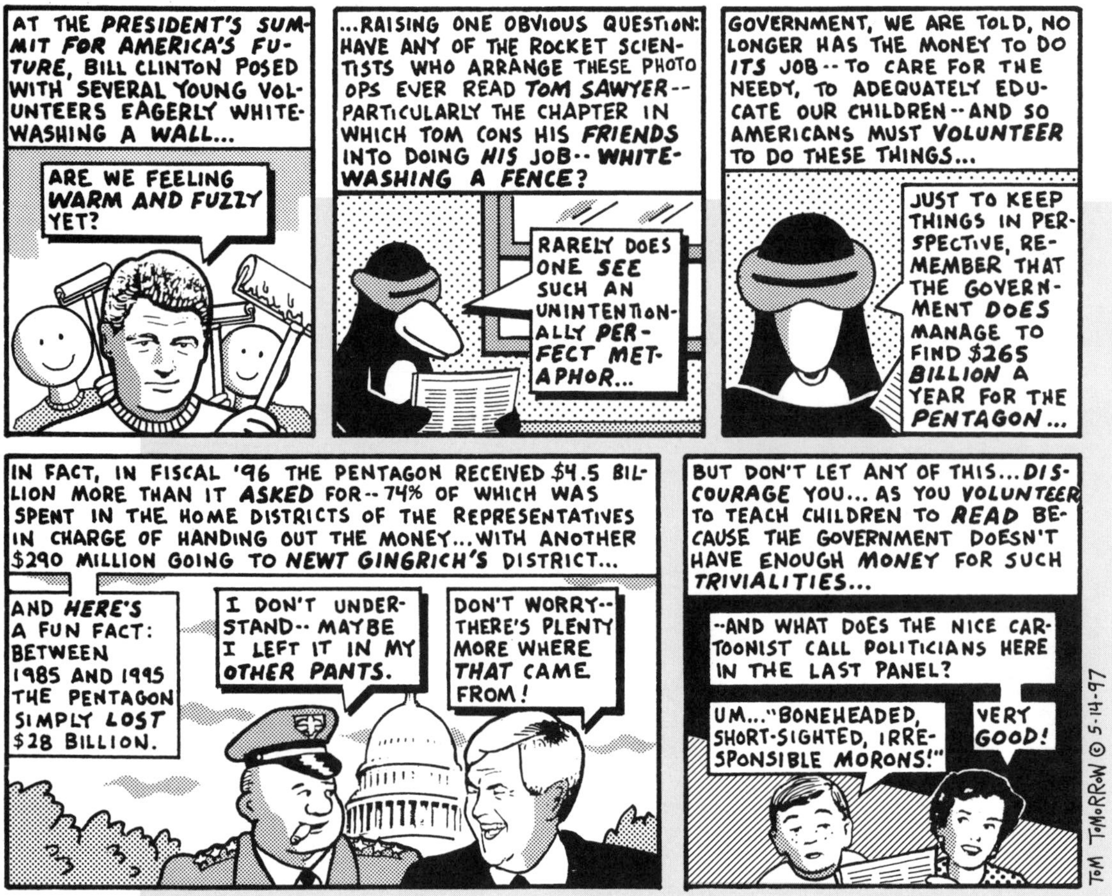

AT THE PRESIDENT'S SUMMIT FOR AMERICA'S FUTURE, BILL CLINTON POSED WITH SEVERAL YOUNG VOLUNTEERS EAGERLY WHITE-WASHING A WALL...
ARE WE FEELING WARM AND FUZZY YET?
...RAISING ONE OBVIOUS QUESTION: HAVE ANY OF THE ROCKET SCIENTISTS WHO ARRANGE THESE PHOTO OPS EVER READ TOM SAWYER--PARTICULARLY THE CHAPTER IN WHICH TOM CONS HIS FRIENDS INTO DOING HIS JOB--WHITE-WASHING A FENCE?
RARELY DOES ONE SEE SUCH AN UNINTENTIONALLY PERFECT METAPHOR...
GOVERNMENT, WE ARE TOLD, NO LONGER HAS THE MONEY TO DO ITS JOB--TO CARE FOR THE NEEDY, TO ADEQUATELY EDUCATE OUR CHILDREN--AND SO AMERICANS MUST VOLUNTEER TO DO THESE THINGS...
JUST TO KEEP THINGS IN PERSPECTIVE, REMEMBER THAT THE GOVERNMENT DOES MANAGE TO FIND $265 BILLION A YEAR FOR THE PENTAGON...
IN FACT, IN FISCAL '96 THE PENTAGON RECEIVED $4.5 BILLION MORE THAN IT ASKED FOR--74% OF WHICH WAS SPENT IN THE HOME DISTRICTS OF THE REPRESENTATIVES IN CHARGE OF HANDING OUT THE MONEY...WITH ANOTHER $290 MILLION GOING TO NEWT GINGRICH'S DISTRICT...
AND HERE'S A FUN FACT: BETWEEN 1985 AND 1995 THE PENTAGON SIMPLY LOST $28 BILLION.
I DON'T UNDERSTAND--MAYBE I LEFT IT IN MY OTHER PANTS.
DON'T WORRY--THERE'S PLENTY MORE WHERE THAT CAME FROM!
BUT DON'T LET ANY OF THIS...DISCOURAGE YOU...AS YOU VOLUNTEER TO TEACH CHILDREN TO READ BECAUSE THE GOVERNMENT DOESN'T HAVE ENOUGH MONEY FOR SUCH TRIVIALITIES...
--AND WHAT DOES THE NICE CARTOONIST CALL POLITICIANS HERE IN THE LAST PANEL?
UM..."BONEHEADED, SHORT-SIGHTED, IRRESPONSIBLE MORONS!"
VERY GOOD!
TOM TOMORROW © 5-14-97

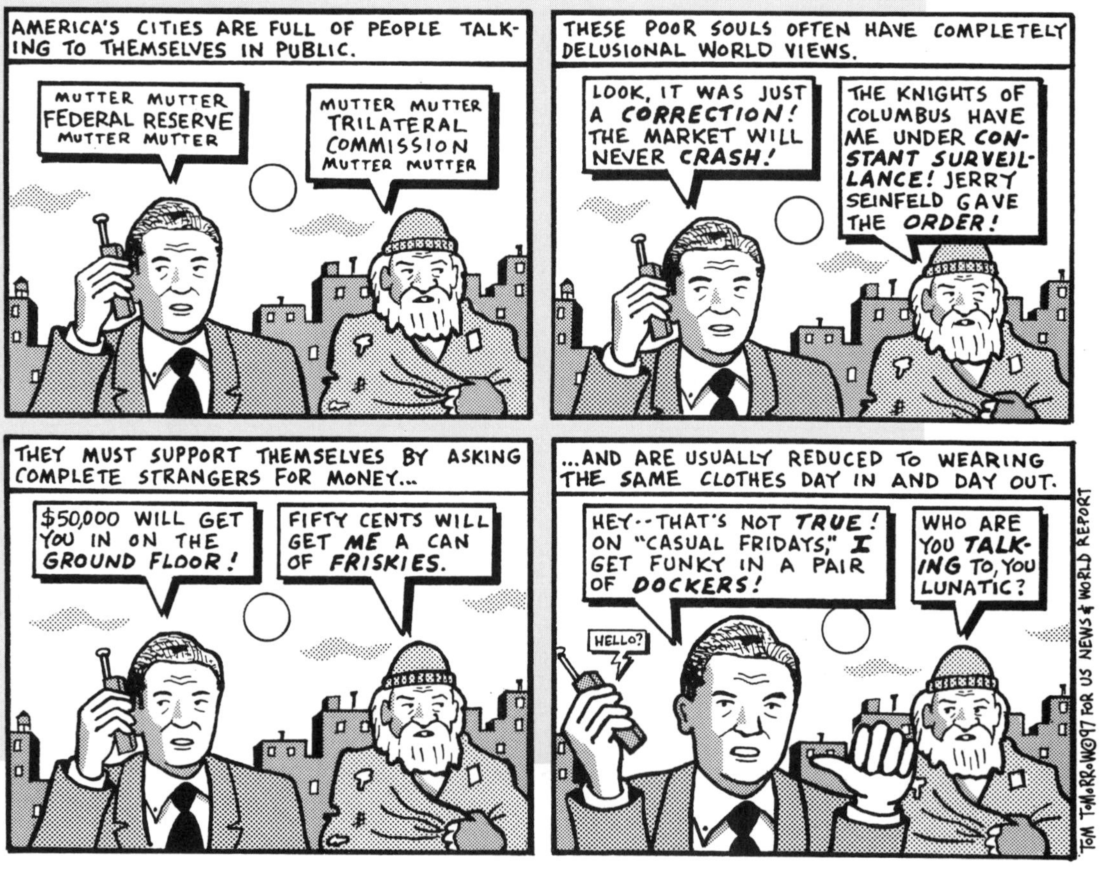

AMERICA'S CITIES ARE FULL OF PEOPLE TALKING TO THEMSELVES IN PUBLIC.
MUTTER MUTTER FEDERAL RESERVE MUTTER MUTTER
MUTTER MUTTER TRILATERAL COMMISSION MUTTER MUTTER
THESE POOR SOULS OFTEN HAVE COMPLETELY DELUSIONAL WORLD VIEWS.
LOOK, IT WAS JUST A CORRECTION! THE MARKET WILL NEVER CRASH!
THE KNIGHTS OF COLUMBUS HAVE ME UNDER CONSTANT SURVEILLANCE! JERRY SEINFELD GAVE THE ORDER!
THEY MUST SUPPORT THEMSELVES BY ASKING COMPLETE STRANGERS FOR MONEY...
$50,000 WILL GET YOU IN ON THE GROUND FLOOR!
FIFTY CENTS WILL GET ME A CAN OF FRISKIES.
...AND ARE USUALLY REDUCED TO WEARING THE SAME CLOTHES DAY IN AND DAY OUT.
HEY--THAT'S NOT TRUE! ON "CASUAL FRIDAYS," I GET FUNKY IN A PAIR OF DOCKERS!
HELLO?
WHO ARE YOU TALKING TO, YOU LUNATIC?
TOM TOMORROW©97 FOR US NEWS & WORLD REPORT

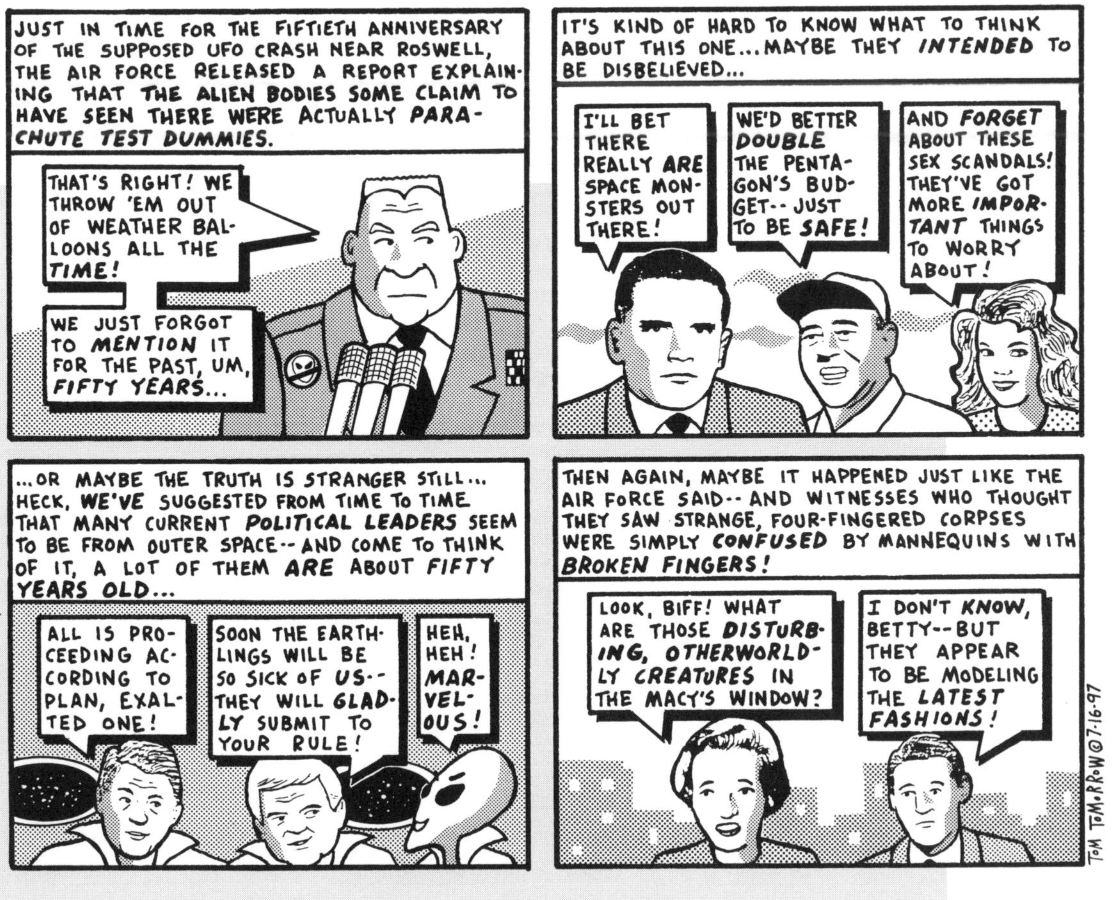
JUST IN TIME FOR THE FIFTIETH ANNIVERSARY OF THE SUPPOSED UFO CRASH NEAR ROSWELL, THE AIR FORCE RELEASED A REPORT EXPLAINING THAT THE ALIEN BODIES SOME CLAIM TO HAVE SEEN THERE WERE ACTUALLY PARACHUTE TEST DUMMIES.
THAT'S RIGHT! WE THROW 'EM OUT OF WEATHER BALLOONS ALL THE TIME!
WE JUST FORGOT TO MENTION IT FOR THE PAST, UM, FIFTY YEARS...
IT'S KIND OF HARD TO KNOW WHAT TO THINK ABOUT THIS ONE... MAYBE THEY INTENDED TO BE DISBELIEVED...
I'LL BET THERE REALLY ARE SPACE MONSTERS OUT THERE!
WE'D BETTER DOUBLE THE PENTAGON'S BUDGET-- JUST TO BE SAFE!
AND FORGET ABOUT THESE SEX SCANDALS! THEY'VE GOT MORE IMPORTANT THINGS TO WORRY ABOUT!
...OR MAYBE THE TRUTH IS STRANGER STILL... HECK, WE'VE SUGGESTED FROM TIME TO TIME THAT MANY CURRENT POLITICAL LEADERS SEEM TO BE FROM OUTER SPACE-- AND COME TO THINK OF IT, A LOT OF THEM ARE ABOUT FIFTY YEARS OLD...
ALL IS PROCEEDING ACCORDING TO PLAN, EXALTED ONE!
SOON THE EARTHLINGS WILL BE SO SICK OF US-- THEY WILL GLADLY SUBMIT TO YOUR RULE!
HEH, HEH! MARVELOUS!
THEN AGAIN, MAYBE IT HAPPENED JUST LIKE THE AIR FORCE SAID-- AND WITNESSES WHO THOUGHT THEY SAW STRANGE, FOUR-FINGERED CORPSES WERE SIMPLY CONFUSED BY MANNEQUINS WITH BROKEN FINGERS!
LOOK, BIFF! WHAT ARE THOSE DISTURBING, OTHERWORLDLY CREATURES IN THE MACY'S WINDOW?
I DON'T KNOW, BETTY--BUT THEY APPEAR TO BE MODELING THE LATEST FASHIONS!
TOM TOMORROW©7-16-97

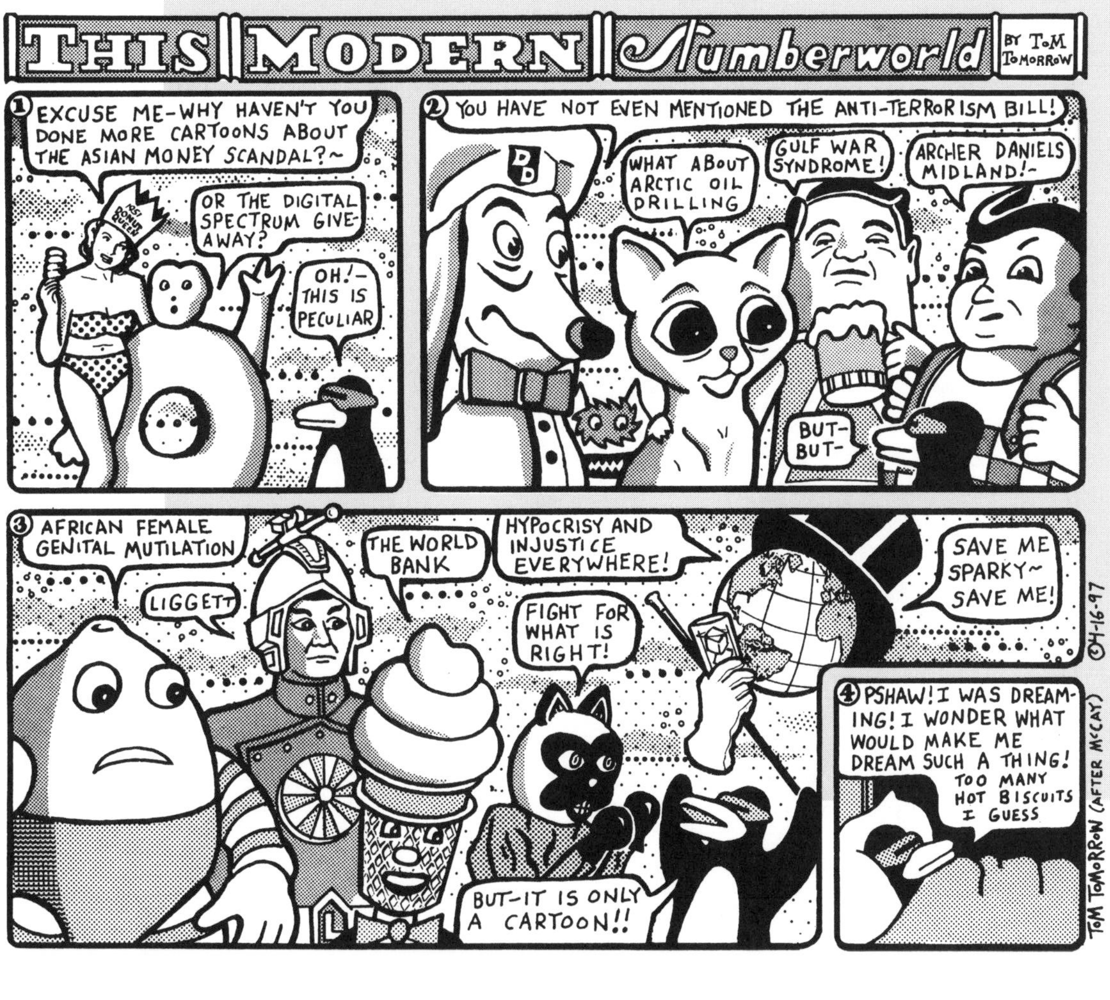
THIS MODERN Slumberworld
BY TOM TOMORROW
1 EXCUSE ME-WHY HAVEN'T YOU DONE MORE CARTOONS ABOUT THE ASIAN MONEY SCANDAL?~
OR THE DIGITAL SPECTRUM GIVE-AWAY?
OH!- THIS IS PECULIAR
2 YOU HAVE NOT EVEN MENTIONED THE ANTI-TERRORISM BILL!
WHAT ABOUT ARCTIC OIL DRILLING
GULF WAR SYNDROME!
ARCHER DANIELS MIDLAND!~
BUT-BUT-
3 AFRICAN FEMALE GENITAL MUTILATION
LIGGETT
THE WORLD BANK
HYPOCRISY AND INJUSTICE EVERYWHERE!
FIGHT FOR WHAT IS RIGHT!
SAVE ME SPARKY~ SAVE ME!
BUT-IT IS ONLY A CARTOON!!
©4-16-97
4 PSHAW! I WAS DREAMING! I WONDER WHAT WOULD MAKE ME DREAM SUCH A THING! TOO MANY HOT BISCUITS I GUESS
TOM TOMORROW (AFTER MCCAY)

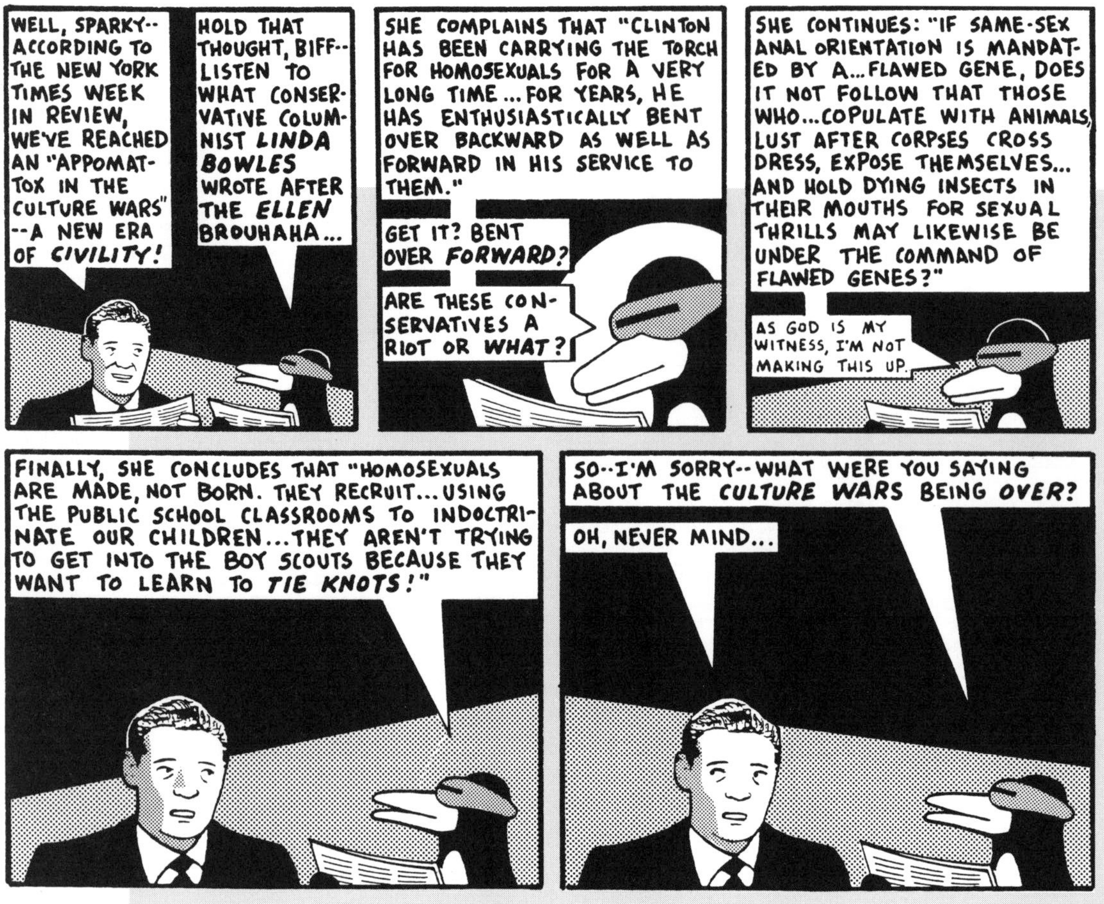
WELL, SPARKY-- ACCORDING TO THE NEW YORK TIMES WEEK IN REVIEW, WE'VE REACHED AN "APPOMATTOX IN THE CULTURE WARS" --A NEW ERA OF CIVILITY!
HOLD THAT THOUGHT, BIFF-- LISTEN TO WHAT CONSERVATIVE COLUMNIST LINDA BOWLES WROTE AFTER THE ELLEN BROUHAHA...
SHE COMPLAINS THAT "CLINTON HAS BEEN CARRYING THE TORCH FOR HOMOSEXUALS FOR A VERY LONG TIME... FOR YEARS, HE HAS ENTHUSIASTICALLY BENT OVER BACKWARD AS WELL AS FORWARD IN HIS SERVICE TO THEM."
GET IT? BENT OVER FORWARD?
ARE THESE CONSERVATIVES A RIOT OR WHAT?
SHE CONTINUES: "IF SAME-SEX ANAL ORIENTATION IS MANDATED BY A... FLAWED GENE, DOES IT NOT FOLLOW THAT THOSE WHO... COPULATE WITH ANIMALS, LUST AFTER CORPSES CROSS DRESS, EXPOSE THEMSELVES... AND HOLD DYING INSECTS IN THEIR MOUTHS FOR SEXUAL THRILLS MAY LIKEWISE BE UNDER THE COMMAND OF FLAWED GENES?"
AS GOD IS MY WITNESS, I'M NOT MAKING THIS UP.
FINALLY, SHE CONCLUDES THAT "HOMOSEXUALS ARE MADE, NOT BORN. THEY RECRUIT... USING THE PUBLIC SCHOOL CLASSROOMS TO INDOCTRINATE OUR CHILDREN... THEY AREN'T TRYING TO GET INTO THE BOY SCOUTS BECAUSE THEY WANT TO LEARN TO TIE KNOTS!"
SO--I'M SORRY--WHAT WERE YOU SAYING ABOUT THE CULTURE WARS BEING OVER?
OH, NEVER MIND...

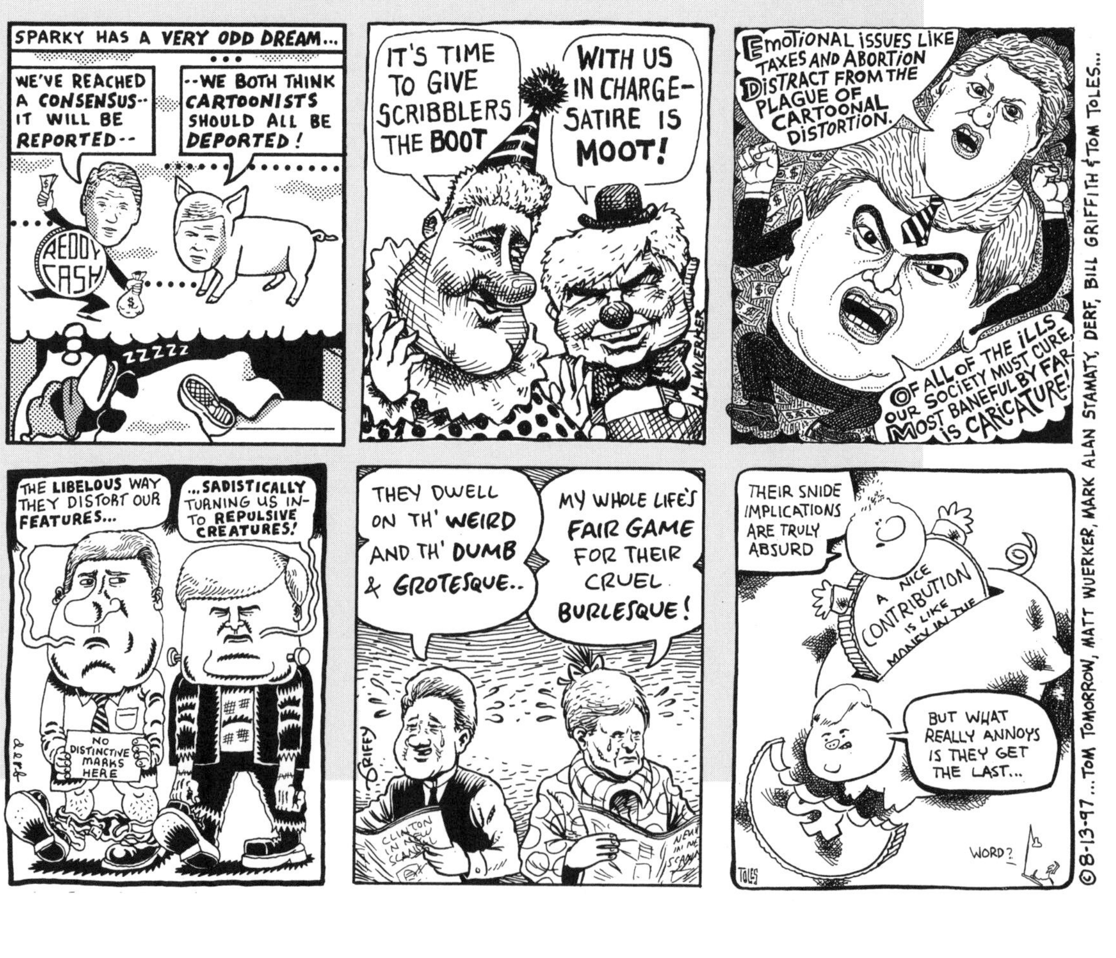
SPARKY HAS A VERY ODD DREAM...
WE'VE REACHED A CONSENSUS-- IT WILL BE REPORTED--
--WE BOTH THINK CARTOONISTS SHOULD ALL BE DEPORTED!
REDDY CASH
ZZZZZ
IT'S TIME TO GIVE SCRIBBLERS THE BOOT
WITH US IN CHARGE- SATIRE IS MOOT!
M. WUERKER
EMOTIONAL ISSUES LIKE TAXES AND ABORTION DISTRACT FROM THE PLAGUE OF CARTOONAL DISTORTION.
OF ALL OF THE ILLS OUR SOCIETY MUST CURE, MOST BANEFUL BY FAR IS CARICATURE!
THE LIBELOUS WAY THEY DISTORT OUR FEATURES...
...SADISTICALLY TURNING US INTO REPULSIVE CREATURES!
NO DISTINCTIVE MARKS HERE
THEY DWELL ON TH' WEIRD AND TH' DUMB & GROTESQUE..
MY WHOLE LIFE'S FAIR GAME FOR THEIR CRUEL BURLESQUE!
CLINTON IN NEW SCANDAL
GRIFFY
THEIR SNIDE IMPLICATIONS ARE TRULY ABSURD
A NICE CONTRIBUTION IS LIKE MONEY IN THE
BUT WHAT REALLY ANNOYS IS THEY GET THE LAST...
WORD?
TOLES
©8-13-97... TOM TOMORROW, MATT WUERKER, MARK ALAN STAMATY, DERF, BILL GRIFFITH & TOM TOLES...

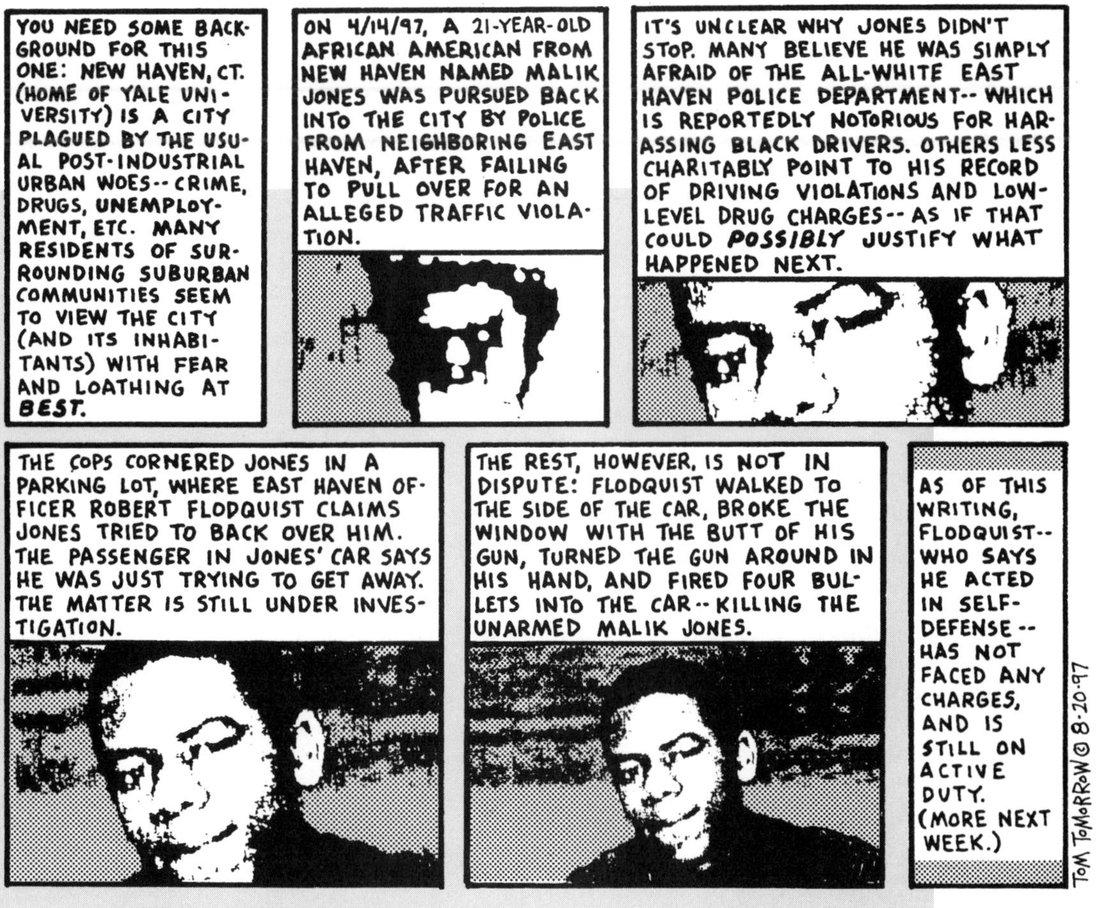
YOU NEED SOME BACKGROUND FOR THIS ONE: NEW HAVEN, CT. (HOME OF YALE UNIVERSITY) IS A CITY PLAGUED BY THE USUAL POST-INDUSTRIAL URBAN WOES--CRIME, DRUGS, UNEMPLOYMENT, ETC. MANY RESIDENTS OF SURROUNDING SUBURBAN COMMUNITIES SEEM TO VIEW THE CITY (AND ITS INHABITANTS) WITH FEAR AND LOATHING AT *BEST*.
ON 4/14/97, A 21-YEAR-OLD AFRICAN AMERICAN FROM NEW HAVEN NAMED MALIK JONES WAS PURSUED BACK INTO THE CITY BY POLICE FROM NEIGHBORING EAST HAVEN, AFTER FAILING TO PULL OVER FOR AN ALLEGED TRAFFIC VIOLATION.
IT'S UNCLEAR WHY JONES DIDN'T STOP. MANY BELIEVE HE WAS SIMPLY AFRAID OF THE ALL-WHITE EAST HAVEN POLICE DEPARTMENT--WHICH IS REPORTEDLY NOTORIOUS FOR HARASSING BLACK DRIVERS. OTHERS LESS CHARITABLY POINT TO HIS RECORD OF DRIVING VIOLATIONS AND LOW-LEVEL DRUG CHARGES--AS IF THAT COULD *POSSIBLY* JUSTIFY WHAT HAPPENED NEXT.
THE COPS CORNERED JONES IN A PARKING LOT, WHERE EAST HAVEN OFFICER ROBERT FLODQUIST CLAIMS JONES TRIED TO BACK OVER HIM. THE PASSENGER IN JONES' CAR SAYS HE WAS JUST TRYING TO GET AWAY. THE MATTER IS STILL UNDER INVESTIGATION.
THE REST, HOWEVER, IS NOT IN DISPUTE: FLODQUIST WALKED TO THE SIDE OF THE CAR, BROKE THE WINDOW WITH THE BUTT OF HIS GUN, TURNED THE GUN AROUND IN HIS HAND, AND FIRED FOUR BULLETS INTO THE CAR--KILLING THE UNARMED MALIK JONES.
AS OF THIS WRITING, FLODQUIST--WHO SAYS HE ACTED IN SELF-DEFENSE--HAS NOT FACED ANY CHARGES, AND IS STILL ON ACTIVE DUTY. (MORE NEXT WEEK.)
TOM TOMORROW © 8-20-97

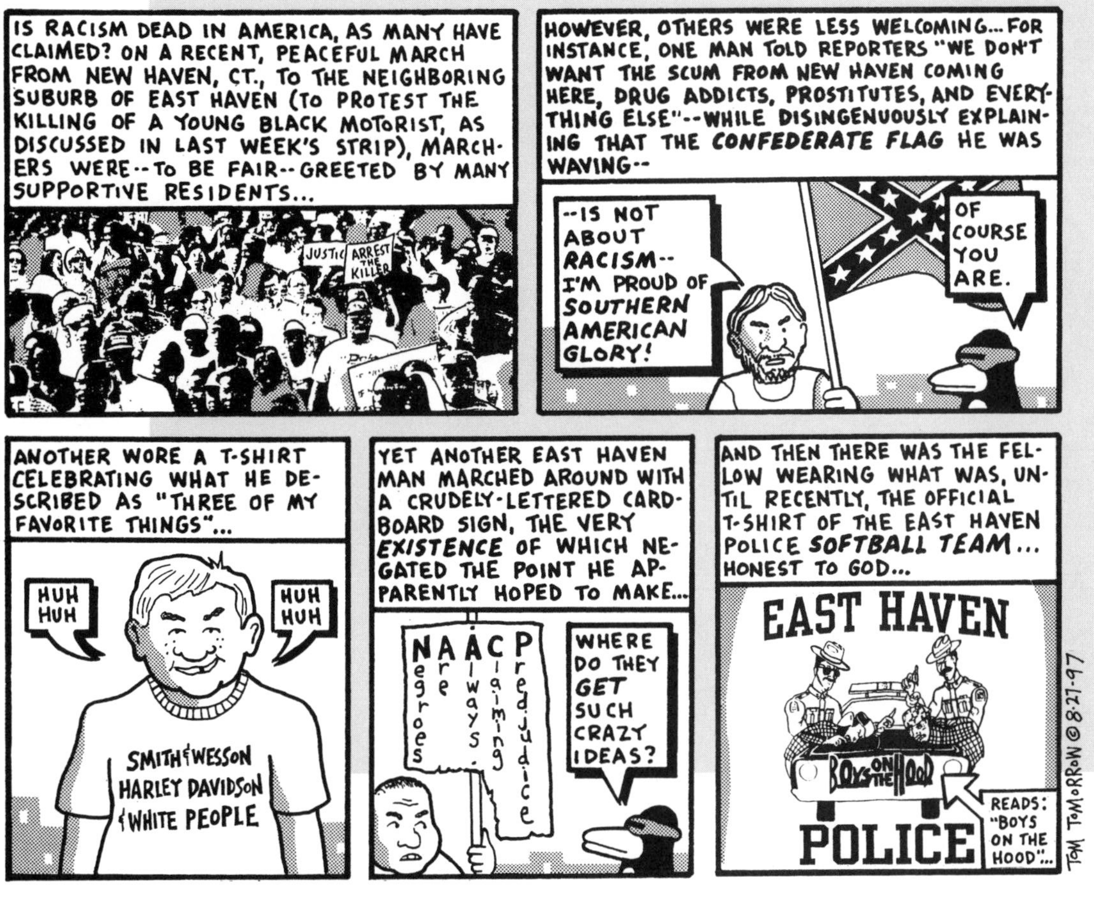
IS RACISM DEAD IN AMERICA, AS MANY HAVE CLAIMED? ON A RECENT, PEACEFUL MARCH FROM NEW HAVEN, CT., TO THE NEIGHBORING SUBURB OF EAST HAVEN (TO PROTEST THE KILLING OF A YOUNG BLACK MOTORIST, AS DISCUSSED IN LAST WEEK'S STRIP), MARCHERS WERE--TO BE FAIR--GREETED BY MANY SUPPORTIVE RESIDENTS...
JUSTIC
ARREST THE KILLER
HOWEVER, OTHERS WERE LESS WELCOMING... FOR INSTANCE, ONE MAN TOLD REPORTERS "WE DON'T WANT THE SCUM FROM NEW HAVEN COMING HERE, DRUG ADDICTS, PROSTITUTES, AND EVERYTHING ELSE"--WHILE DISINGENUOUSLY EXPLAINING THAT THE *CONFEDERATE FLAG* HE WAS WAVING--
--IS NOT ABOUT *RACISM*--I'M PROUD OF *SOUTHERN AMERICAN GLORY!*
OF COURSE YOU ARE.
ANOTHER WORE A T-SHIRT CELEBRATING WHAT HE DESCRIBED AS "THREE OF MY FAVORITE THINGS"...
HUH HUH
HUH HUH
SMITH & WESSON HARLEY DAVIDSON & WHITE PEOPLE
YET ANOTHER EAST HAVEN MAN MARCHED AROUND WITH A CRUDELY-LETTERED CARDBOARD SIGN, THE VERY *EXISTENCE* OF WHICH NEGATED THE POINT HE APPARENTLY HOPED TO MAKE...
Negroes Are Always Claiming Prejudice
WHERE DO THEY *GET* SUCH CRAZY IDEAS?
AND THEN THERE WAS THE FELLOW WEARING WHAT WAS, UNTIL RECENTLY, THE OFFICIAL T-SHIRT OF THE EAST HAVEN POLICE *SOFTBALL TEAM*... HONEST TO GOD...
EAST HAVEN
BOYS ON THE HOOD
POLICE
READS: "BOYS ON THE HOOD"...
TOM TOMORROW © 8-27-97

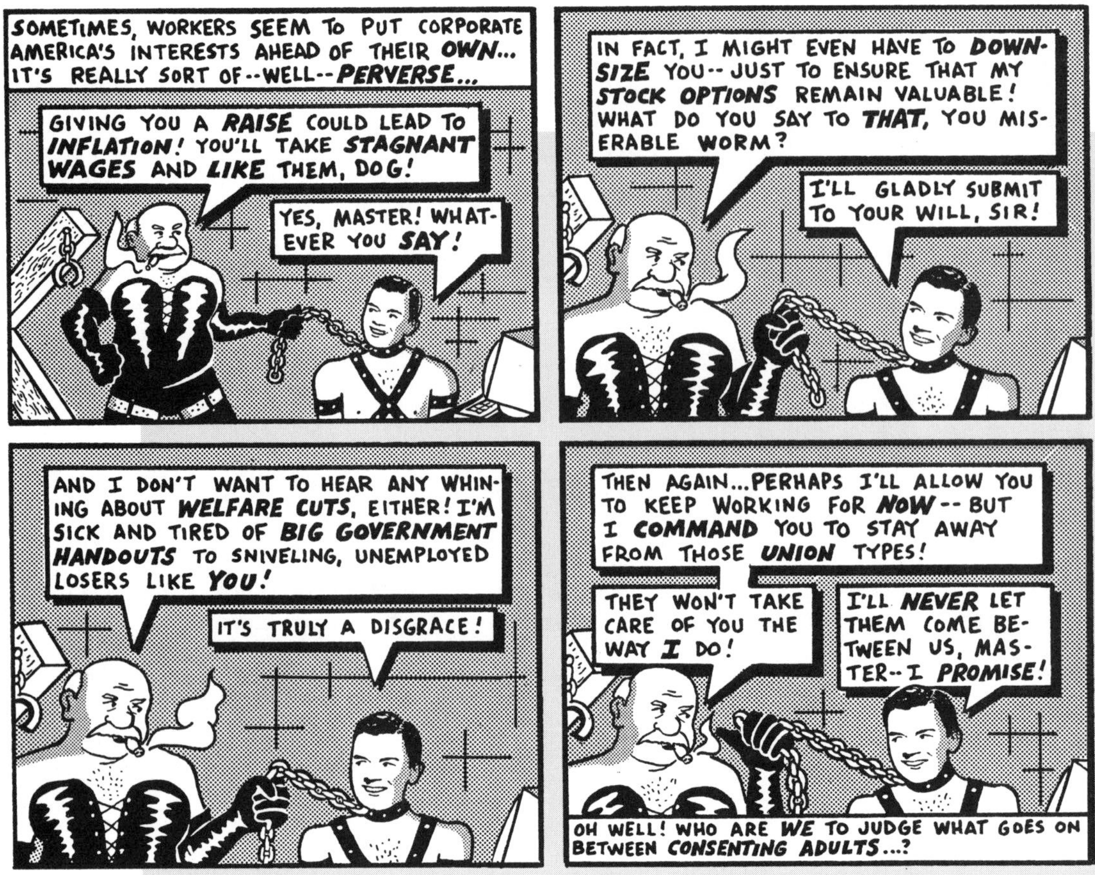
SOMETIMES, WORKERS SEEM TO PUT CORPORATE AMERICA'S INTERESTS AHEAD OF THEIR OWN... IT'S REALLY SORT OF--WELL--PERVERSE...
GIVING YOU A RAISE COULD LEAD TO INFLATION! YOU'LL TAKE STAGNANT WAGES AND LIKE THEM, DOG!
YES, MASTER! WHATEVER YOU SAY!
IN FACT, I MIGHT EVEN HAVE TO DOWNSIZE YOU-- JUST TO ENSURE THAT MY STOCK OPTIONS REMAIN VALUABLE! WHAT DO YOU SAY TO THAT, YOU MISERABLE WORM?
I'LL GLADLY SUBMIT TO YOUR WILL, SIR!
AND I DON'T WANT TO HEAR ANY WHINING ABOUT WELFARE CUTS, EITHER! I'M SICK AND TIRED OF BIG GOVERNMENT HANDOUTS TO SNIVELING, UNEMPLOYED LOSERS LIKE YOU!
IT'S TRULY A DISGRACE!
THEN AGAIN...PERHAPS I'LL ALLOW YOU TO KEEP WORKING FOR NOW -- BUT I COMMAND YOU TO STAY AWAY FROM THOSE UNION TYPES!
THEY WON'T TAKE CARE OF YOU THE WAY I DO!
I'LL NEVER LET THEM COME BETWEEN US, MASTER-- I PROMISE!
OH WELL! WHO ARE WE TO JUDGE WHAT GOES ON BETWEEN CONSENTING ADULTS...?
TOM TOMORROW©9-17-97

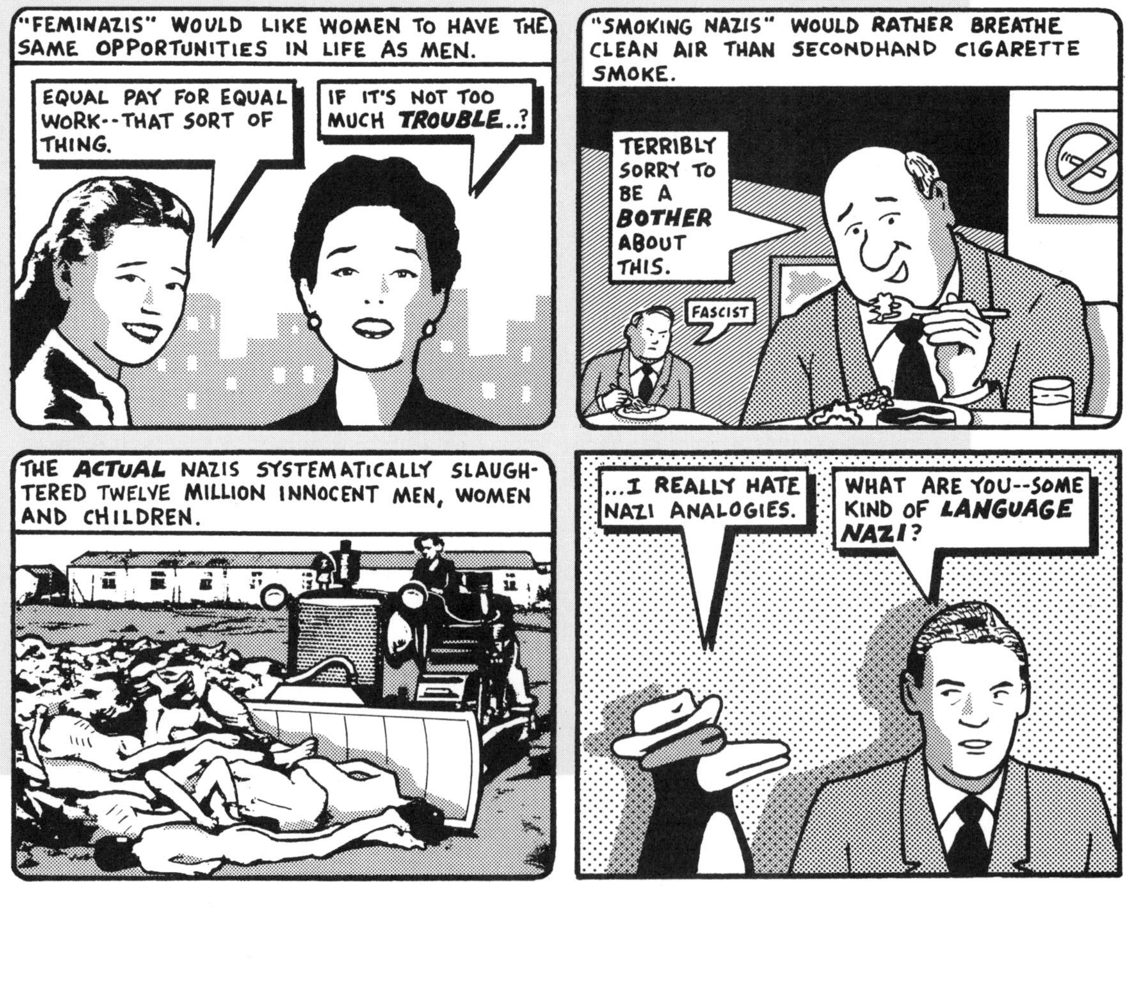
"FEMINAZIS" WOULD LIKE WOMEN TO HAVE THE SAME OPPORTUNITIES IN LIFE AS MEN.
EQUAL PAY FOR EQUAL WORK--THAT SORT OF THING.
IF IT'S NOT TOO MUCH TROUBLE...?
"SMOKING NAZIS" WOULD RATHER BREATHE CLEAN AIR THAN SECONDHAND CIGARETTE SMOKE.
TERRIBLY SORRY TO BE A BOTHER ABOUT THIS.
FASCIST
THE ACTUAL NAZIS SYSTEMATICALLY SLAUGHTERED TWELVE MILLION INNOCENT MEN, WOMEN AND CHILDREN.
...I REALLY HATE NAZI ANALOGIES.
WHAT ARE YOU--SOME KIND OF LANGUAGE NAZI?

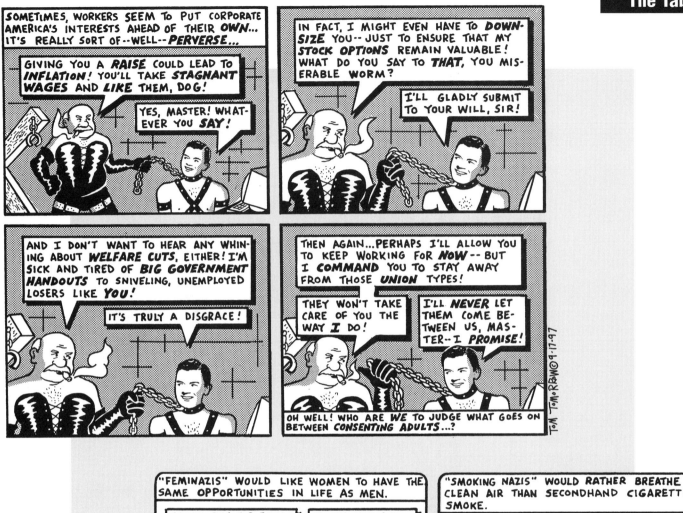

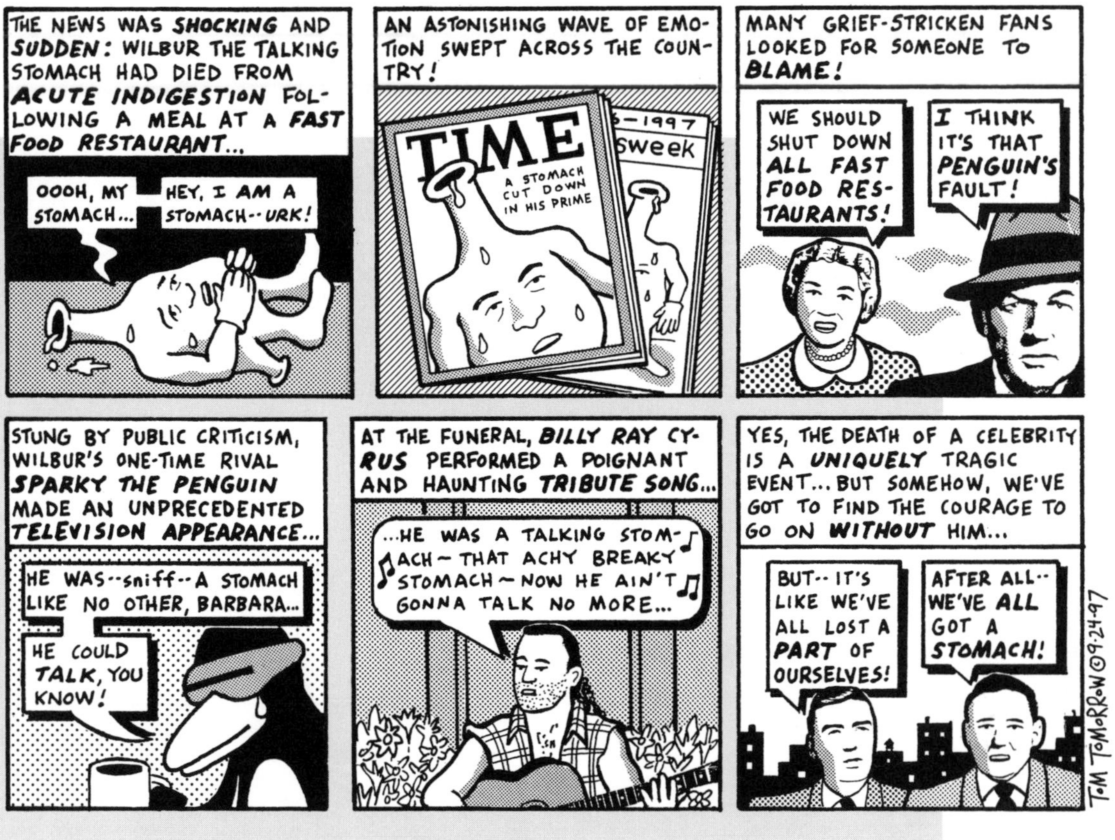
THE NEWS WAS SHOCKING AND SUDDEN: WILBUR THE TALKING STOMACH HAD DIED FROM ACUTE INDIGESTION FOLLOWING A MEAL AT A FAST FOOD RESTAURANT...
OOOH, MY STOMACH...
HEY, I AM A STOMACH--URK!
AN ASTONISHING WAVE OF EMOTION SWEPT ACROSS THE COUNTRY!
TIME
A STOMACH CUT DOWN IN HIS PRIME
MANY GRIEF-STRICKEN FANS LOOKED FOR SOMEONE TO BLAME!
WE SHOULD SHUT DOWN ALL FAST FOOD RESTAURANTS!
I THINK IT'S THAT PENGUIN'S FAULT!
STUNG BY PUBLIC CRITICISM, WILBUR'S ONE-TIME RIVAL SPARKY THE PENGUIN MADE AN UNPRECEDENTED TELEVISION APPEARANCE...
HE WAS--sniff--A STOMACH LIKE NO OTHER, BARBARA...
HE COULD TALK, YOU KNOW!
AT THE FUNERAL, BILLY RAY CYRUS PERFORMED A POIGNANT AND HAUNTING TRIBUTE SONG...
...HE WAS A TALKING STOMACH~THAT ACHY BREAKY STOMACH~NOW HE AIN'T GONNA TALK NO MORE...
YES, THE DEATH OF A CELEBRITY IS A UNIQUELY TRAGIC EVENT... BUT SOMEHOW, WE'VE GOT TO FIND THE COURAGE TO GO ON WITHOUT HIM...
BUT--IT'S LIKE WE'VE ALL LOST A PART OF OURSELVES!
AFTER ALL--WE'VE ALL GOT A STOMACH!
TOM TOMORROW©9·24·97

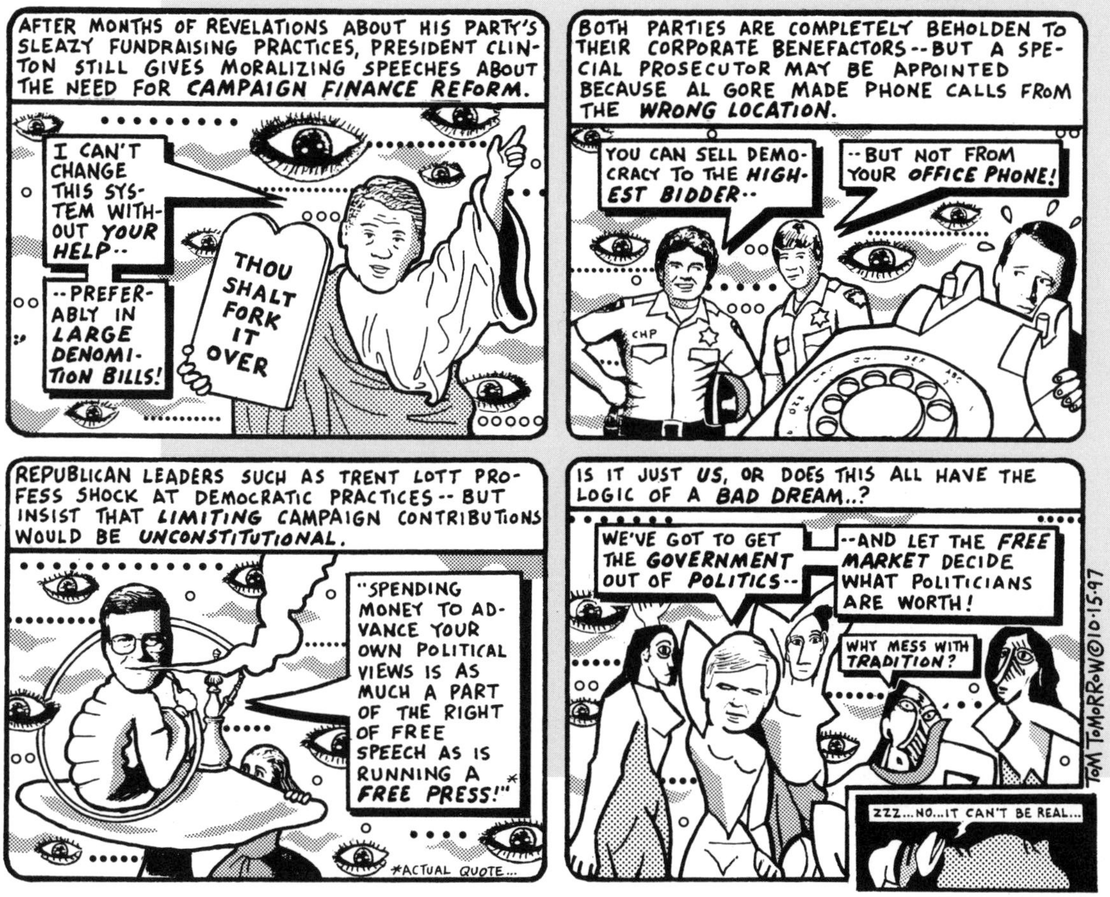
AFTER MONTHS OF REVELATIONS ABOUT HIS PARTY'S SLEAZY FUNDRAISING PRACTICES, PRESIDENT CLINTON STILL GIVES MORALIZING SPEECHES ABOUT THE NEED FOR CAMPAIGN FINANCE REFORM.
I CAN'T CHANGE THIS SYSTEM WITHOUT YOUR HELP--
--PREFERABLY IN LARGE DENOMITION BILLS!
THOU SHALT FORK IT OVER
BOTH PARTIES ARE COMPLETELY BEHOLDEN TO THEIR CORPORATE BENEFACTORS--BUT A SPECIAL PROSECUTOR MAY BE APPOINTED BECAUSE AL GORE MADE PHONE CALLS FROM THE WRONG LOCATION.
YOU CAN SELL DEMOCRACY TO THE HIGHEST BIDDER--
--BUT NOT FROM YOUR OFFICE PHONE!
CHP
REPUBLICAN LEADERS SUCH AS TRENT LOTT PROFESS SHOCK AT DEMOCRATIC PRACTICES--BUT INSIST THAT LIMITING CAMPAIGN CONTRIBUTIONS WOULD BE UNCONSTITUTIONAL.
"SPENDING MONEY TO ADVANCE YOUR OWN POLITICAL VIEWS IS AS MUCH A PART OF THE RIGHT OF FREE SPEECH AS IS RUNNING A FREE PRESS!"*
*ACTUAL QUOTE...
IS IT JUST US, OR DOES THIS ALL HAVE THE LOGIC OF A BAD DREAM..?
WE'VE GOT TO GET THE GOVERNMENT OUT OF POLITICS--
--AND LET THE FREE MARKET DECIDE WHAT POLITICIANS ARE WORTH!
WHY MESS WITH TRADITION?
ZZZ...NO...IT CAN'T BE REAL...
TOM TOMORROW©10·15·97

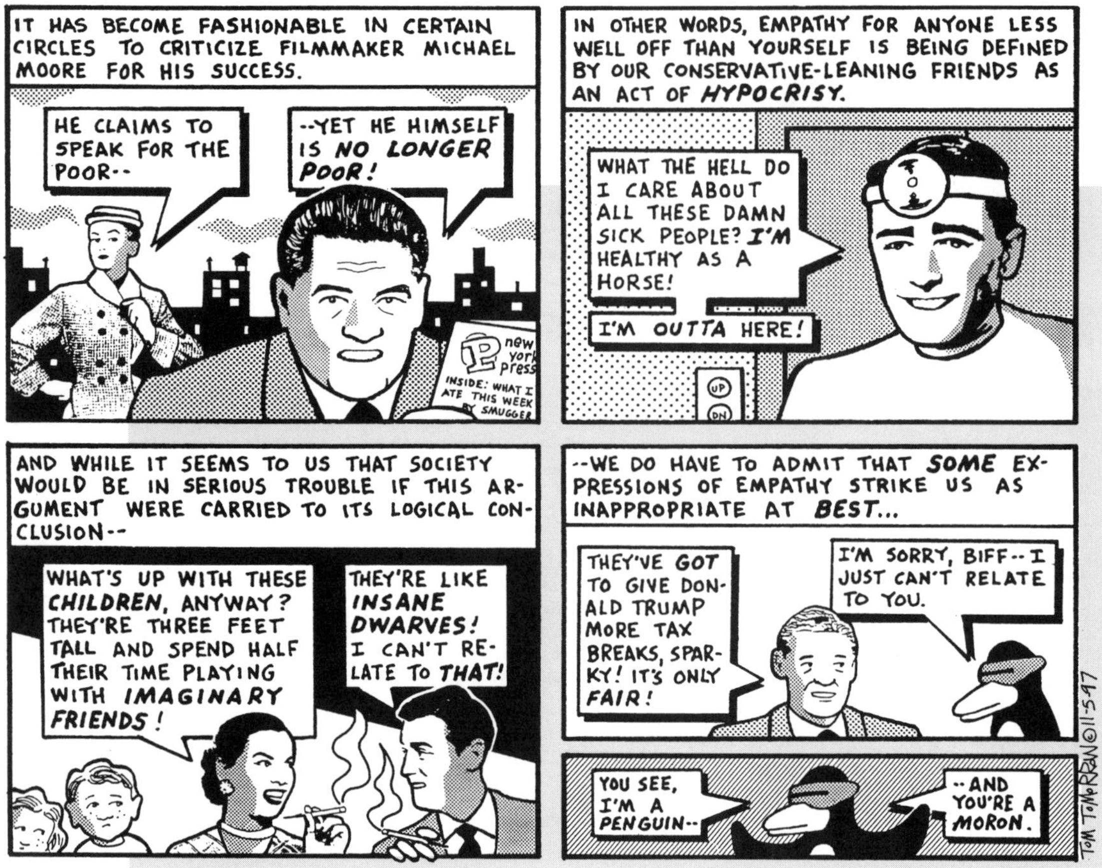
IT HAS BECOME FASHIONABLE IN CERTAIN CIRCLES TO CRITICIZE FILMMAKER MICHAEL MOORE FOR HIS SUCCESS.
HE CLAIMS TO SPEAK FOR THE POOR--
--YET HE HIMSELF IS NO LONGER POOR!
new york press
INSIDE: WHAT I ATE THIS WEEK BY SMUGGER
IN OTHER WORDS, EMPATHY FOR ANYONE LESS WELL OFF THAN YOURSELF IS BEING DEFINED BY OUR CONSERVATIVE-LEANING FRIENDS AS AN ACT OF HYPOCRISY.
WHAT THE HELL DO I CARE ABOUT ALL THESE DAMN SICK PEOPLE? I'M HEALTHY AS A HORSE!
I'M OUTTA HERE!
UP
DN
AND WHILE IT SEEMS TO US THAT SOCIETY WOULD BE IN SERIOUS TROUBLE IF THIS ARGUMENT WERE CARRIED TO ITS LOGICAL CONCLUSION--
WHAT'S UP WITH THESE CHILDREN, ANYWAY? THEY'RE THREE FEET TALL AND SPEND HALF THEIR TIME PLAYING WITH IMAGINARY FRIENDS!
THEY'RE LIKE INSANE DWARVES! I CAN'T RELATE TO THAT!
--WE DO HAVE TO ADMIT THAT SOME EXPRESSIONS OF EMPATHY STRIKE US AS INAPPROPRIATE AT BEST...
THEY'VE GOT TO GIVE DONALD TRUMP MORE TAX BREAKS, SPARKY! IT'S ONLY FAIR!
I'M SORRY, BIFF-- I JUST CAN'T RELATE TO YOU.
YOU SEE, I'M A PENGUIN--
--AND YOU'RE A MORON.
TOM TOMORROW©11-5-97

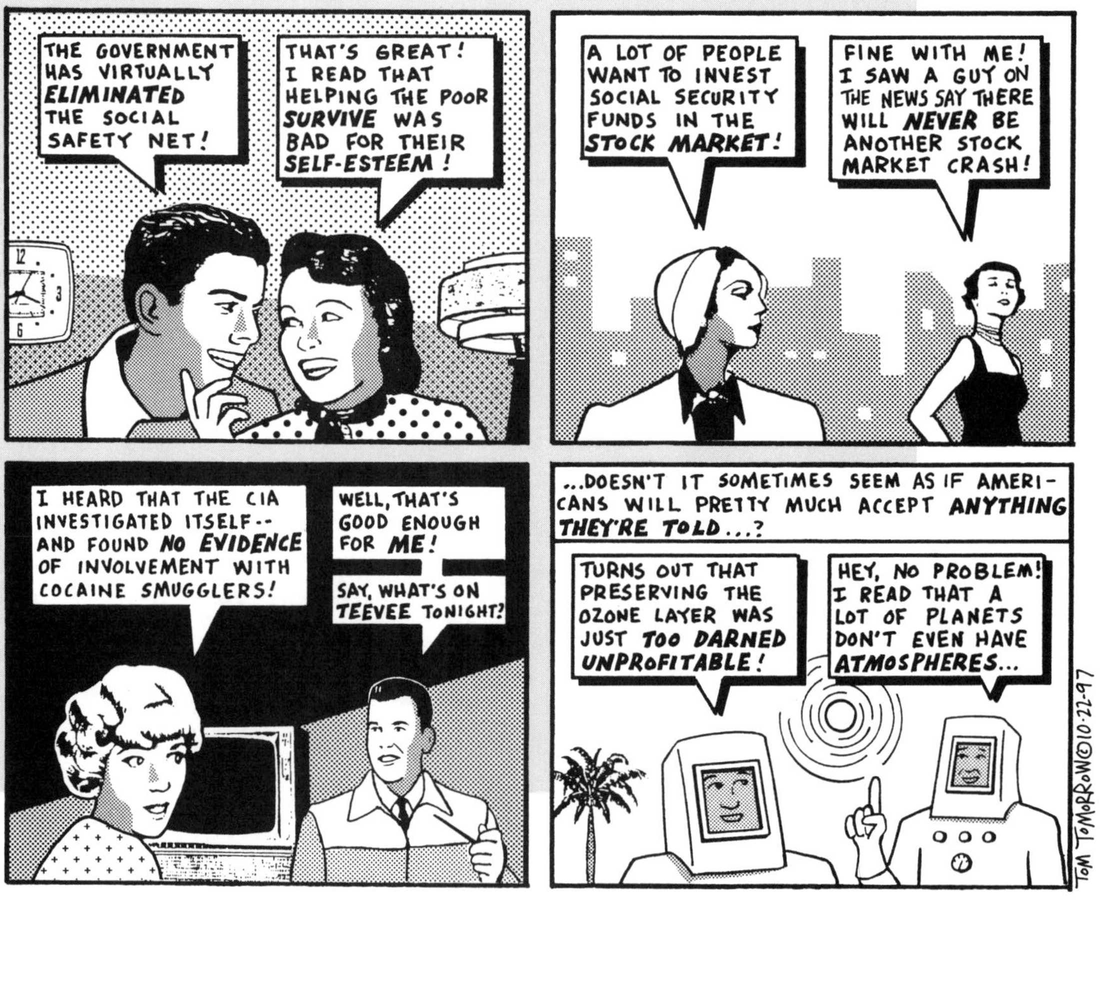
THE GOVERNMENT HAS VIRTUALLY ELIMINATED THE SOCIAL SAFETY NET!
THAT'S GREAT! I READ THAT HELPING THE POOR SURVIVE WAS BAD FOR THEIR SELF-ESTEEM!
A LOT OF PEOPLE WANT TO INVEST SOCIAL SECURITY FUNDS IN THE STOCK MARKET!
FINE WITH ME! I SAW A GUY ON THE NEWS SAY THERE WILL NEVER BE ANOTHER STOCK MARKET CRASH!
I HEARD THAT THE CIA INVESTIGATED ITSELF-- AND FOUND NO EVIDENCE OF INVOLVEMENT WITH COCAINE SMUGGLERS!
WELL, THAT'S GOOD ENOUGH FOR ME!
SAY, WHAT'S ON TEEVEE TONIGHT?
...DOESN'T IT SOMETIMES SEEM AS IF AMERICANS WILL PRETTY MUCH ACCEPT ANYTHING THEY'RE TOLD...?
TURNS OUT THAT PRESERVING THE OZONE LAYER WAS JUST TOO DARNED UNPROFITABLE!
HEY, NO PROBLEM! I READ THAT A LOT OF PLANETS DON'T EVEN HAVE ATMOSPHERES...
TOM TOMORROW©10-22-97

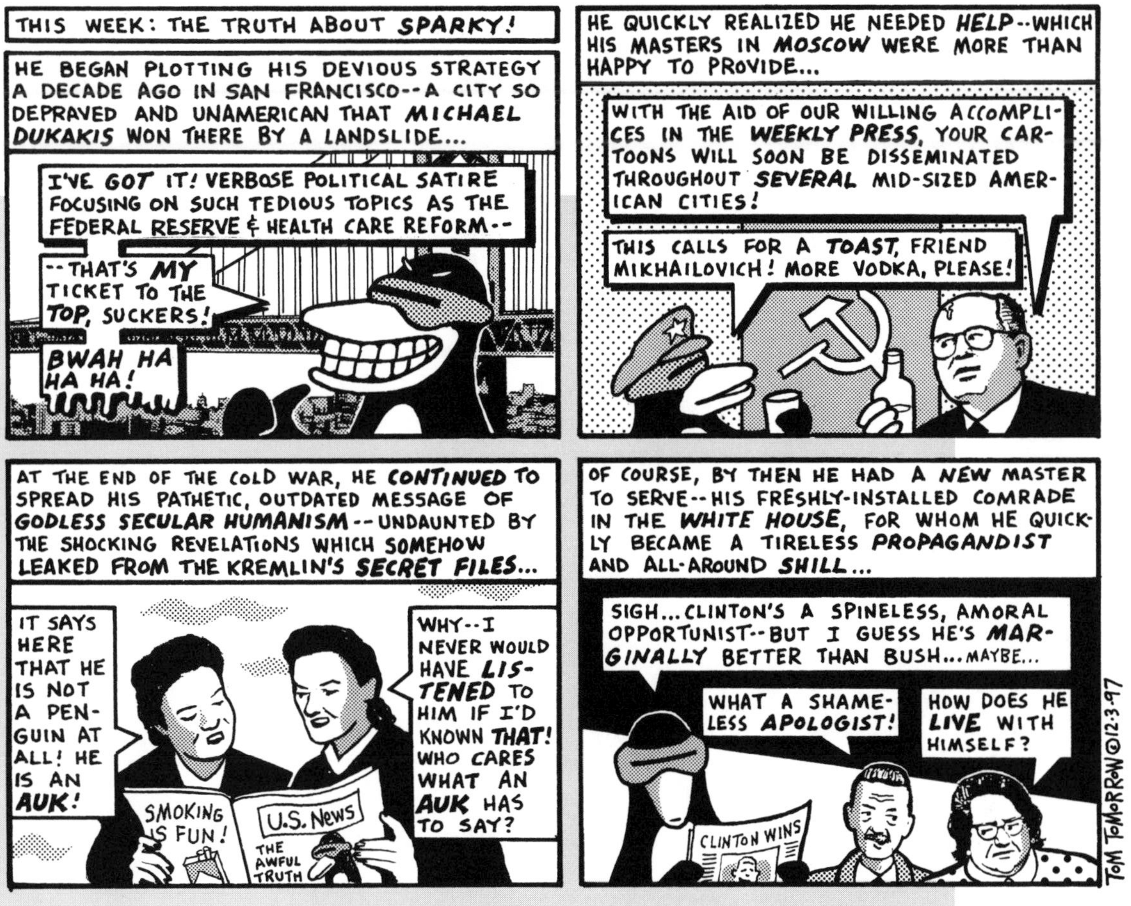
THIS WEEK: THE TRUTH ABOUT SPARKY!
HE BEGAN PLOTTING HIS DEVIOUS STRATEGY A DECADE AGO IN SAN FRANCISCO--A CITY SO DEPRAVED AND UNAMERICAN THAT MICHAEL DUKAKIS WON THERE BY A LANDSLIDE...
I'VE GOT IT! VERBOSE POLITICAL SATIRE FOCUSING ON SUCH TEDIOUS TOPICS AS THE FEDERAL RESERVE & HEALTH CARE REFORM--
--THAT'S MY TICKET TO THE TOP, SUCKERS!
BWAH HA HA HA!
HE QUICKLY REALIZED HE NEEDED HELP--WHICH HIS MASTERS IN MOSCOW WERE MORE THAN HAPPY TO PROVIDE...
WITH THE AID OF OUR WILLING ACCOMPLICES IN THE WEEKLY PRESS, YOUR CARTOONS WILL SOON BE DISSEMINATED THROUGHOUT SEVERAL MID-SIZED AMERICAN CITIES!
THIS CALLS FOR A TOAST, FRIEND MIKHAILOVICH! MORE VODKA, PLEASE!
AT THE END OF THE COLD WAR, HE CONTINUED TO SPREAD HIS PATHETIC, OUTDATED MESSAGE OF GODLESS SECULAR HUMANISM--UNDAUNTED BY THE SHOCKING REVELATIONS WHICH SOMEHOW LEAKED FROM THE KREMLIN'S SECRET FILES...
IT SAYS HERE THAT HE IS NOT A PENGUIN AT ALL! HE IS AN AUK!
WHY--I NEVER WOULD HAVE LISTENED TO HIM IF I'D KNOWN THAT! WHO CARES WHAT AN AUK HAS TO SAY?
SMOKING IS FUN!
U.S. News
THE AWFUL TRUTH
OF COURSE, BY THEN HE HAD A NEW MASTER TO SERVE--HIS FRESHLY-INSTALLED COMRADE IN THE WHITE HOUSE, FOR WHOM HE QUICKLY BECAME A TIRELESS PROPAGANDIST AND ALL-AROUND SHILL...
SIGH...CLINTON'S A SPINELESS, AMORAL OPPORTUNIST--BUT I GUESS HE'S MARGINALLY BETTER THAN BUSH...MAYBE...
WHAT A SHAMELESS APOLOGIST!
HOW DOES HE LIVE WITH HIMSELF?
CLINTON WINS
TOM TOMORROW©12-3-97

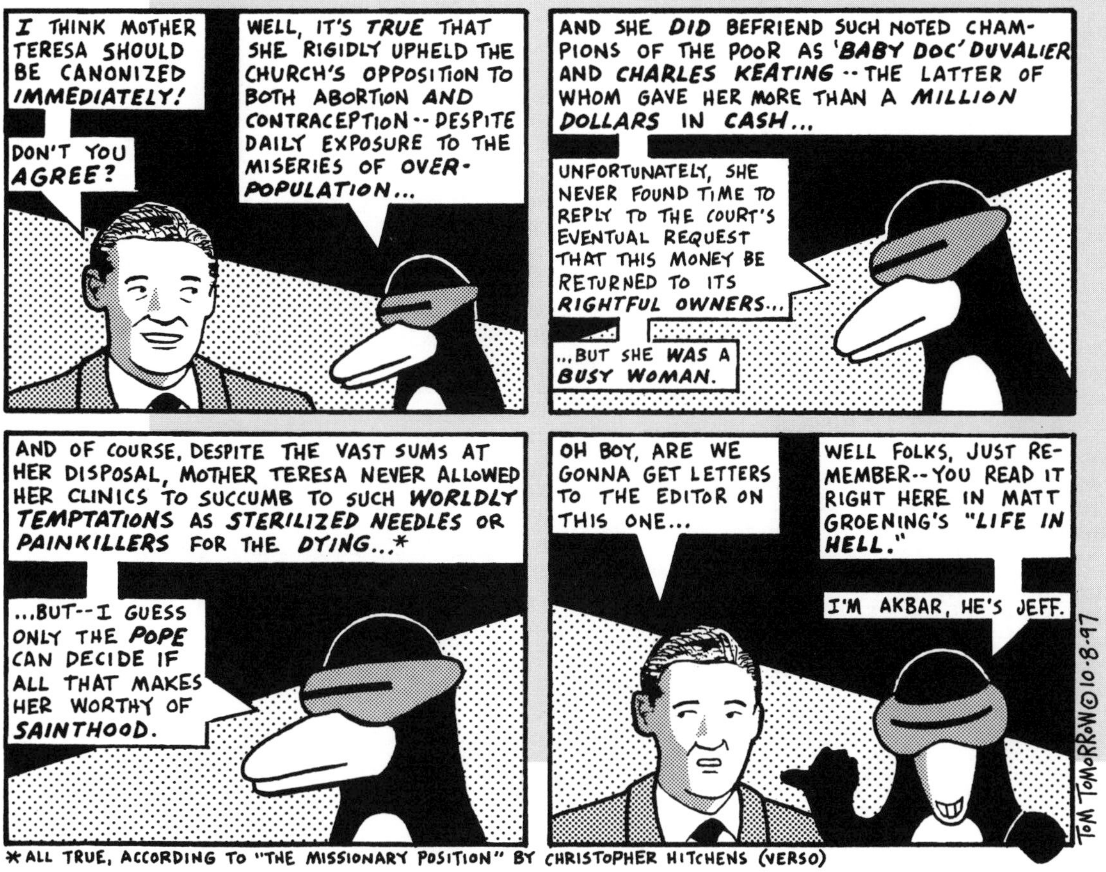
I THINK MOTHER TERESA SHOULD BE CANONIZED IMMEDIATELY!
DON'T YOU AGREE?
WELL, IT'S TRUE THAT SHE RIGIDLY UPHELD THE CHURCH'S OPPOSITION TO BOTH ABORTION AND CONTRACEPTION--DESPITE DAILY EXPOSURE TO THE MISERIES OF OVERPOPULATION...
AND SHE DID BEFRIEND SUCH NOTED CHAMPIONS OF THE POOR AS 'BABY DOC' DUVALIER AND CHARLES KEATING--THE LATTER OF WHOM GAVE HER MORE THAN A MILLION DOLLARS IN CASH...
UNFORTUNATELY, SHE NEVER FOUND TIME TO REPLY TO THE COURT'S EVENTUAL REQUEST THAT THIS MONEY BE RETURNED TO ITS RIGHTFUL OWNERS...
...BUT SHE WAS A BUSY WOMAN.
AND OF COURSE, DESPITE THE VAST SUMS AT HER DISPOSAL, MOTHER TERESA NEVER ALLOWED HER CLINICS TO SUCCUMB TO SUCH WORLDLY TEMPTATIONS AS STERILIZED NEEDLES OR PAINKILLERS FOR THE DYING...*
...BUT--I GUESS ONLY THE POPE CAN DECIDE IF ALL THAT MAKES HER WORTHY OF SAINTHOOD.
OH BOY, ARE WE GONNA GET LETTERS TO THE EDITOR ON THIS ONE...
WELL FOLKS, JUST REMEMBER--YOU READ IT RIGHT HERE IN MATT GROENING'S "LIFE IN HELL."
I'M AKBAR, HE'S JEFF.
TOM TOMORROW©10-8-97

*ALL TRUE, ACCORDING TO "THE MISSIONARY POSITION" BY CHRISTOPHER HITCHENS (VERSO)

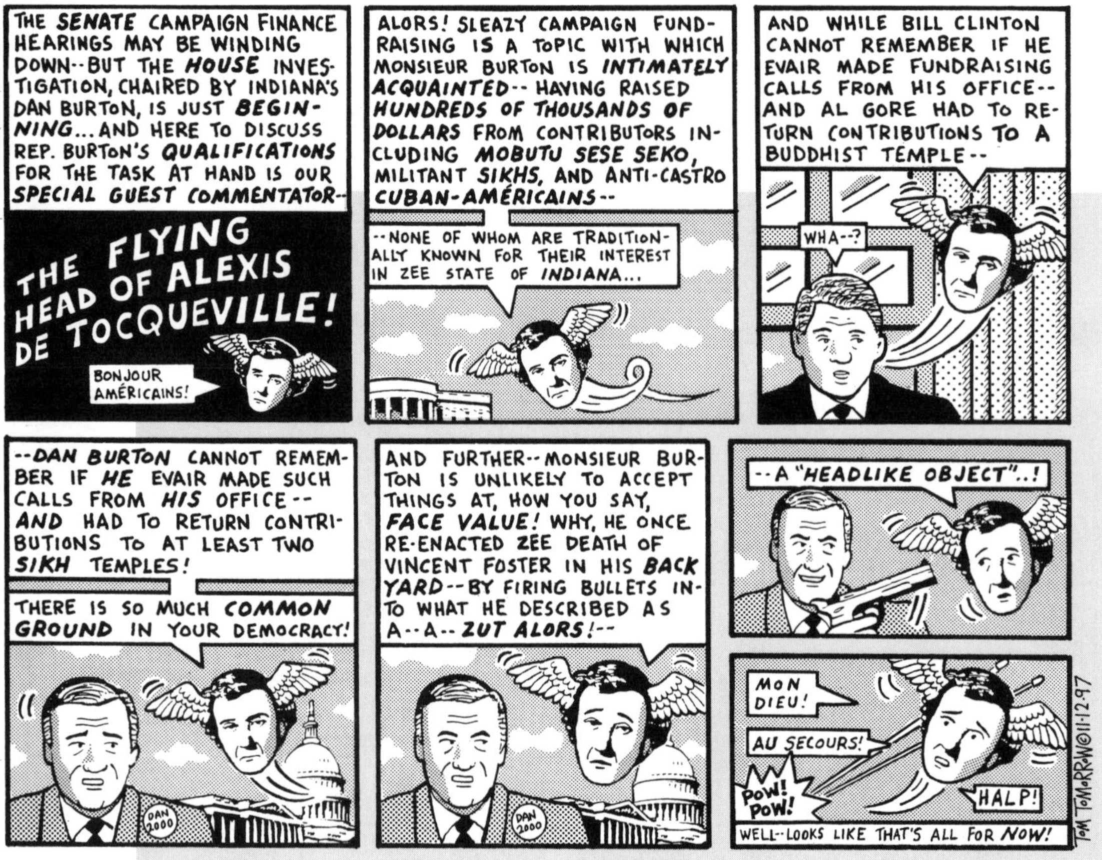
THE SENATE CAMPAIGN FINANCE HEARINGS MAY BE WINDING DOWN--BUT THE HOUSE INVESTIGATION, CHAIRED BY INDIANA'S DAN BURTON, IS JUST BEGINNING... AND HERE TO DISCUSS REP. BURTON'S QUALIFICATIONS FOR THE TASK AT HAND IS OUR SPECIAL GUEST COMMENTATOR--
THE FLYING HEAD OF ALEXIS DE TOCQUEVILLE!
BONJOUR AMÉRICAINS!
ALORS! SLEAZY CAMPAIGN FUND-RAISING IS A TOPIC WITH WHICH MONSIEUR BURTON IS INTIMATELY ACQUAINTED-- HAVING RAISED HUNDREDS OF THOUSANDS OF DOLLARS FROM CONTRIBUTORS INCLUDING MOBUTU SESE SEKO, MILITANT SIKHS, AND ANTI-CASTRO CUBAN-AMÉRICAINS--
--NONE OF WHOM ARE TRADITIONALLY KNOWN FOR THEIR INTEREST IN ZEE STATE OF INDIANA...
AND WHILE BILL CLINTON CANNOT REMEMBER IF HE EVAIR MADE FUNDRAISING CALLS FROM HIS OFFICE-- AND AL GORE HAD TO RETURN CONTRIBUTIONS TO A BUDDHIST TEMPLE--
WHA--?
--DAN BURTON CANNOT REMEMBER IF HE EVAIR MADE SUCH CALLS FROM HIS OFFICE-- AND HAD TO RETURN CONTRIBUTIONS TO AT LEAST TWO SIKH TEMPLES!
THERE IS SO MUCH COMMON GROUND IN YOUR DEMOCRACY!
DAN 2000
AND FURTHER--MONSIEUR BURTON IS UNLIKELY TO ACCEPT THINGS AT, HOW YOU SAY, FACE VALUE! WHY, HE ONCE RE-ENACTED ZEE DEATH OF VINCENT FOSTER IN HIS BACK YARD--BY FIRING BULLETS INTO WHAT HE DESCRIBED AS A--A--ZUT ALORS!--
DAN 2000
--A "HEADLIKE OBJECT"..!
MON DIEU!
AU SECOURS!
POW! POW!
HALP!
WELL--LOOKS LIKE THAT'S ALL FOR NOW!
TOM TOMORROW©11-12-97

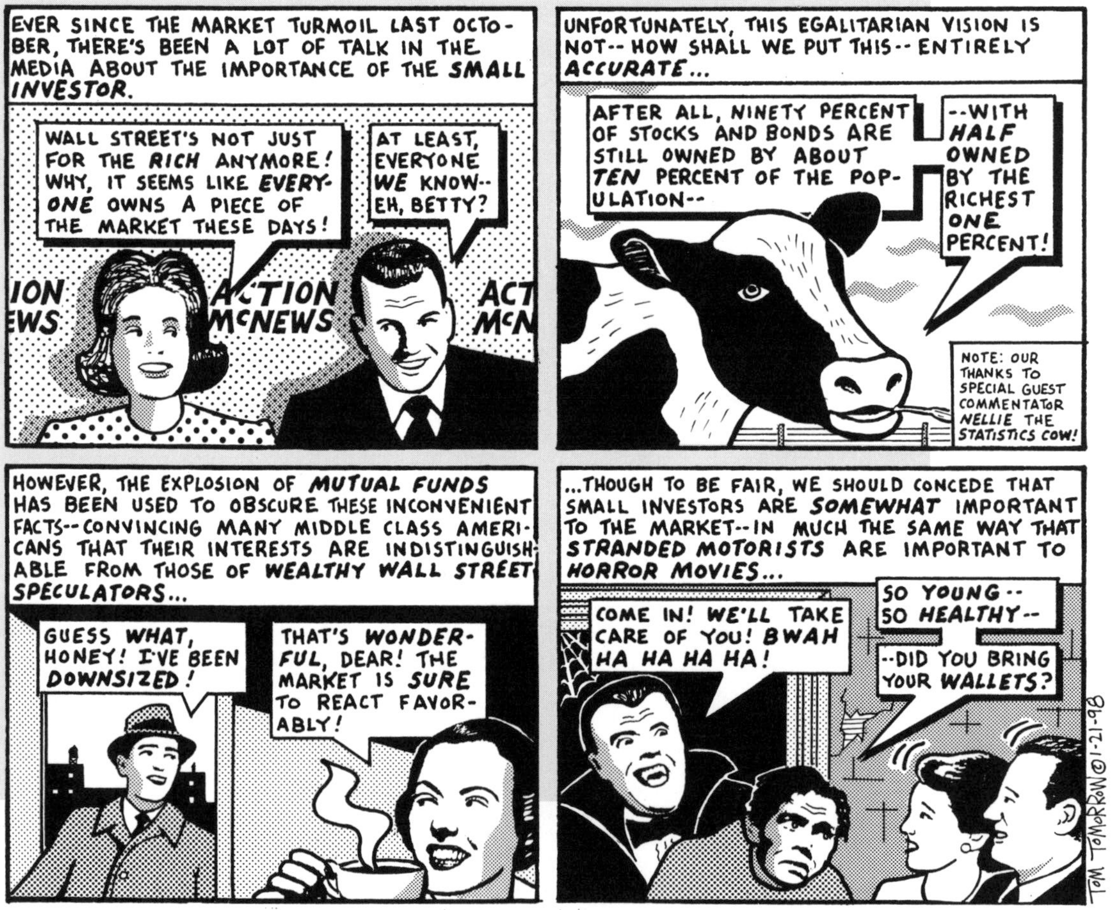
EVER SINCE THE MARKET TURMOIL LAST OCTOBER, THERE'S BEEN A LOT OF TALK IN THE MEDIA ABOUT THE IMPORTANCE OF THE SMALL INVESTOR.
WALL STREET'S NOT JUST FOR THE RICH ANYMORE! WHY, IT SEEMS LIKE EVERYONE OWNS A PIECE OF THE MARKET THESE DAYS!
AT LEAST, EVERYONE WE KNOW-- EH, BETTY?
ACTION McNEWS
UNFORTUNATELY, THIS EGALITARIAN VISION IS NOT-- HOW SHALL WE PUT THIS-- ENTIRELY ACCURATE...
AFTER ALL, NINETY PERCENT OF STOCKS AND BONDS ARE STILL OWNED BY ABOUT TEN PERCENT OF THE POPULATION--
--WITH HALF OWNED BY THE RICHEST ONE PERCENT!
NOTE: OUR THANKS TO SPECIAL GUEST COMMENTATOR NELLIE THE STATISTICS COW!
HOWEVER, THE EXPLOSION OF MUTUAL FUNDS HAS BEEN USED TO OBSCURE THESE INCONVENIENT FACTS--CONVINCING MANY MIDDLE CLASS AMERICANS THAT THEIR INTERESTS ARE INDISTINGUISHABLE FROM THOSE OF WEALTHY WALL STREET SPECULATORS...
GUESS WHAT, HONEY! I'VE BEEN DOWNSIZED!
THAT'S WONDERFUL, DEAR! THE MARKET IS SURE TO REACT FAVORABLY!
...THOUGH TO BE FAIR, WE SHOULD CONCEDE THAT SMALL INVESTORS ARE SOMEWHAT IMPORTANT TO THE MARKET--IN MUCH THE SAME WAY THAT STRANDED MOTORISTS ARE IMPORTANT TO HORROR MOVIES...
COME IN! WE'LL TAKE CARE OF YOU! BWAH HA HA HA HA!
SO YOUNG-- SO HEALTHY--
--DID YOU BRING YOUR WALLETS?
TOM TOMORROW©1-21-98

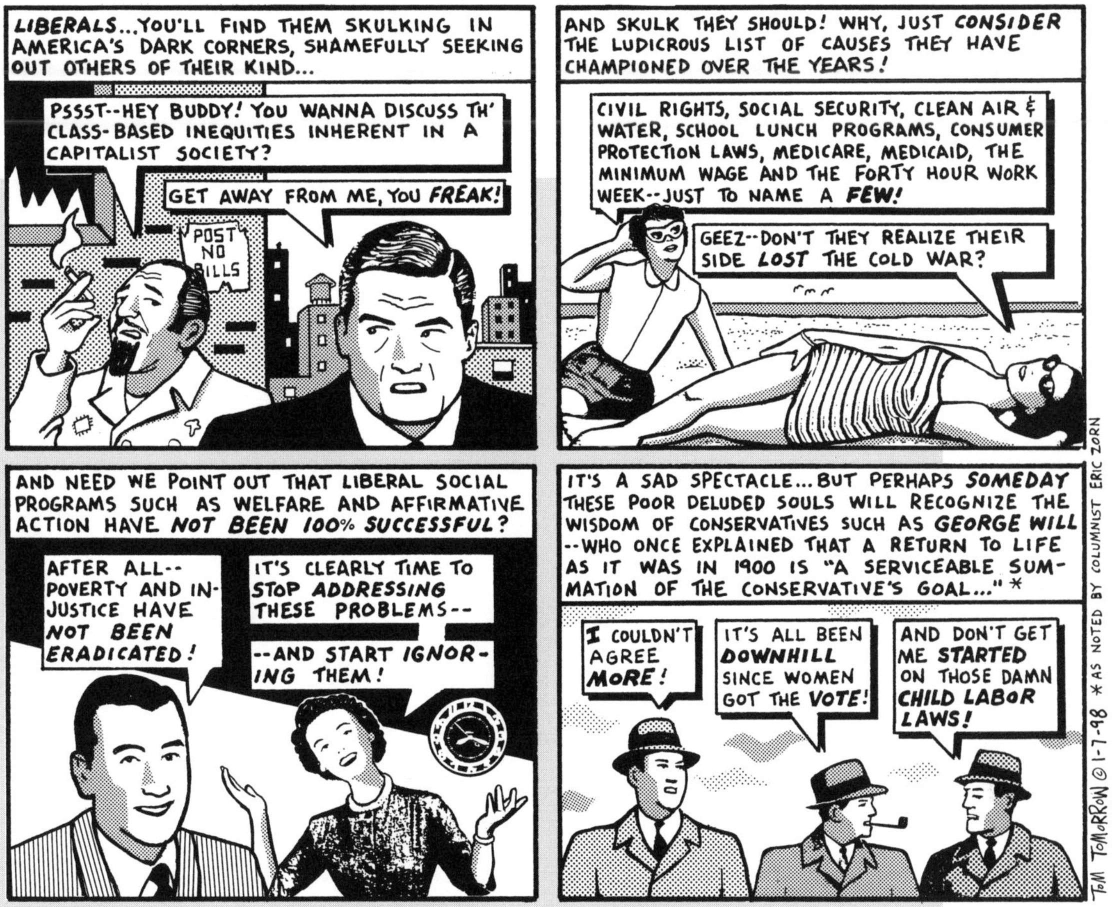
LIBERALS...YOU'LL FIND THEM SKULKING IN AMERICA'S DARK CORNERS, SHAMEFULLY SEEKING OUT OTHERS OF THEIR KIND...
PSSST--HEY BUDDY! YOU WANNA DISCUSS TH' CLASS-BASED INEQUITIES INHERENT IN A CAPITALIST SOCIETY?
GET AWAY FROM ME, YOU FREAK!
POST NO BILLS
AND SKULK THEY SHOULD! WHY, JUST CONSIDER THE LUDICROUS LIST OF CAUSES THEY HAVE CHAMPIONED OVER THE YEARS!
CIVIL RIGHTS, SOCIAL SECURITY, CLEAN AIR & WATER, SCHOOL LUNCH PROGRAMS, CONSUMER PROTECTION LAWS, MEDICARE, MEDICAID, THE MINIMUM WAGE AND THE FORTY HOUR WORK WEEK--JUST TO NAME A FEW!
GEEZ--DON'T THEY REALIZE THEIR SIDE LOST THE COLD WAR?
AND NEED WE POINT OUT THAT LIBERAL SOCIAL PROGRAMS SUCH AS WELFARE AND AFFIRMATIVE ACTION HAVE NOT BEEN 100% SUCCESSFUL?
AFTER ALL--POVERTY AND INJUSTICE HAVE NOT BEEN ERADICATED!
IT'S CLEARLY TIME TO STOP ADDRESSING THESE PROBLEMS--
--AND START IGNORING THEM!
IT'S A SAD SPECTACLE...BUT PERHAPS SOMEDAY THESE POOR DELUDED SOULS WILL RECOGNIZE THE WISDOM OF CONSERVATIVES SUCH AS GEORGE WILL --WHO ONCE EXPLAINED THAT A RETURN TO LIFE AS IT WAS IN 1900 IS "A SERVICEABLE SUMMATION OF THE CONSERVATIVE'S GOAL..." *
I COULDN'T AGREE MORE!
IT'S ALL BEEN DOWNHILL SINCE WOMEN GOT THE VOTE!
AND DON'T GET ME STARTED ON THOSE DAMN CHILD LABOR LAWS!
TOM TOMORROW ©1-7-98 *AS NOTED BY COLUMNIST ERIC ZORN

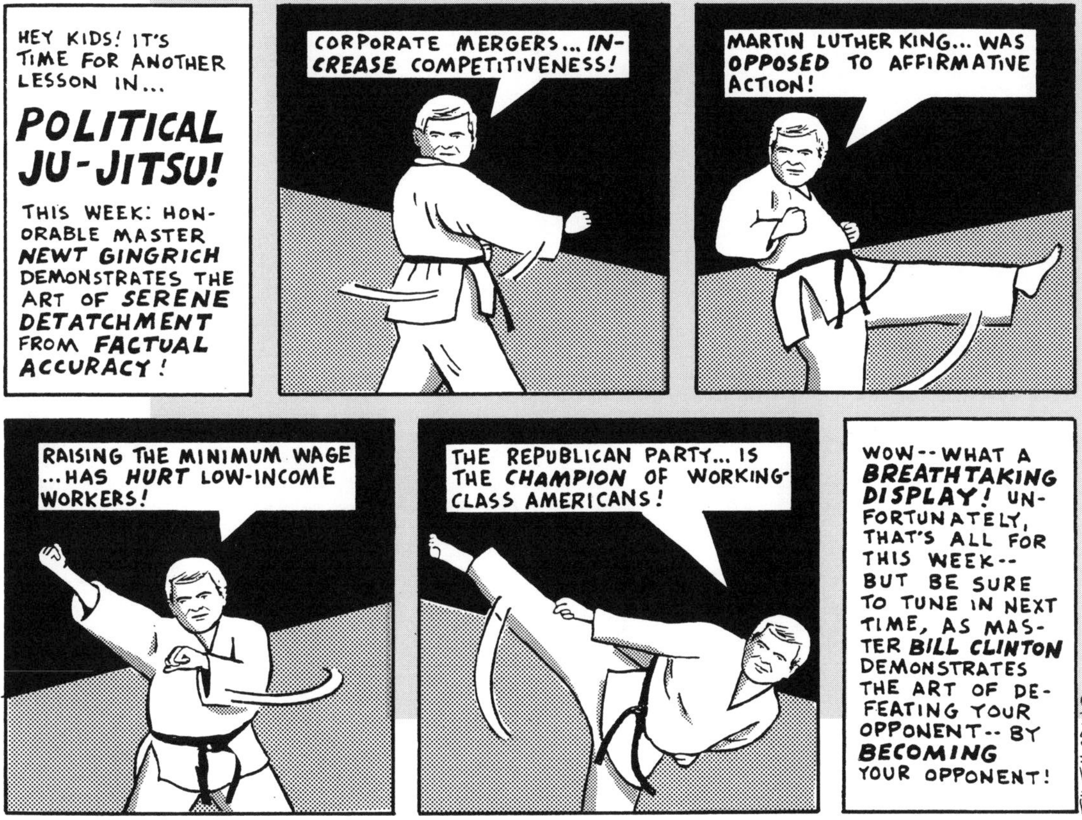
HEY KIDS! IT'S TIME FOR ANOTHER LESSON IN...
POLITICAL JU-JITSU!
THIS WEEK: HONORABLE MASTER NEWT GINGRICH DEMONSTRATES THE ART OF SERENE DETATCHMENT FROM FACTUAL ACCURACY!
CORPORATE MERGERS...INCREASE COMPETITIVENESS!
MARTIN LUTHER KING...WAS OPPOSED TO AFFIRMATIVE ACTION!
RAISING THE MINIMUM WAGE ...HAS HURT LOW-INCOME WORKERS!
THE REPUBLICAN PARTY... IS THE CHAMPION OF WORKING-CLASS AMERICANS!
WOW--WHAT A BREATHTAKING DISPLAY! UNFORTUNATELY, THAT'S ALL FOR THIS WEEK--BUT BE SURE TO TUNE IN NEXT TIME, AS MASTER BILL CLINTON DEMONSTRATES THE ART OF DEFEATING YOUR OPPONENT--BY BECOMING YOUR OPPONENT!
TOM TOMORROW©

Some bonehead transcribed the text to this cartoon and posted it online, sans attribution. Before long, it had been forwarded to pretty much anyone with an email address, and was being reprinted by newspaper columnists around the country, also without attribution. A talk radio station in Seattle even recorded an audio version which they were using as a station ID, at least until I called them and explained the basics of copyright law. The really fun part, of course, was when people started accusing me of having plagiarized—well, myself, basically.

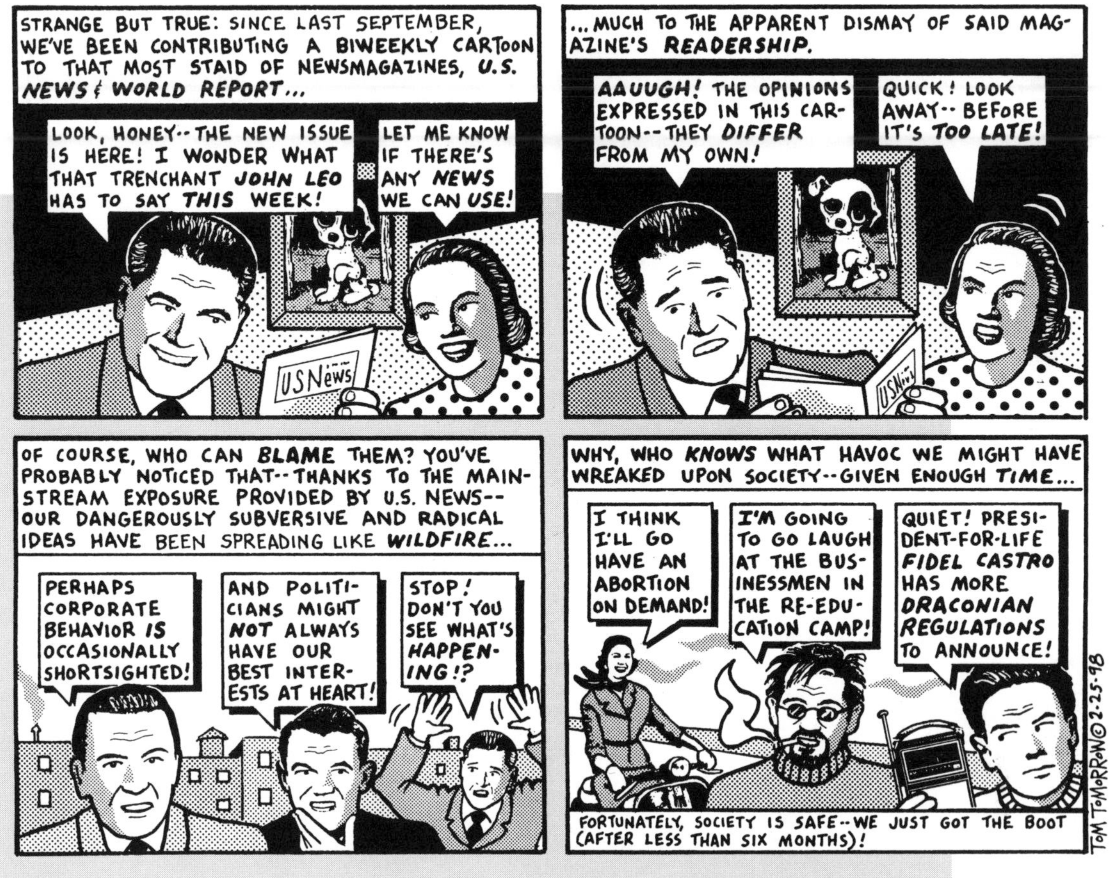
STRANGE BUT TRUE: SINCE LAST SEPTEMBER, WE'VE BEEN CONTRIBUTING A BIWEEKLY CARTOON TO THAT MOST STAID OF NEWSMAGAZINES, U.S. NEWS & WORLD REPORT...
LOOK, HONEY--THE NEW ISSUE IS HERE! I WONDER WHAT THAT TRENCHANT JOHN LEO HAS TO SAY THIS WEEK!
LET ME KNOW IF THERE'S ANY NEWS WE CAN USE!
USNews
...MUCH TO THE APPARENT DISMAY OF SAID MAGAZINE'S READERSHIP.
AAUUGH! THE OPINIONS EXPRESSED IN THIS CARTOON--THEY DIFFER FROM MY OWN!
QUICK! LOOK AWAY--BEFORE IT'S TOO LATE!
OF COURSE, WHO CAN BLAME THEM? YOU'VE PROBABLY NOTICED THAT--THANKS TO THE MAINSTREAM EXPOSURE PROVIDED BY U.S. NEWS--OUR DANGEROUSLY SUBVERSIVE AND RADICAL IDEAS HAVE BEEN SPREADING LIKE WILDFIRE...
PERHAPS CORPORATE BEHAVIOR IS OCCASIONALLY SHORTSIGHTED!
AND POLITICIANS MIGHT NOT ALWAYS HAVE OUR BEST INTERESTS AT HEART!
STOP! DON'T YOU SEE WHAT'S HAPPENING!?
WHY, WHO KNOWS WHAT HAVOC WE MIGHT HAVE WREAKED UPON SOCIETY--GIVEN ENOUGH TIME...
I THINK I'LL GO HAVE AN ABORTION ON DEMAND!
I'M GOING TO GO LAUGH AT THE BUSINESSMEN IN THE RE-EDUCATION CAMP!
QUIET! PRESIDENT-FOR-LIFE FIDEL CASTRO HAS MORE DRACONIAN REGULATIONS TO ANNOUNCE!
FORTUNATELY, SOCIETY IS SAFE--WE JUST GOT THE BOOT (AFTER LESS THAN SIX MONTHS)!
TOM TOMORROW©2-25-98

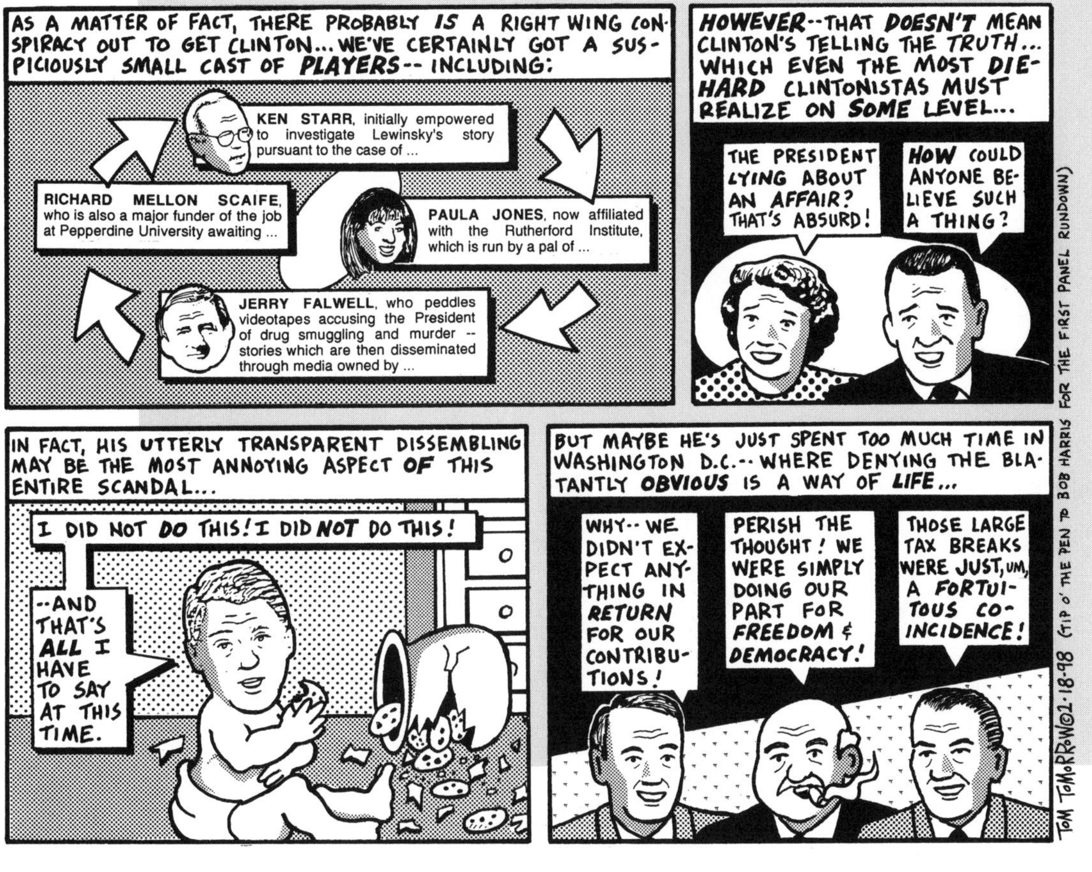
AS A MATTER OF FACT, THERE PROBABLY IS A RIGHT WING CONSPIRACY OUT TO GET CLINTON... WE'VE CERTAINLY GOT A SUSPICIOUSLY SMALL CAST OF PLAYERS-- INCLUDING:
KEN STARR, initially empowered to investigate Lewinsky's story pursuant to the case of ...
PAULA JONES, now affiliated with the Rutherford Institute, which is run by a pal of ...
JERRY FALWELL, who peddles videotapes accusing the President of drug smuggling and murder -- stories which are then disseminated through media owned by ...
RICHARD MELLON SCAIFE, who is also a major funder of the job at Pepperdine University awaiting ...
HOWEVER--THAT DOESN'T MEAN CLINTON'S TELLING THE TRUTH... WHICH EVEN THE MOST DIE-HARD CLINTONISTAS MUST REALIZE ON SOME LEVEL...
THE PRESIDENT LYING ABOUT AN AFFAIR? THAT'S ABSURD!
HOW COULD ANYONE BELIEVE SUCH A THING?
IN FACT, HIS UTTERLY TRANSPARENT DISSEMBLING MAY BE THE MOST ANNOYING ASPECT OF THIS ENTIRE SCANDAL...
I DID NOT DO THIS! I DID NOT DO THIS!
--AND THAT'S ALL I HAVE TO SAY AT THIS TIME.
BUT MAYBE HE'S JUST SPENT TOO MUCH TIME IN WASHINGTON D.C.--WHERE DENYING THE BLATANTLY OBVIOUS IS A WAY OF LIFE...
WHY--WE DIDN'T EXPECT ANYTHING IN RETURN FOR OUR CONTRIBUTIONS!
PERISH THE THOUGHT! WE WERE SIMPLY DOING OUR PART FOR FREEDOM & DEMOCRACY!
THOSE LARGE TAX BREAKS WERE JUST, UM, A FORTUITOUS COINCIDENCE!
TOM TOMORROW©2-18-98 (TIP O' THE PEN TO BOB HARRIS FOR THE FIRST PANEL RUNDOWN)

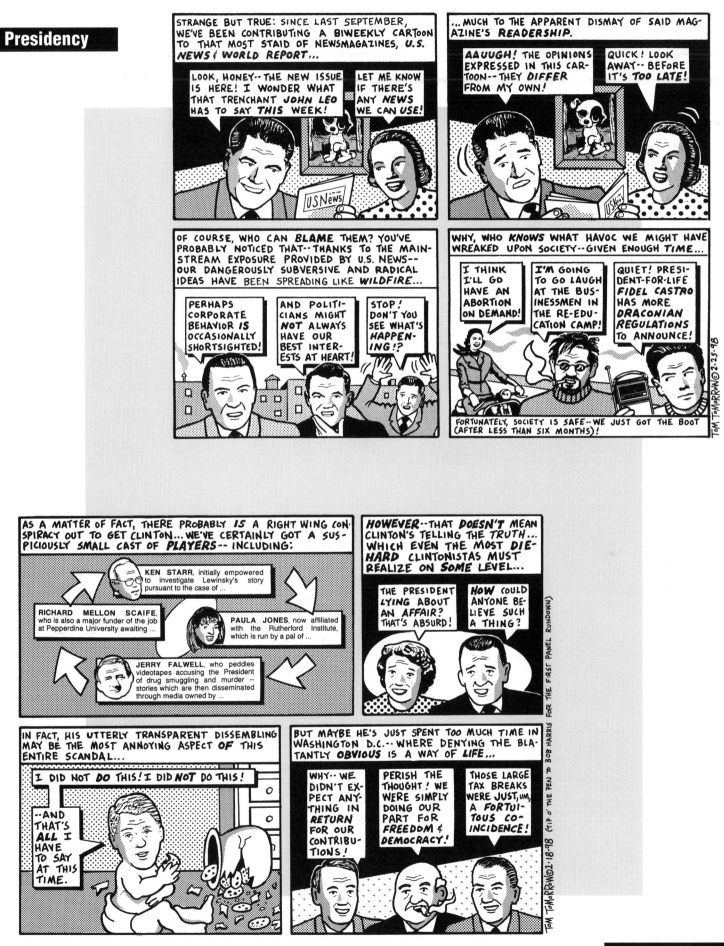

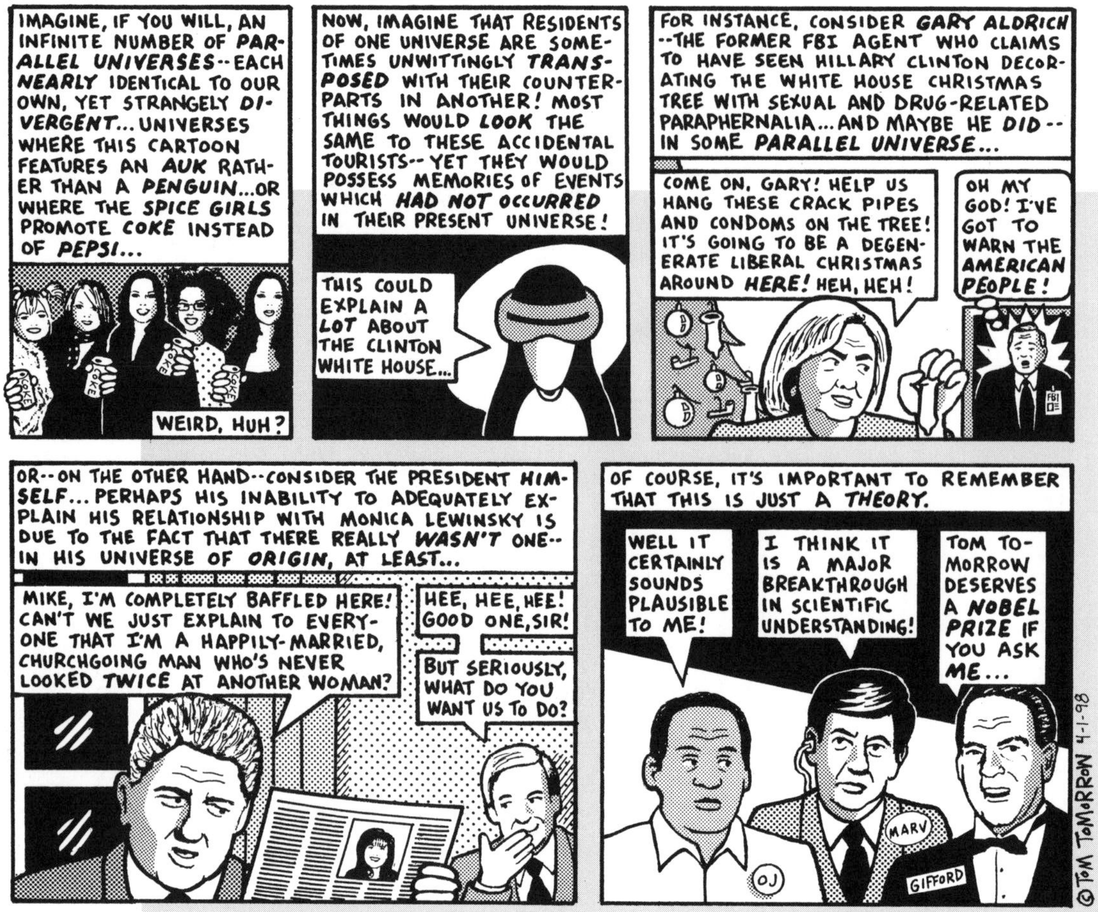
IMAGINE, IF YOU WILL, AN INFINITE NUMBER OF PARALLEL UNIVERSES--EACH NEARLY IDENTICAL TO OUR OWN, YET STRANGELY DIVERGENT... UNIVERSES WHERE THIS CARTOON FEATURES AN AUK RATHER THAN A PENGUIN...OR WHERE THE SPICE GIRLS PROMOTE COKE INSTEAD OF PEPSI...
WEIRD, HUH?
NOW, IMAGINE THAT RESIDENTS OF ONE UNIVERSE ARE SOMETIMES UNWITTINGLY TRANSPOSED WITH THEIR COUNTERPARTS IN ANOTHER! MOST THINGS WOULD LOOK THE SAME TO THESE ACCIDENTAL TOURISTS--YET THEY WOULD POSSESS MEMORIES OF EVENTS WHICH HAD NOT OCCURRED IN THEIR PRESENT UNIVERSE!
THIS COULD EXPLAIN A LOT ABOUT THE CLINTON WHITE HOUSE...
FOR INSTANCE, CONSIDER GARY ALDRICH--THE FORMER FBI AGENT WHO CLAIMS TO HAVE SEEN HILLARY CLINTON DECORATING THE WHITE HOUSE CHRISTMAS TREE WITH SEXUAL AND DRUG-RELATED PARAPHERNALIA... AND MAYBE HE DID--IN SOME PARALLEL UNIVERSE...
COME ON, GARY! HELP US HANG THESE CRACK PIPES AND CONDOMS ON THE TREE! IT'S GOING TO BE A DEGENERATE LIBERAL CHRISTMAS AROUND HERE! HEH, HEH!
OH MY GOD! I'VE GOT TO WARN THE AMERICAN PEOPLE!
OR--ON THE OTHER HAND--CONSIDER THE PRESIDENT HIMSELF... PERHAPS HIS INABILITY TO ADEQUATELY EXPLAIN HIS RELATIONSHIP WITH MONICA LEWINSKY IS DUE TO THE FACT THAT THERE REALLY WASN'T ONE--IN HIS UNIVERSE OF ORIGIN, AT LEAST...
MIKE, I'M COMPLETELY BAFFLED HERE! CAN'T WE JUST EXPLAIN TO EVERYONE THAT I'M A HAPPILY-MARRIED, CHURCHGOING MAN WHO'S NEVER LOOKED TWICE AT ANOTHER WOMAN?
HEE, HEE, HEE! GOOD ONE, SIR!
BUT SERIOUSLY, WHAT DO YOU WANT US TO DO?
OF COURSE, IT'S IMPORTANT TO REMEMBER THAT THIS IS JUST A THEORY.
WELL IT CERTAINLY SOUNDS PLAUSIBLE TO ME!
I THINK IT IS A MAJOR BREAKTHROUGH IN SCIENTIFIC UNDERSTANDING!
TOM TOMORROW DESERVES A NOBEL PRIZE IF YOU ASK ME...
OJ
MARV
GIFFORD
©TOM TOMORROW 4-1-98

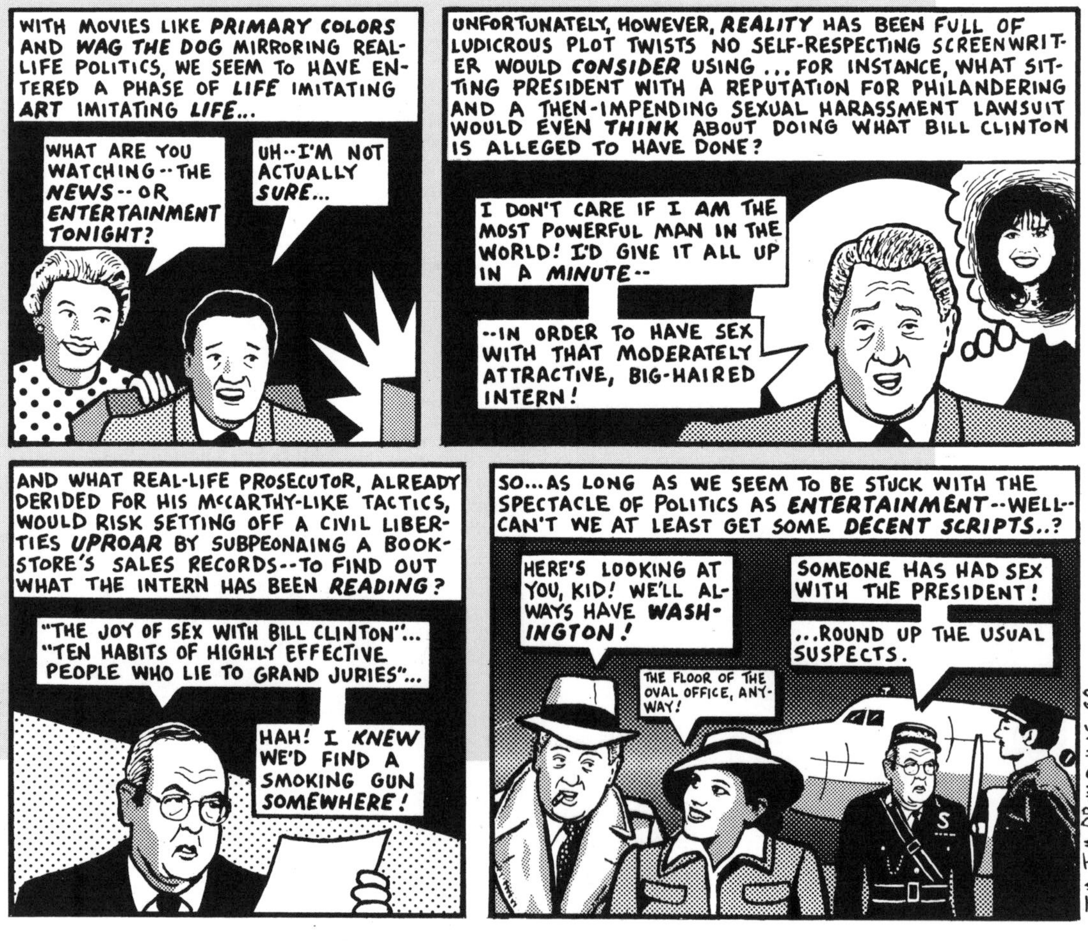
WITH MOVIES LIKE PRIMARY COLORS AND WAG THE DOG MIRRORING REAL-LIFE POLITICS, WE SEEM TO HAVE ENTERED A PHASE OF LIFE IMITATING ART IMITATING LIFE...
WHAT ARE YOU WATCHING--THE NEWS--OR ENTERTAINMENT TONIGHT?
UH--I'M NOT ACTUALLY SURE...
UNFORTUNATELY, HOWEVER, REALITY HAS BEEN FULL OF LUDICROUS PLOT TWISTS NO SELF-RESPECTING SCREENWRITER WOULD CONSIDER USING... FOR INSTANCE, WHAT SITTING PRESIDENT WITH A REPUTATION FOR PHILANDERING AND A THEN-IMPENDING SEXUAL HARASSMENT LAWSUIT WOULD EVEN THINK ABOUT DOING WHAT BILL CLINTON IS ALLEGED TO HAVE DONE?
I DON'T CARE IF I AM THE MOST POWERFUL MAN IN THE WORLD! I'D GIVE IT ALL UP IN A MINUTE--
--IN ORDER TO HAVE SEX WITH THAT MODERATELY ATTRACTIVE, BIG-HAIRED INTERN!
AND WHAT REAL-LIFE PROSECUTOR, ALREADY DERIDED FOR HIS McCARTHY-LIKE TACTICS, WOULD RISK SETTING OFF A CIVIL LIBERTIES UPROAR BY SUBPEONAING A BOOKSTORE'S SALES RECORDS--TO FIND OUT WHAT THE INTERN HAS BEEN READING?
"THE JOY OF SEX WITH BILL CLINTON"... "TEN HABITS OF HIGHLY EFFECTIVE PEOPLE WHO LIE TO GRAND JURIES"...
HAH! I KNEW WE'D FIND A SMOKING GUN SOMEWHERE!
SO...AS LONG AS WE SEEM TO BE STUCK WITH THE SPECTACLE OF POLITICS AS ENTERTAINMENT--WELL--CAN'T WE AT LEAST GET SOME DECENT SCRIPTS..?
HERE'S LOOKING AT YOU, KID! WE'LL ALWAYS HAVE WASHINGTON!
THE FLOOR OF THE OVAL OFFICE, ANYWAY!
SOMEONE HAS HAD SEX WITH THE PRESIDENT!
...ROUND UP THE USUAL SUSPECTS.
TOM TOMORROW© 4-15-98

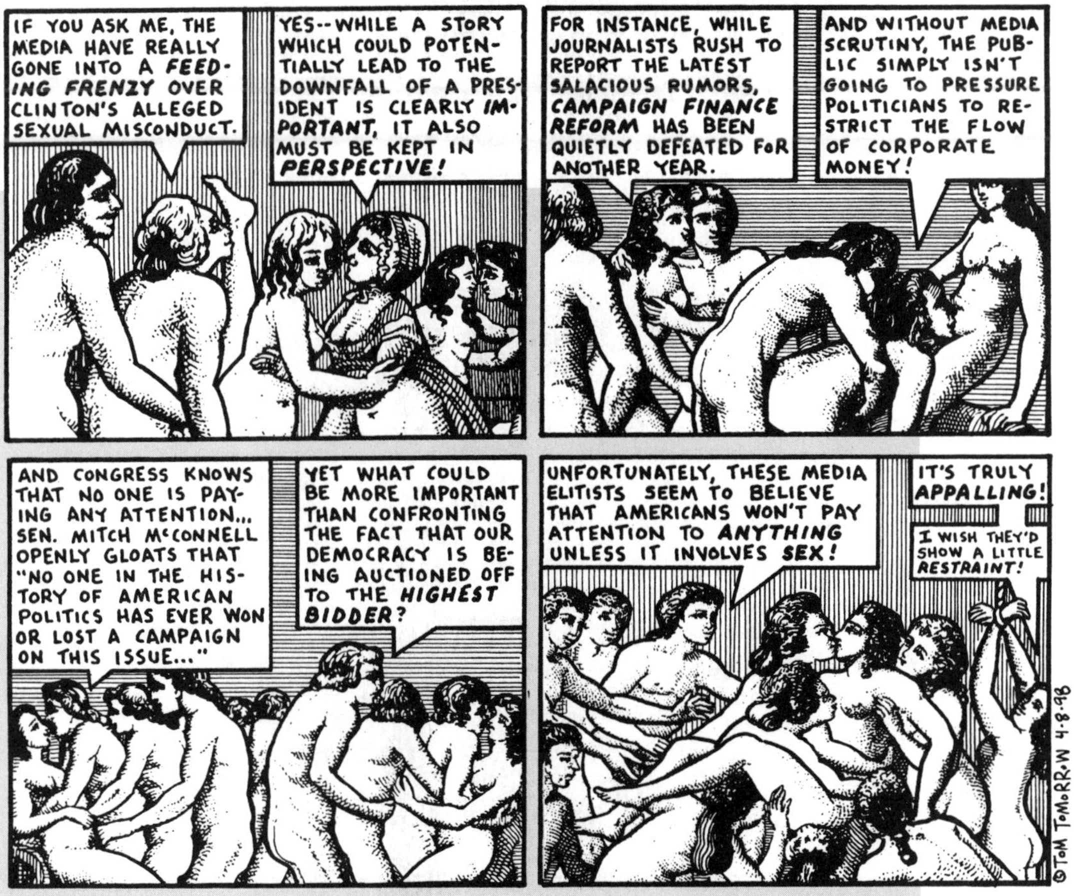
IF YOU ASK ME, THE MEDIA HAVE REALLY GONE INTO A FEEDING FRENZY OVER CLINTON'S ALLEGED SEXUAL MISCONDUCT.
YES--WHILE A STORY WHICH COULD POTENTIALLY LEAD TO THE DOWNFALL OF A PRESIDENT IS CLEARLY IMPORTANT, IT ALSO MUST BE KEPT IN PERSPECTIVE!
FOR INSTANCE, WHILE JOURNALISTS RUSH TO REPORT THE LATEST SALACIOUS RUMORS, CAMPAIGN FINANCE REFORM HAS BEEN QUIETLY DEFEATED FOR ANOTHER YEAR.
AND WITHOUT MEDIA SCRUTINY, THE PUBLIC SIMPLY ISN'T GOING TO PRESSURE POLITICIANS TO RESTRICT THE FLOW OF CORPORATE MONEY!
AND CONGRESS KNOWS THAT NO ONE IS PAYING ANY ATTENTION... SEN. MITCH McCONNELL OPENLY GLOATS THAT "NO ONE IN THE HISTORY OF AMERICAN POLITICS HAS EVER WON OR LOST A CAMPAIGN ON THIS ISSUE..."
YET WHAT COULD BE MORE IMPORTANT THAN CONFRONTING THE FACT THAT OUR DEMOCRACY IS BEING AUCTIONED OFF TO THE HIGHEST BIDDER?
UNFORTUNATELY, THESE MEDIA ELITISTS SEEM TO BELIEVE THAT AMERICANS WON'T PAY ATTENTION TO ANYTHING UNLESS IT INVOLVES SEX!
IT'S TRULY APPALLING!
I WISH THEY'D SHOW A LITTLE RESTRAINT!
©TOM TOMORROW 4-8-98

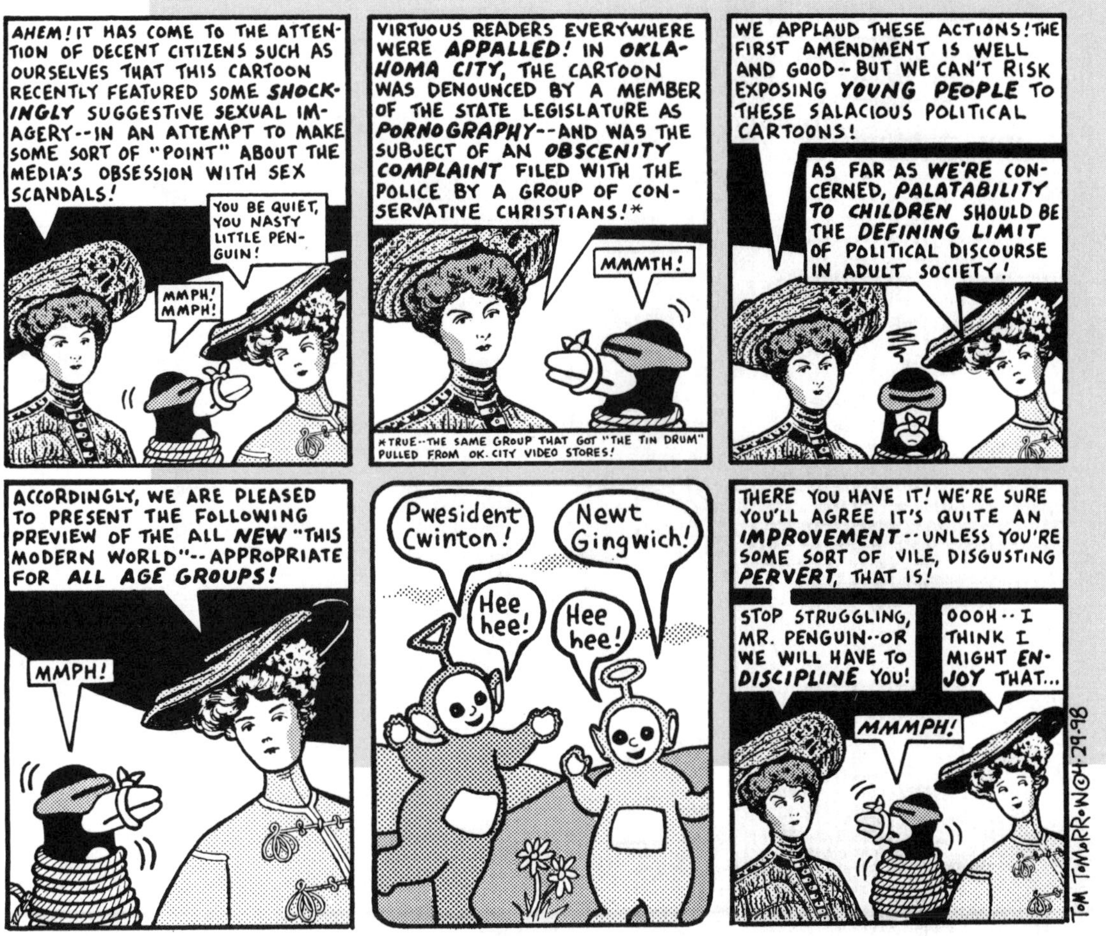
AHEM! IT HAS COME TO THE ATTENTION OF DECENT CITIZENS SUCH AS OURSELVES THAT THIS CARTOON RECENTLY FEATURED SOME SHOCKINGLY SUGGESTIVE SEXUAL IMAGERY--IN AN ATTEMPT TO MAKE SOME SORT OF "POINT" ABOUT THE MEDIA'S OBSESSION WITH SEX SCANDALS!
YOU BE QUIET, YOU NASTY LITTLE PENGUIN!
MMPH! MMPH!
VIRTUOUS READERS EVERYWHERE WERE APPALLED! IN OKLAHOMA CITY, THE CARTOON WAS DENOUNCED BY A MEMBER OF THE STATE LEGISLATURE AS PORNOGRAPHY--AND WAS THE SUBJECT OF AN OBSCENITY COMPLAINT FILED WITH THE POLICE BY A GROUP OF CONSERVATIVE CHRISTIANS!*
MMMTH!
*TRUE--THE SAME GROUP THAT GOT "THE TIN DRUM" PULLED FROM OK. CITY VIDEO STORES!
WE APPLAUD THESE ACTIONS! THE FIRST AMENDMENT IS WELL AND GOOD--BUT WE CAN'T RISK EXPOSING YOUNG PEOPLE TO THESE SALACIOUS POLITICAL CARTOONS!
AS FAR AS WE'RE CONCERNED, PALATABILITY TO CHILDREN SHOULD BE THE DEFINING LIMIT OF POLITICAL DISCOURSE IN ADULT SOCIETY!
ACCORDINGLY, WE ARE PLEASED TO PRESENT THE FOLLOWING PREVIEW OF THE ALL NEW "THIS MODERN WORLD"--APPROPRIATE FOR ALL AGE GROUPS!
MMPH!
Pwesident Cwinton!
Newt Gingwich!
Hee hee!
Hee hee!
THERE YOU HAVE IT! WE'RE SURE YOU'LL AGREE IT'S QUITE AN IMPROVEMENT--UNLESS YOU'RE SOME SORT OF VILE, DISGUSTING PERVERT, THAT IS!
STOP STRUGGLING, MR. PENGUIN--OR WE WILL HAVE TO DISCIPLINE YOU!
OOOH--I THINK I MIGHT ENJOY THAT...
MMMPH!
TOM TOMORROW©4-29-98

This is all true. The director of a group called Oklahomans for Children and Family denounced the cartoon as pornography which might lead teenagers to experiment with deviant sexual behavior, and tried to have me brought up on charges. Fortunately the local district attorney had some passing familiarity with the first amendment and declined to prosecute. Unfortunately the local paper caved under all the pressure and dropped the strip.

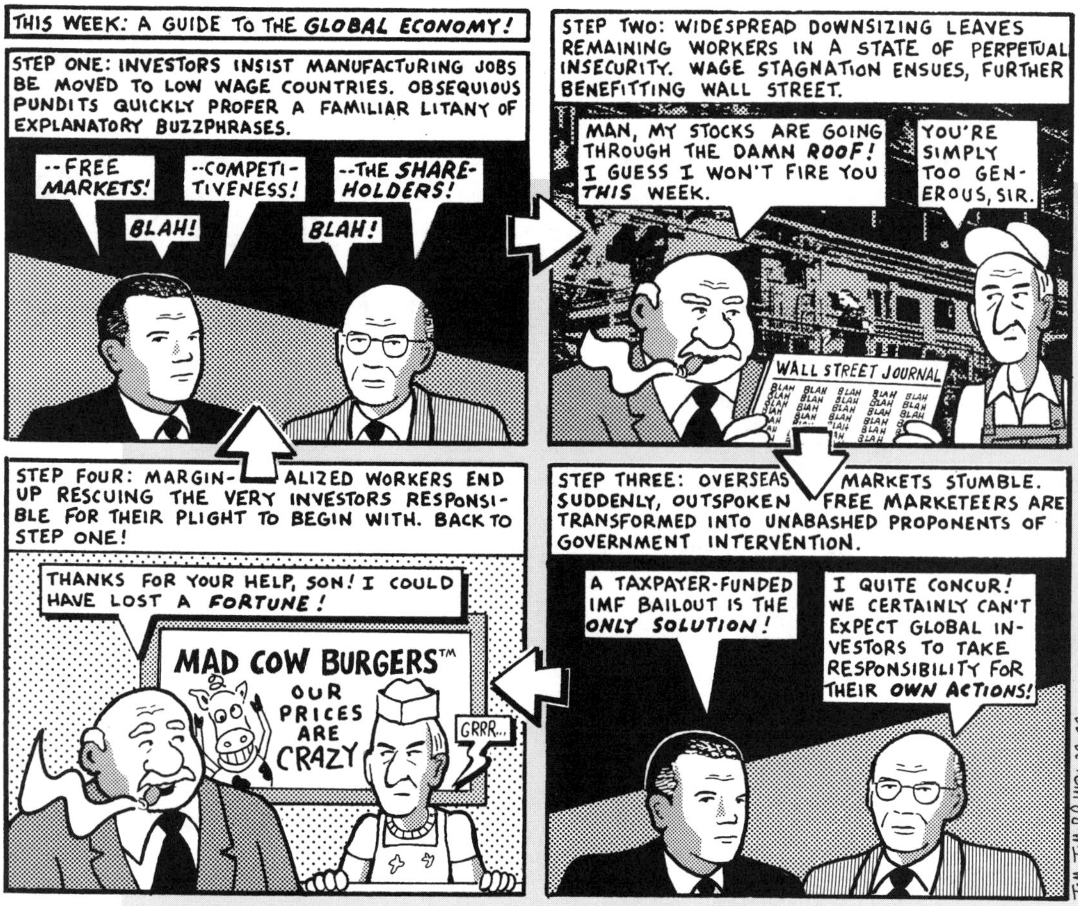
THIS WEEK: A GUIDE TO THE GLOBAL ECONOMY!
STEP ONE: INVESTORS INSIST MANUFACTURING JOBS BE MOVED TO LOW WAGE COUNTRIES. OBSEQUIOUS PUNDITS QUICKLY PROFER A FAMILIAR LITANY OF EXPLANATORY BUZZPHRASES.
--FREE MARKETS!
BLAH!
--COMPETITIVENESS!
BLAH!
--THE SHAREHOLDERS!
STEP TWO: WIDESPREAD DOWNSIZING LEAVES REMAINING WORKERS IN A STATE OF PERPETUAL INSECURITY. WAGE STAGNATION ENSUES, FURTHER BENEFITTING WALL STREET.
MAN, MY STOCKS ARE GOING THROUGH THE DAMN ROOF! I GUESS I WON'T FIRE YOU THIS WEEK.
YOU'RE SIMPLY TOO GENEROUS, SIR.
WALL STREET JOURNAL
STEP THREE: OVERSEAS MARKETS STUMBLE. SUDDENLY, OUTSPOKEN FREE MARKETEERS ARE TRANSFORMED INTO UNABASHED PROPONENTS OF GOVERNMENT INTERVENTION.
A TAXPAYER-FUNDED IMF BAILOUT IS THE ONLY SOLUTION!
I QUITE CONCUR! WE CERTAINLY CAN'T EXPECT GLOBAL INVESTORS TO TAKE RESPONSIBILITY FOR THEIR OWN ACTIONS!
STEP FOUR: MARGINALIZED WORKERS END UP RESCUING THE VERY INVESTORS RESPONSIBLE FOR THEIR PLIGHT TO BEGIN WITH. BACK TO STEP ONE!
THANKS FOR YOUR HELP, SON! I COULD HAVE LOST A FORTUNE!
MAD COW BURGERS™
OUR PRICES ARE CRAZY
GRRR...
TOM TOMORROW©1-28-98

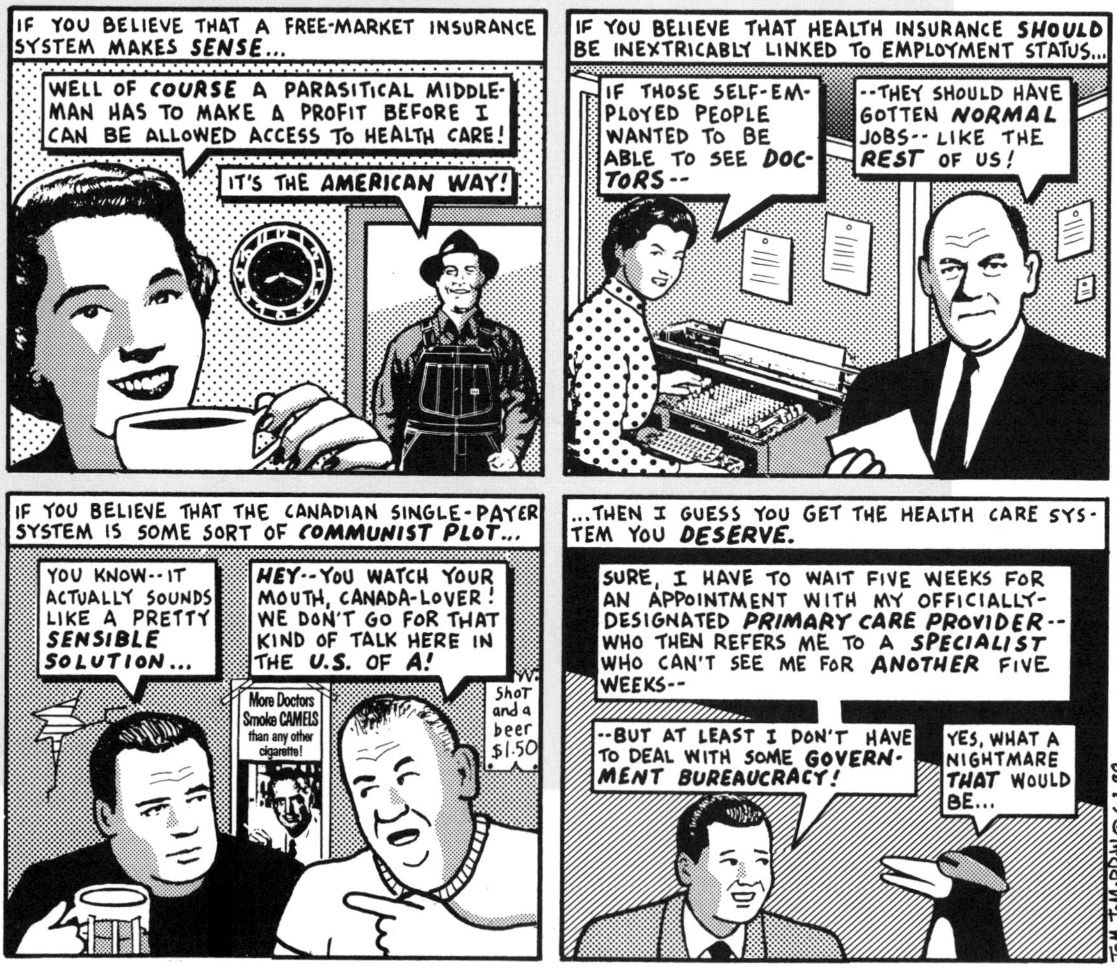
IF YOU BELIEVE THAT A FREE-MARKET INSURANCE SYSTEM MAKES SENSE...
WELL OF COURSE A PARASITICAL MIDDLEMAN HAS TO MAKE A PROFIT BEFORE I CAN BE ALLOWED ACCESS TO HEALTH CARE!
IT'S THE AMERICAN WAY!
IF YOU BELIEVE THAT HEALTH INSURANCE SHOULD BE INEXTRICABLY LINKED TO EMPLOYMENT STATUS...
IF THOSE SELF-EMPLOYED PEOPLE WANTED TO BE ABLE TO SEE DOCTORS--
--THEY SHOULD HAVE GOTTEN NORMAL JOBS--LIKE THE REST OF US!
IF YOU BELIEVE THAT THE CANADIAN SINGLE-PAYER SYSTEM IS SOME SORT OF COMMUNIST PLOT...
YOU KNOW--IT ACTUALLY SOUNDS LIKE A PRETTY SENSIBLE SOLUTION...
HEY--YOU WATCH YOUR MOUTH, CANADA-LOVER! WE DON'T GO FOR THAT KIND OF TALK HERE IN THE U.S. OF A!
More Doctors Smoke CAMELS than any other cigarette!
Shot and a beer $1.50
...THEN I GUESS YOU GET THE HEALTH CARE SYSTEM YOU DESERVE.
SURE, I HAVE TO WAIT FIVE WEEKS FOR AN APPOINTMENT WITH MY OFFICIALLY-DESIGNATED PRIMARY CARE PROVIDER--WHO THEN REFERS ME TO A SPECIALIST WHO CAN'T SEE ME FOR ANOTHER FIVE WEEKS--
--BUT AT LEAST I DON'T HAVE TO DEAL WITH SOME GOVERNMENT BUREAUCRACY!
YES, WHAT A NIGHTMARE THAT WOULD BE...
TOM TOMORROW©6-3-98

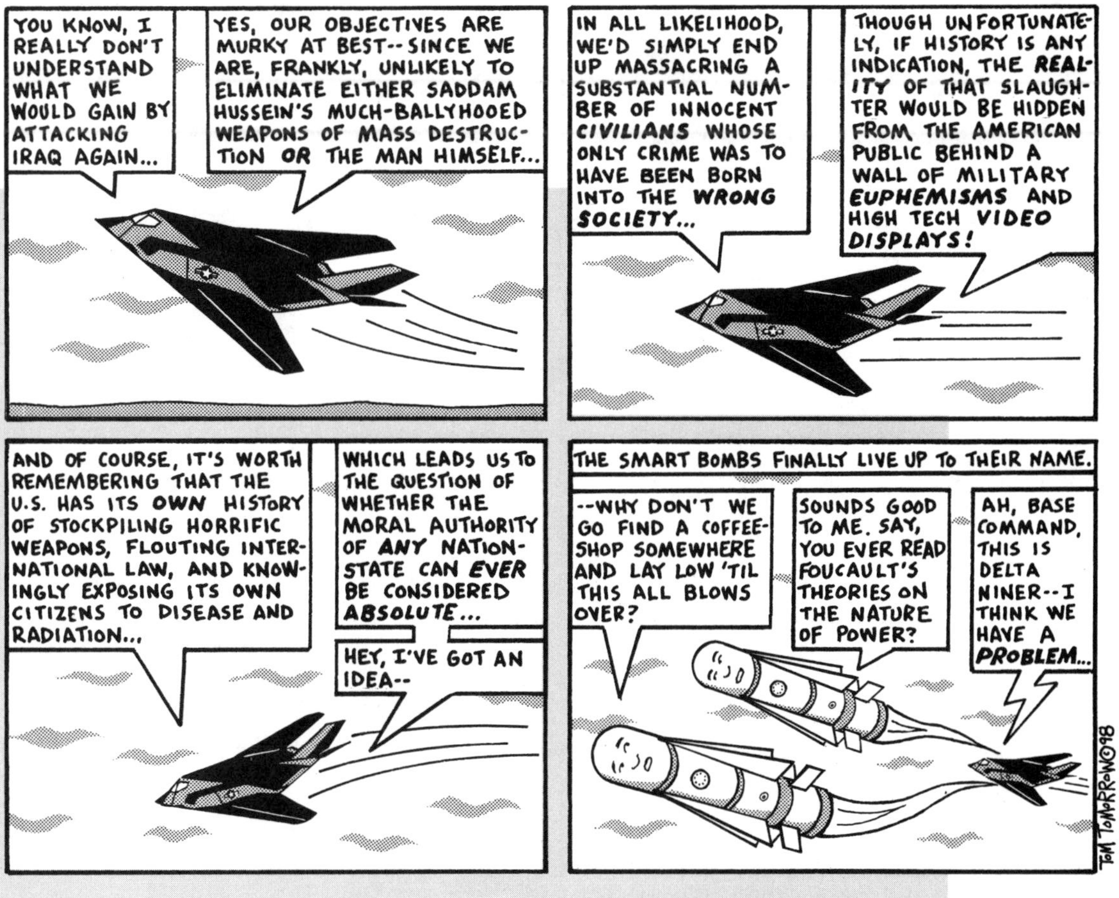
YOU KNOW, I REALLY DON'T UNDERSTAND WHAT WE WOULD GAIN BY ATTACKING IRAQ AGAIN...
YES, OUR OBJECTIVES ARE MURKY AT BEST--SINCE WE ARE, FRANKLY, UNLIKELY TO ELIMINATE EITHER SADDAM HUSSEIN'S MUCH-BALLYHOOED WEAPONS OF MASS DESTRUCTION OR THE MAN HIMSELF...
IN ALL LIKELIHOOD, WE'D SIMPLY END UP MASSACRING A SUBSTANTIAL NUMBER OF INNOCENT CIVILIANS WHOSE ONLY CRIME WAS TO HAVE BEEN BORN INTO THE WRONG SOCIETY...
THOUGH UNFORTUNATELY, IF HISTORY IS ANY INDICATION, THE REALITY OF THAT SLAUGHTER WOULD BE HIDDEN FROM THE AMERICAN PUBLIC BEHIND A WALL OF MILITARY EUPHEMISMS AND HIGH TECH VIDEO DISPLAYS!
AND OF COURSE, IT'S WORTH REMEMBERING THAT THE U.S. HAS ITS OWN HISTORY OF STOCKPILING HORRIFIC WEAPONS, FLOUTING INTERNATIONAL LAW, AND KNOWINGLY EXPOSING ITS OWN CITIZENS TO DISEASE AND RADIATION...
WHICH LEADS US TO THE QUESTION OF WHETHER THE MORAL AUTHORITY OF ANY NATION-STATE CAN EVER BE CONSIDERED ABSOLUTE...
HEY, I'VE GOT AN IDEA--
THE SMART BOMBS FINALLY LIVE UP TO THEIR NAME.
--WHY DON'T WE GO FIND A COFFEE-SHOP SOMEWHERE AND LAY LOW 'TIL THIS ALL BLOWS OVER?
SOUNDS GOOD TO ME. SAY, YOU EVER READ FOUCAULT'S THEORIES ON THE NATURE OF POWER?
AH, BASE COMMAND, THIS IS DELTA NINER--I THINK WE HAVE A PROBLEM...
TOM TOMORROW ©98

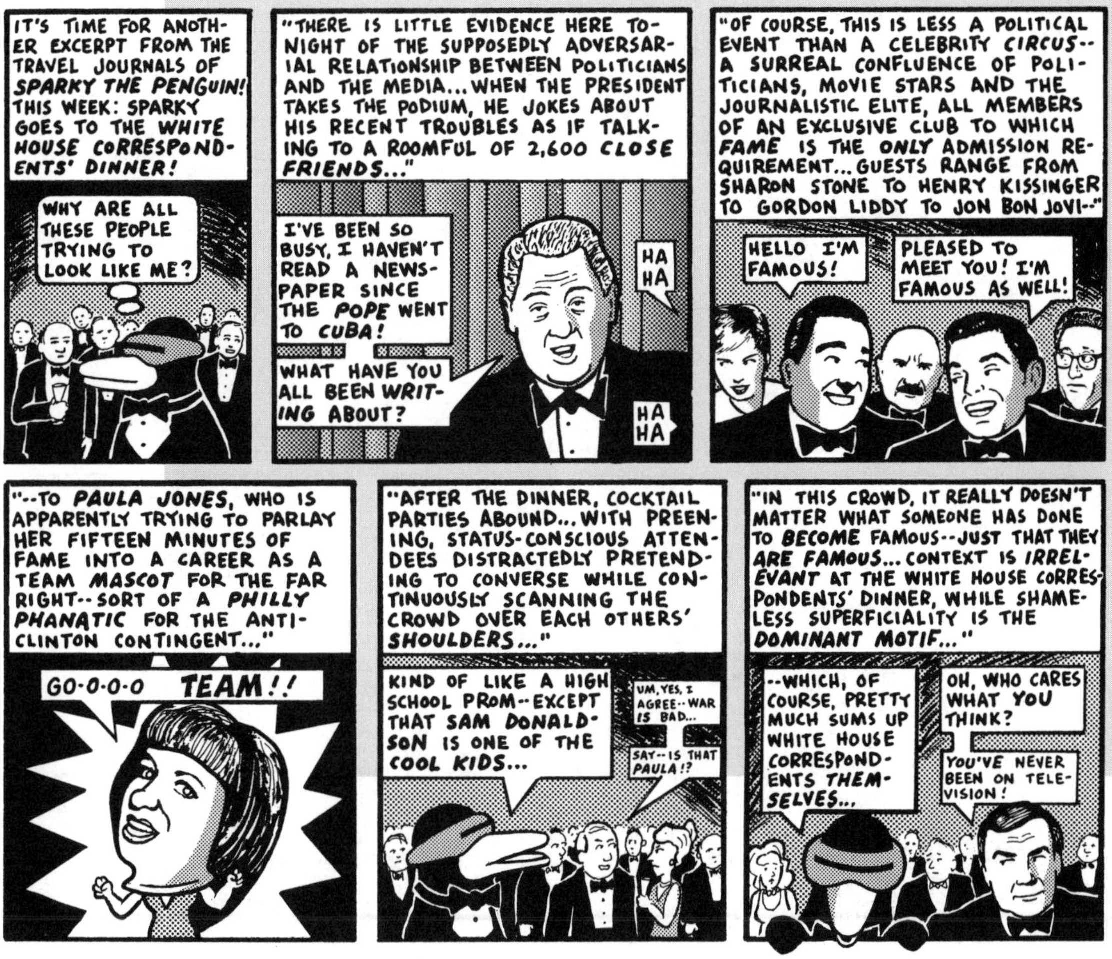
IT'S TIME FOR ANOTHER EXCERPT FROM THE TRAVEL JOURNALS OF SPARKY THE PENGUIN! THIS WEEK: SPARKY GOES TO THE WHITE HOUSE CORRESPONDENTS' DINNER!
WHY ARE ALL THESE PEOPLE TRYING TO LOOK LIKE ME?
"THERE IS LITTLE EVIDENCE HERE TONIGHT OF THE SUPPOSEDLY ADVERSARIAL RELATIONSHIP BETWEEN POLITICIANS AND THE MEDIA... WHEN THE PRESIDENT TAKES THE PODIUM, HE JOKES ABOUT HIS RECENT TROUBLES AS IF TALKING TO A ROOMFUL OF 2,600 CLOSE FRIENDS..."
I'VE BEEN SO BUSY, I HAVEN'T READ A NEWSPAPER SINCE THE POPE WENT TO CUBA!
HA HA
WHAT HAVE YOU ALL BEEN WRITING ABOUT?
HA HA
"OF COURSE, THIS IS LESS A POLITICAL EVENT THAN A CELEBRITY CIRCUS--A SURREAL CONFLUENCE OF POLITICIANS, MOVIE STARS AND THE JOURNALISTIC ELITE, ALL MEMBERS OF AN EXCLUSIVE CLUB TO WHICH FAME IS THE ONLY ADMISSION REQUIREMENT... GUESTS RANGE FROM SHARON STONE TO HENRY KISSINGER TO GORDON LIDDY TO JON BON JOVI--"
HELLO I'M FAMOUS!
PLEASED TO MEET YOU! I'M FAMOUS AS WELL!
"--TO PAULA JONES, WHO IS APPARENTLY TRYING TO PARLAY HER FIFTEEN MINUTES OF FAME INTO A CAREER AS A TEAM MASCOT FOR THE FAR RIGHT--SORT OF A PHILLY PHANATIC FOR THE ANTI-CLINTON CONTINGENT..."
GO-O-O-O TEAM!!
"AFTER THE DINNER, COCKTAIL PARTIES ABOUND... WITH PREENING, STATUS-CONSCIOUS ATTENDEES DISTRACTEDLY PRETENDING TO CONVERSE WHILE CONTINUOUSLY SCANNING THE CROWD OVER EACH OTHERS' SHOULDERS..."
KIND OF LIKE A HIGH SCHOOL PROM--EXCEPT THAT SAM DONALDSON IS ONE OF THE COOL KIDS...
UM, YES, I AGREE--WAR IS BAD...
SAY--IS THAT PAULA!?
"IN THIS CROWD, IT REALLY DOESN'T MATTER WHAT SOMEONE HAS DONE TO BECOME FAMOUS--JUST THAT THEY ARE FAMOUS... CONTEXT IS IRRELEVANT AT THE WHITE HOUSE CORRESPONDENTS' DINNER, WHILE SHAMELESS SUPERFICIALITY IS THE DOMINANT MOTIF..."
--WHICH, OF COURSE, PRETTY MUCH SUMS UP WHITE HOUSE CORRESPONDENTS THEMSELVES...
OH, WHO CARES WHAT YOU THINK?
YOU'VE NEVER BEEN ON TELEVISION!

After publisher Mort Zuckerman reportedly insisted that my brief run at *U.S. News & World Report* be terminated with extreme prejudice, editor Jim Fallows invited me to the White House Correspondents Dinner as a sort of consolation prize. I was coming down with the flu and spent the evening wandering around and taking notes in a feverish daze, and at the end of it, all I could think was—to steal a line from David Foster Wallace—*there's* a supposedly fun thing I'll never do again.

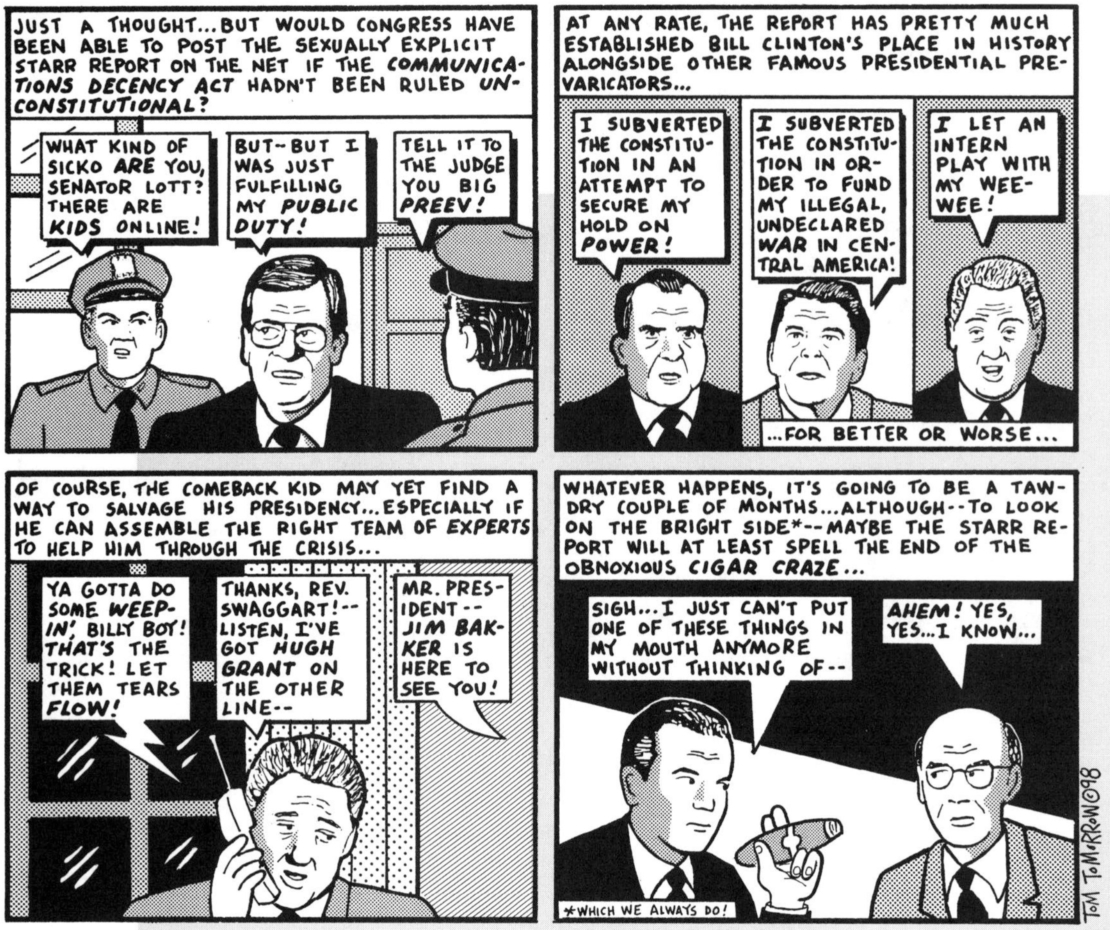
JUST A THOUGHT... BUT WOULD CONGRESS HAVE BEEN ABLE TO POST THE SEXUALLY EXPLICIT STARR REPORT ON THE NET IF THE COMMUNICATIONS DECENCY ACT HADN'T BEEN RULED UNCONSTITUTIONAL?
WHAT KIND OF SICKO ARE YOU, SENATOR LOTT? THERE ARE KIDS ONLINE!
BUT--BUT I WAS JUST FULFILLING MY PUBLIC DUTY!
TELL IT TO THE JUDGE YOU BIG PREEV!
AT ANY RATE, THE REPORT HAS PRETTY MUCH ESTABLISHED BILL CLINTON'S PLACE IN HISTORY ALONGSIDE OTHER FAMOUS PRESIDENTIAL PREVARICATORS...
I SUBVERTED THE CONSTITUTION IN AN ATTEMPT TO SECURE MY HOLD ON POWER!
I SUBVERTED THE CONSTITUTION IN ORDER TO FUND MY ILLEGAL, UNDECLARED WAR IN CENTRAL AMERICA!
I LET AN INTERN PLAY WITH MY WEE-WEE!
...FOR BETTER OR WORSE...
OF COURSE, THE COMEBACK KID MAY YET FIND A WAY TO SALVAGE HIS PRESIDENCY... ESPECIALLY IF HE CAN ASSEMBLE THE RIGHT TEAM OF EXPERTS TO HELP HIM THROUGH THE CRISIS...
YA GOTTA DO SOME WEEPIN', BILLY BOY! THAT'S THE TRICK! LET THEM TEARS FLOW!
THANKS, REV. SWAGGART!-- LISTEN, I'VE GOT HUGH GRANT ON THE OTHER LINE--
MR. PRESIDENT-- JIM BAKKER IS HERE TO SEE YOU!
WHATEVER HAPPENS, IT'S GOING TO BE A TAWDRY COUPLE OF MONTHS... ALTHOUGH--TO LOOK ON THE BRIGHT SIDE*--MAYBE THE STARR REPORT WILL AT LEAST SPELL THE END OF THE OBNOXIOUS CIGAR CRAZE...
SIGH... I JUST CAN'T PUT ONE OF THESE THINGS IN MY MOUTH ANYMORE WITHOUT THINKING OF--
AHEM! YES, YES... I KNOW...
*WHICH WE ALWAYS DO!
TOM TOMORROW©98

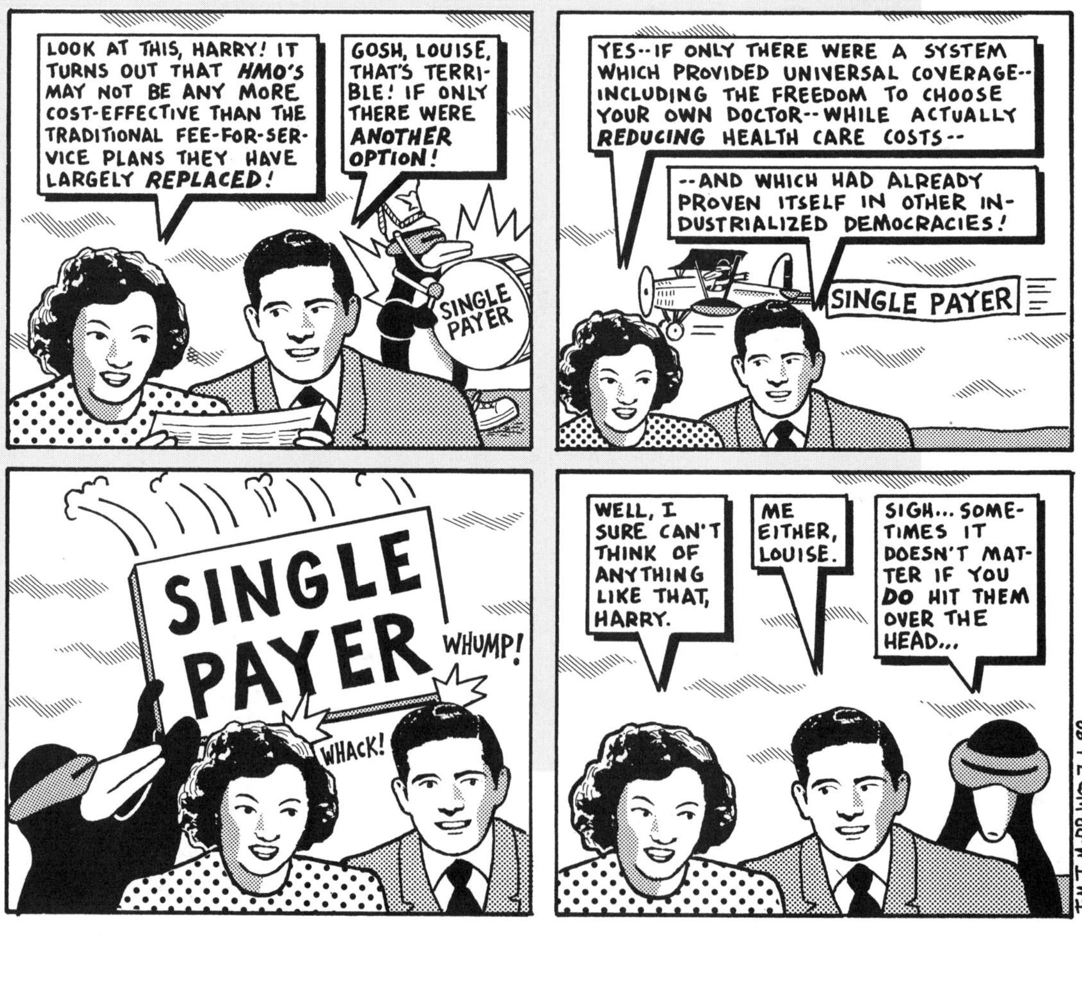
LOOK AT THIS, HARRY! IT TURNS OUT THAT HMO'S MAY NOT BE ANY MORE COST-EFFECTIVE THAN THE TRADITIONAL FEE-FOR-SERVICE PLANS THEY HAVE LARGELY REPLACED!
GOSH, LOUISE, THAT'S TERRIBLE! IF ONLY THERE WERE ANOTHER OPTION!
SINGLE PAYER
YES--IF ONLY THERE WERE A SYSTEM WHICH PROVIDED UNIVERSAL COVERAGE-- INCLUDING THE FREEDOM TO CHOOSE YOUR OWN DOCTOR--WHILE ACTUALLY REDUCING HEALTH CARE COSTS--
--AND WHICH HAD ALREADY PROVEN ITSELF IN OTHER INDUSTRIALIZED DEMOCRACIES!
SINGLE PAYER
SINGLE PAYER
WHUMP!
WHACK!
WELL, I SURE CAN'T THINK OF ANYTHING LIKE THAT, HARRY.
ME EITHER, LOUISE.
SIGH... SOMETIMES IT DOESN'T MATTER IF YOU DO HIT THEM OVER THE HEAD...
TOM TOMORROW© 7-1-98

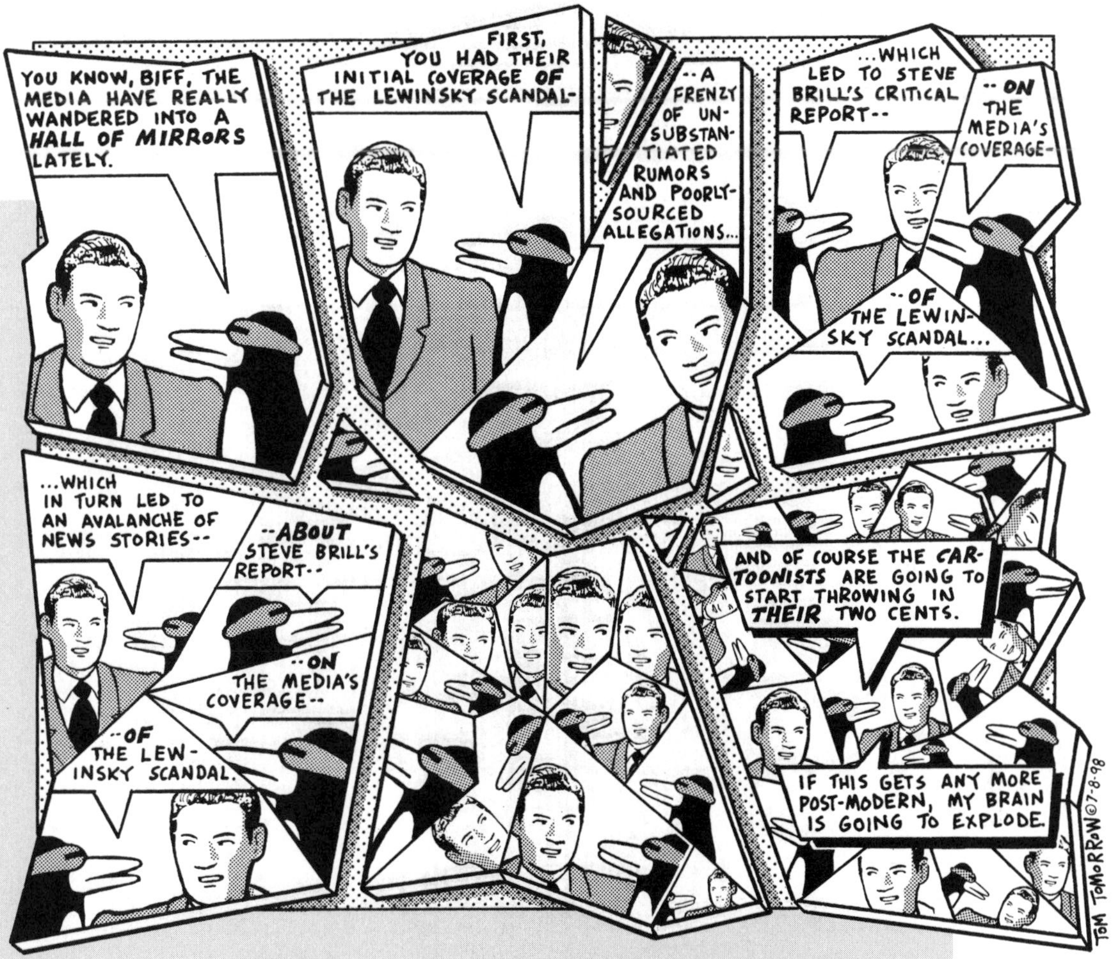
YOU KNOW, BIFF, THE MEDIA HAVE REALLY WANDERED INTO A HALL OF MIRRORS LATELY.
FIRST, YOU HAD THEIR INITIAL COVERAGE OF THE LEWINSKY SCANDAL-
--A FRENZY OF UN-SUBSTAN-TIATED RUMORS AND POORLY-SOURCED ALLEGATIONS...
...WHICH LED TO STEVE BRILL'S CRITICAL REPORT--
--ON THE MEDIA'S COVERAGE-
--OF THE LEWIN-SKY SCANDAL...
...WHICH IN TURN LED TO AN AVALANCHE OF NEWS STORIES--
--ABOUT STEVE BRILL'S REPORT--
--ON THE MEDIA'S COVERAGE--
--OF THE LEW-INSKY SCANDAL.
AND OF COURSE THE CAR-TOONISTS ARE GOING TO START THROWING IN THEIR TWO CENTS.
IF THIS GETS ANY MORE POST-MODERN, MY BRAIN IS GOING TO EXPLODE.
TOM TOMORROW©7-8-98

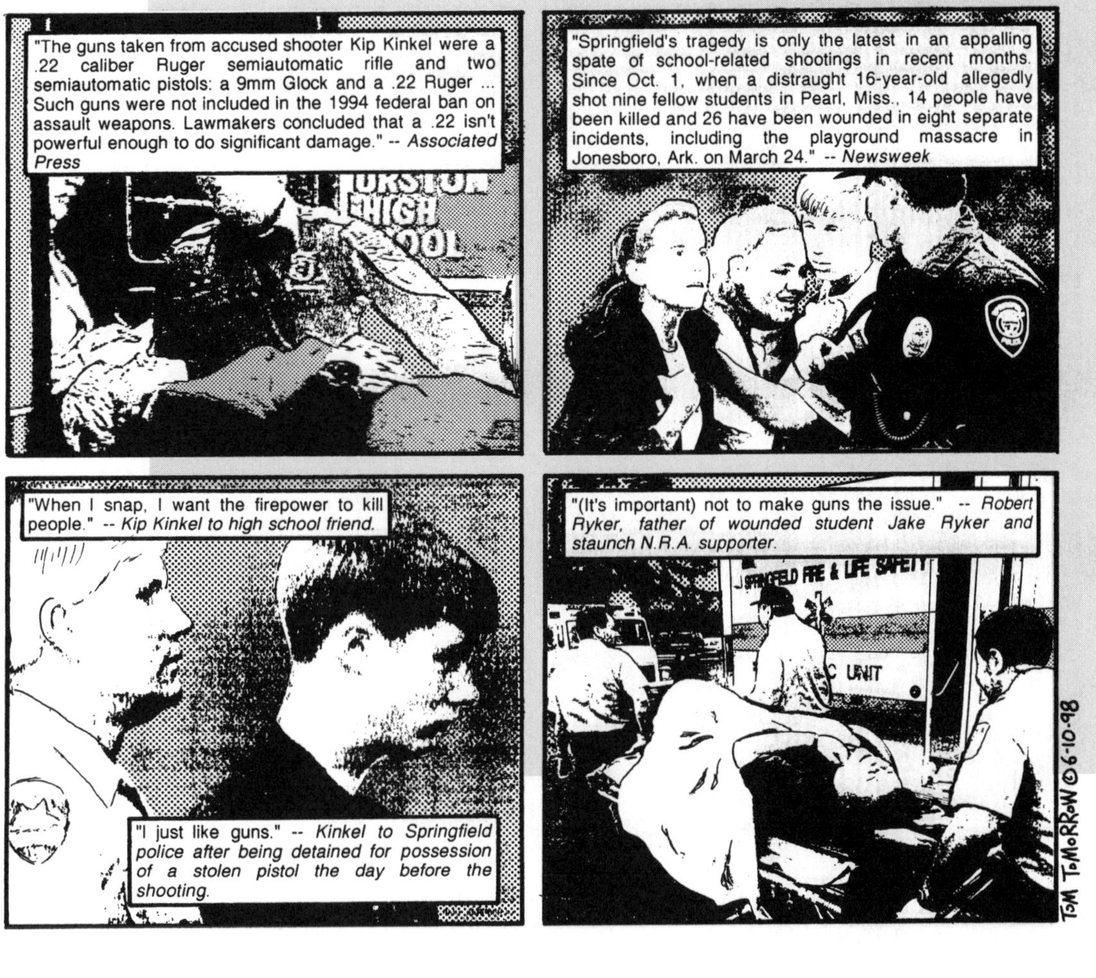
"The guns taken from accused shooter Kip Kinkel were a .22 caliber Ruger semiautomatic rifle and two semiautomatic pistols: a 9mm Glock and a .22 Ruger ... Such guns were not included in the 1994 federal ban on assault weapons. Lawmakers concluded that a .22 isn't powerful enough to do significant damage." -- *Associated Press*
"Springfield's tragedy is only the latest in an appalling spate of school-related shootings in recent months. Since Oct. 1, when a distraught 16-year-old allegedly shot nine fellow students in Pearl, Miss., 14 people have been killed and 26 have been wounded in eight separate incidents, including the playground massacre in Jonesboro, Ark. on March 24." -- *Newsweek*
"When I snap, I want the firepower to kill people." -- *Kip Kinkel to high school friend.*
"I just like guns." -- *Kinkel to Springfield police after being detained for possession of a stolen pistol the day before the shooting.*
"(It's important) not to make guns the issue." -- *Robert Ryker, father of wounded student Jake Ryker and staunch N.R.A. supporter.*
SPRINGFIELD FIRE & LIFE SAFETY
C UNIT
TOM TOMORROW©6-10-98

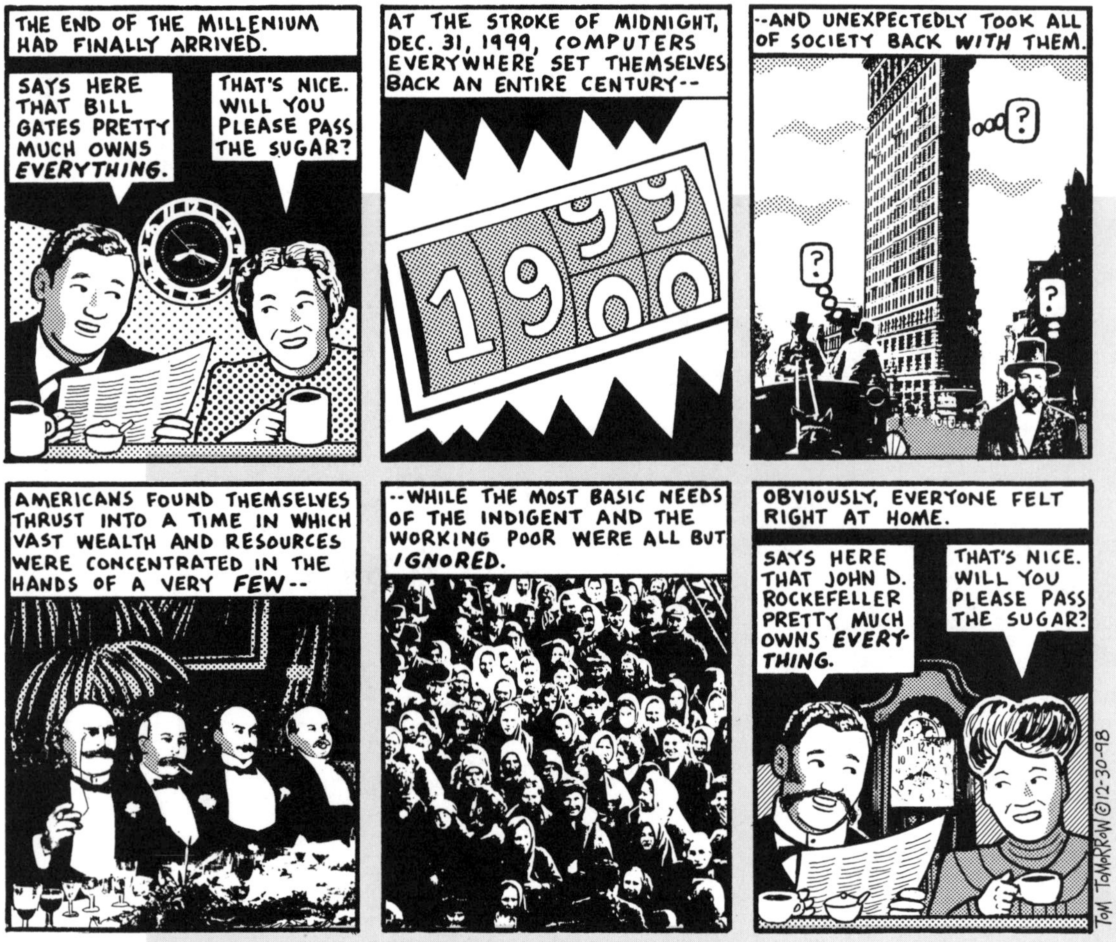
THE END OF THE MILLENIUM HAD FINALLY ARRIVED.
SAYS HERE THAT BILL GATES PRETTY MUCH OWNS EVERYTHING.
THAT'S NICE. WILL YOU PLEASE PASS THE SUGAR?
AT THE STROKE OF MIDNIGHT, DEC. 31, 1999, COMPUTERS EVERYWHERE SET THEMSELVES BACK AN ENTIRE CENTURY--
1999
1900
--AND UNEXPECTEDLY TOOK ALL OF SOCIETY BACK WITH THEM.
?
?
?
AMERICANS FOUND THEMSELVES THRUST INTO A TIME IN WHICH VAST WEALTH AND RESOURCES WERE CONCENTRATED IN THE HANDS OF A VERY FEW--
--WHILE THE MOST BASIC NEEDS OF THE INDIGENT AND THE WORKING POOR WERE ALL BUT IGNORED.
OBVIOUSLY, EVERYONE FELT RIGHT AT HOME.
SAYS HERE THAT JOHN D. ROCKEFELLER PRETTY MUCH OWNS EVERYTHING.
THAT'S NICE. WILL YOU PLEASE PASS THE SUGAR?
TOM TOMORROW ©12-30-98

Just to be clear, this one ran at the very start of 1999. (Remember when all we had to worry about was the "millennium bug"?)

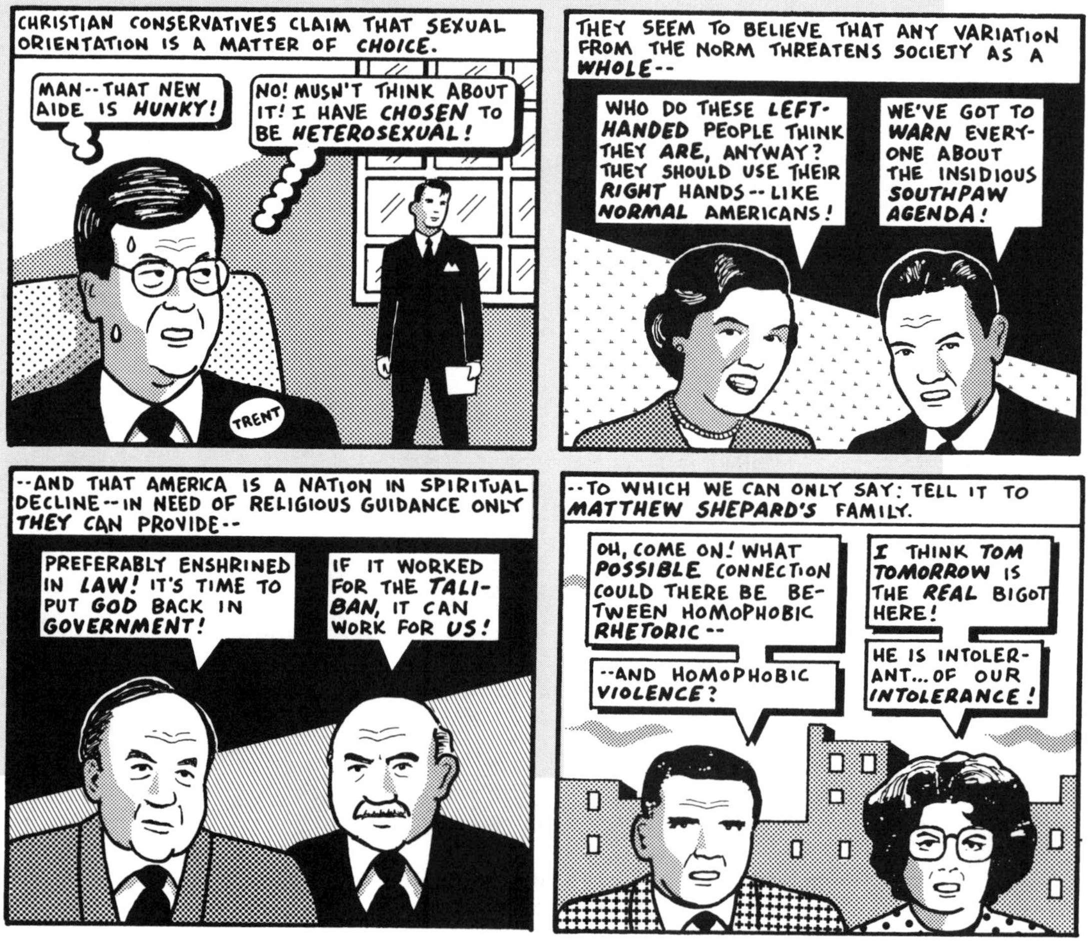
CHRISTIAN CONSERVATIVES CLAIM THAT SEXUAL ORIENTATION IS A MATTER OF CHOICE.
MAN--THAT NEW AIDE IS HUNKY!
NO! MUSN'T THINK ABOUT IT! I HAVE CHOSEN TO BE HETEROSEXUAL!
TRENT
THEY SEEM TO BELIEVE THAT ANY VARIATION FROM THE NORM THREATENS SOCIETY AS A WHOLE--
WHO DO THESE LEFT-HANDED PEOPLE THINK THEY ARE, ANYWAY? THEY SHOULD USE THEIR RIGHT HANDS--LIKE NORMAL AMERICANS!
WE'VE GOT TO WARN EVERYONE ABOUT THE INSIDIOUS SOUTHPAW AGENDA!
--AND THAT AMERICA IS A NATION IN SPIRITUAL DECLINE--IN NEED OF RELIGIOUS GUIDANCE ONLY THEY CAN PROVIDE--
PREFERABLY ENSHRINED IN LAW! IT'S TIME TO PUT GOD BACK IN GOVERNMENT!
IF IT WORKED FOR THE TALIBAN, IT CAN WORK FOR US!
--TO WHICH WE CAN ONLY SAY: TELL IT TO MATTHEW SHEPARD'S FAMILY.
OH, COME ON! WHAT POSSIBLE CONNECTION COULD THERE BE BETWEEN HOMOPHOBIC RHETORIC--
--AND HOMOPHOBIC VIOLENCE?
I THINK TOM TOMORROW IS THE REAL BIGOT HERE!
HE IS INTOLERANT... OF OUR INTOLERANCE!

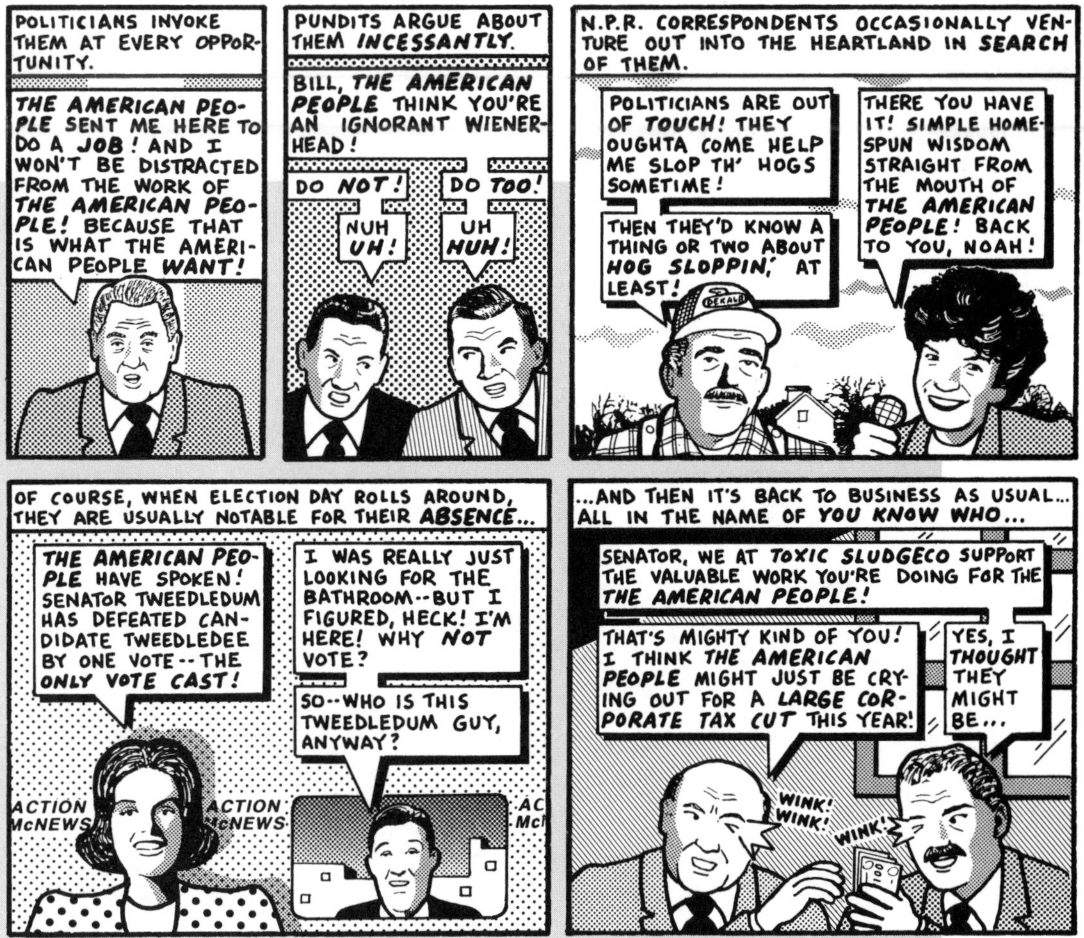
POLITICIANS INVOKE THEM AT EVERY OPPORTUNITY.
THE AMERICAN PEOPLE SENT ME HERE TO DO A JOB! AND I WON'T BE DISTRACTED FROM THE WORK OF THE AMERICAN PEOPLE! BECAUSE THAT IS WHAT THE AMERICAN PEOPLE WANT!
PUNDITS ARGUE ABOUT THEM INCESSANTLY.
BILL, THE AMERICAN PEOPLE THINK YOU'RE AN IGNORANT WIENER-HEAD!
DO NOT!
DO TOO!
NUH UH!
UH HUH!
N.P.R. CORRESPONDENTS OCCASIONALLY VENTURE OUT INTO THE HEARTLAND IN SEARCH OF THEM.
POLITICIANS ARE OUT OF TOUCH! THEY OUGHTA COME HELP ME SLOP TH' HOGS SOMETIME!
THEN THEY'D KNOW A THING OR TWO ABOUT HOG SLOPPIN', AT LEAST!
THERE YOU HAVE IT! SIMPLE HOME-SPUN WISDOM STRAIGHT FROM THE MOUTH OF THE AMERICAN PEOPLE! BACK TO YOU, NOAH!
DEKALB
OF COURSE, WHEN ELECTION DAY ROLLS AROUND, THEY ARE USUALLY NOTABLE FOR THEIR ABSENCE...
THE AMERICAN PEOPLE HAVE SPOKEN! SENATOR TWEEDLEDUM HAS DEFEATED CANDIDATE TWEEDLEDEE BY ONE VOTE--THE ONLY VOTE CAST!
I WAS REALLY JUST LOOKING FOR THE BATHROOM--BUT I FIGURED, HECK! I'M HERE! WHY NOT VOTE?
SO--WHO IS THIS TWEEDLEDUM GUY, ANYWAY?
ACTION McNEWS
...AND THEN IT'S BACK TO BUSINESS AS USUAL... ALL IN THE NAME OF YOU KNOW WHO...
SENATOR, WE AT TOXIC SLUDGECO SUPPORT THE VALUABLE WORK YOU'RE DOING FOR THE THE AMERICAN PEOPLE!
THAT'S MIGHTY KIND OF YOU! I THINK THE AMERICAN PEOPLE MIGHT JUST BE CRYING OUT FOR A LARGE CORPORATE TAX CUT THIS YEAR!
YES, I THOUGHT THEY MIGHT BE...
WINK! WINK!
WINK!

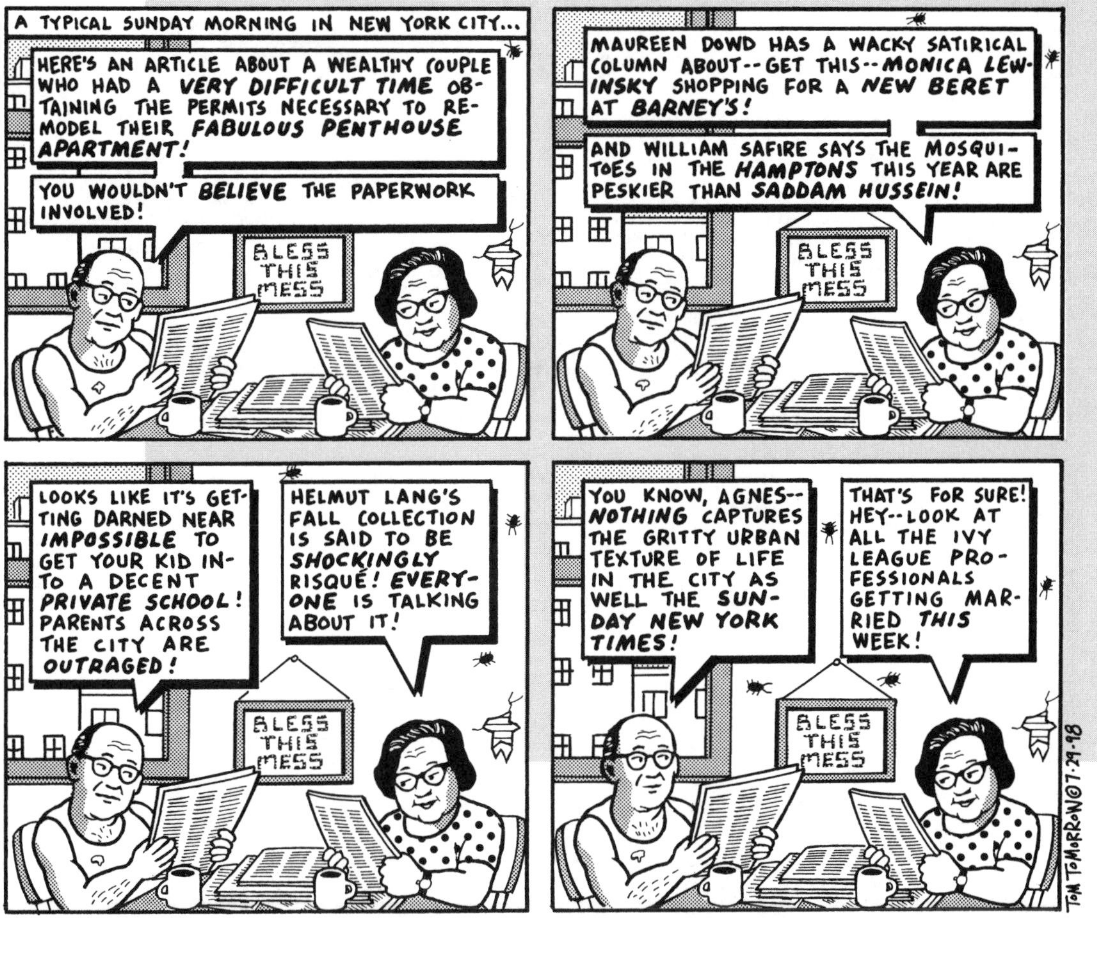
A TYPICAL SUNDAY MORNING IN NEW YORK CITY...
HERE'S AN ARTICLE ABOUT A WEALTHY COUPLE WHO HAD A VERY DIFFICULT TIME OBTAINING THE PERMITS NECESSARY TO REMODEL THEIR FABULOUS PENTHOUSE APARTMENT!
YOU WOULDN'T BELIEVE THE PAPERWORK INVOLVED!
BLESS THIS MESS
MAUREEN DOWD HAS A WACKY SATIRICAL COLUMN ABOUT--GET THIS--MONICA LEWINSKY SHOPPING FOR A NEW BERET AT BARNEY'S!
AND WILLIAM SAFIRE SAYS THE MOSQUITOES IN THE HAMPTONS THIS YEAR ARE PESKIER THAN SADDAM HUSSEIN!
LOOKS LIKE IT'S GETTING DARNED NEAR IMPOSSIBLE TO GET YOUR KID INTO A DECENT PRIVATE SCHOOL! PARENTS ACROSS THE CITY ARE OUTRAGED!
HELMUT LANG'S FALL COLLECTION IS SAID TO BE SHOCKINGLY RISQUÉ! EVERYONE IS TALKING ABOUT IT!
YOU KNOW, AGNES--NOTHING CAPTURES THE GRITTY URBAN TEXTURE OF LIFE IN THE CITY AS WELL THE SUNDAY NEW YORK TIMES!
THAT'S FOR SURE! HEY--LOOK AT ALL THE IVY LEAGUE PROFESSIONALS GETTING MARRIED THIS WEEK!
TOM TOMORROW©7-29-98

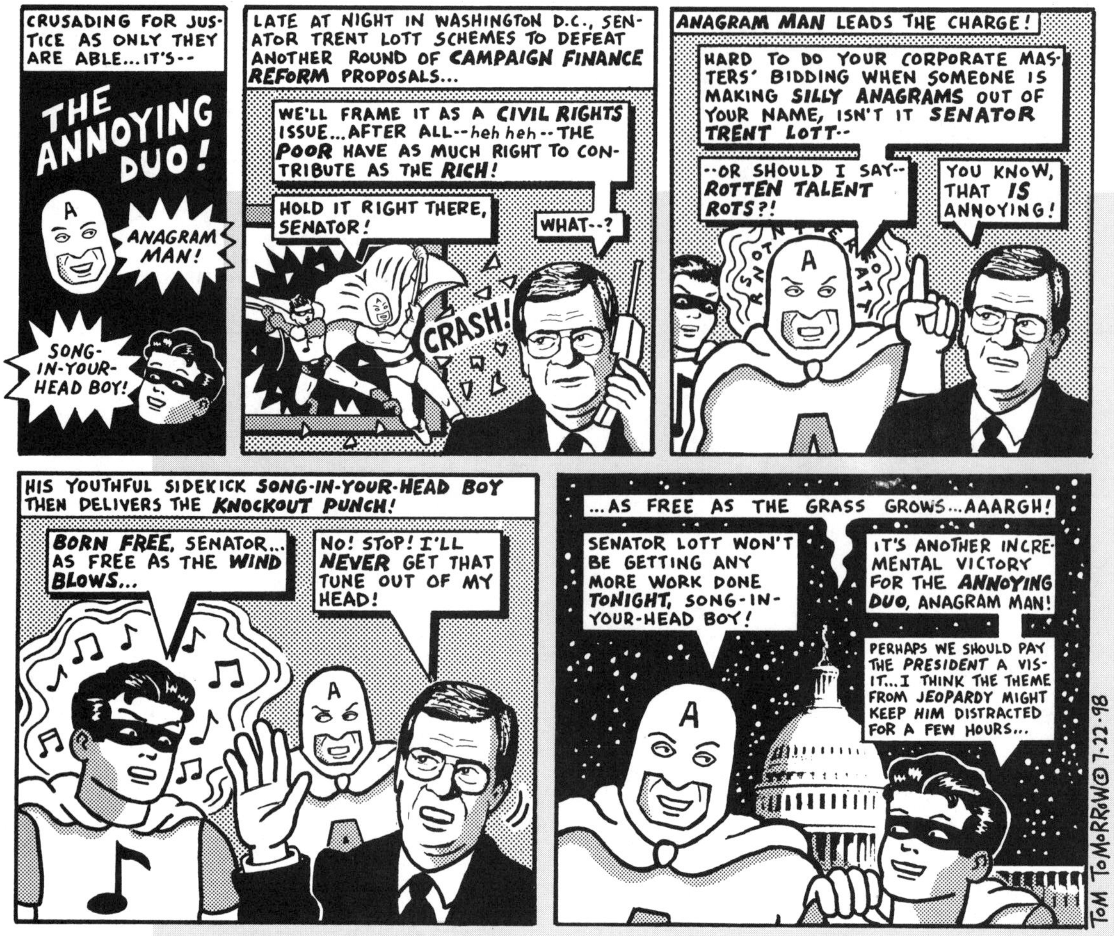
CRUSADING FOR JUSTICE AS ONLY THEY ARE ABLE...IT'S--
THE ANNOYING DUO!
ANAGRAM MAN!
SONG-IN-YOUR-HEAD BOY!
LATE AT NIGHT IN WASHINGTON D.C., SENATOR TRENT LOTT SCHEMES TO DEFEAT ANOTHER ROUND OF CAMPAIGN FINANCE REFORM PROPOSALS...
WE'LL FRAME IT AS A CIVIL RIGHTS ISSUE...AFTER ALL--heh heh--THE POOR HAVE AS MUCH RIGHT TO CONTRIBUTE AS THE RICH!
HOLD IT RIGHT THERE, SENATOR!
WHAT--?
CRASH!
ANAGRAM MAN LEADS THE CHARGE!
HARD TO DO YOUR CORPORATE MASTERS' BIDDING WHEN SOMEONE IS MAKING SILLY ANAGRAMS OUT OF YOUR NAME, ISN'T IT SENATOR TRENT LOTT--
--OR SHOULD I SAY--ROTTEN TALENT ROTS?!
YOU KNOW, THAT IS ANNOYING!
HIS YOUTHFUL SIDEKICK SONG-IN-YOUR-HEAD BOY THEN DELIVERS THE KNOCKOUT PUNCH!
BORN FREE, SENATOR... AS FREE AS THE WIND BLOWS...
NO! STOP! I'LL NEVER GET THAT TUNE OUT OF MY HEAD!
...AS FREE AS THE GRASS GROWS...AAARGH!
SENATOR LOTT WON'T BE GETTING ANY MORE WORK DONE TONIGHT, SONG-IN-YOUR-HEAD BOY!
IT'S ANOTHER INCREMENTAL VICTORY FOR THE ANNOYING DUO, ANAGRAM MAN!
PERHAPS WE SHOULD PAY THE PRESIDENT A VISIT...I THINK THE THEME FROM JEOPARDY MIGHT KEEP HIM DISTRACTED FOR A FEW HOURS...
TOM TOMORROW © 7-22-98

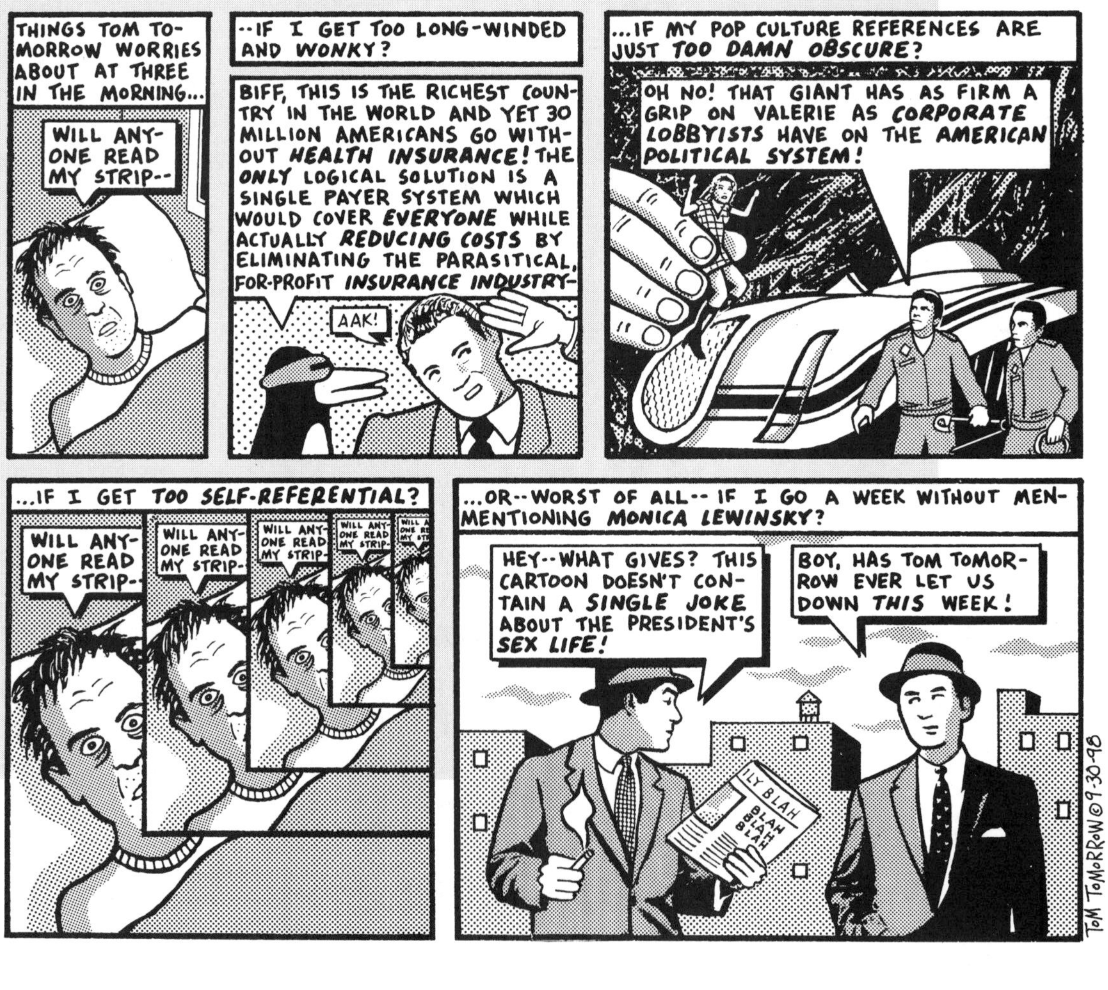
THINGS TOM TOMORROW WORRIES ABOUT AT THREE IN THE MORNING...
WILL ANYONE READ MY STRIP--
--IF I GET TOO LONG-WINDED AND WONKY?
BIFF, THIS IS THE RICHEST COUNTRY IN THE WORLD AND YET 30 MILLION AMERICANS GO WITHOUT HEALTH INSURANCE! THE ONLY LOGICAL SOLUTION IS A SINGLE PAYER SYSTEM WHICH WOULD COVER EVERYONE WHILE ACTUALLY REDUCING COSTS BY ELIMINATING THE PARASITICAL, FOR-PROFIT INSURANCE INDUSTRY--
AAK!
...IF MY POP CULTURE REFERENCES ARE JUST TOO DAMN OBSCURE?
OH NO! THAT GIANT HAS AS FIRM A GRIP ON VALERIE AS CORPORATE LOBBYISTS HAVE ON THE AMERICAN POLITICAL SYSTEM!
...IF I GET TOO SELF-REFERENTIAL?
WILL ANYONE READ MY STRIP--
WILL ANYONE READ MY STRIP--
WILL ANYONE READ MY STRIP--
...OR--WORST OF ALL--IF I GO A WEEK WITHOUT MENMENTIONING MONICA LEWINSKY?
HEY--WHAT GIVES? THIS CARTOON DOESN'T CONTAIN A SINGLE JOKE ABOUT THE PRESIDENT'S SEX LIFE!
BOY, HAS TOM TOMORROW EVER LET US DOWN THIS WEEK!
ILY BLAH
BLAH BLAH BLAH
TOM TOMORROW © 9-30-98

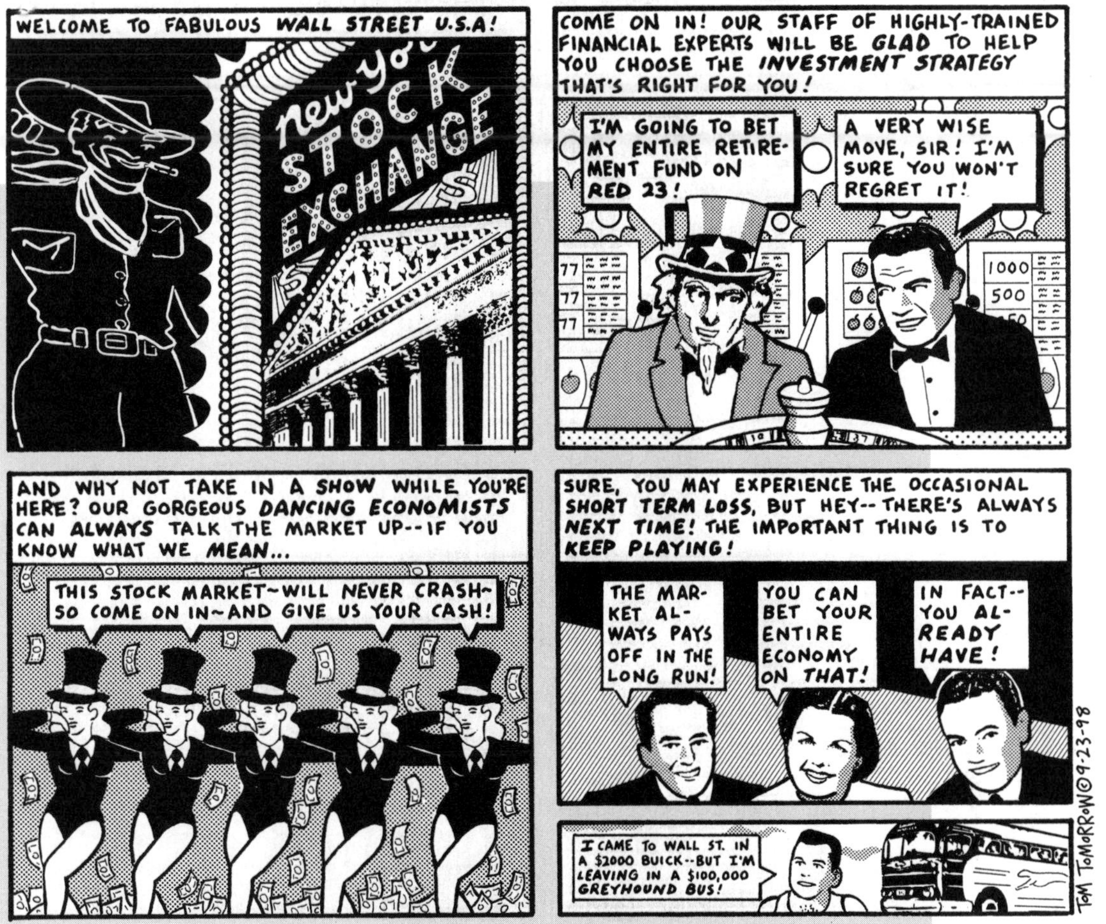
WELCOME TO FABULOUS WALL STREET U.S.A!
NEW YORK STOCK EXCHANGE
COME ON IN! OUR STAFF OF HIGHLY-TRAINED FINANCIAL EXPERTS WILL BE GLAD TO HELP YOU CHOOSE THE INVESTMENT STRATEGY THAT'S RIGHT FOR YOU!
I'M GOING TO BET MY ENTIRE RETIREMENT FUND ON RED 23!
A VERY WISE MOVE, SIR! I'M SURE YOU WON'T REGRET IT!
AND WHY NOT TAKE IN A SHOW WHILE YOU'RE HERE? OUR GORGEOUS DANCING ECONOMISTS CAN ALWAYS TALK THE MARKET UP--IF YOU KNOW WHAT WE MEAN...
THIS STOCK MARKET~WILL NEVER CRASH~SO COME ON IN~AND GIVE US YOUR CASH!
SURE, YOU MAY EXPERIENCE THE OCCASIONAL SHORT TERM LOSS, BUT HEY--THERE'S ALWAYS NEXT TIME! THE IMPORTANT THING IS TO KEEP PLAYING!
THE MARKET ALWAYS PAYS OFF IN THE LONG RUN!
YOU CAN BET YOUR ENTIRE ECONOMY ON THAT!
IN FACT--YOU ALREADY HAVE!
I CAME TO WALL ST. IN A $2000 BUICK--BUT I'M LEAVING IN A $100,000 GREYHOUND BUS!
TOM TOMORROW©9-23-98

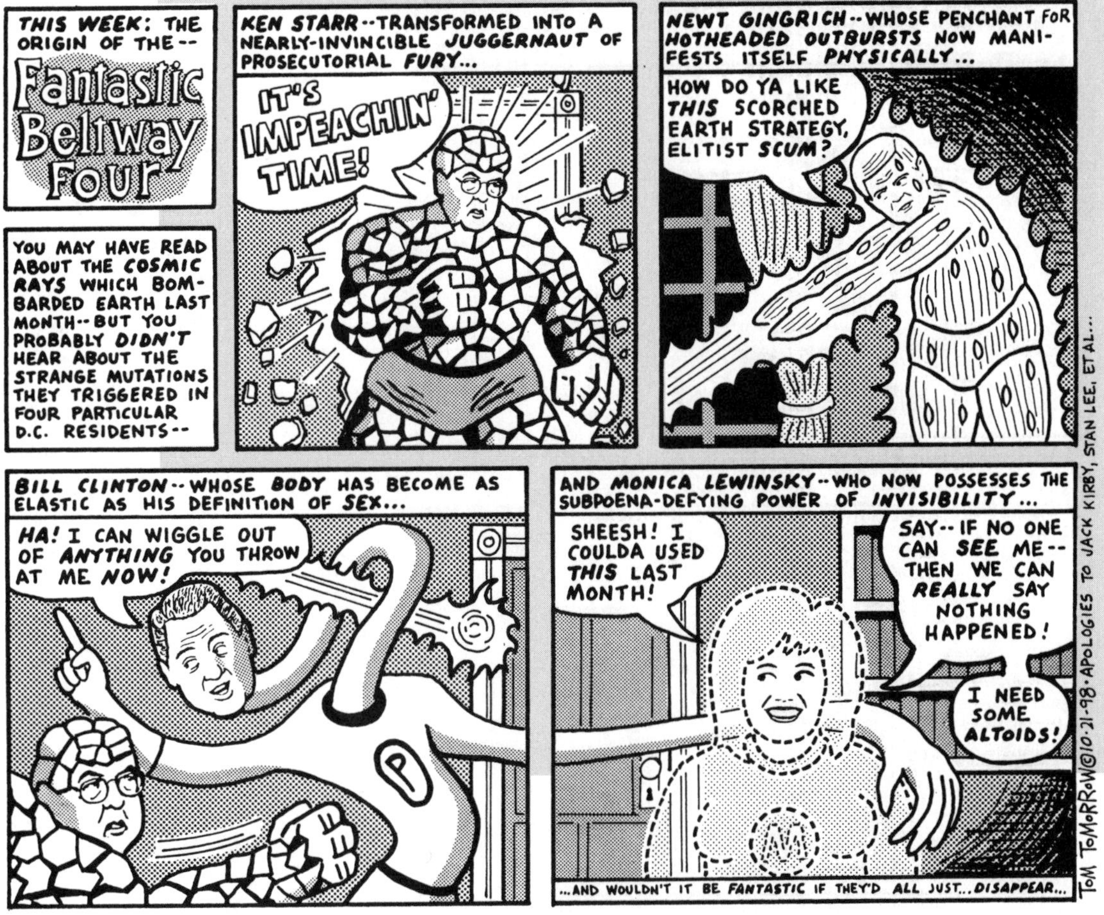
THIS WEEK: THE ORIGIN OF THE--
Fantastic Beltway Four
YOU MAY HAVE READ ABOUT THE COSMIC RAYS WHICH BOMBARDED EARTH LAST MONTH--BUT YOU PROBABLY DIDN'T HEAR ABOUT THE STRANGE MUTATIONS THEY TRIGGERED IN FOUR PARTICULAR D.C. RESIDENTS--
KEN STARR--TRANSFORMED INTO A NEARLY-INVINCIBLE JUGGERNAUT OF PROSECUTORIAL FURY...
IT'S IMPEACHIN' TIME!
NEWT GINGRICH--WHOSE PENCHANT FOR HOTHEADED OUTBURSTS NOW MANIFESTS ITSELF PHYSICALLY...
HOW DO YA LIKE THIS SCORCHED EARTH STRATEGY, ELITIST SCUM?
BILL CLINTON--WHOSE BODY HAS BECOME AS ELASTIC AS HIS DEFINITION OF SEX...
HA! I CAN WIGGLE OUT OF ANYTHING YOU THROW AT ME NOW!
AND MONICA LEWINSKY--WHO NOW POSSESSES THE SUBPOENA-DEFYING POWER OF INVISIBILITY...
SHEESH! I COULDA USED THIS LAST MONTH!
SAY--IF NO ONE CAN SEE ME--THEN WE CAN REALLY SAY NOTHING HAPPENED!
I NEED SOME ALTOIDS!
...AND WOULDN'T IT BE FANTASTIC IF THEY'D ALL JUST...DISAPPEAR...
TOM TOMORROW©10-21-98 · APOLOGIES TO JACK KIRBY, STAN LEE, ET AL...

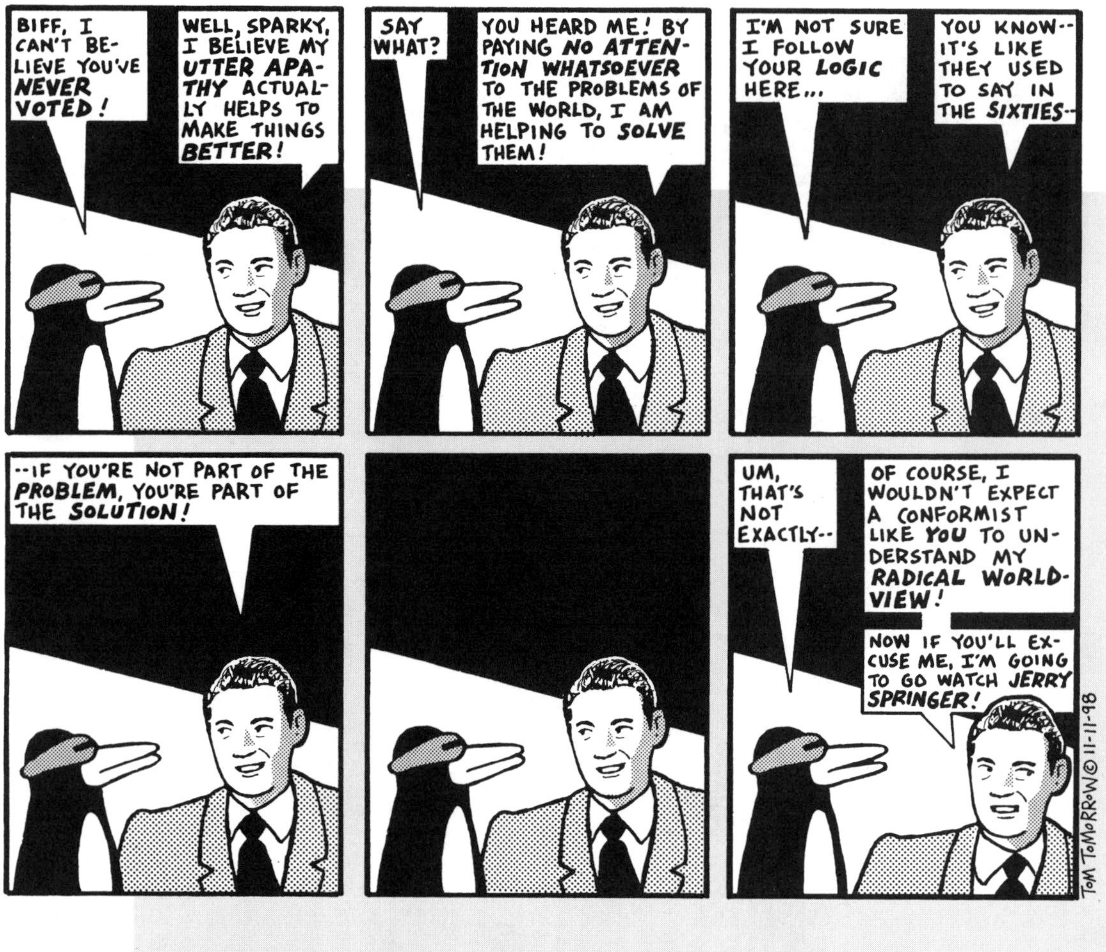
BIFF, I CAN'T BELIEVE YOU'VE NEVER VOTED!
WELL, SPARKY, I BELIEVE MY UTTER APATHY ACTUALLY HELPS TO MAKE THINGS BETTER!
SAY WHAT?
YOU HEARD ME! BY PAYING NO ATTENTION WHATSOEVER TO THE PROBLEMS OF THE WORLD, I AM HELPING TO SOLVE THEM!
I'M NOT SURE I FOLLOW YOUR LOGIC HERE...
YOU KNOW--IT'S LIKE THEY USED TO SAY IN THE SIXTIES--
--IF YOU'RE NOT PART OF THE PROBLEM, YOU'RE PART OF THE SOLUTION!
UM, THAT'S NOT EXACTLY--
OF COURSE, I WOULDN'T EXPECT A CONFORMIST LIKE YOU TO UNDERSTAND MY RADICAL WORLD-VIEW!
NOW IF YOU'LL EXCUSE ME, I'M GOING TO GO WATCH JERRY SPRINGER!
TOM TOMORROW© 11-11-98

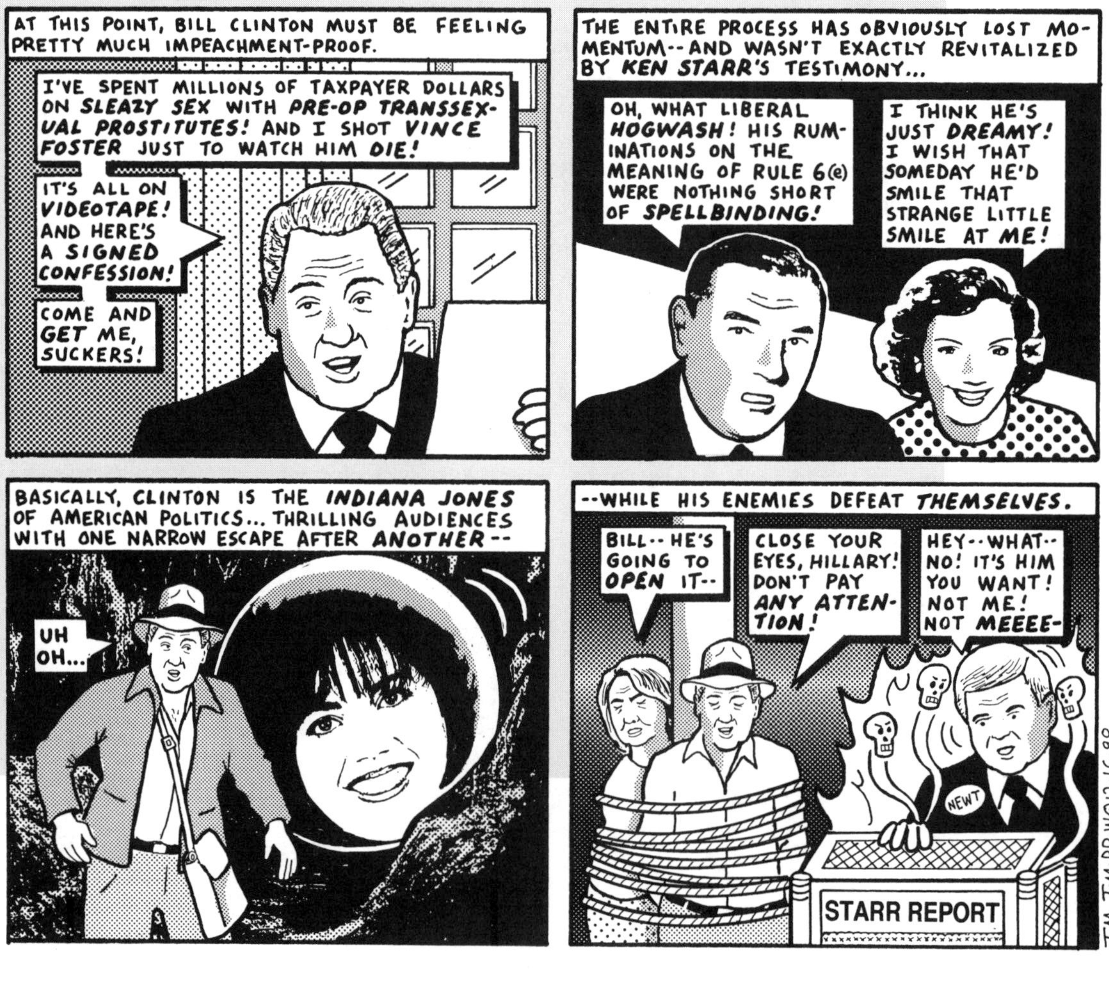
AT THIS POINT, BILL CLINTON MUST BE FEELING PRETTY MUCH IMPEACHMENT-PROOF.
I'VE SPENT MILLIONS OF TAXPAYER DOLLARS ON SLEAZY SEX WITH PRE-OP TRANSSEXUAL PROSTITUTES! AND I SHOT VINCE FOSTER JUST TO WATCH HIM DIE!
IT'S ALL ON VIDEOTAPE! AND HERE'S A SIGNED CONFESSION!
COME AND GET ME, SUCKERS!
THE ENTIRE PROCESS HAS OBVIOUSLY LOST MOMENTUM--AND WASN'T EXACTLY REVITALIZED BY KEN STARR'S TESTIMONY...
OH, WHAT LIBERAL HOGWASH! HIS RUMINATIONS ON THE MEANING OF RULE 6(e) WERE NOTHING SHORT OF SPELLBINDING!
I THINK HE'S JUST DREAMY! I WISH THAT SOMEDAY HE'D SMILE THAT STRANGE LITTLE SMILE AT ME!
BASICALLY, CLINTON IS THE INDIANA JONES OF AMERICAN POLITICS... THRILLING AUDIENCES WITH ONE NARROW ESCAPE AFTER ANOTHER--
UH OH...
--WHILE HIS ENEMIES DEFEAT THEMSELVES.
BILL--HE'S GOING TO OPEN IT--
CLOSE YOUR EYES, HILLARY! DON'T PAY ANY ATTENTION!
HEY--WHAT--NO! IT'S HIM YOU WANT! NOT ME! NOT MEEEE-
NEWT
STARR REPORT
TOM TOMORROW©12-16-98

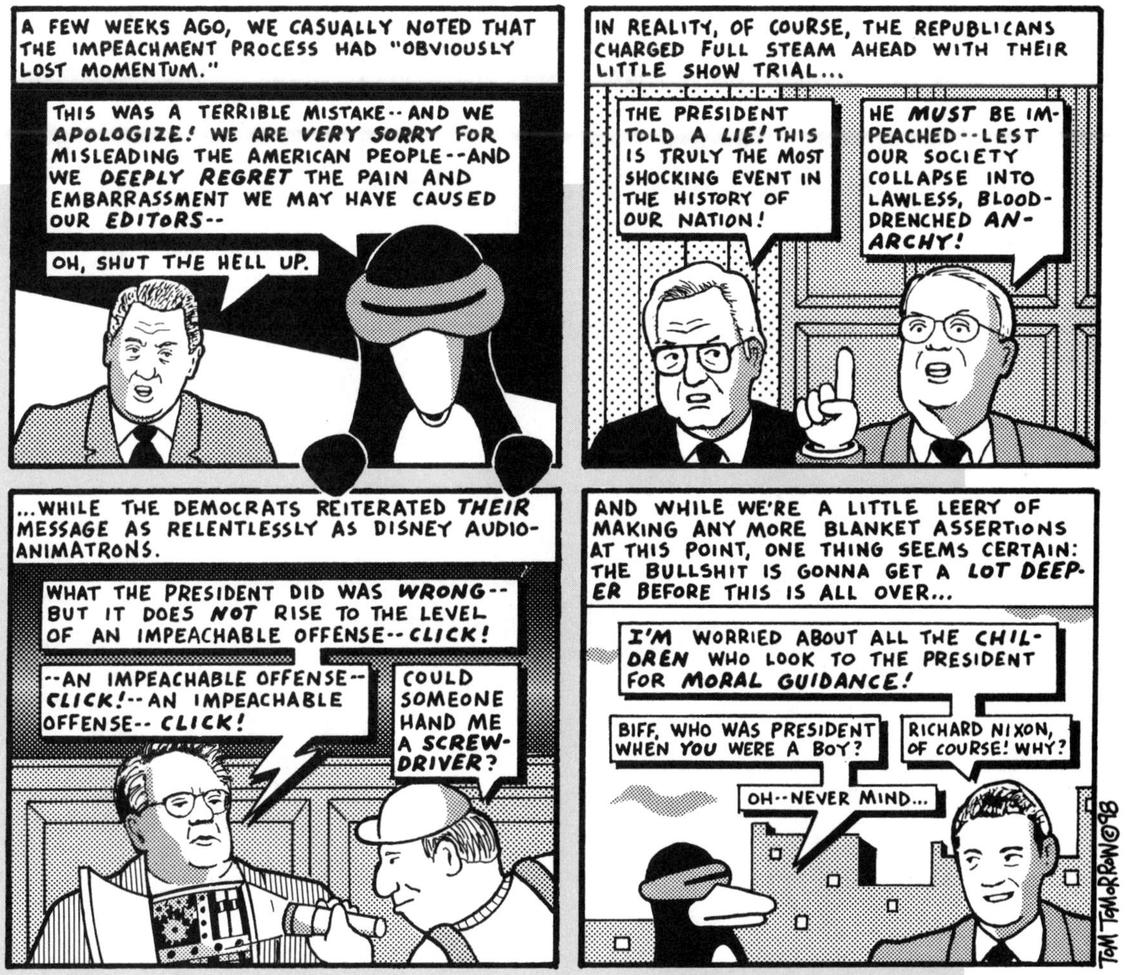
A FEW WEEKS AGO, WE CASUALLY NOTED THAT THE IMPEACHMENT PROCESS HAD "OBVIOUSLY LOST MOMENTUM."
THIS WAS A TERRIBLE MISTAKE-- AND WE APOLOGIZE! WE ARE VERY SORRY FOR MISLEADING THE AMERICAN PEOPLE--AND WE DEEPLY REGRET THE PAIN AND EMBARRASSMENT WE MAY HAVE CAUSED OUR EDITORS--
OH, SHUT THE HELL UP.
IN REALITY, OF COURSE, THE REPUBLICANS CHARGED FULL STEAM AHEAD WITH THEIR LITTLE SHOW TRIAL...
THE PRESIDENT TOLD A LIE! THIS IS TRULY THE MOST SHOCKING EVENT IN THE HISTORY OF OUR NATION!
HE MUST BE IMPEACHED--LEST OUR SOCIETY COLLAPSE INTO LAWLESS, BLOOD-DRENCHED ANARCHY!
...WHILE THE DEMOCRATS REITERATED THEIR MESSAGE AS RELENTLESSLY AS DISNEY AUDIO-ANIMATRONS.
WHAT THE PRESIDENT DID WAS WRONG-- BUT IT DOES NOT RISE TO THE LEVEL OF AN IMPEACHABLE OFFENSE--CLICK!
--AN IMPEACHABLE OFFENSE-- CLICK!--AN IMPEACHABLE OFFENSE-- CLICK!
COULD SOMEONE HAND ME A SCREWDRIVER?
AND WHILE WE'RE A LITTLE LEERY OF MAKING ANY MORE BLANKET ASSERTIONS AT THIS POINT, ONE THING SEEMS CERTAIN: THE BULLSHIT IS GONNA GET A LOT DEEPER BEFORE THIS IS ALL OVER...
I'M WORRIED ABOUT ALL THE CHILDREN WHO LOOK TO THE PRESIDENT FOR MORAL GUIDANCE!
BIFF, WHO WAS PRESIDENT WHEN YOU WERE A BOY?
RICHARD NIXON, OF COURSE! WHY?
OH--NEVER MIND...
TOM TOMORROW©98

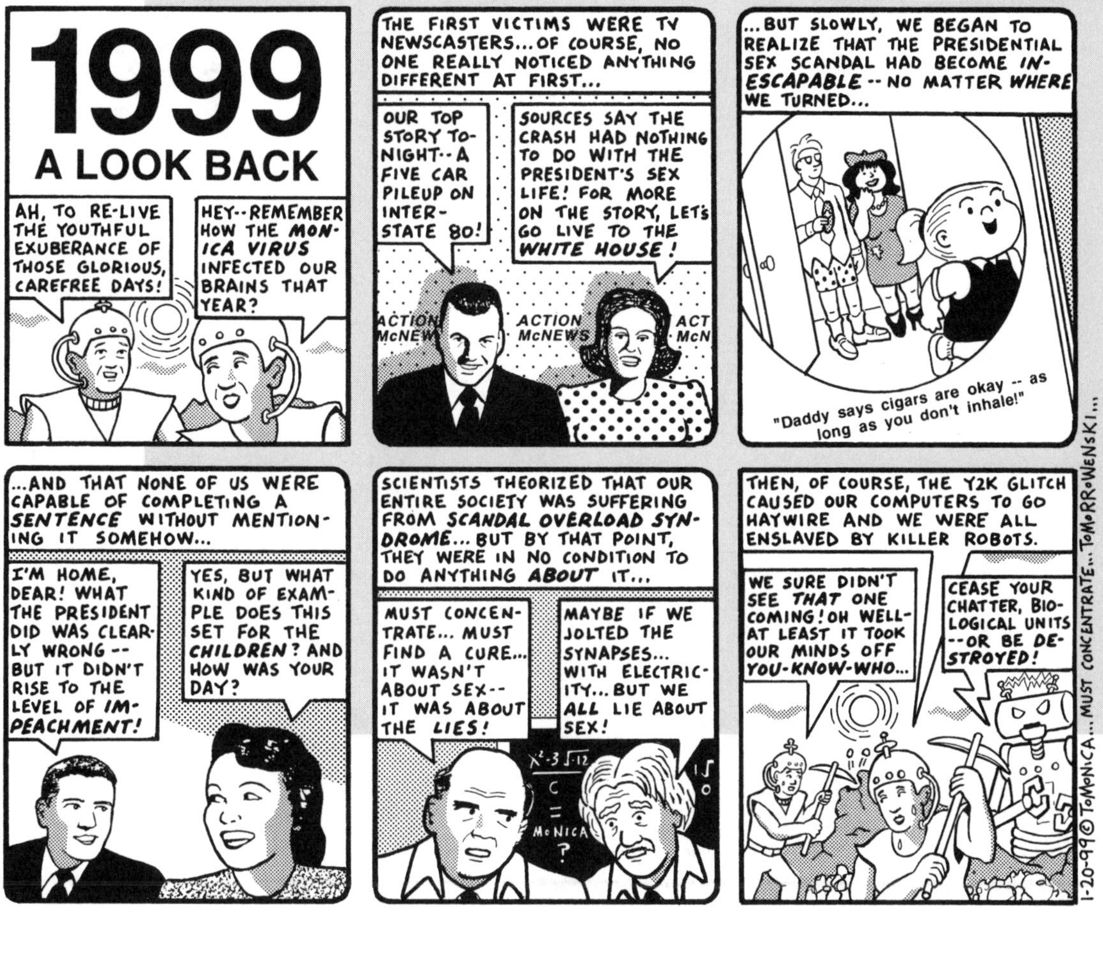
1999
A LOOK BACK
AH, TO RE-LIVE THE YOUTHFUL EXUBERANCE OF THOSE GLORIOUS, CAREFREE DAYS!
HEY--REMEMBER HOW THE MONICA VIRUS INFECTED OUR BRAINS THAT YEAR?
THE FIRST VICTIMS WERE TV NEWSCASTERS...OF COURSE, NO ONE REALLY NOTICED ANYTHING DIFFERENT AT FIRST...
OUR TOP STORY TONIGHT--A FIVE CAR PILEUP ON INTERSTATE 80!
SOURCES SAY THE CRASH HAD NOTHING TO DO WITH THE PRESIDENT'S SEX LIFE! FOR MORE ON THE STORY, LET'S GO LIVE TO THE WHITE HOUSE!
ACTION McNEWS
...BUT SLOWLY, WE BEGAN TO REALIZE THAT THE PRESIDENTIAL SEX SCANDAL HAD BECOME INESCAPABLE -- NO MATTER WHERE WE TURNED...
"Daddy says cigars are okay -- as long as you don't inhale!"
...AND THAT NONE OF US WERE CAPABLE OF COMPLETING A SENTENCE WITHOUT MENTIONING IT SOMEHOW...
I'M HOME, DEAR! WHAT THE PRESIDENT DID WAS CLEARLY WRONG -- BUT IT DIDN'T RISE TO THE LEVEL OF IMPEACHMENT!
YES, BUT WHAT KIND OF EXAMPLE DOES THIS SET FOR THE CHILDREN? AND HOW WAS YOUR DAY?
SCIENTISTS THEORIZED THAT OUR ENTIRE SOCIETY WAS SUFFERING FROM SCANDAL OVERLOAD SYNDROME... BUT BY THAT POINT, THEY WERE IN NO CONDITION TO DO ANYTHING ABOUT IT...
MUST CONCENTRATE... MUST FIND A CURE... IT WASN'T ABOUT SEX-- IT WAS ABOUT THE LIES!
MAYBE IF WE JOLTED THE SYNAPSES... WITH ELECTRICITY... BUT WE ALL LIE ABOUT SEX!
MONICA
THEN, OF COURSE, THE Y2K GLITCH CAUSED OUR COMPUTERS TO GO HAYWIRE AND WE WERE ALL ENSLAVED BY KILLER ROBOTS.
WE SURE DIDN'T SEE THAT ONE COMING! OH WELL-- AT LEAST IT TOOK OUR MINDS OFF YOU-KNOW-WHO...
CEASE YOUR CHATTER, BIOLOGICAL UNITS --OR BE DESTROYED!
1-20-99 © TOMONICA... MUST CONCENTRATE... TOMORROWENSKI...

Despite its title, this one also ran at the beginning of 1999.

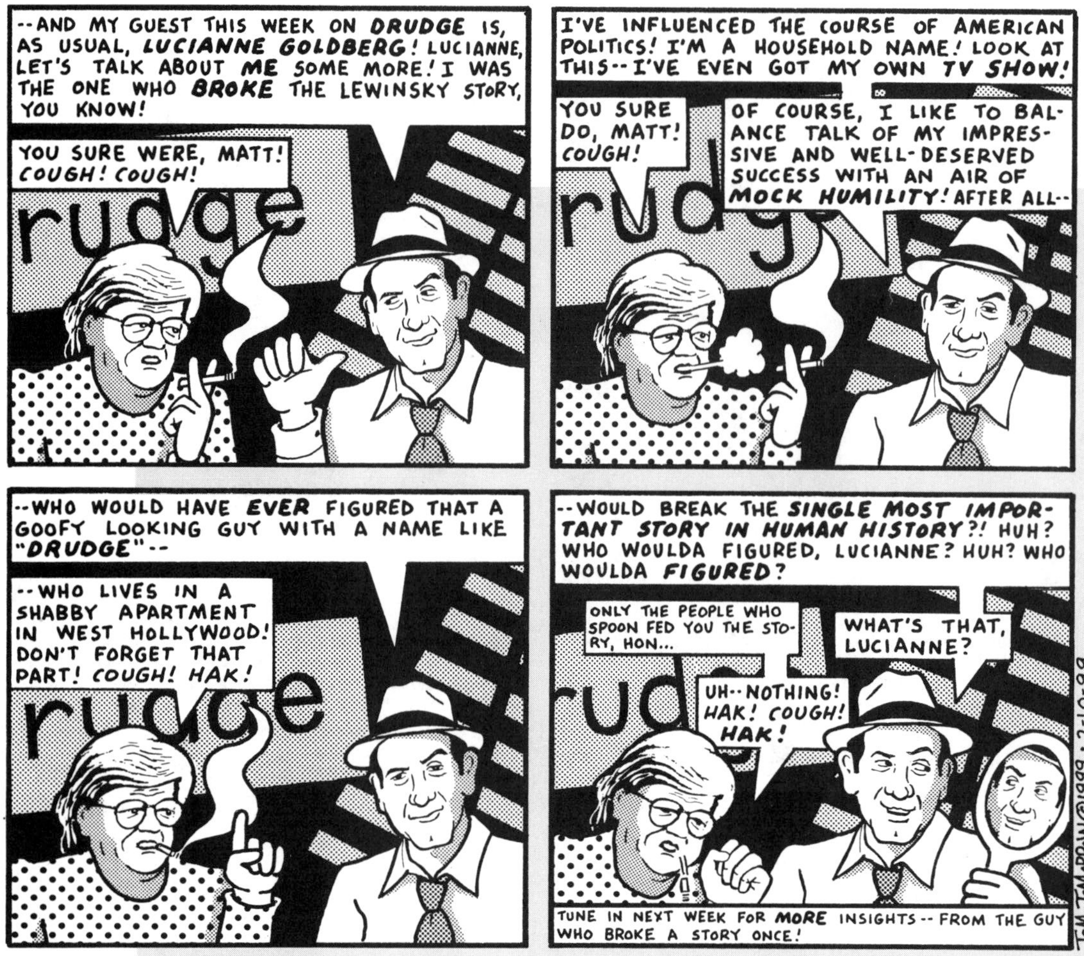
--AND MY GUEST THIS WEEK ON DRUDGE IS, AS USUAL, LUCIANNE GOLDBERG! LUCIANNE, LET'S TALK ABOUT ME SOME MORE! I WAS THE ONE WHO BROKE THE LEWINSKY STORY, YOU KNOW!
YOU SURE WERE, MATT! COUGH! COUGH!
rudge
I'VE INFLUENCED THE COURSE OF AMERICAN POLITICS! I'M A HOUSEHOLD NAME! LOOK AT THIS--I'VE EVEN GOT MY OWN TV SHOW!
YOU SURE DO, MATT! COUGH!
OF COURSE, I LIKE TO BALANCE TALK OF MY IMPRESSIVE AND WELL-DESERVED SUCCESS WITH AN AIR OF MOCK HUMILITY! AFTER ALL--
rudg
--WHO WOULD HAVE EVER FIGURED THAT A GOOFY LOOKING GUY WITH A NAME LIKE "DRUDGE"--
--WHO LIVES IN A SHABBY APARTMENT IN WEST HOLLYWOOD! DON'T FORGET THAT PART! COUGH! HAK!
rudge
--WOULD BREAK THE SINGLE MOST IMPORTANT STORY IN HUMAN HISTORY?! HUH? WHO WOULDA FIGURED, LUCIANNE? HUH? WHO WOULDA FIGURED?
ONLY THE PEOPLE WHO SPOON FED YOU THE STORY, HON...
WHAT'S THAT, LUCIANNE?
UH--NOTHING! HAK! COUGH! HAK!
rud
TUNE IN NEXT WEEK FOR MORE INSIGHTS--FROM THE GUY WHO BROKE A STORY ONCE!
TOM TOMORROW©1999 · 2-10-99

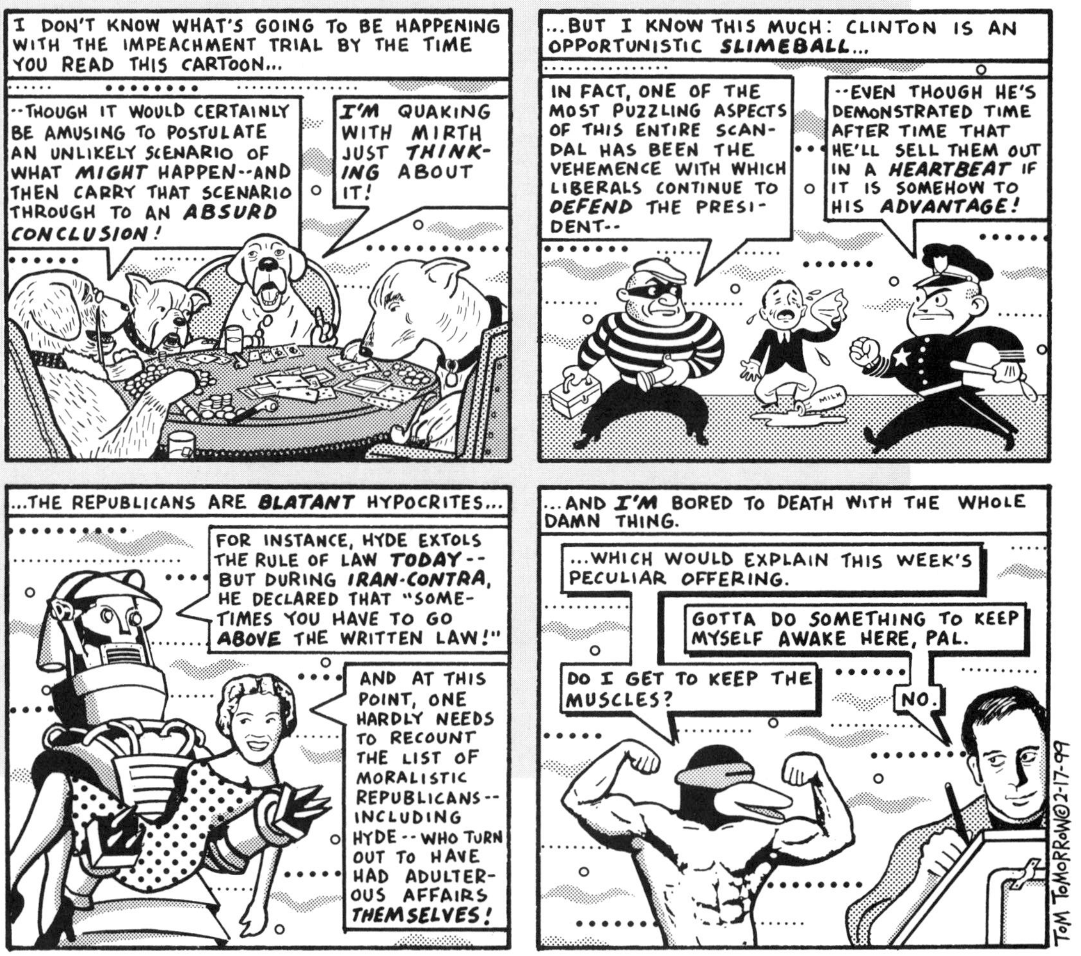
I DON'T KNOW WHAT'S GOING TO BE HAPPENING WITH THE IMPEACHMENT TRIAL BY THE TIME YOU READ THIS CARTOON...
--THOUGH IT WOULD CERTAINLY BE AMUSING TO POSTULATE AN UNLIKELY SCENARIO OF WHAT MIGHT HAPPEN--AND THEN CARRY THAT SCENARIO THROUGH TO AN ABSURD CONCLUSION!
I'M QUAKING WITH MIRTH JUST THINKING ABOUT IT!
...BUT I KNOW THIS MUCH: CLINTON IS AN OPPORTUNISTIC SLIMEBALL...
IN FACT, ONE OF THE MOST PUZZLING ASPECTS OF THIS ENTIRE SCANDAL HAS BEEN THE VEHEMENCE WITH WHICH LIBERALS CONTINUE TO DEFEND THE PRESIDENT--
--EVEN THOUGH HE'S DEMONSTRATED TIME AFTER TIME THAT HE'LL SELL THEM OUT IN A HEARTBEAT IF IT IS SOMEHOW TO HIS ADVANTAGE!
MILK
...THE REPUBLICANS ARE BLATANT HYPOCRITES...
FOR INSTANCE, HYDE EXTOLS THE RULE OF LAW TODAY--BUT DURING IRAN-CONTRA, HE DECLARED THAT "SOMETIMES YOU HAVE TO GO ABOVE THE WRITTEN LAW!"
AND AT THIS POINT, ONE HARDLY NEEDS TO RECOUNT THE LIST OF MORALISTIC REPUBLICANS--INCLUDING HYDE--WHO TURN OUT TO HAVE HAD ADULTEROUS AFFAIRS THEMSELVES!
...AND I'M BORED TO DEATH WITH THE WHOLE DAMN THING.
...WHICH WOULD EXPLAIN THIS WEEK'S PECULIAR OFFERING.
GOTTA DO SOMETHING TO KEEP MYSELF AWAKE HERE, PAL.
DO I GET TO KEEP THE MUSCLES?
NO.
TOM TOMORROW©2-17-99

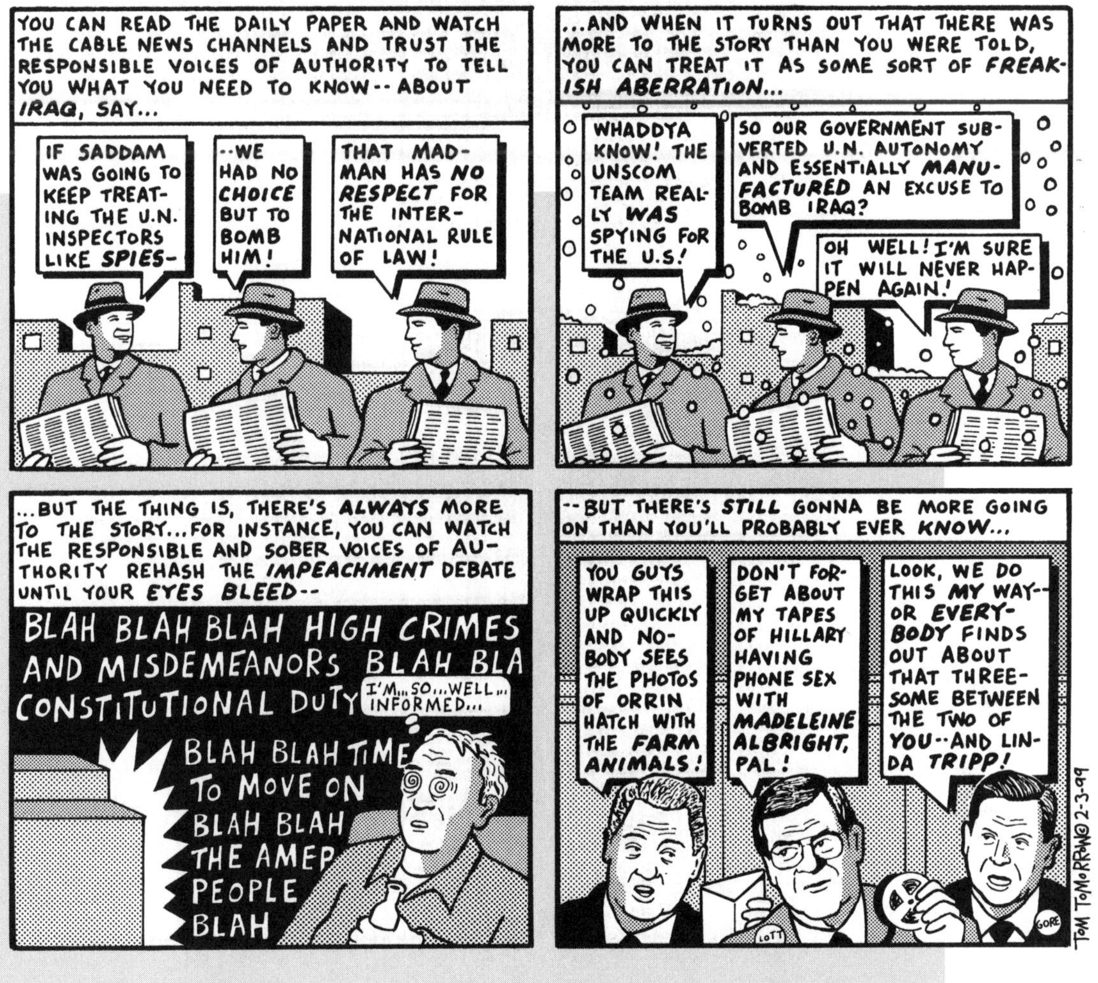
YOU CAN READ THE DAILY PAPER AND WATCH THE CABLE NEWS CHANNELS AND TRUST THE RESPONSIBLE VOICES OF AUTHORITY TO TELL YOU WHAT YOU NEED TO KNOW--ABOUT IRAQ, SAY...
IF SADDAM WAS GOING TO KEEP TREATING THE U.N. INSPECTORS LIKE SPIES-
--WE HAD NO CHOICE BUT TO BOMB HIM!
THAT MADMAN HAS NO RESPECT FOR THE INTERNATIONAL RULE OF LAW!
...AND WHEN IT TURNS OUT THAT THERE WAS MORE TO THE STORY THAN YOU WERE TOLD, YOU CAN TREAT IT AS SOME SORT OF FREAKISH ABERRATION...
WHADDYA KNOW! THE UNSCOM TEAM REALLY WAS SPYING FOR THE U.S.!
SO OUR GOVERNMENT SUBVERTED U.N. AUTONOMY AND ESSENTIALLY MANUFACTURED AN EXCUSE TO BOMB IRAQ?
OH WELL! I'M SURE IT WILL NEVER HAPPEN AGAIN!
...BUT THE THING IS, THERE'S ALWAYS MORE TO THE STORY...FOR INSTANCE, YOU CAN WATCH THE RESPONSIBLE AND SOBER VOICES OF AUTHORITY REHASH THE IMPEACHMENT DEBATE UNTIL YOUR EYES BLEED--
BLAH BLAH BLAH HIGH CRIMES AND MISDEMEANORS BLAH BLA CONSTITUTIONAL DUTY
I'M...SO...WELL...INFORMED...
BLAH BLAH TIME TO MOVE ON BLAH BLAH THE AMER PEOPLE BLAH
--BUT THERE'S STILL GONNA BE MORE GOING ON THAN YOU'LL PROBABLY EVER KNOW...
YOU GUYS WRAP THIS UP QUICKLY AND NOBODY SEES THE PHOTOS OF ORRIN HATCH WITH THE FARM ANIMALS!
DON'T FORGET ABOUT MY TAPES OF HILLARY HAVING PHONE SEX WITH MADELEINE ALBRIGHT, PAL!
LOOK, WE DO THIS MY WAY--OR EVERYBODY FINDS OUT ABOUT THAT THREESOME BETWEEN THE TWO OF YOU--AND LINDA TRIPP!
LOTT
GORE
TOM TOMORROW© 2-3-99

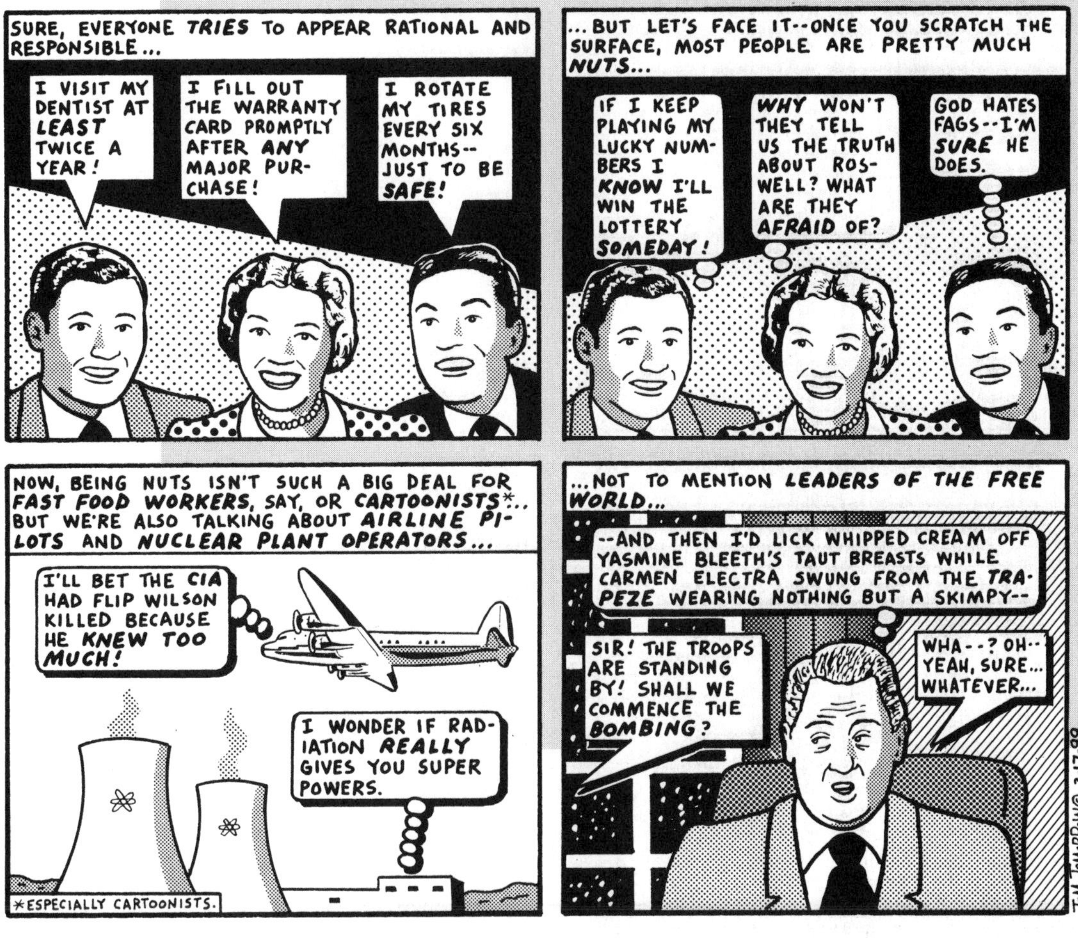
SURE, EVERYONE TRIES TO APPEAR RATIONAL AND RESPONSIBLE...
I VISIT MY DENTIST AT LEAST TWICE A YEAR!
I FILL OUT THE WARRANTY CARD PROMPTLY AFTER ANY MAJOR PURCHASE!
I ROTATE MY TIRES EVERY SIX MONTHS--JUST TO BE SAFE!
...BUT LET'S FACE IT--ONCE YOU SCRATCH THE SURFACE, MOST PEOPLE ARE PRETTY MUCH NUTS...
IF I KEEP PLAYING MY LUCKY NUMBERS I KNOW I'LL WIN THE LOTTERY SOMEDAY!
WHY WON'T THEY TELL US THE TRUTH ABOUT ROSWELL? WHAT ARE THEY AFRAID OF?
GOD HATES FAGS--I'M SURE HE DOES.
NOW, BEING NUTS ISN'T SUCH A BIG DEAL FOR FAST FOOD WORKERS, SAY, OR CARTOONISTS*.. BUT WE'RE ALSO TALKING ABOUT AIRLINE PILOTS AND NUCLEAR PLANT OPERATORS...
I'LL BET THE CIA HAD FLIP WILSON KILLED BECAUSE HE KNEW TOO MUCH!
I WONDER IF RADIATION REALLY GIVES YOU SUPER POWERS.
*ESPECIALLY CARTOONISTS.
...NOT TO MENTION LEADERS OF THE FREE WORLD...
--AND THEN I'D LICK WHIPPED CREAM OFF YASMINE BLEETH'S TAUT BREASTS WHILE CARMEN ELECTRA SWUNG FROM THE TRAPEZE WEARING NOTHING BUT A SKIMPY--
SIR! THE TROOPS ARE STANDING BY! SHALL WE COMMENCE THE BOMBING?
WHA--? OH--YEAH, SURE... WHATEVER...
TOM TOMORROW© 3-17-99

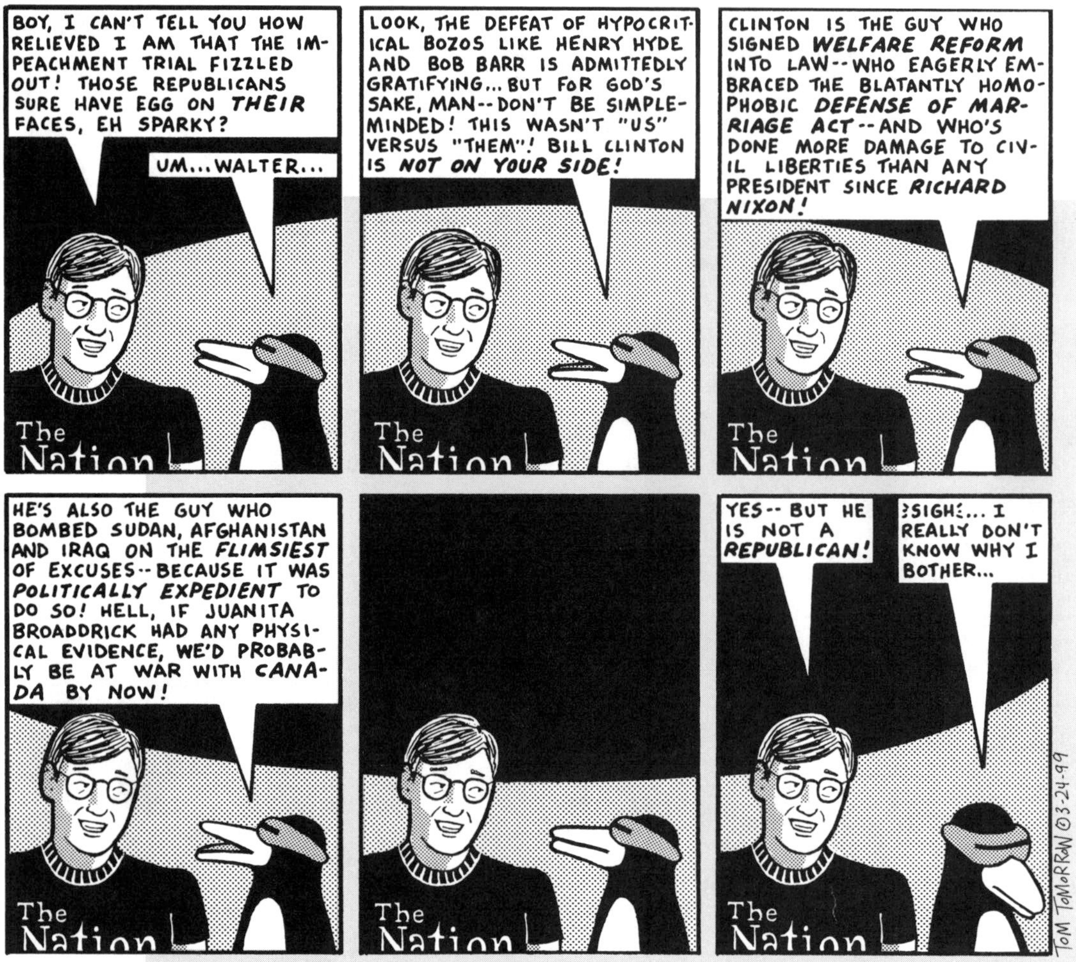
BOY, I CAN'T TELL YOU HOW RELIEVED I AM THAT THE IMPEACHMENT TRIAL FIZZLED OUT! THOSE REPUBLICANS SURE HAVE EGG ON *THEIR* FACES, EH SPARKY?
UM... WALTER...
The Nation
LOOK, THE DEFEAT OF HYPOCRITICAL BOZOS LIKE HENRY HYDE AND BOB BARR IS ADMITTEDLY GRATIFYING... BUT FOR GOD'S SAKE, MAN--DON'T BE SIMPLE-MINDED! THIS WASN'T "US" VERSUS "THEM"! BILL CLINTON IS *NOT ON YOUR SIDE!*
CLINTON IS THE GUY WHO SIGNED *WELFARE REFORM* INTO LAW--WHO EAGERLY EMBRACED THE BLATANTLY HOMOPHOBIC *DEFENSE OF MARRIAGE ACT*--AND WHO'S DONE MORE DAMAGE TO CIVIL LIBERTIES THAN ANY PRESIDENT SINCE *RICHARD NIXON!*
HE'S ALSO THE GUY WHO BOMBED SUDAN, AFGHANISTAN AND IRAQ ON THE *FLIMSIEST* OF EXCUSES--BECAUSE IT WAS *POLITICALLY EXPEDIENT* TO DO SO! HELL, IF JUANITA BROADDRICK HAD ANY PHYSICAL EVIDENCE, WE'D PROBABLY BE AT WAR WITH *CANADA* BY NOW!
YES--BUT HE IS NOT A *REPUBLICAN!*
:SIGH:... I REALLY DON'T KNOW WHY I BOTHER...
TOM TOMORROW ©03-24-99

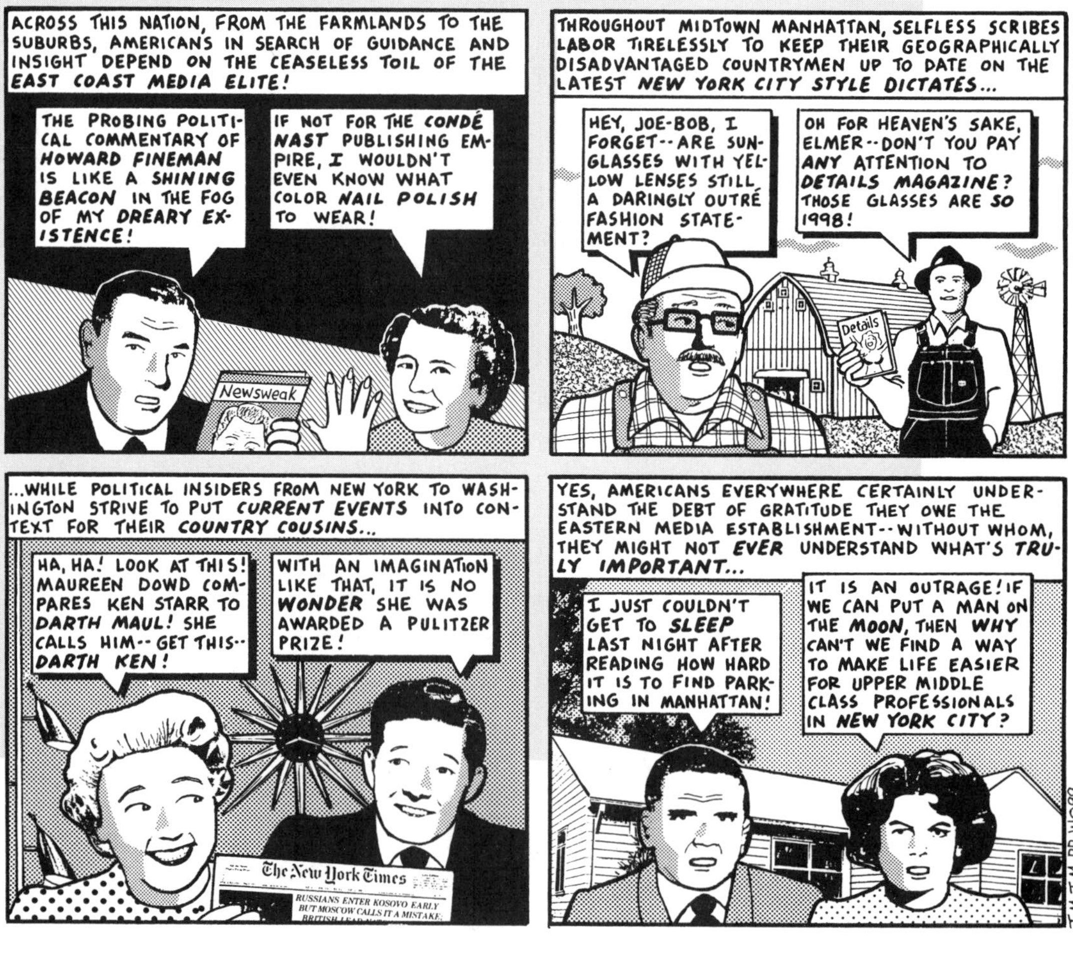
ACROSS THIS NATION, FROM THE FARMLANDS TO THE SUBURBS, AMERICANS IN SEARCH OF GUIDANCE AND INSIGHT DEPEND ON THE CEASELESS TOIL OF THE *EAST COAST MEDIA ELITE!*
THE PROBING POLITICAL COMMENTARY OF *HOWARD FINEMAN* IS LIKE A *SHINING BEACON* IN THE FOG OF MY *DREARY EXISTENCE!*
IF NOT FOR THE *CONDÉ NAST* PUBLISHING EMPIRE, *I* WOULDN'T EVEN KNOW WHAT COLOR *NAIL POLISH* TO WEAR!
Newsweak
THROUGHOUT MIDTOWN MANHATTAN, SELFLESS SCRIBES LABOR TIRELESSLY TO KEEP THEIR GEOGRAPHICALLY DISADVANTAGED COUNTRYMEN UP TO DATE ON THE LATEST *NEW YORK CITY STYLE DICTATES...*
HEY, JOE-BOB, I FORGET--ARE SUNGLASSES WITH YELLOW LENSES STILL A DARINGLY OUTRÉ FASHION STATEMENT?
OH FOR HEAVEN'S SAKE, ELMER--DON'T YOU PAY *ANY* ATTENTION TO *DETAILS MAGAZINE?* THOSE GLASSES ARE *SO* 1998!
Details
...WHILE POLITICAL INSIDERS FROM NEW YORK TO WASHINGTON STRIVE TO PUT *CURRENT EVENTS* INTO CONTEXT FOR THEIR *COUNTRY COUSINS...*
HA, HA! LOOK AT THIS! MAUREEN DOWD COMPARES KEN STARR TO *DARTH MAUL!* SHE CALLS HIM--GET THIS--*DARTH KEN!*
WITH AN IMAGINATION LIKE THAT, IT IS NO *WONDER* SHE WAS AWARDED A PULITZER PRIZE!
The New York Times
RUSSIANS ENTER KOSOVO EARLY BUT MOSCOW CALLS IT A MISTAKE
YES, AMERICANS EVERYWHERE CERTAINLY UNDERSTAND THE DEBT OF GRATITUDE THEY OWE THE EASTERN MEDIA ESTABLISHMENT--WITHOUT WHOM, THEY MIGHT NOT *EVER* UNDERSTAND WHAT'S *TRULY IMPORTANT...*
I JUST COULDN'T GET TO *SLEEP* LAST NIGHT AFTER READING HOW HARD IT IS TO FIND PARKING IN MANHATTAN!
IT IS AN OUTRAGE! IF WE CAN PUT A MAN ON THE *MOON*, THEN *WHY* CAN'T WE FIND A WAY TO MAKE LIFE EASIER FOR UPPER MIDDLE CLASS PROFESSIONALS IN *NEW YORK CITY?*
TOM TOMORROW ©99

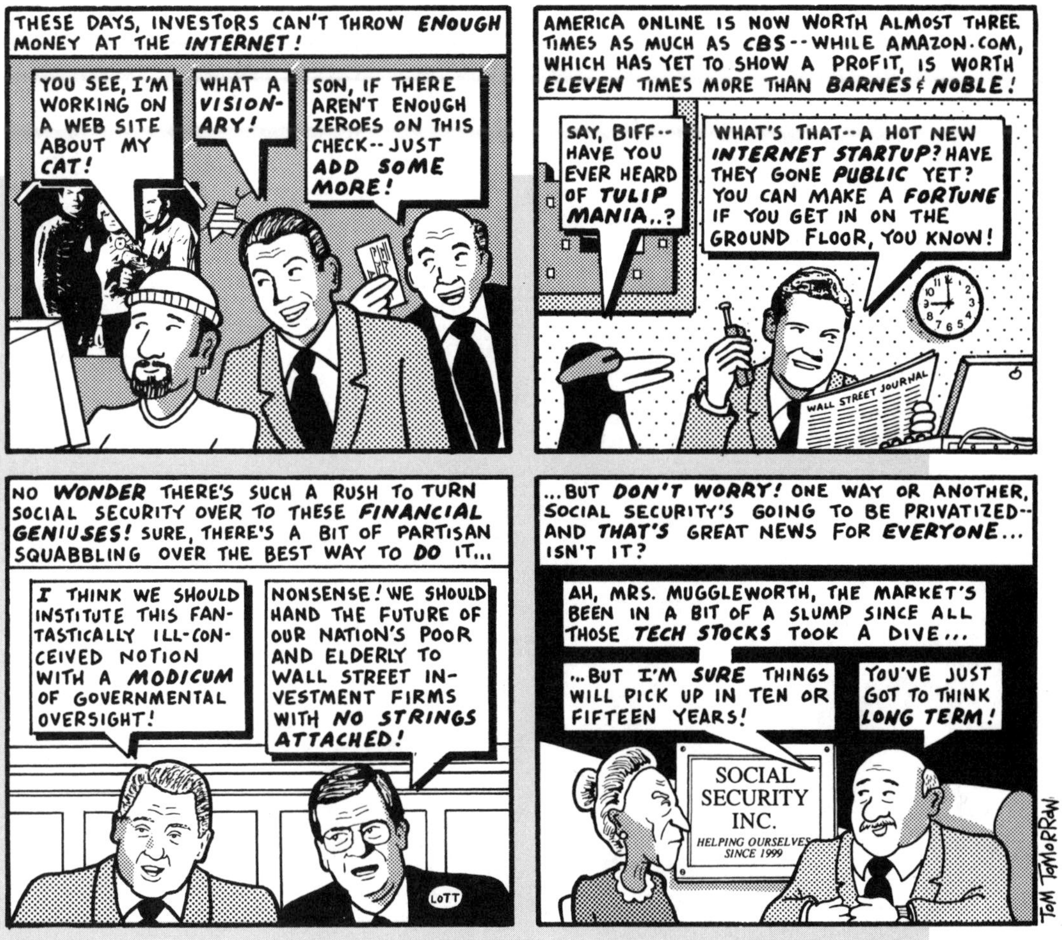
THESE DAYS, INVESTORS CAN'T THROW ENOUGH MONEY AT THE INTERNET!
YOU SEE, I'M WORKING ON A WEB SITE ABOUT MY CAT!
WHAT A VISIONARY!
SON, IF THERE AREN'T ENOUGH ZEROES ON THIS CHECK-- JUST ADD SOME MORE!
AMERICA ONLINE IS NOW WORTH ALMOST THREE TIMES AS MUCH AS CBS--WHILE AMAZON.COM, WHICH HAS YET TO SHOW A PROFIT, IS WORTH ELEVEN TIMES MORE THAN BARNES & NOBLE!
SAY, BIFF-- HAVE YOU EVER HEARD OF TULIP MANIA..?
WHAT'S THAT--A HOT NEW INTERNET STARTUP? HAVE THEY GONE PUBLIC YET? YOU CAN MAKE A FORTUNE IF YOU GET IN ON THE GROUND FLOOR, YOU KNOW!
WALL STREET JOURNAL
NO WONDER THERE'S SUCH A RUSH TO TURN SOCIAL SECURITY OVER TO THESE FINANCIAL GENIUSES! SURE, THERE'S A BIT OF PARTISAN SQUABBLING OVER THE BEST WAY TO DO IT...
I THINK WE SHOULD INSTITUTE THIS FANTASTICALLY ILL-CONCEIVED NOTION WITH A MODICUM OF GOVERNMENTAL OVERSIGHT!
NONSENSE! WE SHOULD HAND THE FUTURE OF OUR NATION'S POOR AND ELDERLY TO WALL STREET INVESTMENT FIRMS WITH NO STRINGS ATTACHED!
LOTT
...BUT DON'T WORRY! ONE WAY OR ANOTHER, SOCIAL SECURITY'S GOING TO BE PRIVATIZED-- AND THAT'S GREAT NEWS FOR EVERYONE... ISN'T IT?
AH, MRS. MUGGLEWORTH, THE MARKET'S BEEN IN A BIT OF A SLUMP SINCE ALL THOSE TECH STOCKS TOOK A DIVE...
...BUT I'M SURE THINGS WILL PICK UP IN TEN OR FIFTEEN YEARS!
YOU'VE JUST GOT TO THINK LONG TERM!
SOCIAL SECURITY INC.
HELPING OURSELVES SINCE 1999
TOM TOMORROW

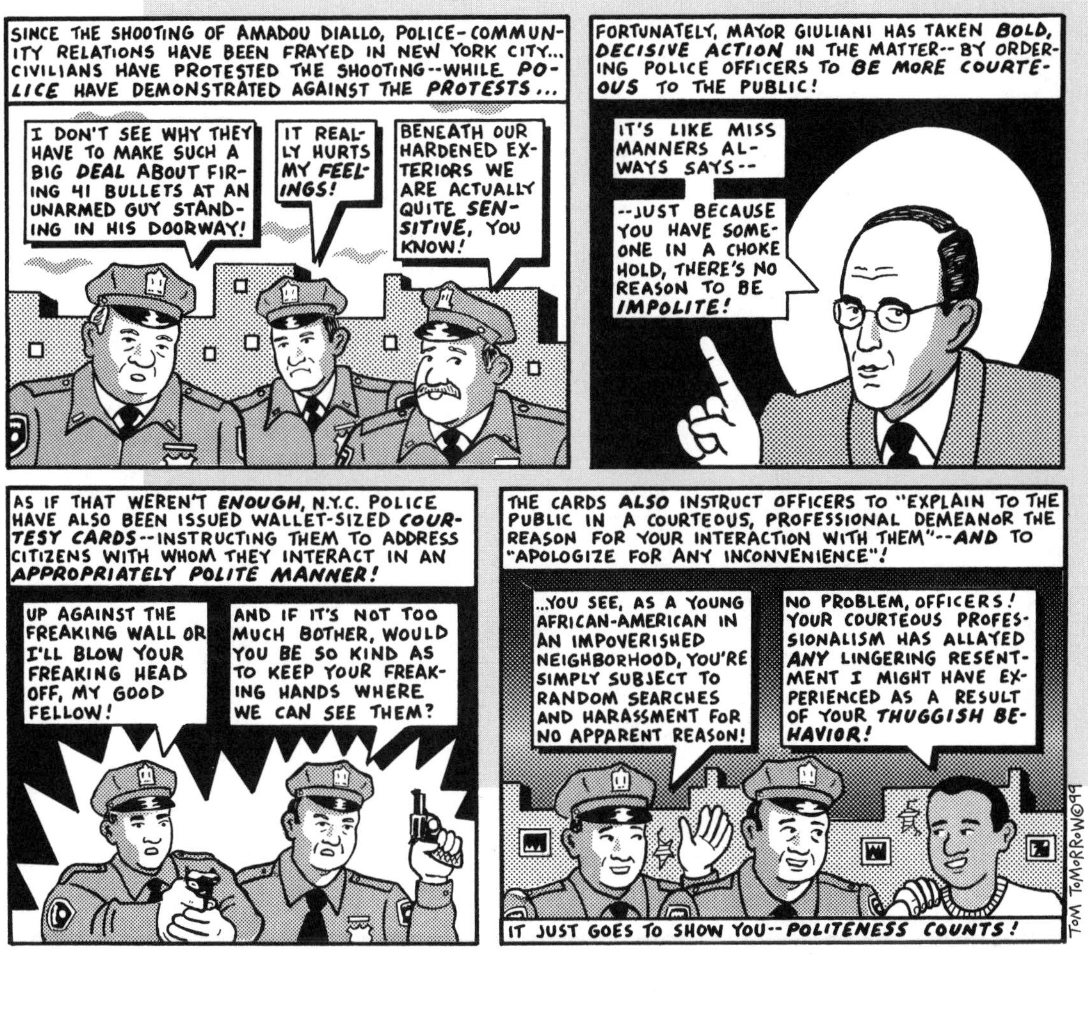
SINCE THE SHOOTING OF AMADOU DIALLO, POLICE-COMMUNITY RELATIONS HAVE BEEN FRAYED IN NEW YORK CITY... CIVILIANS HAVE PROTESTED THE SHOOTING--WHILE POLICE HAVE DEMONSTRATED AGAINST THE PROTESTS...
I DON'T SEE WHY THEY HAVE TO MAKE SUCH A BIG DEAL ABOUT FIRING 41 BULLETS AT AN UNARMED GUY STANDING IN HIS DOORWAY!
IT REALLY HURTS MY FEELINGS!
BENEATH OUR HARDENED EXTERIORS WE ARE ACTUALLY QUITE SENSITIVE, YOU KNOW!
FORTUNATELY, MAYOR GIULIANI HAS TAKEN BOLD, DECISIVE ACTION IN THE MATTER-- BY ORDERING POLICE OFFICERS TO BE MORE COURTEOUS TO THE PUBLIC!
IT'S LIKE MISS MANNERS ALWAYS SAYS--
--JUST BECAUSE YOU HAVE SOMEONE IN A CHOKE HOLD, THERE'S NO REASON TO BE IMPOLITE!
AS IF THAT WEREN'T ENOUGH, N.Y.C. POLICE HAVE ALSO BEEN ISSUED WALLET-SIZED COURTESY CARDS--INSTRUCTING THEM TO ADDRESS CITIZENS WITH WHOM THEY INTERACT IN AN APPROPRIATELY POLITE MANNER!
UP AGAINST THE FREAKING WALL OR I'LL BLOW YOUR FREAKING HEAD OFF, MY GOOD FELLOW!
AND IF IT'S NOT TOO MUCH BOTHER, WOULD YOU BE SO KIND AS TO KEEP YOUR FREAKING HANDS WHERE WE CAN SEE THEM?
THE CARDS ALSO INSTRUCT OFFICERS TO "EXPLAIN TO THE PUBLIC IN A COURTEOUS, PROFESSIONAL DEMEANOR THE REASON FOR YOUR INTERACTION WITH THEM"--AND TO "APOLOGIZE FOR ANY INCONVENIENCE"!
...YOU SEE, AS A YOUNG AFRICAN-AMERICAN IN AN IMPOVERISHED NEIGHBORHOOD, YOU'RE SIMPLY SUBJECT TO RANDOM SEARCHES AND HARASSMENT FOR NO APPARENT REASON!
NO PROBLEM, OFFICERS! YOUR COURTEOUS PROFESSIONALISM HAS ALLAYED ANY LINGERING RESENTMENT I MIGHT HAVE EXPERIENCED AS A RESULT OF YOUR THUGGISH BEHAVIOR!
IT JUST GOES TO SHOW YOU--POLITENESS COUNTS!
TOM TOMORROW©99

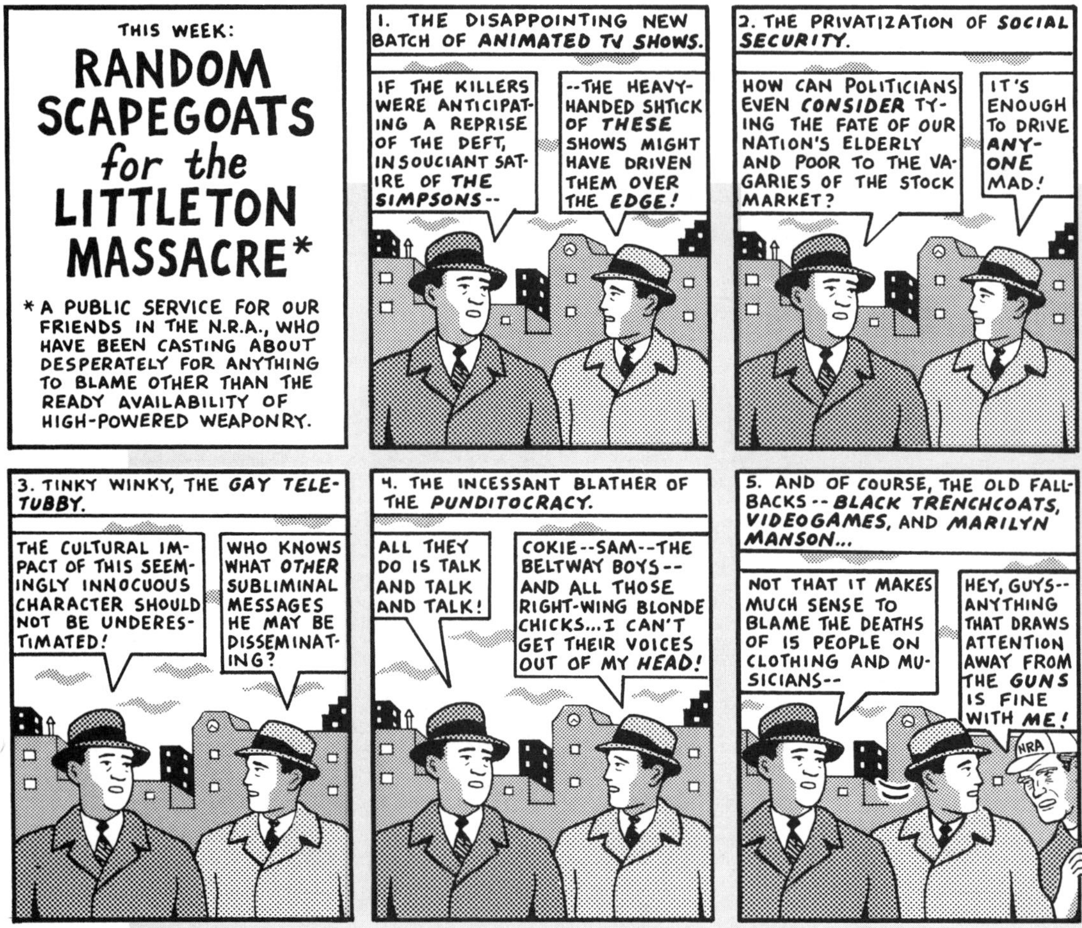
THIS WEEK:
RANDOM SCAPEGOATS for the LITTLETON MASSACRE*
* A PUBLIC SERVICE FOR OUR FRIENDS IN THE N.R.A., WHO HAVE BEEN CASTING ABOUT DESPERATELY FOR ANYTHING TO BLAME OTHER THAN THE READY AVAILABILITY OF HIGH-POWERED WEAPONRY.
1. THE DISAPPOINTING NEW BATCH OF ANIMATED TV SHOWS.
IF THE KILLERS WERE ANTICIPATING A REPRISE OF THE DEFT, INSOUCIANT SATIRE OF THE SIMPSONS--
--THE HEAVY-HANDED SHTICK OF THESE SHOWS MIGHT HAVE DRIVEN THEM OVER THE EDGE!
2. THE PRIVATIZATION OF SOCIAL SECURITY.
HOW CAN POLITICIANS EVEN CONSIDER TYING THE FATE OF OUR NATION'S ELDERLY AND POOR TO THE VAGARIES OF THE STOCK MARKET?
IT'S ENOUGH TO DRIVE ANYONE MAD!
3. TINKY WINKY, THE GAY TELETUBBY.
THE CULTURAL IMPACT OF THIS SEEMINGLY INNOCUOUS CHARACTER SHOULD NOT BE UNDERESTIMATED!
WHO KNOWS WHAT OTHER SUBLIMINAL MESSAGES HE MAY BE DISSEMINATING?
4. THE INCESSANT BLATHER OF THE PUNDITOCRACY.
ALL THEY DO IS TALK AND TALK AND TALK!
COKIE--SAM--THE BELTWAY BOYS--AND ALL THOSE RIGHT-WING BLONDE CHICKS...I CAN'T GET THEIR VOICES OUT OF MY HEAD!
5. AND OF COURSE, THE OLD FALLBACKS--BLACK TRENCHCOATS, VIDEOGAMES, AND MARILYN MANSON...
NOT THAT IT MAKES MUCH SENSE TO BLAME THE DEATHS OF 15 PEOPLE ON CLOTHING AND MUSICIANS--
HEY, GUYS--ANYTHING THAT DRAWS ATTENTION AWAY FROM THE GUNS IS FINE WITH ME!
NRA
TOM TOMORROW©99

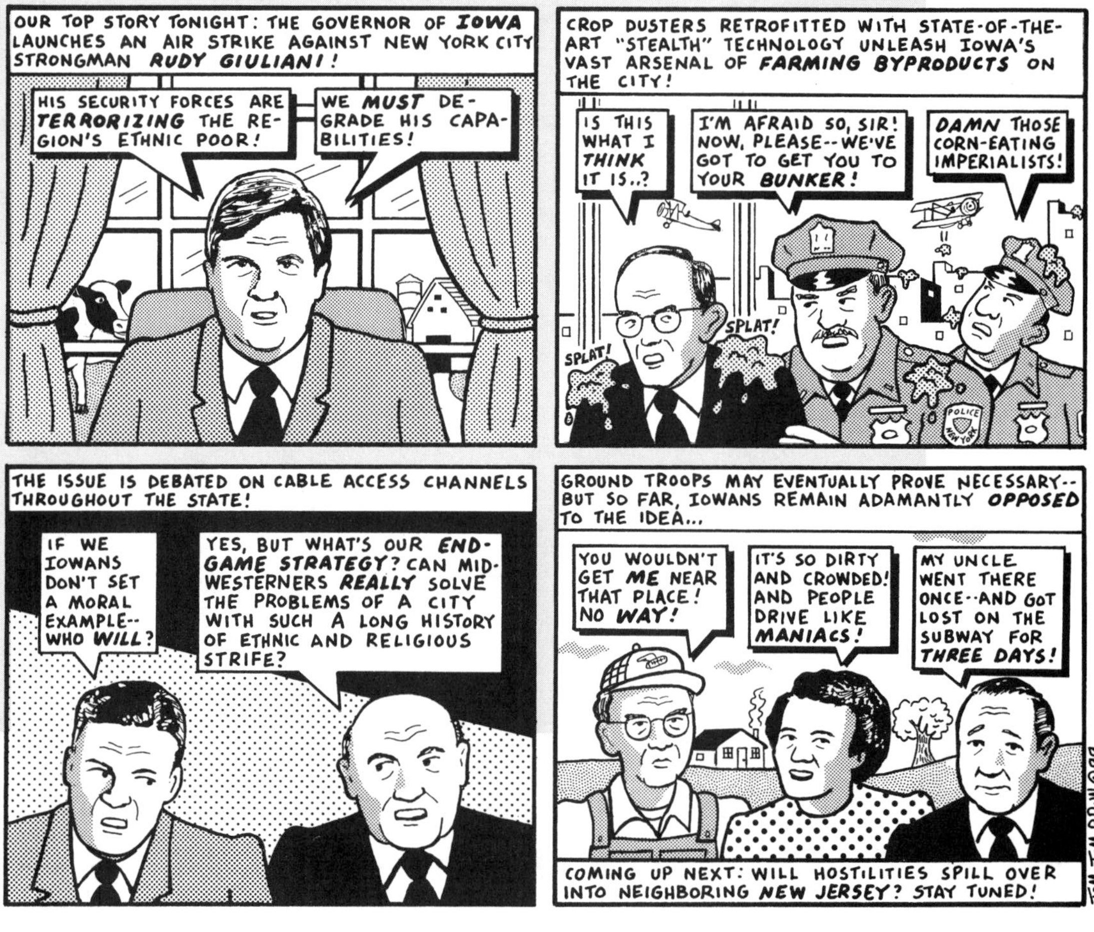
OUR TOP STORY TONIGHT: THE GOVERNOR OF IOWA LAUNCHES AN AIR STRIKE AGAINST NEW YORK CITY STRONGMAN RUDY GIULIANI!
HIS SECURITY FORCES ARE TERRORIZING THE REGION'S ETHNIC POOR!
WE MUST DEGRADE HIS CAPABILITIES!
CROP DUSTERS RETROFITTED WITH STATE-OF-THE-ART "STEALTH" TECHNOLOGY UNLEASH IOWA'S VAST ARSENAL OF FARMING BYPRODUCTS ON THE CITY!
IS THIS WHAT I THINK IT IS..?
I'M AFRAID SO, SIR! NOW, PLEASE--WE'VE GOT TO GET YOU TO YOUR BUNKER!
DAMN THOSE CORN-EATING IMPERIALISTS!
SPLAT!
SPLAT!
POLICE NEW YORK
THE ISSUE IS DEBATED ON CABLE ACCESS CHANNELS THROUGHOUT THE STATE!
IF WE IOWANS DON'T SET A MORAL EXAMPLE--WHO WILL?
YES, BUT WHAT'S OUR ENDGAME STRATEGY? CAN MIDWESTERNERS REALLY SOLVE THE PROBLEMS OF A CITY WITH SUCH A LONG HISTORY OF ETHNIC AND RELIGIOUS STRIFE?
GROUND TROOPS MAY EVENTUALLY PROVE NECESSARY--BUT SO FAR, IOWANS REMAIN ADAMANTLY OPPOSED TO THE IDEA...
YOU WOULDN'T GET ME NEAR THAT PLACE! NO WAY!
IT'S SO DIRTY AND CROWDED! AND PEOPLE DRIVE LIKE MANIACS!
MY UNCLE WENT THERE ONCE--AND GOT LOST ON THE SUBWAY FOR THREE DAYS!
COMING UP NEXT: WILL HOSTILITIES SPILL OVER INTO NEIGHBORING NEW JERSEY? STAY TUNED!
TOM TOMORROW©99

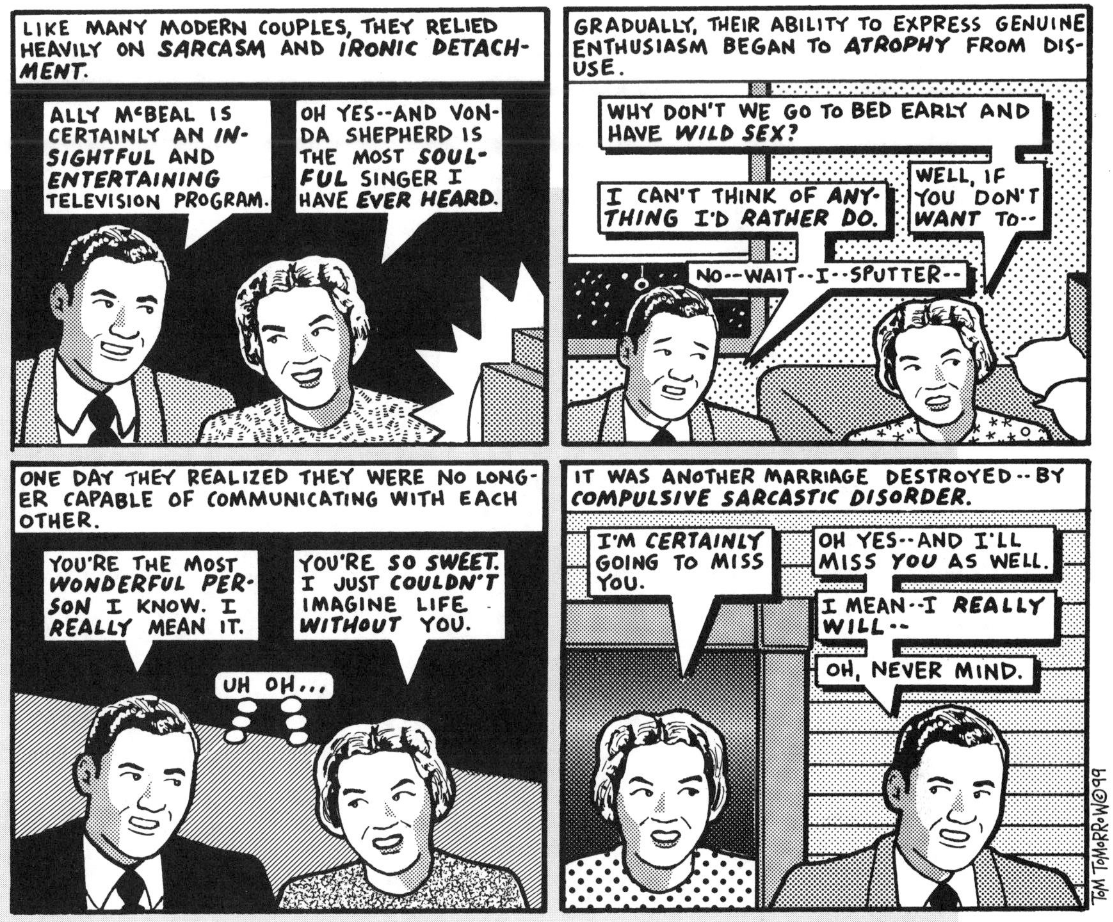
LIKE MANY MODERN COUPLES, THEY RELIED HEAVILY ON SARCASM AND IRONIC DETACHMENT.
ALLY McBEAL IS CERTAINLY AN INSIGHTFUL AND ENTERTAINING TELEVISION PROGRAM.
OH YES--AND VONDA SHEPHERD IS THE MOST SOULFUL SINGER I HAVE EVER HEARD.
GRADUALLY, THEIR ABILITY TO EXPRESS GENUINE ENTHUSIASM BEGAN TO ATROPHY FROM DISUSE.
WHY DON'T WE GO TO BED EARLY AND HAVE WILD SEX?
I CAN'T THINK OF ANYTHING I'D RATHER DO.
WELL, IF YOU DON'T WANT TO--
NO--WAIT--I--SPUTTER--
ONE DAY THEY REALIZED THEY WERE NO LONGER CAPABLE OF COMMUNICATING WITH EACH OTHER.
YOU'RE THE MOST WONDERFUL PERSON I KNOW. I REALLY MEAN IT.
YOU'RE SO SWEET. I JUST COULDN'T IMAGINE LIFE WITHOUT YOU.
UH OH...
IT WAS ANOTHER MARRIAGE DESTROYED--BY COMPULSIVE SARCASTIC DISORDER.
I'M CERTAINLY GOING TO MISS YOU.
OH YES--AND I'LL MISS YOU AS WELL.
I MEAN--I REALLY WILL--
OH, NEVER MIND.
ToM ToMoRRoW©99

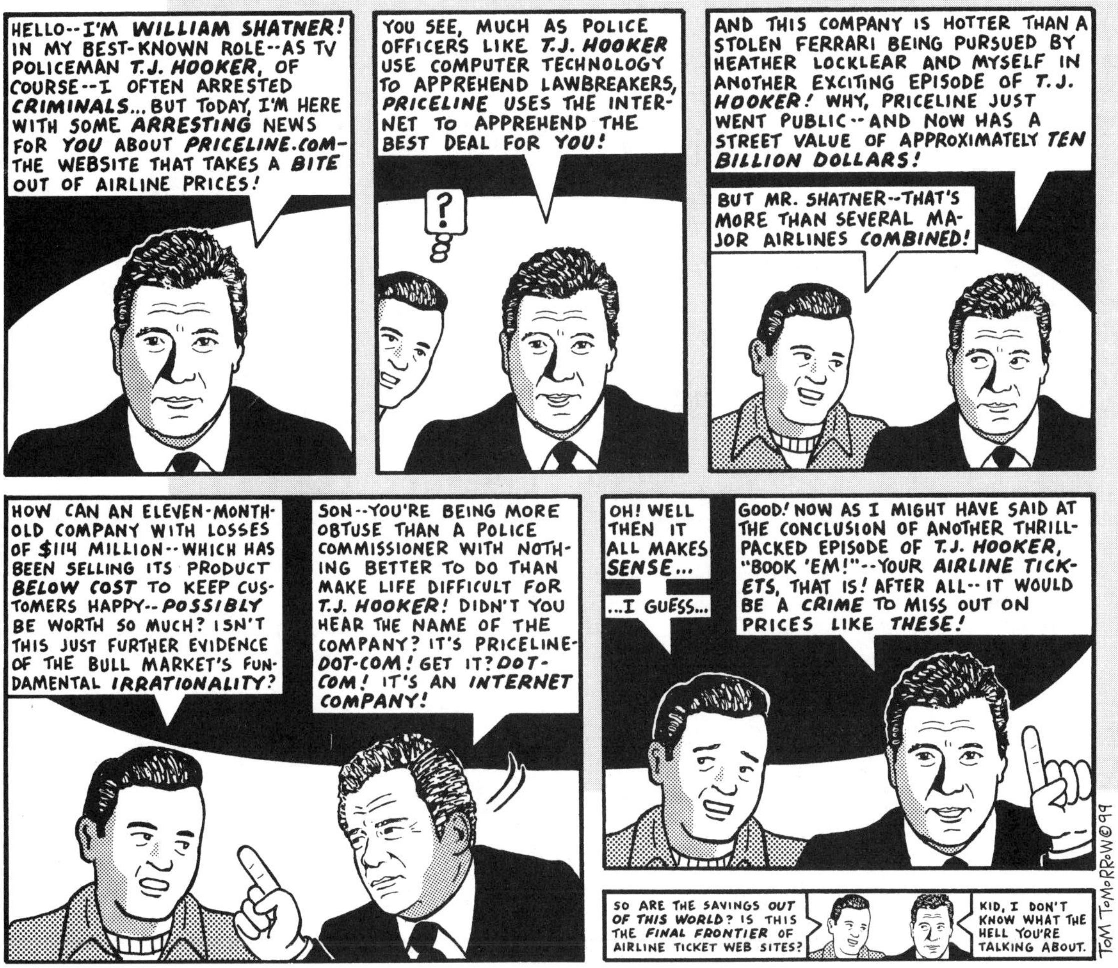
HELLO--I'M WILLIAM SHATNER! IN MY BEST-KNOWN ROLE--AS TV POLICEMAN T.J. HOOKER, OF COURSE--I OFTEN ARRESTED CRIMINALS... BUT TODAY, I'M HERE WITH SOME ARRESTING NEWS FOR YOU ABOUT PRICELINE.COM--THE WEBSITE THAT TAKES A BITE OUT OF AIRLINE PRICES!
YOU SEE, MUCH AS POLICE OFFICERS LIKE T.J. HOOKER USE COMPUTER TECHNOLOGY TO APPREHEND LAWBREAKERS, PRICELINE USES THE INTERNET TO APPREHEND THE BEST DEAL FOR YOU!
?
AND THIS COMPANY IS HOTTER THAN A STOLEN FERRARI BEING PURSUED BY HEATHER LOCKLEAR AND MYSELF IN ANOTHER EXCITING EPISODE OF T.J. HOOKER! WHY, PRICELINE JUST WENT PUBLIC--AND NOW HAS A STREET VALUE OF APPROXIMATELY TEN BILLION DOLLARS!
BUT MR. SHATNER--THAT'S MORE THAN SEVERAL MAJOR AIRLINES COMBINED!
HOW CAN AN ELEVEN-MONTH-OLD COMPANY WITH LOSSES OF $114 MILLION--WHICH HAS BEEN SELLING ITS PRODUCT BELOW COST TO KEEP CUSTOMERS HAPPY--POSSIBLY BE WORTH SO MUCH? ISN'T THIS JUST FURTHER EVIDENCE OF THE BULL MARKET'S FUNDAMENTAL IRRATIONALITY?
SON--YOU'RE BEING MORE OBTUSE THAN A POLICE COMMISSIONER WITH NOTHING BETTER TO DO THAN MAKE LIFE DIFFICULT FOR T.J. HOOKER! DIDN'T YOU HEAR THE NAME OF THE COMPANY? IT'S PRICELINE-DOT-COM! GET IT? DOT-COM! IT'S AN INTERNET COMPANY!
OH! WELL THEN IT ALL MAKES SENSE...
...I GUESS...
GOOD! NOW AS I MIGHT HAVE SAID AT THE CONCLUSION OF ANOTHER THRILL-PACKED EPISODE OF T.J. HOOKER, "BOOK 'EM!"--YOUR AIRLINE TICKETS, THAT IS! AFTER ALL--IT WOULD BE A CRIME TO MISS OUT ON PRICES LIKE THESE!
SO ARE THE SAVINGS OUT OF THIS WORLD? IS THIS THE FINAL FRONTIER OF AIRLINE TICKET WEB SITES?
KID, I DON'T KNOW WHAT THE HELL YOU'RE TALKING ABOUT.
ToM ToMoRRoW©99

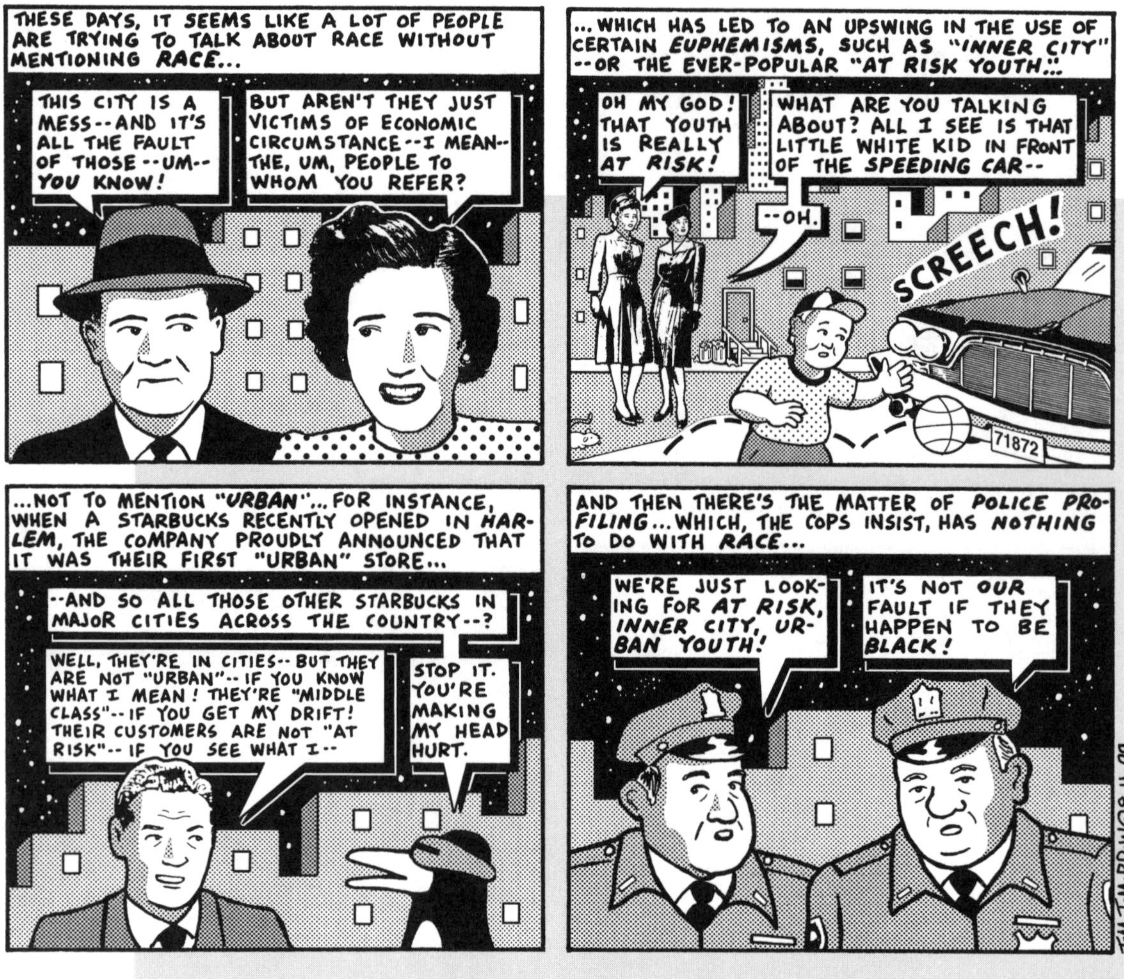
THESE DAYS, IT SEEMS LIKE A LOT OF PEOPLE ARE TRYING TO TALK ABOUT RACE WITHOUT MENTIONING RACE...
THIS CITY IS A MESS--AND IT'S ALL THE FAULT OF THOSE--UM--YOU KNOW!
BUT AREN'T THEY JUST VICTIMS OF ECONOMIC CIRCUMSTANCE--I MEAN--THE, UM, PEOPLE TO WHOM YOU REFER?
...WHICH HAS LED TO AN UPSWING IN THE USE OF CERTAIN EUPHEMISMS, SUCH AS "INNER CITY" --OR THE EVER-POPULAR "AT RISK YOUTH."
OH MY GOD! THAT YOUTH IS REALLY AT RISK!
WHAT ARE YOU TALKING ABOUT? ALL I SEE IS THAT LITTLE WHITE KID IN FRONT OF THE SPEEDING CAR--
--OH.
SCREECH!
71872
...NOT TO MENTION "URBAN"... FOR INSTANCE, WHEN A STARBUCKS RECENTLY OPENED IN HARLEM, THE COMPANY PROUDLY ANNOUNCED THAT IT WAS THEIR FIRST "URBAN" STORE...
--AND SO ALL THOSE OTHER STARBUCKS IN MAJOR CITIES ACROSS THE COUNTRY--?
WELL, THEY'RE IN CITIES--BUT THEY ARE NOT "URBAN"--IF YOU KNOW WHAT I MEAN! THEY'RE "MIDDLE CLASS"--IF YOU GET MY DRIFT! THEIR CUSTOMERS ARE NOT "AT RISK"--IF YOU SEE WHAT I--
STOP IT. YOU'RE MAKING MY HEAD HURT.
AND THEN THERE'S THE MATTER OF POLICE PROFILING... WHICH, THE COPS INSIST, HAS NOTHING TO DO WITH RACE...
WE'RE JUST LOOKING FOR AT RISK, INNER CITY, URBAN YOUTH!
IT'S NOT OUR FAULT IF THEY HAPPEN TO BE BLACK!
TOM TOMORROW©8-11-99

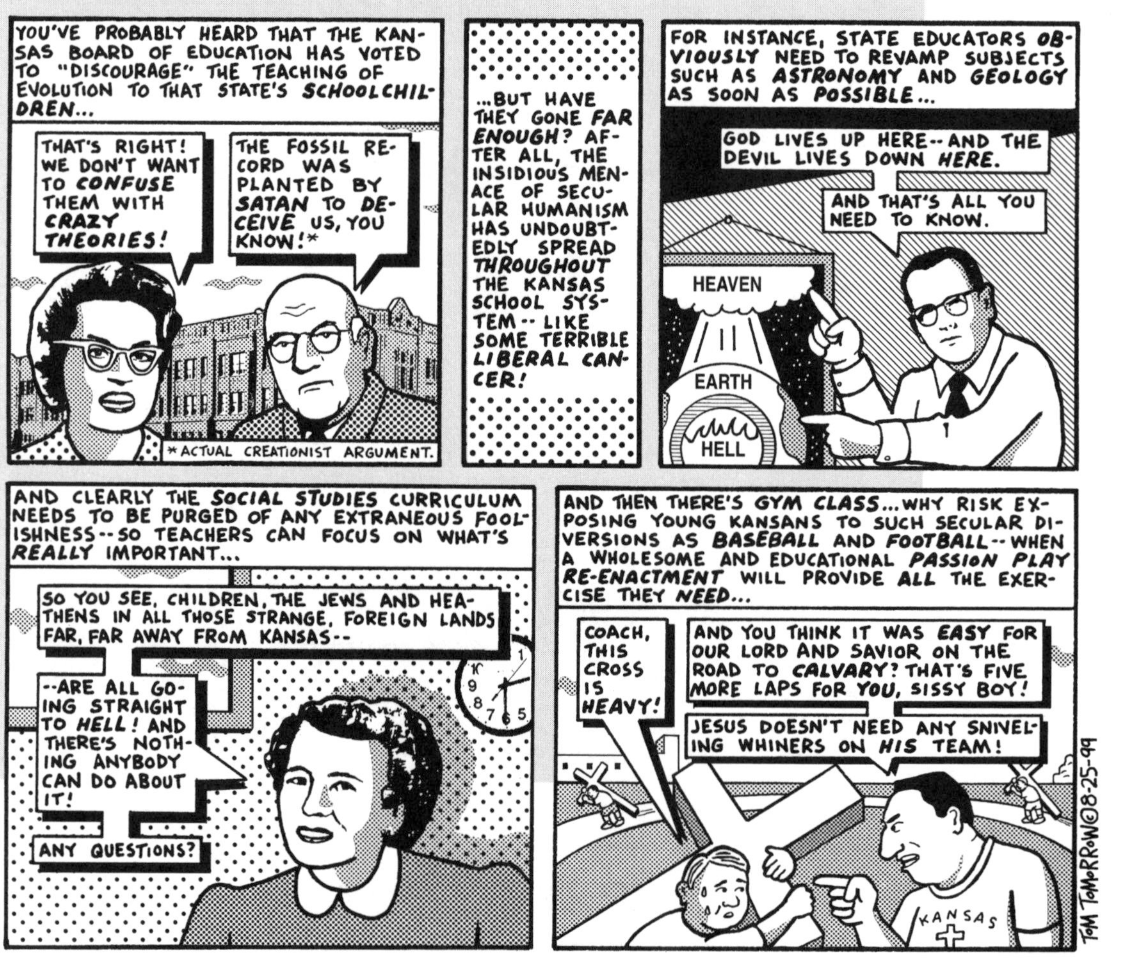
YOU'VE PROBABLY HEARD THAT THE KANSAS BOARD OF EDUCATION HAS VOTED TO "DISCOURAGE" THE TEACHING OF EVOLUTION TO THAT STATE'S SCHOOLCHILDREN...
THAT'S RIGHT! WE DON'T WANT TO CONFUSE THEM WITH CRAZY THEORIES!
THE FOSSIL RECORD WAS PLANTED BY SATAN TO DECEIVE US, YOU KNOW!*
*ACTUAL CREATIONIST ARGUMENT.
...BUT HAVE THEY GONE FAR ENOUGH? AFTER ALL, THE INSIDIOUS MENACE OF SECULAR HUMANISM HAS UNDOUBTEDLY SPREAD THROUGHOUT THE KANSAS SCHOOL SYSTEM--LIKE SOME TERRIBLE LIBERAL CANCER!
FOR INSTANCE, STATE EDUCATORS OBVIOUSLY NEED TO REVAMP SUBJECTS SUCH AS ASTRONOMY AND GEOLOGY AS SOON AS POSSIBLE...
GOD LIVES UP HERE--AND THE DEVIL LIVES DOWN HERE.
AND THAT'S ALL YOU NEED TO KNOW.
HEAVEN
EARTH
HELL
AND CLEARLY THE SOCIAL STUDIES CURRICULUM NEEDS TO BE PURGED OF ANY EXTRANEOUS FOOLISHNESS--SO TEACHERS CAN FOCUS ON WHAT'S REALLY IMPORTANT...
SO YOU SEE, CHILDREN, THE JEWS AND HEATHENS IN ALL THOSE STRANGE, FOREIGN LANDS FAR, FAR AWAY FROM KANSAS--
--ARE ALL GOING STRAIGHT TO HELL! AND THERE'S NOTHING ANYBODY CAN DO ABOUT IT!
ANY QUESTIONS?
AND THEN THERE'S GYM CLASS... WHY RISK EXPOSING YOUNG KANSANS TO SUCH SECULAR DIVERSIONS AS BASEBALL AND FOOTBALL--WHEN A WHOLESOME AND EDUCATIONAL PASSION PLAY RE-ENACTMENT WILL PROVIDE ALL THE EXERCISE THEY NEED...
COACH, THIS CROSS IS HEAVY!
AND YOU THINK IT WAS EASY FOR OUR LORD AND SAVIOR ON THE ROAD TO CALVARY? THAT'S FIVE MORE LAPS FOR YOU, SISSY BOY!
JESUS DOESN'T NEED ANY SNIVELING WHINERS ON HIS TEAM!
KANSAS
TOM TOMORROW©8-25-99

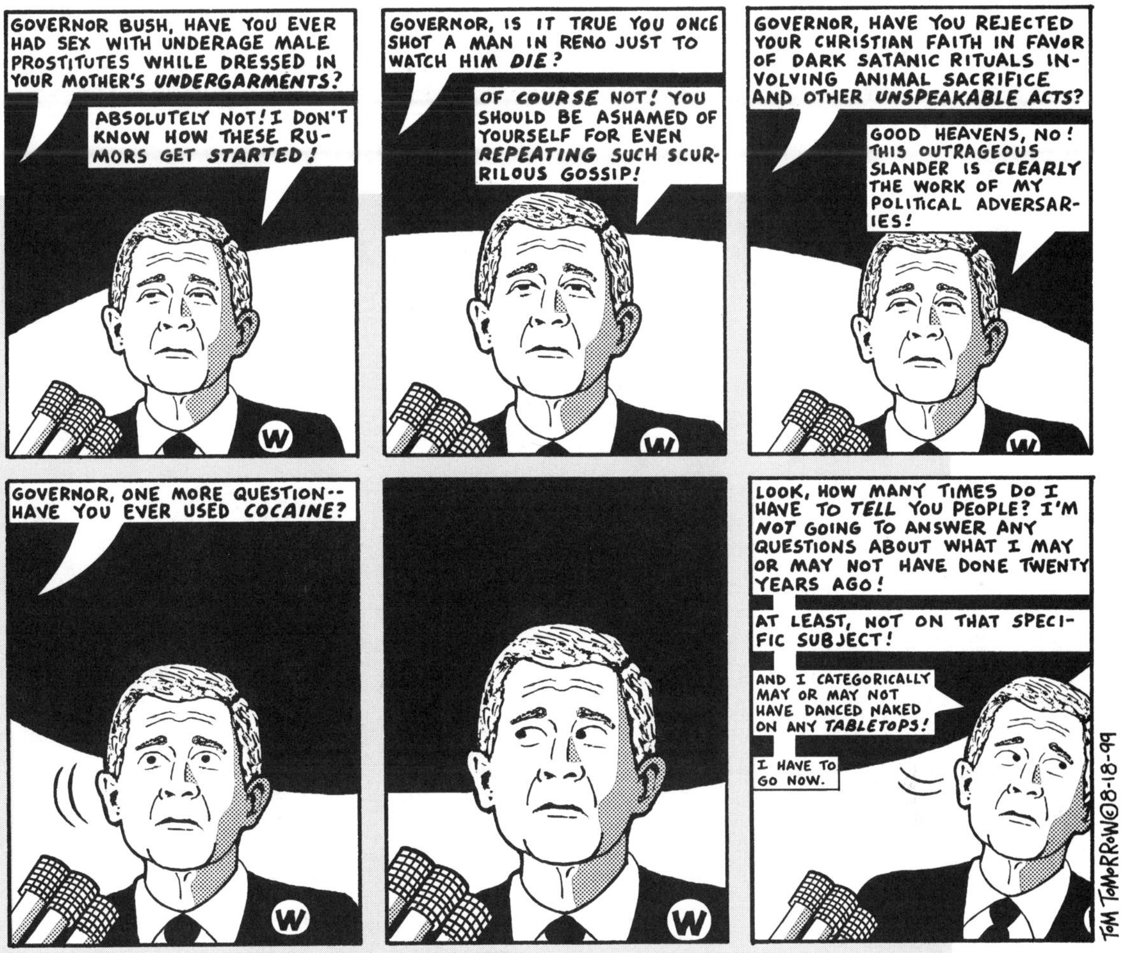
GOVERNOR BUSH, HAVE YOU EVER HAD SEX WITH UNDERAGE MALE PROSTITUTES WHILE DRESSED IN YOUR MOTHER'S UNDERGARMENTS?
ABSOLUTELY NOT! I DON'T KNOW HOW THESE RUMORS GET STARTED!
GOVERNOR, IS IT TRUE YOU ONCE SHOT A MAN IN RENO JUST TO WATCH HIM DIE?
OF COURSE NOT! YOU SHOULD BE ASHAMED OF YOURSELF FOR EVEN REPEATING SUCH SCURRILOUS GOSSIP!
GOVERNOR, HAVE YOU REJECTED YOUR CHRISTIAN FAITH IN FAVOR OF DARK SATANIC RITUALS INVOLVING ANIMAL SACRIFICE AND OTHER UNSPEAKABLE ACTS?
GOOD HEAVENS, NO! THIS OUTRAGEOUS SLANDER IS CLEARLY THE WORK OF MY POLITICAL ADVERSARIES!
W
GOVERNOR, ONE MORE QUESTION-- HAVE YOU EVER USED COCAINE?
LOOK, HOW MANY TIMES DO I HAVE TO TELL YOU PEOPLE? I'M NOT GOING TO ANSWER ANY QUESTIONS ABOUT WHAT I MAY OR MAY NOT HAVE DONE TWENTY YEARS AGO!
AT LEAST, NOT ON THAT SPECIFIC SUBJECT!
AND I CATEGORICALLY MAY OR MAY NOT HAVE DANCED NAKED ON ANY TABLETOPS!
I HAVE TO GO NOW.
TOM TOMORROW©8-18-99

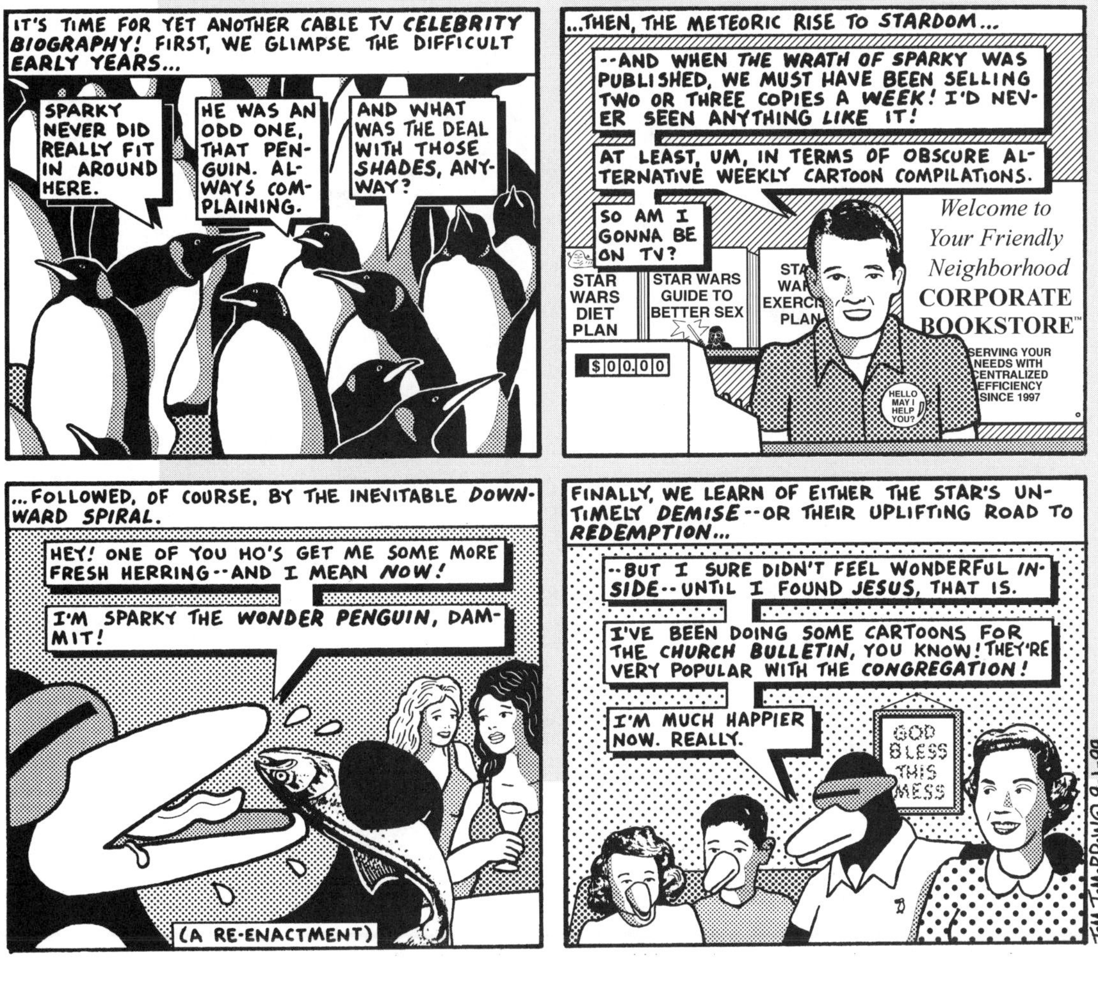
IT'S TIME FOR YET ANOTHER CABLE TV CELEBRITY BIOGRAPHY! FIRST, WE GLIMPSE THE DIFFICULT EARLY YEARS...
SPARKY NEVER DID REALLY FIT IN AROUND HERE.
HE WAS AN ODD ONE, THAT PENGUIN. ALWAYS COMPLAINING.
AND WHAT WAS THE DEAL WITH THOSE SHADES, ANYWAY?
...THEN, THE METEORIC RISE TO STARDOM...
--AND WHEN THE WRATH OF SPARKY WAS PUBLISHED, WE MUST HAVE BEEN SELLING TWO OR THREE COPIES A WEEK! I'D NEVER SEEN ANYTHING LIKE IT!
AT LEAST, UM, IN TERMS OF OBSCURE ALTERNATIVE WEEKLY CARTOON COMPILATIONS.
SO AM I GONNA BE ON TV?
STAR WARS DIET PLAN
STAR WARS GUIDE TO BETTER SEX
Welcome to Your Friendly Neighborhood CORPORATE BOOKSTORE™
SERVING YOUR NEEDS WITH CENTRALIZED EFFICIENCY SINCE 1997
HELLO MAY I HELP YOU?
$00.00
...FOLLOWED, OF COURSE, BY THE INEVITABLE DOWNWARD SPIRAL.
HEY! ONE OF YOU HO'S GET ME SOME MORE FRESH HERRING--AND I MEAN NOW!
I'M SPARKY THE WONDER PENGUIN, DAMMIT!
(A RE-ENACTMENT)
FINALLY, WE LEARN OF EITHER THE STAR'S UNTIMELY DEMISE--OR THEIR UPLIFTING ROAD TO REDEMPTION...
--BUT I SURE DIDN'T FEEL WONDERFUL INSIDE--UNTIL I FOUND JESUS, THAT IS.
I'VE BEEN DOING SOME CARTOONS FOR THE CHURCH BULLETIN, YOU KNOW! THEY'RE VERY POPULAR WITH THE CONGREGATION!
I'M MUCH HAPPIER NOW. REALLY.
GOD BLESS THIS MESS
TOM TOMORROW© 9-1-99

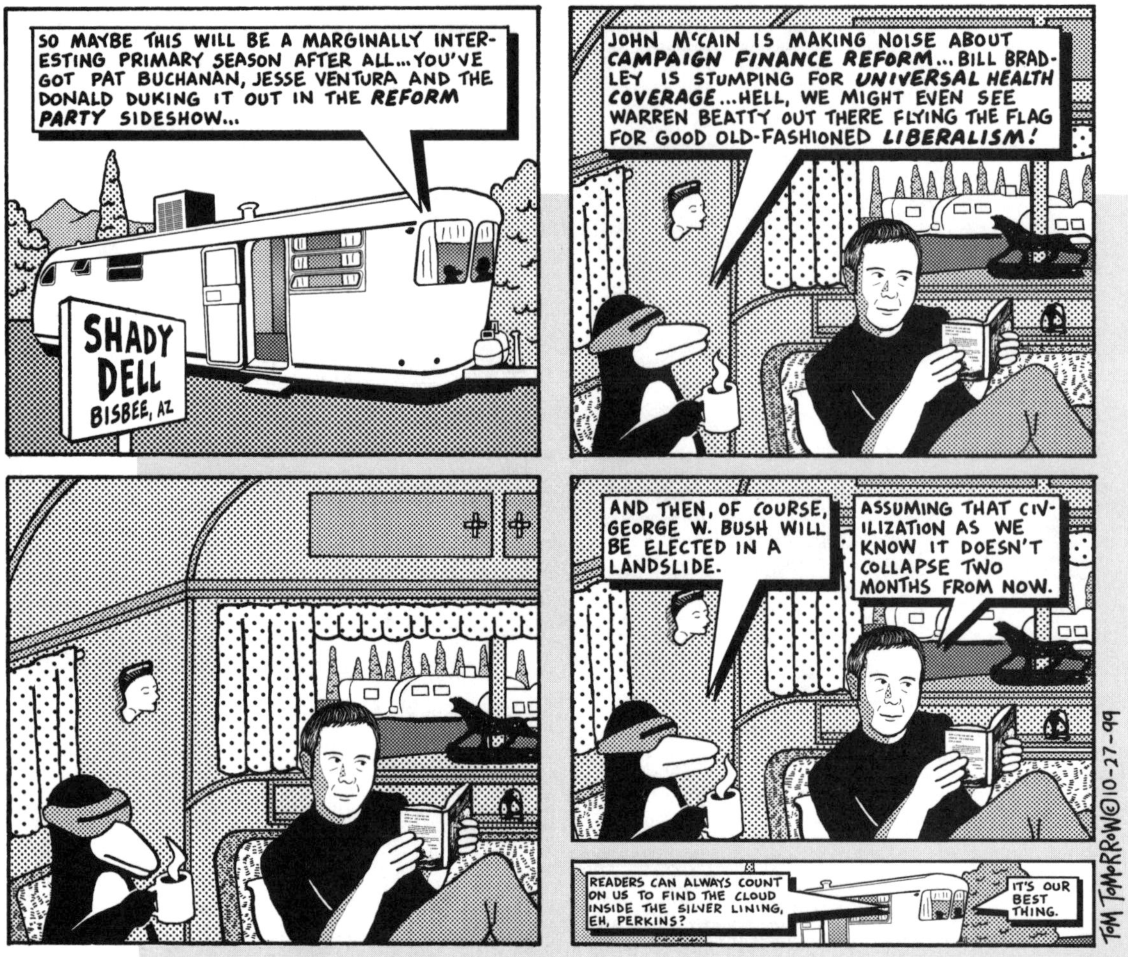
SO MAYBE THIS WILL BE A MARGINALLY INTERESTING PRIMARY SEASON AFTER ALL... YOU'VE GOT PAT BUCHANAN, JESSE VENTURA AND THE DONALD DUKING IT OUT IN THE **REFORM PARTY** SIDESHOW...
SHADY DELL
BISBEE, AZ
JOHN McCAIN IS MAKING NOISE ABOUT **CAMPAIGN FINANCE REFORM**... BILL BRADLEY IS STUMPING FOR **UNIVERSAL HEALTH COVERAGE**... HELL, WE MIGHT EVEN SEE WARREN BEATTY OUT THERE FLYING THE FLAG FOR GOOD OLD-FASHIONED **LIBERALISM!**
AND THEN, OF COURSE, GEORGE W. BUSH WILL BE ELECTED IN A LANDSLIDE.
ASSUMING THAT CIVILIZATION AS WE KNOW IT DOESN'T COLLAPSE TWO MONTHS FROM NOW.
READERS CAN ALWAYS COUNT ON US TO FIND THE CLOUD INSIDE THE SILVER LINING, EH, PERKINS?
IT'S OUR BEST THING.
TOM TOMORROW©10-27-99

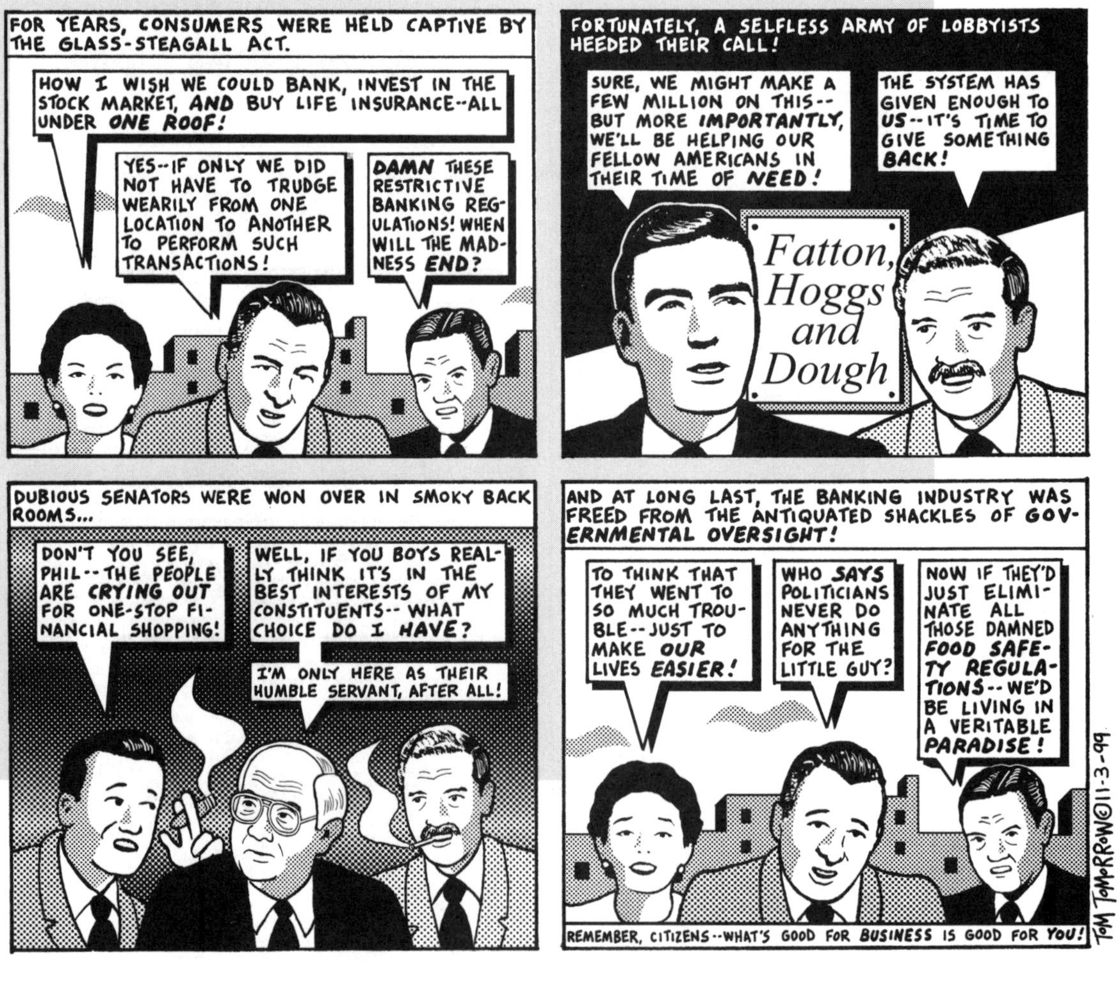
FOR YEARS, CONSUMERS WERE HELD CAPTIVE BY THE GLASS-STEAGALL ACT.
HOW I WISH WE COULD BANK, INVEST IN THE STOCK MARKET, **AND** BUY LIFE INSURANCE--ALL UNDER **ONE ROOF!**
YES--IF ONLY WE DID NOT HAVE TO TRUDGE WEARILY FROM ONE LOCATION TO ANOTHER TO PERFORM SUCH TRANSACTIONS!
DAMN THESE RESTRICTIVE BANKING REGULATIONS! WHEN WILL THE MADNESS **END?**
FORTUNATELY, A SELFLESS ARMY OF LOBBYISTS HEEDED THEIR CALL!
SURE, WE MIGHT MAKE A FEW MILLION ON THIS--BUT MORE **IMPORTANTLY**, WE'LL BE HELPING OUR FELLOW AMERICANS IN THEIR TIME OF **NEED!**
THE SYSTEM HAS GIVEN ENOUGH TO **US**--IT'S TIME TO GIVE SOMETHING **BACK!**
Fatton, Hoggs and Dough
DUBIOUS SENATORS WERE WON OVER IN SMOKY BACK ROOMS...
DON'T YOU SEE, PHIL--THE PEOPLE ARE **CRYING OUT** FOR ONE-STOP FINANCIAL SHOPPING!
WELL, IF YOU BOYS REALLY THINK IT'S IN THE BEST INTERESTS OF MY CONSTITUENTS--WHAT CHOICE DO I **HAVE?**
I'M ONLY HERE AS THEIR HUMBLE SERVANT, AFTER ALL!
AND AT LONG LAST, THE BANKING INDUSTRY WAS FREED FROM THE ANTIQUATED SHACKLES OF **GOVERNMENTAL OVERSIGHT!**
TO THINK THAT THEY WENT TO SO MUCH TROUBLE--JUST TO MAKE **OUR** LIVES **EASIER!**
WHO **SAYS** POLITICIANS NEVER DO ANYTHING FOR THE LITTLE GUY?
NOW IF THEY'D JUST ELIMINATE ALL THOSE DAMNED **FOOD SAFETY REGULATIONS**--WE'D BE LIVING IN A VERITABLE **PARADISE!**
REMEMBER, CITIZENS--WHAT'S GOOD FOR **BUSINESS** IS GOOD FOR **YOU!**
TOM TOMORROW©11-3-99

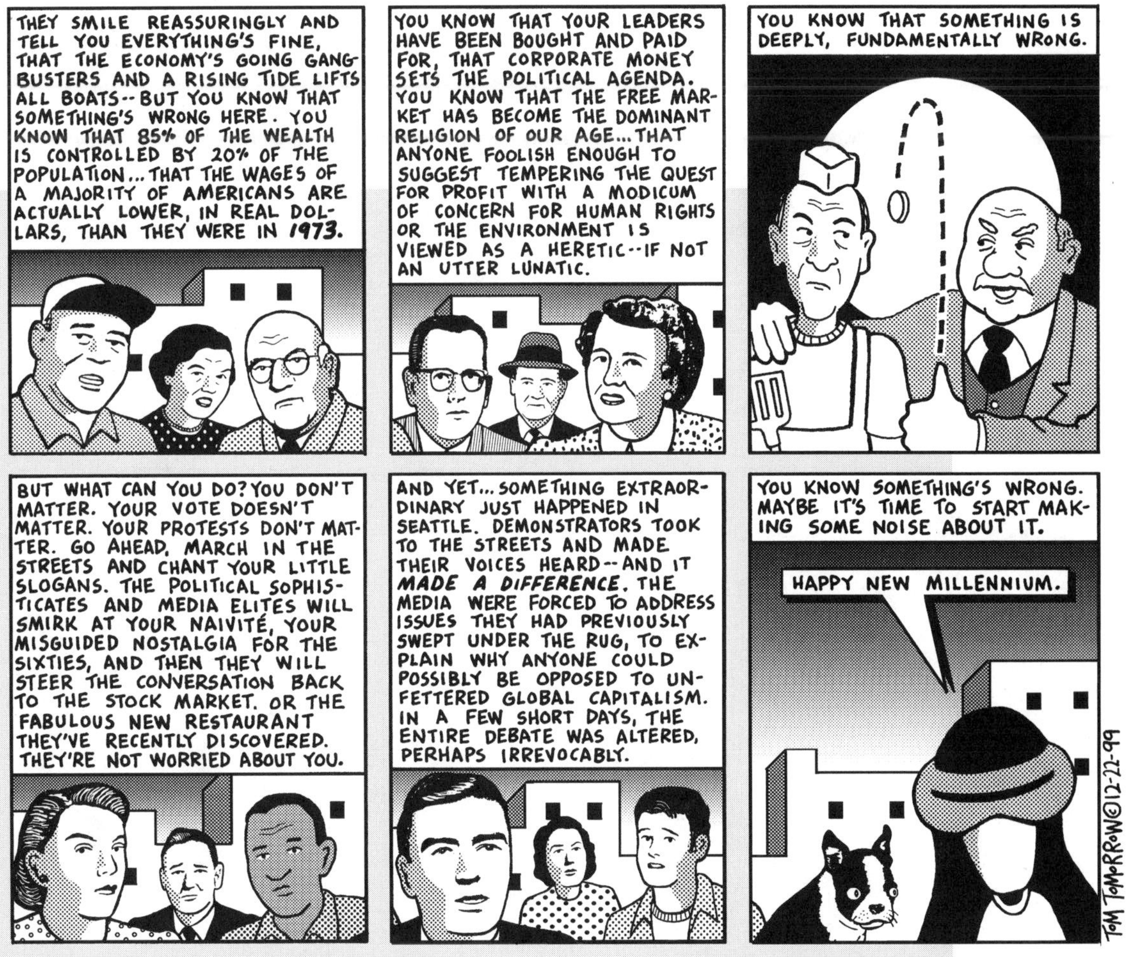
THEY SMILE REASSURINGLY AND TELL YOU EVERYTHING'S FINE, THAT THE ECONOMY'S GOING GANG-BUSTERS AND A RISING TIDE LIFTS ALL BOATS--BUT YOU KNOW THAT SOMETHING'S WRONG HERE. YOU KNOW THAT 85% OF THE WEALTH IS CONTROLLED BY 20% OF THE POPULATION... THAT THE WAGES OF A MAJORITY OF AMERICANS ARE ACTUALLY LOWER, IN REAL DOLLARS, THAN THEY WERE IN 1973.
YOU KNOW THAT YOUR LEADERS HAVE BEEN BOUGHT AND PAID FOR, THAT CORPORATE MONEY SETS THE POLITICAL AGENDA. YOU KNOW THAT THE FREE MARKET HAS BECOME THE DOMINANT RELIGION OF OUR AGE... THAT ANYONE FOOLISH ENOUGH TO SUGGEST TEMPERING THE QUEST FOR PROFIT WITH A MODICUM OF CONCERN FOR HUMAN RIGHTS OR THE ENVIRONMENT IS VIEWED AS A HERETIC--IF NOT AN UTTER LUNATIC.
YOU KNOW THAT SOMETHING IS DEEPLY, FUNDAMENTALLY WRONG.
BUT WHAT CAN YOU DO? YOU DON'T MATTER. YOUR VOTE DOESN'T MATTER. YOUR PROTESTS DON'T MATTER. GO AHEAD, MARCH IN THE STREETS AND CHANT YOUR LITTLE SLOGANS. THE POLITICAL SOPHISTICATES AND MEDIA ELITES WILL SMIRK AT YOUR NAIVITÉ, YOUR MISGUIDED NOSTALGIA FOR THE SIXTIES, AND THEN THEY WILL STEER THE CONVERSATION BACK TO THE STOCK MARKET, OR THE FABULOUS NEW RESTAURANT THEY'VE RECENTLY DISCOVERED. THEY'RE NOT WORRIED ABOUT YOU.
AND YET... SOMETHING EXTRAORDINARY JUST HAPPENED IN SEATTLE. DEMONSTRATORS TOOK TO THE STREETS AND MADE THEIR VOICES HEARD--AND IT MADE A DIFFERENCE. THE MEDIA WERE FORCED TO ADDRESS ISSUES THEY HAD PREVIOUSLY SWEPT UNDER THE RUG, TO EXPLAIN WHY ANYONE COULD POSSIBLY BE OPPOSED TO UNFETTERED GLOBAL CAPITALISM. IN A FEW SHORT DAYS, THE ENTIRE DEBATE WAS ALTERED, PERHAPS IRREVOCABLY.
YOU KNOW SOMETHING'S WRONG. MAYBE IT'S TIME TO START MAKING SOME NOISE ABOUT IT.
HAPPY NEW MILLENNIUM.
TOM TOMORROW©12-22-99

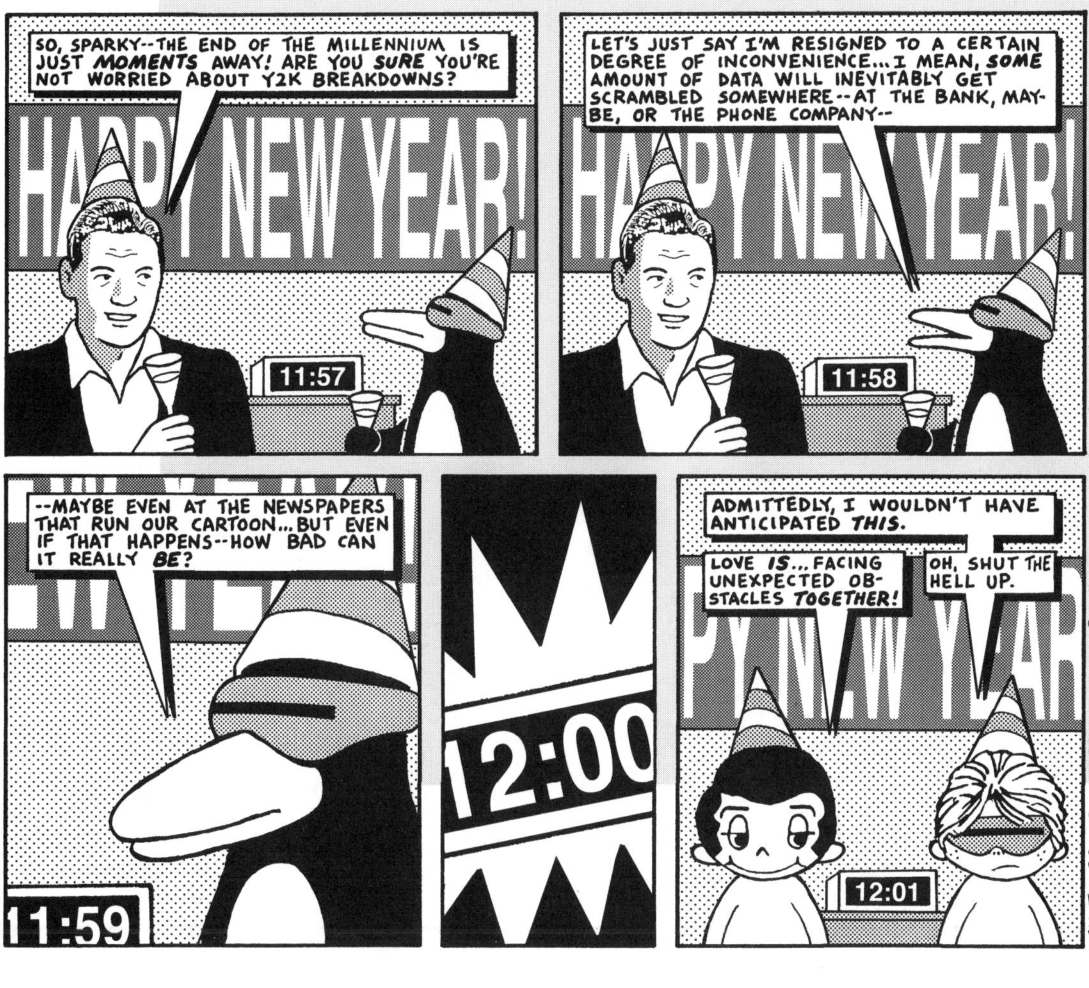
SO, SPARKY--THE END OF THE MILLENNIUM IS JUST MOMENTS AWAY! ARE YOU SURE YOU'RE NOT WORRIED ABOUT Y2K BREAKDOWNS?
11:57
LET'S JUST SAY I'M RESIGNED TO A CERTAIN DEGREE OF INCONVENIENCE... I MEAN, SOME AMOUNT OF DATA WILL INEVITABLY GET SCRAMBLED SOMEWHERE--AT THE BANK, MAYBE, OR THE PHONE COMPANY--
11:58
--MAYBE EVEN AT THE NEWSPAPERS THAT RUN OUR CARTOON... BUT EVEN IF THAT HAPPENS--HOW BAD CAN IT REALLY BE?
11:59
12:00
ADMITTEDLY, I WOULDN'T HAVE ANTICIPATED THIS.
LOVE IS... FACING UNEXPECTED OBSTACLES TOGETHER!
OH, SHUT THE HELL UP.
12:01
TOM TOMORROW©12-29-99

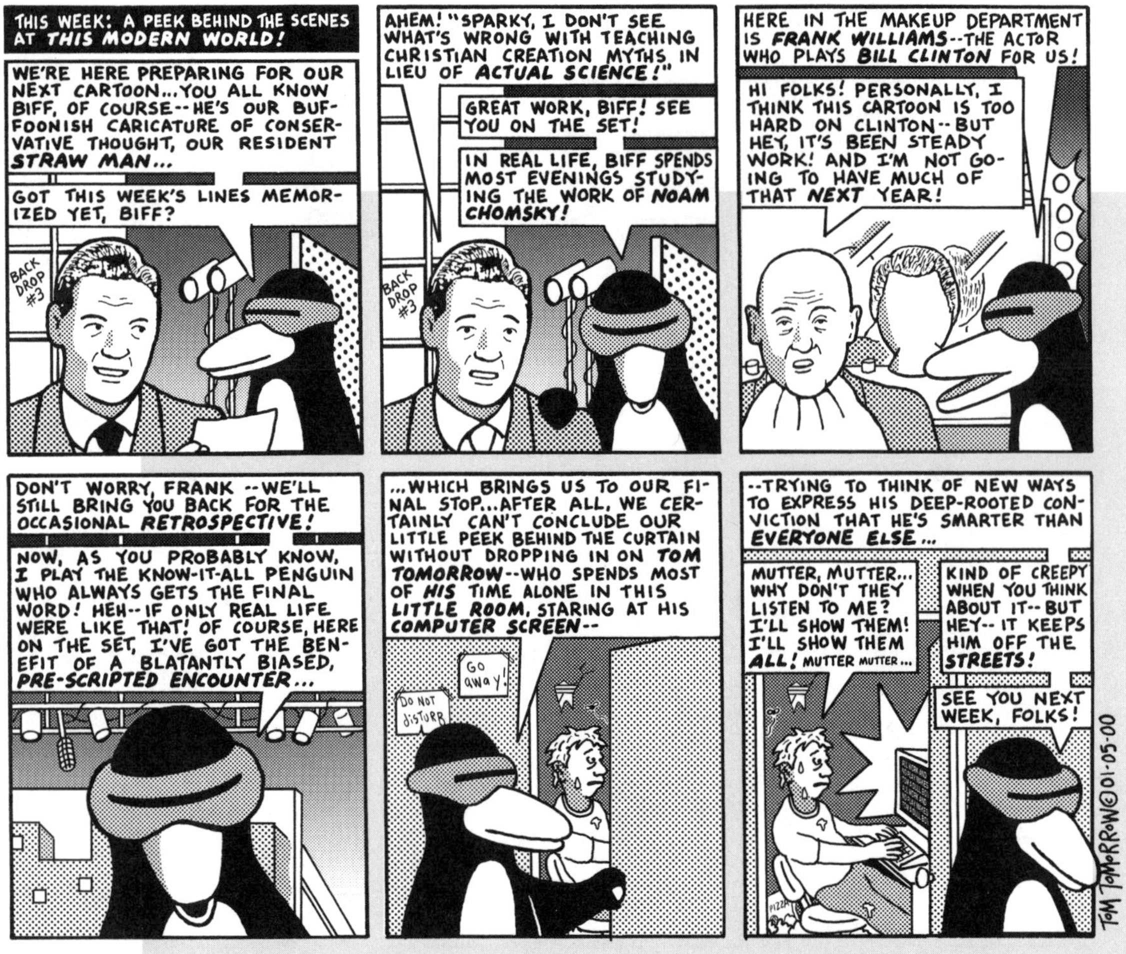
THIS WEEK: A PEEK BEHIND THE SCENES AT THIS MODERN WORLD!
WE'RE HERE PREPARING FOR OUR NEXT CARTOON...YOU ALL KNOW BIFF, OF COURSE--HE'S OUR BUFFOONISH CARICATURE OF CONSERVATIVE THOUGHT, OUR RESIDENT STRAW MAN...
GOT THIS WEEK'S LINES MEMORIZED YET, BIFF?
BACK DROP #3
AHEM! "SPARKY, I DON'T SEE WHAT'S WRONG WITH TEACHING CHRISTIAN CREATION MYTHS IN LIEU OF ACTUAL SCIENCE!"
GREAT WORK, BIFF! SEE YOU ON THE SET!
IN REAL LIFE, BIFF SPENDS MOST EVENINGS STUDYING THE WORK OF NOAM CHOMSKY!
BACK DROP #3
HERE IN THE MAKEUP DEPARTMENT IS FRANK WILLIAMS--THE ACTOR WHO PLAYS BILL CLINTON FOR US!
HI FOLKS! PERSONALLY, I THINK THIS CARTOON IS TOO HARD ON CLINTON--BUT HEY, IT'S BEEN STEADY WORK! AND I'M NOT GOING TO HAVE MUCH OF THAT NEXT YEAR!
DON'T WORRY, FRANK--WE'LL STILL BRING YOU BACK FOR THE OCCASIONAL RETROSPECTIVE!
NOW, AS YOU PROBABLY KNOW, I PLAY THE KNOW-IT-ALL PENGUIN WHO ALWAYS GETS THE FINAL WORD! HEH--IF ONLY REAL LIFE WERE LIKE THAT! OF COURSE, HERE ON THE SET, I'VE GOT THE BENEFIT OF A BLATANTLY BIASED, PRE-SCRIPTED ENCOUNTER...
...WHICH BRINGS US TO OUR FINAL STOP...AFTER ALL, WE CERTAINLY CAN'T CONCLUDE OUR LITTLE PEEK BEHIND THE CURTAIN WITHOUT DROPPING IN ON TOM TOMORROW--WHO SPENDS MOST OF HIS TIME ALONE IN THIS LITTLE ROOM, STARING AT HIS COMPUTER SCREEN--
Go away!
DO NOT DISTURB
--TRYING TO THINK OF NEW WAYS TO EXPRESS HIS DEEP-ROOTED CONVICTION THAT HE'S SMARTER THAN EVERYONE ELSE...
MUTTER, MUTTER... WHY DON'T THEY LISTEN TO ME? I'LL SHOW THEM! I'LL SHOW THEM ALL! MUTTER MUTTER...
KIND OF CREEPY WHEN YOU THINK ABOUT IT--BUT HEY--IT KEEPS HIM OFF THE STREETS!
SEE YOU NEXT WEEK, FOLKS!
PIZZA
TOM TOMORROW©01-05-00

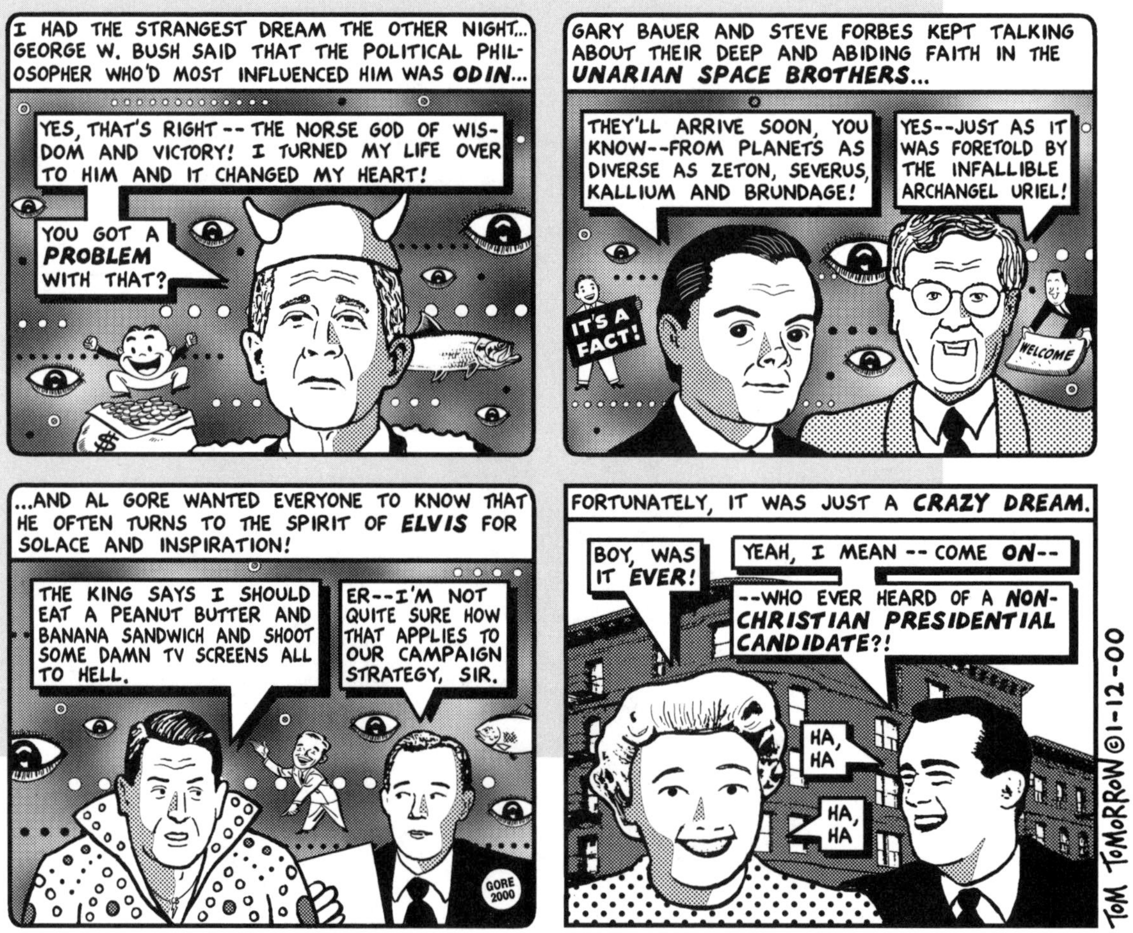
I HAD THE STRANGEST DREAM THE OTHER NIGHT... GEORGE W. BUSH SAID THAT THE POLITICAL PHILOSOPHER WHO'D MOST INFLUENCED HIM WAS ODIN...
YES, THAT'S RIGHT--THE NORSE GOD OF WISDOM AND VICTORY! I TURNED MY LIFE OVER TO HIM AND IT CHANGED MY HEART!
YOU GOT A PROBLEM WITH THAT?
$
GARY BAUER AND STEVE FORBES KEPT TALKING ABOUT THEIR DEEP AND ABIDING FAITH IN THE UNARIAN SPACE BROTHERS...
THEY'LL ARRIVE SOON, YOU KNOW--FROM PLANETS AS DIVERSE AS ZETON, SEVERUS, KALLIUM AND BRUNDAGE!
YES--JUST AS IT WAS FORETOLD BY THE INFALLIBLE ARCHANGEL URIEL!
IT'S A FACT!
WELCOME
...AND AL GORE WANTED EVERYONE TO KNOW THAT HE OFTEN TURNS TO THE SPIRIT OF ELVIS FOR SOLACE AND INSPIRATION!
THE KING SAYS I SHOULD EAT A PEANUT BUTTER AND BANANA SANDWICH AND SHOOT SOME DAMN TV SCREENS ALL TO HELL.
ER--I'M NOT QUITE SURE HOW THAT APPLIES TO OUR CAMPAIGN STRATEGY, SIR.
GORE 2000
FORTUNATELY, IT WAS JUST A CRAZY DREAM.
BOY, WAS IT EVER!
YEAH, I MEAN--COME ON--
--WHO EVER HEARD OF A NON-CHRISTIAN PRESIDENTIAL CANDIDATE?!
HA, HA
HA, HA
TOM TOMORROW©01-12-00

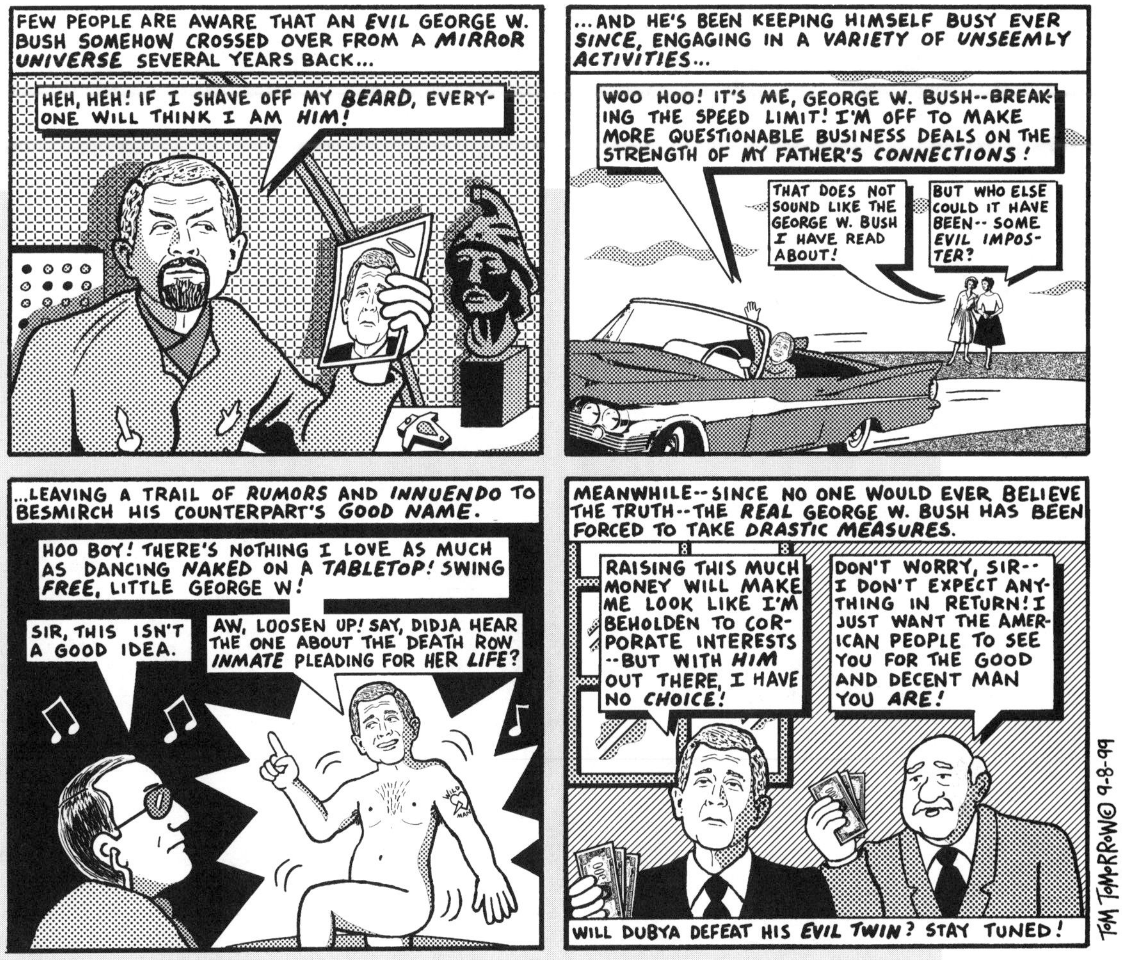
FEW PEOPLE ARE AWARE THAT AN EVIL GEORGE W. BUSH SOMEHOW CROSSED OVER FROM A MIRROR UNIVERSE SEVERAL YEARS BACK...
HEH, HEH! IF I SHAVE OFF MY BEARD, EVERYONE WILL THINK I AM HIM!
...AND HE'S BEEN KEEPING HIMSELF BUSY EVER SINCE, ENGAGING IN A VARIETY OF UNSEEMLY ACTIVITIES...
WOO HOO! IT'S ME, GEORGE W. BUSH--BREAKING THE SPEED LIMIT! I'M OFF TO MAKE MORE QUESTIONABLE BUSINESS DEALS ON THE STRENGTH OF MY FATHER'S CONNECTIONS!
THAT DOES NOT SOUND LIKE THE GEORGE W. BUSH I HAVE READ ABOUT!
BUT WHO ELSE COULD IT HAVE BEEN-- SOME EVIL IMPOSTER?
...LEAVING A TRAIL OF RUMORS AND INNUENDO TO BESMIRCH HIS COUNTERPART'S GOOD NAME.
HOO BOY! THERE'S NOTHING I LOVE AS MUCH AS DANCING NAKED ON A TABLETOP! SWING FREE, LITTLE GEORGE W!
SIR, THIS ISN'T A GOOD IDEA.
AW, LOOSEN UP! SAY, DIDJA HEAR THE ONE ABOUT THE DEATH ROW INMATE PLEADING FOR HER LIFE?
MEANWHILE--SINCE NO ONE WOULD EVER BELIEVE THE TRUTH--THE REAL GEORGE W. BUSH HAS BEEN FORCED TO TAKE DRASTIC MEASURES.
RAISING THIS MUCH MONEY WILL MAKE ME LOOK LIKE I'M BEHOLDEN TO CORPORATE INTERESTS --BUT WITH HIM OUT THERE, I HAVE NO CHOICE!
DON'T WORRY, SIR-- I DON'T EXPECT ANYTHING IN RETURN! I JUST WANT THE AMERICAN PEOPLE TO SEE YOU FOR THE GOOD AND DECENT MAN YOU ARE!
WILL DUBYA DEFEAT HIS EVIL TWIN? STAY TUNED!
TOM TOMORROW© 9-8-99

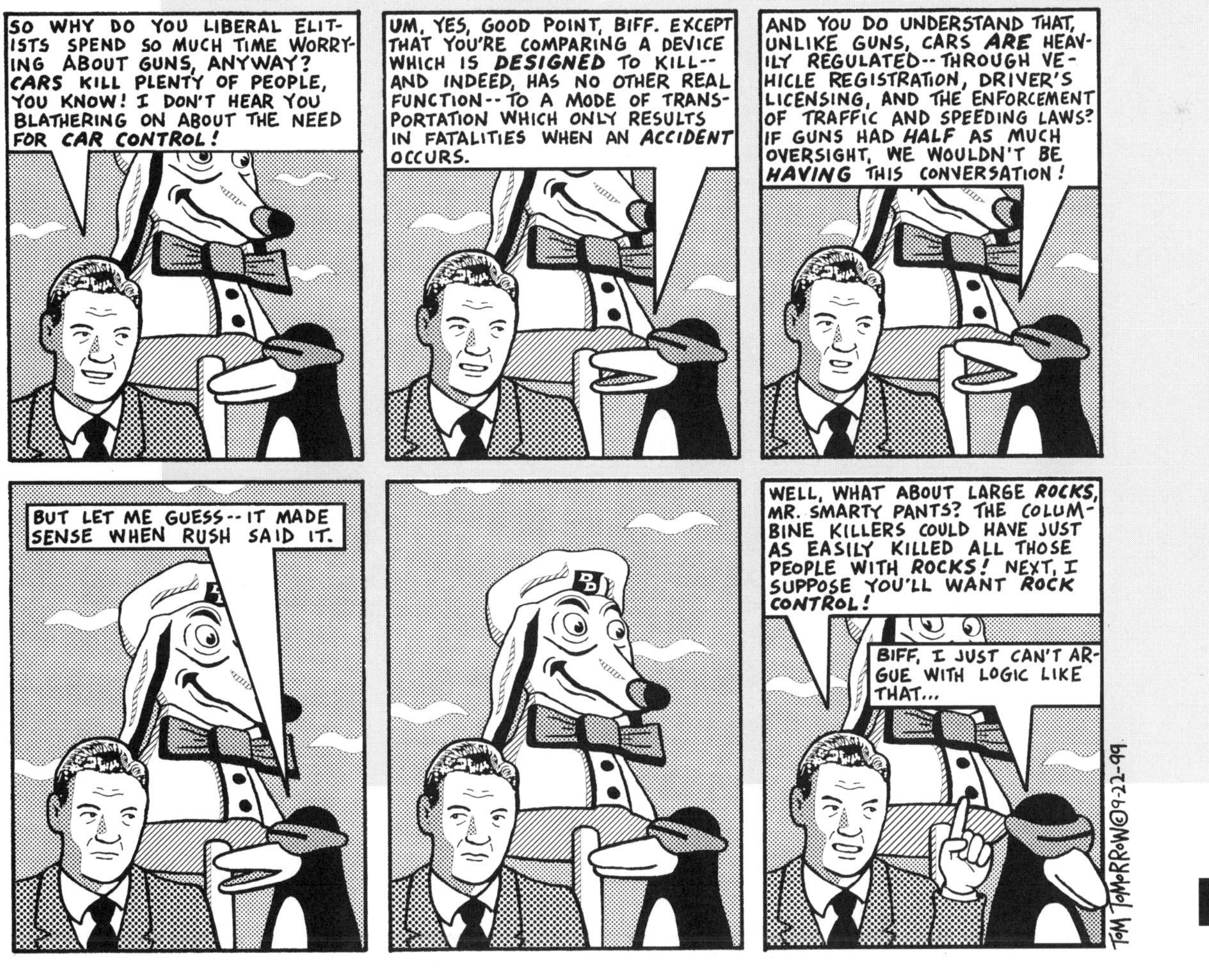
SO WHY DO YOU LIBERAL ELITISTS SPEND SO MUCH TIME WORRYING ABOUT GUNS, ANYWAY? CARS KILL PLENTY OF PEOPLE, YOU KNOW! I DON'T HEAR YOU BLATHERING ON ABOUT THE NEED FOR CAR CONTROL!
UM, YES, GOOD POINT, BIFF. EXCEPT THAT YOU'RE COMPARING A DEVICE WHICH IS DESIGNED TO KILL-- AND INDEED, HAS NO OTHER REAL FUNCTION-- TO A MODE OF TRANSPORTATION WHICH ONLY RESULTS IN FATALITIES WHEN AN ACCIDENT OCCURS.
AND YOU DO UNDERSTAND THAT, UNLIKE GUNS, CARS ARE HEAVILY REGULATED-- THROUGH VEHICLE REGISTRATION, DRIVER'S LICENSING, AND THE ENFORCEMENT OF TRAFFIC AND SPEEDING LAWS? IF GUNS HAD HALF AS MUCH OVERSIGHT, WE WOULDN'T BE HAVING THIS CONVERSATION!
BUT LET ME GUESS-- IT MADE SENSE WHEN RUSH SAID IT.
WELL, WHAT ABOUT LARGE ROCKS, MR. SMARTY PANTS? THE COLUMBINE KILLERS COULD HAVE JUST AS EASILY KILLED ALL THOSE PEOPLE WITH ROCKS! NEXT, I SUPPOSE YOU'LL WANT ROCK CONTROL!
BIFF, I JUST CAN'T ARGUE WITH LOGIC LIKE THAT...
TOM TOMORROW©9-22-99

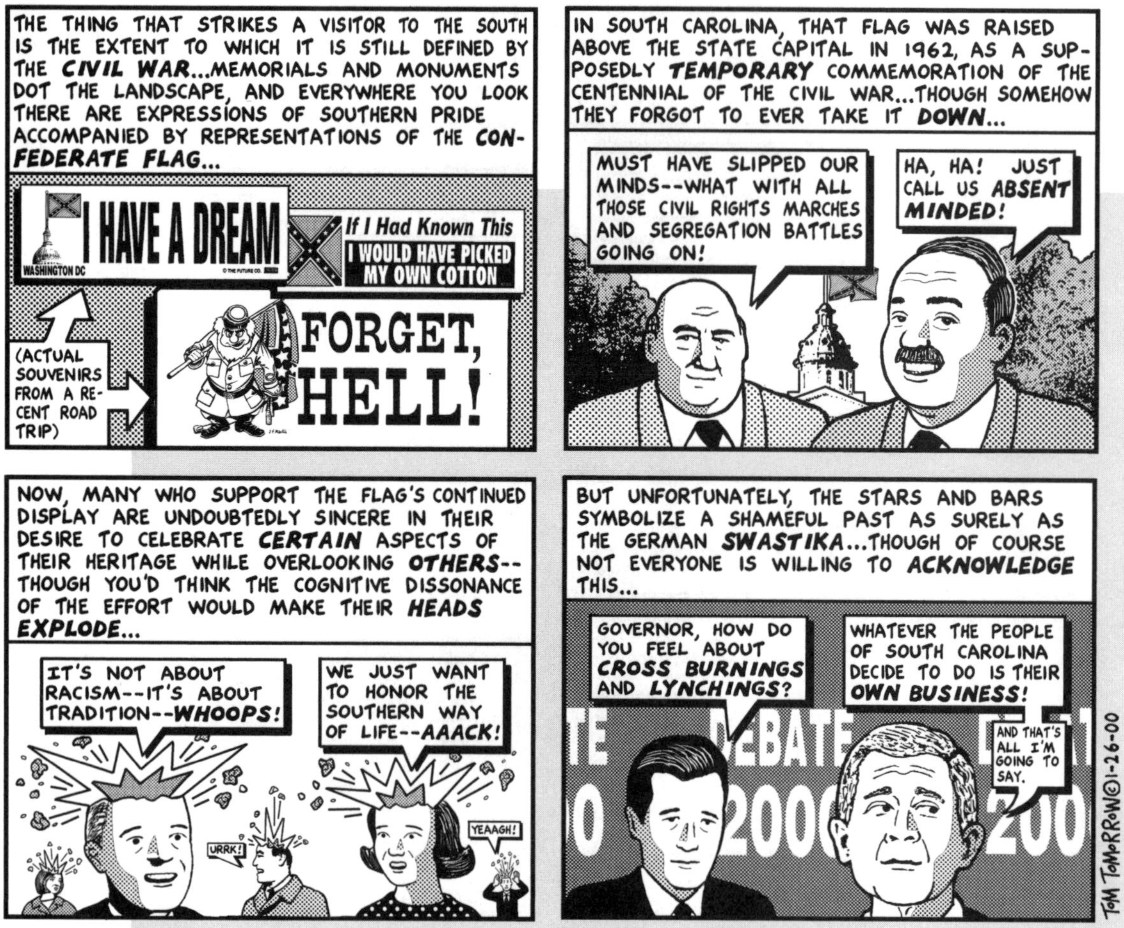
THE THING THAT STRIKES A VISITOR TO THE SOUTH IS THE EXTENT TO WHICH IT IS STILL DEFINED BY THE CIVIL WAR...MEMORIALS AND MONUMENTS DOT THE LANDSCAPE, AND EVERYWHERE YOU LOOK THERE ARE EXPRESSIONS OF SOUTHERN PRIDE ACCOMPANIED BY REPRESENTATIONS OF THE CONFEDERATE FLAG...
I HAVE A DREAM
WASHINGTON DC
If I Had Known This
I WOULD HAVE PICKED MY OWN COTTON
FORGET, HELL!
(ACTUAL SOUVENIRS FROM A RECENT ROAD TRIP)
IN SOUTH CAROLINA, THAT FLAG WAS RAISED ABOVE THE STATE CAPITAL IN 1962, AS A SUPPOSEDLY TEMPORARY COMMEMORATION OF THE CENTENNIAL OF THE CIVIL WAR...THOUGH SOMEHOW THEY FORGOT TO EVER TAKE IT DOWN...
MUST HAVE SLIPPED OUR MINDS--WHAT WITH ALL THOSE CIVIL RIGHTS MARCHES AND SEGREGATION BATTLES GOING ON!
HA, HA! JUST CALL US ABSENT MINDED!
NOW, MANY WHO SUPPORT THE FLAG'S CONTINUED DISPLAY ARE UNDOUBTEDLY SINCERE IN THEIR DESIRE TO CELEBRATE CERTAIN ASPECTS OF THEIR HERITAGE WHILE OVERLOOKING OTHERS--THOUGH YOU'D THINK THE COGNITIVE DISSONANCE OF THE EFFORT WOULD MAKE THEIR HEADS EXPLODE...
IT'S NOT ABOUT RACISM--IT'S ABOUT TRADITION--WHOOPS!
WE JUST WANT TO HONOR THE SOUTHERN WAY OF LIFE--AAACK!
URRK!
YEAAGH!
BUT UNFORTUNATELY, THE STARS AND BARS SYMBOLIZE A SHAMEFUL PAST AS SURELY AS THE GERMAN SWASTIKA...THOUGH OF COURSE NOT EVERYONE IS WILLING TO ACKNOWLEDGE THIS...
GOVERNOR, HOW DO YOU FEEL ABOUT CROSS BURNINGS AND LYNCHINGS?
WHATEVER THE PEOPLE OF SOUTH CAROLINA DECIDE TO DO IS THEIR OWN BUSINESS!
AND THAT'S ALL I'M GOING TO SAY.
DEBATE 2000
TOM TOMORROW©1-26-00

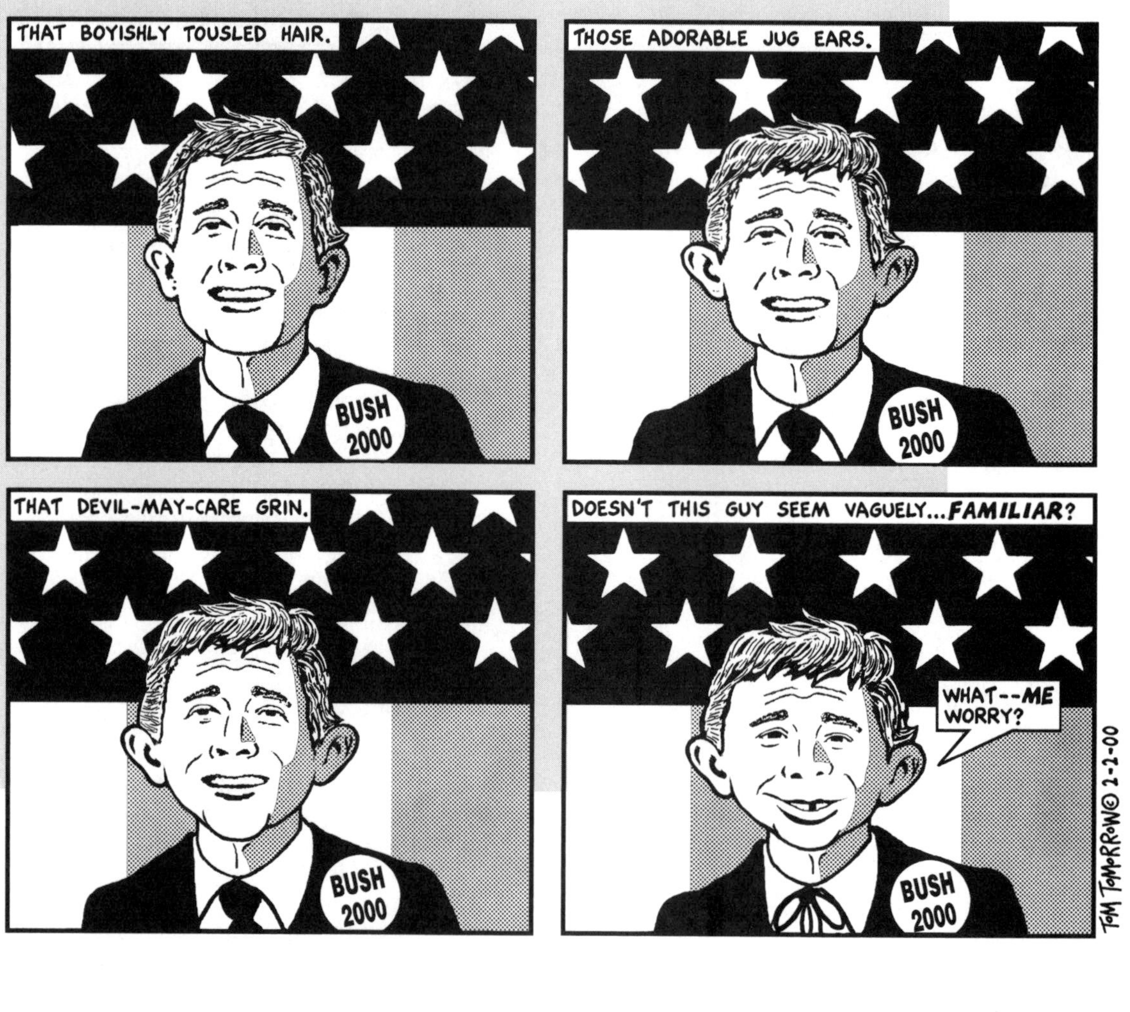
THAT BOYISHLY TOUSLED HAIR.
BUSH 2000
THOSE ADORABLE JUG EARS.
BUSH 2000
THAT DEVIL-MAY-CARE GRIN.
BUSH 2000
DOESN'T THIS GUY SEEM VAGUELY...FAMILIAR?
WHAT--ME WORRY?
BUSH 2000
TOM TOMORROW© 2-2-00

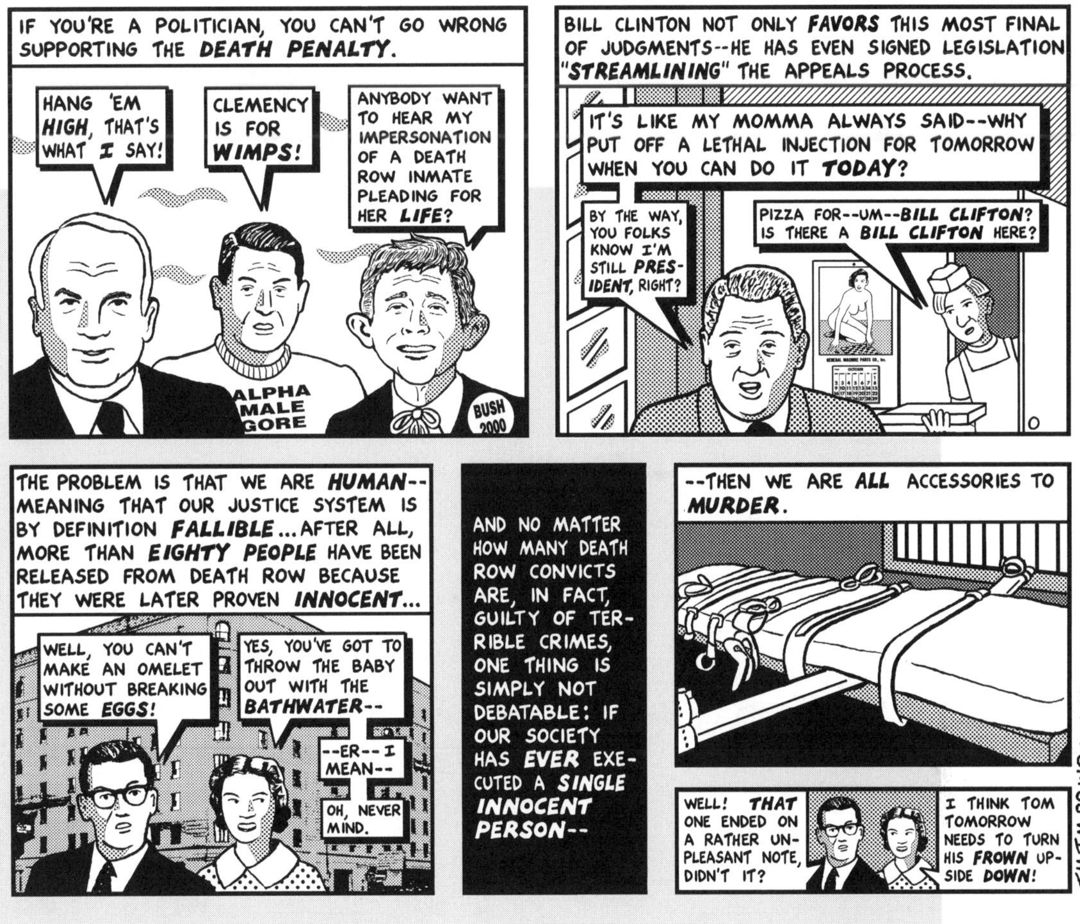
IF YOU'RE A POLITICIAN, YOU CAN'T GO WRONG SUPPORTING THE DEATH PENALTY.
HANG 'EM HIGH, THAT'S WHAT I SAY!
CLEMENCY IS FOR WIMPS!
ANYBODY WANT TO HEAR MY IMPERSONATION OF A DEATH ROW INMATE PLEADING FOR HER LIFE?
ALPHA MALE GORE
BUSH 2000
BILL CLINTON NOT ONLY FAVORS THIS MOST FINAL OF JUDGMENTS--HE HAS EVEN SIGNED LEGISLATION "STREAMLINING" THE APPEALS PROCESS.
IT'S LIKE MY MOMMA ALWAYS SAID--WHY PUT OFF A LETHAL INJECTION FOR TOMORROW WHEN YOU CAN DO IT TODAY?
BY THE WAY, YOU FOLKS KNOW I'M STILL PRESIDENT, RIGHT?
PIZZA FOR--UM--BILL CLIFTON? IS THERE A BILL CLIFTON HERE?
THE PROBLEM IS THAT WE ARE HUMAN--MEANING THAT OUR JUSTICE SYSTEM IS BY DEFINITION FALLIBLE... AFTER ALL, MORE THAN EIGHTY PEOPLE HAVE BEEN RELEASED FROM DEATH ROW BECAUSE THEY WERE LATER PROVEN INNOCENT...
WELL, YOU CAN'T MAKE AN OMELET WITHOUT BREAKING SOME EGGS!
YES, YOU'VE GOT TO THROW THE BABY OUT WITH THE BATHWATER--
--ER--I MEAN--
OH, NEVER MIND.
AND NO MATTER HOW MANY DEATH ROW CONVICTS ARE, IN FACT, GUILTY OF TERRIBLE CRIMES, ONE THING IS SIMPLY NOT DEBATABLE: IF OUR SOCIETY HAS EVER EXECUTED A SINGLE INNOCENT PERSON--
--THEN WE ARE ALL ACCESSORIES TO MURDER.
WELL! THAT ONE ENDED ON A RATHER UNPLEASANT NOTE, DIDN'T IT?
I THINK TOM TOMORROW NEEDS TO TURN HIS FROWN UPSIDE DOWN!
TOM TOMORROW© 2-16-00

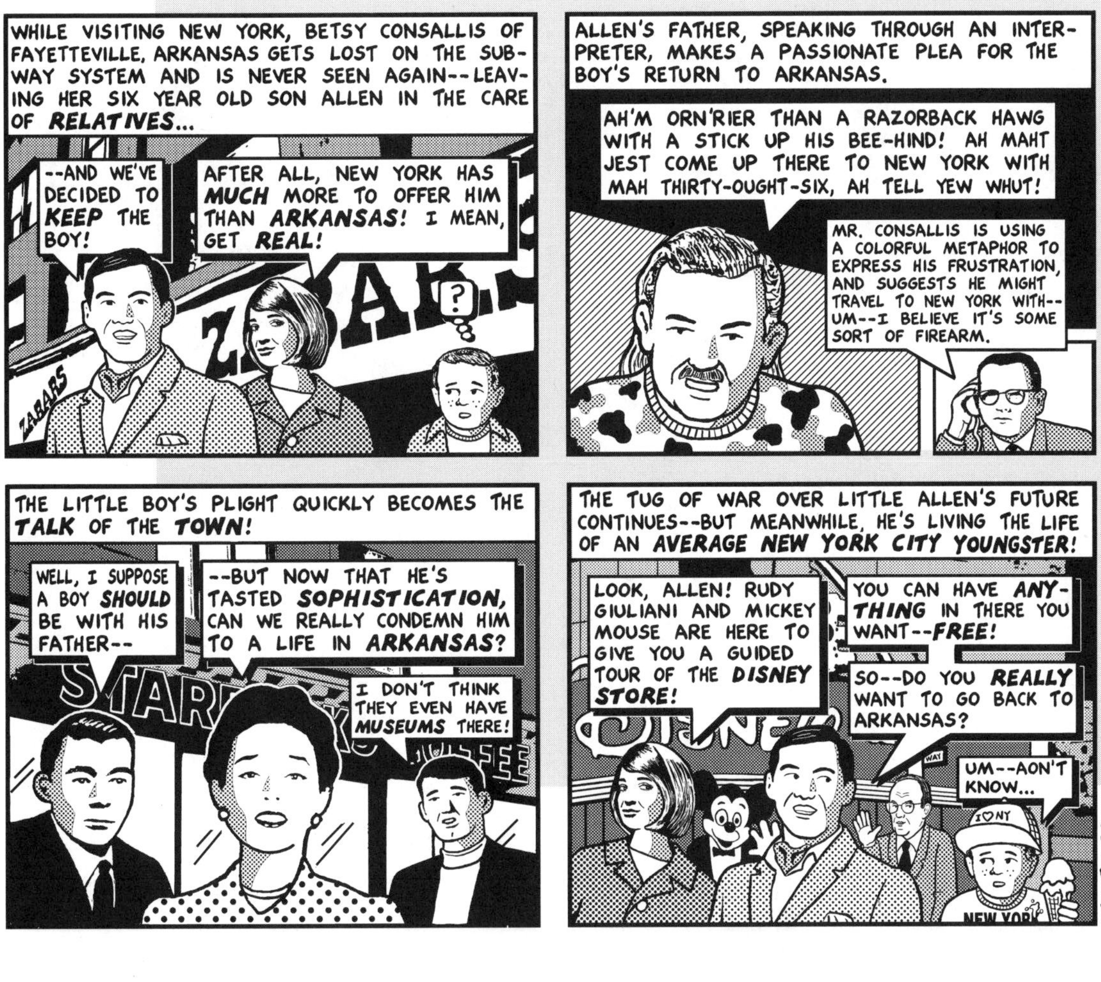
WHILE VISITING NEW YORK, BETSY CONSALLIS OF FAYETTEVILLE, ARKANSAS GETS LOST ON THE SUBWAY SYSTEM AND IS NEVER SEEN AGAIN--LEAVING HER SIX YEAR OLD SON ALLEN IN THE CARE OF RELATIVES...
--AND WE'VE DECIDED TO KEEP THE BOY!
AFTER ALL, NEW YORK HAS MUCH MORE TO OFFER HIM THAN ARKANSAS! I MEAN, GET REAL!
?
ZABARS
ALLEN'S FATHER, SPEAKING THROUGH AN INTERPRETER, MAKES A PASSIONATE PLEA FOR THE BOY'S RETURN TO ARKANSAS.
AH'M ORN'RIER THAN A RAZORBACK HAWG WITH A STICK UP HIS BEE-HIND! AH MAHT JEST COME UP THERE TO NEW YORK WITH MAH THIRTY-OUGHT-SIX, AH TELL YEW WHUT!
MR. CONSALLIS IS USING A COLORFUL METAPHOR TO EXPRESS HIS FRUSTRATION, AND SUGGESTS HE MIGHT TRAVEL TO NEW YORK WITH--UM--I BELIEVE IT'S SOME SORT OF FIREARM.
THE LITTLE BOY'S PLIGHT QUICKLY BECOMES THE TALK OF THE TOWN!
WELL, I SUPPOSE A BOY SHOULD BE WITH HIS FATHER--
--BUT NOW THAT HE'S TASTED SOPHISTICATION, CAN WE REALLY CONDEMN HIM TO A LIFE IN ARKANSAS?
I DON'T THINK THEY EVEN HAVE MUSEUMS THERE!
THE TUG OF WAR OVER LITTLE ALLEN'S FUTURE CONTINUES--BUT MEANWHILE, HE'S LIVING THE LIFE OF AN AVERAGE NEW YORK CITY YOUNGSTER!
LOOK, ALLEN! RUDY GIULIANI AND MICKEY MOUSE ARE HERE TO GIVE YOU A GUIDED TOUR OF THE DISNEY STORE!
YOU CAN HAVE ANYTHING IN THERE YOU WANT--FREE!
SO--DO YOU REALLY WANT TO GO BACK TO ARKANSAS?
UM--AON'T KNOW...
I ♥ NY
NEW YORK
TOM TOMORROW©2-2-00

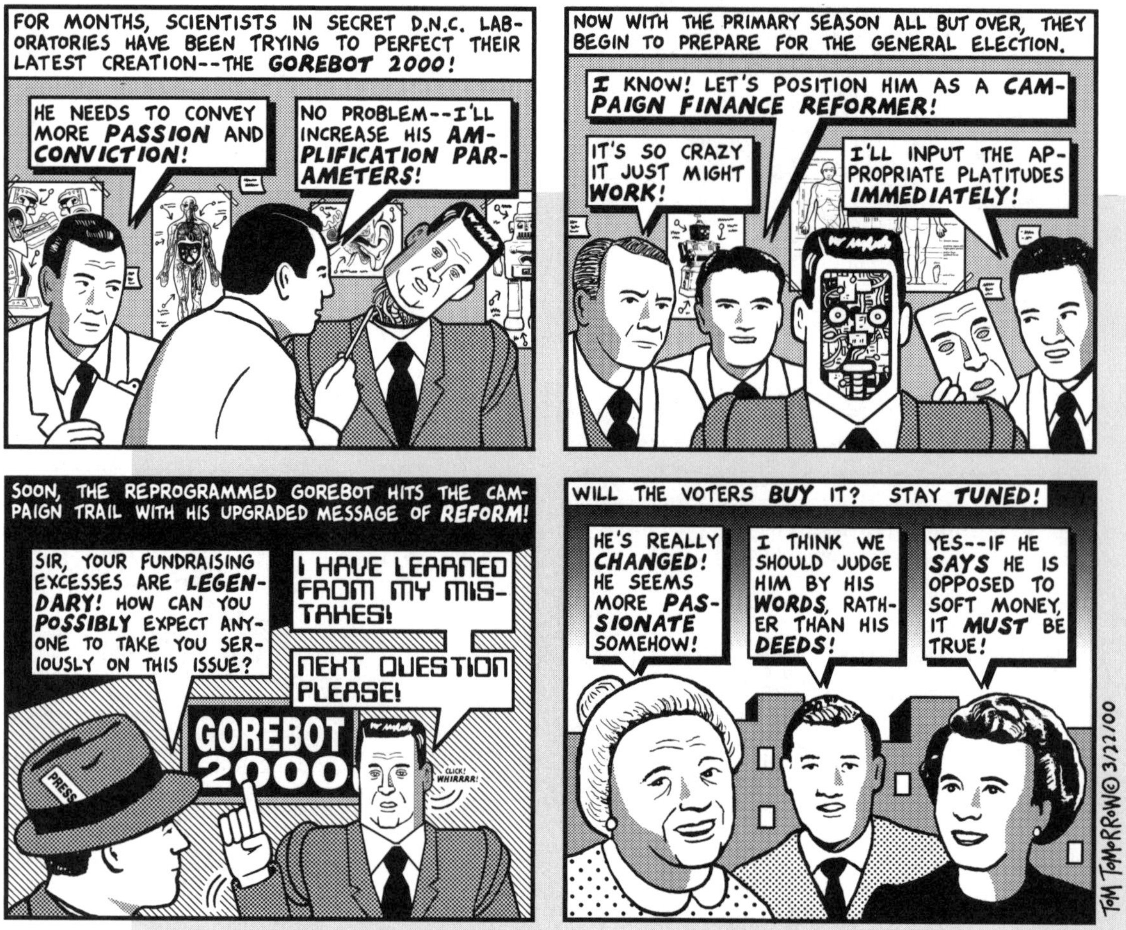
FOR MONTHS, SCIENTISTS IN SECRET D.N.C. LABORATORIES HAVE BEEN TRYING TO PERFECT THEIR LATEST CREATION--THE GOREBOT 2000!
HE NEEDS TO CONVEY MORE PASSION AND CONVICTION!
NO PROBLEM--I'LL INCREASE HIS AMPLIFICATION PARAMETERS!
NOW WITH THE PRIMARY SEASON ALL BUT OVER, THEY BEGIN TO PREPARE FOR THE GENERAL ELECTION.
I KNOW! LET'S POSITION HIM AS A CAMPAIGN FINANCE REFORMER!
IT'S SO CRAZY IT JUST MIGHT WORK!
I'LL INPUT THE APPROPRIATE PLATITUDES IMMEDIATELY!
SOON, THE REPROGRAMMED GOREBOT HITS THE CAMPAIGN TRAIL WITH HIS UPGRADED MESSAGE OF REFORM!
SIR, YOUR FUNDRAISING EXCESSES ARE LEGENDARY! HOW CAN YOU POSSIBLY EXPECT ANYONE TO TAKE YOU SERIOUSLY ON THIS ISSUE?
I HAVE LEARNED FROM MY MISTAKES!
NEXT QUESTION PLEASE!
GOREBOT 2000
PRESS
CLICK! WHIRRRR!
WILL THE VOTERS BUY IT? STAY TUNED!
HE'S REALLY CHANGED! HE SEEMS MORE PASSIONATE SOMEHOW!
I THINK WE SHOULD JUDGE HIM BY HIS WORDS, RATHER THAN HIS DEEDS!
YES--IF HE SAYS HE IS OPPOSED TO SOFT MONEY, IT MUST BE TRUE!
TOM TOMORROW© 3/22/00

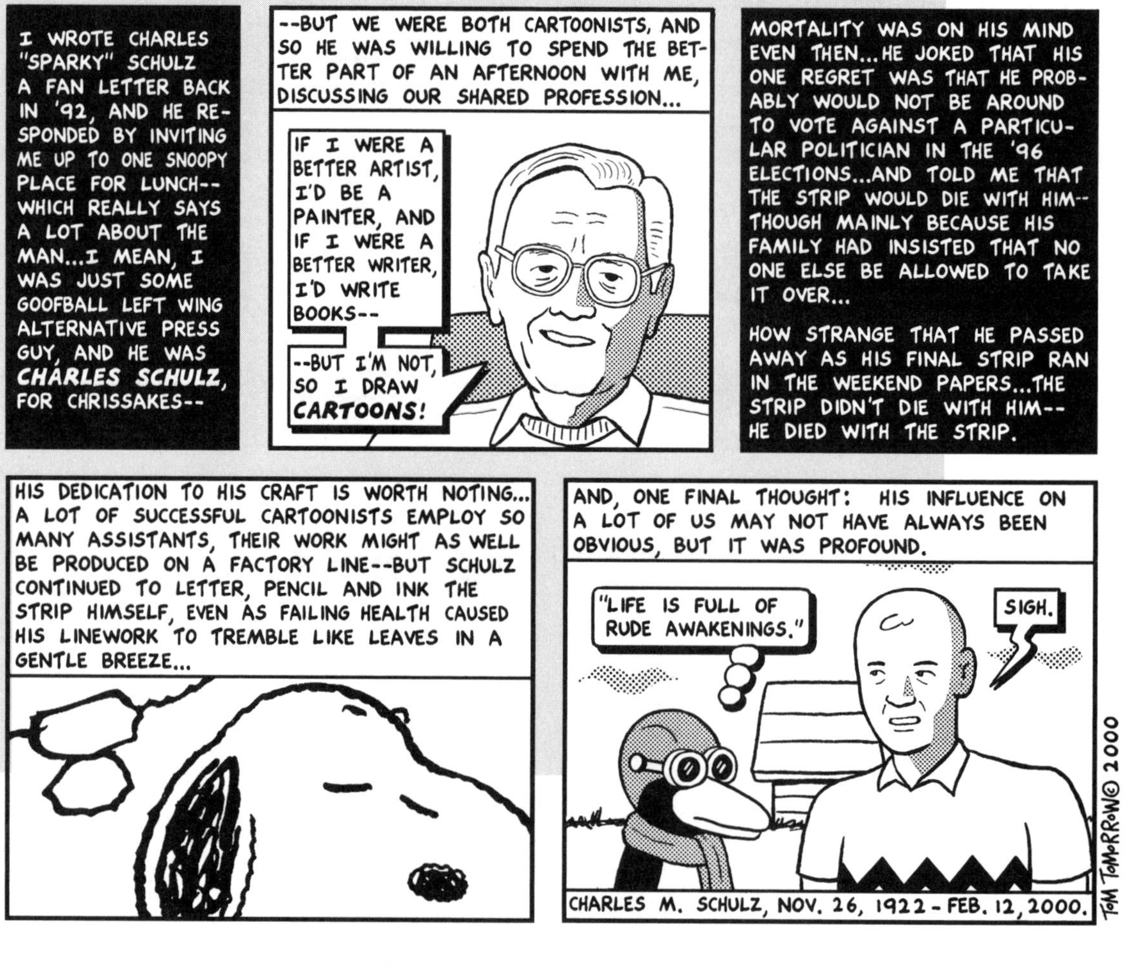
I WROTE CHARLES "SPARKY" SCHULZ A FAN LETTER BACK IN '92, AND HE RESPONDED BY INVITING ME UP TO ONE SNOOPY PLACE FOR LUNCH--WHICH REALLY SAYS A LOT ABOUT THE MAN...I MEAN, I WAS JUST SOME GOOFBALL LEFT WING ALTERNATIVE PRESS GUY, AND HE WAS CHARLES SCHULZ, FOR CHRISSAKES--
--BUT WE WERE BOTH CARTOONISTS, AND SO HE WAS WILLING TO SPEND THE BETTER PART OF AN AFTERNOON WITH ME, DISCUSSING OUR SHARED PROFESSION...
IF I WERE A BETTER ARTIST, I'D BE A PAINTER, AND IF I WERE A BETTER WRITER, I'D WRITE BOOKS--
--BUT I'M NOT, SO I DRAW CARTOONS!
MORTALITY WAS ON HIS MIND EVEN THEN...HE JOKED THAT HIS ONE REGRET WAS THAT HE PROBABLY WOULD NOT BE AROUND TO VOTE AGAINST A PARTICULAR POLITICIAN IN THE '96 ELECTIONS...AND TOLD ME THAT THE STRIP WOULD DIE WITH HIM--THOUGH MAINLY BECAUSE HIS FAMILY HAD INSISTED THAT NO ONE ELSE BE ALLOWED TO TAKE IT OVER...
HOW STRANGE THAT HE PASSED AWAY AS HIS FINAL STRIP RAN IN THE WEEKEND PAPERS...THE STRIP DIDN'T DIE WITH HIM--HE DIED WITH THE STRIP.
HIS DEDICATION TO HIS CRAFT IS WORTH NOTING...A LOT OF SUCCESSFUL CARTOONISTS EMPLOY SO MANY ASSISTANTS, THEIR WORK MIGHT AS WELL BE PRODUCED ON A FACTORY LINE--BUT SCHULZ CONTINUED TO LETTER, PENCIL AND INK THE STRIP HIMSELF, EVEN AS FAILING HEALTH CAUSED HIS LINEWORK TO TREMBLE LIKE LEAVES IN A GENTLE BREEZE...
AND, ONE FINAL THOUGHT: HIS INFLUENCE ON A LOT OF US MAY NOT HAVE ALWAYS BEEN OBVIOUS, BUT IT WAS PROFOUND.
"LIFE IS FULL OF RUDE AWAKENINGS."
SIGH.
CHARLES M. SCHULZ, NOV. 26, 1922 - FEB. 12, 2000.
TOM TOMORROW© 2000

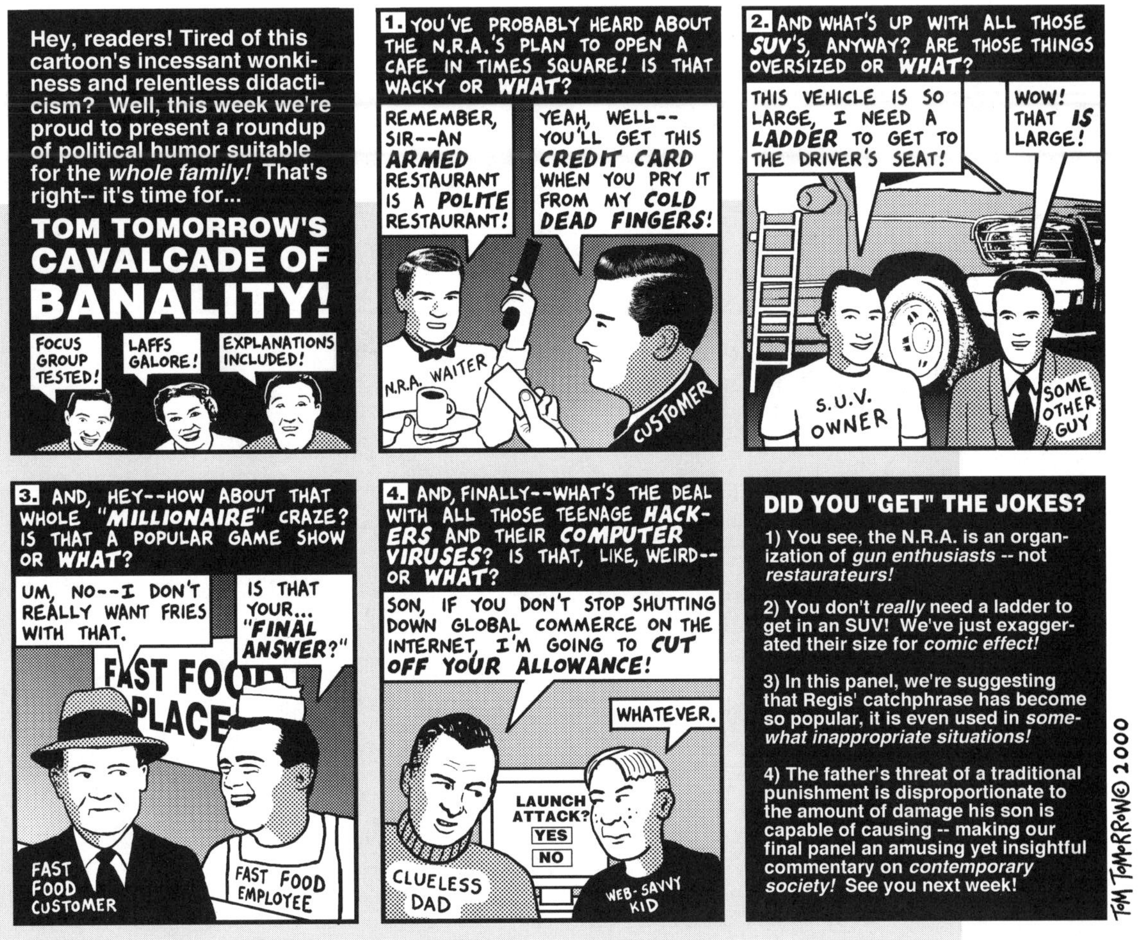
Hey, readers! Tired of this cartoon's incessant wonkiness and relentless didacticism? Well, this week we're proud to present a roundup of political humor suitable for the whole family! That's right-- it's time for...
TOM TOMORROW'S CAVALCADE OF BANALITY!
FOCUS GROUP TESTED!
LAFFS GALORE!
EXPLANATIONS INCLUDED!
1. YOU'VE PROBABLY HEARD ABOUT THE N.R.A.'S PLAN TO OPEN A CAFE IN TIMES SQUARE! IS THAT WACKY OR WHAT?
REMEMBER, SIR--AN ARMED RESTAURANT IS A POLITE RESTAURANT!
YEAH, WELL-- YOU'LL GET THIS CREDIT CARD WHEN YOU PRY IT FROM MY COLD DEAD FINGERS!
N.R.A. WAITER
CUSTOMER
2. AND WHAT'S UP WITH ALL THOSE SUV'S, ANYWAY? ARE THOSE THINGS OVERSIZED OR WHAT?
THIS VEHICLE IS SO LARGE, I NEED A LADDER TO GET TO THE DRIVER'S SEAT!
WOW! THAT IS LARGE!
S.U.V. OWNER
SOME OTHER GUY
3. AND, HEY--HOW ABOUT THAT WHOLE "MILLIONAIRE" CRAZE? IS THAT A POPULAR GAME SHOW OR WHAT?
UM, NO--I DON'T REALLY WANT FRIES WITH THAT.
IS THAT YOUR... "FINAL ANSWER?"
FAST FOOD PLACE
FAST FOOD CUSTOMER
FAST FOOD EMPLOYEE
4. AND, FINALLY--WHAT'S THE DEAL WITH ALL THOSE TEENAGE HACKERS AND THEIR COMPUTER VIRUSES? IS THAT, LIKE, WEIRD--OR WHAT?
SON, IF YOU DON'T STOP SHUTTING DOWN GLOBAL COMMERCE ON THE INTERNET, I'M GOING TO CUT OFF YOUR ALLOWANCE!
WHATEVER.
LAUNCH ATTACK? YES NO
CLUELESS DAD
WEB-SAVVY KID
DID YOU "GET" THE JOKES?
1) You see, the N.R.A. is an organization of gun enthusiasts -- not restaurateurs!
2) You don't really need a ladder to get in an SUV! We've just exaggerated their size for comic effect!
3) In this panel, we're suggesting that Regis' catchphrase has become so popular, it is even used in somewhat inappropriate situations!
4) The father's threat of a traditional punishment is disproportionate to the amount of damage his son is capable of causing -- making our final panel an amusing yet insightful commentary on contemporary society! See you next week!
TOM TOMORROW© 2000

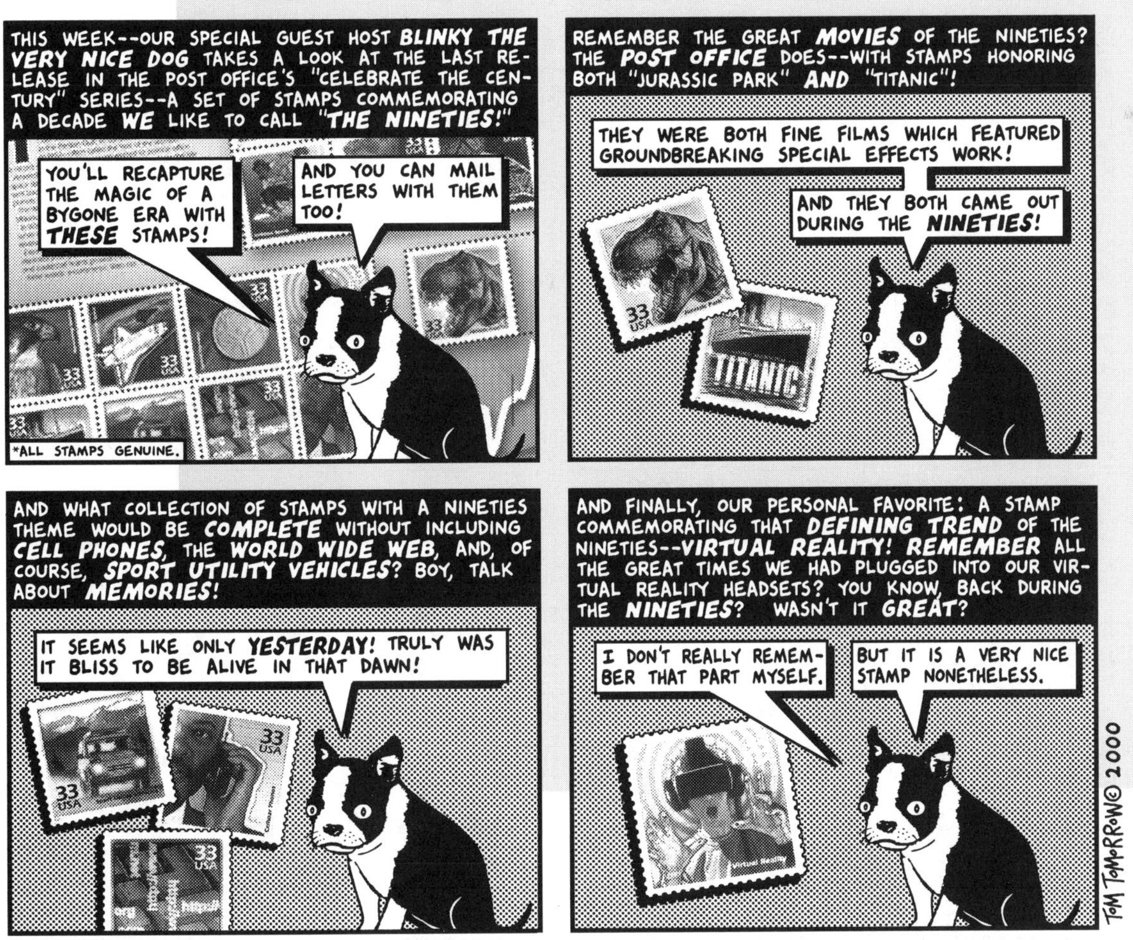
THIS WEEK--OUR SPECIAL GUEST HOST BLINKY THE VERY NICE DOG TAKES A LOOK AT THE LAST RELEASE IN THE POST OFFICE'S "CELEBRATE THE CENTURY" SERIES--A SET OF STAMPS COMMEMORATING A DECADE WE LIKE TO CALL "THE NINETIES!"
YOU'LL RECAPTURE THE MAGIC OF A BYGONE ERA WITH THESE STAMPS!
AND YOU CAN MAIL LETTERS WITH THEM TOO!
*ALL STAMPS GENUINE.
REMEMBER THE GREAT MOVIES OF THE NINETIES? THE POST OFFICE DOES--WITH STAMPS HONORING BOTH "JURASSIC PARK" AND "TITANIC"!
THEY WERE BOTH FINE FILMS WHICH FEATURED GROUNDBREAKING SPECIAL EFFECTS WORK!
AND THEY BOTH CAME OUT DURING THE NINETIES!
TITANIC
AND WHAT COLLECTION OF STAMPS WITH A NINETIES THEME WOULD BE COMPLETE WITHOUT INCLUDING CELL PHONES, THE WORLD WIDE WEB, AND, OF COURSE, SPORT UTILITY VEHICLES? BOY, TALK ABOUT MEMORIES!
IT SEEMS LIKE ONLY YESTERDAY! TRULY WAS IT BLISS TO BE ALIVE IN THAT DAWN!
AND FINALLY, OUR PERSONAL FAVORITE: A STAMP COMMEMORATING THAT DEFINING TREND OF THE NINETIES--VIRTUAL REALITY! REMEMBER ALL THE GREAT TIMES WE HAD PLUGGED INTO OUR VIRTUAL REALITY HEADSETS? YOU KNOW, BACK DURING THE NINETIES? WASN'T IT GREAT?
I DON'T REALLY REMEMBER THAT PART MYSELF.
BUT IT IS A VERY NICE STAMP NONETHELESS.
TOM TOMORROW© 2000

This was a backup cartoon that I never ended up needing to use, so this is the first time it's been published anywhere.

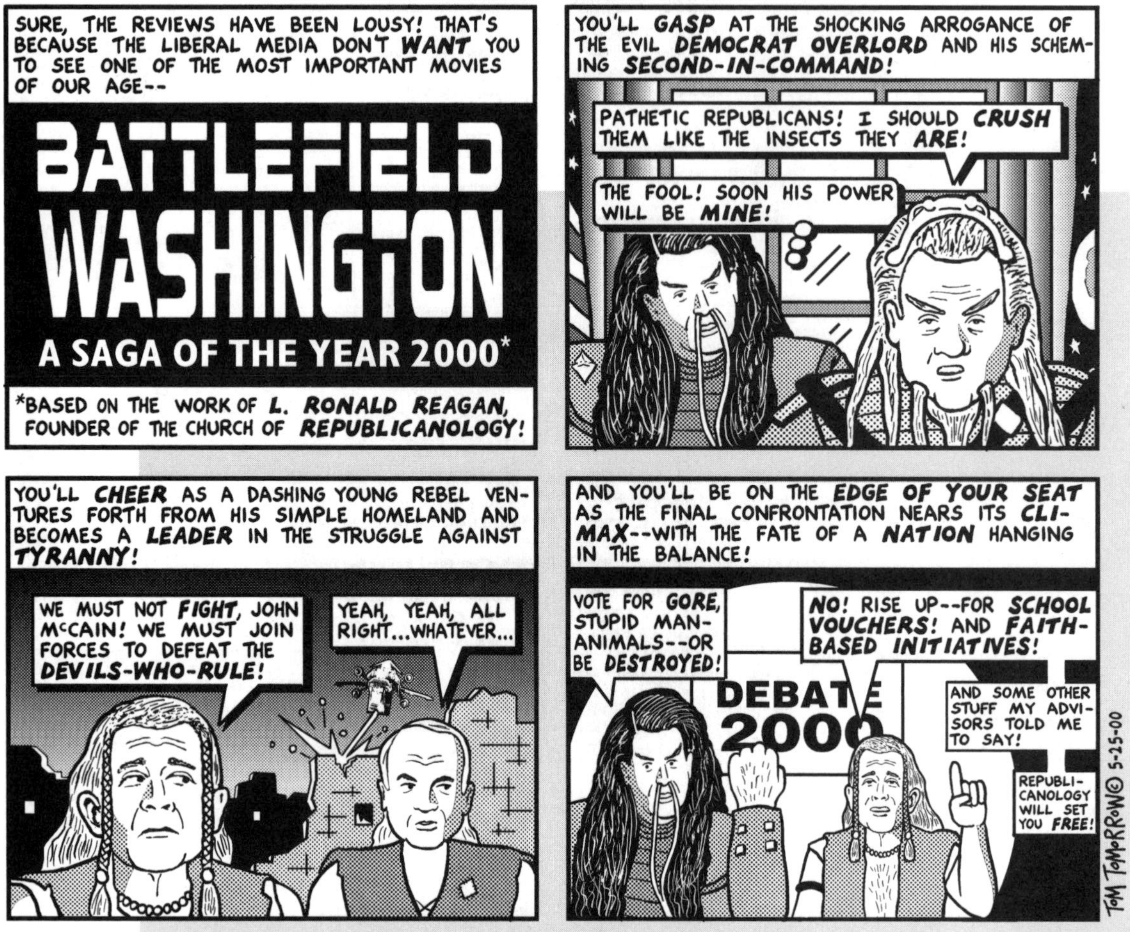
SURE, THE REVIEWS HAVE BEEN LOUSY! THAT'S BECAUSE THE LIBERAL MEDIA DON'T WANT YOU TO SEE ONE OF THE MOST IMPORTANT MOVIES OF OUR AGE--
BATTLEFIELD WASHINGTON
A SAGA OF THE YEAR 2000*
*BASED ON THE WORK OF L. RONALD REAGAN, FOUNDER OF THE CHURCH OF REPUBLICANOLOGY!
YOU'LL GASP AT THE SHOCKING ARROGANCE OF THE EVIL DEMOCRAT OVERLORD AND HIS SCHEMING SECOND-IN-COMMAND!
PATHETIC REPUBLICANS! I SHOULD CRUSH THEM LIKE THE INSECTS THEY ARE!
THE FOOL! SOON HIS POWER WILL BE MINE!
YOU'LL CHEER AS A DASHING YOUNG REBEL VENTURES FORTH FROM HIS SIMPLE HOMELAND AND BECOMES A LEADER IN THE STRUGGLE AGAINST TYRANNY!
WE MUST NOT FIGHT, JOHN McCAIN! WE MUST JOIN FORCES TO DEFEAT THE DEVILS-WHO-RULE!
YEAH, YEAH, ALL RIGHT...WHATEVER...
AND YOU'LL BE ON THE EDGE OF YOUR SEAT AS THE FINAL CONFRONTATION NEARS ITS CLIMAX--WITH THE FATE OF A NATION HANGING IN THE BALANCE!
VOTE FOR GORE, STUPID MAN-ANIMALS--OR BE DESTROYED!
NO! RISE UP--FOR SCHOOL VOUCHERS! AND FAITH-BASED INITIATIVES!
DEBATE 2000
AND SOME OTHER STUFF MY ADVISORS TOLD ME TO SAY!
REPUBLICANOLOGY WILL SET YOU FREE!
TOM TOMORROW© 5-25-00

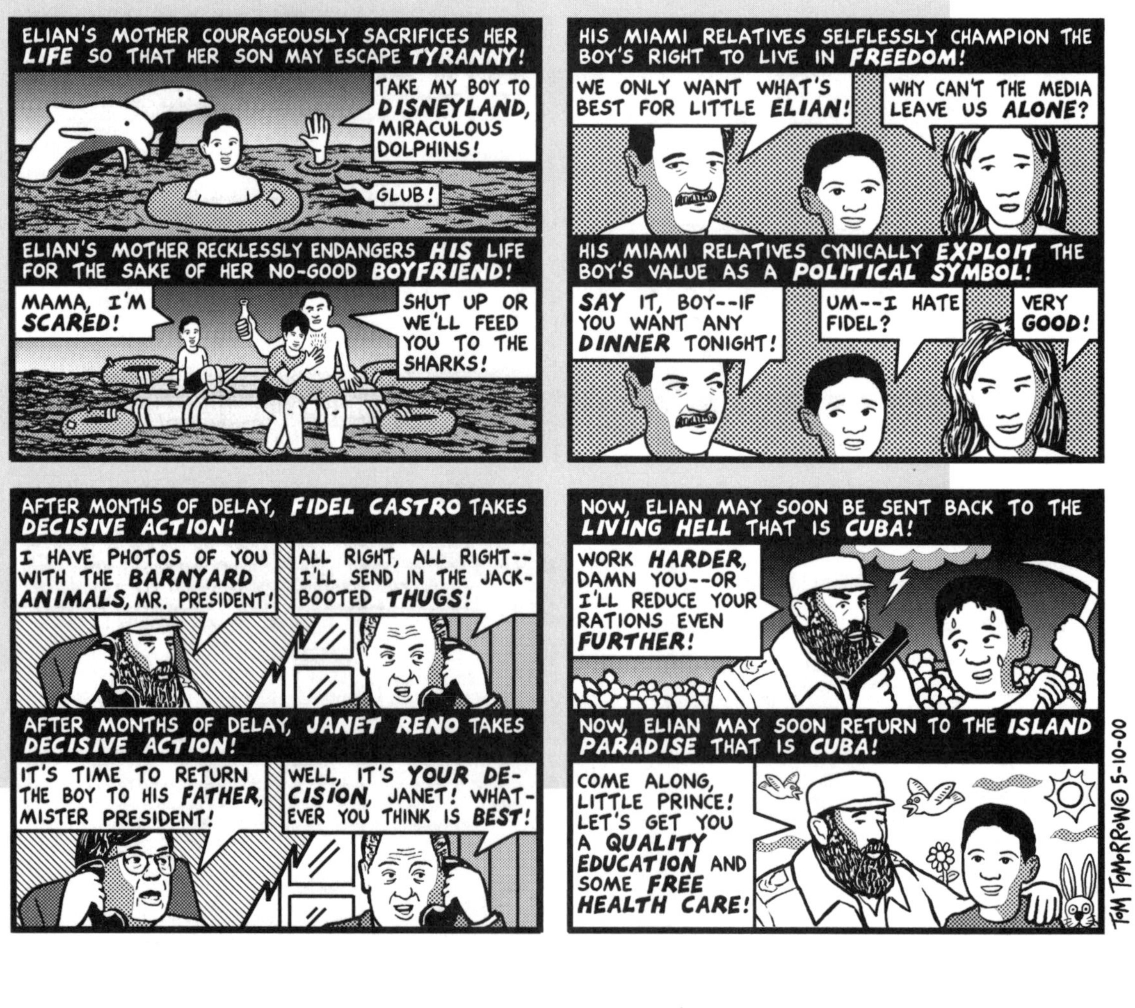
ELIAN'S MOTHER COURAGEOUSLY SACRIFICES HER LIFE SO THAT HER SON MAY ESCAPE TYRANNY!
TAKE MY BOY TO DISNEYLAND, MIRACULOUS DOLPHINS!
GLUB!
ELIAN'S MOTHER RECKLESSLY ENDANGERS HIS LIFE FOR THE SAKE OF HER NO-GOOD BOYFRIEND!
MAMA, I'M SCARED!
SHUT UP OR WE'LL FEED YOU TO THE SHARKS!
HIS MIAMI RELATIVES SELFLESSLY CHAMPION THE BOY'S RIGHT TO LIVE IN FREEDOM!
WE ONLY WANT WHAT'S BEST FOR LITTLE ELIAN!
WHY CAN'T THE MEDIA LEAVE US ALONE?
HIS MIAMI RELATIVES CYNICALLY EXPLOIT THE BOY'S VALUE AS A POLITICAL SYMBOL!
SAY IT, BOY--IF YOU WANT ANY DINNER TONIGHT!
UM--I HATE FIDEL?
VERY GOOD!
AFTER MONTHS OF DELAY, FIDEL CASTRO TAKES DECISIVE ACTION!
I HAVE PHOTOS OF YOU WITH THE BARNYARD ANIMALS, MR. PRESIDENT!
ALL RIGHT, ALL RIGHT--I'LL SEND IN THE JACK-BOOTED THUGS!
AFTER MONTHS OF DELAY, JANET RENO TAKES DECISIVE ACTION!
IT'S TIME TO RETURN THE BOY TO HIS FATHER, MISTER PRESIDENT!
WELL, IT'S YOUR DECISION, JANET! WHATEVER YOU THINK IS BEST!
NOW, ELIAN MAY SOON BE SENT BACK TO THE LIVING HELL THAT IS CUBA!
WORK HARDER, DAMN YOU--OR I'LL REDUCE YOUR RATIONS EVEN FURTHER!
NOW, ELIAN MAY SOON RETURN TO THE ISLAND PARADISE THAT IS CUBA!
COME ALONG, LITTLE PRINCE! LET'S GET YOU A QUALITY EDUCATION AND SOME FREE HEALTH CARE!
TOM TOMORROW© 5-10-00

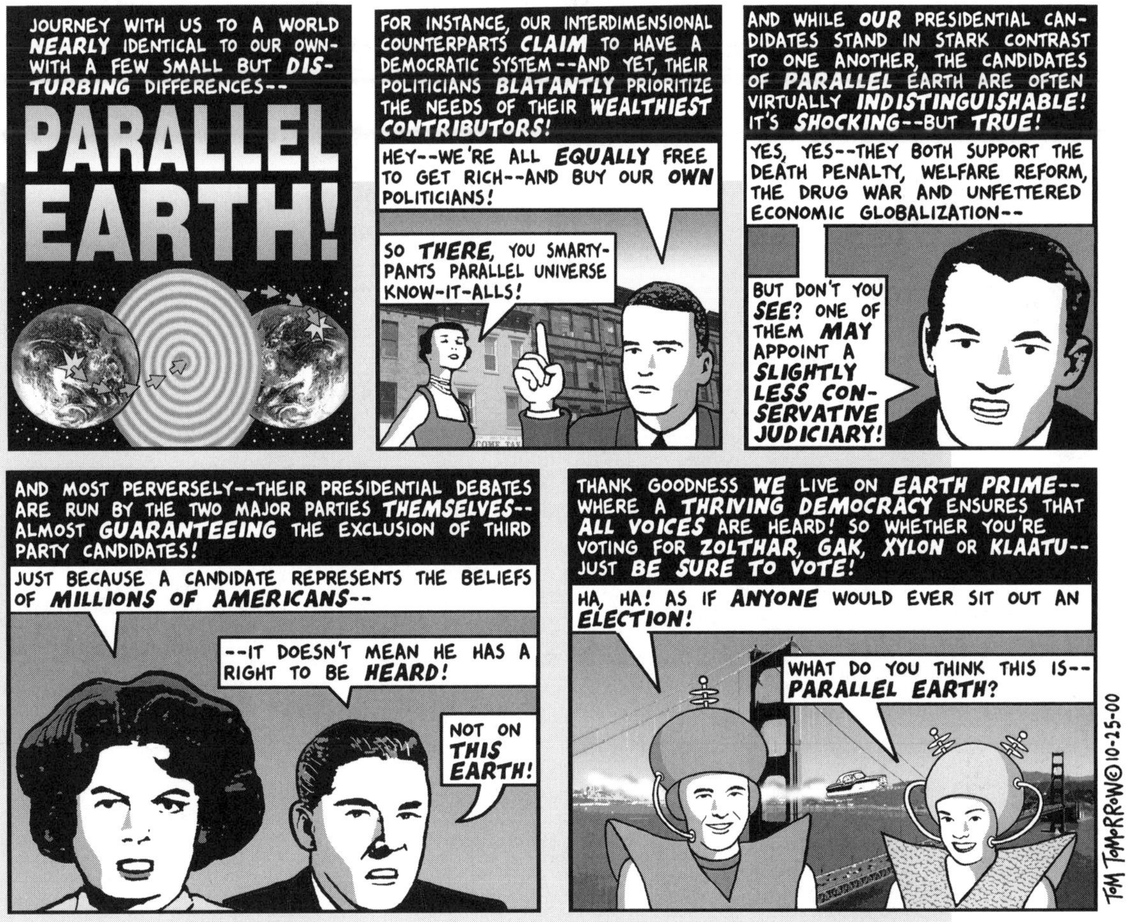
JOURNEY WITH US TO A WORLD NEARLY IDENTICAL TO OUR OWN-WITH A FEW SMALL BUT DISTURBING DIFFERENCES--
PARALLEL EARTH!
FOR INSTANCE, OUR INTERDIMENSIONAL COUNTERPARTS CLAIM TO HAVE A DEMOCRATIC SYSTEM--AND YET, THEIR POLITICIANS BLATANTLY PRIORITIZE THE NEEDS OF THEIR WEALTHIEST CONTRIBUTORS!
HEY--WE'RE ALL EQUALLY FREE TO GET RICH--AND BUY OUR OWN POLITICIANS!
SO THERE, YOU SMARTY-PANTS PARALLEL UNIVERSE KNOW-IT-ALLS!
AND WHILE OUR PRESIDENTIAL CANDIDATES STAND IN STARK CONTRAST TO ONE ANOTHER, THE CANDIDATES OF PARALLEL EARTH ARE OFTEN VIRTUALLY INDISTINGUISHABLE! IT'S SHOCKING--BUT TRUE!
YES, YES--THEY BOTH SUPPORT THE DEATH PENALTY, WELFARE REFORM, THE DRUG WAR AND UNFETTERED ECONOMIC GLOBALIZATION--
BUT DON'T YOU SEE? ONE OF THEM MAY APPOINT A SLIGHTLY LESS CONSERVATIVE JUDICIARY!
AND MOST PERVERSELY--THEIR PRESIDENTIAL DEBATES ARE RUN BY THE TWO MAJOR PARTIES THEMSELVES--ALMOST GUARANTEEING THE EXCLUSION OF THIRD PARTY CANDIDATES!
JUST BECAUSE A CANDIDATE REPRESENTS THE BELIEFS OF MILLIONS OF AMERICANS--
--IT DOESN'T MEAN HE HAS A RIGHT TO BE HEARD!
NOT ON THIS EARTH!
THANK GOODNESS WE LIVE ON EARTH PRIME--WHERE A THRIVING DEMOCRACY ENSURES THAT ALL VOICES ARE HEARD! SO WHETHER YOU'RE VOTING FOR ZOLTHAR, GAK, XYLON OR KLAATU--JUST BE SURE TO VOTE!
HA, HA! AS IF ANYONE WOULD EVER SIT OUT AN ELECTION!
WHAT DO YOU THINK THIS IS--PARALLEL EARTH?
TOM TOMORROW© 10-25-00

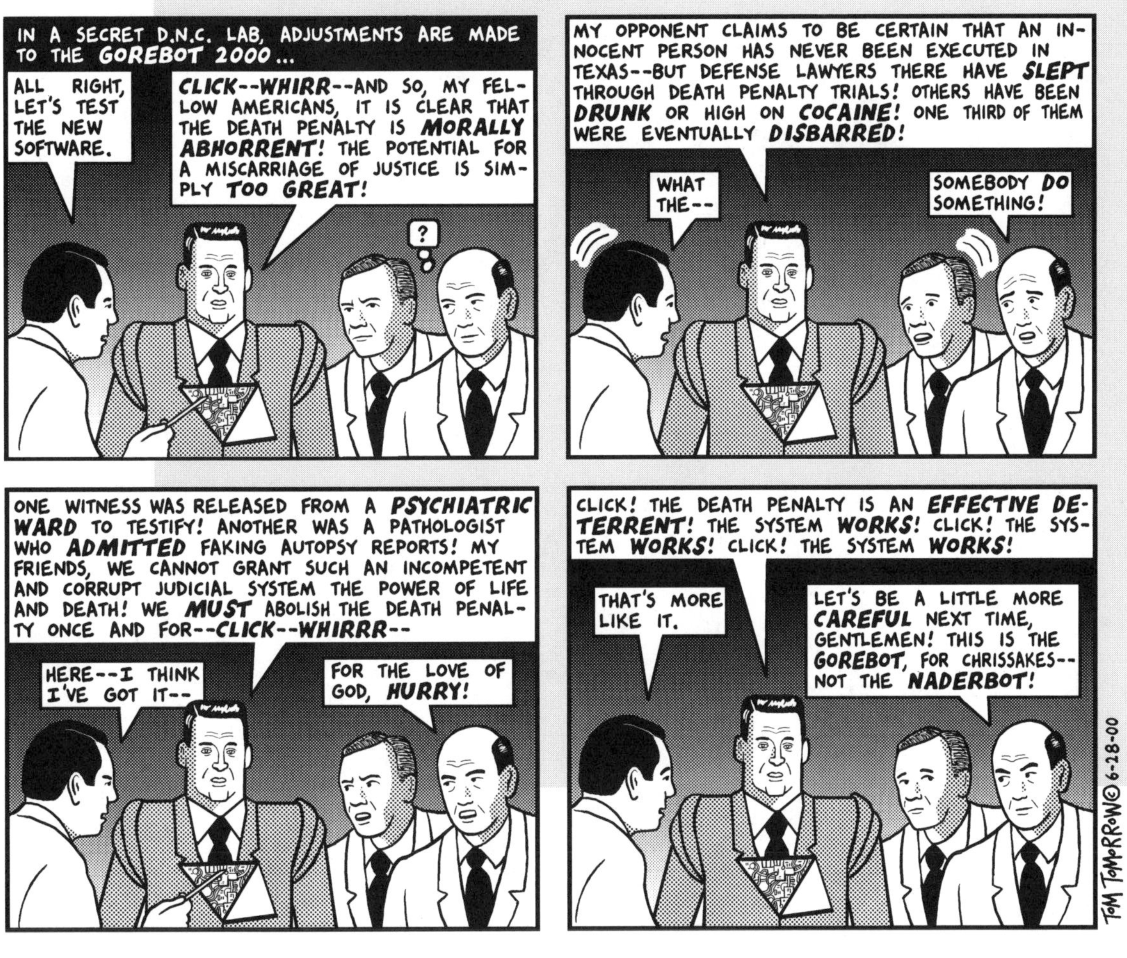
IN A SECRET D.N.C. LAB, ADJUSTMENTS ARE MADE TO THE GOREBOT 2000...
ALL RIGHT, LET'S TEST THE NEW SOFTWARE.
CLICK--WHIRR--AND SO, MY FELLOW AMERICANS, IT IS CLEAR THAT THE DEATH PENALTY IS MORALLY ABHORRENT! THE POTENTIAL FOR A MISCARRIAGE OF JUSTICE IS SIMPLY TOO GREAT!
?
MY OPPONENT CLAIMS TO BE CERTAIN THAT AN INNOCENT PERSON HAS NEVER BEEN EXECUTED IN TEXAS--BUT DEFENSE LAWYERS THERE HAVE SLEPT THROUGH DEATH PENALTY TRIALS! OTHERS HAVE BEEN DRUNK OR HIGH ON COCAINE! ONE THIRD OF THEM WERE EVENTUALLY DISBARRED!
WHAT THE--
SOMEBODY DO SOMETHING!
ONE WITNESS WAS RELEASED FROM A PSYCHIATRIC WARD TO TESTIFY! ANOTHER WAS A PATHOLOGIST WHO ADMITTED FAKING AUTOPSY REPORTS! MY FRIENDS, WE CANNOT GRANT SUCH AN INCOMPETENT AND CORRUPT JUDICIAL SYSTEM THE POWER OF LIFE AND DEATH! WE MUST ABOLISH THE DEATH PENALTY ONCE AND FOR--CLICK--WHIRRR--
HERE--I THINK I'VE GOT IT--
FOR THE LOVE OF GOD, HURRY!
CLICK! THE DEATH PENALTY IS AN EFFECTIVE DETERRENT! THE SYSTEM WORKS! CLICK! THE SYSTEM WORKS! CLICK! THE SYSTEM WORKS!
THAT'S MORE LIKE IT.
LET'S BE A LITTLE MORE CAREFUL NEXT TIME, GENTLEMEN! THIS IS THE GOREBOT, FOR CHRISSAKES--NOT THE NADERBOT!
TOM TOMORROW© 6-28-00

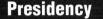

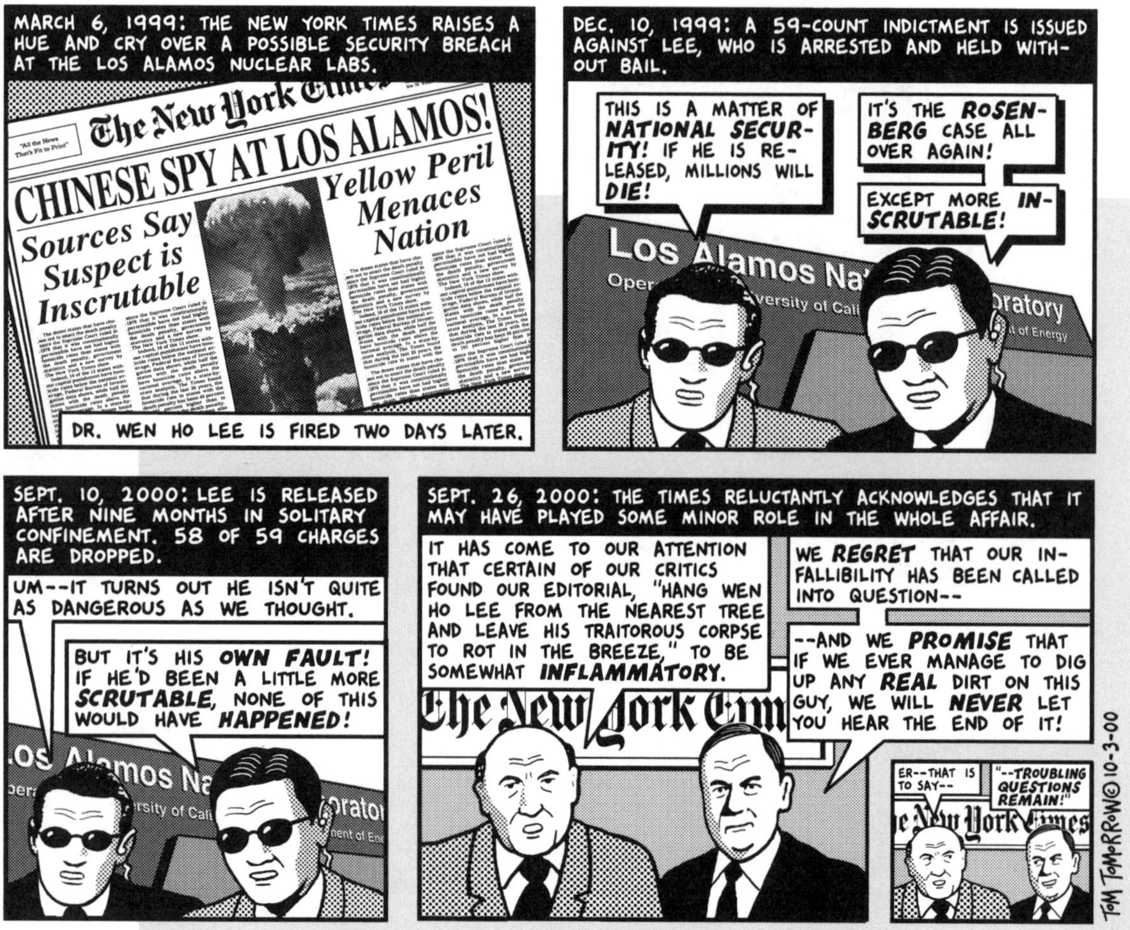
MARCH 6, 1999: THE NEW YORK TIMES RAISES A HUE AND CRY OVER A POSSIBLE SECURITY BREACH AT THE LOS ALAMOS NUCLEAR LABS.
The New York Times
"All the News That's Fit to Print"
CHINESE SPY AT LOS ALAMOS!
Sources Say Suspect is Inscrutable
Yellow Peril Menaces Nation
DR. WEN HO LEE IS FIRED TWO DAYS LATER.
DEC. 10, 1999: A 59-COUNT INDICTMENT IS ISSUED AGAINST LEE, WHO IS ARRESTED AND HELD WITHOUT BAIL.
THIS IS A MATTER OF NATIONAL SECURITY! IF HE IS RELEASED, MILLIONS WILL DIE!
IT'S THE ROSENBERG CASE ALL OVER AGAIN!
EXCEPT MORE INSCRUTABLE!
Los Alamos National Laboratory
SEPT. 10, 2000: LEE IS RELEASED AFTER NINE MONTHS IN SOLITARY CONFINEMENT. 58 OF 59 CHARGES ARE DROPPED.
UM--IT TURNS OUT HE ISN'T QUITE AS DANGEROUS AS WE THOUGHT.
BUT IT'S HIS OWN FAULT! IF HE'D BEEN A LITTLE MORE SCRUTABLE, NONE OF THIS WOULD HAVE HAPPENED!
SEPT. 26, 2000: THE TIMES RELUCTANTLY ACKNOWLEDGES THAT IT MAY HAVE PLAYED SOME MINOR ROLE IN THE WHOLE AFFAIR.
IT HAS COME TO OUR ATTENTION THAT CERTAIN OF OUR CRITICS FOUND OUR EDITORIAL, "HANG WEN HO LEE FROM THE NEAREST TREE AND LEAVE HIS TRAITOROUS CORPSE TO ROT IN THE BREEZE," TO BE SOMEWHAT INFLAMMATORY.
WE REGRET THAT OUR INFALLIBILITY HAS BEEN CALLED INTO QUESTION--
--AND WE PROMISE THAT IF WE EVER MANAGE TO DIG UP ANY REAL DIRT ON THIS GUY, WE WILL NEVER LET YOU HEAR THE END OF IT!
ER--THAT IS TO SAY--
"--TROUBLING QUESTIONS REMAIN!"
TOM TOMORROW © 10-3-00

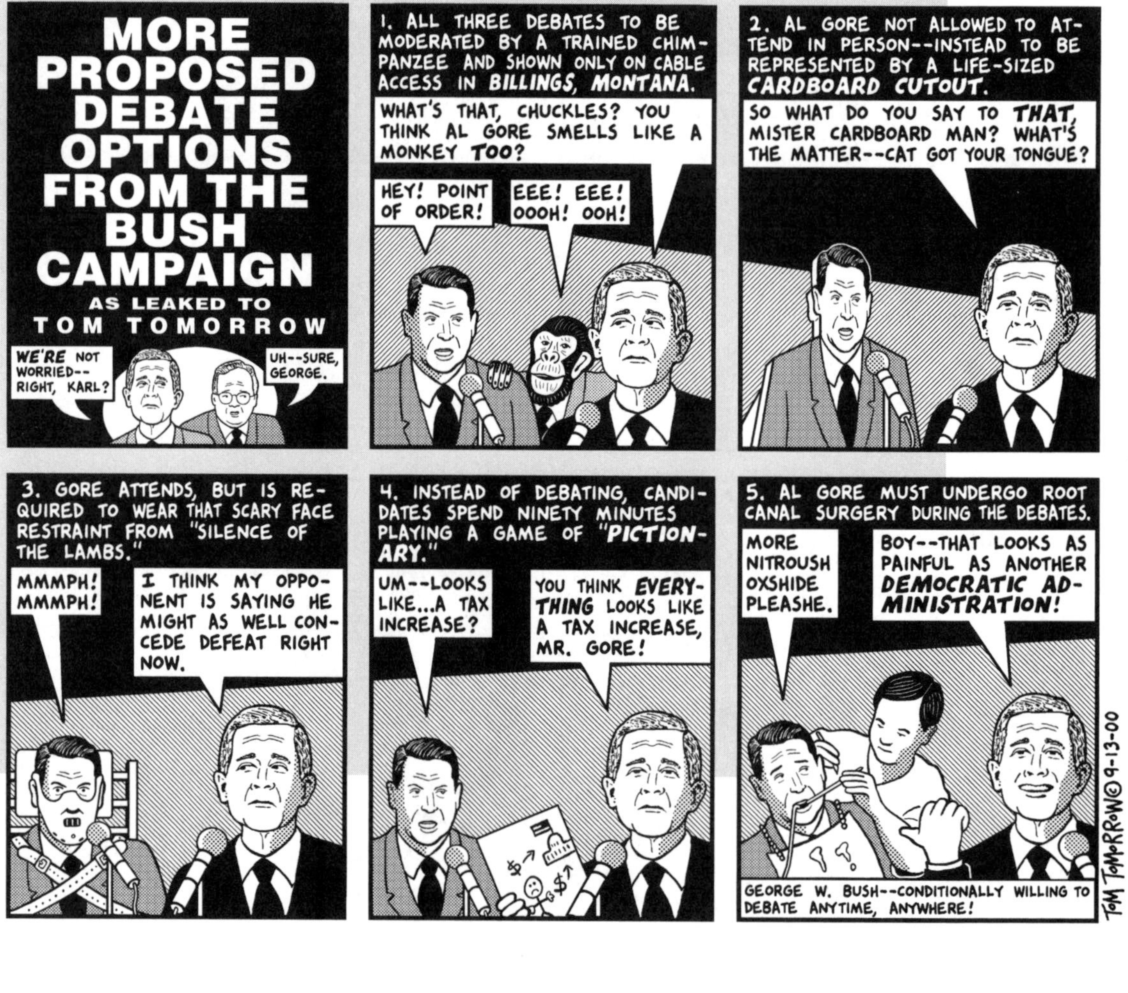
MORE PROPOSED DEBATE OPTIONS FROM THE BUSH CAMPAIGN
AS LEAKED TO TOM TOMORROW
WE'RE NOT WORRIED--RIGHT, KARL?
UH--SURE, GEORGE.
1. ALL THREE DEBATES TO BE MODERATED BY A TRAINED CHIMPANZEE AND SHOWN ONLY ON CABLE ACCESS IN BILLINGS, MONTANA.
WHAT'S THAT, CHUCKLES? YOU THINK AL GORE SMELLS LIKE A MONKEY TOO?
HEY! POINT OF ORDER!
EEE! EEE! OOOH! OOH!
2. AL GORE NOT ALLOWED TO ATTEND IN PERSON--INSTEAD TO BE REPRESENTED BY A LIFE-SIZED CARDBOARD CUTOUT.
SO WHAT DO YOU SAY TO THAT, MISTER CARDBOARD MAN? WHAT'S THE MATTER--CAT GOT YOUR TONGUE?
3. GORE ATTENDS, BUT IS REQUIRED TO WEAR THAT SCARY FACE RESTRAINT FROM "SILENCE OF THE LAMBS."
MMMPH! MMMPH!
I THINK MY OPPONENT IS SAYING HE MIGHT AS WELL CONCEDE DEFEAT RIGHT NOW.
4. INSTEAD OF DEBATING, CANDIDATES SPEND NINETY MINUTES PLAYING A GAME OF "PICTIONARY."
UM--LOOKS LIKE...A TAX INCREASE?
YOU THINK EVERYTHING LOOKS LIKE A TAX INCREASE, MR. GORE!
5. AL GORE MUST UNDERGO ROOT CANAL SURGERY DURING THE DEBATES.
MORE NITROUSH OXSHIDE PLEASHE.
BOY--THAT LOOKS AS PAINFUL AS ANOTHER DEMOCRATIC ADMINISTRATION!
GEORGE W. BUSH--CONDITIONALLY WILLING TO DEBATE ANYTIME, ANYWHERE!
TOM TOMORROW © 9-13-00

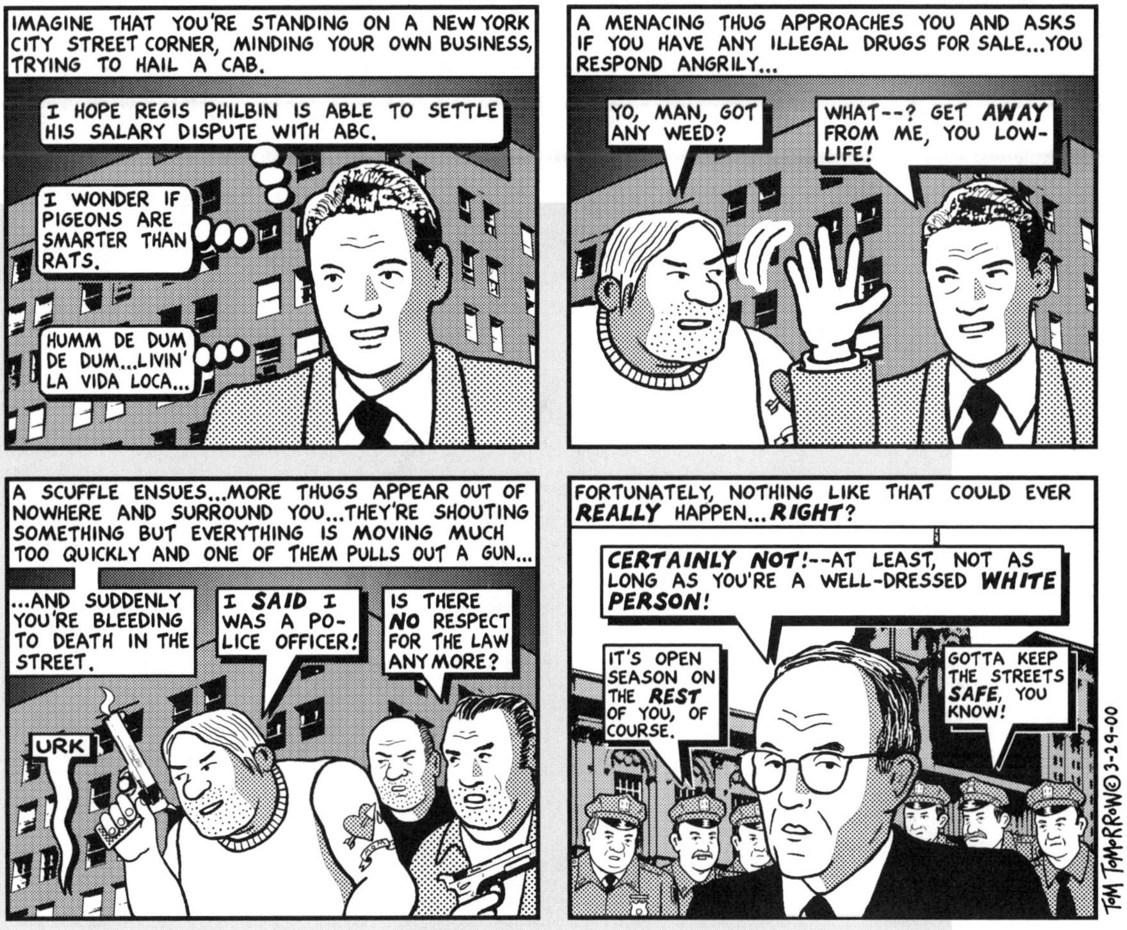
IMAGINE THAT YOU'RE STANDING ON A NEW YORK CITY STREET CORNER, MINDING YOUR OWN BUSINESS, TRYING TO HAIL A CAB.
I HOPE REGIS PHILBIN IS ABLE TO SETTLE HIS SALARY DISPUTE WITH ABC.
I WONDER IF PIGEONS ARE SMARTER THAN RATS.
HUMM DE DUM DE DUM...LIVIN' LA VIDA LOCA...
A MENACING THUG APPROACHES YOU AND ASKS IF YOU HAVE ANY ILLEGAL DRUGS FOR SALE...YOU RESPOND ANGRILY...
YO, MAN, GOT ANY WEED?
WHAT--? GET AWAY FROM ME, YOU LOW-LIFE!
A SCUFFLE ENSUES...MORE THUGS APPEAR OUT OF NOWHERE AND SURROUND YOU...THEY'RE SHOUTING SOMETHING BUT EVERYTHING IS MOVING MUCH TOO QUICKLY AND ONE OF THEM PULLS OUT A GUN...
...AND SUDDENLY YOU'RE BLEEDING TO DEATH IN THE STREET.
I SAID I WAS A PO-LICE OFFICER!
IS THERE NO RESPECT FOR THE LAW ANYMORE?
URK
FORTUNATELY, NOTHING LIKE THAT COULD EVER REALLY HAPPEN... RIGHT?
CERTAINLY NOT!--AT LEAST, NOT AS LONG AS YOU'RE A WELL-DRESSED WHITE PERSON!
IT'S OPEN SEASON ON THE REST OF YOU, OF COURSE.
GOTTA KEEP THE STREETS SAFE, YOU KNOW!
TOM TOMORROW©3-29-00

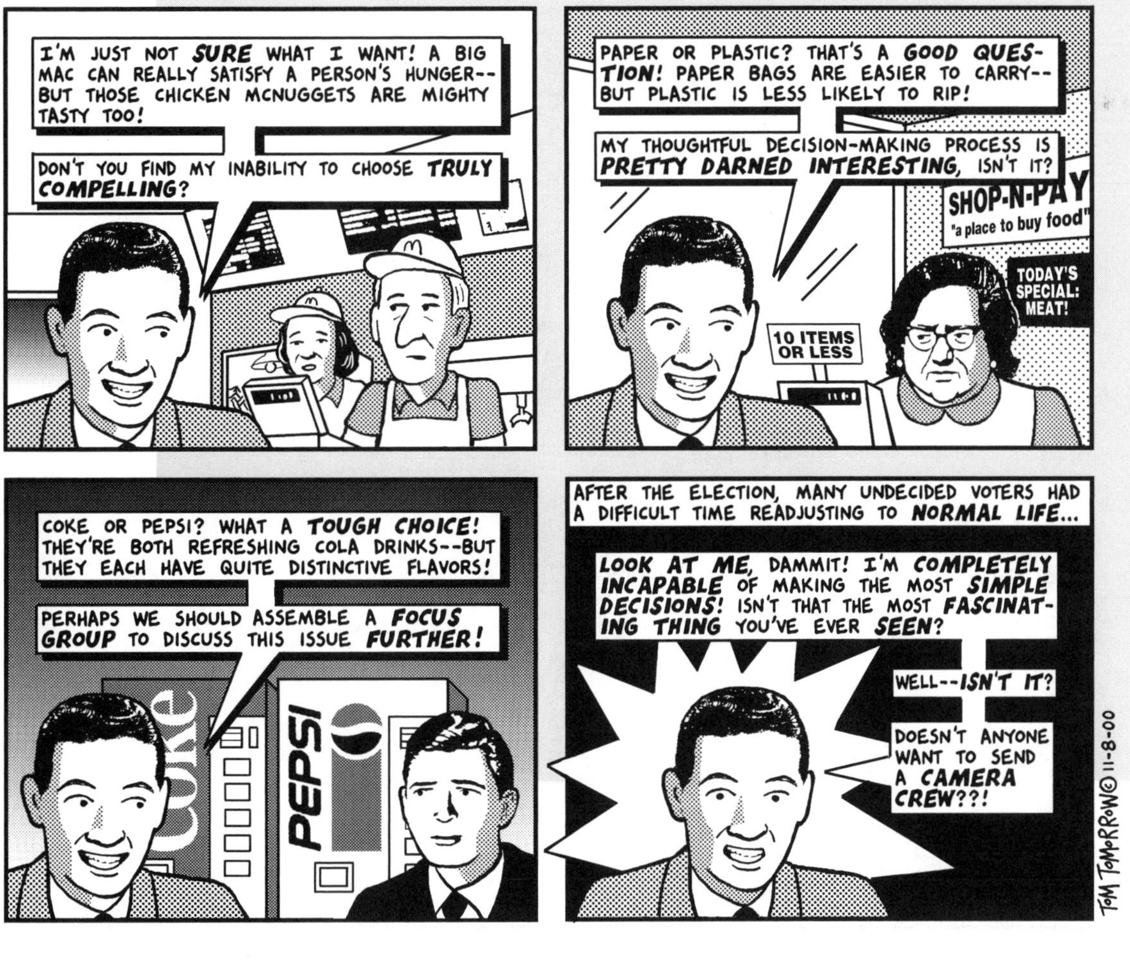
I'M JUST NOT SURE WHAT I WANT! A BIG MAC CAN REALLY SATISFY A PERSON'S HUNGER--BUT THOSE CHICKEN MCNUGGETS ARE MIGHTY TASTY TOO!
DON'T YOU FIND MY INABILITY TO CHOOSE TRULY COMPELLING?
PAPER OR PLASTIC? THAT'S A GOOD QUES-TION! PAPER BAGS ARE EASIER TO CARRY--BUT PLASTIC IS LESS LIKELY TO RIP!
MY THOUGHTFUL DECISION-MAKING PROCESS IS PRETTY DARNED INTERESTING, ISN'T IT?
SHOP-N-PAY
"a place to buy food"
TODAY'S SPECIAL: MEAT!
10 ITEMS OR LESS
COKE OR PEPSI? WHAT A TOUGH CHOICE! THEY'RE BOTH REFRESHING COLA DRINKS--BUT THEY EACH HAVE QUITE DISTINCTIVE FLAVORS!
PERHAPS WE SHOULD ASSEMBLE A FOCUS GROUP TO DISCUSS THIS ISSUE FURTHER!
COKE
PEPSI
AFTER THE ELECTION, MANY UNDECIDED VOTERS HAD A DIFFICULT TIME READJUSTING TO NORMAL LIFE...
LOOK AT ME, DAMMIT! I'M COMPLETELY INCAPABLE OF MAKING THE MOST SIMPLE DECISIONS! ISN'T THAT THE MOST FASCINAT-ING THING YOU'VE EVER SEEN?
WELL--ISN'T IT?
DOESN'T ANYONE WANT TO SEND A CAMERA CREW??!
TOM TOMORROW©11-8-00

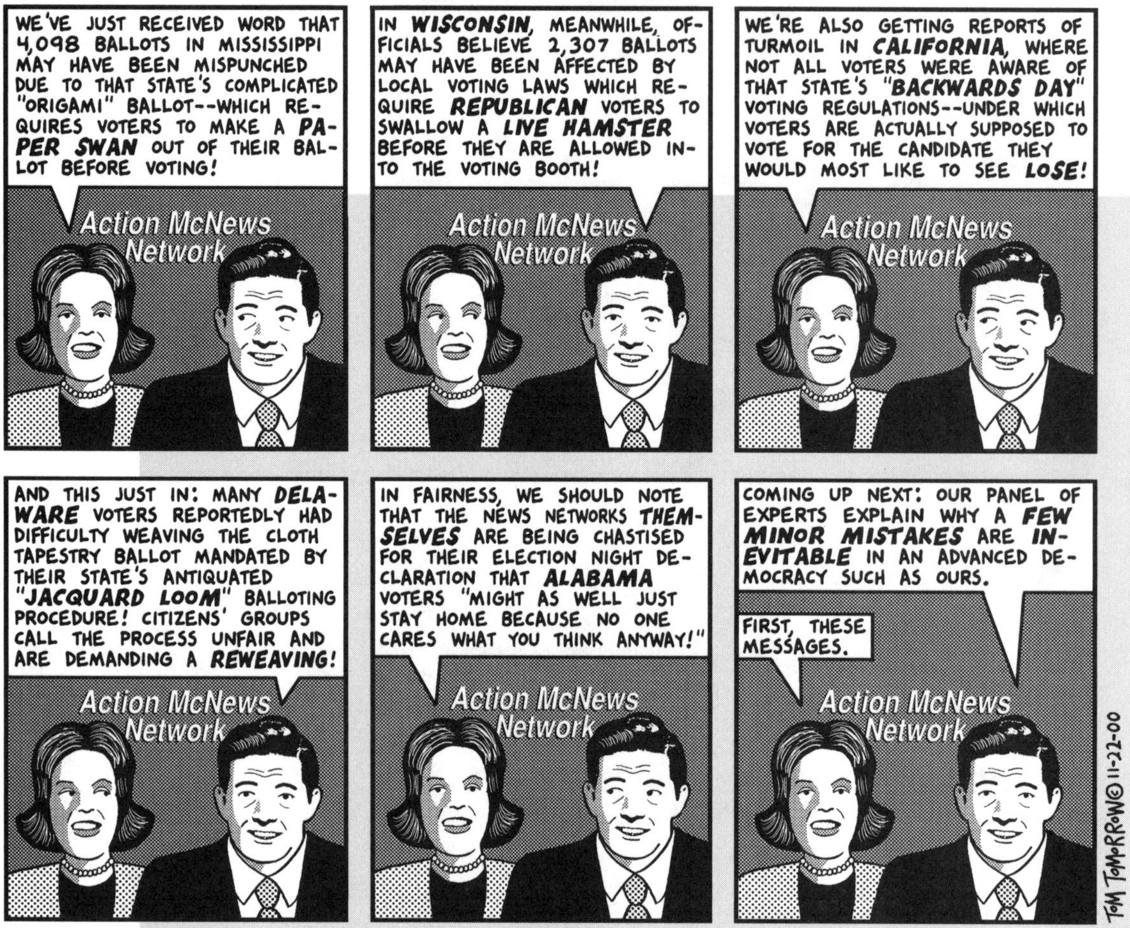
WE'VE JUST RECEIVED WORD THAT 4,098 BALLOTS IN MISSISSIPPI MAY HAVE BEEN MISPUNCHED DUE TO THAT STATE'S COMPLICATED "ORIGAMI" BALLOT--WHICH REQUIRES VOTERS TO MAKE A PAPER SWAN OUT OF THEIR BALLOT BEFORE VOTING!
Action McNews Network
IN WISCONSIN, MEANWHILE, OFFICIALS BELIEVE 2,307 BALLOTS MAY HAVE BEEN AFFECTED BY LOCAL VOTING LAWS WHICH REQUIRE REPUBLICAN VOTERS TO SWALLOW A LIVE HAMSTER BEFORE THEY ARE ALLOWED INTO THE VOTING BOOTH!
Action McNews Network
WE'RE ALSO GETTING REPORTS OF TURMOIL IN CALIFORNIA, WHERE NOT ALL VOTERS WERE AWARE OF THAT STATE'S "BACKWARDS DAY" VOTING REGULATIONS--UNDER WHICH VOTERS ARE ACTUALLY SUPPOSED TO VOTE FOR THE CANDIDATE THEY WOULD MOST LIKE TO SEE LOSE!
Action McNews Network
AND THIS JUST IN: MANY DELAWARE VOTERS REPORTEDLY HAD DIFFICULTY WEAVING THE CLOTH TAPESTRY BALLOT MANDATED BY THEIR STATE'S ANTIQUATED "JACQUARD LOOM" BALLOTING PROCEDURE! CITIZENS' GROUPS CALL THE PROCESS UNFAIR AND ARE DEMANDING A REWEAVING!
Action McNews Network
IN FAIRNESS, WE SHOULD NOTE THAT THE NEWS NETWORKS THEMSELVES ARE BEING CHASTISED FOR THEIR ELECTION NIGHT DECLARATION THAT ALABAMA VOTERS "MIGHT AS WELL JUST STAY HOME BECAUSE NO ONE CARES WHAT YOU THINK ANYWAY!"
Action McNews Network
COMING UP NEXT: OUR PANEL OF EXPERTS EXPLAIN WHY A FEW MINOR MISTAKES ARE INEVITABLE IN AN ADVANCED DEMOCRACY SUCH AS OURS.
FIRST, THESE MESSAGES.
Action McNews Network
TOM TOMORROW© 11-22-00

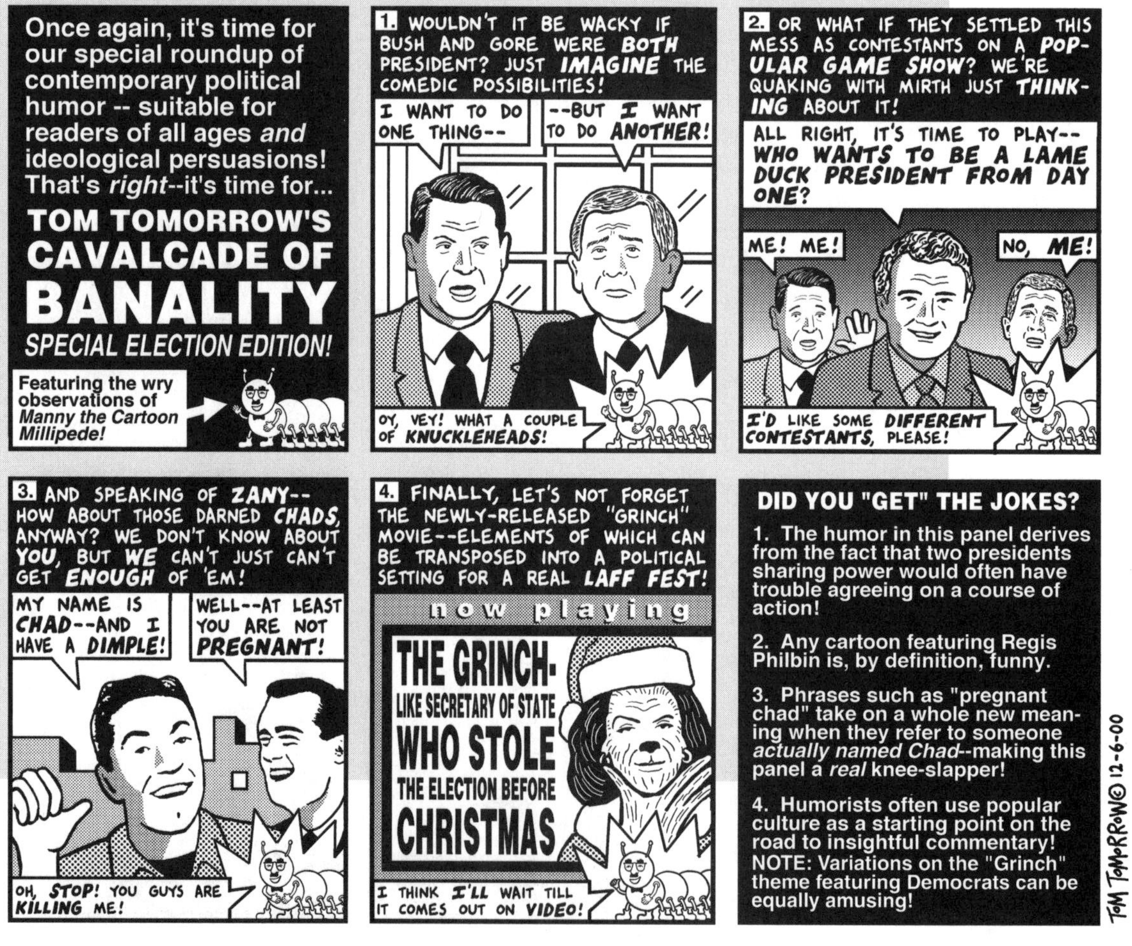
Once again, it's time for our special roundup of contemporary political humor -- suitable for readers of all ages and ideological persuasions! That's right--it's time for...
TOM TOMORROW'S CAVALCADE OF BANALITY
SPECIAL ELECTION EDITION!
Featuring the wry observations of Manny the Cartoon Millipede!
1. WOULDN'T IT BE WACKY IF BUSH AND GORE WERE BOTH PRESIDENT? JUST IMAGINE THE COMEDIC POSSIBILITIES!
I WANT TO DO ONE THING--
--BUT I WANT TO DO ANOTHER!
OY, VEY! WHAT A COUPLE OF KNUCKLEHEADS!
2. OR WHAT IF THEY SETTLED THIS MESS AS CONTESTANTS ON A POPULAR GAME SHOW? WE'RE QUAKING WITH MIRTH JUST THINKING ABOUT IT!
ALL RIGHT, IT'S TIME TO PLAY--WHO WANTS TO BE A LAME DUCK PRESIDENT FROM DAY ONE?
ME! ME!
NO, ME!
I'D LIKE SOME DIFFERENT CONTESTANTS, PLEASE!
3. AND SPEAKING OF ZANY--HOW ABOUT THOSE DARNED CHADS, ANYWAY? WE DON'T KNOW ABOUT YOU, BUT WE CAN'T JUST CAN'T GET ENOUGH OF 'EM!
MY NAME IS CHAD--AND I HAVE A DIMPLE!
WELL--AT LEAST YOU ARE NOT PREGNANT!
OH, STOP! YOU GUYS ARE KILLING ME!
4. FINALLY, LET'S NOT FORGET THE NEWLY-RELEASED "GRINCH" MOVIE--ELEMENTS OF WHICH CAN BE TRANSPOSED INTO A POLITICAL SETTING FOR A REAL LAFF FEST!
now playing
THE GRINCH-LIKE SECRETARY OF STATE WHO STOLE THE ELECTION BEFORE CHRISTMAS
I THINK I'LL WAIT TILL IT COMES OUT ON VIDEO!
DID YOU "GET" THE JOKES?
1. The humor in this panel derives from the fact that two presidents sharing power would often have trouble agreeing on a course of action!
2. Any cartoon featuring Regis Philbin is, by definition, funny.
3. Phrases such as "pregnant chad" take on a whole new meaning when they refer to someone actually named Chad--making this panel a real knee-slapper!
4. Humorists often use popular culture as a starting point on the road to insightful commentary! NOTE: Variations on the "Grinch" theme featuring Democrats can be equally amusing!
TOM TOMORROW© 12-6-00

Hell in a Handbasket

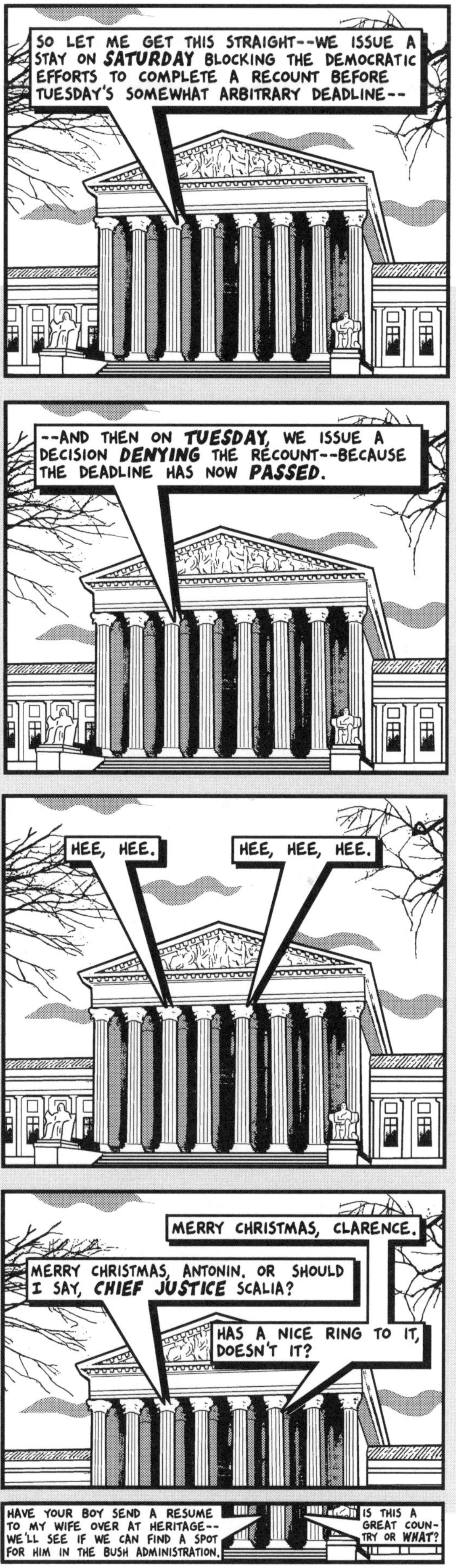

SO LET ME GET THIS STRAIGHT--WE ISSUE A STAY ON SATURDAY BLOCKING THE DEMOCRATIC EFFORTS TO COMPLETE A RECOUNT BEFORE TUESDAY'S SOMEWHAT ARBITRARY DEADLINE--
--AND THEN ON TUESDAY, WE ISSUE A DECISION DENYING THE RECOUNT--BECAUSE THE DEADLINE HAS NOW PASSED.
HEE, HEE.
HEE, HEE, HEE.
MERRY CHRISTMAS, CLARENCE.
MERRY CHRISTMAS, ANTONIN. OR SHOULD I SAY, CHIEF JUSTICE SCALIA?
HAS A NICE RING TO IT, DOESN'T IT?
HAVE YOUR BOY SEND A RESUME TO MY WIFE OVER AT HERITAGE--WE'LL SEE IF WE CAN FIND A SPOT FOR HIM IN THE BUSH ADMINISTRATION.
IS THIS A GREAT COUNTRY OR WHAT?

A n'er-do-well born with a silver spoon in his mouth—and possibly one up his nose—stumbles into the presidency and immediately declares that he has a mandate to to cut taxes for the wealthy, repeal environmental protections, and to keep throwing money at the perennial bipartisan fantasy of missile defense. A year later, we are harshly awakened to the new reality of life in the twenty-first century, and—*quelle surprise!*—it turns out that, in order to fight terrorism, we need to cut taxes for the wealthy, repeal environmental protections, and throw even more money at missile defense.

Meanwhile, crony capitalism begins to implode under the weight of its own corruption and excess, and investors are shocked—*shocked!*—to learn that the actions of corporate executives are not always in the best interests of society as a whole.

Welcome to the twenty-first century, and hang on tight—we're clearly in for a bumpy ride. . .

2000-2002: The Boy King Assumes the Throne

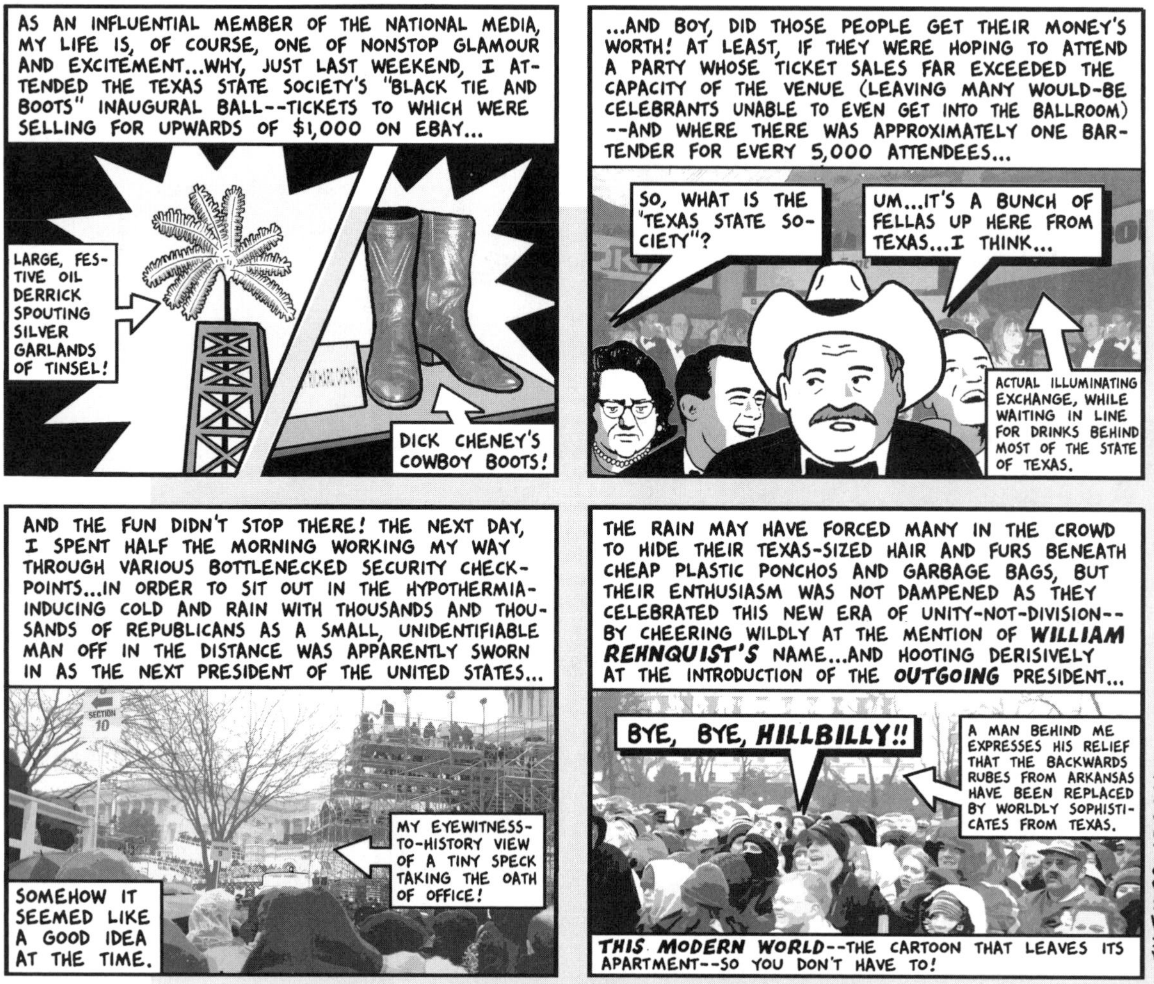
AS AN INFLUENTIAL MEMBER OF THE NATIONAL MEDIA, MY LIFE IS, OF COURSE, ONE OF NONSTOP GLAMOUR AND EXCITEMENT...WHY, JUST LAST WEEKEND, I ATTENDED THE TEXAS STATE SOCIETY'S "BLACK TIE AND BOOTS" INAUGURAL BALL--TICKETS TO WHICH WERE SELLING FOR UPWARDS OF $1,000 ON EBAY...
LARGE, FESTIVE OIL DERRICK SPOUTING SILVER GARLANDS OF TINSEL!
DICK CHENEY'S COWBOY BOOTS!
...AND BOY, DID THOSE PEOPLE GET THEIR MONEY'S WORTH! AT LEAST, IF THEY WERE HOPING TO ATTEND A PARTY WHOSE TICKET SALES FAR EXCEEDED THE CAPACITY OF THE VENUE (LEAVING MANY WOULD-BE CELEBRANTS UNABLE TO EVEN GET INTO THE BALLROOM) --AND WHERE THERE WAS APPROXIMATELY ONE BARTENDER FOR EVERY 5,000 ATTENDEES...
SO, WHAT IS THE "TEXAS STATE SOCIETY"?
UM...IT'S A BUNCH OF FELLAS UP HERE FROM TEXAS...I THINK...
ACTUAL ILLUMINATING EXCHANGE, WHILE WAITING IN LINE FOR DRINKS BEHIND MOST OF THE STATE OF TEXAS.
AND THE FUN DIDN'T STOP THERE! THE NEXT DAY, I SPENT HALF THE MORNING WORKING MY WAY THROUGH VARIOUS BOTTLENECKED SECURITY CHECKPOINTS...IN ORDER TO SIT OUT IN THE HYPOTHERMIA-INDUCING COLD AND RAIN WITH THOUSANDS AND THOUSANDS OF REPUBLICANS AS A SMALL, UNIDENTIFIABLE MAN OFF IN THE DISTANCE WAS APPARENTLY SWORN IN AS THE NEXT PRESIDENT OF THE UNITED STATES...
SECTION 10
MY EYEWITNESS-TO-HISTORY VIEW OF A TINY SPECK TAKING THE OATH OF OFFICE!
SOMEHOW IT SEEMED LIKE A GOOD IDEA AT THE TIME.
THE RAIN MAY HAVE FORCED MANY IN THE CROWD TO HIDE THEIR TEXAS-SIZED HAIR AND FURS BENEATH CHEAP PLASTIC PONCHOS AND GARBAGE BAGS, BUT THEIR ENTHUSIASM WAS NOT DAMPENED AS THEY CELEBRATED THIS NEW ERA OF UNITY-NOT-DIVISION--BY CHEERING WILDLY AT THE MENTION OF WILLIAM REHNQUIST'S NAME...AND HOOTING DERISIVELY AT THE INTRODUCTION OF THE OUTGOING PRESIDENT...
BYE, BYE, HILLBILLY!!
A MAN BEHIND ME EXPRESSES HIS RELIEF THAT THE BACKWARDS RUBES FROM ARKANSAS HAVE BEEN REPLACED BY WORLDLY SOPHISTICATES FROM TEXAS.
THIS MODERN WORLD--THE CARTOON THAT LEAVES ITS APARTMENT--SO YOU DON'T HAVE TO!
TOM TOMORROW© 2001

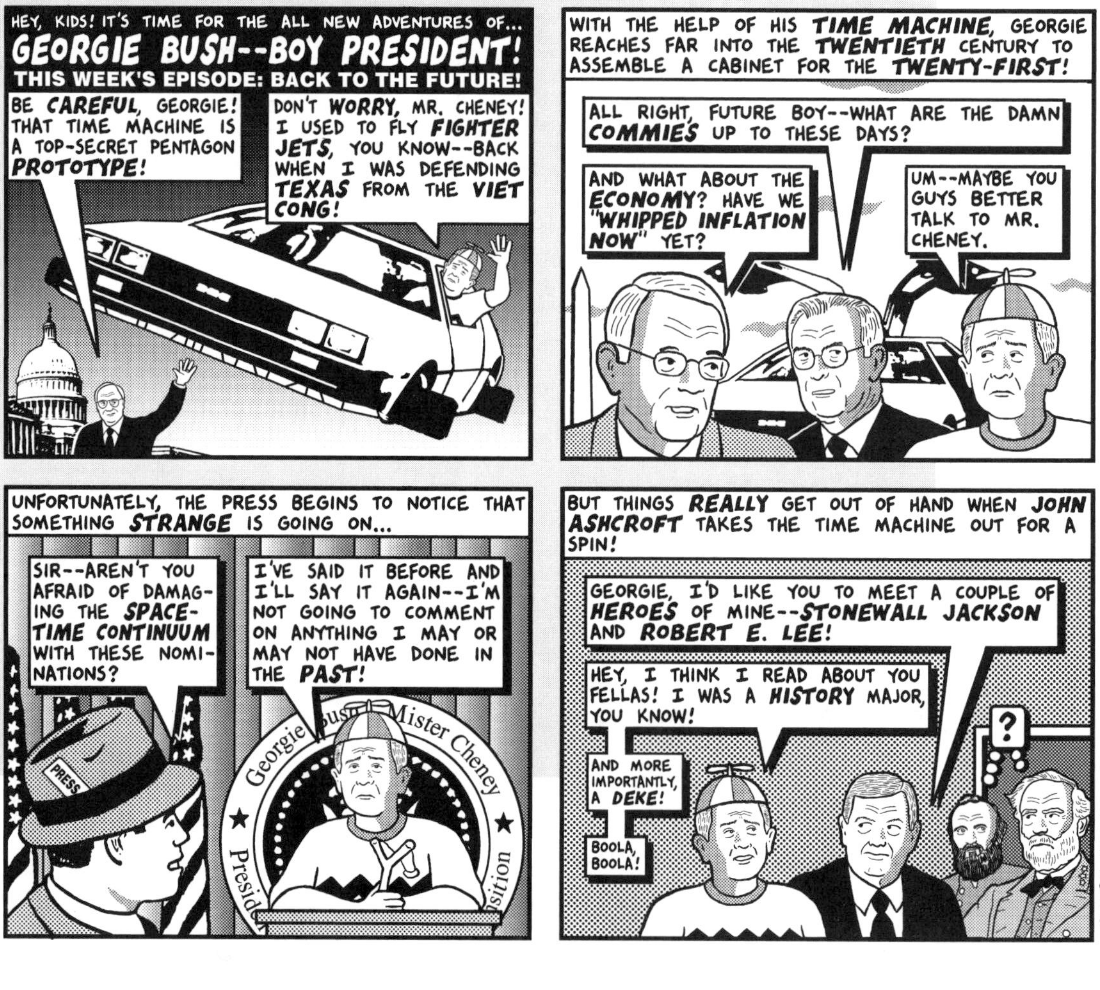
HEY, KIDS! IT'S TIME FOR THE ALL NEW ADVENTURES OF...
GEORGIE BUSH--BOY PRESIDENT!
THIS WEEK'S EPISODE: BACK TO THE FUTURE!
BE CAREFUL, GEORGIE! THAT TIME MACHINE IS A TOP-SECRET PENTAGON PROTOTYPE!
DON'T WORRY, MR. CHENEY! I USED TO FLY FIGHTER JETS, YOU KNOW--BACK WHEN I WAS DEFENDING TEXAS FROM THE VIET CONG!
WITH THE HELP OF HIS TIME MACHINE, GEORGIE REACHES FAR INTO THE TWENTIETH CENTURY TO ASSEMBLE A CABINET FOR THE TWENTY-FIRST!
ALL RIGHT, FUTURE BOY--WHAT ARE THE DAMN COMMIES UP TO THESE DAYS?
AND WHAT ABOUT THE ECONOMY? HAVE WE "WHIPPED INFLATION NOW" YET?
UM--MAYBE YOU GUYS BETTER TALK TO MR. CHENEY.
UNFORTUNATELY, THE PRESS BEGINS TO NOTICE THAT SOMETHING STRANGE IS GOING ON...
SIR--AREN'T YOU AFRAID OF DAMAGING THE SPACE-TIME CONTINUUM WITH THESE NOMINATIONS?
I'VE SAID IT BEFORE AND I'LL SAY IT AGAIN--I'M NOT GOING TO COMMENT ON ANYTHING I MAY OR MAY NOT HAVE DONE IN THE PAST!
PRESS
BUT THINGS REALLY GET OUT OF HAND WHEN JOHN ASHCROFT TAKES THE TIME MACHINE OUT FOR A SPIN!
GEORGIE, I'D LIKE YOU TO MEET A COUPLE OF HEROES OF MINE--STONEWALL JACKSON AND ROBERT E. LEE!
HEY, I THINK I READ ABOUT YOU FELLAS! I WAS A HISTORY MAJOR, YOU KNOW!
AND MORE IMPORTANTLY, A DEKE!
BOOLA, BOOLA!
?
TOM TOMORROW© 1-17-01

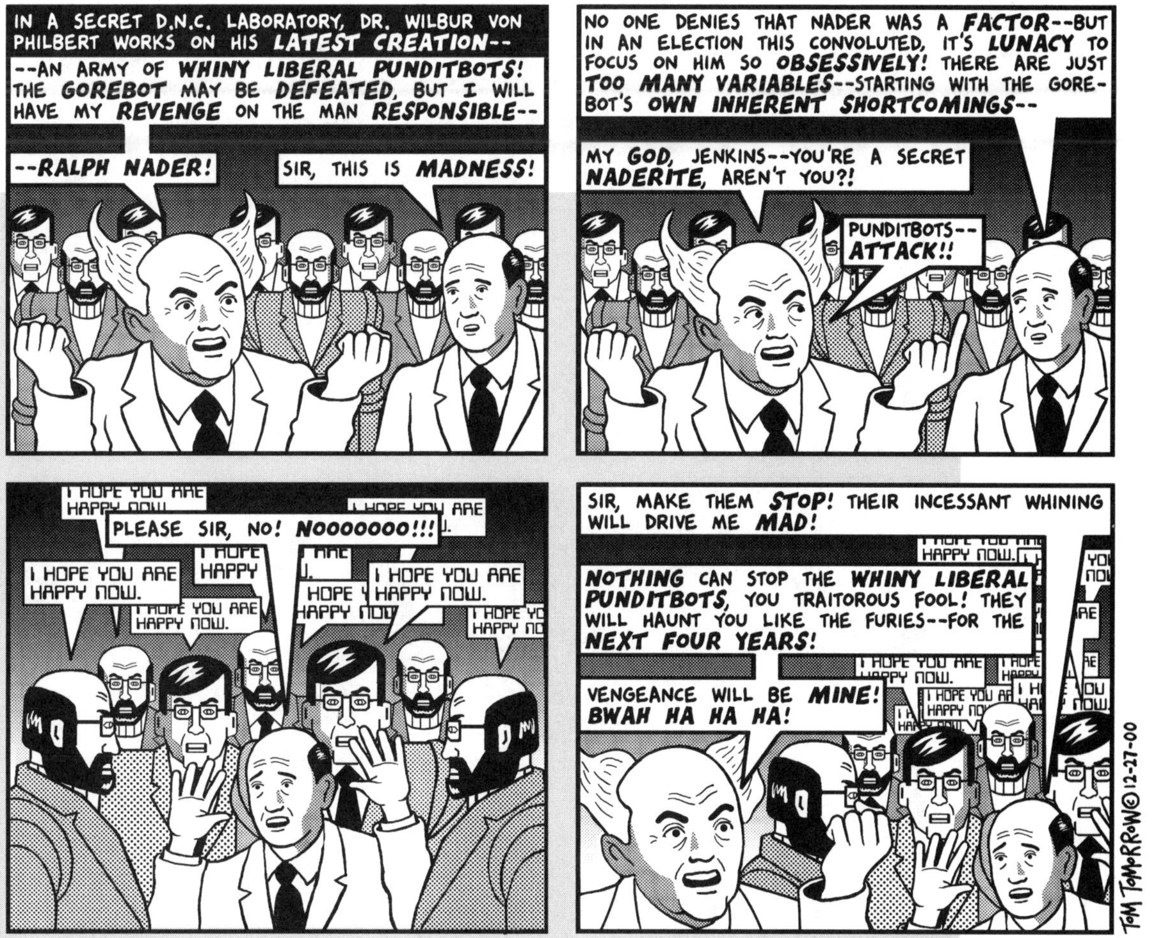
IN A SECRET D.N.C. LABORATORY, DR. WILBUR VON PHILBERT WORKS ON HIS LATEST CREATION--
--AN ARMY OF WHINY LIBERAL PUNDITBOTS! THE GOREBOT MAY BE DEFEATED, BUT I WILL HAVE MY REVENGE ON THE MAN RESPONSIBLE--
--RALPH NADER!
SIR, THIS IS MADNESS!
NO ONE DENIES THAT NADER WAS A FACTOR--BUT IN AN ELECTION THIS CONVOLUTED, IT'S LUNACY TO FOCUS ON HIM SO OBSESSIVELY! THERE ARE JUST TOO MANY VARIABLES--STARTING WITH THE GOREBOT'S OWN INHERENT SHORTCOMINGS--
MY GOD, JENKINS--YOU'RE A SECRET NADERITE, AREN'T YOU?!
PUNDITBOTS--ATTACK!!
PLEASE SIR, NO! NOOOOOOO!!!
I HOPE YOU ARE HAPPY NOW.
I HOPE YOU ARE HAPPY NOW.
I HOPE YOU ARE HAPPY NOW.
SIR, MAKE THEM STOP! THEIR INCESSANT WHINING WILL DRIVE ME MAD!
NOTHING CAN STOP THE WHINY LIBERAL PUNDITBOTS, YOU TRAITOROUS FOOL! THEY WILL HAUNT YOU LIKE THE FURIES--FOR THE NEXT FOUR YEARS!
VENGEANCE WILL BE MINE! BWAH HA HA HA!
TOM TOMORROW©12-27-00

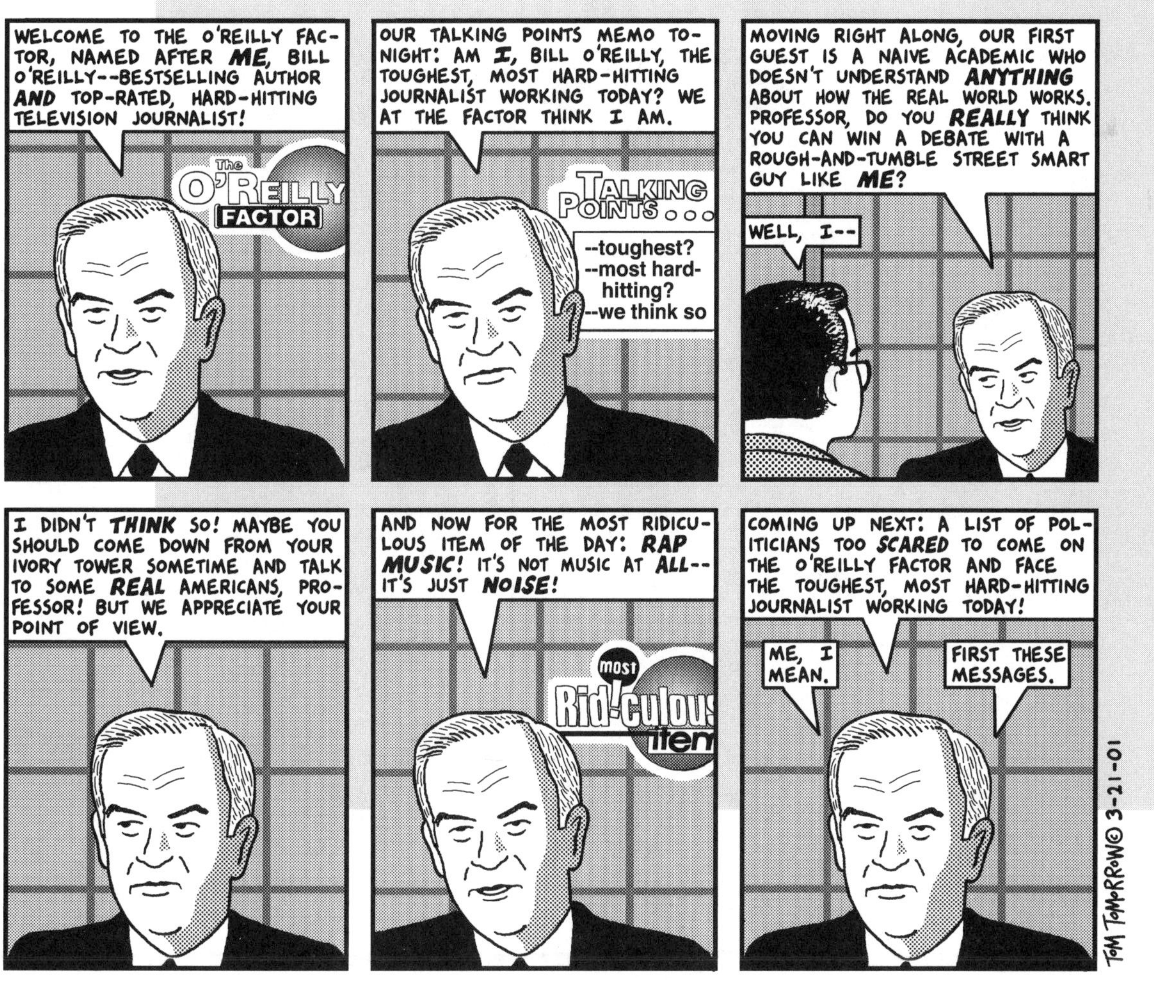
WELCOME TO THE O'REILLY FACTOR, NAMED AFTER ME, BILL O'REILLY--BESTSELLING AUTHOR AND TOP-RATED, HARD-HITTING TELEVISION JOURNALIST!
The O'REILLY FACTOR
OUR TALKING POINTS MEMO TONIGHT: AM I, BILL O'REILLY, THE TOUGHEST, MOST HARD-HITTING JOURNALIST WORKING TODAY? WE AT THE FACTOR THINK I AM.
TALKING POINTS...
--toughest?
--most hard-hitting?
--we think so
MOVING RIGHT ALONG, OUR FIRST GUEST IS A NAIVE ACADEMIC WHO DOESN'T UNDERSTAND ANYTHING ABOUT HOW THE REAL WORLD WORKS. PROFESSOR, DO YOU REALLY THINK YOU CAN WIN A DEBATE WITH A ROUGH-AND-TUMBLE STREET SMART GUY LIKE ME?
WELL, I--
I DIDN'T THINK SO! MAYBE YOU SHOULD COME DOWN FROM YOUR IVORY TOWER SOMETIME AND TALK TO SOME REAL AMERICANS, PROFESSOR! BUT WE APPRECIATE YOUR POINT OF VIEW.
AND NOW FOR THE MOST RIDICULOUS ITEM OF THE DAY: RAP MUSIC! IT'S NOT MUSIC AT ALL--IT'S JUST NOISE!
most Rid!culous item
COMING UP NEXT: A LIST OF POLITICIANS TOO SCARED TO COME ON THE O'REILLY FACTOR AND FACE THE TOUGHEST, MOST HARD-HITTING JOURNALIST WORKING TODAY!
ME, I MEAN.
FIRST THESE MESSAGES.
TOM TOMORROW© 3-21-01

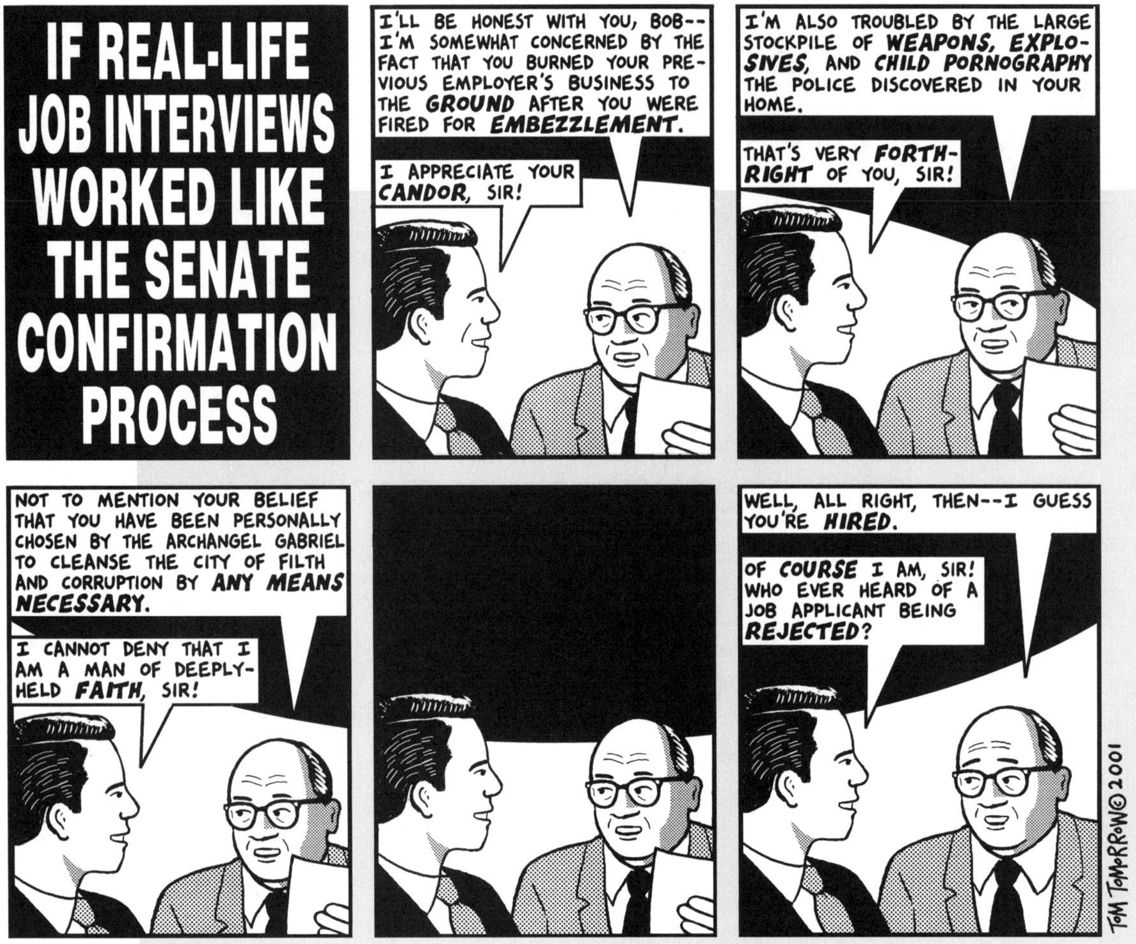
IF REAL-LIFE JOB INTERVIEWS WORKED LIKE THE SENATE CONFIRMATION PROCESS
I'LL BE HONEST WITH YOU, BOB--I'M SOMEWHAT CONCERNED BY THE FACT THAT YOU BURNED YOUR PREVIOUS EMPLOYER'S BUSINESS TO THE GROUND AFTER YOU WERE FIRED FOR EMBEZZLEMENT.
I APPRECIATE YOUR CANDOR, SIR!
I'M ALSO TROUBLED BY THE LARGE STOCKPILE OF WEAPONS, EXPLOSIVES, AND CHILD PORNOGRAPHY THE POLICE DISCOVERED IN YOUR HOME.
THAT'S VERY FORTHRIGHT OF YOU, SIR!
NOT TO MENTION YOUR BELIEF THAT YOU HAVE BEEN PERSONALLY CHOSEN BY THE ARCHANGEL GABRIEL TO CLEANSE THE CITY OF FILTH AND CORRUPTION BY ANY MEANS NECESSARY.
I CANNOT DENY THAT I AM A MAN OF DEEPLY-HELD FAITH, SIR!
WELL, ALL RIGHT, THEN--I GUESS YOU'RE HIRED.
OF COURSE I AM, SIR! WHO EVER HEARD OF A JOB APPLICANT BEING REJECTED?
TOM TOMORROW©2001

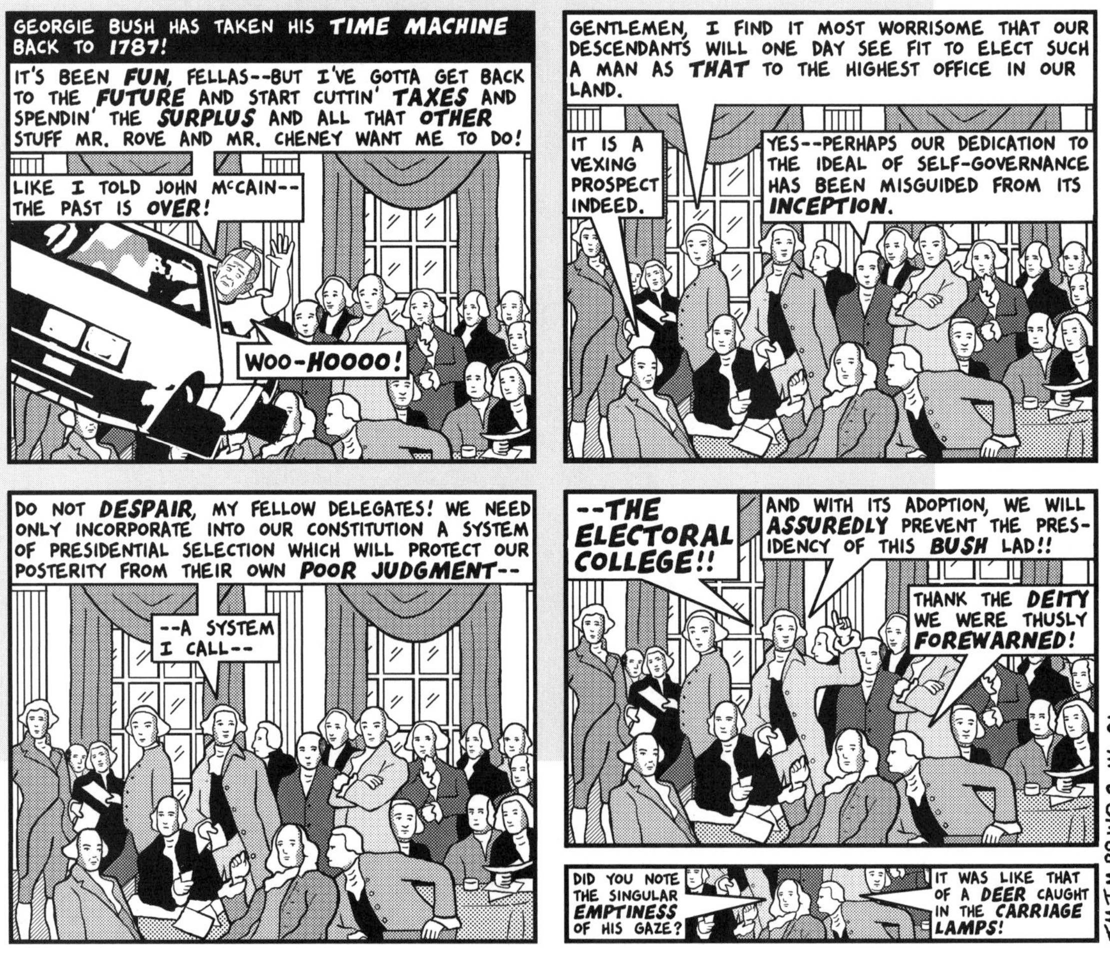
GEORGIE BUSH HAS TAKEN HIS TIME MACHINE BACK TO 1787!
IT'S BEEN FUN, FELLAS--BUT I'VE GOTTA GET BACK TO THE FUTURE AND START CUTTIN' TAXES AND SPENDIN' THE SURPLUS AND ALL THAT OTHER STUFF MR. ROVE AND MR. CHENEY WANT ME TO DO!
LIKE I TOLD JOHN McCAIN--THE PAST IS OVER!
WOO-HOOOO!
GENTLEMEN, I FIND IT MOST WORRISOME THAT OUR DESCENDANTS WILL ONE DAY SEE FIT TO ELECT SUCH A MAN AS THAT TO THE HIGHEST OFFICE IN OUR LAND.
IT IS A VEXING PROSPECT INDEED.
YES--PERHAPS OUR DEDICATION TO THE IDEAL OF SELF-GOVERNANCE HAS BEEN MISGUIDED FROM ITS INCEPTION.
DO NOT DESPAIR, MY FELLOW DELEGATES! WE NEED ONLY INCORPORATE INTO OUR CONSTITUTION A SYSTEM OF PRESIDENTIAL SELECTION WHICH WILL PROTECT OUR POSTERITY FROM THEIR OWN POOR JUDGMENT--
--A SYSTEM I CALL--
--THE ELECTORAL COLLEGE!!
AND WITH ITS ADOPTION, WE WILL ASSUREDLY PREVENT THE PRESIDENCY OF THIS BUSH LAD!!
THANK THE DEITY WE WERE THUSLY FOREWARNED!
DID YOU NOTE THE SINGULAR EMPTINESS OF HIS GAZE?
IT WAS LIKE THAT OF A DEER CAUGHT IN THE CARRIAGE LAMPS!
TOM TOMORROW© 3-14-01

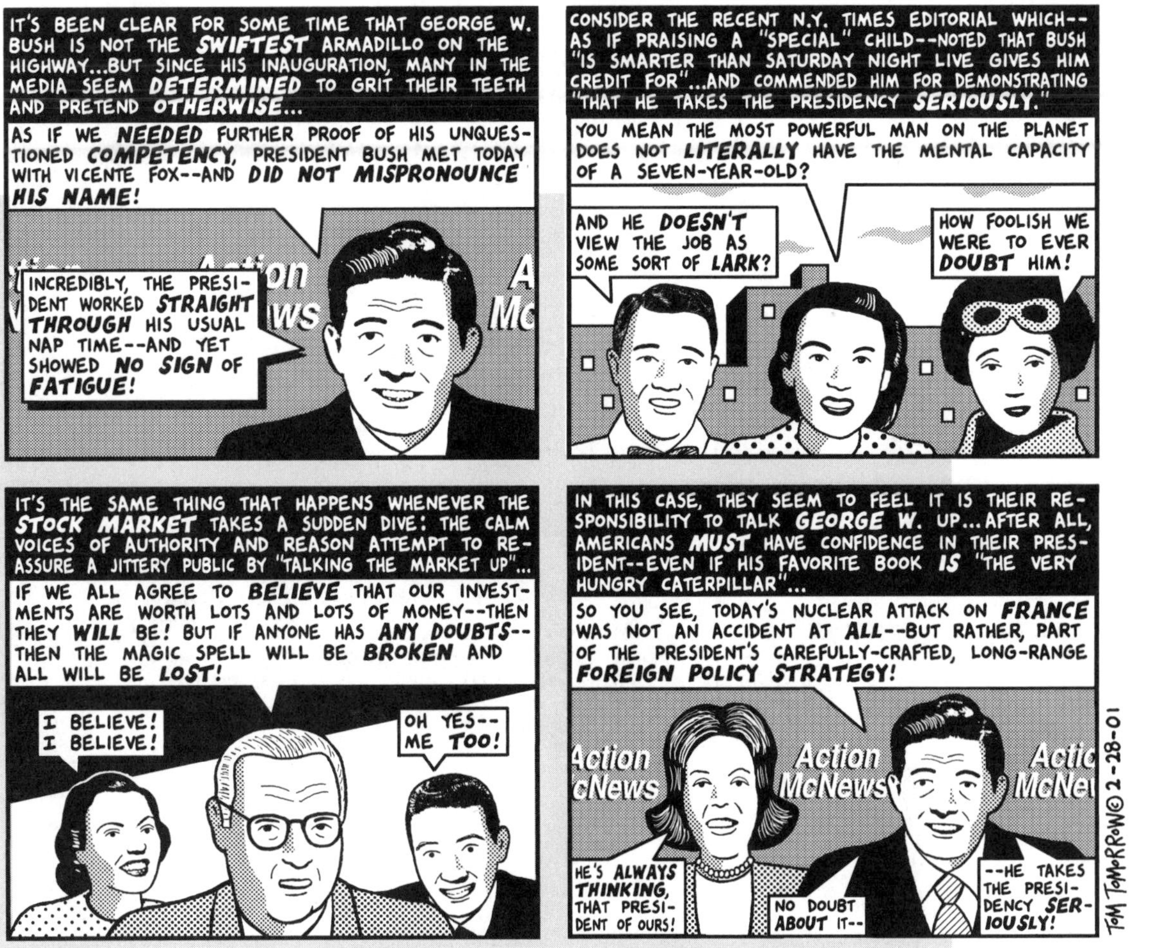
IT'S BEEN CLEAR FOR SOME TIME THAT GEORGE W. BUSH IS NOT THE SWIFTEST ARMADILLO ON THE HIGHWAY...BUT SINCE HIS INAUGURATION, MANY IN THE MEDIA SEEM DETERMINED TO GRIT THEIR TEETH AND PRETEND OTHERWISE...
AS IF WE NEEDED FURTHER PROOF OF HIS UNQUESTIONED COMPETENCY, PRESIDENT BUSH MET TODAY WITH VICENTE FOX--AND DID NOT MISPRONOUNCE HIS NAME!
INCREDIBLY, THE PRESIDENT WORKED STRAIGHT THROUGH HIS USUAL NAP TIME--AND YET SHOWED NO SIGN OF FATIGUE!
CONSIDER THE RECENT N.Y. TIMES EDITORIAL WHICH--AS IF PRAISING A "SPECIAL" CHILD--NOTED THAT BUSH "IS SMARTER THAN SATURDAY NIGHT LIVE GIVES HIM CREDIT FOR"...AND COMMENDED HIM FOR DEMONSTRATING "THAT HE TAKES THE PRESIDENCY SERIOUSLY."
YOU MEAN THE MOST POWERFUL MAN ON THE PLANET DOES NOT LITERALLY HAVE THE MENTAL CAPACITY OF A SEVEN-YEAR-OLD?
AND HE DOESN'T VIEW THE JOB AS SOME SORT OF LARK?
HOW FOOLISH WE WERE TO EVER DOUBT HIM!
IT'S THE SAME THING THAT HAPPENS WHENEVER THE STOCK MARKET TAKES A SUDDEN DIVE: THE CALM VOICES OF AUTHORITY AND REASON ATTEMPT TO REASSURE A JITTERY PUBLIC BY "TALKING THE MARKET UP"...
IF WE ALL AGREE TO BELIEVE THAT OUR INVESTMENTS ARE WORTH LOTS AND LOTS OF MONEY--THEN THEY WILL BE! BUT IF ANYONE HAS ANY DOUBTS--THEN THE MAGIC SPELL WILL BE BROKEN AND ALL WILL BE LOST!
I BELIEVE! I BELIEVE!
OH YES--ME TOO!
IN THIS CASE, THEY SEEM TO FEEL IT IS THEIR RESPONSIBILITY TO TALK GEORGE W. UP...AFTER ALL, AMERICANS MUST HAVE CONFIDENCE IN THEIR PRESIDENT--EVEN IF HIS FAVORITE BOOK IS "THE VERY HUNGRY CATERPILLAR"...
SO YOU SEE, TODAY'S NUCLEAR ATTACK ON FRANCE WAS NOT AN ACCIDENT AT ALL--BUT RATHER, PART OF THE PRESIDENT'S CAREFULLY-CRAFTED, LONG-RANGE FOREIGN POLICY STRATEGY!
Action McNews
HE'S ALWAYS THINKING, THAT PRESIDENT OF OURS!
NO DOUBT ABOUT IT--
--HE TAKES THE PRESIDENCY SERIOUSLY!
TOM TOMORROW© 2-28-01

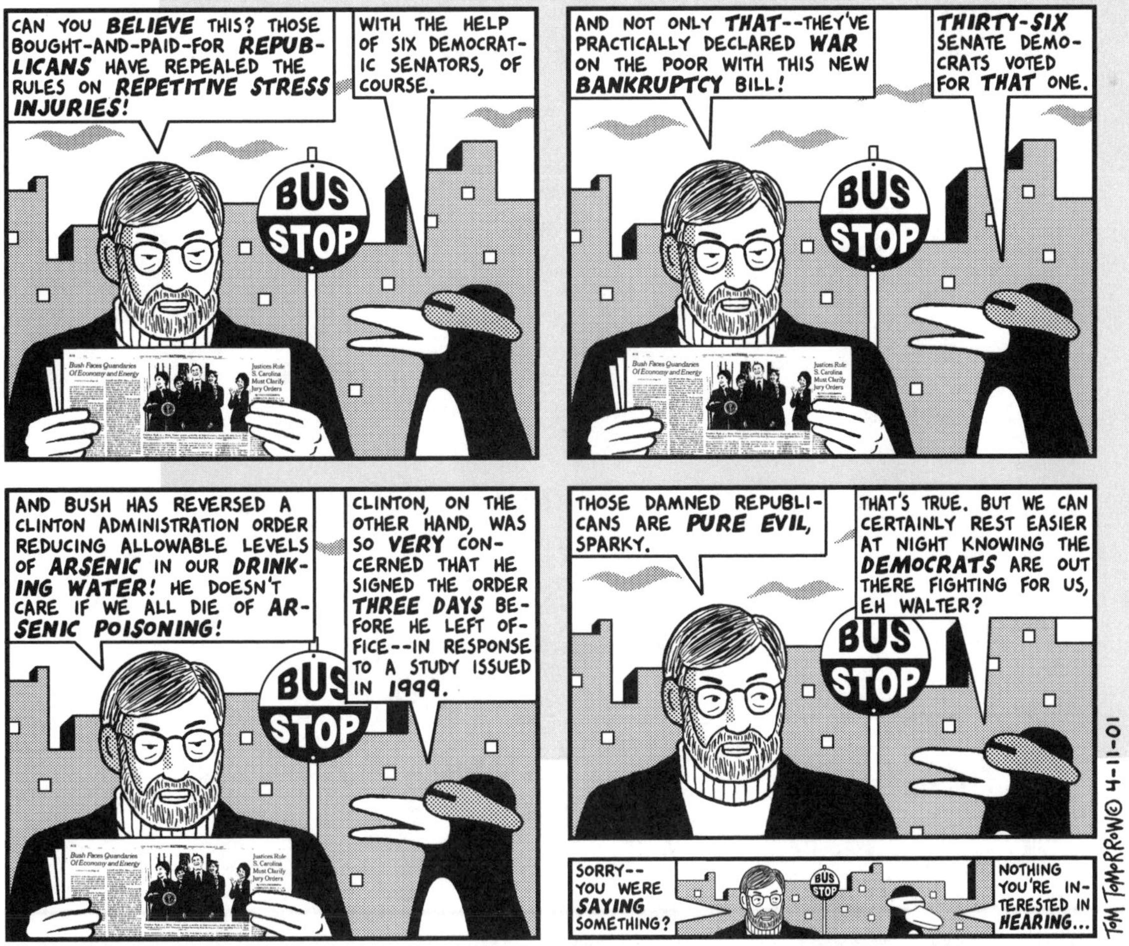
CAN YOU BELIEVE THIS? THOSE BOUGHT-AND-PAID-FOR REPUBLICANS HAVE REPEALED THE RULES ON REPETITIVE STRESS INJURIES!
WITH THE HELP OF SIX DEMOCRATIC SENATORS, OF COURSE.
BUS STOP
Bush Faces Quandaries Of Economy and Energy
Justices Rule S. Carolina Must Clarify Jury Orders
AND NOT ONLY THAT--THEY'VE PRACTICALLY DECLARED WAR ON THE POOR WITH THIS NEW BANKRUPTCY BILL!
THIRTY-SIX SENATE DEMOCRATS VOTED FOR THAT ONE.
BUS STOP
Bush Faces Quandaries Of Economy and Energy
Justices Rule S. Carolina Must Clarify Jury Orders
AND BUSH HAS REVERSED A CLINTON ADMINISTRATION ORDER REDUCING ALLOWABLE LEVELS OF ARSENIC IN OUR DRINKING WATER! HE DOESN'T CARE IF WE ALL DIE OF ARSENIC POISONING!
CLINTON, ON THE OTHER HAND, WAS SO VERY CONCERNED THAT HE SIGNED THE ORDER THREE DAYS BEFORE HE LEFT OFFICE--IN RESPONSE TO A STUDY ISSUED IN 1999.
BUS STOP
Bush Faces Quandaries Of Economy and Energy
Justices Rule S. Carolina Must Clarify Jury Orders
THOSE DAMNED REPUBLICANS ARE PURE EVIL, SPARKY.
THAT'S TRUE. BUT WE CAN CERTAINLY REST EASIER AT NIGHT KNOWING THE DEMOCRATS ARE OUT THERE FIGHTING FOR US, EH WALTER?
BUS STOP
SORRY--YOU WERE SAYING SOMETHING?
NOTHING YOU'RE INTERESTED IN HEARING...
TOM TOMORROW© 4-11-01

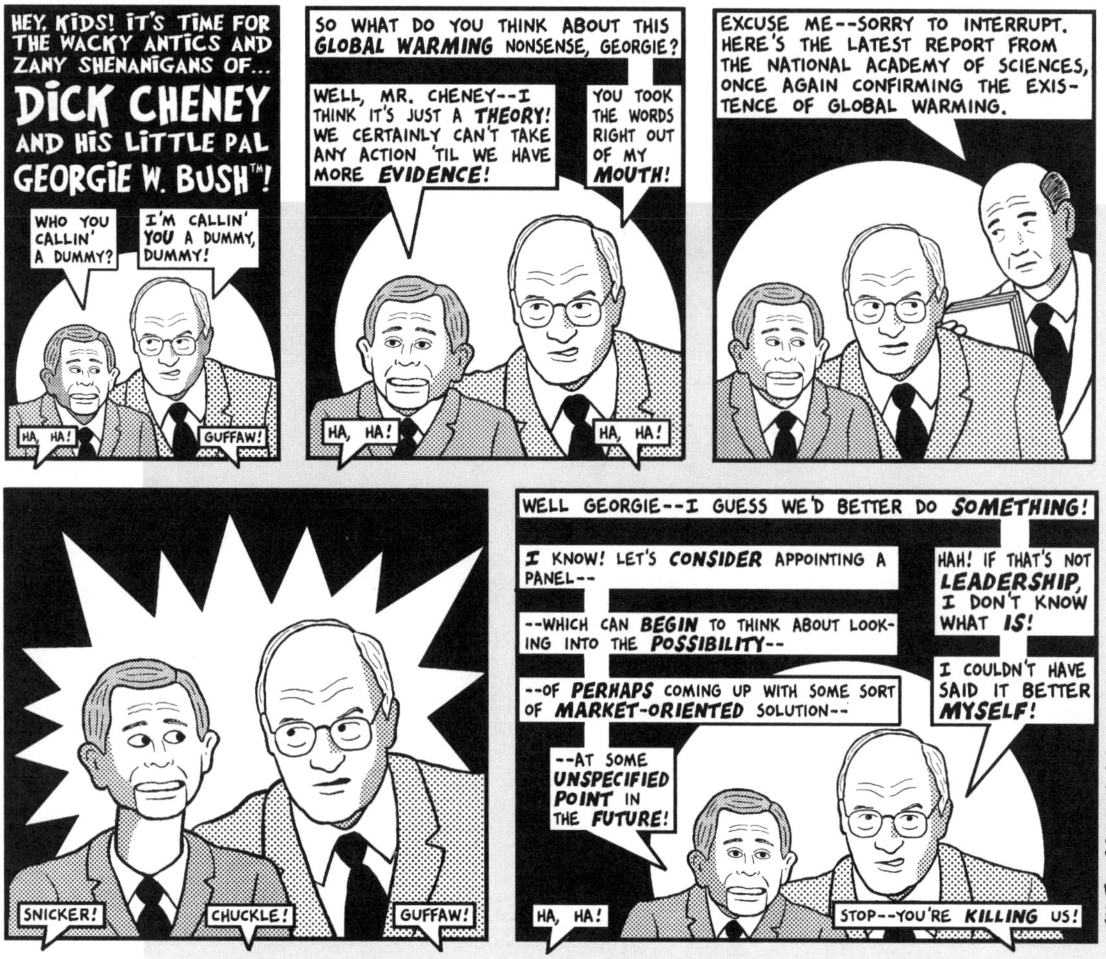
HEY, KIDS! IT'S TIME FOR THE WACKY ANTICS AND ZANY SHENANIGANS OF...
DICK CHENEY AND HIS LITTLE PAL GEORGIE W. BUSH™!
WHO YOU CALLIN' A DUMMY?
I'M CALLIN' YOU A DUMMY, DUMMY!
HA, HA!
GUFFAW!
SO WHAT DO YOU THINK ABOUT THIS GLOBAL WARMING NONSENSE, GEORGIE?
WELL, MR. CHENEY--I THINK IT'S JUST A THEORY! WE CERTAINLY CAN'T TAKE ANY ACTION 'TIL WE HAVE MORE EVIDENCE!
YOU TOOK THE WORDS RIGHT OUT OF MY MOUTH!
HA, HA!
HA, HA!
EXCUSE ME--SORRY TO INTERRUPT. HERE'S THE LATEST REPORT FROM THE NATIONAL ACADEMY OF SCIENCES, ONCE AGAIN CONFIRMING THE EXISTENCE OF GLOBAL WARMING.
SNICKER!
CHUCKLE!
GUFFAW!
WELL GEORGIE--I GUESS WE'D BETTER DO SOMETHING!
I KNOW! LET'S CONSIDER APPOINTING A PANEL--
--WHICH CAN BEGIN TO THINK ABOUT LOOKING INTO THE POSSIBILITY--
--OF PERHAPS COMING UP WITH SOME SORT OF MARKET-ORIENTED SOLUTION--
--AT SOME UNSPECIFIED POINT IN THE FUTURE!
HAH! IF THAT'S NOT LEADERSHIP, I DON'T KNOW WHAT IS!
I COULDN'T HAVE SAID IT BETTER MYSELF!
HA, HA!
STOP--YOU'RE KILLING US!
TOM TOMORROW©6-20-01

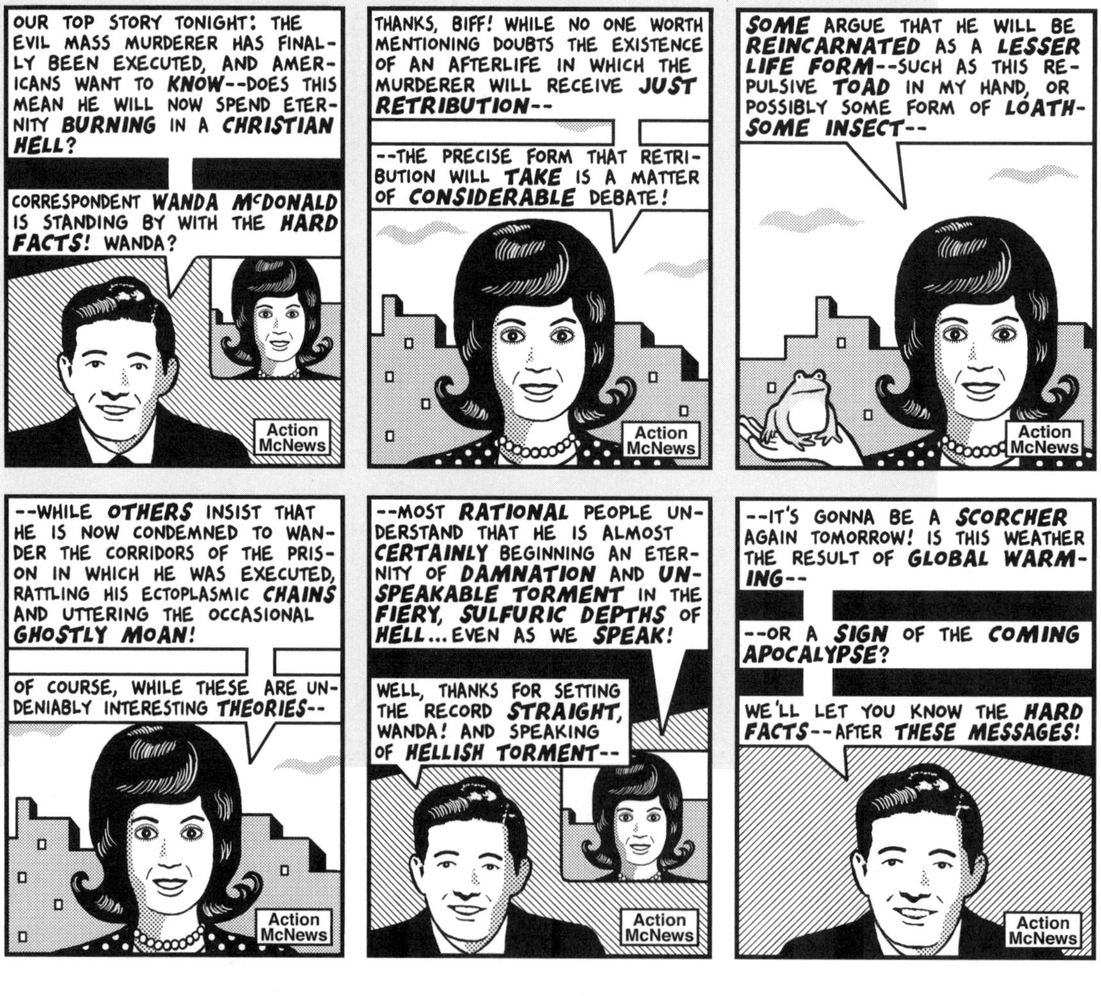
OUR TOP STORY TONIGHT: THE EVIL MASS MURDERER HAS FINALLY BEEN EXECUTED, AND AMERICANS WANT TO KNOW--DOES THIS MEAN HE WILL NOW SPEND ETERNITY BURNING IN A CHRISTIAN HELL?
CORRESPONDENT WANDA McDONALD IS STANDING BY WITH THE HARD FACTS! WANDA?
Action McNews
THANKS, BIFF! WHILE NO ONE WORTH MENTIONING DOUBTS THE EXISTENCE OF AN AFTERLIFE IN WHICH THE MURDERER WILL RECEIVE JUST RETRIBUTION--
--THE PRECISE FORM THAT RETRIBUTION WILL TAKE IS A MATTER OF CONSIDERABLE DEBATE!
Action McNews
SOME ARGUE THAT HE WILL BE REINCARNATED AS A LESSER LIFE FORM--SUCH AS THIS REPULSIVE TOAD IN MY HAND, OR POSSIBLY SOME FORM OF LOATHSOME INSECT--
Action McNews
--WHILE OTHERS INSIST THAT HE IS NOW CONDEMNED TO WANDER THE CORRIDORS OF THE PRISON IN WHICH HE WAS EXECUTED, RATTLING HIS ECTOPLASMIC CHAINS AND UTTERING THE OCCASIONAL GHOSTLY MOAN!
OF COURSE, WHILE THESE ARE UNDENIABLY INTERESTING THEORIES--
Action McNews
--MOST RATIONAL PEOPLE UNDERSTAND THAT HE IS ALMOST CERTAINLY BEGINNING AN ETERNITY OF DAMNATION AND UNSPEAKABLE TORMENT IN THE FIERY, SULFURIC DEPTHS OF HELL... EVEN AS WE SPEAK!
WELL, THANKS FOR SETTING THE RECORD STRAIGHT, WANDA! AND SPEAKING OF HELLISH TORMENT--
Action McNews
--IT'S GONNA BE A SCORCHER AGAIN TOMORROW! IS THIS WEATHER THE RESULT OF GLOBAL WARMING--
--OR A SIGN OF THE COMING APOCALYPSE?
WE'LL LET YOU KNOW THE HARD FACTS--AFTER THESE MESSAGES!
Action McNews
TOM TOMORROW©6-27-01

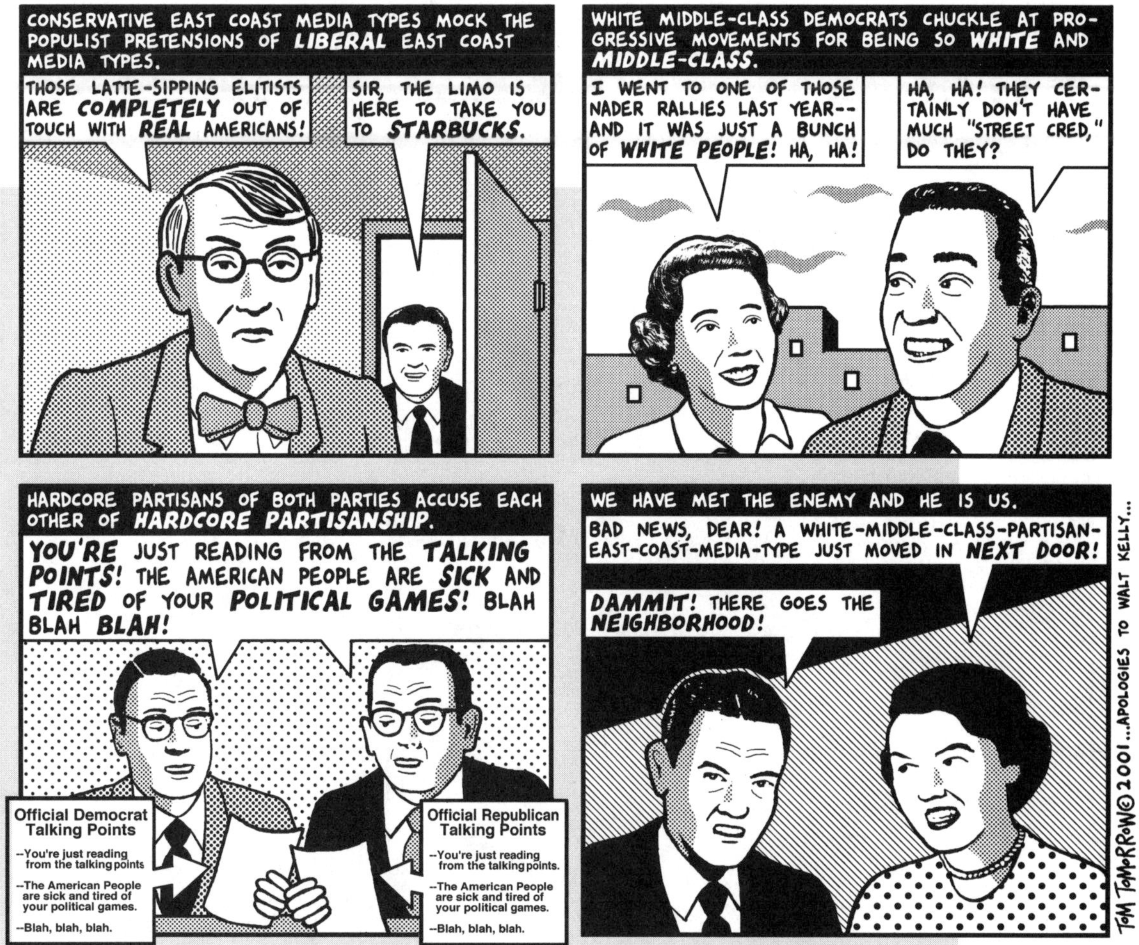
CONSERVATIVE EAST COAST MEDIA TYPES MOCK THE POPULIST PRETENSIONS OF LIBERAL EAST COAST MEDIA TYPES.
THOSE LATTE-SIPPING ELITISTS ARE COMPLETELY OUT OF TOUCH WITH REAL AMERICANS!
SIR, THE LIMO IS HERE TO TAKE YOU TO STARBUCKS.
WHITE MIDDLE-CLASS DEMOCRATS CHUCKLE AT PROGRESSIVE MOVEMENTS FOR BEING SO WHITE AND MIDDLE-CLASS.
I WENT TO ONE OF THOSE NADER RALLIES LAST YEAR--AND IT WAS JUST A BUNCH OF WHITE PEOPLE! HA, HA!
HA, HA! THEY CERTAINLY DON'T HAVE MUCH "STREET CRED," DO THEY?
HARDCORE PARTISANS OF BOTH PARTIES ACCUSE EACH OTHER OF HARDCORE PARTISANSHIP.
YOU'RE JUST READING FROM THE TALKING POINTS! THE AMERICAN PEOPLE ARE SICK AND TIRED OF YOUR POLITICAL GAMES! BLAH BLAH BLAH!
Official Democrat Talking Points
--You're just reading from the talking points
--The American People are sick and tired of your political games.
--Blah, blah, blah.
Official Republican Talking Points
--You're just reading from the talking points.
--The American People are sick and tired of your political games.
--Blah, blah, blah.
WE HAVE MET THE ENEMY AND HE IS US.
BAD NEWS, DEAR! A WHITE-MIDDLE-CLASS-PARTISAN-EAST-COAST-MEDIA-TYPE JUST MOVED IN NEXT DOOR!
DAMMIT! THERE GOES THE NEIGHBORHOOD!
TOM TOMORROW© 2001 ...APOLOGIES TO WALT KELLY...

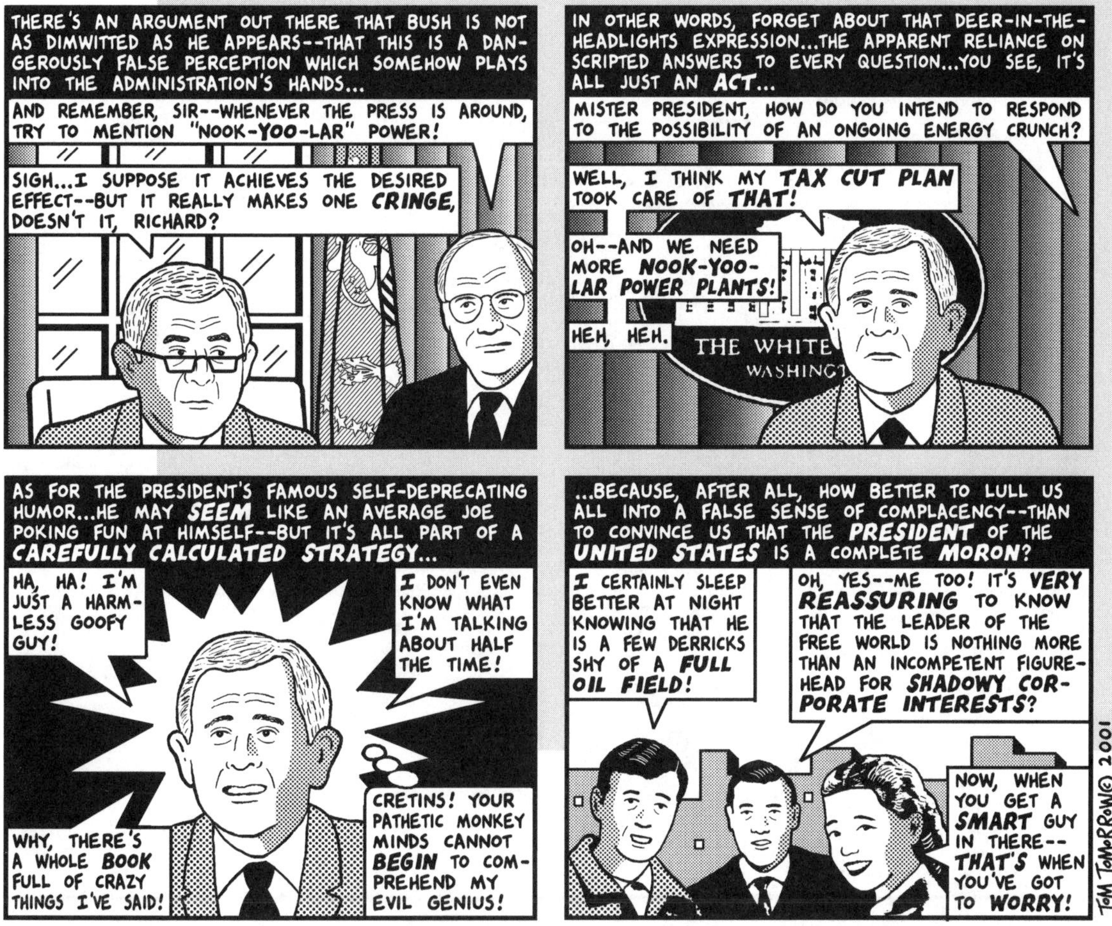
THERE'S AN ARGUMENT OUT THERE THAT BUSH IS NOT AS DIMWITTED AS HE APPEARS--THAT THIS IS A DANGEROUSLY FALSE PERCEPTION WHICH SOMEHOW PLAYS INTO THE ADMINISTRATION'S HANDS...
AND REMEMBER, SIR--WHENEVER THE PRESS IS AROUND, TRY TO MENTION "NOOK-YOO-LAR" POWER!
SIGH...I SUPPOSE IT ACHIEVES THE DESIRED EFFECT--BUT IT REALLY MAKES ONE CRINGE, DOESN'T IT, RICHARD?
IN OTHER WORDS, FORGET ABOUT THAT DEER-IN-THE-HEADLIGHTS EXPRESSION...THE APPARENT RELIANCE ON SCRIPTED ANSWERS TO EVERY QUESTION...YOU SEE, IT'S ALL JUST AN ACT...
MISTER PRESIDENT, HOW DO YOU INTEND TO RESPOND TO THE POSSIBILITY OF AN ONGOING ENERGY CRUNCH?
WELL, I THINK MY TAX CUT PLAN TOOK CARE OF THAT!
OH--AND WE NEED MORE NOOK-YOO-LAR POWER PLANTS!
HEH, HEH.
THE WHITE
WASHINGT
AS FOR THE PRESIDENT'S FAMOUS SELF-DEPRECATING HUMOR...HE MAY SEEM LIKE AN AVERAGE JOE POKING FUN AT HIMSELF--BUT IT'S ALL PART OF A CAREFULLY CALCULATED STRATEGY...
HA, HA! I'M JUST A HARMLESS GOOFY GUY!
I DON'T EVEN KNOW WHAT I'M TALKING ABOUT HALF THE TIME!
WHY, THERE'S A WHOLE BOOK FULL OF CRAZY THINGS I'VE SAID!
CRETINS! YOUR PATHETIC MONKEY MINDS CANNOT BEGIN TO COMPREHEND MY EVIL GENIUS!
...BECAUSE, AFTER ALL, HOW BETTER TO LULL US ALL INTO A FALSE SENSE OF COMPLACENCY--THAN TO CONVINCE US THAT THE PRESIDENT OF THE UNITED STATES IS A COMPLETE MORON?
I CERTAINLY SLEEP BETTER AT NIGHT KNOWING THAT HE IS A FEW DERRICKS SHY OF A FULL OIL FIELD!
OH, YES--ME TOO! IT'S VERY REASSURING TO KNOW THAT THE LEADER OF THE FREE WORLD IS NOTHING MORE THAN AN INCOMPETENT FIGUREHEAD FOR SHADOWY CORPORATE INTERESTS?
NOW, WHEN YOU GET A SMART GUY IN THERE--THAT'S WHEN YOU'VE GOT TO WORRY!
TOM TOMORROW© 2001

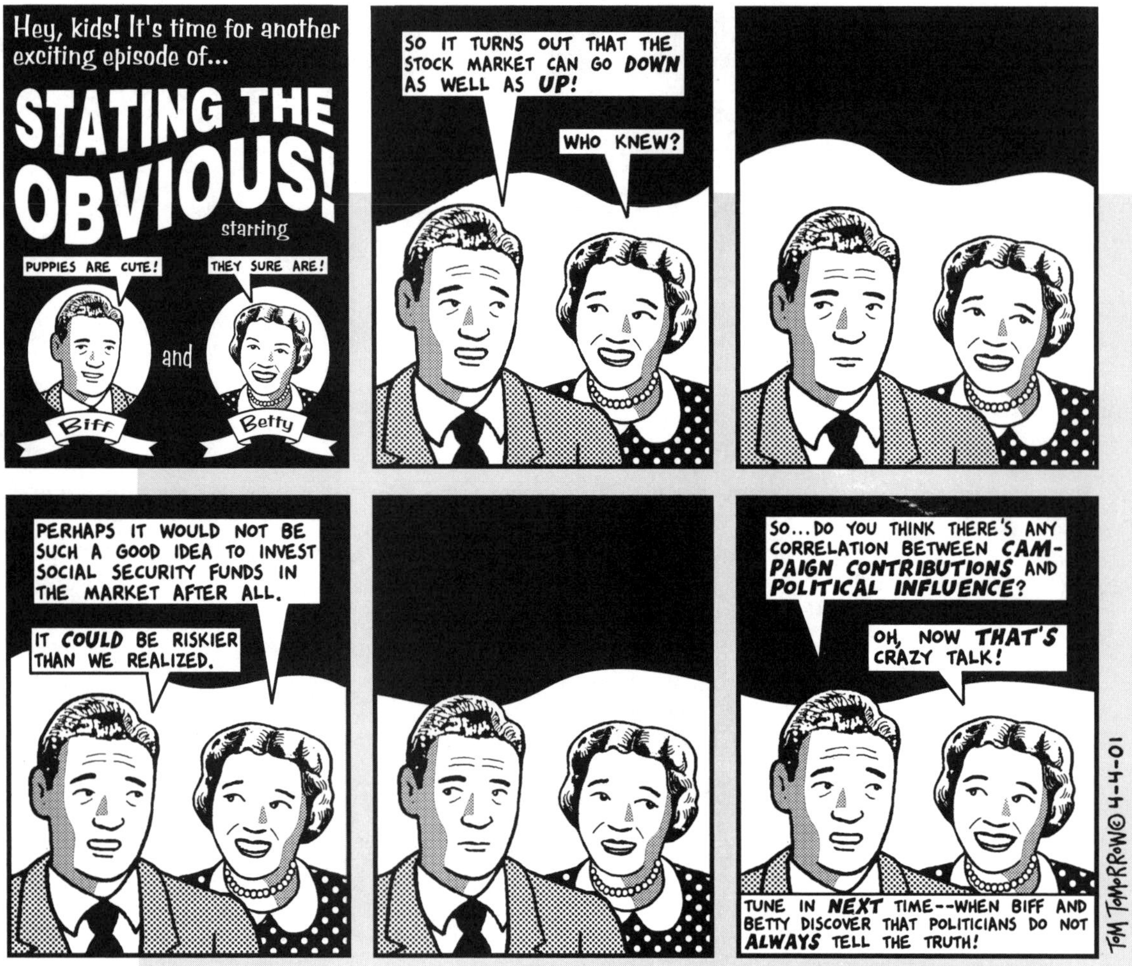
Hey, kids! It's time for another exciting episode of...
STATING THE OBVIOUS!
starring
PUPPIES ARE CUTE!
THEY SURE ARE!
Biff
and
Betty
SO IT TURNS OUT THAT THE STOCK MARKET CAN GO DOWN AS WELL AS UP!
WHO KNEW?
PERHAPS IT WOULD NOT BE SUCH A GOOD IDEA TO INVEST SOCIAL SECURITY FUNDS IN THE MARKET AFTER ALL.
IT COULD BE RISKIER THAN WE REALIZED.
SO... DO YOU THINK THERE'S ANY CORRELATION BETWEEN CAMPAIGN CONTRIBUTIONS AND POLITICAL INFLUENCE?
OH, NOW THAT'S CRAZY TALK!
TUNE IN NEXT TIME--WHEN BIFF AND BETTY DISCOVER THAT POLITICIANS DO NOT ALWAYS TELL THE TRUTH!
TOM TOMORROW© 4-4-01

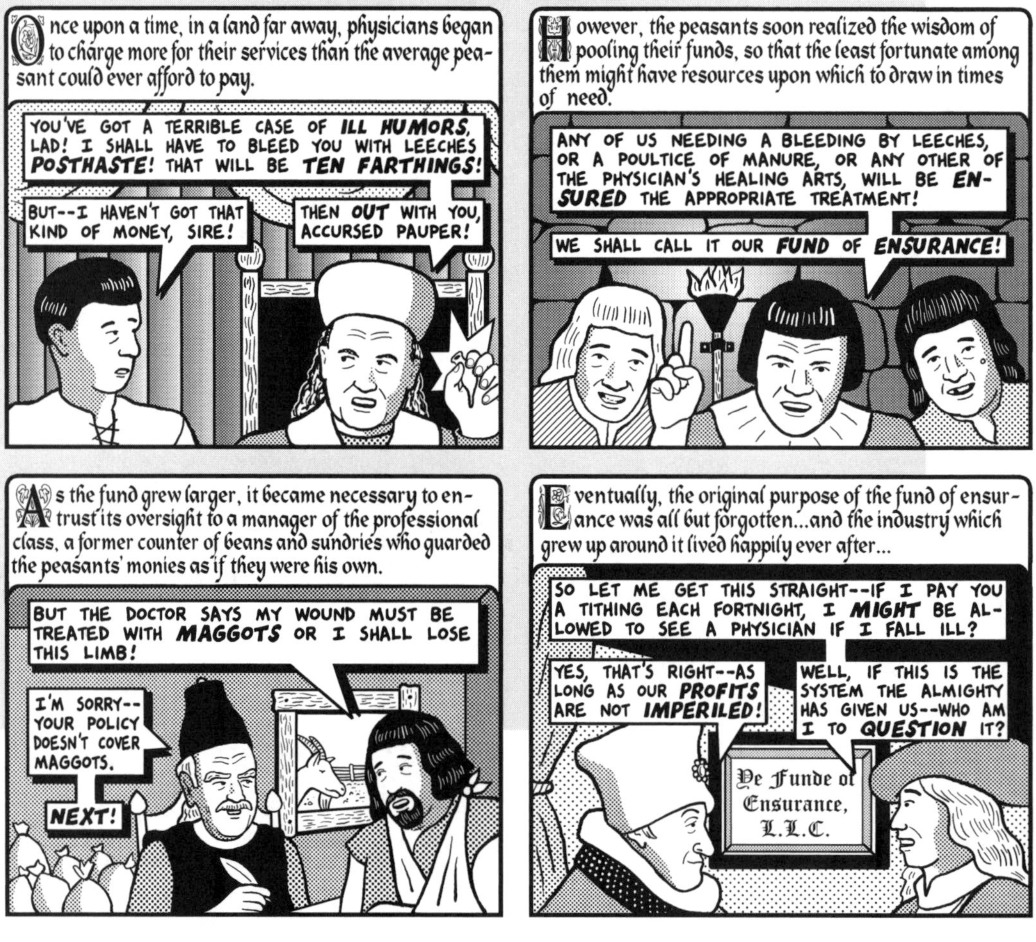
Once upon a time, in a land far away, physicians began to charge more for their services than the average peasant could ever afford to pay.
YOU'VE GOT A TERRIBLE CASE OF ILL HUMORS, LAD! I SHALL HAVE TO BLEED YOU WITH LEECHES POSTHASTE! THAT WILL BE TEN FARTHINGS!
BUT--I HAVEN'T GOT THAT KIND OF MONEY, SIRE!
THEN OUT WITH YOU, ACCURSED PAUPER!
However, the peasants soon realized the wisdom of pooling their funds, so that the least fortunate among them might have resources upon which to draw in times of need.
ANY OF US NEEDING A BLEEDING BY LEECHES, OR A POULTICE OF MANURE, OR ANY OTHER OF THE PHYSICIAN'S HEALING ARTS, WILL BE ENSURED THE APPROPRIATE TREATMENT!
WE SHALL CALL IT OUR FUND OF ENSURANCE!
As the fund grew larger, it became necessary to entrust its oversight to a manager of the professional class, a former counter of beans and sundries who guarded the peasants' monies as if they were his own.
BUT THE DOCTOR SAYS MY WOUND MUST BE TREATED WITH MAGGOTS OR I SHALL LOSE THIS LIMB!
I'M SORRY--YOUR POLICY DOESN'T COVER MAGGOTS.
NEXT!
Eventually, the original purpose of the fund of ensurance was all but forgotten...and the industry which grew up around it lived happily ever after...
SO LET ME GET THIS STRAIGHT--IF I PAY YOU A TITHING EACH FORTNIGHT, I MIGHT BE ALLOWED TO SEE A PHYSICIAN IF I FALL ILL?
YES, THAT'S RIGHT--AS LONG AS OUR PROFITS ARE NOT IMPERILED!
WELL, IF THIS IS THE SYSTEM THE ALMIGHTY HAS GIVEN US--WHO AM I TO QUESTION IT?
Ye Funde of Ensurance, L.L.C.
TOM TOMORROW©7-4-01

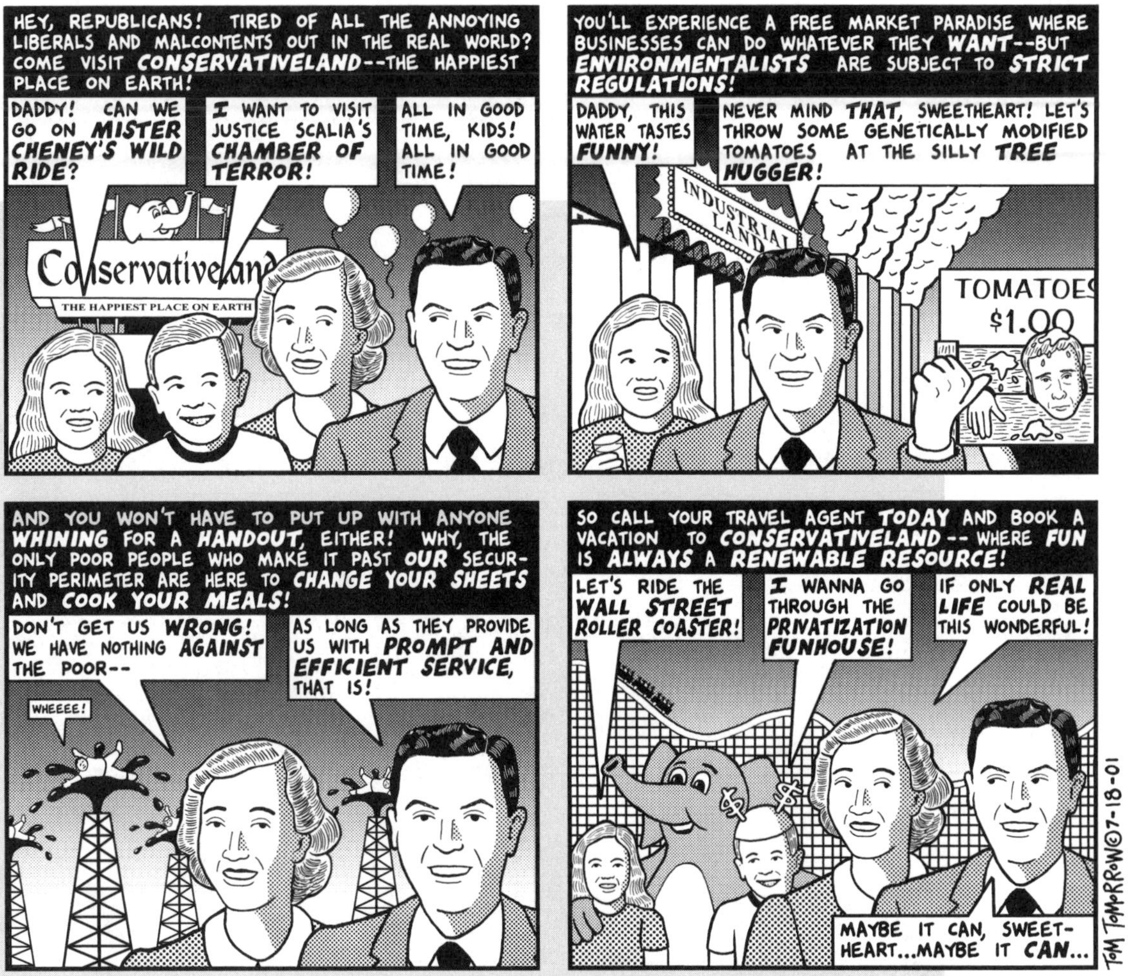
HEY, REPUBLICANS! TIRED OF ALL THE ANNOYING LIBERALS AND MALCONTENTS OUT IN THE REAL WORLD? COME VISIT CONSERVATIVELAND--THE HAPPIEST PLACE ON EARTH!
DADDY! CAN WE GO ON MISTER CHENEY'S WILD RIDE?
I WANT TO VISIT JUSTICE SCALIA'S CHAMBER OF TERROR!
ALL IN GOOD TIME, KIDS! ALL IN GOOD TIME!
Conservativeland
THE HAPPIEST PLACE ON EARTH
YOU'LL EXPERIENCE A FREE MARKET PARADISE WHERE BUSINESSES CAN DO WHATEVER THEY WANT--BUT ENVIRONMENTALISTS ARE SUBJECT TO STRICT REGULATIONS!
DADDY, THIS WATER TASTES FUNNY!
NEVER MIND THAT, SWEETHEART! LET'S THROW SOME GENETICALLY MODIFIED TOMATOES AT THE SILLY TREE HUGGER!
INDUSTRIAL LAND
TOMATOES $1.00
AND YOU WON'T HAVE TO PUT UP WITH ANYONE WHINING FOR A HANDOUT, EITHER! WHY, THE ONLY POOR PEOPLE WHO MAKE IT PAST OUR SECURITY PERIMETER ARE HERE TO CHANGE YOUR SHEETS AND COOK YOUR MEALS!
DON'T GET US WRONG! WE HAVE NOTHING AGAINST THE POOR--
AS LONG AS THEY PROVIDE US WITH PROMPT AND EFFICIENT SERVICE, THAT IS!
WHEEEE!
SO CALL YOUR TRAVEL AGENT TODAY AND BOOK A VACATION TO CONSERVATIVELAND--WHERE FUN IS ALWAYS A RENEWABLE RESOURCE!
LET'S RIDE THE WALL STREET ROLLER COASTER!
I WANNA GO THROUGH THE PRIVATIZATION FUNHOUSE!
IF ONLY REAL LIFE COULD BE THIS WONDERFUL!
MAYBE IT CAN, SWEETHEART...MAYBE IT CAN...
TOM TOMORROW©7-18-01

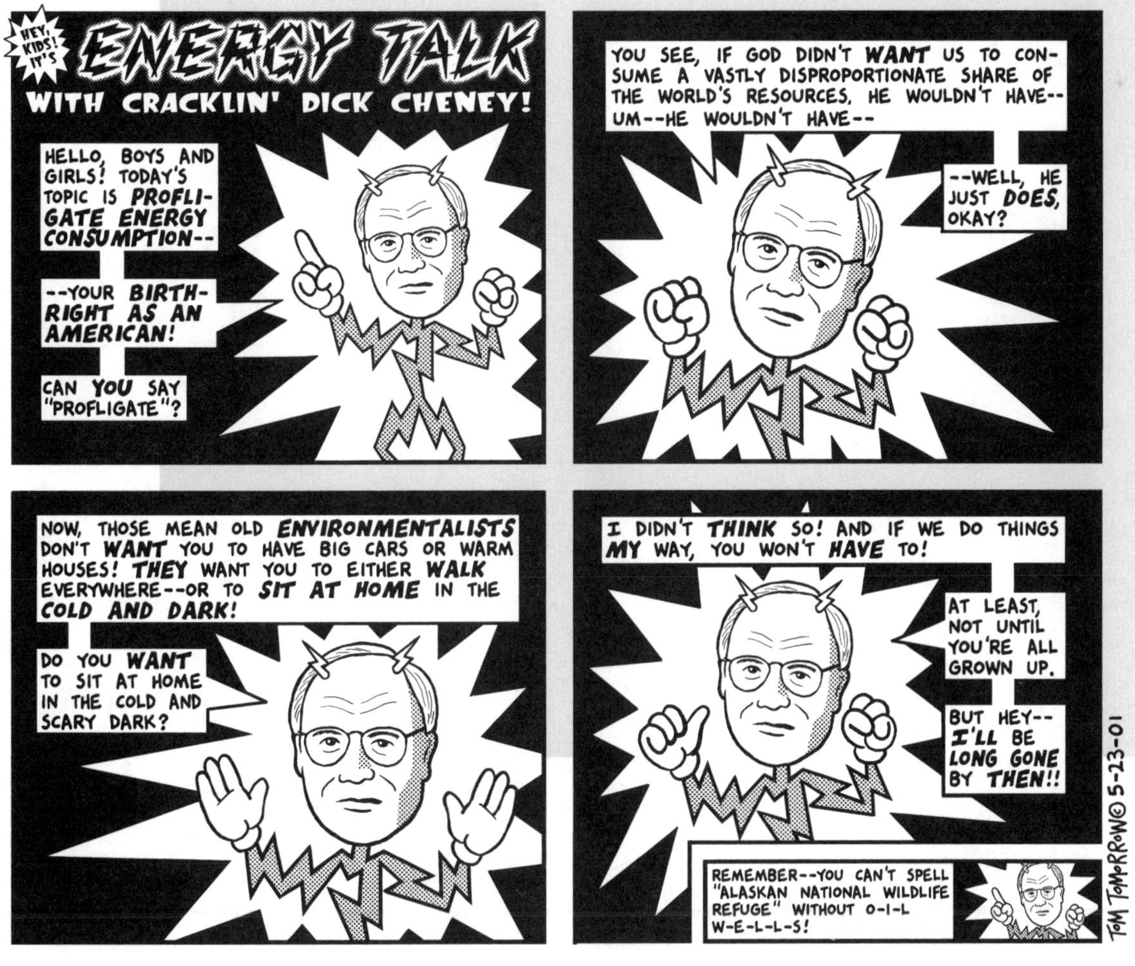
HEY, KIDS! IT'S
ENERGY TALK
WITH CRACKLIN' DICK CHENEY!
HELLO, BOYS AND GIRLS! TODAY'S TOPIC IS PROFLIGATE ENERGY CONSUMPTION--
--YOUR BIRTHRIGHT AS AN AMERICAN!
CAN YOU SAY "PROFLIGATE"?
YOU SEE, IF GOD DIDN'T WANT US TO CONSUME A VASTLY DISPROPORTIONATE SHARE OF THE WORLD'S RESOURCES, HE WOULDN'T HAVE--UM--HE WOULDN'T HAVE--
--WELL, HE JUST DOES, OKAY?
NOW, THOSE MEAN OLD ENVIRONMENTALISTS DON'T WANT YOU TO HAVE BIG CARS OR WARM HOUSES! THEY WANT YOU TO EITHER WALK EVERYWHERE--OR TO SIT AT HOME IN THE COLD AND DARK!
DO YOU WANT TO SIT AT HOME IN THE COLD AND SCARY DARK?
I DIDN'T THINK SO! AND IF WE DO THINGS MY WAY, YOU WON'T HAVE TO!
AT LEAST, NOT UNTIL YOU'RE ALL GROWN UP.
BUT HEY--I'LL BE LONG GONE BY THEN!!
REMEMBER--YOU CAN'T SPELL "ALASKAN NATIONAL WILDLIFE REFUGE" WITHOUT O-I-L W-E-L-L-S!
TOM TOMORROW© 5-23-01

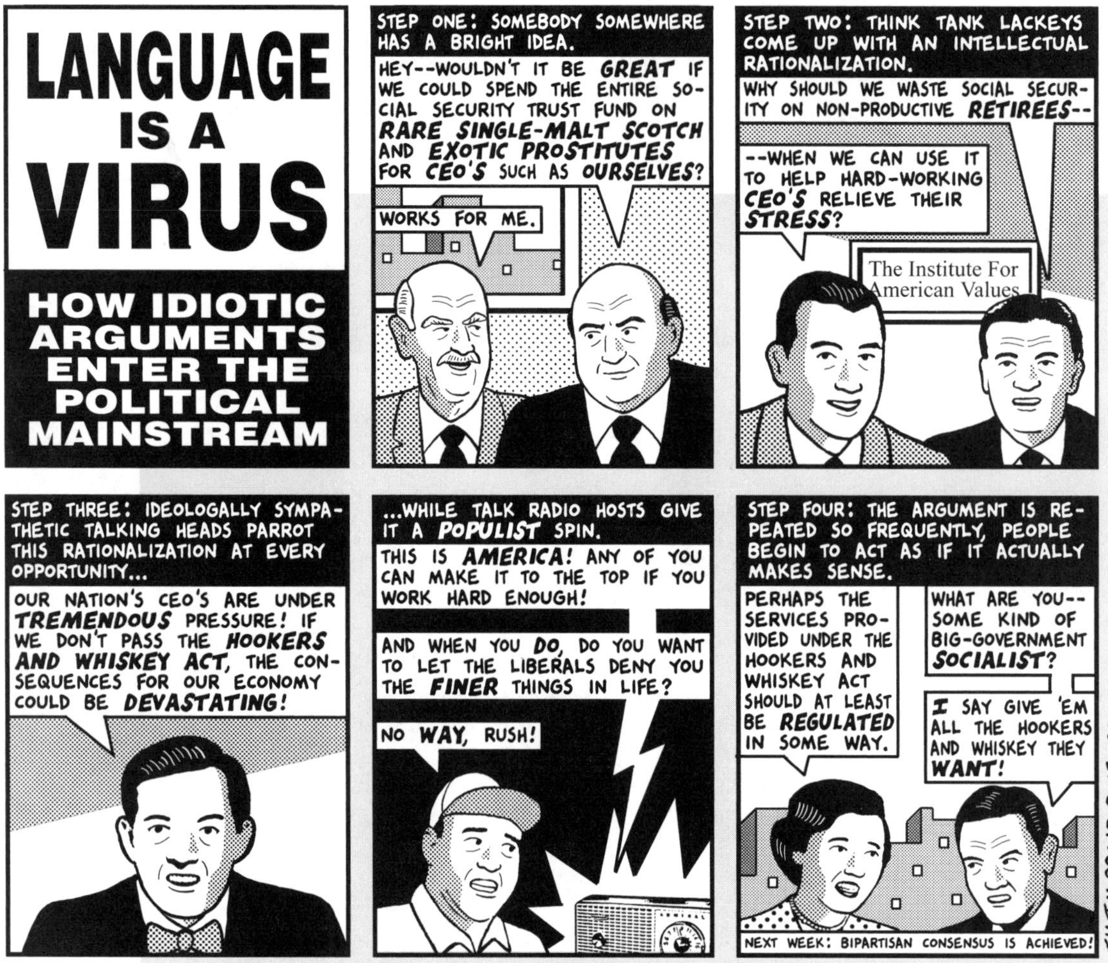
LANGUAGE IS A VIRUS
HOW IDIOTIC ARGUMENTS ENTER THE POLITICAL MAINSTREAM
STEP ONE: SOMEBODY SOMEWHERE HAS A BRIGHT IDEA.
HEY--WOULDN'T IT BE GREAT IF WE COULD SPEND THE ENTIRE SOCIAL SECURITY TRUST FUND ON RARE SINGLE-MALT SCOTCH AND EXOTIC PROSTITUTES FOR CEO'S SUCH AS OURSELVES?
WORKS FOR ME.
STEP TWO: THINK TANK LACKEYS COME UP WITH AN INTELLECTUAL RATIONALIZATION.
WHY SHOULD WE WASTE SOCIAL SECURITY ON NON-PRODUCTIVE RETIREES--
--WHEN WE CAN USE IT TO HELP HARD-WORKING CEO'S RELIEVE THEIR STRESS?
The Institute For American Values
STEP THREE: IDEOLOGALLY SYMPATHETIC TALKING HEADS PARROT THIS RATIONALIZATION AT EVERY OPPORTUNITY...
OUR NATION'S CEO'S ARE UNDER TREMENDOUS PRESSURE! IF WE DON'T PASS THE HOOKERS AND WHISKEY ACT, THE CONSEQUENCES FOR OUR ECONOMY COULD BE DEVASTATING!
...WHILE TALK RADIO HOSTS GIVE IT A POPULIST SPIN.
THIS IS AMERICA! ANY OF YOU CAN MAKE IT TO THE TOP IF YOU WORK HARD ENOUGH!
AND WHEN YOU DO, DO YOU WANT TO LET THE LIBERALS DENY YOU THE FINER THINGS IN LIFE?
NO WAY, RUSH!
STEP FOUR: THE ARGUMENT IS REPEATED SO FREQUENTLY, PEOPLE BEGIN TO ACT AS IF IT ACTUALLY MAKES SENSE.
PERHAPS THE SERVICES PROVIDED UNDER THE HOOKERS AND WHISKEY ACT SHOULD AT LEAST BE REGULATED IN SOME WAY.
WHAT ARE YOU--SOME KIND OF BIG-GOVERNMENT SOCIALIST?
I SAY GIVE 'EM ALL THE HOOKERS AND WHISKEY THEY WANT!
NEXT WEEK: BIPARTISAN CONSENSUS IS ACHIEVED!
TOM TOMORROW© 8-15-01

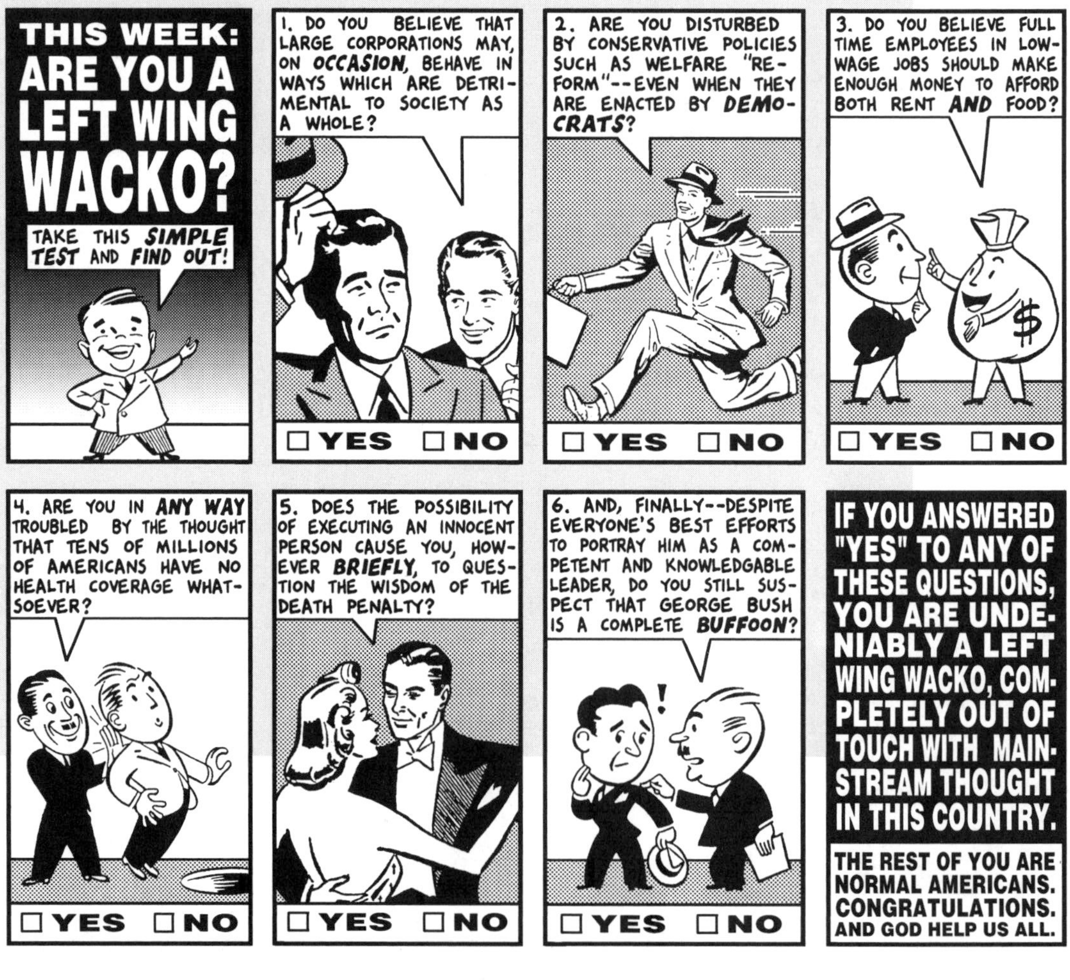
THIS WEEK: ARE YOU A LEFT WING WACKO?
TAKE THIS SIMPLE TEST AND FIND OUT!
1. DO YOU BELIEVE THAT LARGE CORPORATIONS MAY, ON OCCASION, BEHAVE IN WAYS WHICH ARE DETRIMENTAL TO SOCIETY AS A WHOLE?
☐YES ☐NO
2. ARE YOU DISTURBED BY CONSERVATIVE POLICIES SUCH AS WELFARE "REFORM"--EVEN WHEN THEY ARE ENACTED BY DEMOCRATS?
☐YES ☐NO
3. DO YOU BELIEVE FULL TIME EMPLOYEES IN LOW-WAGE JOBS SHOULD MAKE ENOUGH MONEY TO AFFORD BOTH RENT AND FOOD?
☐YES ☐NO
4. ARE YOU IN ANY WAY TROUBLED BY THE THOUGHT THAT TENS OF MILLIONS OF AMERICANS HAVE NO HEALTH COVERAGE WHATSOEVER?
☐YES ☐NO
5. DOES THE POSSIBILITY OF EXECUTING AN INNOCENT PERSON CAUSE YOU, HOWEVER BRIEFLY, TO QUESTION THE WISDOM OF THE DEATH PENALTY?
☐YES ☐NO
6. AND, FINALLY--DESPITE EVERYONE'S BEST EFFORTS TO PORTRAY HIM AS A COMPETENT AND KNOWLEDGABLE LEADER, DO YOU STILL SUSPECT THAT GEORGE BUSH IS A COMPLETE BUFFOON?
☐YES ☐NO
IF YOU ANSWERED "YES" TO ANY OF THESE QUESTIONS, YOU ARE UNDENIABLY A LEFT WING WACKO, COMPLETELY OUT OF TOUCH WITH MAINSTREAM THOUGHT IN THIS COUNTRY.
THE REST OF YOU ARE NORMAL AMERICANS. CONGRATULATIONS. AND GOD HELP US ALL.
TOM TOMORROW© 8-8-01

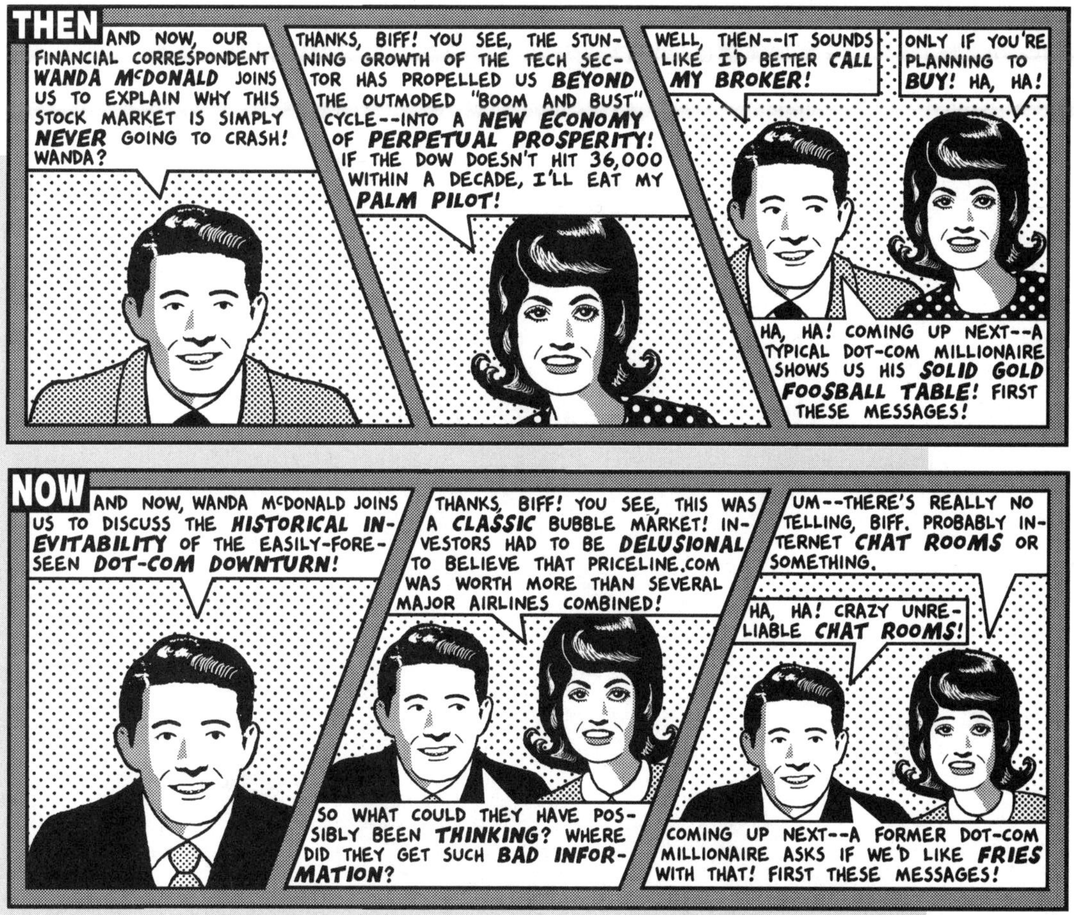
THEN
AND NOW, OUR FINANCIAL CORRESPONDENT WANDA McDONALD JOINS US TO EXPLAIN WHY THIS STOCK MARKET IS SIMPLY NEVER GOING TO CRASH! WANDA?
THANKS, BIFF! YOU SEE, THE STUNNING GROWTH OF THE TECH SECTOR HAS PROPELLED US BEYOND THE OUTMODED "BOOM AND BUST" CYCLE--INTO A NEW ECONOMY OF PERPETUAL PROSPERITY! IF THE DOW DOESN'T HIT 36,000 WITHIN A DECADE, I'LL EAT MY PALM PILOT!
WELL, THEN--IT SOUNDS LIKE I'D BETTER CALL MY BROKER!
ONLY IF YOU'RE PLANNING TO BUY! HA, HA!
HA, HA! COMING UP NEXT--A TYPICAL DOT-COM MILLIONAIRE SHOWS US HIS SOLID GOLD FOOSBALL TABLE! FIRST THESE MESSAGES!
NOW
AND NOW, WANDA McDONALD JOINS US TO DISCUSS THE HISTORICAL INEVITABILITY OF THE EASILY-FORESEEN DOT-COM DOWNTURN!
THANKS, BIFF! YOU SEE, THIS WAS A CLASSIC BUBBLE MARKET! INVESTORS HAD TO BE DELUSIONAL TO BELIEVE THAT PRICELINE.COM WAS WORTH MORE THAN SEVERAL MAJOR AIRLINES COMBINED!
SO WHAT COULD THEY HAVE POSSIBLY BEEN THINKING? WHERE DID THEY GET SUCH BAD INFORMATION?
UM--THERE'S REALLY NO TELLING, BIFF. PROBABLY INTERNET CHAT ROOMS OR SOMETHING.
HA, HA! CRAZY UNRELIABLE CHAT ROOMS!
COMING UP NEXT--A FORMER DOT-COM MILLIONAIRE ASKS IF WE'D LIKE FRIES WITH THAT! FIRST THESE MESSAGES!

A piece for *The New York Times* op-ed page. The humor-impaired editors didn't understand the final punchline—I kid you not—and I had to change it to something like "a former dot-com millionaire shows us the deep fat fryer at his *new* job!"

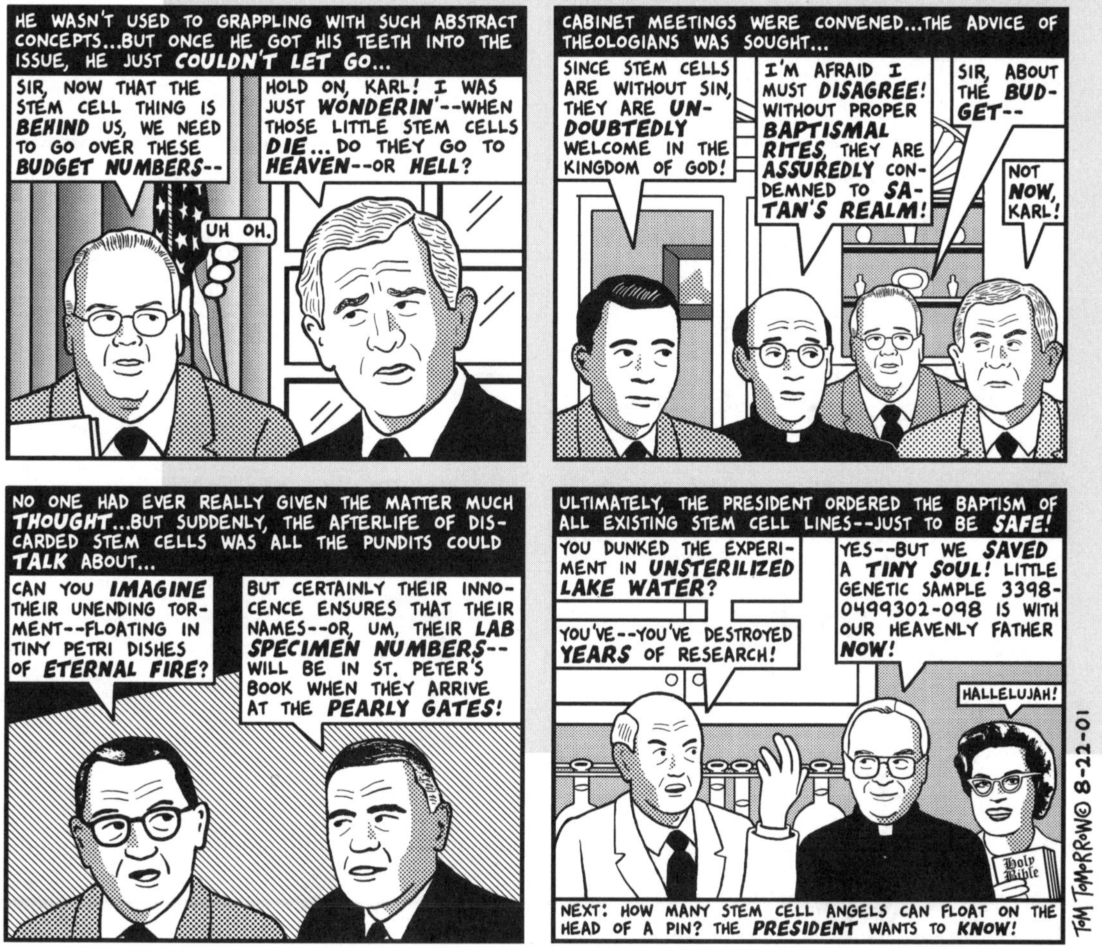
HE WASN'T USED TO GRAPPLING WITH SUCH ABSTRACT CONCEPTS...BUT ONCE HE GOT HIS TEETH INTO THE ISSUE, HE JUST COULDN'T LET GO...
SIR, NOW THAT THE STEM CELL THING IS BEHIND US, WE NEED TO GO OVER THESE BUDGET NUMBERS--
HOLD ON, KARL! I WAS JUST WONDERIN'--WHEN THOSE LITTLE STEM CELLS DIE... DO THEY GO TO HEAVEN--OR HELL?
UH OH.
CABINET MEETINGS WERE CONVENED...THE ADVICE OF THEOLOGIANS WAS SOUGHT...
SINCE STEM CELLS ARE WITHOUT SIN, THEY ARE UNDOUBTEDLY WELCOME IN THE KINGDOM OF GOD!
I'M AFRAID I MUST DISAGREE! WITHOUT PROPER BAPTISMAL RITES, THEY ARE ASSUREDLY CONDEMNED TO SATAN'S REALM!
SIR, ABOUT THE BUDGET--
NOT NOW, KARL!
NO ONE HAD EVER REALLY GIVEN THE MATTER MUCH THOUGHT...BUT SUDDENLY, THE AFTERLIFE OF DISCARDED STEM CELLS WAS ALL THE PUNDITS COULD TALK ABOUT...
CAN YOU IMAGINE THEIR UNENDING TORMENT--FLOATING IN TINY PETRI DISHES OF ETERNAL FIRE?
BUT CERTAINLY THEIR INNOCENCE ENSURES THAT THEIR NAMES--OR, UM, THEIR LAB SPECIMEN NUMBERS--WILL BE IN ST. PETER'S BOOK WHEN THEY ARRIVE AT THE PEARLY GATES!
ULTIMATELY, THE PRESIDENT ORDERED THE BAPTISM OF ALL EXISTING STEM CELL LINES--JUST TO BE SAFE!
YOU DUNKED THE EXPERIMENT IN UNSTERILIZED LAKE WATER?
YOU'VE--YOU'VE DESTROYED YEARS OF RESEARCH!
YES--BUT WE SAVED A TINY SOUL! LITTLE GENETIC SAMPLE 3398-0499302-098 IS WITH OUR HEAVENLY FATHER NOW!
HALLELUJAH!
Holy Bible
NEXT: HOW MANY STEM CELL ANGELS CAN FLOAT ON THE HEAD OF A PIN? THE PRESIDENT WANTS TO KNOW!
TOM TOMORROW© 8-22-01

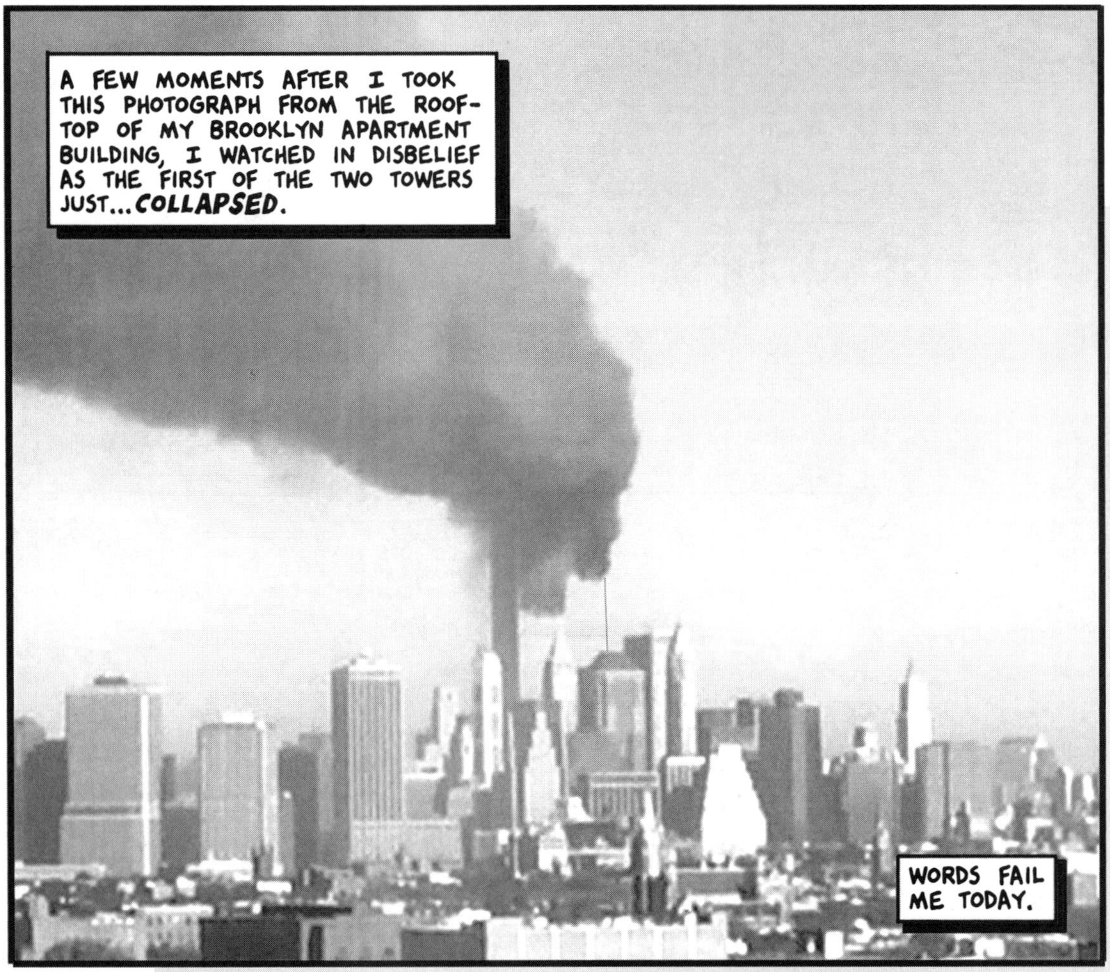
A FEW MOMENTS AFTER I TOOK THIS PHOTOGRAPH FROM THE ROOF-TOP OF MY BROOKLYN APARTMENT BUILDING, I WATCHED IN DISBELIEF AS THE FIRST OF THE TWO TOWERS JUST... COLLAPSED.
WORDS FAIL ME TODAY.

After Sept. 11, a whole lot of hate mail started pouring in from conservatives who seemed to think that anyone who disagreed with their political perspective was aligned with the terrorists. One fellow wrote smugly, after seeing this piece, "I'm a little surprised at your reaction to the Sept. 11 tragedy. Do you suggest you have some sort of deep affection for the country you constantly berate?"

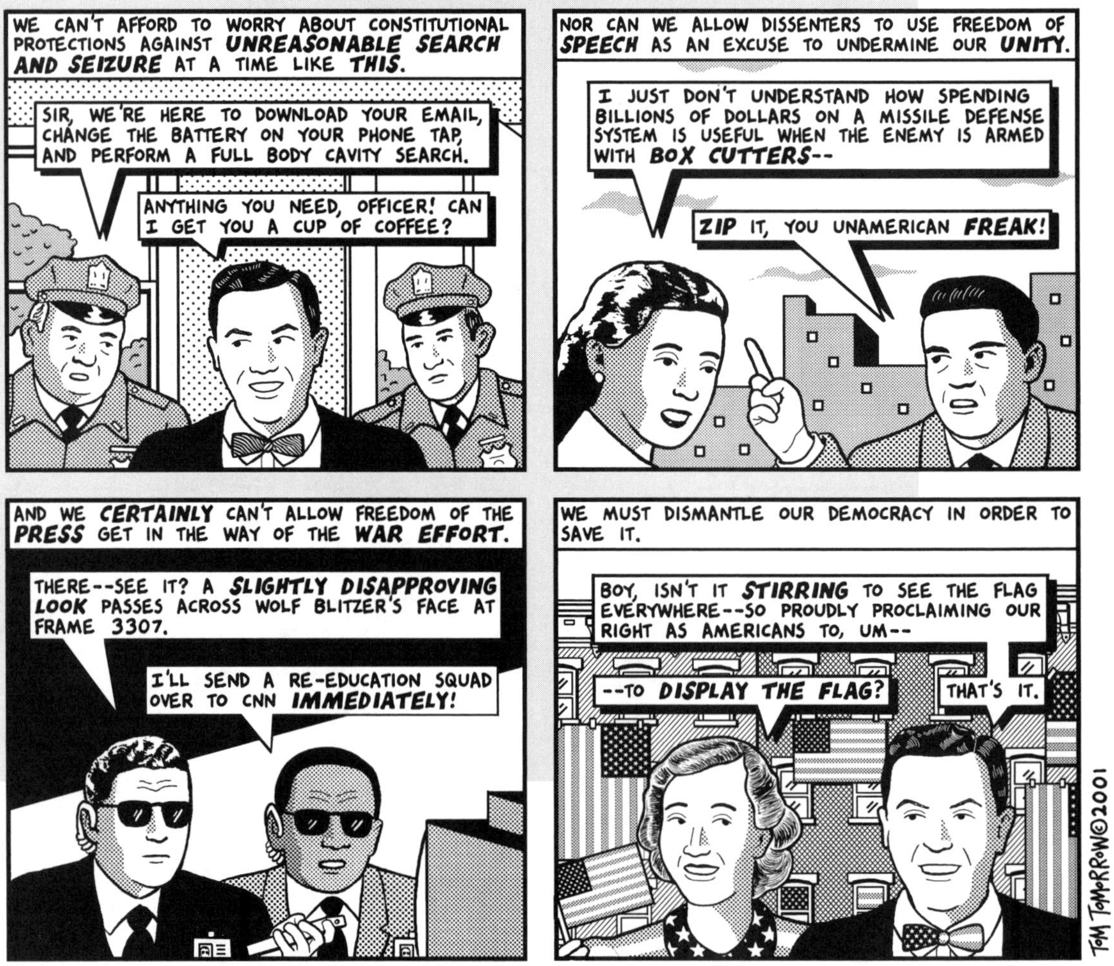
WE CAN'T AFFORD TO WORRY ABOUT CONSTITUTIONAL PROTECTIONS AGAINST UNREASONABLE SEARCH AND SEIZURE AT A TIME LIKE THIS.
SIR, WE'RE HERE TO DOWNLOAD YOUR EMAIL, CHANGE THE BATTERY ON YOUR PHONE TAP, AND PERFORM A FULL BODY CAVITY SEARCH.
ANYTHING YOU NEED, OFFICER! CAN I GET YOU A CUP OF COFFEE?
NOR CAN WE ALLOW DISSENTERS TO USE FREEDOM OF SPEECH AS AN EXCUSE TO UNDERMINE OUR UNITY.
I JUST DON'T UNDERSTAND HOW SPENDING BILLIONS OF DOLLARS ON A MISSILE DEFENSE SYSTEM IS USEFUL WHEN THE ENEMY IS ARMED WITH BOX CUTTERS--
ZIP IT, YOU UNAMERICAN FREAK!
AND WE CERTAINLY CAN'T ALLOW FREEDOM OF THE PRESS GET IN THE WAY OF THE WAR EFFORT.
THERE--SEE IT? A SLIGHTLY DISAPPROVING LOOK PASSES ACROSS WOLF BLITZER'S FACE AT FRAME 3307.
I'LL SEND A RE-EDUCATION SQUAD OVER TO CNN IMMEDIATELY!
WE MUST DISMANTLE OUR DEMOCRACY IN ORDER TO SAVE IT.
BOY, ISN'T IT STIRRING TO SEE THE FLAG EVERYWHERE--SO PROUDLY PROCLAIMING OUR RIGHT AS AMERICANS TO, UM--
--TO DISPLAY THE FLAG?
THAT'S IT.
TOM TOMORROW©2001

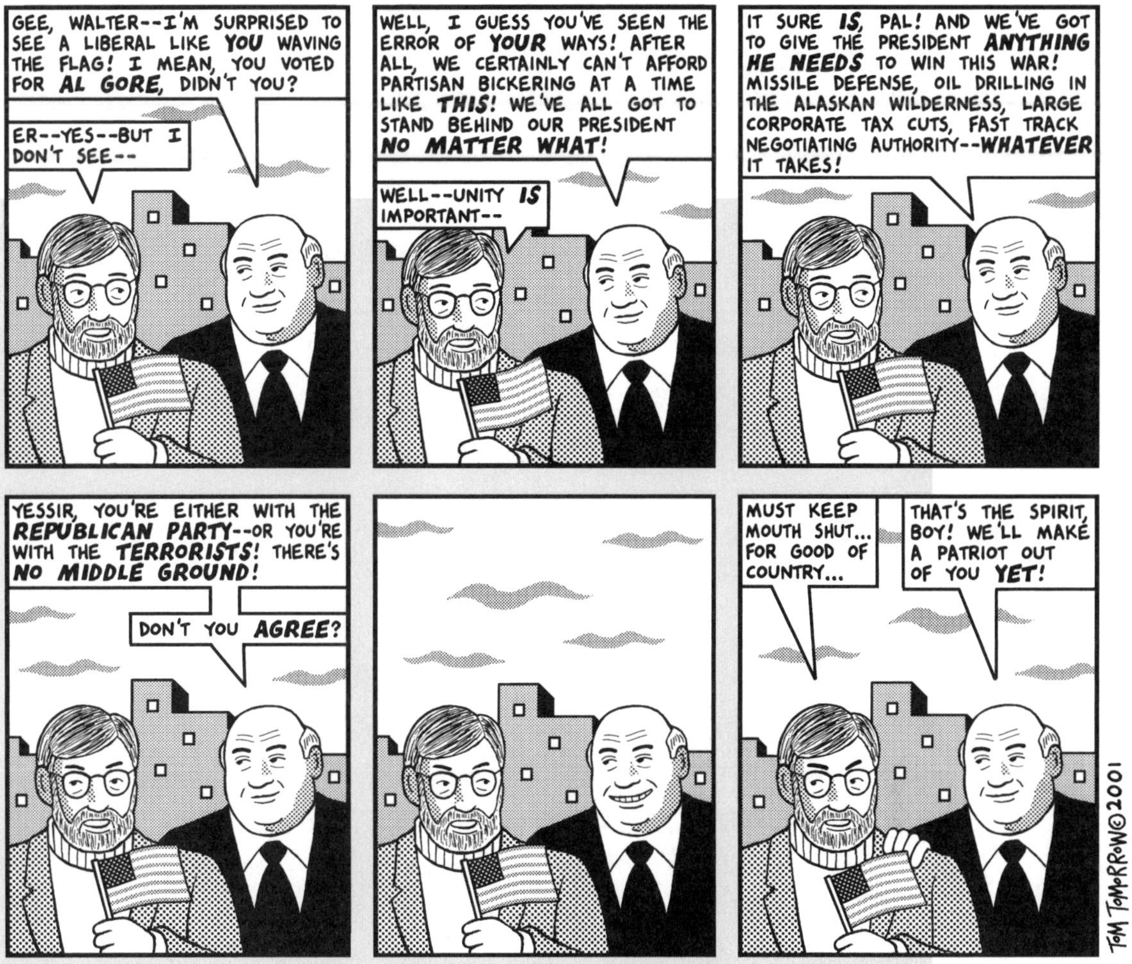
GEE, WALTER--I'M SURPRISED TO SEE A LIBERAL LIKE YOU WAVING THE FLAG! I MEAN, YOU VOTED FOR AL GORE, DIDN'T YOU?
ER--YES--BUT I DON'T SEE--
WELL, I GUESS YOU'VE SEEN THE ERROR OF YOUR WAYS! AFTER ALL, WE CERTAINLY CAN'T AFFORD PARTISAN BICKERING AT A TIME LIKE THIS! WE'VE ALL GOT TO STAND BEHIND OUR PRESIDENT NO MATTER WHAT!
WELL--UNITY IS IMPORTANT--
IT SURE IS, PAL! AND WE'VE GOT TO GIVE THE PRESIDENT ANYTHING HE NEEDS TO WIN THIS WAR! MISSILE DEFENSE, OIL DRILLING IN THE ALASKAN WILDERNESS, LARGE CORPORATE TAX CUTS, FAST TRACK NEGOTIATING AUTHORITY--WHATEVER IT TAKES!
YESSIR, YOU'RE EITHER WITH THE REPUBLICAN PARTY--OR YOU'RE WITH THE TERRORISTS! THERE'S NO MIDDLE GROUND!
DON'T YOU AGREE?
MUST KEEP MOUTH SHUT... FOR GOOD OF COUNTRY...
THAT'S THE SPIRIT, BOY! WE'LL MAKE A PATRIOT OUT OF YOU YET!
TOM TOMORROW©2001

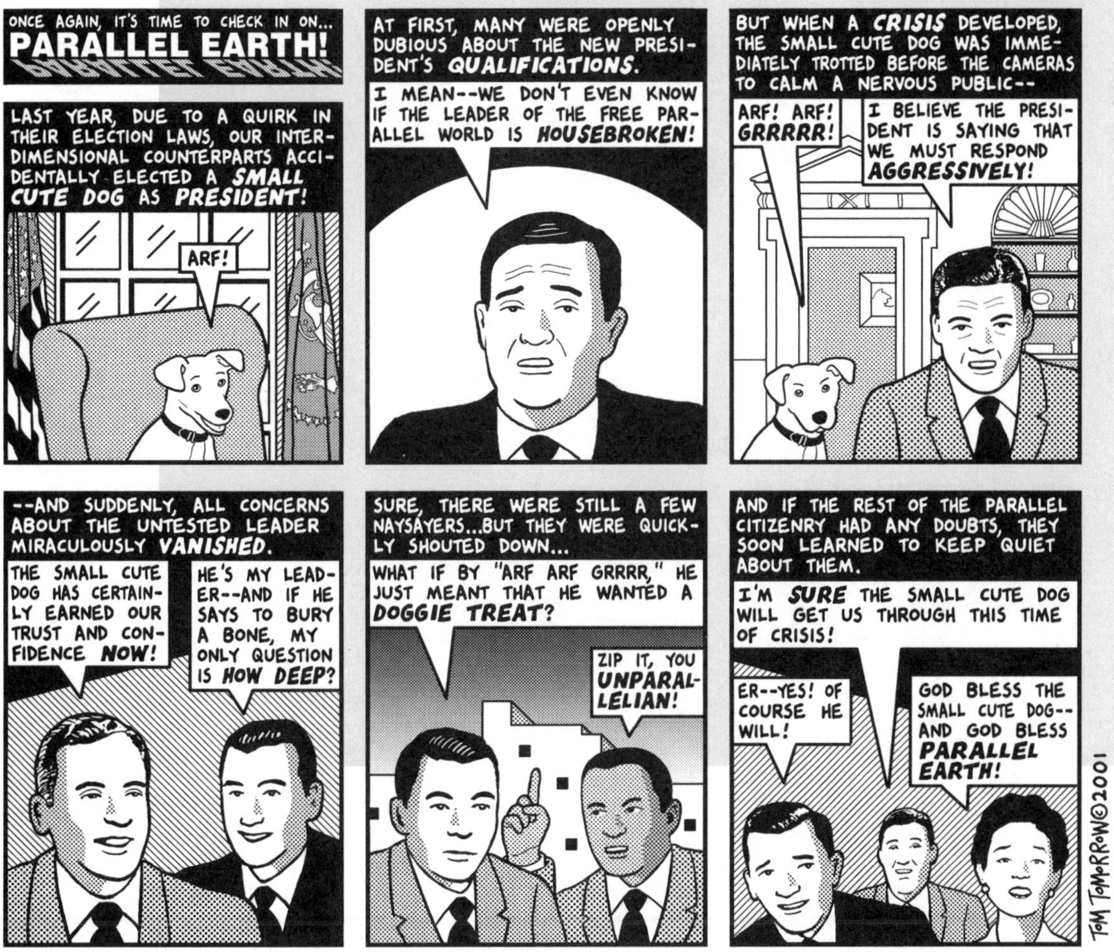
ONCE AGAIN, IT'S TIME TO CHECK IN ON...
PARALLEL EARTH!
LAST YEAR, DUE TO A QUIRK IN THEIR ELECTION LAWS, OUR INTER-DIMENSIONAL COUNTERPARTS ACCIDENTALLY ELECTED A SMALL CUTE DOG AS PRESIDENT!
ARF!
AT FIRST, MANY WERE OPENLY DUBIOUS ABOUT THE NEW PRESIDENT'S QUALIFICATIONS.
I MEAN--WE DON'T EVEN KNOW IF THE LEADER OF THE FREE PARALLEL WORLD IS HOUSEBROKEN!
BUT WHEN A CRISIS DEVELOPED, THE SMALL CUTE DOG WAS IMMEDIATELY TROTTED BEFORE THE CAMERAS TO CALM A NERVOUS PUBLIC--
ARF! ARF! GRRRRR!
I BELIEVE THE PRESIDENT IS SAYING THAT WE MUST RESPOND AGGRESSIVELY!
--AND SUDDENLY, ALL CONCERNS ABOUT THE UNTESTED LEADER MIRACULOUSLY VANISHED.
THE SMALL CUTE DOG HAS CERTAINLY EARNED OUR TRUST AND CONFIDENCE NOW!
HE'S MY LEADER--AND IF HE SAYS TO BURY A BONE, MY ONLY QUESTION IS HOW DEEP?
SURE, THERE WERE STILL A FEW NAYSAYERS...BUT THEY WERE QUICKLY SHOUTED DOWN...
WHAT IF BY "ARF ARF GRRRR," HE JUST MEANT THAT HE WANTED A DOGGIE TREAT?
ZIP IT, YOU UNPARALLELIAN!
AND IF THE REST OF THE PARALLEL CITIZENRY HAD ANY DOUBTS, THEY SOON LEARNED TO KEEP QUIET ABOUT THEM.
I'M SURE THE SMALL CUTE DOG WILL GET US THROUGH THIS TIME OF CRISIS!
ER--YES! OF COURSE HE WILL!
GOD BLESS THE SMALL CUTE DOG--AND GOD BLESS PARALLEL EARTH!
TOM TOMORROW©2001

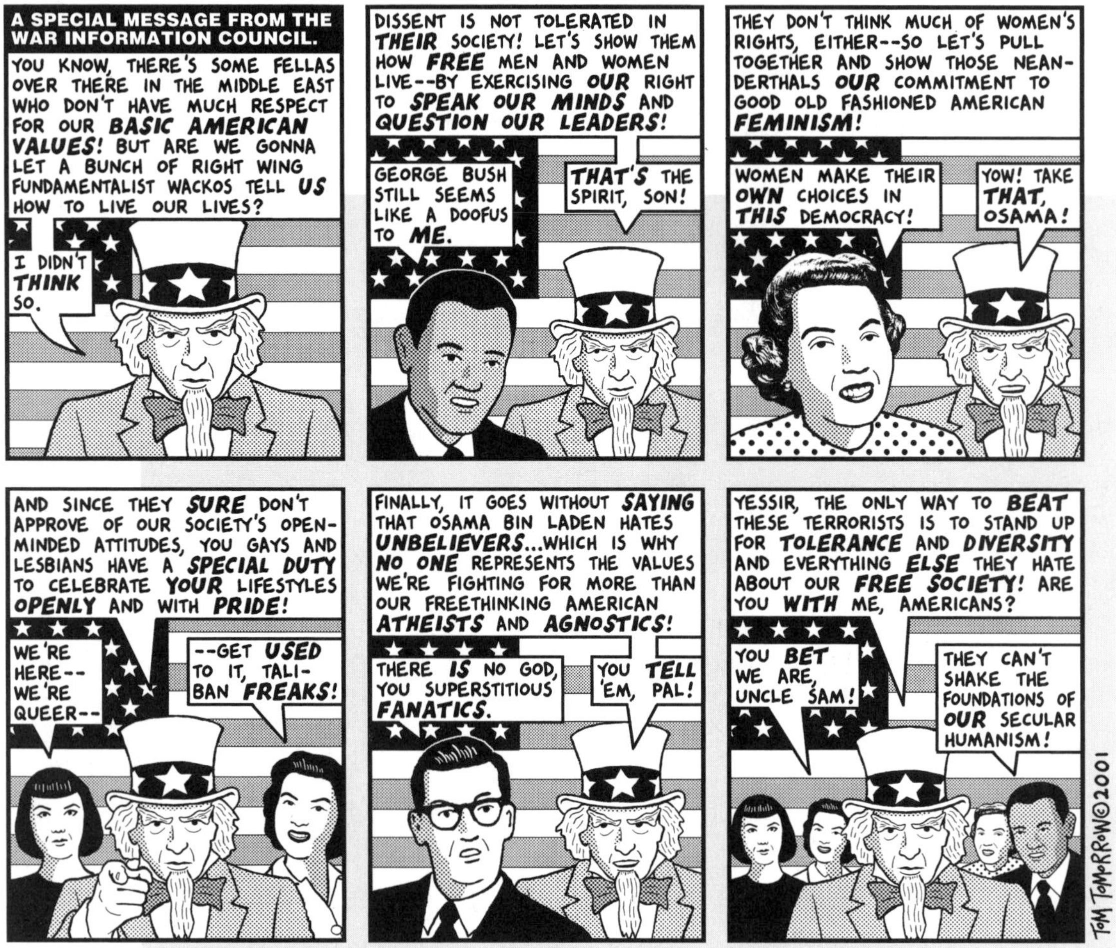
A SPECIAL MESSAGE FROM THE WAR INFORMATION COUNCIL.
YOU KNOW, THERE'S SOME FELLAS OVER THERE IN THE MIDDLE EAST WHO DON'T HAVE MUCH RESPECT FOR OUR BASIC AMERICAN VALUES! BUT ARE WE GONNA LET A BUNCH OF RIGHT WING FUNDAMENTALIST WACKOS TELL US HOW TO LIVE OUR LIVES?
I DIDN'T THINK SO.
DISSENT IS NOT TOLERATED IN THEIR SOCIETY! LET'S SHOW THEM HOW FREE MEN AND WOMEN LIVE--BY EXERCISING OUR RIGHT TO SPEAK OUR MINDS AND QUESTION OUR LEADERS!
GEORGE BUSH STILL SEEMS LIKE A DOOFUS TO ME.
THAT'S THE SPIRIT, SON!
THEY DON'T THINK MUCH OF WOMEN'S RIGHTS, EITHER--SO LET'S PULL TOGETHER AND SHOW THOSE NEANDERTHALS OUR COMMITMENT TO GOOD OLD FASHIONED AMERICAN FEMINISM!
WOMEN MAKE THEIR OWN CHOICES IN THIS DEMOCRACY!
YOW! TAKE THAT, OSAMA!
AND SINCE THEY SURE DON'T APPROVE OF OUR SOCIETY'S OPEN-MINDED ATTITUDES, YOU GAYS AND LESBIANS HAVE A SPECIAL DUTY TO CELEBRATE YOUR LIFESTYLES OPENLY AND WITH PRIDE!
WE'RE HERE--WE'RE QUEER--
--GET USED TO IT, TALIBAN FREAKS!
FINALLY, IT GOES WITHOUT SAYING THAT OSAMA BIN LADEN HATES UNBELIEVERS...WHICH IS WHY NO ONE REPRESENTS THE VALUES WE'RE FIGHTING FOR MORE THAN OUR FREETHINKING AMERICAN ATHEISTS AND AGNOSTICS!
THERE IS NO GOD, YOU SUPERSTITIOUS FANATICS.
YOU TELL 'EM, PAL!
YESSIR, THE ONLY WAY TO BEAT THESE TERRORISTS IS TO STAND UP FOR TOLERANCE AND DIVERSITY AND EVERYTHING ELSE THEY HATE ABOUT OUR FREE SOCIETY! ARE YOU WITH ME, AMERICANS?
YOU BET WE ARE, UNCLE SAM!
THEY CAN'T SHAKE THE FOUNDATIONS OF OUR SECULAR HUMANISM!
TOM TOMORROW©2001

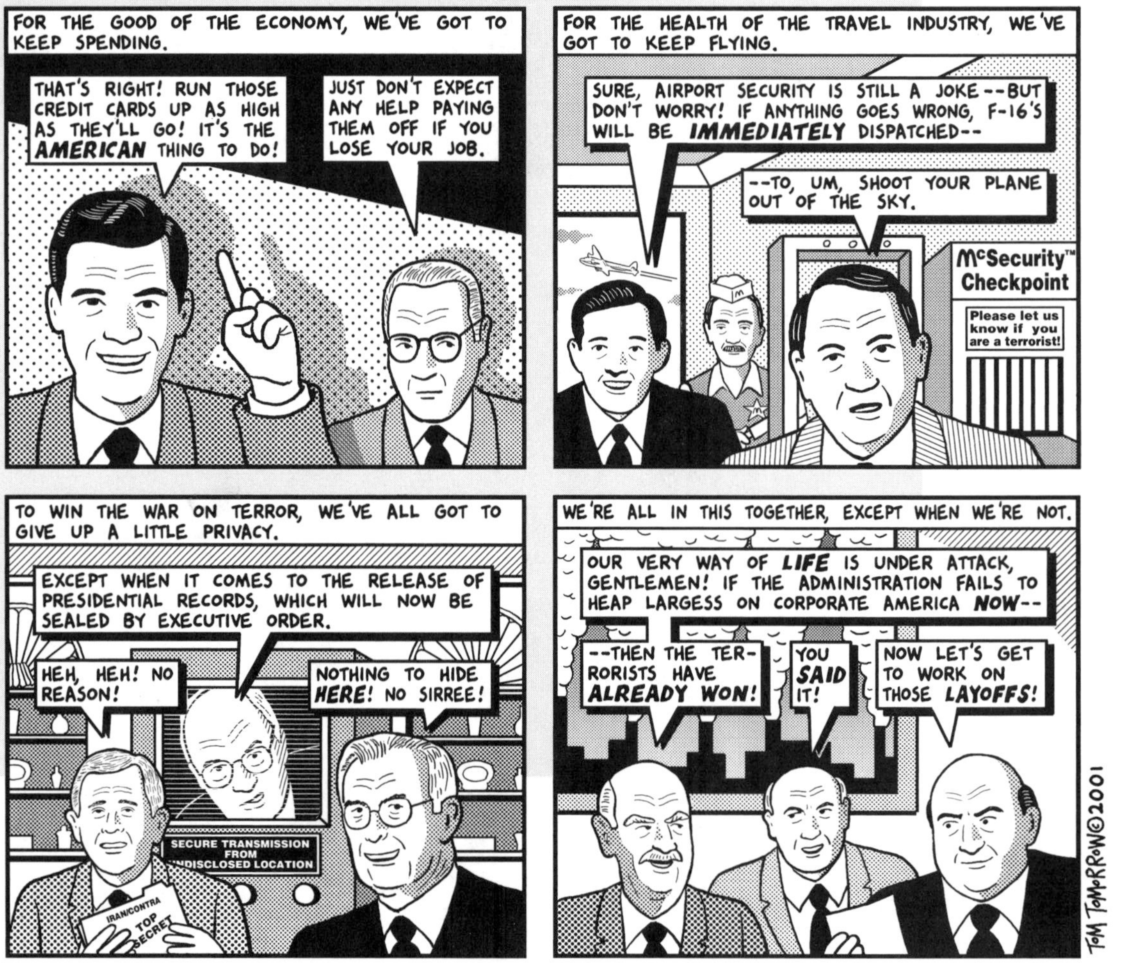
FOR THE GOOD OF THE ECONOMY, WE'VE GOT TO KEEP SPENDING.
THAT'S RIGHT! RUN THOSE CREDIT CARDS UP AS HIGH AS THEY'LL GO! IT'S THE AMERICAN THING TO DO!
JUST DON'T EXPECT ANY HELP PAYING THEM OFF IF YOU LOSE YOUR JOB.
FOR THE HEALTH OF THE TRAVEL INDUSTRY, WE'VE GOT TO KEEP FLYING.
SURE, AIRPORT SECURITY IS STILL A JOKE--BUT DON'T WORRY! IF ANYTHING GOES WRONG, F-16'S WILL BE IMMEDIATELY DISPATCHED--
--TO, UM, SHOOT YOUR PLANE OUT OF THE SKY.
McSecurity™ Checkpoint
Please let us know if you are a terrorist!
TO WIN THE WAR ON TERROR, WE'VE ALL GOT TO GIVE UP A LITTLE PRIVACY.
EXCEPT WHEN IT COMES TO THE RELEASE OF PRESIDENTIAL RECORDS, WHICH WILL NOW BE SEALED BY EXECUTIVE ORDER.
HEH, HEH! NO REASON!
NOTHING TO HIDE HERE! NO SIRREE!
SECURE TRANSMISSION FROM UNDISCLOSED LOCATION
IRAN/CONTRA TOP SECRET
WE'RE ALL IN THIS TOGETHER, EXCEPT WHEN WE'RE NOT.
OUR VERY WAY OF LIFE IS UNDER ATTACK, GENTLEMEN! IF THE ADMINISTRATION FAILS TO HEAP LARGESS ON CORPORATE AMERICA NOW--
--THEN THE TERRORISTS HAVE ALREADY WON!
YOU SAID IT!
NOW LET'S GET TO WORK ON THOSE LAYOFFS!
TOM TOMORROW©2001

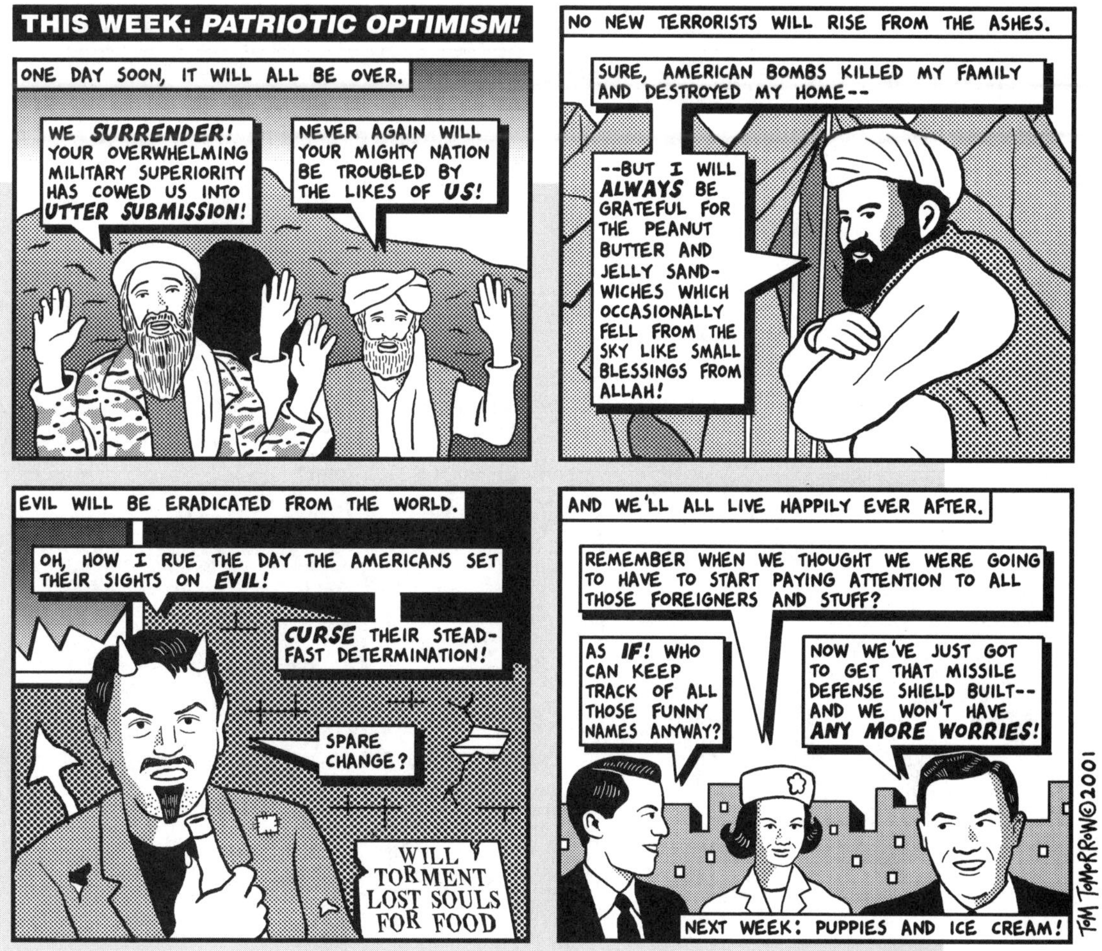
THIS WEEK: PATRIOTIC OPTIMISM!
ONE DAY SOON, IT WILL ALL BE OVER.
WE SURRENDER! YOUR OVERWHELMING MILITARY SUPERIORITY HAS COWED US INTO UTTER SUBMISSION!
NEVER AGAIN WILL YOUR MIGHTY NATION BE TROUBLED BY THE LIKES OF US!
NO NEW TERRORISTS WILL RISE FROM THE ASHES.
SURE, AMERICAN BOMBS KILLED MY FAMILY AND DESTROYED MY HOME--
--BUT I WILL ALWAYS BE GRATEFUL FOR THE PEANUT BUTTER AND JELLY SAND-WICHES WHICH OCCASIONALLY FELL FROM THE SKY LIKE SMALL BLESSINGS FROM ALLAH!
EVIL WILL BE ERADICATED FROM THE WORLD.
OH, HOW I RUE THE DAY THE AMERICANS SET THEIR SIGHTS ON EVIL!
CURSE THEIR STEAD-FAST DETERMINATION!
SPARE CHANGE?
WILL TORMENT LOST SOULS FOR FOOD
AND WE'LL ALL LIVE HAPPILY EVER AFTER.
REMEMBER WHEN WE THOUGHT WE WERE GOING TO HAVE TO START PAYING ATTENTION TO ALL THOSE FOREIGNERS AND STUFF?
AS IF! WHO CAN KEEP TRACK OF ALL THOSE FUNNY NAMES ANYWAY?
NOW WE'VE JUST GOT TO GET THAT MISSILE DEFENSE SHIELD BUILT-- AND WE WON'T HAVE ANY MORE WORRIES!
NEXT WEEK: PUPPIES AND ICE CREAM!
TOM TOMORROW©2001

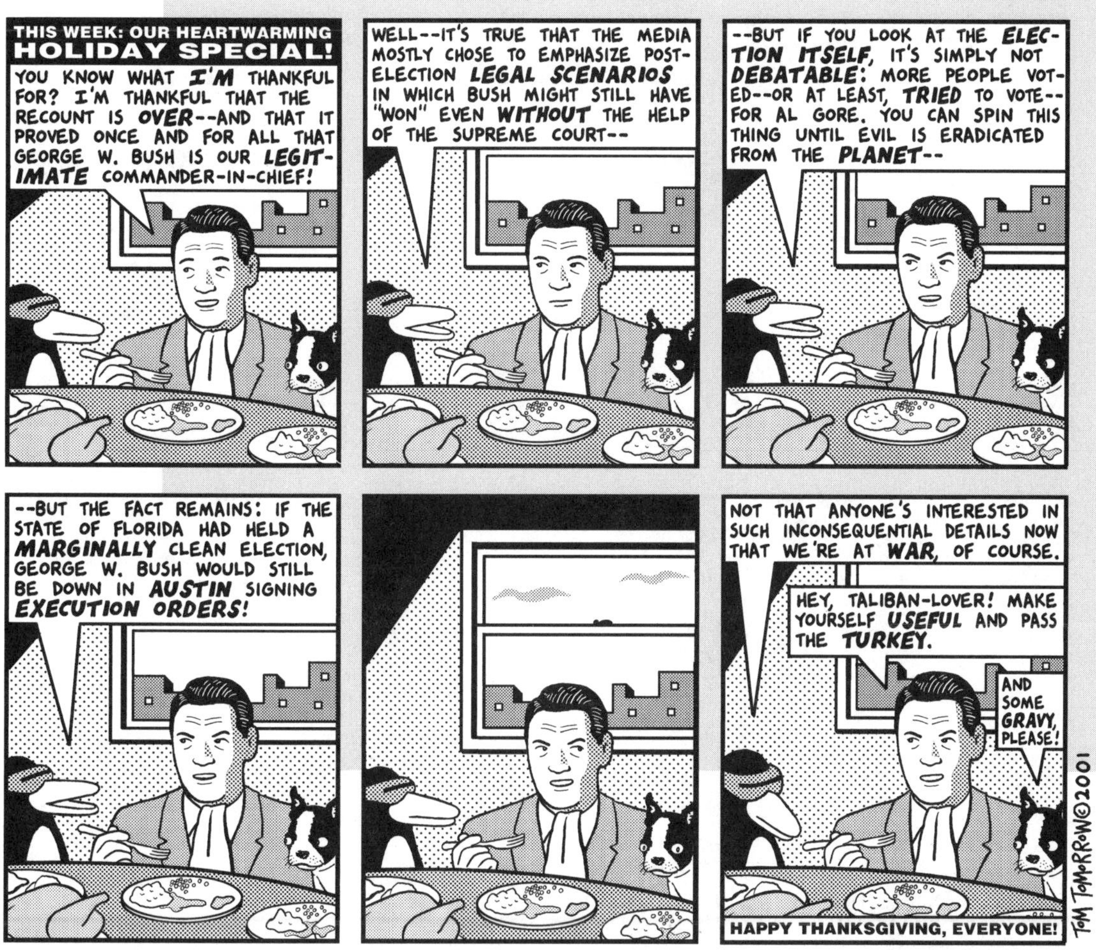
THIS WEEK: OUR HEARTWARMING HOLIDAY SPECIAL!
YOU KNOW WHAT I'M THANKFUL FOR? I'M THANKFUL THAT THE RECOUNT IS OVER--AND THAT IT PROVED ONCE AND FOR ALL THAT GEORGE W. BUSH IS OUR LEGIT-IMATE COMMANDER-IN-CHIEF!
WELL--IT'S TRUE THAT THE MEDIA MOSTLY CHOSE TO EMPHASIZE POST-ELECTION LEGAL SCENARIOS IN WHICH BUSH MIGHT STILL HAVE "WON" EVEN WITHOUT THE HELP OF THE SUPREME COURT--
--BUT IF YOU LOOK AT THE ELEC-TION ITSELF, IT'S SIMPLY NOT DEBATABLE: MORE PEOPLE VOT-ED--OR AT LEAST, TRIED TO VOTE-- FOR AL GORE. YOU CAN SPIN THIS THING UNTIL EVIL IS ERADICATED FROM THE PLANET--
--BUT THE FACT REMAINS: IF THE STATE OF FLORIDA HAD HELD A MARGINALLY CLEAN ELECTION, GEORGE W. BUSH WOULD STILL BE DOWN IN AUSTIN SIGNING EXECUTION ORDERS!
NOT THAT ANYONE'S INTERESTED IN SUCH INCONSEQUENTIAL DETAILS NOW THAT WE'RE AT WAR, OF COURSE.
HEY, TALIBAN-LOVER! MAKE YOURSELF USEFUL AND PASS THE TURKEY.
AND SOME GRAVY, PLEASE!
HAPPY THANKSGIVING, EVERYONE!
TOM TOMORROW©2001

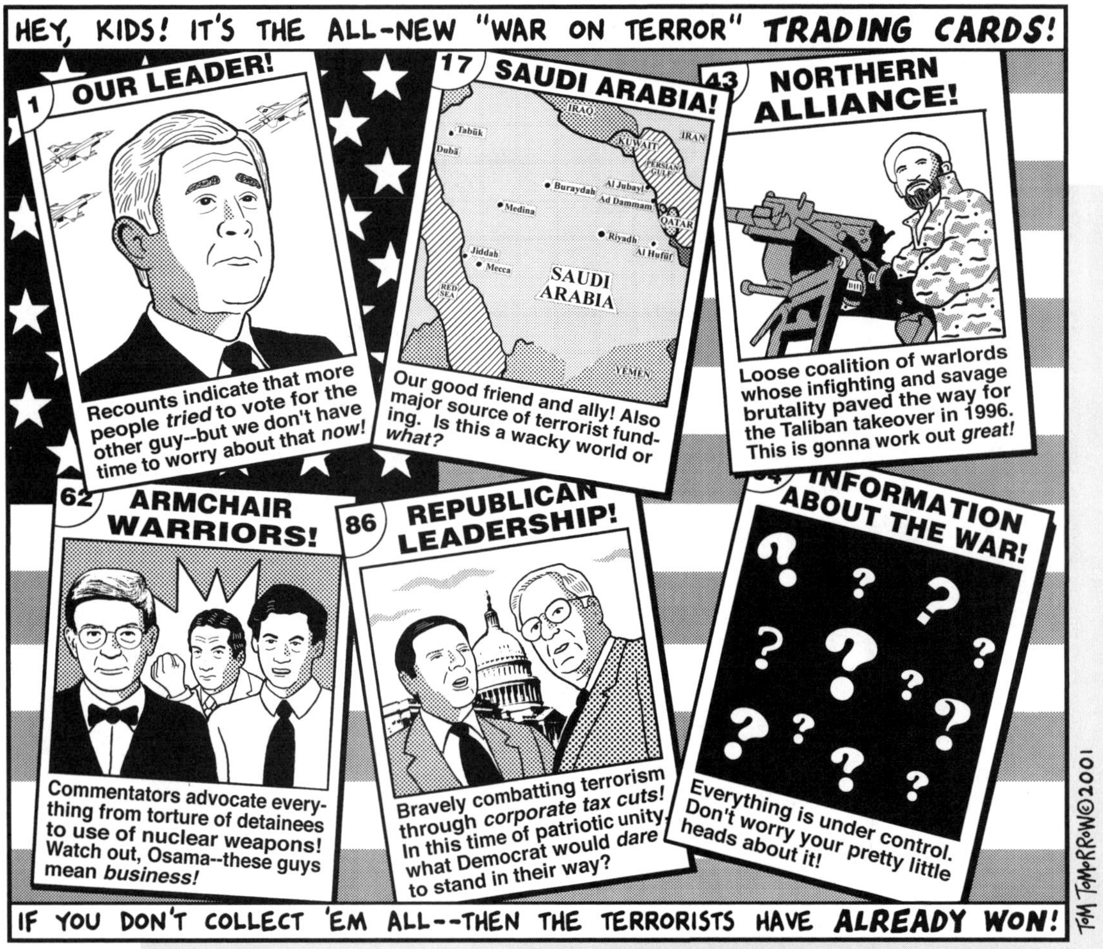
HEY, KIDS! IT'S THE ALL-NEW "WAR ON TERROR" TRADING CARDS!
1 OUR LEADER!
Recounts indicate that more people *tried* to vote for the other guy--but we don't have time to worry about that *now*!
17 SAUDI ARABIA!
Tabūk
Dubā
IRAQ
KUWAIT
IRAN
PERSIAN GULF
Buraydah
Al Jubayl
Ad Dammam
Medina
QATAR
Riyadh
Al Hufūf
Jiddah
Mecca
RED SEA
SAUDI ARABIA
YEMEN
Our good friend and ally! Also major source of terrorist funding. Is this a wacky world or *what?*
43 NORTHERN ALLIANCE!
Loose coalition of warlords whose infighting and savage brutality paved the way for the Taliban takeover in 1996. This is gonna work out *great!*
62 ARMCHAIR WARRIORS!
Commentators advocate everything from torture of detainees to use of nuclear weapons! Watch out, Osama--these guys mean *business!*
86 REPUBLICAN LEADERSHIP!
Bravely combatting terrorism through *corporate tax cuts!* In this time of patriotic unity, what Democrat would *dare* to stand in their way?
INFORMATION ABOUT THE WAR!
Everything is under control. Don't worry your pretty little heads about it!
IF YOU DON'T COLLECT 'EM ALL--THEN THE TERRORISTS HAVE ALREADY WON!
TOM TOMORROW©2001

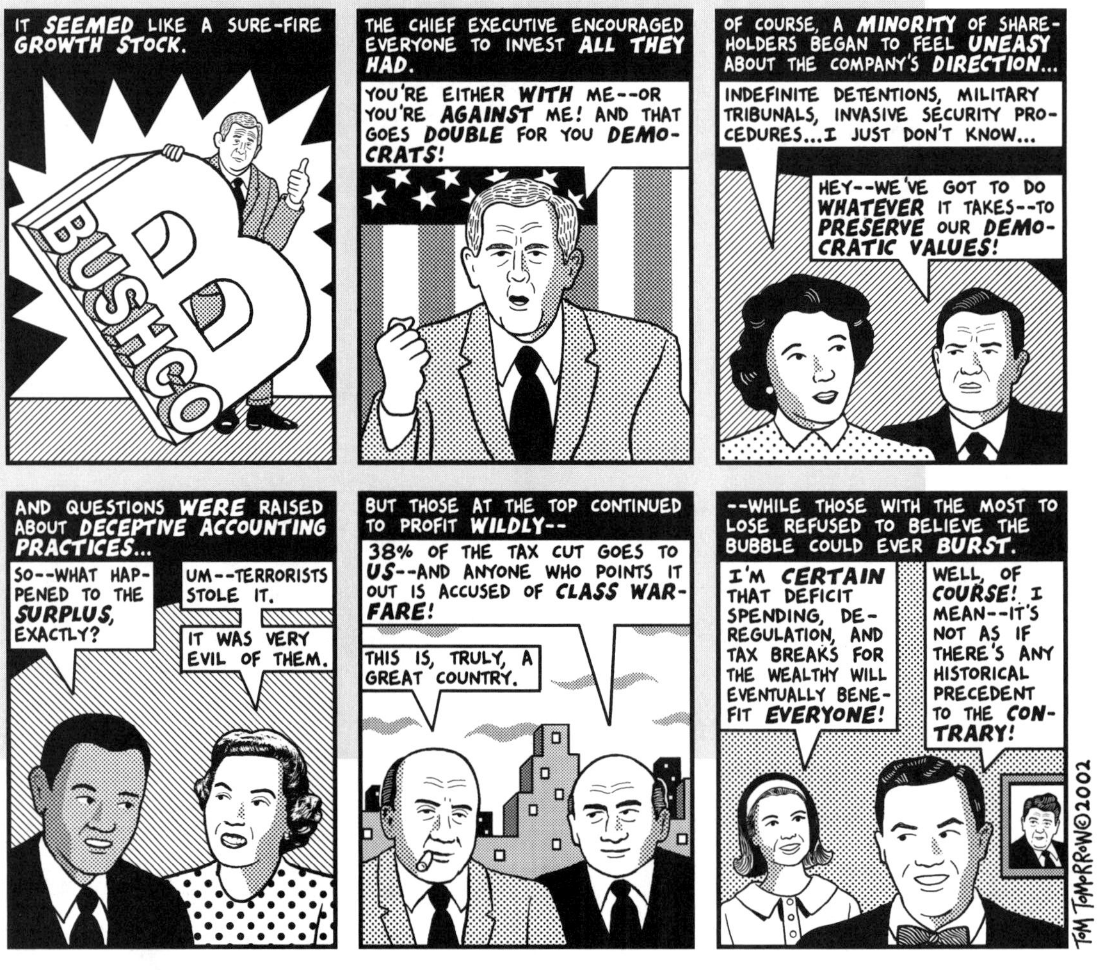
IT SEEMED LIKE A SURE-FIRE GROWTH STOCK.
BUSHCO
THE CHIEF EXECUTIVE ENCOURAGED EVERYONE TO INVEST ALL THEY HAD.
YOU'RE EITHER WITH ME--OR YOU'RE AGAINST ME! AND THAT GOES DOUBLE FOR YOU DEMOCRATS!
OF COURSE, A MINORITY OF SHAREHOLDERS BEGAN TO FEEL UNEASY ABOUT THE COMPANY'S DIRECTION...
INDEFINITE DETENTIONS, MILITARY TRIBUNALS, INVASIVE SECURITY PROCEDURES...I JUST DON'T KNOW...
HEY--WE'VE GOT TO DO WHATEVER IT TAKES--TO PRESERVE OUR DEMOCRATIC VALUES!
AND QUESTIONS WERE RAISED ABOUT DECEPTIVE ACCOUNTING PRACTICES...
SO--WHAT HAPPENED TO THE SURPLUS, EXACTLY?
UM--TERRORISTS STOLE IT.
IT WAS VERY EVIL OF THEM.
BUT THOSE AT THE TOP CONTINUED TO PROFIT WILDLY--
38% OF THE TAX CUT GOES TO US--AND ANYONE WHO POINTS IT OUT IS ACCUSED OF CLASS WARFARE!
THIS IS, TRULY, A GREAT COUNTRY.
--WHILE THOSE WITH THE MOST TO LOSE REFUSED TO BELIEVE THE BUBBLE COULD EVER BURST.
I'M CERTAIN THAT DEFICIT SPENDING, DEREGULATION, AND TAX BREAKS FOR THE WEALTHY WILL EVENTUALLY BENEFIT EVERYONE!
WELL, OF COURSE! I MEAN--IT'S NOT AS IF THERE'S ANY HISTORICAL PRECEDENT TO THE CONTRARY!
TOM TOMORROW©2002

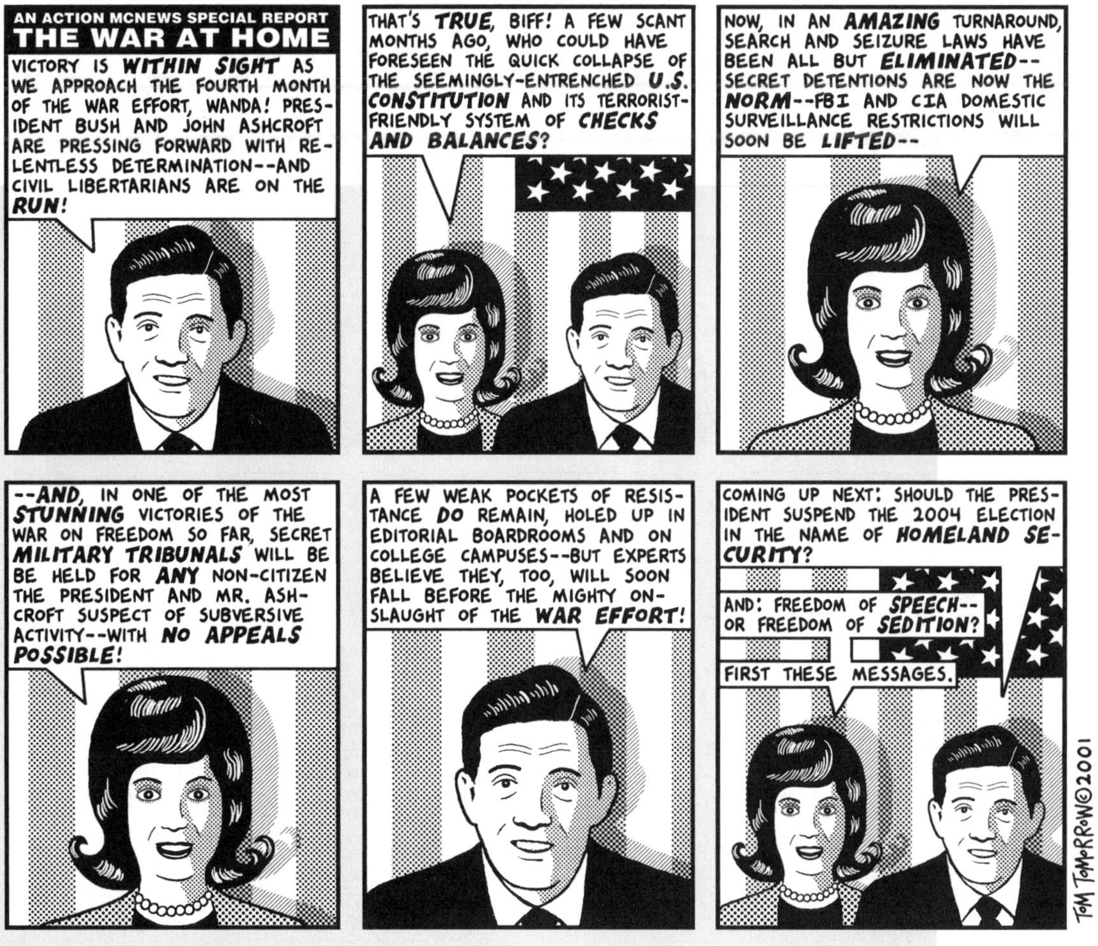
AN ACTION MCNEWS SPECIAL REPORT
THE WAR AT HOME
VICTORY IS WITHIN SIGHT AS WE APPROACH THE FOURTH MONTH OF THE WAR EFFORT, WANDA! PRESIDENT BUSH AND JOHN ASHCROFT ARE PRESSING FORWARD WITH RELENTLESS DETERMINATION--AND CIVIL LIBERTARIANS ARE ON THE RUN!
THAT'S TRUE, BIFF! A FEW SCANT MONTHS AGO, WHO COULD HAVE FORESEEN THE QUICK COLLAPSE OF THE SEEMINGLY-ENTRENCHED U.S. CONSTITUTION AND ITS TERRORIST-FRIENDLY SYSTEM OF CHECKS AND BALANCES?
NOW, IN AN AMAZING TURNAROUND, SEARCH AND SEIZURE LAWS HAVE BEEN ALL BUT ELIMINATED--SECRET DETENTIONS ARE NOW THE NORM--FBI AND CIA DOMESTIC SURVEILLANCE RESTRICTIONS WILL SOON BE LIFTED--
--AND, IN ONE OF THE MOST STUNNING VICTORIES OF THE WAR ON FREEDOM SO FAR, SECRET MILITARY TRIBUNALS WILL BE BE HELD FOR ANY NON-CITIZEN THE PRESIDENT AND MR. ASHCROFT SUSPECT OF SUBVERSIVE ACTIVITY--WITH NO APPEALS POSSIBLE!
A FEW WEAK POCKETS OF RESISTANCE DO REMAIN, HOLED UP IN EDITORIAL BOARDROOMS AND ON COLLEGE CAMPUSES--BUT EXPERTS BELIEVE THEY, TOO, WILL SOON FALL BEFORE THE MIGHTY ONSLAUGHT OF THE WAR EFFORT!
COMING UP NEXT: SHOULD THE PRESIDENT SUSPEND THE 2004 ELECTION IN THE NAME OF HOMELAND SECURITY?
AND: FREEDOM OF SPEECH--OR FREEDOM OF SEDITION?
FIRST THESE MESSAGES.
TOM TOMORROW©2001

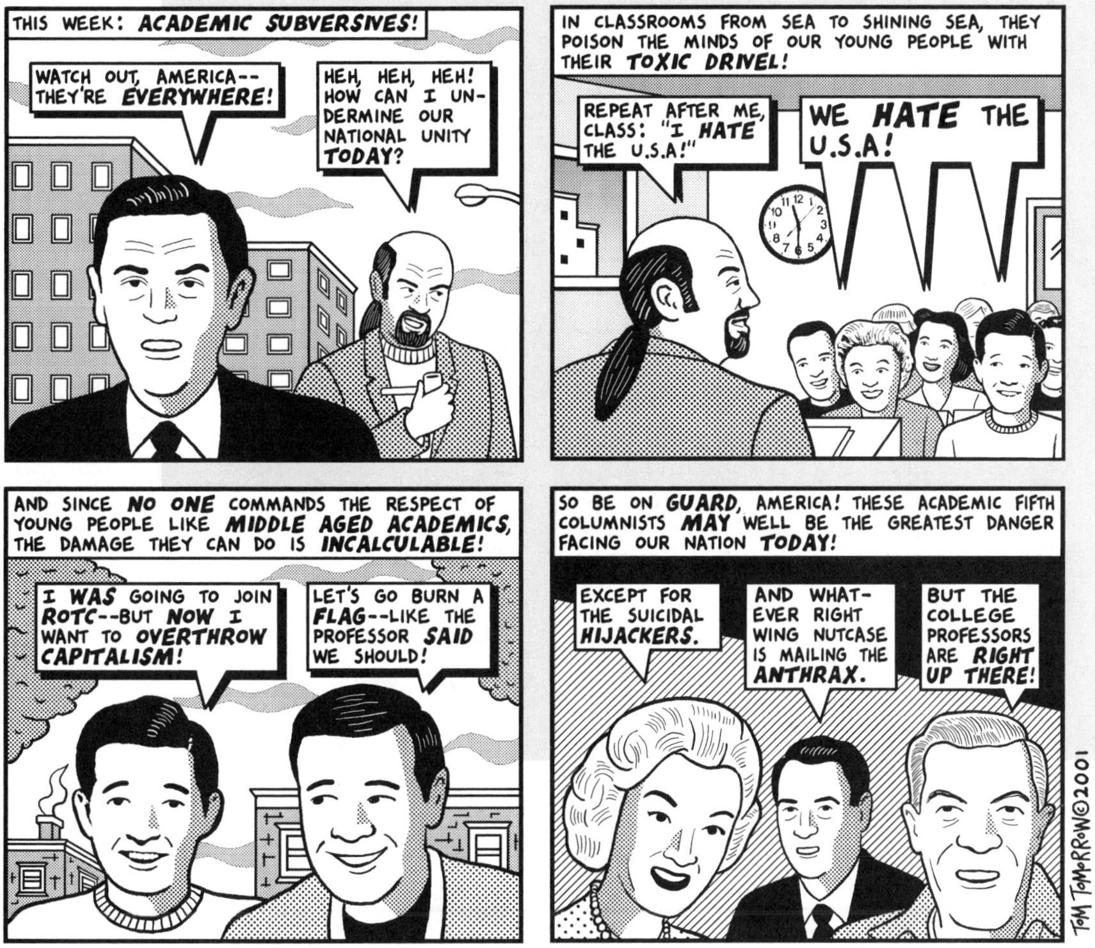
THIS WEEK: ACADEMIC SUBVERSIVES!
WATCH OUT, AMERICA--THEY'RE EVERYWHERE!
HEH, HEH, HEH! HOW CAN I UNDERMINE OUR NATIONAL UNITY TODAY?
IN CLASSROOMS FROM SEA TO SHINING SEA, THEY POISON THE MINDS OF OUR YOUNG PEOPLE WITH THEIR TOXIC DRIVEL!
REPEAT AFTER ME, CLASS: "I HATE THE U.S.A!"
WE HATE THE U.S.A!
AND SINCE NO ONE COMMANDS THE RESPECT OF YOUNG PEOPLE LIKE MIDDLE AGED ACADEMICS, THE DAMAGE THEY CAN DO IS INCALCULABLE!
I WAS GOING TO JOIN ROTC--BUT NOW I WANT TO OVERTHROW CAPITALISM!
LET'S GO BURN A FLAG--LIKE THE PROFESSOR SAID WE SHOULD!
SO BE ON GUARD, AMERICA! THESE ACADEMIC FIFTH COLUMNISTS MAY WELL BE THE GREATEST DANGER FACING OUR NATION TODAY!
EXCEPT FOR THE SUICIDAL HIJACKERS.
AND WHATEVER RIGHT WING NUTCASE IS MAILING THE ANTHRAX.
BUT THE COLLEGE PROFESSORS ARE RIGHT UP THERE!
TOM TOMORROW©2001

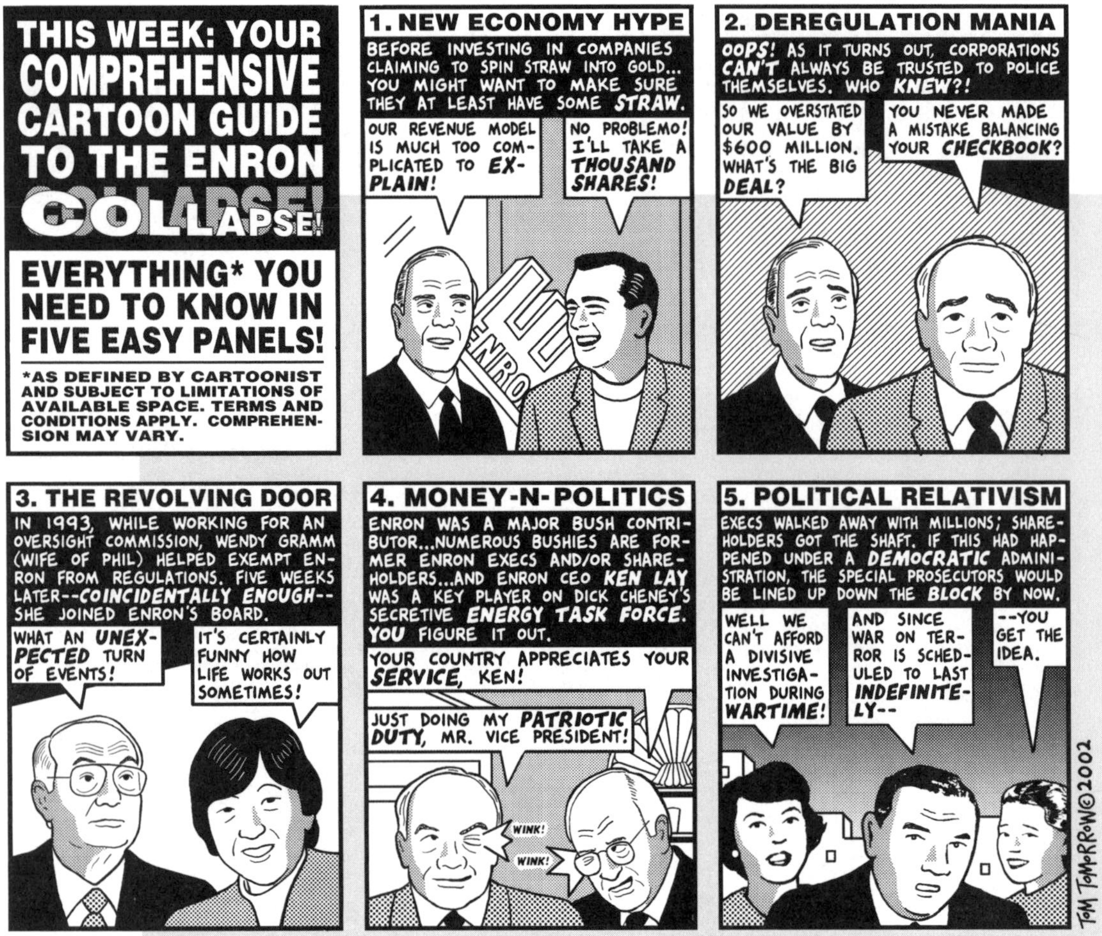
THIS WEEK: YOUR COMPREHENSIVE CARTOON GUIDE TO THE ENRON COLLAPSE!
EVERYTHING* YOU NEED TO KNOW IN FIVE EASY PANELS!
*AS DEFINED BY CARTOONIST AND SUBJECT TO LIMITATIONS OF AVAILABLE SPACE. TERMS AND CONDITIONS APPLY. COMPREHENSION MAY VARY.
1. NEW ECONOMY HYPE
BEFORE INVESTING IN COMPANIES CLAIMING TO SPIN STRAW INTO GOLD... YOU MIGHT WANT TO MAKE SURE THEY AT LEAST HAVE SOME STRAW.
OUR REVENUE MODEL IS MUCH TOO COMPLICATED TO EXPLAIN!
NO PROBLEMO! I'LL TAKE A THOUSAND SHARES!
2. DEREGULATION MANIA
OOPS! AS IT TURNS OUT, CORPORATIONS CAN'T ALWAYS BE TRUSTED TO POLICE THEMSELVES. WHO KNEW?!
SO WE OVERSTATED OUR VALUE BY $600 MILLION. WHAT'S THE BIG DEAL?
YOU NEVER MADE A MISTAKE BALANCING YOUR CHECKBOOK?
3. THE REVOLVING DOOR
IN 1993, WHILE WORKING FOR AN OVERSIGHT COMMISSION, WENDY GRAMM (WIFE OF PHIL) HELPED EXEMPT ENRON FROM REGULATIONS. FIVE WEEKS LATER--COINCIDENTALLY ENOUGH--SHE JOINED ENRON'S BOARD.
WHAT AN UNEXPECTED TURN OF EVENTS!
IT'S CERTAINLY FUNNY HOW LIFE WORKS OUT SOMETIMES!
4. MONEY-N-POLITICS
ENRON WAS A MAJOR BUSH CONTRIBUTOR...NUMEROUS BUSHIES ARE FORMER ENRON EXECS AND/OR SHAREHOLDERS...AND ENRON CEO KEN LAY WAS A KEY PLAYER ON DICK CHENEY'S SECRETIVE ENERGY TASK FORCE. YOU FIGURE IT OUT.
YOUR COUNTRY APPRECIATES YOUR SERVICE, KEN!
JUST DOING MY PATRIOTIC DUTY, MR. VICE PRESIDENT!
WINK!
WINK!
5. POLITICAL RELATIVISM
EXECS WALKED AWAY WITH MILLIONS; SHAREHOLDERS GOT THE SHAFT. IF THIS HAD HAPPENED UNDER A DEMOCRATIC ADMINISTRATION, THE SPECIAL PROSECUTORS WOULD BE LINED UP DOWN THE BLOCK BY NOW.
WELL WE CAN'T AFFORD A DIVISIVE INVESTIGATION DURING WARTIME!
AND SINCE WAR ON TERROR IS SCHEDULED TO LAST INDEFINITELY--
--YOU GET THE IDEA.
TOM TOMORROW©2002

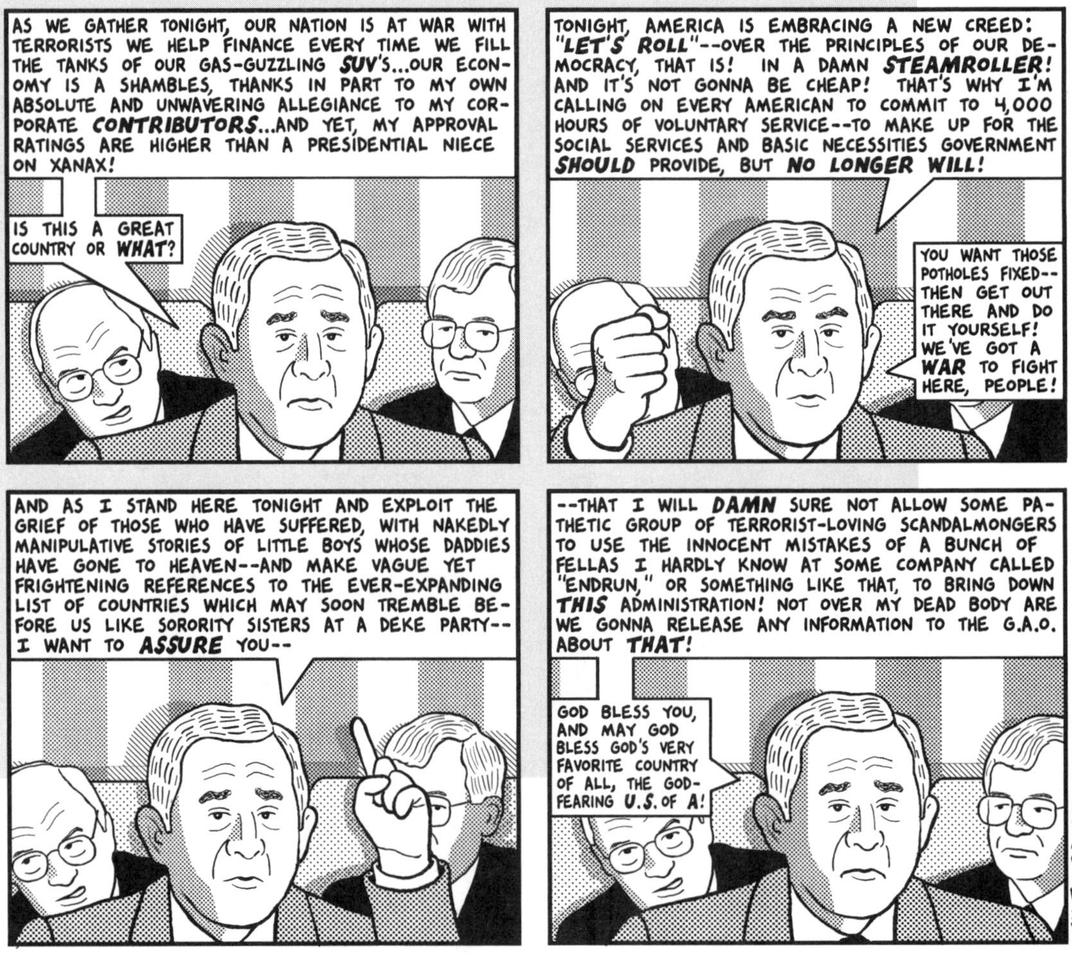
AS WE GATHER TONIGHT, OUR NATION IS AT WAR WITH TERRORISTS WE HELP FINANCE EVERY TIME WE FILL THE TANKS OF OUR GAS-GUZZLING SUV'S...OUR ECONOMY IS A SHAMBLES, THANKS IN PART TO MY OWN ABSOLUTE AND UNWAVERING ALLEGIANCE TO MY CORPORATE CONTRIBUTORS...AND YET, MY APPROVAL RATINGS ARE HIGHER THAN A PRESIDENTIAL NIECE ON XANAX!
IS THIS A GREAT COUNTRY OR WHAT?
TONIGHT, AMERICA IS EMBRACING A NEW CREED: "LET'S ROLL"--OVER THE PRINCIPLES OF OUR DEMOCRACY, THAT IS! IN A DAMN STEAMROLLER! AND IT'S NOT GONNA BE CHEAP! THAT'S WHY I'M CALLING ON EVERY AMERICAN TO COMMIT TO 4,000 HOURS OF VOLUNTARY SERVICE--TO MAKE UP FOR THE SOCIAL SERVICES AND BASIC NECESSITIES GOVERNMENT SHOULD PROVIDE, BUT NO LONGER WILL!
YOU WANT THOSE POTHOLES FIXED--THEN GET OUT THERE AND DO IT YOURSELF! WE'VE GOT A WAR TO FIGHT HERE, PEOPLE!
AND AS I STAND HERE TONIGHT AND EXPLOIT THE GRIEF OF THOSE WHO HAVE SUFFERED, WITH NAKEDLY MANIPULATIVE STORIES OF LITTLE BOYS WHOSE DADDIES HAVE GONE TO HEAVEN--AND MAKE VAGUE YET FRIGHTENING REFERENCES TO THE EVER-EXPANDING LIST OF COUNTRIES WHICH MAY SOON TREMBLE BEFORE US LIKE SORORITY SISTERS AT A DEKE PARTY--I WANT TO ASSURE YOU--
--THAT I WILL DAMN SURE NOT ALLOW SOME PATHETIC GROUP OF TERRORIST-LOVING SCANDALMONGERS TO USE THE INNOCENT MISTAKES OF A BUNCH OF FELLAS I HARDLY KNOW AT SOME COMPANY CALLED "ENDRUN," OR SOMETHING LIKE THAT, TO BRING DOWN THIS ADMINISTRATION! NOT OVER MY DEAD BODY ARE WE GONNA RELEASE ANY INFORMATION TO THE G.A.O. ABOUT THAT!
GOD BLESS YOU, AND MAY GOD BLESS GOD'S VERY FAVORITE COUNTRY OF ALL, THE GOD-FEARING U.S. OF A!
TOM TOMORROW©2002

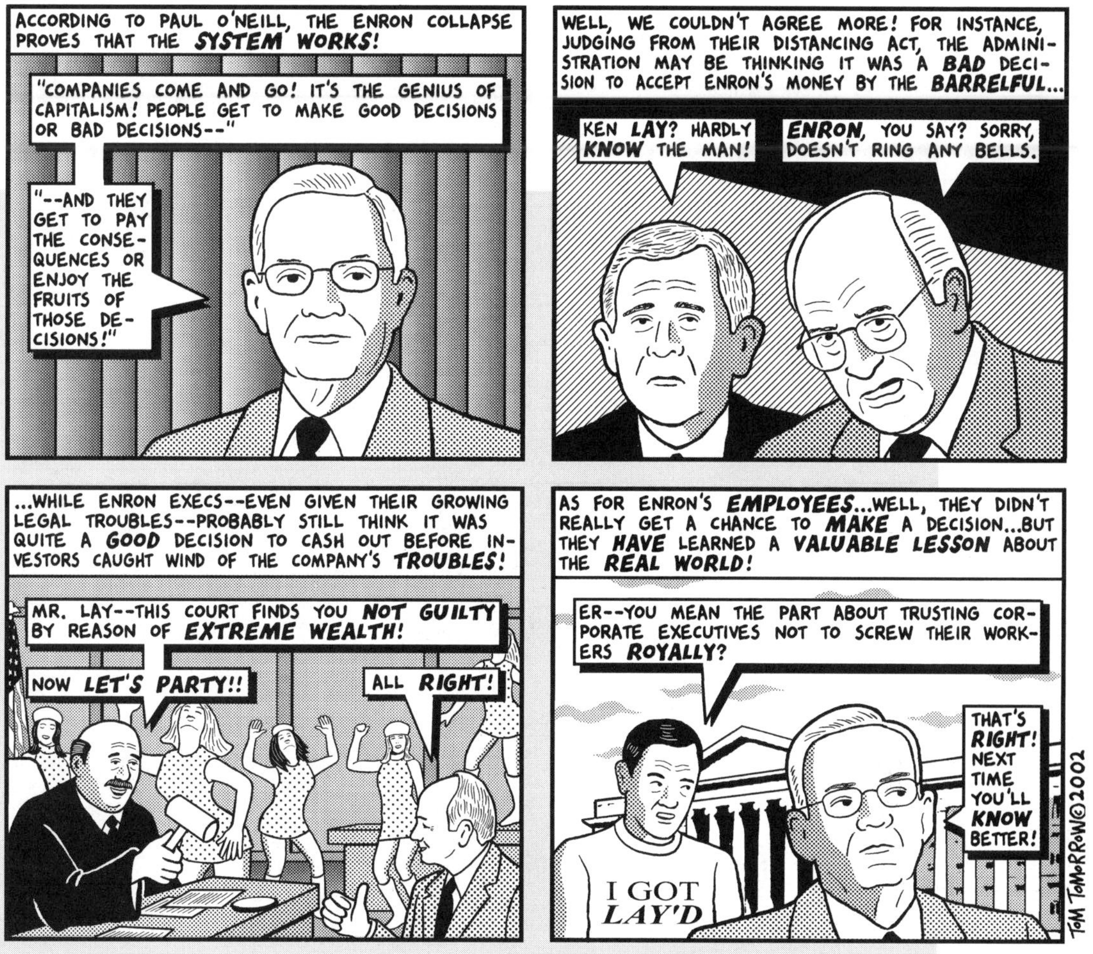
ACCORDING TO PAUL O'NEILL, THE ENRON COLLAPSE PROVES THAT THE SYSTEM WORKS!
"COMPANIES COME AND GO! IT'S THE GENIUS OF CAPITALISM! PEOPLE GET TO MAKE GOOD DECISIONS OR BAD DECISIONS--"
"--AND THEY GET TO PAY THE CONSEQUENCES OR ENJOY THE FRUITS OF THOSE DECISIONS!"
WELL, WE COULDN'T AGREE MORE! FOR INSTANCE, JUDGING FROM THEIR DISTANCING ACT, THE ADMINISTRATION MAY BE THINKING IT WAS A BAD DECISION TO ACCEPT ENRON'S MONEY BY THE BARRELFUL...
KEN LAY? HARDLY KNOW THE MAN!
ENRON, YOU SAY? SORRY, DOESN'T RING ANY BELLS.
...WHILE ENRON EXECS--EVEN GIVEN THEIR GROWING LEGAL TROUBLES--PROBABLY STILL THINK IT WAS QUITE A GOOD DECISION TO CASH OUT BEFORE INVESTORS CAUGHT WIND OF THE COMPANY'S TROUBLES!
MR. LAY--THIS COURT FINDS YOU NOT GUILTY BY REASON OF EXTREME WEALTH!
NOW LET'S PARTY!!
ALL RIGHT!
AS FOR ENRON'S EMPLOYEES...WELL, THEY DIDN'T REALLY GET A CHANCE TO MAKE A DECISION...BUT THEY HAVE LEARNED A VALUABLE LESSON ABOUT THE REAL WORLD!
ER--YOU MEAN THE PART ABOUT TRUSTING CORPORATE EXECUTIVES NOT TO SCREW THEIR WORKERS ROYALLY?
THAT'S RIGHT! NEXT TIME YOU'LL KNOW BETTER!
I GOT LAY'D
TOM TOMORROW©2002

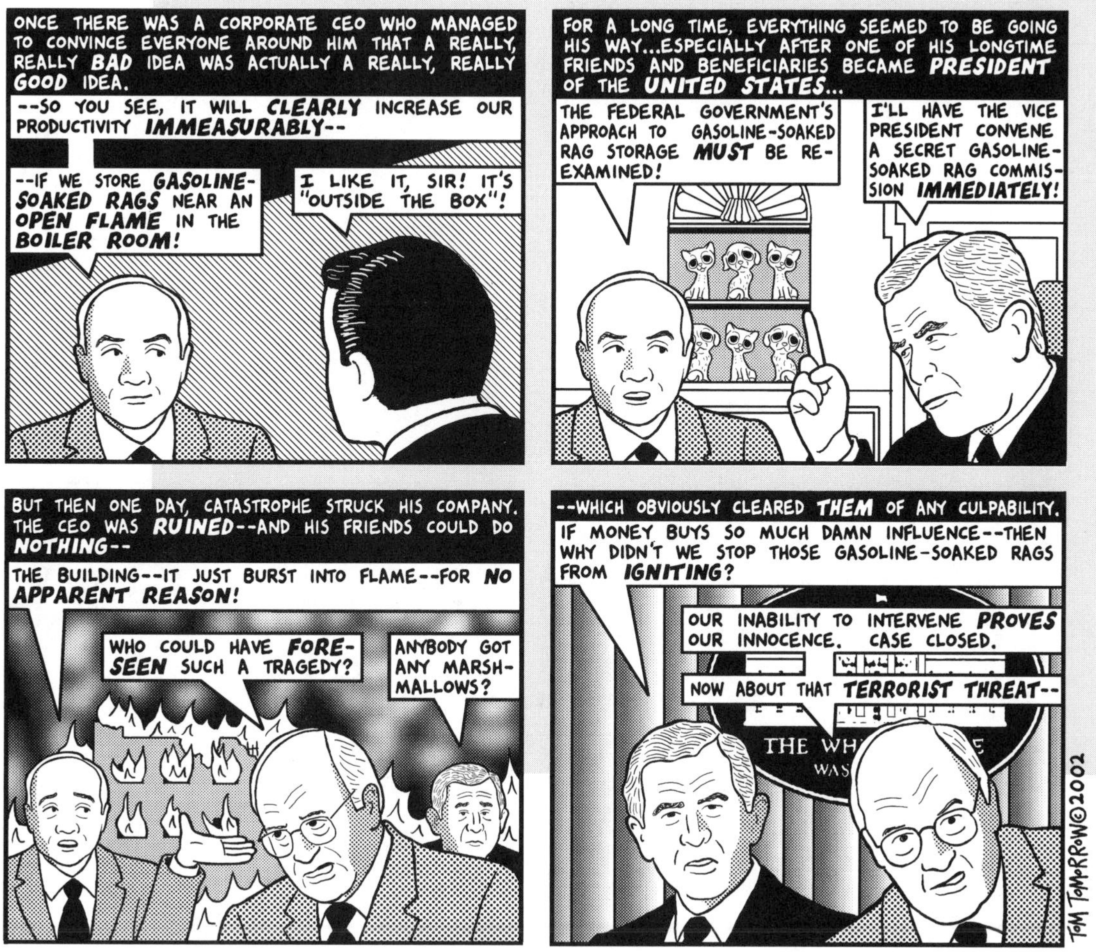
ONCE THERE WAS A CORPORATE CEO WHO MANAGED TO CONVINCE EVERYONE AROUND HIM THAT A REALLY, REALLY BAD IDEA WAS ACTUALLY A REALLY, REALLY GOOD IDEA.
--SO YOU SEE, IT WILL CLEARLY INCREASE OUR PRODUCTIVITY IMMEASURABLY--
--IF WE STORE GASOLINE-SOAKED RAGS NEAR AN OPEN FLAME IN THE BOILER ROOM!
I LIKE IT, SIR! IT'S "OUTSIDE THE BOX"!
FOR A LONG TIME, EVERYTHING SEEMED TO BE GOING HIS WAY...ESPECIALLY AFTER ONE OF HIS LONGTIME FRIENDS AND BENEFICIARIES BECAME PRESIDENT OF THE UNITED STATES...
THE FEDERAL GOVERNMENT'S APPROACH TO GASOLINE-SOAKED RAG STORAGE MUST BE RE-EXAMINED!
I'LL HAVE THE VICE PRESIDENT CONVENE A SECRET GASOLINE-SOAKED RAG COMMISSION IMMEDIATELY!
BUT THEN ONE DAY, CATASTROPHE STRUCK HIS COMPANY. THE CEO WAS RUINED--AND HIS FRIENDS COULD DO NOTHING--
THE BUILDING--IT JUST BURST INTO FLAME--FOR NO APPARENT REASON!
WHO COULD HAVE FORESEEN SUCH A TRAGEDY?
ANYBODY GOT ANY MARSHMALLOWS?
--WHICH OBVIOUSLY CLEARED THEM OF ANY CULPABILITY.
IF MONEY BUYS SO MUCH DAMN INFLUENCE--THEN WHY DIDN'T WE STOP THOSE GASOLINE-SOAKED RAGS FROM IGNITING?
OUR INABILITY TO INTERVENE PROVES OUR INNOCENCE. CASE CLOSED.
NOW ABOUT THAT TERRORIST THREAT--
TOM TOMORROW©2002

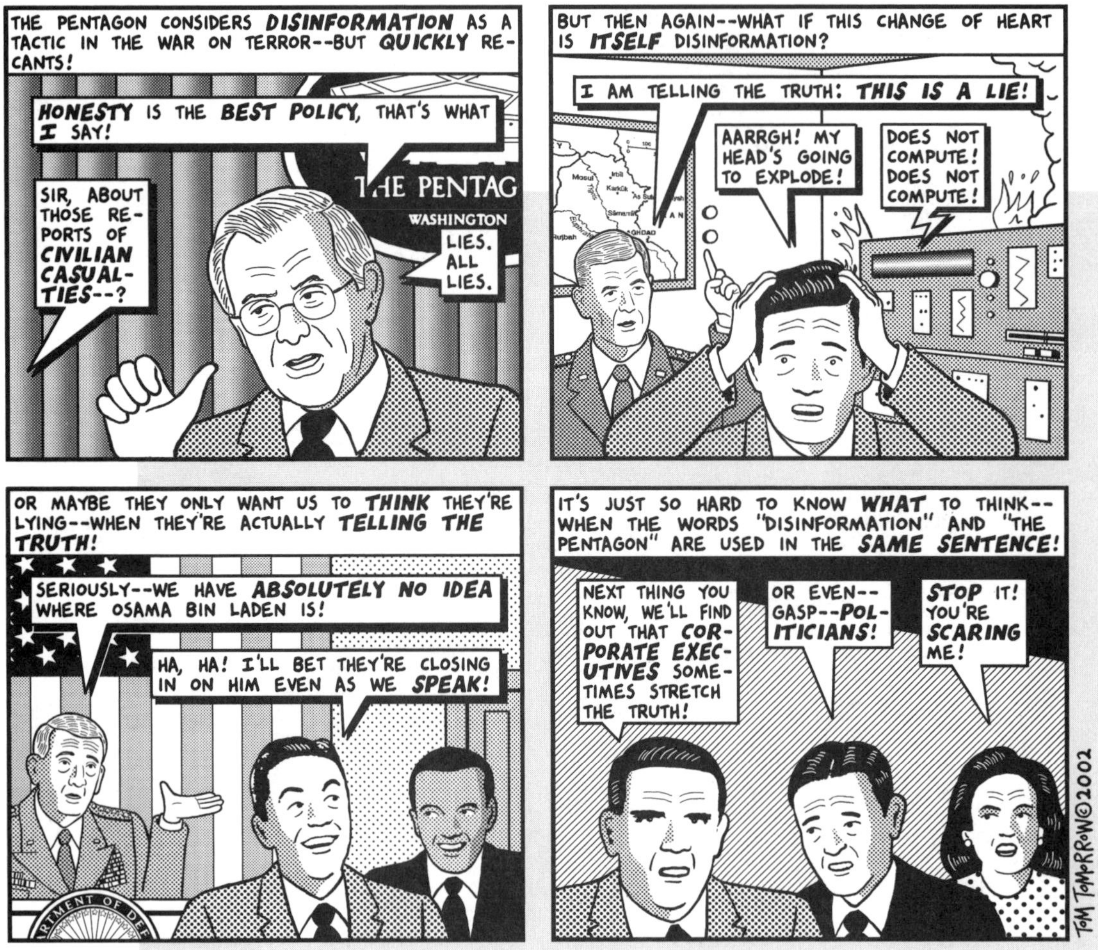
THE PENTAGON CONSIDERS DISINFORMATION AS A TACTIC IN THE WAR ON TERROR--BUT QUICKLY RECANTS!
HONESTY IS THE BEST POLICY, THAT'S WHAT I SAY!
SIR, ABOUT THOSE REPORTS OF CIVILIAN CASUALTIES--?
LIES. ALL LIES.
THE PENTAG
WASHINGTON
BUT THEN AGAIN--WHAT IF THIS CHANGE OF HEART IS ITSELF DISINFORMATION?
I AM TELLING THE TRUTH: THIS IS A LIE!
AARRGH! MY HEAD'S GOING TO EXPLODE!
DOES NOT COMPUTE! DOES NOT COMPUTE!
OR MAYBE THEY ONLY WANT US TO THINK THEY'RE LYING--WHEN THEY'RE ACTUALLY TELLING THE TRUTH!
SERIOUSLY--WE HAVE ABSOLUTELY NO IDEA WHERE OSAMA BIN LADEN IS!
HA, HA! I'LL BET THEY'RE CLOSING IN ON HIM EVEN AS WE SPEAK!
IT'S JUST SO HARD TO KNOW WHAT TO THINK--WHEN THE WORDS "DISINFORMATION" AND "THE PENTAGON" ARE USED IN THE SAME SENTENCE!
NEXT THING YOU KNOW, WE'LL FIND OUT THAT CORPORATE EXECUTIVES SOMETIMES STRETCH THE TRUTH!
OR EVEN--GASP--POLITICIANS!
STOP IT! YOU'RE SCARING ME!
TOM TOMORROW©2002

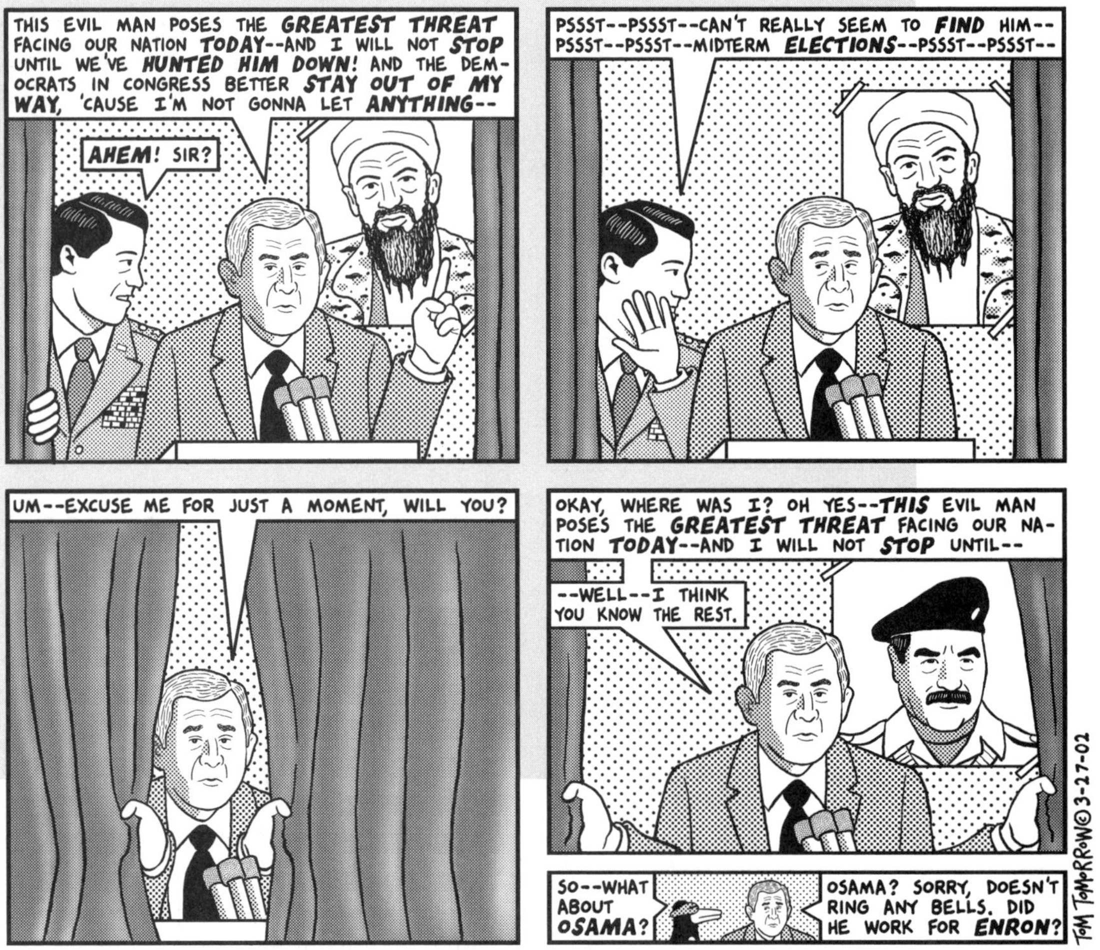
THIS EVIL MAN POSES THE GREATEST THREAT FACING OUR NATION TODAY--AND I WILL NOT STOP UNTIL WE'VE HUNTED HIM DOWN! AND THE DEMOCRATS IN CONGRESS BETTER STAY OUT OF MY WAY, 'CAUSE I'M NOT GONNA LET ANYTHING--
AHEM! SIR?
PSSST--PSSST--CAN'T REALLY SEEM TO FIND HIM--PSSST--PSSST--MIDTERM ELECTIONS--PSSST--PSSST--
UM--EXCUSE ME FOR JUST A MOMENT, WILL YOU?
OKAY, WHERE WAS I? OH YES--THIS EVIL MAN POSES THE GREATEST THREAT FACING OUR NATION TODAY--AND I WILL NOT STOP UNTIL--
--WELL--I THINK YOU KNOW THE REST.
SO--WHAT ABOUT OSAMA?
OSAMA? SORRY, DOESN'T RING ANY BELLS. DID HE WORK FOR ENRON?
TOM TOMORROW©3-27-02

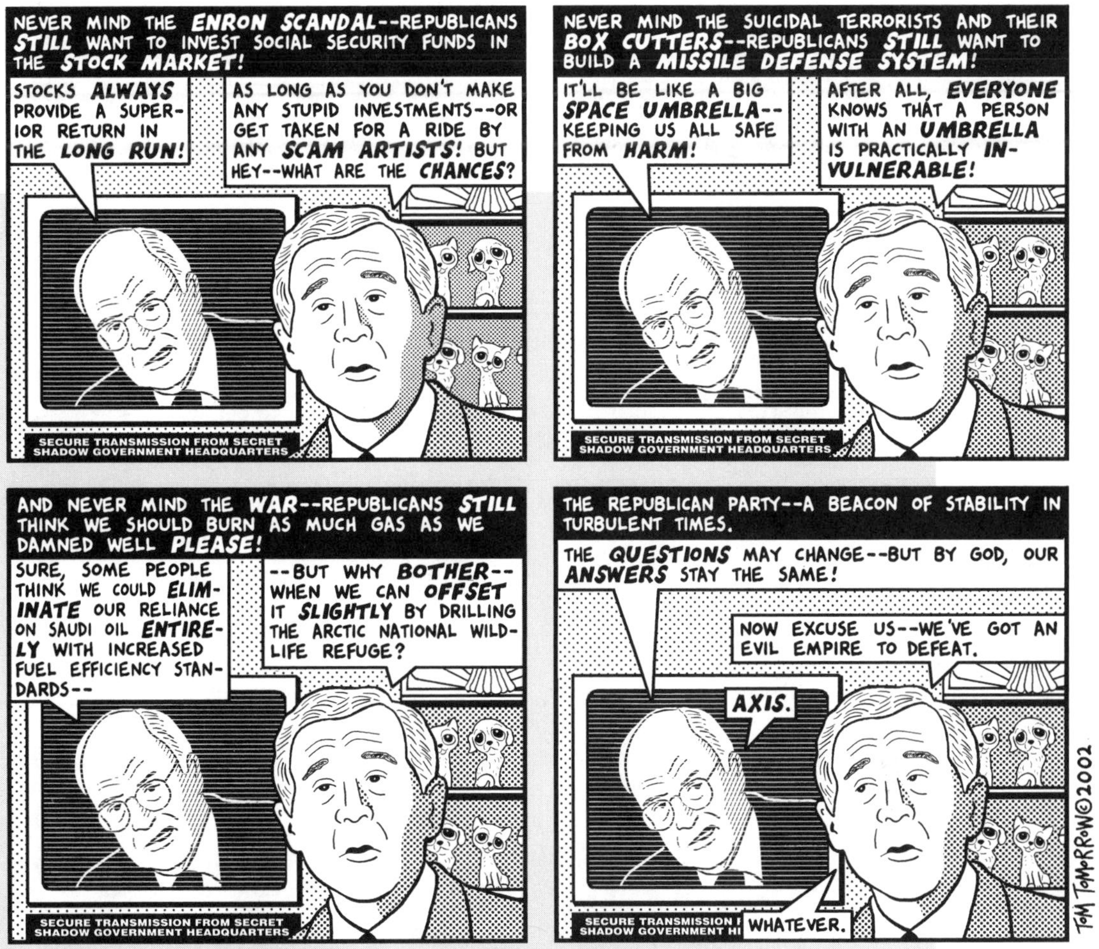
NEVER MIND THE ENRON SCANDAL--REPUBLICANS STILL WANT TO INVEST SOCIAL SECURITY FUNDS IN THE STOCK MARKET!
STOCKS ALWAYS PROVIDE A SUPERIOR RETURN IN THE LONG RUN!
AS LONG AS YOU DON'T MAKE ANY STUPID INVESTMENTS--OR GET TAKEN FOR A RIDE BY ANY SCAM ARTISTS! BUT HEY--WHAT ARE THE CHANCES?
SECURE TRANSMISSION FROM SECRET SHADOW GOVERNMENT HEADQUARTERS
NEVER MIND THE SUICIDAL TERRORISTS AND THEIR BOX CUTTERS--REPUBLICANS STILL WANT TO BUILD A MISSILE DEFENSE SYSTEM!
IT'LL BE LIKE A BIG SPACE UMBRELLA--KEEPING US ALL SAFE FROM HARM!
AFTER ALL, EVERYONE KNOWS THAT A PERSON WITH AN UMBRELLA IS PRACTICALLY INVULNERABLE!
SECURE TRANSMISSION FROM SECRET SHADOW GOVERNMENT HEADQUARTERS
AND NEVER MIND THE WAR--REPUBLICANS STILL THINK WE SHOULD BURN AS MUCH GAS AS WE DAMNED WELL PLEASE!
SURE, SOME PEOPLE THINK WE COULD ELIMINATE OUR RELIANCE ON SAUDI OIL ENTIRELY WITH INCREASED FUEL EFFICIENCY STANDARDS--
--BUT WHY BOTHER--WHEN WE CAN OFFSET IT SLIGHTLY BY DRILLING THE ARCTIC NATIONAL WILDLIFE REFUGE?
SECURE TRANSMISSION FROM SECRET SHADOW GOVERNMENT HEADQUARTERS
THE REPUBLICAN PARTY--A BEACON OF STABILITY IN TURBULENT TIMES.
THE QUESTIONS MAY CHANGE--BUT BY GOD, OUR ANSWERS STAY THE SAME!
NOW EXCUSE US--WE'VE GOT AN EVIL EMPIRE TO DEFEAT.
AXIS.
WHATEVER.
TOM TOMORROW©2002

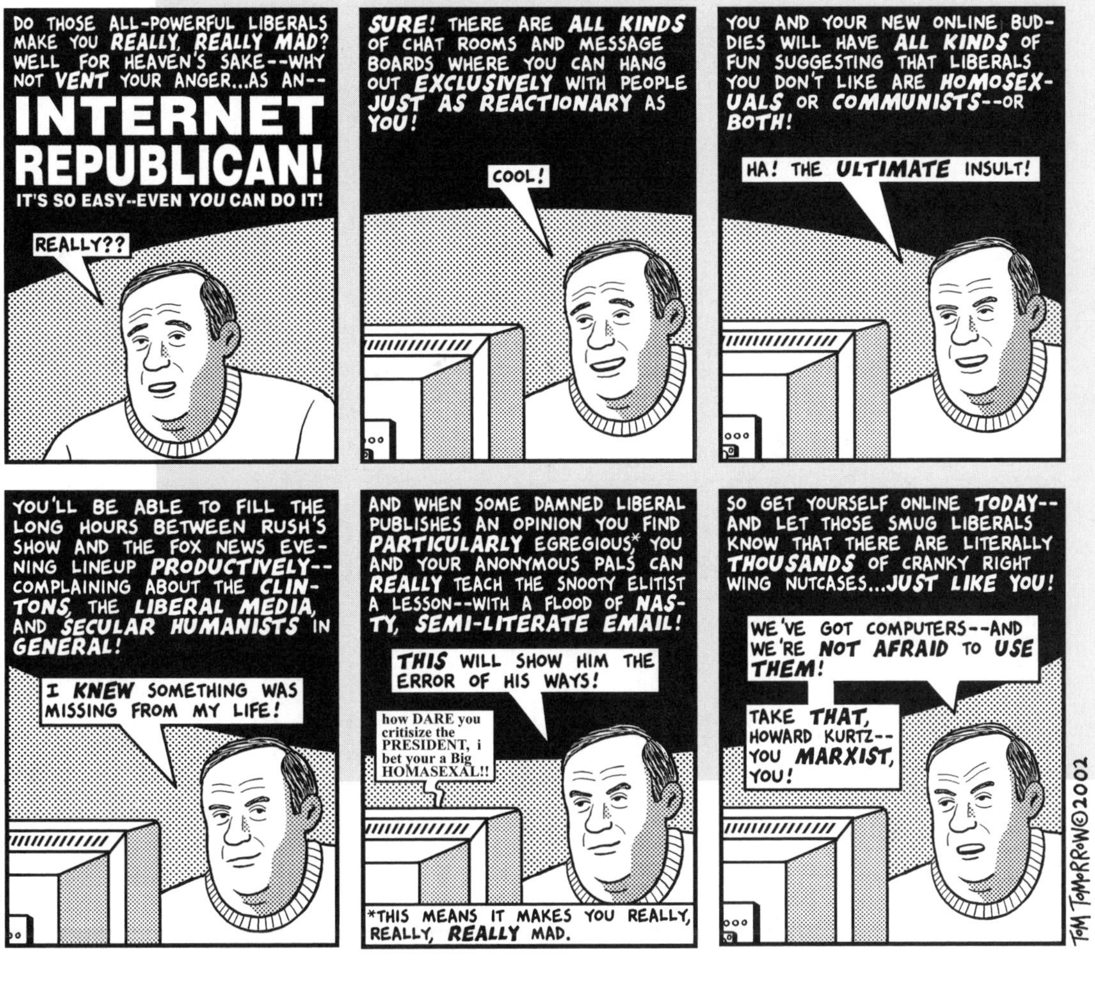
DO THOSE ALL-POWERFUL LIBERALS MAKE YOU REALLY, REALLY MAD? WELL FOR HEAVEN'S SAKE--WHY NOT VENT YOUR ANGER...AS AN--
INTERNET REPUBLICAN!
IT'S SO EASY--EVEN YOU CAN DO IT!
REALLY??
SURE! THERE ARE ALL KINDS OF CHAT ROOMS AND MESSAGE BOARDS WHERE YOU CAN HANG OUT EXCLUSIVELY WITH PEOPLE JUST AS REACTIONARY AS YOU!
COOL!
YOU AND YOUR NEW ONLINE BUDDIES WILL HAVE ALL KINDS OF FUN SUGGESTING THAT LIBERALS YOU DON'T LIKE ARE HOMOSEXUALS OR COMMUNISTS--OR BOTH!
HA! THE ULTIMATE INSULT!
YOU'LL BE ABLE TO FILL THE LONG HOURS BETWEEN RUSH'S SHOW AND THE FOX NEWS EVENING LINEUP PRODUCTIVELY--COMPLAINING ABOUT THE CLINTONS, THE LIBERAL MEDIA, AND SECULAR HUMANISTS IN GENERAL!
I KNEW SOMETHING WAS MISSING FROM MY LIFE!
AND WHEN SOME DAMNED LIBERAL PUBLISHES AN OPINION YOU FIND PARTICULARLY EGREGIOUS,* YOU AND YOUR ANONYMOUS PALS CAN REALLY TEACH THE SNOOTY ELITIST A LESSON--WITH A FLOOD OF NASTY, SEMI-LITERATE EMAIL!
THIS WILL SHOW HIM THE ERROR OF HIS WAYS!
how DARE you critisize the PRESIDENT, i bet your a Big HOMASEXAL!!
*THIS MEANS IT MAKES YOU REALLY, REALLY, REALLY MAD.
SO GET YOURSELF ONLINE TODAY--AND LET THOSE SMUG LIBERALS KNOW THAT THERE ARE LITERALLY THOUSANDS OF CRANKY RIGHT WING NUTCASES...JUST LIKE YOU!
WE'VE GOT COMPUTERS--AND WE'RE NOT AFRAID TO USE THEM!
TAKE THAT, HOWARD KURTZ--YOU MARXIST, YOU!
TOM TOMORROW©2002

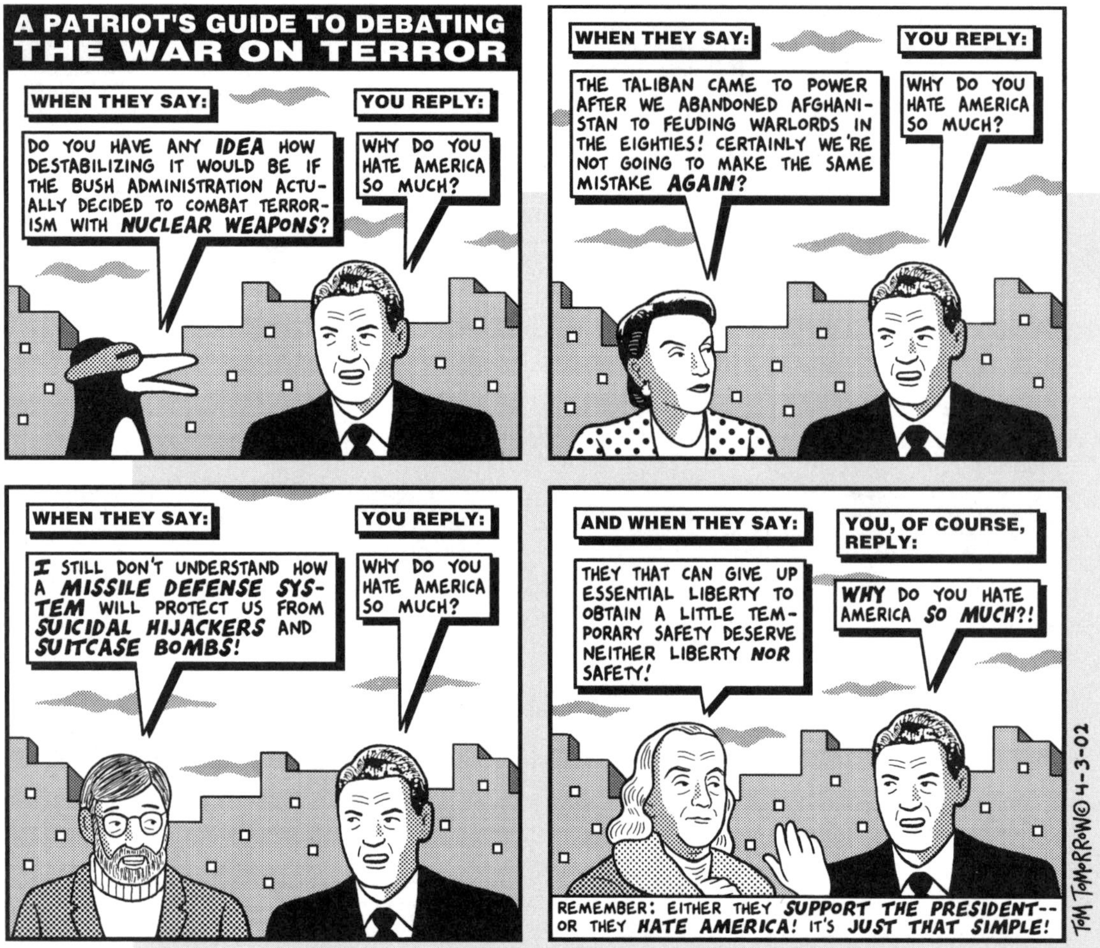
A PATRIOT'S GUIDE TO DEBATING THE WAR ON TERROR
WHEN THEY SAY:
DO YOU HAVE ANY IDEA HOW DESTABILIZING IT WOULD BE IF THE BUSH ADMINISTRATION ACTUALLY DECIDED TO COMBAT TERRORISM WITH NUCLEAR WEAPONS?
YOU REPLY:
WHY DO YOU HATE AMERICA SO MUCH?
WHEN THEY SAY:
THE TALIBAN CAME TO POWER AFTER WE ABANDONED AFGHANISTAN TO FEUDING WARLORDS IN THE EIGHTIES! CERTAINLY WE'RE NOT GOING TO MAKE THE SAME MISTAKE AGAIN?
YOU REPLY:
WHY DO YOU HATE AMERICA SO MUCH?
WHEN THEY SAY:
I STILL DON'T UNDERSTAND HOW A MISSILE DEFENSE SYSTEM WILL PROTECT US FROM SUICIDAL HIJACKERS AND SUITCASE BOMBS!
YOU REPLY:
WHY DO YOU HATE AMERICA SO MUCH?
AND WHEN THEY SAY:
THEY THAT CAN GIVE UP ESSENTIAL LIBERTY TO OBTAIN A LITTLE TEMPORARY SAFETY DESERVE NEITHER LIBERTY NOR SAFETY!
YOU, OF COURSE, REPLY:
WHY DO YOU HATE AMERICA SO MUCH?!
REMEMBER: EITHER THEY SUPPORT THE PRESIDENT-- OR THEY HATE AMERICA! IT'S JUST THAT SIMPLE!
TOM TOMORROW © 4-3-02

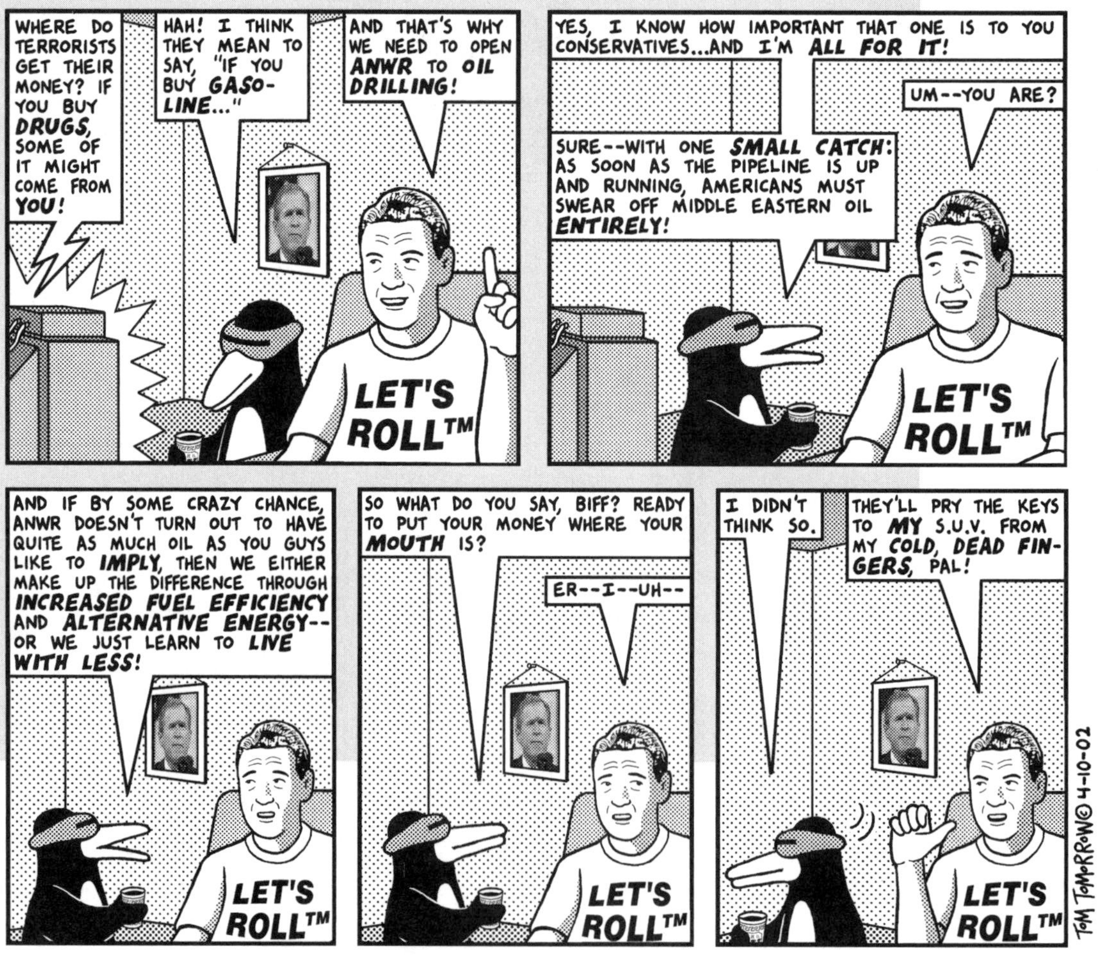
WHERE DO TERRORISTS GET THEIR MONEY? IF YOU BUY DRUGS, SOME OF IT MIGHT COME FROM YOU!
HAH! I THINK THEY MEAN TO SAY, "IF YOU BUY GASOLINE..."
AND THAT'S WHY WE NEED TO OPEN ANWR TO OIL DRILLING!
LET'S ROLL™
YES, I KNOW HOW IMPORTANT THAT ONE IS TO YOU CONSERVATIVES...AND I'M ALL FOR IT!
UM--YOU ARE?
SURE--WITH ONE SMALL CATCH: AS SOON AS THE PIPELINE IS UP AND RUNNING, AMERICANS MUST SWEAR OFF MIDDLE EASTERN OIL ENTIRELY!
LET'S ROLL™
AND IF BY SOME CRAZY CHANCE, ANWR DOESN'T TURN OUT TO HAVE QUITE AS MUCH OIL AS YOU GUYS LIKE TO IMPLY, THEN WE EITHER MAKE UP THE DIFFERENCE THROUGH INCREASED FUEL EFFICIENCY AND ALTERNATIVE ENERGY-- OR WE JUST LEARN TO LIVE WITH LESS!
LET'S ROLL™
SO WHAT DO YOU SAY, BIFF? READY TO PUT YOUR MONEY WHERE YOUR MOUTH IS?
ER--I--UH--
LET'S ROLL™
I DIDN'T THINK SO.
THEY'LL PRY THE KEYS TO MY S.U.V. FROM MY COLD, DEAD FINGERS, PAL!
LET'S ROLL™
TOM TOMORROW © 4-10-02

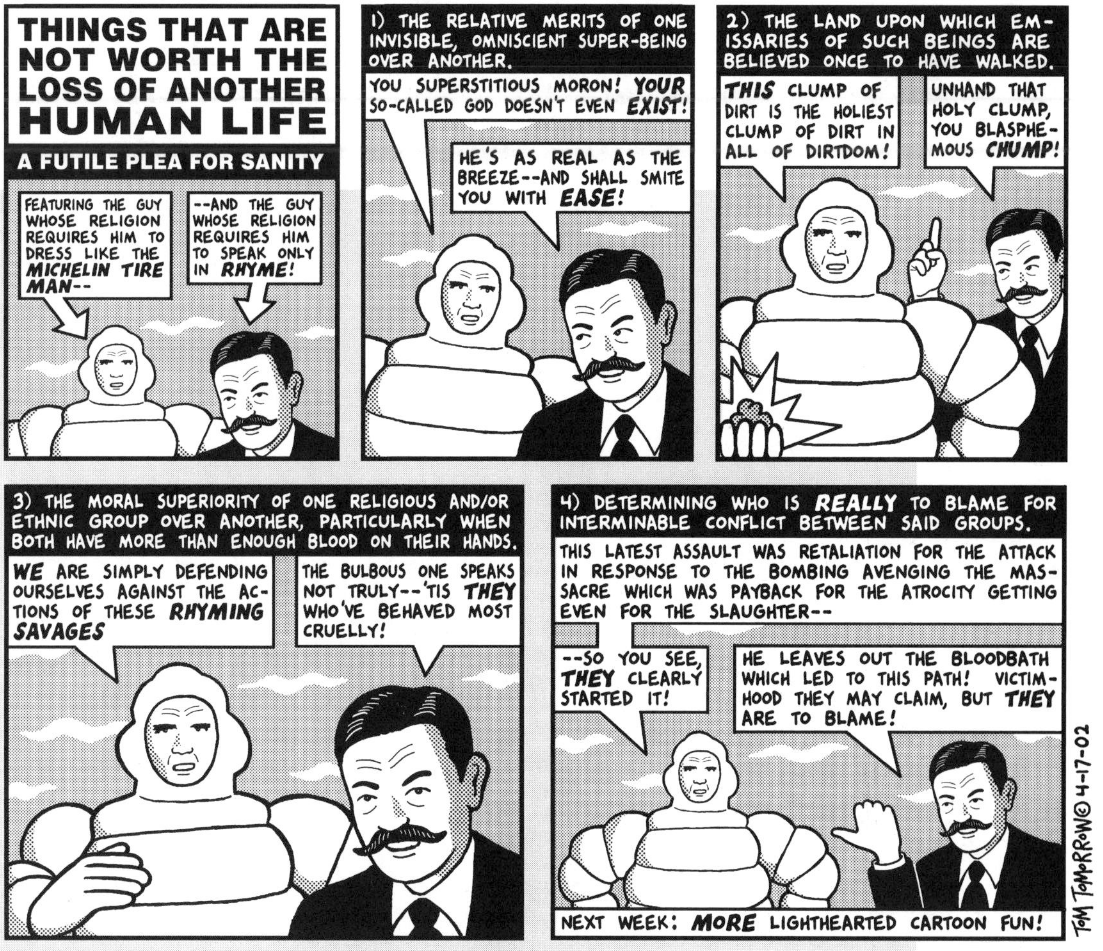
THINGS THAT ARE NOT WORTH THE LOSS OF ANOTHER HUMAN LIFE
A FUTILE PLEA FOR SANITY
FEATURING THE GUY WHOSE RELIGION REQUIRES HIM TO DRESS LIKE THE MICHELIN TIRE MAN--
--AND THE GUY WHOSE RELIGION REQUIRES HIM TO SPEAK ONLY IN RHYME!
1) THE RELATIVE MERITS OF ONE INVISIBLE, OMNISCIENT SUPER-BEING OVER ANOTHER.
YOU SUPERSTITIOUS MORON! YOUR SO-CALLED GOD DOESN'T EVEN EXIST!
HE'S AS REAL AS THE BREEZE--AND SHALL SMITE YOU WITH EASE!
2) THE LAND UPON WHICH EMISSARIES OF SUCH BEINGS ARE BELIEVED ONCE TO HAVE WALKED.
THIS CLUMP OF DIRT IS THE HOLIEST CLUMP OF DIRT IN ALL OF DIRTDOM!
UNHAND THAT HOLY CLUMP, YOU BLASPHEMOUS CHUMP!
3) THE MORAL SUPERIORITY OF ONE RELIGIOUS AND/OR ETHNIC GROUP OVER ANOTHER, PARTICULARLY WHEN BOTH HAVE MORE THAN ENOUGH BLOOD ON THEIR HANDS.
WE ARE SIMPLY DEFENDING OURSELVES AGAINST THE ACTIONS OF THESE RHYMING SAVAGES
THE BULBOUS ONE SPEAKS NOT TRULY--'TIS THEY WHO'VE BEHAVED MOST CRUELLY!
4) DETERMINING WHO IS REALLY TO BLAME FOR INTERMINABLE CONFLICT BETWEEN SAID GROUPS.
THIS LATEST ASSAULT WAS RETALIATION FOR THE ATTACK IN RESPONSE TO THE BOMBING AVENGING THE MASSACRE WHICH WAS PAYBACK FOR THE ATROCITY GETTING EVEN FOR THE SLAUGHTER--
--SO YOU SEE, THEY CLEARLY STARTED IT!
HE LEAVES OUT THE BLOODBATH WHICH LED TO THIS PATH! VICTIMHOOD THEY MAY CLAIM, BUT THEY ARE TO BLAME!
NEXT WEEK: MORE LIGHTHEARTED CARTOON FUN!
TOM TOMORROW© 4-17-02

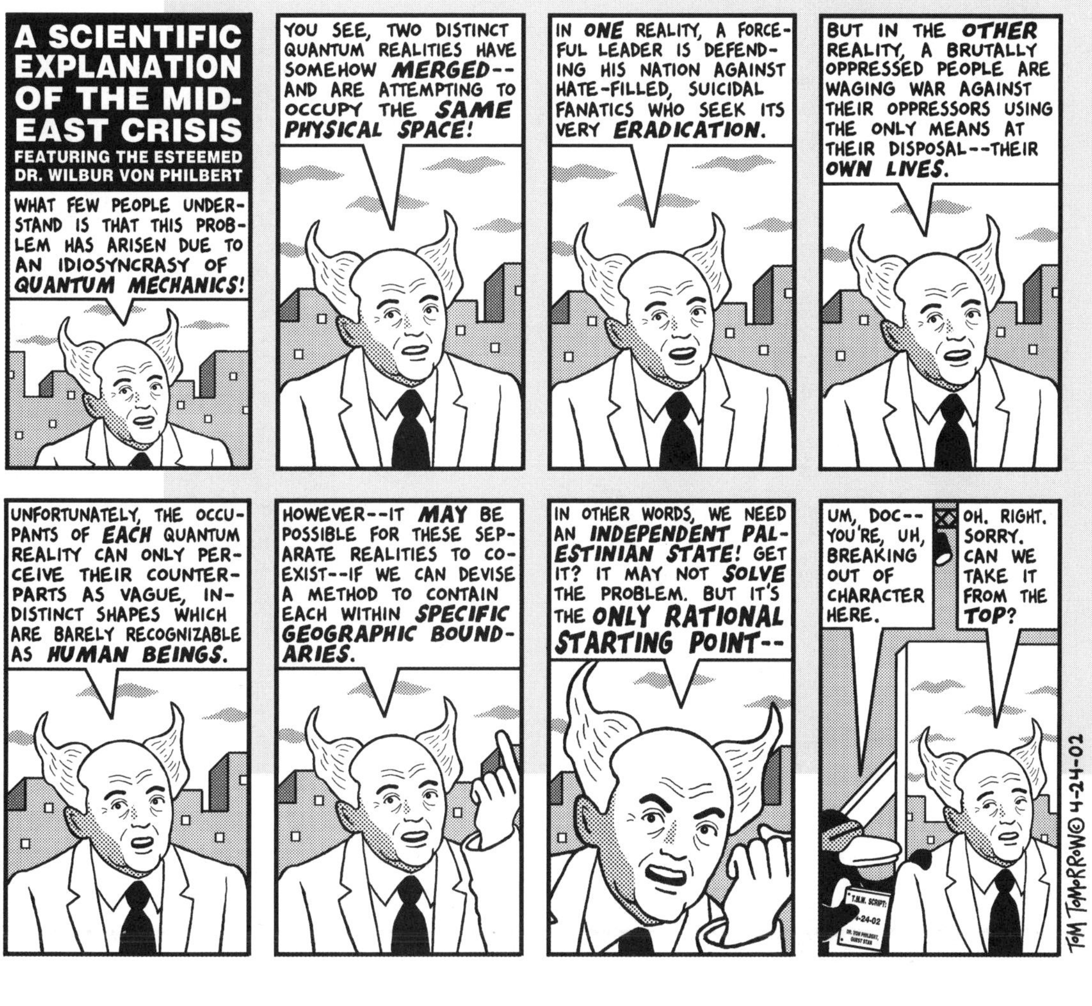
A SCIENTIFIC EXPLANATION OF THE MID-EAST CRISIS
FEATURING THE ESTEEMED DR. WILBUR VON PHILBERT
WHAT FEW PEOPLE UNDERSTAND IS THAT THIS PROBLEM HAS ARISEN DUE TO AN IDIOSYNCRASY OF QUANTUM MECHANICS!
YOU SEE, TWO DISTINCT QUANTUM REALITIES HAVE SOMEHOW MERGED--AND ARE ATTEMPTING TO OCCUPY THE SAME PHYSICAL SPACE!
IN ONE REALITY, A FORCEFUL LEADER IS DEFENDING HIS NATION AGAINST HATE-FILLED, SUICIDAL FANATICS WHO SEEK ITS VERY ERADICATION.
BUT IN THE OTHER REALITY, A BRUTALLY OPPRESSED PEOPLE ARE WAGING WAR AGAINST THEIR OPPRESSORS USING THE ONLY MEANS AT THEIR DISPOSAL--THEIR OWN LIVES.
UNFORTUNATELY, THE OCCUPANTS OF EACH QUANTUM REALITY CAN ONLY PERCEIVE THEIR COUNTERPARTS AS VAGUE, INDISTINCT SHAPES WHICH ARE BARELY RECOGNIZABLE AS HUMAN BEINGS.
HOWEVER--IT MAY BE POSSIBLE FOR THESE SEPARATE REALITIES TO COEXIST--IF WE CAN DEVISE A METHOD TO CONTAIN EACH WITHIN SPECIFIC GEOGRAPHIC BOUNDARIES.
IN OTHER WORDS, WE NEED AN INDEPENDENT PALESTINIAN STATE! GET IT? IT MAY NOT SOLVE THE PROBLEM. BUT IT'S THE ONLY RATIONAL STARTING POINT--
UM, DOC--YOU'RE, UH, BREAKING OUT OF CHARACTER HERE.
OH. RIGHT. SORRY. CAN WE TAKE IT FROM THE TOP?
T.M.W. SCRIPT:
4-24-02
TOM TOMORROW© 4-24-02

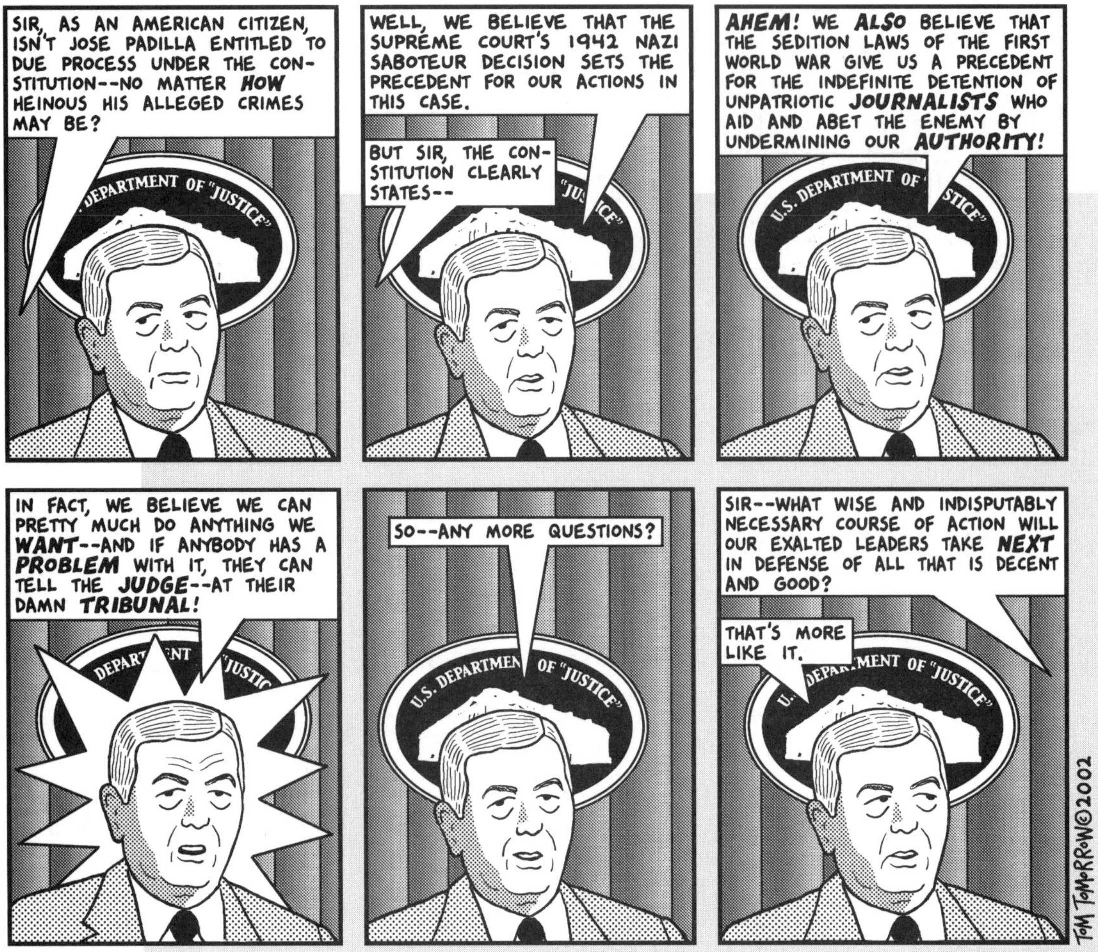
SIR, AS AN AMERICAN CITIZEN, ISN'T JOSE PADILLA ENTITLED TO DUE PROCESS UNDER THE CONSTITUTION--NO MATTER HOW HEINOUS HIS ALLEGED CRIMES MAY BE?
DEPARTMENT OF "JUSTICE"
WELL, WE BELIEVE THAT THE SUPREME COURT'S 1942 NAZI SABOTEUR DECISION SETS THE PRECEDENT FOR OUR ACTIONS IN THIS CASE.
BUT SIR, THE CONSTITUTION CLEARLY STATES--
AHEM! WE ALSO BELIEVE THAT THE SEDITION LAWS OF THE FIRST WORLD WAR GIVE US A PRECEDENT FOR THE INDEFINITE DETENTION OF UNPATRIOTIC JOURNALISTS WHO AID AND ABET THE ENEMY BY UNDERMINING OUR AUTHORITY!
U.S. DEPARTMENT OF "JUSTICE"
IN FACT, WE BELIEVE WE CAN PRETTY MUCH DO ANYTHING WE WANT--AND IF ANYBODY HAS A PROBLEM WITH IT, THEY CAN TELL THE JUDGE--AT THEIR DAMN TRIBUNAL!
SO--ANY MORE QUESTIONS?
U.S. DEPARTMENT OF "JUSTICE"
SIR--WHAT WISE AND INDISPUTABLY NECESSARY COURSE OF ACTION WILL OUR EXALTED LEADERS TAKE NEXT IN DEFENSE OF ALL THAT IS DECENT AND GOOD?
THAT'S MORE LIKE IT.
TOM TOMORROW©2002

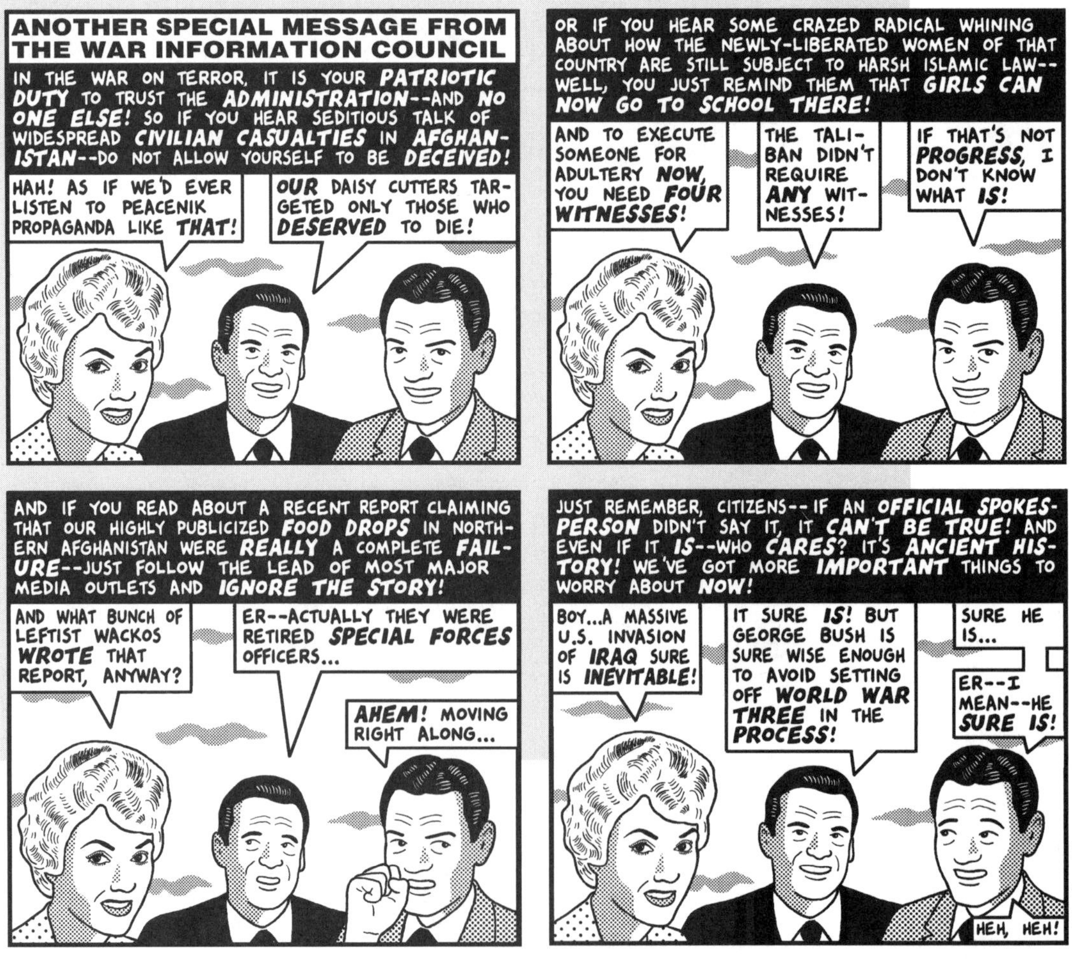
ANOTHER SPECIAL MESSAGE FROM THE WAR INFORMATION COUNCIL
IN THE WAR ON TERROR, IT IS YOUR PATRIOTIC DUTY TO TRUST THE ADMINISTRATION--AND NO ONE ELSE! SO IF YOU HEAR SEDITIOUS TALK OF WIDESPREAD CIVILIAN CASUALTIES IN AFGHANISTAN--DO NOT ALLOW YOURSELF TO BE DECEIVED!
HAH! AS IF WE'D EVER LISTEN TO PEACENIK PROPAGANDA LIKE THAT!
OUR DAISY CUTTERS TARGETED ONLY THOSE WHO DESERVED TO DIE!
OR IF YOU HEAR SOME CRAZED RADICAL WHINING ABOUT HOW THE NEWLY-LIBERATED WOMEN OF THAT COUNTRY ARE STILL SUBJECT TO HARSH ISLAMIC LAW--WELL, YOU JUST REMIND THEM THAT GIRLS CAN NOW GO TO SCHOOL THERE!
AND TO EXECUTE SOMEONE FOR ADULTERY NOW, YOU NEED FOUR WITNESSES!
THE TALIBAN DIDN'T REQUIRE ANY WITNESSES!
IF THAT'S NOT PROGRESS, I DON'T KNOW WHAT IS!
AND IF YOU READ ABOUT A RECENT REPORT CLAIMING THAT OUR HIGHLY PUBLICIZED FOOD DROPS IN NORTHERN AFGHANISTAN WERE REALLY A COMPLETE FAILURE--JUST FOLLOW THE LEAD OF MOST MAJOR MEDIA OUTLETS AND IGNORE THE STORY!
AND WHAT BUNCH OF LEFTIST WACKOS WROTE THAT REPORT, ANYWAY?
ER--ACTUALLY THEY WERE RETIRED SPECIAL FORCES OFFICERS...
AHEM! MOVING RIGHT ALONG...
JUST REMEMBER, CITIZENS--IF AN OFFICIAL SPOKESPERSON DIDN'T SAY IT, IT CAN'T BE TRUE! AND EVEN IF IT IS--WHO CARES? IT'S ANCIENT HISTORY! WE'VE GOT MORE IMPORTANT THINGS TO WORRY ABOUT NOW!
BOY...A MASSIVE U.S. INVASION OF IRAQ SURE IS INEVITABLE!
IT SURE IS! BUT GEORGE BUSH IS SURE WISE ENOUGH TO AVOID SETTING OFF WORLD WAR THREE IN THE PROCESS!
SURE HE IS...
ER--I MEAN--HE SURE IS!
HEH, HEH!
TOM TOMORROW©5-8-02

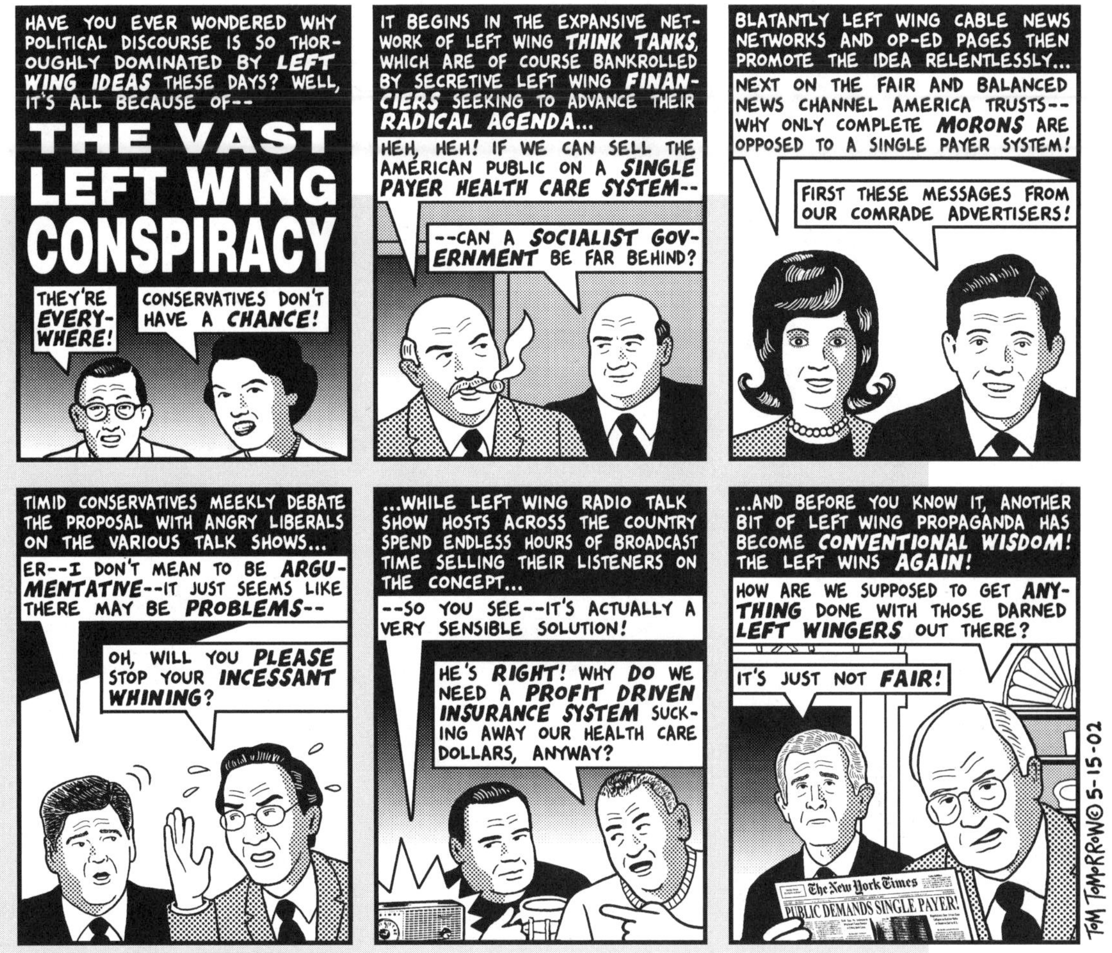
HAVE YOU EVER WONDERED WHY POLITICAL DISCOURSE IS SO THOROUGHLY DOMINATED BY LEFT WING IDEAS THESE DAYS? WELL, IT'S ALL BECAUSE OF--
THE VAST LEFT WING CONSPIRACY
THEY'RE EVERYWHERE!
CONSERVATIVES DON'T HAVE A CHANCE!
IT BEGINS IN THE EXPANSIVE NETWORK OF LEFT WING THINK TANKS, WHICH ARE OF COURSE BANKROLLED BY SECRETIVE LEFT WING FINANCIERS SEEKING TO ADVANCE THEIR RADICAL AGENDA...
HEH, HEH! IF WE CAN SELL THE AMERICAN PUBLIC ON A SINGLE PAYER HEALTH CARE SYSTEM--
--CAN A SOCIALIST GOVERNMENT BE FAR BEHIND?
BLATANTLY LEFT WING CABLE NEWS NETWORKS AND OP-ED PAGES THEN PROMOTE THE IDEA RELENTLESSLY...
NEXT ON THE FAIR AND BALANCED NEWS CHANNEL AMERICA TRUSTS--WHY ONLY COMPLETE MORONS ARE OPPOSED TO A SINGLE PAYER SYSTEM!
FIRST THESE MESSAGES FROM OUR COMRADE ADVERTISERS!
TIMID CONSERVATIVES MEEKLY DEBATE THE PROPOSAL WITH ANGRY LIBERALS ON THE VARIOUS TALK SHOWS...
ER--I DON'T MEAN TO BE ARGUMENTATIVE--IT JUST SEEMS LIKE THERE MAY BE PROBLEMS--
OH, WILL YOU PLEASE STOP YOUR INCESSANT WHINING?
...WHILE LEFT WING RADIO TALK SHOW HOSTS ACROSS THE COUNTRY SPEND ENDLESS HOURS OF BROADCAST TIME SELLING THEIR LISTENERS ON THE CONCEPT...
--SO YOU SEE--IT'S ACTUALLY A VERY SENSIBLE SOLUTION!
HE'S RIGHT! WHY DO WE NEED A PROFIT DRIVEN INSURANCE SYSTEM SUCKING AWAY OUR HEALTH CARE DOLLARS, ANYWAY?
...AND BEFORE YOU KNOW IT, ANOTHER BIT OF LEFT WING PROPAGANDA HAS BECOME CONVENTIONAL WISDOM! THE LEFT WINS AGAIN!
HOW ARE WE SUPPOSED TO GET ANYTHING DONE WITH THOSE DARNED LEFT WINGERS OUT THERE?
IT'S JUST NOT FAIR!
The New York Times
PUBLIC DEMANDS SINGLE PAYER!
TOM TOMORROW©5-15-02

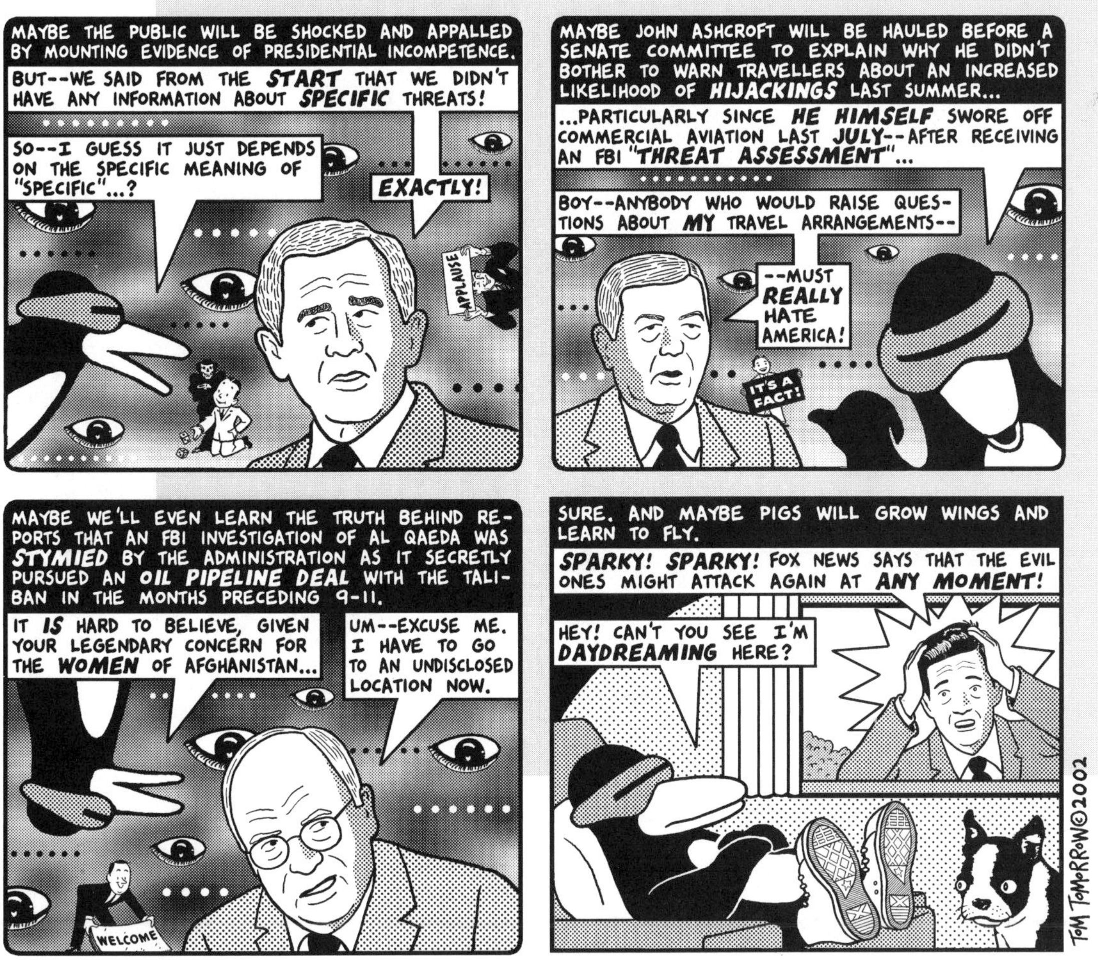
MAYBE THE PUBLIC WILL BE SHOCKED AND APPALLED BY MOUNTING EVIDENCE OF PRESIDENTIAL INCOMPETENCE.
BUT--WE SAID FROM THE START THAT WE DIDN'T HAVE ANY INFORMATION ABOUT SPECIFIC THREATS!
SO--I GUESS IT JUST DEPENDS ON THE SPECIFIC MEANING OF "SPECIFIC"...?
EXACTLY!
APPLAUSE
MAYBE JOHN ASHCROFT WILL BE HAULED BEFORE A SENATE COMMITTEE TO EXPLAIN WHY HE DIDN'T BOTHER TO WARN TRAVELLERS ABOUT AN INCREASED LIKELIHOOD OF HIJACKINGS LAST SUMMER...
...PARTICULARLY SINCE HE HIMSELF SWORE OFF COMMERCIAL AVIATION LAST JULY--AFTER RECEIVING AN FBI "THREAT ASSESSMENT"...
BOY--ANYBODY WHO WOULD RAISE QUESTIONS ABOUT MY TRAVEL ARRANGEMENTS--
--MUST REALLY HATE AMERICA!
IT'S A FACT!
MAYBE WE'LL EVEN LEARN THE TRUTH BEHIND REPORTS THAT AN FBI INVESTIGATION OF AL QAEDA WAS STYMIED BY THE ADMINISTRATION AS IT SECRETLY PURSUED AN OIL PIPELINE DEAL WITH THE TALIBAN IN THE MONTHS PRECEDING 9-11.
IT IS HARD TO BELIEVE, GIVEN YOUR LEGENDARY CONCERN FOR THE WOMEN OF AFGHANISTAN...
UM--EXCUSE ME. I HAVE TO GO TO AN UNDISCLOSED LOCATION NOW.
WELCOME
SURE. AND MAYBE PIGS WILL GROW WINGS AND LEARN TO FLY.
SPARKY! SPARKY! FOX NEWS SAYS THAT THE EVIL ONES MIGHT ATTACK AGAIN AT ANY MOMENT!
HEY! CAN'T YOU SEE I'M DAYDREAMING HERE?
TOM TOMORROW©2002

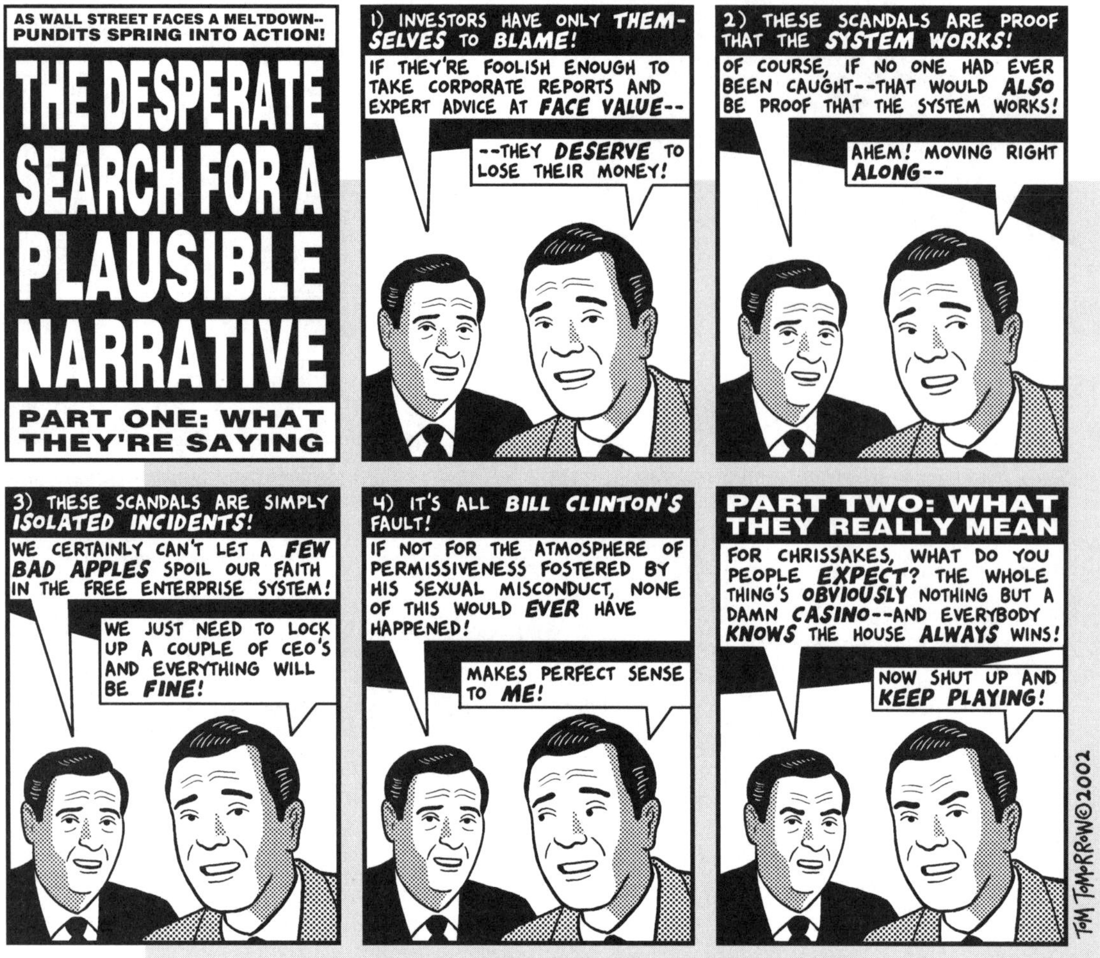
AS WALL STREET FACES A MELTDOWN--PUNDITS SPRING INTO ACTION!
THE DESPERATE SEARCH FOR A PLAUSIBLE NARRATIVE
PART ONE: WHAT THEY'RE SAYING
1) INVESTORS HAVE ONLY THEMSELVES TO BLAME!
IF THEY'RE FOOLISH ENOUGH TO TAKE CORPORATE REPORTS AND EXPERT ADVICE AT FACE VALUE--
--THEY DESERVE TO LOSE THEIR MONEY!
2) THESE SCANDALS ARE PROOF THAT THE SYSTEM WORKS!
OF COURSE, IF NO ONE HAD EVER BEEN CAUGHT--THAT WOULD ALSO BE PROOF THAT THE SYSTEM WORKS!
AHEM! MOVING RIGHT ALONG--
3) THESE SCANDALS ARE SIMPLY ISOLATED INCIDENTS!
WE CERTAINLY CAN'T LET A FEW BAD APPLES SPOIL OUR FAITH IN THE FREE ENTERPRISE SYSTEM!
WE JUST NEED TO LOCK UP A COUPLE OF CEO'S AND EVERYTHING WILL BE FINE!
4) IT'S ALL BILL CLINTON'S FAULT!
IF NOT FOR THE ATMOSPHERE OF PERMISSIVENESS FOSTERED BY HIS SEXUAL MISCONDUCT, NONE OF THIS WOULD EVER HAVE HAPPENED!
MAKES PERFECT SENSE TO ME!
PART TWO: WHAT THEY REALLY MEAN
FOR CHRISSAKES, WHAT DO YOU PEOPLE EXPECT? THE WHOLE THING'S OBVIOUSLY NOTHING BUT A DAMN CASINO--AND EVERYBODY KNOWS THE HOUSE ALWAYS WINS!
NOW SHUT UP AND KEEP PLAYING!
TOM TOMORROW©2002

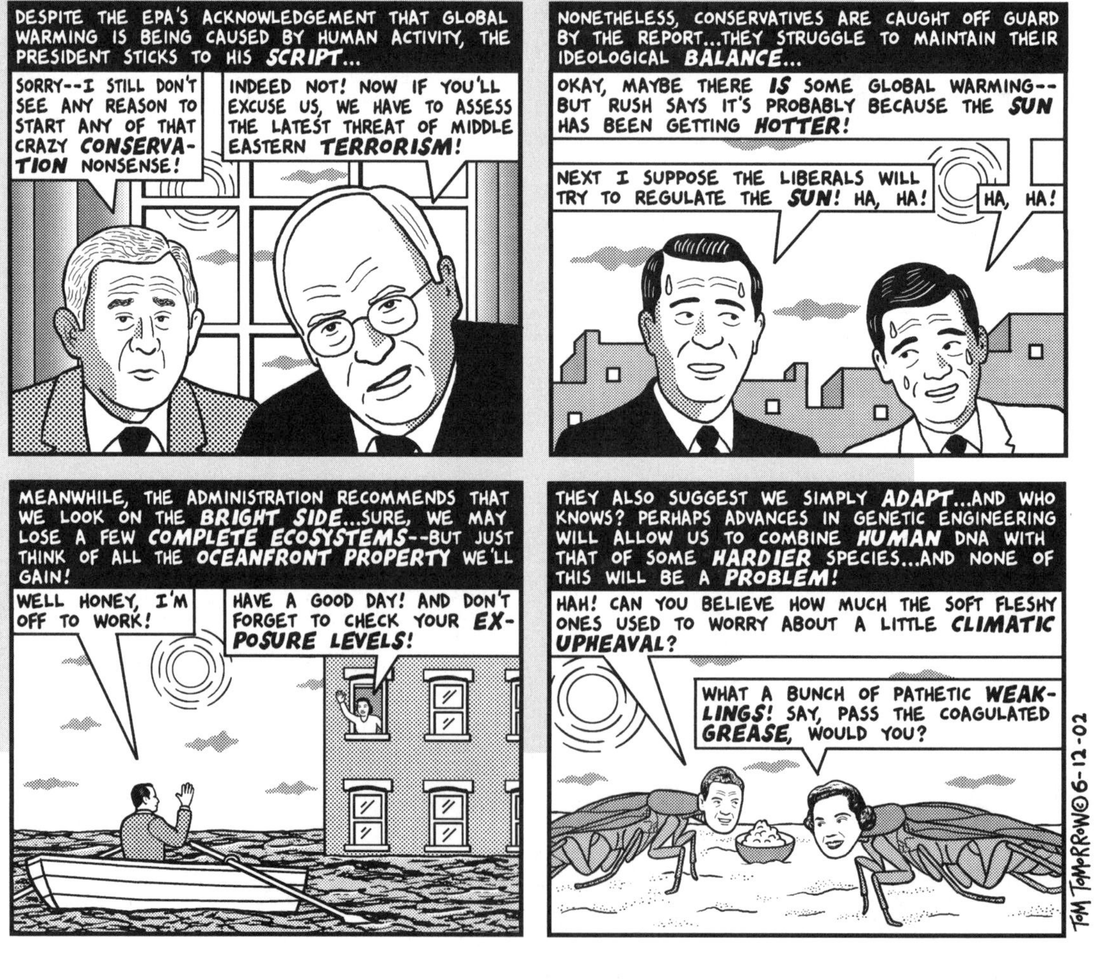
DESPITE THE EPA'S ACKNOWLEDGEMENT THAT GLOBAL WARMING IS BEING CAUSED BY HUMAN ACTIVITY, THE PRESIDENT STICKS TO HIS SCRIPT...
SORRY--I STILL DON'T SEE ANY REASON TO START ANY OF THAT CRAZY CONSERVATION NONSENSE!
INDEED NOT! NOW IF YOU'LL EXCUSE US, WE HAVE TO ASSESS THE LATEST THREAT OF MIDDLE EASTERN TERRORISM!
NONETHELESS, CONSERVATIVES ARE CAUGHT OFF GUARD BY THE REPORT...THEY STRUGGLE TO MAINTAIN THEIR IDEOLOGICAL BALANCE...
OKAY, MAYBE THERE IS SOME GLOBAL WARMING--BUT RUSH SAYS IT'S PROBABLY BECAUSE THE SUN HAS BEEN GETTING HOTTER!
NEXT I SUPPOSE THE LIBERALS WILL TRY TO REGULATE THE SUN! HA, HA!
HA, HA!
MEANWHILE, THE ADMINISTRATION RECOMMENDS THAT WE LOOK ON THE BRIGHT SIDE...SURE, WE MAY LOSE A FEW COMPLETE ECOSYSTEMS--BUT JUST THINK OF ALL THE OCEANFRONT PROPERTY WE'LL GAIN!
WELL HONEY, I'M OFF TO WORK!
HAVE A GOOD DAY! AND DON'T FORGET TO CHECK YOUR EXPOSURE LEVELS!
THEY ALSO SUGGEST WE SIMPLY ADAPT...AND WHO KNOWS? PERHAPS ADVANCES IN GENETIC ENGINEERING WILL ALLOW US TO COMBINE HUMAN DNA WITH THAT OF SOME HARDIER SPECIES...AND NONE OF THIS WILL BE A PROBLEM!
HAH! CAN YOU BELIEVE HOW MUCH THE SOFT FLESHY ONES USED TO WORRY ABOUT A LITTLE CLIMATIC UPHEAVAL?
WHAT A BUNCH OF PATHETIC WEAKLINGS! SAY, PASS THE COAGULATED GREASE, WOULD YOU?
TOM TOMORROW©6-12-02

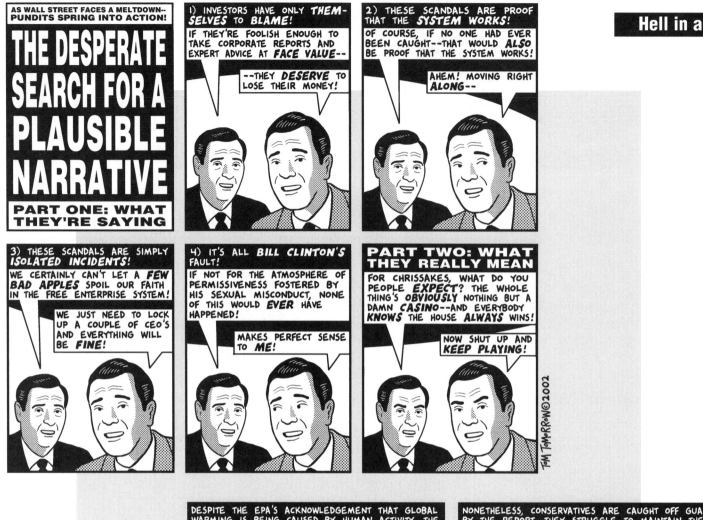

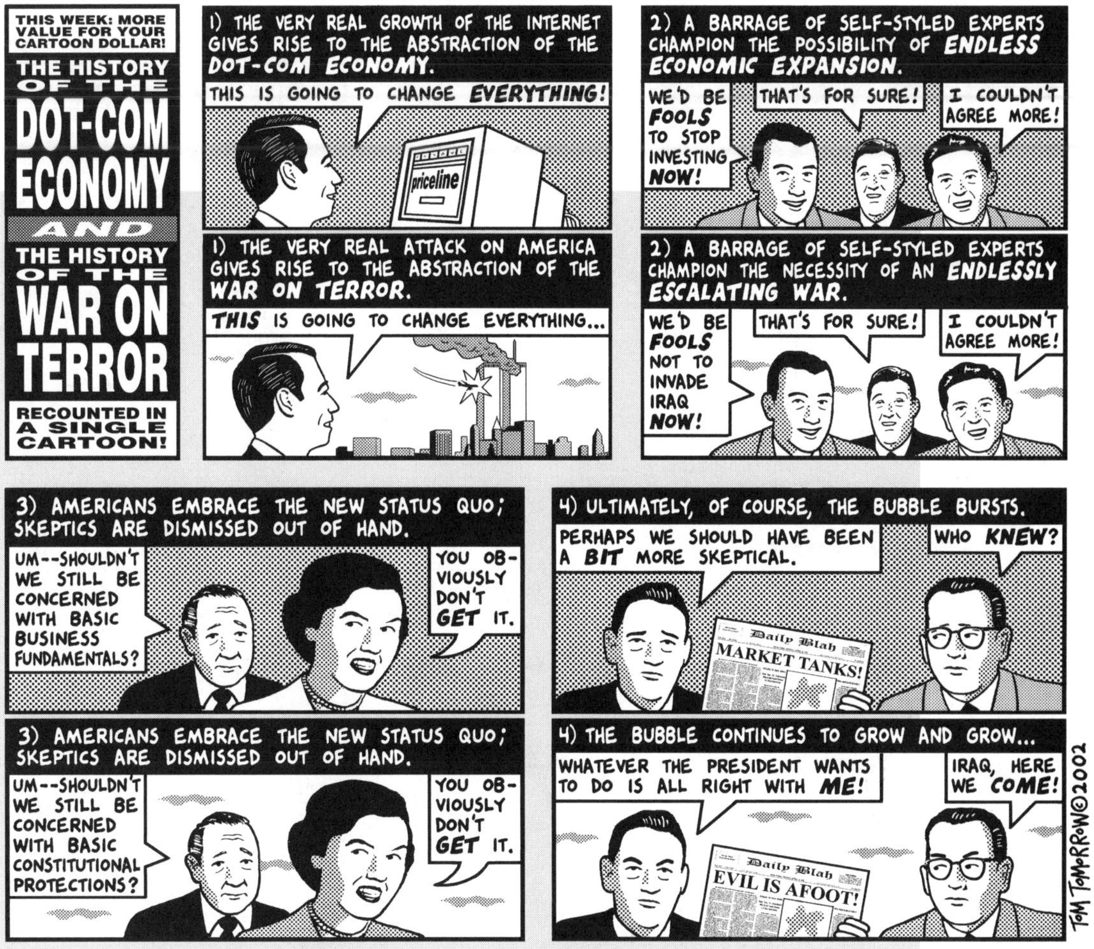
THIS WEEK: MORE VALUE FOR YOUR CARTOON DOLLAR!
THE HISTORY OF THE DOT-COM ECONOMY AND THE HISTORY OF THE WAR ON TERROR RECOUNTED IN A SINGLE CARTOON!
1) THE VERY REAL GROWTH OF THE INTERNET GIVES RISE TO THE ABSTRACTION OF THE DOT-COM ECONOMY.
THIS IS GOING TO CHANGE EVERYTHING!
priceline
2) A BARRAGE OF SELF-STYLED EXPERTS CHAMPION THE POSSIBILITY OF ENDLESS ECONOMIC EXPANSION.
WE'D BE FOOLS TO STOP INVESTING NOW!
THAT'S FOR SURE!
I COULDN'T AGREE MORE!
1) THE VERY REAL ATTACK ON AMERICA GIVES RISE TO THE ABSTRACTION OF THE WAR ON TERROR.
THIS IS GOING TO CHANGE EVERYTHING...
2) A BARRAGE OF SELF-STYLED EXPERTS CHAMPION THE NECESSITY OF AN ENDLESSLY ESCALATING WAR.
WE'D BE FOOLS NOT TO INVADE IRAQ NOW!
THAT'S FOR SURE!
I COULDN'T AGREE MORE!
3) AMERICANS EMBRACE THE NEW STATUS QUO; SKEPTICS ARE DISMISSED OUT OF HAND.
UM--SHOULDN'T WE STILL BE CONCERNED WITH BASIC BUSINESS FUNDAMENTALS?
YOU OBVIOUSLY DON'T GET IT.
4) ULTIMATELY, OF COURSE, THE BUBBLE BURSTS.
PERHAPS WE SHOULD HAVE BEEN A BIT MORE SKEPTICAL.
WHO KNEW?
Daily Blah
MARKET TANKS!
3) AMERICANS EMBRACE THE NEW STATUS QUO; SKEPTICS ARE DISMISSED OUT OF HAND.
UM--SHOULDN'T WE STILL BE CONCERNED WITH BASIC CONSTITUTIONAL PROTECTIONS?
YOU OBVIOUSLY DON'T GET IT.
4) THE BUBBLE CONTINUES TO GROW AND GROW...
WHATEVER THE PRESIDENT WANTS TO DO IS ALL RIGHT WITH ME!
IRAQ, HERE WE COME!
Daily Blah
EVIL IS AFOOT!
TOM TOMORROW©2002

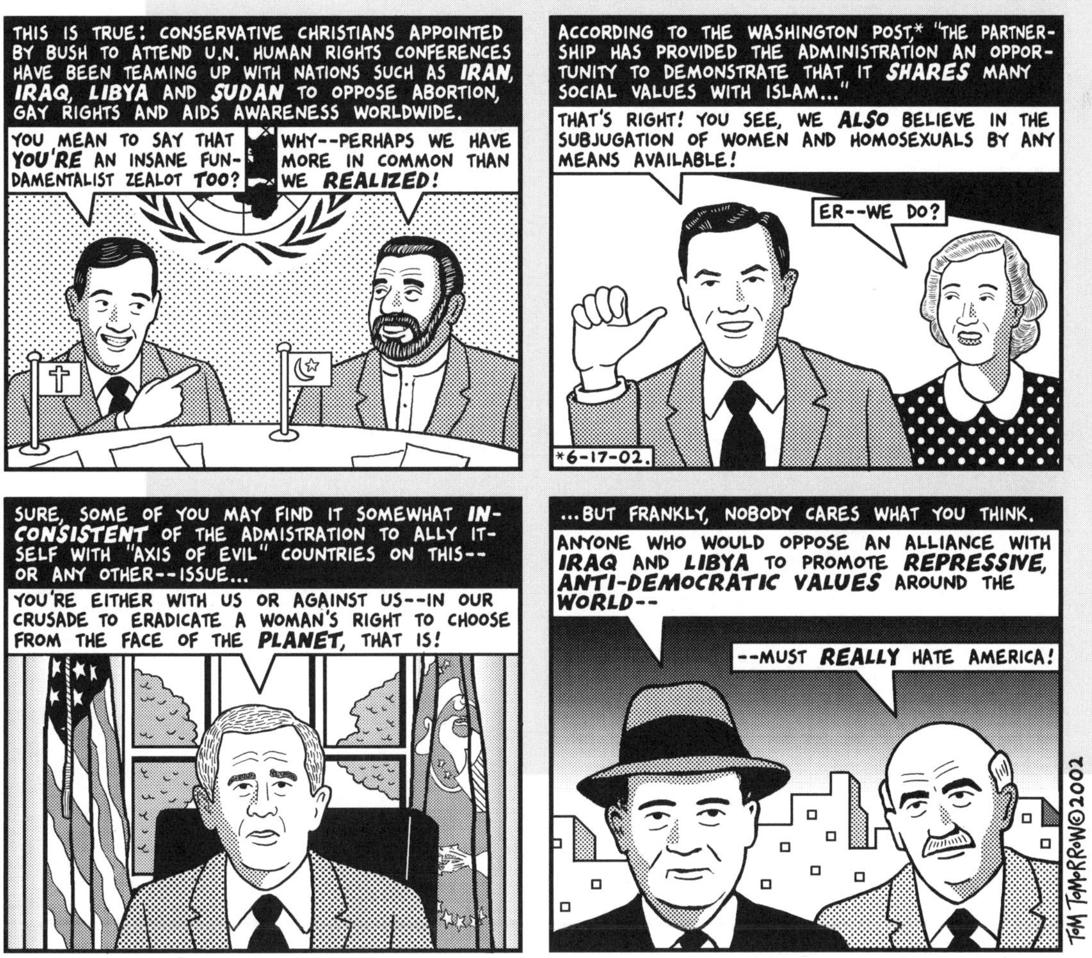
THIS IS TRUE: CONSERVATIVE CHRISTIANS APPOINTED BY BUSH TO ATTEND U.N. HUMAN RIGHTS CONFERENCES HAVE BEEN TEAMING UP WITH NATIONS SUCH AS IRAN, IRAQ, LIBYA AND SUDAN TO OPPOSE ABORTION, GAY RIGHTS AND AIDS AWARENESS WORLDWIDE.
YOU MEAN TO SAY THAT YOU'RE AN INSANE FUNDAMENTALIST ZEALOT TOO?
WHY--PERHAPS WE HAVE MORE IN COMMON THAN WE REALIZED!
ACCORDING TO THE WASHINGTON POST,* "THE PARTNERSHIP HAS PROVIDED THE ADMINISTRATION AN OPPORTUNITY TO DEMONSTRATE THAT IT SHARES MANY SOCIAL VALUES WITH ISLAM..."
THAT'S RIGHT! YOU SEE, WE ALSO BELIEVE IN THE SUBJUGATION OF WOMEN AND HOMOSEXUALS BY ANY MEANS AVAILABLE!
ER--WE DO?
*6-17-02.
SURE, SOME OF YOU MAY FIND IT SOMEWHAT INCONSISTENT OF THE ADMISTRATION TO ALLY ITSELF WITH "AXIS OF EVIL" COUNTRIES ON THIS--OR ANY OTHER--ISSUE...
YOU'RE EITHER WITH US OR AGAINST US--IN OUR CRUSADE TO ERADICATE A WOMAN'S RIGHT TO CHOOSE FROM THE FACE OF THE PLANET, THAT IS!
...BUT FRANKLY, NOBODY CARES WHAT YOU THINK.
ANYONE WHO WOULD OPPOSE AN ALLIANCE WITH IRAQ AND LIBYA TO PROMOTE REPRESSIVE, ANTI-DEMOCRATIC VALUES AROUND THE WORLD--
--MUST REALLY HATE AMERICA!
TOM TOMORROW©2002

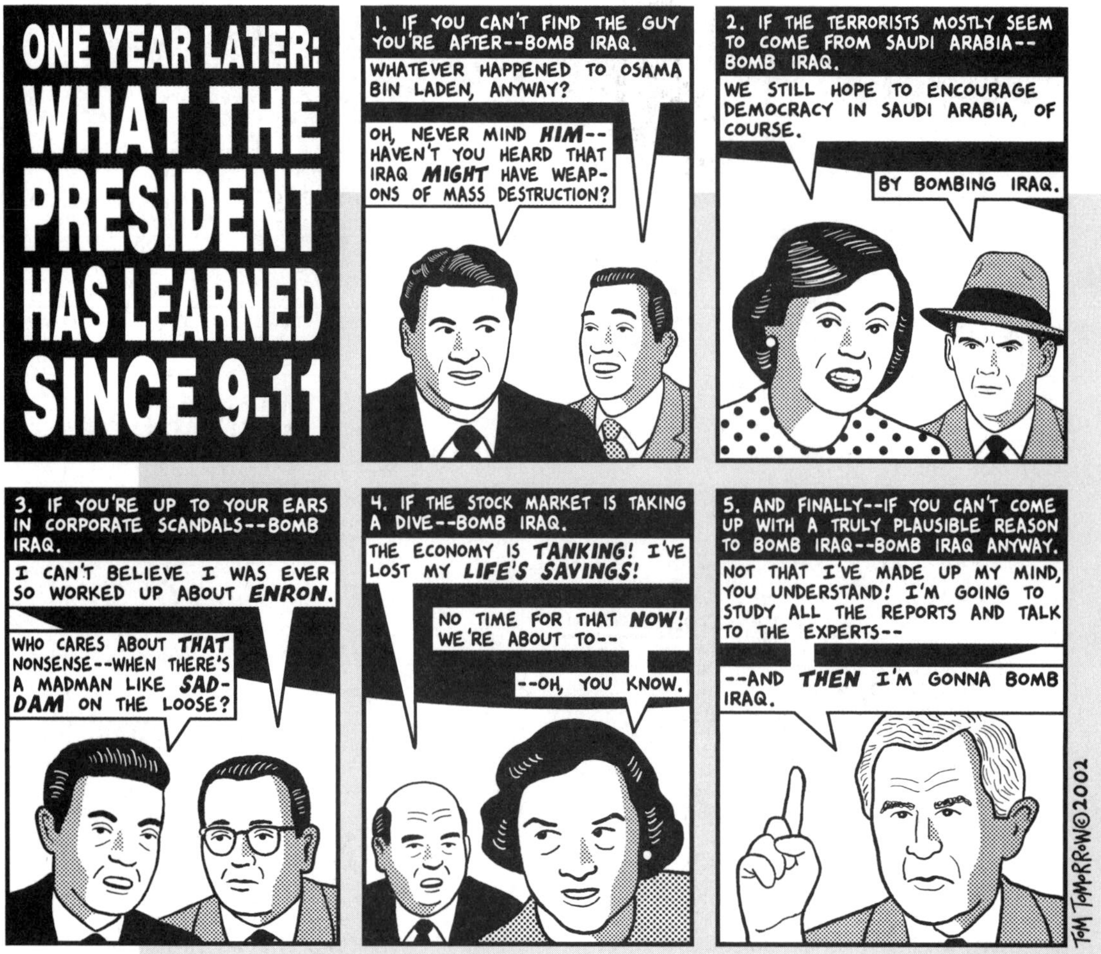
ONE YEAR LATER: WHAT THE PRESIDENT HAS LEARNED SINCE 9-11
1. IF YOU CAN'T FIND THE GUY YOU'RE AFTER--BOMB IRAQ.
WHATEVER HAPPENED TO OSAMA BIN LADEN, ANYWAY?
OH, NEVER MIND HIM--HAVEN'T YOU HEARD THAT IRAQ MIGHT HAVE WEAPONS OF MASS DESTRUCTION?
2. IF THE TERRORISTS MOSTLY SEEM TO COME FROM SAUDI ARABIA--BOMB IRAQ.
WE STILL HOPE TO ENCOURAGE DEMOCRACY IN SAUDI ARABIA, OF COURSE.
BY BOMBING IRAQ.
3. IF YOU'RE UP TO YOUR EARS IN CORPORATE SCANDALS--BOMB IRAQ.
I CAN'T BELIEVE I WAS EVER SO WORKED UP ABOUT ENRON.
WHO CARES ABOUT THAT NONSENSE--WHEN THERE'S A MADMAN LIKE SADDAM ON THE LOOSE?
4. IF THE STOCK MARKET IS TAKING A DIVE--BOMB IRAQ.
THE ECONOMY IS TANKING! I'VE LOST MY LIFE'S SAVINGS!
NO TIME FOR THAT NOW! WE'RE ABOUT TO--
--OH, YOU KNOW.
5. AND FINALLY--IF YOU CAN'T COME UP WITH A TRULY PLAUSIBLE REASON TO BOMB IRAQ--BOMB IRAQ ANYWAY.
NOT THAT I'VE MADE UP MY MIND, YOU UNDERSTAND! I'M GOING TO STUDY ALL THE REPORTS AND TALK TO THE EXPERTS--
--AND THEN I'M GONNA BOMB IRAQ.
TOM TOMORROW©2002

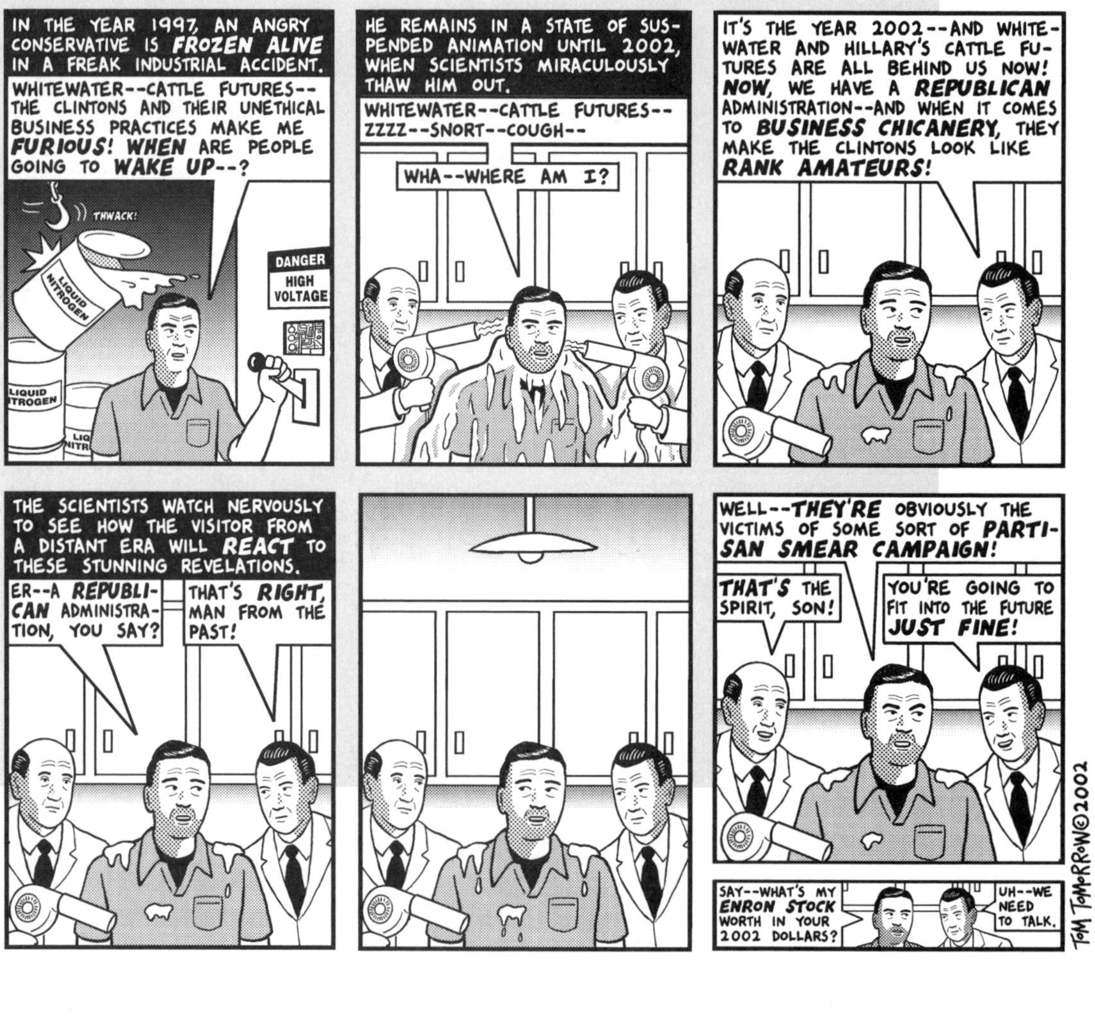
IN THE YEAR 1997, AN ANGRY CONSERVATIVE IS FROZEN ALIVE IN A FREAK INDUSTRIAL ACCIDENT.
WHITEWATER--CATTLE FUTURES--THE CLINTONS AND THEIR UNETHICAL BUSINESS PRACTICES MAKE ME FURIOUS! WHEN ARE PEOPLE GOING TO WAKE UP--?
THWACK!
LIQUID NITROGEN
DANGER
HIGH VOLTAGE
HE REMAINS IN A STATE OF SUSPENDED ANIMATION UNTIL 2002, WHEN SCIENTISTS MIRACULOUSLY THAW HIM OUT.
WHITEWATER--CATTLE FUTURES--ZZZZ--SNORT--COUGH--
WHA--WHERE AM I?
IT'S THE YEAR 2002--AND WHITEWATER AND HILLARY'S CATTLE FUTURES ARE ALL BEHIND US NOW! NOW, WE HAVE A REPUBLICAN ADMINISTRATION--AND WHEN IT COMES TO BUSINESS CHICANERY, THEY MAKE THE CLINTONS LOOK LIKE RANK AMATEURS!
THE SCIENTISTS WATCH NERVOUSLY TO SEE HOW THE VISITOR FROM A DISTANT ERA WILL REACT TO THESE STUNNING REVELATIONS.
ER--A REPUBLICAN ADMINISTRATION, YOU SAY?
THAT'S RIGHT, MAN FROM THE PAST!
WELL--THEY'RE OBVIOUSLY THE VICTIMS OF SOME SORT OF PARTISAN SMEAR CAMPAIGN!
THAT'S THE SPIRIT, SON!
YOU'RE GOING TO FIT INTO THE FUTURE JUST FINE!
SAY--WHAT'S MY ENRON STOCK WORTH IN YOUR 2002 DOLLARS?
UH--WE NEED TO TALK.
TOM TOMORROW©2002

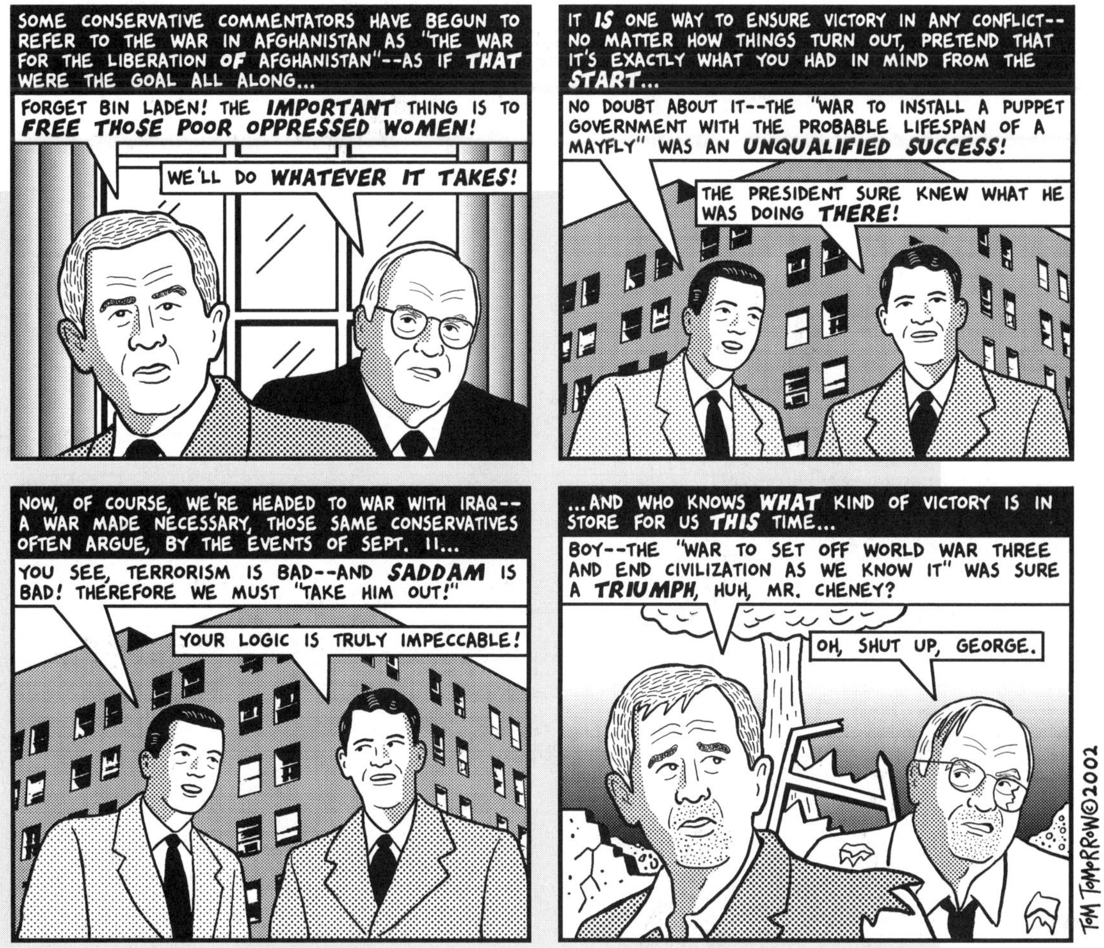
SOME CONSERVATIVE COMMENTATORS HAVE BEGUN TO REFER TO THE WAR IN AFGHANISTAN AS "THE WAR FOR THE LIBERATION OF AFGHANISTAN"--AS IF THAT WERE THE GOAL ALL ALONG...
FORGET BIN LADEN! THE IMPORTANT THING IS TO FREE THOSE POOR OPPRESSED WOMEN!
WE'LL DO WHATEVER IT TAKES!
IT IS ONE WAY TO ENSURE VICTORY IN ANY CONFLICT--NO MATTER HOW THINGS TURN OUT, PRETEND THAT IT'S EXACTLY WHAT YOU HAD IN MIND FROM THE START...
NO DOUBT ABOUT IT--THE "WAR TO INSTALL A PUPPET GOVERNMENT WITH THE PROBABLE LIFESPAN OF A MAYFLY" WAS AN UNQUALIFIED SUCCESS!
THE PRESIDENT SURE KNEW WHAT HE WAS DOING THERE!
NOW, OF COURSE, WE'RE HEADED TO WAR WITH IRAQ--A WAR MADE NECESSARY, THOSE SAME CONSERVATIVES OFTEN ARGUE, BY THE EVENTS OF SEPT. 11...
YOU SEE, TERRORISM IS BAD--AND SADDAM IS BAD! THEREFORE WE MUST "TAKE HIM OUT!"
YOUR LOGIC IS TRULY IMPECCABLE!
...AND WHO KNOWS WHAT KIND OF VICTORY IS IN STORE FOR US THIS TIME...
BOY--THE "WAR TO SET OFF WORLD WAR THREE AND END CIVILIZATION AS WE KNOW IT" WAS SURE A TRIUMPH, HUH, MR. CHENEY?
OH, SHUT UP, GEORGE.
TOM TOMORROW©2002

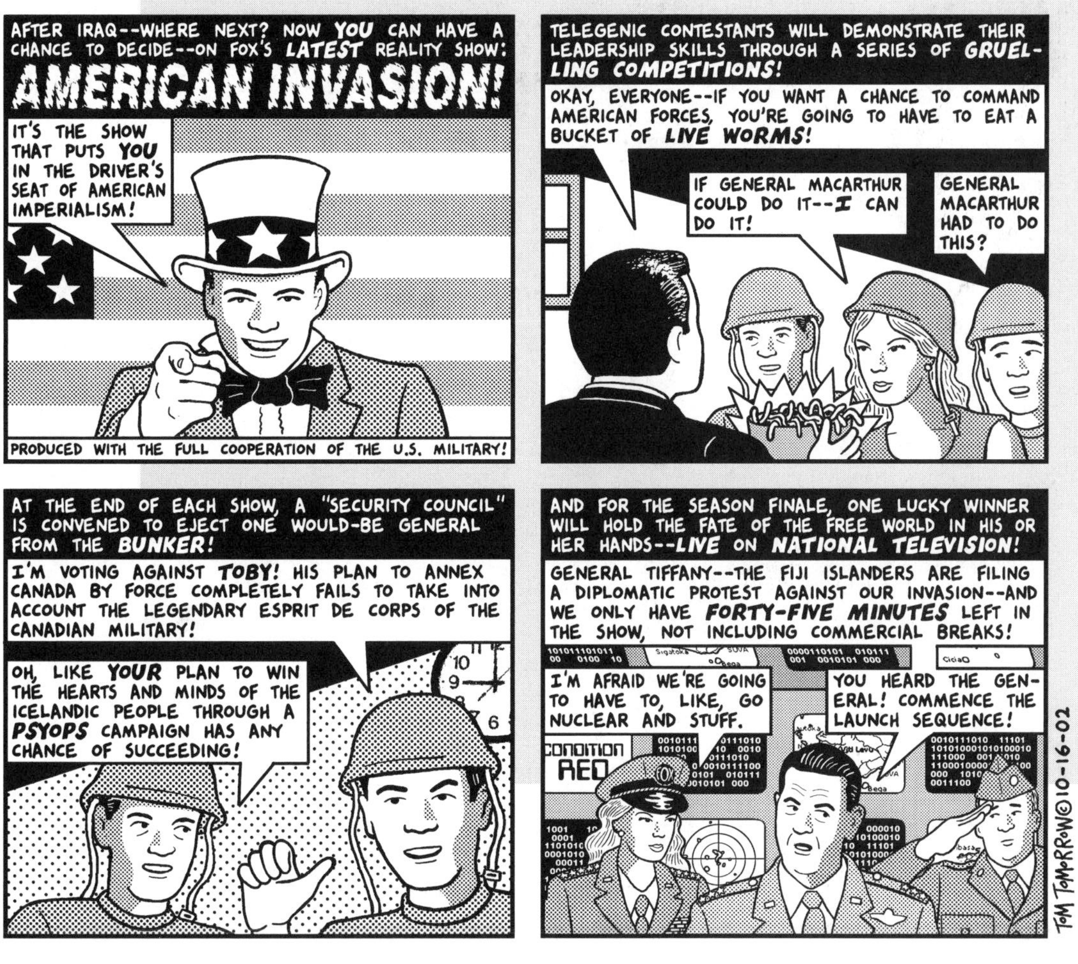
AFTER IRAQ--WHERE NEXT? NOW YOU CAN HAVE A CHANCE TO DECIDE--ON FOX'S LATEST REALITY SHOW:
AMERICAN INVASION!
IT'S THE SHOW THAT PUTS YOU IN THE DRIVER'S SEAT OF AMERICAN IMPERIALISM!
PRODUCED WITH THE FULL COOPERATION OF THE U.S. MILITARY!
TELEGENIC CONTESTANTS WILL DEMONSTRATE THEIR LEADERSHIP SKILLS THROUGH A SERIES OF GRUELLING COMPETITIONS!
OKAY, EVERYONE--IF YOU WANT A CHANCE TO COMMAND AMERICAN FORCES, YOU'RE GOING TO HAVE TO EAT A BUCKET OF LIVE WORMS!
IF GENERAL MACARTHUR COULD DO IT--I CAN DO IT!
GENERAL MACARTHUR HAD TO DO THIS?
AT THE END OF EACH SHOW, A "SECURITY COUNCIL" IS CONVENED TO EJECT ONE WOULD-BE GENERAL FROM THE BUNKER!
I'M VOTING AGAINST TOBY! HIS PLAN TO ANNEX CANADA BY FORCE COMPLETELY FAILS TO TAKE INTO ACCOUNT THE LEGENDARY ESPRIT DE CORPS OF THE CANADIAN MILITARY!
OH, LIKE YOUR PLAN TO WIN THE HEARTS AND MINDS OF THE ICELANDIC PEOPLE THROUGH A PSYOPS CAMPAIGN HAS ANY CHANCE OF SUCCEEDING!
AND FOR THE SEASON FINALE, ONE LUCKY WINNER WILL HOLD THE FATE OF THE FREE WORLD IN HIS OR HER HANDS--LIVE ON NATIONAL TELEVISION!
GENERAL TIFFANY--THE FIJI ISLANDERS ARE FILING A DIPLOMATIC PROTEST AGAINST OUR INVASION--AND WE ONLY HAVE FORTY-FIVE MINUTES LEFT IN THE SHOW, NOT INCLUDING COMMERCIAL BREAKS!
I'M AFRAID WE'RE GOING TO HAVE TO, LIKE, GO NUCLEAR AND STUFF.
YOU HEARD THE GENERAL! COMMENCE THE LAUNCH SEQUENCE!
CONDITION RED
TOM TOMORROW©10-16-02

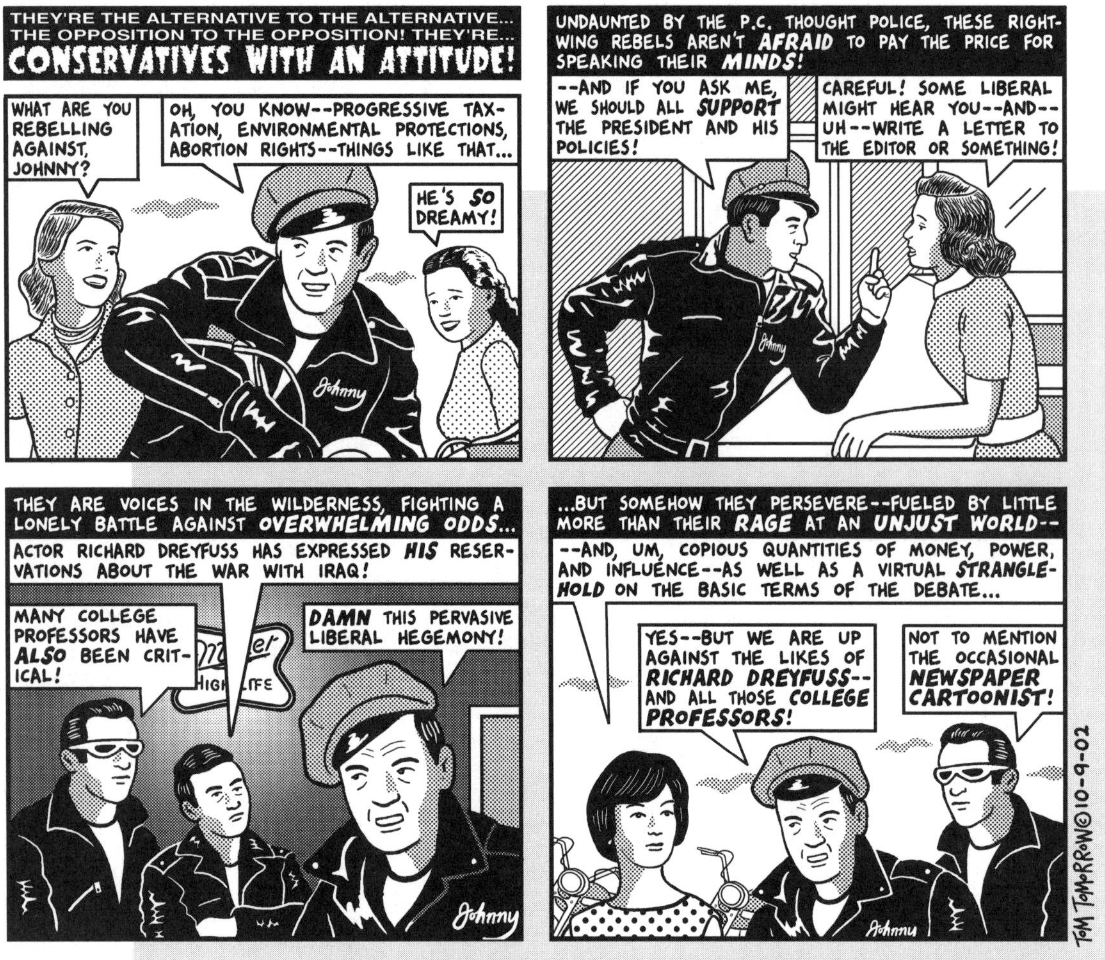
THEY'RE THE ALTERNATIVE TO THE ALTERNATIVE... THE OPPOSITION TO THE OPPOSITION! THEY'RE...
CONSERVATIVES WITH AN ATTITUDE!
WHAT ARE YOU REBELLING AGAINST, JOHNNY?
OH, YOU KNOW--PROGRESSIVE TAXATION, ENVIRONMENTAL PROTECTIONS, ABORTION RIGHTS--THINGS LIKE THAT...
HE'S SO DREAMY!
Johnny
UNDAUNTED BY THE P.C. THOUGHT POLICE, THESE RIGHT-WING REBELS AREN'T AFRAID TO PAY THE PRICE FOR SPEAKING THEIR MINDS!
--AND IF YOU ASK ME, WE SHOULD ALL SUPPORT THE PRESIDENT AND HIS POLICIES!
CAREFUL! SOME LIBERAL MIGHT HEAR YOU--AND--UH--WRITE A LETTER TO THE EDITOR OR SOMETHING!
Johnny
THEY ARE VOICES IN THE WILDERNESS, FIGHTING A LONELY BATTLE AGAINST OVERWHELMING ODDS...
ACTOR RICHARD DREYFUSS HAS EXPRESSED HIS RESERVATIONS ABOUT THE WAR WITH IRAQ!
MANY COLLEGE PROFESSORS HAVE ALSO BEEN CRITICAL!
DAMN THIS PERVASIVE LIBERAL HEGEMONY!
Johnny
...BUT SOMEHOW THEY PERSEVERE--FUELED BY LITTLE MORE THAN THEIR RAGE AT AN UNJUST WORLD--
--AND, UM, COPIOUS QUANTITIES OF MONEY, POWER, AND INFLUENCE--AS WELL AS A VIRTUAL STRANGLEHOLD ON THE BASIC TERMS OF THE DEBATE...
YES--BUT WE ARE UP AGAINST THE LIKES OF RICHARD DREYFUSS--AND ALL THOSE COLLEGE PROFESSORS!
NOT TO MENTION THE OCCASIONAL NEWSPAPER CARTOONIST!
Johnny
TOM TOMORROW©10-9-02

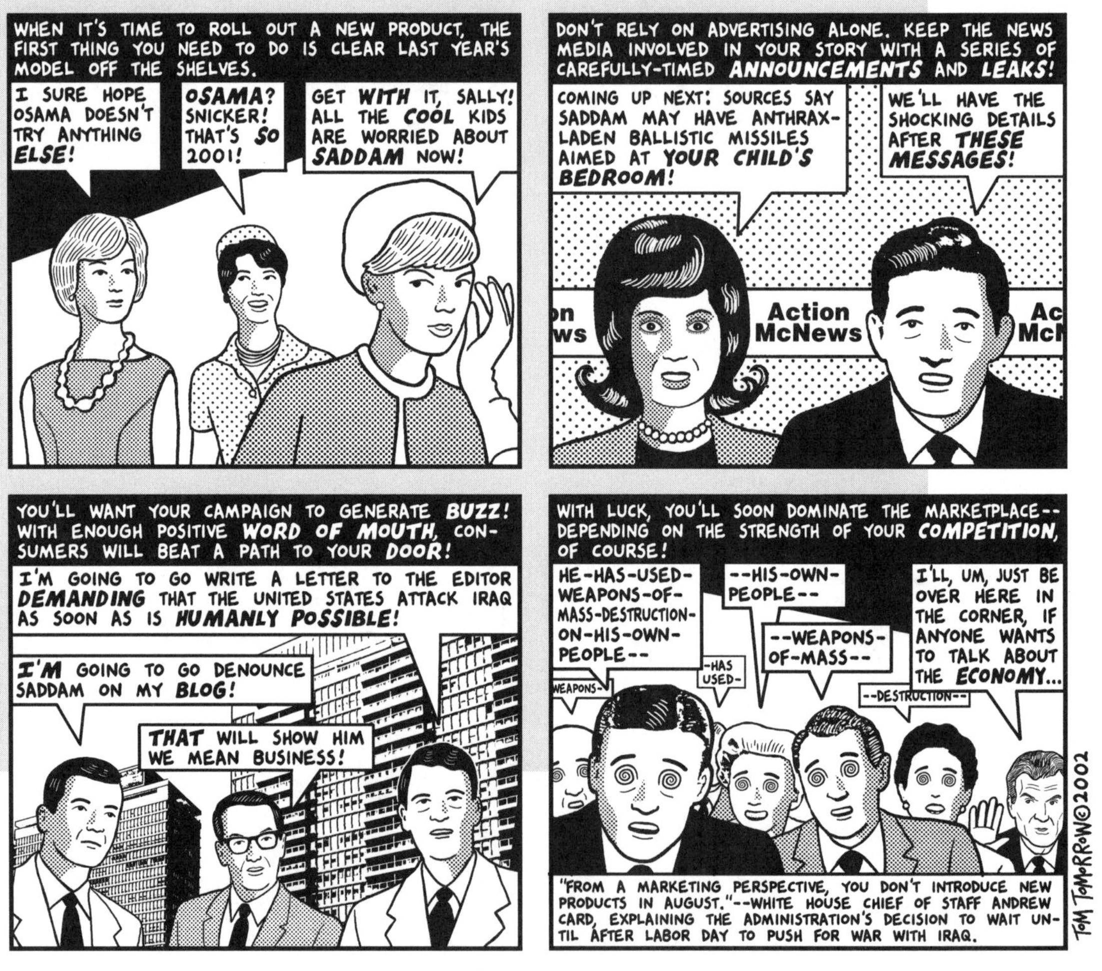
WHEN IT'S TIME TO ROLL OUT A NEW PRODUCT, THE FIRST THING YOU NEED TO DO IS CLEAR LAST YEAR'S MODEL OFF THE SHELVES.
I SURE HOPE OSAMA DOESN'T TRY ANYTHING ELSE!
OSAMA? SNICKER! THAT'S SO 2001!
GET WITH IT, SALLY! ALL THE COOL KIDS ARE WORRIED ABOUT SADDAM NOW!
DON'T RELY ON ADVERTISING ALONE. KEEP THE NEWS MEDIA INVOLVED IN YOUR STORY WITH A SERIES OF CAREFULLY-TIMED ANNOUNCEMENTS AND LEAKS!
COMING UP NEXT: SOURCES SAY SADDAM MAY HAVE ANTHRAX-LADEN BALLISTIC MISSILES AIMED AT YOUR CHILD'S BEDROOM!
WE'LL HAVE THE SHOCKING DETAILS AFTER THESE MESSAGES!
Action McNews
YOU'LL WANT YOUR CAMPAIGN TO GENERATE BUZZ! WITH ENOUGH POSITIVE WORD OF MOUTH, CONSUMERS WILL BEAT A PATH TO YOUR DOOR!
I'M GOING TO GO WRITE A LETTER TO THE EDITOR DEMANDING THAT THE UNITED STATES ATTACK IRAQ AS SOON AS IS HUMANLY POSSIBLE!
I'M GOING TO GO DENOUNCE SADDAM ON MY BLOG!
THAT WILL SHOW HIM WE MEAN BUSINESS!
WITH LUCK, YOU'LL SOON DOMINATE THE MARKETPLACE--DEPENDING ON THE STRENGTH OF YOUR COMPETITION, OF COURSE!
HE-HAS-USED-WEAPONS-OF-MASS-DESTRUCTION-ON-HIS-OWN-PEOPLE--
--HIS-OWN-PEOPLE--
--WEAPONS-OF-MASS--
WEAPONS-
-HAS USED-
--DESTRUCTION--
I'LL, UM, JUST BE OVER HERE IN THE CORNER, IF ANYONE WANTS TO TALK ABOUT THE ECONOMY...
"FROM A MARKETING PERSPECTIVE, YOU DON'T INTRODUCE NEW PRODUCTS IN AUGUST."--WHITE HOUSE CHIEF OF STAFF ANDREW CARD, EXPLAINING THE ADMINISTRATION'S DECISION TO WAIT UNTIL AFTER LABOR DAY TO PUSH FOR WAR WITH IRAQ.
TOM TOMORROW©2002

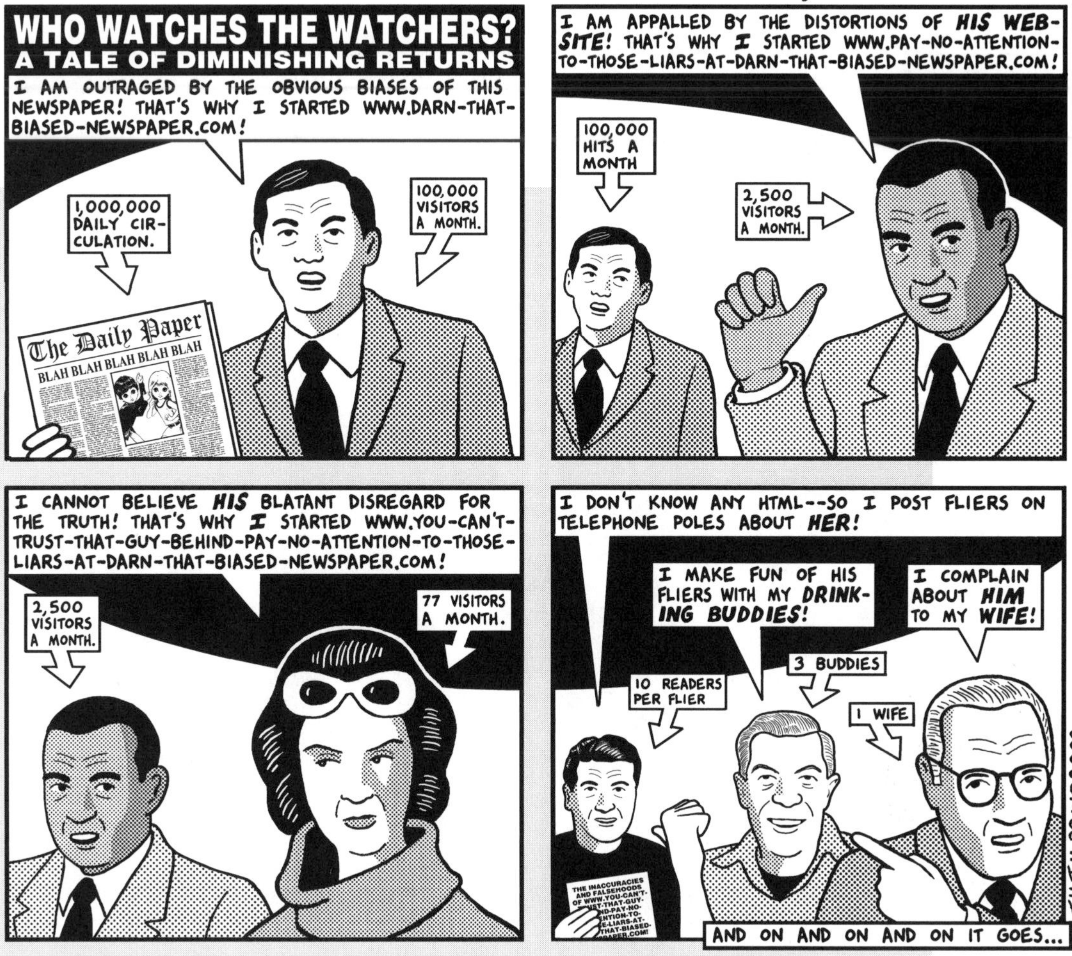
WHO WATCHES THE WATCHERS?
A TALE OF DIMINISHING RETURNS
I AM OUTRAGED BY THE OBVIOUS BIASES OF THIS NEWSPAPER! THAT'S WHY I STARTED WWW.DARN-THAT-BIASED-NEWSPAPER.COM!
1,000,000 DAILY CIRCULATION.
100,000 VISITORS A MONTH.
The Daily Paper
BLAH BLAH BLAH BLAH BLAH
I AM APPALLED BY THE DISTORTIONS OF HIS WEB-SITE! THAT'S WHY I STARTED WWW.PAY-NO-ATTENTION-TO-THOSE-LIARS-AT-DARN-THAT-BIASED-NEWSPAPER.COM!
100,000 HITS A MONTH
2,500 VISITORS A MONTH.
I CANNOT BELIEVE HIS BLATANT DISREGARD FOR THE TRUTH! THAT'S WHY I STARTED WWW.YOU-CAN'T-TRUST-THAT-GUY-BEHIND-PAY-NO-ATTENTION-TO-THOSE-LIARS-AT-DARN-THAT-BIASED-NEWSPAPER.COM!
2,500 VISITORS A MONTH.
77 VISITORS A MONTH.
I DON'T KNOW ANY HTML--SO I POST FLIERS ON TELEPHONE POLES ABOUT HER!
I MAKE FUN OF HIS FLIERS WITH MY DRINKING BUDDIES!
I COMPLAIN ABOUT HIM TO MY WIFE!
10 READERS PER FLIER
3 BUDDIES
1 WIFE
THE INACCURACIES AND FALSEHOODS OF WWW.YOU-CAN'T-
AND ON AND ON AND ON IT GOES...
TOM TOMORROW©2002

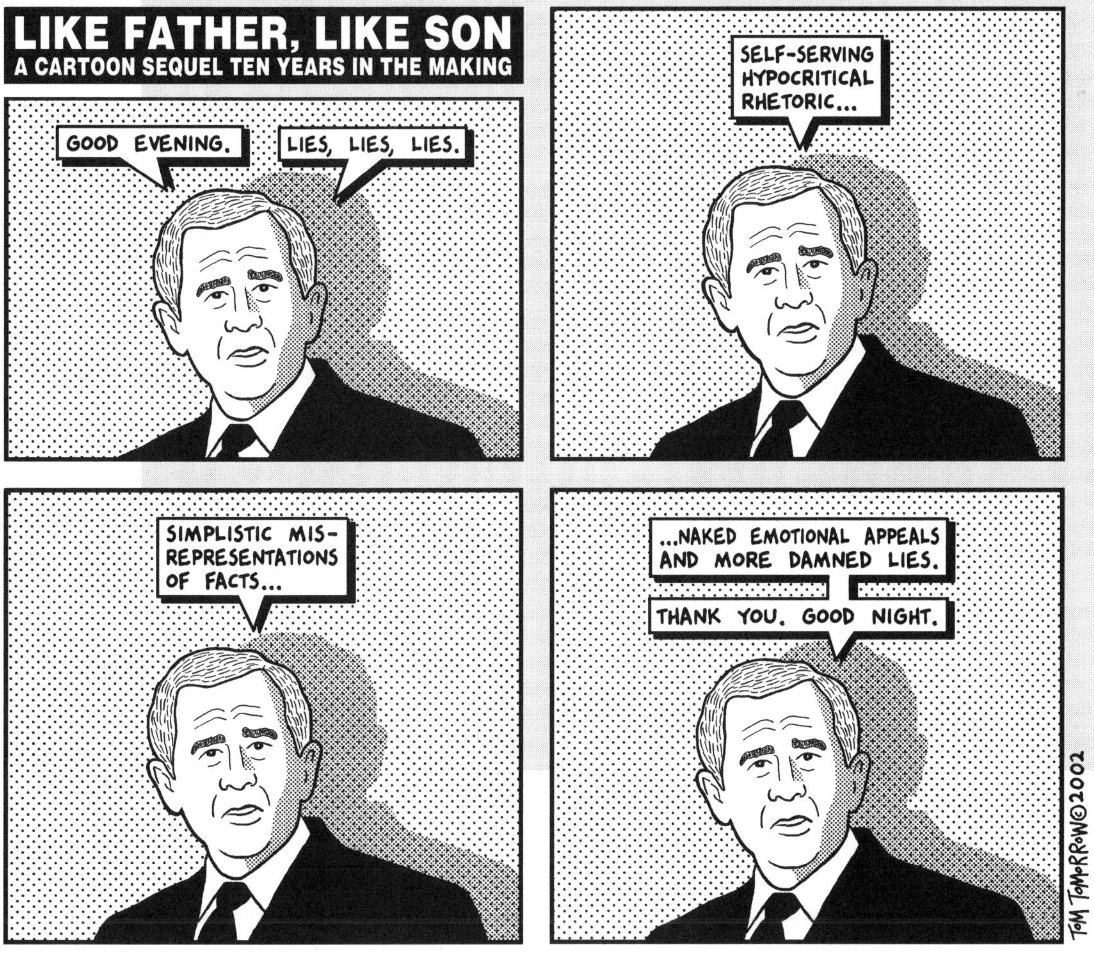
LIKE FATHER, LIKE SON
A CARTOON SEQUEL TEN YEARS IN THE MAKING
GOOD EVENING.
LIES, LIES, LIES.
SELF-SERVING HYPOCRITICAL RHETORIC...
SIMPLISTIC MIS-REPRESENTATIONS OF FACTS...
...NAKED EMOTIONAL APPEALS AND MORE DAMNED LIES.
THANK YOU. GOOD NIGHT.
TOM TOMORROW©2002

Normally, this is the page upon which a small and oddly uninformative paragraph of information about the author would appear. However, because this volume's Foreword already contains more information about its author than most readers are probably interested in knowing, this page will instead be put to other uses, namely:

A note concerning the timeliness of the last few cartoons

Due to the inclusion of a color section, as well as the relatively inflexible release schedule of any large publishing house, this book's deadline falls some nine months before its estimated date of publication—which is why there are no cartoons addressing the imposition of martial law, the great worldwide depression, the roving bands of homicidal cyborgs, the plagues of locusts and blood raining from the sky, and whatever other catastrophes and chaos you people of the future are undoubtedly experiencing. However, if it is still possible for you to somehow gain access to the internet, and if the author has not yet been arrested for sedition or other crimes against the state, his current work can probably be found at www.thismodernworld.com.

Acknowledgments of gratitude

As noted in the Foreword, this book is one of many made possible by the continuing editorial support and guidance of Keith Kahla. Given the author's generally contentious and irritatingly uncompromising nature, this ongoing show of loyalty borders on the inexplicable, but is sincerely appreciated nonetheless.

The author is also extraordinarily grateful to a certain Mr. Kevin Pyle, for his extensive contributions to the design and production of these pages. In real life, Kevin is a frequent contributor to *World War Three Illustrated*, and the author of *Lab USA: Illuminated Documents*, published by Autonomedia.

And at the risk of sounding like an emotionally overwrought actor at an awards ceremony, the author would also like to extend heartfelt thanks to the editors of the many publications in which his cartoons are featured each week, providing him with both a regular soapbox and a reasonable approximation of a steady income.

And finally, a picture of the author's dog

Just because.